KEY TO SOURCE CODES

BiDrLUS	A Biographical Directory of Librarians in the United States and Canada	CnMD	The Concise Encyclopedia of Modern Drama
BiDrUSE	Biographical Directory of the United States Executive Branch 1774-1971	CnMWL	The Concise Encyclopedia of Modern World Literature
		CnThe	A Concise Encyclopedia of the Theatre
BiESc	A Biographical Encyclopedia of Scientists	CngDr	Congressional Directory
BiE&WWA	The Biographical Encyclopaedia and Who's Who of the American Theatre	ConAmA	Contemporary American Authors
		ConAmC	Contemporary American Composers
BiHiMed	A Biographical History of Medicine	ConAmL	Contemporary American Literature
BioIn	Biography Index	ConAmTC	Contemporary American Theater Critics
BioNews	Biography News		
BlkAmWP	Black American Writers Past and Present	ConArch	Contemporary Architects
		ConArt	Contemporary Artists
BlueB	The Blue Book	ConAu	Contemporary Authors
BluesWW	Blues Who's Who	ConDr	Contemporary Dramatists
BkC	The Book of Catholic Authors	ConICB	Contemporary Illustrators of Children's Books
BkCL	A Book of Children's Literature		
BkIE	Book Illustrators in Eighteenth-Century England	ConIsC	Contemporary Issues Criticism
		ConLC	Contemporary Literary Criticism
BkP	Books Are by People	ConLCrt	Contemporary Literary Critics
BnEnAmA	The Britannica Encyclopedia of American Art	ConNov	Contemporary Novelists
		ConPhot	Contemporary Photographers
Br&AmS	British and American Sporting Authors	ConP	Contemporary Poets
		ConSFA	Contemporary Science Fiction Authors
BrAu	British Authors		
BrCA	British Children's Authors	Conv	Conversations
BrWr	British Writers	CorpD	Corpus Delicti of Mystery Fiction
BroadAu	Broadside Authors and Artists	CreCan	Creative Canada
BusPN	Business People in the News	CrtT	The Critical Temper
CabMA	The Cabinetmakers of America	CroCAP	Crowell's Handbook of Contemporary American Poetry
Cald	Caldecott Medal Books: 1938-1957		
CaW	Canada Writes!	CroCD	Crowell's Handbook of Contemporary Drama
CanNov	Canadian Novelists, 1920-1945		
CanWW	The Canadian Who's Who	CroE&S	Crowell's Handbook of Elizabethan and Stuart Literature
CanWr	Canadian Writers		
CarSB	The Carolyn Sherwin Bailey Historical Collection of Children's Books	CurBio	Current Biography Yearbook
		CyAG	Cyclopedia of American Government
		CyAL	Cyclopaedia of American Literature
CasWL	Cassell's Encyclopaedia of World Literature		
		CyEd	Cyclopedia of Education
CathA	Catholic Authors	CyWA	Cyclopedia of World Authors
CelCen	Celebrities of the Century	DcAfL	Dictionary of Afro-Latin American Civilization
CelR	Celebrity Register		
Chambr	Chambers's Cyclopaedia of English Literature	DcAmArt	Dictionary of American Art
		DcAmAu	Dictionary of American Authors
ChiSch	Chicano Scholars and Writers	DcAmB	Dictionary of American Biography
ChhPo	Childhood in Poetry	DcAmDH	Dictionary of American Diplomatic History
ChlLR	Children's Literature Review		
ChrP	The Children's Poets	DcAmLiB	Dictionary of American Library Biography
ChsFB	The Child's First Books		
CivR	Civil Rights	DcAmMeB	Dictionary of American Medical Biography
CivRSt	Civil Rights Struggle: Leaders in Profile		
		DcAmReB	Dictionary of American Religious Biography
CivWDc	Civil War Dictionary		
ClDMEL	Columbia Dictionary of Modern European Literature	DcAmSR	Dictionary of American Social Reform
		DcBiA	A Dictionary of Biographies of Authors Represented in the Authors Digest Series
CmCal	A Companion to California		
CmMov	A Companion to the Movies		
CmpEPM	The Complete Encyclopedia of Popular Music and Jazz	DcBiPP	Dictionary of Biography, Past and Present
CompSN	Composers since 1900: First Supplement	DcBrA	Dictionary of British Artists Working 1900-1950
		DcBrBI	The Dictionary of British Book Illustrators and Caricaturists
CpmDNM	Composium Directory of New Music		
CnDAL	Concise Dictionary of American Literature	DcBrWA	The Dictionary of British Watercolour Artists
		DcCanB	Dictionary of Canadian Biography
CnE&AP	The Concise Encyclopedia of English and American Poets and Poetry		

(Continued on overleaf)

KEY TO SOURCE CODES

DcCathB	Dictionary of Catholic Biography	*EncLatA*	Encyclopedia of Latin America
DcCAA	A Dictionary of Contemporary American Artists	*EncMT*	Encyclopaedia of the Musical Theatre
DcCAr	Dictionary of Contemporary Artists	*EncMys*	Encyclopedia of Mystery and Detection
DcCLAA	A Dictionary of Contemporary Latin American Authors	*EncO&P*	Encyclopedia of Occultism and Parapsychology
DcCM	Dictionary of Contemporary Music	*EncPR&S*	Encyclopedia of Pop, Rock and Soul
DcD&D	Dictionary of Design and Decoration	*EncSF*	The Encyclopedia of Science Fiction
DcEnA	A Dictionary of English Authors		
DcEnL	Dictionary of English Literature	*EncSoA*	Encyclopedia of Southern Africa
DcEuL	A Dictionary of European Literature	*EncSoB*	Encyclopedia of Southern Baptists
		EncSoH	The Encyclopedia of Southern History
DcFM	Dictionary of Film Makers		
DcInB	Dictionary of Indian Biography	*EncTR*	Encyclopedia of the Third Reich
DcInv	Dictionary of Inventions & Discoveries	*EncUrb*	Encyclopedia of Urban Planning
		EncWL	Encyclopedia of World Literature in the 20th Century
DcIrB	A Dictionary of Irish Biography		
DcIrL	Dictionary of Irish Literature	*EncWM*	The Encyclopedia of World Methodism
DcIrW	Dictionary of Irish Writers		
DcItL	Dictionary of Italian Literature	*EncWT*	The Encyclopedia of World Theater
DcLB	Dictionary of Literary Biography	*EuAu*	European Authors, 1000-1900
DcLEL	A Dictionary of Literature in the English Language	*EvEuW*	Everyman's Dictionary of European Writers
DcNiCA	Dictionary of 19th Century Antiques	*EvLB*	Everyman's Dictionary of Literary Biography, English and American
DcNAA	A Dictionary of North American Authors		
DcOrL	Dictionary of Oriental Literatures	*FamA&A*	Famous Actors and Actresses on the American Stage
DcPol	A Dictionary of Politics		
DcRusL	Dictionary of Russian Literature	*FamAIYP*	Famous Author-Illustrators for Young People
DcScB	Dictionary of Scientific Biography		
DcSeaP	Dictionary of Sea Painters	*FamAYP*	Famous Authors for Young People
DcSoc	A Dictionary of Sociology	*FamMS*	Famous Modern Storytellers for Young People
DcSpL	Dictionary of Spanish Literature		
DcVicP	Dictionary of Victorian Painters	*FamPYP*	Famous Poets for Young People
DrAF	A Directory of American Fiction Writers	*FamSYP*	Famous Storytellers for Young People
DrAP	A Directory of American Poets	*FarE&A*	The Far East and Australasia
DrAP&F	A Directory of American Poets and Fiction Writers	*FemPA*	The Female Poets of America
		FifIDA	Fifth International Directory of Anthropologists
DrAS	Directory of American Scholars		
DrBlPA	Directory of Blacks in the Performing Arts	*Film*	Filmarama
		FilmgC	The Filmgoer's Companion
DrInf	The Directory of Infamy	*ForWC*	Foremost Women in Communications
DrLC	Directory of Library Consultants		
DrRegL	Directory of Registered Lobbyists	*ForIl*	Forty Illustrators and How They Work
Dis&D	Disease and Destiny		
Drake	Drake: Dictionary of American Biography	*FourBJA*	Fourth Book of Junior Authors and Illustrators
Dun&B	Dun and Bradstreet Reference Book of Corporate Managements	*Future*	The Future: A Guide to Information Sources
		GolEC	Golombek's Encyclopedia of Chess
EarABI	Early American Book Illustrators and Wood Engravers	*GoodHs*	The Good Housekeeping Woman's Almanac
Ebony	The Ebony Success Library		
EncAAH	Encyclopedia of American Agricultural History	*GrBIl*	The Great Bird Illustrators and Their Art
EncAB-A	Encyclopedia of American Biography (American Historical Society)	*Grk&L*	Greek and Latin Authors: 800 B.C.-A.D.1000
		GuPsyc	A Guide to Psychologists and Their Concepts
EncAB-H	Encyclopedia of American Biography (Harper & Row)	*HarEnUS*	Harper's Encyclopedia of U.S. History
EncAR	Encyclopedia of the American Revolution	*HerW*	Her Way
EncASM	Encyclopedia of American Silver Manufacturers	*HisEWW*	The Historical Encyclopedia of World War II
		HolP	Hollywood Players
EncE	Encyclopedia of Espionage	*HsB&A*	The House of Beadle and Adams and Its Dime and Nickel Novels
EncFCWM	Encyclopedia of Folk, Country and Western Music		
EncJzS	The Encyclopedia of Jazz in the Seventies	*IlBEAAW*	The Illustrated Biographical Encyclopedia of Artists of the American West

(Continued on back endleaf)

WRITERS FOR YOUNG ADULTS:

BIOGRAPHIES
MASTER INDEX

The Gale Biographical Index Series

Biography and Genealogy Master Index
Second Edition and Supplements
(GBIS Number 1)

Children's Authors and Illustrators
Third Edition
(GBIS Number 2)

Author Biographies Master Index
Second Edition
(GBIS Number 3)

Journalist Biographies Master Index
(GBIS Number 4)

Performing Arts Biography Master Index
Second Edition
(GBIS Number 5)

Writers for Young Adults: Biographies Master Index
Second Edition
(GBIS Number 6)

Historical Biographical Dictionaries Master Index
(GBIS Number 7)

Twentieth-Century Author Biographies Master Index
(GBIS Number 8)

Gale Biographical Index Series
Number 6

WRITERS FOR YOUNG ADULTS:
BIOGRAPHIES MASTER INDEX

An index to sources of biographical information about novelists, poets, playwrights, nonfiction writers, songwriters and lyricists, television and screenwriters who are of interest to high school students and to teachers, librarians, and researchers interested in high school reading materials.

SECOND EDITION

Adele Sarkissian, Editor

Gale Research Company • Book Tower • Detroit, Michigan 48226

Editor: Adele Sarkissian
Senior Assistant Editor: Joyce Nakamura
Assistant Editors: Lori J. Bell, Cynthia J. Walker
Research Coordinator: Carolyn Kline
Editorial Assistant: Marilyn O'Connell

Consulting Editor: Barbara McNeil

Production Supervisor: Carol Blanchard
Production Assistant: Dorothy Kalleberg
Art Director: Arthur Chartow
Program Designer: Al Fernandez, Jr.

For their generous assistance in the preparation of this book,
special acknowledgment is due to:

Elizabeth Mulligan, Molly Norris, and Amy Unterburger
of the *Biography and Genealogy Master Index* editorial staff,

Dennis LaBeau, Director of the Editorial Data Systems Department.

Publisher: Frederick G. Ruffner
Executive Vice-President/Editorial: James M. Ethridge
Editorial Director: Dedria Bryfonski
Director, Literature Division: Christine Nasso
Senior Editor, Young People's Literature/
Biography and Genealogy Master Index: Adele Sarkissian

Library of Congress Cataloging in Publication Data

Main entry under title:

Writers for young adults.

(Gale biographical index series; no. 6)
Bibliography: p.
Includes index.
1. Young adult literature—Bio-bibliography—
Indexes. 2. Authors—Biography—Dictionaries—
Indexes. I. Sarkissian, Adele. II. Series.
Z1037.A1W74   1984   016.809   84-21144
[PN497]
ISBN 0-8103-1473-8

Computerized photocomposition by
Computer Composition Corporation
Madison Heights, Michigan

Contents

v

Introduction

Writers for Young Adults (W YA), second edition, expands and updates the index originally published in 1979. Like its predecessor, this new edition aims to simplify biographical research for high school students and others who have an interest in writers for young adults. This index enables a reader to learn quickly and easily where biographical information can be found for any one of approximately 15,000 writers profiled in more than 500 biographical dictionaries.

Students, teachers, and librarians need not waste valuable time and effort in hit-and-miss searching through many reference books. *Writers for Young Adults* provides one convenient location where the reader can determine how many sources of biographical information exist for a given writer. The reader has the option to compare several sources or to choose the most authoritative or accessible source.

Scope

Writers were chosen for this index on the basis of their appeal to the special reading interests and abilities of high school students. These are the writers that young adults are most likely to encounter when fulfilling class assignments or simply reading for their own pleasure. The range of reading represented here, therefore, is a very broad one. Included here are:

--writers of popular teen-age fiction, like Judy Blume, Richard Peck, S.E. Hinton, M.E. Kerr, and Paul Zindel;

--writers of adult fiction and nonfiction whose work has been designated as suitable for young adults in book reviews, library cataloging, publishers' classifications, or in recommended reading lists (like that of the National Council of Teachers of English, for example);

--writers of special interest to young adults in media other than books: songwriters and lyricists (like John Lennon, Bob Dylan, and Stevie Wonder), and television and screenwriters (like Steven Spielberg, George Lucas, and Gene Roddenberry).

The same selection criteria used in the first edition of *WYA* have been used in this new edition. The editors have included here only those writers whose works have been recommended for young adult reading by authorities in the field—librarians, teachers, publishers, book reviewers, or authors themselves. In the absence of authoritative young adult designations for writers in the non-book media, the editors were guided by their own best perception of what screenwriters or lyricists are of interest to young adults.

The biographical sources cited in *WYA* represent a broad range of literary, professional, geographic, and general interest biographical dictionaries. This index has drawn upon all the reference sources contained in Gale's massive *Biography and Genealogy Master Index.* As a result, sources as diverse as the *Directory of American Scholars, Contemporary Authors, The Illustrated Encyclopedia of Rock, Who's Who in America,* and *Who's Who in Science Fiction* are cited in *Writers for Young Adults.*

WYA aims to be comprehensive. No attempt was made to select or reject biographical sources on the basis of their content or point of view, or to rate the usefulness of one source against another. Rather, *WYA* includes *all* citations for a given author that occur in *all* the biographical sources researched for this index. Users' needs for information may vary widely; and some sources may be unavailable in some libraries. Therefore, *WYA* attempts to provide the maximum information from which the user can make his or her own best selection.

This index cites only biographical reference books and excludes most material published in journals, magazines, and newspapers, with the exception of periodicals included in *Biography Index.*

Editorial Practices

The second edition of *WYA* retains all material included in the first edition. Thousands of names were added to those listed in the first edition, and all names were computer-matched against some five million biographical citations in the *Biography and Genealogy Master Index* data bank. The computer-generated information was then refinded "by hand" in order to:

1. Verify in the original reference sources that similar names did, in fact, represent the same individual.

2. Establish standardized forms for names and dates that vary from one biographical source to another. Middle or maiden names have been added when research revealed them. Initials have been expanded to complete given names when it would not hinder the user's locating the name in the original source.

   When discrepancies in birth dates were found among various sources, the editors selected the most commonly-cited date and inserted a question mark after it to indicate some doubt regarding its accuracy.

3. Add cross-references as links between "real names" and

pseudonyms (or name variants) that often did not exist in the original biographical sources.

Cross-references have been used here also to alert the reader to:

a) Name variations in sources cited that do not allow for standardization.

For example,

DeLaMare, Walter and
LaMare, Walter De

b) The names of individual members within a group.

For example, the listing for the Beatles is followed by cross-references to individual listings for George Harrison, John Lennon, Paul McCartney, and Ringo Starr.

Reading a Citation

Each citation gives the writer's name, birth and death dates (if known), and an alphabetically-arranged list of reference sources in which biographical information may be found.

The reference sources cited are given in an abbreviated code form based upon the title of the book. The key to these source codes will be found on the endpapers. Full bibliographic citations, including the codes, begin on page xi.

Any comments or suggestions regarding *Writers for Young Adults* will be most welcome.

Bibliographic Key to Source Codes

Code	Source Indexed
ALA 80	*The ALA Yearbook.* A review of library events 1979. Volume 5, 1980. Chicago: American Library Association, 1980.

Biographies begin on page 73. The Obituary section, indicated in this index by the code *N*, begins on page 227.

AfSS   *Africa South of the Sahara.* London: Europa Publications Ltd., 1978, 1979, 1980, 1981, 1982. Distributed by Gale Research Co., Detroit, Michigan.

AfSS 78	Eighth edition, 1978-1979
AfSS 79	Ninth edition, 1979-1980
AfSS 80	Tenth edition, 1980-1981
AfSS 81	Eleventh edition, 1981-1982
AfSS 82	Twelfth edition, 1982-1983

Biographies are found in the "Who's Who in Africa South of the Sahara" section in each volume.

AfrA   *African Authors: A Companion to Black African Writing.* Volume I: 1300-1973. By Donald E. Herdeck. Washington, D.C.: Black Orpheus Press, 1973.

AfroAA   *Afro-American Artists: A Bio-Bibliographical Directory.* Compiled and edited by Theresa Dickason Cederholm. Boston: Trustees of the Boston Public Library, 1973.

Alli   Allibone, S. Austin. *A Critical Dictionary of English Literature and British and American Authors Living and Deceased from the Earliest Accounts to the Latter Half of the Nineteenth Century.* Containing over 46,000 articles (authors) with 40 indexes of subjects. Three volumes. Philadelphia: J.B. Lippincott & Co., 1858-1871. Reprint. Detroit: Gale Research Co., 1965.

Alli SUP   *A Supplement to Allibone's Critical Dictionary of English Literature and British and American Authors.* Containing over 37,000 articles (authors) and enumerating over 93,000 titles. Two volumes. By John Foster Kirk. Philadelphia: J.B. Lippincott & Co., 1891. Reprint. Detroit: Gale Research Co., 1965.

AlmAP   *The Almanac of American Politics.* The senators, the representatives, the governors--their records, states, and districts. By Michael Barone, Grant Ujifusa, and Douglas Matthews. New York: E.P. Dutton, 1977, 1979.

AlmAP 78	1978 edition, 1977
AlmAP 80	1980 edition, 1979

Use the "Names Index" in each volume to locate biographies.

AlmAP 82   *The Almanac of American Politics 1982.* The president, the senators, the representatives, the governors: their records and election results, their states and districts. By Michael Barone and Grant Ujifusa. Washington, D.C.: Barone & Co., 1981.

Use the "Index of Persons" to locate biographies.

AlmAP 84   *The Almanac of American Politics 1984.* The president, the senators, the representatives, the governors: their records and election results, their states and districts. By Michael Barone and Grant Ujifusa. Washington D.C.:

National Journal, 1983.

Use the "Index of People," beginning on page 1383, to locate biographies.

AmArch 70   *American Architects Directory.* Third edition. Edited by John F. Gane. Published under the sponsorship of American Institute of Architects. New York and London: R.R. Bowker Co., 1970.

AmAu   *American Authors, 1600-1900: A Biographical Dictionary of American Literature.* Edited by Stanley J. Kunitz and Howard Haycraft. New York: H.W. Wilson Co., 1938.

AmAu&B   *American Authors and Books, 1640 to the Present Day.* Third revised edition. By W.J. Burke and Will D. Howe. Revised by Irving Weiss and Anne Weiss. New York: Crown Publishers, Inc., 1972.

AmBench 79   *The American Bench: Judges of the Nation.* Second edition. Edited by Mary Reincke and Nancy Lichterman. Minneapolis: Reginald Bishop Forster & Associates, Inc., 1979.

Use the "Name Index" at the front of the volume to locate biographies.

AmBi   *American Biographies.* By Wheeler Preston. New York and London: Harper & Brothers Publishers, 1940. Reprint. Detroit: Gale Research Co., 1974.

AmCath 80   *The American Catholic Who's Who.* Volume 23, 1980-1981. Edited by Joy Anderson. Washington, D.C.: National Catholic News Service, 1979.

AmEA 74   American Economic Association. *Directory of Members, 1974.* Edited by Rendigs Fels. Published as Volume 64, Number 5, October, 1974 of *The American Economic Review.*

AmLY   *The American Literary Yearbook.* A biographical and bibliographical dictionary of living North American authors; a record of contemporary literary activity; an authors' manual and students' text book. Volume 1, 1919. Edited by Hamilton Traub. Henning, Minnesota: Paul Traub, 1919. Reprint. Detroit: Gale Research Co., 1968.

AmLY	"Biographical and Bibliographical Dictionary of Living North American Authors" begins on page 57.
AmLY X	"Pen-names and Pseudonyms" begins on page 49.

AmM&WS   *American Men and Women of Science.* Edited by Jaques Cattell Press. New York and London: R.R. Bowker Co., 1971-1973, 1976-1978, 1979, 1982.

AmM & WS 73P	Physical & Biological Sciences, 12th edition, 1971-1973
AmM & WS 73S	Social & Behavioral Sciences, 12th edition, 1973
AmM & WS 76P	Physical & Biological Sciences, 13th edition, 1976
AmM & WS 78S	Social & Behavioral Sciences, 13th edition, 1978
AmM & WS 79P	Physical & Biological Sciences, 14th edition, 1979
AmM & WS 82P	Physical & Biological Sciences, 15th edition, 1982

AmNov   *American Novelists of Today.* By Harry R. Warfel. New York: American Book Co., 1951. Reprint. Westport, Connecticut: Greenwood Press, 1976.

The "Index of Married Names and Pseudonyms," indicated in this index by the code *X*, begins on page 477.

AmPB   *American Picturebooks from Noah's Ark to The Beast Within.* By Barbara Bader. New York: Macmillan Publishing Co., Inc.; London: Collier Macmillian Publishers, 1976.

Use the Index to locate biographies.

AmPolW	*American Political Women: Contemporary and Historical Profiles.* By Esther Stineman. Littleton, Colorado: Libraries Unlimited, Inc., 1980.	

        AmPolW 80   Profiles

        AmPolW 80A   Appendix I: "Women of the Congress 1917-1980" begins on page 191.

        AmPolW 80B   Appendix II: "Women Ambassadors of the United States Currently Serving" begins on page 198.

        AmPolW 80C   Appendix III: "Women Chiefs of Mission 1933-1980" begins on page 199.

AmPS   *American Popular Songs from the Revolutionary War to the Present.* Edited by David Ewen. New York: Random House, 1966.

        AmPS   "American Popular Songs" begins on page 1.

        AmPS A   "All-Time Best-Selling Popular Recordings" begins on page 485.

        AmPS B   "Some American Performers of the Past and Present" begins on page 499.

AmSCAP 66   *The ASCAP Biographical Dictionary of Composers, Authors and Publishers.* Third edition, 1966. Compiled and edited by The Lynn Farnol Group, Inc. New York: American Society of Composers, Authors and Publishers.

AmWom   *American Women.* A revised edition of *Woman of the Century,* 1,500 biographies with over 1,400 portraits; a comprehensive encyclopedia of the lives and achievements of American women during the nineteenth century. Two volumes. Edited by Frances E. Willard and Mary A. Livermore. New York: Mast, Crowell & Kirkpatrick, 1897. Reprint. Detroit: Gale Research Co., 1973.

AmWomWr   *American Women Writers: A Critical Reference Guide from Colonial Times to the Present.* Four volumes. Edited by Lina Mainiero. New York: Frederick Ungar Publishing Co., 1979-1982.

AmWr   *American Writers: A Collection of Literary Biographies.* Four volumes and supplement. Edited by Leonard Unger. New York: Charles Scribner's Sons, 1974, 1979. Originally published as the *University of Minnesota Pamphlets on American Writers.*

        AmWr   Volumes I-IV, 1974

        AmWr SUP   Supplement I, 1979

AnObit   *The Annual Obituary.* New York: St. Martin's Press, 1981, 1982, 1983.

        AnObit 1980   *1980,* edited by Roland Turner, 1981

        AnObit 1981   *1981,* edited by Janet Podell, 1982

        AnObit 1982   *1982,* edited by Janet Podell, 1983

        Use the "Alphabetical Index of Entrants" at the front of each volume to locate biographies.

AnCL   *Anthology of Children's Literature.* Fourth edition. Edited by Edna Johnson, Evelyn R. Sickels, and Frances Clarke Sayers. Boston: Houghton Mifflin Co., 1970.

        Biographies begin on page 1217.

AnMV 1926   *Anthology of Magazine Verse for 1926 and Yearbook of American Poetry.* Edited by William Stanley Braithwaite. New York: G. Sully, 1926. Reprint. Granger Index Reprint Series. Freeport, New York: Books for Libraries Press, 1972.

        "Biographical Dictionary of Poets in the United States" begins on page 3 of part IV.

AntBDN   *The Antique Buyer's Dictionary of Names.* By A.W. Coysh. Newton Abbot, England: David & Charles, 1970.

AntBDN A	"Art Nouveau" begins on page 13.
AntBDN B	"Book Illustrations and Prints" begins on page 23.
AntBDN C	"Bronzes" begins on page 48.
AntBDN D	"Clocks and Barometers" begins on page 59.
AntBDN E	"Fashion Plates" begins on page 81.
AntBDN F	"Firearms" begins on page 86.
AntBDN G	"Furniture" begins on page 98.
AntBDN H	"Glass" begins on page 123.
AntBDN I	"Maps, Charts, and Globes" begins on page 137.
AntBDN J	"Miniatures" begins on page 148.
AntBDN K	"Musical Instruments" begins on page 170.
AntBDN L	"Netsuke" begins on page 179.
AntBDN M	"Pottery and Porcelain" begins on page 185.
AntBDN N	"Sheffield Plate" begins on page 224.
AntBDN O	"Silhouettes or Profiles" begins on page 231.
AntBDN P	"Silk Pictures, Portraits, and Bookmarks" begins on page 243.
AntBDN Q	"Silver" begins on page 250.

ApCAB   *Appleton's Cyclopaedia of American Biography.* Six volumes. Edited by James Grant Wilson and John Fiske. New York: D. Appleton & Co., 1888-1889. Reprint. Detroit: Gale Research Co., 1968.

ApCAB SUP   *Appleton's Cyclopaedia of American Biography.* Volume seven, Supplement. Edited by James Grant Wilson. New York: D. Appleton & Co., 1901. Reprint. Detroit: Gale Research Co., 1968.

ApCAB X   *A Supplement to Appleton's Cyclopaedia of American Biography.* Six volumes. Originally published as *The Cyclopaedia of American Biography, Supplementary Edition.* Edited by L.E. Dearborn. New York: Press Association Compilers, Inc., 1918-1931.

ArizL   *Arizona in Literature: A Collection of the Best Writings of Arizona Authors from Early Spanish Days to the Present Time.* By Mary G. Boyer. Glendale, California: Arthur H. Clark Co., 1935. Reprint. Ann Arbor: Gryphon Books, 1971.

               Use the Index to locate biographies.

ArtCS   *The Art of the Comic Strip.* By Judith O'Sullivan. College Park: University of Maryland, Department of Art, 1971.

               Biographies begin on page 60.

ArtsAmW   *Artists of the American West: A Biographical Dictionary.* By Doris Ostrander Dawdy. Chicago: Swallow Press, Inc., 1974.

ArtsCL   *Artists of a Certain Line: A Selection of Illustrators for Children's Books.* By John Ryder. London: The Bodley Head, 1960.

               Biographies begin on page 43.

ArtsNiC   *Artists of the Nineteenth Century and Their Works.* A handbook containing 2,050 biographical sketches. Revised edition. By Clara Erskine Clement and Laurence Hutton. Boston: J.R. Osgood & Co., 1885. Reprint, two volumes in one. St. Louis: North Point, Inc., 1969.

AsBiEn   *Asimov's Biographical Encyclopedia of Science and Technology.* The lives and achievements of 1,195 great scientists from ancient times to the present, chronologically arranged. New revised edition. By Isaac Asimov. New York: Avon, 1976.

               Use the "Alphabetic List of Biographical Entries" at the front of the book to locate biographies.

AtlBL   *Atlantic Brief Lives: A Biographical Companion to the Arts.* Edited by Louis Kronenberger. Boston: Little, Brown & Co., 1971.

ASpks   *The Author Speaks: Selected "PW" Interviews, 1967-1976.* By *Publishers Weekly* editors and contributors. New York and London: R.R. Bowker Co., 1977.

Au&ICB   *Authors and Illustrators of Children's Books: Writings on Their Lives and Works.* By Miriam Hoffman and Eva Samuels. New York and London: R.R. Bowker Co., 1972.

Au&Wr 6   *The Author's and Writer's Who's Who.* Sixth edition. Darien, Connecticut: Hafner Publishing Co., Inc., 1971.

AuBYP   *Authors of Books for Young People.* By Martha E. Ward and Dorothy A. Marquardt. Metuchen, New Jersey: Scarecrow Press Inc., 1971, 1979.

   AuBYP   Second edition, 1971
   AuBYP SUP   Supplement to the second edition, 1979
   AuBYP SUPA   Addendum to the Supplement
                    begins on page 301.

AuNews   *Authors in the News.* A compilation of news stories and feature articles from American newspapers and magazines covering writers and other members of the communications media. Two volumes. Edited by Barbara Nykoruk. Detroit: Gale Research Co., 1976.

   AuNews 1   Volume 1
   AuNews 2   Volume 2

Baker 78   *Baker's Biographical Dictionary of Musicians.* Sixth edition. Revised by Nicolas Slonimsky. New York: Schirmer Books; London: Collier Macmillan Publishers, 1978.

BbD   *The Bibliophile Dictionary.* A biographical record of the great authors, with bibliographical notices of their principal works from the beginning of history. Originally published as Volumes 29 and 30 of *The Bibliophile Library of Literature, Art, and Rare Manuscripts.* Compiled and arranged by Nathan Haskell Dole, Forrest Morgan, and Caroline Ticknor. New York and London: International Bibliophile Society, 1904. Reprint. Detroit: Gale Research Co., 1966.

BbtC   *Bibliotheca Canadensis: Or, A Manual of Canadian Literature.* By Henry J. Morgan. Ottawa: G.E. Desbarats, 1867. Reprint. Detroit: Gale Research Co., 1968.

BiAUS   *Biographical Annals of the Civil Government of the United States, during Its First Century.* From original and official sources. By Charles Lanman. Washington, D.C.: James Anglim, 1876. Reprint. Detroit: Gale Research Co., 1976.

   "Additional Facts," indicated in this index by the code *SUP*, begins on page 633.

BiCAW   *The Biographical Cyclopaedia of American Women.* Two volumes. Volume I: Compiled under the supervision of Mabel Ward Cameron. New York: Halvord Publishing Co., Inc., 1924. Volume II: Compiled under the supervision of Erma Conkling Lee. New York: Franklin W. Lee Publishing Corp., 1925. Reprint (both volumes). Detroit: Gale Research Co., 1974.

   Use the Indexes to locate biographies.

BiDAfM   *Biographical Dictionary of Afro-American and African Musicians.* By Eileen Southern. Westport, Connecticut and London: Greenwood Press, 1982.

BiDAmAr   *Biographical Dictionary of American Architects, Deceased.* By Henry F. Withey and Elsie Rathburn Withey. Los Angeles: New Age Publishing Co., 1956.

BiDAmBL 83   *Biographical Dictionary of American Business Leaders.* By John N. Ingham. Westport, Connecticut and London: Greenwood Press, 1983.

Use the Index to locate biographies.

BiDAmEd   *Biographical Dictionary of American Educators.* Three volumes. Edited by John F. Ohles. Westport, Connecticut and London: Greenwood Press, 1978.

BiDAmLL   *Biographical Dictionary of American Labor Leaders.* Edited by Gary M. Fink. Westport, Connecticut and London: Greenwood Press, 1974.

BiDAmM   *Biographical Dictionary of American Music.* By Charles Eugene Claghorn. West Nyack, New York: Parker Publishing Co., Inc., 1973.

BiDAmS   *Biographical Dictionary of American Science, the Seventeenth through the Nineteenth Centuries.* By Clark A. Elliott. Westport, Connecticut and London: Greenwood Press, 1979.

BiD&SB   *Biographical Dictionary and Synopsis of Books Ancient and Modern.* Edited by Charles Dudley Warner. Akron, Ohio: Werner Co., 1902. Reprint. Detroit: Gale Research Co., 1965.

BiDBrA   *A Biographical Dictionary of British Architects 1600-1840.* By Howard Colvin. New York: Facts on File, Inc., 1980.

"Appendix A," indicated in this index by the code *A*, begins on page 969.

BiDFedJ   *Biographical Dictionary of the Federal Judiciary.* Compiled by Harold Chase, Samuel Krislov, Keith O. Boyum, and Jerry N. Clark. Detroit: Gale Research Co., 1976.

The Addendum, indicated in this index by the code *A*, begins on page 319.

BiDFilm   *A Biographical Dictionary of Film.* By David Thomson. First edition. New York: William Morrow & Co., Inc., 1976.

BiDJaL   *Biographical Dictionary of Japanese Literature.* By Sen'ichi Hisamatsu. Tokyo: Kodansha International Ltd., 1976. Distributed by Harper & Row, New York, New York.

Use the Index to locate biographies.

BiDLA   *A Biographical Dictionary of the Living Authors of Great Britain and Ireland.* Comprising literary memoirs and anecdotes of their lives; and a chronological register of their publications, with the number of editions printed; including notices of some foreign writers whose works have been occasionally published in England. London: Printed for Henry Colburn, Public Library, Hanover Square, 1816. Reprint. Detroit: Gale Research Co., 1966.

The "Supplement of Additions and Corrections," indicated in this index by the code *SUP*, begins on page 407.

BiDPara   *Biographical Dictionary of Parapsychology, with Directory and Glossary, 1964-1966.* Edited by Helene Pleasants. New York: Garrett Publications, Helix Press, 1964.

BiDSA   *Biographical Dictionary of Southern Authors.* Originally published as *Library of Southern Literature, Volume 15, Biographical Dictionary of Authors.* Compiled by Lucian Lamar Knight. Atlanta: Martin & Hoyt Co., 1929. Reprint. Detroit: Gale Research Co., 1978.

BiDrACP 79   *Biographical Directory of the American College of Physicians, 1979.* Compiled by Jaques Cattell Press. New York and London: R.R. Bowker Co., 1979.

Use the Index, beginning on page 1789, to locate biographies.

BiDrAC   *Biographical Directory of the American Congress 1774-1971.* The Continental Congress (September 5, 1774 to October 21, 1788) and The Congress of the United States (From the first through the ninety-first Congress March 4,

1789, to January 3, 1971, inclusive), Washington, D.C.: United States Government Printing Office, 1971.

Biographies begin on page 487.

BiDrAPA 77　　*Biographical Directory of the Fellows and Members of the American Psychiatric Association.* Compiled by Jaques Cattell Press. New York and London: R.R. Bowker Co., 1977.

BiDrAPH 79　　*Biographical Directory of the American Public Health Association, 1979.* Compiled by Jaques Cattell Press. New York and London: R.R. Bowker Co., 1979.

BiDrGov　　*Biographical Directory of the Governors of the United States, 1789-1978.* Four volumes. Edited by Robert Sobel and John Raimo. Westport, Connecticut: Microform Review, Inc., Meckler Books, 1978.

Use the Index in each volume to locate biographies.

BiDrLUS 70　　*A Biographical Directory of Librarians in the United States and Canada.* Fifth edition. Edited by Lee Ash. Chicago: American Library Association, 1970.

BiDrUSE　　*Biographical Directory of the United States Executive Branch 1774-1971.* Edited by Robert Sobel. Westport, Connecticut: Greenwood Publishing Co., 1971.

BiESc　　*A Biographical Encyclopedia of Scientists.* Two volumes. Edited by John Daintith, Sarah Mitchell, and Elizabeth Tootill. New York: Facts on File, Inc., 1981.

BiE&WWA　　*The Biographical Encyclopaedia and Who's Who of the American Theatre.* Edited by Walter Rigdon. New York: James H. Heineman, Inc., 1966. Revised edition published as *Notable Names in the American Theatre* (see below).

"Biographical Who's Who" begins on page 227.

BiHiMed　　*A Biographical History of Medicine: Excerpts and Essays on the Men and Their Work.* By John H. Talbott. New York: Grune & Stratton, 1970.

Use the "Name Index," beginning on page 1193, to locate biographies.

BioIn　　*Biography Index.* A cumulative index to biographical material in books and magazines. New York: H.W. Wilson Co., 1949-1983.

BioIn 1	Volume 1: January, 1946- July, 1949; 1949
BioIn 2	Volume 2: August, 1949- August, 1952; 1953
BioIn 3	Volume 3: September, 1952- August, 1955; 1956
BioIn 4	Volume 4: September, 1955- August, 1958; 1960
BioIn 5	Volume 5: September, 1958- August, 1961; 1962
BioIn 6	Volume 6: September, 1961- August, 1964; 1965
BioIn 7	Volume 7: September, 1964- August, 1967; 1968
BioIn 8	Volume 8: September, 1967- August, 1970; 1971
BioIn 9	Volume 9: September, 1970- August, 1973; 1974
BioIn 10	Volume 10: September, 1973- August, 1976; 1977
BioIn 11	Volume 11: September, 1976- August, 1979; 1980

	BioIn 12	Volume 12: September, 1979- August, 1982; 1983

BioNews   *Biography News.* A compilation of news stories and feature articles from American news media covering personalities of national interest in all fields. Edited by Frank E. Bair. Detroit: Gale Research Co., 1974-1975.

	BioNews 74	Volume 1, Numbers 1-12, 1974
	BioNews 75	Volume 2, Number 1, January-February, 1975

BlkAmWP   *Black American Writers Past and Present: A Biographical and Bibliographical Dictionary.* Two volumes. By Theressa Gunnels Rush, Carol Fairbanks Myers, and Esther Spring Arata. Metuchen, New Jersey: Scarecrow Press, Inc., 1975.

BlueB 76   *The Blue Book: Leaders of the English-Speaking World.* 1976 edition. London: St. James Press; New York: St. Martin's Press, 1976. Republished in two volumes by Gale Research Co., Detroit, Michigan, 1979.

         The "Obituary" section, indicated in this index by the code *N*, begins on page 1837.

BluesWW   *Blues Who's Who: A Biographical Dictionary of Blues Singers.* By Sheldon Harris. New Rochelle, New York: Arlington House Publishers, 1979.

BkC   *The Book of Catholic Authors: Informal Self-Portraits of Famous Modern Catholic Writers.* Edited by Walter Romig. Detroit: Walter Romig & Co., 1942-?

	BkC 1	First series, 1942
	BkC 2	Second series, 1943
	BkC 3	Third series, 1945
	BkC 4	Fourth series (n.d.)
	BkC 5	Fifth series (n.d.)
	BkC 6	Sixth series (n.d.)

BkCL   *A Book of Children's Literature.* Third edition. Edited by Lillian Hollowell. New York: Holt, Rinehart & Winston, Inc., 1966.

         Biographies begin on page 553.

BkIE   *Book Illustrators in Eighteenth-Century England.* By Hanns Hammelmann. Edited and completed by T.S.R. Boase. New Haven, Connecticut: Yale University Press (for The Paul Mellon Centre for Studies in British Art, London), 1975.

BkP   *Books Are by People: Interviews with 104 Authors and Illustrators of Books for Young Children.* By Lee Bennett Hopkins. New York: Citation Press, 1969.

BnEnAmA   *The Britannica Encyclopedia of American Art.* Chicago: Encyclopaedia Britannica Educational Corp., 1973. World Book Trade Distribution by Simon & Schuster, New York.

Br&AmS   *British and American Sporting Authors: Their Writings and Biographies.* By A. Henry Higginson. London: Hutchinson & Co., Ltd., 1951.

         Use the Index to locate biographies.

BrAu   *British Authors before 1800: A Biographical Dictionary.* Edited by Stanley J. Kunitz and Howard Haycraft. New York: H.W. Wilson Co., 1952.

BrAu 19   *British Authors of the Nineteenth Century.* Edited by Stanley J. Kunitz. New York: H.W. Wilson Co., 1936.

BrCA   *British Children's Authors: Interviews at Home.* By Cornelia Jones and Olivia R. Way. Chicago: American Library Association, 1976.

BrWr   *British Writers.* Edited under the auspices of the British Council, Ian Scott-Kilvert, General Editor. New York: Charles Scribner's Sons, 1979-1983.

	BrWr 1	Volume I: William Langland to

	The English Bible, 1979
BrWr 2	Volume II: Thomas Middleton to George Farquhar, 1979
BrWr 3	Volume III: Daniel Defoe to The Gothic Novel, 1980
BrWr 4	Volume IV: William Wordsworth to Robert Browning, 1981
BrWr 5	Volume V: Elizabeth Gaskell to Francis Thompson, 1982
BrWr 6	Volume VI: Thomas Hardy to Wilfred Owen, 1983

Use the "List of Subjects" at the front of each volume to locate biographies.

BroadAu   *Broadside Authors and Artists: An Illustrated Biographical Directory.* Compiled and edited by Leaonead Pack Bailey. Detroit: Broadside Press, 1974.

BusPN   *Business People in the News.* A compilation of news stories and feature articles from American newspapers and magazines covering people in industry, finance, and labor. Volume 1. Edited by Barbara Nykoruk. Detroit: Gale Research Co., 1976.

CabMA   *The Cabinetmakers of America.* Revised and corrected edition. By Ethel Hall Bjerkoe. Exton, Pennsylvania: Schiffer Ltd., 1978. Originally published by Doubleday & Co., Inc., 1957.

Biographies begin on page 19.

Cald 1938   *Caldecott Medal Books: 1938-1957.* With the artist's acceptance papers and related material chiefly from the *Horn Book Magazine.* Horn Book Papers, Volume II. Edited by Bertha Mahony Miller and Elinor Whitney Field. Boston: Horn Book, Inc., 1957.

CaW   *Canada Writes!* The members' book of the Writers' Union of Canada. Edited by K.A. Hamilton. Toronto: Writers' Union of Canada, 1977.

"Additional Members," indicated in this index by the code *A*, begins on page 387.

CanNov   *Canadian Novelists, 1920-1945.* By Clara Thomas. Toronto: Longmans, Green & Co., 1946. Reprint. Folcroft, Pennsylvania: Folcroft Library Editions, 1970.

CanWW 70   *The Canadian Who's Who.* A biographical dictionary of notable living men and women. Volume 12, 1970-1972. Toronto: Who's Who Canadian Publications, 1972.

CanWW   *Canadian Who's Who.* A biographical dictionary of notable living men and women. Edited by Kieran Simpson. Toronto: University of Toronto Press, 1979, 1980, 1981, 1983.

CanWW 79	Volume XIV, 1979
CanWW 80	Volume XV, 1980
CanWW 81	Volume XVI, 1981
CanWW 83	Volume XVIII, 1983

CanWr   *Canadian Writers: A Biographical Dictionary.* New edition, revised and enlarged. Edited by Guy Sylvestre, Brandon Conron, and Carl F. Klinck. Toronto: Ryerson Press, 1966.

CarSB   *The Carolyn Sherwin Bailey Historical Collection of Children's Books: A Catalogue.* Edited and compiled by Dorothy R. Davis. New Haven, Connecticut: Southern Connecticut State College, 1966.

Not in strict alphabetic sequence.

CasWL   *Cassell's Encyclopaedia of World Literature.* Edited by S.H. Steinberg in two
               volumes. Revised and enlarged in three volumes by J. Buchanan-Brown. New
               York: William Morrow & Co., Inc., 1973.

               Biographies are found in Volumes 2 and 3.

CathA   *Catholic Authors: Contemporary Biographical Sketches.* Edited by Matthew
               Hoehn. Newark, New Jersey: St. Mary's Abbey, 1948, 1952. Reprint (first
               volume). Detroit: Gale Research Co., 1981.

               CathA 1930   First volume: 1930-1947, 1948
               CathA 1952   Second volume, 1952

CelCen   *Celebrities of the Century.* Being a dictionary of men and women of the
               nineteenth century. Two volumes. Edited by Lloyd C. Sanders. London:
               Cassell & Co., Ltd., 1887. Reprint. Ann Arbor: Gryphon Books, 1971.

CelR   *Celebrity Register.* Third edition. Edited by Earl Blackwell. New York: Simon &
               Schuster, 1973.

Chambr   *Chambers's Cyclopaedia of English Literature.* A history critical and
               biographical of authors in the English tongue from the earliest times till the
               present day with specimens of their writings. Three volumes. Edited by David
               Patrick, revised by J. Liddell Geddie. Philadelphia: J.B. Lippincott, Co.,
               1938. Reprint. Detroit: Gale Research Co., 1978.

               Chambr 1   Volume I: 7th-17th Century
               Chambr 2   Volume II: 18th Century
               Chambr 3   Volume III: 19th-20th Century

               Use the Index in each volume to locate biographies.

ChiSch   *Chicano Scholars and Writers: A Bio-Bibliographical Directory.* Edited and
               compiled by Julio A. Martinez. Metuchen, New Jersey and London:
               Scarecrow Press, Inc., 1979.

ChhPo   *Childhood in Poetry.* A catalogue, with biographical and critical annotations, of
               the books of English and American poets comprising the Shaw Childhood in
               Poetry Collection in the Library of the Florida State University. By John
               Mackay Shaw. Detroit: Gale Research Co., 1967, 1972, 1976, 1980.

               ChhPo   Original Volumes, 1967
               ChhPo S1   First Supplement, 1972
               ChhPo S2   Second Supplement, 1976
               ChhPo S3   Third Supplement, 1980

ChlLR   *Children's Literature Review.* Excerpts from reviews, criticism, and commentary
               on books for children. Detroit: Gale Research Co., 1976-1984.

               ChlLR 1   Volume 1, 1976
               ChlLR 2   Volume 2, 1976
               ChlLR 3   Volume 3, 1978
               ChlLR 4   Volume 4, 1982
               ChlLR 5   Volume 5, 1983
               ChlLR 6   Volume 6, 1984

ChrP   *The Children's Poets: Analyses and Appraisals of the Greatest English and
               American Poets for Children.* By Walter Barnes. Yonkers-on-Hudson, New
               York: World Book Co., 1924.

ChsFB   *The Child's First Books: A Critical Study of Pictures and Texts.* By Donnarae
               MacCann and Olga Richard. New York: H.W. Wilson Co., 1973.

               ChsFB A   "Author Biographies" begins on page 96.
               ChsFB I   "Illustrator Biographies" begins on page 47.

CivR 74   *Civil Rights: A Current Guide to the People, Organizations, and Events.* A CBS
               News Reference Book. Second edition. By Joan Martin Burke. New York:
               R.R. Bowker Co., 1974.

               Biographies begin on page 21.

CivRSt	*The Civil Rights Struggle: Leaders in Profile.* By John D'Emilio. New York: Facts on File, 1979.
CivWDc	*The Civil War Dictionary.* By Mark Mayo Boatner, III. New York: David McKay Co., Inc., 1959.
ClDMEL	*Columbia Dictionary of Modern European Literature.* First edition. Edited by Horatio Smith. New York: Columbia University Press, 1947.
CmCal	*A Companion to California.* By James D. Hart. New York: Oxford University Press, 1978.
CmMov	*A Companion to the Movies: From 1903 to the Present Day.* A guide to the leading players, directors, screenwriters, composers, cameramen and other artistes who have worked in the English-speaking cinema over the last 70 years. By Roy Pickard. New York: Hippocrene Books, Inc., 1972.
	Use the "Who's Who Index" to locate biographies.
CmpEPM	*The Complete Encyclopedia of Popular Music and Jazz, 1900-1950.* Three volumes. By Roger D. Kinkle. New Rochelle, New York: Arlington House Publishers, 1974.
	Biographies are located in Volumes 2 and 3.
CompSN SUP	*Composers since 1900: First Supplement.* A biographical and critical guide. Compiled and edited by David Ewen. New York: H.W. Wilson Co., 1981.
CpmDNM	*Composium Directory of New Music.* Annual index of contemporary compositions. Sedro Woolley, Washington: Crystal Musicworks: 1981, 1983.

CpmDNM 81		1981 edition
CpmDNM 82		1982/83 edition

CnDAL	*Concise Dictionary of American Literature.* Edited by Robert Fulton Richards. New York: Philosophical Library, Inc., 1955. Reprint. New York: Greenwood Press, 1969.
CnE&AP	*The Concise Encyclopedia of English and American Poets and Poetry.* Edited by Stephen Spender and Donald Hall. New York: Hawthorn Books, Inc., 1963.
CnMD	*The Concise Encyclopedia of Modern Drama.* By Siegfried Melchinger. Translated by George Wellwarth. Edited by Henry Popkin. New York: Horizon Press, 1964.
	Biographies begin on page 159. "Additional Entries," indicated in this index by the code *SUP*, begins on page 287.
CnMWL	*The Concise Encyclopedia of Modern World Literature.* Second edition. Edited by Geoffrey Grigson. London: Hutchinson & Co., Ltd., 1970.
	Biographies begin on page 29.
CnThe	*A Concise Encyclopedia of the Theatre.* By Robin May. Reading, England: Osprey Publishing Ltd., 1974.
	Use the Index to locate biographies.
CngDr	*Congressional Directory.* Washington, D.C.: United States Government Printing Office, 1974, 1977, 1979, 1981, 1983.

CngDr 74	93rd Congress, 2nd Session, 1974
CngDr 77	95th Congress, 1st Session, 1977
CngDr 79	96th Congress, 1st Session, 1979
CngDr 81	97th Congress, 1st Session, 1981
CngDr 83	98th Congress, 1st Session, 1983

Use the "Individual Index" in each volume to locate biographies.

ConAmA	*Contemporary American Authors: A Critical Survey and 219 Bio-Bibliographies.* By Fred B. Millett. New York: Harcourt, Brace & World, Inc., 1940. Reprint. New York: AMS Press, Inc., 1970.
	Biographies begin on page 207.

ConAmC   *Contemporary American Composers: A Biographical Dictionary.* Compiled by E. Ruth Anderson. Boston: G.K. Hall & Co., 1976.

        The Addendum, indicated in this index by the code *A*, begins on page 495.

ConAmL   *Contemporary American Literature: Bibliographies and Study Outlines.* By John Matthews Manly and Edith Rickert. Revised by Fred B. Millett. New York: Harcourt, Brace, 1929. Reprint. New York: Haskell House Publishers Ltd., 1974.

        Biographies begin on page 101.

ConAmTC   *Contemporary American Theater Critics: A Directory and Anthology of Their Works.* Compiled by M.E. Comtois and Lynn F. Miller. Metuchen, New Jersey and London: Scarecrow Press, Inc., 1977.

ConArch   *Contemporary Architects.* Edited by Muriel Emanuel. New York: St. Martin's Press, 1980.

        "Notes on Advisors and Contributors," indicated in this index by the code *A*, begins on page 927.

ConArt   *Contemporary Artists.* Edited by Colin Naylor and Genesis P-Orridge. London: St. James Press; New York: St. Martin's Press, 1977.

ConArt 83   *Contemporary Artists.* Second edition. Edited by Muriel Emanuel et al. New York: St. Martin's Press, 1983.

ConAu   *Contemporary Authors.* A bio-bibliographical guide to current writers in fiction, general nonfiction, poetry, journalism, drama, motion pictures, television, and other fields. Detroit: Gale Research Co., 1967-1984.

ConAu 1R	Volumes 1-4, 1st revision, 1967
ConAu 5R	Volumes 5-8, 1st revision, 1969
ConAu 9R	Volumes 9-12, 1st revision, 1974
ConAu 13R	Volumes 13-16, 1st revision, 1975
ConAu 17R	Volumes 17-20, 1st revision, 1976
ConAu 21R	Volumes 21-24, 1st revision, 1977
ConAu 25R	Volumes 25-28, 1st revision, 1977
ConAu 29R	Volumes 29-32, 1st revision, 1978
ConAu 33R	Volumes 33-36, 1st revision, 1978
ConAu 37R	Volumes 37-40, 1st revision, 1979
ConAu 41R	Volumes 41-44, 1st revision, 1979
ConAu 45	Volumes 45-48, 1974
ConAu 49	Volumes 49-52, 1975
ConAu 53	Volumes 53-56, 1975
ConAu 57	Volumes 57-60, 1976
ConAu 61	Volumes 61-64, 1976
ConAu 65	Volumes 65-68, 1977
ConAu 69	Volumes 69-72, 1978
ConAu 73	Volumes 73-76, 1978
ConAu 77	Volumes 77-80, 1979
ConAu 81	Volumes 81-84, 1979
ConAu 85	Volumes 85-88, 1980
ConAu 89	Volumes 89-92, 1980
ConAu 93	Volumes 93-96, 1980
ConAu 97	Volumes 97-100, 1981
ConAu 101	Volume 101, 1981
ConAu 102	Volume 102, 1981
ConAu 103	Volume 103, 1982
ConAu 104	Volume 104, 1982
ConAu 105	Volume 105, 1982
ConAu 106	Volume 106, 1982
ConAu 107	Volume 107, 1983
ConAu 108	Volume 108, 1983
ConAu 109	Volume 109, 1983

| ConAu 110 | Volume 110, 1984 |
| ConAu X | This code refers to pseudonym |

entries which appear only as cross-references in the cumulative index to *Contemporary Authors.*

ConAu NR　　*Contemporary Authors, New Revision Series.* A bio-bibliographical guide to current writers in fiction, general nonfiction, poetry, journalism, drama, motion pictures, television, and other fields. Detroit: Gale Research Co., 1981-1984.

ConAu 1NR	Volume 1, 1981
ConAu 2NR	Volume 2, 1981
ConAu 3NR	Volume 3, 1981
ConAu 4NR	Volume 4, 1981
ConAu 5NR	Volume 5, 1982
ConAu 6NR	Volume 6, 1982
ConAu 7NR	Volume 7, 1982
ConAu 8NR	Volume 8, 1983
ConAu 9NR	Volume 9, 1983
ConAu 10NR	Volume 10, 1983
ConAu 11NR	Volume 11, 1984

ConAu P-　　*Contemporary Authors, Permanent Series.* A bio-bibliographical guide to current authors and their works. Detroit: Gale Research Co., 1975-1978.

| ConAu P-1 | Volume 1, 1975 |
| ConAu P-2 | Volume 2, 1978 |

ConDr　　*Contemporary Dramatists.* Edited by James Vinson. London: St. James Press; New York: St. Martin's Press, 1973, 1977, 1982.

ConDr 73	First edition, 1973
ConDr 77	Second edition, 1977, "Contemporary Dramatists" begins on page 9.
ConDr 77A	Second edition, "Screen Writers" begins on page 893.
ConDr 77B	Second edition, "Radio Writers" begins on page 903.
ConDr 77C	Second edition, "Television Writers" begins on page 915.
ConDr 77D	Second edition, "Musical Librettists" begins on page 925.
ConDr 77E	Second edition, "The Theatre of the Mixed Means" begins on page 941.
ConDr 77F	Second edition, Appendix begins on page 969.
ConDr 82	Third edition, 1982, "Contemporary Dramatists" begins on page 9.
ConDr 82A	Third edition, "Screen Writers" begins on page 887.
ConDr 82B	Third edition, "Radio Writers" begins on page 899.
ConDr 82C	Third edition, "Television Writers" begins on page 911.
ConDr 82D	Third edition, "Musical Librettists" begins on page 921.
ConDr 82E	Third edition, Appendix begins on page 951.

ConICB　　*Contemporary Illustrators of Children's Books.* Compiled by Bertha E. Mahony and Elinor Whitney. Boston: Bookshop for Boys and Girls, Women's Educational and Industrial Union, 1930. Reprint. Detroit: Gale Research Co., 1978.

ConIsC	*Contemporary Issues Criticism.* Excerpts from criticism of contemporary writings in sociology, economics, politics, psychology, anthropology, education, history, law, theology, and related fields. Detroit: Gale Research Co., 1982-1984.

ConIsC 1	Volume 1, 1982
ConIsC 2	Volume 2, 1984

ConLC	*Contemporary Literary Criticism.* Excerpts from criticism of the works of today's novelists, poets, playwrights, short story writers, filmmakers, scriptwriters, and other creative writers. Detroit: Gale Research Co., 1973-1984.

ConLC 1	Volume 1, 1973
ConLC 2	Volume 2, 1974
ConLC 3	Volume 3, 1975
ConLC 4	Volume 4, 1975
ConLC 5	Volume 5, 1976
ConLC 6	Volume 6, 1976
ConLC 7	Volume 7, 1977
ConLC 8	Volume 8, 1978
ConLC 9	Volume 9, 1978
ConLC 10	Volume 10, 1979
ConLC 11	Volume 11, 1979
ConLC 12	Volume 12, 1980
ConLC 13	Volume 13, 1980
ConLC 14	Volume 14, 1980
ConLC 15	Volume 15, 1980
ConLC 16	Volume 16, 1981
ConLC 17	Volume 17, 1981
ConLC 18	Volume 18, 1981
ConLC 19	Volume 19, 1981
ConLC 20	Volume 20, 1982
ConLC 21	Volume 21, 1982
ConLC 22	Volume 22, 1982
ConLC 23	Volume 23, 1983
ConLC 24	Volume 24, 1983
ConLC 25	Volume 25, 1983
ConLC 26	Volume 26, 1983
ConLC 27	Volume 27, 1984

ConLCrt	*Contemporary Literary Critics.* By Elmer Borklund. London: St. James Press; New York: St. Martin's Press, 1977.
ConLCrt 82	*Contemporary Literary Critics.* Second edition. By Elmer Borklund. Detroit: Gale Research Co., 1982.
ConNov	*Contemporary Novelists.* Edited by James Vinson. London: St. James Press; New York: St. Martin's Press, 1972, 1976, 1982.

ConNov 72	First edition, 1972
ConNov 76	Second edition, 1976
ConNov 82	Third edition, 1982

Deceased novelists are listed in the Appendix at the end of each volume.

ConPhot	*Contemporary Photographers.* Edited by George Walsh, Colin Naylor, and Michael Held. New York: St. Martin's Press, 1982.
ConP	*Contemporary Poets.* London: St. James Press; New York: St. Martin's Press, 1970, 1975, 1980.

ConP 70	First edition, edited by Rosalie Murphy, 1970
ConP 75	Second edition, edited by James Vinson, 1975
ConP 80	Third edition, edited by James Vinson, 1980

Deceased poets are listed in the Appendix at the end of each volume.

ConSFA   *Contemporary Science Fiction Authors.* First edition. Compiled and edited by R. Reginald. New York: Arno Press, 1975. Previously published as *Stella Nova: The Contemporary Science Fiction Authors.* Los Angeles: Unicorn & Son, Publishers, 1970.

Conv   *Conversations.* Conversations series. Detroit: Gale Research Co., 1977-1978.

Conv 1	Volume 1: *Conversations with Writers*, 1977
Conv 2	Volume 2: *Conversations with Jazz Musicians*, 1977
Conv 3	Volume 3: *Conversations with Writers II*, 1978

CorpD   *Corpus Delicti of Mystery Fiction: A Guide to the Body of the Case.* By Linda Herman and Beth Stiel. Metuchen, New Jersey: Scarecrow Press, Inc., 1974.

Biographies begin on page 31.

CreCan   *Creative Canada: A Biographical Dictionary of Twentieth-Century Creative and Performing Artists.* Compiled by the Reference Division, McPherson Library, University of Victoria, British Columbia. Toronto: University of Toronto Press, 1971, 1972.

CreCan 1	Volume 1, 1971
CreCan 2	Volume 2, 1972

CrtT   *The Critical Temper: A Survey of Modern Criticism on English and American Literature from the Beginnings to the Twentieth Century.* Four volumes. Edited by Martin Tucker. A Library of Literary Criticism. New York: Frederick Ungar Publishing Co., 1969, 1979.

CrtT 1	Volume I: From Old English to Shakespeare, 1969
CrtT 2	Volume II: From Milton to Romantic Literature, 1969
CrtT 3	Volume III: Victorian Literature and American Literature, 1969
CrtT 4	Volume IV: Supplement, 1979

Authors are listed alphabetically within each period or division of literature.

CroCAP   *Crowell's Handbook of Contemporary American Poetry.* By Karl Malkoff. New York: Thomas Y. Crowell Co., 1973.

Biographies begin on page 43.

CroCD   *Crowell's Handbook of Contemporary Drama.* By Michael Anderson, et al. New York: Thomas Y. Crowell Co., 1971.

CroE&S   *Crowell's Handbook of Elizabethan & Stuart Literature.* By James E. Ruoff. New York: Thomas Y. Crowell Co., 1975.

CurBio   *Current Biography Yearbook.* New York: H.W. Wilson Co., 1940-1984.

Number after the source code indicates the year covered by the yearbook. Obituaries, located in the back of some volumes, are indicated in this index by the code *N*.

CyAG   *Cyclopedia of American Government.* Three volumes. Edited by Andrew C. McLaughlin and Albert Bushnell Hart. New York: D. Appleton & Co., 1914. Reprint. Gloucester, Massachusetts: Peter Smith, 1963.

CyAL   *Cyclopaedia of American Literature.* Embracing personal and critical notices of authors, and selections from their writings, from the earliest period to the present day; with portraits, autographs, and other illustrations. Two volumes. By Evert A. Duyckinck and George L. Duyckinck. Philadelphia: William Rutter & Co., 1875. Reprint. Detroit: Gale Research Co., 1965.

Use the Index in Volume 2 to locate biographies.

CyEd   *A Cyclopedia of Education.* Five volumes. Edited by Paul Monroe. New York: Macmillan Co., 1911. Reprint. Detroit: Gale Research Co., 1968.

CyWA   *Cyclopedia of World Authors.* Edited by Frank N. Magill. New York and London: Harper & Row, Publishers, 1958. Also published as *Masterplots Cyclopedia of World Authors.*

DcAfL   *Dictionary of Afro-Latin American Civilization.* By Benjamin Nunez with the assistance of the African Bibliographic Center. Westport, Connecticut and London: Greenwood Press, 1980.

DcAmArt   *Dictionary of American Art.* By Matthew Baigell. New York: Harper & Row Publishers, 1979.

DcAmAu   *A Dictionary of American Authors.* Fifth edition, revised and enlarged. By Oscar Fay Adams. New York: Houghton Mifflin Co., 1904. Reprint. Detroit: Gale Research Co., 1969.

                Biographies are found in the "Dictionary of American Authors" section beginning on page 1 and in the "Supplement" beginning on page 441.

DcAmB   *Dictionary of American Biography.* 20 volumes and seven supplements. Edited under the auspices of the American Council of Learned Societies. New York: Charles Scribner's Sons, 1928-1936, 1944, 1958, 1973, 1974, 1977, 1980, 1981.

DcAmB	Volumes 1-20, 1928-1936
DcAmB S1	Supplement 1, 1944
DcAmB S2	Supplement 2, 1958
DcAmB S3	Supplement 3, 1973
DcAmB S4	Supplement 4, 1974
DcAmB S5	Supplement 5, 1977
DcAmB S6	Supplement 6, 1980
DcAmB S7	Supplement 7, 1981

DcAmDH   *Dictionary of American Diplomatic History.* By John E. Findling. Westport, Connecticut and London: Greenwood Press, 1980.

DcAmLiB   *Dictionary of American Library Biography.* Edited by Bohdan S. Wynar. Littleton, Colorado: Libraries Unlimited, Inc., 1978.

DcAmMeB   *Dictionary of American Medical Biography.* Lives of eminent physicians of the United States and Canada, from the earliest times. By Howard A. Kelly and Walter L. Burrage. New York: D. Appleton & Co., 1928. Reprint. Road Town, Tortola, British Virgin Islands: Longwood Press Ltd., 1979.

DcAmReB   *Dictionary of American Religious Biography.* By Henry Warner Bowden. Westport, Connecticut and London: Greenwood Press, 1977.

DcAmSR   *A Dictionary of American Social Reform.* By Louis Filler. New York: Philosophical Library, 1963.

DcBiA   *A Dictionary of Biographies of Authors Represented in the Authors Digest Series.* With a supplemental list of later titles and a supplementary biographical section. Edited by Rossiter Johnson. New York: Authors Press, 1927. Reprint. Detroit: Gale Research Co., 1974.

                "Biographies of Authors" begins on page 3 and "Biographies of Authors Whose Works Are in Volume XVIII" begins on page 437.

DcBiPP   *A Dictionary of Biography, Past and Present.* Containing the chief events in the lives of eminent persons of all ages and nations. Preceded by the biographies and genealogies of the chief representatives of the royal houses of the world. Edited by Benjamin Vincent. Haydn Series. London: Ward, Lock, & Co., 1877. Reprint. Detroit: Gale Research Co., 1974.

                The Addenda, indicated in this index by the code *A*, begins on page 638.

DcBrA	*Dictionary of British Artists Working 1900-1950.* Two volumes. By Grant M. Waters. Eastbourne, England: Eastbourne Fine Art Publications, 1975, 1976.

DcBrA 1	Volume I, 1975
DcBrA 2	Volume II, 1976

DcBrBI	*The Dictionary of British Book Illustrators and Caricaturists, 1800-1914.* With introductory chapters on the rise and progress of the art. By Simon Houfe. Woodbridge, England: Baron Publishing (for The Antique Collectors' Club), 1978.

Biographies begin on page 215.

DcBrWA	*The Dictionary of British Watercolour Artists up to 1920.* By H.L. Mallalieu. Woodbridge, England: Baron Publishing (for The Antique Collectors' Club), 1976.

DcCanB	*Dictionary of Canadian Biography.* Toronto: University of Toronto Press, 1966-1982.

DcCanB 9	*Volume IX: 1861 to 1870,* edited by Francess G. Halpenny, 1976
DcCanB 11	*Volume XI: 1881 to 1890,* edited by Henri Pilon, 1982

DcCathB	*Dictionary of Catholic Biography.* By John J. Delaney and James Edward Tobin. Garden City, New York: Doubleday & Co., Inc., 1961.

DcCAA	*A Dictionary of Contemporary American Artists.* By Paul Cummings. London: St. James Press; New York: St. Martin's Press, 1971, 1977.

DcCAA 71	Second edition, 1971
DcCAA 77	Third edition, 1977

DcCAr 81	*Dictionary of Contemporary Artists.* Edited by V. Babington Smith. Oxford, England and Santa Barbara, California: Clio Press, 1981.
DcCLAA	*A Dictionary of Contemporary Latin American Authors.* Compiled by David William Foster. Tempe, Arizona: Center for Latin American Studies, Arizona State University, 1975.
DcCM	*Dictionary of Contemporary Music.* Edited by John Vinton. New York: E.P. Dutton & Co., Inc., 1974.

This book ignores prefixes in filing surnames.

DcD&D	*Dictionary of Design & Decoration.* A Studio Book. New York: Viking Press, 1973.
DcEnA	*A Dictionary of English Authors, Biographical and Bibliographical.* Being a compendious account of the lives and writings of upwards of 800 British and American writers from the year 1400 to the present time. New edition, revised with an appendix bringing the whole up to date and including a large amount of new matter. By R. Farquharson Sharp. London: Kegan Paul, Trench, Trubner & Co., Ltd., 1904. Reprint. Detroit: Gale Research Co., 1978.

The Appendix, indicated in this index by the code *AP*, begins on page 311.

DcEnL	*Dictionary of English Literature: Being a Comprehensive Guide to English Authors and Their Works.* Second edition. By W. Davenport Adams. London: Cassell Petter & Galpin (n.d.). Reprint. Detroit: Gale Research Co., 1966.
DcEuL	*A Dictionary of European Literature.* Designed as a companion to English studies. Second, revised edition. By Laurie Magnus. London: George Routledge & Sons, Ltd.; New York: E.P. Dutton & Co., 1927. Reprint. Detroit: Gale Research Co., 1974.

The Appendix begins on page 595.

World War II. Two volumes. Edited by Stanley Weintraub, 1982.

DcLB 14	Volume 14: *British Novelists since 1960.* Two volumes. Edited by Jay L. Halio, 1983.
DcLB 15	Volume 15: *British Novelists, 1930-1959.* Two volumes. Edited by Bernard Oldsey, 1983.
DcLB 16	Volume 16: *The Beats: Literary Bohemians in Postwar America.* Two volumes. Edited by Ann Charters, 1983.
DcLB 17	Volume 17: *Twentieth-Century American Historians.* Edited by Clyde N. Wilson, 1983.
DcLB 18	Volume 18: *Victorian Novelists after 1885.* Edited by Ira B. Nadel and William E. Fredeman, 1983.
DcLB 19	Volume 19: *British Poets, 1880-1914.* Edited by Donald E. Stanford, 1983.
DcLB 20	Volume 20: *British Poets, 1914-1945.* Edited by Donald E. Stanford, 1983.
DcLB 21	Volume 21: *Victorian Novelists before 1885.* Edited by Ira B. Nadel and William E. Fredeman, 1983.
DcLB 22	Volume 22: *American Writers for Children, 1900-1960.* Edited by John Cech, 1983.
DcLB 23	Volume 23: *American Newspaper Journalists, 1873-1900.* Edited by Perry J. Ashley, 1983.
DcLB 24	Volume 24: *American Colonial Writers, 1606-1734.* Edited by Emory Elliott, 1984.
DcLB 25	Volume 25: *American Newspaper Journalists, 1901-1925.* Edited by Perry J. Ashley, 1984.
DcLB 26	Volume 26: *American Screenwriters.* Edited by Robert E. Morsberger, Stephen O. Lesser, and Randall Clark, 1984.

DcLB DS   *Dictionary of Literary Biography Documentary Series: An Illustrated Chronicle.* Detroit, Gale Research Co., 1982-1984.

DcLB DS1	Volume 1, edited by Margaret A. Van Antwerp, 1982
DcLB DS2	Volume 2, edited by Margaret A. Van Antwerp, 1982
DcLB DS3	Volume 3, edited by Mary Bruccoli, 1983
DcLB DS4	Volume 4, edited by Margaret A. Van Antwerp and Sally Johns, 1984

DcLB Y-   *Dictionary of Literary Biography Yearbook.* Detroit: Gale Research Co., 1981-1984.

DcLB Y80A	Yearbook: 1980. Edited by Karen L. Rood, Jean W. Ross, and Richard Ziegfeld, 1981. "Updated Entries" begin on page 3.
DcLB Y80B	Yearbook: 1980. "New Entries" begin on page 127.
DcLB Y81A	Yearbook: 1981. Edited by Karen L. Rood, Jean W. Ross, and Richard Ziegfeld, 1982. "Updated Entries" begin on page 21.
DcLB Y81B	Yearbook: 1981. "New Entries" begin on page 139.
DcLB Y82A	Yearbook: 1982. Edited by Richard Ziegfeld, 1983. "Updated Entries" begin on page 121.

	DcLB Y82B	Yearbook: 1982. "New Entries" begin on page 203.
	DcLB Y83A	Yearbook: 1983. Edited by Mary Bruccoli and Jean W. Ross, 1984. "Updated Entries" begin on page 155.
	DcLB Y83B	Yearbook: 1983. "New Entries" begin on page 175.
	DcLB Y83N	Yearbook: 1983. "Obituaries" begin on page 103.

DcLEL   *A Dictionary of Literature in the English Language.* Compiled and edited by Robin Myers. Oxford and New York: Pergamon Press, 1970, 1978.

DcLEL	*From Chaucer to 1940*, 1970
DcLEL 1940	*From 1940 to 1970*, 1978

DcNiCA   *Dictionary of 19th Century Antiques and Later Objets d'Art.* By George Savage. London: Barrie & Jenkins Ltd., 1978.

DcNAA   *A Dictionary of North American Authors Deceased before 1950.* Compiled by W. Stewart Wallace. Toronto: Ryerson Press, 1951. Reprint. Detroit: Gale Research Co., 1968.

DcOrL   *Dictionary of Oriental Literatures.* Three volumes. Jaroslav Prusek, general editor. New York: Basic Books, Inc., 1974.

DcOrL 1	Volume I: East Asia, edited by Zbigniew Slupski
DcOrL 2	Volume II: South and South-East Asia, edited by Dusan Zbavitel
DcOrL 3	Volume III: West Asia and North Africa, edited by Jiri Becka

DcPol   *A Dictionary of Politics.* Revised edition. Edited by Walter Laqueur. New York: Macmillan Publishing Co., Free Press, 1974.

DcRusL   *Dictionary of Russian Literature.* By William E. Harkins. New York: Philosophical Library, Inc., 1956. Reprint. Westport, Connecticut: Greenwood Press, 1971.

DcScB   *Dictionary of Scientific Biography.* 14 volumes and supplement. Edited by Charles Coulston Gillispie. New York: Charles Scribner's Sons, 1970-1976, 1978.

DcScB	Volumes I-XIV, 1970-1976
DcScB S1	Volume XV, Supplement I, 1978

DcSeaP   *Dictionary of Sea Painters.* By E.H.H. Archibald. Woodbridge, England: Antique Collectors' Club, Ltd., 1980.

Biographies begin on page 59.

DcSoc   *A Dictionary of Sociology.* Edited by G. Duncan Mitchell. Chicago: Aldine Publishing Co., 1968.

DcSpL   *Dictionary of Spanish Literature.* By Maxim Newmark. New York: Philosophical Library, Inc., 1956. Reprint. Totowa, New Jersey: Littlefield, Adams & Co., 1970.

DcVicP   *Dictionary of Victorian Painters.* By Christopher Wood. Suffolk, England: Baron Publishing (for The Antique Collectors' Club), 1971.

DrAF 76   *A Directory of American Fiction Writers.* Names and addresses of more than 800 contemporary fiction writers whose work has been published in the United States. 1976 edition. New York: Poets & Writers, Inc., 1976.

Use the Index to locate listings.

DrAP 75   *A Directory of American Poets.* Names and addresses of more than 1,500 contemporary poets whose work has been published in the United States. 1975 edition. New York: Poets & Writers, Inc., 1974.

           Use the Index, beginning on page vii, to locate listings.

DrAP&F 83   *A Directory of American Poets and Fiction Writers.* Names and addresses of 5,533 contemporary poets and fiction writers whose work has been published in the United States. 1983-1984 edition. New York: Poets & Writers, Inc., 1983.

           Use the Index to locate listings.

DrAS   *Directory of American Scholars.* Edited by Jaques Cattell Press. New York and London: R.R. Bowker Co., 1974, 1978, 1982.

DrAS 74H	Sixth edition, Volume 1: History
DrAS 74E	Sixth edition, Volume 2: English, Speech, & Drama
DrAS 74F	Sixth edition, Volume 3: Foreign Languages, Linguistics, & Philology
DrAS 74P	Sixth edition, Volume 4: Philosophy, Religion, & Law
DrAS 78H	Seventh edition, Volume 1: History
DrAS 78E	Seventh edition, Volume 2: English, Speech, & Drama
DrAS 78F	Seventh edition, Volume 3: Foreign Languages, Linguistics, & Philology
DrAS 78P	Seventh edition, Volume 4: Philosophy, Religion, & Law
DrAS 82H	Eighth edition, Volume 1: History
DrAS 82E	Eighth edition, Volume 2: English, Speech, & Drama
DrAS 82F	Eighth edition, Volume 3: Foreign Languages, Linguistics, & Philology
DrAS 82P	Eighth edition, Volume 4: Philosophy, Religion, & Law

DrBlPA   *Directory of Blacks in the Performing Arts.* By Edward Mapp. Metuchen, New Jersey: Scarecrow Press, Inc., 1978.

DrInf   *The Directory of Infamy: The Best of the Worst.* An illustrated compendium of over 600 of the all-time great crooks. By Jonathon Green. London: Mills & Boon, 1980.

           Use the Index to locate biographies.

DrLC 69   *Directory of Library Consultants.* Edited by John N. Berry, III. New York and London: R.R. Bowker Co., 1969.

DrRegL 75   *Directory of Registered Lobbyists and Lobbyist Legislation.* Second edition. Chicago: Marquis Academic Media, 1975.

           Use the "Lobbyist Index," beginning on page 451, to locate listings.

Dis&D   *Disease and Destiny: A Bibliography of Medical References to the Famous.* By Judson Bennett Gilbert. Additions and introduction by Gordon E. Mestler. London: Dawsons of Pall Mall, 1962.

Drake   Drake, Francis S. *Dictionary of American Biography, including Men of the Time.* Containing nearly 10,000 notices of persons of both sexes, of native and foreign birth, who have been remarkable, or prominently connected with the arts, sciences, literature, politics, or history, of the American continent. Giving also the pronunciation of many of the foreign and peculiar American names, a key to the assumed names of writers, and a supplement. Boston: James R. Osgood & Co., 1872. Reprint. Detroit: Gale Research Co., 1974.

           The Supplement, indicated in this index by the code *SUP*, begins on page 1015.

Dun&B 79   *Dun & Bradstreet Reference Book of Corporate Managements, 1979-1980.*
                 13th edition. New York: Dun & Bradstreet, Inc., 1979.

                       Use the Index to locate biographies.

EarABI   *Early American Book Illustrators and Wood Engravers, 1670-1870.* A
                 catalogue of a collection of American books illustrated for the most part with
                 woodcuts and wood engravings in the Princeton University Library with
                 supplement. By Sinclair Hamilton. Princeton, New Jersey: Princeton
                 University Press, 1958, 1968.

EarABI	Volume I: Main Catalogue, 1958
EarABI SUP	Volume II: Supplement, 1968

Ebony   *The Ebony Success Library.* Three volumes. By the Editors of *Ebony.* Volume 1:
                 1,000 Successful Blacks. Nashville: Southwestern Co., 1973.

EncAAH   *Encyclopedia of American Agricultural History.* By Edward L. Schapsmeier and
                 Frederick H. Schapsmeier. Westport, Connecticut and London: Greenwood
                 Press, 1975.

EncAB-A   *Encyclopedia of American Biography.* New Series. 40 volumes. New York and
                 West Palm Beach, Florida: The American Historical Society, 1934-1970.

                       Number after the source code indicates volume number. Use the Index
                       in each volume to locate biographies.

EncAB-H   *Encyclopedia of American Biography.* Edited by John A. Garraty. New York:
                 Harper & Row, Publishers, 1974.

EncAR   *Encyclopedia of the American Revolution.* By Mark Mayo Boatner, III. New
                 York: David McKay Co., Inc., 1966.

EncASM   *Encyclopedia of American Silver Manufacturers.* By Dorothy T. Rainwater.
                 New York: Crown Publishers, Inc., 1975.

EncE 75   *Encyclopedia of Espionage.* New edition. By Ronald Seth. London: New English
                 Library, 1975.

EncFCWM 69 *Encyclopedia of Folk, Country and Western Music.* By Irwin Stambler and
                 Grelun Landon. New York: St. Martin's Press, 1969.

EncJzS 70 *The Encyclopedia of Jazz in the Seventies.* By Leonard Feather and Ira Gitler.
                 New York: Horizon Press, 1976.

EncLatA   *Encyclopedia of Latin America.* Edited by Helen Delpar. New York: McGraw-
                 Hill Book Co., 1974.

EncMT   *Encyclopaedia of the Musical Theatre.* By Stanley Green. New York: Dodd,
                 Mead & Co., 1976.

EncMys   *Encyclopedia of Mystery and Detection.* By Chris Steinbrunner and Otto
                 Penzler. New York: McGraw-Hill Book Co., 1976.

EncO&P   *Encyclopedia of Occultism & Parapsychology.* A compendium of information on
                 the occult sciences, magic, demonology, superstitions, spiritism, mysticism,
                 metaphysics, psychical science, and parapsychology, with biographical and
                 bibliographical notes and comprehensive indexes. Two volumes and
                 supplements. Edited by Leslie Shepard. Detroit: Gale Research Co., 1978,
                 1980, 1981.

EncO & P 78	Main volumes, 1978
EncO & P 78S1	Occultism Update, Issue Number 1, 1978
EncO & P 80	Occultism Update, Issue Number 2, 1980
EncO & P 81	Occultism Update, Issue Numbers 3-4, 1981

EncPR&S   *Encyclopedia of Pop, Rock and Soul.* By Irwin Stambler. New York: St.
                 Martin's Press; London: St. James Press, 1974, 1977.

EncPR & S	1974 edition
EncPR & S 77	1977 edition

| | **EncPR & S 77S** | "Supplement" begins on page xvii. |

EncSF   *The Encyclopedia of Science Fiction: An Illustrated A to Z.* Edited by Peter Nicholls. London: Granada Publishing Ltd., 1979.

EncSoA   *Encyclopaedia of Southern Africa.* Sixth edition. Compiled and edited by Eric Rosenthal. London and New York: Frederick Warne & Co., Ltd., 1973.

EncSoB   *Encyclopedia of Southern Baptists.* Two volumes and supplement. Nashville: Broadman Press, 1958, 1971.

| | **EncSoB** | Two volumes, 1958 |
| | **EncSoB SUP** | Volume III, Supplement, 1971 |

EncSoH   *The Encyclopedia of Southern History.* Edited by David C. Roller and Robert W. Twyman. Baton Rouge and London: Louisiana State University Press, 1979.

EncTR   *Encyclopedia of the Third Reich.* By Louis L. Snyder. New York: McGraw-Hill Book Co., 1976.

EncUrb   *Encyclopedia of Urban Planning.* Edited by Arnold Whittick. New York: McGraw-Hill Book Co., 1974.

EncWL   *Encyclopedia of World Literature in the 20th Century.* Three volumes and supplement. Edited by Wolfgang Bernard Fleischmann. New York: Frederick Ungar Publishing Co., 1967, 1975. An enlarged and updated edition of the Herder *Lexikon der Weltliteratur im 20. Jahrhundert.*

EncWL 2   *Encyclopedia of World Literature in the 20th Century.* Revised edition. Four volumes. Volume 2: E to K, Volume 3: L to Q. Edited by Leonard S. Klein. New York: Frederick Ungar Publishing Co., 1982-1983.

Volume 4 forthcoming.

EncWM   *The Encyclopedia of World Methodism.* Two volumes. Edited by Nolan B. Harmon. Nashville: United Methodist Publishing House, 1974.

EncWT   *The Encyclopedia of World Theater.* Translated by Estella Schmid, edited by Martin Esslin. New York: Charles Scribner's Sons, 1977. Based on *Friedrichs Theaterlexikon*, by Karl Groning and Werner Kliess.

EuAu   *European Authors, 1000-1900: A Biographical Dictionary of European Literature.* Edited by Stanley J. Kunitz and Vineta Colby. New York: H.W. Wilson Co., 1967.

EvEuW   *Everyman's Dictionary of European Writers.* By W.N. Hargreaves-Mawdsley. London: J.M. Dent & Sons Ltd.; New York: E.P. Dutton & Co., Inc., 1968.

EvLB   *Everyman's Dictionary of Literary Biography, English and American.* Revised edition. Compiled after John W. Cousin by D.C. Browning. London: J.M. Dent & Sons Ltd; New York: E.P. Dutton & Co., Inc., 1960.

FamA&A   *Famous Actors and Actresses on the American Stage: Documents of American Theater History.* Two volumes. By William C. Young. New York and London: R.R. Bowker Co., 1975.

FamAIYP   *Famous Author-Illustrators for Young People.* By Norah Smaridge. New York: Dodd, Mead & Co., 1973.

FamAYP   *Famous Authors for Young People.* By Ramon P. Coffman and Nathan G. Goodman. New York: Dodd, Mead & Co., 1943.

FamMS   *Famous Modern Storytellers for Young People.* By Norah Smaridge. New York: Dodd, Mead & Co., 1969.

FamPYP   *Famous Poets for Young People.* By Laura Benet. New York: Dodd, Mead & Co., 1964.

FamSYP	*Famous Storytellers for Young People.* By Laura Benet. New York: Dodd, Mead & Co., 1968.
FarE&A	*The Far East and Australasia: A Survey and Directory of Asia and the Pacific.* London: Europa Publications Ltd., 1978, 1979, 1980, 1981. Distributed by Gale Research Co., Detroit, Michigan.

        FarE & A 78   1978-1979 edition
        FarE & A 79   1979-1980 edition
        FarE & A 80   1980-1981 edition
        FarE & A 81   1981-1982 edition

        Biographies are found in "Who's Who in the Far East and Australasia" at the back of each volume.

FemPA	*The Female Poets of America.* With portraits, biographical notices, and specimens of their writings. Seventh edition, revised. By Thomas Buchanan Read. Philadelphia: E.H. Butler & Co., 1857. Reprint. Detroit: Gale Research Co., 1978.
FifIDA	*Fifth International Directory of Anthropologists.* Current Anthropology Resource Series, edited by Sol Tax. Chicago: University of Chicago Press, 1975.
Film	*Filmarama.* Compiled by John Stewart. Metuchen, New Jersey: Scarecrow Press, Inc., 1975, 1977.

        Film 1   Volume I: *The Formidable Years, 1893-1919,* 1975

        Film 2   Volume II: *The Flaming Years, 1920-1929,* 1977

FilmgC	*The Filmgoer's Companion.* Fourth edition. By Leslie Halliwell. New York: Hill & Wang, 1974.
ForWC 70	*Foremost Women in Communications.* A biographical reference work on accomplished women in broadcasting, publishing, advertising, public relations, and allied professions. New York: Foremost Americans Publishing Corp., in association with R.R. Bowker Co., 1970.
ForIl	*Forty Illustrators and How They Work.* By Ernest W. Watson. Cincinnati: Watson-Guptill Publications, Inc., 1946. Reprinted by Books for Libraries Press, Freeport, N.Y., 1970.
FourBJA	*Fourth Book of Junior Authors and Illustrators.* Edited by Doris De Montreville and Elizabeth D. Crawford. New York: H.W. Wilson Co., 1978.
Future	*The Future: A Guide to Information Sources.* Second edition. Edited by Edward S. Cornish. Washington, D.C.: World Future Society, 1979.

        Biographies begin on page 125.

GolEC	*Golombek's Encyclopedia of Chess.* Edited by Harry Golombek. New York: Crown Publishers, Inc., 1977.
GoodHs	*The Good Housekeeping Woman's Almanac.* Edited by Barbara McDowell and Hana Umlauf. New York: Newspaper Enterprise Association, Inc., 1977.

        Use the Index to locate biographies.

GrBIl	*The Great Bird Illustrators and Their Art, 1730-1930.* By Peyton Skipwith. New York and London: Hamlyn Publishing Group Ltd., 1979.
Grk&L	*Greek and Latin Authors, 800 B.C.-A.D. 1000.* By Michael Grant. New York: H.W. Wilson Co., 1980.
GuPsyc	*A Guide to Psychologists and Their Concepts.* By Vernon J. Nordby and Calvin S. Hall. San Francisco: W.H. Freeman & Co., 1974.

HarEnUS   *Harper's Encyclopaedia of United States History: From 458 A.D. to 1915.* New edition entirely revised and enlarged. 10 volumes. By Benson John Lossing. New York and London: Harper & Brothers Publishers, 1915. Reprint. Detroit: Gale Research Co., 1974.

HerW   *Her Way: Biographies of Women for Young People.* By Mary-Ellen Kulkin. Chicago: American Library Association, 1976.

HisEWW   *The Historical Encyclopedia of World War II.* Edited by Marcel Baudot, et al. New York: Facts on File, Inc., 1980. Originally published as *Encyclopedie de la Guerre 1939-1945.* Paris and Tournai: Editions Casterman, 1977.

HolP   *Hollywood Players: The Forties.* By James Robert Parish and Lennard DeCarl. New Rochelle, New York: Arlington House Publishers, 1976.

HsB&A   *The House of Beadle and Adams and Its Dime and Nickel Novels: The Story of a Vanished Literature.* Two volumes and supplement. By Albert Johannsen. Norman, Oklahoma: University of Oklahoma Press, 1950, 1962.

    HsB & A   Volumes I-II, 1950, biographies are found in volume II.

    HsB & A SUP   Volume III, Supplement, Addenda, Corrigenda, 1962

IIBEAAW   *The Illustrated Biographical Encyclopedia of Artists of the American West.* By Peggy and Harold Samuels. Garden City, New York: Doubleday & Co., Inc., 1976.

IlDcG   *An Illustrated Dictionary of Glass.* 2,442 entries, including definitions of wares, materials, processes, forms, and decorative styles, and entries on principal glass-makers, decorators, and designers, from antiquity to the present. By Harold Newman. London: Thames & Hudson, Ltd., 1977.

IlEncJ   *The Illustrated Encyclopedia of Jazz.* By Brian Case and Stan Britt. New York: Harmony Books, 1978.

IlEncMy   *An Illustrated Encyclopaedia of Mysticism and the Mystery Religions.* By John Ferguson. London: Thames & Hudson Ltd., 1976.

IlEncRk   *The Illustrated Encyclopedia of Rock.* Compiled by Nick Logan and Bob Woffinden. London: Hamlyn Publishing Group Ltd., 1976; New York: Harmony Books, 1977.

IlrAm   *The Illustrator in America, 1900-1960's.* Compiled and edited by Walt Reed. New York: Reinhold Publishing Corp., 1966.

    IlrAm A   The Decade: 1900-1910, by Harold Von Schmidt
    IlrAm B   The Decade: 1910-1920, by Arthur William Brown
    IlrAm C   The Decade: 1920-1930, by Norman Rockwell
    IlrAm D   The Decade: 1930-1940, by Floyd Davis
    IlrAm E   The Decade: 1940-1950, by Al Parker
    IlrAm F   The Decade: 1950-1960, by Austin Briggs
    IlrAm G   The Decade: 1960's, by Bernard Fuchs
    Each article includes the signature of the biographee.

IlsBYP   *Illustrators of Books for Young People.* Second edition. By Martha E. Ward and Dorothy A. Marquardt. Metuchen, New Jersey: Scarecrow Press, Inc., 1975.

IlsCB   *Illustrators of Children's Books.* Boston: Horn Book, Inc., 1947, 1958, 1968, 1978.

    IlsCB 1744   *1744-1945.* Compiled by Bertha E. Mahony, Louise Payson Latimer, and Beulah Folmsbee, 1947. Biographies begin on page 267.

    IlsCB 1946   *1946-1956.* Compiled by Ruth Hill Viguers, Marcia Dalphin, and

	Bertha Mahony Miller, 1958. Biographies begin on page 62.
IlsCB 1957	*1957-1966.* Compiled by Lee Kingman, Joanna Foster, and Ruth Giles Lontoft, 1968. Biographies begin on page 70.
IlsCB 1967	*1967-1976.* Compiled by Lee Kingman, Grace Allen Hogarth, and Harriet Quimby, 1978. Biographies begin on page 93.

InB&W 80   *In Black and White.* A guide to magazine articles, newspaper articles, and books concerning more than 15,000 Black individuals and groups. Third edition. Two volumes. Edited by Mary Mace Spradling. Detroit: Gale Research Co., 1980.

InSci   *Index to Scientists of the World from Ancient to Modern Times: Biographies and Portraits.* By Norma Olin Ireland. Boston: F.W. Faxon Co., Inc., 1962.

InWom   *Index to Women of the World from Ancient to Modern Times: Biographies and Portraits.* By Norma Olin Ireland. Westwood, Massachusetts: F.W. Faxon Co., Inc., 1970.

IndAu 1816   *Indiana Authors and Their Books, 1816-1916.* Biographical sketches of authors who published during the first century of Indiana statehood with lists of their books. Compiled by R.E. Banta. Crawfordsville, Indiana: Wabash College, 1949.

IndAu 1917   *Indiana Authors and Their Books, 1917-1966.* A continuation of *Indiana Authors and Their Books, 1816-1916*, and containing additional names from the earlier period. Compiled by Donald E. Thompson. Crawfordsville, Indiana: Wabash College, 1974.

IntAu&W 76   *The International Authors and Writers Who's Who.* Seventh edition. Edited by Ernest Kay. Cambridge, England: Melrose Press, 1976.

IntAu & W 76	Biographical Section
IntAu & W 76A	Addendum begins on page 641.
IntAu & W 76X	"Pseudonyms of Included Authors" begins on page 645.

IntAu&W   *The International Authors and Writers Who's Who.* Edited by Adrian Gaster. Cambridge, England: International Biographical Centre, 1977, 1982. 1982 edition is combined with *International Who's Who in Poetry* (see below).

IntAu & W 77	Eighth edition, 1977, Biographical Section
IntAu & W 77X	"Pseudonyms of Included Authors" begins on page 1131.
IntAu & W 82	Ninth edition, 1982, Biographical Section
IntAu & W 82X	"Pseudonyms of Included Authors" begins on page 719.

IntDcWB   *The International Dictionary of Women's Biography.* Compiled and edited by Jennifer S. Uglow. New York: Continuum Publishing Co., 1982.

IntEnSS 79   *International Encyclopedia of the Social Sciences.* Volume 18: Biographical Supplement. Edited by David L. Sills. New York: Macmillan Publishing Co., Free Press, 1979.

IntMed 80   *International Medical Who's Who: A Biographical Guide in Medical Research.* First edition. Two volumes. Harlow, United Kingdom: Longman Group Ltd., Francis Hodgson, 1980. Distributed by Gale Research Co., Detroit, Michigan.

IntMPA   *International Motion Picture Almanac.* Edited by Richard Gertner. New York
                  and London: Quigley Publishing Co., Inc., 1975, 1976, 1977, 1978, 1979,
                  1981, 1982, 1984.

IntMPA 75	1975 edition
IntMPA 76	1976 edition
IntMPA 77	1977 edition
IntMPA 78	1978 edition
IntMPA 79	1979 edition
IntMPA 81	1981 edition
IntMPA 82	1982 edition
IntMPA 84	1984 edition

Biographies are found in the "Who's Who in Motion Pictures and
Television" section in each volume. The listings are identical to those
found in *The International Television Almanac.*

IntWW   *The International Who's Who.* London: Europa Publications Ltd., 1974, 1975,
                  1976, 1977, 1978, 1979, 1980, 1981, 1982, 1983. Distributed by Gale
                  Research Co., Detroit, Michigan.

IntWW 74	38th edition, 1974-1975
IntWW 75	39th edition, 1975-1976
IntWW 76	40th edition, 1976-1977
IntWW 77	41st edition, 1977-1978
IntWW 78	42nd edition, 1978-1979
IntWW 79	43rd edition, 1979-1980
IntWW 80	44th edition, 1980-1981
IntWW 81	45th edition, 1981-1982
IntWW 82	46th edition, 1982-1983
IntWW 83	47th edition, 1983-1984

The Obituary section, indicated in this index by the code *N*, is located at
the front of each volume.

IntWWE   *International Who's Who in Energy and Nuclear Sciences.* Compiled by the
                  Longman Editorial Team. Harlow, United Kingdom: Longman Group Ltd.,
                  1983. Distributed by Gale Research Co., Detroit, Michigan.

IntWWM 77   *International Who's Who in Music and Musicians' Directory.* Eighth edition.
                  Edited by Adrian Gaster. Cambridge, England: International Who's Who in
                  Music, 1977. Distributed by Gale Research Co., Detroit, Michigan. Earlier
                  editions published as *Who's Who in Music and Musicians' International
                  Directory* (see below).

IntWWP   *International Who's Who in Poetry.* Edited by Ernest Kay. Cambridge,
                  England: International Biographical Centre, 1977, 1982. 1982 edition is
                  combined with *International Authors and Writers Who's Who* (see above).

IntWWP 77	Fifth edition, 1977, Biographical Section
IntWWP 77A	Addendum begins on page 470.
IntWWP 77X	"Pseudonyms and Pen Names of Included Authors" begins on page 702.
IntWWP 82	Sixth edition, 1982, Biographical Section begins on page 759.
IntWWP 82X	"Pseudonyms of Included Poets" begins on page 1035.

IntYB   *The International Year Book and Statesmen's Who's Who.* West Sussex,
                  England: Kelly's Directories Ltd., 1978, 1979, 1980, 1981. Distributed by
                  Gale Research Co., Detroit, Michigan.

IntYB 78	1978 edition
IntYB 79	1979 edition
IntYB 80	1980 edition
IntYB 81	1981 edition

Biographies are found in Part 3 of each volume.

IntYB 82   *The International Yearbook and Statesmen's Who's Who.* West Sussex, England: Thomas Skinner Directories Ltd., 1982. Distributed by Gale Research Co., Detroit, Michigan.

Biographies are found in Part 3.

The "Late Information" section, indicated in this index by the code *A*, begins on page 749 of Part 3.

JBA 34   *The Junior Book of Authors.* An introduction to the lives of writers and illustrators for younger readers from Lewis Carroll and Louisa Alcott to the present day. First edition. Edited by Stanley J. Kunitz and Howard Haycraft. New York: H.W. Wilson Co., 1934.

JBA 51   *The Junior Book of Authors.* Second edition, revised. Edited by Stanley J. Kunitz and Howard Haycraft. New York: H.W. Wilson Co., 1951.

Law&B 80   *Law and Business Directory of Corporate Counsel, 1980-81.* New York: Harcourt Brace Jovanovich, Law & Business, Inc., 1980.

Entries are by corporation. Use the "Individual Name Index," beginning on page 1014, to locate listings.

LEduc 74   *Leaders in Education.* Fifth edition. Edited by Jaques Cattell Press. New York and London: R.R. Bowker Co., 1974.

LElec   *Leaders in Electronics.* New York: McGraw-Hill Book Co., 1979.

Title page reads *McGraw-Hill's Leaders in Electronics.*

LesBEnT   *Les Brown's Encyclopedia of Television.* By Les Brown. New York: New York Zoetrope, 1982. Previous edition published as *The New York Times Encyclopedia of Television* (see below).

LibW   *Liberty's Women.* Edited by Robert McHenry. Springfield, Massachusetts: G. & C. Merriam Co., 1980.

LinLib L   *The Lincoln Library of Language Arts.* Third edition. Two volumes. Columbus, Ohio: Frontier Press Co., 1978.

Biographies begin on page 345 of Volume 1 and are continued in Volume 2. The "Pen Names" section, indicated in this index by the code *LP*, begins on page 331.

LinLib S   *The Lincoln Library of Social Studies.* Eighth edition. Three volumes. Columbus, Ohio: Frontier Press Co., 1978.

Biographies begin on page 865 of Volume 3.

LivgBAA   *Living Black American Authors: A Biographical Directory.* By Ann Allen Shockley and Sue P. Chandler. New York and London: R.R. Bowker Co., 1973.

LongCEL   *Longman Companion to English Literature.* Second edition. By Christopher Gillie. London: Longman Group Ltd., 1977. Also published as *A Companion to British Literature.* Detroit: Grand River Books, 1980.

LongCTC   *Longman Companion to Twentieth Century Literature.* By A.C. Ward. London: Longman Group Ltd., 1970.

LuthC 75   *Lutheran Cyclopedia.* Revised edition. Edited by Erwin L. Lueker. St. Louis and London: Concordia Publishing House, 1975.

MGM   *The MGM Stock Company: The Golden Era.* By James Robert Parish and Ronald L. Bowers. New Rochelle, New York: Arlington House, 1973.

The "Capsule Biographies of MGM Executives," indicated in this index by the code *A*, begins on page 796.

MacDCB 78   *The Macmillan Dictionary of Canadian Biography.* Edited by W. Stewart Wallace. Fourth edition, revised, enlarged, and updated by W.A. McKay. Toronto: Macmillan of Canada, 1978.

MakMC   *Makers of Modern Culture.* Edited by Justin Wintle. New York: Facts on File, Inc., 1981.

McGDA   *McGraw-Hill Dictionary of Art.* Five volumes. Edited by Bernard S. Myers. New York: McGraw-Hill Book Co., 1969.

McGEWB   *The McGraw-Hill Encyclopedia of World Biography.* An international reference work in 12 volumes including an index. New York: McGraw-Hill Book Co., 1973.

McGEWD   *McGraw-Hill Encyclopedia of World Drama.* New York: McGraw-Hill Book Co., 1972, 1984.

McGEWD	First edition, an international reference work in four volumes, 1972
McGEWD 84	Second edition, an international reference work in five volumes, 1984

McGMS 80   *McGraw-Hill Modern Scientists and Engineers.* Three volumes. New York: McGraw-Hill Book Co., 1980.

MedHR   *Medal of Honor Recipients, 1863-1978.* Prepared by the Committee on Veterans' Affairs, United States Senate. 96th Congress, 1st Session, Senate Committee Print No. 3. Washington, D.C.: United States Government Printing Office, 1979.

　　　　　　　　Use the "Medal of Honor Alphabetical Index," beginning on page 1023, to locate biographies.

MnBBF   *The Men behind Boys' Fiction.* By W.O.G. Lofts and D.J. Adley. London: Howard Baker Publishers Ltd., 1970.

MichAu 80   *Michigan Authors.* Second edition. By the Michigan Association for Media in Education. Ann Arbor: Michigan Association for Media in Education, 1980.

　　　　　　　　The Addendum, indicated in this index by the code *A*, begins on page 339.

MidE   *The Middle East and North Africa.* London: Europa Publications Ltd., 1978, 1979, 1980, 1981, 1982. Distributed by Gale Research Co., Detroit, Michigan.

MidE 78	25th edition, 1978-1979
MidE 79	26th edition, 1979-1980
MidE 80	27th edition, 1980-1981
MidE 81	28th edition, 1981-1982
MidE 82	29th edition, 1982-1983

　　　　　　　　Biographies are found in "Who's Who in the Middle East and North Africa" at the end of each volume.

MinnWr   *Minnesota Writers: A Collection of Autobiographical Stories by Minnesota Prose Writers.* Edited and annotated by Carmen Nelson Richards. Minneapolis: T.S. Denison & Co., Inc., 1961.

　　　　　　　　Use the Table of Contents to locate biographies.

ModAL   *Modern American Literature.* Fourth enlarged edition. Four volumes. Compiled and edited by Dorothy Nyren Curley, Maurice Kramer, and Elaine Fialka Kramer. A Library of Literary Criticism. New York: Frederick Ungar Publishing Co., 1969, 1976.

ModAL	Volumes 1-3, 1969
ModAL SUP	Volume 4, Supplement, 1976

ModBlW   *Modern Black Writers.* Compiled and edited by Michael Popkin. A Library of Literary Criticism. New York: Frederick Ungar Publishing Co., 1978.

ModBrL   *Modern British Literature.* Four volumes. A Library of Literary Criticism. New York: Frederick Ungar Publishing Co., 1966, 1975.

ModBrL	Volumes I-III, compiled and edited by Ruth

		Z. Temple and Martin Tucker, 1966
	ModBrL SUP	Volume IV, Supplement, compiled and edited by Martin Tucker and Rita Stein, 1975

ModCmwL   *Modern Commonwealth Literature.* Compiled and edited by John H. Ferres and Martin Tucker. A Library of Literary Criticism. New York: Frederick Ungar Publishing Co., 1977.

ModFrL   *Modern French Literature.* Two volumes. Compiled and edited by Debra Popkin and Michael Popkin. A Library of Literary Criticism. New York: Frederick Ungar Publishing Co., 1977.

ModGL   *Modern German Literature.* Two volumes. Compiled and edited by Agnes Korner Domandi. A Library of Literary Criticism. New York: Frederick Ungar Publishing Co., 1972.

ModLAL   *Modern Latin American Literature.* Two volumes. Compiled and edited by David William Foster and Virginia Ramos Foster. A Library of Literary Criticism. New York: Frederick Ungar Publishing Co., 1975.

ModRL   *Modern Romance Literatures.* Compiled and edited by Dorothy Nyren Curley and Arthur Curley. A Library of Literary Criticism. New York: Frederick Ungar Publishing Co., 1967.

ModSL   *Modern Slavic Literatures.* Two volumes. A Library of Literary Criticism. New York: Frederick Ungar Publishing Co., 1972, 1976.

	ModSL 1	Volume I: Russian Literature, compiled and edited by Vasa D. Mihailovich, 1972
	ModSL 2	Volume II: Bulgarian, Czechoslovak, Polish, Ukrainian and Yugoslav Literatures, compiled and edited by Vasa D. Mihailovich, et al., 1976

Use the alphabetic listing of authors at the front of each volume to locate biographies.

ModWD   *Modern World Drama: An Encyclopedia.* By Myron Matlaw. New York: E.P. Dutton & Co., Inc., 1972.

MorBMP   *More Books by More People: Interviews with Sixty-Five Authors of Books for Children.* By Lee Bennett Hopkins. New York: Citation Press, 1974.

MorJA   *More Junior Authors.* Edited by Muriel Fuller. New York: H.W. Wilson Co., 1963.

MotPP   *Motion Picture Performers: A Bibliography of Magazine and Periodical Articles, 1900-1969.* Compiled by Mel Schuster. Metuchen, New Jersey: Scarecrow Press, Inc., 1971.

MouLC   *Moulton's Library of Literary Criticism of English and American Authors through the Beginning of the Twentieth Century.* Four volumes. Abridged, revised, and with additions by Martin Tucker. New York: Frederick Ungar Publishing Co., 1966.

	MouLC 1	Volume I: The Beginnings to the Seventeenth Century
	MouLC 2	Volume II: Neo-Classicism to the Romantic Period
	MouLC 3	Volume III: The Romantic Period to the Victorian Age
	MouLC 4	Volume IV: The Mid-Nineteenth Century to Edwardianism

Use the alphabetic listings at the front of each volume to locate biographies.

MovMk	*The Movie Makers.* By Sol Chaneles and Albert Wolsky. Secaucus, New Jersey: Derbibooks Inc., 1974.
	The "Directors" begins on page 506.
MugS	*Mug Shots: Who's Who in the New Earth.* By Jay Acton, Alan Le Mond, and Parker Hodges. New York: World Publishing Co., 1972.
MusSN	*Musicians since 1900: Performers in Concert and Opera.* Compiled and edited by David Ewen. New York: H.W. Wilson Co., 1978.
NamesHP	*Names in the History of Psychology: A Biographical Sourcebook.* By Leonard Zusne. Washington, D.C.: Hemisphere Publishing Corp., 1975. Distributed by John Wiley & Sons, Halstead Press, New York, New York.
	Use the "Alphabetic List of Names," beginning on page ix, to locate biographies.
NatCAB	*The National Cyclopaedia of American Biography.* 61 volumes. New York and Clifton, New Jersey: James T. White & Co., 1892-1982. Reprint. Volumes 1-50. Ann Arbor: University Microfilms, 1967-1971.
	Number after the source code indicates volume number. Use the Index in each volume to locate biographies.
NatPD	*National Playwrights Directory.* Edited by Phyllis Johnson Kaye. Waterford, Connecticut: The O'Neill Theater Center, 1977, 1981. Distributed by Gale Research Co., Detroit, Michigan.

NatPD	First edition, 1977
NatPD 81	Second edition, 1981

NegAl 76	*The Negro Almanac: A Reference Work on the Afro American.* Third edition. Edited by Harry A. Ploski and Warren Marr, II. New York: Bellwether Co., 1976.
	Use the Index to locate biographies.
NegAl 83	*The Negro Almanac: A Reference Work on the Afro-American.* Fourth edition. Compiled and edited by Harry A. Ploski and James Williams. New York and Toronto: John Wiley & Sons, 1983.
	Use the Index to locate biographies.
NewC	*The New Century Handbook of English Literature.* Revised edition. Edited by Clarence L. Barnhart with the assistance of William D. Halsey. New York: Appleton-Century-Crofts, 1967.
NewCBMT	*New Complete Book of the American Musical Theater.* By David Ewen. New York: Holt, Rinehart & Winston, 1970.
	Biographies are found in "Librettists, Lyricists and Composers" beginning on page 607.
NewEOp 71	*The New Encyclopedia of the Opera.* By David Ewen. New York: Hill & Wang, 1971.
NewRR 83	*The New Rock 'n' Roll.* By Stuart Coupe and Glenn A. Baker. New York: St. Martin's Press, 1983.
	Use the Index to locate biographies.
New YHSD	*The New-York Historical Society's Dictionary of Artists in America, 1564-1860.* By George C. Groce and David H. Wallace. New Haven, Connecticut and London: Yale University Press, 1957.
New YTBE	*The New York Times Biographical Edition: A Compilation of Current Biographical Information of General Interest.* New York: Arno Press, 1970-1973. Continued by *The New York Times Biographical Service* (see below).

NewYTBE 70	Volume 1, Numbers 1-12, 1970
NewYTBE 71	Volume 2, Numbers 1-12, 1971

NewYTBE 72	Volume 3, Numbers 1-12, 1972
NewYTBE 73	Volume 4, Numbers 1-12, 1973

Use the "Annual Index" to locate biographies.

New YTBS   *The New York Times Biographical Service: A Compilation of Current Biographical Information of General Interest.* New York: Arno Press, 1974-1981. A continuation of *The New York Times Biographical Edition* (see above).

NewYTBS 74	Volume 5, Numbers 1-12, 1974
NewYTBS 75	Volume 6, Numbers 1-12, 1975
NewYTBS 76	Volume 7, Numbers 1-12, 1976
NewYTBS 77	Volume 8, Numbers 1-12, 1977
NewYTBS 78	Volume 9, Numbers 1-12, 1978
NewYTBS 79	Volume 10, Numbers 1-12, 1979
NewYTBS 80	Volume 11, Numbers 1-12, 1980
NewYTBS 81	Volume 12, Numbers 1-12, 1981

Use the "Annual Index" to locate biographies.

New YTBS   *The New York Times Biographical Service: A Compilation of Current Biographical Information of General Interest.* Sanford, North Carolina: Microfilming Corp. of America, 1982-1983.

NewYTBS 82	Volume 13, Numbers 1-12, 1982
NewYTBS 83	Volume 14, Numbers 1-12, 1983

Use the "Annual Index" to locate biographies.

New YTET   *The New York Times Encyclopedia of Television.* By Les Brown. New York: New York Times Book Co., Inc., 1977. Expanded edition published as *Les Brown's Encyclopedia of Television* (see above).

NewbC   *Newbery and Caldecott Medal Books.* With acceptance papers, biographies and related material chiefly from the *Horn Book Magazine.* Edited by Lee Kingman. Boston: Horn Book, Inc., 1965, 1975.

NewbC 1956	*1956-1965*, 1965
NewbC 1966	*1966-1975*, 1975

Newb 1922   *Newbery Medal Books, 1922-1955.* With their authors' acceptance papers and related material chiefly from the *Horn Book Magazine.* Horn Book Papers, Volume 1. Edited by Bertha Mahony Miller and Elinor Whitney Field. Boston: Horn Book, Inc., 1955.

NotAW   *Notable American Women, 1607-1950: A Biographical Dictionary.* Three volumes. Edited by Edward T. James. Cambridge, Massachusetts: Harvard University Press, Belknap Press, 1971.

NotAW MOD   *Notable American Women: The Modern Period.* A biographical dictionary. Edited by Barbara Sicherman and Carol Hurd Green. Cambridge, Massachusetts and London: Harvard University Press, Belknap Press, 1980.

NotNAT   *Notable Names in the American Theatre.* Clifton, New Jersey: James T. White & Co., 1976. First edition published as *The Biographical Encyclopaedia and Who's Who of the American Theatre* (see above).

NotNAT	"Notable Names in the American Theatre" begins on page 489.
NotNAT A	"Biographical Bibliography" begins on page 309.
NotNAT B	"Necrology" begins on page 343.

This book often alphabetizes by titles of address, e.g.: Dr., Mrs., and Sir.

Novels   *Novels and Novelists: A Guide to the World of Fiction.* Edited by Martin Seymour-Smith. New York: St. Martin's Press, 1980.

Biographies are located in the "Novelists: An Alphabetical Guide" section beginning on page 87.

ObitOF 79	*Obituaries on File.* Two volumes. Compiled by Felice Levy. New York: Facts on File, 1979.
ObitT	*Obituaries from the Times.* Compiled by Frank C. Roberts. Reading, England: Newspaper Archive Developments Ltd., 1975, 1978, 1979. Distributed by Meckler Books, Westport, Connecticut.

ObitT 1951   *1951-1960,* 1979
ObitT 1961   *1961-1970,* 1975
ObitT 1971   *1971-1975,* 1978

ODwPR 79	*O'Dwyer's Directory of Public Relations Executives, 1979.* Edited by Jack O'Dwyer. New York: J.R. O'Dwyer Co., Inc., 1979.
OhA&B	*Ohio Authors and Their Books: Biographical Data and Selective Bibliographies for Ohio Authors, Native and Resident, 1796-1950.* Edited by William Coyle. Cleveland and New York: World Publishing Co., 1962.
OxAmH	*The Oxford Companion to American History.* By Thomas H. Johnson. New York: Oxford University Press, 1966.
OxAmL	*The Oxford Companion to American Literature.* Fourth edition. By James D. Hart. New York: Oxford University Press, 1965.
OxArt	*The Oxford Companion to Art.* Edited by Harold Osborne. Oxford: Oxford University Press, Clarendon Press, 1970.
OxCan	*The Oxford Companion to Canadian History and Literature.* Toronto: Oxford University Press, 1967, 1973.

OxCan   Original volume, by Norah Story, 1967, reprinted with corrections, 1968
OxCan SUP   Supplement, edited by William Toye, 1973

OxEng	*The Oxford Companion to English Literature.* Compiled and edited by Sir Paul Harvey. Fourth edition, revised by Dorothy Eagle. New York and Oxford: Oxford University Press, 1967.
OxFilm	*The Oxford Companion to Film.* Edited by Liz-Anne Bawden. New York and London: Oxford University Press, 1976.
OxFr	*The Oxford Companion to French Literature.* Compiled and edited by Sir Paul Harvey and J.E. Heseltine. Oxford: Oxford University Press, Clarendon Press, 1959. Reprinted with corrections, 1966.
OxGer	*The Oxford Companion to German Literature.* By Henry Garland and Mary Garland. Oxford: Oxford University Press, Clarendon Press, 1976.
OxLaw	*The Oxford Companion to Law.* By David M. Walker. Oxford: Oxford University Press, Clarendon Press, 1980.
OxMus	*The Oxford Companion to Music.* By Percy A. Scholes. 10th edition (corrected). Edited by John Owen Ward. London: Oxford University Press, 1974.
OxShips	*The Oxford Companion to Ships and the Sea.* Edited by Peter Kemp. London and New York: Oxford University Press, 1976.
OxSpan	*The Oxford Companion to Spanish Literature.* Edited by Philip Ward. Oxford: Oxford University Press, Clarendon Press, 1978.
OxThe	*The Oxford Companion to the Theatre.* Third edition. Edited by Phyllis Hartnoll. London: Oxford University Press, 1967.
OxTwCA	*The Oxford Companion to Twentieth-Century Art.* Edited by Harold Osborne. Oxford and New York: Oxford University Press, 1981.
PenC	*The Penguin Companion to World Literature.* New York: McGraw-Hill Book Co., 1969, 1971.

PenC AM   *The Penguin Companion to American Literature.* Edited by Malcolm Bradbury,

Eric Mottram, and Jean Franco, 1971.
Biographies are found in the "U.S.A."
and "Latin America" sections.

PenC CL

*The Penguin Companion to Classical,
Oriental and African Literature.* Edited
by D.M. Lang and D.R. Dudley, 1969.
Biographies are found in the "Classical,"
"Byzantine," "Oriental," and
"African" sections.

PenC ENG

*The Penguin Companion to English
Literature.* Edited by David Daiches, 1971.

PenC EUR

*The Penguin Companion to European
Literature.* Edited by Anthony Thorlby, 1969.

PhDcTCA 77   *Phaidon Dictionary of Twentieth-Century Art.* Second edition. Oxford: Phaidon Press Ltd.; New York: E.P. Dutton, 1977.

PiP   *The Pied Pipers: Interviews with the Influential Creators of Children's Literature.* By Justin Wintle and Emma Fisher. New York: Paddington Press Ltd., 1974.

Use the Table of Contents to locate biographies.

PlP&P   *Plays, Players, and Playwrights: An Illustrated History of the Theatre.* By Marion Geisinger. Updated by Peggy Marks. New York: Hart Publishing Co., Inc., 1975.

Use the Index, beginning on page 575, to locate biographies in the main section of the book. A Supplemental Index to the last chapter "The Theatre of the Seventies" begins on page 797, and is indicated in this index by the code *A*.

PoChrch   *The Poets of the Church: A Series of Biographical Sketches of Hymn-Writers with Notes on Their Hymns.* By Edwin F. Hatfield. New York: Anson D.F. Randolph & Co., 1884. Reprint. Detroit: Gale Research Co., 1978.

PoIre   *The Poets of Ireland: A Biographical and Bibliographical Dictionary of Irish Writers of English Verse.* By D.J. O'Donoghue. Dublin: Hodges Figgis & Co., Ltd.; London: Henry Frowde, Oxford University Press, 1912. Reprint. Detroit: Gale Research Co., 1968.

"The Poets of Ireland" begins on page 5. The Appendices begin on page 495.

PoLE   *The Poets Laureate of England.* Being a history of the office of poet laureate, biographical notices of its holders, and a collection of the satires, epigrams, and lampoons directed against them. By Walter Hamilton. London: Elliot Stock, 1879. Reprint. Detroit: Gale Research Co., 1968.

Use the Index to locate biographies.

Po&Wr 77   *The Poets & Writers, Inc. 1977 Supplement.* A complete update to *A Directory of American Poets* (1975) and *A Directory of American Fiction Writers* (1976). New York: Poets & Writers, Inc., 1977.

Use the Index to locate listings.

PolProf   *Political Profiles.* New York: Facts on File, Inc., 1976-1979.

PolProf E

The Eisenhower Years. Edited by
Eleanora W. Schoenebaum, 1977.

PolProf J

The Johnson Years. Edited by
Nelson Lichtenstein, 1976.

PolProf K

The Kennedy Years. Edited by
Nelson Lichtenstein, 1976.

PolProf NF

The Nixon/Ford Years. Edited by
Eleanora W. Schoenebaum, 1979.

PolProf T

The Truman Years. Edited by

Eleanora W. Schoenebaum, 1978.

Profile   *Profiles.* (Articles from *In Review: Canadian Books for Children,* published quarterly by the Ontario Provincial Library Service.) Revised edition. Edited by Irma McDonough. Ottawa: Canadian Library Association, 1975.

PrintW 83   *The Printworld Directory.* Edited by Selma Smith. Bala Cynwyd, Pennsylvania: Printworld, Inc., 1983.

Not in strict alphabetical order.

PseudAu   *Pseudonyms of Authors; Including Anonyms and Initialisms.* By John Edward Haynes. New York: John Edward Haynes, 1882. Reprint. Detroit: Gale Research Co., 1969.

The Addenda, indicated in this index by the code *A,* begin on page 104. Pseudonyms are given exactly as written by the author and are filed under the first letter of the pseudonym including the articles "a," "an," and "the."

PueRA   *Puerto Rican Authors: A Biobibliographic Handbook.* By Marnesba D. Hill and Harold B. Schleifer. Translation of entries into Spanish by Daniel Maratos. Metuchen, New Jersey: Scarecrow Press, Inc., 1974.

RAdv 1   *The Reader's Adviser: A Layman's Guide to Literature.* 12th edition. Volume 1: *The Best in American and British Fiction, Poetry, Essays, Literary Biography, Bibliography, and Reference.* Edited by Sarah L. Prakken. New York and London: R.R. Bowker Co., 1974.

Use the "Author Index," beginning on page 741, to locate biographies and bibliographies.

RComWL   *The Reader's Companion to World Literature.* Second edition. Revised and updated by Lillian Herlands Hornstein, Leon Edel, and Horst Frenz. New York and Scarborough, Ontario: New American Library, 1973.

REn   *The Reader's Encyclopedia.* Second edition. By William Rose Benet. New York: Thomas Y. Crowell Co., 1965.

REnAL   *The Reader's Encyclopedia of American Literature.* By Max J. Herzberg. New York: Thomas Y. Crowell Co., 1962.

REnAW   *The Reader's Encyclopedia of the American West.* Edited by Howard R. Lamar. New York: Thomas Y. Crowell Co., 1977.

REnWD   *The Reader's Encyclopedia of World Drama.* Edited by John Gassner and Edward Quinn. New York: Thomas Y. Crowell Co., 1969.

RGAfL   *A Reader's Guide to African Literature.* Compiled and edited by Hans M. Zell and Helene Silver. New York: Africana Publishing Corp., 1971.

Biographies begin on page 113.

RkOn   *Rock On: The Illustrated Encyclopedia of Rock 'n' Roll.* By Norm N. Nite. New York: Thomas Y. Crowell Co., 1974, 1978, 1982, 1984.

RkOn 74	Volume 1: *The Solid Gold Years,* 1974
RkOn 78	Volume 2: *The Modern Years: 1964-Present,* 1978
RkOn 78A	Volume 2: Appendix begins on page 543.
RkOn 82	Volume 1: *The Solid Gold Years,* Updated Edition, 1982
RkOn 84	Volume 2: *The Years of Change: 1964-1978,* Updated Edition, 1984.

Rk 100   *Rock 100.* By David Dalton and Lenny Kaye. New York: Grosset & Dunlap, 1977.

RolSEnR 83   *The Rolling Stone Encyclopedia of Rock & Roll.* Edited by Jon Pareles. New York: Rolling Stone Press/Summit Books, 1983.

ScF&FL	*Science Fiction and Fantasy Literature.* A checklist, 1700-1974, with *Contemporary Science Fiction Authors II.* By R. Reginald. Detroit: Gale Research Co., 1979.

ScF & FL 1	Volume 1: "Author Index" begins on page 3.
ScF & FL 1A	Volume 1: Addendum begins on page 581.
ScF & FL 2	Volume 2: *Contemporary Science Fiction Authors II*

SingR	*The Singing Roads: A Guide to Australian Children's Authors and Illustrators.* Arranged and edited by Hugh Anderson. Surry Hills: Wentworth Books.

SingR1	Part 1, fourth edition, 1972
SingR2	Part 2, 1970

SelBAA	*Selected Black American Authors: An Illustrated Bio-Bibliography.* Compiled by James A. Page. Boston: G.K. Hall & Co., 1977.
SenS	*A Sense of Story: Essays on Contemporary Writers for Children.* By John Rowe Townsend. London: Longman Group Ltd., 1971.
SixAP	*Sixty American Poets, 1896-1944.* Revised edition. Selected, with preface and critical notes by Allen Tate. Washington, D.C.: Library of Congress, 1954. Reprint. Detroit: Gale Research Co., 1969.
SmATA	*Something about the Author.* Facts and pictures about authors and illustrators of books for young people. Edited by Anne Commire. Detroit: Gale Research Co., 1971-1984.

SmATA 1	Volume 1, 1971
SmATA 2	Volume 2, 1971
SmATA 3	Volume 3, 1972
SmATA 4	Volume 4, 1973
SmATA 5	Volume 5, 1973
SmATA 6	Volume 6, 1974
SmATA 7	Volume 7, 1975
SmATA 8	Volume 8, 1976
SmATA 9	Volume 9, 1976
SmATA 10	Volume 10, 1976
SmATA 11	Volume 11, 1977
SmATA 12	Volume 12, 1977
SmATA 13	Volume 13, 1978
SmATA 14	Volume 14, 1978
SmATA 15	Volume 15, 1979
SmATA 16	Volume 16, 1979
SmATA 17	Volume 17, 1979
SmATA 18	Volume 18, 1980
SmATA 19	Volume 19, 1980
SmATA 20	Volume 20, 1980
SmATA 20N	Volume 20, Obituary Notices
SmATA 21	Volume 21, 1980
SmATA 21N	Volume 21, Obituary Notices
SmATA 22	Volume 22, 1981
SmATA 22N	Volume 22, Obituary Notices
SmATA 23	Volume 23, 1981
SmATA 23N	Volume 23, Obituary Notices
SmATA 24	Volume 24, 1981
SmATA 24N	Volume 24, Obituary Notices
SmATA 25	Volume 25, 1981
SmATA 25N	Volume 25, Obituary Notices
SmATA 26	Volume 26, 1982
SmATA 26N	Volume 26, Obituary Notices
SmATA 27	Volume 27, 1982
SmATA 27N	Volume 27, Obituary Notices
SmATA 28	Volume 28, 1982
SmATA 28N	Volume 28, Obituary Notices

SmATA 29	Volume 29, 1982
SmATA 29N	Volume 29, Obituary Notices
SmATA 30	Volume 30, 1983
SmATA 30N	Volume 30, Obituary Notices
SmATA 31	Volume 31, 1983
SmATA 31N	Volume 31, Obituary Notices
SmATA 32	Volume 32, 1983
SmATA 32N	Volume 32, Obituary Notices
SmATA 33	Volume 33, 1983
SmATA 33N	Volume 33, Obituary Notices
SmATA 34	Volume 34, 1984
SmATA 34N	Volume 34, Obituary Notices
SmATA 35	Volume 35, 1984
SmATA 35N	Volume 35, Obituary Notices
SmATA 36	Volume 36, 1984
SmATA 36N	Volume 36, Obituary Notices
SmATA 37	Volume 37, 1984
SmATA 37N	Volume 37, Obituary Notices
SmATA X	This code refers to pseudonym entries

which appear only as cross-references in the cumulative index to *Something about the Author.*

St&PR 75   *Standard and Poor's Register of Corporations, Directors and Executives.* Three volumes. Volume 2: *Directors and Executives.* New York: Standard & Poor's Corp., 1975.

Str&VC   *Story and Verse for Children.* Third edition. By Miriam Blanton Huber. New York: Macmillan Co., 1965.
Biographies begin on page 793.

TelT   *Tellers of Tales: British Authors of Children's Books from 1800 to 1964.* Revised edition. By Roger Lancelyn Green. New York: Franklin Watts, Inc., 1964.

TexWr   *Texas Writers of Today.* By Florence Elberta Barns. Dallas: Tardy Publishing Co., 1935. Reprint. Ann Arbor: Gryphon Books, 1971.

ThFT   *They Had Faces Then: Super Stars, Stars and Starlets of the 1930's.* By John Springer and Jack Hamilton. Secaucus, New Jersey: Citadel Press, 1974.

ThrBJA   *Third Book of Junior Authors.* Edited by Doris De Montreville and Donna Hill. New York: H.W. Wilson Co., 1972.

TwCA   *Twentieth Century Authors: A Biographical Dictionary of Modern Literature.* New York: H.W. Wilson Co., 1942, 1955.

TwCA	Original volume, edited by Stanley J. Kunitz and Howard Haycraft, 1942
TwCA SUP	First Supplement, edited by Stanley J. Kunitz, 1955

TwCBDA   *The Twentieth Century Biographical Dictionary of Notable Americans.* Brief biographies of authors, administrators, clergymen, commanders, editors, engineers, jurists, merchants, officials, philanthropists, scientists, statesmen, and others who are making American history. 10 volumes. Edited by Rossiter Johnson. Boston: The Biographical Society, 1904. Reprint. Detroit: Gale Research Co., 1968.

TwCCW   *Twentieth-Century Children's Writers.* Edited by D.L. Kirkpatrick. New York: St. Martin's Press, 1978, 1983.

TwCCW 78	"Twentieth-Century Children's Writers" begins on page 9.
TwCCW 78A	Appendix begins on page 1391.
TwCCW 78B	"Children's Books in Translation" begins on page 1481.

	TwCWW 83	"Twentieth-Century Children's Writers" begins on page 11.
	TwCWW 83A	Appendix begins on page 859.
	TwCWW 83B	"Foreign-Language Writers" begins on page 893.

TwCCr&M *Twentieth-Century Crime and Mystery Writers.* Edited by John M. Reilly. New York: St. Martin's Press, 1980.

	TwCCr & M 80	"Twentieth-Century Crime and Mystery Writers"
	TwCCr & M 80A	"Nineteenth-Century Writers" begins on page 1525.
	TwCCr & M 80B	"Foreign-Language Writers" begins on page 1537.

TwCLC *Twentieth-Century Literary Criticism.* Excerpts from criticism of the works of novelists, poets, playwrights, short story writers, and other creative writers who died between 1900 and 1960, from the first published critical appraisals to current evaluations. Detroit: Gale Research Co., 1978-1984.

TwCLC 1	Volume 1, 1978
TwCLC 2	Volume 2, 1979
TwCLC 3	Volume 3, 1980
TwCLC 4	Volume 4, 1981
TwCLC 5	Volume 5, 1981
TwCLC 6	Volume 6, 1982
TwCLC 7	Volume 7, 1982
TwCLC 8	Volume 8, 1982
TwCLC 9	Volume 9, 1983
TwCLC 10	Volume 10, 1983
TwCLC 11	Volume 11, 1983
TwCLC 12	Volume 12, 1984

TwCWr *Twentieth Century Writing: A Reader's Guide to Contemporary Literature.* Edited by Kenneth Richardson. Levittown, New York: Transatlantic Arts, Inc., 1971.

TwYS *Twenty Years of Silents, 1908-1928.* Compiled by John T. Weaver. Metuchen, New Jersey: Scarecrow Press, Inc., 1971.

TwYS	"The Players" begin on page 27
TwYS A	"Directors" begin on page 407

UFOEn *The UFO Encyclopedia.* By Margaret Sachs. New York: G.P. Putnam's Sons, 1980.

USBiR 74 United States. Department of State. *The Biographic Register, July, 1974.* Washington, D.C.: United States Government Printing Office, 1974.

Vers *The Versatiles.* A study of supporting character actors and actresses in the American motion picture, 1930-1955. By Alfred E. Twomey and Arthur F. McClure. South Brunswick, New Jersey and New York: A.S. Barnes & Co.; London: Thomas Yoseloff, Ltd., 1969.

Vers A	"Biographical Section" begins on page 25.
Vers B	"Non-Biographical Section" begins on page 249.

Ward *1977 Ward's Who's Who among U.S. Motor Vehicle Manufacturers.* Detroit: Ward's Communications, Inc., 1977.

Ward 77	"U.S. Big Four Biographical Section" begins on page 61.
Ward 77A	"The Independent Truck, Off-Highway and Farm Vehicle Manufacturers" begins on page 335.
Ward 77B	"The Importers" begins on page 355.
Ward 77C	"United Auto Workers" begins on page 371.

Ward 77D	"Government Agencies" begins on page 372.
Ward 77E	"Auto Associations" begins on page 376.
Ward 77F	"The Automotive Press" begins on page 387.
Ward 77G	"Where Are They Now?" begins on page 404.
Ward 77H	"Automotive Suppliers' Section" begins on page 449.

WebAB   *Webster's American Biographies.* Edited by Charles Van Doren. Springfield, Massachusetts: G. & C. Merriam Co., 1974, 1979.

WebAB	1974 edition
WebAB 79	1979 edition

WebAMB   *Webster's American Military Biographies.* Springfield, Massachusetts: G. & C. Merriam Co., 1978.

WebE&AL   *Webster's New World Companion to English and American Literature.* Edited by Arthur Pollard. New York: World Publishing Co., 1973.

WhDW   *Who Did What.* The lives and achievements of the 5000 men and women -- leaders of nations, saints and sinners, artists and scientists -- who shaped our world. Edited by Gerald Howat. New York: Crown Publishers, Inc., 1974.

WhAm HS   *Who Was Who in America, Historical Volume, 1607-1896.* A component volume of *Who's Who in American History.* Revised edition. Chicago: Marquis Who's Who, Inc., 1967.

   The Addendum, indicated in this index by the code *A*, begins on page 677.

WhAm 1   *Who Was Who in America, Volume I, 1897-1942.* A component volume of *Who's Who in American History.* Chicago: A.N. Marquis Co., 1943.

   The Corrigenda, indicated in this index by the code *C*, begin on page x.

WhAm 2   *Who Was Who in America, Volume II, 1943-1950.* A companion biographical reference work to *Who's Who in America.* Chicago: A.N. Marquis Co., 1963.

WhAm 2A	Addendum begins on page 12.
WhAm 2C	Corrigenda begin on page 5.

WhAm 3   *Who Was Who in America, Volume III, 1951-1960.* A component of *Who's Who in American History.* Chicago: Marquis Who's Who, Inc., 1966.

   The Addendum, indicated in this index by the code *A*, begins on page 952.

WhAm 4   *Who Was Who in America with World Notables, Volume IV, 1961-1968.* A component volume of *Who's Who in American History.* Chicago: Marquis-Who's Who, Inc., 1968.

   The Addendum, indicated in this index by the code *A*, begins on page 1049.

WhAm 5   *Who Was Who in America with World Notables, Volume V, 1969-1973.* Chicago: Marquis Who's Who, Inc., 1973.

WhAm 6   *Who Was Who in America with World Notables, Volume VI, 1974-1976.* Chicago: Marquis Who's Who, Inc., 1976.

WhAm 7   *Who Was Who in America with World Notables, Volume VII, 1977-1981.* Chicago: Marquis Who's Who, Inc., 1981.

WhAmP   *Who Was Who in American Politics.* A biographical dictionary of over 4,000 men and women who contributed to the United States political scene from colonial days up to and including the immediate past. By Dan and Inez Morris. New York: Hawthorn Books, Inc., 1974.

WhE&EA   *Who Was Who among English and European Authors, 1931-1949.* Based on entries which first appeared in *The Author's and Writer's Who's Who and Reference Guide*, originally compiled by Edward Martell and L.G. Pine, and in *Who's Who among Living Authors of Older Nations*, originally compiled by Alberta Lawrence. Three volumes. Gale Composite Biographical Dictionary Series, Number 2. Detroit: Gale Research Co., 1978.

WhFla   *Who Was Who in Florida.* Written and compiled by Henry S. Marks. Huntsville, Alabama: Strode Publishers, 1973.

WhJnl   *Who Was Who in Journalism, 1925-1928.* A consolidation of all material appearing in the 1928 edition of *Who's Who in Journalism*, with unduplicated biographical entries from the 1925 edition of *Who's Who in Journalism*, originally compiled by M.N. Ask (1925 and 1928 editions) and S. Gershanek (1925 edition). Gale Composite Biographical Dictionary Series, Number 4. Detroit: Gale Research Co., 1978.

         The "1925 Supplement," indicated in this index by the code *SUP*, begins on page 639.

WhLit   *Who Was Who in Literature, 1906-1934.* Based on entries that first appeared in *Literary Yearbook* (1906-1913), *Literary Yearbook and Author's Who's Who* (1914-1917), *Literary Yearbook* (1920-1922), and *Who's Who in Literature* (1924-1934). Two volumes. Gale Composite Biographical Dictionary Series, Number 5. Detroit: Gale Research Co., 1979.

WhNAA   *Who Was Who among North American Authors, 1921-1939.* Compiled from *Who's Who among North American Authors*, Volumes 1-7, 1921-1939. Two volumes. Gale Composite Biographical Dictionary Series, Number 1. Detroit: Gale Research Co., 1976.

WhScrn   *Who Was Who on Screen.* By Evelyn Mack Truitt. New York and London: R.R. Bowker Co., 1974, 1977.

         WhScrn   First edition, 1974
         WhScrn 2   Second edition, 1977

WhThe   *Who Was Who in the Theatre: 1912-1976.* A biographical dictionary of actors, actresses, directors, playwrights, and producers of the English-speaking theatre. Compiled from *Who's Who in the Theatre*, Volumes 1-15 (1912-1972). Four volumes. Gale Composite Biographical Dictionary Series, Number 3. Detroit: Gale Research Co., 1978.

WhWW-II   *Who Was Who in World War II.* Edited by John Keegan. London: Arms & Armour Press, 1978.

Who   *Who's Who.* An annual biographical dictionary. New York: St. Martin's Press; London: Adam & Charles Black Ltd., 1974, 1982, 1983.

         Who 74   126th Year of Issue, 1974-1975
         Who 82   134th Year of Issue, 1982-1983
         Who 83   135th Year of Issue, 1983-1984

         Each volume contains an Obituary section, indicated in this index by the code *N*, "The Royal Family" section, indicated in this index by the code *R*, and a Supplement, indicated in this index by the code *S*. The Supplement may contain up to three parts: "Additions," "Members of Parliament," and "New Year Honours List."

WhoAdv 72   *Who's Who in Advertising.* Second edition. Edited by Robert S. Morgan. Rye, New York: Redfield Publishing Co., 1972.

         Biographies are found in "U.S. Advertising Executives" beginning on page 1, "Canadian Advertising Executives" beginning on page 585, and the Addendum beginning on page 637.

WhoAdv 80   *Who's Who in Advertising.* Third edition. Edited by Catherine Quinn Serie. Monroe, New York: Redfield Publishing Co., Inc., 1980.

WhoAm	*Who's Who in America.* Chicago: Marquis Who's Who, Inc., 1974, 1976, 1978, 1980, 1982.	

WhoAm 74	38th edition, 1974-1975
WhoAm 76	39th edition, 1976-1977
WhoAm 78	40th edition, 1978-1979
WhoAm 80	41st edition, 1980-1981
WhoAm 82	42nd edition, 1982-1983

WhoAmA   *Who's Who in American Art.* Edited by Jaques Cattell Press. New York and London: R.R. Bowker Co., 1973, 1976, 1978, 1980, 1982.

WhoAmA 73	1973 edition
WhoAmA 76	1976 edition
WhoAmA 78	1978 edition
WhoAmA 80	1980 edition
WhoAmA 82	1982 edition

The Necrology, indicated in this index by the code *N*, is found at the end of each volume.

WhoAmJ 80   *Who's Who in American Jewry.* Incorporating *The Directory of American Jewish Institutions.* 1980 edition. Los Angeles: Standard Who's Who, 1980.

WhoAmL   *Who's Who in American Law.* Chicago: Marquis Who's Who, Inc., 1978, 1979, 1983.

WhoAmL 78	First edition, 1978
WhoAmL 79	Second edition, 1979
WhoAmL 83	Third edition, 1983

WhoAmM 83   *Who's Who in American Music: Classical.* First edition. Edited by Jaques Cattell Press. New York and London: R.R. Bowker Co., 1983.

WhoAmP   *Who's Who in American Politics.* Edited by Jaques Cattell Press. New York and London: R.R. Bowker Co., 1973, 1975, 1977, 1979, 1981, 1983.

WhoAmP 73	Fourth edition, 1973-1974
WhoAmP 75	Fifth edition, 1975-1976
WhoAmP 77	Sixth edition, 1977-1978
WhoAmP 79	Seventh edition, 1979-1980
WhoAmP 81	Eighth edition, 1981-1982
WhoAmP 83	Ninth edition, 1983-1984

Biographies in the later editions are divided by geographical areas. Use the Index to locate biographies.

WhoAmW   *Who's Who of American Women.* Chicago: Marquis Who's Who, Inc., 1958, 1961, 1963, 1965, 1967, 1969, 1971, 1973, 1975, 1978, 1979, 1981, 1983.

WhoAmW 58	First edition, 1958-1959
WhoAmW 61	Second edition, 1961-1962
WhoAmW 64	Third edition, 1964-1965
WhoAmW 66	Fourth edition, 1966-1967
WhoAmW 68	Fifth edition, 1968-1969
WhoAmW 70	Sixth edition, 1970-1971
WhoAmW 72	Seventh edition, 1972-1973
WhoAmW 74	Eighth edition, 1974-1975
WhoAmW 75	Ninth edition, 1975-1976
WhoAmW 77	Tenth edition, 1977-1978
WhoAmW 79	Eleventh edition, 1979-1980
WhoAmW 81	Twelfth edition, 1981-1982
WhoAmW 83	Thirteenth edition, 1983-1984

Earlier editions have Addenda, indicated in this index by the code *A*.

WhoArab 81   *Who's Who in the Arab World.* Sixth edition, 1981-1982. Edited by Gabriel M. Bustros. Beirut, Lebanon: Publitec Publications, 1981.

Biographies are located in Part III, beginning on page 651.

WhoArt	*Who's Who in Art.* Havant, England: Art Trade Press, Ltd., 1980, 1982. Distributed by Gale Research Co., Detroit, Michigan.

WhoArt 80	19th Edition, 1980
WhoArt 82	20th Edition, 1982

The Obituary section, indicated in this index by the code *N*, is located at the back of each volume.

WhoAtom 77   *Who's Who in Atoms.* Sixth edition. Edited by Ann Pernet. Guernsey, British Isles: Francis Hodgson, 1977.

WhoBbl 73   *Who's Who in Basketball.* By Ronald L. Mendell. New Rochelle, New York: Arlington House, 1973.

WhoBlA   *Who's Who among Black Americans.* Northbrook, Illinois: Who's Who among Black Americans, Inc., 1976, 1978, 1981.

WhoBlA 75	First edition, 1975-1976
WhoBlA 77	Second edition, 1977-1978
WhoBLA 80	Third edition, 1980-1981

WhoBox 74   *Who's Who in Boxing.* By Bob Burrill. New Rochelle, New York: Arlington House, 1974.

WhoBW&I   *Who's Who of Boys' Writers and Illustrators, 1964.* Edited and compiled by Brian Doyle. London: published by the author, 1964.

WhoBWI A	Author biographies begin on page 5.
WhoBWI I	Illustrator biographies begin on page 79.

WhoCan   *Who's Who in Canada.* An illustrated biographical record of men and women of the time in Canada. Toronto: International Press Ltd., 1973, 1975, 1977, 1980, 1982.

WhoCan 73	1973-1974 edition
WhoCan 75	1975-1976 edition
WhoCan 77	1977-1978 edition
WhoCan 80	1980-1981 edition
WhoCan 82	1982-1983 edition

Use the Index at the front of each volume to locate biographies.

WhoChL   *The Who's Who of Children's Literature.* Compiled and edited by Brian Doyle. New York: Schocken Books, 1968.

Biographies are found in "The Authors" beginning on page 1, and "The Illustrators" beginning on page 303.

WhoColR   *Who's Who of the Colored Race.* A general biographical dictionary of men and women of African descent. Volume one. Edited by Frank Lincoln Mather. Chicago: 1915. Reprint. Detroit: Gale Research Co., 1976.

The Addenda, indicated in this index by the code *A*, begin on page xxvi.

WhoCon 73   *Who's Who in Consulting.* A reference guide to professional personnel engaged in consultation for business, industry and government. Second edition. Edited by Paul Wasserman. Detroit: Gale Research Co., 1973.

WhoCtE 79   *Who's Who in Continuing Education: Human Resources in Continuing Library-Information-Media Education, 1979.* Compiled by CLENE, Inc. (The Continuing Library Education Network and Exchange.) New York and London: K.G. Saur, 1979. Distributed by Gale Research Co., Detroit, Michigan.

WhoE   *Who's Who in the East.* Chicago: Marquis Who's Who, Inc., 1974, 1975, 1977, 1979, 1981, 1983.

WhoE 74	14th edition, 1974-1975
WhoE 75	15th edition, 1975-1976
WhoE 77	16th edition, 1977-1978
WhoE 79	17th edition, 1979-1980
WhoE 81	18th edition, 1981-1982

	WhoE 83	19th edition, 1983-1984

WhoEc   *Who's Who in Economics: A Biographical Dictionary of Major Economists 1700-1981.* Edited by Mark Blaug and Paul Sturges. Cambridge, Massachusetts: MIT Press, 1983.

WhoEng 80   *Who's Who in Engineering.* Fourth edition. Edited by Jean Gregory. New York: American Association of Engineering Societies, Inc., 1980.

WhoF&I   *Who's Who in Finance and Industry.* Chicago: Marquis Who's Who, Inc., 1974, 1975, 1977, 1979, 1981, 1983.

WhoF & I 74	18th edition, 1974-1975
WhoF & I 75	19th edition, 1975-1976
WhoF & I 77	20th edition, 1977-1978
WhoF & I 79	21st edition, 1979-1980
WhoF & I 81	22nd edition, 1981-1982
WhoF & I 83	23rd edition, 1983-1984

WhoFla   *Who's Who in Florida, 1973/74.* A composite of biographical sketches of outstanding men and women of the State of Florida. First edition. Lexington, Kentucky and Acworth, Georgia: Names of Distinction, Inc., 1974.

WhoFtbl 74   *Who's Who in Football.* By Ronald L. Mendell and Timothy B. Phares. New Rochelle, New York: Arlington House, 1974.

WhoFr 79   *Who's Who in France: Qui est Qui en France.* 14th edition, 1979-1980. Dictionnaire biographique de personnalites francaises vivant en France, dans les territoires d'Outre-Mer ou a l'etranger et de personnalites etrangeres residant en France. Paris: Editions Jacques Lafitte, 1979.

"Liste des Personnalites Decedees," indicated in this index by the code *N*, begins on page cviii.

WhoGen 81   *Who's Who in Genealogy & Heraldry.* Volume 1. Edited by Mary Keysor Meyer and P. William Filby. Detroit: Gale Research Co., 1981.

"Late Additions," indicated in this index by the code *A*, begins on page 231.

WhoGolf   *Who's Who in Golf.* By Len Elliott and Barbara Kelly. New Rochelle, New York: Arlington House Publishers, 1976.

WhoGov   *Who's Who in Government.* Chicago: Marquis Who's Who, Inc., 1972, 1975.

WhoGov 72	First edition, 1972-1973
WhoGov 75	Second edition, 1975-1976

WhoGrA   *Who's Who in Graphic Art.* An illustrated book of reference to the world's leading graphic designers, illustrators, typographers and cartoonists. First edition. Edited by Walter Amstutz. Zurich: Amstutz & Herdeg Graphis Press, 1962. Distributed by Gale Research Co., Detroit, Michigan.

Use the "Index of Artists' Names," beginning on page 576, to locate biographies.

WhoGrA 82   *Who's Who in Graphic Art.* An illustrated world review of the leading contemporary graphic and typographic designers, illustrators and cartoonists. Volume Two. Edited and designed by Walter Amstutz. Dubendorf, Switzerland: De Clivo Press, 1982. Distributed by Gale Research Co., Detroit, Michigan.

Use the "Index of Artists' Names," beginning on page 886, to locate biographies.

WhoHcky 73   *Who's Who in Hockey.* By Harry C. Kariher. New Rochelle, New York: Arlington House, 1973.

WhoHol   *Who's Who in Hollywood, 1900-1976.* By David Ragan. New Rochelle, New York: Arlington House, 1976.

WhoHol A	"Living Players" begins on page 11.

| | WhoHol B | "Late Players (1900-1974)" begins on page 539. |
| | WhoHol C | "Players Who Died in 1975 and 1976" begins on page 845. |

WhoHr&F   Who's Who in Horror and Fantasy Fiction. By Mike Ashley. London: Elm Tree Books Ltd., 1977.

WhoIns   Who's Who in Insurance. Englewood, New Jersey: Underwriter Printing & Publishing Co., 1976, 1977, 1978, 1979, 1980, 1981, 1982, 1984.

WhoIns 76	1976 edition
WhoIns 77	1977 edition
WhoIns 78	1978 edition
WhoIns 79	1979 edition
WhoIns 80	1980 edition
WhoIns 81	1981 edition
WhoIns 82	1982 edition
WhoIns 84	1984 edition

The Addenda, indicated in this index by the code A, are located at the back of each volume.

WhoJazz 72   Who's Who of Jazz: Storyville to Swing Street. By John Chilton. Philadelphia: Chilton Book Co., 1972.

WhoLab 76   Who's Who in Labor. New York: Arno Press, 1976.

WhoLib 54   Who's Who in Librarianship. Edited by Thomas Landau. Cambridge, England: Bowes & Bowes Ltd., 1954.

WhoLib 72   Who's Who in Librarianship and Information Science. Second edition. Edited by T. Landau. London and New York: Abelard-Schuman, 1972.

WhoLibI 82   Who's Who in Library and Information Services. Edited by Joel M. Lee. Chicago: American Library Association, 1982.

WhoLibS 55   Who's Who in Library Service. A biographical directory of professional librarians of the United States and Canada. Third edition. Edited by Dorothy Ethlyn Cole. New York: Grolier Society, Inc., 1955.

WhoLibS 66   Who's Who in Library Service. A biographical directory of professional librarians in the United States and Canada. Fourth edition. Edited by Lee Ash. Hamden, Connecticut: Shoe String Press, Inc., 1966.

WhoLA   Who's Who among Living Authors of Older Nations. Covering the literary activities of living authors and writers of all countries of the world except the United States of America, Canada, Mexico, Alaska, Hawaii, Newfoundland, the Philippine Islands, the West Indies, and Central America. These countries are covered by our Who's Who among North American Authors. Volume 1, 1931-1932. Edited by A. Lawrence. Los Angeles: Golden Syndicate Publishing Co., 1931. Reprint. Detroit: Gale Research Co., 1966.

WhoMW   Who's Who in the Midwest. Chicago: Marquis Who's Who, Inc., 1974, 1976, 1978, 1980, 1982.

WhoMW 74	14th edition, 1974-1975
WhoMW 76	15th edition, 1976-1977
WhoMW 78	16th edition, 1978-1979
WhoMW 80	17th edition, 1980-1981
WhoMW 82	18th edition, 1982-1983

WhoMilH 76   Who's Who in Military History: From 1453 to the Present Day. By John Keegan and Andrew Wheatcroft. New York: William Morrow & Co., Inc., 1976.

WhoMus 72   Who's Who in Music and Musicians' International Directory. Sixth edition. New York: Hafner Publishing Co., Inc., 1972. Later editions published as International Who's Who in Music and Musicians' Directory (see above).

Key to Source Codes

WhoOcn 78   *Who's Who in Ocean and Freshwater Science.* First edition. Edited by Allen Varley. Essex, England: Longman Group Ltd., Francis Hodgson, 1978. Distributed by Gale Research Co., Detroit, Michigan.

WhoOp 76   *Who's Who in Opera.* An international biographical directory of singers, conductors, directors, designers, and administrators. Also including profiles of 101 opera companies. Edited by Maria F. Rich. New York: Arno Press, 1976.

WhoPNW   *Who's Who among Pacific Northwest Authors.* Second edition. Edited by Frances Valentine Wright. Missoula, Montana: Pacific Northwest Library Association, Reference Division, 1969.

Biographies are arranged alphabetically by state. Use the "Index of Authors" to locate listings.

WhoPRCh   *Who's Who in the People's Republic of China.* By Wolfgang Bartke. Armonk, New York: M.E. Sharpe Inc., 1981.

WhoPRCh 81	Biographical section
WhoPRCh 81A	Wade-Giles/Pinyin Conversion Table begins on page 719.
WhoPRCh 81B	"Biographies of Important Deceased and Purged Cadres" begins on page 573.

WhoPolA   *Who's Who in Polish America.* A biographical directory of Polish-American leaders and distinguished Poles resident in the Americas. Third edition. Edited by Francis Bolek. New York: Harbinger House, 1943. Reprint, The American Immigration Collection - Series II. New York: Arno Press and The New York Times, 1970.

WhoProB 73   *Who's Who in Professional Baseball.* By Gene Karst and Martin J. Jones, Jr. New Rochelle, New York: Arlington House, 1973.

WhoPubR   *Who's Who in Public Relations (International).* Edited by Adrian A. Paradis. Meriden, New Hampshire: PR Publishing Co., Inc., 1972, 1976.

WhoPubR 72	Fourth edition, 1972
WhoPubR 76	Fifth edition, 1976

WhoReal 83   *Who's Who in Real Estate: The Directory of the Real Estate Professions.* Boston and New York: Warren, Gorham & Lamont, Inc., 1983.

WhoRel   *Who's Who in Religion.* Chicago: Marquis Who's Who, Inc., 1975, 1977.

WhoRel 75	First edition, 1975-1976
WhoRel 77	Second edition, 1977

WhoRocM 82   *Who's Who in Rock Music.* By William York. New York: Charles Scribner's Sons, 1982.

WhoSciF   *Who's Who in Science Fiction.* By Brian Ash. London: Elm Tree Books Ltd., 1976.

WhoSocC 78   *Who's Who in the Socialist Countries.* A biographical encyclopedia of 10,000 leading personalities in 16 communist countries. First edition. Edited by Borys Lewytzkyj and Juliusz Stroynowski. New York: K.G. Saur Publishing, Inc., 1978. Distributed by Gale Research Co., Detroit, Michigan.

The Appendix, indicated in this index by the code *A*, begins on page 713.

WhoS&SW   *Who's Who in the South and Southwest.* Chicago: Marquis Who's Who, Inc., 1973, 1975, 1976, 1978, 1980, 1982.

WhoS & SW 73	13th edition, 1973-1974
WhoS & SW 75	14th edition, 1975-1976
WhoS & SW 76	15th edition, 1976-1977
WhoS & SW 78	16th edition, 1978-1979
WhoS & SW 80	17th edition, 1980-1981
WhoS & SW 82	18th edition, 1982-1983

WhoSpyF   *Who's Who in Spy Fiction.* By Donald McCormick. London: Elm Tree Books Ltd., 1977.

WhoStg 1906 *Who's Who on the Stage.* The dramatic reference book and biographical dictionary of the theatre. Containing records of the careers of actors, actresses, managers and playwrights of the American stage. Edited by Walter Browne and F.A. Austin. New York: Walter Browne & F.A. Austin, 1906.

               Some entries are not in alphabetic sequence.

WhoStg 1908 *Who's Who on the Stage, 1908.* The dramatic reference book and biographical dictionary of the theatre. Containing careers of actors, actresses, managers and playwrights of the American stage. Edited by Walter Browne and E. De Roy Koch. New York: B.W. Dodge & Co., 1908.

               Some entries are not in alphabetic sequence.

WhoTech 82   *Who's Who in Technology Today.* Third edition. Four volumes. Edited by Jan W. Churchwell. Highland Park, Illinois: J. Dick & Co., 1982.

               Use the "Index of Names," beginning on page 667 of Volume 4, to locate biographies.

WhoThe   *Who's Who in the Theatre: A Biographical Record of the Contemporary Stage.* London: Pitman Publishing Ltd.; Detroit: Gale Research Co., 1972, 1977, 1981.

WhoThe 15	15th edition, compiled by John Parker, 1972
WhoThe 16	16th edition, edited by Ian Herbert, 1977
WhoThe 81	17th edition, edited by Ian Herbert, 1981
WhoThe 81N	17th edition, Obituary section begins on page 743.

WhoTr&F 73   *Who's Who in Track and Field.* By Reid M. Hanley. New Rochelle, New York: Arlington House, 1973.

WhoTran   *Who's Who in Translating and Interpreting.* Compiled by A. Flegon. London: Flegon Press, 1967.

WhoTran AFR	Afrikaans section begins on page 5.
WhoTran ALB	Albanian section begins on page 5.
WhoTran ARB	Arabic section begins on page 5.
WhoTran BEL	Belorussian section begins on page 9.
WhoTran BUL	Bulgarian section begins on page 9.
WhoTran CHI	Chinese section begins on page 11.
WhoTran CZE	Czech section begins on page 12.
WhoTran DAN	Danish section begins on page 16.
WhoTran DUT	Dutch section begins on page 18.
WhoTran ESP	Esperanto section begins on page 29.
WhoTran EST	Estonian section begins on page 29.
WhoTran FIN	Finnish section begins on page 30.
WhoTran FLE	Flemish section begins on page 30.
WhoTran FRE	French section begins on page 32.
WhoTran GER	German section begins on page 70.
WhoTran GRE	Greek section begins on page 110.
WhoTran HEB	Hebrew section begins on page 112.
WhoTran HIN	Hindi section begins on page 112.
WhoTran HUN	Hungarian section begins on page 113.
WhoTran ICE	Icelandic section begins on page 116.
WhoTran IND	Indonesian section begins on page 116.
WhoTran INT	Interlingua section begins on page 116.
WhoTran IRI	Irish section begins on page 117.
WhoTran ITA	Italian section begins on page 118.
WhoTran JAP	Japanese section begins on page 130.
WhoTran LAT	Latvian section begins on page 132.
WhoTran LIT	Lithuanian section begins on page 133.

WhoTran MLY	Malay section begins on page 133.
WhoTran MLT	Maltese section begins on page 134.
WhoTran NOR	Norwegian section begins on page 136.
WhoTran POL	Polish section begins on page 137.
WhoTran POR	Portuguese section begins on page 143.
WhoTran RUM	Rumanian section begins on page 146.
WhoTran RUS	Russian section begins on page 148.
WhoTran SAN	Sanskrit section begins on page 162.
WhoTran SCA	Scandinavian section begins on page 162.
WhoTran SER	Serbo-Croat section begins on page 162.
WhoTran SPA	Spanish section begins on page 164.
WhoTran SWA	Swahili section begins on page 182.
WhoTran SWE	Swedish section begins on page 183.
WhoTran TUR	Turkish section begins on page 187.
WhoTran UKR	Ukranian section begins on page 188.

WhoTwCL   *Who's Who in Twentieth Century Literature.* By Martin Seymour-Smith. New York: Holt, Rinehart & Winston, 1976.

WhoUN 75   *Who's Who in the United Nations and Related Agencies.* New York: Arno Press, 1975.

WhoWest   *Who's Who in the West.* Chicago: Marquis Who's Who, Inc., 1974, 1976, 1978, 1980, 1982, 1983.

WhoWest 74	14th edition, 1974-1975
WhoWest 76	15th edition, 1976-1977
WhoWest 78	16th edition, 1978-1979
WhoWest 80	17th edition, 1980-1981
WhoWest 82	18th edition, 1982-1983
WhoWest 84	19th edition, 1984-1985

WhoWor   *Who's Who in the World.* Chicago: Marquis Who's Who, Inc., 1973, 1976, 1978, 1980, 1982.

WhoWor 74	Second edition, 1974-1975
WhoWor 76	Third edition, 1976-1977
WhoWor 78	Fourth edition, 1978-1979
WhoWor 80	Fifth edition, 1980-1981
WhoWor 82	Sixth edition, 1982-1983

WhoWorJ 72   *Who's Who in World Jewry: A Biographical Dictionary of Outstanding Jews.* Edited by I.J. Carmin Karpman. New York: Pitman Publishing Corp., Inc., 1972.

WhoWorJ 78   *Who's Who in World Jewry: A Biographical Dictionary of Outstanding Jews.* Edited by I.J. Carmin Karpman. Tel-Aviv, Israel: Olive Books of Israel, 1978.

WisWr   *Wisconsin Writers: Sketches and Studies.* By William A. Titus. Chicago: 1930. Reprint. Detroit: Gale Research Co., 1974.
Use the Table of Contents to locate biographies.

WomArt   *Women Artists: An Historical, Contemporary and Feminist Bibliography.* By Donna G. Bachmann and Sherry Piland. Metuchen, New Jersey and London: Scarecrow Press, Inc., 1978.
Use the Table of Contents to locate biographies which begin on page 47. The Addenda, indicated in this index by the code *A*, begin on page 322.

WomPO 76   *Women in Public Office: A Biographical Directory and Statistical Analysis.* Compiled by Center for the American Woman and Politics. New York and London: R.R. Bowker Co., 1976.
Use the "Name Index" to locate listings.

WomPO 78   *Women in Public Office: A Biographical Directory and Statistical Analysis.* Second edition. Compiled by Center for the American Woman and Politics.

        Metuchen, New Jersey and London: Scarecrow Press, Inc., 1978.

        Use the "Name Index" to locate listings.

WomWMM   *Women Who Make Movies.* Cinema Study Series. By Sharon Smith. New York: Hopkinson & Blake, 1975.

            WomWMM   "Overview" section. Biographies can be located through the index beginning on page 299.

            WomWMM A   "The New Filmmakers" begins on page 145.

            WomWMM B   "Directory" begins on page 221.

WomWWA 14   *Woman's Who's Who of America.* A biographical dictionary of contemporary women of the United States and Canada, 1914-1915. Edited by John William Leonard. New York: American Commonwealth Co., 1914. Reprint. Detroit: Gale Research Co., 1976.

        The "Addenda and Corrections" and "Deaths during Printing" sections, indicated in this index by the code *A*, begin on page 29.

WorAl   *The World Almanac Book of Who.* Edited by Hana Umlauf Lane. New York: World Almanac Publications, 1980.

        Use the "Name Index," beginning on page 326, to locate biographies.

WorAu   *World Authors.* A volume in the Wilson Authors Series. Edited by John Wakeman. New York: H.W. Wilson Co., 1975, 1980.

            WorAu   1950-1970, 1975

            WorAu 1970   1970-1975, 1980

WorDWW   *World Defence Who's Who.* Edited by Paul Martell and Grace P. Hayes. London: Macdonald & Jane's, 1974.

WorECar   *The World Encyclopedia of Cartoons.* Two volumes. Edited by Maurice Horn. Detroit: Gale Research Co., 1980. Published in association with Chelsea House Publishers, New York and London.

        The "Notes on the Contributors" section, indicated in this index by the code *A*, begins on page 631.

WorECom   *The World Encyclopedia of Comics.* Two volumes. Edited by Maurice Horn. New York: Chelsea House Publishers, 1976.

        Biographies begin on page 65.

WorEFlm   *The World Encyclopedia of the Film.* Edited by John M. Smith and Tim Cawkwell. New York: A. & W. Visual Library, 1972.

WorFshn   *World of Fashion: People, Places, Resources.* By Eleanor Lambert. New York and London: R.R. Bowker Co., 1976.

        Use the "Name Index," beginning on page 351, to locate biographies.

WrDr   *The Writers Directory.* London: St. James Press; New York: St. Martin's Press, 1976, 1979.

            WrDr 76   1976-1978 edition

            WrDr 80   1980-1982 edition

WrDr 82   *The Writers Directory.* 1982-1984 edition. Detroit: Gale Research Co., 1981.

WrDr 84   *The Writers Directory.* 1984-1986 edition. Chicago: St. James Press, 1983. Distributed by Gale Research Co., Detroit, Michigan.

YABC   *Yesterday's Authors of Books for Children.* Facts and pictures about authors and illustrators of books for young people, from early times to 1960. Edited by Anne Commire. Detroit: Gale Research Co., 1977-1978.

            YABC 1   Volume 1, 1977

            YABC 2   Volume 2, 1978

YABC X

This code refers to pseudonym entries which appear only as cross-references in the cumulative index to *Yesterday's Authors of Books for Children.*

WRITERS FOR YOUNG ADULTS:
BIOGRAPHIES
MASTER INDEX

A

Aaron, Chester 1923- *AuBYP SUP*,
BioIn 11, *ConAu 8NR*, *-21R*,
SmATA 9, *TwCCW 83*, *WhoWest 74*
Aaron, Hank 1934- *BioIn 12*, *BioNews 74*,
BlueB 76, *CelR 73*, *ConAu X*,
CurBio 58, *NegAl 76 [port]*, *-83 [port]*
Aaron, Hank *see also* Aaron, Henry
Aaron, Henry 1934- *BioIn 4*, *-5*, *-6*, *-7*, *-8*, *-9*,
-10, *-11*, *-12*, *ConAu 104*, *CurBio 58*,
Ebony 1, *InB&W 80*, *NewYTBE 72*, *-73*,
NewYTBS 74, *-75*, *-76*, *WebAB*, *-79*,
WhoAm 74, *-76*, *-78*, *-80*, *-82*, *WhoBlA 75*,
-77, *-80*, *WhoProB 73*, *WorAl*
Aaron, Henry *see also* Aaron, Hank
Aaseng, Nate 1953- *ConAu X*
Aaseng, Nathan 1953- *ConAu 106*
Abbey, Edward 1927- *BioIn 10*, *-11*, *-12*,
ConAu 2NR, *-45*, *DrAF 76*, *DrAP&F 83*,
WrDr 80, *-82*, *-84*
Abbott, Berenice 1898- *AmAu&B*, *BioIn 1*, *-7*,
-9, *-10*, *-11*, *-12*, *BnEnAmA*, *ConAu 106*,
ConPhot, *CurBio 42*, *GoodHs*, *InWom*,
IntDcWB, *NewYTBS 80[port]*, *-83[port]*,
WhoAm 82, *WhoAmW 58*, *WomArt*,
WorAl
Abbott, Edwin Abbott 1838-1926 *Alli SUP*,
CelCen, *EncSF*, *NewC*, *ScF&FL 1*,
WhLit
Abbott, Frank Frost 1860-1924 *AmLY*,
DcAmAu, *DcNAA*, *WhAm 1*
Abbott, Jack Henry 1944- *BioIn 12*, *ConAu X*,
ConIsC 2[port]
Abbott, R Tucker 1919- *ConAu 4NR*, *-9R*,
IntAu&W 76, *-77*, *WrDr 82*, *-84*
Abbott, Robert Tucker 1919- *AmM&WS 73P*,
-76P, *-79P*, *AuBYP SUP*, *ConAu 9R*,
WhoAm 76, *-80*, *-82*, *WhoE 74*,
WhoOcn 78, *WrDr 76*, *-80*
Abdul, Raoul 1929- *BioIn 11*, *ChhPo S2*,
ConAu 29R, *DrBlPA*, *InB&W 80*,
SelBAA, *SmATA 12*, *WhoBlA 75*, *-77*,
-80, *WhoE 77*, *-79*, *-81*
Abdul-Jabbar, Kareem 1947- *BioIn 9*, *-10*, *-11*,
-12, *CelR 73*, *CmCal*, *Ebony 1*,
NegAl 76, *-83[port]*, *NewYTBS 74*, *-76*,
-82[port], *WhoAm 74*, *-76*, *-78*, *-80*, *-82*,
WhoBbl 73, *WhoBlA 80*, *WorAl*
Abe, Kobo 1924- *BioIn 7*, *-10*, *-12*, *CasWL*,

ConAu 65, *ConLC 8*, *-22[port]*, *DcOrL 1*,
EncSF, *EncWL*, *-81*, *FarE&A 78*, *-79*,
-80, *-81*, *IntAu&W 76*, *-77*, *IntWW 74*,
-75, *-76*, *-77*, *-78*, *-79*, *-80*, *-81*, *-82*, *-83*,
MakMC, *McGEWD 84*, *NewYTBS 74*,
-79, *ScF&FL 1*, *WhoSciF*, *WhoWor 74*,
-76, *-78*, *-82*, *WorAu*
Abel, Elie 1920- *CanWW 70*, *-79*, *-80*, *-81*,
-83, *ConAu 8NR*, *-61*, *LEduc 74*,
LesBEnT[port], *WhoAm 74*, *-76*, *-78*, *-80*,
-82, *WhoE 74*, *WhoWor 74*, *-76*,
WhoWorJ 72
Abell, George Ogden 1927- *AmM&WS 73P*,
-76P, *-79P*, *-82P*, *ConAu 3NR*, *-9R*,
WhoAm 74, *-76*, *-78*, *-80*, *-82*,
WhoWest 82, *-84*, *WhoWor 74*, *WrDr 76*,
-80, *-82*, *-84*
Abels, Jules 1913- *ConAu 61*, *WhoAm 74*,
-76
Abercrombie, Barbara 1939- *BioIn 12*,
ConAu 81, *SmATA 16*
Abernethy, Robert Gordon 1927- *BioIn 10*,
ConAu 21R, *SmATA 5*, *WhoAm 74*, *-76*,
-78, *-80*, *-82*
Abodaher, David J 1919- *AuBYP SUP*,
BioIn 12, *ConAu 10NR*, *-17R*,
MichAu 80, *SmATA 17*
Abrahams, Peter 1919- *AfrA*, *Au&Wr 6*,
BioIn 3, *-4*, *-8*, *-9*, *-10*, *-12*, *CasWL*,
ConAu 57, *ConLC 4*, *ConNov 76*, *-82*,
CurBio 57, *DcLEL 1940*, *EncWL 81*,
InB&W 80, *IntAu&W 76*, *-77*, *ModBlW*,
Novels, *PenC ENG*, *RGAfL*, *TwCWr*,
WebE&AL, *WhE&EA*, *WhoWor 74*,
WorAu, *WrDr 76*, *-80*, *-82*, *-84*
Abrahams, Robert David 1905- *AmAu&B*,
AuBYP, *BioIn 8*, *-9*, *ConAu P-2*,
SmATA 4, *WhE&EA*, *WhoAm 74*, *-76*,
-78, *-80*, *-82*, *WhoAmL 83*, *WhoE 74*,
WhoWor 76, *-82*, *WhoWorJ 72*, *-78*
Abrahams, Roger David 1933- *ConAu 5NR*,
-9R, *DrAS 74E*, *-78E*, *-82E*, *FifIDA*,
IntAu&W 76, *-77*, *WhoAm 76*, *-78*, *-80*,
-82, *WhoWor 78*, *WrDr 76*, *-80*, *-82*, *-84*
Abramovitz, Anita Zeltner Brooks 1914-
ConAu 97, *WhoAmW 74*, *-66*, *-68*, *-70*,
-72, *-79*, *-81*, *WhoE 81*, *-83*
Abrams, Joy 1941- *BioIn 12*, *ConAu 77*,

1

SmATA 16
Abzug, Robert Henry 1945- ConAu 104,
  DrAS 78H, -82H
Achebe, Chinua 1930- AfSS 78, -79, -80, -81,
  -82, AfrA, Au&Wr 6, BioIn 7, -8, -9,
  -10, -12, CasWL, ConAu 1R, -6NR,
  ConLC 1, -3, -5, -7, -11, -26[port],
  ConNov 72, -76, -82, ConP 75, -80,
  DcLEL 1940, EncWL, -81[port],
  InB&W 80, IntAu&W 76, -77, -82,
  IntWW 74, -75, -76, -77, -78, -79, -80, -81,
  -82, -83, LinLib L, LongCTC, McGEWB,
  ModBlW, ModCmwL, Novels, PenC CL,
  -ENG, RGAfL, TwCCW 83, TwCWr,
  WebE&AL, Who 74, -82, -83, WhoTwCL,
  WhoWor 74, -80, -82, WorAu, WrDr 76,
  -80, -82, -84
Acheson, Patricia Castles 1924- AuBYP,
  BioIn 8, ConAu 1R
Ackart, Robert 1921- ConAu 109
Ackerman, Diane 1948- ConAu 57, DrAP 75,
  DrAP&F 83, DrAS 82E, IntWWP 77,
  -82, WhoE 83
Ackley, Edith Flack InWom
Acton, Jay 1949- ConAu X, -45
Adair, Margaret Weeks d1971 BioIn 11,
  ConAu P-1, SmATA 10
Adam, Helen 1909- ChhPo S2, ConAu 7NR,
  -17R, ConP 70, -80, DrAP 75,
  IntWWP 77, WhoAm 82, WrDr 82, -84
Adams, Alice 1926- BioIn 7, -11, ConAu 81,
  ConLC 6, -13, WhoAm 80, -82, WrDr 84
Adams, Andy 1859-1935 AmAu&B, AmLY,
  BiDSA, BioIn 2, -7, -8, -11, CnDAL,
  DcAmAu, DcAmB S1, DcLEL, DcNAA,
  EncAAH, IndAu 1816, JBA 34, -51,
  OxAmH, OxAmL, REnAL, REnAW,
  TexWr, WebAB, -79, WhAm 2, WhNAA,
  YABC 1
Adams, Ansel 1902-1984 AuNews 1, BioIn 4,
  -6, -7, -8, -10, -11, -12, BioNews 74,
  BlueB, BnEnAmA, CmCal,
  ConAu 10NR, -21R, ConPhot, CurBio 77,
  DcAmArt, DcCAr 81, WebAB, -79,
  WhoAm 74, -76, -78, -80, -82,
  WhoAmA 76, -78, -80, -82, WorAl,
  WrDr 80, -82, -84
Adams, Bryan NewRR 83
Adams, Charlotte 1899- AuBYP SUP,
  ConAu 107, WhoAmW 58, -61, -64
Adams, Douglas 1952- ConDr 82B
Adams, Douglas Noel 1952- ConAu 106,
  ConLC 27[port], DcLB Y83B[port],
  WrDr 82, -84
Adams, Harriet S 1893?-1982 AmAu&B,
  AmWomWr, AnObit 1982[port],
  AuNews 2, BioIn 12, ConAu 106, -17R,
  EncMys, NewYTBS 82[port], SmATA 1,
  -29N, WhoAm 78, -80, -82
Adams, Harriet S see also Appleton, Victor, II
Adams, Harriet S see also Dixon, Franklin W
Adams, Harriet S see also Hope, Laura Lee

Adams, Harriet S see also Keene, Carolyn
Adams, Hazard 1926- BioIn 10, ConAu 9R,
  DrAS 74E, -78E, -82E, IntAu&W 76, -77,
  IntWWP 77, LEduc 74, ScF&FL 1,
  SmATA 6, WhoAm 74, -76, -78, -80, -82,
  WhoWest 74, -76, WrDr 76, -80, -82, -84
Adams, Henry Brooks 1838-1918 Alli SUP,
  AmAu, AmAu&B, AmBi, AmWr,
  ApCAB, AtlBL, BbD, BiDAmEd,
  BiD&SB, BioIn 1, -2, -3, -4, -5, -6, -7, -8,
  -9, -10, -11, -12, CasWL, CnDAL,
  ConAu 104, CyWA, DcAmAu, DcAmB,
  DcAmSR, DcBiA, DcLB 12[port],
  DcLEL, DcNAA, EncAB-H, EncWL 81,
  EvLB, HarEnUS, LinLib L, -S,
  LongCTC, McGEWB, ModAL,
  ModAL SUP, NatCAB 11, Novels,
  OxAmH, OxAmL, OxEng, PenC AM,
  RAdv 1, RComWL, REn, REnAL,
  TwCBDA, TwCLC 4[port], TwCWr,
  WebAB, -79, WebE&AL, WhAm HSA,
  -1, -4A, WhAmP, WhoTwCL, WorAl
Adams, Laurie 1941- ConAu 53, SmATA 33,
  WhoAmW 83, WrDr 76, -80, -82, -84
Adams, Richard 1920- AuBYP SUP,
  AuNews 1, -2, BioIn 10, -11, -12,
  ChhPo S2, ConAu 3NR, -49, ConLC 4,
  -5, -18, CurBio 78, IntAu&W 77,
  IntWW 78, -79, -80, -81, -82, -83,
  Novels[port], PiP, ScF&FL 1, -2,
  SmATA 7, TwCCW 78, -83, Who 82,
  -83, WhoAm 80, -82, WhoWor 82,
  WorAu 1970, WrDr 76, -80, -82, -84
Adamson, Joe 1945- ConAu X
Adamson, Joseph, III 1945- ConAu 1NR, -45
Adamson, Joy 1910-1980 AnObit 1980[port],
  -1981, Au&Wr 6, BioIn 7, -8, -9, -11,
  -12, ConAu 69, -93, ConLC 17,
  CurBio 72, -80N, FourBJA, GoodHs,
  IntAu&W 76, -77, IntDcWB, LinLib L,
  NewYTBS 80[port], SmATA 11, -22N,
  WhAm 7, Who 74, WhoAm 74, -76, -78,
  WhoAmW 74
Adamson, Wendy Wriston 1942- ConAu 53,
  SmATA 22[port]
Addams, Charles Samuel 1912- AmAu&B,
  BioIn 2, -3, -6, -7, -8, -10, BlueB 76,
  CelR 73, ConAu 61, CurBio 54,
  IntWW 74, -75, -76, -77, -78, -79, -80, -81,
  -82, -83, LinLib L, WebAB, -79, WhDW,
  WhoAm 74, -76, -78, -80, -82,
  WhoAmA 73, -76, -78, -80, -82,
  WhoWor 74, -76, -78, -80, -82, WorAl,
  WrDr 76, -80, -82, -84
Adelberg, Roy P 1928- ConAu 17R
Adelman, Janet Ann 1941- ConAu 61,
  DrAS 74E, -78E, -82E
Adkins, Jan 1944- AuBYP SUP, BioIn 11,
  -12, ConAu 33R, SmATA 8, WhoE 77
Adlard, Mark 1932- ConAu 65, EncSF,
  IntAu&W 76, -77, ScF&FL 1, -2,
  WhoSciF, WrDr 84

Adler, Bill 1929- *BioIn 7, ConAu X, WhoE 74*

Adler, Bill *see also* Adler, William

Adler, C S 1932- *ConAu 89, DrAP&F 83, SmATA 26[port]*

Adler, Freda 1934- *ConAu 11NR, –69, WhoAm 82, WhoAmW 77, –79, –81, –83, WhoE 77, –79, –81*

Adler, Helmut E 1920- *AmM&WS 73S, –78S, ConAu 33R, WhoE 83, WhoWorJ 72, WrDr 76, –80, –82, –84*

Adler, Irene *AuBYP SUP, ConAu X, SmATA X*

Adler, Irene *see also* Penzler, Otto M

Adler, Irene *see also* Storr, Catherine

Adler, Irving 1913- *AmAu&B, Au&Wr 6, AuBYP, BioIn 7, –9, ConAu 2NR, –5R, SmATA 1, –29[port], ThrBJA*

Adler, Larry 1939- *ConAu 105, SmATA 36*

Adler, Mortimer Jerome 1902- *AmAu&B, BioIn 2, –3, –4, –5, –11, –12, ConAu 7NR, –65, CurBio 40, –52, DrAS 74P, –78P, –82P, LinLib L, NewYTBS 82, OxAmL, REnAL, TwCA SUP, WebAB, –79, WhNAA, WhoAm 76, –78, –80, –82, WhoWor 74, –76, WrDr 82, –84*

Adler, William 1929- *ConAu 7NR, –9R*

Adler, William *see also* Adler, Bill

Adoff, Arnold 1935- *AuBYP, AuNews 1, BioIn 10, ChhPo S1, –S2, –S3, ConAu 41R, FourBJA, MorBMP, SmATA 5, TwCCW 83*

Adshead, Gladys L 1896- *AmAu&B, BioIn 2, –6, –9, ConAu 29R, MorJA, SmATA 3, WhAm 7, WhoAmW 58, –64, –66*

Agassi, Joseph 1927- *ConAu 41R, DrAS 74P, –78P, –82P, WhoAm 74, –76, –78, –80, –82, WhoAmJ 80, WhoE 83, WhoWorJ 78*

Agee, James 1909-1955 *AmAu&B, AmWr, AuNews 1, BioIn 3, –4, –5, –6, –7, –8, –9, –10, –12, BioNews 74, CasWL, ConAu 108, DcAmB S5, DcLB 2, –26[port], EncAAH, EncSoH, EncWL, –2, FilmgC, LinLib L, –S, ModAL, ModAL SUP, NatCAB 42, NewYTBS 81[port], Novels, ObitOF 79, OxAmL, OxFilm, PenC AM, RAdv 1, REn, REnAL, SixAP, TwCA SUP, TwCLC 1, TwCWr, WebAB, –79, WebE&AL, WhAm HSA, –4, WhoTwCL, WorEFlm*

Agee, Joel 1940- *BioIn 12, ConAu 105, DrAP&F 83, NewYTBS 81[port]*

Agel, Jerome *ScF&FL 1*

Agnelli, Susanna 1922- *BioIn 10, ConAu 109, NewYTBS 75, –83[port]*

Agonito, Rosemary 1937- *DrAS 78P, –82P, WrDr 82, –84*

Ahern, James F 1932- *ConAu 41R, IntAu&W 77, NewYTBE 70, WhoAm 74, –76, –78, –80, WhoIns 76, –77, –78, –79, –80, –81, –82, –84, WhoWor 76, –78, –80,*

–82

Ahnstrom, Doris Newell 1915- *AuBYP, BioIn 8, ConAu 5R, WhoAmW 61, –64, –68, –70, –77, –79, –81, WhoE 81, –83, WhoS&SW 76, –78*

Aiken, Conrad Potter 1889-1973 *AmAu&B, AmLY, –XR, AmWr, AnCL, ApCAB X, AuBYP, BioIn 1, –2, –3, –4, –5, –6, –7, –8, –9, –10, –11, –12, CasWL, Chambr 3, ChhPo, –S1, –S2, –S3, CnDAL, CnE&AP, CnMD, CnMWL, ConAmA, ConAmL, ConAu 4NR, –5R, –45, ConLC 1, –3, –5, –10, ConNov 72, ConP 70, CurBio 70, –73, –73N, DcLB 9[port], DcLEL, EncWL, –81, EvLB, IntAu&W 76, –77, –82, IntWWP 77, LinLib L, –S, LongCTC, MakMC, ModAL, ModAL SUP, ModWD, NewYTBE 73, Novels, ObitOF 79, ObitT 1971, OxAmL, OxEng, PenC AM, RAdv 1, REn, REnAL, SixAP, SmATA 3, –30[port], TwCA, TwCA SUP, TwCWr, WebAB, –79, WebE&AL, WhDW, WhAm 6, WhE&EA, WhNAA, WhoAm 74, WhoE 74, WhoTwCL, WhoWor 74, –76, WorAl*

Aiken, Joan 1924- *Au&Wr 6, AuBYP, BioIn 8, –9, –10, –11, BrCA, ChlLR 1, ChhPo S3, ConAu 4NR, –9R, IntAu&W 76, –82, PiP, ScF&FL 1, –1A, –2, SenS, SmATA 2, –30[port], ThrBJA, TwCCW 78, –83, TwCCr&M 80, Who 82, –83, WhoHr&F, WrDr 76, –80, –82, –84*

Ainsworth, Ruth Gallard 1908- *Au&Wr 6, BioIn 8, –10, ChhPo, –S1, ConAu X, ScF&FL 1, –2, SmATA 7, TwCCW 78, –83, WhoChL, WrDr 76, –80, –82, –84*

Ainsworth, Ruth Gallard *see also* Gilbert, Ruth Gallard

Aitmatov, Chingiz 1928- *Au&Wr 6, BioIn 10, ConAu 103, FarE&A 78, –79, –80, –81, IntAu&W 76, –77, IntWW 74, –75, –76, –77, –78, –79, –80, –81, –82, –83, TwCCW 78B, –83B, WhoSocC 78, WhoWor 74, –82*

Ajar, Emile 1940?- *BioIn 11*

Akens, David S 1921- *ConAu 25R, WhoAm 78, –80*

Akers, Charles Wesley 1920- *ConAu 13R, DrAS 74H, –78H, –82H, IndAu 1917*

Akhmatova, Anna 1888?-1966 *AtlBL, BioIn 1, –2, –7, –8, –9, –10, –11, –12, CasWL, CIDMEL, ConAu 25R, ConAu P-1, ConLC 11, –25[port], DcRusL, EncWL, –81[port], EvEuW, IntDcWB, LinLib L, LongCTC, McGEWB, ModSL 1, ObitOF 79, ObitT 1961, PenC EUR, REn, TwCWr, WhDW, WhoTwCL, WorAl, WorAu*

Alajalov, Constantin 1900- *BioIn 1, –2, –5, CurBio 42, ForIl, IlrAm D, IlsBYP, IlsCB 1744, –1946, WhoAm 74, –76, –78,*

-80, -82, WhoAmA 73, -76, -78, -80, -82,
WorECar
Albee, Edward 1928- *AmAu&B, AmWr,*
AuNews 1, BiDAmM, BiE&WWA,
BioIn 5, -6, -7, -8, -9, -10, -11, -12,
BlueB 76, CasWL, CelR 73, CnMD,
CnThe, ConAu 5R, -8NR, ConDr 73, -77,
-82, ConLC 1, -2, -3, -5, -9, -11, -13,
-25[port], CroCD, DcLB 7[port],
DcLEL 1940, EncAB-H, EncWL,
-81[port], EncWT, FilmgC, IntAu&W 76,
-77, IntWW 74, -75, -76, -77, -78, -79,
-80, -81, -82, -83, LinLib L, LongCTC,
MakMC, McGEWD, -84[port], ModAL,
ModAL SUP, ModWD, NatPD, -81[port],
NotNAT, -A, OxAmL, OxThe,
PenC AM, PIP&P, -A, RComWL, REn,
REnAL, REnWD, TwCWr, WebAB, -79,
WebE&AL, WhDW, Who 74, -82, -83,
WhoAm 74, -76, -78, -80, -82, WhoE 77,
-79, -81, -83, WhoThe 15, -16, -81,
WhoTwCL, WhoWor 78, -80, -82, WorAl,
WorAu, WrDr 76, -80, -82, -84
Albert, Louise 1928- *ConAu 69*
Albert, Marvin H *AuBYP, BioIn 8,*
ConAu 73, ScF&FL 1, WrDr 84
Albery, Nobuko *ConAu 81*
Albion, Robert Greenhalgh 1896-1983
AmAu&B, BioIn 3, -10, BlueB 76,
ConAu 1R, -3NR, -110, CurBio 54, -83N,
DrAS 74H, -78H, IntYB 78, -79, -80, -81,
-82, NewYTBS 83, WhE&EA,
WhoAm 74, -76, -78, -80, WrDr 76, -80,
-82, -84
Albrand, Martha 1914?-1981 *AmAu&B,*
AmNov, AnObit 1981[port], Au&W 6,
BioIn 1, -2, -4, -6, -7, -12, ConAu 108,
-11NR, -13R, EncMys, InWom,
IntAu&W 76, Novels, TwCA SUP,
TwCCr&M 80, WhoAm 74, -76, -78, -80,
-82, WhoAmW 74, -58, -61, -64, -66, -68,
-70, -72, WhoE 74, WhoSpyF,
WhoWor 78, -80, WrDr 82, -84
Alcock, Vivien 1924?- *ConAu 110,*
TwCCW 83
Alcorn, Robert Hayden 1909- *ConAu 5R,*
WhoE 75
Alcott, Louisa May 1832-1888 *Alli SUP,*
AmAu, AmAu&B, AmBi, AmWom,
AmWomWr, AmWr SUP, ApCAB,
AtlBL, AuBYP, BbD, BiD&SB, BioIn 1,
-2, -3, -4, -5, -6, -7, -8, -9, -10, -11, -12,
CarSB, CasWL, CelCen, Chambr 3,
ChlLR 1, ChhPo, -S3, CivWDc, CnDAL,
CrtT 3, -4, CyAL 2, CyWA, DcAmAu,
DcAmB, DcBiA, DcBiPP, DcEnL,
DcLB 1, DcLEL, DcNAA, EncAB-H,
EvLB, FamAYP, FilmgC, GoodHs,
HarEnUS, HerW, InWom, IntDcWB,
JBA 34, LibW, LinLib L, -S, McGEWB,
MouLC 4, NatCAB 1, NotAW, Novels,
OxAmH, OxAmL, OxEng, PenC AM,

REn, REnAL, Str&VC, TwCBDA,
TwCCW 78A, -83A, WebAB, -79,
WhAm HS, WhoChL, WorAl, YABC 1
Aldan, Daisy 1923- *AmAu&B, ConAu 8NR,*
-13R, DrAP 75, DrAP&F 83,
ForWC 70, WhoAmW 70, WomWMM B
Alderman, Clifford Lindsey 1902- *AuBYP,*
BioIn 8, -9, ConAu 1R, -3NR,
IntAu&W 76, SmATA 3
Alderson, William Thomas, Jr. 1926-
BiDrLUS 70, ConAu 9R, DrAS 74H,
-78H, -82H, EncAB 32[port], St&PR 75,
WhoAm 74, -76, -78, -80, -82, WhoE 83,
WhoLibI 82, WhoLibS 66,
WhoS&SW 73
Aldiss, Brian 1925- *Au&Wr 6, BioIn 11, -12,*
BlueB 76, ConAu 5R, -5NR, ConLC 5,
-14, ConNov 72, -76, -82, ConSFA,
DcLB 14[port], DcLEL 1940, EncSF,
IntAu&W 76, -77, -82, IntWW 74, -75,
-76, -77, -78, -79, -80, -81, -82, -83,
LinLib L, Novels, ScF&FL 1, -2,
SmATA 34[port], TwCWr, Who 74, -82,
-83, WhoSciF, WhoWor 74, -76, -78, -82,
WorAl, WorAu 1970, WrDr 76, -80, -82,
-84
Aldrich, Bess Streeter 1881-1954 *AmAu&B,*
AmNov, AmWomWr, BioIn 2, -3, -4, -6,
DcAmB S5, EncAB 6, InWom, LibW,
NatCAB 46, ObitOF 79, OxAmL, REn,
REnAL, TwCA, TwCA SUP, WhAm 3,
WhE&EA, WhLit, WhNAA
Aldridge, James 1918- *Au&Wr 6, BioIn 2, -4,*
-6, -10, ConAu 61, ConNov 72, -76, -82,
CurBio 43, IntAu&W 77, IntWW 83,
Novels, TwCA SUP, Who 74, -82, -83,
WrDr 76, -80, -82, -84
Aldrin, Edwin Eugene, Jr. 1930-
AmM&WS 73P, BioIn 7, -8, -9, -10, -12,
BioNews 74, BlueB 76, CelR 73,
ConAu 89, IntWW 74, -75, -76, -77, -78,
-79, -80, -81, -82, -83, LinLib S,
NewYTBE 71, UFOEn, Who 74, -82, -83,
WhoAm 74, -76, -78, -80, -82,
WhoWest 78, -80, WhoWor 74, -78,
WorAl
Aleichem, Sholom 1859-1916 *AmAu&B,*
AtlBL, ConAu X, LinLib L, NotNAT B,
OxThe, TwCLC 1, WorAl
Aleksin, Anatoli Georgievich 1924- *BioIn 11,*
SmATA 36
Alexander, Anna Barbara Cooke 1913- *BioIn 9,*
ConAu 5R, -57, SmATA 1
Alexander, Anna Barbara Cooke *see also*
Alexander, Anne
Alexander, Anna Barbara Cooke *see also* Cooke,
Barbara
Alexander, Anne 1913- *AuBYP, ConAu 57*
Alexander, Anne *see also* Alexander, Anna
Barbara Cooke
Alexander, David M 1945- *ConAu 81*
Alexander, Lloyd 1924- *AnCL, Au&Wr 6,*

AuBYP, BioIn 5, –9, –10, ChlLR 1, –5[port], ConAu 1R, –1NR, MorBMP, PiP, ScF&FL 1, –2, NewbC 1966, SmATA 3, ThrBJA, TwCCW 78, –83, WhoAm 74, –76, –78, –80, –82, WhoE 74, WhoHr&F, WhoWor 78, WrDr 80, –82, –84

Alexander, Patrick James 1926- WrDr 80, –82, –84

Alexander, Raymond Pace 1898-1974 BioIn 8, –10, BioNews 75, ConAu 97, Ebony 1, InB&W 80, ObitOF 79, SmATA 22[port], WhAm 6, WhAmP, WhoAm 74, WhoAmP 73, WhoBlA 75

Alexander, Shana 1925- BioIn 6, –8, ConAu 61, ConIsC 2[port], ForWC 70, St&PR 75, WhoAm 74, –76, –78, –80, –82, WhoAmW 74, –72, –77, –79, –81, –83, WhoF&I 74, WhoWor 80, WorAl, WrDr 76, –80, –82, –84

Alexander, Sue 1933- BioIn 11, ConAu 4NR, –53, SmATA 12

Alexander, Taylor Richard 1915- AmM&WS 73P, –76P, –79P, –82P, ConAu 107

Alexander, Thomas W, Jr. 1930- ConAu 9R

Alfven, Hannes Olof Gosta 1908- BiESc, BioIn 12, ConAu 29R, IntWW 74, –75, –76, –77, –78, –79, –80, –81, –82, –83, LuthC 75, McGMS 80[port], Who 74, –82, –83, WhoAm 82, WhoWor 74, –78, –80, –82

Alfven, Hannes Olof Gosta see also Johannesson, Olof

Algren, Nelson 1909-1981 AmAu&B, AmNov, AnObit 1981[port], BioIn 2, –4, –5, –7, –8, –10, –12, BlueB 76, CasWL, CnDAL, CnMWL, ConAu 103, –13R, ConLC 4, –10, ConNov 72, –76, DcLB Y81A, –Y82A[port], –9[port], DcLEL, DrAF 76, EncWL, –81, FilmgC, IntAu&W 76, –77, LinLib L, ModAL, ModAL SUP, NewYTBS 81[port], Novels, OxAmL, PenC AM, RAdv 1, REn, REnAL, TwCA SUP, TwCWr, WebE&AL, WhAm 7, WhoAm 74, –76, –80, WhoTwCL, WhoWor 74, WorAl, WrDr 76, –80, –82

Ali, Muhammad 1942- BioIn 8, –9, –10, –11, –12, BioNews 74, BlueB 76, CurBio 63, –78, Ebony 1, EncAB-H, InB&W 80, IntWW 76, –77, –78, –79, –80, –81, –82, –83, NegAl 76, NewYTBS 80[port], PolProf J, UFOEn[port], WebAB, –79, WhoAm 74, –76, –78, –80, –82, WhoBlA 75, –77, –80, WhoBox 74, WhoWor 78, WorAl

Ali, Muhammad see also Muhammad Ali

Ali, Tariq 1943- Au&Wr 6, BioIn 10, ConAu 10NR, –25R, IntAu&W 77

Aliav, Ruth 1914?-1980 BioIn 10, ConAu X, WhoPubR 76, WhoWorJ 72, –78, WrDr 76, –80

Aliav, Ruth see also Kluger, Ruth

Alkema, Chester Jay 1932- BioIn 11, ConAu 53, MichAu 80, SmATA 12

Allan, Mabel Esther 1915- Au&Wr 6, AuBYP, BioIn 7, –10, ConAu 2NR, –5R, IntAu&W 76, –77, –82, ScF&FL 1, SmATA 32[port], –5, TwCCW 78, –83, WrDr 76, –80, –82, –84

Allan, Mabel Esther see also Estoril, Jean

Allan, Mabel Esther see also Hagon, Priscilla

Allan, Mabel Esther see also Pilgrim, Anne

Allan, Mea 1909-1982 Au&Wr 6, ConAu 2NR, –5R, –107, IntAu&W 76, –77, –82, ScF&FL 1, –2, WrDr 76, –80, –82

Allbeury, Ted 1917- ConAu X, Novels, TwCCr&M 80, WhoSpyF, WrDr 76, –80, –82, –84

Allbeury, Theodore 1917- ConAu 5NR, –53

Alldritt, Keith 1935- ConAu 25R, DcLB 14[port]

Allee, Marjorie Hill 1890-1945 AmAu&B, AmWomWr, BioIn 1, –2, –12, DcNAA, InWom, IndAu 1917, JBA 34, –51, SmATA 17, WhAm 2, –2C, WhNAA

Allegro, John Marco 1923- Au&Wr 6, BioIn 9, BlueB 76, ConAu 4NR, –9R, CurBio 70, DcLEL 1940, EncO&P 78, IntAu&W 76, –77, –82, IntWW 74, –75, –76, –77, –78, –79, –80, –81, –82, –83, MidE 78, –79, –80, –81, –82, Who 74, –82, –83, WhoWor 74, –76, –78, –80, –82, WrDr 76, –80, –82, –84

Allen, Adam AuBYP, ConAu X, MorJA, SmATA X

Allen, Adam see also Epstein, Beryl Williams

Allen, Adam see also Epstein, Samuel

Allen, Betsy 1909- AuBYP, BioIn 6, –7, –9, ConAu X, CurBio 50, SmATA X, –1, TwCCW 83, WrDr 80

Allen, Betsy see also Cavanna, Betty

Allen, Chris 1929- ConAu 29R, DrRegL 75, MnBBF

Allen, Donald M 1912- AmAu&B, ConAu 17R

Allen, Durward Leon 1910- AmM&WS 73P, –76P, –79P, –82P, ConAu 41R, –41R, MichAu 80, WhoAm 74, –76, –78, –80, –82, WhoGov 77, –72, –75, WhoWor 76, WrDr 82, –84

Allen, Elizabeth 1914- MichAu 80

Allen, Ethan 1904- BioIn 3, CurBio 54, OhA&B, WhoProB 73

Allen, Henry Wilson 1912- ConAu 89, EncSF, ScF&FL 1, WrDr 84

Allen, Hervey 1889-1949 AmAu&B, AmNov, AnMV 1926, BioIn 1, –2, –3, –4, –5, –12, Chambr 3, ChhPo, –S1, –S2, CnDAL, ConAmA, ConAmL, ConAu 108, CyWA, DcAmB S4, DcLB 9[port], DcLEL, DcNAA, EncWL, LinLib L, LongCTC, NatCAB 37, Novels, ObitOF 79, OxAmL, PenC AM,

REn, REnAL, TwCA, TwCA SUP,
TwCWr, WhAm 2, WhNAA
Allen, Heywood 1935- *ConAu 33R*
Allen, Heywood *see also* Allen, Woody
Allen, Janet Crouse Stewart 1904-
WhoAmW 58, –66, –68, –70
Allen, Lee 1915-1969 *AuBYP, BioIn 8,*
ConAu 1R, –1NR, OhA&B
Allen, Maury 1932- *ConAu 11NR, –17R,*
IntAu&W 76A, SmATA 26[port]
Allen, Merritt Parmelee 1892-1954 *AuBYP,*
BioIn 2, –3, –7, JBA 51, SmATA 22,
WhE&EA, WhNAA
Allen, Michael 1939- *ConAu 77*
Allen, Richard J *AuBYP*
Allen, Rodney F 1938- *ConAu 61,*
SmATA 27[port]
Allen, Samuel 1917- *BioIn 11, BlkAWP,*
BroadAu, ChhPo S2, ConAu 49,
DrAP 75, DrAP&F 83, DrAS 74E, –78E,
–82E, InB&W 80, IntAu&W 82,
IntWWP 82, LivgBAA, SmATA 9,
WhoAm 76, –78, –80, –82, WhoBlA 77, –80
Allen, Steve 1921- *AmAu&B, AmSCAP 66,*
AuBYP SUP, BiE&WWA, BioIn 2, –3, –4,
–5, –6, –8, –10, –12, BioNews 75, CelR 73,
CmpEPM, ConAu 25R, –25R, CurBio 51,
–82[port], EncJzS 70, FilmgC,
IntAu&W 76, IntMPA 77, –75, –76, –78,
–79, –81, –82, –84, IntWWP 77,
LesBEnT[port], NewYTBS 81[port],
NewYTET, REnAL, WebAB, –79,
WhoHol A, WorAl, WrDr 76, –82, –84
Allen, T D 1908- *AmAu&B, ConAu X,*
DrAP&F 83
Allen, Terril Diener 1908- *ConAu 2NR, –5R,*
WhoAmW 68, –70, WhoWest 74, –76, –78,
–80, –82, –84
Allen, Terry D 1908- *AmAu&B, ConAu X*
Allen, Thomas Benton 1929- *ConAu 5NR,*
–13R
Allen, William 1940- *ConAu 65*
Allen, Woody 1935- *AmAu&B, BioIn 6, –7,*
–8, –9, –10, –11, –12, CelR 73, ConAu X,
ConDr 82A, ConLC 16, CurBio 66, –79,
FilmgC, IntMPA 77, –75, –76, –78, –79, –81,
–82, –84, IntWW 79, –80, –81, –82, –83,
MovMk, NatPD 81[port], NewYTBE 73,
NewYTBS 75, –79, –80[port], NotNAT, –A,
Who 82, –83, WhoAm 74, –76, –78, –80,
–82, WhoAmJ 80, WhoHol A,
WhoThe 16, –81, WorAl, WrDr 76, –80,
–82, –84
Allen, Woody *see also* Allen, Heywood
Allende, Salvador 1908?-1973 *BioIn 9, –10, –11,*
–12, CurBio 71, –73, –73N, EncLatA[port],
NewYTBE 70, ObitT 1971, WhoGov 72,
WhoWor 74
Alliluyeva, Svetlana 1926- *ASpks, CelR 73,*
ConAu 57, CurBio 68, InWom, LinLib L,
WhoAmW 74, –68A, –70, –77, WhoWor 74
Allingham, Margery 1904-1966 *BioIn 1, –2, –4,*

–7, –9, –12, ConAu 4NR, –5R, –25R,
ConLC 19, CorpD, DcLEL, EncMys,
EncSF, EvLB, LongCTC, MnBBF,
NewC, Novels[port], ObitOF 79,
ObitT 1961, ScF&FL 1, –2, TwCA,
TwCA SUP, TwCCr&M 80, TwCWr,
WhE&EA, WhoSpyF, WorAl
Allison, Bob *AuBYP, BioIn 8, –12,*
SmATA 14
Allmendinger, David Frederick, Jr. 1938-
ConAu 61, DrAS 74H, –78H, –82H,
SmATA 35
Almedingen, E M 1898-1971 *Au&Wr 6,*
AuBYP SUP, ConAu X, –1R, ConLC 12,
LongCTC, SmATA 3, ThrBJA,
TwCCW 78, –83, WorAu
Almedingen, E M *see also* Almedingen, Martha
Edith·Von
Almedingen, E M *see also* VonAlmedingen,
Martha Edith
Almedingen, Martha Edith Von 1898-1971
BioIn 2, –3, –6, –8, –9, –10, ConAu 1NR,
SmATA 3
Almedingen, Martha Edith Von *see also*
Almedingen, E M
Alonso, Ricardo *DrAP&F 83*
Alotta, Robert Ignatius 1937- *ConAu 65,*
WhoE 79, –81
Alpenfels, Ethel J *WhoAmW 74, –68, –70, –72*
Alpert, Helen *WhoAmW 66, –68, –70, –77*
Alsop, Joseph Wright 1910- *AmAu&B,*
BioIn 1, –2, –3, –4, –5, –6, –7, –8, –9, –10,
–11, BlueB 76, CelR 73, CurBio 52,
IntAu&W 76, –77, IntWW 74, –75, –76,
–77, –78, –79, –80, –81, –82, –83, LinLib L,
NewYTBE 71, PolProf E, PolProf K,
PolProf T, REn, REnAL, WhoAm 74,
–76, –78, –80, –82, WhoS&SW 73,
WhoWor 74, –78, WorAl, WorAu
Alsop, Mary O'Hara 1885-1980 *BioIn 9, –12,*
ConAu 4NR, –9R, –102,
NewYTBS 80[port], SmATA 2, –24N,
–34[port], WrDr 80, –82
Alsop, Mary O'Hara *see also* O'Hara, Mary
Alter, Dinsmore 1888-1968 *BioIn 8, –10,*
NatCAB 54, ObitOF 79, WhAm 5,
WhNAA
Alter, Judy *ConAu X*
Alth, Max O 1927- *ConAu 41R*
Alther, Lisa 1944- *BioIn 12, ConAu 65,*
ConLC 7, Novels, WrDr 80, –82, –84
Altick, Richard Daniel 1915- *ChhPo, –S3,*
ConAu 1R, –4NR, DrAS 74E, –78E, –82E,
OhA&B, WrDr 76, –80, –82, –84
Altman, Nathaniel 1948- *ConAu 6NR, –57*
Altsheler, Joseph Alexander 1862-1919
AmAu&B, AuBYP, BiDSA, BioIn 7, –11,
DcAmAu, DcAmB, DcNAA, JBA,
LinLib L, NatCAB 11, REnAL, TwCA,
TwCA SUP, TwCBDA, TwCCW 83,
WhAm 1, WhE&EA, YABC 1
Alvarez, Joseph A 1930- *BioIn 12,*

ConAu 33R, SmATA 18

Amado, Jorge 1912- BioIn 5, -10, -12, CasWL, CelR 73, ConAu 77, ConLC 13, CyWA, EncLatA, EncWL, -81, IntAu&W 76, -77, IntWW 74, -75, -76, -77, -78, -79, -80, -81, -82, -83, LinLib L, McGEWB, ModLAL, Novels, PenC AM, REn, TwCWr, WhoWor 74, -76, -78, -82, WorAu

Ambler, Eric 1909- AmAu&B, Au&Wr 6, BioIn 4, -5, -10, -12, BlueB 76, CnMWL, ConAu 7NR, -9R, ConLC 4, -6, -9, ConNov 72, -76, -82, CorpD, CurBio 75, DcLEL, EncMys, FilmgC, IntAu&W 76, -82, IntWW 83, LinLib L, LongCTC, NewC, NewYTBS 81[port], Novels, OxFilm, REn, ScF&FL 1, TwCCr&M 80, TwCWr, Who 74, -83, WhoSpyF, WhoWor 74, -76, -82, WorAl, WrDr 76, -80, -82, -84

Ambrose, Stephen E 1936- ConAu 1R, -3NR, DrAS 74H, -78H, -82H, IntAu&W 76

Ambrus, Gyozo Laszlo 1935- ConAu 11NR, -25R, IntAu&W 77

Ambrus, Gyozo Laszlo see also Ambrus, Victor G

Ambrus, Victor G 1935- BioIn 7, -8, -9, -11, -12, BrCA, ChhPo S1, -S2, ConAu X, IlsBYP, IlsCB 1957, -1967, IntAu&W 77X, SmATA 1, ThrBJA, WhoArt 80, -82, WhoChL

Ambrus, Victor G see also Ambrus, Gyozo Laszlo

America BiDAmM, EncPR&S, IlEncRk, RkOn 78, WhoRocM 82

America see also Beckley, Gerry

America see also Bunnell, Dewey

America see also Peek, Dan

Amerman, Lockhart 1911-1969 AuBYP, BioIn 8, -9, ConAu P-2, SmATA 3

Ames, Delano 1906- Au&Wr 6, ConAu 107, MnBBF, OhA&B, ScF&FL 1, WhLit

Ames, Evelyn 1908- ConAu 57, SmATA 13, WhoAmW 58, -61

Ames, Lee Judah 1921- AuBYP, BioIn 5, -8, -9, ConAu 1R, -3NR, IlsCB 1946, -1957, -1967, SmATA 3, WhoAmA 73, -76, -78, -80, -82

Ames, Mildred 1919- ConAu 11NR, -69, SmATA 22[port]

Amis, Kingsley 1922- Au&Wr 6, AuNews 2, BioIn 3, -4, -5, -6, -8, -9, -10, -11, -12, BlueB 76, CasWL, ChhPo S3, CnMWL, ConAu 8NR, -9R, ConLC 1, -2, -3, -5, -8, -13, ConNov 72, -76, -82, ConP 70, -75, -80, ConSFA, CurBio 58, DcLB 15[port], DcLEL 1940, EncMys, EncSF, EncWL, -81, FilmgC, IntAu&W 76, -77, IntWW 74, -75, -76, -77, -78, -79, -80, -81, -82, -83, IntWWP 77, LinLib L, LongCEL, LongCTC, MakMC, ModBrL, ModBrL SUP, NewC, Novels[port], PenC ENG, RAdv 1, REn, ScF&FL 1, -2, TwCCr&M 80, TwCWr, WebE&AL, WhDW, Who 74, -82, -83, WhoAm 74,

-76, -78, -80, -82, WhoSciF, WhoSpyF, WhoTwCL, WorAu, WrDr 76, -80, -82, -84

Ammerman, Gale Richard 1923- AmM&WS 73P, ConAu 107, IntAu&W 76, -77

Ammons, A R 1926- AmAu&B, AuNews 1, BlueB 76, ConAu 6NR, -9R, ConLC 2, -3, -5, -8, -9, -25[port], ConP 70, -75, -80, CroCAP, CurBio 82[port], DcLB 5[port], DrAP 75, DrAP&F 83, EncWL 81, IntWWP 77, LinLib L, ModAL SUP, RAdv 1, WorAu, WrDr 76, -80, -82, -84

Amon, Aline 1928- AuBYP SUP, BioIn 11, ConAu 8NR, -61, SmATA 9

Amory, Cleveland 1917- AmAu&B, AuNews 1, BioIn 2, -4, -5, -7, -10, -11, -12, BioNews 75, CelR 73, ConAu 69, LinLib L, -S, REnAL, TwCA SUP, WhoAm 74, -76, -78, -80, -82, WhoWor 74, WrDr 76, -80, -82, -84

Amoss, Berthe 1920?- BioIn 10, ConAu 21R, SmATA 5, WhoAmA 78, -80, -82, WhoAmW 74

Anaya, Rudolfo A 1937- ChiSch, ConAu 1NR, -45, ConLC 23[port], DrAF 76, DrAP&F 83

Anckarsvard, Karin 1915-1969 AuBYP, BioIn 7, -9, -10, ConAu 9R, -103, SmATA 6, ThrBJA

Ancona, George 1929- AuBYP SUP, BioIn 11, ConAu 4NR, -53, SmATA 12, WhoAm 76, -78, -80, -82

Andersen, Yvonne 1932- AuBYP SUP, BioIn 10, ConAu 29R, SmATA 27[port], WomWMM A, -B

Anderson, Alan H, Jr. 1943- ConAu 69, WrDr 82, -84

Anderson, Bernard E AmEA 74, AmM&WS 73S, -78S, WhoBlA 77, -80, WhoCon 73

Anderson, Bernice G 1894- ConAu 101, SmATA 33[port], WhNAA

Anderson, Brad 1924- AmAu&B, ConAu 106, SmATA 31, -33[port], WhoAmA 73, -76, -78, -80, -82

Anderson, C W 1891-1971 BkP, JBA 51, LinLib L, SmATA 11, Str&VC, ThrBJA, TwCCW 83

Anderson, C W see also Anderson, Clarence William

Anderson, Chester Grant 1923- ConAu 25R, DrAS 74E, -78E, -82E, WhoAm 80, -82

Anderson, Chuck 1933- ConAu 49

Anderson, Clarence William 1891-1971 ArtsAmW, AuBYP, BioIn 1, -2, -5, -7, -8, -9, -11, ConAu 29R, -73, IlBEAAW, IlsCB 1744, -1946, -1957

Anderson, Clarence William see also Anderson, C W

Anderson, Clary NewYTBE 72

Anderson, Dave 1929- AuNews 2, ConAu X

Anderson, David Poole 1929- *BioIn 11,*
ConAu 89, IntAu&W 82, WhoAm 76,
–78, –80, –82
Anderson, Edna A *BioIn 6, MinnWr*
Anderson, Ella 1916- *IntAu&W 76X, –82X,*
SmATA X, WrDr 76, –80, –82
Anderson, Ella *see also* MacLeod, Ellen Jane
Anderson, J R L 1911-1981 *ConAu 104, –25R,*
SmATA 15, –27N
Anderson, J R L *see also* Anderson, John Richard
Lane
Anderson, Jack Northman 1922- *AuNews 1,*
BioIn 6, –8, –9, –10, –11, –12, BlueB 76,
CelR 73, ConAu 6NR, –57, CurBio 72,
PolProf J, PolProf NF, WhoAm 74, –76,
–78, –80, –82, WhoS&SW 73, –75, –76,
WhoWor 74, –76, WorAl, WrDr 76, –80,
–82, –84
Anderson, Jean 1930?- *AuBYP SUP,*
ConAu 41R, ForWC 70, WhoAmW 77,
–79, –81, –83, WhoE 77, –79, –81, –83
Anderson, Johannes Carl 1873-1959 *DcLEL*
Anderson, John Richard Lane 1911-1981
Au&Wr 6, BioIn 12, IntAu&W 76, –77,
–82, WhoWor 76, WrDr 76, –80, –82
Anderson, John Richard Lane *see also* Anderson,
J R L
Anderson, LaVere Francis Shoenfelt 1907-
ConAu 101, SmATA 27, WhoAmW 77,
–79, –81, WhoS&SW 76, –78, –80
Anderson, Madelyn Klein *ConAu 11NR, –69,*
SmATA 28
Anderson, Margaret J 1909- *ConAu 1R, –3NR,*
WhoAmW 81
Anderson, Marian 1902- *AmWomWr,*
Baker 78, BiDAfM, BiDAmM, BioIn 3,
–4, –5, –6, –7, –8, –9, –10, –11, –12, CelR 73,
CurBio 40, –50, DrBlPA, EncAB-H,
GoodHs, HerW, InWom, IntDcWB,
IntWW 74, –75, –76, –77, –78, –79, –80, –81,
–82, –83, LibW, LinLib L, –S, McGEWB,
MusSN, NegAl 76, –83, NewEOp 71,
NewYTBE 72, REn, SelBAA, WebAB,
–79, Who 82, –83, WhoAm 74, –76, –78,
–80, –82, WhoAmW 77, –81, –83,
WhoBlA 75, –77, –80, WhoGov 72,
WhoMus 72, WhoWor 74, –78, WorAl
Anderson, Mary 1939- *AuBYP SUP, BioIn 10,*
ConAu 1NR, –49, IntAu&W 76, –77, –82,
SmATA 7
Anderson, Mary Desiree 1902- *Au&Wr 6,*
ConAu 9R
Anderson, Maxwell 1888-1959 *AmAu&B,*
AmSCAP 66, BiDAmM, BioIn 1, –2, –3,
–4, –5, –6, –7, –8, –9, –10, –11, –12, CasWL,
CmpEPM, CnDAL, CnMD, CnThe,
ConAmA, ConAmL, ConAu 105, CroCD,
CurBio 42, –53, –59, CyWA, DcAmB S6,
DcLB 7[port], DcLEL, EncAB-H,
EncMT, EncWL, EncWT, EvLB, FilmgC,
LinLib L, –S, LongCTC, McGEWB,
McGEWD, –84[port], ModAL, ModWD,

NatCAB 60, NewCBMT, NotNAT A, –B,
ObitOF 79, ObitT 1951, OxAmL, OxThe,
PenC AM, PIP&P, REn, REnAL,
REnWD, TwCA, TwCA SUP, TwCLC 2,
TwCWr, WebAB, –79, WebE&AL,
WhDW, WhAm 3, WhJnl, WhThe,
WorAl, WorEFlm
Anderson, Norman Dean 1928- *ConAu 33R,*
LEduc 74, SmATA 22[port]
Anderson, Patrick 1936- *AmAu&B,*
ConAu 33R
Anderson, Paul Lewis 1880-1956 *BioIn 4,*
WhAm 3, WhNAA
Anderson, Peggy 1938- *ConAu 93,*
NewYTBS 79, WrDr 76, –80, –82, –84
Anderson, Poul 1926- *AmAu&B,*
AuBYP SUP, BioIn 3, –10, –12,
ConAu 1R, –2NR, ConLC 15, ConSFA,
DcLB 8[port], DcLEL 1940, DrAP&F 83,
EncSF, IntAu&W 82, LinLib L, Novels,
ScF&FL 1, –2, WhoAm 74, –76, –78, –80,
–82, WhoHr&F, WhoSciF, WorAl,
WorAu, WrDr 76, –80, –82, –84
Anderson, Rachel 1943- *ConAu 9NR, –21R,*
SmATA 34[port], WrDr 76, –80, –82, –84
Anderson, Robert 1917- *AmAu&B, AuNews 1,*
BiE&WWA, BioIn 2, –3, –8, –10, –11, –12,
BlueB 76, CelR 73, CnMD, ConAu 21R,
ConDr 73, –77, –82, ConLC 23[port],
CroCD, DcLB 7[port], DcLEL 1940,
EncWT, IntAu&W 76, –77, –82, LinLib L,
McGEWD, –84[port], ModAL, ModWD,
NatPD, –81[port], NotNAT, OxAmL,
PenC AM, REn, REnAL, Who 74, –82,
–83, WhoAm 74, –76, –78, –80, –82,
WhoThe 15, –16, –81, WhoWor 74, –76,
WorAl, WorAu, WrDr 76, –80, –82, –84
Anderson, Sherwood 1876-1941 *AmAu&B,*
AmWr, ApCAB X, AtlBL, BioIn 1, –2,
–3, –4, –5, –6, –7, –8, –9, –10, –11, –12,
CasWL, Chambr 3, CnDAL, CnMWL,
ConAmA, ConAmL, ConAu 104,
CurBio 41, CyWA, DcAmB S3,
DcLB DS1[port], –4, –9[port], DcLEL,
DcNAA, EncAB 14[port], EncWL,
–81[port], EvLB, LinLib L, –S, LongCTC,
MakMC, McGEWB, ModAL,
ModAL SUP, NatCAB 36, NotNAT B,
Novels, ObitOF 79, OhA&B, OxAmL,
OxEng, PenC AM, RAdv 1, REn,
REnAL, TwCA, TwCA SUP, TwCLC 1,
–10[port], TwCWr, WebAB, –79,
WebE&AL, WhDW, WhAm 1, WhJnl,
WhLit, WhNAA, WhoTwCL, WorAl
Anderson, William Carl 1943- *WhoF&I 81*
Anderson, William Charles 1920- *ConAu 5R*
Anderson, William Robert 1921- *BiDrAC,*
BioIn 5, –6, –9, BlueB 76, ConAu 5R,
IntWW 74, –75, –76, –77, –78, –79, –80, –81,
–82, –83, WhoAm 74, –76, –78, –80, –82,
WhoAmP 73, –75, –77, –79, WhoGov 72,
–75, WhoS&SW 73

Andrew, Prudence 1924- *Au&Wr 6,
ConAu 1R, -1NR, TwCCW 78, -83,
WrDr 76, -80, -82, -84*

Andrews, Allen 1913- *ConAu 1NR, -49,
IntAu&W 77, -82, WrDr 76, -80, -82, -84*

Andrews, Bart 1945- *ConAu 9NR, -65*

Andrews, F Emerson 1902-1978 *AmAu&B,
BioIn 11, ConAu 1R, -1NR, -81,
NewYTBS 78, ScF&FL 1, -2,
SmATA 22[port], WhAm 7, WhoAm 74,
-76, -78*

Andrews, Mary Raymond Shipman 1865?-1936
*AmAu&B, AmWomWr, ChhPo,
ConAmA, ConAmL, InWom, JBA 34,
NotAW, REnAL, TwCA, WhAm 1,
WhNAA*

Andrews, Michael Frank 1916- *ConAu 49,
IntAu&W 77, LEduc 74, WhoAm 74,
WhoAmA 76, -78, -80, -82, WhoWor 74*

Andrews, V C *ConAu 97, NewYTBS 80[port]*

Andrist, Ralph K 1914- *AuBYP SUP,
ConAu 5NR, -9R*

Anema, Durlynn Carol 1935- *WhoWest 84*

Angel, Heather 1941- *ConAu 69, WrDr 80,
-82, -84*

Angeli, Marguerite De 1889- *JBA 51*

Angeli, Marguerite De *see also* DeAngeli,
Marguerite Lof

Angell, Judie 1937- *ConAu 77,
SmATA 22[port]*

Angell, Madeline 1919- *BioIn 12,
ConAu 10NR, -65, SmATA 18,
WhoMW 80, -82*

Angell, Roger 1920- *BioIn 9, -11, ConAu 57,
ConLC 26[port], DrAF 76, DrAP&F 83,
WhoAm 74, -76, -78, -80, -82*

Angelou, Maya 1928- *AmWomWr, BioIn 8,
-9, -10, -11, -12, BlkAWP, ConAu 65,
ConLC 12, CurBio 74, DrAP 75,
DrAP&F 83, DrBlPA, Ebony 1, HerW,
InB&W 80, LivgBAA, NegAl 83[port],
NewYTBE 72, NotNAT A, SelBAA,
WhoAm 74, -76, -78, -80, -82,
WhoAmW 72, -79, -81, -83, WhoBlA 77,
-80, WomWMM, WrDr 76, -80, -82, -84*

Angier, Bradford *AuBYP SUP, BioIn 11,
ConAu 5R, -7NR, SmATA 12*

Anglund, Joan Walsh 1926- *AmAu&B,
Au&Wr 6, AuBYP, BioIn 6, -7, -8, -9,
-10, ChlLR 1, ChhPo S1, -S2, -S3,
ConAu 5R, FamAIYP, IlsCB 1957,
LinLib L, SmATA 2, ThrBJA,
TwCCW 78, WhoAm 74, -76, -78, -80,
WhoAmW 74, -61, -64, -66, -68, -70, -83,
WrDr 80, -82, -84*

Angrist, Stanley W 1933- *AmM&WS 73P,
-79P, -82P, BioIn 9, ConAu 25R,
SmATA 4*

Angus, Douglas Ross 1909- *ConAu 1R, -3NR,
DrAS 74E, -78E, -82E*

Angus, Sylvia 1921-1982 *ConAu 10NR, -61,
WrDr 84*

Anka, Paul 1941- *AmPS, Baker 78,
BiDAmM, BioIn 5, -6, -7, -9, -10, -12,
CanWW 70, -79, -80, -81, -83, CelR 73,
CreCan 2, EncPR&S 77, FilmgC, MotPP,
RkOn 74, -78, -82, -84, RolSEnR 83,
WhoAm 74, -76, -78, -80, -82,
WhoArab 81, WhoHol A, WhoRocM 82,
WorAl*

Annixter, Jane *AuBYP, BioIn 8, -9,
ConAu X, ForWC 70, MichAu 80,
SmATA 1*

Annixter, Jane *see also* Sturtzel, Jane Levington

Annixter, Paul *BioIn 6, -9, ConAu X,
SmATA X*

Annixter, Paul *see also* Sturtzel, Howard A

Anno, Mitsumasa 1920?- *BioIn 10, -12,
ChlLR 2, ConAu 4NR, -49, FourBJA,
IlsBYP, IlsCB 1967, IntAu&W 77,
SmATA 5, TwCCW 83B*

Anobile, Richard J 1947- *ConAu 5NR, -53*

Anouilh, Jean 1910- *Au&Wr 6, BiE&WWA,
BioIn 3, -4, -5, -6, -7, -8, -9, -12, CasWL,
CnMD, CnMWL, CnThe, ConAu 17R,
ConLC 1, -3, -8, -13, CroCD, CurBio 54,
CyWA, DcFM, EncWL, -81[port],
EncWT, EvEuW, FilmgC, IntAu&W 76,
-77, IntWW 74, -75, -76, -77, -78, -79,
-80, -81, -82, -83, LinLib L, -S,
LongCTC, MakMC, McGEWB,
McGEWD, -84[port], ModFrL, ModRL,
ModWD, NotNAT, -A, OxEng, OxFilm,
OxFr, OxThe, PenC EUR, PIP&P,
RComWL, REn, REnWD, TwCA SUP,
TwCWr, WhDW, Who 74, -82, -83,
WhoFr 79, WhoThe 15, -16, -81,
WhoTwCL, WhoWor 74, WorAl,
WorEFlm*

Anson, Jay 1921?-1980 *BioIn 12, ConAu 81,
-97, NewYTBS 80*

Anthony, Earl 1941- *BlkAWP, CivR 74,
InB&W 80, LivgBAA, NatPD*

Anthony, Evelyn 1928- *Au&Wr 6, ConAu X,
IntAu&W 76, -77, -82, Novels,
TwCCr&M 80, Who 82, -83, WhoSpyF,
WorAl, WrDr 76, -80, -82, -84*

Anthony, Evelyn *see also* Ward-Thomas, Evelyn
Bridget

Anthony, Piers 1934- *AmAu&B, Au&Wr 6,
BioIn 12, ConAu X, ConSFA,
DcLB 8[port], EncSF, Novels,
ScF&FL 1, -2, WhoSciF, WrDr 76, -80,
-82, -84*

Anthony, Piers *see also* Jacob, Piers A D

Antoncich, Betty 1913- *AuBYP, BioIn 8,
ConAu 13R*

Apel, Willi 1893- *AmAu&B, AmCath 80,
Au&Wr 6, Baker 78, BlueB 76,
ConAu 1R, -2NR, DrAS 74H, -78H, -82H,
IntWW 74, -75, -76, -77, -78, -79, -80, -81,
-82, -83, IntWWM 77, OxMus, REnAL,
WhoAm 74, -76, -78, -80*

Apfel, Necia H 1930- *ConAu 107*

Appel, Benjamin 1907-1977 *AmAu&B,
AmNov, BioIn 1, -2, -4, -11, -12,
ConAu 6NR, -13R, -69, DcLEL, EncSF,
IntAu&W 77, NewYTBS 77, OxAmL,
ScF&FL 1, -2, SmATA 21N, TwCA,
TwCA SUP, WhAm 7, WhoAm 74, -76*
Appel, Martin E 1948- *ConAu 85*
Appelfeld, Aharon 1932- *BioIn 12, CasWL,
ConLC 23[port], NewYTBS 80[port]*
Appiah, Peggy 1921- *Au&Wr 6, BioIn 12,
ConAu 41R, IntAu&W 76, SmATA 15,
TwCCW 78, -83, WrDr 76, -80, -82, -84*
Apple, Max 1941- *BioIn 12, ConAu 81,
ConLC 9, DrAF 76, DrAP&F 83,
DrAS 74E, -78E, -82E,
NewYTBS 81[port]*
Appleton, Victor *AmAu&B, ConAu P-2,
ScF&FL 1, -1A, SmATA 1, WebAB 79*
Appleton, Victor *see also* Stratemeyer, Edward L
Appleton, Victor, II *AmAu&B, ConAu X,
-17R, ScF&FL 1, SmATA X, -1*
Appleton, Victor, II *see also* Adams, Harriet S
Appleton, Victor, II *see also* Stratemeyer, Edward L
Apsler, Alfred 1907- *AuBYP SUP, BioIn 11,
ConAu 3NR, -5R, IntAu&W 76, -77,
SmATA 10, WhoPNW, WrDr 76, -80,
-82, -84*
Aptheker, Herbert 1915- *AmAu&B, BioIn 10,
ConAu 5R, -6NR, DrAS 74H, -78H, -82H,
EncAAH, IntAu&W 76, WhoAm 74, -76,
-78, -80, -82, WhoWor 74, WhoWorJ 72,
-78*
Aragones, Sergio 1937- *WhoAm 82,
WorECom*
Arbeiter, Jean S *AuBYP SUP*
Arbib, Michael A 1940- *AmM&WS 73P, -76P,
-79P, -82P, WhoAm 74, -76, -78, -80, -82*
Arbuckle, Wanda Rector 1910- *ConAu 41R,
WhoAmW 74, -72, WhoWest 74, -76*
Archer, Jeffrey 1940- *BioIn 12, ConAu 77,
IntAu&W 82, IntWW 83,
NewYTBS 80[port], Novels, Who 74, -82,
-83, WhoWor 80, WrDr 82, -84*
Archer, Jules 1915- *AuBYP, BioIn 8, -9,
ConAu 6NR, -9R, ConLC 12,
IntAu&W 76, -77, SmATA 4, WrDr 80,
-82, -84*
Archer, Myrtle 1926- *ConAu 102,
IntWWP 77X, -82X*
Archibald, Joe 1898- *AuBYP, ConAu X*
Archibald, Joseph S 1898- *BioIn 7, -9,
ConAu 5NR, -9R, SmATA 3*
Arden, John 1930- *Au&Wr 6, BioIn 7, -8, -9,
-10, -12, BlueB 76, CasWL, CnMD,
CnThe, ConAu 13R, ConDr 73, -77, -82,
ConLC 6, -13, -15, CroCD,
DcLB 13[port], DcLEL 1940, EncWL 81,
EncWT, IntAu&W 76, -77, IntWW 74,
-75, -76, -77, -78, -79, -80, -81, -82, -83,
LongCEL, LongCTC, McGEWD, -84,
ModBrL SUP, ModWD, NewC, NotNAT,*

*OxThe, PenC ENG, PIP&P, REnWD,
TwCWr, WebE&AL, WhDW, Who 74,
-82, -83, WhoThe 15, -16, -81,
WhoTwCL, WhoWor 74, WorAu,
WrDr 76, -80, -82, -84*
Arden, William *ConAu X, EncMys,
TwCCr&M 80, WrDr 82, -84*
Arden, William *see also* Lynds, Dennis
Ardizzone, Edward 1900-1979 *ArtsCL,
Au&ICB, Au&Wr 6, AuBYP, BioIn 1,
-4, -5, -6, -7, -8, -9, -10, -11, -12,
BlueB 76, BrCA, ChlLR 3, ChhPo, -S1,
-S2, -S3, ConArt, ConAu 5R, -8NR, -89,
CurBio 64, -80N, DcBrA 1, IlsCB 1744,
-1946, -1957, -1967, IntAu&W 76,
IntWW 74, -75, -76, -77, -78, -79,
LinLib L, LongCTC, MorJA,
NewYTBS 79, PhDcTCA 77, PiP,
SmATA 1, -21N, -28[port], TwCCW 78,
-83, WhE&EA, Who 74, WhoAmA 80N,
-82N, WhoArt 80, -82N, WhoChL,
WhoWor 74, -76, -78, WrDr 76*
Ardrey, Robert 1908-1980 *AmAu&B,
AnObit 1980[port], BiE&WWA, BioIn 4,
-9, -10, -12, BioNews 74, BlkAWP,
CelR 73, CnMD, ConAu 33R, -93,
ConDr 73, -77, CurBio 73, -80N, EncSF,
LinLib L, ModWD, NewYTBS 80,
NotNAT, PIP&P, ScF&FL 1, -2,
TwCA SUP, WhDW, WhAm 7, WhThe,
WhoAm 74, -76, -78, -80, WhoThe 81N,
WhoWor 74, -76, -78, WorEFlm,
WrDr 76, -80*
Arehart-Treichel, Joan 1942- *ConAu 6NR, -57,
SmATA 22[port]*
Argenzio, Victor 1902- *ConAu 53*
Arkin, Frieda 1917- *ConAu 11NR, -65,
DrAF 76, DrAP&F 83*
Arlen, Michael J 1930- *AmAu&B, ASpks,
BioIn 8, -10, -11, ConAu 61,
DcLEL 1940, WhoAm 74, -76, -78, -80,
-82, WhoE 74, WrDr 80, -82, -84*
Armah, Ayi Kwei 1939- *AfrA, CasWL,
ConAu 61, ConLC 5, ConNov 76, -82,
DcLEL 1940, EncWL, -81, InB&W 80,
IntAu&W 76, -77, ModBlW, ModCmwL,
RGAfL, WrDr 76, -80, -82, -84*
Armer, Alberta Roller 1904- *BioIn 11,
ConAu 5R, ForWC 70, IndAu 1917,
SmATA 9*
Armer, Laura Adams 1874-1963 *AmAu&B,
AuBYP, BioIn 1, -2, -4, -6, -7, ConAmA,
ConAu 65, IlsCB 1744, InWom, JBA 34,
-51, Newb 1922, SmATA 13,
TwCCW 83*
Armes, Roy 1937- *ConAu 73, IntAu&W 82,
WrDr 76, -80, -82, -84*
Armour, Richard 1906- *AmAu&B, AnCL,
Au&Wr 6, AuBYP, BioIn 2, -5, -7, -8,
-12, ChhPo, -S1, -S2, -S3, ConAu 1R,
-4NR, CurBio 58, DrAS 74E, -78E, -82E,
IntAu&W 76, -77, -82, REnAL,*

SmATA 14, TwCCW 78, WhE&EA,
WhoAm 74, –76, –78, –80, –82,
WhoWor 74, –76, –78, –80, –82, WorAl,
WrDr 76, –80, –82, –84

Armstrong, Charlotte 1905-1969 AmAu&B,
AmWomWr, BioIn 1, –8, –10, ConAu 1R,
–3NR, –25R, CorpD, CurBio 46, –69,
EncMys, InWom, Novels, ObitOF 79,
TwCCr&M 80, WhAm 5, WhoAmW 58,
–66, –68, –70, WorAu

Armstrong, Diana 1943- ConAu 107

Armstrong, Karen BioIn 12

Armstrong, Louise AuBYP SUP, SmATA 33

Armstrong, Neil A 1930- AmM&WS 73P,
–79P, –82P, AsBiEn, BioIn 7, –8, –9, –10,
–12, BlueB 76, CelR 73, CurBio 69,
IntWW 74, –75, –76, –77, –78, –79, –80, –81,
–82, –83, LinLib S, McGEWB,
PolProf NF, UFOEn, WebAB, –79,
WebAMB, WhDW, Who 74, –82, –83,
WhoAm 74, –76, –78, –80, –82, WhoEng 80,
WhoGov 72, WhoMW 74, –76, –78,
WhoS&SW 73, WhoWor 74, –78, –80, –82,
WorAl

Armstrong, Richard 1903- Au&Wr 6, AuBYP,
BioIn 2, –8, –9, –11, ConAu 77,
SmATA 11, ThrBJA, TwCCW 78, –83,
WhoChL, WrDr 80, –82, –84

Armstrong, William Howard 1914- AuBYP,
AuNews 1, BioIn 8, –9, –10, BioNews 74,
ChlLR 1, ConAu 9NR, –17R, MorBMP,
NinCLC 1966, SmATA 4, ThrBJA,
TwCCW 78, –83, WhoAm 74, –76, –78,
–80, –82, WhoE 74, WrDr 76, –80, –82,
–84

Arnason, H Harvard 1909- ConAu 61,
WhoAmA 73, –76, –78, –80, –82

Arneson, D J 1935- ConAu 106, ScF&FL 1,
SmATA 37

Arnett, Caroline 1902- BioIn 11, ConAu X,
SmATA X

Arnett, Caroline see also Cole, Lois Dwight

Arno, Enrico 1913-1981 BioIn 4, –5, –8,
ChhPo S1, –S2, –S3, FourBJA, IlsBYP,
IlsCB 1946, –1957, –1967, SmATA 28N

Arnold, Alan 1922- ConAu 5R, WhE&EA

Arnold, Arnold 1921- ChhPo S2,
ConAu 10NR, –17R

Arnold, Caroline 1944- ConAu 107,
SmATA 34, –36

Arnold, Eddy 1918- AmPS A, –B, BioIn 1, –4,
–7, –8, –9, –10, –12, CelR 73, CmpEPM,
CurBio 70, EncFCWM 69, IntMPA 77,
–75, –76, –78, –79, –81, –82, –84, RkOn 74,
WhoAm 74, –76, –78, –80, –82, WorAl

Arnold, Edmund Clarence 1913- BlueB 76,
ConAu 1R, –3NR, MichAu 80,
WhoCon 73, WhoWor 74, WrDr 76, –80,
–82, –84

Arnold, Elliott 1912-1980 AmAu&B, AmNov,
AnObit 1980[port], Au&Wr 6, AuBYP,
BioIn 2, –4, –8, –10, –12, BlueB 76,

ConAu 17R, –97, NewYTBS 80,
SmATA 22N, –5, TwCA SUP, WhAm 7,
WhoAm 74, –76, –78, –80, WhoWest 74,
–76, –78, –80, WhoWor 74, –76, –78, –80,
WrDr 76, –80

Arnold, Emily 1939- ConAu 109

Arnold, Eve 1913- BioIn 10, –12, ConPhot,
WomWMM A, –B

Arnold, Francena H 1888- ConAu P-1

Arnold, Harry L, Jr. 1912- BiDrACP 79,
BlueB 76, WhoAm 74, –76, –78, –80, –82,
WhoWor 74, –76, –78, –80, –82, WrDr 76,
–80, –82, –84

Arnold, Lois B ConAu 107

Arnold, Margot ConAu X, IntAu&W 82X

Arnold, Oren 1900- BioIn 3, –9, –10,
ConAu 2NR, –5R, SmATA 4

Arnold, Pauline 1894-1974 ConAu 1R, –2NR,
InWom

Arnold, Peter 1943- ConAu 1NR, –49,
IntAu&W 77, WrDr 76, –80, –82, –84

Arnold, Richard 1912- Au&Wr 6,
ConAu 3NR, –9R

Arnold, William Van 1941- ConAu 110

Arnold-Forster, Mark 1920-1981 ConAu 105,
–65

Arnosky, Jim 1946- ConAu 69,
SmATA 22[port]

Arnothy, Christine 1930- Au&Wr 6,
ConAu 10NR, –65, IntAu&W 76, –77,
REn, ScF&FL 1, WhoFr 79

Arnott, Kathleen 1914- BioIn 12, ConAu 57,
SmATA 20

Arnov, Boris, Jr. 1926- AuBYP, BioIn 7, –11,
ConAu 1R, –3NR, SmATA 12

Arnow, Harriette 1908- AmAu&B, AmNov,
AmWomWr, BioIn 2, –3, –4, –10, –11,
ConAu 9R, ConLC 2, –7, –18, ConNov 76,
–82, CurBio 54, DcLB 6[port], InWom,
IntAu&W 76, MichAu 80, WhoAmW 66,
WorAu, WrDr 76, –80, –82, –84

Arntson, Herbert Edward 1911- BioIn 11,
ConAu 17R, DrAS 74E, –78E, –82E,
SmATA 12, WhoPNW

Arquette, Lois S 1934- BioIn 9, –12, ConAu X,
SmATA 1

Arquette, Lois S see also Cardozo, Lois S

Arquette, Lois S see also Duncan, Lois

Arquette, Lois S see also Kerry, Lois

Arr, E H 1831-1881 Alli SUP, DcAmAu,
DcNAA

Arr, E H see also Rollins, Ellen Chapman Hobbs

Arre, John 1926- ConAu X

Arre, John see also Holt, John Robert

Arthur, Robert 1909-1969 AuBYP SUP,
BioIn 8, ConAu X, FilmgC, IntMPA 77,
–75, –76, –78, –79, –84, ScF&FL 1,
WhoHr&F

Arthur, Ruth M 1905-1979 Au&Wr 6,
AuBYP SUP, BioIn 10, –11, BrCA,
ChhPo, ConAu 4NR, –9R, –85, ConLC 12,
IntAu&W 76, –77, ScF&FL 1, –1A, –2,

SmATA 26N, –7, TwCCW 78, –83,
WrDr 80

Artzybasheff, Boris 1899-1965 *AmAu&B,*
AmPB, AnCL, AuBYP, BioIn 1, –2, –3,
–5, –7, –8, –12, ChhPo S2, ConICB,
CurBio 45, –65, DcAmB S7, ForII,
IlrAm D, IlsCB 1744, JBA 34, –51,
LinLib L, SmATA 14, Str&VC,
WhAm 4, WhoAmA 78N, WhoGrA

Arundel, Honor 1919-1973 *Au&Wr 6,*
AuBYP SUP, BioIn 9, –10, ConAu 41R,
ConAu P-2, ConLC 17, FourBJA,
SmATA 24N, –4, TwCCW 78, –83

Arvio, Raymond Paavo 1930- *ConAu 77*

Ash, Brian 1936- *EncSF, WrDr 80, –82, –84*

Ashabranner, Brent 1921- *BioIn 9, BlueB 76,*
ConAu 5R, –10NR, SmATA 1,
WhoAm 74, –76, –78, –80

Ashbery, John 1927- *AmAu&B, BioIn 8, –10,*
–11, –12, BlueB 76, ChhPo S3,
ConAu 5R, –9NR, ConLC 2, –3, –4, –6, –9,
–13, –15, –25[port], ConP 70, –75, –80,
CroCAP, CurBio 76, DcLB Y81A[port],
–5[port], DcLEL 1940, DrAP 75,
DrAP&F 83, IntAu&W 82, IntWWP 77,
LinLib L, ModAL SUP, NewYTBS 76,
PenC AM, RAdv 1, WebE&AL,
WhoAm 74, –76, –78, –80, –82,
WhoAmA 78, –80, –82, WhoE 77, –79, –81,
–83, WhoWor 80, –82, WorAu, WrDr 76,
–80, –82, –84

Ashe, Arthur 1943- *BioIn 6, –7, –8, –9, –10,*
–11, –12, BioNews 74, BlueB 76,
CelR 73, ConAu 65, CurBio 66, Ebony 1,
InB&W 80, IntWW 78, –79, –80, –81, –82,
–83, NegAl 76, –83[port], NewYTBS 77,
–79, WebAB, –79, WhoAm 74, –76, –78,
–80, –82, WhoBlA 75, –77, –80,
WhoS&SW 73, –75, –76, WhoTech 82,
WorAl

Asher, Sandy 1942- *ConAu 105,*
DcLB Y83B[port], SmATA 34, –36

Ashford, Jeffrey 1926- *Au&Wr 6, AuBYP,*
BioIn 8, –9, ConAu X, –1R, EncMys,
IntAu&W 76, TwCCr&M 80, WrDr 76,
–80, –82, –84

Ashford, Jeffrey *see also* Jeffries, Roderic

Ashley, Bernard 1935- *ChlLR 4[port],*
ConAu 93, IntAu&W 82, TwCCW 78,
–83, WrDr 80, –82, –84

Ashner, Sonie Shapiro 1938- *ConAu 57*

Ashton, Dore 1928- *AmAu&B, ConAu 2NR,*
–5R, IntAu&W 77, –82, WhoAm 74, –76,
–78, –80, –82, WhoAmA 73, –76, –78, –80,
–82, WhoAmW 58, –61, –64, –66, –68, –83,
WhoE 75, –77, WrDr 76, –80, –82, –84

Ashton-Warner, Sylvia 1908-1978 *BioIn 8, –9,*
–10, –12, BlueB 76, ConAu 69,
ConLC 19, ConNov 72, –76, –82,
DcLEL 1940, IntAu&W 76, –77,
IntDcWB, LongCTC, ModCmwL, Novels,
PenC ENG, RAdv 1, TwCWr, WorAu,

WrDr 76, –80, –82, –84

Ashworth, Mae Hurley *IndAu 1917*

Asimov, Isaac 1920- *AmAu&B,*
AmM&WS 73P, –76P, –79P, –82P, AsBiEn,
Au&Wr 6, AuBYP, BioIn 3, –7, –8, –9,
–10, –11, –12, BlueB 76, CasWL,
CelR 73, ConAu 1R, –2NR, ConLC 1, –3,
–9, –19, –26[port], ConNov 72, –76, –82,
ConSFA, CurBio 53, –68, DcLB 8[port],
DcLEL 1940, DrAF 76, DrAP&F 83,
EncMys, EncSF, Future, IntAu&W 76,
–77, –82, IntWW 74, –75, –76, –77, –78,
–79, –80, –81, –82, –83, LinLib L, –S,
LongCTC, MakMC, Novels[port],
PenC AM, REn, REnAL, ScF&FL 1, –2,
SmATA 1, –26[port], ThrBJA,
TwCCr&M 80, TwCWr, WebAB, –79,
WebE&AL, Who 82, –83, WhoAm 74,
–76, –78, –80, –82, WhoAmJ 80, WhoE 74,
–81, –83, WhoSciF, WhoWor 74, –76, –78,
–80, –82, WhoWorJ 78, WorAl, WorAu,
WrDr 76, –80, –82, –84

Asinof, Eliot 1919- *ConAu 7NR, –9R,*
SmATA 6, WrDr 76, –80, –82, –84

Asprin, Robert 1946- *ConAu 85, WrDr 84*

Atkinson, Brooks 1894- *BiE&WWA, BioIn 1,*
–4, –5, –6, –7, –10, BlueB 76, CelR 73,
ConAu 61, CurBio 42, –61, EncWT,
IntAu&W 77, LinLib L, –S,
NewYTBE 73, NotNAT, OxAmL,
OxThe, REnAL, TwCA, TwCA SUP,
WebAB, –79, WhNAA, Who 74, –82, –83,
WhoThe 81, WorAl, WrDr 76, –80, –82

Atkinson, Margaret Fleming *AuBYP, BioIn 8,*
–12, ConAu 73, SmATA 14

Atmore, Anthony 1932- *ConAu 25R*

Attenborough, David Frederick 1926-
Au&Wr 6, BioIn 12, BlueB 76,
ConAu 1R, –6NR, CurBio 83[port],
IntAu&W 77, IntMPA 77, –75, –76, –78,
–79, –81, –82, –84, IntWW 75, –76, –77,
–78, –79, –80, –81, –82, –83, Who '74, –82,
–83, WhoWor 76, –78, –82, WrDr 76, –80,
–82, –84

Atticus *ConAu X, SmATA X*

Atticus *see also* Fleming, Ian

Atwater, Constance Elizabeth 1923-
ConAu 13R

Atwater, James David 1928- *ConAu 101,*
WhoAm 74, –76, –78, –80, –82

Atwood, Ann Margaret 1913- *AuBYP SUP,*
BioIn 10, ConAu 41R, FourBJA,
IntAu&W 82, SmATA 7, WhoAm 74,
–76, –78, –80, –82, WhoAmW 74,
WrDr 82, –84

Atwood, Margaret Eleanor 1939- *Au&Wr 6,*
BioIn 10, –11, –12, CaW, CanWW 70, –79,
–80, –81, –83, ConAu 3NR, –49, ConLC 2,
–3, –4, –8, –13, –15, –25[port], ConNov 76,
–82, ConP 70, –75, –80, DcLEL 1940,
DrAF 76, DrAP 75, EncWL 81,
IntAu&W 76, –77, –82, IntDcWB,

IntWWP 77, –82, ModCmwL,
NewYTBS 82[port], Novels, OxCan,
OxCan SUP, WhoAm 74, –76, –78, –80,
WhoAmW 81, –83, WhoWor 80, –82,
WorAu 1970, WrDr 76, –80, –82, –84

Auchincloss, Louis 1917- *AmAu&B,*
Au&Wr 6, BioIn 3, –4, –5, –6, –7, –8, –10,
–11, –12, BlueB 76, CelR 73, ConAu 1R,
–6NR, ConLC 4, –6, –9, –18, ConLCrt,
–82, ConNov 72, –76, –82, CurBio 54, –78,
DcLB Y80A[port], –2, DcLEL 1940,
DrAF 76, DrAP&F 83, IntAu&W 76,
–77, IntWW 74, –75, –76, –77, –78, –79,
–80, –81, –82, –83, LinLib L, ModAL,
ModAL SUP, NewYTBS 79, Novels,
OxAmL, PenC AM, RAdv 1, REn,
REnAL, TwCWr, WebE&AL, Who 74,
–82, –83, WhoAm 74, –76, –78, –80, –82,
WhoAmL 78, –79, –83, WhoWor 74, –78,
–80, –82, WorAl, WorAu, WrDr 76, –80,
–82, –84

Auden, W H 1907-1973 *AmAu&B,*
AmSCAP 66, Au&Wr 6, BiE&WWA,
CasWL, CelR 73, Chambr 3, ChhPo, –S1,
–S2, CnE&AP, CnMD, CnMWL,
ConAu 5NR, –9R, –45, ConDr 73,
ConLC 1, –2, –3, –4, –6, –9, –11, –14,
ConLCrt, –82, ConP 70, –75, –80A,
CurBio 71, –73, –73N, CyWA,
DcLB 10[port], –20[port], DcLEL,
EncWL, –81[port], EvLB, LinLib L, –S,
LongCTC, McGEWD, –84[port], ModAL,
ModAL SUP, ModBrL, ModBrL SUP,
ModWD, NewC, NewEOp 71,
NewYTBE 71, –72, –73, ObitOF 79,
ObitT 1971, OxAmL, OxEng,
PenC ENG, PIP&P, RAdv 1, RComWL,
REn, REnAL, TwCA, TwCA SUP,
TwCWr, WebE&AL, WhThe,
WhoThe 15, WhoTwCL, WorAl

Auel, Jean M 1936- *BioIn 12, ConAu 103,*
NewYTBS 80[port]

Auerbach, Arnold 1917- *BioIn 6, –7, –8, –9, –10,*
–11, –12, CelR 73, CurBio 69,
WhoAm 74, –76, –78, –80, –82, WhoBbl 73,
WhoE 74, –79, –81, –83

Auerbach, Arnold *see also* Auerbach, Red

Auerbach, Red 1917- *BioIn 6, –7, –8, –9, –10,*
–11, –12, CurBio 69

Auerbach, Red *see also* Auerbach, Arnold

Ault, Phil H 1914- *BioIn 1, ConAu X,*
SmATA X

Ault, Phillip H 1914- *AuBYP SUP,*
ConAu 101, IntYB 78, –79, –80, –81, –82,
SmATA 23[port], WhoAm 74, –76, –78,
–80, WhoMW 74, –76, –78

Auslander, Joseph 1897-1965 *AmAu&B,*
BioIn 4, –5, –7, ChhPo, –S1, CnDAL,
ObitOF 79, OxAmL, REn, REnAL,
TwCA, TwCA SUP, WhJnl, WhNAA

Austen, Jane 1775-1817 *Alli, AtlBL, BbD,*
BiD&SB, BioIn 1, –2, –3, –4, –5, –6, –7, –8,

–9, –10, –11, –12, BrAu 19, BrWr 4,
CelCen, Chambr 2, CrtT 2, –4, CyWA,
DcBiA, DcBiPP, DcEnA, DcEnL, DcEuL,
DcLEL, Dis&D, EvLB, GoodHs, HerW,
InWom, IntDcWB[port], LinLib L, –S,
LongCEL, McGEWB, MouLC 2, NewC,
Novels[port], OxEng, PenC ENG,
RAdv 1, RComWL, REn, WebE&AL,
WhDW, WorAl

Austin, Elizabeth S 1907- *AuBYP SUP,*
BioIn 10, ConAu P-2, IntAu&W 77,
SmATA 5, WhoAmW 72

Austin, Oliver Luther, Jr. 1903-
AmM&WS 73P, –76P, –79P, –82P,
AuBYP SUP, BioIn 10, ConAu 49,
SmATA 7, WhoS&SW 73

Austin, Paul Britten *ChhPo S3*

Avallone, Michael 1924- *Au&Wr 6, BioIn 7,*
–11, ConAu 4NR, –5R, EncMys, EncSF,
IntAu&W 76, –77, Novels, ScF&FL 1, –2,
TwCCr&M 80, WhoAm 82, WhoE 83,
WhoHr&F, WrDr 76, –80, –82, –84

Avery, Gillian Elise 1926- *AuBYP, BioIn 8,*
–10, ConAu 4NR, –9R, FourBJA,
IntAu&W 77, –82, SmATA 7,
TwCCW 78, –83, Who 82, –83, WhoChL,
WhoWor 80, WrDr 80, –82, –84

Avery, Ira 1914- *ConAu 81, WhoE 81*

Avery, Lynn *AuBYP, BioIn 11, ConAu X,*
SmATA X

Avery, Lynn *see also* Cole, Lois Dwight

Avery, Virginia Turner 1912- *WhoAmW 81*

Avi *ConAu X, SmATA X*

Awad, Elias Michael 1934- *ConAu 11NR,*
–17R, WhoCon 73, WhoMW 74, –76

Axelrod, Herbert Richard 1927- *Au&Wr 6,*
BioIn 7, ConAu 85

Axtell, James Lewis 1941- *ConAu 108,*
DrAS 78H, –82H

Axthelm, Pete 1943- *WhoAm 80, –82*

Ayars, Albert Lee 1917- *AmM&WS 73S,*
BlueB 76, ConAu 29R, IntAu&W 77,
LEduc 74, WhoAm 74, –76, –78, –80, –82,
WhoPubR 72, –76, WhoS&SW 80, –82,
WhoWor 74, –76, WrDr 76, –80, –82, –84

Ayars, James Sterling 1898- *AuBYP, BioIn 8,*
–9, ConAu 2NR, –5R, IntAu&W 77, –82,
MichAu 80, SmATA 4, WhoMW 74, –82,
WrDr 76, –80, –82, –84

Ayensu, Edward Solomon 1935- *BioIn 11,*
WhoBlA 75, –77, –80, WhoGov 77, –75,
WhoS&SW 73, –75, –76, WhoWor 78

Ayer, Margaret *BioIn 5, –6, –12, ConAu 65,*
ForWC 70, IlsBYP, IlsCB 1946, MorJA,
SmATA 15, WhoAmW 58, –61

Aylesworth, Thomas Gibbons 1927-
AmM&WS 73P, –76P, –79P, –82P,
AuBYP SUP, BioIn 9, ChlLR 6[port],
ConAu 10NR, –25R, IndAu 1917,
LEduc 74, ScF&FL 1, –2, SmATA 4,
WhoE 74, –75, –77, –79, –81, –83

Ayling, Keith 1898-1976 *BioIn 11, ConAu 69,*

−73, NewYTBS 76
Aymar, Brandt 1911- *ConAu 1R,*
  SmATA 22[port], WhNAA
Azuela, Mariano 1873-1952 *BioIn 1, −2, −3, −5,*
  −9, −10, CasWL, ConAu 104, CyWA,
  DcSpL, EncLatA, EncWL, −81, LinLib L,
  McGEWB, ModLAL, ObitOF 79,
  OxSpan, PenC AM, REn, TwCLC 3,
  TwCWr, WhAm 5, WhE&EA, WhNAA,
  WorAu

B

Baastad, Babbis Friis 1921-1970 *ConAu X, SmATA X*
Baastad, Babbis Friis *see also* Friis-Baastad, Babbis El
Babbis, Eleanor 1921-1970 *AuBYP SUP, ConAu X, SmATA X, ThrBJA*
Babbis, Eleanor *see also* Friis-Baastad, Babbis Ellinor
Babbitt, Natalie 1932- *AuBYP SUP, BioIn 10, -12, ChlLR 2, ChhPo S2, -S3, ConAu 2NR, -49, FourBJA, IlsCB 1967, IntAu&W 77, MorBMP, SmATA 6, TwCCW 78, -83, WhoAm 82, WrDr 76, -80, -82, -84*
Babel, Isaac 1894-1941 *LinLib L, -S, McGEWB, WorAl*
Babson, Marian *ConAu 102, IntAu&W 76, TwCCr&M 80, WrDr 80, -82, -84*
Bacall, Lauren 1924- *BiDFilm, BiE&WWA, BioIn 1, -3, -4, -5, -7, -8, -9, -10, -11, -12, BlueB 76, CelR 73, CmMov, ConAu 93, CurBio 70, EncMT, FilmgC, GoodHs, InWom, IntDcWB, IntMPA 77, -75, -76, -78, -79, -81, -82, -84, IntWW 74, -75, -76, -77, -78, -79, -80, -81, -82, -83, MotPP, MovMk, NewYTBE 70, NewYTBS 79, -80[port], NotNAT, OxFilm, WhoAm 74, -76, -78, -80, -82, WhoAmJ 80, WhoAmW 74, -58, -61, -64, -66, -68, -70, -72, -79, -81, -83, WhoHol A, WhoThe 15, -16, -81, WhoWor 74, -78, WorAl, WorEFlm, WrDr 82, -84*
Bach, Alice 1942- *AuBYP SUP, ConAu 101, ForWC 70, SmATA 27, -30[port]*
Bach, Mickey 1909- *WhoAmA 76, -78*
Bach, Richard 1936- *AuNews 1, BioIn 9, -10, -11, BioNews 74, ConAu 9R, ConLC 14, CurBio 73, EncO&P 78S1, Novels, ScF&FL 1, -2, SmATA 13, WhoAm 76, -78, -80, WorAl, WrDr 76, -80, -82, -84*
Bacher, June Masters 1918- *ConAu 108*
Backus, Richard Haven 1922- *AmM&WS 73P, -76P, -79P, -82P*
Bacon, Margaret Hope 1921- *BioIn 10, ConAu 25R, SmATA 6, WrDr 76*
Bacon, Martha 1917-1981 *AuBYP SUP, BioIn 12, ChlLR 3, ChhPo S1,*

ConAu 104, -85, ScF&FL 1, SmATA 18, -27N, TwCCW 78, -83
Baen, James 1943- *EncSF*
Baender, Margaret Woodruff 1921- *WhoWest 84*
Baer, Edith Ruth 1920- *Au&Wr 6, ConAu 104, IntAu&W 76, -77*
Baer, Jean L 1926- *ConAu 9NR, -13R, WhoAmW 61, -64, -66, -68, -70, -77, -79, -81, -83, WhoE 74*
Baez, Joan 1941- *Baker 78, BiDAmM, BioIn 6, -7, -8, -9, -10, -11, -12, BioNews 74, BlueB 76, CelR 73, ChiSch, CivR 74, CmCal, ConAu 21R, CurBio 63, EncFCWM 69, EncPR&S 77, GoodHs, InWom, IntAu&W 76, IntDcWB, IntWW 76, -77, -78, -79, -80, -81, -82, -83, IntWWM 77, LibW, MugS, NewYTBE 72, PolProf J, RkOn 78, -84, RolSEnR 83, WebAB, -79, WhoAm 74, -76, -78, -80, -82, WhoAmW 74, -66, -68, -70, -72, -81, -83, WhoRocM 82, WhoWest 74, -76, -78, WhoWor 74, -78, -80, -82, WorAl*
Bagdikian, Ben Haig 1920- *AmAu&B, BioIn 7, -11, ConAu 6NR, -9R, DrAS 78E, -82E, IntAu&W 77, -82, WhoAm 74, -76, -78, -80, -82, WhoS&SW 73, WhoWor 74, -82, WrDr 76, -80, -82, -84*
Baginski, Frank 1938- *ConAu 93*
Bagley, Desmond 1923-1983 *Au&Wr 6, ConAu 109, -17R, DcLEL 1940, IntAu&W 76, -77, Novels, TwCCr&M 80, Who 82, -83, WhoWor 78, WrDr 76, -80, -82, -84*
Bagley, John Joseph 1908- *Au&Wr 6, ConAu 5R, IntAu&W 76, -77, -82, WhoWor 76, WrDr 76, -80, -82, -84*
Bagni, Gwen *ConAu X*
Bagnold, Enid 1889-1981 *AnObit 1981[port], AuBYP, BiE&WWA, BioIn 2, -4, -6, -7, -8, -9, -10, -12, BlueB 76, ChhPo S2, CnMD, ConAu 5R, -5NR, -103, ConDr 73, -77, ConLC 25[port], ConNov 76, CurBio 64, -81N, DcLB 13[port], DcLEL, EncWT, EvLB, FourBJA, InWom, IntAu&W 76, -77,*

IntWW 78, –79, –80, –81, –81N, *LinLib* L,
LongCTC, *ModWD*, *NewC*,
NewYTBS 81[port], *NotNAT*, –A, *Novels*,
OxEng, *PIP&P*, *REn*, *SmATA* 1,
–25[port], *TwCA*, *TwCA SUP*,
TwCCW 83, *TwCWr*, *WhAm* 7,
WhE&EA, *Who* 74, –82N, *WhoAmW* 74,
–66, –68, –70, –72, *WhoChL*, *WhoThe* 15,
–16, –81, *WhoWor* 74, –76, –78, *WorAl*,
WrDr 76, –80, –82
Bailey, Anthony 1933- *BioIn* 12, *ConAu* 1R,
–3NR
Bailey, Bernadine Freeman 1901- *AuBYP*,
BioIn 7, *ConAu* 5R, –7NR, *ForWC* 70,
IntAu&W 76, –77, *SmATA* 14,
WhoAmW 74, –58, –68, –72
Bailey, Charles Waldo, II 1929- *BioIn* 7,
ConAu 1R, –1NR, *ScF&FL* 1, –2,
WhoAm 74, –76, –78, –80, –82, *WrDr* 76,
–80, –82, –84
Bailey, F Lee 1933- *BioIn* 7, –8, –9, –10, –11,
CelR 73, *ConAu* 89, *CurBio* 67,
NewYTBE 70, *WebAB*, –79, *WhoAm* 74,
–76, –78, –80, –82, *WhoAmL* 78, –79,
WhoE 74, *WorAl*
Bailey, Jane H 1916- *BioIn* 11, *ConAu* 4NR,
–53, *SmATA* 12, *WhoAmW* 77
Bailey, Maralyn Collins 1941- *BioIn* 11,
ConAu 53, *IntAu&W* 77, *SmATA* 12
Bailey, Maurice Charles 1932- *BioIn* 11,
ConAu 53, *SmATA* 12
Bailey, Pearl 1918- *AmPS* B, *AmSCAP* 66,
BiDAfM, *BiDAmM*, *BiE&WWA*,
BioIn 3, –4, –6, –8, –9, –10, –11, –12,
CelR 73, *CmpEPM*, *ConAu* 61,
CurBio 55, –69, *DrBlPA*, *Ebony* 1,
EncJzS 70, *EncMT*, *FilmgC*, *HerW*,
InB&W 80, *InWom*, *IntMPA* 77, –75, –76,
–78, –79, –81, –82, –84, *LivgBAA*, *MotPP*,
MovMk, *NegAl* 76, –83[port],
NewYTBE 71, *NotNAT*, –A, *SelBAA*,
WhoAm 74, –76, –78, –80, –82,
WhoAmW 74, –58, –64, –66, –68, –70, –72,
–77, –83, *WhoBlA* 75, –77, –80,
WhoHol A, *WhoThe* 15, –16, –81,
WhoWor 74, *WorAl*, *WrDr* 80, –82, –84
Bailey, Ralph Edgar 1893- *BioIn* 11,
ConAu P-1, *SmATA* 11
Bainbridge, Beryl 1934- *ASpks*, *BioIn* 10, –11,
–12, *ConAu* 21R, –21R, *ConLC* 4, –5, –8,
–10, –14, –18, –22[port], *ConNov* 76, –82,
DcLB 14[port], *EncWL* 81, *IntAu&W* 76,
IntWW 81, –82, –83, *NewYTBS* 81[port],
Novels, *Who* 82, –83, *WorAu* 1970,
WrDr 76, –80, –82, –84
Baird, Bil 1904- *BiE&WWA*, *BioIn* 1, –3, –5,
–10, *BioNews* 74, *CelR* 73, *ChhPo* S2,
ConAu 106, *CurBio* 54, *NotNAT*,
SmATA 30[port], *WhoThe* 81, *WorAl*
Baird, Eva-Lee *AuBYP SUP*
Baird, Marie-Terese 1918- *ConAu* 57
Baird, Thomas 1923- *Alli*, *AmAu&B*,

ConAu 4NR, –53, *WrDr* 76, –80, –82, –84
Baity, Elizabeth Chesley 1907- *AmAu&B*,
AnCL, *BioIn* 3, –6, –9, *ConAu* 29R,
MorJA, *SmATA* 1
Bakeless, John Edwin 1894-1978 *AmAu&B*,
Au&Wr 6, *AuBYP*, *BioIn* 4, –7, –11,
ConAu 5R, –5NR, *DrAS* 74E, *REnAL*,
IntAu&W 76, *NatCAB* 61[port], *REnAL*,
SmATA 9, *TwCA*, *TwCA SUP*,
WhAm 7, *WhE&EA*, *WhNAA*,
WhoAm 74, –76, –78, *WhoWor* 74,
WrDr 76
Bakeless, Katherine Little 1895- *Au&Wr* 6,
BioIn 11, *ConAu* 5R, *IntAu&W* 76,
SmATA 9, *WhoAmW* 64, –66, *WhoE* 74,
WrDr 76, –80, –82, –84
Baker, Betty 1928- *AmAu&B*, *AuBYP*,
BioIn 8, –9, –10, *ConAu* 1R, –2NR,
ScF&FL 1, –2, *SmATA* 5, *ThrBJA*,
TwCCW 78, –83, *WhoAmW* 74, –64, –66,
–68, –70, –72, *WhoWest* 74, –76, *WrDr* 84
Baker, Betty *see also* Venturo, Betty Lou Baker
Baker, Carlos 1909- *AmAu&B*, *ASpks*,
BioIn 10, –11, *BlueB* 76, *ChhPo*, –S3,
ConAu 3NR, –5R, *ConLCrt*, –82,
DcLEL 1940, *DrAS* 74E, –78E, –82E,
IntAu&W 77, –82, *IntWW* 74, –75, –76,
–77, –78, –79, –80, –81, –82, –83, *LinLib* L,
REnAL, *WhNAA*, *WhoAm* 74, –76, –78,
–80, *WhoWor* 74, *WorAu*, *WrDr* 76, –80,
–82, –84
Baker, Charlotte 1910- *AuBYP*, *BioIn* 5, –7,
–9, *ConAu* 17R, *IlsCB* 1946,
IntAu&W 77X, *SmATA* 2, *WhoAmW* 58,
–61, –64, –66
Baker, Elizabeth 1923- *AuBYP SUP*,
BioIn 10, *ConAu* 1R, –3NR, *SmATA* 7,
WrDr 76, –80, –82, –84
Baker, Ivon Robert 1928- *ConAu* 73,
WhoWor 80
Baker, Jeffrey John Wheeler 1931-
AmM&WS 73P, –76P, –79P, –82P,
BioIn 10, *ConAu* 1NR, –49, *SmATA* 5,
WhoE 83
Baker, Jerry *AuNews* 2, *BioIn* 11, *BusPN*,
ConAu 105
Baker, Jim *ConAu* X, *SmATA* X
Baker, Laura Nelson 1911- *Au&Wr* 6,
AuBYP, *BioIn* 6, –8, –9, *ConAu* 5R,
–5NR, *ForWC* 70, *MinnWr*, *SmATA* 3,
WrDr 76, –80, –84
Baker, Leonard 1931- *Alli SUP*,
AmM&WS 79P, *ConAu* 21R,
WhoAm 80, –82, *WhoAmJ* 80,
WhoS&SW 73, –75, –76, *WrDr* 76, –80,
–82, –84
Baker, Lucinda 1916- *ConAu* 65,
WhoAmW 77, –79, –81, *WrDr* 80, –82, –84
Baker, Marilyn 1929- *BioIn* 10, *BioNews* 75,
WhoAm 76, –78, –80, –82, *WhoAmW* 77,
–79, *WhoWor* 78
Baker, Nina 1888-1957 *AmAu&B*, *AuBYP*,

Balliett, Whitney 1926- *AmAu&B,*
ConAu 17R, DcLEL 1940, WhoAm 74,
−76, −78, −80, −82, WrDr 76, −80, −82, −84
Ballou, Arthur W 1915- *ConAu 25R,*
ScF&FL 1, −2
Ballou, Robert O 1892-1977 *AmAu&B,*
BioIn 11
Balmer, Edwin 1883-1959 *AmAu&B, EncMys,*
EncSF, ObitOF 79, REnAL, ScF&FL 1,
TwCCr&M 80, WhAm 3, WhNAA
Balsdon, John Percy Vyvian Dacre 1901-1977
Au&Wr 6, BioIn 12, BlueB 76,
ConAu 5R, −73, WhE&EA, Who 74,
WrDr 76
Balukas, Jean 1959- *BioIn 11, −12, GoodHs,*
WhoAm 80, −82, WorAl
Balzac, Honore De 1799-1850 *AtlBL, BbD,*
BiD&SB, BioIn 1, −2, −3, −4, −5, −6, −7, −8,
−9, −10, −11, −12, CasWL, CelCen,
ChhPo S2, CyWA, DcBiA, DcBiPP,
DcEuL, Dis&D, EncMys, EncSF,
EncWT, EuAu, EvEuW, LinLib L, −S,
McGEWB, McGEWD, −84[port], NewC,
NotNAT B, Novels[port], OxEng, OxFr,
OxThe, PenC EUR, RComWL, REn,
ScF&FL 1, WhDW, WorAl
Bambara, Toni Cade 1939- *BlkAWP,*
ConAu 29R, ConLC 19, DrAP&F 83,
InB&W 80, LivgBAA, SelBAA,
WhoBlA 75, −77, −80
Bambara, Toni Cade *see also* Cade, Toni
Bamman, Henry A 1918- *BioIn 11,*
ConAu 5R, −7NR, LEduc 74, ScF&FL 1,
−2, SmATA 12
Bancroft, Griffing 1907- *AuBYP, AuNews 1,*
BioIn 10, ConAu 29R, SmATA 6
Bane, Michael 1950- *ConAu 108*
Baner, Skulda Vanadis 1897-1964 *BioIn 11,*
ConAu P-1, SmATA 10
Banister, Manly 1914- *ConAu 41R, EncSF,*
ScF&FL 1, −2
Banks, Carolyn 1941- *ConAu 105*
Banks, Lynne Reid 1929- *ConLC 23[port],*
ConNov 72, −76, DcLEL 1940,
IntAu&W 82, Novels, TwCCW 83,
TwCWr, WhoWor 76
Banks, Oliver 1941- *ConAu 107*
Banner, Lois W 1939- *ConAu 1NR, −49,*
DrAS 74H, −78H, −82H
Banning, Evelyn Irene 1903- *ConAu 73,*
SmATA 36, WhoAmW 79, WrDr 76, −80,
−82, −84
Bannister, Roger 1929- *Au&Wr 6, BioIn 3,*
−4, −5, −6, −7, −8, −9, −10, −12, BlueB 76,
CurBio 56, InSci, IntWW 79, −80, −81,
−82, −83, WhDW, Who 74, −82, −83,
WhoTr&F 73, WhoWor 74, −76, WorAl,
WrDr 76, −80, −82, −84
Bar-Zohar, Michael J 1938- *ConAu 21R,*
WhoWorJ 72, −78
Baraheni, Reza 1935- *ConAu 69, WhoE 79*
Baraka, Amiri 1934- *BioIn 12, ConDr 82,*

ConNov 82, ConP 80, DcLB 5[port], −7,
−16[port], DrAP&F 83, EncWL 81,
ModBlW, WebE&AL
Baraka, Amiri *see also* Jones, LeRoi
Barbary, James *BioIn 11, ConAu X,*
SmATA X
Barbary, James *see also* Baumann, Amy
Beeching
Barbary, James *see also* Beeching, Jack
Barber, D F 1940- *ConAu 61*
Barber, D F *see also* Fletcher, David
Barber, Elsie Oakes 1914- *AmAu&B, AmNov,*
BioIn 2, InWom, WhoAmW 58
Barber, James David 1930- *AmM&WS 73S,*
−78S, BioIn 8, −12, BlueB 76,
ConAu 6NR, −13R, WhoAm 74, −76, −78,
−80, −82, WrDr 76, −80, −82, −84
Barber, Richard 1941- *ConAu 33R,*
IntAu&W 82, SmATA 35, WrDr 80, −82,
−84
Barclay, Glen St. John 1930- *ConAu 77*
Bardi, Pietro Maria 1900- *ConAu 85,*
WhoWor 74, −76, −78, −80, −82
Barfield, Arthur Owen 1898- *Au&Wr 6,*
ConAu 5R, DcLEL, IntAu&W 76,
WhE&EA, WrDr 76
Barker, A J 1918-1981 *ConAu 7NR, −104,*
−13R
Barker, Arthur James 1918-1981 *IntAu&W 76,*
−77, Who 74, −82N, WhoWor 76, −80
Barker, Carol 1938- *BioIn 6, −8, ChhPo S1,*
ConAu 107, IlsBYP, IlsCB 1957, −1967,
InWom, SmATA 31[port]
Barker, Eric 1905-1973 *BioIn 9, −10,*
ConAu 1R, −41R, ConP 70, IntWWP 77
Barker, Mildred Joy 1900- *ForWC 70*
Barkley, James Edward 1941- *BioIn 10, −12,*
IlsBYP, IlsCB 1967, SmATA 6
Barkow, Al 1932- *ConAu 4NR, −53,*
WrDr 76, −80, −82, −84
Barlow, Judith Ellen 1946- *ConAu 107,*
DrAS 82E
Barnaby, Frank 1927- *ConAu 33R*
Barnaby, Ralph S 1893- *AuBYP SUP,*
ConAu 61, SmATA 9
Barnard, Charles Nelson 1924- *ConAu 1NR,*
−49, WhoAm 74, −76, −78, −80, −82
Barnard, Robert 1936- *ConAu 77,*
IntAu&W 82, WhoWor 80
Barne, Kitty 1883-1957 *AuBYP SUP, BioIn 2,*
−8, JBA 51, TwCCW 78, −83, WhoChL
Barnes, Ben E 1933- *InB&W 80*
Barnes, Clive 1927- *AmAu&B, AuNews 2,*
BioIn 7, −8, −9, −10, −11, BlueB 76,
CelR 73, ConAmTC, ConAu 77,
CurBio 72, IntAu&W 77, IntWW 74, −75,
−76, −77, −78, −79, −80, −81, −82, −83,
NotNAT, Who 82, −83, WhoAm 74, −76,
−78, −80, −82, WhoE 74, WhoThe 16, −81,
WhoWor 78, WrDr 80, −82, −84
Barnes, Eric Wollencott 1907-1962 *AmAu&B,*
AuBYP, BioIn 6, −8, SmATA 22[port],

WhAm 4

Barnes, Gregory Allen 1934- *ConAu 10NR, –25R*

Barnes, Leola Christie 1889- *TexWr, WhE&EA*

Barnes, Margaret Campbell 1891-1962 *BioIn 3, –6, CurBio 53, InWom, WhAm 4, WhE&EA*

Barness, Richard 1917- *ConAu 65*

Barnett, Correlli 1927- *Au&Wr 6, ConAu 13R, IntAu&W 76, –82, Who 82, –83, WrDr 76, –80, –82, –84*

Barnett, Lincoln Kinnear 1909-1979 *AmAu&B, BioIn 10, –12, ConAu 102, –89, NewYTBS 79, SmATA 36, WhAm 7, WorAu*

Barnett, Samuel Anthony 1915- *Au&Wr 6, ConAu 13R, IntAu&W 76, –77, WrDr 76*

Barnhart, Clarence Lewis 1900- *AmAu&B, BioIn 2, –3, –11, BlueB 76, ConAu 13R, CurBio 54, DrAS 74F, NewYTBS 77, WhoAm 74, –76, –78, –80, –82, WhoWor 74, WorAl*

Barnouw, Erik 1908- *AmAu&B, ConAu 13R, CurBio 40, DrAS 74E, –78E, –82E, LesBEnT[port], NewYTET, WhoAm 74, –76, –78, –80, –82, WrDr 84*

Barnouw, Victor 1915- *AmM&WS 73S, –76P, ConAu 85, FifIDA, SmATA 28, WhoAm 74, WhoWor 76*

Barnstone, Aliki 1956- *ChhPo S1, ConAu 105, DrAP&F 83, IntWWP 82, Po&Wr 77*

Barnstone, Willis 1927- *BioIn 12, ConAu 17R, DrAP 75, DrAP&F 83, DrAS 74F, –78F, –82F, IntWWP 82, SmATA 20, WhoAm 78, –80, –82*

Barnwell, William Curtis 1943- *ConAu 103, DrAS 78E*

Baron, Richard Warren 1923- *WhoAm 74, –76, –78, –80, –82*

Baron, Robert Alex 1920-1980 *BiE&WWA, BioIn 12, ConAu 41R, NotNAT, WhoE 77, –79*

Baron, Virginia Olsen 1931- *AuBYP SUP, ConAu 25R, SmATA 28*

Barr, Alfred Hamilton, Jr. 1902-1981 *AmAu&B, AnObit 1981[port], BioIn 3, –5, –6, –7, –8, –9, –12, BlueB 76, ConAu 105, –49, CurBio 61, –81N, IntWW 74, –75, –76, –77, –78, –79, –80, –81, –82N, LinLib L, NewYTBS 81[port], OxAmH, WhE&EA, Who 74, –82N, WhoAm 74, –76, –78, WhoAmA 73, –76, –78, –80, –82N, WhoArt 80, –82*

Barr, Stephen 1904- *ConAu P-1*

Barraclough, Elmer Davies 1920- *DrAS 74E, –82E*

Barraclough, Geoffrey 1908- *BioIn 10, ConAu 101, Who 74, –82, –83, WhoAm 76, –78, WhoWor 74, –76, WorAu, WrDr 80, –82, –84*

Barrett, Bob 1925- *ConAu 73*

Barrett, Eugene F 1921- *ConAu 57*

Barrett, Stephen Melvil 1865- *AmAu&B, WhAm 4, WhNAA*

Barrett, William Edmund 1900- *AmAu&B, AmCath 80, Au&Wr 6, BioIn 3, –4, BkC 5, CathA 1952, ConAu 5R, ConSFA, EncSF, IntAu&W 76, REnAL, ScF&FL 1, –2, WhoAm 74, –76, WhoWor 74, –76, –78*

Barrie, Alexander 1923- *Au&Wr 6, ConAu 1R, –5NR, IntAu&W 76, –77, –82, WhoWor 76, –78, WrDr 76, –80, –82, –84*

Barrie, J M 1860-1937 *ConAu 104, Novels, ScF&FL 1, TwCCW 83, TwCLC 2, WorAl*

Barrie, Sir James Matthew 1860-1937 *Alli SUP, AtlBL, BbD, BiD&SB, BioIn 1, –2, –3, –4, –5, –6, –8, –9, –10, –11, –12, CarSB, CasWL, Chambr 3, ChhPo, –S1, –S2, –S3, CnMD, CnThe, CyWA, DcBiA, DcEnA, –AP, DcLB 10[port], DcLEL, Dis&D, EncWL, –81, EncWT, EvLB, FamAYP, FilmgC, JBA 34, LinLib L, –S, LongCEL, LongCTC, McGEWB, McGEWD, –84[port], ModBrL, ModWD, NewC, NotNAT A, –B, OxEng, OxThe, PenC ENG, PIP&P, RAdv 1, REn, REnWD, TelT, TwCA, TwCA SUP, TwCCW 78, TwCWr, WebE&AL, WhDW, WhE&EA, WhLit, WhScrn 2, WhThe, WhoChL, WhoStg 1906, –1908, WhoTwCL, YABC 1*

Barrio, Raymond 1921- *ChiSch, ConAu 11NR, –25R, DrAF 76, DrAP&F 83, WhoAm 74, –76, –78, –80, –82, WhoAmA 76, –78, –80, –82, WrDr 76, –80, –82, –84*

Barroll, Clare *BioIn 10*

Barron, Greg 1952- *ConAu 110*

Barrow, John V *ApCAB X*

Barrows, Marjorie 1892?-1983 *AmAu&B, AuBYP, BioIn 2, –7, ChhPo, –S1, –S3, ConAu 109, ConAu P-2, ScF&FL 1, –2, WhJnl, WhNAA, WhoAm 74, –76, –78, –80, –82, WhoAmW 74, –58, –64, –66, –68, –70, –72*

Barry, Anne Meredith 1932- *WhoAmA 78, –80, –82, WhoAmW 77*

Barry, James P 1918- *BioIn 12, ConAu 37R, IntAu&W 76, –77, –82, SmATA 14, WhoMW 76, –78, –80, –82, WrDr 76, –80, –82, –84*

Barry, Jane 1925- *ConAu 5R, ForWC 70, IntAu&W 76, –77, –82, WrDr 76, –80, –82, –84*

Barry, Joseph 1917- *ConAu 57*

Bart, Peter 1932- *ConAu 93, IntMPA 77, –75, –76, –78, –79, –81, –82, –84*

Barth, Alan 1906-1979 *AmAu&B, Au&Wr 6, BioIn 12, BlueB 76, ConAu 1R, –5NR, –104, IntAu&W 76, IntYB 78, –79, –80, –81, –82, NewYTBS 79, WhAm 7,*

WhoAm 74, -76, -78, WhoS&SW 73,
WhoWor 74, WhoWorJ 72, WrDr 80, -82,
-84

Barth, John 1930- *AmAu&B, AmWr,*
Au&Wr 6, AuNews 1, -2, BioIn 6, -7, -8,
-9, -10, -11, -12, BioNews 74, BlueB 76,
CasWL, ConAu 1R, -5NR, ConLC 1, -2,
-3, -5, -7, -9, -10, -14, -27[port],
ConNov 72, -76, -82, CurBio 69, DcLB 2,
DcLEL 1940, DrAF 76, DrAP&F 83,
DrAS 74E, -78E, -82E, EncSF, EncWL,
-81[port], IntAu&W 76, IntWW 74, -75,
-76, -77, -78, -79, -80, -81, -82, -83,
LinLib L, -S, ModAL, ModAL SUP,
NewYTBS 82[port], Novels[port],
OxAmL, PenC AM, RAdv 1, ScF&FL 1,
-2, TwCWr, WebAB, -79, WebE&AL,
WhoAm 74, -76, -78, -80, -82, WhoTwCL,
WhoWor 74, -78, -80, -82, WorAl,
WorAu, WrDr 76, -80, -82, -84

Barthelme, Donald 1931- *AmArch 70,*
AmAu&B, AuBYP SUP, BioIn 9, -10,
-11, -12, BlueB 76, CelR 73,
ConAu 21R, ConLC 1, -2, -3, -5, -6, -8,
-13, -23[port], ConNov 72, -76, -82,
CurBio 76, DcLB Y80A[port], -2,
DcLEL 1940, DrAF 76, DrAP&F 83,
EncSF, EncWL 81, IntAu&W 76, -77,
ModAL SUP, Novels, PenC AM,
RAdv 1, SmATA 7, WhoAm 74, -76, -78,
-80, WhoE 75, -77, WorAl, WorAu,
WrDr 76, -80, -82, -84

Bartlett, Irving Henry 1923- *ConAu 9NR,*
-21R, DrAS 74H, -78H, -82H,
WhoAm 74, -76, -78, -80, -82

Bartos-Hoeppner, Barbara 1923- *Au&Wr 6,*
BioIn 10, ConAu 10NR, -25R, FourBJA,
SmATA 5, TwCCW 78B

Baruch, Grace Kestenman 1936-
AmM&WS 73S, -78S

Barzun, Jacques 1907- *AmAu&B, Au&Wr 6,*
Baker 78, BioIn 2, -4, -7, -9, -11,
BlueB 76, CelR 73, -73, ConAu 61,
CurBio 64, DrAS 74H, -78H, -82H,
EncMys, IntAu&W 76A, -77, -82,
IntWW 74, -75, -76, -77, -78, -79, -80, -81,
-82, -83, LinLib L, -S, NewYTBS 75,
OxAmL, RAdv 1, REn, REnAL, TwCA,
TwCA SUP, WebAB, -79, WhE&EA,
Who 74, -82, -83, WhoAm 74, -76, -78,
-80, -82, WhoAmA 73, -76, -78, -80, -82,
WhoMus 72, WhoWor 74, -78, -80, -82,
WrDr 76, -80, -82, -84

Bascom, Willard 1916- *AmM&WS 73P, -76P,*
-79P, -82P, BioIn 6, -12, ConAu 1R,
-6NR, WhoOcn 78, WhoWest 74, -76,
-78

Basinger, Jeanine 1936- *ConAu 97,*
ForWC 70

Baskin, John Roland 1916- *WhoAmL 83*

Bass, Althea 1892- *ConAu P-2, WhoAmW 58,*
-61, -64

Bass, Ellen 1947- *ConAu 2NR, -49, DrAP 75,*
DrAP&F 83, IntWWP 77

Bass, George Fletcher 1932- *BioIn 8, -9,*
DrAS 74H, -78H, -82H

Bassani, Giorgio 1916- *BioIn 9, -10, CasWL,*
ConAu 65, ConLC 9, DcItL, EncWL,
-81, EvEuW, IntAu&W 76, -77,
IntWW 74, -75, -76, -77, -78, -79, -80, -81,
-82, -83, ModRL, Novels, PenC EUR,
REn, TwCWr, WhoTwCL, WhoWor 74,
-76, -78, WorAu

Bates, Betty 1921- *BioIn 12, ConAu X,*
SmATA 19

Bathgate, Andy 1932- *BioIn 6, -9, CurBio 64,*
WhoHcky 73

Battcock, Gregory 1938?-1980 *AnObit 1980,*
BioIn 12, BlueB 76, ConAu 105, -11NR,
-21R, WhoAm 80, -82, WhoAmA 73, -76,
-78, -80, WhoE 74, WrDr 76, -80, -82

Batten, Mary 1937- *AuBYP SUP, BioIn 10,*
ConAu 41R, SmATA 5

Batterberry, Ariane Ruskin 1935- *ConAu 69,*
SmATA 13, WhoAmW 77, -79

Batterberry, Michael Carver 1932-
AuBYP SUP, ConAu 77, SmATA 32

Baudouy, Michel-Aime 1909- *ConAu P-2,*
IntAu&W 82, SmATA 7, ThrBJA

Bauer, Marion Dane 1938- *BioIn 12,*
ConAu 11NR, -69, SmATA 20

Bauer, Steven *DrAP&F 83*

Bauer, William Waldo 1892-1967 *BioIn 4, -5,*
-8, -9, -10, ConAu 5R, -7NR,
NatCAB 53, -54, WhAm 4A, WhE&EA

Baum, Daniel 1934- *ConAu 6NR*

Baum, Patricia *AuBYP SUP*

Baumann, Amy Beeching 1922- *BioIn 11,*
ConAu 21R, SmATA 10

Baumann, Elwood D *AuBYP SUP,*
SmATA 33

Baumann, Hans 1914- *Au&Wr 6, BioIn 9,*
ConAu 3NR, -5R, IntAu&W 77, -82,
SmATA 2, ThrBJA, TwCCW 78B, -83B,
WhoWor 74, WorDWW

Baur, John Edward 1922- *ConAu 9R,*
DrAS 74H, -78H, -82H, WrDr 76, -80,
-82, -84

Bawden, Nina 1925- *Au&Wr 6, AuBYP SUP,*
BioIn 9, -10, -11, BrCA, ChlLR 2,
ConAu X, ConNov 72, -76, -82,
DcLB 14[port], DcLEL 1940, FourBJA,
IntAu&W 76, -77, -82, Novels, SmATA 4,
TwCCW 78, -83, TwCCr&M 80, Who 74,
-82, -83, WhoWor 78, WrDr 76, -80, -82,
-84

Bawden, Nina *see also* Kark, Nina Mary

Baxter, Anne 1923- *BiDFilm, BiE&WWA,*
BioIn 9, -10, -11, CelR 73, CurBio 72,
FilmgC, InWom, IntMPA 77, -75, -76,
-78, -79, -81, -82, -84, MotPP, MovMk,
NewYTBE 71, NewYTBS 82[port],
NotNAT, WhoAm 74, -76, -78, -80, -82,
WhoAmW 74, -58, -64, -66, -68, -70, -72,

−83, WhoHol A, WhoThe 16, −81, WomPO 78, WorAl, WorEFlm

Bayley, Barrington John 1937- ConAu 37R, EncSF, IntAu&W 76, −77, −82, ScF&FL 1, −2, WhoSciF, WrDr 76, −80, −82, −84

Baylor, Byrd 1924- AuBYP SUP, BioIn 12, ChlLR 3, ChhPo S3, ConAu 81, FourBJA, SmATA 16

Bayly, Joseph 1920- ConAu 17R, IntAu&W 77, St&PR 75, WrDr 76, −80, −82, −84

Bayne-Jardine, C C 1932- ConAu 25R

Bayrd, Edwin 1944- ConAu 97

Beach, Edward Latimer 1918- Au&Wr 6, BioIn 3, −5, −6, −11, ConAu 5R, −6NR, DrAP&F 83, Novels, SmATA 12, WebAMB, WhoAmP 73, −75, −77, WhoGov 77, −72, −75, WrDr 76, −80, −82, −84

Beach Boys, The CmCal, EncPR&S, −77, IlEncRk, RkOn 74, −82, RkOneH, RolSEnR 83, WorAl

Beach Boys, The see also Chaplin, Blondie

Beach Boys, The see also Fataar, Ricky

Beach Boys, The see also Love, Mike

Beach Boys, The see also Wilson, Brian

Beach Boys, The see also Wilson, Carl

Beach Boys, The see also Wilson, Dennis

Beachcroft, Nina 1931- BioIn 12, ConAu 97, ScF&FL 1, SmATA 18, TwCCW 78, −83, WrDr 80, −82, −84

Beagle, Peter S 1939- BioIn 12, ConAu 4NR, −9R, ConLC 7, ConSFA, DcLB Y80B[port], DrAF 76, DrAP&F 83, EncSF, ScF&FL 1, −2, WhoAm 74, −76, −78, −80, −82, WhoHr&F, WhoSciF, WrDr 76, −80, −82, −84

Beal, Merrill D 1898- ConAu 1R, −5NR, DrAS 74H, −78H, −82H, EncAAH, WhoPNW

Beals, Carleton 1893-1979 AmAu&B, Au&Wr 6, AuBYP, BioIn 1, −4, −5, −7, −11, −12, BlueB 76, ConAu 1R, −3NR, −77, IntWW 74, −75, −76, −77, −78, −79, OxAmL, REnAL, ScF&FL 1, −2, SmATA 12, TwCA, TwCA SUP, WhAm 7, WhNAA, WhoAm 74, −76, −78, WhoWor 74, WrDr 76, −80

Beaman, Joyce Proctor 1931- ConAu 29R, IntAu&W 77, WrDr 76, −80, −82, −84

Bear, Greg 1951- WrDr 84

Bear, John 1938- BioIn 9, ConAu 73

Beard, Alice Gamble 1919- WhoS&SW 75, −76

Beard, Annie E S d1930 DcNAA

Beard, Charles Austin 1874-1948 AmAu&B, BiDAmEd, BioIn 1, −2, −3, −4, −6, −7, −8, −9, −10, −11, −12, ConAmA, CurBio 41, −48, DcAmB S4, DcAmDH, DcAmSR, DcLB 17[port], DcLEL, DcNAA, EncAAH, EncAB-H, EvLB, IndAu 1816,

LinLib L, −S, LongCTC, McGEWB, ObitOF 79, OxAmH, OxAmL, PenC AM, REn, REnAL, SmATA 18, TwCA, TwCA SUP, WebAB, −79, WebE&AL, WhAm 2, −2C, WorAl

Beard, Peter Hill 1938- BioIn 6, −8, −10, −12, ConAu 13R, ConPhot, WhoAm 76, −78

Beard, William 1907- AmAu&B, WhoAm 74, −76, −78, −80

Bearden, Romare 1914- AfroAA, AmSCAP 66, BioIn 8, −9, −10, −11, −12, BlueB 76, ConArt, −83, ConAu 102, CurBio 72, DcAmArt, DcCAA 71, −77, DcCAr 81, Ebony 1, InB&W 80, McGEWB, NegAl 76, −83, OxTwCA, PrintW 83, SmATA 22, WhoAm 74, −76, −78, −80, −82, WhoAmA 73, −76, −78, −80, −82, WhoWor 74

Beardsley, Aubrey Vincent 1872-1898 AntBDN A, −B, AtlBL, BioIn 1, −2, −3, −6, −7, −8, −9, −10, −11, −12, BrAu 19, ChhPo, −S2, DcBrBI, DcBrWA, DcCathB, DcLEL, DcNiCA, Dis&D, LinLib L, −S, LongCEL, McGDA, McGEWB, NewC, OxArt[port], PhDcTCA 77, REn, ScF&FL 1, WebE&AL, WhDW, WorAl

Beardsley, Charles Noel 1914- ConAu 1R, −2NR, IntAu&W 76

Beatles, The EncPR&S, −77, FilmgC, IlEncRk, MakMC, MotPP, MovMk, NewYTBS 75, OxFilm, RkOn 78, −84, RkOneH, RolSEnR 83, WorEFlm

Beatles, The see also Harrison, George

Beatles, The see also Lennon, John

Beatles, The see also McCartney, Paul

Beatles, The see also Starr, Ringo

Beattie, Ann 1947- BioIn 12, ConAu 81, ConLC 8, −13, −18, DcLB Y82B[port], DrAP&F 83, NewYTBS 80[port], WhoAm 82

Beatty, Jerome, Jr. 1918- AuBYP, BioIn 8, −10, ConAu 3NR, −9R, ScF&FL 1, −2, SmATA 5

Beatty, John 1922-1975 BioIn 7, −9, −10, ConAu 4NR, −5R, −57, DrAS 74H, SmATA 25N, −6, ThrBJA, TwCCW 78, −83

Beatty, Patricia Robbins 1922- AuBYP, ConAu 1R, −3NR, ForWC 70, SmATA 1, −30[port], ThrBJA, TwCCW 78, −83, WrDr 82, −84

Beaty, David 1919- Au&Wr 6, ConAu 1R, −2NR, ConNov 72, −76, −82, IntAu&W 76, −77, −82, WrDr 76, −80, −82, −84

Beaty, John Yocum 1884- AuBYP, BioIn 2, −7, WhAm 3, WhE&EA

Beaufort, John 1912- ConAmTC, ConAu 104, IntAu&W 77, −82, NotNAT, WhoAm 78, −80, −82, WhoThe 15, −16, −81

Beauvoir, Simone De 1908- BioIn 1, −3, −4, −5, −6, −7, −8, −9, −10, −11, −12, CasWL,

–83

Behn, Noel 1928- *BiE&WWA, NotNAT, TwCCr&M 80, WrDr 82, –84*

Behnke, Frances L *BioIn 11, ConAu 33R, SmATA 8*

Behrman, Carol H 1925- *BioIn 12, ConAu 7NR, –61, IntWWP 77, SmATA 14, WhoAmW 77, –79*

Behrman, Daniel 1923- *ConAu 65*

Beichman, Arnold 1913- *ConAu 49, IntAu&W 76*

Beier, Ulli 1922- *ConAu 4NR, –9R, IntAu&W 77, TwCWr, WhoWor 74, WrDr 76, –80, –82, –84*

Beim, Lorraine 1909-1951 *BioIn 2, JBA 51*

Beiser, Arthur 1931- *AuBYP, BioIn 7, ConAu 93, SmATA 22*

Beiser, Germaine 1931- *AuBYP, BioIn 11, SmATA 11, WhoAmW 58, –64A*

Beitler, Ethel Jane 1906- *ConAu 2NR, –5R*

Belden, Wilanne Schneider 1925- *ConAu 106*

Belfield, Eversley Michael Gallimore 1918- *Au&Wr 6, ConAu 11NR, –25R, IntAu&W 76, –77, –82, WrDr 76, –80, –82, –84*

Belfrage, Sally 1936- *Au&Wr 6, BioIn 5, ConAu 105*

Bell, Adrian Hanbury 1901-1980 *AnObit 1980, BioIn 4, –6, ConAu 102, –97, DcLEL, EvLB, IntAu&W 76, –77, LongCTC, TwCA, TwCA SUP, WhE&EA, Who 74*

Bell, Eric Temple 1883-1960 *AmAu&B, BioIn 3, –4, –5, –10, –12, DcAmB S6, DcScB, EncSF, NatCAB 54, ObitOF 79, REnAL, ScF&FL 1, TwCA SUP, WhAm 4, WhE&EA, WhNAA, WhoRocM 82*

Bell, Joseph Newton 1921- *AuBYP, BioIn 7, ConAu 5R, IndAu 1917, WhoWest 74, –76*

Bell, Margaret Elizabeth 1898- *AmAu&B, AuBYP, BioIn 2, –3, –6, –7, –9, ConAu 1R, –1NR, CurBio 52, InWom, IntAu&W 76, MorJA, SmATA 2*

Bell, Marvin 1937- *AmAu&B, BioIn 9, –10, –12, ConAu 21R, ConLC 8, ConP 70, –75, –80, CroCAP, DcLB 5[port], DrAP 75, DrAP&F 83, IntWWP 77, –82, WorAu 1970, WrDr 76, –80, –82, –84*

Bell, R C 1917- *ConAu 7NR, –17R*

Bell, R C *see also* Bell, Robert Charles

Bell, Raymond Martin 1907- *AmM&WS 73P, –76P, –79P, –82P, ConAu 29R, SmATA 13, WhoGen 81, WrDr 76, –80, –82, –84*

Bell, Robert Charles 1917- *IntAu&W 77, –82, WhoWor 76, WrDr 76, –80, –82, –84*

Bell, Robert Charles *see also* Bell, R C

Bell, Sallie Lee *ConAu 1R, –1NR, ForWC 70, WhoAmW 58, –61*

Bell, Thomas 1903-1961 *AmAu&B, BioIn 5, ObitOF 79, REnAL*

Bellairs, John 1938- *BioIn 9, ConAu 8NR, –21R, IntAu&W 82, ScF&FL 1, –2, SmATA 2, WhoE 74, WrDr 76, –80, –82, –84*

Bellamy, Edward 1850-1898 *Alli SUP, AmAu, AmAu&B, AmBi, ApCAB SUP, BbD, BiD&SB, BioIn 1, –2, –3, –5, –8, –10, –12, CasWL, CnDAL, CyWA, DcAmAu, DcAmB, DcAmSR, DcBiA, DcEnA AP, DcLB 12[port], DcLEL, DcNAA, EncAB-H, EncSF, EncUrb, EvLB, HarEnUS, LinLib L, –S, LuthC 75, McGEWB, MouLC 4, NatCAB 1, Novels, OxAmH, OxAmL, OxEng, PenC AM, RAdv 1, REn, REnAL, ScF&FL 1, TwCBDA, WebAB, –79, WebE&AL, WhAm HS, WhAmP, WorAl*

Bellamy, Francis Rufus 1886-1972 *AmAu&B, AmNov, BioIn 2, –9, ConAu 33R, EncSF, NewYTBE 72, ScF&FL 1, WhAm 5, WhLit*

Bellegarde, Ida Rowland 1904- *IntWWP 77A, –82*

Beller, William Stern 1919- *ConAu 5R, WhoE 74*

Belli, Melvin Mouron 1907- *AmAu&B, BioIn 3, –4, –5, –6, –7, –10, –11, –12, CelR 73, ConAu 104, CurBio 79, WhoAm 74, –76, –78, –80, –82, WhoAmL 78, –79, WhoWest 74, –76, –78, WhoWor 74, WorAl*

Bellow, Saul 1915- *AmAu&B, AmNov, AmWr, AuNews 2, BioIn 2, –3, –4, –7, –8, –9, –10, –11, –12, BlueB 76, CasWL, CelR 73, CnMWL, ConAu 5R, ConDr 73, –77, –82, ConLC 1, –2, –3, –6, –8, –10, –13, –15, –25[port], ConNov 72, –76, –82, CroCD, CurBio 65, DcLB DS3[port], –Y82A[port], –2, DcLEL 1940, DrAF 76, DrAP&F 83, DrAS 74E, –78E, –82E, EncAB-H, EncSF, EncWL, –81[port], IntAu&W 76, –77, IntWW 74, –75, –76, –77, –78, –79, –80, –81, –82, –83, LinLib L, –S, LongCTC, MakMC, McGEWB, ModAL, ModAL SUP, NewYTBE 71, NewYTBS 76, –81[port], NotNAT, Novels[port], OxAmL, PenC AM, RAdv 1, REn, REnAL, TwCA SUP, TwCWr, WebAB, –79, WebE&AL, WhDW, Who 74, –82, –83, WhoAm 74, –76, –78, –80, –82, WhoAmJ 80, WhoMW 78, –80, –82, WhoTwCL, WhoWor 74, –78, –80, –82, WhoWorJ 72, –78, WorAl, WrDr 76, –80, –82, –84*

Belote, James Hine 1922- *ConAu 33R, DrAS 74H, –78H, –82H*

Belote, William Milton 1922- *ConAu 49, DrAS 74H, –78H, –82H, WhoE 77, –79, –81, –83*

Belous, Russell E 1925- *ConAu 25R*

Belpre, Pura 1899-1982 *AuBYP, BioIn 7, –12,
BkP, ConAu 109, –73, FourBJA,
SmATA 16, –30N*
Belting, Natalia Maree 1915- *AuBYP, BioIn 7,
–9, –10, ChhPo S2, ConAu 1R, –3NR,
DrAS 74H, –78H, –82H, IntAu&W 76,
SmATA 6, ThrBJA*
Benagh, Jim 1937- *AuBYP SUP,
ConAu 9NR, –57, MichAu 80*
Benarde, Melvin Albert 1923?-
*AmM&WS 73P, –76P, –79P, –82P,
ConAu 25R, WhoAm 82, WhoE 74, –81,
–83, WrDr 76, –80, –82, –84*
Benary-Isbert, Margot 1889-1979 *AnCL,
AuBYP, BioIn 6, –7, –9, –12, ConAu 4NR,
–5R, –89, ConLC 12, MorJA, ScF&FL 1,
SmATA 2, –21N, WhoAmW 58, –61*
Benatar, Pat 1953?- *BioIn 12, RolSEnR 83*
Benchley, Nathaniel 1915-1981 *AmAu&B,
AnObit 1981, Au&Wr 6, AuBYP SUP,
BiE&WWA, BioIn 3, –4, –9, –10, –11, –12,
BlueB 76, CelR 73, ConAu 1R, –2NR,
–105, CurBio 53, –82N, FourBJA,
IntAu&W 82, NewYTBS 81[port],
NotNAT, ScF&FL 1A, SmATA 25[port],
–28N, –3, TwCCW 78, –83, WhoAm 74,
–76, –78, –80, WhoWor 74, WorAl,
WorAu, WrDr 76, –80, –82*
Benchley, Peter 1940- *AuNews 2, BioIn 9,
–10, –11, –12, ConAu 17R, ConLC 4, –8,
CurBio 76, IntAu&W 76, –77,
NewYTBS 79, Novels, SmATA 3,
WhoAm 76, –78, –80, –82, WorAl,
WrDr 80, –82, –84*
Bender, Lucy Ellen 1942- *ConAu 25R*
Bender, Marylin 1925- *ConAu 21R,
WhoAmW 70, –72*
Bendick, Jeanne 1919- *AmPB, AuBYP,
BioIn 2, –5, –6, –8, –9, BkP,
ChlLR 5[port], ConAu 2NR, –5R,
ForWC 70, IlsCB 1946, –1957, MorJA,
SmATA 2, WhoAmW 58*
Bendick, Robert 1917- *AuBYP, BioIn 6, –8,
–11, ConAu 61, IntMPA 77, –75, –76, –78,
–79, –81, –82, –84, LesBEnT, MorJA,
NewYTET, SmATA 11*
Bendiner, Elmer 1916- *ConAu 7NR, –57*
Benedict, Dorothy Potter 1889-1979 *BioIn 11,
ConAu 93, ConAu P-1, SmATA 11, –23N*
Benedict, Rex Arthur 1920- *AuBYP SUP,
BioIn 11, ConAu 17R, IntAu&W 77,
IntWWP 77, SmATA 8, TwCCW 78, –83,
WhoE 74, WrDr 76, –80, –82, –84*
Benedict, Ruth Fulton 1887-1948 *AmAu&B,
AmWomWr, BiDAmEd, BioIn 1, –2, –4,
–5, –6, –10, –12, CurBio 41, –48,
DcAmB S4, DcNAA, DcSoc, EncAAH,
EncAB-H, GoodHs, InSci, InWom,
IntDcWB, LibW, LinLib L, LuthC 75,
McGEWB, NamesHP, NatCAB 36,
NotAW, ObitOF 79, OxAmH, REnAL,
TwCA SUP, WebAB, –79, WhDW,*

WhAm 2, WorAl
Benedict, Stewart Hurd 1924- *ConAu 13R,
IntAu&W 76, –77, ScF&FL 1,
SmATA 26[port], WhoE 74*
Benedikt, Michael 1935?- *AmAu&B, BioIn 9,
–10, –12, ConAu 7NR, –13R, ConLC 4,
–14, ConP 70, –75, –80, CroCAP,
DcLB 5[port], DcLEL 1940, DrAF 76,
DrAP 75, DrAP&F 83, IntAu&W 76,
–77, –82, IntWWP 77, –82, RAdv 1,
WhoAm 76, –78, –80, –82, WhoAmA 76,
–78, –80, –82, WhoE 75, –77, WrDr 76,
–80, –82, –84*
Benet, Laura 1884-1979 *AmAu&B,
AmWomWr, AuBYP, BioIn 2, –8, –9, –10,
–11, ChhPo, –S3, ConAu 6NR, –9R, –85,
InWom, JBA 51, LinLib L, REn,
REnAL, ScF&FL 1, –2, SmATA 23N, –3,
WhAm 7, WhE&EA, WhoAm 74,
WhoAmW 74, –58, –61, –64, –66, –68, –70,
–72, WhoE 74*
Benet, Stephen Vincent 1898-1943 *AmAu&B,
AnCL, ApCAB X, AuBYP SUP, BioIn 1,
–2, –3, –4, –5, –6, –7, –10, –11, –12, BkCL,
CasWL, Chambr 3, ChhPo, –S1, –S2, –S3,
CnDAL, CnE&AP, CnMWL, ConAmL,
ConAu 104, CurBio 43, CyWA,
DcAmB S3, DcLB 4, DcLEL, DcNAA,
EncAAH, EncAB 29, EncSF, EncWL,
–81, EvLB, FamPYP, LinLib L, –S,
LongCTC, McGEWB, ModAL,
NatCAB 33, NotNAT B, Novels,
ObitOF 79, OxAmH, OxAmL, OxEng,
PenC AM, RAdv 1, REn, REnAL,
ScF&FL 1, SixAP, Str&VC, TwCA,
TwCA SUP, TwCLC 7[port], TwCWr,
WebAB, –79, WebE&AL, WhDW,
WhAm 2, WhE&EA, WhLit, WhNAA,
WhoHr&F, WhoTwCL, WorAl, YABC 1*
Benet, William Rose 1886-1950 *AmAu&B,
ApCAB X, BioIn 1, –2, –3, –4, –10, –12,
ChhPo, –S1, –S2, –S3, CnDAL, ConAmA,
ConAmL, DcAmB S4, DcLEL, LinLib L,
LongCTC, NatCAB 37, ObitOF 79,
OxAmL, OxEng, PenC AM, REn,
REnAL, TwCA, TwCA SUP, WebAB,
–79, WhAm 3, WhE&EA, WhLit,
WhNAA, WorAl*
Benford, Gregory 1941- *BioIn 12, ConAu 69,
DcLB Y82B[port], EncSF, IntAu&W 82,
WhoAm 78, –80, –82, WhoSciF,
WhoTech 82, WrDr 84*
Bennett, Deborah Elizabeth 1932- *Au&Wr 6*
Bennett, Dorothea *ConAu X, SmATA X*
Bennett, Dorothea *see also* Young, Dorothea
Bennett
Bennett, George 1920- *ConAu 5R*
Bennett, Hal 1936- *ConLC 5, DrAP&F 83,
WrDr 80, –82, –84*
Bennett, Jack 1927- *AmM&WS 73P*
Bennett, Jay 1912- *AuBYP SUP, BioIn 10,
ConAu 11NR, –69, SmATA 27,*

*–83[port], OxFilm, OxThe, PIP&P A,
REn, WhDW, Who 74, –82, –83,
WhoAm 80, –82, WhoWor 74, –76, –78,
–80, –82, WorAl, WorEFlm*
Bergman, Jules 1929- *ConAu 108, LesBEnT,
NewYTET, WhoAm 80, –82*
Bergonzi, Bernard 1929- *Au&Wr 6, BlueB 76,
ConAu 8NR, –17R, DcLEL 1940,
IntAu&W 76, –77, –82, ScF&FL 1, –2,
Who 83, WrDr 76, –80, –82, –84*
Berkeley, Ellen Perry 1931- *ConAu 110,
ForWC 70*
Berkman, Edward O 1914- *ConAu 9NR, –61,
WhoWorJ 78*
Berkman, Ted *ConAu X*
Berkman, Ted *see also* Berkman, Edward O
Berkow, Ira 1940- *BioIn 10, ConAu 97,
IntAu&W 82*
Berkowitz, Freda Pastor 1910- *AuBYP,
BioIn 8, –11, ConAu P-1, SmATA 12,
WhoAmW 66A*
Berland, Theodore 1929- *ConAu 2NR, –5R,
IntAu&W 77, WhoMW 74, –76, –78, –80,
–82*
Berle, Milton 1908- *AmAu&B, AmPS B,
AmSCAP 66, AuNews 1, BiDAmM,
BiE&WWA, BioIn 1, –2, –3, –4, –5, –6, –7,
–8, –10, –12, BioNews 75, CelR 73,
CmpEPM, ConAu 77, CurBio 49,
EncMT, Film 1, –2, FilmgC, IntMPA 77,
–75, –76, –78, –79, –81, –82, –84,
LesBEnT[port], MovMk, NewYTET,
NotNAT, –A, PIP&P, TwYS, WebAB,
–79, WhoAm 74, –76, –78, –80, –82,
WhoHol A, WhoThe 15, –16, –81,
WhoWor 74, WorAl*
Berlitz, Charles 1914- *AmAu&B, BioIn 4,
ConAu 5R, –9NR, CurBio 57,
SmATA 32[port], UFOEn, WhoAm 74,
–76, –78, –80, –82, WhoWor 74*
Berman, Arthur Irwin 1925- *AmM&WS 73P,
–76P, –79P, BlueB 76, ConAu 97,
WhoAm 74, –76, –78, –80, WhoWor 74,
–76, WrDr 76, –80, –82, –84*
Berman, Connie 1949- *ConAu 93*
Bermant, Chaim 1929- *Au&Wr 6, BioIn 11,
ConAu 6NR, –57, ConNov 76, –82,
IntAu&W 76, –77, –82, Novels, Who 82,
–83, WrDr 76, –80, –82, –84*
Berna, Paul 1910?- *Au&Wr 6, AuBYP,
BioIn 8, –9, –12, ConAu 73, ScF&FL 1,
SmATA 15, ThrBJA, TwCCW 78B, –83B*
Bernard, Christine 1926- *ScF&FL 1, –2*
Bernard, Jacqueline 1921- *AuBYP SUP,
BioIn 11, ConAu 21R, SmATA 8*
Bernays, Anne 1930- *AmWomWr, ConAu X,
DrAF 76, DrAP&F 83, ForWC 70,
IntAu&W 77, –82, SmATA X*
Bernays, Anne *see also* Kaplan, Anne Bernays
Bernays, Edward L 1891- *AmAu&B,
BiDAmBL 83, BioIn 2, –4, –5, –7, –11,
ConAu 17R, CurBio 42, –60,*

*IntAu&W 77, REnAL, WhE&EA,
WhNAA, WhoAm 74, –76, –78, –80, –82,
WhoAmJ 80, WhoE 79, –81, –83,
WhoPubR 72, –76, WhoWor 74, –76,
WhoWorJ 72, –78, WrDr 76, –80, –82, –84*
Berne, Eric L 1910-1970 *AmAu&B, BioIn 7,
–8, –9, ConAu 4NR, –5R, –25R,
NewYTBE 70, ObitOF 79, WhAm 5*
Bernhardsen, Bris 1923- *AuBYP SUP,
ConAu X*
Bernhardsen, Bris *see also* Bernhardsen, Christian
Bernhardsen, Christian 1923- *AuBYP SUP,
ConAu 29R*
Bernheim, Evelyne 1935- *ConAu 21R*
Bernheim, Marc 1924- *ConAu 21R*
Bernikow, Louise 1940- *DrAP&F 83,
WhoAm 82, WhoAmW 70, –72*
Bernstein, Burton 1932- *BioIn 12, ConAu 1R,
–4NR, DrAP&F 83, IntAu&W 77, –82,
WrDr 76, –80, –82, –84*
Bernstein, Carl 1944- *AuNews 1, BioIn 9, –10,
–11, –12, BioNews 74, ConAu 81,
CurBio 76, WhoAm 74, –76, –78, –80, –82,
WorAl, WrDr 80, –82, –84*
Bernstein, Jane 1949- *ConAu 104,
DrAP&F 83*
Bernstein, Jeremy 1929- *AmM&WS 73P, –76P,
–79P, –82P, BioIn 8, –12, ConAu 13R,
NewYTBS 82[port], WhoAm 76, –78, –80*
Bernstein, Joanne E 1943- *BioIn 12,
ConAu 77, SmATA 15*
Bernstein, Leonard 1918- *AmAu&B, AmPS,
AmSCAP 66, Baker 78, BiDAmM,
BiE&WWA, BioIn 1, –2, –3, –4, –5, –6, –7,
–8, –9, –10, –11, –12, BlueB 76, CelR 73,
CmpEPM, CompSN SUP, CpmDNM 82,
ConAmC, ConAu 1R, –2NR, CurBio 44,
–60, DcCM, EncAB-H, EncMT, EncWT,
FilmgC, IntAu&W 77, –82, IntWW 74,
–75, –76, –77, –78, –79, –80, –81, –82, –83,
IntWWM 77, LesBEnT[port], LinLib L,
–S, McGEWB, McGEWD, –84, MusSN,
NewCBMT, NewEOp 71, NewYTBE 71,
–72, NewYTET, NotNAT, OxAmH,
OxAmL, OxFilm, OxMus, PIP&P, –A,
REn, REnAL, WebAB, –79, WhDW,
Who 74, –82, –83, WhoAm 74, –76, –78,
–80, –82, WhoAmJ 80, WhoAmM 83,
WhoE 74, –79, –81, –83, WhoMus 72,
WhoOp 76, WhoThe 15, –16, –81,
WhoWor 74, –76, –78, –80, –82,
WhoWorJ 72, –78, WorAl, WorEFlm,
WrDr 80, –82, –84*
Bernstein, Theodore Menline 1904-1979 *BioIn 6,
–11, –12, ConAu 1R, –3NR,
NewYTBE 72, NewYTBS 79, SmATA 12,
–27N, WhAm 7, WhJnl, WhNAA,
WhoAm 74, –76, –78, WhoWorJ 72, –78*
Berri, Claude 1934- *FilmgC, NewYTBE 70,
WhoFr 79, WhoWor 74*
Berrien, Edith Heal 1903- *BioIn 10, ConAu X,
ForWC 70, SmATA X*

Berrien, Edith Heal *see also* Heal, Edith
Berrigan, Daniel 1921- *AmAu&B,*
AmCath 80, ASpks, BioIn 7, -8, -9, -10,
-11, -12, CelR 73, ConAu 11NR, -33R,
ConLC 4, ConP 70, -75, -80,
DcLB 5[port], DrAP 75, DrAP&F 83,
IntWWP 77, LinLib L, MugS, PolProf J,
PolProf NF, WhoAm 74, -76, -78, -80, -82,
WhoRel 77, WrDr 76, -80, -82, -84
Berrill, Jacquelyn 1905- *AuBYP, BioIn 7, -8,*
-11, ConAu 17R, IlsCB 1957,
SmATA 12
Berrill, N J   *WhoOcn 78*
Berrill, N J 1903- *AmM&WS 73P,*
ConAu 17R
Berrill, Norman John 1903- *AmM&WS 76P,*
BlueB 76, CanWW 70, -79, -80, -81, -83,
IntAu&W 77, -82, IntWW 74, -75, -76,
-77, -78, -79, -80, -81, -82, -83, Who 74,
-82, -83, WhoWor 74, WrDr 80, -82, -84
Berry, Adrian M 1937- *ConAu 9NR, -57,*
Future, IntAu&W 77, WrDr 76, -80, -82,
-84
Berry, Barbara J 1937- *BioIn 10, ConAu 33R,*
SmATA 7, WrDr 76, -80, -82, -84
Berry, Chuck 1926- *Baker 78, BioIn 8, -9,*
-11, -12, ConLC 17, CurBio 77, DrBlPA,
EncPR&S, -77, IlEncRk, RkOn 74, -82,
RkOneH, RolSEnR 83, WhoAm 74, -76,
-78, -80, -82, WhoBlA 75, -77,
WhoRocM 82, WorAl
Berry, Erick 1892-1974 *AmPB, AuBYP,*
BioIn 1, -2, -5, -7, -9, ChhPo, ConAu X,
ConICB, DcNAA, IlsCB 1946, JBA 34,
-51, SmATA X
Berry, Erick *see also* Best, Allena Champlin
Berry, Frederic Aroyce, Jr. 1906-1978
ConAu 77
Berry, I William 1934- *ConAu 105,*
IntAu&W 82
Berry, James 1932- *AuBYP SUP, BioIn 7,*
ConAu 21R
Berry, Wendell 1934- *AuNews 1, BioIn 10,*
-11, -12, ConAu 73, ConLC 4, -6, -8,
-27[port], ConP 70, -75, -80,
DcLB 5[port], -6[port], DrAF 76,
DrAP 75, DrAP&F 83, IntWWP 77, -82,
Novels[port], PenC AM, RAdv 1,
WhoAm 74, -76, -78, -80, -82,
WhoS&SW 73, WrDr 76, -80, -82, -84
Berton, Ralph 1910- *ConAu 49*
Bessette, Gerard 1920- *CanWW 70, -79, -80,*
-81, -83, CanWr, CasWL, ConAu 37R,
CreCan 1, DrAS 74F, -78F, -82F, OxCan,
OxCan SUP, WhoE 74, WhoWor 74, -76
Best, Allena Champlin 1892-1974 *AuBYP,*
BioIn 1, -2, -5, -7, -9, ConAu P-2,
IlsCB 1744, -1946, InWom, JBA 34, -51,
SmATA 2, -25N, WhoAmW 58, -61
Best, Allena Champlin *see also* Berry, Erick
Best, Herbert 1894-1981 *AmAu&B, AmNov,*
AuBYP, BioIn 2, -8, -9, ConAu P-2,

EncSF, JBA 34, -51, ScF&FL 1, -2,
SmATA 2, TwCCW 78, -83, WhE&EA,
WrDr 80, -82, -84
Bester, Alfred 1913- *AmAu&B, BioIn 11, -12,*
ConAu 13R, ConSFA, DcLB 8[port],
DcLEL 1940, EncSF, Novels, ScF&FL 1,
-2, WhoSciF, WrDr 76, -80, -82, -84
Betenson, Lula Parker 1884- *ConAu 61*
Beth, Mary *ConAu X, SmATA X*
Beth, Mary *see also* Miller, Mary Beth
Bethancourt, T Ernesto 1932- *ChlLR 3,*
ConAu X, SmATA 11
Bethancourt, T Ernesto *see also* Paisley, Tom
Bettenbender, John I 1921- *DrAS 74E, -78E,*
-82E
Bettmann, Otto Ludwig 1903- *BiE&WWA,*
BioIn 1, -5, -6, -10, -12, ConAu 17R,
CurBio 61, NewYTBS 81[port], NotNAT,
WhoAm 74, -76, -78, -80, -82,
WhoAmA 76, -78, -80, -82, WhoWor 74,
-76
Beyer, Audrey White 1916- *BioIn 11,*
ConAu 13R, ForWC 70, SmATA 9
Bhatia, June 1919- *Au&Wr 6, ConAu X,*
IntAu&W 76X, -77X, OxCan SUP,
WrDr 76, -80, -82, -84
Bhatia, June *see also* Forrester, Helen
Bibby, Cyril 1914- *Au&Wr 6, ConAu 7NR,*
-13R, IntAu&W 76, -77, -82, Who 74,
-82, -83, WrDr 76, -80, -82, -84
Bibby, Dause L 1911- *EncAB 31, IntYB 78,*
-79, -80, -81, -82, WhoAm 74, -76, -78,
WhoF&I 74, -75
Bibby, Thomas Geoffrey 1917- *Au&Wr 6,*
ConAu 1R, IntAu&W 77, -82,
WhoWor 76
Bibby, Violet 1908- *AuBYP SUP, ConAu 102,*
SmATA 24[port], TwCCW 78, -83,
WrDr 80, -82, -84
Bichler, Joyce 1954- *ConAu 107*
Bickel, Lennard 1923- *WrDr 82, -84*
Bickham, Jack M 1930- *AmAu&B,*
AmCath 80, ConAu 5R, -8NR,
IntAu&W 82, WhoAm 74, WrDr 76, -80,
-82, -84
Biemiller, Carl Ludwig 1912-1979 *AuBYP SUP,*
BioIn 12, ConAu 106, ScF&FL 1, -2,
SmATA 21N
Bierce, Ambrose 1842-1914? *AmAu,*
AmAu&B, AmBi, AmWr, ApCAB SUP,
AtlBL, BioIn 1, -2, -3, -4, -5, -6, -7, -8, -9,
-10, -11, -12, CasWL, Chambr 3, ChhPo,
-S1, -S3, CmCal, CnDAL, ConAu 104,
CrtT 3, -4, CyWA, DcAmAu, DcAmB,
DcLB 11[port], -12[port], -23[port],
DcLEL, DcNAA, EncAB-H, EncMys,
EncSF, EvLB, LinLib L, -S, LongCTC,
McGEWB, ModAL, ModAL SUP,
NatCAB 14, Novels, OhA&B, OxAmL,
OxEng, PenC AM, RAdv 1, REn,
REnAL, REnAW, ScF&FL 1, TwCLC 1,
-7[port], WebAB, -79, WebE&AL,

WhDW, WhAm HSA, –4, WhoHr&F,
WhoSciF, WorAl
Bierhorst, John 1936- *AuBYP SUP, BioIn 10,*
ConAu 33R, IntAu&W 77, SmATA 6,
WhoE 83, WrDr 76, –80, –82, –84
Biggle, Lloyd, Jr. 1923- *BioIn 12,*
ConAu 5NR, –13R, ConSFA,
DcLB 8[port], EncSF, ScF&FL 1, –2,
WhoSciF, WrDr 84
Biko, Steve 1947-1977 *InB&W 80*
Billings, Henry 1901- *AmAu&B, BioIn 1, –5,*
–6, IlsCB 1946, MorJA, WhoAmA 73,
–76, –78, –80, –82
Billings, Peggy 1928- *ConAu 25R*
Billingsley, Andrew 1926- *ConAu 57, Ebony 1,*
InB&W 80, LivgBAA, NegAl 76, –83,
SelBAA, WhoBlA 75, –77, –80
Billington, Elizabeth T *ConAu 101*
Bing, Rudolf 1902- *Baker 78, BiDAmM,*
BioIn 1, –2, –3, –4, –5, –6, –7, –8, –9, –10,
BlueB 76, CelR 73, ConAu 89,
CurBio 50, IntWW 74, –75, –76, –77, –78,
–79, –80, –81, –82, –83, IntWWM 77,
LinLib S, NewEOp 71, NewYTBE 71,
–72, –73, REn, Who 74, –82, –83,
WhoAm 74, –76, –78, –80, –82,
WhoMus 72, WhoOp 76, WhoWor 74,
–78, –80, –82
Bingham, Caroline 1938- *ConAu 10NR, –57,*
IntAu&W 76, –77, –82, Who 82, –83,
WrDr 76, –80, –82, –84
Binns, Archie 1899-1971 *AmAu&B, AmNov,*
BioIn 2, –4, ConAu 73, LinLib L,
OxAmL, REnAL, TwCA, TwCA SUP,
WhAm 5, WhoPNW
Bioy Casares, Adolfo 1914- *BioIn 12,*
ConAu 29R, ConLC 4, –8, –13, DcCLAA,
EncLatA, EncSF, EncWL 81,
IntAu&W 77, –82, ModLAL, OxSpan,
PenC AM, ScF&FL 1, –2, WhoWor 74,
–76
Birch, Cyril 1925- *ConAu 85, DrAS 74F,*
–78F, –82F
Bird, Anthony Cole 1917- *Au&Wr 6,*
ConAu 13R
Bird, Caroline 1915- *BioIn 10, –11,*
ConAu 11NR, –17R, CurBio 76,
ForWC 70, IntAu&W 77, WhoAm 76,
–78, –80, –82, WhoAmW 74, –61, –64, –66,
–68, –70, –72, –77, –79, WhoE 75,
WrDr 76, –80, –82, –84
Birley, Anthony Richard 1937- *Au&Wr 6,*
IntAu&W 76
Birmingham, John 1951- *ConAu 45*
Birnbach, Lisa *BioIn 12*
Bischoff, David F 1951- *ConAu 81, WrDr 84*
Bishop, Claire Huchet *AmPB, AmWomWr,*
AuBYP, BioIn 1, –2, –3, –7, –8, –12, BkP,
CathA 1952, ConAu 73, FamMS,
JBA 51, SmATA 14, TwCCW 78, –83,
WhoAmW 58, –61, –64, WrDr 80, –82, –84
Bishop, Curtis Kent 1912-1967 *AuBYP,*

BioIn 7, –10, ConAu P-1, EncAB 39[port],
SmATA 6
Bishop, Elizabeth 1911-1979 *AmAu&B,*
AmWomWr, AmWr SUP, Au&Wr 6,
AuBYP SUP, BioIn 4, –7, –8, –10, –11, –12,
BlueB 76, CelR 73, ChhPo, –S1, –S3,
CnE&AP, ConAu 5R, –89, ConLC 1, –4,
–9, –13, –15, ConP 70, –75, –80, CroCAP,
CurBio 77, –79N, DcLB 5[port],
DcLEL 1940, DrAP 75, EncWL, –81,
FourBJA, IntAu&W 77, IntDcWB,
IntWW 74, –75, –76, –77, –78, –79,
IntWWP 77, LibW, LinLib L, MakMC,
ModAL, ModAL SUP, NewYTBS 79,
OxAmL, PenC AM, RAdv 1, REn,
REnAL, SmATA 24N, TwCA SUP,
TwCWr, WebE&AL, WhAm 7,
WhoAm 74, –76, –78, WhoAmW 74, –58,
–64, –66, –68, –70, –72, WhoE 74,
WhoWor 74, WrDr 76, –80
Bishop, James Alonzo 1907- *AuNews 1,*
BioIn 3, –4, –8, –10, BioNews 74,
ConAu 17R
Bishop, James Alonzo *see also* Bishop, Jim
Bishop, Jim 1907- *AmAu&B, AuNews 1, –2,*
BioIn 11, –12, CelR 73, ConAu X,
CurBio 69, DrAP 75, LinLib L, REnAL,
WhoAm 74, –76, –78, –80, –82,
WhoS&SW 73, –75, –76, WhoWor 74, –76,
–78, WorAl
Bishop, Jim *see also* Bishop, James Alonzo
Bishop, Michael 1945- *AuNews 2, BioIn 11,*
ConAu 9NR, –61, EncSF, IntAu&W 82,
WrDr 84
Bishop, Morris Gilbert 1893?-1973 *AmAu&B,*
BioIn 4, –10, ChhPo, –S1, –S2, ConAu 1R,
–6NR, –45, ObitOF 79, OxAmL, REnAL,
ScF&FL 1, –2, TwCA SUP, WhAm 6,
WhLit, WhoAm 74
Bishop, W Arthur 1923- *ConAu 21R*
Bixby, William Courtney 1920- *AmAu&B,*
AuBYP, BioIn 8, –10, ConAu 1R, –6NR,
SmATA 6, WhoAm 74
Bjorklund, Karna L *AuBYP SUP*
Bjorn, Thyra Ferre 1905-1975 *AmAu&B,*
BioIn 3, –7, –10, ConAu 3NR, –5R, –57,
WhoAmW 61, –64, –68, –72
Black, Bonnie Lee 1945- *ConAu 107*
Black, Cyril Edwin 1915- *AmAu&B,*
ConAu 1R, –3NR, DrAS 74H, –78H, –82H,
WhoAm 74, –76, –78, –80, –82, WhoE 74,
WhoWor 74, –76
Black, Hallie 1943- *ConAu 108*
Black, Hugo LaFayette 1886-1971 *BiDFedJ,*
BiDrAC, BioIn 1, –2, –4, –5, –6, –7, –8, –9,
–10, –11, –12, ConAu 33R, CurBio 41, –64,
–71N, DcAmSR, EncAB-H, EncSoH,
LinLib L, –S, McGEWB, NewYTBE 71,
ObitOF 79, ObitT 1971, OxAmH,
PolProf E, PolProf J, PolProf K,
PolProf NF, PolProf T, WebAB, –79,
WhAm 5, WhAmP, WorAl

Black, Hugo LaFayette, Jr. 1922- *WhoAm 80,*
–82, WhoAmL 78, –79
Black, Laura *WrDr 84*
Black, Max 1909- *AmAu&B, ConAu 61,*
DrAS 74P, –78P, –82P, WhoAm 74, –76,
–78, –80, –82, WhoAmJ 80, WhoE 74,
WhoWorJ 72, –78
Black, Susan Adams 1953- *ConAu 105*
Blackbeard, Bill 1926- *ConAu 97,*
WhoWest 80, WorECar A
Blackburn, Graham 1940- *ConAu 69*
Blackburn, Joyce Knight 1920- *ConAu 17R,*
IndAu 1917, SmATA 29[port],
WhoAmW 74
Blackmore, Michael 1916- *WhE&EA*
Blackmore, Richard Doddridge 1825-1900
Alli SUP, BbD, BiD&SB, BioIn 1, –2, –3,
–4, –5, –10, –11, –12, BrAu 19, CelCen,
Chambr 3, ChhPo, –S1, –S2, –S3, CyWA,
DcBiA, DcEnA, –AP, DcEnL, DcEuL,
DcLEL, EvLB, JBA 34, LinLib L, –S,
MouLC 4, NewC, OxEng, PenC ENG,
REn, TelT, WebE&AL
Blackwell, Elizabeth 1821-1910 *Alli, Alli SUP,*
AmBi, AmWom, AmWomWr, ApCAB,
BiD&SB, BiHiMed, BioIn 1, –2, –3, –4, –5,
–6, –7, –8, –9, –10, –11, –12, CelCen,
CivWDc, DcAmAu, DcAmB, DcAmMeB,
DcBiPP, DcNAA, Drake, EncAB-H,
GoodHs, HarEnUS, HerW, InSci,
InWom, IntDcWB, LibW, LinLib S,
McGEWB, NatCAB 9, NotAW, OhA&B,
OxAmH, TwCBDA, WebAB, –79,
WhDW, WhAm 1, WhLit, WorAl
Blackwood, Alan 1932- *ConAu 110*
Blackwood, Paul Everett 1913-
AmM&WS 73P, ConAu 102, LEduc 74,
WhoGov 77, –72, –75
Blair, Clay Drewry, Jr. 1925- *AmAu&B,*
AuNews 2, BioIn 4, –8, –10, –11,
ConAu 77, IntAu&W 76, –77, IntWW 74,
WhoAm 76, –78, –80, –82
Blair, Lucile *ConAu X*
Blair, Lucile *see also* Yeakley, Marjorie Hall
Blair, William Robert 1928- *WhoAm 82*
Blake, Howard E 1922- *DrAS 74E, –78E, –82E,*
LEduc 74
Blake, Peter Jost 1920- *AmArch 70,*
AmAu&B, BioIn 4, –10, ConArch,
ConAu 65, McGDA, WhoAm 80, –82,
WhoAmA 73, –76, –78, –80, –82, WhoE 74,
WrDr 82, –84
Blake, Walker E *AuBYP SUP, ConAu X*
Blake, Walker E *see also* Butterworth, W E
Blake, William 1757-1827 *Alli, AnCL,*
AntBDN B, AtlBL, AuBYP SUP, BbD,
BiD&SB, BiDLA, BioIn 1, –2, –3, –4, –5,
–6, –7, –8, –9, –10, –11, –12, BkIE,
BrAu 19, BrWr 3, CarSB, CasWL,
CelCen, Chambr 2, ChrP, ChhPo, –S1,
–S2, –S3, CnE&AP, CrtT 2, –4, CyWA,
DcBiPP, DcBrBI, DcBrWA, DcEnA, –AP,

DcEnL, DcEuL, DcLEL, DcNiCA,
Dis&D, EncO&P 78, EvLB, FamPYP,
IlEncMy, LinLib L, –S, LongCEL,
LuthC 75, McGDA, McGEWB,
MouLC 3, NewC, OxArt, OxEng,
OxMus, PenC ENG, RAdv 1, RComWL,
REn, SmATA 30[port], Str&VC,
WebE&AL, WhDW, WorAl
Blakemore, Colin Brian 1944- *ConAu 85,*
IntWW 76, –77, –78, –79, –80, –81, –82, –83,
Who 82, –83, WhoWor 78
Blaker, Charles William 1918- *WhoS&SW 82*
Blanco, Richard L 1926- *ConAu 57,*
DrAS 74H
Blanpied, Pamela Wharton 1937- *ConAu 102,*
DrAP&F 83
Blanton, Catherine 1907- *AuBYP, BioIn 8,*
ConAu 1R
Blanzaco, Andre Charles 1934- *ConAu 29R,*
WhoE 79, –81
Blassingame, John W 1940- *ConAu 49,*
ConIsC 1[port], DrAS 74H, –78H, –82H,
InB&W 80, LivgBAA, NegAl 83,
WhoBlA 75, –77, –80
Blassingame, Wyatt Rainey 1909- *AuBYP,*
BioIn 8, –9, ConAu 1R, –3NR,
IntAu&W 77, –82, SmATA 1, –34[port],
WhoHr&F, WhoS&SW 76, WrDr 76, –80,
–82, –84
Blatter, Dorothy 1901- *ConAu P-1*
Blatty, William Peter 1928- *BioIn 8, –9, –10,*
–11, ConAu 5R, –9NR, ConLC 2,
CurBio 74, FilmgC, IntAu&W 76, –77,
IntMPA 77, –75, –76, –78, –79, –81, –82, –84,
ScF&FL 1, –2, WhoAm 76, –78, –80, –82,
WrDr 76, –80, –82, –84
Blaushild, Babette 1927- *ConAu 29R,*
WhoAmP 73, –75
Blaylock, James P 1950- *ConAu 110*
Bleeck, Oliver *ConAu X, EncMys,*
TwCCr&M 80, WrDr 76, –80, –82, –84
Bleeck, Oliver *see also* Thomas, Ross Elmore
Bleich, Alan R 1913- *BiDrAPH 79,*
ConAu 13R
Bleiler, E F 1920- *ChhPo S2, WhoSciF*
Bleiler, Everett Franklin 1920- *ScF&FL 1,*
WhoAm 76, –78, –80
Bligh, William 1754-1817 *Alli, BiDLA,*
BioIn 2, –3, –4, –6, –7, –8, –9, –10, –11,
CelCen, DcBiPP, McGEWB, NewC,
OxShips, REn, WhDW, WorAl
Blinn, William *LesBEnT, NewYTET*
Blish, James 1921-1975 *AmAu&B, Au&Wr 6,*
BioIn 10, –12, ConAu 1R, –3NR, –57,
ConLC 14, ConNov 76, ConSFA,
DcLB 8[port], DcLEL 1940, EncSF,
IntAu&W 76, LinLib L, NewYTBS 75,
Novels, ObitT 1971, ScF&FL 1, –2,
WhoSciF, WorAl, WorAu, WrDr 76
Blishen, Edward 1920- *Au&Wr 6, BioIn 11,*
ChhPo, ConAu 11NR, –17R,
IntAu&W 77, ScF&FL 1, –2, SmATA 8,

Who 82, –83, WrDr 76, –80, –82, –84

Blitzer, Charles 1927- *WhoAm 74, –76, –78, –80, –82, WhoGov 77, –72, –75*

Blixen, Karen Christentze Dinesen 1885-1962 *BioIn 12, CasWL, ConAu P-2, ConLC 10, EncWL, InWom, IntDcWB, LongCTC, Novels[port], ObitT 1961, PenC ENG, –EUR, REn, ScF&FL 1, TwCA, TwCA SUP, WhoTwCL*

Blixen, Karen Christentze Dinesen *see also* Dinesen, Isa

Bloch, Marie Halun 1910- *Au&Wr 6, AuBYP, BioIn 7, –10, ConAu 1R, –4NR, ForWC 70, FourBJA, IntAu&W 76, SmATA 6, TwCCW 78, WrDr 76, –80, –82, –84*

Bloch, Robert 1917- *AmAu&B, BioIn 7, –11, ConAu 5R, –5NR, ConSFA, DrAF 76, EncMys, EncSF, FilmgC, IntAu&W 76, –82, IntMPA 77, –75, –76, –78, –79, –81, –82, –84, LinLib L, Novels, ScF&FL 1, –2, SmATA 12, TwCCr&M 80, WhoAm 82, WhoHr&F, WhoSciF, WrDr 76, –80, –82, –84*

Block, Eugene B 1890- *ConAu 2NR, –5R, WhoWorJ 72*

Block, Herbert Lawrence 1909- *AmAu&B, BioIn 1, –2, –3, –4, –5, –6, –9, –10, –11, CurBio 54, EncAB-H, IntWW 83, WebAB, –79, WhoAm 74, –76, –78, –80, –82, WhoAmA 78, –80, –82, WhoS&SW 73, –75, WhoWor 74, WorAl, WorECar*

Block, Irvin 1917- *BioIn 11, ConAu 17R, SmATA 12*

Block, Joel D 1943- *ConAu 89*

Block, Lawrence 1938- *ConAu 1R, –6NR, DrAP&F 83, TwCCr&M 80, WhoAm 82, WrDr 82, –84*

Block, Thomas H 1945- *ConAu 101*

Bloom, Claire 1931- *BiDFilm, BioIn 3, –4, –6, –7, –8, –9, –11, –12, BlueB 76, CelR 73, CnThe, FilmgC, InWom, IntMPA 77, –75, –76, –78, –79, –81, –82, –84, IntWW 74, –75, –76, –77, –78, –79, –80, –81, –82, –83, MovMk, NotNAT, Who 74, –82, –83, WhoAm 74, –76, –78, –80, –82, WhoAmW 83, WhoThe 15, –16, –81, WhoWor 78, WorAl, WorEFlm*

Bloom, Edward Alan 1914- *ConAu 1R, –2NR, DrAS 74E, –78E, –82E, IndAu 1917, WhoAm 74, –76, –78, –80, –82, WrDr 82, –84*

Bloom, Harold 1930- *AmAu&B, BlueB 76, ChhPo, ConAu 13R, ConLC 24[port], ConLCrt, –82, DcLEL 1940, DrAS 74E, –78E, –82E, IntAu&W 77, –82, WhoAm 74, –76, –78, –80, –82, WhoAmJ 80, WhoE 83, WhoWorJ 72, –78, WorAu 1970, WrDr 76, –80, –82, –84*

Bloomfield, Harold H 1944- *BiDrAPA 77, ConAu 9NR, –57*

Bloomstein, Morris J 1928- *ConAu 25R*

Blos, Joan W 1928- *AuBYP SUP, BioIn 12, ConAu 101, SmATA 27, –33[port], TwCCW 83, WhoAm 82, WhoAmW 81, WrDr 84*

Blotnick, Elihu 1939- *ConAu 106*

Blount, Roy, Jr. 1941- *ConAu 10NR, –53*

Blue, Betty A 1922- *ConAu 1NR, –45, DrAS 74F, –78F, –82F*

Blue, Rose 1931- *AuBYP SUP, ConAu 41R, IntAu&W 76, SmATA 5, WhoAmW 74, –77, –79, –81, –83, WhoE 75, –77, –79, –81, –83*

Bluebond-Langner, Myra 1948- *AmM&WS 76P, ConAu 81*

Bluestone, George 1928- *ConAu 1R, –1NR, DrAS 74E*

Bluestone, Naomi 1936- *BiDrAPH 79*

Blum, Arlene 1945- *BioIn 11, IntDcWB*

Blumberg, Gary 1938- *ConAu 2NR, –45*

Blumberg, Rhoda 1917- *ConAu 9NR, –65, SmATA 35, WhoAmW 79, –81, –83, WhoE 81, –83*

Blume, Judy 1938- *AuBYP SUP, BioIn 9, –10, –11, –12, ChlLR 2, ConAu 29R, ConLC 12, CurBio 80[port], FourBJA, NewYTBS 82[port], PiP, SmATA 2, –31[port], TwCCW 78, –83, WhoAm 76, –78, –80, –82, WhoAmW 74, –81, –83, WorAl, WrDr 76, –80, –82, –84*

Blumenthal, Lassor Agoos 1926- *ConAu 25R, WhoE 74*

Blumenthal, Shirley 1943- *ConAu 108*

Bly, Robert 1926- *AmAu&B, BioIn 10, –12, BlueB 76, ConAu 5R, ConLC 1, –2, –5, –10, –15, ConP 70, –75, –80, CroCAP, DcLB 5[port], DcLEL 1940, DrAP 75, DrAP&F 83, EncWL 81, IntWWP 77, LinLib L, ModAL SUP, PenC AM, RAdv 1, WebE&AL, WhoAm 74, –76, –78, –80, –82, WhoTwCL, WhoWor 74, WorAl, WorAu, WrDr 76, –80, –82, –84*

Blyth, Alan Geoffrey 1929- *ConAu 1NR, –49, IntAu&W 77, IntWWM 77, WhoMus 72, WhoWor 76, WrDr 76, –80, –82, –84*

Boardman, Fon Wyman, Jr. 1911- *BioIn 10, ConAu 1R, –3NR, IntAu&W 82, SmATA 6, WrDr 76, –80, –82, –84*

Boardman, Peter 1950-1982 *AnObit 1982[port], ConAu 108, –97*

Bobbe, Dorothie 1905-1975 *BioIn 9, ConAu 57, ConAu P-2, SmATA 1, –25N*

Bock, Hal 1939- *ConAu X, SmATA X*

Bock, Hal *see also* Bock, Harold I

Bock, Harold I 1939- *BioIn 11, ConAu 29R, SmATA 10, WhoE 75, –77*

Boddy, William Charles 1913- *Au&Wr 6, ConAu 101*

Bode, Janet 1943- *ConAu 69, WhoAmW 81, –83*

Bodecker, N M 1922- *ConAu 4NR, IntAu&W 76, TwCCW 78, –83, WrDr 80,*

−82, −84

Boden, Hilda *AuBYP SUP, ConAu X, SmATA X*

Boden, Hilda *see also* Bodenham, Hilda Morris

Bodenham, Hilda Morris 1901- *AuBYP SUP, ConAu 6NR, −9R, SmATA 13*

Bodey, Hugh 1939- *ConAu 61, IntAu&W 77, WrDr 76, −80, −82, −84*

Bodger, Joan *BioIn 8, ChhPo S1, ConAu X*

Bodie, Idella F 1925- *BioIn 11, ConAu 41R, SmATA 12*

Bodker, Cecil 1927- *BioIn 12, CasWL, ConAu 73, ConLC 21[port], IntAu&W 77, −82, SmATA 14*

Bodo, Peter T 1949- *ConAu 85*

Bodsworth, Fred 1918- *Au&Wr 6, CaW, ConAu 1R, −3NR, ConNov 72, −76, −82, CreCan 2, OxCan, OxCan SUP, SmATA 27[port], WrDr 76, −80, −82, −84*

Boeckman, Charles 1920- *AuBYP SUP, BioIn 11, ConAu 13R, SmATA 12*

Boell, Heinrich 1917- *ConAu 21R*

Boell, Heinrich *see also* Boll, Heinrich

Boesch, Mark J 1917- *BioIn 11, ConAu 21R, SmATA 12, WhoPNW*

Boesen, Victor 1908- *AuBYP SUP, BioIn 12, ConAu 37R, IndAu 1917, IntAu&W 77, SmATA 16, WhoWest 76, −78, −80, −82, −84*

Bogan, Louise 1897-1970 *AmAu&B, AmWomWr, AuBYP, BioIn 4, −8, −10, −12, ChhPo, −S3, CnDAL, CnE&AP, ConAmA, ConAu 25R, −73, ConLC 4, ConP 70, DcLEL, EncWL, −81, InWom, LibW, LinLib L, ModAL, ModAL SUP, NewYTBE 70, NotAW MOD, ObitOF 79, OxAmL, PenC AM, RAdv 1, REn, REnAL, SixAP, TwCA, TwCA SUP, TwCWr, WhAm 5, WhE&EA, WhoAmW 58, −64, −66, −68, −70, −72*

Bogdanovich, Peter 1939- *BiDFilm, BioIn 9, −10, −11, −12, BioNews 74, CelR 73, ConAu 5R, CurBio 72, IntAu&W 82, IntMPA 77, −75, −76, −78, −79, −81, −82, −84, IntWW 75, −76, −77, −78, −79, −80, −81, −82, −83, MovMk, NewYTBS 77, OxFilm, Who 82, −83, WhoAm 74, −76, −78, −80, −82, WhoWest 78, WhoWor 76, −78, WorAl, WrDr 76*

Bogen, Constance *AuBYP SUP*

Bogle, Donald *AuNews 1, BioIn 10, SelBAA*

Bograd, Larry 1953- *ConAu 93, SmATA 33[port]*

Bohannan, Paul 1920- *AmM&WS 73S, −76P, ConAu 9R, FifIDA, IntAu&W 82, WhoAm 74, −76, −78, WhoWor 74, −76, WrDr 76, −80, −82, −84*

Bohle, Bruce William 1918- *ConAu 9NR, −21R, WhoAm 74, −76, −78, −80, −82*

Boland, Charles Michael 1917- *ConAu 9R*

Boles, Paul Darcy 1916?-1984 *Au&Wr 6, BioIn 3, −4, −11, ConAu 4NR, −9R,*

CurBio 56, IndAu 1917, SmATA 9, WhoS&SW 73, −75, −76, −78, −80

Bolitho, Henry Hector 1897?-1974 *Au&Wr 6, ConAu 53, ConAu P-1, DcLEL, EvLB, IntWW 74, −75N, LongCTC, NewC, PenC ENG, TwCA, TwCA SUP, WhE&EA, WhLit, Who 74, WhoWor 74*

Boll, Heinrich 1917- *BioIn 5, −9, −10, −12, CasWL, CelR 73, ConAu X, ConLC 2, −3, −6, −9, −11, −15, −27[port], CurBio 72, EncWL, −81[port], EvEuW, IntAu&W 76, −77, IntWW 74, −75, −76, −77, −78, −79, −80, −81, −82, −83, LinLib L, −S, MakMC, ModGL, NewYTBE 72, NewYTBS 74, Novels[port], OxGer, PenC EUR, REn, TwCWr, WhDW, Who 74, −82, −83, WhoAm 76, −78, −80, −82, WhoTwCL, WhoWor 74, −78, −80, −82, WorAl, WorAu*

Boll, Heinrich *see also* Boell, Heinrich

Boller, Paul Franklin, Jr. 1916- *ConAu 1R, −3NR, DrAS 74H, −78H, −82H*

Bolles, Richard Nelson 1927- *BioIn 12, ConAu 1NR, −45, IntAu&W 76, WhoAm 80, −82, WhoRel 75, −77, WhoWest 78, −80, −82, −84*

Bolognese, Don 1934- *ConAu X, FourBJA, SmATA 24*

Bolognese, Donald Alan 1934- *BioIn 8, ChhPo S1, −S2, ConAu 97, IlsBYP, IlsCB 1957, −1967*

Bolt, Robert 1924- *BiE&WWA, BioIn 6, −7, −8, −9, −10, −11, −12, BlueB 76, CasWL, CelR 73, CnThe, ConAu 17R, ConDr 73, −77, −82, ConLC 14, CroCD, CurBio 63, DcLB 13[port], DcLEL 1940, EncWL 81, EncWT, FilmgC, IntAu&W 76, −77, −82, IntMPA 77, −78, −79, −81, −82, −84, IntWW 74, −75, −76, −77, −78, −79, −80, −81, −82, −83, LinLib L, LongCTC, McGEWD, −84[port], ModBrL SUP, ModWD, NewC, NotNAT, OxThe, PenC ENG, REnWD, TwCWr, WebE&AL, Who 74, −82, −83, WhoThe 15, −16, −81, WhoWor 74, −76, −78, −82, WorAu, WorEFlm, WrDr 76, −80, −82, −84*

Bolton, Carole 1926- *AuBYP SUP, BioIn 10, ConAu 1NR, −49, ForWC 70, SmATA 6*

Bolton, Ivy May 1879- *AuBYP, BioIn 7*

Bolton, Sarah Knowles 1841-1916 *Alli SUP, AmAu, AmAu&B, AmBi, AmWom, AmWomWr, ApCAB, BbD, BiD&SB, CarSB, ChhPo, −S1, −S2, DcAmAu, DcAmB, DcNAA, HarEnUS, NatCAB 1, OhA&B, TwCBDA, WhAm 1, WomWWA 14*

Bombaugh, Charles Carroll 1828-1906 *Alli SUP, ChhPo S2, −S3, DcAmAu, DcNAA, NatCAB 7*

Bombeck, Erma 1927- *AmCath 80, AuNews 1, BioIn 8, −9, −10, −11, −12,*

ConAu 21R, CurBio 79, ForWC 70,
LibW, WhoAm 76, -78, -80, -82,
WhoAmW 74, -72, -79, -81, -83, WorAl,
WrDr 80, -82, -84
Bonavia, David Michael 1940- *ConAu 106*
Bond, Michael 1926- *Au&Wr 6,*
AuBYP SUP, BioIn 8, -9, -10, -11, BrCA,
ChlLR 1, ConAu 4NR, -5R,
IntAu&W 76, -77, -82, MorBMP,
SmATA 6, ThrBJA, TwCCW 78, -83,
Who 74, -82, -83, WhoChL, WrDr 76,
-80, -82, -84
Bond, Nancy 1945- *AuBYP SUP,*
ConAu 9NR, -65, SmATA 22[port],
TwCCW 83
Bonderoff, Jason 1946- *ConAu 97*
Bone, Stephen 1904-1958 *BioIn 5, DcBrA 1,*
DcSeaP, IlsBYP, IlsCB 1946, LongCTC,
ObitOF 79, ObitT 1951, WhE&EA
Boney, Mary Lily 1918- *ConAu 13R*
Boney, Mary Lily *see also* Sheats, Mary Boney
Bonfiglioli, Kyril *WhoSciF*
Bongar, Emmet W 1919- *ConAu 33R*
Bonham, Barbara 1926- *BioIn 10,*
ConAu 7NR, -17R, SmATA 7, WrDr 76,
-80, -82, -84
Bonham, Frank 1914- *AuBYP, BioIn 8, -9,*
-10, ConAu 4NR, -9R, ConLC 12,
MorBMP, SmATA 1, ThrBJA,
TwCCW 78, -83, WrDr 80, -82, -84
Bonington, Christian 1934- *BioIn 10, -11,*
ConAu 1NR, -45, IntAu&W 76, -77, -82,
Who 74, -82, -83, WhoWor 76, -80,
WrDr 76, -80, -82, -84
Bonner, John Tyler 1920- *AmM&WS 73P,*
-76P, -79P, -82P, ConAu 49, WhoAm 74,
-76, -78, -80, -82, WhoAtom 77
Bono, Philip 1921- *ConAu 101, WhoAm 74,*
-76, -78, -80, -82, WhoF&I 74, -75, -77,
-79, -81, WhoWest 78, -80, -82, -84,
WhoWor 74, -76, -82
Bontemps, Arna Wendell 1902-1973 *AmAu&B,*
AmNov, AnMV 1926, Au&Wr 6,
AuBYP, BioIn 1, -2, -7, -8, -9, -10, -12,
BkCL, BlkAWP, BroadAu,
ChlLR 6[port], ChhPo S1, -S3,
ConAu 1R, -4NR, -41R, ConLC 1, -18,
ConP 70, CurBio 46, -73, -73N,
DcAmLiB, Ebony 1, InB&W 80, JBA 51,
LinLib L, ModBlW, MorBMP,
NatCAB 61, NegAl 76[port], -83[port],
NewYTBE 73, Novels, ObitOF 79,
OxAmL, REnAL, SelBAA, SmATA 2,
-24N, Str&VC, WebE&AL, WhAm 5,
WhoAm 74, WhoBlA 75, WhoLibS 55,
WhoWor 74, WorAu 1970
Bonzon, Paul-Jacques 1908-1978 *Au&Wr 6,*
AuBYP, BioIn 7, ConAu 93, FourBJA,
SmATA 22[port], WhoWor 74
Booher, Dianna Daniels 1948- *ConAu 103,*
SmATA 33[port]
Bookbinder, David J 1951- *ConAu 101*

Bookspan, Martin 1926- *ConAu 41R,*
IntAu&W 76, WhoAmJ 80,
WhoAmM 83, WhoE 74, WhoWorJ 72,
-78
Boorstin, Daniel J 1914- *AmAu&B,*
AuNews 2, BioIn 6, -7, -8, -10, -11, -12,
BlueB 76, ConAu 1R, -1NR, CurBio 68,
DcLB 17[port], DcLEL 1940, DrAS 74H,
-78H, -82H, EncAAH, IntAu&W 77, -82,
IntWW 74, -75, -76, -77, -78, -79, -80, -81,
-82, -83, LinLib L, Who 82, -83,
WhoAm 74, -76, -78, -80, -82,
WhoAmJ 80, WhoE 81, -83, WhoGov 77,
-72, WhoLibI 82, WhoS&SW 73, -75,
-76, WhoWor 76, -78, -80, -82,
WhoWorJ 72, -78, WorAl, WorAu,
WrDr 76, -80, -82, -84
Booth, George 1926- *WhoAm 82, WorECar*
Borden, Charles A 1912-1968 *AuBYP, BioIn 8,*
ConAu 5R
Borek, Ernest 1911- *AmM&WS 73P, -76P,*
-79P, ConAu 106
Borges, Jorge Luis 1899- *BioIn 1, -5, -6, -7, -8,*
-9, -10, -11, -12, CasWL, CelR 73,
ConAu 21R, ConLC 1, -2, -3, -4, -6, -8,
-9, -10, -13, -19, CurBio 70, DcCLAA,
DcSpL, EncLatA, EncSF, EncWL,
-81[port], IntAu&W 77, IntWW 74, -75,
-76, -77, -78, -79, -80, -81, -82, -83,
IntWWP 77, LinLib L, -S, MakMC,
McGEWB, ModLAL, NewYTBE 71,
Novels[port], OxSpan, PenC AM, REn,
TwCCr&M 80B, TwCWr, WhDW,
Who 74, -82, -83, WhoTwCL,
WhoWor 74, -78, -80, -82, WorAl,
WorAu
Borgese, Elisabeth Mann 1918- *ConAu 73,*
Future, IntAu&W 76, ScF&FL 1,
WhoAm 78, -80, -82, WhoAmW 70, -83
Boring, Mel 1939- *ConAu 106, SmATA 35*
Borkin, Joseph 1911-1979 *AmEA 74, BioIn 12,*
ConAu 89, -97, NewYTBS 79,
WhoAmL 78, -79
Borland, Hal 1900-1978 *AmAu&B, Au&Wr 6,*
BioIn 4, -5, -6, -8, -10, -11, ChhPo,
ConAu X, NewYTBS 78, ObitOF 79,
REnAL, SmATA 24N, -5, WhAm 7,
WhoAm 74, -76, -78, WhoWor 74,
WorAu, WrDr 84
Borland, Hal *see also* Borland, Harold Glen
Borland, Harold Glen 1900-1978 *ConAu 1R,*
-6NR, -77, SmATA X
Borland, Harold Glen *see also* Borland, Hal
Borland, Harold Glen *see also* West, Ward
Borland, Kathryn Kilby 1916- *BioIn 12,*
ConAu 4NR, -53, IndAu 1917,
MichAu 80, SmATA 16, WhoAm 74, -76,
-78, -80, -82, WrDr 84
Borton, Elizabeth 1904- *BioIn 7, -8, -9, -10,*
-11, ConAu X, SmATA X, ThrBJA
Borton DeTrevino, Elizabeth 1904-
NinCLC 1966, WhoAmW 68A, -70, -72

Borton DeTrevino, Elizabeth *see also* DeTrevino, Elizabeth Borton
Borton DeTrevino, Elizabeth *see also* Trevino, Elizabeth Borton De
Bortstein, Larry 1942- *BioIn 12, ConAu 33R, SmATA 16*
Bosco, Henri 1888-1976 *BioIn 7, -10, CasWL, ConAu 65, -69, EvEuW, ObitOF 79, OxFr, PenC EUR, REn, WorAu*
Bossard, James Herbert Siward 1888-1960 *AmAu&B, BioIn 5, ObitOF 79, WhAm 3, WhE&EA, WhNAA*
Bosse, Malcolm J 1933- *ConAu 106, DrAP&F 83, SmATA 35, WhoE 77, -79, -83*
Boston, L M 1892- *ChlLR 3, ScF&FL 1, WrDr 80, -82, -84*
Boswell, James 1740-1795 *Alli, AtlBL, BbD, BiD&SB, BioIn 1, -2, -3, -4, -5, -6, -7, -8, -9, -10, -11, -12, BrAu, BrWr 3, CasWL, Chambr 2, ChhPo S2, -S3, CrtT 2, -4, CyWA, DcBiPP, DcEnA, DcEnL, DcEuL, DcLEL, Dis&D, EvLB, IlsCB 1957, LinLib L, -S, LongCEL, LongCTC, McGEWB, MnBBF, MouLC 2, NewC, OxEng, OxLaw, OxMus, PenC ENG, RAdv 1, RComWL, REn, WebE&AL, WhDW, WorAl*
Bosworth, Allan R 1901?- *ASpks, BioIn 8, -11, ConAu 1R, WrDr 84*
Bosworth, J Allan 1925- *AuBYP, BioIn 8, -12, SmATA 19*
Bothmer, Bernard V 1912- *DrAS 74H, -78H, -82H, WhoAm 74, -76, -78, -80, -82, WhoAmA 73, -76, -78, -80, -82, WhoE 83, WhoWor 74*
Bothwell, Jean d1977 *AuBYP, BioIn 1, -2, -7, -9, ConAu 1R, -3NR, CurBio 46, InWom, JBA 51, SmATA 2*
Botjer, George 1937- *ConAu 97*
Botkin, Benjamin Albert 1901-1975 *AmAu&B, Au&W 6, BioIn 4, -10, ConAu 57, ConAu P-1, DrAS 74E, NewYTBS 75, REnAL, TwCA SUP, WhAm 6, WhoAm 74, WhoWorJ 72, -78*
Bottel, Helen 1914- *BioIn 4, ConAu 25R, ForWC 70, IntAu&W 76, -77, WhoAm 80, -82, WhoAmW 74, -70, -70A, -72, -77, WhoWest 78, -82, WrDr 76, -80, -82, -84*
Boucher, Alan Estcourt 1918- *Au&Wr 6, ConAu 5R, -9NR, WhoWor 80, -82*
Boucher, Anthony 1911-1968 *AmAu&B, BioIn 1, -4, -6, -8, -12, ConAu X, CurBio 62, -68, DcLB 8, EncMys, EncSF, LinLib L, Novels, ObitOF 79, ScF&FL 1, -2, TwCA SUP, TwCCr&M 80, WhAm 5, WhoSciF*
Boucher, Anthony *see also* White, William Anthony Parker
Boucher, John G 1930- *ConAu 37R*
Boulle, Pierre 1912- *Au&Wr 6, BioIn 5, -8,*

-10, CasWL, ConAu 9R, EncSF, LinLib L, Novels, REn, ScF&FL 1, -2, SmATA 22[port], TwCCr&M 80B, TwCWr, WhoFr 79, WhoSciF, WhoWor 74, -76, WorAl, WorAu
Bourdeaux, Michael Alan 1934- *Au&Wr 6, ConAu 33R, IntAu&W 76, -77, -82, Who 83, WhoWor 78, -80, -82, WrDr 76, -80, -82, -84*
Bourdon, David 1934- *ConAu 37R, WhoAm 76, -78, -80, -82, WhoAmA 76, -78, -80, -82, WhoE 79*
Bourke-White, Margaret 1906?-1971 *AmAu&B, AmWomWr, BioIn 1, -2, -3, -4, -5, -6, -7, -8, -9, -10, -11, -12, ConAu 29R, ConAu P-1, ConPhot, CurBio 40, -71, -71N, GoodHs, HerW, InWom, IntDcWB, LibW, LinLib L, -S, NewYTBE 71, NotAW MOD, REn, REnAL, WebAB, -79, WhAm 5, WhoAmW 58, -64, -66, -68, -70, -72, WomArt, WorAl*
Bourliaguet, Leonce 1895-1965 *ConAu 102, FourBJA*
Bourne, Eulalia *BioIn 7, -10, ConAu 97*
Bourne, Miriam Anne 1931- *AuBYP SUP, BioIn 12, ConAu 10NR, -21R, SmATA 16*
Bouton, Jim 1939- *BioIn 12, CelR 73, ConAu X, CurBio 71, NewYTBE 70, WhoHol A, WorAl*
Bova, Ben W 1932- *BioIn 10, ChlLR 3, ConAu 1R, -5R, -11NR, ConSFA, DcLB Y81B[port], EncSF, IntAu&W 76, -77, Novels, ScF&FL 1, -2, SmATA 6, WhoSciF, WrDr 76, -80, -82, -84*
Bova, Benjamin William 1932- *AuBYP SUP, WhoAm 74, -76, -78, -82, WhoE 74, -75, -77, WhoWor 82*
Bowe, Frank 1947- *ConAu 104*
Bowen, Catherine Drinker 1897-1973 *AmAu&B, AmWomWr, BioIn 2, -4, -5, -6, -8, -10, -12, ConAu 5R, -45, CurBio 44, -73, -73N, InWom, LinLib L, NatCAB 58[port], NewYTBE 73, NotAW MOD, ObitOF 79, OxAmL, REn, REnAL, SmATA 7, TwCA SUP, WhAm 6, WhE&EA, Who 74, WhoAm 74, WhoAmW 74, -58, -64, -66, -68, -70, -72, WhoGov 72, WhoWor 74*
Bowen, Elizabeth 1899-1973 *Au&Wr 6, AuBYP, BioIn 1, -2, -3, -4, -5, -6, -7, -8, -9, -10, -11, -12, CasWL, ConAu 41R, ConAu P-2, ConLC 1, -3, -6, -11, -15, -22[port], ConNov 72, CyWA, DcIrB, DcIrL, DcIrW 1, -2, DcLB 15[port], DcLEL, EncWL, -81[port], EvLB, InWom, IntAu&W 76, -77, IntDcWB, LinLib L, LongCTC, McGEWB, ModBrL, ModBrL SUP, NewC, NewYTBE 73, Novels, ObitOF 79, ObitT 1971, OxEng, PenC ENG,*

RAdv 1, REn, TwCA, TwCA SUP,
TwCWr, WebE&AL, WhDW, WhAm 5,
WhE&EA, WhoAmW 74, –64, –66, –68,
–70, –72, WhoHr&F, WhoTwCL, WorAl
Bowen, Ezra 1927- *ConAu 85*
Bowen, Joshua David 1930- *AuBYP, BioIn 8,*
ConAu 105, SmATA 22[port]
Bowen, Robert Sidney 1900-1977 *AuBYP,*
BioIn 8, –11, –12, ConAu 69, –73,
ScF&FL 1, SmATA 21N
Bower, Louise 1900- *ConAu P-2*
Bowie, David 1947- *BioIn 9, –10, –11, –12,*
BioNews 74, ConAu X, ConLC 17,
CurBio 76, EncPR&S, –77, IlEncRk,
RkOn 78, –84, RkOneH, RolSEnR 83,
Who 83, WhoAm 78, –80, –82,
WhoHol A, WhoRocM 82, WorAl
Bowie, David *see also* Jones, David Robert
Bowles, Paul 1910- *AmAu&B, AmSCAP 66,*
Au&Wr 6, Baker 78, BiDAmM,
BiE&WWA, BioIn 1, –2, –4, –8, –9, –10,
–12, BlueB 76, ConAmC, ConAu 1R,
–1NR, ConLC 1, –2, –19, ConNov 72, –76,
–82, DcLB 5[port], –6[port], DcLEL 1940,
DrAF 76, DrAP&F 83, EncWL 81,
IntAu&W 76, –77, –82, IntWW 74, –75,
–76, –77, –78, –79, –80, –81, –82, –83,
IntWWM 77, LinLib L, ModAL,
ModAL SUP, NotNAT, Novels, OxAmL,
OxMus, PenC AM, RAdv 1, REnAL,
TwCA SUP, TwCWr, WhoAm 74, –76,
–78, –80, –82, WhoAmM 83, WhoE 74,
WhoTwCL, WhoWor 74, –76, –78, –82,
WrDr 76, –80, –82, –84
Bowman, Bruce 1938- *ConAu 65,*
WhoAmA 78, –80, –82, WhoWest 80, –82
Bowman, Gerald d1967 *MnBBF,*
WhoBW&I A
Bowman, James Cloyd 1880-1961 *AmAu&B,*
AnCL, AuBYP, BioIn 2, –6, –8,
ConAu 97, JBA 51, OhA&B,
SmATA 23[port], Str&VC, WhAm 4,
WhNAA
Bowman, John S 1931- *Au&Wr 6,*
AuBYP SUP, BioIn 12, ConAu 5NR,
–9R, ScF&FL 1, –2, SmATA 16
Bowra, Sir Cecil Maurice 1898-1970?
Au&Wr 6, BioIn 4, –7, ConAu 1R, –29R,
DcLEL, EvLB, LongCTC, ModBrL,
NewC, NewYTBE 71, REn, TwCA SUP,
WhAm 5, WhE&EA
Bowskill, Derek 1928- *ConAu 77,*
IntAu&W 76, –77
Boyarsky, Bill 1936- *ConAu 25R*
Boyd, James 1888-1944 *AmAu&B, BioIn 2, –3,*
–4, –5, –9, –11, –12, CnDAL, ConAmA,
ConAmL, CurBio 44, CyWA,
DcAmB S3, DcLB 9[port], DcLEL,
DcNAA, LinLib L, LongCTC,
NatCAB 35, Novels, ObitOF 79, OxAmL,
PenC AM, REnAL, TwCA, TwCA SUP,
WhAm 2, WhLit, WhNAA

Boyd, Jessie Edna 1899- *BiDrLUS 70,*
WhoLibS 55, –66
Boyd, John 1919- *ConAu X, ConSFA,*
DcLB 8[port], EncSF, ScF&FL 1, –2,
WhoSciF, WrDr 76, –80, –82, –84
Boyd, John *see also* Upchurch, Boyd
Boyd, Malcolm 1923- *AmAu&B, ASpks,*
Au&Wr 6, BioIn 6, –7, –8, –10, –11,
BlueB 76, CelR 73, ConAu 4NR, –5R,
CurBio 68, IntAu&W 76, –77, –82,
IntWWM 77, ScF&FL 1, –2, WhoAm 74,
–76, –78, –80, –82, WhoE 74, WhoRel 75,
–77, WhoWor 74, –76, WorAl, WrDr 76,
–80, –82, –84
Boyd, Mildred 1921- *AuBYP SUP,*
ConAu 17R, ForWC 70
Boyd, Waldo T 1918- *AuBYP SUP, BioIn 12,*
ConAu 29R, SmATA 18, WrDr 76, –80,
–82, –84
Boyd, William C 1903-1983 *AmM&WS 73P,*
–76P, –79P, AsBiEn, BiESc, BioIn 1,
ConAu 109, McGMS 80[port],
NewYTBS 83, WhoAm 74, –76, –78, –80,
–82
Boyer, Elizabeth 1913- *ConAu 81,*
WhoAmW 61
Boyer, Paul S 1935- *ConAu 1NR, –49,*
DrAS 74H, –78H, –82H
Boyer, Robert E 1929- *AmM&WS 73P, –76P,*
–79P, –82P, BioIn 12, ConAu 41R,
LEduc 74, SmATA 22[port], WhoAm 76,
–78, –80, –82, WhoS&SW 82
Boyington, Gregory 1912- *AmAu&B, BioIn 1,*
–5, –10, –12, MedHR, WebAMB
Boyle, Sarah Patton 1906- *ConAu P-1,*
WhoAmW 66, –68
Boylston, Helen Dore 1895- *AmWomWr,*
AuBYP, BioIn 2, –7, –8, ConAu 73,
CurBio 42, InWom, JBA 51,
SmATA 23[port], TwCCW 78, –83,
WhoChL, WrDr 80, –82, –84
Boyne, Walter J 1929- *ConAu 107*
Bracegirdle, Cyril 1920- *Au&Wr 6,*
ConAu 45, IntAu&W 76, WrDr 76, –80
Bracewell, Ronald Newbold 1921-
AmM&WS 76P, –79P, –82P, ConAu 57,
LElec, WhoAm 74, –76, –78, –80,
WhoTech 82
Bracken, Peg 1918- *AmWomWr, BioIn 11,*
–12, ConAu 1R, –6NR, WhoAm 78, –80,
–82, WhoAmW 74, –58, –61, –68A, –70,
–72, –77, –83, WhoWest 74, –76
Brackett, Leigh 1915-1978 *BioIn 11, –12,*
CmMov, ConAu 1R, –1NR, –77, ConSFA,
DcLB 8[port], –26[port], EncSF, FilmgC,
ForWC 70, Novels, OhA&B, ScF&FL 1,
–2, WhoSciF, WomWMM, WrDr 76
Bradbury, Bianca 1908- *AmAu&B, AuBYP,*
BioIn 8, –9, ConAu 5NR, –13R,
ForWC 70, FourBJA, SmATA 3,
WhoAmW 68, –70, WhoE 75, –77, –79, –81
Bradbury, Ray 1920- *AmAu&B, Au&Wr 6,*

*AuNews 1, –2,. BioIn 2, –3, –4, –7, –8, –10,
–11, –12, BioNews 74, BlueB 76, CasWL,
CelR 73, CmCal, CmMov, CnMWL,
ConAu 1R, –2NR, ConLC 1, –3, –10, –15,
ConNov 72, –76, –82, ConSFA, CurBio 53,
–82[port], DcLB 2, –8[port], DcLEL 1940,
DrAF 76, DrAP&F 83, EncSF, FilmgC,
IntAu&W 76, –77, LinLib L, LongCTC,
Novels[port], OxAmL, PenC AM, REn,
REnAL, ScF&FL 1, –2, SmATA 11,
TwCA SUP, TwCCr&M 80, TwCWr,
WebAB, –79, Who 74, –82, –83,
WhoAm 74, –76, –78, –80, –82, WhoHr&F,
WhoSciF, WhoWor 74, WorAl,
WorEFlm, WrDr 76, –80, –82, –84*

Braden, Thomas Wardell 1918- *BioIn 8, –10,
WhoAm 74, –76, –78, –80, –82*

Braden, Vic 1929?- *BioIn 10, –12*

Bradford, Richard 1932- *BioIn 8,
ConAu 2NR, –49, WhoAm 74, –76, –78,
–80, –82, WhoHol A, WrDr 84*

Bradley, Bill 1943- *AlmAP 80, –82[port],
–84[port], BioIn 7, –8, –9, –10, –11, –12,
CelR 73, CngDr 79, –81, –83, ConAu X,
CurBio 82[port], NewYTBS 83[port],
WhoAm 80, –82, WhoAmP 79, –81, –83,
WhoBbl 73, WhoE 81, –83, WhoWor 80,
–82, WorAl*

Bradley, David Henry, Jr. 1950- *BioIn 12,
ConAu 104, ConLC 23[port], InB&W 80,
NegAl 83, NewYTBS 81[port],
WhoBlA 77, –80*

Bradley, Duane 1914- *AuBYP, BioIn 8,
ConAu X*

Bradley, Duane *see also* Sanborn, Duane

Bradley, James Howard, Jr. 1936- *WhoBlA 80*

Bradley, James Vandiver 1924-
*AmM&WS 73S, –78S, ConAu 37R,
WrDr 76, –80, –82, –84*

Bradley, Marion Zimmer 1930- *BioIn 12,
ConAu 7NR, –57, ConSFA, DcLB 8[port],
DrAP&F 83, EncSF, ScF&FL 1, –2,
WhoSciF, WhoWest 84, WrDr 84*

Bradley, Michael *ConAu X*

Bradley, Michael *see also* Blumberg, Gary

Bradley, Virginia 1912- *ConAu 8NR, –61,
SmATA 23[port], WhoWest 78, –80, –82,
–84*

Bradshaw, Gillian 1956- *ConAu 103*

Brady, Esther Wood 1905- *ConAu 93,
SmATA 31*

Brady, Irene 1943- *BioIn 9, –12, ConAu 33R,
IlsCB 1967, SmATA 4*

Brady, Joan *BioIn 12*

Brady, Maxine L 1941- *AuBYP SUP,
ConAu 69*

Bragdon, Elspeth 1897- *BioIn 10, ConAu 5R,
–5NR, SmATA 6*

Brahs, Stuart J 1940- *ConAu 57*

Braider, Donald 1923-1976 *BioIn 10,
ConAu 33R, –65, ConAu P-2,
NewYTBS 76, WhAm 7, WhoAm 74, –76,*

*WhoAmA 78N, –80N, –82N, WrDr 76,
–80, –82*

Brainerd, John W 1918- *AmM&WS 73P, –76P,
–79P, –82P, ConAu 57*

Braithwaite, E R 1912?- *ConAu 106,
ConNov 72, WrDr 76, –80, –82, –84*

Braithwaite, Edward R 1912?- *BioIn 5, –7, –8,
–9, –10*

Braithwaite, Edward R *WhoWor 74*

Braly, Malcolm 1925-1980 *ASpks, BioIn 8,
–10, –11, –12, ConAu 17R, –97,
NewYTBS 80*

Brancato, Robin F 1936- *ConAu 11NR, –69,
SmATA 23[port]*

Brand, Max 1892-1944 *AmAu&B, BioIn 1, –3,
–4, –8, CmCal, ConAu X, CurBio 44,
DcAmB S3, DcLEL, DcNAA, EncMys,
FilmgC, LongCTC, MnBBF, ObitOF 79,
REn, REnAL, REnAW, ScF&FL 1,
TwCA, TwCA SUP, TwCCr&M 80,
WebAB, –79, WhLit, WorAl*

Brand, Max *see also* Faust, Frederick

Brand, Millen 1906-1980 *AmAu&B, AmNov,
BioIn 2, –4, –10, –12, ChhPo S3,
ConAu 21R, –97, ConLC 7, DrAF 76,
DrAP 75, IntAu&W 76, IntWWP 77,
NewYTBS 80[port], REnAL, TwCA,
TwCA SUP, WrDr 76, –80*

Brand, Oscar 1920- *AmAu&B, AuBYP,
BiDAmM, BioIn 6, –8, BlueB 76,
CanWW 70, –79, –80, –81, –83, ConAu 1R,
–4NR, CurBio 62, EncFCWM 69,
IntAu&W 77, NatPD, –81[port], NotNAT,
WhoAm 74, –76, –78, –80, –82,
WhoWor 74, –76, WhoWorJ 72, –78,
WrDr 76, –80, –82, –84*

Branden, Nathaniel 1930- *ConAu 33R,
IntAu&W 76, –77, WhoWest 78, –82,
WrDr 76, –80, –82, –84*

Brandon, James R 1927- *ConAu 11NR, –69,
DrAS 74E, –78E, –82E*

Brandon, William 1914- *ConAu 77,
IndAu 1917*

Brandreth, Gyles D 1948- *BioIn 9, ConAu 65,
IntAu&W 77, –82, SmATA 28[port],
Who 82, –83, WhoWor 80, WrDr 76, –80,
–82, –84*

Brandys, Marian 1912- *ConAu 57,
WhoSocC 78, WhoWor 74, –76*

Branfield, John 1931- *Au&Wr 6,
AuBYP SUP, BioIn 11, ConAu 41R,
IntAu&W 76, –77, –82, SmATA 11,
TwCCW 83, WrDr 76, –80, –82, –84*

Branley, Franklyn M 1915- *AmM&WS 73P,
–76P, –79P, –82P, Au&Wr 6, AuBYP,
BioIn 6, –7, –9, BlueB 76, BkP,
ConAu 33R, ConLC 21[port],
IntAu&W 76, MorJA, ScF&FL 1, –2,
SmATA 4, WhoAm 74, –76, –78, –80*

Branscum, Robbie 1937- *ConAu 8NR, –61,
SmATA 23[port]*

Brant, Charles S 1919- *AmM&WS 73S, –76P,*

ConAu 25R, FifIDA

Brant, Irving Newton 1885-1976 *AmAu&B,
BioIn 2, –4, –11, ConAu 9R, –69,
NewYTBS 76, REnAL, TwCA SUP,
WhAm 7, WhoAm 74, –76*

Brasch, Rudolph 1912- *Au&Wr 6,
ConAu 8NR, –21R, IntAu&W 76,
WhoWor 74, –76, WhoWorJ 72, –78,
WrDr 76, –80, –82, –84*

Brashler, William 1947- *BioIn 11,
ConAu 2NR, –45*

Brauer, Earle William 1918- *WhoE 74, –75,
–77*

Braun, Wernher Von 1912-1977 *AsBiEn,
AuBYP, BiESc, BioIn 2, –3, –4, –5, –6, –7,
–8, –9, –10, –11, –12, CurBio 52, EncTR,
HisEWW, InSci, IntAu&W 77,
IntWW 74, –75, –76, –78N, LinLib L, –S,
NewYTBE 70, NewYTBS 77, ScF&FL 1,
WebAB, –79, WebAMB, WhDW,
WhWW-II, WhoMilH 76, WorAl*

Braun, Wernher Von *see also* VonBraun,
Wernher

Brautigan, Richard 1935?- *AmAu&B, BioIn 9,
–10, –12, BlueB 76, CelR 73, CmCal,
ConAu 53, ConLC 1, –3, –5, –9, –12,
ConNov 72, –76, –82, ConP 70, –75, –80,
DcLB Y80A[port], –2, –5, DcLEL 1940,
DrAF 76, DrAP 75, DrAP&F 83, EncSF,
IntAu&W 76, –77, IntWWP 77,
ModAL SUP, MugS, Novels, PenC AM,
ScF&FL 1, WhoAm 74, –76, –78, –80, –82,
WorAu 1970, WrDr 76, –80, –82, –84*

Bray, Warwick 1936- *ConAu 25R, FifIDA*

Braymer, Marjorie Elizabeth 1911- *AnCL,
BioIn 10, ConAu 1R, SmATA 6,
WhoAm 74, –76, –78, –80, WhoAmW 74,
–64, –66, –68, –70, –72, WhoWest 74*

Brecher, Edward Moritz 1911- *ConAu 7NR,
–13R, WhoAm 76, –78, –80, –82*

Brecht, Bertolt 1898-1956 *AtlBL, BioIn 1, –2,
–3, –4, –5, –6, –7, –8, –9, –10, –11, –12,
CasWL, ClDMEL, CnMD, CnMWL,
CnThe, ConAu 104, CroCD, CyWA,
DcFM, EncTR, EncWL, –81[port],
EncWT, EvEuW, FilmgC, LinLib L, –S,
LongCTC, MakMC, McGEWB,
McGEWD, –84[port], ModGL, ModWD,
NewEOp 71, NotNAT A, –B, OxEng,
OxFilm, OxGer, OxThe, PenC EUR,
PIP&P, RComWL, REn, REnWD,
TwCA, TwCA SUP, TwCLC 1, –6[port],
TwCWr, WhDW, WhAm HSA, –4,
WhoTwCL, WorAl, WorEFlm*

Breck, Vivian 1895- *AmAu&B, AuBYP,
BioIn 6, –8, –9, ConAu X, MorJA,
SmATA 1*

Breck, Vivian *see also* Breckenfeld, Vivian
Gurney

Breckenfeld, Vivian Gurney 1895- *AmAu&B,
AuBYP, BioIn 6, –8, –9, ConAu 5R,
ForWC 70, SmATA 1*

Breckenfeld, Vivian Gurney *see also* Breck,
Vivian

Breckler, Rosemary 1920- *ConAu 101*

Bredes, Don 1947- *ConAu 110, DrAP&F 83*

Bree, Germaine 1907- *AmWomWr, BioIn 9,
–10, BlueB 76, ConAu 1R, –4NR,
DrAS 74F, –78F, –82F, IntAu&W 77, –82,
WhoAm 74, –76, –78, –80, –82,
WhoAmW 74, –58, –61, –64, –66, –68, –70,
–72, WhoFr 79, WhoWor 74, WorAu,
WrDr 76, –80, –82, –84*

Breihan, Carl W 1916- *Au&Wr 6, ConAu 1R,
–1NR*

Breisky, William J 1928- *ConAu 53,
SmATA 22*

Breitman, George 1916- *ConAu 7NR, –61*

Breland, Osmond Philip 1910- *AmM&WS 73P,
–76P, –79P, ConAu 9R, IntAu&W 76,
–82, WrDr 76, –80, –82, –84*

Breman, Paul 1931- *BroadAu, ConAu 21R*

Brennan, Joseph Lomas 1903- *BioIn 10,
ConAu 2NR, –5R, IntAu&W 77,
SmATA 6*

Brennan, Joseph Lomas *see also* Lomas, Steve

Brennan, Joseph Payne 1918- *ChhPo S1,
ConAu 1R, –4NR, DrAP&F 83, EncMys,
IntAu&W 77, –82, IntWWP 77, –82,
Po&Wr 77, ScF&FL 1, –2, WhoE 77, –79,
–83, WhoHr&F, WrDr 76, –80, –82, –84*

Brennan, Louis A 1911-1983 *BioIn 3,
ConAu 109, –17R, NewYTBS 83,
WhoE 74*

Brenner, Barbara 1925- *AuBYP, BioIn 8, –9,
ConAu 9R, ForWC 70, FourBJA,
SmATA 4*

Brent, Madeleine *WrDr 84*

Brent, Peter 1931- *ConAu 65, IntAu&W 77,
–82, WrDr 76, –80, –82, –84*

Breslin, Herbert H 1924- *ConAu 53*

Breslin, James 1930- *ConAu 73*

Breslin, Jimmy 1930- *AmAu&B, AuNews 1,
BioIn 6, –7, –8, –10, –11, CelR 73,
ConAu X, –73, ConLC 4, CurBio 73,
LinLib L, WhoAm 74, –76, –78, –80, –82,
WhoE 74, WhoWor 74, WorAl,
WrDr 76, –80, –82, –84*

Bretnor, Reginald 1911- *ConAu 10NR, –65,
EncSF, ScF&FL 1, –2, WrDr 84*

Brett, Bernard 1925- *BioIn 12, ConAu 97,
IlsCB 1967, SmATA 22[port]*

Brett, Simon 1945- *ConAu 69,
TwCCr&M 80, WrDr 82, –84*

Breunig, Charles 1920- *DrAS 74H, –78H,
–82H*

Brewton, John Edmund 1898- *BioIn 10, BkP,
ChhPo, –S1, –S2, –S3, ConAu 3NR, –5R,
SmATA 5*

Brewton, Sara W *BkP*

Brian, Denis 1923- *BioIn 8, ConAu 25R*

Brick, John 1922-1973 *AmAu&B, AuBYP,
BioIn 3, –7, –10, –11, ConAu 45,
ConAu P-1, CurBio 53, –73, –73N,*

SmATA 10

Brickhill, Paul Chester Jerome 1916- *Au&Wr 6,*
BioIn 6, ConAu 9R, DcLEL 1940, EvLB,
IntAu&W 76, -77, TwCWr, Who 74, -82,
-83

Bridenbaugh, Carl 1903- *AmAu&B,*
ConAu 4NR, -9R, DrAS 74H, -78H, -82H,
WhoAm 74, -76, -78, -80, WhoWor 74

Bridge, Raymond 1943- *ConAu 69*

Bridgeman, William Barton 1917?-1968 *BioIn 2,*
-3, -6, -8, -12, ConAu 9R

Bridgers, Sue Ellen 1942- *ConAu 11NR, -65,*
ConLC 26[port], DrAP&F 83,
SmATA 22[port]

Bridges, William 1901- *AmAu&B, AuBYP,*
BioIn 7, -10, ConAu 33R, IndAu 1917,
IntAu&W 77, -82, SmATA 5,
WhoAm 74, -76, -78, -80, -82, WrDr 76,
-80, -82, -84

Briggs, Katharine Mary 1898-1980 *Au&Wr 6,*
BioIn 12, ChhPo S2, ConAu 9R, -102,
EncO&P 78, IntAu&W 76, -82,
SmATA 25N, TwCCW 83, WhoWor 76,
-78, WrDr 76, -80, -82

Briggs, Mitchell Pirie 1892- *AmAu&B*

Briggs, Peter 1921-1975 *BioIn 10, ConAu 57,*
ConAu P-2, NewYTBS 75, SmATA 31N,
WhoE 74

Briggs, Raymond 1934- *Au&Wr 6, BioIn 6,*
-8, -9, -10, -12, BkP, ChhPo, -S1, -S2,
ConAu 73, IlsBYP, IlsCB 1957,
SmATA 23[port], ThrBJA, TwCCW 83,
Who 82, -83, WrDr 82, -84

Brill, Steven *ConAu 85*

Brilliant, Moshe D 1915- *WhoWorJ 72, -78*

Brin, David 1950- *ConAu 102*

Brin, Ruth F 1921- *ConAu 8NR, -17R,*
SmATA 22[port]

Brindel, June Rachuy 1919- *AuBYP SUP,*
BioIn 10, ConAu 49, DrAP&F 83,
IntWWP 77, -82, SmATA 7

Brindze, Ruth 1903- *AuBYP, BioIn 6, -8,*
ConAu 73, MorJA, SmATA 23[port]

Brinkley, William 1917- *AmAu&B,*
Au&Wr 6, BioIn 4, ConAu 11NR, -21R,
WhoAm 74, -76, -78, -80, -82,
WhoWor 82

Brinley, Bertrand R 1917- *ConAu 29R*

Brinnin, John Malcolm 1916- *AmAu&B,*
Au&Wr 6, BioIn 4, -10, -12, ChhPo,
ConAu 1R, -1NR, ConP 70, -75, -80,
DcLEL 1940, DrAP 75, DrAP&F 83,
DrAS 74E, -78E, -82E, IntWW 77, -78,
-79, -80, -81, -82, -83, IntWWP 77,
LinLib L, OxAmL, PenC AM, REn,
REnAL, TwCA SUP, WhoAm 74, -76,
-78, -80, -82, WhoTwCL, WhoWor 74,
-76, WrDr 76, -80, -82, -84

Brinsmead, H F 1922- *ConAu 10NR, -21R,*
ConLC 21[port], SmATA 18,
TwCCW 78, WrDr 82, -84

Brinsmead, Hesba Fay 1922- *BioIn 12,*

Brickhill, Paul Chester Jerome *ConAu 21R,*
FourBJA, IntAu&W 77,
SenS, SingR 2, TwCCW 83, WrDr 76,
-80

Brinton, Henry 1901-1977 *Au&Wr 6,*
ConAu 1R, -4NR, EncSF, ScF&FL 1, -2,
WhE&EA

Brisco, Patty 1927- *ConAu X, -69,*
SmATA X, WrDr 84

Brisco, Patty *see also* Matthews, Patricia

Briskin, Jacqueline 1927- *ConAu 29R,*
WhoAmW 83, WrDr 80, -82, -84

Brister, C W, Jr. 1926- *ConAu 7NR, -13R*

Bristow, Gwen 1903-1980 *AmAu&B, AmNov,*
AmWomWr, Au&Wr 6, BioIn 2, -4,
ConAu 102, -17R, CurBio 40, EncMys,
ForWC 70, InWom, IntAu&W 77,
REnAL, TwCA, TwCA SUP, WhAm 7,
WhNAA, WhoAm 74, -76, -78, -80,
WhoAmW 74, -61, -64, -66, -70, -72,
WhoWor 76, -78, -80, WrDr 76, -80, -82,
-84

Britt, Katrina *WrDr 84*

Britton, Dorothy 1922- *ConAmC, ConAu 107*

Brock, Edwin 1927- *ConP 70, -75, -80,*
DcLEL 1940, IntWWP 77, WorAu 1970,
WrDr 76, -80, -82, -84

Brock, Stanley E 1936?- *BioIn 9, ConAu 57*

Brockett, Oscar Gross 1923- *ConAu 7NR,*
-13R, DrAS 74E, -78E, -82E,
IntAu&W 77, -82, WhoAm 80, -82,
WhoAmA 80, WhoMW 74, -76,
WhoThe 81, WrDr 76, -80, -82, -84

Brockman, C Frank 1902- *ConAu 5R,*
SmATA 26

Brockway, Edith 1914- *ConAu 17R,*
ForWC 70

Broder, Bill *DrAP&F 83*

Broderick, Dorothy M 1929- *AuBYP,*
BiDrLUS 70, BioIn 8, -10, ConAu 13R,
SmATA 5, WhoLibS 66

Broderick, Richard L 1927- *ConAu 1NR, -45*

Brodeur, Paul 1931- *ConAu 5R, ConNov 72,*
-76, DcLEL 1940, IntAu&W 76, -77,
WrDr 76, -80, -82, -84

Brodie, Fawn McKay 1915-1981 *AnObit 1981,*
Au&Wr 6, BioIn 1, -12, ConAu 10NR,
-102, -17R, DrAS 74H, -78H, ForWC 70,
NewYTBS 81, WhAm 7, WhoAm 78, -80,
WhoAmW 74, -70, -72, -77

Brodkin, Sylvia Z *ScF&FL 1*

Brodsky, Joseph 1940- *AuNews 1, BioIn 12,*
ConAu X, ConLC 4, -6, -13,
CurBio 82[port], EncWL 81, IntWW 76,
-77, IntWWP 82, NewYTBS 80[port],
WorAu

Brody, Jane Ellen 1941?- *BioIn 7, -12,*
ConAu 102, NewYTBS 81[port],
WhoAm 80, -82

Brokhin, Yuri 1934- *ConAu 57*

Bromige, Iris 1910- *Au&Wr 6, IntAu&W 76,*
WrDr 84

Bromley, Dudley 1948- *ConAu 77,*

IntAu&W 82

Brommer, Gerald F 1927- *ConAu 105,*
SmATA 28[port], WhoAmA 76, -78, -80,
-82, WhoWest 78, -84

Brondfield, Jerome 1913- *ConAu 73,*
IntMPA 77, -75, -76, -78, -79, -81, -82, -84,
SmATA 22[port]

Brondfield, Jerry 1913- *ConAu X, SmATA X*

Brondfield, Jerry *see also* Brondfield, Jerome

Bronowski, Jacob 1908-1974 *AmAu&B, AnCL,*
AuBYP SUP, BioIn 2, -4, -5, -7, -10, -11,
-12, BlueB 76N, ConAu 1R, -3NR, -53,
CurBio 74, DcLEL, InSci, IntAu&W 76,
IntWW 74, -75N, LinLib L, -S,
NewYTBS 74, ObitOF 79, ObitT 1971,
WhAm 6, Who 74, WhoAm 74,
WhoWor 74, WorAl, WorAu

Bronson, Wilfrid Swancourt 1894- *AmAu&B,*
AuBYP, BioIn 1, -2, -5, -7, ConAu 73,
IlsCB 1744, -1946, JBA 34, -51, Str&VC

Bronson, William Knox 1926-1976 *ConAu 41R,*
-65, WhoWest 74, -76

Bronte, Charlotte 1816-1855 *Alli, AtlBL, BbD,*
BiD&SB, BioIn 1, -2, -3, -4, -5, -6, -7, -8,
-9, -10, -11, -12, BrAu 19, BrWr 5,
CasWL, Chambr 3, ChhPo, -S1, -S2, -S3,
CrtT 3, -4, CyWA, DcBiA, DcBiPP,
DcEnA, -AP, DcEnL, DcEuL,
DcLB 21[port], DcLEL, Dis&D, EvLB,
FilmgC, GoodHs, HerW, HsB&A,
InWom, IntDcWB[port], LinLib L, -S,
LongCEL, McGEWB, MouLC 3,
NotNAT B, Novels[port], OxEng,
PenC ENG, RAdv 1, RComWL,
ScF&FL 1, WebE&AL, WhDW, WorAl

Bronte, Emily 1818-1848 *AtlBL, BbD,*
BiD&SB, BioIn 1, -2, -3, -4, -5, -6, -7, -8,
-9, -10, -11, -12, BrAu 19, BrWr 5,
CasWL, Chambr 3, ChhPo, -S1, -S2, -S3,
CnE&AP, CrtT 3, -4, CyWA, DcBiA,
DcBiPP, DcEnA, -AP, DcEnL, DcEuL,
DcLB 21[port], DcLEL, Dis&D, EvLB,
FilmgC, GoodHs, HerW, InWom,
IntDcWB[port], LinLib L, LongCEL,
McGEWB, MouLC 3, Novels[port],
OxEng, PenC ENG, RAdv 1, RComWL,
WebE&AL, WhDW, WorAl

Brook, George Leslie 1910- *Au&Wr 6,*
IntAu&W 76, -77, Who 74, -82, -83,
WrDr 76, -80, -82, -84

Brooke, Joshua *ConAu X*

Brooke, Joshua *see also* Miller, Victor

Brookins, Dana 1931- *ConAu 69,*
SmATA 28[port]

Brooks, Anne Tedlock 1905- *ConAu 1R, -1NR,*
WhoAmW 58, -61, -64, -68, -72

Brooks, Charlotte K *AuBYP, ConAu 89,*
InB&W 80, LivgBAA, SmATA 24,
WhoBlA 77, -80

Brooks, David H 1929- *ConAu 61*

Brooks, Gwendolyn 1917- *AmAu&B,*
AmWomWr, AuNews 1, -1, BioIn 2, -4,

-6, -7, -8, -9, -10, -11, -12, BioNews 74,
BlueB 76, BkCL, BlkAWP,
BroadAu[port], CasWL, CelR 73, ChhPo,
-S1, -S2, -S3, ConAu 1R, -1NR,
ConLC 1, -2, -4, -5, -15, ConP 70, -75,
-80, CroCAP, CurBio 50, -77,
DcLB 5[port], DcLEL 1940, DrAP 75,
Ebony 1, EncAB-H, EncWL 81,
FourBJA, GoodHs, InWom,
IntAu&W 77, IntDcWB, IntWW 74, -75,
-76, -77, -78, -79, -80, -81, -82, -83,
IntWWP 77, LibW, LinLib L, LivgBAA,
ModAL, ModAL SUP, ModBlW,
NegAl 76[port], -83[port], OxAmL,
PenC AM, RAdv 1, REnAL, SelBAA,
SmATA 6, TwCA SUP, WebAB, -79,
WhoAm 74, -76, -78, -80, -82,
WhoAmW 74, -58, -64, -66, -68, -70, -72,
-77, -79, -81, -83, WhoBlA 75, -77, -80,
WhoWor 74, -76, -78, -80, -82, WorAl,
WrDr 76, -80, -82, -84

Brooks, Janice Young 1943- *ConAu 9NR, -65*

Brooks, Jerome 1931- *ConAu 2NR, -49,*
SmATA 23[port]

Brooks, Lester 1924- *AuBYP SUP, BioIn 10,*
ConAu 33R, SmATA 7, WhoPubR 72

Brooks, Maurice Graham 1900- *WhoAm 74*

Brooks, Mel 1926- *BiE&WWA, BioIn 7, -8,*
-10, -11, -12, ConAu 65, ConLC 12,
CurBio 74, DcLB 26[port], FilmgC,
IntMPA 77, -75, -76, -78, -79, -81, -82, -84,
IntWW 82, -83, LesBEnT, MovMk,
NewYTBS 75, NewYTET, Who 82, -83,
WhoAm 74, -76, -78, -80, -82,
WhoAmJ 80, WhoWest 78, -80, -82,
WorAl

Brooks, Paul 1909- *ConAu 7NR, -13R,*
WhoAm 74, -76, -78, -80, WhoE 74,
WrDr 80, -82, -84

Brooks, Polly 1912- *BioIn 11, ConAu 1R,*
SmATA 12

Brooks, Stewart M 1923- *ConAu 9NR, -17R,*
WhoE 74

Brooks, Terry 1944- *ConAu 77, DrAP&F 83,*
IntAu&W 82, WhoAm 78, -80, -82,
WhoMW 80

Brooks, Tim 1942- *ConAu 102*

Brooks, Van Wyck 1886-1963 *AmAu&B,*
AmLY, AmWr, AtlBL, CasWL,
Chambr 3, CnDAL, ConAmA, ConAmL,
ConAu 1R, ConLCrt, -82, CurBio 41, -60,
-63, DcLEL, EvLB, LinLib L, LongCTC,
ModAL, ObitOF 79, OxAmL, PenC AM,
RAdv 1, REn, REnAL, TwCA,
TwCA SUP, TwCWr, WebE&AL,
WhLit, WhNAA

Brophy, Ann 1931- *ConAu 106*

Brophy, Brigid 1929- *Au&Wr 6, BioIn 9, -10,*
-11, BlueB 76, CasWL, ConAu 5R,
ConDr 73, -77, ConLC 6, -11,
ConNov 72, -76, -82, DcLB 14[port],
DcLEL 1940, EncWL 81, IntAu&W 76,

-77, -82, IntWW 74, -75, -76, -77, -78,
-79, -80, -81, -82, -83, LinLib L,
LongCTC, ModBrL, ModBrL SUP,
NewC, Novels, ScF&FL 1, TwCWr,
Who 74, -82, -83, WhoAmW 74, -68, -70,
-70A, -72, WhoTwCL, WhoWor 74, -76,
-78, WorAu, WrDr 76, -80, -82, -84

Brophy, Donald 1934- AmCath 80,
ConAu 10NR, -21R

Broughton, James 1913- AmAu&B, BioIn 11,
-12, ChhPo, CmCal, ConAu 2NR, -49,
ConP 70, -75, -80, DcLB 5[port],
DcLEL 1940, DrAP 75, DrAP&F 83,
IntAu&W 76, -77, -82, IntWWP 77, -82,
PenC AM, WhoAm 76, -78, -80, -82,
WorEFlm, WrDr 76, -80, -82, -84

Broughton, T Alan 1936- ConAu 2NR, -45,
ConLC 19, DrAF 76, DrAP 75,
DrAP&F 83, IntWWP 77, -82, WrDr 80,
-82, -84

Broun, Heywood 1888-1939 AmAu&B, AmBi,
ApCAB X, AuBYP SUP, BiDAmLL,
BioIn 1, -2, -3, -4, -5, -6, -10, CathA 1930,
ConAmA, CurBio 40, DcAmB S2,
DcAmSR, DcCathB, DcLEL, DcNAA,
LinLib L, -S, NatCAB 30, NotNAT B,
OxAmH, OxAmL, PIP&P, REn, REnAL,
ScF&FL 1, TwCA, TwCA SUP, WebAB,
-79, WhAm 1, WhJnl, WhThe, WorAl

Broun, Heywood Hale 1918- BiE&WWA,
BioIn 1, -3, -7, -8, -10, -12, BioNews 74,
ConAu 17R, NewYTBS 75, NotNAT, -A,
PIP&P, WhoAm 80, -82

Browder, Walter Everett 1939- ConAu 53

Brower, David Ross 1912- BioIn 7, -8, -9, -10,
-11, -12, CelR 73, CmCal, ConAu 9NR,
-61, CurBio 73, PolProf J, PolProf K,
PolProf NF, WhoAm 74, -76, -78, -80, -82,
WhoWest 82, -84, WhoWor 74

Brower, Kenneth 1944- ConAu 10NR, -25R

Browin, Frances 1898- AuBYP, BioIn 8, -10,
ConAu P-1, SmATA 5

Brown, Beth AmSCAP 66, ConAu P-2,
ScF&FL 1, -2, WhoAmW 72

Brown, Bob 1886-1959 AmAu&B, ConAu X,
DcLB 4, SmATA X, WhNAA, WhoE 74

Brown, Bob see also Brown, Robert Joseph

Brown, Christy 1932-1981 AnObit 1981,
BioIn 8, -9, -10, -12, ConAu 104, -105,
DcIrL, DcIrW 2, DcLB 14[port],
NewYTBE 70, -71, NewYTBS 81[port],
Novels, WrDr 76, -80, -82, -84

Brown, Claude 1937- AmAu&B, BioIn 7, -8,
BlkAWP, CivR 74, ConAu 73,
CurBio 67, DrAF 76, LinLib L,
LivgBAA, SelBAA, WhoAm 74

Brown, Curtis F 1925- ConAu 61

Brown, David 1916- ConAu 13R, IntMPA 77,
-75, -76, -78, -79, -81, -82, -84, WhE&EA,
WhoAm 74, -76, -78, -80, -82, WhoE 74,
WhoF&I 74, -75, -77, -79, -81, -83,
WhoWor 74, -76, -78, -80, -82

Brown, Dee 1908- AuBYP SUP, BiDrLUS 70,
BioIn 10, -11, -12, ConAu 11NR, -13R,
ConLC 18, CurBio 79, DcLB Y80B[port],
DrAS 78H, -82H, NewYTBS 80[port],
REnAW, SmATA 5, WhoAm 74, -76, -78,
-80, -82, WhoLibS 66, WhoMW 74,
WrDr 76, -80, -82, -84

Brown, E K 1905-1951 ConAu 107

Brown, Fern G 1918- ConAu 97,
SmATA 34[port]

Brown, Fredric 1906-1972 AmAu&B,
Au&Wr 6, BioIn 9, -10, -12, ConSFA,
EncMys, EncSF, ObitOF 79, ScF&FL 1,
-2, TwCCr&M 80, WhAm 5, WhoSciF,
WorAu

Brown, H Rap 1943- BioIn 8, -9, -10, -11,
CivR 74, CivRSt, LivgBAA, NegAl 76,
-83, PolProf J, WhoBlA 77, -80

Brown, H Rap see also Brown, Hubert Rap

Brown, Harrison 1917- AmAu&B,
AmM&WS 73P, -76P, -79P, -82P, BioIn 1,
-3, -4, BlueB 76, ConAu 69, ConSFA,
CurBio 55, EncSF, Future, InSci,
IntWW 74, -75, -76, -77, -78, -79, -80, -81,
-82, -83, McGMS 80[port], ScF&FL 1,
-2, WhoAm 74, -78, -80, -82, WhoGov 72,
-75, WhoWor 74, -82, WrDr 80, -82, -84

Brown, Harry Peter McNab, Jr. 1917-
AmAu&B, AmNov, BioIn 2, -4,
ChhPo S3, CmMov, ConAu 69, DcLB 26,
DcLEL 1940, FilmgC, IntMPA 77, -75,
-76, -78, -79, -81, -82, -84, OxAmL,
REnAL, TwCA SUP, WhoAm 74, -76,
-78, -80, -82

Brown, Himan 1910- BioIn 10, IntMPA 77,
-75, -76, -78, -79, -81, -82, WhoWorJ 72,
-78

Brown, Hubert Rap 1943- AmAu&B

Brown, Hubert Rap see also Brown, H Rap

Brown, Ida Mae 1908- ConAu P-2

Brown, Irene Bennett 1932- BioIn 9,
ConAu 29R, SmATA 3

Brown, Ivor John Carnegie 1891-1974
Au&Wr 6, BiE&WWA, BioIn 2, -3, -4,
-10, ConAu 9R, -49, DcLEL, EncWT,
EvLB, IntAu&W 76, -77, LongCTC,
ModBrL, NewC, NewYTBS 74,
ObitT 1971, OxThe, PenC ENG,
SmATA 26N, -5, TwCA SUP, WhAm 6,
WhE&EA, WhLit, WhThe, Who 74,
WhoThe 15, WhoWor 74

Brown, J P S 1930- ConAu 61

Brown, Jamie 1945- ConAu 101

Brown, Jim 1936- BioNews 74, CelR 73,
CurBio 64, FilmgC, IntMPA 77, -75, -76,
-78, -79, -81, -82, -84, MotPP, MovMk,
NegAl 83[port], NewYTBE 73,
WhoAm 74, -76, -78, -80, -82, WhoBlA 75,
-77, -80, WhoHol A, WorAl

Brown, Jimmy 1936- BioIn 6, -7, -8, -9, -10,
-11, -12, CurBio 64, NegAl 76[port]

Brown, Joe David 1915-1976 AmAu&B,

AmNov, BioIn 2, –10, ConAu 13R, –65, NewYTBS 76

Brown, John Mason 1900-1969 *AmAu&B, BiE&WWA, BioIn 1, –2, –3, –4, –5, –8, –9, –10, CnDAL, ConAu 9R, –25R, CurBio 42, –69, EncO&P 78, LinLib L, –S, LongCTC, NotNAT A, –B, ObitOF 79, OxAmL, OxThe, PenC AM, PIP&P, REnAL, TwCA, TwCA SUP*

Brown, John Russell 1923- *ConAu 11NR, –21R, Who 74, –82, –83, WhoThe 15, –16, –81, WhoWor 74, –76, WrDr 76, –80, –82, –84*

Brown, Joseph E 1929- *ConAu 6NR, –53*

Brown, LeRoy 1908- *ConAu P-1, DrAS 74E, –78E, –82E, IndAu 1917*

Brown, Lester Russell 1934- *AmM&WS 82P, BioIn 7, –10, –12, Future, WhoAm 74, –76, –78, –80, –82, WhoWor 74*

Brown, Lloyd Arnold 1907-1966 *AuBYP, BioIn 4, –7, ConAu P-1, SmATA 36, WhAm 4*

Brown, Marian A 1911- *ConAu 73, WhoAmW 83*

Brown, Marion Marsh 1908- *AuBYP, BioIn 7, –10, ConAu 1R, –3NR, DrAS 74E, –78E, –82E, IntAu&W 76, –77, SmATA 6, WhoAmW 58, –61*

Brown, Morna Doris 1907- *ConAu 5R, –5NR, EncMys*

Brown, Norman D 1935- *ConAu 53, DrAS 74H, –78H, –82H, IntAu&W 77*

Brown, Norman O 1913- *AmAu&B, BioIn 10, ConAu 21R, DrAS 74F, –78F, –82F, LinLib L, MugS, PenC AM, WorAu*

Brown, Peter Lancaster 1927- *ConAu 4NR, –53*

Brown, Ralph Adams 1908- *ConAu 33R, DrAS 74H, –78H, –82H, WhoE 79, WrDr 76, –80, –82, –84*

Brown, Richard C 1919- *ConAu 2NR, –5R, DrAS 74H, –78H, –82H*

Brown, Richard Maxwell 1927- *ConAu 11NR, –17R, DrAS 74H, –78H, –82H, WhoAm 76, –78*

Brown, Rita Mae 1944- *AmWomWr, BioIn 10, –11, ConAu 2NR, –11NR, –45, DrAF 76, DrAP 75, DrAP&F 83, ForWC 70, IntAu&W 77, IntWWP 77, NewYTBS 77, WhoAmW 81, –83*

Brown, Robert Joseph 1907- *BioIn 12, ConAu P-1, SmATA 14*

Brown, Robert Joseph *see also* Brown, Bob

Brown, Robert McAfee 1920- *AmAu&B, BioIn 6, –7, –9, –10, BlueB 76, ConAu 7NR, –13R, CurBio 65, DrAS 74P, –78P, –82P, WhoAm 74, –76, –78, –80, –82, WhoRel 75, –77, WhoWest 74, –76, WhoWor 74, WrDr 76, –80, –82, –84*

Brown, Robin 1937- *ConAu 97, IntAu&W 82*

Brown, Rosellen 1939- *ConAu 77, DrAF 76, DrAP 75, DrAP&F 83*

Brown, Rosemary 1917- *EncO&P 78, –80, IntDcWB*

Brown, Roy Allen 1921- *WhoE 74, –75, –77, –79*

Brown, Roy Frederick 1921-1982 *Au&Wr 6, ConAu 65, FourBJA, IntAu&W 82, TwCCW 78, –83, WrDr 80, –82, –84*

Brown, Seyom 1933- *ConAu 65, Future*

Brown, Sterling A 1901- *AmAu&B, BioIn 2, –10, –11, –12, BlkAWP, BroadAu, ChhPo S3, ConAu 85, ConLC 1, –23[port], ConP 80, CurBio 82[port], DrAP 75, DrAP&F 83, InB&W 80, LinLib L, LivgBAA, ModBlW, NegAl 76, –83, REnAL, SelBAA, WhoBlA 77, –80, WorAu 1970, WrDr 82, –84*

Brown, Theo W 1934- *ConAu 8NR, –61*

Brown, Vinson 1912- *AuBYP, BioIn 7, –12, ConAu 1R, –1NR, IntAu&W 76, SmATA 19, WhoWest 74, –76, –78, WrDr 82, –84*

Brown, Walter R 1929- *ConAu 2NR, –45, SmATA 19*

Browne, Dik 1917- *AuNews 1, BioIn 10, –11, WhoAm 76, –78, –80, –82, WorECom*

Browne, Gerald A *Novels, ScF&FL 1*

Browne, Jackson 1948?- *BioIn 9, –11, –12, ConLC 21, EncPR&S 77, RkOn 78, –84, RolSEnR 83, WhoRocM 82, WorAl*

Browne, Malcolm Wilde 1931- *ConAu 17R, WhoAm 74, –76, –78, –80, –82*

Browne, Rose Butler 1893?- *InB&W 80, WhoBlA 77, –80*

Browning, Elizabeth Barrett 1806-1861 *Alli, Alli SUP, AtlBL, BbD, BiD&SB, BioIn 1, –2, –3, –4, –5, –6, –7, –8, –9, –10, –11, –12, BrAu 19, BrWr 4, CasWL, CelCen, Chambr 3, ChhPo, –S1, –S2, –S3, CnE&AP, ConAu 57, CrtT 3, CyWA, DcBiPP, DcEnA AP, DcEnL, DcEuL, DcLEL, Dis&D, EvLB, GoodHs, HerW, InWom, IntDcWB, LinLib L, –S, LongCEL, LuthC 75, McGEWB, MouLC 3, NewC, OxEng, PenC ENG, RAdv 1, RComWL, REn, WebE&AL, WhDW, WorAl*

Browning, Frank 1946- *ConAu 107*

Browning, Robert 1812-1889 *Alli, Alli SUP, AnCL, AtlBL, BiD&SB, BioIn 1, –2, –3, –4, –5, –6, –7, –8, –9, –10, –11, –12, BrAu 19, BrWr 4, CasWL, CelCen, Chambr 3, ChhPo, –S1, –S2, –S3, CnE&AP, CnThe, CrtT 3, –4, CyWA, DcBiPP, DcEnA, –AP, DcEnL, DcEuL, DcLEL, Dis&D, EncO&P 78, EncWT, EvLB, IlEncMy, LinLib L, –S, LongCEL, LuthC 75, McGEWB, McGEWD, –84[port], MouLC 4, NewC, OxEng, OxMus, OxThe, PenC ENG, PIP&P, RAdv 1, RComWL, REn, REnWD, Str&VC, WebE&AL, WhDW, WorAl, YABC 1*

Brownlee, Walter 1930- *ConAu 57*
Brownlow, Kevin 1938- *Au&Wr 6,*
ConAu 25R, FilmgC, IntAu&W 76,
OxFilm, Who 82, –83, WhoWor 76,
WrDr 76, –80, –82, –84
Brownmiller, Susan 1935- *BioIn 10, –11, –12,*
ConAu 103, CurBio 78, ForWC 70,
GoodHs, WhoAm 78, –80, WhoAmW 79,
–81, –83, WorAl
Brownstein, Samuel C 1909- *ConAu 5R,*
WrDr 76, –80, –82
Brownstone, David M 1928- *ConAu 104*
Bruccoli, Matthew J 1931- *BioIn 11,*
ChhPo S1, –S3, ConAu 7NR, –9R,
DrAS 74E, –78E, –82E, IntAu&W 77,
NewYTBS 77, WhoAm 80, –82,
WhoS&SW 73, –75, WrDr 76, –80, –82,
–84
Bruce, Leo 1903-1979 *ConAu X,*
TwCCr&M 80
Bruch, Hilde 1904- *AmM&WS 73P, –76P,*
–79P, AuNews 1, BiDrAPA 77, BioIn 10,
–11, ConAu 53, InWom, WhoAm 74, –76,
–78, –80, –82, WhoAmJ 80, WhoAmW 74,
–58, –61, –68, –72, WhoWorJ 72, –78
Bruchac, Joseph, III 1942- *ConAu 33R,*
DrAF 76, DrAP 75, DrAP&F 83,
IntAu&W 82, IntWWP 77, –82, WrDr 76,
–80, –82, –84
Brucker, Roger Warren 1929- *ConAu 11NR,*
–65, IntAu&W 77, WhoAdv 80,
WhoF&I 75, WhoMW 74, –76
Bruemmer, Fred 1929- *BioIn 12, CanWW 81,*
–83, ConAu 102, IntAu&W 77,
OxCan SUP, WhoAm 82, WrDr 76, –80,
–82, –84
Brumbaugh, Robert Sherrick 1918-
ConAu 3NR, –5R, DrAS 74P, –78P, –82P,
WhoAm 74, –76, –78, –80, –82, WrDr 76,
–80, –82, –84
Bruner, Richard W 1926- *AuBYP SUP,*
ConAu 49, NatPD
Brunetti, Cledo 1910-1971 *BioIn 1,*
ConAu P-2
Brunhouse, Robert Levere 1908- *ConAu 2NR,*
–49, DrAS 74H, –78H
Bruning, Nancy P 1948- *ConAu 106*
Brunner, John 1934- *Au&Wr 6, BioIn 12,*
ConAu 1R, –2NR, ConLC 8, –10,
ConSFA, EncSF, IntAu&W 76, –77, –82,
LinLib L, Novels, ScF&FL 1, –2,
WhoSciF, WorAl, WrDr 76, –80, –82, –84
Brunvand, Jan Harold 1933- *ConAu 108,*
DrAS 74E, –78E, –82E
Bruton, Eric Moore 1915- *Au&Wr 6,*
ConAu 5NR, –13R, IntAu&W 77, –82,
TwCCr&M 80, WhE&EA, WrDr 76, –80,
–84
Bruun, Ruth Dowling 1937- *BiDrAPA 77,*
ConAu 108, WhoAmW 74, –77, –79,
WhoE 75, –77, –79, –81
Bryan, C D B 1936- *AmAu&B, ConAu 73,*

DrAF 76, DrAP&F 83
Bryan, C D B *see also* Bryan, Courtlandt Dixon
Barnes
Bryan, Christopher 1935- *ConAu 104*
Bryan, Courtlandt Dixon Barnes 1936-
WhoAm 74, –76, –78, –80, –82, WhoE 74
Bryan, Courtlandt Dixon Barnes *see also* Bryan,
C D B
Bryan, J, III 1904- *ConAu 11NR,*
IntAu&W 82, WhoAm 80, –82
Bryant, Anita 1940- *AmPS A, –B,*
AmWomWr, BiDAmM, BioIn 9, –10, –11,
–12, ConAu X, CurBio 75, InWom,
NewYTBS 78, RkOn 74, WhoAm 74, –76,
–78, –80, –82, WhoAmW 74, –72, –79, –81,
–83, WorAl
Bryant, Dorothy 1930- *ConAu 4NR, –53,*
WrDr 80, –82, –84
Bryant, Edward 1945- *ConAu 1NR, –45,*
EncSF, IntAu&W 76, –77, ScF&FL 1, –2,
WrDr 80, –82, –84
Bryant, Paul 1913-1983 *BioIn 2, –6, –7, –9, –10,*
–11, –12, BioNews 75, CelR 73,
ConAu 108, CurBio 80[port], –83N,
NewYTBS 79, –81[port], –82, –83[port],
WhoAm 74, –76, –78, –82, WhoFtbl 74,
WhoS&SW 73, WorAl
Bryson, Bernarda 1903?- *BioIn 4, –5, –8, –9,*
–11, ChhPo, ConAu 49, IlsBYP,
IlsCB 1946, –1957, –1967, SmATA 9,
ThrBJA
Buban, Peter, Sr. 1920- *LEduc 74,*
WhoMW 76
Buchan, John 1875-1940 *BioIn 1, –2, –3, –4, –5,*
–6, –7, –9, –10, –11, –12, CasWL,
Chambr 3, ChhPo, –S1, –S2, –S3,
CnMWL, ConAu 108, CorpD, CurBio 40,
CyWA, DcLEL, EncMys, EncSoA, EvLB,
FilmgC, JBA 34, LinLib S, LongCTC,
MacDCB 78, MnBBF, ModBrL, NewC,
Novels, OxCan, OxEng, PenC ENG,
REn, ScF&FL 1, TelT, TwCA,
TwCA SUP, TwCCr&M 80, TwCWr,
WebE&AL, WhDW, WhE&EA, WhLit,
WhoBW&I A, WhoHr&F, WhoSpyF,
YABC 2
Buchan, Stuart 1942- *ConAu 57*
Buchanan, William J 1926- *ConAu 73*
Buchenholz, Bruce 1916- *BiDrAPA 77*
Buchman, Dian Dincin 1922- *BiDrAPH 79,*
ConAu 8NR, –61, IntAu&W 76
Buchsbaum, Ralph 1907- *AmM&WS 73P,*
–76P, –79P, –82P, WhoAm 74, –76, –78,
–80, –82, WhoOcn 78
Buchwald, Ann 1921?- *AuBYP SUP,*
BioIn 12
Buchwald, Art 1925- *AmAu&B, AuBYP SUP,*
AuNews 1, BioIn 3, –4, –5, –6, –7, –8, –9,
–10, –11, –12, BioNews 74, BlueB 76,
CelR 73, ConAu 5R, CurBio 60,
IntAu&W 77, –82, IntWW 74, –75, –76,
–77, –78, –79, –80, –81, –82, –83,

*NewYTBE 72, NewYTBS 79, PenC AM,
SmATA 10, Who 74, –82, –83,
WhoAm 74, –76, –78, –80, –82,
WhoS&SW 73, –75, –76, WhoWor 74, –76,
–78, –80, –82, WorAl, WorAu, WrDr 76,
–80, –82, –84*

Buck, Pearl S 1892-1973 *AmAu&B, AmNov,
AmWomWr, Au&Wr 6, AuBYP,
AuNews 1, BiE&WWA, BioIn 1, –2, –3,
–4, –5, –6, –7, –8, –9, –10, –11, –12, CasWL,
CnDAL, ConAmA, ConAu 1R, –1NR,
–41R, ConLC 7, –11, –18, ConNov 72,
CurBio 56, –73, –73N, CyWA,
DcLB 9[port], DcLEL, EncWL, EvLB,
FilmgC, GoodHs, HerW, InWom,
IntDcWB, LibW, LinLib L, –S,
LongCTC, McGEWB, ModAL,
NewYTBE 73, NotAW MOD,
Novels[port], ObitOF 79, ObitT 1971,
OxAmH, OxAmL, PenC AM, REn,
REnAL, SmATA 1, –25[port], TwCA,
TwCA SUP, TwCWr, WebAB, –79,
WhDW, WhAm 5, WhE&EA, WhNAA,
WhoAmW 74, –58, –61, –64, –66, –66A, –68,
–70, –72, WorAl*

Buck, Sir Peter Henry 1880-1951 *BioIn 1, –2,
–3, –9, ObitOF 79, ObitT 1951,
WhAm 3*

Buck, William Ray 1930- *AuBYP, ConAu 1R,
WrDr 76, –80, –82, –84*

Buckingham, James William 1932- *ConAu 29R*

Buckingham, James William *see also*
Buckingham, Jamie

Buckingham, Jamie 1932- *Au&Wr 6,
ConAu X*

Buckingham, Jamie *see also* Buckingham, James
William

Buckler, William Earl 1924?- *AmCath 80,
ConAu 1R, –5NR, DrAS 74E, –78E, –82E,
WhoAm 74, WhoE 83*

Buckley, Jerome Hamilton 1917- *AmAu&B,
CanWW 70, –79, –80, –81, –83, ChhPo,
ConAu 1R, –3NR, DrAS 74E, –78E, –82E,
WhoAm 74, –76, –78, –80, –82,
WhoWor 74, –76*

Buckley, Shawn 1943- *ConAu 93,
WhoTech 82*

Buckley, William F, Jr. 1925- *AmAu&B,
AmCath 80, AuNews 1, BioIn 3, –5, –6,
–7, –8, –9, –10, –11, –12, BioNews 74,
BlueB 76, CelR 73, ConAu 1R, –1NR,
ConIsC 1[port], ConLC 7, –18, CurBio 62,
–82[port], DcAmSR, DcBrWA,
DcLB Y80B[port], DcLEL 1940, Film 2,
IntAu&W 76, –77, –82, IntWW 74, –75,
–76, –77, –78, –79, –80, –81, –82, –83,
LinLib L, –S, NewYTBE 70,
NewYTBS 80[port], Novels, PolProf E,
PolProf J, PolProf K, PolProf NF,
St&PR 75, WebAB, –79, WhoAm 74, –76,
–78, –80, –82, WhoAmP 73, –75, –77, –79,
–81, –83, WhoE 74, –75, –77, WhoF&I 74,*

*WhoGov 77, –72, –75, WhoWor 74, –76,
–78, –80, –82, WorAl, WorAu, WrDr 76,
–80, –82, –84*

Buckmaster, Henrietta 1909-1983 *AmAu&B,
AmNov, AmWomWr, Au&Wr 6,
BioIn 1, –2, –10, ConAu X, –69,
CurBio 46, –83N, InWom, IntAu&W 76,
–77, NewYTBS 83, OhA&B, ScF&FL 1,
–2, SmATA 6, WhoAmW 77, WorAu*

Buckmaster, Henrietta *see also* Stephens,
Henrietta Henk

Bucknall, Barbara Jane 1933- *ConAu 33R,
DrAS 74F, –78F, –82F, WrDr 76, –80, –82,
–84*

Buckvar, Felice 1938- *ConAu 107,
DrAP&F 83*

Budbill, David 1940- *ConAu 73, DrAP&F 83,
IntWWP 77, –82, Po&Wr 77*

Budd, Lillian 1897- *AuBYP, BioIn 7, –10,
ConAu 1R, –4NR, IntAu&W 77, –82,
SmATA 7, WhoAmW 58, –61, –68,
WrDr 76, –80, –82, –84*

Budoff, Penny Wise 1939- *ConAu 110,
WhoAmW 70*

Budrys, Algis 1931- *ConAu X, ConSFA,
EncSF, Novels, ScF&FL 1, –2, WhoSciF,
WrDr 76, –82, –84*

Budzik, Richard Steven 1938- *WhoMW 76*

Buehr, Walter Franklin 1897-1971 *AuBYP,
BioIn 5, –7, –8, –9, ConAu 3NR, –5R,
–33R, IlsCB 1946, –1957, SmATA 3,
ThrBJA*

Buell, Frederick Henderson 1942- *ConAu 33R,
DrAP 75, DrAP&F 83, DrAS 78E, –82E,
IntWWP 77, –82, WrDr 76, –80, –82, –84*

Buell, Harold G 1931- *AuBYP SUP,
WhoAm 78, –80, –82*

Buell, John 1927- *Au&Wr 6, BioIn 11,
ConAu 1R, ConLC 10, CreCan 1, NewC,
OxCan, OxCan SUP, ScF&FL 1*

Buell, Lawrence 1939- *ConAu 49, DrAS 74E,
–78E, –82E*

Bugbee, Emma 1888?-1981 *AuBYP, BioIn 7,
–10, –12, ConAu 105, InWom,
NewYTBS 81, SmATA 29N*

Bugliosi, Vincent 1934- *BioIn 12, ConAu 73,
WhoAm 76, –78, –80, –82*

Bulfinch, Thomas 1796-1867 *Alli, Alli SUP,
AmAu, AmAu&B, AmBi, ApCAB,
BiD&SB, BioIn 3, CarSB, ChhPo, –S3,
DcAmAu, DcAmB, DcNAA, Drake,
OxAmL, REn, REnAL, SmATA 35,
WebAB, –79, WhAm HS*

Bulgakov, Mikhail 1891-1940 *BioIn 1, –8, –9,
–10, –11, CasWL, ClDMEL, CnMD,
CnThe, ConAu 105, DcRusL, EncWL,
–81, EncWT, EvEuW, McGEWB,
McGEWD, –84, ModSL 1, ModWD,
NotNAT B, Novels, PenC EUR, REn,
REnWD, ScF&FL 1, TwCLC 2, TwCWr,
WhDW, WhoTwCL, WorAl, WorAu*

Bull, Angela 1936- *ConAu 9NR, –21R,*

IntAu&W 82, TwCCW 78, –83, WrDr 80, –82, –84

Bulla, Clyde Robert 1914- *Au&ICB, AuBYP, BioIn 6, –7, –9, BkP, ConAu 3NR, –5R, MorJA, SmATA 2, TwCCW 78, –83, WhoWest 74, –76, WrDr 80, –82, –84*

Bullard, Pamela 1948- *ConAu 106*

Bunin, Ivan 1870-1953 *BioIn 1, –2, –3, –4, –5, –8, –9, –12, CasWL, ClDMEL, CnMWL, ConAu 104, CyWA, DcRusL, EncWL, –81, EvEuW, LinLib L, –S, LongCTC, McGEWB, ModSL 1, Novels, ObitOF 79, ObitT 1951, PenC EUR, REn, TwCA, TwCA SUP, TwCLC 6[port], TwCWr, WhDW, WhAm 3, WhE&EA, WhoLA, WhoTwCL, WorAl*

Bunnell, Dewey *WhoRocM 82*

Bunnell, Dewey *see also* America

Bunting, A E 1928- *AuBYP SUP, ConAu X, SmATA X, TwCCW 83*

Bunting, Anne Evelyn 1928- *AuBYP SUP, BioIn 12, ConAu 5NR, –53, SmATA 18, WhoAm 78, –80, –82, WhoWor 82*

Bunting, Eve 1928- *AuBYP SUP, ConAu X, SmATA X, TwCCW 83*

Bunting, Eve *see also* Bunting, A E

Bunting, Eve *see also* Bunting, Anne Evelyn

Bunting, Glenn 1957- *SmATA 22*

Bunyan, John 1628-1668 *Alli, AtlBL, BbD, BiD&SB, BioIn 1, –2, –3, –4, –5, –6, –7, –8, –9, –10, –11, –12, BrAu, BrWr 2, CarSB, CasWL, Chambr 1, ChhPo, –S1, –S2, –S3, CroE&S, CrtT 2, CyWA, DcBiPP, DcEnA, DcEnL, DcEuL, DcLEL, Dis&D, EncSoB, EvLB, LinLib L, –S, LongCEL, LuthC 75, McGEWB, MouLC 1, NewC, NewEOp 71, Novels[port], OxEng, OxMus, PenC ENG, RAdv 1, RComWL, REn, WebE&AL, WhDW, WorAl*

Burack, Abraham S 1908-1978 *AmAu&B, BioIn 4, –11, ConAu 4NR, –9R, –77, WhoAdv 72, WhoE 75, WhoWorJ 72, –78*

Buranelli, Vincent 1919- *ConAu 5NR, –9R, DrAS 74H, –78H, –82H, IntAu&W 76, –77, WhoE 75, WrDr 76, –80, –82, –84*

Burch, Gladys 1899- *AuBYP, BioIn 8*

Burch, Robert 1925- *AuBYP, BioIn 7, –8, –9, –10, ConAu 2NR, –5R, IntAu&W 82, MorBMP, SmATA 1, ThrBJA, TwCCW 78, –83, WrDr 76, –80, –82, –84*

Burchard, Peter Duncan 1921- *Au&Wr 6, AuBYP, BioIn 5, –8, –9, –10, –12, ConAu 3NR, –5R, IlsCB 1946, –1957, –1967, SmATA 5, ThrBJA, WhoAmA 78, –80, –82, WhoE 75, –77, WhoWest 80*

Burchard, S H *ConAu X*

Burchell, Mary *Au&Wr 6, WrDr 84*

Burdick, Eugene 1918-1965 *AmAu&B, BioIn 5, –6, –7, –10, ConAu 5R, –25R, DcAmB S7, EncSF, ObitOF 79, SmATA 22[port], TwCWr, WhAm 4, WhoSciF, WorAl, WorAu*

Burford, Lolah 1931- *BioIn 9, ConAu 41R, ScF&FL 1, –2, WrDr 76, –80, –82, –84*

Burgess, Alan 1915- *WhE&EA*

Burgess, Anthony 1917- *Alli, Au&Wr 6, AuNews 1, Baker 78, BioIn 7, –8, –9, –10, –12, BlueB 76, CasWL, CelR 73, ConAu X, –1R, ConLC 1, –2, –4, –5, –8, –10, –13, –15, –22[port], ConNov 72, –76, –82, ConSFA, CurBio 72, DcLB 14[port], DcLEL 1940, DrAF 76, EncSF, EncWL, –81, IntAu&W 76, –77, IntWW 74, –75, –76, –77, –78, –79, –80, –81, –82, –83, LinLib L, LongCTC, MakMC, ModBrL, ModBrL SUP, NewC, Novels, PenC ENG, RAdv 1, ScF&FL 1, –2, TwCWr, WebE&AL, Who 74, –82, –83, WhoAm 76, –78, –80, –82, WhoFr 79, WhoSciF, WhoTwCL, WhoWor 74, –76, –78, –80, –82, WorAl, WorAu, WrDr 76, –80, –82, –84*

Burgess, Anthony *see also* Wilson, John Burgess

Burgess, Linda Cannon 1911- *ConAu 73*

Burgess, Mary 1916- *BioIn 12, ConAu 61, SmATA 18*

Burgess, Robert F 1927- *AuBYP SUP, BioIn 9, ConAu 11NR, –25R, SmATA 4*

Burgess-Kohn, Jane 1928- *ConAu 73*

Burgoyne, Arthur Gordon d1914 *DcNAA*

Burke, Alan Dennis 1949- *ConAu 106*

Burke, Carl F 1917- *ConAu 25R*

Burke, Fred George 1926- *AmAu&B, AmM&WS 73S, ConAu 13R, LEduc 74, WhoAm 78, –80, –82, WhoE 74, –79, –81, –83, WhoGov 77, –75*

Burke, John 1915-1975 *ConAu X*

Burke, John *see also* O'Connor, Richard

Burke, John Frederick 1922- *Au&Wr 6, ConAu 5R, –9NR, IntAu&W 76, –77, –82, ScF&FL 1, –2, TwCCr&M 80, WhoHr&F, WhoSciF, WrDr 82, –84*

Burkert, Nancy Ekholm 1933- *BioIn 8, –9, –11, –12, ChhPo S1, IlsBYP, IlsCB 1957, –1967, SmATA 24[port], ThrBJA*

Burkhart, Kathryn Watterson 1942- *BioIn 10, ConAu 45, WhoAm 76, –78, –80*

Burkholz, Herbert 1932?- *Au&Wr 6, BioIn 8, –11, ConAu 11NR, –25R, DrAP&F 83*

Burland, C A 1905- *ConAu X, EncO&P 78, SmATA 5*

Burland, C A *see also* Burland, Cottie Arthur

Burland, Cottie Arthur 1905- *Au&Wr 6, AuBYP, BioIn 8, –9, –10, ConAu 5R, –5NR, FifIDA, IntAu&W 76, –77, –82, SmATA 5, WhoArt 80, –82*

Burland, Cottie Arthur *see also* Burland, C A

Burley, W J 1914- *ConAu 33R, TwCCr&M 80, WrDr 82, –84*

Burlingame, Roger 1889-1967 *AmAu&B, AuBYP SUP, BioIn 4, –5, –7, –9, ConAu 5R, REn, REnAL, SmATA 2, TwCA, TwCA SUP, WhAm 4*

Burman, Ben Lucien 1895- *AmAu&B, AmNov,*

ModAL SUP, Novels, OxAmL,
PenC AM, RAdv 1, REn, REnAL,
ScF&FL 1, –2, TwCWr, WebAB, –79,
WebE&AL, WhDW, WhoAm 74, –76, –78,
–80, –82, WhoSciF, WhoTwCL,
WhoWor 74, WorAu, WrDr 76, –80, –82,
–84

Burrow, John W 1935- *ConAu 21R*

Burt, Jesse Clifton 1921-1976 *BioIn 12,*
ConAu 4NR, –9R, SmATA 20N

Burt, Olive Woolley 1894- *AuBYP, BioIn 7,*
–9, ChhPo S2, ConAu 5R, –5NR,
ForWC 70, IntAu&W 76, –77, SmATA 4,
WhoAmW 58

Burt, William Henry 1903- *AmM&WS 73P,*
–76P, –79P, ConAu 106, WhoAm 74, –76,
–78, –80, WhoWor 76

Burton, Anthony 1933- *ConAu 61*

Burton, Elizabeth 1908- *Au&Wr 6, AuBYP,*
BioIn 8, ConAu 65, ScF&FL 1,
WrDr 82, –84

Burton, Hester 1913- *Au&Wr 6,*
AuBYP SUP, BioIn 8, –9, –10, ChlLR 1,
ConAu 9R, –10NR, IntAu&W 82,
SmATA 7, ThrBJA, TwCCW 78, –83,
WhoChL, WrDr 76, –80, –82, –84

Burton, Maurice 1898- *Au&Wr 6, BlueB 76,*
ConAu 9NR, –65, IntAu&W 76, –77, –82,
SmATA 23[port], Who 74, –82, –83,
WrDr 80, –82, –84

Buscema, John 1927- *WorECom*

Busch, Frederick 1941- *ConAu 33R,*
ConLC 7, –10, –18, ConNov 76, –82,
DcLB 6[port], DrAF 76, DrAS 74E, –78E,
–82E, WrDr 76, –80, –82, –84

Busch, Noel Fairchild 1906- *AmAu&B,*
BlueB 76, ConAu 49, WhoAm 74, –76,
–78, –80, –82, WhoWor 74, –76, WrDr 80,
–82, –84

Busch, Phyllis S 1909- *ConAu 107,*
SmATA 30[port], WhoAmW 70

Bush, Douglas 1896-1983 *AmAu&B, BioIn 4,*
BlueB 76, CanWr, ConAu 109, –37R,
DcLEL, DrAS 74E, –78E, –82E, LongCTC,
NewYTBS 83, RAdv 1, TwCA SUP,
Who 74, –82, –83, WrDr 76, –80, –82, –84

Bush, George P 1892- *ConAu 17R*

Bush, Jim 1926- *ConAu 57*

Bushnell, Geoffrey Hext Sutherland 1903-1978
Au&Wr 6, BioIn 12, FifIDA,
IntAu&W 76, –77, Who 74, WhoWor 74,
–76, WrDr 76, –80

Bushyager, Linda E 1947- *ConAu 93*

Busoni, Rafaello 1900-1962 *AmAu&B,*
AuBYP, BioIn 1, –2, –3, –5, –6, –7, –8, –12,
IlsCB 1744, –1946, –1957, JBA 51,
SmATA 16

Butkus, Dick 1942- *BioIn 8, –9, –10, CelR 73,*
NewYTBS 74, WhoAm 74, –76, –78, –80,
–82, WhoFtbl 74, WhoWor 78, WorAl

Butler, Beverly Kathleen 1932- *AuBYP,*
BioIn 7, –10, ChhPo S2, ConAu 1R,

–4NR, ForWC 70, SmATA 7,
WhoAmW 58, –61

Butler, Bonnie Marie 1941- *LEduc 74*

Butler, Gwendoline 1922- *Au&Wr 6,*
ConAu 6NR, –9R, DcLEL 1940,
IntAu&W 76, –77, Novels, TwCCr&M 80,
WrDr 76, –80, –82, –84

Butler, Gwendoline *see also* Melville, Jennie

Butler, Hal 1913- *AuBYP, BioIn 8,*
ConAu 57, MichAu 80

Butler, Mildred Allen 1897- *AuBYP SUP,*
ConAu 29R, ConAu P-2, WhoPNW

Butler, Octavia E 1947- *ConAu 73,*
InB&W 80, WrDr 80, –82, –84

Butler, Samuel 1835-1902 *Alli SUP, AtlBL,*
BbD, BioIn 1, –2, –3, –4, –5, –6, –7, –8, –9,
–10, –11, –12, BrAu 19, CasWL,
CnMWL, ConAu 104, CrtT 3, CyWA,
DcBrA 2, DcEnA, –AP, DcEuL,
DcLB 18[port], DcLEL, DcVicP, EncSF,
EvLB, LinLib L, –S, LongCEL,
LongCTC, McGEWB, ModBrL, NewC,
Novels[port], OxEng, OxMus, PenC ENG,
RAdv 1, REn, ScF&FL 1, TwCLC 1,
WebE&AL, WhDW, WorAl

Butler, William 1929- *Au&Wr 6,*
AuBYP SUP, ConAu 107, EncSF,
ScF&FL 1

Butterfield, Roger Place 1907-1981 *AmAu&B,*
BioIn 1, –12, ConAu 103, ConAu P-1,
CurBio 48, LinLib L, REnAL

Butters, Dorothy Gilman 1923- *AmAu&B,*
AuBYP, BioIn 7, –8, –10, –12, ConAu 1R,
–2NR, ForWC 70, SmATA 5,
WhoAmW 66, –68, –70, WrDr 82, –84

Butters, Dorothy Gilman *see also* Gilman,
Dorothy

Butterworth, Emma Macalik 1928- *ConAu 105*

Butterworth, Michael 1924?- *ConAu 10NR,*
–25R, WrDr 76, –80, –82, –84

Butterworth, W E 1929- *ConAu 1R, –2NR,*
IntAu&W 76, SmATA 5

Butterworth, W E *see also* Beech, Webb

Butterworth, W E *see also* Blake, Walker E

Butterworth, W E *see also* Butterworth, William
Edmund, III

Butterworth, W E *see also* Douglas, James McM

Butterworth, W E *see also* Scholefield, Edmund
O

Butterworth, W E *see also* Williams, Patrick J

Butterworth, William Edmund, III 1929-
AuBYP SUP, WhoS&SW 73, –75, –76

Butterworth, William Edmund, III *see also*
Butterworth, W E

Butti, Ken 1950- *ConAu 104*

Buxbaum, Robert C 1930- *BiDrACP 79,*
BiDrAPH 79, ConAu 97

Buzan, Tony 1942- *IntAu&W 77,*
IntWWP 82, WrDr 76, –80, –82, –84

Byars, Betsy 1928- *AuBYP, BioIn 8, –9, –10,*
–12, ChlLR 1, ConAu 33R, MorBMP,
NinCLC 1966, SmATA 4, ThrBJA,

TwCCW 78, –83, WrDr 80, –82, –84
Bykov, Vasilii Vladimirovich 1924-
  WhoSocC 78
Byrd, Elizabeth 1912- *Au&Wr 6, BioIn 8,
  ConAu 5R, –5NR, SmATA 34[port],
  WhoAmW 58*
Byrd, Richard Evelyn 1888-1957 *AmAu&B,
  AsBiEn, BiESc, BioIn 1, –2, –3, –4, –5, –6,
  –7, –8, –9, –11, –12, CurBio 42, –56, –57,
  DcAmB S6, EncAB-H, InSci, LinLib L,
  –S, McGEWB, MedHR, NatCAB 46,
  ObitOF 79, OxAmH, OxAmL, REn,
  REnAL, TwCA, TwCA SUP, WebAB,
  –79, WebAMB, WhDW, WhAm 3,
  WhNAA, WorAl*
Byrne, Donn 1931- *AmM&WS 73S, –78S,
  BioIn 12, ConAu 5NR, –9R,
  IntAu&W 77, –82, WhoAm 80, –82,
  WhoMW 78, WrDr 76, –80, –82, –84*

C

Cable, Mary 1920- *BioIn 11, ConAu 11NR, −25R, DrAF 76, DrAP&F 83, SmATA 9, WhoAmW 74, −70, −72*

Cabral, Olga 1909- *ConAu 10NR, −25R, DrAP 75, DrAP&F 83*

Cade, Toni 1939- *BlkAWP, ConAu X*

Cade, Toni *see also* Bambara, Toni Cade

Cadell, Elizabeth 1903- *Au&Wr 6, BioIn 2, ConAu 11NR, −57, CurBio 51, InWom, ScF&FL 1, −2, WrDr 76, −80, −82, −84*

Cadwallader, Sharon 1936- *BioIn 10, ConAu 1NR, −49, SmATA 7*

Cady, Edwin Harrison 1917- *AmAu&B, BlueB 76, ConAu 1R, −4NR, DrAS 74E, −78E, −82E, WhoAm 74, −76, −78, −80, −82, WhoWor 74, −76, −78, −80, −82, WrDr 80, −82, −84*

Cady, Steve 1927- *ConAu 45*

Caffrey, Kate *ConAu 1NR, −49, IntAu&W 76, −77, −82, WrDr 76, −80, −82, −84*

Cagle, Malcolm W 1918- *ConAu 108, SmATA 32, WhoAm 74, WorDWW*

Cahill, James Francis 1926- *ConAu 1R, −6NR, DrAS 74H, −78H, −82H, WhoAm 74, −76, −78, −80, −82, WhoAmA 73, −76, −78, −80, −82*

Cahill, Susan 1940- *BioIn 11, ConAu 37R*

Cahill, Thomas 1940- *ConAu 49*

Cahn, Edgar S 1935- *ConAu 29R, WhoS&SW 75, −76*

Cahn, Rhoda 1922- *ConAu 81, SmATA 37*

Cahn, William 1912-1976 *BioIn 11, ConAu 21R, −69, NewYTBS 76, SmATA 37, WhoAdv 72*

Caidin, Martin 1927- *AmAu&B, AuNews 2, BioIn 6, −10, −11, −12, ConAu 1R, −2NR, ConSFA, EncSF, LinLib L, ScF&FL 1, −2, WhoSciF, WrDr 84*

Cain, Arthur H 1913- *AuBYP SUP, BioIn 9, ConAu 1R, −4NR, SmATA 3*

Cain, Michael Peter 1941- *ConAu 93, WhoAmA 73, −76*

Caine, Lynn 1927?- *ASpks, BioIn 10, −11, WhoAm 78, −80*

Caird, Janet 1913- *Au&Wr 6, ConAu 2NR, −49, IntAu&W 76, −77, −82, ScF&FL 1, −2, TwCCr&M 80, WrDr 76, −80, −82,*

−84

Cairns, Trevor 1922- *BioIn 12, ConAu 33R, IntAu&W 77, −82, SmATA 14, WrDr 76, −80, −82, −84*

Calahan, Harold Augustin 1889-1965 *BioIn 7, −8, NatCAB 50*

Calde, Mark A 1945- *ConAu 69*

Caldecott, Moyra 1927- *ConAu 77, SmATA 22*

Calder, Jenni 1941- *ConAu 1NR, −45*

Calder, Nigel 1931- *Au&Wr 6, ConAu 11NR, −21R, DcLEL 1940, Future, IntAu&W 76, −77, Who 74, −82, −83, WhoWor 76, −80, WrDr 76, −80, −82, −84*

Calder, Robert Lorin 1941- *ConAu 65, −69, DrAS 74E, −78E, −82E*

Calder-Marshall, Arthur 1908- *Au&Wr 6, BioIn 2, −10, BlueB 76, ChhPo S3, ConAu 61, ConNov 72, −76, −82, DcLEL, IntAu&W 76, −77, ScF&FL 1, −2, WhE&EA, Who 74, −82, −83, WorAu, WrDr 76, −80, −82, −84*

Calderone, Mary Steichen 1904- *AuNews 1, BiDAmEd, BioIn 8, −10, −11, −12, BioNews 74, ConAu 104, CurBio 67, InWom, LibW, WhoAm 74, −76, −78, −80, −82, WhoAmW 74, −58, −61, −66, −68, −70, −72, −75, −79, −81, −83, WhoWor 74*

Calderwood, James Dixon 1917- *AmEA 74, AmM&WS 73S, −78S, ConAu 3NR, −5R, IntAu&W 77, WhoCon 73*

Caldwell, John 1928- *BioIn 12, ConAu 73, WhoWor 74, −76*

Caldwell, John Cope 1913- *AuBYP, BioIn 7, −10, ConAu 21R, SmATA 7*

Caldwell, Taylor 1900- *AmAu&B, AmCath 80, AmNov, AmWomWr, Au&Wr 6, BioIn 1, −2, −5, −6, −9, −11, −12, BlueB 76, CelR 73, ConAu 5R, −5NR, ConLC 2, CurBio 40, EncSF, ForWC 70, InWom, IntAu&W 77, LibW, LinLib LP, LongCTC, NewYTBS 76, −81[port], Novels, OxAmL, REn, REnAL, ScF&FL 1, −2, Who 74, −82, −83, WhoAm 80, −82, WhoAmW 58, −58A, −64, −66, −68, −70, −72, −81, WhoWor 80, −82, WorAl, WrDr 76, −80, −82, −84*

Calhoun, Mary 1926- *AuBYP, BioIn 7, −9,*

81 331670

ConAu X, –5R, ForWC 70, ScF&FL 1,
–2, SmATA 2, ThrBJA

Call, Hughie Florence 1890-1969 BioIn 9,
ConAu 5R, SmATA 1, WhoAmW 66,
WhoPNW

Callahan, Dorothy Louise 1920- AuBYP,
BioIn 8, WhoAmW 74, –58, –61, –64, –66,
–68, –70, –75

Callahan, Philip S 1923- AmM&WS 73P, –76P,
–79P, –82P, AuBYP SUP, ConAu 102,
SmATA 25[port]

Callan, Jamie 1954- ConAu 109, DrAP&F 83

Callaway, Kathy 1943- ConAu 107,
DrAP&F 83, SmATA 36

Callen, Larry 1927- ConAu X, SmATA X

Callen, Larry see also Callen, Lawrence Willard,
Jr.

Callen, Lawrence Willard, Jr. 1927- BioIn 12,
ConAu 73, SmATA 19

Callenbach, Ernest William, Jr. 1929-
ConAu 6NR, –57, WhoWest 74, –76, –78

Calley, William L, Jr. 1943- BioIn 8, –9, –10,
–11, –12, NewYTBS 74, PolProf NF

Callison, Brian 1934- Au&Wr 6, ConAu 29R,
WrDr 76, –80, –82, –84

Callum, Myles 1934- ConAu 9R, WhoAm 74,
–76, –78, –80, –82, WhoWor 78

Calter, Paul 1934- ConAu 41R, WhoE 77,
–79, –81

Calvert, James Francis 1920- AuBYP, BioIn 5,
–6, –8, Dun&B 79, WhoAm 74, –76, –78,
–80, –82, WhoF&I 83, WhoGov 72,
WorDWW

Calvert, Patricia 1931- ConAu 105

Calvino, Italo 1923- BioIn 10, –12, CasWL,
ConAu 85, ConLC 5, –8, –11, –22[port],
DcItL, EncSF, EncWL, –81[port],
IntAu&W 76, –77, –82, IntWW 74, –75,
–76, –77, –78, –79, –80, –81, –82, –83,
ModRL, NewYTBS 81, –83[port], Novels,
PenC EUR, ScF&FL 1, TwCWr,
Who 83, WhoTwCL, WhoWor 74, –76,
–78, –82, WorAu

Calvocoressi, Peter 1912- BlueB 76,
ConAu 65, IntAu&W 76, –77, –82,
IntWW 74, –75, –76, –77, –78, –79, –80, –81,
–82, –83, Who 74, –82, –83, WrDr 80, –82,
–84

Cameron, Anne InWom

Cameron, Betsy 1949?- BioIn 12, ConAu 101

Cameron, Eleanor 1912- AuBYP, BioIn 6, –8,
–9, ChLR 1, ChhPo, ConAu 1R, –2NR,
IntAu&W 82, ScF&FL 1, –2, SmATA 1,
–25[port], ThrBJA, TwCCW 78, –83,
WhoAm 76, –78, –80, –82, WhoAmW 81,
–83, WrDr 80, –82, –84

Cameron, Ian 1924- ConAu X, ConSFA,
EncSF, IntAu&W 76X, –77X, –82X,
ScF&FL 1, WrDr 76, –80, –82, –84

Cameron, Ian see also Payne, Donald Gordon

Cameron, Kenneth Neill 1908- ChhPo S2,
ConAu 3NR, –9R, DrAS 74E, –78E, –82E,

NatPD

Camner, James 1950- ConAu 108

Camp, Walter Chauncey 1859-1925 AmAu&B,
AmBi, AmLY, BiD&SB, BioIn 2, –3, –5,
–6, –9, –11, –12, ChhPo, DcAmAu,
DcAmB, DcNAA, JBA 34, –51, LinLib S,
NatCAB 21, OxAmH, REnAL, WebAB,
–79, WhAm 1, WhNAA, WhoFtbl 74,
WorAl, YABC 1

Campanella, Roy 1921- BioIn 1, –2, –3, –4, –5,
–6, –7, –8, –9, –10, –11, CelR 73,
CurBio 53, InB&W 80, NegAl 76, –83,
NewYTBS 77, WhoAm 74, –76, –78,
WhoBlA 75, –77, –80, WhoProB 73,
WorAl

Campbell, Ann R 1925- BioIn 11, ConAu 21R,
SmATA 11

Campbell, Archibald Bruce 1881-1966 BioIn 2,
–3, –7, ConAu P-1

Campbell, Bruce AuBYP, ConAu X, MorJA,
SmATA X

Campbell, Bruce see also Epstein, Samuel

Campbell, Hannah ConAu 9R

Campbell, Hope 1925- BioIn 12,
ConAu 10NR, –61, SmATA 20,
WhoAmW 83

Campbell, Jane 1932- ConAu X, SmATA X,
WomWWA 14

Campbell, Jane see also Edwards, Jane Campbell

Campbell, Jane C AmWomWr

Campbell, John W 1910-1971 AmAu&B,
BioIn 7, –9, –10, –12, ConAu 29R,
ConAu P-2, ConSFA, DcLB 8[port],
EncSF, LinLib L, NewYTBE 71, Novels,
ObitOF 79, ScF&FL 1, –2, WhoSciF,
WorAl, WorAu

Campbell, Joseph 1904- AmAu&B, BioIn 4,
–11, –12, ConAu 1R, –3NR, DrAS 74P,
–78P, LinLib L, REnAL, TwCA SUP,
WhoAm 74, –76, –78, –80, –82, WhoE 74

Campbell, Judith 1914- ConAu X,
IntAu&W 82X, WrDr 76, –80, –82, –84

Campbell, Judith see also Pares, Marion
Stapylton

Campbell, Patricia J 1930- ConAu 103

Campbell, Ramsey 1946- ConAu 7NR, –57,
IntAu&W 77, –82, ScF&FL 1, –2,
WhoHr&F, WhoWor 78

Campbell, Walter Stanley 1887-1957 AmAu&B,
BioIn 4, CnDAL, OxAmL, REn, REnAL,
REnAW, TwCA, TwCA SUP, WhAm 3,
WhE&EA, WhNAA

Campbell, Walter Stanley see also Vestal, Stanley

Campbell, Will 1924?- BioIn 8, –9, –11,
ConAu 5R, –7NR

Campbell, William Edward March 1893-1954
AmAu&B, AmNov X, BioIn 2, –3, –4, –5,
–12, ConAmA, ConAu 108, DcAmB S5,
ObitOF 79, REn, REnAL, TwCA SUP

Campbell, William Edward March see also
March, William

Campion, Nardi Reeder 1917- AuBYP,

*BioIn 7, ConAu 1R, –6NR,
SmATA 22[port], WhoAmW 58, –61*

Camus, Albert 1913-1960 *AtlBL, BioIn 1, –3,
–4, –5, –6, –7, –8, –9, –10, –11, –12, CasWL,
CIDMEL, CnMD, CnMWL, CnThe,
ConAu 89, ConLC 1, –2, –4, –9, –11, –14,
CroCD, CyWA, EncWL, –81[port],
EncWT, EvEuW, LinLib L, –S,
LongCTC, MakMC, McGEWB,
McGEWD, –84[port], ModFrL, ModRL,
ModWD, NotNAT A, –B, Novels[port],
ObitOF 79, ObitT 1951, OxEng, OxFr,
OxThe, PenC EUR, RComWL, REn,
REnWD, TwCA SUP, TwCWr, WhDW,
WhAm 3, WhoTwCL, WorAl*

Camuti, Louis J 1893-1981 *BioIn 12,
ConAu 101, –103, NewYTBS 81,
WhoE 74, –75, –77, –79, –81*

Canada, Lena 1942- *ConAu 93*

Canaday, John E 1907- *AmAu&B, BioIn 6, –9,
–10, ConAu 7NR, –13R, DrAS 74H,
EncMys, TwCCr&M 80, WhoAm 74, –76,
–78, –80, WhoAmA 73, –76, –78, –80, –82,
WhoE 74, WorAu, WrDr 82, –84*

Canfield, Dorothy 1879-1958 *AmAu&B,
AmNov, BioIn 2, –3, –4, –11, –12,
Chambr 3, CnDAL, ConAmA, ConAmL,
DcBiA, DcLEL, JBA 34, LongCTC,
NotAW MOD, OxAmL, REn, REnAL,
TwCA, TwCA SUP, WhNAA*

Canfield, Kenneth French 1909- *ConAu P-1*

Canning, Victor 1911- *Au&Wr 6, BioIn 10,
ConAu 6NR, –13R, EncMys,
IntAu&W 76, –77, LongCTC, MnBBF,
Novels, ScF&FL 1, TwCCr&M 80,
WhE&EA, Who 74, –82, –83, WhoSpyF,
WorAu, WrDr 76, –80, –82, –84*

Cannon, Grant G 1911?-1969 *BioIn 8,
WhAm 5*

Cannon, Jimmy 1909-1973 *ConAu 104,
NewYTBE 73, ObitOF 79, REnAL,
WhAm 6*

Cannon, LeGrand, Jr. 1899-1979 *AmAu&B,
AmNov, Au&Wr 6, BioIn 2, –4, CnDAL,
ConAu 93, CurBio 43, NewYTBS 79,
REnAL, TwCA SUP, WhAm 7,
WhoAm 74, –76, –78*

Cantor, Muriel G 1923- *ConAu 33R,
WhoAm 82, WhoE 81, –83*

Cantwell, Robert Emmett 1908-1978 *AmAu&B,
Au&Wr 6, BioIn 4, –9, –10, –11,
ConAmA, ConAu 4NR, –5R, –81,
ConNov 72, –76, –82, DcLB 9,
IntAu&W 76, –77, NewYTBS 78, Novels,
OxAmL, REnAL, TwCA, TwCA SUP,
TwCWr, WhAm 7, WhE&EA,
WhoAm 74, –76, –78, WhoE 74, WrDr 76,
–82, –84*

Canutt, Yakima 1895- *BioIn 7, –8, –12,
CmMov, Film 2, FilmgC, IntMPA 77,
–75, –76, –78, –79, –81, –82, –84, OxFilm,
TwYS, WhoHol A, WorEFlm*

Capek, Josef 1887-1945 *BioIn 1, CasWL,
CIDMEL, CnThe, EncSF, EncWT,
NotNAT B, OxTwCA, PhDcTCA 77,
REnWD, ScF&FL 1*

Capek, Karel 1890-1938 *BioIn 1, –5, –6, –7, –12,
CasWL, CIDMEL, CnMD, CnThe,
ConAu 104, CyWA, EncSF, EncWL,
–81[port], EncWT, EvEuW, LinLib L,
LongCTC, MakMC, McGEWB,
McGEWD, –84[port], ModSL 2, ModWD,
NotNAT B, OxThe, PenC EUR, REn,
REnWD, ScF&FL 1, TwCA,
TwCA SUP, TwCLC 6[port], TwCWr,
WhDW, WhE&EA, WhThe, WhoSciF,
WhoTwCL, WorAl*

Capizzi, Michael 1941- *ConAu 41R*

Capote, Truman 1924-1984 *AmAu&B, AmNov,
AmSCAP 66, Au&Wr 6, BiE&WWA,
BioIn 1, –2, –3, –4, –7, –8, –9, –10, –11, –12,
BlueB 76, CasWL, CelR 73, CnDAL,
CnMD, ConAu 5R, ConDr 73, –77D,
–82D, ConLC 1, –3, –8, –13, –19,
ConNov 72, –76, –82, CurBio 51, –68,
DcLB Y80A[port], –2, DcLEL 1940,
DrAF 76, DrAP&F 83, EncWL, –81,
FilmgC, IntAu&W 76, –77, –82,
IntWW 74, –75, –76, –77, –78, –79, –80, –81,
–82, –83, LinLib L, LongCTC, MakMC,
ModAL, ModAL SUP, ModWD,
NewYTBE 71, NewYTBS 78, NotNAT,
Novels[port], OxAmL, OxFilm,
PenC AM, RAdv 1, REn, REnAL,
TwCA SUP, TwCWr, WebAB, –79,
WebE&AL, WhDW, Who 74, –82, –83,
WhoAm 74, –76, –78, –80, –82, WhoHol A,
WhoTwCL, WhoWor 74, –78, WorAl,
WrDr 76, –80, –82, –84*

Capps, Benjamin 1922- *BioIn 11, –12,
ConAu 5R, –7NR, SmATA 9,
WhoAm 74, –76, –78, –80, WrDr 76, –80*

Capron, Jean F 1924- *ConAu 21R*

Caputo, Philip 1941- *BioIn 12, ConAu 73,
NewYTBS 81[port], WhoAm 74, –76, –78,
–80, –82, WhoWor 80, –82*

Caras, Roger A 1928- *AmAu&B, BioIn 11,
ConAu 1R, –5NR, IntAu&W 76, –77, –82,
ScF&FL 1, SmATA 12, WhoAm 74, –76,
–78, –80, –82, WhoE 74, WhoWor 74,
WhoWorJ 72, –78, WrDr 76, –80, –82, –84*

Carawan, Candie *ConAu X*

Carawan, Candie *see also* Carawan, Carolanne M

Carawan, Carolanne M 1939- *ConAu 17R*

Carawan, Guy 1927- *BiDAmM, ConAu 17R,
EncFCWM 69*

Carbonnier, Jeanne 1894-1974 *BioIn 9,
ConAu P-2, SmATA 3, –34N*

Card, Orson Scott 1951- *ConAu 102*

Cardenal, Ernesto 1925- *BioIn 8, –12, CasWL,
ConAu 2NR, –49, DcCLAA, OxSpan,
PenC AM, WhoTwCL, WorAu 1970*

Cardozo, Lois S 1934- *AuBYP, ConAu 1R*

Cardozo, Lois S *see also* Arquette, Lois S

Cardozo, Peter 1916- *ConAu 61*
Cardwell, Paul *AuBYP SUP*
Carefoot, Thomas Henry 1938-
  AmM&WS 73P
Carew, Dorothy 1910?-1973 *BioIn 9,*
  ConAu 41R, NewYTBE 73
Carey, Ernestine Gilbreth 1908- *Au&Wr 6,*
  BioIn 1, -2, -9, ConAu 5R, ConLC 17,
  CurBio 49, InWom, IntAu&W 77,
  ScF&FL 1, -2, SmATA 2, WhoAm 74,
  -76, -78, -80, -82, WhoAmW 74, -58, -61,
  -64, -66, -68, -70, -72, -79, -81, -83,
  WhoWor 74, -82, WorAl, WrDr 76, -80,
  -82, -84
Carliner, David 1918- *WhoAm 76, -78, -80,*
  -82, WhoS&SW 73, WhoWor 82
Carlinsky, Dan 1944- *ConAu 8NR, -21R,*
  IntAu&W 77, WhoE 74, -75
Carlisle, Olga Andreyev 1930- *AuBYP SUP,*
  BioIn 12, ConAu 7NR, -13R,
  IntAu&W 77, SmATA 35
Carlsen, G Robert 1917- *ConAu 8NR, -17R,*
  IntAu&W 77, SmATA 30[port],
  WrDr 76, -80, -82, -84
Carlsen, Ruth C 1918- *ConAu 8NR*
Carlsen, Ruth Christoffer 1918- *AuBYP SUP,*
  BioIn 9, ConAu 17R, IntAu&W 77,
  ScF&FL 1, SmATA 2, WhoAmW 75,
  WrDr 76, -80, -82, -84
Carlson, Avis D 1896- *ConAu 73*
Carlson, Bernice Wells 1910- *AuBYP, BioIn 7,*
  -11, ConAu 2NR, -5R, ForWC 70,
  IntAu&W 77, -82, MichAu 80,
  SmATA 8, WrDr 76, -80, -82, -84
Carlson, Dale Bick 1935- *AuBYP SUP,*
  BioIn 9, ConAu 3NR, -9R, IntAu&W 76,
  ScF&FL 1, -2, SmATA 1, WhoAmW 74,
  -72, -75, -77, -79, -81, -83, WhoE 74, -75,
  -77, -81, -83
Carlyle, Thomas 1795-1881 *Alli, Alli SUP,*
  AtlBL, BbD, BiD&SB, BioIn 1, -2, -3, -4,
  -5, -6, -7, -8, -9, -10, -11, -12, BrAu 19,
  BrWr 4, CasWL, CelCen, Chambr 3,
  ChhPo, -S1, -S2, -S3, CrtT 3, -4,
  CyEd[port], CyWA, DcAmSR, DcBiPP,
  DcEnA, DcEnL, DcEuL, DcLEL, Dis&D,
  EvLB, FamAYP, LinLib L, -S, LongCEL,
  LuthC 75, McGEWB, MouLC 3, NewC,
  OxEng, OxMus, PenC ENG, RAdv 1,
  RComWL, REn, WebE&AL, WhDW,
  WorAl
Carmer, Carl Lamson 1893-1976 *AmAu&B,*
  Au&Wr 6, AuBYP, BioIn 2, -3, -4, -7,
  -11, ChhPo, -S1, -S2, -S3, ConAu 4NR,
  -5R, -69, LinLib L, -S, NewYTBS 76,
  OxAmL, REn, REnAL, ScF&FL 1, -2,
  SmATA 30N, Str&VC, TwCA,
  TwCA SUP, WhAm 7, WhoAm 74, -76,
  WhoWor 74
Carmichael, Joel 1915- *AuBYP SUP,*
  ConAu 1R, -2NR

Caroselli, Remus Francis 1916-
  AmM&WS 73P, -76P, -79P, -82P,
  ConAu 97, SmATA 36
Carpenter, Frances 1890-1972 *AmAu&B,*
  Au&Wr 6, AuBYP, BioIn 6, -8, -9,
  ConAu 4NR, -5R, -37R, ForWC 70,
  MorJA, SmATA 27N, -3
Carpenter, Humphrey 1946- *ChhPo S3,*
  ConAu 89, WrDr 84
Carpentier, Alejo 1904-1980 *AnObit 1980,*
  BioIn 5, -7, -10, CasWL, ConAu 11NR,
  -65, -97, ConLC 8, -11, DcAfL,
  DcCLAA, EncLatA, EncWL, -81,
  ModLAL, Novels, OxSpan, PenC AM,
  ScF&FL 1, TwCWr, WorAu
Carpozi, George, Jr. 1920- *ConAu 11NR, -13R*
Carr, Albert Z 1902-1971 *AmAu&B, BioIn 9,*
  ConAu 1R, -1NR, -33R, NewYTBE 71,
  WhAm 5
Carr, Archie F, Jr. 1909- *AmM&WS 73P,*
  -76P, -79P, -82P, BioIn 12, ConAu 13R,
  WhoAm 74, -76, -78, -80, -82,
  WhoWor 74
Carr, John Dickson 1905?-1977 *AmAu&B,*
  Au&Wr 6, BioIn 2, -4, -5, -11,
  ConAu 3NR, -49, -69, ConLC 3, CorpD,
  DcLEL, EncMys, EncSF, EvLB,
  IntAu&W 76, -77, LongCTC, NewC,
  NewYTBS 77, Novels, ObitOF 79,
  PenC ENG, REn, REnAL, ScF&FL 1,
  -2, TwCA, TwCA SUP, TwCCr&M 80,
  TwCWr, WhAm 7, WhE&EA, Who 74,
  WhoAm 74, -76, WhoWor 74, WorAl
Carr, Mary Jane 1899- *AmCath 80, AuBYP,*
  BioIn 2, -3, -7, -9, BkC 1, CathA 1952,
  ChhPo S2, ConAu P-1, JBA 51,
  SmATA 2, WhoAmW 61, -64
Carr, Philippa 1906- *ConAu X,*
  IntAu&W 77X, NewYTBS 77, Novels,
  Who 74, -82, -83, WrDr 76, -80, -82, -84
Carr, Philippa *see also* Hibbert, Eleanor
Carr, Rachel *AuBYP SUP*
Carr, Terry 1937- *ConAu 81, ConSFA,*
  EncSF, ScF&FL 1, -2, WhoSciF,
  WrDr 84
Carra, Andrew Joseph 1943- *WhoAm 76, -78,*
  -80, -82
Carrick, Donald 1929- *BioIn 10, -12,*
  ConAu 5NR, -53, FourBJA, IlsBYP,
  IlsCB 1967, MichAu 80, SmATA 7
Carrico, John P 1938- *AmM&WS 73P*
Carrier, Jean-Guy 1945- *ConAu 101*
Carrier, Roch 1937?- *ConLC 13, CreCan 2,*
  ModCmwL, OxCan SUP
Carrighar, Sally 1905?- *AmWomWr, AnCL,*
  BioIn 3, ConAu 93, OhA&B,
  SmATA 24[port], WhoAmW 58, -61
Carrington, Richard 1921- *Au&Wr 6,*
  ConAu 9R
Carris, Joan Davenport 1938- *ConAu 106*
Carrison, Daniel Jordan 1917- *ConAu 37R,*
  WhoAmP 73, WhoGov 72,

WhoS&SW 76

Carroll, Gladys Hasty 1904- AmAu&B,
AmNov, AmWomWr, Au&Wr 6,
BioIn 2, –4, –6, –12, BlueB 76, ConAu 1R,
–5NR, DcLB 9, ForWC 70, InWom,
LinLib L, OxAmL, REnAL, ScF&FL 1,
–2, TwCA, TwCA SUP, WhE&EA,
WhNAA, WhoAm 74, –76, –78, –80, –82,
WhoAmW 74, –58, –61, –64, –66, –68, –70,
–72, WhoE 74, WhoWor 74, WrDr 76,
–80, –82, –84

Carroll, James 1943- WhoAm 82, WrDr 82,
–84

Carroll, Jim 1950?- BioIn 12, ConAu 45,
DrAP 75, DrAP&F 83, NewRR 83,
RolSEnR 83, WhoRocM 82

Carroll, John 1925- AmM&WS 73P, –79P,
–82P, ConAu 5R, –8NR, WhoLibI 82,
WhoMW 74

Carroll, Jonathan 1949- ConAu 105

Carroll, Joseph T 1935- Au&Wr 6,
ConAu 102

Carroll, Lewis 1832-1898 Alli SUP, AnCL,
AtlBL, AuBYP, BbD, BiD&SB, BioIn 1,
–2, –3, –4, –5, –6, –7, –8, –9, –10, –11, –12,
BrAu 19, BrWr 5, CasWL, CelCen,
Chambr 3, ChlLR 2, ChrP, ChhPo, –S1,
–S2, –S3, CnE&AP, CrtT 3, –4, CyWA,
DcEnA, DcEnL, DcEuL, DcLB 18[port],
DcLEL, EncSF, EvLB, FamAYP,
FamPYP, FilmgC, InSci, JBA 34,
LinLib L, –LP, –S, LongCEL, McGEWB,
NewC, NewYTBE 71, Novels[port],
OxEng, PenC ENG, RAdv 1, REn,
ScF&FL 1, Str&VC, TelT,
TwCCW 78A, –83A, WebE&AL, WhDW,
WhoChL, WorAl, YABC X

Carroll, Lewis see also Dodgson, Charles
Lutwidge

Carroll, Paul 1927- ConAu 25R, ConP 70,
–75, –80, CroCAP, DcLB 16[port],
DcLEL 1940, DrAP 75, IntAu&W 77,
IntWWP 77, WrDr 76, –80, –82, –84

Carroll, Theodus 1928- ConAu 69,
WhoAmW 79, –81

Carruth, Estelle 1910- ConAu 9R

Carruth, Hayden 1921- AmAu&B, BioIn 12,
ConAu 4NR, –9R, ConLC 4, –7, –10, –18,
ConP 70, –75, –80, DcLB 5[port],
DcLEL 1940, DrAP 75, DrAP&F 83,
IntAu&W 77, –82, IntWWP 77, LinLib L,
RAdv 1, REnAL, WhoAm 74, –76, –78,
–80, –82, WhoE 74, WhoWor 74, –76,
WorAu, WrDr 76, –80, –82, –84

Carse, Robert 1902-1971 BioIn 9, –10,
ConAu 1R, –1NR, –29R, NewYTBE 71,
ObitOF 79, SmATA 5

Carson, John F 1920- AuBYP, BioIn 8, –9,
ConAu 9R, –13R, IndAu 1917,
MichAu 80, ScF&FL 1, –2, SmATA 1

Carson, Josephine 1919- BioIn 4

Carson, Julia M 1899- AuBYP, BioIn 8,

InB&W 80, OhA&B, WhoAmP 81,
WhoAmW 58, –61

Carson, Rachel Louise 1907-1964 AmAu&B,
AmWomWr, AnCL, BioIn 2, –3, –4, –5, –6,
–7, –8, –9, –10, –11, –12, ConAu 77,
ConISC 2[port], CurBio 51, –64,
DcAmB S7, EncAAH, EncAB-H, EvLB,
GoodHs, HerW, InSci, InWom,
IntDcWB, LibW, LinLib L, –S,
LongCTC, McGEWB, NatCAB 51,
NewYTBS 82[port], NotAW MOD,
ObitOF 79, OxAmL, REn,
SmATA 23[port], TwCA SUP, TwCWr,
WebAB, –79, WhAm 4, WhoAmW 58,
–61, –64

Carson, Robert 1909-1983 AmAu&B,
Au&Wr 6, BioIn 3, ConAu 108, –21R,
IntMPA 77, –75, –76, –78, –79, –81, –82,
WhoAm 74, –76, –78, –80, –82, WhoHol A

Carter, Anne 1905- ConAu X

Carter, Anne see also Brooks, Anne Tedlock

Carter, Bruce 1922- AuBYP, BioIn 6, –12,
ConAu X, ScF&FL 1, –2, SmATA X,
TwCCW 78, –83, Who 74, –82, –83,
WrDr 80, –82, –84

Carter, Bruce see also Hough, Richard Alexander

Carter, Dorothy Sharp 1921- ConAu 49,
IntAu&W 77, SmATA 8, WhoAmW 77,
–79

Carter, Ernest Frank 1899- Au&Wr 6

Carter, Ernestine Marie d1983 Au&Wr 6,
BlueB 76, ConAu 110, Who 74, –82, –83,
WrDr 76, –80, –82, –84

Carter, Forest Charles 1922- WhoAm 74, –76,
–78, –80, WhoE 74

Carter, Forrest Bedford 1926?-1979 BioIn 11,
ConAu 107, SmATA 32[port]

Carter, Howard 1874-1939 BioIn 2, –4, –6, –8,
–9, –11, –12, DcBrA 1, InSci, LongCTC,
WhDW

Carter, Joseph 1912- ConAu 49

Carter, Lin 1930- ConAu 41R, ConSFA,
DcLB Y81B[port], EncSF, ScF&FL 1, –2,
WhoHr&F, WhoSciF, WrDr 84

Carter, Paul Allen 1926- ConAu 33R,
DrAS 74H, –78H, –82H

Carter, Peter 1929- ConAu 69, TwCCW 78,
–83, WrDr 80, –82, –84

Carter, Richard 1918- AmAu&B,
ConAu 8NR, –61, WhoAm 74, –76, –78,
–80, –82, WhoE 74

Carter, Robert F 1930- DrAS 74H, –78H,
–82H

Carter, Rubin 1937- BioIn 6, –7, –10, –11, –12,
InB&W 80, NewYTBE 72, NewYTBS 74,
PolProf NF, SelBAA

Carter, Samuel, III 1904- ConAu 57,
SmATA 37, WhoAm 76, –78, –80, –82,
WrDr 80, –82, –84

Carter, William E 1926?-1983 AmM&WS 73S,
–76P, AuBYP, BioIn 8, –9, ConAu 110,
–17R, FifIDA, SmATA 1, –35N, WhoFla,

WhoS&SW 75, –76, –78
Cartey, Wilfred G 1931- *ConAu 73,*
InB&W 80, WhoAm 82, WhoBlA 80,
WhoWor 82
Cartland, Barbara 1900?- *BioIn 1, –5, –8, –9,*
–10, –11, –12, BlueB 76, ConAu 6NR,
–9R, CurBio 79, IntAu&W 76, –77, –82,
IntDcWB, LinLib L, LongCTC,
NewYTBE 73, NewYTBS 81[port],
Novels, TwCWr, WhE&EA, WhLit,
Who 74, –82, –83, WhoAm 78, –80, –82,
WhoAmW 79, –81, –83, WhoE 83,
WhoWor 78, –80, –82, WorAl, WrDr 76,
–80, –82, –84
Cartwright, Rosalind Dymond 1922-
AmM&WS 73S, –78S, ConAu 81,
WhoAmW 74, –58, –68, –70, –72
Caruso, John Anthony 1907- *ConAu 33R,*
WrDr 76, –80, –82, –84
Cary, Diana Serra 1918- *BioIn 7, ConAu 57,*
WhoAmW 77
Casady, Jack 1944- *BioIn 9, WhoRocM 82*
Casady, Jack *see also* Jefferson Airplane
Casals, Pablo 1876-1973 *AmSCAP 66,*
Baker 78, BiDAmM, BioIn 1, –2, –3, –4,
–5, –6, –7, –8, –9, –10, –11, –12, CelR 73,
ConAu X, CurBio 50, –64, –73, –73N,
LinLib S, MusSN, NewYTBE 73,
ObitOF 79, ObitT 1971, REn, WhDW,
WhAm 6, WhScrn 2, Who 74,
WhoMus 72, WhoWor 74, WorAl
Casals, Pau Carlos Salvador Defillo De
1876-1973 *ConAu 45, –93, OxMus, REn*
Case, Victoria 1897- *ConAu 5R,*
WhoAmW 58, –61, –64, –66, WhoPNW
Casewit, Curtis 1922- *BioIn 9, ConAu 6NR,*
–13R, ConSFA, EncSF, ScF&FL 1, –2,
SmATA 4, WhoWest 76, –78
Casey, Warren 1935- *BioIn 12, ConAu 101,*
ConDr 82D, WhoAm 78, –80, –82
Cash, Johnny 1932- *Baker 78, BioIn 5, –8, –9,*
–10, –12, CelR 73, –73, ConAu 110,
CurBio 69, EncFCWM 69, FilmgC,
NewYTBE 73, RkOn 74, –82,
RolSEnR 83, WebAB, –79, WhoAm 74,
–76, –78, –80, –82, WhoHol A,
WhoRocM 82, WhoS&SW 73, –75,
WorAl
Cashin, Edward 1927- *ConAu X, –9NR, –21R,*
DrAS 82H
Cass, James 1915- *ConAu 101*
Cassedy, Sylvia 1930- *AuBYP SUP,*
ChhPo S2, ConAu 105, SmATA 27[port]
Cassel, Virginia Cunningham *ConAu 105*
Cassiday, Bruce 1920- *ConAu 1R, –4NR,*
ScF&FL 1, –2
Cassidy, Vincent H 1923- *ConAu 21R,*
DrAS 74H, –78H, –82H
Cassill, Kay 1930- *ConAu 89, Po&Wr 77,*
WhoAmW 77, –79
Casson, Lionel 1914- *Au&Wr 6, ConAu 3NR,*
–9R, DrAS 74H, –78H, –82H

Castaneda, Carlos 1931- *BioIn 9, –10, –11, –12,*
ConAu 25R, ConLC 12, EncO&P 78,
MakMC, NewYTBE 72, WhoAm 74, –76,
–78, –80, –82, WorAl, WorAu 1970,
WrDr 76, –80, –82, –84
Castex, Pierre-Georges 1915- *IntAu&W 76,*
–77, –82, WhoFr 79
Castor, Henry 1909- *AuBYP, BioIn 8,*
ConAu 17R
Castro, Antonio 1946- *ConAu 53*
Castro, Tony 1946- *ConAu X, WrDr 76, –80,*
–82, –84
Casty, Alan Howard 1929- *ConAu 1R, –4NR,*
IntAu&W 77, WhoWest 78, WrDr 76,
–80, –82, –84
Catchpole, Clive E 1938- *AmM&WS 73P*
Cate, Dick 1932- *ConAu X, –73, SmATA X*
Cather, Willa Sibert 1873-1947 *AmAu&B,*
AmWomWr, AmWr, ApCAB X, AtlBL,
BioIn 1, –2, –3, –4, –5, –6, –7, –8, –9, –10,
–11, –12, CasWL, Chambr 3, ChhPo, –S1,
–S3, CnDAL, ConAmA, ConAmL,
ConAu 104, CyWA, DcAmB S4, DcBiA,
DcLB DS1[port], –9[port], DcLEL,
DcNAA, EncAAH, EncAB-H, EncWL,
–81, EvLB, GoodHs, HerW, InWom,
IntDcWB, JBA 34, LibW, LinLib L, –S,
LongCTC, McGEWB, ModAL,
ModAL SUP, NatCAB 44, NotAW,
Novels, ObitOF 79, OxAmH, OxAmL,
OxCan, OxEng, PenC AM, RAdv 1,
RComWL, REn, REnAL, REnAW,
SmATA 30[port], TwCA, TwCA SUP,
TwCLC 1, –11[port], TwCWr, WebAB,
–79, WebE&AL, WhDW, WhAm 2,
WhE&EA, WhNAA, WhoTwCL,
WomWWA 14, WorAl
Catherall, Arthur 1906-1980 *Au&Wr 6,*
AuBYP, BioIn 8, –9, ConAu 5R,
IntAu&W 76, –77, –82, MnBBF,
SmATA 3, TwCCW 78, –83, WrDr 76,
–80
Catto, Max 1909- *Au&Wr 6, ConAu 105*
Catton, Bruce 1899-1978 *Alli SUP, AmAu&B,*
AuNews 1, BioIn 3, –4, –5, –6, –7, –8, –9,
–10, –11, –12, BioNews 74, BlueB 76,
CelR 73, ConAu 5R, –7NR, –81,
CurBio 54, –78, –78N, DcLB 17[port],
DcLEL 1940, EncSoH, IntAu&W 76, –77,
IntWW 74, –75, –76, –77, –78, –79N,
LinLib L, –S, MichAu 80, NewYTBS 78,
ObitOF 79, OxAmL, PenC AM, REn,
REnAL, SmATA 2, –24N, TwCA SUP,
WebAB, –79, WhAm 7, Who 74,
WhoAm 74, –76, –78, WhoWor 74, –78,
WorAl, WrDr 76
Catton, William R, Jr. 1926- *ConAu 109*
Caudill, Harry Monroe 1922- *AmAu&B,*
BioIn 8, ConAu 33R, WhoAm 78, –80
Caudill, Rebecca 1899- *AmAu&B, AuBYP,*
BioIn 2, –6, –7, –9, –10, ChhPo S1,
ConAu 2NR, –5R, CurBio 50, ForWC 70,

InWom, MorJA, SmATA 1, TwCCW 78,
–83, WhoAm 74, –76, –78, –80, –82,
WhoAmW 74, –58, –61, –64, –66, –68, –70,
–72, WrDr 76, –80, –82, –84
Cauman, Samuel 1909?-1971 *BioIn 9,*
ConAu P-2, NewYTBE 71
Causley, Charles 1917- *Au&Wr 6, AuBYP,*
BioIn 8, –9, –10, –12, BlueB 76, ChhPo,
–S1, –S2, –S3, CnE&AP, ConAu 5NR,
–9R, ConLC 7, ConP 70, –75, –80,
DcLEL 1940, IntAu&W 76, –77, –82,
IntWWP 77, LongCTC, NewC,
SmATA 3, TwCCW 78, –83, WebE&AL,
WhDW, Who 74, –82, –83, WhoWor 74,
–76, WorAu, WrDr 76, –80, –82, –84
Cavallaro, Ann 1918- *ConAu 5R*
Cavallo, Robert M 1932- *ConAu 10NR, –65,*
WhoAmL 78, –79, –83, WhoE 79
Cavanagh, Helen 1939- *ConAu 104,*
SmATA 37
Cavanah, Frances 1899-1982 *AuBYP, BioIn 2,*
–3, –6, –7, –9, ConAu 13R, CurBio 54,
ForWC 70, InWom, IndAu 1917,
IntAu&W 76, –77, MorJA, SmATA 1,
–31[port], WhNAA, WhoAmW 74, –70,
–72, –75, WhoS&SW 73
Cavanna, Betty 1909- *Au&Wr 6, AuBYP,*
BioIn 2, –6, –7, –9, ConAu 6NR, –9R,
ConLC 12, CurBio 50, InWom,
IntAu&W 76, –77, –82, MorJA,
SmATA 1, –30[port], TwCCW 78, –83,
WhoAmW 58, –61, WrDr 76, –80, –82, –84
Cavanna, Betty *see also* Allen, Betsy
Cavanna, Betty *see also* Harrison, Elizabeth
Cavanna
Cavanna, Betty *see also* Headley, Elizabeth
Cave, Hugh Barnett 1910- *Au&Wr 6,*
ConAu 2NR, –5R, WhNAA, WhoHr&F
Cavendish, Richard 1930- *ConAu 5NR, –9R,*
IntAu&W 82, WrDr 80, –82, –84
Cavett, Dick 1936?- *BioIn 7, –8, –9, –10, –11,*
–12, BioNews 74, BlueB 76, CelR 73,
ConAu X, CurBio 70, IntMPA 77, –75,
–76, –78, –79, –81, –82, –84, LesBEnT[port],
NewYTBS 77, –81[port], NewYTET,
WhoAm 74, –76, –78, –80, –82, WhoE 74,
WorAl
Cavin, Ruth 1918- *ConAu 8NR, –61*
Cazeau, Charles J 1931- *AmM&WS 73P, –76P,*
–79P, –82P, ConAu 104, WhoE 75, –77,
–79
Cazzola, Gus 1934- *ConAu 108*
Cebulash, Mel 1937- *BioIn 11, ConAu 29R,*
IntAu&W 77, ScF&FL 1, –2, SmATA 10,
WhoE 75, WrDr 76, –80, –82, –84
Cepeda, Orlando 1937- *BioIn 4, –5, –6, –8, –11,*
CmCal, CurBio 68, InB&W 80,
NewYTBS 77, WhoAm 74, WhoProB 73
Ceram, C W 1915-1972 *AmAu&B, BioIn 3, –4,*
–9, –10, ConAu X, CurBio 57, –72, –72N,
LinLib L, NewYTBE 72, ObitOF 79,
WorAu

Ceram, C W *see also* Marek, Kurt W
Cerf, Bennett Alfred 1898-1971 *AmAu&B,*
Au&Wr 6, AuBYP, BiE&WWA, BioIn 1,
–2, –3, –4, –5, –6, –7, –8, –9, –10, –11, –12,
ConAu 29R, ConAu P-2, CurBio 41, –58,
–71, –71N, LinLib L, –S, NewYTBE 71,
ObitOF 79, PIP&P, REn, REnAL,
ScF&FL 1, –2, SmATA 7, WebAB, –79,
WhAm 5, WhE&EA, WorAl
Cerf, Christopher 1941- *BioIn 9, ConAu 25R,*
ConSFA, ScF&FL 1, –2, SmATA 2,
WhoE 83
Cermack, Laird S 1942- *ConAu 53*
Cervantes, Miguel De 1547-1616 *AtlBL,*
BiD&SB, CasWL, ChhPo S2, CnThe,
CyWA, DcBiA, DcEuL, DcSpL, EuAu,
EvEuW, McGEWD, –84[port], NewC,
NewEOp 71, Novels[port], OxEng,
PenC EUR, RComWL, REn, REnWD
Cervantes Saavedra, Miguel De 1547-1616
AtlBL, BbD, BiD&SB, BioIn 1, –2, –3, –4,
–5, –6, –7, –8, –9, –10, –11, –12, CasWL,
CyWA, DcBiA, DcBiPP, DcCathB,
DcEuL, DcSpL, Dis&D, EncWT, EuAu,
EvEuW, LinLib L, –S, LongCEL,
McGEWB, NotNAT B, OxEng, OxSpan,
OxThe, PenC EUR, RComWL, WorAl
Cervon, Jacqueline 1924- *ConAu X,*
SmATA X
Cervon, Jacqueline *see also* Moussard, Jacqueline
Cetera, Peter 1944- *BioNews 74,*
WhoRocM 82
Cetera, Peter *see also* Chicago
Chaber, M E *ConAu X, TwCCr&M 80,*
WrDr 82, –84
Chaber, M E *see also* Crossen, Kendell Foster
Chadwick, Lee 1909- *Au&Wr 6, ConAu 69*
Chadwick, William Owen 1916- *Au&Wr 6,*
ConAu 1R, DcLEL 1940, IntWW 74, –75,
–76, –77, –78, –79, Who 74, –82,
WhoWor 74, –76, –78
Chaikin, Miriam 1928- *ConAu 81, ForWC 70,*
SmATA 24[port]
Chalk, Ocania 1927- *ConAu 1NR, –45,*
LivgBAA
Chalker, Jack L 1944- *ConAu 73, ConSFA,*
EncSF, IntAu&W 82, ScF&FL 1, –2,
WrDr 84
Challans, Mary 1905-1983 *BioIn 5, –6, –8, –9,*
–10, ConAu 81, IntAu&W 76X, –77X,
NewC, SmATA 23[port], –36N, Who 74,
–82, –83, WorAu, WrDr 76, –80, –82, –84
Challans, Mary *see also* Renault, Mary
Chamberlain, William 1878-1967 *WhAm 4*
Chamberlain, Wilt 1936- *BioIn 12, CelR 73,*
CmCal, ConAu 103, CurBio 60, Ebony 1,
NegAl 76[port], –83, NewYTBE 72, –73,
NewYTBS 75, WebAB 79, WhoBbl 73,
WhoBlA 75, –77, –80, WorAl
Chamberlin, Eric Russell 1926- *Au&Wr 6,*
ConAu 97, IntAu&W 76
Chamberlin, Jo Hubbard *AuBYP, BioIn 8*

Chamberlin, M Hope 1920-1974 *ConAu 45, –49*

Chambers, Aidan 1934- *Au&Wr 6, BioIn 9, ChhPo S2, –S3, ConAu 25R, IntAu&W 76, –77, –82, ScF&FL 1, –2, SmATA 1, TwCCW 83, WrDr 84*

Chambers, Bradford *AuBYP SUP*

Chambers, Henry Alban 1902- *WhoMus 72*

Chambers, Margaret Ada Eastwood 1911-1965 *BioIn 9, ConAu 9R, Film 2, IntAu&W 76, –77, SmATA 2, WhScrn, –2, WhoHol B*

Chambers, Margaret Ada Eastwood *see also* Chambers, Peggy

Chambers, Peggy 1911-1965 *Au&Wr 6, ConAu X, IntAu&W 76X, –77X, SmATA 2, WhE&EA*

Chambers, Peggy *see also* Chambers, Margaret Ada Eastwood

Chambers, Robert Hunter, III 1939- *DrAS 82E, LEduc 74, WhoE 75, –77*

Chambers, Robert Warner 1924- *AmM&WS 76P, –79P, –82P, AuBYP, BioIn 8, WhoAm 76, –78, –80, –82*

Chambliss, William C 1908?-1975 *ConAu 57*

Champion, Frances 1909- *WhoAmW 58, –61, –64, –68*

Champlin, Tim *ConAu X*

Chance, Stephen 1925- *ConAu X, IntAu&W 77X, –82X, TwCCW 78, –83, WrDr 80, –82, –84*

Chance, Stephen *see also* Turner, Philip

Chancellor, John 1900-1971 *Au&Wr 6, AuNews 1, BioNews 74, ConAu P-2, CurBio 62, MnBBF, WhE&EA*

Chand, Meira 1942- *ConAu 106*

Chandler, A Bertram 1912- *ConAu 21R, ConSFA, EncSF, IntAu&W 82, ScF&FL 1, –2, WhoSciF, WrDr 76, –80, –82, –84*

Chandler, Anna Curtis 1890?-1969 *BioIn 8, ChhPo, InWom, WhAm 5*

Chandler, Caroline A 1906-1979 *AmAu&B, AmCath 80, AmM&WS 73S, –78S, AuBYP, BiDrAPA 77, BioIn 1, –8, BkC 4, CathA 1930, ConAu 17R, –93, SmATA 22N, –24, WhAm 7, WhoAm 74, –76, –78, –80, WhoAmW 74, –58, –64, –66, –68, –70, –72*

Chandler, David Geoffrey 1934- *ConAu 11NR, IntAu&W 76, –77, –82, WrDr 76, –80, –82, –84*

Chandler, David L 1937?- *ConAu 1NR, –49, DrAS 74H, –78H, –82H, WhoAm 82*

Chandler, Edna Walker 1908-1982 *AuBYP, BioIn 8, –11, ConAu 1R, –4NR, –108, SmATA 11, –31N, WhoAmW 58, –75, –77*

Chandler, Raymond 1888-1959 *AmAu&B, BioIn 1, –4, –5, –6, –7, –9, –10, –11, –12, CasWL, CmCal, CmMov, CnMWL, ConAu 104, CorpD, CurBio 46, –59, DcAmB S6, DcFM, DcLEL, EncMys, FilmgC, LinLib L, LongCTC, MakMC,*

ModAL, ModAL SUP, NewYTBE 73, Novels, ObitOF 79, ObitT 1951, OxAmL, OxEng, OxFilm, PenC AM, REn, REnAL, TwCA SUP, TwCCr&M 80, TwCLC 1, –7[port], TwCWr, WebAB, –79, WebE&AL, WhAm 3, WhE&EA, WhoTwCL, WorAl, WorEFlm

Chaneles, Sol 1926- *AmM&WS 73S, –78S, AuBYP SUP, ConAu 41R*

Chang, Diana *DrAF 76, DrAP 75*

Chanover, Hyman 1920- *ConAu 2NR, –49, IntAu&W 77, WhoAmJ 80, WhoWorJ 72, –78*

Chant, Joy 1945- *ConAu X, ScF&FL 1, –2*

Chapin, Harry 1942-1981 *AnObit 1981[port], BioIn 11, –12, ConAu 104, –105, NewYTBS 81[port], RkOn 78, –84, RolSEnR 83, WhoAm 76, –78, –80, WhoRocM 82*

Chapin, Henry 1893-1983 *Au&Wr 6, AuBYP, ConAu 110, –93*

Chapin, Kim 1942- *ConAu 9NR, –53, MichAu 80*

Chaplin, Blondie *WhoRocM 82*

Chaplin, Blondie *see also* Beach Boys, The

Chapman, Abraham 1915-1976 *BioIn 11, ConAu 45, DrAS 74E*

Chapman, Clark Russell 1945- *AmM&WS 76P, –79P, –82P, ConAu 110*

Chapman, Hester W 1899-1976 *Au&Wr 6, ConAu 9R, –9NR, –65, WhE&EA, Who 74*

Chapman, Sydney 1888-1970 *BiESc, BioIn 1, –2, –3, –4, –8, –9, ConAu 106, CurBio 57, –70, InSci, McGEWB, McGMS 80[port], NewYTBE 70, ObitOF 79, ObitT 1961, WhE&EA, WhoLA*

Chapman, Vera 1898- *ConAu 81, SmATA 33[port]*

Chapman, Walker 1935- *ConAu X, DcLEL 1940, SmATA X, ThrBJA, WorAu 1970*

Chapman, Walker *see also* Silverberg, Robert

Chapple, Steve 1949- *ConAu 77*

Charles, Sharon Ashenbrenner 1947- *WhoLibI 82*

Charren, Peggy 1928- *BioIn 12, LesBEnT, NewYTET, PolProf NF, WhoAm 76, –78, –80, –82, WhoAmW 79, –81*

Charriere, Henri 1906?-1973 *ASpks, BioIn 8, –9, –10, –11, ConAu 101, –45, NewYTBE 73, ObitOF 79, ObitT 1971, WhScrn 2*

Charry, Elias 1906- *ConAu 69, WhoWorJ 72, –78*

Charters, Ann 1936- *ConAu 9NR, –17R, WhoAmW 83, WrDr 76, –80, –82, –84*

Charyn, Jerome 1937- *AmAu&B, ConAu 5R, –7NR, ConLC 5, –8, –18, ConNov 72, –76, –82, DcLB Y83B[port], DcLEL 1940, DrAF 76, DrAP&F 83, DrAS 74E, –78E, –82E, IntAu&W 76, –77, –82, WhoAm 74,*

-76, -78, -80, -82, WrDr 76, -80, -82, -84

Chasan, Daniel Jack 1943- ConAu 29R

Chase, Alice Elizabeth 1906- Au&Wr 6,
AuBYP, AuBYP SUP, BioIn 8, -9,
ConAu X, ConAu P-1, DrAS 74H, -78H,
-82H, ForWC 70, IntAu&W 76,
SmATA 4, WhoAmA 73, -76, -78, -80,
-82, WhoAmW 58, -61, -64, WomPO 76,
-78

Chase, Alice Elizabeth see also McHargue,
Georgess

Chase, Chris AuNews 1, BioIn 10, -12

Chase, Joan Barbara 1936- LEduc 74,
WhoAmW 74, -75, -77

Chase, Mary Ellen 1887-1973 AmAu&B,
AmNov, AmWomWr, AuBYP, BioIn 1,
-2, -3, -4, -5, -7, -8, -10, -11, BlueB 76N,
ChhPo, ConAmA, ConAu 41R,
ConAu P-1, ConLC 2, CurBio 40, -45,
-73, -73N, DcLEL, FourBJA, InWom,
LibW, LinLib L, LongCTC,
NewYTBE 73, Novels, ObitOF 79,
OxAmL, PenC AM, REn, REnAL,
ScF&FL 1A, SmATA 10, TwCA,
TwCA SUP, WhAm 5, WhLit, WhNAA,
Who 74, WhoAmW 74, -58, -64, -66, -68,
-70, -72

Chase, Naomi Feigelson 1932- ConAu 104,
DrAP&F 83

Chase, Stuart 1888- AmAu&B, BioIn 2, -3,
-4, BlueB 76, ChhPo S2, ConAmA,
ConAu 65, CurBio 40, DcAmSR, DcLEL,
Future, IntAu&W 77, -82, IntWW 74,
-75, -76, -77, -78, -79, -80, -81, -82, -83,
LinLib L, -S, LongCTC, OxAmH,
OxAmL, REn, REnAL, TwCA,
TwCA SUP, WebAB, -79, WhNAA,
Who 74, -82, -83, WhoAm 74, -76, -78,
WhoWor 74

Chase-Riboud, Barbara 1939- AfroAA,
BioIn 12, ConArt, WhoAm 78, -80, -82,
WhoAmA 73, -76, -78, -80, -82,
WhoBlA 77, -80, WhoWor 78

Chatwin, Bruce 1940- BioIn 12, ConAu 85

Chaucer, Geoffrey 1340?-1400? Alli, AnCL,
AtlBL, BbD, BiD&SB, BioIn 1, -2, -3, -4,
-5, -6, -7, -8, -9, -10, -11, -12, BrAu,
BrWr 1, CasWL, Chambr 1, ChhPo, -S1,
-S2, -S3, CnE&AP, CrtT 1, -4, CyWA,
DcBiPP, DcCathB, DcEnA, DcEnL,
DcEuL, DcLEL, DcScB, Dis&D, EvLB,
LinLib L, -S, LongCEL, LuthC 75,
McGEWB, MouLC 1, NewC,
NewEOp 71, OxEng, OxMus,
PenC ENG, PoLE, RAdv 1, RComWL,
REn, WebE&AL, WhDW, WorAl

Chayefsky, Paddy 1923-1981 AmAu&B,
AmSCAP 66, AnObit 1981[port],
BiE&WWA, BioIn 3, -4, -10, -11, -12,
BlueB 76, CelR 73, CnMD, CnThe,
ConAu 9R, -104, ConDr 73, -77,
ConLC 23[port], CroCD, CurBio 57,

-81N, DcFM, DcLB Y81A[port], -7[port],
DcLEL 1940, EncSF, EncWT,
IntAu&W 76, -77, -82, IntMPA 77, -75,
-76, -78, -79, -81, IntWW 74, -75, -76,
-77, -78, -79, -80, -81, -82N, LesBEnT,
LinLib L, McGEWD, -84, ModWD,
NewYTBS 81[port], NotNAT, OxAmL,
OxFilm, PenC AM, PIP&P, REnAL,
WebAB, -79, WhoAm 74, -76, -78, -80,
WhoE 74, WhoThe 15, -16, -81,
WhoTwCL, WhoWor 74, -78, -80, WorAl,
WorAu, WorEFlm, WrDr 76, -80, -82

Cheatham, K Follis 1943- ConAu 81,
DrAP&F 83

Cheever, John 1912-1982 AmAu&B,
AmWr SUP, AnObit 1982[port], BioIn 3,
-4, -5, -6, -8, -10, -11, -12, BlueB 76,
CasWL, CelR 73, ConAu 5R, -5NR, -106,
ConLC 3, -7, -8, -11, -15, -25[port],
ConNov 72, -76, -82, CurBio 75, -82N,
DcLB Y80A[port], -Y82A[port], -2,
DcLEL 1940, DrAF 76, EncWL, -81,
IntAu&W 76, -77, IntWW 74, -75, -76,
-77, -78, -79, -80, -81, -82, -83N,
LinLib L, ModAL, ModAL SUP,
NewYTBS 78, -79, -82[port], Novels,
OxAmL, PenC AM, Po&Wr 77, RAdv 1,
REn, REnAL, TwCWr, WebE&AL,
Who 74, -82, -83N, WhoAm 74, -76, -78,
-80, -82, WhoTwCL, WhoWor 74, -76,
-78, WorAl, WorAu, WrDr 76, -80, -82

Chekhov, Anton Pavlovich 1860-1904 AtlBL,
BioIn 1, -2, -3, -4, -5, -6, -7, -8, -9, -10,
-11, -12, CasWL, ClDMEL, CnMD,
CnThe, ConAu 104, CyWA, DcEuL,
DcRusL, Dis&D, EncWL, -81[port],
EncWT, EuAu, EvEuW, InSci, LinLib L,
-S, LongCEL, McGEWB,
McGEWD, -84[port], ModSL 1, ModWD,
NewC, NotNAT A, -B, Novels[port],
OxEng, OxThe, PenC EUR, PIP&P, -A,
RComWL, REn, REnWD, TwCLC 3,
-10[port], WhDW, WorAl

Chekhov, Anton Pavlovich see also Tchekhov,
Anton Pavlovich

Chen, Jack 1908- BioIn 9, ConAu 41R,
IntAu&W 77, -82

Chen, Jo-Hsi 1938- IntAu&W 77X, -82

Chen, Yuan-Tsung 1932- BioIn 12,
ConAu 106, NewYTBS 80[port]

Cheney, Cora 1916- AuBYP, BioIn 8, -9,
ConAu 1R, -4NR, SmATA 3,
WhoAmW 58, -61

Cheney, David M ScF&FL 1

Cheney, Glenn Alan 1951- ConAu 109

Cheney, Sheldon 1886-1980 AmAu&B,
AnObit 1980, Au&Wr 6, BiE&WWA,
BioIn 4, -12, ConAu 102, IntAu&W 76,
NewYTBS 80, NotNAT, REnAL, TwCA,
TwCA SUP, WhAm 7, WhE&EA,
WhThe, WhoAm 74, -76, -78,
WhoAmA 73, -76, -78, -80, -82N,

WhoWor 74, –76

Chennault, Anna Chan 1925- *AmAu&B, BioIn 6, –11, –12, BlueB 76, ConAu 61, ForWC 70, IntAu&W 76, WhoAm 74, –76, –78, –80, –82, WhoAmP 73, –75, –77, –79, –81, –83, WhoAmW 74, –66, –68, –70, –72, –75, –77, –79, –81, –83, WhoS&SW 73, –75, –76, WhoWor 80, –82*

Cherryh, C J 1942- *BioIn 12, ConAu X, –65, DcLB Y80B[port], EncSF, WrDr 84*

Chesher, Richard 1940- *BioIn 10, ConAu 106*

Cheshire, Maxine 1930- *BioIn 8, –9, –11, CelR 73, ConAu 108, GoodHs, WhoAm 74, –76, –78, –80, –82, WhoAmW 74, –70A, –72, –75, –79, –83*

Chesler, Phyllis 1940- *AmWomWr, BioIn 11, ConAu 4NR, –49*

Chesnut, Mary Boykin 1823-1886 *AmWomWr, BioIn 2, –4, –10, –12, InWom, LibW, NotAW, OxAmL, REnAL*

Chester, Deborah 1957- *ConAu 102*

Chester, Laura 1949- *ConAu 9NR, –65, DrAP 75, DrAP&F 83, IntWWP 77*

Chester, Michael 1928- *AuBYP, BioIn 8, ConAu 1R, –1NR, ScF&FL 1, –2*

Chester, William L 1907- *EncSF, ScF&FL 1*

Chesterton, Gilbert Keith 1874-1936 *AnCL, AtlBL, BioIn 1, –2, –3, –4, –5, –6, –7, –8, –9, –10, –11, –12, BkC 6, CasWL, CathA 1930, Chambr 3, ChhPo, –S1, –S2, –S3, CorpD, DcBrBI, DcCathB, DcLEL, EvLB, LinLib L, –S, LongCEL, LuthC 75, MakMC, McGEWB, NotNAT B, OxEng, PenC ENG, TwCA, TwCA SUP, TwCWr, WhDW, WhE&EA, WhLit, WhoLA*

Chetin, Helen 1922- *BioIn 10, ConAu 29R, SmATA 6*

Chevigny, Bell Gale 1936- *ConAu 57, WhoAmW 74, –72*

Chew, Ruth 1920- *BioIn 10, ConAu 41R, IntAu&W 82, SmATA 7*

Chicago *BiDAmM, BioNews 74, EncJzS 70, EncPR&S, –77, IlEncRk, RkOn 78, –84, RolSEnR 83, WhoRocM 82*

Chicago *see also* Cetera, Peter

Chicago *see also* Kath, Terry

Chicago *see also* Lamm, Robert

Chicago *see also* Loughnane, Lee

Chicago *see also* Pankow, James

Chicago *see also* Parazaider, Walt

Chicago *see also* Seraphine, Dan

Chicago, Judy 1939- *BioIn 9, –10, –12, ConArt, –83, ConAu 85, CurBio 81[port], DcCAr 81, IntDcWB, NewYTBS 79, PrintW 83, WhoAm 76, –78, –80, –82, WhoAmA 73, –76, –78, –80, –82, WhoAmW 75, –77, –79, –81, –83, WomWMM B*

Chichester, Sir Francis 1901-1972 *Au&Wr 6, BioIn 6, –7, –8, –9, –10, ConAu 37R, ConAu P-1, CurBio 67, –72, –72N,*

LinLib L, NewYTBE 72, ObitOF 79, ObitT 1971, OxShips, WhDW, WhAm 5, WhE&EA

Chidsey, Donald Barr 1902-1981 *AmAu&B, AmNov, Au&Wr 6, BioIn 2, –4, –9, ConAu 2NR, –5R, –103, REnAL, SmATA 27N, –3, TwCA SUP*

Child, John 1922- *ConAu 93, WrDr 76, –80, –82, –84*

Childers, Erskine 1905-1974 *BioIn 10, –11, BlueB 76N, DcIrB, IntWW 74, –75N, NewYTBE 73, ObitT 1971, Who 74, WhoWor 74*

Childress, Alice 1920- *AuBYP SUP, BioIn 10, –12, BlkAWP, ConAu 3NR, –45, ConDr 77, –82, ConLC 12, –15, DcLB 7[port], DrAP&F 83, DrBlPA, InB&W 80, LivgBAA, McGEWD 84, NegAl 83, NotNAT, PlP&P A, SelBAA, SmATA 7, WhoAm 74, –76, –82, WhoAmW 74, –72, WhoBlA 75, –77, –80, WrDr 80, –82, –84*

Chilton, Irma 1930- *ConAu 103, ScF&FL 1, –2*

Chin, Richard 1932- *WhoAmP 73*

Chinery, Michael 1938- *ConAu 103, IntAu&W 77, SmATA 26, WrDr 76, –80, –82, –84*

Chinn, William G 1919- *ConAu 33R, LEduc 74, WhoWest 76, –78*

Chipman, Bruce Lewis 1946- *ConAu 37R, WhoE 83, WrDr 76, –80, –82, –84*

Chipperfield, Joseph Eugene 1912-1976 *Au&Wr 6, AuBYP, BioIn 6, –8, –9, ConAu 6NR, –9R, IntAu&W 76, MorJA, SmATA 2, TwCCW 78, –83, WrDr 80*

Chipperfield, Joseph Eugene *see also* Craig, John Eland

Chisholm, Shirley 1924- *AlmAP 78, –80, –82[port], AmAu&B, AmPolW 80, –80A, BiDrAC, BioIn 8, –9, –10, –11, –12, BlueB 76, CelR 73, CivR 74, CngDr 74, –77, –79, –81, ConAu 29R, ConIsC 2[port], CurBio 69, Ebony 1, GoodHs, HerW, InB&W 80, IntDcWB, LibW, LinLib S, LivgBAA, NegAl 76, –83[port], NewYTBE 70, PolProf NF, SelBAA, WhoAm 74, –76, –78, –80, –82, WhoAmP 73, –75, –77, –79, –81, –83, WhoAmW 66A, –68, –70, –72, –75, –77, –79, –81, –83, WhoBlA 75, –77, –80, WhoE 74, –75, –77, –79, –81, –83, WhoGov 77, –72, –75, WomPO 76, –78, WorAl, WrDr 76, –80, –82, –84*

Chissell, Joan Olive 1919- *Au&Wr 6, ConAu 61, IntAu&W 76, IntWWM 77, WhoMus 72, WhoWor 78, WrDr 76, –80, –82, –84*

Chittenden, Elizabeth F 1903- *BioIn 11, ConAu 61, SmATA 9*

Chittum, Ida 1918- *AuBYP SUP, BioIn 10, ConAu 37R, IntAu&W 77, SmATA 7,*

WhoAmW 81, WrDr 76, –80, –82, –84

Chopin, Kate 1851-1904 *AmAu, AmAu&B, AmWomWr, AmWr SUP, BbD, BiDSA, BioIn 8, –10, –12, CasWL, CnDAL, ConAu 104, CrtT 4, DcAmAu, DcAmB, DcLB 12[port], DcLEL, DcNAA, EncSoH, GoodHs, IntDcWB, LibW, ModAL, ModAL SUP, NatCAB 25, NotAW, Novels, OxAmL, PenC AM, REn, REnAL, TwCLC 5[port], WebAB, –79, WhAm 1, WorAl*

Choron, Jacques 1904-1972 *AuBYP, BioIn 8, –9, ConAu 33R, ConAu P-1, NewYTBE 72, WhoAm 74*

Chrisman, Harry E 1906- *ConAu 1R*

Christ, Henry I 1915- *ConAu 2NR, –5R, IntAu&W 76, WrDr 76, –80, –82, –84*

Christensen, Jo I 1943- *ConAu X, –57*

Christensen, Jo I *see also* Christensen, Yolanda Maria Ippolito

Christensen, Yolanda Maria Ippolito 1943- *ConAu 7NR, WhoAmW 77, –79*

Christensen, Yolanda Maria Ippolito *see also* Christensen, Jo I

Christgau, Robert 1942- *BioIn 10, –11, ConAu 65, MugS, WhoE 81*

Christian, Catherine 1901- *ScF&FL 1, WhE&EA*

Christian, Mary Blount 1933- *BioIn 11, ConAu 1NR, –45, IntAu&W 77, SmATA 9, WhoAmW 83, WrDr 76, –80, –82, –84*

Christian, Samuel Terry 1937- *AmM&WS 73P, –76P, –79P, –82P, AuBYP SUP*

Christie, Agatha 1890?-1976 *Au&Wr 6, AuBYP, AuNews 1, –2, BiE&WWA, BioIn 1, –2, –4, –6, –7, –8, –9, –11, –12, BioNews 74, BlueB 76, CasWL, CelR 73, CnThe, ConAu 10NR, –17R, –61, ConDr 73, –77, ConLC 1, –6, –8, –12, ConNov 72, –76, CorpD, CurBio 40, –64, –76, –76N, DcLB 13[port], DcLEL, EncMys, EncWT, EvLB, FilmgC, GoodHs, InWom, IntAu&W 76X, IntDcWB, IntWW 74, –75, –76N, LinLib L, –LP, –S, LongCTC, MnBBF, NewC, NewYTBS 76, Novels, ObitOF 79, OxEng, PenC ENG, PIP&P, REn, ScF&FL 1, –2, SmATA 36, TwCA, TwCA SUP, TwCCr&M 80, TwCWr, WhAm 6, WhE&EA, Who 74, WhoAmW 74, –61, –66, –68, –70, –72, –75, WhoHr&F, WhoThe 15, –16, –81N, WhoWor 74, WorAl, WrDr 76*

Christie, Ian Ralph 1919- *Au&Wr 6, ConAu 2NR, –5R, IntAu&W 76, –77, –82, Who 82, –83, WhoWor 82, WrDr 76, –80, –82, –84*

Christie, Trevor L 1905?-1969 *BioIn 8, ConAu P-2*

Christman, Elizabeth 1914- *ConAu 89*

Christopher, John 1922- *BioIn 4, –10,*

ChlLR 2, ConAu X, –73, –77, ConSFA, DcLEL 1940, EncSF, FourBJA, LElec, LinLib L, Novels, ScF&FL 1, –2, SenS, SmATA X, TwCCW 78, –83, WhoSciF, WorAu, WrDr 80, –82, –84

Christopher, John *see also* Youd, Samuel

Christopher, Matt 1917- *ConAu 1R, –5NR, IntAu&W 77X, –82X, SmATA 2*

Christopher, Matthew F 1917- *AuBYP, BioIn 8, –9, –10, ConAu 1R, IntAu&W 77, –82, MorBMP, SmATA 2, WrDr 76, –80, –82, –84*

Christopher, Milbourne *BioIn 5, –10, BioNews 74, ConAu 105, EncO&P 78*

Chrystie, Frances Nicholson 1904- *AuBYP, BioIn 3, –7*

Chu, Daniel 1933- *BioIn 11, ConAu 13R, SmATA 11*

Chu, Louis H 1913?-1970 *BioIn 8, ConAu 13R*

Chu, Samuel C 1929- *ConAu 69, DrAS 74H, –78H, –82H*

Chubb, Thomas Caldecot 1899-1972 *AmAu&B, Au&Wr 6, BioIn 9, ChhPo, –S1, –S2, ConAu 1R, –6NR, –33R, NewYTBE 72, REn, REnAL, WhAm 5, WhE&EA, WhNAA*

Chukovsky, Kornei 1882-1969 *ConAu 4NR, –25R, ObitOF 79, SmATA 34[port], TwCCW 78B, –83B*

Church, Alfred John 1829-1912 *Alli SUP, AuBYP, BioIn 2, –8, ChhPo S2, JBA 34, –51, ScF&FL 1, TelT, WhLit*

Church, Carol Bauer *AuBYP SUP*

Church, Richard 1893-1972 *Alli, Au&Wr 6, BioIn 4, –6, –7, –8, –9, ChhPo, –S1, –S2, –S3, ConAu 1R, –3NR, –33R, ConNov 72, ConP 70, DcLEL, EvLB, LongCTC, ModBrL, MorJA, NewC, NewYTBE 72, Novels, ObitT 1971, PenC ENG, REn, ScF&FL 1, SmATA 3, TwCA, TwCA SUP, TwCCW 78, –83, TwCWr, WhE&EA, WhLit, WhoChL*

Churchill, E Richard 1937- *BioIn 11, ConAu 11NR, –17R, SmATA 11, WrDr 76, –80, –82, –84*

Churchill, Linda R 1938- *ConAu 11NR, –21R, WhoAmW 74*

Churchill, Winston 1871-1947 *AmAu&B, AmLY, ApCAB SUP, ApCAB X, BbD, BiD&SB, BiDSA, BioIn 1, –2, –4, –5, –10, –12, CarSB, CasWL, Chambr 3, CnDAL, ConAmA, ConAmL, CurBio 40, –42, –53, –65, CyWA, DcAmAu, DcAmB S4, DcAmSR, DcBiA, DcLEL, DcNAA, EvLB, JBA 34, LinLib L, –S, LongCTC, McGEWB, NatCAB 10, NotNAT B, Novels, ObitOF 79, OxAmL, OxEng, PenC AM, REn, REnAL, TwCA SUP, TwCBDA, TwCWr, WebE&AL, WhAm 2, WhE&EA, WhLit, WhNAA, WhThe*

Chute, B J 1913- *AmAu&B, ConAu 1R, DrAP&F 83, IntAu&W 77X, -82X, MnBBF, MorJA, SmATA 2, WhoAmW 74, -58, -61, -66, -68, -70, -72, WrDr 76, -80, -82, -84*

Chute, Beatrice Joy 1913- *AmWomWr, BioIn 1, -2, -6, -9, CurBio 50, InWom, IntAu&W 77, -82*

Chute, Marchette 1909- *AmAu&B, AmWomWr, Au&Wr 6, AuBYP, BiE&WWA, BioIn 2, -3, -4, -5, -6, -7, -9, BkCL, ChhPo, -S1, -S2, ConAu 1R, -5NR, CurBio 50, DrAS 74H, -78H, -82H, EvLB, InWom, IntAu&W 76, -77, -82, IntWWP 77, LinLib L, MinnWr, MorJA, NotNAT, RAdv 1, REnAL, SmATA 1, TwCA SUP, TwCCW 78, -83, Who 74, -82, -83, WhoAm 74, -76, -78, -80, -82, WhoAmW 74, -58, -64, -66, -68, -70, -72, -83, WrDr 76, -80, -82, -84*

Ciardi, John 1916- *AmAu&B, AuBYP, BioIn 2, -4, -5, -6, -7, -8, -9, -12, BlueB 76, BkCL, BkP, CasWL, CelR 73, ChhPo, -S1, -S2, -S3, CnDAL, ConAu 5R, -5NR, ConLC 10, ConP 70, -75, -80, CurBio 67, DcLB 5[port], DcLEL 1940, DrAP 75, DrAS 74E, -78E, -82E, IntWWP 77, LinLib L, ModAL, OxAmL, PenC AM, RAdv 1, REn, REnAL, SmATA 1, Str&VC, ThrBJA, TwCA SUP, TwCCW 78, -83, WebAB, -79, WebE&AL, WhoAm 74, -76, -78, -80, -82, WhoE 74, WhoWor 74, WorAl, WrDr 76, -80, -82, -84*

Cipriano, Anthony 1941- *ConAu 102*

Cirino, Robert 1937- *ConAu 61*

Citron, Samuel J 1908-1979 *BioIn 12, WhoWorJ 72, -78*

Claflin, Edward 1949- *AuBYP SUP, ConAu 97*

Clagett, John 1916- *AmAu&B, AuBYP, BioIn 3, -8, ConAu 5R, -6NR, DrAS 74E, -78E, -82E*

Claiborne, Robert 1919- *ConAu 29R, IntAu&W 77*

Claire, Keith 1940- *Au&Wr 6, ConAu X, ScF&FL 1*

Clampett, Bob 1959?- *AuNews 1, BioIn 10, -11, NewYTBS 78, NewYTET, WhoAm 80, -82*

Clampitt, Amy *ConAu 110, DrAP&F 83*

Clapp, Patricia 1912- *BioIn 9, ConAu 10NR, -25R, IntAu&W 82, ScF&FL 1, -2, SmATA 4, TwCCW 78, -83, WhoE 83, WrDr 76, -80, -82, -84*

Clapton, Eric 1945- *BioIn 8, -9, -10, -11, -12, CelR 73, EncPR&S, -77, IlEncRk, RkOn 78, -84, RolSEnR 83, WhoAm 74, -76, -78, -80, -82, WhoRocM 82, WhoWor 78, WorAl*

Clare, George 1920- *WrDr 84*

Clarens, Carlos 1936- *ConAu 21R,*

ScF&FL 1, -2

Clark, Ann Nolan 1898- *AmAu&B, AmCath 80, AmPB, AmWomWr, AnCL, Au&ICB, AuBYP, BioIn 2, -3, -4, -6, -7, -9, -10, ChhPo, ConAu 2NR, -5R, IntAu&W 76, JBA 51, LinLib L, MorBMP, Newb 1922, SmATA 4, Str&VC, TwCCW 78, -83, WhoAm 74, -76, -78, -80, -82, WhoAmW 74, -58, -61, -64, -66, -68, -70, -72, WrDr 80, -82, -84*

Clark, Billy Curtis 1928- *BioIn 4, -8, ConAu 1R, WhoS&SW 73*

Clark, Brian 1932- *ConAu 41R, ConDr 77C, -82, WhoThe 81, WrDr 84*

Clark, Dick 1929- *AlmAP 78, BioIn 5, -10, -11, CmpEPM, CngDr 77, CurBio 59, IntMPA 77, -75, -76, -78, -79, -81, -82, -84, IntWW 74, -75, -76, -77, -78, LesBEnT[port], NewYTET, WhoAm 74, -76, -78, -80, -82, WhoAmP 75, WhoHol A*

Clark, Dorothy Park 1899- *AmAu&B, AmNov X, BioIn 2, -4, ConAu 5R, CurBio 57, InWom, WhoAmW 58*

Clark, Eleanor 1913- *AmAu&B, AmWomWr, BioIn 2, -4, -11, ConAu 9R, ConLC 5, -19, ConNov 72, -76, -82, CurBio 78, DcLB 6[port], DcLEL 1940, DrAF 76, IntAu&W 76, -77, -82, NewYTBS 77, REnAL, TwCA SUP, WhoAm 74, -76, -78, -80, -82, WhoAmW 58, -68, WrDr 76, -80, -82, -84*

Clark, Eric 1911- *Au&Wr 6, ConAu 9NR, -13R, WhE&EA, WhoWor 76, WrDr 76, -80, -82, -84*

Clark, Eugenie 1922- *AmM&WS 73P, -76P, -79P, -82P, BioIn 2, -3, -5, -7, -8, -9, -11, -12, ConAu 49, CurBio 53, HerW, InSci, InWom, WhoAm 76, -78, -80, -82, WhoAmW 74, -66, -66A, -68, -70, -72, -75, -77, WhoS&SW 73, -75, WhoWor 74*

Clark, Frank J 1922- *AmSCAP 66, AuBYP, BioIn 8, -12, ConAu 13R, SmATA 18*

Clark, Kenneth M 1903- *Au&Wr 6, BioIn 2, -3, -4, -6, -8, -9, -10, -11, -12, BlueB 76, CasWL, ConAu 93, CurBio 63, IntAu&W 77, IntMPA 75, IntWW 75, -76, -77, -78, -79, -80, -81, LinLib L, LongCTC, NewYTBE 70, TwCA SUP, Who 74, WhoWor 74, -76, -78, -82, WrDr 82*

Clark, LaVerne Harrell 1929- *ConAu 11NR, -13R, DrAF 76, DrAP&F 83, ForWC 70, IntAu&W 77, -82, IntWWP 77, -82, WhoAmW 75, -77, -81, WrDr 76, -80, -82, -84*

Clark, Margaret Goff 1913- *AuBYP, BioIn 8, -11, ConAu 1R, -5NR, ForWC 70, IntAu&W 76, SmATA 8, WhoAmW 75, -77*

Clark, Mary Higgins 1929?- *BioIn 11, –12,
ConAu 81, IntAu&W 82, WhoAm 82,
WrDr 80, –82, –84*

Clark, Mavis Thorpe 1912?- *BioIn 11,
ConAu 8NR, –57, ConLC 12, FourBJA,
SingR 1, SmATA 8, TwCCW 78, –83,
WrDr 80, –82, –84*

Clark, Ramsey 1927- *AmAu&B, BioIn 5, –7,
–8, –9, –10, –11, –12, BioNews 74,
BlueB 76, CelR 73, ConAu 29R,
CurBio 67, IntWW 74, –75, –76, –77, –78,
–79, –80, –81, –82, –83, NewYTBS 74,
PolProf J, PolProf NF, Who 74, –82, –83,
WhoAm 74, –76, –78, –80, –82,
WhoAmL 78, –79, –83, WhoAmP 73, –75,
–77, –79, –81, –83, WhoWor 74, –78, –80*

Clark, Ronald William 1916- *Au&Wr 6,
AuBYP, BioIn 7, –9, ConAu 25R,
ConSFA, EncSF, ScF&FL 1, –2,
SmATA 2*

Clark, Sue C 1935- *ConAu 41R*

Clark, Walter VanTilburg 1909-1971 *AmAu&B,
AmNov, BioIn 1, –2, –4, –5, –8, –9, –10, –11,
–12, CmCal, CnDAL, ConAu 9R, –33R,
ConNov 72, –76, –82A, CyWA,
DcLB 9[port], DcLEL 1940, LinLib L,
ModAL, NatCAB 57, NewYTBE 71,
Novels, ObitOF 79, OxAmL, PenC AM,
RAdv 1, REn, REnAL, REnAW,
SmATA 8, TwCA SUP, WhAm 5,
WorAl*

Clarke, Arthur Charles 1917- *Au&Wr 6,
AuBYP, BioIn 3, –4, –6, –7, –8, –10, –11,
–12, BlueB 76, CelR 73, ConAu 1R,
–2NR, ConLC 1, –4, –13, –18, ConNov 72,
–76, –82, ConSFA, CurBio 66,
DcLEL 1940, EncSF, EvLB, FourBJA,
Future, IntAu&W 76, –77, –82,
IntWW 74, –75, –76, –77, –78, –79, –80, –81,
–82, –83, LinLib L, LongCTC, NewC,
NewYTBS 83[port], Novels[port],
ScF&FL 1, –2, SmATA 13, TwCA SUP,
TwCWr, WebE&AL, Who 74, –82, –83,
WhoSciF, WhoWor 74, –76, –78, –82,
WorAl, WrDr 76, –80, –82*

Clarke, James 1934- *Au&Wr 6*

Clarke, Joan B 1921- *ScF&FL 1, SmATA 27,
TwCCW 78, WrDr 76, –80, –82*

Clarke, John 1907- *BioIn 10, ConAu X,
IntAu&W 77X, SmATA 5*

Clarke, John *see also* Laklan, Virginia Carli

Clarke, John Henrik 1915- *AfroAA,
AmAu&B, AuNews 1, BioIn 4, –5, –10,
BioNews 74, BlkAWP, CivR 74,
ConAu 53, Ebony 1, InB&W 80,
LinLib L, LivgBAA, NegAl 76, –83,
SelBAA, WhoAm 74, –76, WhoE 74, –75*

Clarke, Mary Stetson 1911- *BioIn 10,
ConAu 8NR, –21R, SmATA 5,
WhoAmW 74, –75, –77, WhoE 83,
WrDr 76, –80, –82, –84*

Clarke, Robin Harwood 1937- *Au&Wr 6,*

ConAu 9NR, –13R, IntAu&W 76

Clarke, Ron 1937- *BioIn 7, –8, –9, –10, –12,
ConAu 107, CurBio 71, WhoTr&F 73*

Clarke, Thurston 1946- *ConAu 77*

Clarke, Tom E 1915- *ConAu 5R, WhoPNW*

Clarkson, E Margaret 1915- *ConAu 1R, –5NR,
IntAu&W 76, –77, SmATA 37, WrDr 76,
–80, –82, –84*

Clarkson, Ewan 1929- *BioIn 11, ConAu 25R,
SmATA 9, TwCCW 78, WhoWor 76, –78,
WrDr 76, –80, –82, –84*

Clarkson, Philip B 1924- *DrAS 74E, –78E,
–82E, WhoAm 74, –76, –78, –80*

Clary, Jack 1932- *ConAu 57, WhoAmL 83*

Clason, Clyde B *ScF&FL 1*

Claster, Jill Nadell 1932- *DrAS 74H, –78H,
WhoAm 80*

Clause, Frank *BioIn 6*

Clauser, Suzanne 1929- *ConAu 37R*

Clavel, Bernard 1923- *ConAu 2NR, –45,
IntAu&W 76, –77, –82, IntWW 74, –75,
–76, –77, –78, –79, –80, –81, –82, –83,
WhoFr 79, WhoWor 74, –82*

Clavell, James 1924- *BioIn 7, –12,
ConAu 25R, ConLC 6, –25[port],
CurBio 81[port], FilmgC, IntMPA 75,
NewYTBS 81[port], Novels, WhoAm 74,
–76, –78, –80, –82, WhoWor 74, WorAl,
WorEFlm, WrDr 80, –82, –84*

Clay, Patrice 1947- *ConAu 106*

Claypool, Jane 1933- *ConAu X*

Claypool, Jane *see also* Miner, Jane Claypool

Clayton, Jo 1939- *ConAu 81, EncSF*

Clayton, Keith 1928- *Au&Wr 6,
ConAu 11NR, –21R, Who 82, –83*

Clayton, Richard Henry Michael 1907- *BioIn 7,
–11, ConAu 4NR, –5R, EncMys,
IntAu&W 76, –77, Who 74, –82, –83,
WhoSpyF, WrDr 76, –80, –82*

Clayton, Thompson B 1904- *ConAu 57*

Cleare, John 1936- *ConAu 65, IntAu&W 77,
WrDr 76, –80, –82, –84*

Cleary, Beverly Atlee 1916- *AmAu&B,
AmWomWr, Au&ICB, AuBYP, BioIn 6,
–7, –8, –9, –10, –12, ChlLR 2, ConAu 1R,
–2NR, IntAu&W 77, –82, MorBMP,
MorJA, SmATA 2, TwCCW 78, –83,
WhoAm 74, –76, –78, –80, –82,
WhoAmW 74, –58, –61, –64, –66, –68, –70,
–72, –75, –77, –83, WrDr 76, –80, –82, –84*

Cleary, David Powers 1915- *ConAu 106*

Cleary, Jon 1917- *Au&Wr 6, BioIn 3, –6, –10,
ConAu 1R, –3NR, ConNov 72, –76, –82,
DcLEL 1940, IntAu&W 76, –77, –82,
Novels, TwCCr&M 80, Who 74, –82, –83,
WhoAm 78, –80, WhoWor 74, –76, –78,
–80, WorAu, WrDr 76, –80, –82, –84*

Cleaver, Bill 1920-1981 *BioIn 8,
ChlLR 6[port], ConAu 73, FourBJA,
SmATA 22[port], –27N, TwCCW 78, –83*

Cleaver, Bill *see also* Cleaver, William

Cleaver, Eldridge 1935- *AmAu&B, BioIn 8,*

–9, –10, –11, –12, *BlkAWP, CelR 73,*
CivR 74, CmCal, ConAu 21R,
CurBio 70, DcLEL 1940, LinLib L,
LivgBAA, MugS, NegAl 76[port],
–83[port], NewYTBS 77, PenC AM,
PolProf NF, WebE&AL, WhoBlA 77, –80,
WrDr 76, –80, –82, –84

Cleaver, Vera 1919- *AuBYP, BioIn 8,*
ChlLR 6[port], ConAu 73, FourBJA,
SmATA 22[port], TwCCW 78, –83,
WhoAm 78, –80, –82, WrDr 84

Cleaver, William 1920-1981 *AuBYP, BioIn 12,*
ConAu 104, FourBJA, WhoAm 78, –80,
–82

Cleaver, William *see also* Cleaver, Bill

Cleeve, Brian 1921- *Au&Wr 6, ConAu 1NR,*
–49, DclrL, DcIrW 1, IntAu&W 76, –77,
TwCCr&M 80, WrDr 76, –80, –82, –84

Clegg, John 1909- *Au&Wr 6, IntAu&W 76,*
WrDr 76, –80, –82, –84

Clemeau, Carol *ConAu X, DrAP&F 83*

Clemens, Samuel Langhorne 1835-1910
Alli SUP, AmAu, AmAu&B, AmBi,
AnCL, ApCAB, ArizL, AuBYP, BbD,
BiD&SB, BiDPara, BiDSA, BioIn 1, –2,
–3, –4, –5, –6, –7, –8, –9, –10, –11, –12,
CarSB, CasWL, CelCen, Chambr 3,
ChhPo, –S1, CmCal, CnDAL, ConAu 104,
CyAL 2, DcAmAu, DcAmB, DcAmSR,
DcBiPP, DcEnA, DcEnL, DcLB 12[port],
–23[port], DcLEL, DcNAA, Dis&D,
Drake, EncAAH, EncAB-H, EncMys,
EncO&P 78, EncSoH, EncWL, EvLB,
HarEnUS[port], JBA 34, LinLib L, –S,
LongCTC, NatCAB 6, OxAmH, OxAmL,
OxEng, PenC AM, RComWL, REn,
REnAL, REnAW, ScF&FL 1, TwCA,
TwCBDA, WebAB, –79, WhAm 1,
WhLit, YABC 2

Clemens, Samuel Langhorne *see also* Mark
Twain

Clemens, Samuel Langhorne *see also* Twain,
Mark

Clemens, Virginia Phelps 1941- *ConAu 85,*
SmATA 35

Clement, Hal 1922- *AmAu&B, BioIn 12,*
ConAu X, ConSFA, DcLB 8[port],
EncSF, Novels, ScF&FL 1, –2, WhoSciF,
WrDr 84

Clements, Bruce 1931- *AuBYP SUP,*
ConAu 5NR, –53, ScF&FL 1, –2,
SmATA 27[port], TwCCW 83

Cleminshaw, Clarence Higbee 1902-
ConAu 106, WhoAm 74, –76, –78, –80

Clerk, N W *ConAu X, SmATA X*

Clerk, N W *see also* Lewis, C S

Clery, Val 1924- *ConAu 3NR, –49*

Clewes, Dorothy 1907- *Au&Wr 6, AuBYP,*
BioIn 8, –9, ConAu 3NR, –5R, SmATA 1,
TwCCW 78, –83, WrDr 80, –82, –84

Clifford, Eth 1915- *AuBYP SUP, ConAu X,*
SmATA 3, WhoAmW 79

Clifford, Eth *see also* Rosenberg, Ethel

Clifford, Francis 1917-1975 *Alli, Au&Wr 6,*
BioIn 10, ConAu X, ConNov 76,
DcIrW 1, IntAu&W 76, Novels,
TwCCr&M 80, WhoSpyF, WhoWor 74,
WorAu 1970

Clifford, Francis *see also* Thompson, Arthur
Leonard Bell

Clifford, Martin 1910- *ConAu 11NR, –25R,*
WhoE 74

Clifford, Mary Louise 1926- *AuBYP SUP,*
ConAu 3NR, –5R, IntAu&W 77,
SmATA 23, WrDr 76, –80, –82, –84

Clifton, Lucille 1936- *BioIn 10, –11, –12,*
BlkAWP, ChlLR 5[port], ChhPo S1,
ConAu 2NR, –49, ConLC 19, ConP 75,
–80, DcLB 5[port], DrAP 75,
DrAP&F 83, SelBAA, SmATA 20,
TwCCW 78, –83, WhoAm 76, –78, –80,
–82, WhoBlA 77, –80, WrDr 76, –80, –82,
–84

Cline, C Terry, Jr. 1935- *BioIn 10,*
ConAu 8NR, –61

Cline, Linda 1941- *ConAu 65, WrDr 80, –82,*
–84

Cline, Ray Steiner 1918- *ConAu 106,*
WhoAm 74, –76, –78, –80, –82, WhoGov 72,
WhoWor 76, –82

Clinton-Baddeley, V C 1900?-1970 *ConAu 104,*
TwCCr&M 80

Clipman, William 1954- *ConAu 106*

Clissold, John Stephen Hallett 1913- *Au&Wr 6,*
IntAu&W 76, –77, –82

Clor, Harry M 1929- *ConAu 53*

Clurman, Harold 1901-1980 *AmAu&B,*
AnObit 1980[port], Au&Wr 6,
BiE&WWA, BioIn 2, –5, –8, –9, –10, –11,
–12, BlueB 76, CnThe, ConAmTC,
ConAu 1R, –2NR, –101, CurBio 59, –80N,
DcLEL 1940, EncWT, FilmgC,
IntAu&W 76, –77, –82, IntWW 74, –75,
–76, –77, –78, –79, –80, –81N,
NewYTBS 79, –80[port], NotNAT, –A,
OxThe, PenC AM, PIP&P, REnAL,
WhAm 7, WhoAm 78, –80, WhoAmJ 80,
WhoThe 15, –16, –81, WhoWor 74, –76,
–78, WhoWorJ 72, –78, WorEFlm,
WrDr 76, –80

Clymer, Eleanor 1906- *AuBYP, BioIn 7, –11,*
ConAu 9NR, –61, FourBJA,
IntAu&W 82, SmATA 9, TwCCW 78,
–83, WhoAm 78, –80, –82, WhoAmW 61,
WrDr 76, –80, –82, –84

Coan, Howard Charles 1940- *WhoE 81, –83*

Coates, Belle 1896- *BioIn 9, ConAu 5R,*
ForWC 70, SmATA 2

Coatsworth, Elizabeth 1893- *AmAu&B,*
AmNov, AmWomWr, AnCL, Au&ICB,
AuBYP, BioIn 2, –4, –7, –8, –9, –10, –11,
BkCL, ChlLR 2, ChhPo, –S1, –S2, –S3,
ConAu 4NR, –5R, DcLB 22[port],
FamMS, InWom, IntAu&W 76, JBA 34,

–51, LinLib L, MorBMP, Newb 1922,
OxAmL, REnAL, ScF&FL 1, –2,
SmATA 2, Str&VC, TwCA, TwCA SUP,
TwCCW 78, –83, WhE&EA, WhLit,
WhoAm 74, –76, –78, –80, –82,
WhoAmW 74, –58, –64, –66, –68, –70, –72,
WhoChL, WhoWor 74, WrDr 80, –82, –84

Cobb, Vicki 1938- AuBYP SUP, BioIn 11,
ChlLR 2, ConAu 33R, SmATA 8,
WrDr 76, –80, –82, –84

Coblentz, Stanton A 1896- AmAu&B,
AnMV 1926, Au&Wr 6, BioIn 3, –5,
ChhPo, –S1, –S2, –S3, ConAu 5R,
ConSFA, CurBio 54, DrAP&F 83,
EncSF, IntAu&W 77, –82, IntWWP 77,
REnAL, ScF&FL 1, –2, WhNAA,
WhoAm 74, –76, –78, –80, –82, WhoSciF,
WrDr 76, –80, –82, –84

Cocker, Joe 1944?- BioIn 8, –9, –11,
EncPR&S, –77, IlEncRk, RkOn 78, –84,
RolSEnR 83, WhoRocM 82, WorAl

Cockett, Mary 1915- Au&Wr 6, BioIn 9,
ConAu 4NR, –9R, IntAu&W 76, –77, –82,
SmATA 3, TwCCW 78, –83, WrDr 80,
–82, –84

Cockrell, Marian 1909- AmAu&B, AmNov,
BioIn 2, ConAu P-2, InWom, ScF&FL 1,
WrDr 84

Cody, William Frederick 1846-1917 AmAu&B,
AmBi, ApCAB, ApCAB X, BioIn 1, –2,
–3, –4, –5, –6, –7, –8, –9, –10, –11, –12,
DcAmB, DcCathB, DcNAA, EncAAH,
EncAB-H, FilmgC, HarEnUS, HsB&A,
LinLib L, –S, NatCAB B, NotNAT B,
OxAmH, OxAmL, OxFilm, OxThe, REn,
REnAL, TwCBDA, WebAB, –79,
WebAMB, WhDW, WhAm 1, WhScrn 2,
WorAl

Coe, Douglas AuBYP, ConAu X, OhA&B,
SmATA X

Coe, Douglas see also Epstein, Beryl Williams

Coe, Douglas see also Epstein, Samuel

Coe, Michael Douglas 1929- AmM&WS 73S,
–76P, ConAu 1R, –4NR, WhoAm 74, –76,
–78, –80, –82, WhoE 74, –75, –77,
WrDr 76, –80, –82, –84

Coen, Rena Neumann 1925- BioIn 12,
ConAu 13R, ForWC 70, SmATA 20,
WhoAmW 75, –77, WrDr 76, –80, –84

Coens, Mary Xavier 1918- ConAu 21R,
DrAS 74E, –78E, –82E, WhoAmW 74, –70,
WomPO 78

Coerr, Eleanor 1922- AuBYP SUP, BioIn 9,
ConAu 11NR, –25R, SmATA 1,
WhoAmW 77, –79, –83, WrDr 76, –80, –82,
–84

Coffey, Dairine 1933- AuBYP SUP,
ChhPo S1, ConAu 21R

Coffin, Geoffrey AuBYP, BioIn 1, –2, –9,
ConAu X, EncMys, SmATA X, –3,
WhoSpyF

Coffin, Geoffrey see also Mason, F VanWyck

Coffin, Robert Peter Tristram 1892-1955
AmAu&B, AnMV 1926, BioIn 1, –3, –4,
–5, –6, –7, –8, –9, –11, ChhPo, –S1, –S2, –S3,
CnDAL, ConAmA, DcAmB S5, DcLEL,
LongCTC, NatCAB 45, ObitOF 79,
OxAmL, PenC AM, REn, REnAL,
Str&VC, TwCA, TwCA SUP, WhAm 3,
WhNAA

Coffman, Ramon P 1896- AmAu&B,
Au&Wr 6, BioIn 9, ConAu P-2,
IndAu 1917, SmATA 4

Coggins, Jack Banham 1914- AuBYP, BioIn 6,
–7, –9, ConAu 2NR, –5R, IntAu&W 77,
–82, MorJA, SmATA 2, WhoAm 74, –76,
–78, –80, –82, WhoAmA 82, WrDr 76,
–80, –82, –84

Cogswell, Theodore R 1918- ConAu 1R, –4NR,
ConSFA, DrAS 74E, –78E, –82E, EncSF,
IntAu&W 76, ScF&FL 1, –2, WhoE 75,
WhoSciF, WrDr 76, –80, –82, –84

Cohen, Barbara 1932- AuBYP SUP, BioIn 11,
ConAu 4NR, –53, CurBio 57, SmATA 10

Cohen, Daniel 1936- AuBYP SUP, BioIn 11,
ChlLR 3, ConAu 1NR, –45,
IntAu&W 77, –82, SmATA 8

Cohen, Florence Chanock 1927- ConAu 5R,
IntAu&W 76, WhoAmW 68

Cohen, Joel H AuBYP SUP

Cohen, Leonard 1934- BioIn 8, –9, –10, –11,
–12, BlueB 76, CanWW 79, –80, –81, –83,
CanWr, CasWL, CelR 73, ChhPo S1,
ConAu 21R, ConLC 3, ConNov 72, –76,
–82, ConP 70, –75, –80, CreCan 1,
CurBio 69, DcLEL 1940, EncPR&S 77,
EncWL 81, IntAu&W 76, –77,
IntWWP 77, ModCmwL, OxCan,
OxCan SUP, RolSEnR 83, WebE&AL,
WhoAm 74, –76, –78, –80, –82, WorAl,
WorAu 1970, WrDr 76, –80, –82, –84

Cohen, Peter Zachary 1931- BioIn 9,
ConAu 33R, IntAu&W 82, SmATA 4,
WrDr 76, –80, –82, –84

Cohen, Richard Murry 1938- ConAu 103

Cohn, Angelo 1914- BioIn 12, ConAu 4NR,
–5R, IntAu&W 77, SmATA 19

Cohn, Nik 1946- Au&Wr 6, AuBYP SUP,
ConAu 102

Coit, Margaret Louise 1919?- AmAu&B,
AmWomWr, Au&Wr 6, AuBYP, BioIn 2,
–3, –4, –7, –9, ConAu 1R, –5NR,
CurBio 51, DrAS 74H, EncAAH,
ForWC 70, InWom, IntAu&W 77,
OxAmL, REnAL, SmATA 2,
TwCA SUP, WhoAm 74, –76, –78, –80,
–82, WhoAmW 74, –58, –64, –66, –68, –70,
–72

Coker, Jerry 1932- BiDAmM, ConAu 6NR,
–9R, IndAu 1917

Colbert, Edwin Harris 1905- AmM&WS 73P,
–76P, –79P, –82P, BioIn 2, –3, –7,
BlueB 76, ConAu 8NR, –61, CurBio 65,
IntWW 74, –75, –76, –77, –78, –79, –80, –81,

−82, −83, WhoAm 74, −76, −78, −80, −82, WrDr 76, −80, −82, −84

Colby, C B 1904-1977 *ConAu 1R, −6NR, IntAu&W 77, SmATA 3, −35*

Colby, Carroll Burleigh 1904-1977 *AuBYP, BioIn 6, −7, −9, ConAu 1R, MorJA, SmATA 3, WhAm 7, WhoAm 74, −76, −78*

Colby, Jean Poindexter 1970?- *AuBYP SUP, BioIn 2, ChhPo S1, ConAu 1R, −5NR, ForWC 70, IntAu&W 77, SmATA 23[port], WhoAmW 74, −58, −61, −64, −70, −72, −75, WrDr 76, −80, −82, −84*

Cole, Ernest *InB&W 80*

Cole, Joanna 1944- *SmATA 37*

Cole, Lewis 1946- *ConAu 109*

Cole, Lois Dwight 1902?-1979 *AmAu&B, AuBYP, BioIn 8, −11, ConAu 1R, −4NR, −104, SmATA 10, −26N, WhoAmW 58, −61, −68, −70, −72*

Cole, Lois Dwight *see also* Avery, Lynn

Cole, Lois Dwight *see also* Dudley, Nancy

Cole, Lois Dwight *see also* Dwight, Allan

Cole, Lois Dwight *see also* Eliot, Anne

Cole, Sheila R 1939- *ConAu 4NR, −53, SmATA 24[port], WrDr 76, −80, −82, −84*

Cole, William 1919- *AuBYP, BioIn 8, −11, BkP, ChhPo, −S1, −S2, −S3, ConAu 7NR, −9R, DrAP 75, FourBJA, IntWWP 77, SmATA 9, WrDr 76, −80, −82, −84*

Coleman, Eleanor 1901- *WhoAmW 61, −64*

Coleman, John Royston 1921- *AmEA 74, AmM&WS 73S, −78S, AuNews 1, BioIn 9, −10, CanWW 70, −79, −80, −81, ConAu 1R, −1NR, CurBio 74, LEduc 74, WhoAm 74, −76, −78, −80, −82, WhoE 74*

Coleman, Lonnie 1920-1982 *AmAu&B, AmNov, BiE&WWA, BioIn 2, −4, −5, ConAu 107, −77, CurBio 58, −82N, NewYTBS 82, NotNAT*

Coleman, Ronny Jack 1940- *WhoGov 77*

Colen, B D 1946- *ConAu 65*

Coleridge, Samuel Taylor 1771?-1834 *Alli, AtlBL, BbD, BiD&SB, BiDLA, BioIn 1, −2, −3, −4, −5, −6, −7, −8, −9, −10, −11, −12, BrAu 19, BrWr 4, CasWL, CelCen, Chambr 3, ChhPo, −S1, −S2, −S3, CnE&AP, CrtT 2, −4, CyWA, DcBiPP, DcEnA, DcEnL, DcEuL, DcLEL, Dis&D, EncO&P 78, EncWT, EvLB, LinLib L, −S, LongCEL, LuthC 75, McGEWB, MouLC 3, NewC, NotNAT B, OxEng, OxMus, OxThe, PenC ENG, RAdv 1, RComWL, REn, WebE&AL, WhDW, WorAl*

Coles, Robert 1929- *AmAu&B, AmM&WS 79P, −82P, Au&Wr 6, AuBYP SUP, BiDrAPA 77, BioIn 8, −9, −10, −11, BlueB 76, CelR 73, ConAu 3NR, −45, CurBio 69, IntAu&W 76, NewYTBS 78, SmATA 23[port], WhoAm 74, −76, −82,*

WhoE 83, WorAu 1970, WrDr 80, −82, −84

Colford, William E 1908-1971 *BioIn 9, −11, ConAu 5R, −33R, NatCAB 56, NewYTBE 71, WhAm 5*

Collett, Rosemary K 1931- *ConAu 69*

Collier, Christopher 1930- *AuBYP SUP, BioIn 11, −12, ConAu 33R, DrAS 74H, −78H, −82H, SmATA 16, WhoE 75*

Collier, James Lincoln 1928- *AuBYP SUP, BioIn 7, −11, ChlLR 3, ConAu 4NR, −9R, SmATA 8*

Collier, John 1901-1980 *AnObit 1980, BioIn 2, −4, −11, −12, ConAu 10NR, −65, −97, ConNov 72, −76, DcLEL, EncMys, FilmgC, IntAu&W 76, −77, LongCTC, NewC, NewYTBS 80, Novels, PenC AM, REn, REnAL, ScF&FL 1, TwCA, TwCA SUP, TwCCr&M 80, WhoHr&F, WrDr 76, −80*

Collier, Peter 1929?- *ConAu 65, WrDr 82, −84*

Collier, Richard 1924- *Au&Wr 6, BioIn 5, ConAu 1R, −5NR, IntAu&W 76, −77, −82, WhoWor 76, −78, WrDr 76, −80, −82, −84*

Collier, Zena 1926- *ConAu X, −3NR, DrAP&F 83, IntAu&W 77X, −82X, SmATA 23[port], WhoAm 80, WhoAmW 81, WrDr 76, −80, −82, −84*

Collins, David R 1940- *AuBYP SUP, BioIn 10, ConAu 11NR, −29R, IntAu&W 76A, SmATA 7, WhoMW 74, −76, −78, −80, −82, WrDr 76, −80, −82, −84*

Collins, Gary Ross 1934- *AmM&WS 73S, −78S, ConAu 7NR, −57, WhoMW 74, −76, −78*

Collins, Henry Hill 1907-1961 *AuBYP, BioIn 5, −8*

Collins, Jean E 1948- *ConAu 110*

Collins, Judy 1939- *BiDAmM, BioIn 7, −8, −10, −11, −12, CelR 73, ConAu 103, CurBio 69, EncFCWM 69, EncPR&S 77, GoodHs, NewYTBS 76, RkOn 78, −84, RolSEnR 83, WhoAm 74, −76, −78, −80, −82, WhoAmW 74, −66, −68, −70, −72, −75, −77, −79, −81, −83, WhoRocM 82, WhoWor 74, WorAl*

Collins, Larry 1929- *AmAu&B, BioIn 9, −12, CelR 73, ConAu 65, EncFCWM 69, NewYTBS 80[port], WhoAm 74, −76, −78, −80, −82, WhoWor 74, −76, −78, WrDr 84*

Collins, Max, Jr. 1948- *ConAu 103*

Collins, Meghan 1926- *ConAu 101*

Collins, Michael 1924- *ConAu X, EncMys, ScF&FL 1, −2, TwCCr&M 80, WrDr 82*

Collins, Michael 1930- *AmM&WS 73P, −79P, ASpks, BioIn 7, −8, −9, −10, −11, −12, BlueB 76, CelR 73, ConAu 5NR, −53, CurBio 75, EncSF, IntWW 74, −75, −76, −77, −78, −79, −80, −81, −82, −83, LinLib S, UFOEn, WebAMB, Who 74, −82, −83, WhoAm 74, −76, −78, −80, −82,*

ConAu 33R, SmATA 6, TwCCW 83,
WrDr 76, –80, –82, –84

Conigliaro, Tony 1945- CurBio 71,
NewYTBE 71, NewYTBS 83[port],
WhoProB 73

Conklin, Barbara P 1927- ConAu 109

Conklin, Gladys Plemon 1903- AuBYP,
BiDrLUS 70, BioIn 8, –9, ConAu 1R,
–4NR, ForWC 70, FourBJA, SmATA 2,
WhoAmW 64, –66, –75, –77, WhoLibS 55,
–66

Conklin, Groff 1904-1968 AmAu&B, BioIn 8,
ConAu 1R, –3NR, EncSF, ScF&FL 1, –2,
WhoSciF

Conly, Robert L 1918-1973 AuBYP SUP,
BioIn 9, ConAu 41R, –73, ScF&FL 1,
SmATA 23[port]

Conly, Robert L see also O'Brien, Robert C

Conn, Frances G 1925- AuBYP SUP,
ConAu 33R

Conn, Martha Orr 1935- ConAu 93

Connell, Evan S, Jr. 1924- AmAu&B,
Au&Wr 6, BioIn 12, CmCal, ConAu 1R,
–2NR, ConLC 4, –6, ConNov 72, –76, –82,
DcLB Y81A[port], –2, DcLEL 1940,
DrAF 76, IntAu&W 76, –77, LinLib L,
ModAL SUP, OxAmL, PenC AM,
RAdv 1, REnAL, WhoAm 74, –76, –78,
–80, –82, WhoTwCL, WhoWor 74,
WorAu, WrDr 76, –80, –82, –84

Connell, Richard 1893-1949 Alli, AmAu&B,
BioIn 2, –4, DcNAA, EncMys, LinLib L,
NatCAB 36, ObitOF 79, REnAL, TwCA,
TwCA SUP, WhAm 2, WhE&EA,
WhNAA

Connelly, John Peter 1926- WhoE 74,
WhoMW 74, –76, –78, –80, –82

Connelly, Marcus Cook 1890- AmAu&B,
BiE&WWA, Chambr 3, CnDAL, CnMD,
CnThe, ConAmA, ConAmL, ConDr 73,
CurBio 69, DcLEL, IntAu&W 76,
IntWW 74, LongCTC, McGEWD,
ModAL, ModWD, OxAmL, PenC AM,
REn, REnAL, REnWD, TwCA,
TwCA SUP, Who 74, WhoAm 74,
WhoThe 15, WhoWor 74, WrDr 76

Conner, Patrick 1947- ConAu 106, WrDr 82

Conners, Bernard F 1926- BioIn 9,
ConAu 41R, IntAu&W 76, WhoE 75, –77

Connolly, Ray 1940- ConAu 101,
IntAu&W 77, –82, WrDr 76, –80, –82, –84

Connor, Ralph 1860-1937 BioIn 1, –2, –11,
CanWr, CasWL, Chambr 3, ChhPo,
ConAu X, CreCan 1, DcBiA, DcLEL,
DcNAA, EvLB, LinLib LP, –S,
LongCTC, MacDCB 78, NewC, OxAmL,
OxCan, REnAL, TwCA, TwCA SUP,
TwCCW 78, TwCWr, WhLit, WhNAA

Connor, Ralph see also Gordon, Charles William

Conot, Robert E 1929- AmAu&B,
ConAu 2NR, –45, WrDr 76, –80, –82, –84

Conquest, Robert 1917- BioIn 8, –10,

BlueB 76, ConAu 9NR, –13R, ConNov 72,
ConP 70, –75, –80, ConSFA, EncSF,
IntAu&W 76, –77, –82, IntWWP 77, –82,
LinLib L, LongCTC, RAdv 1,
ScF&FL 1, –2, TwCWr, Who 74, –82, –83,
WhoSciF, WorAu, WrDr 76, –80, –82, –84

Conrad, Joseph 1857-1924 AtlBL, BbD,
BiD&SB, BioIn 1, –2, –3, –4, –5, –6, –7, –8,
–9, –10, –11, –12, BrWr 6, CasWL,
Chambr 3, CnMD, CnMWL, ConAu 104,
CyWA, DcEnA AP, DcEuL,
DcLB 10[port], DcLEL, Dis&D, EncMys,
EncSF, EncWL, –81[port], EvLB, FilmgC,
JBA 34, LinLib L, –S, LongCEL,
LongCTC, MakMC, McGEWB, ModBrL,
ModBrL SUP, ModWD, NewC,
Novels[port], OxEng, OxShips,
PenC ENG, RAdv 1, RComWL, REn,
ScF&FL 1, SmATA 27[port], TwCA,
TwCA SUP, TwCLC 1, –6[port], TwCWr,
WebE&AL, WhDW, WhoSpyF,
WhoTwCL, WorAl

Conrad, Sybil 1921- AuBYP, BioIn 8,
ConAu 21R

Conroy, Frank 1936- AmAu&B, BioIn 8, –9,
–11, ConAu 77, WhoAm 74

Conroy, Pat 1945?- AuNews 1, BioIn 9, –10,
–12, BioNews 74, ConAu 85,
DcLB 6[port]

Considine, Bob 1906-1975 AmAu&B,
AuNews 2, BioIn 1, –5, –7, –10, –11,
CathA 1930, CelR 73, –73, ConAu X, –61,
–93, CurBio 47, –75, –75N, NewYTBS 75,
ObitOF 79, REnAL, WhAm 6, –7,
WhoAm 74, –76, WhoWor 74, –76,
WorAl

Constable, Trevor James 1925- ConAu 89,
UFOEn[port]

Constant, Alberta Wilson 1908-1981
AuBYP SUP, BioIn 3, ConAu 1R, –4NR,
–109, SmATA 22[port], –28N

Conze, Edward 1904- Au&Wr 6, BioIn 12,
ConAu 13R, IntAu&W 76

Cook, Ann Turner GoodHs

Cook, Bob 1957?-1981 BioIn 12

Cook, Bruce 1932- ConAu 33R

Cook, David 1929- ConAu 107

Cook, Fred James 1911- AmAu&B, AuBYP,
BioIn 4, –5, –7, –9, ConAu 3NR, –9R,
DcAmAu, SmATA 2, WhoAm 74, –76,
–78, –80, –82, WhoWor 74

Cook, Glen 1944- ScF&FL 1, –2

Cook, James Gordon 1916- ConAu 9R

Cook, Marjorie 1920- ConAu 81

Cook, Paul H 1950- ConAu 106, IntWWP 77,
–82

Cook, Robert William Arthur 1931- Au&Wr 6,
ConAu 25R

Cook, Robert William Arthur see also Cook,
Robin

Cook, Robin 1931- ConAu X, DcLEL 1940,
ScF&FL 1, –2, WrDr 76, –80, –82, –84

Cook, Robin *see also* Cook, Robert William Arthur

Cook, Stephani 1944?- *BioIn 12, ConAu 106*

Cook, Terry 1942- *ConAu 73*

Cooke, Alistair 1908- *AmAu&B, AuNews 1, BioIn 2, -3, -4, -8, -9, -10, -11, -12, BlueB 76, CelR 73, ConAu 9NR, -57, CurBio 52, -74, IntAu&W 77, IntMPA 77, -75, -76, -78, -79, -81, -82, -84, IntWW 74, -75, -76, -77, -78, -79, -80, -81, -82, -83, LesBEnT, LongCTC, NewYTET, OxAmL, REnAL, TwCA SUP, Who 74, -82, -83, WorAl, WrDr 76, -80, -82, -84*

Cooke, Barbara 1913- *AuBYP, BioIn 7, ConAu 57*

Cooke, Barbara *see also* Alexander, Anna Barbara Cooke

Cooke, David Coxe 1917- *AuBYP, BioIn 8, -9, ConAu 1R, -2NR, SmATA 2*

Cooke, Donald Ewin 1916- *AuBYP, BioIn 7, -9, ConAu 1R, -4NR, ScF&FL 1, SmATA 2, WhoAmA 73, -76, -78, -80, WhoE 75, -77*

Cookson, Catherine 1906- *Au&Wr 6, BioIn 8, -9, -10, -11, ConAu 9NR, -13R, IntAu&W 76, Novels, SmATA 9, Who 83, WrDr 76, -80, -82, -84*

Coolidge, Olivia 1908- *AuBYP, BioIn 6, -7, -9, BkCL, ConAu 2NR, -5R, MorJA, ScF&FL 1, SmATA 1, -26[port], TwCCW 78, WhoAmW 61, -64, WrDr 80, -82, -84*

Coombs, Charles Ira 1914- *AuBYP, BioIn 7, -9, ConAu 4NR, -5R, ScF&FL 1, -2, SmATA 3*

Coon, Carleton Stevens 1904-1981 *AmAu&B, AmM&WS 73S, -76P, AnObit 1981[port], Au&Wr 6, BioIn 4, -5, -10, -12, BlueB 76, ConAu 2NR, -5R, -104, CurBio 55, -81N, FifIDA, InSci, IntAu&W 76, -77, -82, IntWW 74, -75, -76, -77, -78, -79, -80, -81, -82N, McGMS 80[port], WhAm 7, WhoAm 74, -76, -78, -80, WhoWor 74, -76, -78, WorAu*

Cooney, Caroline B 1947- *ConAu 97*

Cooney, Timothy J 1929?- *BioIn 9, ConAu 107, WhoE 74*

Coontz, Otto 1946- *ConAu 105, SmATA 33[port]*

Cooper, Alice 1948- *BioIn 9, -10, -11, -12, BioNews 74, CelR 73, -73, ConAu 106, EncPR&S, -77, IllEncRk, RkOn 78, -84, RkOneH, RolSEnR 83, WhoAm 74, -76, -78, -80, -82, WhoRocM 82, WorAl*

Cooper, Alice *see also* Furnier, Vincent

Cooper, Darien B 1937- *ConAu 1NR, -49*

Cooper, Elizabeth Keyser 1910?- *ConAu 1R, -1NR, FourBJA, WhoAmW 61*

Cooper, Gale S 1946- *BiDrAPA 77*

Cooper, Gordon 1932- *AuBYP SUP,*

ConAu 61, IntAu&W 77, SmATA 23[port], TwCCW 78, -83, WrDr 76, -80, -82, -84

Cooper, Harold Eugene 1928- *AmM&WS 73P, -76P, -79P, ConAu 45*

Cooper, Harold R 1910?-1978 *BioIn 11, ConAu 77*

Cooper, Henry Spotswood Fenimore, Jr. 1933- *ConAu 69, WhoE 75, -77*

Cooper, Irving Spencer 1922- *AmM&WS 73P, -76P, -79P, -82P, BioIn 7, -10, -11, -12, ConAu 69, CurBio 74, WhoAm 74, -76, -78, -80, -82, WhoE 74, WhoWor 76, -78*

Cooper, James Fenimore 1789-1851 *Alli, AmAu, AmAu&B, AmBi, AmWr, ApCAB, AtlBL, AuBYP, BbD, BiD&SB, BioIn 1, -2, -3, -4, -5, -6, -7, -8, -9, -10, -11, -12, CasWL, CelCen, Chambr 3, CnDAL, CrtT 3, -4, CyAL 1, CyWA, DcAmAu, DcAmB, DcBiA, DcBiPP, DcEnA, DcEnL, DcLB 3, DcLEL, DcNAA, EncAAH, EncAB-H, EvLB, FilmgC, HarEnUS[port], HsB&A, LinLib L, -S, McGEWB, MnBBF, MouLC 3, NatCAB 1, Novels[port], OxAmH, OxAmL, OxEng, OxShips, PenC AM, RAdv 1, RComWL, REn, REnAL, REnAW, SmATA 19, TwCBDA, WebAB, -79, WebE&AL, WhDW, WhAm HS, WhoBW&I A, WhoChL, WhoSpyF, WorAl*

Cooper, Jamie Lee *ConAu 9R, IndAu 1917*

Cooper, Lettice 1897- *Au&Wr 6, ConAu 5NR, -9R, ConNov 72, -76, -82, IntAu&W 76, -77, -82, SmATA 35, TwCCW 78, -83, WhE&EA, WhLit, WrDr 76, -80, -82, -84*

Cooper, Louise Field 1905- *AmAu&B, AmNov, BioIn 2, -4, ConAu 1R, -4NR, -107, CurBio 50, InWom, REnAL, ScF&FL 1, -2, TwCA SUP, WhoAm 74, -76, -78, -80, -82, WhoAmW 74, -58, -66, -68, -70, -72, WhoHr&F*

Cooper, Lynna 1911- *ConAu X*

Cooper, Margaret 1893- *ChhPo S2, WhE&EA*

Cooper, Paulette 1944?- *ConAu 37R, IntAu&W 76, -77, WhoAmW 75, -83, WhoE 77, -79, -81, -83, WrDr 76, -80, -82, -84*

Cooper, Susan 1935- *Au&Wr 6, AuBYP SUP, BioIn 9, -11, ChlLR 4[port], ConAu 29R, EncSF, FourBJA, IntAu&W 82, ScF&FL 1, -2, SmATA 4, TwCCW 78, -83, WhoAm 76, -78, -80, -82, WrDr 76, -80, -82, -84*

Coover, Robert 1932- *AmAu&B, BioIn 10, ConAu 3NR, -45, ConLC 3, -7, -15, ConNov 72, -76, -82, DcLB Y81A[port], -2, DcLEL 1940, DrAF 76, DrAP&F 83, EncSF, IntAu&W 76, -77, -82, ModAL SUP, Novels, PenC AM,*

RAdv 1, WhoAm 74, –76, –78, –80, –82,
WhoE 74, –75, WorAu 1970, WrDr 76,
–80, –82, –84
Cope, Myron 1929- ConAu 57, WhoE 77
Coppel, Alfred 1921- ConAu 10NR, –17R,
ConSFA, DcLB Y83B[port], DrAF 76,
EncSF, ScF&FL 1, –2, WhoAm 82,
WhoSciF, WhoWest 74, –76, –78,
WrDr 76, –80, –82, –84
Coppel, Alfred see also Gilman, Robert Cham
Copper, Basil 1924- Au&Wr 6, IntAu&W 76,
ScF&FL 1, –2, TwCCr&M 80,
WhoHr&F, WrDr 76, –80, –82, –84
Copper, Marcia S 1934- ConAu 53
Corbett, James Edward 1875-1955 AuBYP,
BioIn 1, –3, –4, –8, –12, CurBio 46, –55
Corbett, Scott 1913- Au&Wr 6, AuBYP,
BioIn 8, –9, ChlLR 1, ConAu 1R, –1NR,
FourBJA, IntAu&W 76, –77, –82,
ScF&FL 1, –2, SmATA 2, TwCCW 78,
–83, WhoAm 80, –82, WrDr 80, –82, –84
Corbin, Richard 1911- ConAu 3NR, –5R,
DrAS 74E, –78E, –82E, WhoE 75, –77
Corcoran, Barbara 1911- AuBYP SUP,
BioIn 9, ConAu 11NR, –21R,
ConLC 17, DrAP&F 83, IntAu&W 82,
SmATA 3, WhoAm 78, –80, –82,
WrDr 76, –80, –82, –84
Corcoran, Barbara see also Dixon, Paige
Corcoran, Barbara see also Hamilton, Gail
Cordwell, Miriam 1908- ConAu 89,
WhoAmW 74, –58, –61, –64, –66, –68, –70,
–72, –75, –77, –79, WhoE 74, –79, –81
Corle, Edwin 1906-1956 AmAu&B, BioIn 4,
–6, –7, CmCal, NatCAB 46, OxAmL,
REnAL, TwCA SUP, WhAm 3,
WhNAA
Corlett, William 1938- ConAu 103,
TwCCW 78, –83, WhoS&SW 76, –78, –80,
WhoTech 82, WrDr 80, –82, –84
Corley, Edwin 1931-1981 BioIn 8, –12,
ConAu 105, –25R, EncSF, ScF&FL 1, –2,
WhoAm 74
Corliss, William R 1926- ConAu 1NR, –45
Cormack, Margaret L 1912- AmM&WS 73S,
–78S, ConAu 1R
Cormack, Maribelle 1902- AuBYP, BioIn 2,
–7, JBA 51, ScF&FL 1, WhoAmW 58,
–61, –64, –66, –68, –72
Cormier, Robert 1925- BioIn 11, –12,
ConAu 1R, –5NR, ConLC 12,
SmATA 10, TwCCW 83, WhoAm 82,
WrDr 84
Corn, Ira George, Jr. 1921-1982 BioIn 12,
ConAu 106, –85, Dun&B 79,
NewYTBE 70, NewYTBS 82[port],
St&PR 75, WhoAm 74, –76, –78, –80, –82,
WhoF&I 74, –75, –77, –79, –81,
WhoS&SW 78, –82, WhoWor 78, –80
Cornelisen, Ann 1926- BioIn 9, ConAu 25R
Cornelius, Temple H 1891-1964 BioIn 7,
ConAu P-1

Cornell, James 1938- ConAu 11NR, –69,
SmATA 27[port]
Cornell, Jean Gay 1920- ConAu 1NR, –45,
SmATA 23, WhoAmW 77
Cornell, William Ainsworth 1923- WhoAm 76,
–78
Corner, George Washington 1889-1981
AmM&WS 73P, –76P, –79P,
AnObit 1981[port], BioIn 3, –4, –12,
BlueB 76, ConAu 102, –104, IntWW 74,
–75, –76, –77, –78, –79, –80, –81, –82N,
McGMS 80[port], NewYTBS 81[port],
WhNAA, Who 74, –82N, WhoAm 74, –76,
–78, –80
Cornish, Samuel 1935- BlkAWP, ChhPo S3,
ConAu 41R, ConP 70, –75, –80,
DcLEL 1940, DrAP 75, IntWWP 77,
LivgBAA, SelBAA, SmATA X, –23[port],
WrDr 76, –80, –82, –84
Cornwall, Ian Wolfran 1909- Au&Wr 6,
BioIn 5, ConAu 9R, IntAu&W 76, –77,
ScF&FL 1, Who 74, –82, –83
Cornwell, David John Moore 1931- Au&Wr 6,
BioIn 6, –7, –10, –11, –12, BlueB 76,
ConAu 5R, ConLC 9, –15, EncMys,
IntAu&W 76, –77, IntWW 74, –75, –76,
–77, –78, –79, –80, –81, –82, –83, NewC,
NewYTBS 74, Who 74, –82, –83,
WhoAm 80, –82, WhoSpyF, WhoWor 74,
–76, –78, –82, WorAu, WrDr 76, –80, –82,
–84
Cornwell, David John Moore see also LeCarre,
John
Correy, Lee 1928- BioIn 11, ConAu X, –65,
EncSF, ScF&FL 1, –2, SmATA X,
WrDr 84
Correy, Lee see also Stine, George Harry
Corrigan, Barbara 1922- BioIn 11, ChhPo,
ConAu 57, SmATA 8
Corrigan, Robert W 1927- BiE&WWA,
BlueB 76, ConAu 5R, –6NR, DrAS 74E,
–78E, –82E, NotNAT, WhoAm 74, –76,
–78, –80, –82, WhoWor 74, WrDr 76, –80,
–82, –84
Corsaro, Maria C 1949- ConAu 107
Cortesi, Lawrence ConAu X
Corwen, Leonard 1921- ConAu 93
Cosman, Madeleine Pelner 1937- ConAu 105,
DrAS 74E, –78E, –82E
Costain, Thomas Bertram 1885-1965 AmAu&B,
AmNov, AuBYP, BioIn 2, –3, –4, –7, –8,
–12, CanWr, ConAu 5R, –25R, CreCan 2,
CurBio 53, –65, DcAmB S7,
DcLB 9[port], DcLEL, –1940, LinLib L,
–S, LongCTC, MacDCB 78, ObitOF 79,
OxAmL, OxCan, REn, REnAL,
ScF&FL 1, –2, TwCA SUP, TwCWr,
WhAm 4, WhJnl, WorAl
Costello, David F 1904- AmM&WS 73P,
–76P, –79P, –82P, ConAu 33R,
SmATA 23[port], WhoPNW, WrDr 76,

WrDr 80, –82, –84
Costello, John Edmond 1943- *ConAu 85,*
WhoE 81, –83
Cott, Nancy Falik 1945- *ConAu 81,*
DrAS 78H, –82H, WhoAmW 79
Cotten, Sallie Southall 1846-1929 *BiDSA,*
BioIn 3, ChhPo, –S1, EncSoH, NotAW,
WhAm 1, WomWWA 14
Cotterell, Arthur George 1917- *WhoArt 80, –82*
Cottler, Joseph 1899- *ConAu P-2,*
SmATA 22[port]
Cottrell, Leonard 1913-1974 *Au&Wr 6,*
AuBYP, BioIn 8, –10, BlueB 76N,
ConAu 4NR, –5R, DcLEL 1940,
FourBJA, IntAu&W 76, –77, IntWW 74,
–75, SmATA 24[port], TwCWr,
WhAm 6, Who 74, WhoWor 74, WorAu,
WrDr 76
Couffer, Jack C 1924- *Au&Wr 6, ConAu 1R,*
–1NR, FilmgC
Cougar, John *WhoRocM 82*
Coughlan, Robert 1914- *AmAu&B, ConAu 65,*
IndAu 1917, WhoAm 78, –80, –82,
WrDr 76, –80, –82, –84
Coughlin, George G 1900- *ConAu 107,*
WhoE 74
Coulson, Juanita 1933- *ConAu 9NR, –25R,*
ConSFA, EncSF, IntAu&W 77, –82,
ScF&FL 1, –2, WhoHr&F, WhoSciF,
WrDr 76, –80, –82, –84
Counsilman, James Edward 1920- *BioIn 10, –12,*
WhoAm 82
Couper, John Mill 1914- *Au&Wr 6,*
ConAu 45, ConP 70, IntWWP 77
Courlander, Harold 1908- *AnCL, AuBYP,*
BioIn 6, –8, –10, –11, BkCL, ConAu 3NR,
–9R, IndAu 1917, IntAu&W 76, –77, –82,
MichAu 80, MorJA, SmATA 6
Cournos, John 1881-1966 *AmAu&B, BioIn 4,*
–7, –11, ConAmL, ConAu P-2, DcLEL,
LongCTC, OxAmL, REnAL, ScF&FL 1,
TwCA, TwCA SUP, WhE&EA, WhLit,
WhoLA
Courter, Gay 1944- *ConAu 7NR, –57,*
WrDr 84
Courthion, Pierre-Barthelemy 1902- *ConAu 81,*
IntAu&W 77, –82, IntWW 74, –75, –76,
–77, –78, –79, –80, –81, –82, –83, WhoFr 79,
WhoWor 74, –76, –78
Cousins, Norman 1912?- *AmAu&B, BioIn 3,*
–4, –8, –9, –10, –11, –12, BlueB 76,
CelR 73, ChhPo, ConAu 17R, CurBio 43,
–77, DcLEL 1940, IntAu&W 76, –77,
IntWW 74, –75, –76, –77, –78, –79, –80, –81,
–82, –83, LinLib L, –S, NewYTBE 71,
NewYTBS 79, OxAmL, PolProf E,
PolProf K, REn, REnAL, TwCA SUP,
WebAB, –79, Who 74, –82, –83,
WhoAm 74, –76, –78, –80, –82, WhoE 74,
–79, WhoF&I 74, WhoWor 74, WorAl,
WrDr 76, –80, –82, –84
Cousteau, Jacques-Yves 1910- *AnCL, AsBiEn,*

BiESc, BioIn 1, –2, –3, –4, –5, –6, –7, –8, –9,
–10, –11, –12, BioNews 74, CelR 73,
ConAu 65, CurBio 76, DcFM, FilmgC,
InSci, IntAu&W 77, –82, IntMPA 84,
IntWW 74, –75, –76, –77, –78, –79, –80, –81,
–82, –83, LinLib L, NewYTBE 72,
OxFilm, OxShips, REn, WhDW,
Who 74, –82, –83, WhoAm 80, –82,
WhoFr 79, WhoOcn 78, WhoUN 75,
WhoWor 74, –76, –78, –80, –82, WorAl,
WorEFlm
Coville, Bruce 1950- *ConAu 97,*
SmATA 32[port]
Cowden, Jeanne 1918- *ConAu 85*
Cowell, Cyril 1888- *ChhPo S2, ConAu P-2*
Cowell, Frank Richard 1897- *Au&Wr 6,*
AuBYP, BioIn 8, ConAu 8NR,
IntAu&W 76, –77, WhE&EA, Who 74,
WrDr 76, –80
Cowell, Frank Richard *see also* Cowell, Richard
Cowell, Richard 1897- *ConAu 53*
Cowell, Richard *see also* Cowell, Frank Richard
Cowen, Eve *ConAu X*
Cowie, Leonard W 1919- *ConAu 9NR*
Cowie, Leonard Wallace 1919- *Au&Wr 6,*
BioIn 9, ConAu 13R, IntAu&W 76, –77,
–82, SmATA 4, WrDr 76, –80, –82,
–84
Cowles, Virginia 1912-1983 *Au&Wr 6,*
ConAu 110, –65, CurBio 42, –83N,
InWom, IntAu&W 76, –77, –82,
NewYTBS 83, Who 74, –82, –83
Cowley, Joy 1936- *AuBYP SUP, BioIn 9,*
ConAu 11NR, –25R, SmATA 4
Cowley, Malcolm 1898- *AmAu&B, Au&Wr 6,*
BioIn 1, –2, –4, –6, –7, –10, –11, –12,
BlueB 76, CelR 73, ChhPo, –S3, CnDAL,
ConAmA, ConAu 3NR, –5R, ConLCrt,
–82, ConP 70, –75, –80, CurBio 79,
DcLB Y81A[port], –4, DcLEL, EncWL,
–81, IntAu&W 76, –77, –82, IntWW 74,
–75, –76, –77, –78, –79, –80, –81, –82, –83,
IntWWP 77, –82, LinLib L, –S, ModAL,
ModAL SUP, NewYTBS 77, OxAmL,
PenC AM, RAdv 1, REn, REnAL,
SixAP, TwCA, TwCA SUP, WebAB, –79,
WhNAA, WhoAm 74, –76, –78, –80, –82,
WhoE 83, WhoWor 74, WrDr 76, –80,
–82, –84
Cowling, Elizabeth 1910- *ConAu 110,*
DrAS 74H, –78H, –82H, WhoAmW 70,
–72
Cowper, Richard 1926- *Au&Wr 6, ConAu X,*
ConSFA, EncSF, IntAu&W 76, –76X, –77,
–82, Novels, ScF&FL 2, WhoSciF,
WrDr 76, –80, –82, –84
Cox, Barry 1931- *ConAu 103*
Cox, Charles Brian 1928- *Au&Wr 6,*
ConAu 25R, IntAu&W 76, –77, –82,
Who 82, –83, WrDr 76, –80, –82, –84
Cox, Donald William 1921- *ConAu 1R, –4NR,*
SmATA 23[port]

Cox, William Robert 1901- *AuBYP,*
ConAu 6NR, –9R, SmATA 31, WrDr 84

Coxe, Louis Osborne 1918- *AmAu&B,*
BiE&WWA, BioIn 6, –10, –12, ChhPo,
–S1, –S3, ConAu 13R, ConP 70, –75, –80,
DcLB 5[port], DcLEL 1940, DrAP 75,
DrAP&F 83, IntWWP 77, –82,
McGEWD, –84, NotNAT, OxAmL,
WhoAm 74, –76, –78, –80, –82,
WhoWor 74, WorAu, WrDr 76, –80, –82,
–84

Coy, Harold 1902- *AuBYP, BioIn 7, –9,*
ConAu 4NR, –5R, IntAu&W 76, –77,
SmATA 3, WrDr 76, –80, –82, –84

Coyle, David Cushman 1887-1969 *ConAu 1R,*
–103, WhAm 5

Coyne, John R, Jr. 1935- *ConAu 37R*

Cozzens, James Gould 1903-1978 *AmAu&B,*
AmNov, AmWr, BioIn 1, –2, –4, –5, –7, –8,
–9, –10, –11, –12, BlueB 76, CasWL,
CnDAL, ConAmA, ConAu 9R, –81,
ConLC 1, –4, –11, ConNov 72, –76,
CurBio 49, –78, –78N, CyWA,
DcLB DS2[port], –9[port], DcLEL,
DrAF 76, EncWL, –81, IntAu&W 76, –77,
IntWW 74, –75, –76, –77, –78, –79N,
LinLib L, –S, LongCTC, ModAL,
NatCAB 61, NewYTBS 78, Novels,
ObitOF 79, OxAmL, PenC AM, RAdv 1,
REn, REnAL, ScF&FL 1, –2, TwCA,
TwCA SUP, TwCWr, WebAB, –79,
WebE&AL, WhAm 7, WhE&EA,
Who 74, WhoAm 74, –76, –78,
WhoWor 74, WorAl, WrDr 76

Crabb, Cecil VanMeter, Jr. 1924-
AmM&WS 73S, –78S, ConAu 13R,
WhoAm 74, –76

Cragg, Kenneth 1913- *ConAu 7NR, –17R,*
IntAu&W 76, –77, Who 74, –82, –83,
WrDr 76, –80, –82, –84

Craig, Eleanor 1929- *ConAu 93*

Craig, John Eland 1912-1980? *ConAu X,*
IntAu&W 76X, SmATA 2, WrDr 80

Craig, John Eland *see also* Chipperfield, Joseph
Eugene

Craig, John Ernest 1921-1982 *BioIn 10, CaW,*
ConAu 101, SmATA 23[port],
TwCCW 78, –83, WhoAm 74, WrDr 80,
–82, –84

Craig, Margaret Maze 1911-1964 *BioIn 6, –7,*
–11, ConAu 1R, MorJA, SmATA 9,
WhoAmW 61, –64, –66, –66A, –68

Craig, Mary Francis 1923- *BioIn 9, –10, –12,*
ConAu 1R, –4NR, IntAu&W 77, –82,
SmATA 6, ThrBJA, WhoAmW 74, –70,
–72, –75, –77, –79, WrDr 76, –80, –82, –84

Craig, Mary Francis *see also* Shura, Mary
Francis

Craig, Robert Wallace 1924- *BioIn 12,*
WhoWest 80, –82, –84

Craighead, Frank Cooper, Jr. 1916- *ConAu 97,*
WhoWest 74, –76, –78

Cramer, Kathryn 1943- *ConAu 25R*

Crane, Caroline 1930- *AuBYP SUP, BioIn 11,*
ConAu 3NR, –9R, ForWC 70,
SmATA 11, WhoE 83, WrDr 76, –80, –82,
–84

Crane, Milton 1917- *DrAS 74E, –78E, –82E*

Crane, Stephen 1871-1900 *AmAu, AmAu&B,*
AmBi, AmWr, ApCAB SUP, AtlBL,
BbD, BiD&SB, BioIn 1, –2, –3, –4, –5, –6,
–7, –8, –9, –10, –11, –12, CasWL,
Chambr 3, ChhPo, –S3, CnDAL,
CnE&AP, ConAu 109, CrtT 3, –4,
CyWA, DcAmAu, DcAmB,
DcLB 12[port], DcLEL, DcNAA,
EncAAH, EncAB-H, EvLB, HarEnUS,
LinLib L, LongCTC, McGEWB, ModAL,
NatCAB 10, Novels, OxAmL, OxEng,
PenC AM, RAdv 1, RComWL, REn,
REnAL, TwCBDA, TwCLC 11[port],
WebAB, –79, WebE&AL, WhDW,
WhAm 1, WhFla, WorAl, YABC 2

Crane, William B 1904-1981 *ConAu 107,*
DrRegL 75

Crane, William D 1892- *BioIn 9, ConAu 5R,*
SmATA 1

Crary, Margaret Coleman 1906- *AuBYP,*
BioIn 8, –11, ConAu 5R, ForWC 70,
SmATA 9

Craven, Margaret 1901-1980 *AmWomWr,*
BioIn 10, –12, ConAu 103, ConLC 17,
IntAu&W 76, –77, WhAm 7, WhoAm 76,
–78, –80, WrDr 76, –80, –82

Craven, Thomas 1889-1969 *AmAu&B, AuBYP,*
BioIn 8, ConAu 97, CurBio 44, –69,
ObitOF 79, REnAL, SmATA 22[port],
TwCA, TwCA SUP, WhAm 5

Crawford, Alan 1953- *ConAu 101*

Crawford, Char 1935- *ConAu 57*

Crawford, Char *see also* Johnson, Charlene

Crawford, Charles P 1945- *ConAu 45,*
SmATA 28

Crawford, Deborah 1922- *BioIn 10,*
ConAu 49, IntAu&W 77, SmATA 6

Crawford, F Marion 1854-1909 *ConAu 107,*
Novels, ScF&FL 1, TwCLC 10[port],
WhLit, WhoHr&F

Crawford, Joanna 1941- *ConAu 9R,*
WomWMM

Crawford, Richard 1935- *ConAu 9NR, –57,*
DrAS 78H, –82H, WhoAm 78, –80, –82,
WhoAmM 83

Crawford, Thomas Edgar 1867-1941 *BioIn 6*

Crawshaw, Alwyn 1934- *WhoArt 80, –82,*
WhoWor 80, –82

Crayder, Dorothy 1906- *AuBYP SUP,*
BioIn 10, ConAu 33R, ScF&FL 1,
SmATA 7

Crayder, Teresa *ConAu X, SmATA 1*

Crayder, Teresa *see also* Colman, Hila

Creamer, Robert W 1922- *BioIn 10,*
ConAu 21R, WhoE 83, WrDr 76, –80,
–82, –84

Creasey, John 1908-1973 *Au&Wr 6, BioIn 4, -5, -6, -7, -8, -9, -10, ConAu 5R, -8NR, -41R, ConLC 11, CorpD, CurBio 63, -73, -73N, EncMys, EncSF, LongCTC, MnBBF, NewYTBE 73, Novels[port], ObitT 1971, REn, ScF&FL 1, -1A, -2, TwCCr&M 80, TwCWr, WhAm 6, WhE&EA, WhoBW&I A, WhoSpyF, WorAl, WorAu*

Credle, Ellis 1902- *AuBYP, BioIn 1, -2, -3, -4, -5, -7, -9, ConAu 9NR, -13R, IlsCB 1744, -1946, InWom, JBA 51, LinLib L, SmATA 1, Str&VC*

Creekmore, Hubert 1907-1966 *AmAu&B, AmNov, BioIn 2, -4, -7, REnAL, TwCA SUP*

Creeley, Robert White 1926- *AmAu&B, Au&Wr 6, BioIn 8, -10, -11, -12, BlueB 76, CasWL, ConAu 1R, ConLC 1, -2, -4, -8, -11, -15, ConP 70, -75, -80, CroCAP, DcLB 5[port], -16[port], DcLEL 1940, DrAF 76, DrAP 75, DrAP&F 83, EncWL 81, IntAu&W 76, -77, -82, IntWW 74, -75, -76, -77, -78, -79, -80, -81, -82, -83, IntWWP 77, LinLib L, ModAL, ModAL SUP, Novels, PenC AM, RAdv 1, REnAL, WebE&AL, WhoAm 74, -76, -78, -80, -82, WhoTwCL, WhoWor 74, -80, -82, WorAu, WrDr 76, -80, -82, -84*

Creighton, Luella Sanders Bruce 1901- *BioIn 2, -10, ConAu P-1, CreCan 2, OxCan, OxCan SUP, WhoAm 76, -78, -80*

Crenshaw, Marshall *NewRR 83*

Crenshaw, Mary Ann 1929- *ConAu 8NR, -57, WhoAmW 77, -79, -81, WhoE 79, -81*

Cresswell, Helen 1936?- *Au&Wr 6, AuBYP, BioIn 9, ConAu 8NR, -17R, FourBJA, IntAu&W 76, -77, -82, ScF&FL 1, -2, SenS, SmATA 1, TwCCW 78, -83, WrDr 76, -80, -82, -84*

Crews, Frederick C 1933- *AmAu&B, ConAu 1R, -1NR, ConLCrt, -82, DrAS 74E, -78E, -82E, IntAu&W 82, WhoAm 78, -80, -82, WrDr 80, -82, -84*

Crews, Harry 1935- *AuNews 1, BioIn 8, -10, -11, -12, BioNews 74, ConAu 25R, ConLC 6, -23[port], ConNov 82, DcLB 6[port], DrAF 76, DrAP&F 83, NewYTBS 78, WhoAm 74, -76, -78, -80, -82, WorAu 1970, WrDr 84*

Crichton, Michael 1942- *AmAu&B, Au&Wr 6, AuNews 2, BioIn 8, -9, -10, -11, -12, CelR 73, ConAu 25R, ConLC 2, -6, ConNov 76, -82, CurBio 76, DcLB Y81B[port], EncSF, FilmgC, IntMPA 77, -75, -76, -78, -79, -81, -82, -84, LinLib L, NewYTBE 70, NewYTBS 81[port], Novels, ScF&FL 1, -2, SmATA 9, TwCCr&M 80, WhoSciF, WorAl, WorAu 1970, WrDr 76, -80, -82, -84*

Crichton, Robert 1925- *AuNews 1, BioIn 7, -8, -10, BioNews 74, ConAu 17R, IntAu&W 76, WrDr 76, -80, -82, -84*

Crick, Bernard R 1929- *Au&Wr 6, ConAu 1R, -5NR, IntAu&W 76, -77, -82, Who 74, -82, -83, WrDr 76, -80, -82, -84*

Crick, Francis Harry Compton 1916- *AsBiEn, BiESc, BioIn 5, -6, -8, -9, -11, -12, BlueB 76, CelR 73, CurBio 83[port], IntWW 74, -75, -76, -77, -78, -79, -80, -81, -82, -83, McGEWB, McGMS 80[port], WhDW, Who 74, -82, -83, WhoWor 74, -78, -80, -82, WorAl*

Criner, Beatrice Hall 1915- *AuBYP SUP, WhoAmW 64, -66, -68, -75, -77, WhoS&SW 78, -80, -82*

Criner, Calvin *AuBYP SUP*

Crispin, Edmund 1921-1978 *Au&Wr 6, BioIn 1, -2, -10, ConAu X, ConLC 22[port], ConSFA, CurBio 49, EncMys, EncSF, Novels, ScF&FL 1, -2, TwCCr&M 80, WhoSciF, WorAl, WorAu*

Crispin, Edmund see also Montgomery, Robert Bruce

Crist, Judith 1922- *AmAu&B, AmWomWr, AuNews 1, BioIn 7, -8, -9, -10, -12, BlueB 76, CelR 73, ConAu 81, ForWC 70, IntMPA 77, -75, -76, -78, -79, -81, -82, -84, WhoAm 74, -76, -78, -80, -82, WhoAmW 74, -61, -64, -66, -68, -70, -72, -75, -83, WhoE 74, WhoWorJ 72, -78, WrDr 76, -80, -82, -84*

Critchfield, Richard Patrick 1931- *BlueB 76, ConAu 41R, IntAu&W 82, WhoAm 74, -76, -78, -80, -82, WhoS&SW 73, WhoWor 80, -82, WrDr 80, -82, -84*

Croce, Arlene Louise 1934- *ConAu 104, WhoAm 80, -82, WhoAmW 81, -83*

Croce, Jim 1943-1973 *BioIn 10, -11, -12, BioNews 74, EncPR&S, -77, IlEncRk, ObitOF 79, RkOn 78, -84, RolSEnR 83, WhoRocM 82, WorAl*

Croft-Cooke, Rupert 1903-1979 *Au&Wr 6, BioIn 3, -4, -6, -7, -8, -10, BlueB 76, CathA 1952, ChhPo, -S1, ConAu 4NR, -9R, -89, IntAu&W 76, -77, IntWW 74, -75, -76, -77, -78, -79N, IntWWP 77, LongCTC, NewC, TwCA, TwCA SUP, TwCCr&M 80, WhE&EA, WhLit, Who 74, WhoWor 74, -76, -78, WrDr 76, -80*

Crofts, Dash *WhoAm 78, -80, -82, WhoRocM 82*

Crofts, Dash see also Seals & Crofts

Crofts, Freeman Wills 1879-1957 *BioIn 4, DcIrB, DcLEL, EncMys, EvLB, LongCTC, NewC, Novels, ObitOF 79, PenC ENG, REn, TwCA, TwCA SUP, TwCCr&M 80, TwCWr, WhE&EA, WhLit, WorAl*

Cromie, William Joseph 1930- *AuBYP SUP,*

BioIn 8, *–12*, *ConAu 73*, *SmATA 14*,
WrDr 76, *–80*, *–82*, *–84*

Croy, Homer 1883-1965 *AmAu&B*, *AmNov*,
BioIn 2, *–4*, *–7*, *–8*, *–10*, *–12*, *ConAu 110*,
–89, *DcAmB S7*, *DcLB 4*, *NatCAB 51*,
ObitOF 79, *REnAL*, *REnAW*, *TwCA*,
TwCA SUP, *WhAm 4*, *–5*, *WhScrn 2*

Cruise O'Brien, Conor 1917- *Au&Wr 6*,
IntAu&W 76

Crume, Vic *ScF&FL 1*

Cruse, Heloise 1920?- *AmAu&B*, *BioIn 5*, *–6*,
–7, *ForWC 70*, *WhoAmW 74*, *–68*, *–70*

Cruz, Nicky 1938- *BioIn 12*, *WhoRel 75*

Cuadra, Pablo Antonio 1912- *BioIn 8*,
DcCLAA, *OxSpan*, *PenC AM*

Cudahy, Brian J 1936- *AmCath 80*,
ConAu 41R, *DrAS 74P*, *WhoE 74*, *–75*

Culliney, John L 1942- *ConAu 65*

Cumming, Patricia Arenas 1932- *ConAu 11NR*,
–61, *DrAP&F 83*, *IntWWP 82*,
Po&Wr 77

Cumming, Patricia Arens 1932- *ForWC 70*,
IntAu&W 77, *–82*, *IntWWP 77*

Cumming, Primrose Amy 1915- *Au&Wr 6*,
ConAu 33R, *IntAu&W 76*, *SmATA 24*,
TwCCW 83, *WhE&EA*, *WrDr 76*, *–80*,
–82, *–84*

Cumming, Robert 1945- *ConAu 106*

Cummings, Betty Sue 1918- *BioIn 12*,
ConAu 73, *SmATA 15*

Cummings, E E 1894-1962 *AmAu&B*, *AmWr*,
AnCL, *AtlBL*, *AuBYP*, *CasWL*, *ChhPo*,
CnDAL, *CnE&AP*, *CnMD*, *CnMWL*,
ConAmA, *ConAmL*, *ConAu 73*,
ConLC 1, *–3*, *–8*, *–12*, *–15*, *CyWA*,
DcAmB S7, *DcLB 4*, *DcLEL*, *EncWL*,
–81, *EvLB*, *LinLib L*, *–S*, *LongCTC*,
McGEWD, *–84[port]*, *ModAL*,
ModAL SUP, *ModWD*, *ObitT 1961*,
OxAmL, *OxEng*, *PenC AM*, *RAdv 1*,
REn, *REnAL*, *SixAP*, *TwCA*,
TwCA SUP, *TwCWr*, *WebE&AL*,
WhoTwCL, *WorAl*

Cummings, Richard *AuBYP*, *BioIn 8*,
ConAu X, *SmATA X*, *WrDr 76*, *–80*, *–82*

Cummings, Richard *see also* Gardner, Richard M

Cuneo, John Robert 1911- *ConAu 53*,
WhoE 83

Cunliffe, Marcus Falkner 1922- *AmAu&B*,
Au&Wr 6, *BlueB 76*, *ConAu 10NR*,
–21R, *IntAu&W 82*, *SmATA 37*,
Who 74, *–82*, *–83*, *WrDr 76*, *–80*, *–82*, *–84*

Cunningham, Chet 1928- *ConAu 4NR*, *–49*,
SmATA 23, *WrDr 84*

Cunningham, E V 1914- *AuBYP*, *BioIn 10*,
–11, *–12*, *ConAu X*, *ConNov 72*, *–76*, *–82*,
EncSF, *IntAu&W 76X*, *–77X*, *Novels*,
SmATA 7, *TwCCr&M 80*, *WrDr 76*, *–80*,
–82, *–84*

Cunningham, E V *see also* Fast, Howard

Cunningham, Glenn 1910- *BioIn 2*, *–3*, *–5*, *–6*,
–7, *–9*, *–10*, *–12*, *WorAl*

Cunningham, John Donoven 1933-
AmM&WS 73P, *LEduc 74*

Cunningham, Julia Woolfolk 1916- *AmAu&B*,
AuBYP, *BioIn 7*, *–9*, *–10*, *ConAu 4NR*,
–9R, *ConLC 12*, *MorBMP*, *SmATA 1*,
–26[port], *ThrBJA*, *TwCCW 78*, *–83*,
WhoAm 74, *–76*, *–78*, *–80*, *–82*,
WhoAmW 74, *–68*, *–70*, *–72*, *WrDr 80*, *–82*,
–84

Curie, Eve 1904- *AmAu&B*, *AnCL*,
Au&Wr 6, *BioIn 3*, *–6*, *–9*, *ConAu P-1*,
CurBio 40, *InWom*, *IntAu&W 76*, *–77*,
IntWW 74, *–75*, *–76*, *–77*, *–78*, *–79*, *–80*, *–81*,
–82, *–83*, *LinLib L*, *–S*, *SmATA 1*,
WhE&EA, *Who 74*, *–83*, *WhoAm 74*, *–76*,
–78, *–80*, *–82*, *WhoAmW 74*, *–61*, *–64*, *–66*,
–68, *–70*, *–72*, *–75*, *–79*, *–81*, *–83*, *WhoFr 79*,
WhoWor 74, *–76*, *–78*, *–80*

Curley, Daniel 1918- *ConAu 3NR*, *–9R*,
DrAF 76, *DrAP&F 83*, *IntAu&W 76*,
–82, *SmATA 23[port]*, *WrDr 76*, *–80*, *–82*,
–84

Currier, Richard L 1940- *ConAu 57*

Curry, Jane Louise 1932- *AuBYP*, *BioIn 8*, *–9*,
ConAu 7NR, *–17R*, *FourBJA*,
IntAu&W 82, *ScF&FL 1*, *–2*, *SmATA 1*,
TwCCW 78, *–83*, *WhoAm 82*,
WhoAmW 83, *WrDr 80*, *–82*, *–84*

Curtis, Anthony 1926?- *ConAu 101*,
IntAu&W 77, *–82*, *WhoAm 74*, *–76*,
WhoWor 74, *WrDr 76*, *–80*, *–82*, *–84*

Curtis, Edward S 1868-1952 *AmAu&B*,
BioIn 3, *–10*, *–11*, *–12*, *CmCal*, *DcAmB S5*,
ObitOF 79, *REnAW*, *WhAm 4*

Curtis, Patricia 1921?- *ConAu 69*,
SmATA 23[port]

Curtis, Richard 1937- *AuBYP SUP*,
ConAu 106, *ConSFA*, *EncSF*, *ScF&FL 1*,
–2, *SmATA 29*

Curtis, Robert H *AuBYP SUP*

Curtis, Will *ConAu X*, *IntAu&W 76X*, *–82X*,
WrDr 76, *–80*, *–82*, *–84*

Curtis, Will *see also* Nunn, William Curtis

Curtiss, Ursula Reilly 1923- *AmAu&B*,
AmWomWr, *Au&Wr 6*, *ConAu 1R*,
–5NR, *EncMys*, *IntAu&W 76*, *–77*,
TwCCr&M 80, *WhoAm 78*, *–80*, *–82*,
WhoAmW 74, *–66*, *–68*, *–70*, *–72*, *–75*, *–77*,
WrDr 82, *–84*

Cusack, Anne E *DrAP&F 83*

Cusack, Michael Joseph 1928- *ConAu 69*,
WhoAm 78, *–80*, *–82*

Cussler, Clive 1931- *BioIn 12*, *ConAu 1NR*,
–45, *NewYTBS 81[port]*, *Novels*,
WhoAm 78, *–80*, *–82*, *WhoF&I 75*,
WrDr 80, *–82*, *–84*

Custer, Elizabeth Bacon 1842?-1933 *Alli SUP*,
AmAu&B, *AmBi*, *AmWom*, *AmWomWr*,
ApCAB, *BiD&SB*, *BioIn 2*, *–6*, *–7*, *–10*,
–11, *DcAmAu*, *DcNAA*, *HarEnUS*,
HerW, *InWom*, *REnAL*, *WhAm 1*

Cuthbertson, Tom 1945- *ConAu 1NR*, *–45*

Cutler, Ebbitt 1923- *AuBYP SUP,*
  ConAu 4NR, –49, IntAu&W 82,
  SmATA 9
Cuyler, Margery S 1948- *WhoAmW 77,*
  WhoLibI 82

D

Dace, Letitia 1941- *ConAu 106, DrAS 74E, –78E*

Dace, Wallace 1920- *ConAu 61, DrAS 74E, –78E, –82E, NatPD, –81[port]*

Dachs, David 1922-1980 *ConAu 11NR, –69*

DaCruz, Daniel 1921- *ConAu 3NR, –5R, IntAu&W 76, WrDr 76, –80, –82, –84*

Dade, George C 1912?- *BioIn 12*

Dahl, Borghild 1890-1984 *AuBYP, BioIn 6, –8, –9, –10, ConAu 1R, –2NR, IntAu&W 82, MinnWr, SmATA 37N, –7, ThrBJA, WhoAmW 58, –61, –64, –66, –68, –70, –72, WrDr 76, –80, –84*

Dahl, Roald 1916- *Au&Wr 6, AuBYP, BioIn 5, –6, –8, –9, –10, –11, –12, BioNews 74, ChlLR 1, ConAu 1R, –6NR, ConLC 1, –6, –18, ConNov 72, –76, –82, DcLEL 1940, DrAF 76, DrAP&F 83, EncSF, IntAu&W 76, –77, –82, IntWW 82, –83, LinLib L, MorBMP, NewC, NewYTBS 77, Novels, PiP, RAdv 1, REn, REnAL, ScF&FL 1, –2, SmATA 1, –26[port], ThrBJA, TwCCW 78, –83, TwCCr&M 80, WhE&EA, Who 82, –83, WhoAm 74, –76, –78, –80, –82, WhoHr&F, WhoSciF, WhoWor 74, –76, –78, WorAl, WorAu, WrDr 76, –80, –82, –84*

Daiches, David 1912- *Au&Wr 6, BioIn 4, BlueB 76, ChhPo S1, –S3, ConAu 5R, –7NR, ConLCrt, –82, DcLEL, EvLB, IntAu&W 76, –77, IntWW 74, –75, –76, –77, –78, –79, –80, –81, –82, –83, LinLib L, LongCTC, ModBrL, RAdv 1, REn, TwCA SUP, Who 74, –82, –83, WhoAm 74, –76, –78, WhoWor 74, –76, –78, WhoWorJ 78, WrDr 76, –80, –82, –84*

Daigon, Arthur 1928- *ConAu 33R, LEduc 74*

Dale, Margaret J Miller 1911- *Au&Wr 6, ConAu 3NR, –5R*

Dale, Margaret J Miller *see also* Miller, Margaret J

Dale, Margaret Jessy 1911- *Au&Wr 6, ConAu 5R, IntAu&W 76, –77, –82*

Daley, Arthur 1904-1974 *AmAu&B, BioIn 4, –10, ConAu 45, ConAu P-2, CurBio 56, –74, –74N*

Daley, Robert 1930- *ConAu 1R, –2NR, IntMPA 84, WhoAm 74, –76, –78, –80, WhoE 74, WrDr 80, –82, –84*

Dalrymple, Byron W 1910- *ConAu 6NR, –57*

Dalton, David 1944- *ConAu 97*

Daltrey, Roger 1944- *WhoAm 80, –82, WhoHol A, WhoRocM 82*

Daltrey, Roger *see also* Who, The

Daly, Donald F 1904- *ConAu 69, WhoWest 80, –82, –84*

Daly, Elizabeth 1878-1967 *AmAu&B, BioIn 4, –8, ConAu P-2, DcLEL 1940, EncMys, Novels, REnAL, TwCA SUP, TwCCr&M 80*

Daly, Jay 1946- *WhoE 83, WhoLibI 82*

Daly, Maureen 1921- *AmAu&B, AmNov, AuBYP, BioIn 1, –2, –6, –7, –9, BkC 4, CathA 1930, ConAu X, ConLC 17, CurBio 46, MorJA, REnAL, SmATA 2, TwCCW 78, –83, WhoAmW 58, –61, WrDr 80, –82, –84*

Daly, Maureen *see also* McGivern, Maureen Daly

Daly, Sheila John 1927?- *AuBYP, BioIn 2, –3, –8, CathA 1952*

D'Amato, Alex 1919- *AuBYP SUP, BioIn 12, ConAu 81, SmATA 20*

D'Amato, Janet Potter 1925- *AuBYP SUP, BioIn 11, ConAu 1NR, –49, SmATA 9, WhoAmA 78, –80, –82*

D'Ambrosio, Richard A 1927- *ConAu 102, WhoE 74*

Damsker, Matt 1951- *ConAu 108*

Dana, Barbara 1940- *ConAu 8NR, –17R, ForWC 70, SmATA 22[port], WhoHol A*

Dana, Richard Henry, Jr. 1815-1882 *Alli, Alli SUP, AmAu, AmAu&B, AmBi, ApCAB, BbD, BiAUS SUP, BiD&SB, BioIn 1, –2, –3, –5, –6, –8, –9, –12, CarSB, CasWL, Chambr 3, CivWDc, CmCal, CnDAL, CrtT 3, CyAL 2, CyWA, DcAmAu, DcAmB, DcAmSR, DcBiPP, DcEnL, DcLB 1, DcLEL, DcNAA, Drake, EncAB-H, EvLB, HarEnUS, LinLib L, –S, McGEWB, MouLC 4, OxAmH, OxAmL, OxEng, OxLaw, OxShips, PenC AM, REn, REnAL, REnAW, SmATA 26[port], TwCBDA, WebAB, –79, WebE&AL, WhDW,*

WhAm HS, WhAmP, WorAl
Dance, Stanley Frank 1910- *Au&Wr 6,*
ConAu 8NR, -17R, IntAu&W 76, -77, -82,
WhoE 74, -75, WrDr 76, -80, -82, -84
Daniel, Anita 1893?-1978 *AuBYP, BioIn 8,*
-11, ConAu 77, ForWC 70, SmATA 23,
-24N
Daniel, Ralph T 1921- *ConAu 53,*
IntWWM 77
Daniels, Dorothy 1915- *AmWomWr,*
ConAu 89, ScF&FL 1, WhoAmW 83,
WrDr 82, -84
Daniels, Jonathan 1902-1981 *AmAu&B,*
AnObit 1981[port], Au&Wr 6, AuBYP,
BioIn 2, -3, -4, -5, -7, -10, -12, BlueB 76,
CnDAL, ConAu 105, -49, CurBio 42,
-82N, EncSoH, IntAu&W 76, IntYB 78,
-79, -80, -81, -82, LinLib L,
NewYTBS 81[port], OxAmL, REn,
REnAL, ScF&FL 1, -2, TwCA,
TwCA SUP, WhoAm 74, -76, -78, -80,
WhoAmP 73, -75, -77, -79, WhoS&SW 73,
WhoWor 74, WrDr 80, -82
Daniken, Erich Von 1935- *BioIn 10, -11, -12,*
CurBio 76, IntAu&W 82, UFOEn
Dank, Milton 1920- *AmM&WS 73P, -76P,*
-79P, -82P, ConAu 11NR, -69,
SmATA 31[port]
Dann, Colin 1943- *ConAu 108, WrDr 82, -84*
Dann, Jack 1945- *ConAu 2NR, -49, DrAF 76,*
DrAP&F 83, EncSF, IntAu&W 82,
ScF&FL 1, -2, WrDr 84
Dannay, Frederic 1905-1982 *AmAu&B,*
AnObit 1982[port], ASpks, AuBYP,
BioIn 2, -3, -4, -8, -10, -11, -12,
ConAu 1R, -1NR, -107, ConLC 11,
CurBio 40, -82N, DcLEL, EncMys,
EvLB, IntAu&W 76, -77, IntWW 74, -75,
-76, -77, -78, -79, -80, -81, -82, -83N,
LongCTC, NewYTBS 82[port], PenC AM,
REn, ScF&FL 1, TwCA, TwCA SUP,
TwCCr&M 80, WebAB, -79, Who 74,
-82, -83N, WhoAm 74, -76, -78, -80, -82,
WhoWor 74, WrDr 76, -80, -82
Dannay, Frederic *see also* Queen, Ellery
Dannett, Sylvia G L 1909- *ConAu 1R, -4NR,*
WhoAmW 74, -72, -75, -77, -79,
WhoWorJ 72, -78
Danziger, Paula 1944- *ConLC 21[port],*
SmATA 30, -36
Darack, Arthur J 1918- *Ward 77F,*
WhoAm 74, -76, -78, -80, -82
Darby, Patricia *AuBYP, BioIn 12,*
ConAu 73, SmATA 14
Darby, Ray 1912- *AmSCAP 66, AuBYP,*
BioIn 8, -10, ConAu 17R, SmATA 7,
WhoWest 74, -76, -78
Darcy, Clare *ConAu 102, Novels, WrDr 76,*
-80, -82, -84
Dardis, Tom 1926- *ConAu 9NR, -65*
Dareff, Hal 1920- *AmAu&B, AuBYP,*
BioIn 8, ConAu 65, WhoAm 74, -76, -78,

-80, -82, WhoE 74
Daringer, Helen Fern 1892- *BioIn 2, -6, -9,*
ConAu P-2, CurBio 51, InWom, MorJA,
SmATA 1
Darion, Joe 1917- *EncMT, NewCBMT,*
WhoAm 74, -76, -78, -80, -82
Darion, Joseph 1917- *AmSCAP 66, BioIn 10,*
-12
Darke, Marjorie 1929- *BioIn 12, ConAu 81,*
IntAu&W 82, SmATA 16, TwCCW 78,
-83, Who 82, -83, WrDr 80, -82, -84
Darling, Kathy 1943- *BioIn 11, ConAu X,*
SmATA X
Darling, Lois MacIntyre 1917- *AmAu&B,*
AuBYP, BioIn 8, -9, -12, ConAu 3NR,
-5R, IlsCB 1967, SmATA 3, WhoAm 74,
-76, -78, -80, -82, WhoAmW 74, -66, -68,
-70, -72, WhoE 74, -83, WrDr 76, -80,
-82, -84
Darling, Louis 1916-1970 *AmAu&B, AuBYP,*
BioIn 5, -6, -8, -9, ConAu 3NR, -5R, -89,
IlsCB 1946, -1957, -1967, MorJA,
NewYTBE 70, SmATA 23N, -3,
WhAm 5
Darr, John C 1929- *ConAu 53*
Darrow, Whitney, Jr. 1909- *AmAu&B,*
AuBYP SUP, BioIn 2, -5, ConAu 61,
CurBio 58, LinLib L, SmATA 13,
WhoAm 74, -76, -78, -80, -82,
WhoAmA 73, -76, -78, -80, -82,
WhoWor 74, WorECar
Darwin, Charles Robert 1809-1882 *Alli,*
Alli SUP, ApCAB SUP, AsBiEn, AtlBL,
BbD, BiD&SB, BiESc, BioIn 1, -2, -3, -4,
-5, -6, -7, -8, -9, -10, -11, -12, BrAu 19,
CarSB, CasWL, CelCen, Chambr 3,
CyEd[port], CyWA, DcBiPP, DcEnA,
-AP, DcEnL, DcEuL, DcInv, DcLEL,
DcScB, Dis&D, EvLB, InSci, LinLib L,
LongCEL, LuthC 75, McGEWB,
MouLC 4, NamesHP[port], NewC,
OxEng, OxShips, PenC ENG, RComWL,
REn, WebE&AL, WhDW, WorAl
Dary, David Archie 1934- *ConAu 29R,*
IntAu&W 76, WhoAm 80, -82,
WhoMW 74, -76, -78, -80, WhoWor 80,
-82, WrDr 76, -80, -82, -84
Dasmann, Raymond Fredric 1919-
AmM&WS 73P, -76P, -79P, -82P,
ConAu 2NR, -5R, WhoAm 74, -76, -78,
-80, -82, WhoTech 82, WhoWor 74
Daudet, Alphonse 1840-1897 *AtlBL,*
AuBYP SUP, BbD, BiD&SB, BioIn 1, -2,
-3, -4, -5, -6, -7, -10, -11, CelCen, ChhPo,
-S2, ClDMEL, CyWA, DcBiA, DcEuL,
Dis&D, EvEuW, LinLib L, -S,
McGEWB, McGEWD, -84[port], NewC,
NewEOp 71, NotNAT B, Novels[port],
OxEng, OxFr, OxMus, PenC EUR,
RComWL, REn, WhDW, WorAl
Daugherty, Charles Michael 1914- *AuBYP,*
BioIn 5, -8, -12, ConAu 73, IlsCB 1946,

SmATA 16
Daugherty, James Henry 1889-1974 AmAu&B,
AmLY, AmPB, AnCL, AuBYP, BioIn 1,
-2, -3, -4, -5, -7, -8, -10, BkP, ChhPo, -S1,
ConAu 49, -73, CurBio 40, -74, -74N,
IlBEAAW, IlsCB 1744, -1946, -1957,
-1967, JBA 34, -51, NewYTBS 74,
Newb 1922, SmATA 13, Str&VC,
TwCCW 78, -83, WhAm 6, WhoAm 74,
WhoAmA 73, -76N, -78N, -80N, -82N
Daugherty, Richard Deo 1922- AmM&WS 73S,
-76P, ConAu 108, SmATA 35,
WhoAm 74, -76, -78, -80
Daugherty, Sonia Medwedeff d1971
ConAu 104, SmATA 27N
Daveluy, Paule Cloutier 1919- BioIn 10, -11,
ConAu 9R, OxCan SUP, Profile,
SmATA 11
Daves, Jessica 1898-1974 BioIn 10, ConAu 53,
NewYTBS 74, WhAm 6, WhoAm 74,
WhoAmW 74, -58, -64, -66, -68, -70, -72,
WorFshn
David, Jay ConAu X
David, Jay see also Adler, William
David, Jonathan SmATA X
David, Jonathan see also Ames, Lee Judah
David-Neel, Alexandra 1868-1969 BioIn 8, -9,
ConAu 25R, EncO&P 78, ObitOF 79,
WhE&EA
Davidson, Basil 1914- AfSS 78, -79, -80, -81,
-82, AmAu&B, Au&Wr 6, BioIn 10,
ConAu 1R, -1NR, IntAu&W 76, -77, -82,
IntWW 81, -82, -83, SmATA 13, Who 74,
-82, -83, WhoWor 74, -76, WorAu,
WrDr 76, -80, -82, -84
Davidson, Bill 1918- AuBYP, BiE&WWA,
BioIn 8, ConAu X
Davidson, Donald 1925- NewYTBE 71,
WhoProB 73
Davidson, H R Ellis 1914- ConAu 11NR, -17R
Davidson, Jessica 1915- BioIn 10, ConAu 41R,
SmATA 5
Davidson, Lionel 1922- Au&Wr 6, ConAu 1R,
-1NR, DcLB 14[port], DcLEL 1940,
EncSF, IntAu&W 77, -82, Novels,
TwCCr&M 80, WrDr 76, -80, -82, -84
Davidson, Margaret 1936- AuBYP SUP,
BioIn 10, ConAu 25R, SmATA 5
Davidson, Mary S 1940- ConAu 107
Davidson, Robyn 1949?- BioIn 11, ConAu X
Davidson, T Whitfield NewYTBS 74
Davies, Andrew 1936- ConAu 105,
IntAu&W 77, -82, SmATA 27,
TwCCW 83
Davies, Bettilu D 1942- ConAu 101,
SmATA 33[port]
Davies, Hunter 1936- ConAu 57, Who 82,
-83, WhoWor 74, -76, WrDr 76, -80, -82,
-84
Davies, L P 1914- ConAu 9NR, -21R,
ConSFA, EncSF, ScF&FL 1, -2,
TwCCr&M 80, WrDr 82, -84

Davies, Leslie Purnell 1914- ConAu 21R,
IntAu&W 76, -77, WhoWor 76, WrDr 76,
-80
Davies, Paul 1946- BioIn 12, ConAu 106
Davies, Peter 1937- BioIn 10, ConAu 53,
Profile
Davies, Robertson 1913- Au&Wr 6, BioIn 6,
-9, -10, -11, -12, BlueB 76, CaW,
CanWr 70, -79, -80, -81, -83, CanWr,
CasWL, CnThe, ConAu 33R, ConDr 73,
-77, -82, ConLC 2, -7, -13, -25[port],
ConNov 72, -76, -82, CreCan 1,
CurBio 75, DcLEL, -1940, DrAS 74E,
-78E, -82E, IntAu&W 76, -77, -82,
IntWW 77, -78, -79, -80, -81, -82, -83,
LongCTC, McGEWD, -84, ModCmwL,
Novels, OxCan, OxCan SUP, PenC ENG,
REnAL, REnWD, TwCWr, WhoAm 74,
-76, -78, -80, -82, WhoThe 81,
WhoWor 74, -82, WorAu, WrDr 76, -80,
-82, -84
Davies, Valentine 1905-1961 AmAu&B,
AmNov, BioIn 2, -6, -8, NatCAB 50,
ObitOF 79, ScF&FL 1, WhAm 4
Davis, Angela 1944- BioIn 8, -9, -10, -11, -12,
BioNews 74, CelR 73, CivR 74, CmCal,
ConAu 10NR, -57, ConInSC 1[port],
CurBio 72, GoodHs, HerW, InB&W 80,
IntDcWB, MugS, NegAl 76, -83,
NewYTBE 70, -71, -72, PolProf NF,
SelBAA, WhoAm 76, WhoAmW 79,
WorAl
Davis, Burke 1913- AmAu&B, AuBYP,
BioIn 3, -4, -5, -7, -9, ConAu 1R, -4NR,
DrAP&F 83, SmATA 4, WhoAm 74, -76,
-78, -80, -82, WrDr 76, -80, -82, -84
Davis, Clive E 1914- AuBYP, BioIn 8,
ConAu 17R
Davis, Daniel S 1936- BioIn 11, ConAu 45,
IntAu&W 77, SmATA 12, WhoE 77
Davis, Dorothy Salisbury 1916- AmAu&B,
Au&Wr 6, BioIn 10, -12, ConAu 37R,
EncMys, IntAu&W 77, -82, Novels,
TwCCr&M 80, WhoAm 74, -76, -78, -80,
-82, WhoAmW 74, -58, -64, -66, -68, -70,
-72, WorAu, WrDr 76, -80, -82, -84
Davis, Flora 1934- ConAu 10NR, -65
Davis, Grania 1943- ConAu 85
Davis, Gwen 1936- AmAu&B, AuNews 1,
BioIn 10, -12, BioNews 74, ConAu 1R,
-2NR, ScF&FL 1, -2
Davis, Harriet Eager 1892?-1974 ConAu 49
Davis, James Warren 1935- AmM&WS 73S,
-78S, ConAu 29R
Davis, Jim 1946?- BioIn 12, ConAu X,
SmATA X
Davis, Kenneth Sydney 1912- AmAu&B,
AmNov, BioIn 2, ConAu 13R,
IntAu&W 77
Davis, Mac 1942?- BioIn 11, -12, EncPR&S,
-77, IntMPA 84, NewYTBS 79,
RkOn 78, -84, RolSEnR 83, WhoAm 78,

–80
Davis, Mary Gould 1882-1956 *AmAu&B,*
AnCL, AuBYP, BioIn 2, –4, –8, ChhPo,
–S1, –S3, JBA 34, –51, WhAm 3
Davis, Morton David 1930- *AmM&WS 73P,*
–76P, –79P, –82P, ConAu 65, WhoE 83,
WhoTech 82
Davis, Ossie 1917- *AmAu&B, BiE&WWA,*
BioIn 5, –6, –8, –9, –10, –12, BlkAWP,
BroadAu[port], CelR 73, CivR 74,
ConDr 73, –77, –82, CurBio 69,
DcLB 7[port], DrBIPA, Ebony 1, FilmgC,
InB&W 80, IntMPA 77, –75, –76, –78, –79,
–81, –82, –84, LinLib L, LivgBAA,
McGEWB, MotPP, MovMk,
NatPD 81[port], NegAl 76[port], –83,
NotNAT, PIP&P A, SelBAA,
WhoAm 76, –82, WhoBlA 77, –80,
WhoHol A, WhoThe 15, –16, –81,
WhoWor 74, WorAl, WorAu 1970,
WrDr 76, –80, –82, –84
Davis, Paxton 1925- *BioIn 12, ConAu 3NR,*
–9R, SmATA 16
Davis, Philip Edward 1927- *ConAu 49,*
DrAS 74P, –78P, –82P, WhoWest 74, –76,
–80, –82
Davis, Richard 1945- *Au&Wr 6,*
ConAu 7NR, –53, IntAu&W 76, –77,
ScF&FL 1, –2, WhoHr&F, WrDr 76, –80,
–82, –84
Davis, Richard Harding 1864-1916 *AmAu&B,*
AmBi, ApCAB X, BbD, BiD&SB,
BioIn 3, –4, –5, –6, –8, –9, –10, –12, CarSB,
CasWL, Chambr 3, CnDAL, DcAmAu,
DcAmB, DcAmDH, DcBiA, DcEnA AP,
DcLB 23[port], DcLEL, DcNAA,
EncMys, EvLB, JBA 34, LinLib L, –S,
LongCTC, McGEWB, NatCAB 8,
NotNAT B, OxAmH, OxAmL,
PenC AM, REn, REnAL, ScF&FL 1,
TwCA, TwCA SUP, TwCBDA, WebAB,
WebE&AL, WhAm 1, WhLit, WhThe,
WhoStg 1906, –1908
Davis, Robert Con 1948- *ConAu 104*
Davis, Robert Prunier 1929- *ConAu 3NR, –5R,*
WhoF&I 74, –75, WrDr 76, –80, –82, –84
Davis, Roy Eugene 1931- *ConAu 6NR, –9R*
Davis, Russell Gerard 1922- *BioIn 9,*
ConAu 5R, SmATA 3, WhoAm 74, –76,
–78, –80
Davis, Sammy, Jr. 1925- *AmPS B, BiDAfM,*
BiDAmM, BiE&WWA, BioIn 3, –4, –5, –6,
–7, –8, –9, –10, –11, –12, BioNews 74,
CelR 73, CivR 74, ConAu 108,
CurBio 56, –78, DrBIPA, Ebony 1,
EncMT, EncPR&S, –77, FilmgC,
InB&W 80, IntMPA 77, –75, –76, –78, –79,
–81, –82, –84, IntWW 79, –80, –81, –82,
–83, MotPP, MovMk, NegAl 76[port],
–83[port], NewYTBE 71, –72, NotNAT,
–A, OxFilm, RkOn 74, –82, WebAB, –79,
WhoAm 74, –76, –78, –80, WhoBlA 75, –77,

–80, WhoHol A, WhoThe 15, –16, –81,
WhoWor 74, –76, WorAl
Davis, William C 1946- *ConAu 8NR, –61*
Davis, William Stearns 1877-1930 *AmAu&B,*
ApCAB X, CarSB, DcAmAu, DcNAA,
JBA 34, NatCAB 24, OxAmL,
ScF&FL 1, TwCA, WhAm 1, WhNAA
Davis-Gardner, Angela 1942- *ConAu 110,*
DrAP&F 83
Davison, Jane 1932?-1981 *BioIn 12,*
ConAu 104
Davison, Jean 1937- *ConAu 10NR, –65*
Dawood, N J 1927- *ConAu 49,*
WhoTran ARB
Dawson, A J 1872?-1951 *BbD, BiD&SB,*
BioIn 8, NewC, ScF&FL 1, WhLit,
WhoChL
Dawson, Christopher Henry 1889-1970 *BioIn 1,*
–4, –6, CathA 1930, ChhPo, ConAu 1R,
–6NR, –29R, LinLib L, ObitT 1961,
PoIre, TwCA SUP, WhE&EA
Dawson, Fielding 1930- *ConAu 85, ConLC 6,*
DrAF 76, DrAP&F 83, IntAu&W 76
Dawson, Will *OxCan*
Day, A Grove 1904- *AmAu&B, ConAu 8NR,*
–21R, DrAS 74E, WhNAA, WhoAm 74
Day, Beth Feagles 1924- *AuBYP SUP,*
ChhPo S2, ConAu 3NR, –9R, ForWC 70,
SmATA 33[port], WhoAmW 74, –58, –61,
–72, –75, –77
Day, Clarence Shepard, Jr. 1874-1935
AmAu&B, BioIn 3, –4, –5, –6, ChhPo, –S1,
–S3, ConAmA, ConAu 108, CyWA,
DcAmB S1, DcLB 11[port], DcLEL,
DcNAA, EvLB, LinLib L, LongCTC,
NatCAB 28, OxAmL, PenC AM, REn,
REnAL, TwCA, TwCA SUP, TwCWr,
WebAB, –79, WhAm 1, WorAl
Day, Ingeborg 1940- *BioIn 12*
Day, Michael Herbert 1927- *Au&Wr 6,*
FifIDA, IntAu&W 76, –77, –82,
IntMed 80, WhoWor 76, WrDr 76, –80,
–82, –84
Day, Robert S 1941- *WrDr 84*
Day-Lewis, Cecil 1904-1972 *Au&Wr 6,*
BioIn 3, –4, –5, –6, –8, –9, –10, –12, CasWL,
ChhPo, –S1, –S3, CnE&AP, CnMWL,
ConAu 33R, ConAu P-1, ConLC 1, –6,
–10, ConLCrt, –82, ConNov 72, ConP 70,
–75, CurBio 40, –69, –72, –72N, DcIrB,
DcIrL, DcIrW 1, DcLB 15[port],
–20[port], DcLEL, EncMys, EncWL, –81,
LinLib L, –S, LongCEL, LongCTC,
ModBrL, ModBrL SUP, NewC, Novels,
ObitOF 79, ObitT 1971, OxEng,
PenC ENG, RAdv, –1, REn, ScF&FL 1,
TwCA, TwCA SUP, TwCCW 78, –83,
TwCCr&M 80, TwCWr, WebE&AL,
WhDW, WhAm 5, WhoTwCL
Day-Lewis, Cecil *see also* Lewis, C Day
Da·y-Lewis, Cecil *see also* Lewis, Cecil Day
Dayan, Moshe 1915-1981 *AnObit 1981[port],*

BioIn 4, -7, -8, -9, -10, -11, -12, CelR 73, ConAu 105, -21R, CurBio 57, -82N, DcPol, IntAu&W 77, IntWW 74, -75, -76, -77, -78, -79, -80, -81, -82N, IntYB 78, -79, -80, -81, LinLib L, McGEWB, MidE 78, -79, -80, -81, NewYTBE 70, NewYTBS 78, -80[port], -81[port], WhDW, WhoMilH 76, WhoWor 74, -78, -80, WhoWorJ 72, -78, WorAl, WorDWW

Deal, Borden 1922- AmAu&B, Au&Wr 6, BioIn 5, ConAu 1R, -2NR, DcLB 6, DrAP&F 83, IntAu&W 76, -77, -82, REnAL, WrDr 76, -80, -82, -84

Dean, Anabel 1915- BioIn 11, ConAu 37R, IntAu&W 77, SmATA 12, WhoAmW 83, WrDr 76, -80, -82, -84

Dean, John Wesley, III 1938- BioIn 9, -10, -11, -12, ConAu 105, NewYTBE 73, PolProf NF, WhoAm 74, -76, -78, -80, WhoAmP 73, WhoGov 72, WorAl

Dean, Karen Strickler 1923- ConAu 109

DeAndrea, William L 1952- ConAu 81

DeAngeli, Marguerite Lofft 1889- AmAu&B, AmWomWr, Au&ICB, Au&Wr 6, AuBYP, AuNews 2, BioIn 1, -2, -3, -4, -5, -7, -8, -9, -10, -11, -12, BkCL, ChlLR 1, ChhPo, -S1, ConAu 3NR, -5R, ConICB, CurBio 47, DcLB 22[port], FamMS, HerW, IlsCB 1744, -1946, -1957, -1967, InWom, JBA 51, LinLib L, MichAu 80, MorBMP, Newb 1922, SmATA 1, -27[port], TwCCW 78, -83, WhoAm 74, WhoAmA 73, -76, WhoAmW 74, -58, -64, -66, -70, -72, WrDr 80, -82, -84

DeAngeli, Marguerite Lofft see also Angeli, Marguerite

DeBeauvoir, Simone 1908- Au&Wr 6, ConAu X, IntDcWB[port], ModRL, ScF&FL 1, WhoWor 78, -80, -82

DeBeauvoir, Simone see also Beauvoir, Simone De

Debo, Angie 1890- BioIn 4, ConAu 69, ConIsC 1[port], TexWr, WhoAm 74, -76, -78, WhoAmW 58, WhoLibS 55

DeBorhegyi, Suzanne Sims 1926- AuBYP, BioIn 8, ConAu 5R, ForWC 70, WhoAmA 73, -78, -80, WhoAmW 74, -70, -72, -75

Debray, Regis 1940?- BioIn 8, -9, -12, ConAu 21R, CurBio 82[port], EncLatA, NewYTBE 70, WhoAm 74, -76

DeCamp, L Sprague 1907- AuBYP, ConAu 1R, -1NR, -9NR, ConSFA, DcLB 8[port], EncSF, IntAu&W 77, -82, LinLib L, Novels, ScF&FL 1, -2, SmATA 9, WhoAm 78, -80, -82, WhoHr&F, WhoSciF, WorAl, WorAu, WrDr 76, -80, -82, -84

DeCamp, L Sprague see also Lyon, Lyman R

DeCamp, L Sprague see also Wells, J Wellington

DeCamp, Lyon Sprague 1907- BioIn 7, -8, -10,

-11, -12, DrAS 74H, -78H, -82H, WhoAm 76, WhoE 75, -77

Decker, Duane Walter 1910-1964 AuBYP, BioIn 2, -7, -10, ConAu 5R, SmATA 5

Decker, William B 1926- ASpks, BioIn 8, -11, DrAP&F 83, WrDr 84

DeClements, Barthe 1920- ConAu 105, SmATA 35

Dee, Ruby 1924?- BiE&WWA, BioIn 5, -6, -9, -10, -12, BlkAWP, CelR 73, ChhPo S2, CivR 74, CurBio 70, DrBlPA, Ebony 1, FilmgC, InB&W 80, IntMPA 82, -84, MotPP, MovMk, NegAl 76, -83, NewYTBE 70, NotNAT, WhoAm 74, -76, -78, -80, -82, WhoAmW 74, -66, -68, -70, -72, -75, WhoBlA 75, -77, -80, WhoHol A, WhoThe 15, -16, -81, WomWMM, WorAl

Deedy, John Gerard, Jr. 1923- AmCath 80, ConAu 33R, SmATA 24[port], WhoAm 74, -76, -78, -80, -82, WhoE 74, WhoF&I 74

Deegan, Paul Joseph 1937- ConAu 102

DeFelitta, Frank Paul 1921- ConAu 61, WhoAm 74, -76, -78, -80, -82, WhoWest 74, -76, -78, WhoWor 74

Defoe, Daniel 1660?-1731 Alli, AtlBL, BbD, BiD&SB, BioIn 1, -2, -3, -4, -5, -6, -7, -8, -9, -10, -11, -12, BrAu, BrWr 3, CarSB, CasWL, Chambr 2, ChhPo S1, -S3, CrtT 2, -4, CyEd[port], CyWA, DcBiA, DcBiPP, DcEnA, DcEnL, DcEuL, DcLEL, Dis&D, EncE 75, EncSF, EvLB, FilmgC, HsB&A, LinLib L, -S, LongCEL, LuthC 75, McGEWB, MnBBF, MouLC 2, NewC, Novels[port], OxEng, OxShips, PenC ENG, RAdv 1, RComWL, REn, ScF&FL 1, SmATA 22[port], WebE&AL, WhDW, WhoChL, WhoHr&F, WorAl

Deford, Frank 1938- BioIn 10, ConAu 33R, WrDr 76, -80, -82, -84

Degani, Meir H 1909- AmM&WS 73P, -76P, -79P, -82P, ConAu 102, WhoAmJ 80, WhoWorJ 72, -78

Degler, Carl Neumann 1921- ConAu 3NR, -5R, DrAS 74H, -78H, -82H, WhoAm 74, -76, -78, -80, -82

DeGraft-Johnson, John Coleman 1919- ConAu 21R, IntAu&W 76A, WrDr 76

DeGramont, Sanche 1932- AmAu&B, BioIn 9, ConAu 45, WhoSpyF

DeGramont, Sanche see also Morgan, Ted

DeGrummond, Lena Young AuBYP, BiDrLUS 70, BioIn 8, -10, ConAu 1R, -1NR, SmATA 6, WhoAmW 66, WhoLibS 55, -66

Deighton, Len 1929- BioIn 6, -7, -9, -10, -12, ConAu 9R, ConLC 4, -7, -22[port], ConNov 72, -76, -82, CorpD, DcLEL 1940, EncMys, EncSF, IntAu&W 76, -77, IntMPA 77, -75, -76,

Delton, Jina 1961- *ConAu 106*
DeLuca, A Michael 1912- *ConAu 21R,*
DrAS 74F
Delving, Michael 1914-1978 *AmAu&B,*
BioIn 11, ConAu X, IntAu&W 76X,
-77X, SmATA X, -3, TwCCr&M 80,
WorAu, WrDr 76
Delving, Michael *see also* Williams, Jay
DeMare, Eric S 1910- *Au&Wr 6, ConArch A,*
ConAu 6NR, -9R, IntAu&W 76, -77
DeMarinis, Rick 1934- *BioIn 10,*
ConAu 9NR, -57
Demas, Vida 1927- *BioIn 11, ConAu 49,*
SmATA 9
DeMaupassant, Guy 1850-1893 *EuAu, FilmgC,*
ScF&FL 1, WhoHr&F
DeMaupassant, Guy *see also* Maupassant, Guy
De
DeMessieres, Nicole 1930- *ConAu 107*
DeMille, Agnes 1905?- *AmAu&B,*
AmWomWr, BiE&WWA, BioIn 1, -2, -3,
-4, -5, -6, -7, -8, -9, -10, -11, -12,
BioNews 74, CelR 73, ConAu X,
CurBio 43, EncMT, GoodHs, HerW,
InWom, LibW, NewYTBS 76, NotNAT,
-A, OxAmH, REnAL, WebAB, -79,
Who 74, -82, -83, WhoAm 74, -76, -78,
-80, -82, WhoAmW 74, -58, -58A, -64,
-64A, -66, -68, -70, -72, -81, -83,
WhoThe 15, -16, -81, WhoWor 74, -78,
WorAl
DeMille, Agnes *see also* Prude, Agnes George
DeMille, Nelson Richard 1943- *ConAu 6NR,*
-57, WhoE 77, -79, -81, -83
Deming, Richard 1915- *AuBYP SUP,*
ConAu 3NR, -9R, IntAu&W 76, -77, -82,
SmATA 24[port], TwCCr&M 80,
WrDr 76, -80, -82, -84
Dempsey, Hugh Aylmer 1929- *ConAu 11NR,*
-69, OxCan SUP
Dengler, Dieter 1938- *BioIn 7, -9, ConAu 102*
Dengler, Marianna 1935- *ConAu 102*
Denham, Bertie 1927- *ConAu 93*
Denisoff, R Serge 1939- *AmM&WS 73S, -78S,*
ConAu 33R, WrDr 76, -80, -82, -84
Denker, Henry 1912- *AmAu&B, AmNov,*
AuNews 1, BiE&WWA, BioIn 10,
CnMD SUP, ConAu 33R, NotNAT,
WhoAm 74, -76, -78, -80, -82, WhoThe 81,
WhoWor 82, WrDr 80, -82, -84
Dennis, Henry Charles 1918- *AmM&WS 73S,*
ConAu 41R, WhoF&I 74, -75, -77,
WhoWest 74, -76, -78
Dennis, Patrick 1921-1976 *AmAu&B, BioIn 4,*
-5, -6, -7, -10, -11, ConAu X, CurBio 59,
-77N, NewYTBS 76, ObitOF 79,
WhoAm 74, -76, WhoThe 81N, WorAl,
WorAu, WrDr 76
Dennis, Patrick *see also* Tanner, Edward Everett,
III
Dennis, Peggy 1909- *BioIn 11, ConAu 77*
Dennys, Rodney Onslow 1911- *ConAu 85,*

Who 74, -82, -83, WhoGen 81
Densen-Gerber, Judianne 1934- *AuBYP SUP,*
BiDrAPA 77, BioIn 9, -12, ConAu 37R,
CurBio 83[port], NewYTBE 70,
WhoAm 76, -78, -80, -82, WhoAmL 83,
WhoAmW 74, -70, -72, -75, -77, -79, -81,
-83, WhoE 74, -77, -79, -81, -83,
WomPO 78, WrDr 76, -80, -82, -84
Denver, John 1943- *BioIn 10, -11, -12,*
BioNews 74, ChhPo S2, CurBio 75,
EncPR&S, -77, IlEncRk, NewYTBE 73,
RkOn 78, -84, RolSEnR 83, WhoAm 76,
-78, -80, -82, WhoRocM 82, WorAl
Denzel, Justin F 1917- *ConAu 4NR, -53*
DePauw, Linda Grant 1940- *AuBYP SUP,*
ConAu 9NR, -21R, DrAS 74H, -78H,
-82H, SmATA 24[port], WhoAmW 83,
WhoE 83
Derby, Pat 1942- *BioIn 10, ConAu 69*
Derleth, August 1909-1971 *AmAu&B, AmNov,*
AuBYP, BioIn 2, -3, -4, -6, -7, -8, -9, -10,
-12, BkC 6, ChhPo, -S2, CnDAL,
ConAu 1R, -4NR, -29R, ConNov 72,
DcLB 9[port], DcLEL, EncMys, EncSF,
NewYTBE 71, Novels, OxAmL, REn,
REnAL, ScF&FL 1, -2, SmATA 5,
TwCA, TwCA SUP, TwCCr&M 80,
WhAm 5, WhNAA, WhoHr&F,
WhoSciF
DeRopp, Robert Sylvester 1913- *Au&Wr 6,*
ConAu 17R
Desai, Anita 1937- *CasWL, ConAu 81,*
ConLC 19, ConNov 72, -76, -82,
DcLEL 1940, IntAu&W 76, -77, -82,
Novels, REn, WrDr 76, -80, -82, -84
DeSaint-Exupery, Antoine 1900-1944 *ModRL,*
ObitOF 79, ScF&FL 1, WhAm 2
DeSaint-Exupery, Antoine *see also*
Saint-Exupery, Antoine De
Desbarats, Peter 1933- *CanWW 79, -80, -81,*
-83, ConAu 10NR, -17R, OxCan
Deschin, Celia Spalter 1903- *ConAu 104,*
WhoAmW 74, -72, -75
DeSchweinitz, Karl 1887-1975 *AuBYP SUP,*
BioIn 10, ConAu 57, -61, ObitOF 79,
WhAm 6
DeShields, James Thomas 1891- *TexWr*
Desmond, Adrian J 1947- *ConAu 8NR, -61*
Desmond, Alice Curtis 1897- *AmAu&B,*
AuBYP, BioIn 7, -11, ConAu 1R, -2NR,
SmATA 8, WhoAm 74, -76,
WhoAmW 74, -58, -61, -64, -66, -68, -70,
-72, -75, -77, WhoE 74, -75, -77
Desoutter, Denis Marcel 1919- *Au&Wr 6*
DesPres, Terrence 1939- *ConAu 73,*
DrAS 82E
Dethier, Vincent Gaston 1915- *AmM&WS 76P,*
-79P, -82P, BlueB 76, ConAu 9NR, -65,
IntAu&W 76, -77, IntWW 74, -75, -76,
-77, -78, -79, -80, -81, -82, -83,
McGMS 80[port], WhoAm 74, -76,
WhoE 74, WrDr 76, -80, -82, -84

DeTocqueville, Alexis 1805-1859 *OxAmL,*
REnAL, WhAm HS
DeTocqueville, Alexis *see also* Tocqueville,
Alexis, Com
DeToledano, Ralph 1916- *AmAu&B,*
AuNews 1, BioIn 3, –5, –6, –10,
CurBio 62, DrAP&F 83, WhoAm 74, –76,
–78
DeTrevino, Elizabeth Borton 1904- *Au&ICB,*
BioIn 10, –11, ForWC 70, MorBMP,
ScF&FL 1, NewbC 1966, TwCCW 78,
–83, WrDr 80, –82, –84
DeTrevino, Elizabeth Borton *see also* Trevino,
Elizabeth
Deutsch, Babette 1895-1982 *AmAu&B,*
AmWomWr, AnObit 1982[port], AnCL,
Au&Wr 6, BioIn 4, –6, –9, –12, BlueB 76,
ChhPo, –S1, –S2, –S3, ConAmL,
ConAu 1R, –4NR, –108, ConLC 18,
ConP 70, –75, –80, DcLEL, DrAP 75,
DrAS 74E, EvLB, IntAu&W 76, –77, –82,
IntWW 74, –75, –76, –77, –78, –79, –80, –81,
–82, –83N, IntWWP 77, –82, LinLib L,
LongCTC, MorJA, NewYTBS 82, Novels,
OxAmL, PenC AM, RAdv 1, REn,
REnAL, SmATA 1, –33N, TwCA,
TwCA SUP, TwCWr, WhE&EA,
WhNAA, WhoAm 74, –76, –78, –80,
WhoAmW 74, –58, –64, –66, –68, –70,
WhoWor 74, WhoWorJ 72, WrDr 76, –80,
–82
Deutsch, Ronald M 1928- *ConAu 1R, –4NR*
DeValois, Ninette 1898- *Au&Wr 6, BioIn 1,*
–2, –3, –4, –5, –6, –8, –9, –11, BlueB 76,
CurBio 49, InWom, IntDcWB,
IntWW 74, –75, –76, –77, –78, –79, –80, –81,
–82, –83, PIP&P, WhThe, Who 74, –82,
–83, WhoAmW 74, –68, –70, –72, WorAl
Devaney, John 1926- *AuBYP SUP, BioIn 11,*
ConAu 7NR, –17R, SmATA 12
DeVeaux, Alexis *ConAu 65, DrAF 76,*
DrAP&F 83, NatPD
Devereux, Frederick Leonard, Jr. 1914-
BioIn 11, ConAu 1NR, –49, SmATA 9,
WhoE 77, –79, –81
Devi, Shakuntala 1932?- *BioIn 2*
Devine, D M 1920- *ConAu 1NR,*
TwCCr&M 80, WrDr 82
Devine, D M *see also* Devine, Dominic
Devine, Dominic 1920- *ConAu X, EncMys,*
WrDr 76, –80
Devine, Dominic *see also* Devine, D M
Devlin, Bernadette 1947- *BioIn 8, –9, –10, –11,*
–12, BlueB 76, CelR 73, ConAu 105,
CurBio 70, HerW, Who 74, –82, –83,
WhoAmW 74, –72, WhoWor 74, WorAl
DeVries, Peter 1910- *AmAu&B, Au&Wr 6,*
BiE&WWA, BioIn 4, –5, –6, –8, –10, –12,
BlueB 76, CelR 73, CnDAL, ConAu 17R,
ConLC 1, –2, –3, –7, –10, ConNov 72, –76,
–82, CurBio 59, DcLB Y82A[port], –6,
DcLEL 1940, DrAF 76, DrAP&F 83,

EncWL, IntAu&W 76, –77, –82,
IntWW 74, –75, –76, –77, –78, –79, –80, –81,
–82, –83, LinLib L, ModAL,
ModAL SUP, NewYTBS 83[port],
NotNAT, Novels[port], OxAmL,
PenC AM, REnAL, Who 74, –82, –83,
WhoAm 74, –76, –78, –80, –82, WhoTwCL,
WhoWor 74, WorAu, WrDr 76, –80, –82,
–84
DeWeese, Gene 1934- *ConAu X, EncSF,*
WrDr 84
Dewhurst, Keith 1931- *BioIn 10, ConAu 61,*
ConDr 73, –77, –82, WhoThe 81,
WhoWor 76, WrDr 76, –80, –82, –84
Dewitz, Ludwig Richard Max 1916- *DrAS 74P,*
–78P, –82P
Dexter, Pat Egan *ConAu 81*
Deyneka, Anita 1943- *ConAu 11NR, –61,*
SmATA 24[port]
Dhondy, Farrukh 1944- *TwCCW 83*
Diamond, Neil 1941- *BiDAmM, BioIn 8, –9,*
–10, –11, –12, BioNews 74, CelR 73,
ConAu 108, CurBio 81[port], EncPR&S,
–77, IlEncRk, IntMPA 84, NewYTBE 72,
RkOn 78, –84, RolSEnR 83, WhoAm 74,
–76, –78, –80, –82, WhoRocM 82, WorAl
Diamonstein, Barbaralee D *ConAu 85,*
IntAu&W 82, WhoAm 76, –78, –80, –82,
WhoAmA 82, WhoAmW 68, –70, –75, –77,
WhoE 77
Dibdin, Michael 1947- *ConAu 77*
Dibner, Bern 1897- *BioIn 10, –11, –12,*
ConAu 107, LElec, St&PR 75,
WhoAm 74, –76, –78, –80, WhoEng 80,
WhoTech 82
DiCerto, J J 1933- *ConAu 21R, WrDr 76,*
–80, –82, –84
Dick, Philip K 1928-1982 *AmAu&B,*
AnObit 1982, BioIn 12, ConAu 2NR,
–106, –49, ConLC 10, ConNov 76, –82,
ConSFA, DcLB 8[port], DrAF 76,
EncSF, LinLib L, Novels, ScF&FL 1, –2,
WhoAm 82, WhoSciF, WorAl, WrDr 76,
–80, –82
Dickens, Charles 1812-1870 *Alli, Alli SUP,*
AtlBL, AuBYP, BbD, BiD&SB, BioIn 1,
–2, –3, –4, –5, –6, –7, –8, –9, –10, –11, –12,
BrAu 19, BrWr 5, CarSB, CasWL,
CelCen, Chambr 3, ChhPo, –S1, –S2, –S3,
CrtT 3, –4, CyEd, CyWA, DcAmSR,
DcBiA, DcBiPP, DcEnA, –AP, DcEnL,
DcEuL, DcLB 21[port], DcLEL, Dis&D,
EncMys, EncO&P 78, EvLB, FamAYP,
FilmgC, HsB&A, JBA 34, LinLib L, –S,
LongCEL, McGEWB, MnBBF,
MouLC 3, NewC, NewEOp 71,
NotNAT B, Novels[port], OxAmH,
OxAmL, OxEng, OxFilm, OxMus,
OxThe, PenC AM, –ENG, PIP&P,
RAdv 1, RComWL, REn, ScF&FL 1,
SmATA 15, Str&VC, TelT,
TwCCr&M 80A, WebE&AL, WhDW,

*WhAm HS, WhoChL, WhoHr&F,
WhoSpyF, WorAl*
Dickens, Monica Enid 1915- *Au&Wr 6,
AuBYP SUP, BioIn 1, -2, -3, -4, -5, -6, -7,
-9, -10, -11, CathA 1930, ConAu 2NR,
-5R, ConNov 72, -76, -82, DcLEL, EvLB,
ForWC 70, IntAu&W 76, -77, -82,
IntWW 77, -78, -79, -80, -81, -82, -83,
LongCTC, NewC, NewYTBS 77, Novels,
PenC ENG, REn, SmATA 4, TwCWr,
WhE&EA, Who 74, -82, -83,
WhoAmW 74, -58, -61, -68, -70, -72, -75,
WorAu, WrDr 76, -80, -82, -84*
Dicker, Eva Barash 1936- *ConAu 107*
Dickerson, Robert B, Jr. 1955- *ConAu 106*
Dickerson, Roy Ernest 1886-1965 *AmAu&B,
Au&Wr 6, ConAu 5R, -103, CurBio 44,
IndAu 1917, OhA&B, SmATA 26N,
WhAm 4, -7, WhE&EA, WhLit,
WhNAA*
Dickey, Glenn Ernest, Jr. 1936- *ConAu 4NR,
-53, WhoAm 80, -82, WhoWest 76, -78*
Dickey, James 1923- *AmAu&B, AnCL,
AuNews 1, -2, BioIn 8, -9, -10, -11, -12,
BlueB 76, CelR 73, ConAu 9R, -10NR,
ConLC 1, -2, -4, -7, -10, -15, ConP 70,
-75, -80, Conv 1, CroCAP, CurBio 68,
DcLB Y82A[port], -5[port], DcLEL 1940,
DrAF 76, DrAP 75, DrAP&F 83,
DrAS 74E, -78E, -82E, EncWL, -81,
IntAu&W 77, IntWW 74, -75, -76, -77,
-78, -79, -80, -81, -82, -83, IntWWP 77,
-82, LinLib L, ModAL, ModAL SUP,
Novels, OxAmL, PenC AM, RAdv 1,
WebAB, -79, WebE&AL, WhoAm 74,
-76, -78, -80, -82, WhoS&SW 73, -75, -76,
WhoTwCL, WhoWor 74, -76, -78, -80, -82,
WorAu, WrDr 76, -80, -82, -84*
Dickinson, Emily 1830-1886 *AmAu, AmAu&B,
AmBi, AmWomWr, AmWr, AnCL,
AtlBL, BiD&SB, BioIn 1, -2, -3, -4, -5, -6,
-7, -8, -9, -10, -11, -12, CasWL,
Chambr 3, ChhPo, -S1, -S2, -S3, CnDAL,
CnE&AP, CrtT 3, -4, CyWA, DcAmAu,
DcAmB, DcLB 1, DcLEL, DcNAA,
EncAB-H, EvLB, GoodHs, HerW,
IlEncMy, InWom, IntDcWB, LibW,
LinLib L, -S, McGEWB, ModAL,
ModAL SUP, NatCAB 11, -23,
NewYTBE 73, OxAmH, OxAmL, OxEng,
PenC AM, RAdv 1, RComWL, REn,
REnAL, SmATA 29[port], Str&VC,
TwCBDA, WebAB, -79, WebE&AL,
WhDW, WhAm HS, WorAl*
Dickinson, Peter 1927- *Au&Wr 6,
AuBYP SUP, BioIn 10, ConAu 41R,
ConLC 12, EncMys, EncSF, FourBJA,
IntAu&W 76, -77, -82, Novels,
ScF&FL 1, -2, SmATA 5, TwCCW 78,
-83, TwCCr&M 80, Who 82, -83,
WhoWor 74, -76, WorAu 1970, WrDr 76,
80, -82, -84*

Dicks, Terrance *ScF&FL 1*
Dickson, Gordon R 1923- *BioIn 12,
ConAu 6NR, -9R, ConSFA,
DcLB 8[port], EncSF, IntAu&W 77,
Novels, ScF&FL 1, -2, WhoSciF, WorAl,
WrDr 80, -82, -84*
Dickson, Lovat 1902- *Au&Wr 6, BioIn 1, -5,
-6, BlueB 76, CaW, CanNov,
CanWW 70, -79, -80, ChhPo S2,
ConAu 13R, CurBio 62, IntAu&W 76,
-77, -82, IntYB 78, -79, -80, -81, -82,
Who 74, -82, -83, WrDr 76, -80, -82, -84*
Dickson, Naida 1916- *BioIn 11, ConAu 37R,
IntAu&W 77, SmATA 8, WhoAmW 75,
-77, -79, WhoWest 80, -82, -84, WrDr 76,
-80, -82, -84*
Dickson, Paul 1939- *ConAu 33R, Future,
IntAu&W 77, WrDr 76, -80, -82, -84*
Didinger, Ray 1946- *ConAu 93*
Diederich, Bernard 1926- *ConAu 77,
IntAu&W 82*
Dietz, Betty Warner 1908- *AuBYP,
AuBYP SUP, ConAu X, WhoAmW 66*
Dietz, Betty Warner *see also* Dietz, Elisabeth H
Dietz, David 1897- *AmM&WS 73P, -76P,
-79P, -82P, Au&Wr 6, BioIn 5, -11,
BlueB 76, ConAu 1R, -2NR, CurBio 40,
InSci, IntAu&W 76, -77, -82, IntWW 74,
-75, -76, -77, -78, -79, -80, -81, -82, -83,
IntYB 78, -79, -80, -81, -82, OhA&B,
REnAL, SmATA 10, WhE&EA,
WhoAm 74, -76, -78, -80, WhoAmJ 80,
WhoWorJ 72, -78*
Dietz, Elisabeth H 1908- *AuBYP SUP,
BioIn 8, ConAu 29R, LEduc 74,
WhoAmW 74, -68, -70, -72, -75, -77*
Dietz, Elisabeth H *see also* Dietz, Betty Warner
Dietz, Lew 1907- *AuBYP, BioIn 8, -11,
ConAu 3NR, -5R, SmATA 11,
WhoAmP 73, -75, -77, -79, WrDr 76, -80,
-82 -84*
DiFate, Vincent 1945- *EncSF, WhoAmA 82*
Diggins, Julia E *AuBYP, BioIn 8*
D'Ignazio, Fred 1949- *ConAu 110,
SmATA 35*
Dillard, Annie 1945- *AmWomWr, BioIn 10,
-11, -12, BlueB 76, ConAu 3NR, -49,
ConLC 9, CurBio 83[port],
DcLB Y80B[port], DrAP 75,
DrAP&F 83, IntAu&W 77, -82,
NewYTBS 77, SmATA 10, WhoAm 76,
-78, -80, -82, WhoAmW 81, WrDr 76,
-80, -82, -84*
Dillard, J L 1924- *ConAu 41R*
Dille, Robert Crabtree 1924?-1983 *ConAu 109,
IntYB 78, -79, -80, -81, -82, WhoAm 74,
-76, -78, WhoF&I 74, -75, -77*
Dillon, Eilis 1920- *Au&Wr 6, AuBYP,
ConAu 4NR, -9R, ConLC 17, DcIrL,
DcIrW 1, IntAu&W 76, SmATA 2,
ThrBJA, TwCCW 78, -83, WrDr 80, -82,
-84*

Dillon, Richard Hugh 1924- *AmAu&B, BiDrLUS 70, CmCal, ConAu 8NR, -17R, WhoAm 74, -76, -78, -80, -82, WhoLibS 55, WhoWest 74, -76, -78*

Dilson, Jesse 1914- *ConAu 25R, IntAu&W 76, SmATA 24, WhoE 74, WrDr 76, -80, -82, -84*

Dinesen, Isak 1885-1962 *AtlBL, BioIn 2, -3, -4, -5, -6, -7, -8, -9, -10, -12, CasWL, ConAu X, ConLC 10, CyWA, EncWL, -81, EvEuW, InWom, IntDcWB, LinLib L, LongCTC, McGEWB, Novels, ObitOF 79, PenC EUR, REn, ScF&FL 1, -2, TwCA, TwCA SUP, TwCWr, WomWMM, WorAl*

Dinesen, Isak *see also* Blixen, Karen Christentze Dinese

Dingwell, Joyce *WrDr 84*

Dinneen, Betty 1929- *ConAu 8NR, -57*

Dinsdale, Tim 1924- *BioIn 11, ConAu 1R, -2NR, SmATA 11, WrDr 76, -80, -82, -84*

Diole, Philippe Victor 1908-1977 *ConAu 53, IntAu&W 76, -77, WhoFr 79N*

DiPersio, Michael S 1934- *ConAu 110*

Disch, Thomas M 1940- *BioIn 12, ConAu 21R, ConLC 7, ConSFA, DcLB 8[port], DcLEL 1940, DrAP&F 83, EncSF, Po&Wr 77, ScF&FL 1, -2, WhoAm 82, WhoE 74, WhoSciF, WrDr 84*

Disney, Doris Miles 1907-1976 *AmAu&B, AmCath 80, AmWomWr, ASpks, Au&Wr 6, BioIn 3, -10, -11, ConAu 3NR, -5R, -65, CurBio 54, EncMys, InWom, NewYTBS 76, TwCCr&M 80, WhAm 7, WhoAm 74, WhoAmW 74, -58, -64, -66, -68, -70, -72*

Disraeli, Robert 1903- *ConAu P-1*

Ditmars, Raymond Lee 1876-1942 *AmAu&B, AuBYP, BioIn 2, -5, -7, CurBio 40, -42, DcAmB S3, DcNAA, InSci, JBA 34, -51, LinLib L, -S, NatCAB 10, ObitOF 79, REnAL, TwCA, TwCA SUP, WhAm 2, WhNAA*

DiValentin, Maria Amelia Messuri 1911- *BioIn 10, ConAu 5R, -5NR, ForWC 70, SmATA 7, WhoAmW 74, -68, -70, -72, WhoE 74, -75, -77*

Divoky, Diane 1939- *ConAu 33R, WhoAmW 75*

Dixon, Bernard 1938- *ConAu 10NR, -65, IntAu&W 77, -82, Who 74, -82, -83, WhoWor 80, -82, WrDr 80, -82, -84*

Dixon, Franklin W *BioIn 9, -10, -11, -12, CarSB, ConAu X, -17R, EncMys, SmATA X, -1, -2, WebAB, -79*

Dixon, Franklin W *see also* Adams, Harriet S

Dixon, Franklin W *see also* Stratemeyer, Edward L

Dixon, Franklin W *see also* Svenson, Andrew E

Dixon, Jeanne 1936- *ConAu 105, SmATA 31*

Dixon, P A 1924- *Dun&B 79*

Dixon, Paige 1911- *AuBYP SUP, ConAu X, DrAP&F 83, IntAu&W 82X, WrDr 76, -80, -82, -84*

Dixon, Paige *see also* Corcoran, Barbara

Dixon, Peter Lee 1931- *BioIn 10, ConAu 2NR, -45, SmATA 6, WhoAm 74, -76, -78, -80, -82*

Djilas, Milovan 1911- *Au&Wr 6, BioIn 1, -4, -5, -6, -7, -8, -9, -10, -11, -12, CurBio 58, DcPol, IntAu&W 76, -77, IntWW 74, -75, -76, -77, -78, -79, -80, -81, -82, -83, LinLib L, McGEWB, WhDW, WhoAm 74, -76, -78, WhoSocC 78, WhoWor 74, WorAu*

Doan, Eleanor Lloyd *ConAu 1R, -1NR, IntAu&W 77, WhoAmW 74, -61, -64, -66, -68, -70, -72, -75, -77, -79, -81, WrDr 76, -80, -82, -84*

Dobie, J Frank 1888-1964 *AmAu&B, ConAu 1R, -6NR, CurBio 45, -64, DcAmB S7, DcLEL, LinLib L, -S, ObitOF 79, OxAmL, REn, REnAL, TexWr, TwCA SUP*

Dobie, James Frank 1888-1964 *BioIn 1, -2, -3, -4, -5, -7, -8, -9, -10, -11, EncAAH, REnAW, WebAB, -79, WhAm 4, WhE&EA, WorAl*

Dobkin, Kaye *ConAu X*

Dobler, Lavinia G 1910- *BioIn 10, ConAu 1R, -2NR, ForWC 70, MorBMP, SmATA 6, WhoAmW 74, -70, -75, -77, WhoLibS 55, -66*

Dobrin, Arnold Jack 1928- *AuBYP SUP, BioIn 7, -8, -9, ConAu 11NR, -25R, IlsCB 1957, -67, SmATA 4, WhoAmA 78, -80, WhoE 74*

Dobson, James Clayton, Jr. 1936- *AmM&WS 73S, -78S, ConAu 29R, WhoWest 78, -80, -82, -84, WrDr 76, -80, -82, -84*

Dobson, Terry 1937- *ConAu 81*

Dobyns, Henry F 1925- *AmM&WS 73S, -76P, ConAu 37R, DrAS 74H, FifIDA, IntAu&W 77, -82, WhoAm 74, -76, -78, WhoWest 76, WrDr 76, -80, -82, -84*

Doctorow, E L 1931- *ASpks, AuNews 2, ConAu 2NR, -45, ConLC 6, -11, -15, -18, ConNov 82, CurBio 76, DcLB Y80A[port], -2, DrAF 76, DrAP&F 83, EncSF, EncWL 81, IntAu&W 77, ModAL SUP, Novels[port], ScF&FL 1, -2, WorAl, WorAu 1970, WrDr 80, -82, -84*

Dodd, Ed 1902- *SmATA 4, WhoAm 76, -80, -82, WhoAmA 78, -80, -82*

Dodd, Wayne D 1930- *BioIn 12, ConAu 33R, DrAP 75, DrAP&F 83, DrAS 74E, -78E, -82E, IntAu&W 82, IntWWP 77, -82, WrDr 76, -80, -82, -84*

Dodds, John Wendell 1902- *Au&Wr 6,*

AuBYP SUP, BlueB 76, ConAu 5R,
DrAS 74E, –78E, –82E, IntAu&W 76, –77,
–82, WhoAm 74, –76, –78, –80, WrDr 76,
–80, –82, –84

Dodge, Bertha Sanford 1902- *AuBYP, BioIn 8,*
–11, ConAu 2NR, –5R, SmATA 8,
WhoAmW 58, –61, WrDr 76, –80, –82, –84

Dodge, Ernest Stanley 1913-1980 *BioIn 12,*
ConAu 1R, –2NR, –97, DrAS 74H, –78H,
FifIDA, IntAu&W 76, –77, –82,
NewYTBS 80, OxCan, WhAm 7,
WhoAm 74, –76, –78, –80, WhoAmA 73,
WhoOcn 78

Dodgson, Charles Lutwidge 1832-1898
Alli SUP, AnCL, AtlBL, AuBYP,
BiD&SB, BioIn 1, –2, –3, –4, –5, –6, –7, –8,
–9, –10, –11, –12, BrAu 19, CarSB,
CasWL, CelCen, Chambr 3, ChhPo, –S1,
DcBrBI, DcEnA, –AP, DcEnL, DcEuL,
DcLEL, DcScB, Dis&D, EvLB, InSci,
JBA 34, LinLib S, MouLC 4, NewC,
OxEng, PenC ENG, RComWL, REn,
ScF&FL 1, TelT, WhDW, WhoChL,
YABC 2

Dodgson, Charles Lutwidge *see also* Carroll,
Lewis

Dodson, Fitzhugh James 1923- *ConAu 29R,*
IntAu&W 76, WhoWest 74, –76

Dodson, Kenneth M 1907- *BioIn 11,*
ConAu 1R, IntAu&W 76, SmATA 11,
WrDr 76, –80, –82, –84

Dodson, Owen 1914-1983 *AmAu&B,*
BiE&WWA, BioIn 1, –12, BlkAWP,
BroadAu[port], ConAu 110, –65, DrAF 76,
DrAP 75, DrAP&F 83, DrBlPA,
InB&W 80, LinLib L, LivgBAA,
NegAl 76, –83, NewYTBS 83[port],
NotNAT, Novels, PenC AM, SelBAA,
WhoAm 78, –80

Dodson, Susan 1941- *ConAu 97*

Doerflinger, William Main 1910- *AmAu&B,*
WhoAm 74, –76

Dohan, Mary Helen 1914- *ConAu 85,*
WrDr 76, –80, –82, –84

Doherty, Anna Marie 1929- *ForWC 70,*
WhoAmW 75, –77, –79, –81, –83, WhoE 79,
–81, –83

Doherty, John Stephen *AuBYP, BioIn 7*

Doig, Desmond 1921- *ConAu 69*

Doig, Ivan 1939- *ConAu 81*

Dolan, Edward F, Jr. 1924- *AuBYP SUP,*
ConAu 33R, SmATA 31

Dolan, John Richard 1893- *ConAu 9R*

Dolce, Philip Charles 1941- *ConAu 57,*
DrAS 74H, –78H, –82H, WhoE 77

Dolim, Mary Nuzum 1925- *AuBYP, BioIn 8,*
ConAu 17R

Dolson, Hildegarde 1908-1981 *BioIn 1, –10, –12,*
ConAu X, –5R, ForWC 70, InWom,
SmATA 5, TwCCr&M 80, WhoAmW 58,
–61, WrDr 82, –84

Doming, Eric 1918- *ConAu 9R*

Donaldson, Frances 1907- *ConAu 61, Who 82,*
–83, WrDr 76, –80, –82, –84

Donaldson, Margaret 1926- *ConAu 103*

Donaldson, Stephen R 1947- *BioIn 12,*
ConAu 89, WhoAm 82, WrDr 84

Donleavy, J P 1926- *AmAu&B, Au&Wr 6,*
AuNews 2, BlueB 76, CnMD, ConAu 9R,
ConDr 73, –77, –82, ConLC 1, –4, –6, –10,
ConNov 72, –76, –82, CurBio 79, DcIrL,
DcLB 6, DrAF 76, DrAP&F 83,
IntAu&W 76, LinLib L, ModAL,
ModWD, Novels, OxAmL, PenC AM,
RAdv 1, TwCWr, WebE&AL,
WhoThe 15, –16, –81, WhoTwCL, WorAl,
WorAu, WrDr 76, –80, –82, –84

Donleavy, James Patrick 1926- *BioIn 8, –9, –10,*
–11, –12, DcLEL 1940, IntAu&W 77, –82,
IntWW 74, –75, –76, –77, –78, –79, –80, –81,
–82, –83, Who 74, –82, –83, WhoAm 74,
–76, –78, –80, –82, WhoWor 74, –76, –78,
–80, –82

Donnan, Marcia Jeanne 1932- *ConAu 104,*
WhoLab 76, WomPO 76

Donnelly, Elfie *TwCCW 83B*

Donovan 1946- *AntBDN M, BioIn 8,*
EncFCWM 69, EncPR&S, –77, IlEncRk,
RkOn 78, –84, RolSEnR 83, WhoHol A,
WhoRocM 82, WorAl

Donovan, Frank Robert 1906-1975 *AuBYP,*
BioIn 8, –10, ConAu 1R, –6NR, –61,
SmATA 30N

Donovan, John 1928- *ChlLR 3, ConAu 97,*
SmATA 29, TwCCW 78, –83, WrDr 84

Donovan, Robert John 1912- *AmAu&B,*
Au&Wr 6, BioIn 9, BlueB 76,
ConAu 1R, –2NR, WhoAm 74, –76, –78,
–80, –82, WhoWor 74, –76

Doob, Leonard W 1909- *AmAu&B,*
AmM&WS 73S, –78S, AuBYP SUP,
BioIn 11, BlueB 76, ConAu 2NR, –5R,
IntWW 74, –75, –76, –77, –78, –79, –80, –81,
–82, –83, SmATA 8, WhoAm 74, –76, –78,
–80, –82, WhoWor 74, WrDr 76, –80, –82,
–84

Doody, Margaret Anne 1939- *ConAu 11NR,*
–69, DrAS 82E, WhoAmW 79, –81, –83

Dooley, Thomas Anthony 1927-1961 *AmAu&B,*
BioIn 4, –5, –6, –7, –8, –9, –10, –11, –12,
ConAu 93, CurBio 57, –61, DcAmB S7,
DcCathB, InSci, LinLib L, LuthC 75,
ObitOF 79, WebAB, –79, WebAMB,
WhAm 4A

Doone, Jice 1887-1964 *ConAu X*

Doone, Jice *see also* Marshall, James Vance

Doray, Maya 1922- *ConAu 45*

Dore, Ronald Philip 1925- *ConAu 89,*
Who 82, –83

Dorman, Michael 1932- *AuBYP SUP,*
BioIn 10, ConAu 5NR, –13R,
IntAu&W 77, SmATA 7, WhoE 74, –75,
WrDr 76, –80, –82, –84

Dorman, N B 1927- *ConAu 106*

Dorman, Sonya 1924- *ConAu 73, DrAF 76, DrAP 75, DrAP&F 83, EncSF, WhoSciF, WrDr 84*

Dornberg, John Robert 1931- *AuBYP SUP, ConAu 1R, –1NR, IntAu&W 77, –82, WrDr 76, –80, –82, –84*

Dorson, Richard M 1916-1981 *BioIn 12, ChhPo S3, ConAu 105, –106, DrAS 74H, –78H, NewYTBS 81, SmATA 30[port], WhoAm 76, –78, WhoWor 78, –80*

DosPassos, John 1896-1970 *AmAu&B, AmNov, AmWr, AtlBL, Au&Wr 6, BiE&WWA, BioIn 1, –2, –3, –4, –5, –6, –7, –8, –9, –10, –11, –12, CasWL, Chambr 3, CnDAL, CnMD, ConAmA, ConAmL, ConAu 3NR, –29R, ConLC 1, –4, –8, –11, –25[port], CurBio 40, –70, CyWA, DcAmSR, DcLB DS1[port], –4, –9[port], DcLEL, EncAB-H, EncWL, –81[port], EvLB, LinLib L, –S, LongCTC, MakMC, McGEWB, ModAL, ModAL SUP, ModWD, NewYTBE 70, Novels[port], ObitOF 79, OxAmL, OxEng, PenC AM, RAdv 1, REn, REnAL, TwCA, TwCA SUP, TwCWr, WebAB, –79, WebE&AL, WhDW, WhAm 5, WhE&EA, WhNAA, WhoTwCL, WorAl*

DosPassos, John *see also* Passos, John Dos

Doss, Helen 1918?- *AuBYP, BioIn 8, –12, ConAu 6NR, –9R, SmATA 20, WhoAmW 61*

Doster, William Clark 1921- *ConAu 13R, DrAS 74E, –78E, –82E*

Doster, William Ernst 1941- *WhoAmL 79*

Dostoyevsky, Fyodor Mikhailovich 1821-1881 *AtlBL, AuBYP SUP, BbD, BiD&SB, CasWL, CIDMEL, CyWA, DcEuL, DcRusL, EncMys, EncSF, EncWT, EuAu, EvEuW, McGEWB, NewC, Novels[port], OxEng, PenC EUR, RComWL, REn, WhDW, WorAl*

Doty, Jean Slaughter 1929- *AuBYP SUP, ConAu 2NR, –45, SmATA 28[port]*

Doubtfire, Dianne Joan 1918- *Au&Wr 6, ConAu 1R, –1NR, IntAu&W 76, –77, –82, SmATA 29[port], WhoWor 76, –78, WrDr 76, –80, –82, –84*

Doughty, Wayne Dyre 1929-1968 *IndAu 1917*

Douglas, Carole Nelson 1944- *ConAu 107*

Douglas, James McM *ConAu X, SmATA 5*

Douglas, James McM *see also* Butterworth, W E

Douglas, John Scott 1905- *AuBYP, BioIn 8, WhNAA*

Douglas, Lloyd Cassel 1877-1951 *AmAu&B, AmNov, BioIn 1, –2, –3, –4, –5, –10, CyWA, DcAmB S5, EvLB, FilmgC, IndAu 1917, LinLib L, LongCTC, MichAu 80, Novels, ObitOF 79, OhA&B, OxAmL, PenC AM, REn, REnAL, TwCA, TwCA SUP, TwCWr, WebAB, –79, WhAm 3, WhNAA, WorAl*

Douglas, Martha Carol 1937- *WhoWest 84*

Douglas, Mike 1925- *AmPS B, BioIn 7, –8, –9, –10, –11, –12, BioNews 75, CelR 73, CmpEPM, ConAu 89, CurBio 68, IntMPA 79, –81, –82, –84, LesBEnT, NewYTET, RkOn 78, WhoAm 74, –76, –78, –80, –82, WhoE 74, WhoHol A, WhoRocM 82, WorAl*

Douglas, William Orville 1898-1980 *AmAu&B, AmBench 79, AnObit 1980[port], Au&Wr 6, AuBYP, BiDFedJ, BioIn 1, –2, –3, –4, –5, –6, –7, –8, –9, –10, –11, –12, BlueB 76, CelR 73, CngDr 74, –77, –79, ConAu 9R, –93, ConISC 1[port], CurBio 41, –50, –80N, DcAmSR, DcLEL 1940, DcPol, DrAS 74P, –78P, EncAAH, EncAB-H, IntAu&W 77, IntWW 74, –75, –76, –77, –78, –79, LinLib L, –S, McGEWB, MinnWr, NewYTBE 70, NewYTBS 75, –80[port], OxAmH, OxAmL, OxLaw, PolProf E, PolProf J, PolProf K, PolProf NF, PolProf T, REn, REnAL, TwCA SUP, WebAB, –79, WhAm 7, Who 74, WhoAm 74, –76, –78, –80, WhoAmL 78, –79, WhoAmP 73, –75, –77, –79, WhoGov 77, –72, –75, WhoPNW, WhoS&SW 73, –75, WhoWest 74, –76, WhoWor 74, –78, WorAl, WrDr 76*

Douglass, Frederick 1817-1895 *Alli SUP, AmAu, AmAu&B, AmBi, ApCAB, BbD, BiD&SB, BiDSA, BioIn 1, –2, –3, –4, –5, –6, –7, –8, –9, –10, –11, –12, BlkAWP, CelCen, Chambr 3, CivWDc, CyAG, DcAmAu, DcAmB, DcAmDH, DcAmSR, DcBiPP, –A, DcLB 1, DcNAA, Drake, EncAAH, EncAB-H, EncSoH, HarEnUS[port], InB&W 80, LinLib L, –S, McGEWB, NatCAB 2, NegAl 76[port], –83[port], OxAmH, OxAmL, REn, REnAL, SelBAA, SmATA 29[port], TwCBDA, WebAB, –79, WebE&AL, WhAm HS, WhAmP, WorAl*

Douty, Esther M 1911-1978 *AuBYP SUP, BioIn 11, ConAu 3NR, –5R, –85, SmATA 23N, –8*

Dowd, David L 1918-1968 *WhAm 5*

Dowdell, Dorothy Florence Karns 1910- *BioIn 11, ConAu 5NR, –9R, ForWC 70, SmATA 12, WhoAmW 74, –68, –70, –72, –75, –77*

Dowden, Anne Ophelia Todd 1907- *AuBYP, BioIn 8, –10, –12, ConAu 3NR, –9R, IlsCB 1967, SmATA 7, WhoAmA 73, –76, –78, –80, –82, WhoAmW 83, WrDr 76, –80, –82, –84*

Dowden, Anne Ophelia Todd *see also* Todd, Anne Ophelia

Dowdey, Clifford 1904- *AmAu&B, AmNov, BioIn 2, –4, ConAu 9R, EncSoH, REnAL, TwCA, TwCA SUP, WhoAm 74, –76, –78, –80*

Down, Goldie 1918- *ConAu 11NR, –25R*

Downer, Marion 1892?-1971 *AuBYP, BioIn 8, –9, ConAu 33R, SmATA 25[port]*

Downey, Fairfax Davis 1893- *AmAu&B, AmSCAP 66, AuBYP, BioIn 1, –2, –8, –9, ChhPo, ConAu 1R, –1NR, CurBio 49, IntAu&W 76, –82, OxCan, REnAL, SmATA 3, WhE&EA, WhNAA, WhoAm 74, –76, –78, –80, WrDr 76, –80, –82, –84*

Downey, Glanville 1908- *ConAu 1R, –1NR, DrAS 74H, –78H, –82H, WhoAm 74, –76, –78, –80*

Downie, John 1931- *AmM&WS 73P, –79P, –82P, ConAu 108, OxCan SUP*

Downie, Leonard, Jr. 1942- *ConAu 1NR, –49, WrDr 76, –80, –82, –84*

Downie, Mary Alice 1934- *CaW, CanWW 83, ConAu 10NR, –25R, IntAu&W 76, –82, OxCan SUP, SmATA 13, TwCCW 78, –83, WrDr 76, –80, –82, –84*

Downs, Robert C S 1937- *ConAu 1NR, –45, DrAF 76, DrAP&F 83, WrDr 80, –82, –84*

Doyle, Sir Arthur Conan 1859-1930 *Alli SUP, AtlBL, AuBYP, BbD, BiD&SB, BiDPara, BiHiMed, BioIn 1, –2, –3, –4, –5, –6, –7, –8, –9, –10, –11, –12, CarSB, CasWL, Chambr 3, ChhPo, –S1, ConAu 104, CyWA, DcBiA, DcEnA AP, DcLB 18[port], DcLEL, Dis&D, EncMys, EncO&P 78, EncSF, EvLB, FilmgC, JBA 34, LinLib L, –S, LongCEL, LongCTC, McGEWB, MnBBF, ModBrL, NewC, NotNAT B, Novels[port], OxEng, PenC ENG, PIP&P, PoIre, RAdv 1, REn, ScF&FL 1, SmATA 24[port], TelT, TwCA, TwCA SUP, TwCCr&M 80, TwCLC 7[port], TwCWr, WebE&AL, WhDW, WhE&EA, WhLit, WhThe, WhoBW&I A, WhoChL, WhoHr&F, WhoSciF, WhoSpyF, WhoTwCL, WorAl*

Doyle, Sir Arthur Conan *see also* Conan Doyle, Arthur

Doyle, Robert V 1916- *ConAu 9NR, –65*

Dozois, Gardner R 1947- *ConAu 108, EncSF, ScF&FL 1, WhoSciF, WrDr 84*

Drabble, Margaret 1939- *Au&Wr 6, BioIn 10, –11, –12, BlueB 76, ConAu 13R, ConLC 2, –3, –5, –8, –10, –22[port], ConNov 72, –76, –82, CurBio 81[port], DcLB 14[port], DcLEL 1940, EncWL 81, IntAu&W 76, –77, IntDcWB, IntWW 74, –75, –76, –77, –78, –79, –80, –81, –82, –83, LongCTC, ModBrL SUP, NewYTBS 77, Novels, RAdv 1, TwCWr, Who 74, –82, –83, WhoAm 74, –76, –78, –82, WhoAmW 74, –70, –72, –75, WhoTwCL, WhoWor 78, –80, –82, WomWMM, WorAl, WorAu 1970, WrDr 76, –80, –82, –84*

Drackett, Phil 1922- *Au&Wr 6, ConAu 3NR, –9R, IntAu&W 76, –77, WrDr 76, –80,*

–82, –84

Drago, Harry Sinclair 1888-1979 *AmAu&B, BioIn 3, –12, ConAu 89, NewYTBS 79, OhA&B, REnAW*

Dragonwagon, Crescent 1952- *BioIn 11, ConAu 65, DrAP&F 83, SmATA 11*

Drake, Elizabeth 1948- *ConAu 109*

Drake, George Randolph 1938- *ConAu 11NR, –69*

Drake, Samuel Adams 1833-1905 *Alli, Alli SUP, AmAu, AmAu&B, AmBi, ApCAB, BbD, BiD&SB, ChhPo S1, CyAL 2, DcAmAu, DcAmB, DcNAA, HarEnUS, NatCAB 25, TwCBDA, WhAm 1*

Draper, Cena Christopher 1907- *ConAu 10NR, –17R, IntAu&W 77, WrDr 76, –80, –82, –84*

Dreifus, Claudia 1944- *BioIn 10, ConAu 1NR, –45, ForWC 70, MugS, WhoAmW 75, –77*

Dreiser, Theodore 1871-1945 *AmAu&B, AmLY, AmWr, ApCAB X, AtlBL, BioIn 1, –2, –3, –4, –5, –6, –7, –8, –9, –10, –11, –12, CasWL, Chambr 3, CnDAL, CnMD, CnMWL, ConAmA, ConAmL, ConAu 106, CurBio 46, CyWA, DcAmAu, DcAmB S3, DcAmSR, DcBiA, DcLB DS1[port], –9[port], –12[port], DcLEL, DcNAA, EncAB-H, EncMys, EncWL, –81[port], EvLB, FilmgC, IndAu 1816, LinLib L, –S, LongCTC, ModAL, ModAL SUP, ModWD, NatCAB 15, –18, –34, NotNAT B, Novels[port], ObitOF 79, OxAmH, OxAmL, OxEng, PenC AM, RAdv 1, RComWL, REn, REnAL, TwCA, TwCA SUP, TwCLC 10[port], TwCWr, WebAB, –79, WebE&AL, WhDW, WhAm 2, WhE&EA, WhLit, WhNAA, WhThe, WhoTwCL, WorAl*

Dresang, Eliza 1941- *BiDrLUS 70, BioIn 12, ConAu 69, SmATA 19, WhoLibI 82*

Drew, Elizabeth 1887-1965 *ChhPo, ConAu 5R*

Drew, Wayland *CaW*

Dribben, Judith Strick 1923- *BioIn 9, ConAu 37R*

Driggs, Howard Roscoe 1873-1963 *AmAu&B, EncAB 34, WhAm 4, WhLit, WhNAA*

Driggs, Peter 1921-1975 *ConAu 25R*

Drimmer, Frederick 1916- *ConAu 7NR, –61*

Drinkwater, John 1882-1937 *Alli, BiDLA, BioIn 1, –2, –7, –9, CasWL, Chambr 3, ChhPo, –S1, –S2, –S3, CnMD, CnThe, ConAu 109, DcLB 10[port], –19[port], DcLEL, EncWT, EvLB, JBA 34, LinLib L, –S, LongCTC, McGEWD, –84[port], ModBrL, ModWD, NewC, NotNAT A, –B, OxEng, OxMus, OxThe, PenC ENG, PIP&P, REn, Str&VC, TwCA, TwCA SUP, WebE&AL, WhE&EA, WhLit, WhThe, WhoLA*

Driver, Tom Faw 1925- *BiE&WWA,*
ConAu 1R, –1NR, DrAS 74P, –78P, –82P,
NotNAT, WhoAm 74, –76, –78, –80, –82,
WhoE 74, WhoRel 75, –77
Droescher, Vitus B 1925- *ConAu 33R*
Drotning, Phillip Thomas 1920- *ConAu 10NR,*
–25R, WhoMW 74, –76, –78, –80, –82,
WhoPubR 72, –76
Drucker, Malka 1945- *ConAu 81, SmATA 29*
Drummond, Walter 1935- *AuBYP, ConAu X,*
DcLEL 1940, SmATA X, ThrBJA,
WorAu 1970
Drummond, Walter *see also* Silverberg, Robert
Drury, Allen 1918- *AmAu&B, BioIn 5, –10,*
BlueB 76, CelR 73, ConAu 57,
ConNov 72, –76, –82, DcLEL 1940,
EncSF, IntAu&W 76, –77, –82,
IntWW 74, –75, –76, –77, –78, –79, –80, –81,
–82, –83, LinLib L, Novels, OxAmL,
REnAL, ScF&FL 1, –2, TwCWr,
Who 74, –82, –83, WhoAm 74, –76, –78,
–80, –82, WhoWor 74, –78, –80, –82,
WorAl, WorAu, WrDr 76, –80, –82, –84
Drury, John 1898-1972 *Au&Wr 6, BioIn 9,*
ConAu 5R, –33R, WhAm 5
Druxman, Michael B 1941- *ConAu 1NR, –49,*
IntMPA 77, –75, –76, –78, –79, –81, –82, –84,
WhoWest 84
Dryden, Ken 1947- *BioIn 9, –10, –11, –12,*
ConAu 105, NewYTBE 71, WhoE 74,
–75, WhoHcky 73
Dryden, Pamela *SmATA X*
Dryden, Pamela *see also* Johnston, Norma
Dryden, Spencer *WhoRocM 82*
Dryden, Spencer *see also* Jefferson Airplane
Duane, Diane Elizabeth 1952- *WhoAmW 83*
DuBois, Shirley Graham 1907?-1977 *BiDAfM,*
BioIn 11, –12, BlkAWP, ConAu 69, –77,
CurBio 77, –77N, InB&W 80,
IndAu 1917, NewYTBS 77, ObitOF 79,
ScF&FL 1, SmATA 24[port], WrDr 76
DuBois, Shirley Graham *see also* Graham,
Shirley
DuBois, W E B 1868-1963 *AmAu&B,*
ConAu 85, ConLC 1, –2, –13, CurBio 40,
–63, DcAmSR, LinLib L,
NegAl 76[port], ObitT 1961, WhLit,
WorAl
DuBois, William Edward Burghardt 1868-1963
BiDAmEd, BiDSA, BioIn 1, –2, –3, –4, –5,
–6, –7, –8, –9, –10, –11, –12, BlkAWP,
CasWL, ChhPo S3, ConAmL, DcAmAu,
DcAmB S7, DcLEL, EncAB-H, EncSoH,
HarEnUS, InB&W 80, LinLib S,
LongCTC, LuthC 75, McGEWB,
NatCAB 13, Novels, ObitOF 79,
OxAmH, OxAmL, PenC AM, REn,
REnAL, SelBAA, TwCA, TwCA SUP,
TwCBDA, WebAB, –79, WebE&AL,
WhAm 4, WhAmP, WhE&EA, WhJnl,
WhNAA, WhoColR
Dubos, Rene Jules 1901-1982 *AmAu&B,*

AmM&WS 73P, –76P, –79P,
AnObit 1982[port], AsBiEn, BiESc,
BioIn 3, –5, –7, –9, –10, –12, BlueB 76,
CelR 73, ConAu 5R, –106, CurBio 52,
–73, –82N, Future, InSci, IntEnSS 79,
IntWW 74, –75, –76, –77, –78, –79, –80, –81,
–82N, McGEWB, McGMS 80[port],
NewYTBE 70, –71, NewYTBS 82[port],
WebAB, –79, WhoAm 74, –76, –78, –80,
–82, WhoE 74, WhoWor 74, WrDr 80,
–82
Duboscq, Genevieve *BioIn 12*
Dubov, Paul d1979 *BioIn 12, ConAu 89, –97*
DuBroff, Sidney 1929- *Au&Wr 6,*
ConAu 9NR, –21R, IntAu&W 76
Duckat, Walter Benjamin 1911- *ConAu 29R*
Duckett, Alfred 1917?- *BlkAWP, ConAu 45,*
InB&W 80, SelBAA
Dudley, Geoffrey Arthur 1917- *Au&Wr 6,*
ConAu 6NR, –13R, IntAu&W 76, –77, –82,
WhoWor 76, –78, WrDr 76, –80, –82, –84
Dudley, Nancy 1902- *AuBYP, BioIn 8, –11,*
ConAu X, SmATA X, WomPO 78
Dudley, Nancy *see also* Cole, Lois Dwight
Due, Linnea A 1948- *ConAu 105*
Duff, Annis *BioIn 5, ChhPo*
Duffy, Maureen 1933- *Au&Wr 6, BioIn 10,*
BlueB 76, ConAu 25R, ConDr 73, –77,
–82, ConNov 72, –76, –82, DcLB 14[port],
DcLEL 1940, IntAu&W 76, –77, –82,
IntWWP 77, –82, Novels, TwCWr,
Who 82, –83, WhoTwCL, WhoWor 80,
WrDr 76, –80, –82, –84
Dugan, James 1912-1967 *AnCL, BioIn 7,*
ConAu 4NR, –5R, ObitOF 79, WhAm 4
Duggan, Alfred Leo 1903-1964 *AnCL, AuBYP,*
BioIn 3, –4, –6, –7, –8, ConAu 73,
FourBJA, LongCTC, ModBrL,
ObitOF 79, SmATA 25[port],
TwCA SUP, TwCWr
DuJardin, Rosamond Neal 1902-1963 *AmAu&B,*
AmWomWr, AuBYP SUP, BioIn 2, –3, –6,
–7, –9, ConAu 1R, –103, CurBio 53,
InWom, LinLib L, MorJA, REnAL,
SmATA 2, WhAm 4, WhE&EA,
WhoAmW 58, –61, –64
Dukert, Joseph Michael 1929- *AuBYP,*
BioIn 7, ConAu 3NR, –5R, IntAu&W 77,
WhoAmP 73, –75, –77, –79, –81, –83,
WhoE 83, WrDr 76, –80, –82, –84
Dulles, Allen Welsh 1893-1969 *AmAu&B,*
BioIn 1, –2, –3, –4, –5, –6, –8, –9, –11, –12,
ConAu P-2, CurBio 49, –69, EncE 75,
EncTR, HisEWW, LinLib L, –S,
NatCAB 58[port], ObitOF 79,
ObitT 1961, PolProf E, PolProf K,
PolProf T, WhAm 5, WhE&EA,
WhWW-II, WorAl
Dumas, Alexandre, Fils 1824-1895 *AtlBL, BbD,*
BiD&SB, BioIn 1, –2, –4, –5, –6, –7, –9, –11,
CasWL, CelCen, CnThe, CyWA, DcBiA,
DcBiPP, DcEuL, DrBlPA, EncWT,

EuAu, EvEuW, FilmgC, HsB&A, InB&W 80, LinLib L, –S, McGEWD, –84[port], NewC, NewEOp 71, NotNAT A, –B, OxEng, OxFr, OxThe, PenC EUR, RComWL, REn, REnWD, ScF&FL 1, WorAl

Dumas, Alexandre, Pere 1802-1870 *AtlBL, BbD, BiD&SB, BioIn 1, –2, –3, –4, –5, –6, –7, –9, –10, –11, –12, CarSB, CasWL, CelCen, CmCal, CnThe, CyWA, DcBiPP, DcEuL, Dis&D, EncWT, EuAu, EvEuW, FilmgC, HsB&A, InB&W 80, LinLib L, –S, McGEWB, McGEWD, –84[port], MnBBF, NewC, NewEOp 71, NotNAT A, –B, Novels, OxEng, OxFr, OxThe, PenC EUR, PIP&P, RComWL, REn, REnWD, ScF&FL 1, SmATA 18, WhDW, WhoChL, WhoHr&F, WorAl*

Dumas, Frederic 1913- *ConAu 69*

DuMaurier, Daphne 1907- *Au&Wr 6, BiE&WWA, BioIn 1, –2, –4, –5, –8, –9, –11, BlueB 76, ConAu 5R, –6NR, ConLC 6, –11, ConNov 72, –76, –82, CurBio 40, CyWA, DcLEL, EncMys, EncSF, EncWT, EvLB, FilmgC, InWom, IntAu&W 76, –77, –82, IntWW 74, –75, –76, –77, –78, –79, –80, –81, –82, –83, LinLib L, –LP, –S, LongCTC, ModBrL, NewC, NotNAT, Novels[port], OxThe, PenC ENG, RAdv 1, REn, ScF&FL 1, –2, SmATA 27[port], TwCA, TwCA SUP, TwCCr&M 80, TwCWr, WhE&EA, WhThe, Who 74, –82, –83, WhoAmW 74, –66, –68, –70, –72, –75, WhoHr&F, WhoWor 74, –76, –78, WorAl, WrDr 76, –80, –82, –84*

DuMaurier, Daphne *see also* Maurier, Daphne Du

Dunaway, David King 1948- *ConAu 107*

Dunbar, Paul Laurence 1872-1906 *AmAu, AmAu&B, AmBi, ApCAB SUP, BiDAfM, BiDAmM, BiD&SB, BioIn 1, –2, –3, –5, –6, –7, –8, –9, –11, –12, BkCL, BlkAWP, CasWL, Chambr 3, ChhPo, –S1, –S2, –S3, CnDAL, ConAu 104, DcAmAu, DcAmB, DcNAA, Dis&D, InB&W 80, LinLib L, –S, McGEWB, ModBlW, NatCAB 9, NegAl 76[port], –83[port], OhA&B, OxAmL, PenC AM, RAdv 1, REn, REnAL, SelBAA, SmATA 34[port], TwCBDA, TwCLC 2, –12[port], WebAB, –79, WebE&AL, WhAm 1, WhFla, WorAl*

Dunbar, Robert E 1926- *ConAu 85, SmATA 32[port], WhoE 77, –79, –81, WhoF&I 74, WhoMW 74*

Duncan, Frances 1942- *ConAu 97*

Duncan, Isadora 1878-1927 *AmAu&B, AmBi, AmWomWr, BioIn 1, –2, –3, –4, –5, –6, –7, –8, –9, –10, –11, –12, CmCal, DcAmB, Dis&D, EncAB-H, GoodHs, InWom, IntDcWB, LibW, LinLib L, –S,*

McGEWB, NatCAB 22, NotAW, NotNAT B, OxAmH, OxAmL, OxMus, REn, REnAL, WebAB, –79, WhDW, WhAm HSA, –4, WhThe, WorAl

Duncan, Lois 1934- *AuBYP, BioIn 8, –9, –12, ConAu X, –2NR, ConLC 26[port], IntAu&W 82, ScF&FL 1, –2, SmATA 1, –36, TwCCW 83, WrDr 76, –80, –82, –84*

Duncan, Lois *see also* Arquette, Lois S

Duncan, Robert L 1927- *ConAu 106, ScF&FL 1, TwCCr&M 80, WrDr 82, –84*

Duncan, Sylvia 1916- *Au&Wr 6*

Duncombe, Frances 1900- *ConAu 25R, SmATA 25*

Dunham, John L 1939- *BioIn 9, ConAu 29R, EncASM, WhoBlA 75, –77, –80, WhoMW 74, –76, –78, –80*

Dunham, Katherine 1910- *AmSCAP 66, BiDAfM, BiE&WWA, BioIn 1, –2, –3, –4, –5, –6, –8, –9, –10, –11, –12, BlkAWP, ConAu 65, CurBio 41, DrBlPA, Ebony 1, GoodHs, HerW, InB&W 80, InWom, IntWW 74, –75, –76, –77, –78, –79, –80, –81, –82, –83, LibW, LivgBAA, NegAl 76, –83, NotNAT, –A, REnAL, SelBAA, WebAB, –79, WhDW, WhoAm 74, –76, –78, WhoAmW 74, –58, –64, –66, –68, –70, –72, WhoBlA 75, –77, –80, WhoE 74, WhoHol A, WhoThe 15, –16, –81, WhoWor 74, WomPO 76, WorAl*

Dunkling, Leslie Alan 1935- *ConAu 81*

Dunlap, Orrin Elmer, Jr. 1896-1970 *AmAu&B, BioIn 8, ConAu P-1, NewYTBE 70, WhAm 5*

Dunlop, Agnes Mary Robinson d1982 *Au&Wr 6, AuBYP, BioIn 6, –7, –8, –9, BlueB 76, ConAu 9NR, –13R, SmATA 3, Who 74, –82, WrDr 76, –80, –82*

Dunlop, Agnes Mary Robinson *see also* Kyle, Elisabeth

Dunlop, Eileen 1938- *ConAu 73, SmATA 24[port], WhoWor 80, WrDr 80, –82, –84*

Dunlop, Richard 1921- *ConAu 7NR, –17R, WrDr 76, –80, –82, –84*

Dunn, Judy 1942- *BioIn 10, ConAu X, SmATA 5*

Dunn, Judy *see also* Spangenburg, Judith Dunn

Dunn, Mary Lois 1930- *AuBYP SUP, BiDrLUS 70, BioIn 4, –10, ConAu 61, SmATA 6, WhoLibS 66*

Dunn, Paul Harold 1924- *WhoWest 74*

Dunn, Stephen 1939- *ConAu 33R, ConP 80, DrAP 75, DrAP&F 83, IntAu&W 77, WrDr 76, –80, –82, –84*

Dunnahoo, Terry 1927- *BioIn 10, ConAu 41R, IntAu&W 77, –82, SmATA 7, WhoAm 74, –76, –78, –80, –82*

Dunne, John Gregory 1932- *AuNews 1, BioIn 9, –10, –12, CmCal, ConAu 25R, CurBio 83[port], DcLB Y80B[port], TwCCr&M 80, WorAl, WrDr 82, –84*

Dunne, Mary Collins 1914- *AuBYP SUP,*
BioIn 11, ConAu 41R, SmATA 11,
WhoAmW 75, –77, –79
Dunnett, Alastair MacTavish 1908- *Au&Wr 6,*
BlueB 76, ConAu 65, IntAu&W 76, –77,
–82, IntWW 74, –75, –76, –77, –78, –79,
–80, –81, –82, –83, IntYB 78, –79, –80, –81,
–82, Who 74, –82, –83, WhoWor 74, –76,
–78
Dunnett, Dorothy 1923- *Au&Wr 6,*
ConAu 1R, –3NR, IntAu&W 76, –77, –82,
Novels, TwCCr&M 80, WhoWor 76, –78,
WrDr 76, –80, –82, –84
Dunnett, Margaret 1909- *ConAu 108*
Dunning, Arthur Stephen 1924- *AuBYP SUP,*
DrAS 74E
Dunning, Arthur Stephen *see also* Dunning,
Stephen
Dunning, Stephen 1924- *ChhPo S1,*
ConAu 25R, DrAP&F 83, LEduc 74,
MichAu 80
Dunning, Stephen *see also* Dunning, Arthur
Stephen
Dunsany, Baron Edward J M Drax Plunkett
1878-1957 *Alli SUP, AtlBL, BioIn 1, –3,*
–4, –5, –9, CasWL, ChhPo, –S1, –S2, –S3,
CnMD, CnThe, ConAu 104, DcIrW 1,
DcLB 10[port], DcLEL, EncMys, EvLB,
JBA 34, LinLib L, –S, LongCTC,
McGEWD, ModBrL, ModWD, NewC,
OxEng, OxThe, PenC ENG, PIP&P,
REn, REnWD, TwCA, TwCA SUP,
TwCWr, WhDW, WhE&EA, WhThe
Dunsheath, Percy 1886- *Au&Wr 6, BioIn 10,*
ConAu 107, IntAu&W 76, –77,
IntWW 74, –75, –76, –77, –78, –79,
WhE&EA, Who 74
Dupuy, R Ernest 1887-1975 *ConAu 1R, –6NR,*
–57, NewYTBS 75, ObitOF 79,
WhAm 6, WhoWor 74
Dupuy, Richard Ernest 1887-1975 *AmAu&B,*
BioIn 10, ConAu 1R, –57, DrAS 74H,
WhoAm 74
Dupuy, Trevor Nevitt 1916- *AuBYP, BioIn 8,*
–9, ConAu 1R, DrAS 74H,
IntAu&W 77, SmATA 4, WhoAm 74,
–76, –78, –80, –82, WhoWor 74, WrDr 76,
–80, –82, –84
Durant, John 1902- *AmAu&B, AuBYP,*
BioIn 7, ConAu 5NR, –9R,
SmATA 27[port], WhoAm 74, –76, –78,
–80, –82, WhoS&SW 73
Durant, Will 1885-1981 *AmAu&B,*
AnObit 1981[port], ASpks, BlueB 76,
CelR 73, ConAu 4NR, –9R, –105,
CurBio 64, –82N, DcAmSR, DcLEL,
EvLB, IntWW 74, –75, –76, –77, –78, –79,
–80, –81, –82N, LinLib L, –S, LongCTC,
NewYTBS 75, –81[port], OxAmL, REn,
REnAL, TwCA, TwCA SUP, WebAB,
–79, WhNAA, WhoWest 74, –76,
WhoWor 74, –76, –78, –80

Durfee, David Arthur 1929- *ConAu 29R,*
IntAu&W 77, WhoE 75, WrDr 76, –80,
–82, –84
Durgnat, Raymond Eric 1932- *Au&Wr 6,*
ConAu 17R, DcLEL 1940, IntAu&W 76,
–77, WhoWor 76, WrDr 76, –80, –82, –84
Durham, John 1925- *ConAu 107, DrAS 74E,*
–78E
Durham, Marilyn 1930- *BioIn 9, –10,*
ConAu 49, DrAF 76, DrAP&F 83,
WrDr 84
Durham, Philip 1912-1977 *ConAu 7NR, –9R,*
DrAS 74E, –78E, WhAm 7, WhoAm 76
Durrell, Gerald Malcolm 1925- *Au&Wr 6,*
AuBYP, BioIn 5, –8, –9, –10, –11, –12,
BlueB 76, ConAu 4NR, –5R,
DcLEL 1940, IntAu&W 76, –77, –82,
IntWW 74, –75, –76, –77, –78, –79, –80, –81,
–82, –83, LongCTC, NewC, REn,
ScF&FL 1, –2, SmATA 8, TwCWr,
Who 74, –82, –83, WhoWor 74, –76, –78,
WorAu, WrDr 76, –80, –82, –84
Durrell, Lawrence 1912- *ASpks, Au&Wr 6,*
BioIn 4, –5, –6, –7, –8, –9, –10, –11,
BlueB 76, CasWL, ChhPo, –S3, CnE&AP,
CnMD, CnMWL, ConAu 9R, ConDr 73,
–77, –82, ConLC 1, –4, –6, –8, –13,
–27[port], ConNov 72, –76, –82, ConP 70,
–75, –80, CurBio 63, DcLB 15[port],
DcLEL, EncSF, EncWL, –81[port], EvLB,
IntAu&W 76, –77, IntWW 74, –75, –76,
–77, –78, –79, –80, –81, –82, –83,
IntWWP 77, LinLib L, –S, LongCEL,
LongCTC, ModBrL, ModBrL SUP,
ModWD, NewC, Novels, OxEng,
PenC ENG, RAdv 1, REn, ScF&FL 1,
–2, TwCA SUP, TwCWr, WebE&AL,
WhDW, Who 74, –82, –83, WhoFr 79,
WhoTwCL, WhoWor 74, –78, –80, –82,
WorAl, WrDr 76, –80, –82, –84
D'Urso, Joseph 1943- *BioIn 12*
Durst, Paul 1921- *Au&Wr 6, BioIn 11,*
ConAu 21R, IntAu&W 76, –77, –82,
WrDr 84
Dutta, Reginald 1914- *ConAu 61*
Dutton, Mary 1922- *Au&Wr 6, ConAu 33R*
Duvall, Evelyn Millis 1906- *AmAu&B,*
AmM&WS 73S, –78S, BioIn 1, –11,
ConAu 1R, –1NR, CurBio 47, ForWC 70,
InWom, SmATA 9, WhoAm 74, –76, –78,
WhoAmW 74, –58, –61, –64, –66, –68, –70,
–72, WhoWor 74, WrDr 76, –80, –82, –84
Duvoison, Roger Antoine 1904-1968 *AmAu&B,*
AmPB, Au&ICB, Au&Wr 6, AuBYP,
BkP, Cald 1938, ChhPo, –S1, –S2,
ConAu 13R, FamAIYP, IlsBYP,
IlsCB 1744, –1946, –1957, SmATA 2,
Str&VC, WhoAmA 73, WhoChL,
WhoGrA
Dwiggins, Don 1913- *AuBYP SUP, BioIn 9,*
ConAu 8NR, –17R, SmATA 4
Dwight, Allan 1902?-1979 *BioIn 8, –11,*

ConAu X, SmATA X

Dwight, Allan *see also* Cole, Lois Dwight

Dwyer-Joyce, Alice 1913- *Au&Wr 6,*
ConAu 4NR, -53, IntAu&W 76, -77, -82,
WrDr 82, -84

Dybek, Stuart 1942- *ConAu 97, DrAF 76,*
DrAP 75, DrAP&F 83, IntWWP 77, -82

Dyer, T A 1947- *ConAu 101*

Dygard, Thomas J 1931- *ConAu 85,*
SmATA 24[port]

Dyke, Henry Van 1852-1933 *Chambr 3,*
DrAP&F 83, JBA 34, ScF&FL 1

Dyke, Henry Van *see also* VanDyke, Henry

Dykeman, Wilma 1920- *AmWomWr, BioIn 4,*
-7, ConAu X, -1NR, DrAS 82H,
ForWC 70, InWom, IntAu&W 77,
WhoAmW 74, -58, -61, -75, -77, -83,
WhoS&SW 75, -76, -78, WrDr 76, -80,
-82, -84

Dykeman, Wilma *see also* Stokely, Wilma
Dykeman

Dylan, Bob 1941- *AmAu&B, AmSCAP 66,*
Baker 78, BiDAmM, BioIn 6, -7, -8, -9,
-10, -11, -12, BioNews 74, BlueB 76,
CelR 73, ConAu 41R, ConLC 3, -4, -6,
-12, ConP 70, -75, -80, CurBio 65,
DcLB 16[port], DcLEL 1940, EncAB-H,
EncFCWM 69, EncPR&S, -77, IlEncRk,
IntAu&W 76, -77, -82, IntWW 74, -75,
-76, -77, -78, -79, -80, -81, -82, -83,
IntWWP 77, -82, LinLib L, MakMC,
MugS, NewYTBE 71, -72, PolProf J,
RkOn 78, -84, RkOneH, RolSEnR 83,
WebAB, -79, WhoAm 74, -76, -78, -80,
-82, WhoE 74, -75, -77, WhoRocM 82,
WhoWor 74, -76, -78, -80, -82,
WhoWorJ 78, WorAl, WrDr 76, -80, -82,
-84

Dylan, Bob *see also* Zimmerman, Robert

Dyson, Freeman John 1923- *AmM&WS 73P,*
-76P, -79P, -82P, BiESc, BioIn 7, -11, -12,
BlueB 76, ConAu 89, CurBio 80[port],
EncSF, IntWW 74, -75, -76, -77, -78, -79,
-80, -81, -82, -83, McGMS 80[port],
Who 74, -82, -83, WhoAm 74, -76, -78,
-80, -82, WhoE 74, WhoTech 82,
WrDr 82, -84

E

Eagan, Andrea Boroff 1943- *ConAu 73*
Eagar, Frances 1940- *BioIn 11, ConAu 61,
IntAu&W 77, SmATA 11*
Eager, George Boardman 1925- *WhoE 83*
Eagles, The *EncPR&S, -77, IlEncRk,
RkOn 78, -84, RolSEnR 83*
Eagles, The *see also* Frey, Glenn
Eagles, The *see also* Henley, Don
Eagles, The *see also* Meisner, Randy
Eareckson, Joni 1960- *BioIn 11, -12*
Earhart, Amelia 1898-1937 *AmBi, BioIn 1, -2,
-3, -4, -5, -6, -7, -8, -9, -10, -11, -12,
ChhPo, DcAmB S2, DcNAA, EncAB 2,
GoodHs, HerW, InSci, InWom,
IntDcWB, LibW, LinLib L, -S, NotAW,
OxAmH, REn, WebAB, -79, WhAm 1,
WomWMM, WorAl*
Earl, Lawrence 1915- *Au&Wr 6, ConAu 9R*
Earle, Alice Morse 1853?-1911 *AmAu&B,
AmBi, AmWomWr, ApCAB SUP,
AuBYP SUP, BbD, BiD&SB, BioIn 1,
-12, ChhPo S1, DcAmAu, DcAmB,
DcLEL, DcNAA, HarEnUS, InWom,
LibW, NatCAB 13, NotAW, OxAmL,
REnAL, TwCBDA, WhAm 1, WhLit*
Earle, Olive Lydia 1888- *Au&Wr 6, BioIn 5,
-6, -8, -10, -12, ConAu 21R, IlsBYP,
IlsCB 1946, -1957, -1967, IntAu&W 76,
-77, MorJA, SmATA 7, WhoAmW 58,
-61*
Earle, Peter G 1923- *ConAu 17R, DrAS 74F,
-78F, -82F*
Earle, Sylvia A 1935- *AmM&WS 73P,
BioIn 10, -11, -12, WhoAm 82,
WhoAmW 72, -77, -83, WhoWest 82, -84*
Earle, William Alexander 1919- *ConAu 85,
DrAS 74P, -78P, -82P, WhoAm 80, -82*
East, Ben 1898- *ConAu 33R, MichAu 80*
Eastlake, William 1917- *AmAu&B,
Au&Wr 6, BioIn 9, -10, BlueB 76,
ConAu 5R, -5NR, ConLC 8, ConNov 72,
-76, -82, DcLB 6[port], DrAF 76,
DrAP&F 83, IntAu&W 76, -77, -82,
ModAL SUP, Novels, OxAmL,
PenC AM, REnAL, WhoAm 74, -76, -78,
-80, -82, WhoWor 74, WorAu, WrDr 76,
-80, -82, -84*

Eastman, Charles Alexander 1858-1939
*AmAu&B, AmLY, BioIn 2, -3, -7, -8, -9,
-11, -12, ConAmL, DcAmAu, InSci,
JBA 34, -51, NatPD, OxAmL, REnAL,
WhAm 4, YABC 1*
Easton, Carol 1933- *ConAu 65*
Easton, Robert 1915- *ConAu 7NR, -13R,
WhoWest 76, -78, -82, -84, WrDr 76, -80,
-82, -84*
Eaton, Jeanette 1885?-1968 *AmAu&B, AnCL,
AuBYP SUP, BioIn 2, -8, ConAu 73,
JBA 34, -51, LinLib L, OhA&B,
SmATA 24[port], Str&VC, WhoAmW 58,
-61, -64*
Eaton, Tom 1940- *ConAu 41R, IlsBYP,
SmATA 22[port]*
Ebenstein, William 1910-1976 *AmAu&B,
AmM&WS 73S, -78S, BioIn 10, -12,
ConAu 1R, -6NR, -65, NatCAB 59[port],
NewYTBS 76, WhAm 7, WhoAm 74, -76,
WhoWorJ 72, -78, WrDr 76*
Eber, Dorothy Harley 1930- *ConAu 41R,
IntAu&W 76, -76X, -77, SmATA 27*
Eberhard, Wolfram 1909- *AmM&WS 73S,
-78S, ConAu 2NR, -49, FifIDA,
IntWW 74, -75, -76, -77, -78, -79, -80, -81,
-82, -83, WhoAm 74, -76, -78, -80,
WhoWor 74, -76, -78*
Eberhart, Mignon Good 1899- *AmAu&B,
AmWomWr, ASpks, AuNews 2, BioIn 4,
-5, -10, -11, ConAu 73, CorpD, EncMys,
LinLib L, LongCTC, Novels, REnAL,
TwCA, TwCA SUP, TwCCr&M 80,
WhNAA, WhoAm 74, -76, -78, -80, -82,
WhoAmW 74, -61, -64, -66, -68, -70, -72,
WhoWor 74, -76, WorAl, WrDr 82, -84*
Eberhart, Richard 1904- *AmAu&B, AmWr,
BiE&WWA, BioIn 3, -4, -5, -6, -7, -8, -9,
-10, -11, -12, BlueB 76, CasWL, ChhPo,
-S3, CnE&AP, ConAu 1R, -2NR,
ConLC 3, -11, -19, ConP 70, -75, -80,
CurBio 61, DcLEL, DrAP 75,
DrAP&F 83, DrAS 74E, -78E, -82E,
IntAu&W 77, -82, IntWW 74, -75, -76,
-77, -78, -79, -80, -81, -82, -83,
IntWWP 77, LinLib L, LongCTC,
ModAL, ModAL SUP, NotNAT,
OxAmL, PenC AM, RAdv 1, REn,*

REnAL, SixAP, TwCA SUP, TwCWr,
WebE&AL, Who 74, -82, -83,
WhoAm 74, -76, -78, -80, -82, WhoE 74,
WhoTwCL, WhoWor 74, -76, -78, -80, -82,
WorAl, WrDr 76, -80, -82, -84

Ebersohn, Wessel 1940- *ConAu 97*

Ebon, Martin 1917- *ConAu 10NR, -21R,*
EncO&P 78, WrDr 80, -82, -84

Echewa, T Obinkaram 1940- *ConAu 73*

Ecke, Wolfgang 1927-1983 *AuBYP SUP,*
SmATA 37N

Eckel, Malcolm William 1912- *ConAu 61,*
WhoRel 75, -77

Eckert, Allan W 1931- *AuBYP SUP,*
ConAu 13R, ConLC 17, FourBJA,
SmATA 27, -29[port], WhoAm 74, -76,
-78, -80, -82, WhoS&SW 73

Eckholm, Erik P 1949- *ConAu 6NR, -57,*
Future

Eddings, David 1931- *ConAu 110*

Edel, Leon 1907- *AmAu&B, BioIn 3, -6, -9,*
-10, -11, -12, BlueB 76, CanWW 70, -79,
-80, -81, -83, ConAu 1R, -1NR, ConLCrt,
-82, CurBio 63, DrAS 74E, -78E, -82E,
IntWW 74, -75, -76, -77, -78, -79, -80, -81,
-82, -83, LinLib L, NewYTBE 72,
NewYTBS 76, -80[port], OxAmL,
RAdv 1, REn, Who 74, -82, -83,
WhoAmJ 80, WhoWor 74, -76, -78, -80,
-82, WorAu, WrDr 76, -80, -82, -84

Edelman, Maurice 1911-1975 *Au&Wr 6,*
BioIn 3, -6, -8, -10, -11, ChhPo S3,
ConAu 61, -65, ConNov 72, -76,
CurBio 54, -76, -76N, DcLEL 1940,
IntAu&W 76, LongCTC, ObitT 1971,
TwCWr, WhAm 6, WhE&EA, Who 74,
WhoSpyF, WhoWor 74, WorAu,
WrDr 76

Edelson, Edward 1932- *AuBYP SUP,*
ConAu 17R, ScF&FL 1, -2, WhoAm 76,
-78, WhoE 74, -75, -77, -83

Eden, Dorothy 1912-1982 *AnObit 1982[port],*
BioIn 12, ConAu 106, -81, CorpD,
TwCCr&M 80, WhE&EA, WrDr 76, -80,
-82

Edens, David 1926- *AmM&WS 73S,*
ConAu 108

Edlin, Herbert Leeson 1913-1976 *Au&Wr 6,*
ConAu 9NR, -61, -69, IntAu&W 76, -77,
WhoWor 76, WrDr 76, -80

Edmonds, I G 1917- *AuBYP SUP,*
ConAu 33R, SmATA 8

Edmonds, Ivy Gordon 1917- *BioIn 11,*
WhoWest 76, -78, -80, -82, -84

Edmonds, Walter Dumaux 1903- *AfroAA,*
AmAu&B, AmNov, AuBYP, BioIn 1, -2,
-4, -5, -6, -7, -9, -10, -12, CnDAL,
ConAmA, ConAu 2NR, -5R, CurBio 42,
CyWA, DcLB 9[port], DcLEL,
IntAu&W 82, LinLib L, ModAL,
MorBMP, MorJA, Newb 1922, Novels,
OxAmL, PenC AM, REn, REnAL,

ScF&FL 1A, SmATA 1, -27[port],
TwCA, TwCA SUP, TwCCW 78, -83,
WhoAm 74, -76, -78, -80, -82, WrDr 76,
-80, -82, -84

Edmondson, Madeleine *AuBYP SUP*

Edmonson, Harold Arthur 1937- *ConAu 41R,*
WhoMW 76, -78, -80

Edson, Russell 1935- *ConAu 33R, ConLC 13,*
ConP 75, -80, DrAP 75, DrAP&F 83,
Po&Wr 77, WrDr 76, -80, -82, -84

Edwardes, Michael 1923- *Au&Wr 6,*
ConAu 10NR, -57

Edwards, Anne 1927- *Au&Wr 6, BioIn 10,*
-11, -12, ConAu 61, SmATA 35,
WhoOp 76, WrDr 76, -80, -82, -84

Edwards, Audrey 1947- *ConAu 81,*
SmATA 31

Edwards, Dorothy 1914-1982 *Au&Wr 6,*
BioIn 9, ConAu 107, -25R, IntAu&W 76,
-77, SmATA 31N, -4, TwCCW 78, -83,
WhoBlA 77, WrDr 76, -80, -82

Edwards, Frank 1908-1967 *BioIn 2, -4, -7, -8,*
BluesWW, ConAu 1R, -1NR, ObitOF 79,
UFOEn, WhAm 4

Edwards, G B 1899-1976 *ConAu 110,*
ConLC 25

Edwards, Iorwerth Eiddon Stephen 1909-
Au&Wr 6, BlueB 76, ConAu 13R,
IntAu&W 76, -77, -82, Who 74, -82, -83,
WhoArt 80, -82, WhoWor 74, -76, -82,
WrDr 76, -80, -82, -84

Edwards, Jane Campbell 1932- *BioIn 11,*
ConAu 13R, ForWC 70, SmATA 10

Edwards, Jane Campbell *see also* Campbell, Jane

Edwards, Ronald George 1930- *IntAu&W 77,*
WrDr 76, -80, -82, -84

Effinger, George Alec 1947- *BioIn 12,*
ConAu 37R, DcLB 8[port], EncSF,
ScF&FL 1, -2, WhoE 75, -77, -79,
WhoSciF, WhoS&SW 78, -80, -82,
WrDr 76, -80, -82, -84

Efron, Alexander 1897- *ConAu P-2*

Efron, Marshall *NewYTBE 71*

Ehrlich, Max 1909- *ConAu 1R, -1NR, EncSF,*
IntAu&W 77, -82, ScF&FL 1, -2,
WrDr 76, -80, -82, -84

Ehrlich, Paul Ralph 1932- *AmM&WS 73P,*
-76P, -79P, -82P, BioIn 9, ConAu 8NR,
-65, CurBio 70, IntAu&W 77,
IntWW 74, -75, -76, -77, -78, -79, -80, -81,
-82, -83, WhoAm 74, -76, -78, -80, -82,
WhoWest 82, -84, WhoWor 74, -78, -80,
-82, WrDr 76, -80, -82, -84

Eichenberg, Fritz 1901- *AnCL, BioIn 1, -3, -4,*
-5, -6, -8, -10, -11, -12, ChhPo S2,
ConAu 6NR, -57, IlsBYP, IlsCB 1744,
-1946, -1957, -1967, McGDA, MorJA,
SmATA 9, Str&VC, WhoAm 74, -76, -78,
-80, -82, WhoAmA 73, -76, -78, -80, -82,
WhoGrA, -82[port]

Eichner, James A 1927- *BioIn 9, ConAu 13R,*
SmATA 4, WhoAmL 83

Eifert, Virginia Snider 1911-1966 *AmAu&B,*
Au&Wr 6, AuBYP, BioIn 7, –9,
ConAu 1R, SmATA 2, WhAm 4,
WhoAmW 58, –64, –66

Eimerl, Sarel 1925- *ConAu 21R,*
WhoWest 74

Einstein, Charles 1926- *ConAu 65, ConSFA,*
EncSF, ScF&FL 1, –2

Eiseley, Loren Corey 1907-1977 *AmAu&B,*
AmM&WS 73S, –76P, ASpks, Au&Wr 6,
BioIn 1, –5, –6, –7, –9, –10, –11, BlueB 76,
CelR 73, ChhPo S3, ConAu 1R, –6NR,
–73, ConLC 7, CurBio 60, –77, –77N,
DcLEL 1940, FifIDA, InSci, LinLib L,
NewYTBS 77, ObitOF 79, REnAL,
WebAB, –79, WhAm 7, WhoAm 74, –76,
–78, WhoE 74, WhoGov 77, –72, –75,
WhoWor 74, –76, WorAu, WrDr 80

Eisenberg, Azriel 1903- *AuBYP, BioIn 7, –11,*
ConAu 10NR, –49, LEduc 74,
SmATA 12, WhoAmJ 80, WhoWorJ 72,
–78

Eisenberg, Dennis Harold 1929- *ConAu 25R,*
IntAu&W 77, WhoWor 76, WrDr 76, –80,
–82, –84

Eisenberg, Lisa 1949- *ConAu 110*

Eisenstein, Phyllis 1946- *ConAu 85, WrDr 84*

Elbert, Virginie Fowler 1912- *AuBYP SUP,*
ConAu 8NR, –61

Elbert, Virginie Fowler *see also* Fowler, Virginie

Elder, Lauren 1947?- *BioIn 11*

Elder, Lonne, III 1931- *BioIn 10, –12,*
BlkAWP, ConAu 81, ConDr 73, –77, –82,
DcLB 7[port], DcLEL 1940, DrBlPA,
Ebony 1, InB&W 80, LesBEnT,
LivgBAA, NatPD, NewYTBS 75,
NewYTET, NotNAT, PlP&P A, SelBAA,
WhoAm 80, –82, WhoBlA 75, –77, –80,
WhoThe 16, –81, WrDr 76, –80, –82, –84

Elfman, Blossom 1925- *BioIn 11,*
ConAu 2NR, –45, SmATA 8

Elgin, Suzette Haden 1936- *ConAu 8NR, –61,*
EncSF, ScF&FL 1, –2, WhoWest 78,
WrDr 84

Eliot, Anne 1902?-1979 *BioIn 11, ConAu X,*
SmATA X

Eliot, Anne *see also* Cole, Lois Dwight

Eliot, George 1819-1880 *Alli SUP, AtlBL,*
BbD, BiD&SB, BioIn 1, –2, –3, –4, –5, –6,
–7, –8, –9, –10, –11, –12, BrAu 19, BrWr 5,
CasWL, CelCen, Chambr 3, ChhPo, –S2,
–S3, CrtT 3, –4, CyWA, DcBiA, DcEnA,
–AP, DcEnL, DcEuL, DcLB 21[port],
DcLEL, Dis&D, EvLB, GoodHs, HerW,
HsB&A, InWom, IntDcWB[port],
LinLib L, –LP, –S, LongCEL, McGEWB,
MnBBF, MouLC 3, NewC, Novels[port],
OxEng, PenC ENG, RAdv 1, RComWL,
REn, WebE&AL, WhDW, WorAl

Eliot, George *see also* Evans, Mary Ann

Eliot, T S 1888-1965 *AmAu&B, AmWr,*
AnCL, AtlBL, BiE&WWA, CasWL,

Chambr 3, ChhPo, –S1, –S2, CnDAL,
CnE&AP, CnMD, CnMWL, CnThe,
ConAmL, ConAu 5R, –25R, ConLC 1, –2,
–3, –6, –9, –10, –13, –15, –24[port],
ConLCrt, –82, CroCD, CyWA,
DcAmB S7, DcLB 7[port], –10[port],
DcLEL, EncWL, –2[port], EvLB,
LinLib L, LongCTC, McGEWD, ModAL,
ModAL SUP, ModBrL, ModBrL SUP,
ModWD, NewC, NotNAT A, ObitOF 79,
ObitT 1961, OxAmH, OxAmL, OxEng,
PenC AM, –ENG, PlP&P, RAdv 1,
RComWL, REn, REnAL, REnWD,
SixAP, TwCA, TwCA SUP, TwCWr,
WebE&AL, WhE&EA, WhNAA,
WhThe, WhoChL, WhoTwCL, WorAl

Eliot, Thomas Stearns 1888-1965 *BioIn 1, –2,*
–3, –4, –5, –6, –7, –8, –9, –10, –11, –12,
ChhPo S3, CnMD, CurBio 62, –65,
EncWT, LinLib S, LongCEL, LuthC 75,
MakMC, McGEWB, McGEWD 84[port],
NotNAT B, OxThe, WebAB, –79,
WhDW, WhAm 4, WhLit

Elkin, Stanley 1930- *AmAu&B, BioIn 8, –10,*
–12, ConAu 8NR, –9R, ConLC 4, –6, –9,
–14, –27[port], ConNov 72, –76, –82,
DcLB Y80A[port], –2, DrAF 76,
DrAP&F 83, DrAS 74E, –78E, –82E,
EncWL, IntAu&W 76, –77, Novels,
PenC AM, WhoAm 74, –76, –78, –80, –82,
WorAu 1970, WrDr 76, –80, –82, –84

Elkins, Dov Peretz 1937- *AuBYP, BioIn 8,*
–10, ConAu 29R, SmATA 5,
WhoAmJ 80, WhoWorJ 78, WrDr 76,
–80, –82, –84

Elkon, Juliette *ConAu X*

Elkon-Hamelecourt, Juliette 1912- *ConAu 57*

Ellacott, S E 1911- *ConAu 3NR, –5R,*
SmATA 19, WrDr 82, –84

Ellacott, Samuel Ernest 1911- *Au&Wr 6,*
BioIn 12, ConAu 5R, IntAu&W 76, –77,
–82, WrDr 76, –80

Ellington, Duke 1899-1974 *AmPS,*
AmSCAP 66, BiE&WWA, BioIn 1, –2, –3,
–4, –5, –6, –7, –8, –9, –10, –11, –12,
BioNews 74, CelR 73, CmpEPM,
ConAu X, –49, CurBio 41, –70, –74, –74N,
DrBlPA, EncJzS 70, FilmgC, IlEncJ,
MakMC, NegAl 76[port], –83[port],
NewYTBE 72, NewYTBS 74,
NotNAT A, –B, ObitT 1971, OxAmH,
OxMus, WebAB, –79, WhScrn 2,
WhoE 74, WhoGov 72, WhoHol B,
WhoMus 72, WhoWor 74, WorAl

Ellington, Duke *see also* Ellington, Edward
Kennedy

Ellington, Edward Kennedy 1899-1974 *Baker 78,*
BiDAfM, BiDAmM, BioIn 1, –8, –9, –10,
–11, –12, ConAmC, ConAu 49, –97,
Ebony 1, EncAB-H, EncJzS 70,
InB&W 80, McGEWB, ObitOF 79,
SelBAA, WhDW, WhAm 6, Who 74,

WhoAm 74, WhoBlA 75, WhoJazz 72
Ellington, Edward Kennedy *see also* Ellington,
Duke
Elliot, Ian Douglas 1925- *ConAu 69,
WhoE 79, –83*
Elliott, Bob 1923- *BioIn 3, –4, –5, –9, –10,
CelR 73, ConAu 109, CurBio 57*
Elliott, Charles Newton 1906- *WhE&EA,
WhoS&SW 76, –78*
Elliott, David William 1939- *ConAu 45,
WhoE 77, –79, –81*
Elliott, Janice 1931- *ConAu 8NR, –13R,
DcLB 14[port], IntAu&W 76, –77, –82,
WhoWor 78, WrDr 76, –80, –82, –84*
Elliott, Lawrence 1924- *ConAu 3NR, –5R,
WhoAm 74, –76, –78, –80, –82, WhoE 74*
Ellis, Ella Thorp 1928- *AuBYP SUP,
BioIn 10, ConAu 2NR, –49, DrAP&F 83,
IntAu&W 77, –82, SmATA 7,
WhoAmW 77, –79, WrDr 76, –80, –82, –84*
Ellis, Harry Bearse 1921- *AmAu&B, AuBYP,
BioIn 8, –11, BlueB 76, ConAu 1R, –2NR,
IntAu&W 77, –82, SmATA 9,
WhoAm 74, –76, –78, –80, –82,
WhoWor 74, –76, WrDr 76, –80, –82, –84*
Ellis, Melvin Richard 1912- *BioIn 10,
ConAu 13R, SmATA 7*
Ellis, R Hobart, Jr. 1918- *AmM&WS 73P*
Ellis, Richard 1938- *BioIn 12, ConAu 104,
WhoAmA 78, –80, –82*
Ellison, Harlan 1934- *BioIn 10, –12,
ConAu 5NR, ConLC 1, –13, ConSFA,
DcLB 8[port], DrAF 76, DrAP&F 83,
EncSF, IntAu&W 76X, LinLib L, Novels,
ScF&FL 1, –2, WhoAm 76, –78, –80, –82,
WhoSciF, WorAl, WorAu 1970,
WrDr 76, –80, –82, –84*
Ellison, Ralph 1914- *AmAu&B, BioIn 2, –3,
–4, –5, –6, –7, –8, –9, –10, –11, –12,
BlueB 76, BlkAWP, CasWL, CivR 74,
CnDAL, ConAu 9R, ConLC 1, –3, –11,
ConNov 72, –76, –82, CurBio 68,
DcAmSR, DcLB 2, DcLEL 1940,
DrAF 76, DrAP&F 83, Ebony 1,
EncAB-H, EncSoH, EncWL, –2,
InB&W 80, IntAu&W 76, –77,
IntWW 74, –75, –76, –77, –78, –79, –80, –81,
–82, –83, LinLib L, –S, LivgBAA,
McGEWB, ModAL, ModAL SUP,
ModBlW, NegAl 76[port], –83[port],
Novels, OxAmL, PenC AM, RAdv 1,
REn, REnAL, SelBAA, TwCWr,
WebAB, –79, WebE&AL, WhoAm 74,
–76, –78, –80, –82, WhoBlA 75, –77, –80,
WhoE 74, WhoGov 72, –75, WhoTwCL,
WhoWor 74, –78, WorAl, WorAu,
WrDr 76, –80, –82, –84*
Ellsberg, Daniel 1931- *BioIn 9, –10, –12,
BioNews 74, ConAu 69, CurBio 73,
LinLib S, NewYTBE 71, PolProf NF,
WhoAm 74, –76, –78, –80, –82,
WhoWor 80, –82, WorAl*

Ellsberg, Edward 1891-1983 *AmAu&B,
AmNov, Au&Wr 6, AuBYP, BioIn 2, –3,
–4, –6, –7, –8, –10, ConAu 5R, CurBio 42,
JBA 34, –51, LinLib L, NewYTBS 83,
REnAL, SmATA 7, TwCA, TwCA SUP,
WebAMB, WhE&EA, WhoAm 74, –76,
–78, –80, –82*
Elman, Robert 1930- *ConAu 3NR, –45,
WhoE 77, –79*
Elmblad, Mary 1927- *ConAu 108*
Elmore, Patricia 1933- *DrAP&F 83,
SmATA 35*
Elting, Mary 1906- *AuBYP, BioIn 6, –8, –9,
ConAu 4NR, –9R, ForWC 70, MorJA,
SmATA 2, WhoAmW 79, –81*
Elwood, Roger 1943- *AuBYP SUP,
ConAu 10NR, –57, ConSFA, EncSF,
ScF&FL 1, –2, WhoSciF*
Emanuel, James A 1921- *BioIn 10, BlkAWP,
BroadAu[port], ConAu 29R, ConP 75, –80,
CroCAP, DrAP 75, DrAP&F 83,
DrAS 74E, –78E, –82E, InB&W 80,
IntAu&W 77, IntWWP 77, LinLib L,
LivgBAA, SelBAA, WrDr 76, –80, –82,
–84*
Embery, Joan 1949- *BioIn 12*
Emboden, William Allen, Jr. 1935-
*AmM&WS 73P, –76P, –79P, –82P,
ConAu 41R, IntAu&W 82*
Embry, Margaret Jacob 1919-1975
*AuBYP SUP, BioIn 10, ConAu 1R,
–3NR, ForWC 70, SmATA 5*
Emecheta, Buchi 1944- *BioIn 12, ConAu 81,
ConLC 14, InB&W 80, IntAu&W 82,
Who 83, WrDr 76, –80, –82, –84*
Emerson, Ralph Waldo 1803-1882 *Alli,
Alli SUP, AmAu, AmAu&B, AmBi,
AmWr, AnCL, ApCAB, AtlBL, BbD,
BiDAmM, BiD&SB, BioIn 1, –2, –3, –4, –5,
–6, –7, –8, –9, –10, –11, –12, CasWL,
CelCen, Chambr 3, ChhPo, –S1, –S3,
CnDAL, CnE&AP, CrtT 3, –4, CyAL 2,
CyEd, CyWA, DcAmAu, DcAmB,
DcAmReB, DcAmSR, DcBiPP, DcEnA,
–AP, DcEnL, DcLB 1, DcLEL, DcNAA,
Dis&D, Drake, EncAAH, EncAB-H,
EvLB, HarEnUS[port], LinLib L, –S,
LuthC 75, McGEWB, MouLC 4,
NatCAB 3, OxAmH, OxAmL, OxEng,
PenC AM, RAdv 1, RComWL, REn,
REnAL, Str&VC, TwCBDA, WebAB,
–79, WebE&AL, WhDW, WhAm HS,
WorAl*
Emery, Anne 1907- *AuBYP, BioIn 2, –3, –6,
–7, –9, ConAu 1R, –2NR, CurBio 52,
ForWC 70, InWom, MorJA, SmATA 1,
–33[port], WhoAmW 58, –61, –64, –66, –68,
–70, –72*
Emmens, Carol Ann 1944- *ConAu 106,
WhoAmW 77, –79*
Emmet, Eric Revell 1909- *Au&Wr 6,
IntAu&W 76, –77, –82, WhoWor 78,*

WrDr 76, –80
Emmitt, Robert 1925- *ConAu 29R*
Emrich, Duncan 1908-197-? *AuBYP SUP,*
AuBYP SUPA, BioIn 3, –4, –11,
ChhPo S1, –S2, ConAu 9NR, –61,
CurBio 55, SmATA 11, WhAm 7,
WhoAm 74, –76
Endacott, M Violet 1915- *ConAu 9R*
Enderle, Judith 1941- *ConAu 106*
Engdahl, Sylvia Louise 1933- *AuBYP SUP,*
BioIn 9, ChlLR 2, ConAu 29R, EncSF,
FourBJA, IntAu&W 76, –77, ScF&FL 1,
–2, SmATA 4, TwCCW 78, –83,
WrDr 76, –80, –82, –84
Engebrecht, P A 1935- *ConAu 57*
Engel, Lehman 1910-1982 *AmAu&B,*
AnObit 1982[port], Baker 78,
BiE&WWA, BioIn 1, –2, –4, –5, –10,
ChhPo S3, ConAmC, ConAu 107, –41R,
DcCM, IntWWM 77, NewYTBS 82[port],
NotNAT, –A, WhoAm 74, –76, –78, –80,
–82, WhoAmJ 80, WhoAmM 83,
WhoMus 72, WhoWor 74, –76, –78,
WhoWorJ 72, –78
Engel, Leonard 1916-1964 *AmAu&B, BioIn 7,*
EncSF, ScF&FL 1
Engel, Lyle Kenyon 1915- *BioIn 11, –12,*
ConAu 85, EncSF, WhoAm 82
Engeman, John T 1901- *AuBYP, BioIn 8*
Engle, Eloise 1923- *BioIn 11, ConAu 1R,*
–2NR, ForWC 70, IntAu&W 77, –82X,
ScF&FL 1, –2, SmATA 9, WhoAmW 74,
–66, –68, –70, –72, –75, –79, –81, WrDr 76,
–80, –82, –84
Engle, Paul 1908- *AmAu&B, BioIn 4, –5, –7,*
–10, –12, BlueB 76, ChhPo, –S1, –S2,
CnDAL, ConAmA, ConAu 1R, –5NR,
ConP 70, –75, –80, CurBio 42, DcLEL,
DrAP 75, DrAP&F 83, DrAS 74E, –78E,
–82E, IntWWP 77, –82, LinLib L,
OxAmL, REnAL, SixAP, WhE&EA,
WhoAm 74, –76, –78, –80, –82,
WhoWor 74, –76, WorAu, WrDr 76, –80,
–82, –84
Englebardt, Stanley L 1925- *IntAu&W 82*
Englebert, Victor 1933- *BioIn 11, ConAu 57,*
SmATA 8
Engler, Larry 1949- *ConAu 53, WhoE 77*
English, Urma Mae Peterson 1910-
WhoAmW 74, –66, –72
Enright, D J 1920- *BlueB 76, ConAu 1NR,*
ConLC 8, ConLCrt, –82, ConP 80,
EncWL 2, IntWWP 77, –82, Novels,
SmATA 25[port], WrDr 80, –82, –84
Enright, Dennis Joseph 1920- *Au&Wr 6,*
BioIn 8, –10, ChhPo S2, ConAu 1R,
ConLC 4, ConNov 72, –76, ConP 70, –75,
DcLEL 1940, IntAu&W 76, –77, –82,
IntWW 74, –75, –76, –77, –78, –79, –80, –81,
–82, –83, LongCTC, ModBrL,
ModBrL SUP, NewC, PenC ENG,
TwCWr, Who 74, –82, –83, WhoTwCL,

WhoWor 74, –76, –78, –80, WorAu,
WrDr 76
Entwistle, John 1944- *BioIn 11, WhoAm 80,*
–82
Entwistle, John *see also* Who, The
Epand, Len 1950- *ConAu 85*
Ephron, Delia 1944- *BioIn 11, –12, ConAu 97,*
NewYTBS 78
Epp, Margaret A 1913- *BioIn 12,*
ConAu 3NR, –9R, IntAu&W 77, –82,
SmATA 20, WhoAmW 74, –70, –72, –75,
–83, WhoWest 74, –76, –78, WrDr 76, –80,
–82, –84
Epstein, Anne Merrick 1931- *BioIn 12,*
ConAu 69, SmATA 20
Epstein, Beryl Williams 1910- *AuBYP,*
BioIn 6, –7, –9, ConAu 2NR, –5R, MorJA,
OhA&B, SmATA 1, –31[port]
Epstein, Cynthia Fuchs 1933- *AmM&WS 73S,*
–78S, ConAu 29R, IntAu&W 77,
WrDr 76, –80, –82, –84
Epstein, Edward Jay 1935- *BioIn 8, –11,*
ConAu 17R, WhoWorJ 72, –78
Epstein, Helen 1947- *ConAu 89, WrDr 82,*
–84
Epstein, Jacob 1956?- *BioIn 12, ConLC 19*
Epstein, Joseph 1937- *WhoAm 82*
Epstein, Leslie 1938- *BioIn 11, ConAu 73,*
ConLC 27[port], DrAF 76, DrAP&F 83
Epstein, Morris 1921-1973 *BioIn 10,*
ConAu P-1, NewYTBE 73, WhoWorJ 72
Epstein, Perle S 1938- *AuBYP SUP, BioIn 12,*
ConAu 9NR, –65, SmATA 27[port]
Epstein, Samuel 1909- *AuBYP, BioIn 6, –7,*
–9, ConAu 4NR, –9R, MorJA,
SmATA 1, –31[port], WhoWorJ 72, –78
Erdman, Loula Grace d1976 *AmAu&B,*
AmNov, AuBYP, BioIn 2, –6, –7, –9,
ConAu 5R, –10NR, DrAS 74E,
ForWC 70, InWom, MorJA, SmATA 1,
TexWr, WhoAmW 58, –61, –64, –66, –68,
–72
Erdoes, Richard 1912- *BioIn 1, –3, –8,*
ConAu 77, IlsBYP, IlsCB 1957,
SmATA 33[port]
Erhard, Thomas A 1923- *ConAu 33R,*
DrAS 74E, –78E, –82E, WrDr 76
Erickson, Sabra Rollins 1912- *ConAu 5R,*
–5NR, SmATA 35, WhoAmW 74, –72,
–75, –77
Erickson, Sabra Rollins *see also* Holbrook, Sabra
Erlanger, Ellen 1950- *ConAu 85,*
WhoAmW 81
Erlich, Lillian 1910- *AuBYP, BioIn 7, –11,*
ConAu 1R, –5NR, ForWC 70,
SmATA 10, WhoAmW 74, –75
Erno, Richard B 1923- *BioIn 3, ConAu 13R,*
DrAS 74E, –78E, –82E, MichAu 80,
WrDr 80, –82, –84
Ernst, John 1940- *ConAu 45*
Ernst, Margaret 1894?-1964 *BioIn 7,*
ConAu P-1

Erskine, Albert Russel, Jr. 1911- *WhoAm 74,*
–76, –78
Erskine, Jim 1956- *ConAu 107*
Eshmeyer, R E 1898- *ConAu X,*
SmATA 29[port]
Eskenazi, Gerald 1936- *ConAu 7NR, –61,*
WhoAmJ 80, WhoE 79
Esposito, Phil 1942- *BioIn 8, –9, –10, –11, –12,*
ConAu 108, CurBio 73, NewYTBS 79,
–81[port], WhoHcky 73, WorAl
Esposito, Tony 1943- *BioIn 8, –9, –10,*
WhoAm 74, WhoHcky 73
Espy, Willard R 1910- *BioIn 2, –11,*
ConAu 2NR, –49, IntAu&W 76, –77,
WhoAm 76, –78, –80, –82, WhoWor 78,
–80, –82
Esslin, Martin 1918- *BiE&WWA, BlueB 76,*
ConAu 85, ConLCrt, –82, DcLEL 1940,
DrAS 82E, NotNAT, Who 74, –82, –83,
WhoThe 16, –81, WhoWor 76,
WorAu 1970, WrDr 80, –82, –84
Esterow, Milton 1928- *ConAu 17R,*
WhoAm 74, –76, –78, –80, –82,
WhoAmA 76, –78, –80, –82, WhoE 83
Estes, Winston 1917- *ConAu 29R,*
WhoS&SW 75, –76
Estes, Winston M 1917- *BioIn 8, ConAu 29R,*
IntAu&W 76, –77, WrDr 76, –80, –82, –84
Estleman, Loren D 1952- *ConAu 85,*
WrDr 84
Estoril, Jean *AuBYP, ConAu X,*
IntAu&W 76X, –77X, –82X, SmATA X,
TwCCW 83, WrDr 76, –80, –82, –84
Estoril, Jean *see also* Allan, Mabel Esther
Etchison, Birdie L 1937- *ConAu 106*
Etter, Les 1904- *ConAu 25R*
Ettinger, Blanche 1922- *WhoE 81*
Euller, John E 1926- *ConAu 9R*
Eulo, Ken 1939- *ConAu 109, IntAu&W 76,*
NatPD
Eunson, Dale 1904- *AmAu&B, AmNov,*
BiE&WWA, BioIn 2, –10, ConAu 41R,
IntAu&W 82, NotNAT, SmATA 5
Eunson, Roby *AuBYP SUP*
Eustis, Helen 1916- *BioIn 3, –4, CurBio 55,*
EncMys, InWom, OhA&B,
TwCCr&M 80, WrDr 82, –84
Evanoff, Vlad 1916- *ConAu 5R, –6NR,*
IntAu&W 77, WrDr 76, –80, –82, –84
Evans, Sir Anthony 1922- *Au&Wr 6, Who 74,*
–82, –83
Evans, Arthur L 1931- *WhoBlA 75, –77, –80*
Evans, Barbara Lloyd *ConAu X*
Evans, Bergen 1904-1978 *AmAu&B,*
Au&Wr 6, BioIn 3, –4, –5, –11, –12,
CelR 73, ConAu 4NR, –5R, –77,
CurBio 55, –78, –78N, DcLEL 1940,
DrAS 74E, LesBEnT, LinLib L,
NatCAB 60[port], NewYTET, ObitOF 79,
OhA&B, WhAm 7, WhoAm 74, –76,
WhoWor 74, WorAl
Evans, Christopher 1931-1979 *ConAu 102,*

EncO&P 81, IntAu&W 76, ScF&FL 1,
–2
Evans, Edna Hoffman 1913- *AuBYP, BioIn 7,*
ForWC 70, WhoAmW 66, –68, –70, –72
Evans, Elizabeth 1932- *ConAu 53*
Evans, Gareth Lloyd 1923- *Au&Wr 6*
Evans, Harold Matthew 1928- *BioIn 10, –12,*
BlueB 76, ConAu 41R, IntAu&W 77, –82,
IntWW 75, –76, –77, –78, –79, –80, –81, –82,
–83, Who 74, –82, –83, WhoWor 74, –76,
–78, WrDr 76, –80, –82, –84
Evans, Howard Ensign 1919- *AmM&WS 73P,*
–76P, –79P, –82P, ConAu 5R, –6NR,
WhoAm 74, –76, –78, –80, –82
Evans, Humphrey 1914- *ConAu 29R*
Evans, Idrisyn Oliver 1894- *Au&Wr 6,*
ConAu 13R, IntAu&W 76, –77,
WhE&EA, WrDr 76, –80, –82, –84
Evans, Larry Melvyn 1932- *GolEC,*
WhoAm 74, –76, –78, –80, –82
Evans, Mari 1923- *AuBYP SUP, BioIn 10,*
–11, BlkAWP, BroadAu[port],
ConAu 2NR, –49, ConP 75, –80, CroCAP,
DrAP 75, DrAP&F 83, Ebony 1,
InB&W 80, LinLib L, LivgBAA,
NegAl 76, –83, SelBAA, SmATA 10,
WhoAm 76, –78, –80, –82, WhoBlA 75, –77,
–80, WrDr 76, –80, –82, –84
Evans, Mary Ann 1819-1880 *BiD&SB,*
BrAu 19, CarSB, DcLEL, Dis&D, EvLB,
GoodHs, InWom, IntDcWB, LinLib S,
NewC, OxEng, PenC ENG, REn,
WhDW
Evans, Mary Ann *see also* Eliot, George
Evans, Max 1925- *Au&Wr 6, ConAu 1R,*
–1NR, IntAu&W 76, WrDr 84
Evans, Richard 1939- *ConAu 106*
Evans, Rowland, Jr. 1921- *BioIn 7, CelR 73,*
ConAu 21R, WhoAm 74, –76, –78, –80,
–82, WhoS&SW 73, WhoWor 74,
WrDr 76, –80, –82, –84
Evans, Shirlee 1931- *ConAu 61*
Evans, Walker 1903-1975 *AmAu&B, BioIn 1,*
–4, –7, –9, –10, –11, –12, BnEnAmA,
ConAu 89, ConPhot, CurBio 71, –75,
–75N, DcAmArt, EncAB-H,
NewYTBS 75, ObitOF 79, WebAB, –79,
WhAm 6, WhoAm 74, WhoWor 74
Evans, William Eugene 1930- *AmM&WS 73P*
Evarts, Hal G 1915- *AuBYP SUP, BioIn 10,*
ConAu 2NR, –49, SmATA 6,
WhoWest 78, –80, –82, –84, WrDr 84
Evelyn, John Michael 1916- *ConAu 5R,*
WrDr 82, –84
Everson, William K 1929- *AuBYP, BioIn 8,*
–10, ConAu 1R, IntMPA 77, –75, –76, –78,
–79, –84, ScF&FL 1, –2, WhoAm 74, –76
Evslin, Bernard 1922- *AuBYP SUP,*
ConAu 9NR, –21R, SmATA 28
Ewart, William Dunlop 1923- *Au&Wr 6*
Ewen, David 1907- *AmAu&B, Au&Wr 6,*
AuBYP, BiE&WWA, BioIn 8, –9, –10,

ConAu 1R, –2NR, IntAu&W 77, REnAL,
SmATA 4, WhE&EA, WhoAm 74, –76,
–78, –80, –82, WhoMus 72,
WhoS&SW 73, WhoWor 74, –76,
WhoWorJ 72, –78, WrDr 76, –80, –82, –84

Ewen, Robert B 1940- *AmM&WS 73S,*
ConAu 37R, WhoS&SW 82

Ewen, Stuart Baer 1945- *AmM&WS 78S,*
ConAu 69, DrAS 78H, –82H

Eyerly, Jeanette Hyde 1908- *AuBYP SUP*

Eyerly, Jeannette Hyde 1908- *AmCath 80,*
AuBYP SUP, BioIn 9, ConAu 1R, –4NR,
ForWC 70, SmATA 4, WhoAm 74, –76,
–78, –80, –82, WhoAmW 74, –66, –68, –70,
–72, –75, –77, –79

Eyre, Katherine Wigmore 1901-1970 *AmAu&B,*
BioIn 2, –4, –6, –8, ConAu 104,
CurBio 49, –57, InWom, MorJA,
ScF&FL 1, SmATA 26[port]

Eyre, Ronald 1929- *ConAu 104, EncWT,*
IntAu&W 82, Who 83, WhoThe 15, –16,
–81

Ezzell, Marilyn 1937- *ConAu 109*

F

TwCCr&M 80, TwCWr, WebAB, –79, WebE&AL, WhDW, WhAm 4, WhE&EA, WhoTwCL, WorAl, WorEFlm

Faust, Frederick 1892-1944 *AmAu&B, BioIn 1, –3, –4, –8, ChhPo, CmCal, ConAu 108, CurBio 44, DcAmB S3, DcLEL, DcNAA, EncMys, LongCTC, MnBBF, NatCAB 33, ObitOF 79, REn, REnAL, REnAW, ScF&FL 1, TwCA, TwCA SUP, WebAB, –79, WhoBW&I A, WhoHr&F*

Faust, Frederick *see also* Brand, Max

Fax, Elton Clay 1909- *AfroAA, BioIn 10, ConAu 13R, IlsCB 1967, InB&W 80, LivgBAA, NegAl 76[port], –83[port], SmATA 25[port], WhoAm 76, –78, –80, –82, WhoAmA 73, –76, –78, –80, –82, WhoBlA 75, –77, –80, WhoWor 78*

Fay, Frederic L 1890- *ConAu P-2*

Fay, Gordon S 1912- *ConAu 53*

Feagles, Anita M 1926- *AuBYP, BioIn 8, –11, ConAu 1R, –4NR, ForWC 70, FourBJA, SmATA 9, WhoAmW 64*

Feagles, Elizabeth *ConAu X, SmATA X*

Feagles, Elizabeth *see also* Day, Beth Feagles

Feather, Leonard Geoffrey 1914- *AmAu&B, AmSCAP 66, Baker 78, CmpEPM, ConAu 61, IntWWM 77, WhoAm 74, –76, –78, –80, –82, WhoWor 74, –76*

Featherstone, Helen 1944- *ConAu 102*

Fecher, Constance 1911- *Au&Wr 6, AuBYP SUP, BioIn 10, ConAu X, –49, IntAu&W 77X, SmATA 7, WrDr 76, –80, –82, –84*

Fecher, Constance *see also* Heaven, Constance

Fedder, Ruth 1907- *AmM&WS 73S, ConAu 2NR, –5R, LEduc 74, WhoAmW 66, –68, –70, –72, WhoWest 74*

Feegel, John R 1932- *ConAu 9NR, –57*

Feelings, Thomas 1933- *ConAu 49, InB&W 80, SmATA 8, WhoBlA 77, –80, WhoE 77, –79*

Feelings, Tom 1933- *AfroAA, BioIn 8, –9, –11, –12, BkP, ChlLR 5[port], ConAu 49, IlsBYP, IlsCB 1967, LivgBAA, SelBAA, SmATA 8, ThrBJA*

Fehrenbach, T R 1925- *ConAu 1R, –1NR, IntAu&W 76, –77, –82, SmATA 33[port], WhoS&SW 73, –75, –76, WhoWor 78, –80, WrDr 82, –84*

Fehrenbacher, Don Edward 1920- *ConAu 1R, –2NR, DrAS 74H, –78H, –82H, WhoAm 74, –76, –78, –80, –82, WrDr 76, –80, –82, –84*

Feibleman, James Kern 1904- *AmAu&B, Au&Wr 6, AuNews 2, BioIn 2, –4, –8, –11, BlueB 76, ConAu 5R, –7NR, DrAS 74P, –78P, –82P, IntAu&W 76, TwCA SUP, WhoAm 74, –76, –78, –80, –82, WhoWor 74, WhoWorJ 72, –78*

Feifel, Herman 1915- *AmM&WS 73S, –78S, ConAu 101, WhoAm 80, WhoWest 74,*

–76, –78, –82

Feiffer, Jules 1929- *AmAu&B, ArtCS, Au&Wr 6, BioIn 5, –6, –7, –8, –9, –10, –11, –12, BlueB 76, CelR 73, CnThe, ConAu 17R, ConDr 73, –77, –82, ConLC 2, –8, CroCD, CurBio 61, DcLB 7[port], DcLEL 1940, EncWT, FilmgC, IntAu&W 76, –77, IntWW 74, –75, –76, –77, –78, –79, –80, –81, –82, –83, LinLib L, McGEWD, –84, NatPD 81[port], NewYTBS 76, –81[port], NotNAT, SmATA 8, WhoAm 74, –76, –78, –80, –82, WhoAmA 76, –78, –80, –82, WhoAmJ 80, WhoThe 15, –16, –81, WhoWor 74, –78, WhoWorJ 72, –78, WorAl, WorAu 1970, WorECom, WrDr 76, –80, –82, –84*

Feil, Hila 1942- *BioIn 11, ConAu 37R, SmATA 12*

Feinbloom, Deborah Heller 1940- *ConAu 65*

Feingold, S Norman 1914- *AmM&WS 73S, –78S, ConAu 13R, LEduc 74, WhoAm 76, –78, –80, –82, WhoAmJ 80, WhoE 79, WhoS&SW 73, –75, –76, WhoWor 82, WhoWorJ 72, –78*

Feininger, Andreas 1906- *AmAu&B, BioIn 2, –4, –12, ConAu 85, ConPhot, CurBio 57, LinLib L, WhoAm 74, –76, –78, –80, –82, WhoWor 74, –76*

Feinman, Jeffrey Paul 1943- *ConAu 10NR, –65, WhoAdv 72, WhoCon 73, WhoE 83*

Feirer, John Louis 1915- *LEduc 74, WhoAm 76, –78, –80, –82*

Fejes, Claire 1920- *ConAu 21R, WhoAmA 82, WhoAmW 74, –75*

Feldman, Annette Gerber 1913- *ConAu 69, WhoAmW 81*

Feldman, Charles K 1904?-1968 *BioIn 2, –8, FilmgC, NotNAT B, ObitOF 79, WhAm 5, WorEFlm*

Feldman, Samuel Nathan 1931- *BiDrAPA 77, ConAu 25R*

Feldman, Silvia 1928- *ConAu 97*

Feldstein, Albert B 1925- *WhoAm 76, –78, –80, –82, WhoAmJ 80, WhoWor 80, –82, WorECom*

Felice, Cynthia 1942- *ConAu 107*

Feller, Bob 1918- *CurBio 41, NewYTBS 75*

Feller, Robert William Andrew 1918- *AuBYP, BioIn 1, –2, –3, –4, –5, –6, –7, –8, –9, –10, WebAB, –79, WhoProB 73, WorAl*

Fellini, Federico 1920- *BiDFilm, BioIn 4, –5, –6, –7, –8, –9, –10, –11, –12, BioNews 75, CelR 73, ConAu 65, ConLC 16, CurBio 57, –80[port], DcFM, FilmgC, IntMPA 77, –75, –76, –78, –79, –81, –82, –84, IntWW 74, –75, –76, –77, –78, –80, –81, –82, –83, MakMC, McGEWB, MovMk, OxFilm, REn, WhDW, Who 74, –82, –83, WhoAm 80, –82, WhoWor 74, –78, –80, –82, WomWMM, WorAl, WorEFlm*

Fellows, Lawrence Perry 1924- *ConAu 49,*

WhoE 77, –79

Felsen, Henry Gregor 1916- *AuBYP, BioIn 2, –7, –9, ConAu 1R, –1NR, ConLC 17, ScF&FL 1, –2, SmATA 1*

Felt, W Mark 1913- *BioIn 12, WhoAm 74, WhoGov 72, WhoS&SW 73*

Felton, Harold William 1902- *AuBYP, BioIn 6, –8, –9, ChhPo S2, ConAu 1R, –1NR, MorJA, SmATA 1*

Felton, Ronald Oliver 1909-1982 *Au&Wr 6, BioIn 8, –9, ConAu 3NR, –9R, IntAu&W 77, SmATA 3, WrDr 82*

Felton, Ronald Oliver *see also* Welch, Ronald

Fenady, Andrew J 1928- *ConAu 77, IntMPA 77, –75, –76, –78, –79, –81, –82, –84*

Fendell, Bob 1925- *ConAu 57*

Fenderson, Lewis H 1907-1983 *ConAu 106, DrAS 74E, SmATA 37N*

Fenelon, Fania 1918-1983 *ConAu 77, NewYTBS 78, –83[port], WhoWor 80*

Fenin, George N 1916- *ConAu 9R*

Fenner, Phyllis Reid 1899-1982 *AuBYP, BioIn 3, –7, –9, –12, ConAu 2NR, –5R, –106, ForWC 70, ScF&FL 1, –2, SmATA 1, –29N, WhoAmW 74, –58, –61, –64, –66, –68, –70, –72, –75, –77, WhoLibS 66*

Fenten, Barbara D 1935- *ConAu 5NR, –53, SmATA 26*

Fenten, D X 1932- *AuBYP SUP, BioIn 9, ConAu 5NR, –33R, SmATA 4, WhoE 75, –77, –79, WrDr 76, –80, –82, –84*

Fenton, Carroll Lane 1900-1969 *AmAu&B, AuBYP, BioIn 6, –7, –8, –10, ConAu 1R, –6NR, –29R, MorJA, NatCAB 55, SmATA 5, WhE&EA*

Fenton, Edward 1917- *Au&Wr 6, AuBYP, BioIn 9, –10, ConAu 9R, ScF&FL 1, SmATA 7, ThrBJA, TwCCW 78, –83, WrDr 80, –82, –84*

Fenton, Mildred Adams 1899- *Au&Wr 6, BioIn 6, –7, –12, ConAu 77, MorJA, SmATA 21[port]*

Fenwick, Elizabeth 1920- *Au&Wr 6, TwCCr&M 80, WrDr 82, –84*

Fenwick, Sheridan 1942- *ConAu 69*

Feola, Jose M 1926- *AmM&WS 79P, –82P, BiDPara, ConAu 69, EncO&P 78*

Ferber, Edna 1887-1968 *AmAu&B, AmNov, AmWomWr, ApCAB X, AuNews 1, BiE&WWA, BioIn 1, –2, –3, –4, –5, –6, –8, –9, –10, –11, –12, Chambr 3, CnDAL, CnMD, CnThe, ConAmA, ConAmL, ConAu 5R, –25R, ConLC 18, DcLB 9[port], DcLEL, EncWL, EncWT, EvLB, FilmgC, GoodHs, InWom, LibW, LinLib L, –S, LongCTC, McGEWB, McGEWD, –84[port], ModAL, ModWD, NatCAB 60, NotAW MOD, NotNAT A, –B, Novels, ObitOF 79, ObitT 1961, OxAmL, OxThe, PenC AM, PIP&P, REn, REnAL, REnAW, SmATA 7,*

TwCA, TwCA SUP, TwCWr, WebAB, –79, WhAm 5, WhE&EA, WhNAA, WhThe, WhoAmW 58, –61, –64, –66, –68, –70, WisWr, WorAl

Ferencz, Benjamin B 1920- *ConAu 97, WhoAmJ 80, WhoWorJ 72, –78*

Ferguson, Annabelle Evelyn 1923- *ConAu 102, WhoAmW 74, –64, –66, –68, –72, –75, –77, –79, WhoE 81*

Ferguson, Bob *ConAu X, SmATA X*

Ferguson, Bob *see also* Ferguson, Robert Bruce

Ferguson, Robert Bruce 1927- *BiDAmM, ConAu 69, SmATA 13*

Fergusson, Erna 1888-1964 *AmAu&B, BioIn 3, –4, –7, –9, –10, ConAu P-1, CurBio 55, InWom, SmATA 5, WhE&EA*

Fergusson, Harvey 1890-1971 *AmAu&B, AmNov, BioIn 2, –4, –8, –9, –10, CmCal, CnDAL, ConAu 33R, OxAmL, REnAL, REnAW, TwCA, TwCA SUP, WhLit, WhNAA*

Ferlinghetti, Lawrence 1919?- *AmAu&B, BioIn 8, –10, –12, BlueB 76, CasWL, CelR 73, CmCal, ConAu 3NR, –5R, ConDr 73, –77, –82, ConLC 2, –6, –10, –27[port], ConP 70, –75, –80, CroCAP, CroCD, DcLB 5, –16[port], DcLEL 1940, DrAP 75, DrAP&F 83, IntAu&W 77, IntWW 74, –75, –76, –77, –78, –79, –80, –81, –82, –83, IntWWP 77, ModAL, OxAmL, PenC AM, RAdv 1, REn, REnAL, TwCWr, WebE&AL, WhoAm 74, –76, –78, –80, –82, WhoTwCL, WhoWest 74, WhoWor 74, –78, –80, –82, WorAl, WorAu, WrDr 76, –80, –82, –84*

Ferman, Edward L 1937- *ConAu 106, ConSFA, EncSF, ScF&FL 1, –2, WhoAm 82, WhoSciF*

Fermi, Laura 1907-1977 *AmAu&B, AuBYP, BioIn 3, –4, –5, –7, –10, –11, BlueB 76, ConAu 1R, –6NR, CurBio 58, InWom, IntAu&W 77, SmATA 28N, –6, WhAm 7, WhoAm 74, –76, –78, WhoAmW 74, –58, –61, –64, –66, –68, –70, –72, –75, WhoWor 74, WrDr 76, –80, –82, –84*

Ferrara, Peter J 1955- *WhoAmP 83*

Ferrigno, Lou 1952?- *BioIn 12, NewYTBS 76*

Ferris, Paul 1929- *Au&Wr 6, BlueB 76, ConAu 3NR, –5R, DcLEL 1940, IntAu&W 76, –77, ScF&FL 1, –2, Who 74, –82, –83, WhoWor 74, –76, WrDr 76, –80, –82, –84*

Ferris, Timothy 1944- *ConAu 11NR, –69, WhoE 81*

Ferry, Charles 1927- *ConAu 97*

Fetterman, John 1920-1975 *BioIn 10, ConAu 61, –93, NewYTBS 75, ObitOF 79, WhAm 6, WhoAm 74, WhoS&SW 73, –75, –76*

Feuerlicht, Roberta Strauss 1931- *ConAu 17R*

Ffrench Blake, R L V 1913- *ConAu 61*

Fichter, George S 1922- *AuBYP SUP,*
BioIn 2, –10, ConAu 7NR, –17R,
IntAu&W 82, SmATA 7, WhoS&SW 73,
–75, –76, WrDr 76, –80, –82, –84
Fichter, George S *see also* Warner, Matt
Fidrych, Mark 1954- *BioIn 11, –12,*
CurBio 78, NewYTBS 76, –77, –80[port],
–82, –83[port], WhoAm 78, –80
Fiedler, Jean Feldman 1923- *BioIn 9,*
ConAu 11NR, –29R, DrAP&F 83,
ForWC 70, SmATA 4, WhoAmW 74, –66,
–68, –70, –72, –75, –77
Field, Eugene 1850-1895 *Alli SUP, AmAu,*
AmAu&B, AmBi, AmSCAP 66,
ApCAB SUP, AuBYP, BbD, BiDAmM,
BiD&SB, BiDSA, BioIn 1, –2, –3, –4, –5,
–6, –7, –8, –9, –10, –11, –12, CarSB,
CasWL, Chambr 3, ChrP, ChhPo, –S1,
–S2, –S3, CnDAL, DcAmAu, DcAmB,
DcLB 23[port], DcLEL, DcNAA, EvLB,
FamPYP, HarEnUS, JBA 34, LinLib L,
–S, NatCAB 1, OxAmL, OxEng,
PenC AM, RAdv 1, REn, REnAL,
ScF&FL 1, SmATA 16, Str&VC,
TwCBDA, WebAB, –79, WhAm HS,
WorAl
Field, Frank 1942- *IntYB 80, –81, –82,*
Who 74, –82, –83
Field, Michael 1915-1971 *BiDAmM, BioIn 7,*
–8, –9, ConAu 29R, NewYTBE 71
Field, Rachel 1894-1942 *AmAu&B,*
AmWomWr, AnCL, AuBYP, BioIn 1, –2,
–4, –6, –7, –12, BkCL, CarSB, ChhPo, –S1,
–S2, –S3, CnDAL, ConAmA, ConAu 109,
ConICB, CurBio 42, DcLB 9, –22[port],
DcNAA, FamPYP, FilmgC, InWom,
JBA 34, –51, LinLib L, LongCTC,
NatCAB 33, Newb 1922, NotAW,
NotNAT B, OxAmL, REnAL,
ScF&FL 1, SmATA 15, Str&VC, TwCA,
TwCA SUP, TwCCW 78, –83, TwCWr,
WhAm 2, WorAl
Fielding, Henry 1707-1754 *Alli, AtlBL, BbD,*
BiD&SB, BioIn 1, –2, –3, –4, –5, –6, –7, –8,
–9, –10, –11, –12, BrAu, BrWr 3, CasWL,
Chambr 2, ChhPo, –S1, CnThe, CrtT 2,
–4, CyWA, DcBiA, DcBiPP, DcEnA,
DcEnL, DcEuL, DcLEL, Dis&D,
EncWT, EvLB, LinLib L, –S, LongCEL,
McGEWB, McGEWD, –84[port],
MouLC 2, NewC, NotNAT B,
Novels[port], OxEng, OxThe, PenC ENG,
PIP&P, RAdv 1, RComWL, REn,
REnWD, ScF&FL 1, WebE&AL,
WhDW, WorAl
Fielding, Raymond 1931- *ConAu 8NR, –17R,*
DrAS 74E, –78E, –82E, IntAu&W 77, –82,
WhoE 75, WhoEng 80, WrDr 76, –80,
–82, –84
Fields, Jeff 1938?- *AuNews 2, BioIn 10, –11*
Fife, Dale 1910- *AuBYP SUP, BioIn 12,*
ConAu 85, FourBJA, SmATA 18

Fijan, Carol 1918- *BioIn 11, ConAu 53,*
SmATA 12
Filosa, Gary Fairmont 1931- *ConAu 65,*
WhoAm 74, –76, –78, –80, –82,
WhoF&I 79, –81, –83, WhoWest 74, –78,
–80, –82, –84, WhoWor 76, –78, –80, –82,
WrDr 80, –82, –84
Filson, Brent *DrAP&F 83*
Filson, Floyd Vivian 1896- *AmAu&B,*
ConAu 61, WhoAm 74, –76
Finch, Christopher 1939- *WrDr 76, –80, –82,*
–84
Finch, Donald George 1937- *ConAu 53,*
WhoMW 78, –80, –82
Fincher, Ernest B 1910- *ConAu 9NR, –53*
Findley, Timothy 1930- *BioIn 12, CaW,*
CanWW 79, –80, –81, –83, ConAu 25R,
ConLC 27[port], OxCan SUP, WhoE 74
Fine, Anne 1947- *ConAu 105, SmATA 29,*
TwCCW 83
Fine, Benjamin 1905-1975 *AmAu&B, BioIn 2,*
–3, –4, –5, –6, –10, BlueB 76N,
ConAu 4NR, –5R, –57, CurBio 61,
IntAu&W 77, NewYTBS 75, ObitOF 79,
WhAm 6, WhoAm 74, WhoWorJ 72, –78
Finger, Charles Joseph 1869-1941 *AmAu&B,*
AnCL, AuBYP, BioIn 4, –6, –7, BkCL,
ChhPo S3, CurBio 41, DcNAA, JBA 34,
NatCAB 46, Newb 1922, OhA&B,
REnAL, ScF&FL 1, TwCA, TwCCW 83,
WebE&AL, WhAm 1
Fink, Augusta 1916- *ConAu 33R,*
IntAu&W 77, –82, WhoAmW 75,
WrDr 76, –80, –82, –84
Finke, Blythe Foote 1922- *ConAu 65,*
IntAu&W 82, SmATA 26[port],
USBiR 74, WhoE 81, –83, WhoPubR 72,
–76
Finlay, Winifred Lindsay 1910- *Au&Wr 6,*
ConAu 9R, IntAu&W 76, –77, –82,
SmATA 23[port], TwCCW 78, –83,
WhoAmW 74, –75, WhoWor 74, –76,
WrDr 76, –80, –82, –84
Finlayson, Ann 1925- *BioIn 11, ConAu 29R,*
SmATA 8, WhoAmW 74, –75
Finley, M I 1912- *ConAu 10NR, WhoWor 74,*
–76
Finney, Charles G 1905- *AmAu&B, BioIn 4,*
ConAu P-2, ConSFA, EncSF, ScF&FL 1,
–2, TwCA, TwCA SUP, WhoHr&F
Finney, Gertrude Elva 1892- *AuBYP, BioIn 4,*
–8, ConAu P-1, CurBio 57, InWom,
IndAu 1917, WhoAmW 58, –61, –70, –72,
WhoPNW
Finney, Jack 1911- *Au&Wr 6, BioIn 12,*
ConAu X, ConSFA, DcLB 8, EncSF,
ScF&FL 1, TwCCr&M 80, WhoSciF,
WorAl, WrDr 82, –84
Fiore, Edith Anne 1930- *ConAu 85,*
WhoWest 78, –80, –84
Fiorina, Morris Paul 1946- *AmM&WS 73S,*
–78S, ConAu 85

Fischer, Bobby 1943- *BioIn 9, –10, –11, –12,
CelR 73, ConAu X, CurBio 63,
NewYTBE 73, WhDW, WhoAm 74, –76,
–78, –80, –82, WhoWor 74*

Fischer, John 1910-1978 *AmAu&B,
BiDrLUS 70, BioIn 1, –3, –11,
ConAu 4NR, –9R, –81, CurBio 53, –78,
–78N, IntWW 74, –75, –76, –77, –78, –79N,
IntYB 78, ObitOF 79, WhAm 7,
Who 74, WhoAm 74, –76, –78,
WhoWor 74, WrDr 80*

Fischler, Stan *SmATA 36*

Fish, Byron Morris 1908- *ConAu 45,
WhoPNW, WhoWest 76*

Fish, Helen Dean 1890-1953 *AmAu&B,
BioIn 3, ChhPo, ObitOF 79*

Fish, Robert L 1912-1981 *AnObit 1981[port],
Au&Wr 6, BioIn 12, ConAu 103,
DrAP&F 83, EncMys, IntAu&W 76, –77,
Novels, WhoAm 74, –76, –78, –80,
WrDr 82*

Fisher, Aileen Lucia 1906- *AuBYP, BioIn 6,
–9, BkCL, BkP, ChhPo, –S1, –S2,
ConAu 2NR, –5R, ForWC 70, MorJA,
SmATA 1, –25[port], TwCCW 78, –83,
WhoAmW 58, –61, –83, WrDr 80, –82, –84*

Fisher, David E 1932- *AmM&WS 73P, –76P,
–79P, –82P, ConAu 4NR, –53, WrDr 76,
–80, –82, –84*

Fisher, Douglas 1934- *AmEA 74,
AmM&WS 73S, ConAu 102, WhoE 74*

Fisher, John 1909- *Au&Wr 6, BioIn 12*

Fisher, Leonard Everett 1924- *AuBYP,
BioIn 3, –5, –7, –8, –9, –10, –12, ConAu 1R,
–2NR, IlsCB 1946, –1957, –1967,
IntAu&W 82, MorBMP,
SmATA 34[port], –4, ThrBJA,
WhoAmA 73, –76, –78, –80, –82,
WhoAmJ 80, WhoE 74, WhoWorJ 72,
–78, WrDr 76, –80, –82, –84*

Fisher, Lois I 1948- *SmATA 35*

Fisher, Margery 1913- *Au&Wr 6, AuBYP,
BioIn 8, –12, ChhPo, –S3, ConAu 73,
IntAu&W 77, –82, SmATA 20, Who 82,
–83, WhoChL*

Fisher, Vardis 1895-1968 *AmAu&B, AmNov,
Au&Wr 6, BioIn 1, –2, –4, –5, –7, –8, –9,
–10, –12, CnDAL, ConAmA, ConAu 5R,
–25R, ConLC 7, CyWA, DcLB 9[port],
DcLEL, EncSF, LinLib L, LongCTC,
ModAL, Novels, ObitOF 79, OxAmL,
PenC AM, REn, REnAL, REnAW,
ScF&FL 1, –2, TwCA, TwCA SUP,
WhAm 5, WhNAA, Who 74*

Fisher, Welthy Honsinger 1879-1980 *AmAu&B,
Au&Wr 6, BioIn 6, –7, –8, –12,
ConAu 1R, –2NR, –102, CurBio 69, –81N,
EncWM, ForWC 70, InWom,
IntAu&W 77, –82, NewYTBS 74, –80,
WhoAmW 74, –58, –61, –68, –70, –72, –75,
–77, –81*

Fisk, Nicholas 1923- *ConAu 11NR, –65,*

*ConSFA, IlsBYP, ScF&FL 1, –2,
SmATA 25[port], TwCCW 78, –83,
WrDr 80, –82, –84*

Fitch, Florence Mary 1875-1959 *AmAu&B,
AuBYP, BioIn 5, –6, –7, MorJA,
ObitOF 79, OhA&B, WhAm 3,
WhoAmW 58, WomWWA 14*

Fitts, Dudley 1903-1968 *AmAu&B,
BiE&WWA, BioIn 4, –8, ConAu 25R, –93,
LinLib L, ModAL, NotNAT B, OxAmL,
PenC AM, REnAL, TwCA, TwCA SUP,
WhAm 5*

Fitz-Randolph, Jane 1915- *ConAu 103*

Fitzgerald, Barbara *WrDr 76, –80, –82, –84*

FitzGerald, C P 1902- *ConAu 11NR, –17R*

FitzGerald, Charles Patrick 1902- *Au&Wr 6,
BioIn 7, WhE&EA, Who 74, –82, –83,
WrDr 76, –80, –82, –84*

Fitzgerald, Edward Earl 1919- *AmAu&B,
AuBYP, BioIn 8, –12, ConAu 73,
SmATA 20, WhoAm 74, –76, –78, –80, –82,
WhoF&I 74, WhoWor 78, –80, –82*

Fitzgerald, F Scott 1896-1940 *AmAu&B,
AmWr, AtlBL, AuNews 1, BioIn 12,
BioNews 74, CasWL, Chambr 3, CmCal,
CnDAL, CnMD, CnMWL, ConAmA,
ConAmL, ConAu 110, CurBio 41,
CyWA, DcLB DS1[port], –Y81A[port], –4,
–9[port], DcLEL, DcNAA, EncMys,
EncWL, –2[port], EvLB, FilmgC,
LinLib L, –S, LongCTC, ModAL,
ModAL SUP, NotNAT B, Novels[port],
ObitOF 79, OxAmL, OxEng, OxFilm,
PenC AM, RAdv 1, RComWL, REn,
REnAL, TwCA, TwCA SUP, TwCLC 1,
–6[port], TwCWr, WebAB, –79,
WebE&AL, WhDW, WhLit, WhNAA,
WhoTwCL, WorAl*

FitzGerald, Gregory 1923- *ConAu 1NR, –49,
DrAF 76, DrAP&F 83, ScF&FL 1, –2*

Fitzgerald, John D 1907- *AuBYP SUP,
BioIn 12, ChlLR 1, ConAu 93,
SmATA 20, TwCCW 83*

Fitzgerald, Nancy 1951- *ConAu 85*

Fitzgerald, Zelda 1900-1948 *AmAu&B,
AmWomWr, AuNews 1, BioIn 1, –6, –8,
–9, –10, –12, IntDcWB*

FitzGibbon, Constantine 1919-1983 *AmAu&B,
Au&Wr 6, BlueB 76, ConAu 1R, –2NR,
–109, DcIrL, EncSF, IntAu&W 76, –77,
–82, IntWW 74, –75, –76, –77, –78, –79,
–80, –81, –82, –83, –83N, Novels,
ScF&FL 1, –2, Who 74, –82, –83,
WhoWor 74, –78, WorAu, WrDr 76, –80,
–82, –84*

Fitzhardinge, Joan Margaret 1912- *Au&Wr 6,
AuBYP, BioIn 9, ConAu 6NR, –13R,
IntAu&W 76, –77, –82, ScF&FL 1,
SmATA 2, ThrBJA*

Fitzhardinge, Joan Margaret *see also* Phipson,
Joan

Fitzhugh, Louise 1928-1974 *AuBYP, BioIn 8,*

–9, –10, ChlLR 1, ConAu 53, ConAu P-2,
IntAu&W 76, NewYTBS 74, SmATA 1,
–24N, ThrBJA, TwCCW 78, –83

Fitzsimons, Raymund ConAu 33R,
IntAu&W 76, WrDr 76, –80, –84

Fixx, James F 1932-1984 BioIn 11, –12,
ConAu 73, NewYTBS 78, WhoAm 74,
–76, –78, –80, –82, WrDr 80, –82, –84

Flagg, Fannie 1941?- BioIn 12, ForWC 70,
WhoHol A

Flagler, John J 1927- WhoCon 73

Flanagan, Geraldine Lux AuBYP SUP

Flanagan, Thomas 1923- ConNov 82,
DcLB Y80B[port]

Flaubert, Gustave 1821-1880 AtlBL, BbD,
BiD&SB, BioIn 1, –2, –3, –4, –5, –6, –7, –8,
–9, –10, –11, –12, CasWL, CelCen,
ClDMEL, CyWA, DcBiA, DcEuL,
Dis&D, EncWT, EuAu, EvEuW,
LinLib L, –S, LongCEL, McGEWB,
NewC, NewEOp 71, Novels[port], OxEng,
OxFr, PenC EUR, RComWL, REn,
ScF&FL 1, WhDW, WorAl

Flayderman, Phillip C 1930-1969 ConAu P-2

Fleetwood, Mick 1947- BioIn 11, WhoAm 78,
–80, –82, WhoRocM 82

Fleetwood, Mick see also Fleetwood Mac

Fleetwood Mac BioIn 11, EncPR&S, –77,
IlEncRk, RkOn 78, –84, RolSEnR 83,
WhoRocM 82

Fleetwood Mac SA Fleetwood, Mick

Fleetwood Mac SA McVie, Christine Perfect

Fleetwood Mac SA McVie, John

Fleetwood Mac SA Spencer, Jeremy

Fleetwood Mac SA Welch, Bob

Fleischer, Leonore BioIn 12, ConAu 109

Fleischman, Albert Sidney 1920- AuBYP,
BioIn 8, –11, ConAu 1R, WhoAm 82

Fleischman, Albert Sidney see also Fleischman,
Sid

Fleischman, Paul SmATA 32

Fleischman, Sid 1920- AnCL, BioIn 9,
ChlLR 1, ConAu X, –5NR, SmATA 8,
ThrBJA, TwCCW 78, –83, WrDr 80, –82,
–84

Fleischman, Sid see also Fleischman, Albert
Sidney

Fleischmann, Glen Harvey 1909- AuBYP SUP,
BioIn 2, ConAu 33R, WhoAm 74, –76,
–78, –80, –82, WhoE 74, WhoWor 74, –76,
–78, –80, –82

Fleissner, Else Mentz 1900- DrAS 74F,
WhoAmW 58

Fleming, Alice Carew Mulcahey 1928- AuBYP,
BioIn 8, –11, ConAu 1R, –2NR,
ForWC 70, SmATA 9, WhoAmW 74, –66,
–68, –70, –75, –77, –79, –83, WhoE 74, –79,
–81, WrDr 76, –80, –82, –84

Fleming, Gordon Howard 1920- DrAS 78E,
–82E

Fleming, Ian 1908-1964 AuBYP, BioIn 5, –6,
–7, –8, –10, –11, ConAu 5R, ConLC 3,

CorpD, CurBio 64, DcLEL 1940,
EncMys, EncSF, LinLib L, LongCTC,
NewC, Novels[port], ObitOF 79,
ObitT 1961, PenC ENG, REn,
SmATA 9, TwCA, TwCCr&M 80,
TwCWr, WhDW, WhAm 4, WhoSpyF,
WorAl, WorAu

Fleming, June 1935- ConAu 110

Fleming, Thomas James 1927- AmAu&B,
AuBYP SUP, BioIn 11, ConAu 5R,
–10NR, SmATA 8, WhoAm 74, –76, –78,
–80, –82, WhoWor 74, –76

Flender, Harold 1924- AuBYP SUP,
ConAu 49, DrAF 76

Fles, Barthold 1902- ScF&FL 1, –2

Fletcher, Adele Whitely 1897?- BioIn 12,
ConAu P-1, ForWC 70, WhNAA

Fletcher, Alan Mark 1928- AuBYP SUP,
ConAu 73, WrDr 76, –80, –82, –84

Fletcher, Charlie May Hogue 1897-1977
AuBYP, BioIn 9, –11, –12, ConAu 9R,
SmATA 3

Fletcher, Charlie May Hogue see also Simon,
Charlie May

Fletcher, Colin 1922- AuNews 1, BioIn 10,
–12, ConAu 11NR, –13R, SmATA 28,
WhoAm 74, –76, –78, –80, –82, WrDr 76,
–80, –82, –84

Fletcher, David 1940- ConAu X,
IntAu&W 82X, WrDr 76, –80, –82, –84

Fletcher, David see also Barber, D F

Fletcher, Helen Jill 1911- AuBYP, BioIn 8,
ConAu 9R, ForWC 70, SmATA 13

Flexner, Eleanor 1908- AmWomWr, BioIn 12,
ConAu 45

Flexner, James Thomas 1908- AmAu&B,
Au&Wr 6, BioIn 1, –11, –12, ConAu 1R,
–2NR, IntAu&W 76, NewYTBE 73,
SmATA 9, WhNAA, WhoAm 74, –76,
–78, –80, –82, WhoAmA 73, –76, –78, –80,
–82, WhoE 74, WorAu 1970, WrDr 76,
–80, –82, –84

Flexner, Stuart B 1928- ConAu 11NR, –13R,
DrAS 82F, WrDr 80, –82, –84

Flink, James John 1932- DrAS 74H, –78H,
–82H

Floethe, Louise Lee 1913- AuBYP, BioIn 9,
ConAu 1R, –2NR, ForWC 70, SmATA 4,
WhoAmW 58

Floherty, John Joseph 1882-1964 AmAu&B,
AuBYP, BioIn 2, –7, JBA 51,
SmATA 25[port], WhAm 4

Flood, Charles Bracelen 1929- AmAu&B,
AmCath 80, ConAu 41R, ScF&FL 1, –2,
WhoAm 74, –76, –78, WhoE 74, WrDr 80,
–82, –84

Flood, Curt 1938- AfroAA, NewYTBE 70,
NewYTBS 81[port], WorAl

Flores, Angel 1900- AmAu&B, ConAu 103,
DcSpL, DrAS 74F, –78F, –82F,
ScF&FL 1, WhoE 83

Florescu, Radu R 1925- ConAu 41R,

DrAS 74H, –78H, –82H

Flory, Jane Trescott 1917- *AuBYP SUP,*
ConAu 3NR, –9R, SmATA 22[port]

Flower, Dean Scott 1938- *ConAu 21R,*
DrAS 74E, –78E, –82E

Flower, Desmond John Newman 1907-
Au&Wr 6, ChhPo, –S2, ConAu 9R,
IntAu&W 76, –77, –82, IntYB 78, –79, –80,
–81, –82, WhE&EA, Who 74, –82, –83

Flower, Raymond 1921- *ConAu 108*

Flumiani, Carlo M 1911- *ConAu 9NR, –13R*

Flynn, Bethine *BioIn 12*

Flynn, James J 1911-1977 *AuBYP SUP,*
BioIn 11, ConAu 21R, DrAS 74H, –78H,
NewYTBS 77, WhoE 74

Flynn, Robert 1932- *ConAu 29R, DrAF 76,*
DrAP&F 83, WrDr 84

Fodor, Eugene 1905- *AmAu&B, BioIn 5,*
ConAu 21R, CurBio 76, IntAu&W 76,
NewYTBS 74, WhoAm 74, –76, –78, –80,
–82, WhoWor 74

Fogelberg, Dan 1951- *RkOn 78, –84,*
RolSEnR 83, WhoRocM 82

Foley, June 1944- *ConAu 109*

Foley, Louise Munro 1933- *AuBYP SUP,*
ConAu 37R, IntAu&W 77X, WrDr 76,
–80, –82, –84

Foley, Martha 1897-1977 *AmAu&B, BioIn 11,*
ConAu 73, CurBio 41, –77, –77N, InWom,
NewYTBS 77, –79, ObitOF 79, REnAL,
WhoAmW 74, –58, –64, –66, –68, –70, –72

Foley, Rae 1900-1978 *ConAu X, SmATA X,*
TwCCr&M 80

Foley, Scott *ConAu X*

Foley, Scott *see also* Dareff, Hal

Follett, James 1939- *EncSF*

Follett, Ken 1949- *BioIn 11, ConAu 81,*
ConLC 18, DcLB Y81B[port], Novels

Folsom, Franklin Brewster 1907- *AuBYP,*
BioIn 8, –10, ConAu 1R, –2NR,
IntAu&W 82, SmATA 5, WhoAm 76,
–78, –80, –82, WrDr 76, –80, –82, –84

Fon Eisen, Anthony 1917- *ConAu 13R,*
ScF&FL 2

Fonarow, Jerry 1935- *ConAu 4NR, –53*

Foner, Eric 1943- *ConAu 29R, DrAS 74H,*
–78H, –82H, WhoAm 82, WrDr 76, –80,
–82, –84

Foner, Philip S 1910- *AmAu&B, BlueB 76,*
ConAu 3NR, –9R, DrAS 74H, –78H, –82H,
IntYB 78, –79, –80, –81, –82, WhoAm 76,
–78, –80, –82, WhoE 74, –79, WhoWor 74,
WrDr 80, –82, –84

Fontane, Theodor 1819-1898 *BiD&SB, BioIn 1,*
–3, –5, –7, –11, –12, CasWL, ChhPo S2,
CIDMEL, CyWA, EncWT, EuAu,
EvEuW, LinLib L, McGEWB, Novels,
OxGer, PenC EUR, REn, WhDW

Fonteyn, Margot 1919- *BioIn 1, –2, –3, –4, –5,*
–6, –7, –8, –9, –10, –11, –12, BlueB 76,
CelR 73, ConAu X, CurBio 49, –72,
GoodHs, InWom, IntDcWB, IntWW 74,

–75, –76, –77, –78, –79, –80, –81, –82, –83,
LinLib S, NewYTBE 72, NewYTBS 74,
–80[port], WhDW, WhThe, Who 74, –82,
–83, WhoAmW 75, WhoWor 74, WorAl

Fooner, Michael *AuBYP SUP, ConAu 81,*
SmATA 22[port]

Footman, David John 1895- *Au&Wr 6,*
ConAu 97, IntAu&W 76, –77, –82,
ScF&FL 1, WhE&EA, Who 74, –82, –83

Forbes, Colin 1923- *Au&Wr 6, ConAu X,*
IntAu&W 76, WrDr 80, –82, –84

Forbes, Colin *see also* Sawkins, Raymond

Forbes, Esther 1894?-1967 *AmAu&B, AmNov,*
AmWomWr, AnCL, AuBYP, BioIn 1, –2,
–3, –4, –5, –6, –7, –8, –9, –11, –12,
ChhPo S2, ConAu 25R, ConAu P-1,
ConLC 12, CyWA, DcLB 22[port],
DcLEL, InWom, MorJA, NatCAB 53,
Newb 1922, NotAW MOD, ObitOF 79,
OxAmL, REn, REnAL, ScF&FL 1, –2,
SmATA 2, TwCA, TwCA SUP,
TwCCW 78, –83, WhAm 4,
WhoAmW 58, –64, –66, –68

Forbes, Kathryn 1909-1966 *AmAu&B, AmNov,*
BioIn 2, –7, –11, CmCal, ConAu X,
CurBio 44, –66, InWom, ObitOF 79,
REn, REnAL, SmATA X, WorAl

Forbes, Kathryn *see also* McLean, Kathryn

Forbis, William Hunt 1918- *ConAu 37R,*
WhoAm 74, –76, –78, –80, –82

Ford, Barbara *SmATA 34*

Ford, Betty 1918- *BioIn 12, BioNews 74,*
ConAu X, CurBio 75, NewYTBE 73,
NewYTBS 74, –75, –77, –78, WhoAm 76,
–78, –80, –82, WhoWest 78, WhoWor 76,
–78, –80, –82

Ford, Brian J 1939- *ConAu 41R,*
IntAu&W 77, –82, WrDr 76, –80, –82, –84

Ford, Corey 1902-1969 *AmAu&B, BioIn 5, –8,*
ConAu 25R, DcLB 11[port], EncMys,
ObitOF 79, REnAL, WhAm 5,
WhE&EA, WhNAA

Ford, Jesse Hill 1928- *AmAu&B, BioIn 5, –9,*
ConAu 1R, –1NR, ConNov 72, –76, –82,
DcLB 6[port], DcLEL 1940,
IntAu&W 76, –77, PenC AM,
WhoAm 74, –76, –78, –80, –82,
WhoWor 82, WrDr 76, –80, –82, –84

Ford, Paul Leicester 1865-1902 *Alli SUP,*
AmAu, AmAu&B, AmBi, ApCAB, BbD,
BiD&SB, BioIn 11, CarSB, Chambr 3,
ChhPo S1, CnDAL, DcAmAu, DcAmB,
DcBiA, DcLEL, DcNAA, EvLB,
HarEnUS, JBA 34, LinLib L, –S,
McGEWB, NatCAB 13, OxAmL, REn,
REnAL, TwCBDA, WebAB, –79,
WhAm 1

Ford, Richard *DrAP&F 83*

Forde-Johnston, James 1927- *Au&Wr 6,*
ConAu 3NR, –9R, IntAu&W 76, –77, –82,
WhoWor 78, WrDr 76, –80, –82, –84

Fordin, Hugh 1935- *BiE&WWA, ConAu 57,*

NotNAT, WrDr 76, –80, –82, –84

Forer, Lois Goldstein 1914- AmBench 79,
BioIn 3, ConAu 29R, WhoAm 74, –76,
WhoAmL 78, –79, WhoAmW 74, –58, –68,
–70, –72, WomPO 76, –78

Forest, Antonia ConAu 103,
SmATA 29[port], TwCCW 78, –83,
WrDr 76, –80, –82, –84

Forester, C S 1899-1966 ConAu 25R, –73,
EncSF, FilmgC, LinLib L, –S, Novels,
ObitOF 79, ObitT 1961, ScF&FL 1,
SmATA 13, WhE&EA, WorAl

Forester, Cecil Scott 1899-1966 AmAu&B,
BioIn 1, –2, –3, –4, –5, –7, –8, –9,
ConAu 25R, CyWA, DcLEL, EncMys,
EvLB, LongCTC, MnBBF, ModBrL,
NatCAB 53, NewC, OxShips, RAdv 1,
REn, REnAL, SmATA 13, TwCA,
TwCA SUP, TwCWr, WebE&AL,
WhAm 4, WhLit, WhoChL

Forkner, Benjamin Sands, III 1944-
WhoWor 82

Forman, Brenda 1936- Au&Wr 6, AuBYP,
BioIn 8, –9, ConAu 6NR, –9R, ForWC 70,
SmATA 4, WhoAmW 75

Forman, James Douglas 1932- AuBYP,
BioIn 8, –9, –11, ConAu 4NR, –9R,
ConLC 21[port], IntAu&W 76, –77, –82,
SmATA 8, ThrBJA

Forrest, David ConAu X, IntAu&W 77X,
–82X, ScF&FL 1, WrDr 82, –84

Forrest, Richard S 1932- ConAu 9NR, –57

Forrester, Helen ConAu X, IntAu&W 76X,
–77X, WrDr 76, –80, –82, –84

Forrester, Helen see also Bhatia, June

Forsee, Aylesa AuBYP SUP, ConAu 1R,
–1NR, InWom, IntAu&W 76, –77, –82,
SmATA 1, WhoAm 74, –76, –78, –80, –82,
WhoAmW 74, –70A, –72, –75, WrDr 76,
–80, –82, –84

Forster, E M 1879-1970 AtlBL, BrWr 6,
CasWL, Chambr 3, ChhPo S2, –S3,
CnMWL, ConAu 25R, ConAu P-1,
ConLC 1, –2, –3, –4, –9, –10, –13, –15,
–22[port], ConLCrt, –82, CyWA, DcLEL,
EncSF, EncWL, –2[port], EvLB,
LinLib L, –S, LongCEL, LongCTC,
ModBrL, ModBrL SUP, NewC,
Novels[port], ObitOF 79, ObitT 1961,
OxEng, PenC ENG, RAdv 1, RComWL,
REn, ScF&FL 1, TwCA, TwCA SUP,
TwCWr, WebE&AL, WhAm 5,
WhoTwCL, WorAl

Forsyth, Frederick 1938- BioIn 9, –11, –12,
ConAu 85, ConLC 2, –5, ConNov 82,
IntAu&W 76, –77, NewYTBS 80[port],
Novels[port], TwCCr&M 80, WhoAm 74,
–76, –78, –80, WhoSpyF, WorAl,
WrDr 76, –80, –82, –84

Forsythe, George Elmer 1917-1972
AmM&WS 73P, –76P, BioIn 9,
NewYTBE 72, WhAm 5

Forte, David F 1941- ConAu 53

Forten, Charlotte L 1837-1914 InB&W 80,
NegAl 76

Forward, Robert L 1932- AmM&WS 73P,
–76P, –79P, –82P, ConAu 103,
WhoTech 82, WhoWest 84

Fosdick, Harry Emerson 1878-1969 AmAu&B,
ApCAB X, AuBYP, BiDAmM, BioIn 1,
–2, –3, –4, –6, –7, –8, –9, –10, –11,
ConAu 25R, CurBio 40, –69, DcAmReB,
LinLib L, –S, LuthC 75, McGEWB,
NatCAB 55, ObitOF 79, OxAmH,
REnAL, TwCA SUP, WebAB, –79,
WhLit, WhNAA, WorAl

Foss, William O 1918- AuBYP, BioIn 8,
ConAu 17R

Foster, Alan Dean 1946- ConAu 5NR, –53,
EncSF, IntAu&W 77, –82, ScF&FL 1, –2,
WrDr 84

Foster, F Blanche 1919- BiDrLUS 70,
BioIn 11, ConAu 61, SmATA 11,
WhoAmW 83, WhoMW 78, –80, –82

Foster, G Allen 1907-1969 BioIn 8, ConAu 9R,
SmATA 26

Foster, Genevieve 1893-1979 AmAu&B, AnCL,
Au&ICB, AuBYP, BioIn 2, –5, –8, –9, –10,
–12, ConAu 4NR, –5R, –89, IlsCB 1946,
–1957, –1967, JBA 51, MorBMP,
NewYTBS 79, SmATA 2, –23N,
WhoAmA 80N, –82N, WrDr 76, –80

Foster, John T 1925- AuBYP SUP, BioIn 11,
ConAu 33R, SmATA 8

Foster, M A 1939- ConAu 9NR, –57, EncSF

Foster, Robert 1949- ConAu 81, ScF&FL 1

Foulds, Elfrida Vipont 1902- BioIn 2, –8,
ConAu 4NR, –53, IntAu&W 76, –77, –82,
WrDr 76, –80, –82, –84

Foulds, Elfrida Vipont see also Vipont, Charles

Foulds, Elfrida Vipont see also Vipont, Elfrida

Fountaine, Margaret 1862-1940 BioIn 12

Fowke, Edith Margaret 1913- BioIn 10, –12,
CaW, CanWW 70, –79, –80, –81, –83,
ChhPo S1, –S2, –S3, ConAu 37R, –37R,
DrAS 74E, –78E, –82E, IntAu&W 76, –77,
–82, OxCan, OxCan SUP, Profile,
SmATA 14, WhoAm 80, –82,
WhoAmW 75, –77, –79, –81, –83, WrDr 76,
–80, –82, –84

Fowler, Francis George 1870-1918 DcLEL,
LongCTC, TwCA, TwCA SUP

Fowler, H W 1858-1933 LinLib L, LongCTC,
PenC ENG

Fowler, Henry Watson 1858-1933 BioIn 2, –3,
–4, –7, DcLEL, EvLB, NewC, REn,
TwCA, TwCA SUP

Fowler, Raymond E 1933- ConAu 85,
UFOEn[port]

Fowler, Robert Howard 1926- CanWW 79,
ConAu 73, WhoAm 74, –76, –78, –80, –82,
WhoE 74, WhoF&I 74, WhoWor 74

Fowler, Virginie BioIn 3, ConAu X

Fowler, Virginie see also Elbert, Virginie Fowler

Fowles, John 1926- *ASpks, Au&Wr 6,*
AuBYP SUP, BioIn 7, –8, –10, –11, –12,
CelR 73, ConAu 5R, ConLC 1, –2, –3, –4,
–6, –9, –10, –15, ConNov 72, –76, –82,
CurBio 77, DcLB 14[port], DcLEL 1940,
EncWL, –2, IntAu&W 76, –77,
IntWW 74, –75, –76, –77, –78, –79, –80, –81,
–82, –83, IntWWP 77, LinLib L,
ModBrL SUP, NewC, NewYTBS 74, –77,
Novels[port], RAdv 1, SmATA 22[port],
TwCWr, WebE&AL, Who 82, –83,
WhoAm 80, –82, WhoWor 74, –76, –78,
–80, –82, WorAl, WorAu, WrDr 76, –80,
–82, –84

Fox, Aileen 1907- *Au&Wr 6, ConAu 5R,*
–5NR, WrDr 76, –80, –82, –84

Fox, Anthony 1934- *ConAu X, WhoLib 72,*
WrDr 82, –84

Fox, Larry 1942- *AuBYP SUP, ConAu 106,*
SmATA 30, WhoMW 74, –76, –78

Fox, Mary Virginia 1919- *AuBYP, BioIn 7,*
ConAu 29R

Fox, Michael Wilson 1937- *AmM&WS 73S,*
–76P, –78S, –79P, –82P, AuBYP SUP,
BioIn 12, ConAu 73, CurBio 77,
SmATA 15, WhoAm 78, –80, –82,
WhoWor 82, WrDr 76, –80

Fox, Paula 1923- *AmWomWr, AuBYP SUP,*
BioIn 10, –11, –12, ChlLR 1, ConAu 73,
ConLC 2, –8, DrAF 76, DrAP&F 83,
FourBJA, IntAu&W 76,
NewYTBS 81[port], SenS, NewbC 1966,
SmATA 17, TwCCW 78, –83,
WhoAm 74, –76, –78, –80, –82, WhoE 75,
–77, WrDr 76, –80, –82, –84

Fox, Ray Errol 1941- *ConAu 85,*
IntAu&W 82, NatPD, –81[port]

Fox, Robert J 1927- *AmCath 80,*
ConAu 1NR, –45, SmATA 33[port]

Fox, William Price 1926- *BioIn 11,*
ConAu 11NR, –17R, ConLC 22[port],
Conv 1, DcLB Y81A[port], –2

Foyt, Anthony Joseph 1935- *BioIn 6, –7, –8, –9,*
–10, –11, BusPN, WebAB, –79

Frame, Donald Murdoch 1911- *ConAu 17R,*
DrAS 74F, –78F, –82F, IntAu&W 76, –77,
–82, WhoAm 74, –76, –78, –80, WhoE 74,
WhoWor 78, WrDr 76, –80, –82, –84

Frame, Paul 1913- *BioIn 8, IlsBYP,*
IlsCB 1957, –1967, SmATA 33

Frampton, Peter 1950- *BioIn 10, –11, –12,*
CurBio 78, EncPR&S, –77S, IlEncRk,
NewYTBS 76, RkOn 78, –84,
RolSEnR 83, WhoAm 78, –80, –82,
WhoRocM 82, WorAl

France, Anatole 1844-1924 *AtlBL, BbD,*
BiD&SB, BioIn 1, –2, –3, –4, –5, –6, –8, –9,
–10, CasWL, CIDMEL, ConAu X,
CyWA, DcBiA, DcEuL, Dis&D, EncSF,
EncWL, –2[port], EvEuW, InWom,
LinLib L, –LP, –S, LongCTC, McGEWB,
ModFrL, ModRL, NewC, NewEOp 71,

Novels, OxEng, OxFr, PenC EUR,
PIP&P, RComWL, REn, ScF&FL 1,
TwCA, TwCA SUP, TwCLC 9[port],
TwCWr, WhDW, WhThe, WhoTwCL,
WorAl

Franchere, Ruth 1906- *BioIn 12, ConAu 73,*
FourBJA, SmATA 18, WhoPNW

Francis, Clare 1946- *ConAu 77, IntDcWB,*
Who 82, –83, WhoWor 80, WrDr 84

Francis, Dick 1920- *ASpks, Au&Wr 6,*
BioIn 8, –9, –10, –11, –12, ConAu 5R,
–9NR, ConLC 2, –22[port], ConNov 76,
–82, CorpD, CurBio 81[port], EncMys,
IntAu&W 76X, –77, NewYTBS 80[port],
–82[port], Novels[port], TwCCr&M 80,
Who 74, –82, –83, WhoAm 82, WorAl,
WorAu 1970, WrDr 76, –80, –82, –84

Francis, Dorothy Brenner 1926- *BioIn 11,*
ConAu 9NR, –21R, SmATA 10,
WhoAmW 74, –75, WomPO 76, –78,
WrDr 76, –80, –82, –84

Francis, H E 1924- *ConAu 10NR, WrDr 84*

Francis, Philip Sheridan 1918- *ConAu 17R*

Francke, Linda Bird 1939- *ConAu 85,*
WhoAm 78, –80, –82, WhoAmW 77

Franco, Jean 1924- *ConAu 9NR, –21R,*
DrAS 74F, –78F, –82F

Franco, Johan 1908- *Baker 78, BioIn 1,*
CpmDNM 82, ConAmC, ConAu 97,
DcCM, IntWWM 77, WhoAm 74, –76,
–78, –80, –82, WhoAmM 83, WhoMus 72,
WhoS&SW 73, –75, –76

Frank, Anne 1929-1945 *BioIn 2, –3, –4, –5, –7,*
–8, –10, –11, –12, DcAmSR, EncTR,
GoodHs, HerW, HisEWW, InWom,
IntDcWB, LinLib L, REn, TwCWr,
WhWW-II, WorAl

Frank, Gerold 1907- *Au&Wr 6, BioIn 5, –7,*
–8, –9, ConAu 109, IntAu&W 76,
WhoAm 74, –76, –78, –80, –82,
WhoWor 80, –82, WorAl

Frank, Pat 1907-1964 *AmNov, BioIn 1, –2, –3,*
–5, –7, ConAu 5R, EncSF, ScF&FL 1, –2,
WhAm 4, WhoAmP 77, –79, WhoSciF

Franke, Herbert W 1927- *BioIn 11,*
ConAu 110, EncSF, ScF&FL 1,
WhoSciF, WhoWor 78

Frankel, Edward 1910- *AuBYP, BioIn 8,*
ConAu 85, LEduc 74

Frankel, Haskel 1926- *ConAu 89*

Frankel, Sandor 1943- *ConAu 33R,*
IntAu&W 82, WhoAm 74, –76, –78, –80,
–82, WhoAmJ 80, WhoAmL 83,
WhoE 83, WrDr 76, –80, –82, –84

Frankenberg, Lloyd d1975 *ObitOF 79*

Frankenberg, Lloyd 1907-1975 *AmAu&B,*
BioIn 4, –10, ChhPo S1, –S3, ConAu 1R,
–6NR, –57, NewYTBS 75, REnAL,
TwCA SUP, WhAm 6, WhoAm 74

Frankenberg, Robert Clinton 1911- *BioIn 5, –8,*
IlsBYP, IlsCB 1946, –1957, –1967,
SmATA 22[port], WhoAmA 78, –80, –82

Frankenstein, Alfred 1906-1981 *AmAu&B, AnObit 1981, Baker 78, BioIn 12, CmCal, ConAu 1R, -2NR, -104, DrAS 74H, -78H, NewYTBS 81[port], WhoAm 74, -76, -78, -80, WhoAmA 73, -76, -78, -80, -82N, WhoMus 72, WhoWest 74, WhoWor 74, WrDr 82*

Franklin, Benjamin 1706-1790 *Alli, AmAu, AmAu&B, AmBi, AmWr, ApCAB, AsBiEn, AtlBL, Baker 78, BbD, BiAUS, BiDAmEd, BiDAmS, BiD&SB, BiDrAC, BiESc, BioIn 1, -2, -3, -4, -5, -6, -7, -8, -9, -10, -11, -12, BnEnAmA, CasWL, Chambr 3, ChhPo, -S1, -S2, -S3, CnDAL, CrtT 3, -4, CyAG, CyAL 1, CyEd[port], CyWA, DcAmAu, DcAmB, DcAmDH, DcAmLiB, DcAmMeB, DcAmSR, DcBiPP, DcEnL, DcInv, DcLB 24[port], DcLEL, DcNAA, DcScB, Dis&D, Drake, EncAAH, EncAB-H, EncAR, EncO&P 78S1, EvLB, GolEC, HarEnUS[port], InSci, LinLib L, -S, McGEWB, MouLC 2, NamesHP[port], NatCAB 1, NewC, NewYHSD 57, OxAmH, OxAmL, OxEng, OxMus, PenC AM, RComWL, REn, REnAL, REnAW, TwCBDA, WebAB, -79, WebE&AL, WhDW, WhAm HS, WhAmP, WhoEc, WorAl*

Franklin, H Bruce 1934- *BioIn 9, -11, ConAu 5R, -9NR, ConSFA, DrAS 74E, -78E, -82E, EncSF, IntAu&W 77, -82, NewYTBE 72, ScF&FL 1, -2, WhE&EA, WhoE 77, WhoSciF*

Franklin, Harold 1920- *ConAu 29R, SmATA 13, WhoBlA 75, -77, -80*

Franklin, John Hope 1915- *AmAu&B, BioIn 5, -6, -8, -9, -11, -12, BlueB 76, ConAu 1R, -1NR, -3NR, -5R, CurBio 63, DcLEL 1940, DrAS 74H, -78H, -82H, Ebony 1, EncAAH, EncSoH, InB&W 80, IntAu&W 82, IntWW 83, LinLib L, -S, LivgBAA, NegAl 76[port], -83[port], SelBAA, WebAB, -79, Who 83, WhoAm 74, -76, -78, -80, -82, WhoBlA 75, -77, -80, WhoWor 74, -78, -80, -82, WrDr 76, -80, -82, -84*

Franklin, Jon Daniel 1942- *BioIn 10, ConAu 104, WhoAm 80, -82*

Franklin, Miles 1879-1954 *BioIn 1, -6, -8, -9, -12, CasWL, ConAu 104, IntDcWB, McGEWB, ModCmwL, TwCLC 7[port], TwCWr*

Franks, Arthur Henry 1907- *WhE&EA*

Franks, Lucinda Laura 1946- *ConAu 53, WhoAm 74, -76, -78, -80, -82, WhoAmW 74, -81*

Franz, Barbara E 1946- *ConAu 110*

Franz, William S 1945- *ConAu 110*

Franzen, Nils-Olof 1916- *BioIn 11, ConAu 29R, SmATA 10*

Fraser, Amy Stewart 1892- *ConAu 9NR, -49,*

IntAu&W 76, -77, WrDr 76, -80, -82, -84

Fraser, Lady Antonia 1932- *BioIn 8, -10, -11, -12, BlueB 76, ChhPo S3, ConAu 85, CurBio 74, DcLEL 1940, IntAu&W 76, IntWW 74, -75, -76, -77, -78, -79, -80, -81, -82, -83, NewYTBS 79, SmATA 32, TwCCr&M 80, Who 74, -82, -83, WhoAmW 74, WhoWor 74, -76, -78, WorAl, WorAu 1970, WrDr 76, -80, -82, -84*

Fraser, Conon 1930- *Au&Wr 6, ConAu P-1, IntAu&W 76, -77, WrDr 76, -80, -82, -84*

Fraser, G S 1915-1980 *AnObit 1980, BioIn 10, ConAu 105, -85, ConLCrt, -82, ConP 70, -75, -80, ModBrL, PenC ENG, REn, WorAu*

Frassanito, William A 1946- *ConAu 9NR, -57*

Frayn, Michael 1933- *Au&Wr 6, BioIn 10, ConAu 5R, ConDr 73, -77, -82, ConLC 7, ConNov 72, -76, -82, ConSFA, DcLB 13[port], -14[port], DcLEL 1940, EncSF, IntAu&W 76, -77, -82, ModBrL SUP, NewC, Novels, ScF&FL 1, -2, Who 74, -82, -83, WhoThe 16, -81, WhoWor 76, WorAu, WrDr 76, -80, -82, -84*

Frazer, Sir James George 1854-1941 *Alli, Alli SUP, AtlBL, BioIn 1, -2, -3, -5, -6, -9, -10, -11, CasWL, Chambr 3, CurBio 41, DcEnA AP, DcLEL, DcScB, DcSoc, EvLB, InSci, LinLib L, -S, LongCEL, LongCTC, LuthC 75, McGEWB, NewC, ObitOF 79, OxEng, PenC ENG, REn, TwCA, TwCA SUP, WebE&AL, WhDW, WhE&EA, WhLit, WorAl*

Frazier, Kendrick Crosby 1942- *ConAu 101, WhoAm 78, -80, -82, WhoWest 82*

Frazier, Neta Lohnes 1890- *AuBYP, BioIn 7, -10, ConAu 1R, -1NR, ForWC 70, SmATA 7, WhoAmW 58, -61, -64, -66, -70, -72, WhoPNW, WrDr 76, -80, -82, -84*

Frazier, Walt 1945- *BioIn 8, -9, -10, -11, -12, CelR 73, ConAu 103, CurBio 73, NewYTBE 72, -73, NewYTBS 74, -75, -76, -77, -78, WhoAm 74, -76, -78, -80, -82, WhoBbl 73, WhoBlA 75, -77, -80, WorAl*

Freas, Frank Kelly 1922- *ConAu 102, EncSF, WhoAm 78, -80, -82, WhoSciF*

Fredericks, Fred 1929- *ArtCS*

Frederikson, Edna 1904- *ConAu 49*

Freed, Alvyn M 1913- *AmM&WS 73S, -78S, ConAu 8NR, -61, SmATA 22[port]*

Freedgood, Lillian 1911- *ConAu 13R*

Freedland, Michael 1934- *ConAu 11NR, -65, IntAu&W 77, -82, WhoWor 80, WrDr 76, -80, -82, -84*

Freedley, George 1904-1967 *AmAu&B, BiE&WWA, BioIn 1, -4, -8, ConAu 4NR, -5R, CurBio 47, -67, NotNAT B, OxThe,*

*WhAm 4, WhE&EA, WhThe,
WhoLibS 55*

Freedman, Benedict 1919- *AmAu&B, AmNov,
BioIn 1, –2, –3, ConAu 69, CurBio 47,
SmATA 27[port], WhoAm 74, –76*

Freedman, Nancy 1920- *AmAu&B, AmNov,
BioIn 1, –2, –3, ConAu 1NR, –45,
CurBio 47, EncSF, ForWC 70, InWom,
ScF&FL 1, –2, SmATA 27[port],
WhoAm 74, –76, –78, –80, WhoAmW 74,
–64, –66, –68, –70, –72, WrDr 80, –82, –84*

Freedman, Russell 1929- *AuBYP, BioIn 8, –12,
ConAu 7NR, –17R, ScF&FL 1, –2,
SmATA 16, WhoE 74*

Freehan, Bill 1941- *WhoAm 74, WhoProB 73*

Freehof, Solomon B 1892- *ConAu 93,
WhoWorJ 72*

Freeling, Nicolas 1927- *ASpks, BioIn 7, –10,
–11, ConAu 1NR, –49, ConNov 72, –76,
–82, EncMys, IntAu&W 76, –82, Novels,
TwCCr&M 80, TwCWr, Who 74, –82,
–83, WhoAm 74, WorAl, WorAu,
WrDr 76, –80, –82, –84*

Freeman, Barbara C 1906- *Au&Wr 6,
ConAu 73, IntAu&W 76, –77,
SmATA 28, TwCCW 78, –83, WrDr 76,
–80, –82, –84*

Freeman, Don 1908-1978 *AmPB, AuBYP,
BioIn 2, –3, –5, –6, –8, –11, –12, BkP,
ConAu 77, IlsCB 1946, –1957, –1967,
MorJA, NewYTBS 78, SmATA 17,
TwCCW 78, –83, WhoAmA 78N, –80N,
–82N*

Freeman, Douglas Southall 1886-1953
*AmAu&B, BioIn 1, –2, –3, –4, –5, –11, –12,
ConAu 109, CyWA, DcAmB S5,
DcLB 17[port], EncSoH, LinLib L,
McGEWB, NatCAB 58[port], ObitOF 79,
ObitT 1951, OxAmH, OxAmL, REn,
REnAL, TwCA, TwCA SUP,
TwCLC 11[port], WebAB, –79, WhAm 3,
WhJnl*

Freeman, Ira M 1905- *AmAu&B,
AmM&WS 73P, –76P, –79P, AuBYP,
BioIn 6, –7, –12, ConAu 73, MorJA,
SmATA 21[port]*

Freeman, James Montague 1936-
AmM&WS 73S, ConAu 102

Freeman, Leslie Jane 1944- *ConAu 106,
DrAS 78E, –82E*

Freeman, Lucy 1916- *AmAu&B, BioIn 2, –3,
–12, ConAu 3NR, –5R, CurBio 53,
ForWC 70, InWom, SmATA 24[port],
WhoAm 74, –76, –78, –80, –82,
WhoAmJ 80, WhoAmW 74, –58, –61, –64,
–66, –68, –70, –72, WhoWorJ 72, –78,
WrDr 76, –80, –82, –84*

Freeman, Mae 1907- *BioIn 6, –8, ConAu 73,
MorJA, SmATA 25[port], WhoAmW 58,
–61*

Freeman, Mary E Wilkins 1852-1930 *AmAu&B,
AmBi, AmLY, AmWomWr, BioIn 1, –4,*

*–8, –9, –11, –12, CarSB, CasWL, ChhPo,
–S1, –S2, CnDAL, ConAmL, ConAu 106,
DcAmAu, DcAmB, DcEnA AP,
DcLB 12[port], DcLEL, DcNAA,
HarEnUS, InWom, LibW, LinLib L, –S,
LongCTC, NotAW, Novels, OxAmL,
OxEng, PenC AM, REn, REnAL,
ScF&FL 1, TwCA, TwCLC 9[port],
WebAB, –79, WhAm 1, WhoHr&F,
WomWWA 14*

Freeman, Warren Samuel 1911- *ConAu 5R,
WhoAm 74, –76, –78, –80, –82*

Freemantle, Brian 1936- *TwCCr&M 80,
WrDr 82*

Freese, Arthur S 1917- *ConAu 77*

Fregosi, Claudia 1946- *AuBYP SUP,
ConAu 69, SmATA 24[port]*

Freidel, Frank Burt, Jr. 1916- *AmAu&B,
ConAu 1R, –5NR, DrAS 78H, –82H,
WhoAm 74, –76, –78, –80, –82*

Fremantle, Anne 1910- *AmAu&B,
AmWomWr, BioIn 3, –4, –9, –12, BkC 5,
CathA 1952, ConAu 13R, LongCTC,
REnAL, TwCA SUP, WhoAmW 58, –61,
–64, WrDr 80, –82, –84*

French, Allen 1870-1946 *AmAu&B, BioIn 1,
–2, –11, CarSB, ChhPo, DcAmAu,
JBA 34, –51, MnBBF, NatCAB 34,
REnAL, WhAm 2, YABC 1*

French, Bevan Meredith 1937- *AmM&WS 73P,
–76P, –79P, –82P, ConAu 97, WhoAm 78,
–80, –82, WhoTech 82*

French, Dorothy Kayser 1926- *AuBYP,
BioIn 8, –10, ConAu 3NR, –9R,
ForWC 70, IntAu&W 76, –77, –82,
SmATA 5, WhoAmW 75, –77, –79*

French, Michael Raymond 1944- *ConAu 89,
IntAu&W 82*

Frese, Dolores Warwick 1936- *ConAu 5R,
–9NR, DrAS 78E, –82E*

Frewer, Glyn 1931- *Au&Wr 6, AuBYP,
BioIn 8, –11, ConAu 10NR, –13R,
IntAu&W 76, –77, –82, ScF&FL 1, –2,
SmATA 11, WhoWor 76, WrDr 76, –80,
–82, –84*

Frey, Glenn 1948- *WhoAm 80, –82,
WhoRocM 82*

Frey, Glenn *see also* Eagles, The

Frey, Shaney *AuBYP, BioIn 8*

Fribourg, Marjorie G 1920- *AuBYP, BioIn 8,
ConAu 1R, –4NR*

Frick, C H *ConAu X, IntAu&W 77X, –82X,
SmATA 6, WrDr 76, –80, –82, –84*

Frick, C H *see also* Irwin, Constance Frick

Frick, Constance 1913- *BioIn 3, ConAu X,
SmATA 6, WhoLibS 55*

Frick, Constance *see also* Irwin, Constance Frick

Friday, Nancy 1937- *BioIn 12, ConAu 77,
WhoAm 80, –82, WrDr 82, –84*

Fried, John J 1940- *ConAu 33R*

Fried, Joseph P 1939- *ConAu 37R, WhoE 75,
WrDr 76, –80, –82, –84*

Fried, Martha Nemes 1923- *WhoAmW 61*
Friedan, Betty 1921- *AmAu&B, AmWomWr,*
BioIn 6, -9, -10, -11, -12, BlueB 76,
CelR 73, ConAu 65, ConIsC 2[port],
CurBio 70, EncAB-H, ForWC 70,
GoodHs, IntDcWB, IntWW 74, -75, -76,
-77, -78, -79, -80, -81, -82, -83, LibW,
LinLib L, MakMC, NewYTBE 70, -71,
PolProf J, PolProf NF, WebAB, -79,
WhoAm 74, -76, -78, -80, -82,
WhoAmJ 80, WhoAmW 74, -66, -68, -72,
-75, -77, -79, -81, -83, WhoWor 78, -80,
-82, WorAl, WrDr 76, -80, -82, -84
Friedberg, Maurice 1929- *ConAu 1R, -5NR,*
DrAS 74F, -78F, -82F, IntAu&W 76, -77,
WhoAm 74, -76, -78, -80, -82,
WhoAmJ 80, WhoMW 74, -76, -78,
WhoWor 78, WhoWorJ 72, -78, WrDr 76,
-80, -82, -84
Friedland, Ronald Lloyd 1937-1975 *BioIn 9,*
ConAu 57, ConAu P-2
Friedlander, Saul 1932- *BioIn 12,*
WhoWorJ 72
Friedman, Albert Barron 1920- *ConAu 1R,*
DrAS 74E, -78E, -82E, LElec,
WhoAm 74, -76, -78, -80, -82,
WhoWest 74, WhoWorJ 72, -78
Friedman, Bruce Jay 1930- *AmAu&B, BioIn 7,*
-8, -9, -10, -11, ConAu 9R, ConDr 73,
-77, -82, ConLC 3, -5, ConNov 72, -76,
-82, CurBio 72, DcLB 2, DcLEL 1940,
DrAF 76, DrAP&F 83, IntAu&W 76,
-77, LinLib L, McGEWD, -84, ModAL,
ModAL SUP, NatPD, -81[port], Novels,
PenC AM, RAdv 1, WhoAm 74, -76, -78,
-80, WhoThe 81, WorAl, WorAu,
WrDr 76, -80, -82, -84
Friedman, Estelle Ehrenwald 1920- *AuBYP,*
BioIn 8, -10, ConAu 5R, ForWC 70,
SmATA 7
Friedman, Ina R 1926- *AuBYP SUP,*
ConAu 53
Friedman, Judi 1935- *AuNews 2, BioIn 11,*
ConAu 65
Friedman, Leon 1933- *ConAu 81,*
WhoAmL 78, -79, WhoWorJ 72, -78
Friedman, Marcia 1925- *ConAu 57*
Friedman, Milton 1912-1983 *AmAu&B,*
AmEA 74, AmM&WS 73S, -78S,
Au&Wr 6, BioIn 6, -7, -8, -9, -10, -11,
-12, BlueB 76, CelR 73, ConAu 1R,
-1NR, ConIsC 1[port], EncAB-H,
IntAu&W 76, -77, -82, IntWW 74, -75,
-76, -77, -78, -79, -80, -81, -82, -83,
LinLib L, MakMC, NewYTBS 76,
-80[port], -83, PolProf J, PolProf NF,
WebAB, -79, Who 74, -82, -83,
WhoAm 74, -76, -78, -80, -82,
WhoAmJ 80, WhoEc, WhoF&I 79, -81,
-83, WhoWest 80, -82, -84, WhoWor 74,
-78, -80, -82, WhoWorJ 72, -78, WorAl,
WrDr 76, -80, -82, -84

Friedman, Myra *BioIn 10, BioNews 74*
Friedman, Paul 1899-1972 *BioIn 9,*
ConAu 37R, DrAF 76
Friedman, Philip 1944- *WhoE 83*
Friedman, Rose *BioIn 12, ConAu 101,*
NewYTBS 80[port]
Friedman, Sara Ann 1935- *ConAu 77*
Friedrich, Otto Alva 1929- *AmAu&B, AmPB,*
ConAu 3NR, -5R, SmATA 33[port],
WhoAm 74, -76, -78, -80, -82
Friel, Brian 1929- *Au&Wr 6, BioIn 10,*
CnThe, ConAu 21R, ConDr 73, -77, -82,
ConLC 5, CurBio 74, DcIrL, DcIrW 1,
DcLB 13[port], DcLEL 1940,
IntAu&W 76, -77, -82, McGEWD, -84,
ModBrL SUP, ModWD, NotNAT,
REnWD, Who 74, -82, -83, WhoAm 76,
-78, -80, -82, WhoThe 15, -16, -81,
WhoWor 74, -76, WorAu, WrDr 76, -80,
-82, -84
Friendlich, Dick 1909- *AuBYP, BioIn 8, -11,*
ConAu X, SmATA X
Friendlich, Richard J 1909- *ConAu P-1,*
SmATA 11
Friendly, Fred W 1915- *AmAu&B, BioIn 3,*
-4, -5, -6, -7, -10, BlueB 76, ConAu 21R,
CurBio 57, IntAu&W 77, IntMPA 75,
-76, IntWW 74, -75, -76, -77, -78, -79,
-80, -81, -82, -83, LesBEnT[port],
NewYTET, WhoAm 74, -76, -78, -80, -82,
WorAl
Friermood, Elisabeth Hamilton 1903- *AuBYP,*
BioIn 6, -8, -10, ConAu 1R, -1NR,
ForWC 70, IndAu 1917, MorJA,
SmATA 5, WhoAmW 58, -68, -70, -72,
WrDr 76, -80, -82, -84
Friis, Babbis *ConAu X, SmATA 7, ThrBJA*
Friis-Baastad, Babbis Ellinor 1921-1970
AuBYP SUP, BioIn 9, -10, ConAu 17R,
ConLC 12, SmATA 7, ThrBJA
Frimmer, Steven 1928- *AuBYP SUP,*
ConAu 33R, SmATA 31
Frisch, Otto Robert 1904-1979 *AsBiEn,*
AuBYP, BiESc, BioIn 1, -8, -12,
BlueB 76, ConAu 9R, InSci, IntWW 74,
-75, -76, -77, -78, -79, Who 74,
WhoWor 74, -76, WorAl, WrDr 76, -80
Friskey, Margaret 1901- *AuBYP, BioIn 2, -4,*
-8, -10, ConAu 2NR, -5R, ForWC 70,
SmATA 5
Fritz, Jean 1915- *AuBYP, BioIn 4, -7, -9, -10,*
-12, ChlLR 2, ChhPo S2, ConAu 1R,
-5NR, ForWC 70, MorBMP,
ScF&FL 1A, SmATA 1, -29[port],
ThrBJA, TwCCW 78, -83, WhoAmW 83,
WrDr 80, -82, -84
Fritz, Leah 1931- *ConAu 93*
Froehlich, Walter 1921- *AmEA 74,*
USBiR 74, WhoE 77, -79, -81
Frolov, Vadim 1913- *AuBYP SUP,*
TwCCW 78B, -83B
Froman, Robert 1917- *AuBYP, BioIn 8, -11,*

ConAu 1R, -1NR, FourBJA, SmATA 8

Frome, Michael 1920- *BioIn 10, ConAu 1R, -1NR, IntAu&W 82, WrDr 76, -80, -82, -84*

Fromm, Erich 1900-1980 *AmAu&B, AmM&WS 73S, -78S, AnObit 1980[port], Au&Wr 6, BioIn 4, -5, -7, -8, -9, -10, -11, -12, BlueB 76, ConAu 73, -97, CurBio 67, -80N, EncAB-H, EncTR, GuPsyc[port], InSci, IntAu&W 82, IntEnSS 79, IntWW 74, -75, -76, -77, -78, -79, LinLib L, MakMC, NewYTBS 80[port], PenC AM, REn, REnAL, TwCA SUP, WebAB, -79, WhDW, WhAm 7, WhoAm 74, -76, -78, -80, WhoE 74, WhoS&SW 73, WhoTwCL, WhoWor 74, -78, WorAl, WrDr 76, -80*

Frommer, Harvey 1937- *ConAu 103*

Frost, David 1939- *BioIn 12, IntWW 83, LesBEnT[port], Who 83, WhoWor 82, WrDr 84*

Frost, Kelman *ScF&FL 1*

Frost, Lawrence A 1907- *ConAu 11NR, -69*

Frost, Robert 1874?-1963 *AmAu&B, AmLY, AmWr, AnCL, ApCAB X, AtlBL, BioIn 1, -2, -3, -4, -5, -6, -7, -8, -9, -10, -11, -12, CasWL, Chambr 3, ChhPo, -S1, -S2, -S3, CnDAL, CnE&AP, CnMWL, ConAmA, ConAmL, ConAu 89, ConLC 1, -3, -4, -9, -10, -13, -15, -26[port], CurBio 42, -63, CyWA, DcAmB S7, DcLEL, EncAAH, EncAB-H, EncWL, -2[port], EvLB, FamPYP, LinLib L, -S, LongCTC, MakMC, McGEWB, ModAL, ModAL SUP, NatCAB 58, NewYTBE 72, NewYTBS 74, ObitOF 79, ObitT 1961, OxAmH, OxAmL, OxEng, PenC AM, RAdv 1, RComWL, REn, REnAL, SixAP, SmATA 14, Str&VC, TwCA, TwCA SUP, TwCWr, WebAB, -79, WebE&AL, WhDW, WhAm 4, WhLit, WhNAA, WhoTwCL, WorAl*

Froud, Brian *IlsCB 1967*

Fry, Christopher 1907- *Au&Wr 6, AuBYP, BiE&WWA, BioIn 2, -3, -4, -5, -6, -8, -9, -10, BlueB 76, CasWL, CnMD, CnMWL, CnThe, ConAu 9NR, -17R, ConDr 73, -77, -82, ConLC 2, -10, -14, ConP 70, -75, -80, CroCD, CurBio 51, CyWA, DcLB 13[port], DcLEL, EncWL, -2, EncWT, EvLB, IntAu&W 76, IntWW 74, -75, -76, -77, -78, -79, -80, -81, -82, -83, IntWWP 77, LinLib L, -S, LongCTC, McGEWD, -84[port], ModBrL, ModBrL SUP, ModWD, NewC, NotNAT, -A, OxEng, OxThe, PenC ENG, PIP&P, REn, TwCA SUP, TwCWr, WebE&AL, Who 74, -82, -83, WhoThe 15, -16, -81, WhoWor 74, -76, -78, WorAl, WorEFlm, WrDr 76, -80, -82, -84*

Fry, Edward Bernard 1925- *SmATA 35*

Fry, Ronald W 1949- *ConAu 57, WrDr 80, -82, -84*

Fryatt, Norma R *AuBYP, BioIn 8, ConAu 57*

Frye, John 1910- *ConAu 49*

Fuchs, Lawrence H 1927- *AmM&WS 73S, -78S, ConAu 1R, -5NR, DrAS 74H, -78H, -82H, IntAu&W 76, -77, WhoAm 74, -76, -78, -80, WhoAmJ 80, WhoWor 74, WhoWorJ 72, -78*

Fuentes, Carlos 1928?- *AuNews 2, BioIn 7, -8, -9, -10, -11, -12, CasWL, ConAu 10NR, -69, ConLC 3, -8, -10, -13, -22[port], CurBio 72, DcCLAA, EncLatA, EncWL, -2[port], IntAu&W 76, -77, -82, IntWW 74, -75, -76, -77, -78, -79, -80, -81, -82, -83, McGEWB, ModLAL, Novels[port], OxSpan, PenC AM, TwCWr, WhoAm 78, -80, -82, WhoS&SW 73, WhoTwCL, WhoWor 78, -80, -82, WorAl, WorAu*

Fugard, Athol 1932- *AfSS 78, -79, -80, -81, -82, BioIn 10, CasWL, CnThe, ConAu 85, ConDr 73, -77, -82, ConLC 5, -9, -14, -25[port], CurBio 75, DcLEL 1940, EncSoA, EncWL 2, EncWT, IntAu&W 76, -77, IntWW 74, -75, -76, -77, -78, -79, -80, -81, -82, -83, McGEWD 84, ModCmwL, NewYTBE 70, NotNAT, PIP&P A, TwCWr, Who 82, -83, WhoThe 15, -16, -81, WhoTwCL, WhoWor 78, -80, -82, WorAu 1970, WrDr 76, -80, -82, -84*

Fuja, Abayomi *AuBYP SUP*

Fukei, Arlene 1920- *BiDrLUS 70, WhoLibS 66*

Fukei, Arlene *see also* Fukei, Gladys Arlene Harper

Fukei, Gladys Arlene Harper 1920- *ConAu 13R*

Fukei, Gladys Arlene Harper *see also* Fukei, Arlene

Fulks, Bryan 1897- *AuBYP SUP, ConAu 97*

Fuller, Charles 1939- *BioIn 12, ConAu 108, ConLC 25[port], InB&W 80, McGEWD 84, NatPD 81[port], NegAl 83[port], NewYTBS 82[port], WhoAm 82, WhoBlA 80*

Fuller, Edmund 1914- *AmAu&B, AuBYP, BioIn 8, -10, -12, ChhPo S1, ConAu 77, ConNov 72, -76, DcLEL 1940, DrAS 74E, IntAu&W 76, -77, SmATA 21[port], WorAu, WrDr 76, -80, -82, -84*

Fuller, Iola 1906- *AmNov, BioIn 2, -7, -9, ConAu X, ForWC 70, InWom, MichAu 80, REnAL, SmATA 3, WhoAmW 58*

Fuller, Iola *see also* McCoy, Iola Fuller

Fuller, John Grant, Jr. 1913- *Alli, AmAu&B, BiDLA, BiE&WWA, ChhPo S3, ConAu 1R, -2NR, NotNAT, WhoAm 74, -76, -78, -80, -82, WhoAmP 81, -83,*

WhoWor 74

Fuller, R Buckminster 1895-1983 *BioNews 74,
BnEnAmA, CelR 73, ConAu 9R, -109,
CurBio 76, -83N, Future, LinLib S,
ModAL SUP, MugS, NewYTBS 78,
-83[port], PenC AM, WhoAmA 78, -80,
-82, WhoEng 80, WorAl, WorAu 1970*

Fuller, Roy Broadbent 1912- *Au&Wr 6,
BioIn 4, -8, -10, -12, BlueB 76, CasWL,
ChhPo S1, -S2, -S3, CnE&AP,
ConAu 5R, ConLC 4, ConNov 72, -76,
-82, ConP 70, -75, -80, DcLB 15[port],
-20[port], EncWL 2, IntAu&W 76,
IntWW 74, -75, -76, -77, -78, -79, -80, -81,
-82, -83, IntWWP 77, LinLib L,
LongCTC, MakMC, ModBrL,
ModBrL SUP, NewC, Novels,
PenC ENG, RAdv 1, REn, TwCA SUP,
TwCCW 78, -83, TwCCr&M 80, TwCWr,
WebE&AL, WhE&EA, Who 74, -82, -83,
WhoChL, WhoTwCL, WhoWor 74, -76,
-78, WrDr 76, -80, -82, -84*

Funk, Charles Earle 1881-1957 *AmAu&B,
BioIn 1, -4, -6, CurBio 47, -57,
NatCAB 45, OhA&B, WhAm 3*

Funk, Peter V K 1921- *ConAu 21R,
St&PR 75, WhoE 74*

Furer, Howard B 1934- *ConAu 33R,
DrAS 74H, -78H, -82H*

Furlong, William Rea 1881-1976 *WhAm 6, -7,
WhoAm 74*

Furneaux, Rupert 1908- *ConAu 1R, -1NR*

Furness, Edna L 1906- *ConAu 37R,
DrAS 74E, -78E, -82E, ForWC 70,
IntAu&W 77, -82, WhoAmW 58,
WrDr 76, -80, -82*

Furnier, Vincent 1948- *BioIn 9, -10, -11, -12*

Furnier, Vincent *see also* Cooper, Alice

Furniss, Tim 1948- *ConAu 109*

Fussell, Paul 1924- *BioIn 12, ChhPo S1,
ConAu 8NR, -17R, DrAS 74E, -78E, -82E,
IntWW 83, WhoAm 78, -80, -82*

Fyodorova, Victoria 1946- *GoodHs,
NewYTBS 77*

G

Gaan, Margaret 1914- *ConAu 81*

Gabriel, Roman 1940- *BioIn 8, –9, –10, ConAu 107, CurBio 75, NewYTBS 83[port], WhoAm 74, –76, –78, WhoFtbl 74*

Gaddis, Vincent Hayes 1913- *ConAu 13R, IntAu&W 77, SmATA 35, WrDr 76, –80, –82, –84*

Gaddis, William 1922- *AmAu&B, BioIn 3, –8, –10, –12, ConAu 17R, ConLC 1, –3, –6, –8, –10, –19, ConNov 72, –76, –82, DcLB 2, DcLEL 1940, DrAF 76, DrAP&F 83, EncWL 2, IntAu&W 76, –77, ModAL SUP, Novels, PenC AM, RAdv 1, WhoAm 74, –76, –78, –80, –82, WorAu, WrDr 76, –80, –82, –84*

Gaeddert, Lou Ann 1931- *BioIn 12, BkP, ConAu 73, SmATA 20*

Gaer, Joseph 1897-1969 *AmAu&B, AuBYP, BioIn 2, –6, –8, –10, ConAu 9R, CurBio 51, MorJA, NatCAB 55, WhoAm 74, –76, WhoWorJ 72, –78*

Gage, Edwin 1943- *ConAu 85*

Gage, Wilson 1922- *AuBYP, BioIn 8, –9, –11, ConAu X, SmATA 3, ThrBJA, WrDr 76, –80, –82, –84*

Gage, Wilson *see also* Steele, Mary Quintard

Gaines, Charles Ellis 1924- *WhoAmP 81*

Gaines, Charles F 1944- *WhoBlA 80*

Gaines, Ernest J 1933- *AuBYP SUP, AuNews 1, BioIn 10, –11, –12, BlkAWP, CivR 74, CmCal, ConAu 6NR, –9R, ConLC 3, –11, –18, ConNov 72, –76, –82, DcLB Y80A[port], –2, DrAF 76, DrAP&F 83, InB&W 80, IntAu&W 76, –77, –82, LivgBAA, ModBlW, NegAl 76[port], –83[port], SelBAA, WhoAm 74, –76, –78, –80, –82, WhoBlA 75, –77, –80, WorAu 1970, WrDr 76, –80, –82, –84*

Gaines, William Maxwell 1922- *ConAu 108, WhoAm 76, –78, –80, –82, WhoWor 78, WorECom*

Gainham, Sarah 1922- *AmAu&B, ConAu X, DcLEL 1940, IntAu&W 76, –77, TwCCr&M 80, Who 74, –82, –83, WhoSpyF, WrDr 76, –80, –82, –84*

Galanoy, Terry 1927- *ConAu 4NR, –45*

Galarza, Ernesto 1905- *BiDAmLL, ChiSch*

Galbraith, John Kenneth 1908- *AmAu&B, AmEA 74, AmM&WS 73S, BioIn 5, –6, –7, –8, –9, –10, –11, –12, CanWW 70, –79, –80, –81, –83, CelR 73, ConAu 21R, ConIsC 1[port], CurBio 59, –75, DcAmDH, EncAB-H, IntEnSS 79, LongCTC, MakMC, NewYTBE 73, NewYTBS 79, OxAmH, PolProf E, PolProf J, PolProf K, PolProf NF, PolProf T, REnAL, ScF&FL 1, –2, WebAB, –79, Who 74, –82, –83, WhoAm 78, –80, –82, WhoAmP 81, –83, WhoEc, WhoF&I 83, WorAl, WorAu, WrDr 76, –84*

Gale, Elizabeth *WhNAA*

Gallagher, Mary 1947- *ConAu 97, NatPD 81*

Gallagher, Thomas *ConAu 1R, –5NR, IntAu&W 76*

Gallant, Roy A 1924- *AuBYP, BioIn 8, –9, ConAu 4NR, –5R, ConLC 17, SmATA 4, WrDr 76, –80, –82, –84*

Gallico, Paul 1897-1976 *AmAu&B, AmNov, ASpks, Au&Wr 6, AuBYP SUP, AuNews 1, BioIn 1, –2, –4, –6, –9, –10, –11, –12, BlueB 76, ConAu 5R, –65, –69, ConLC 2, ConNov 72, –76, CurBio 46, –76, –76N, DcLB 9[port], DcLEL, EncSF, EvLB, FilmgC, IntAu&W 76, –77, IntWW 74, –75, –76, –77N, NatCAB 59[port], NewYTBS 76, Novels, ObitOF 79, REnAL, ScF&FL 1, –1A, –2, SmATA 13, TwCA SUP, TwCWr, WhAm 7, Who 74, WhoAm 74, –76, WhoThe 81N, WhoWor 74, –76, WorAl, WrDr 76*

Galston, Arthur William 1920- *AmM&WS 73P, –76P, –79P, –82P, ConAu 102, McGMS 80[port], WhoAm 74, –76, –78, –80, –82, WhoAmJ 80, WhoE 74, WhoWor 74, WhoWorJ 72, –78*

Galsworthy, John 1867-1933 *AtlBL, BioIn 1, –2, –3, –4, –5, –6, –8, –9, –10, –11, –12, BrWr 6, CasWL, Chambr 3, ChhPo, –S1, –S2, –S3, CnMD, CnMWL, CnThe, ConAu 104, CyWA, DcAmSR, DcBiA, DcLB 10[port], DcLEL, EncSoA, EncWL,*

−2, EncWT, EvLB, FilmgC, LinLib L,
−S, LongCEL, LongCTC, MakMC,
McGEWB, McGEWD, −84[port], ModBrL,
ModBrL SUP, ModWD, NewC,
NotNAT A, −B, Novels[port], OxEng,
OxThe, PenC ENG, PlP&P, RAdv 1,
RComWL, REn, REnWD, TwCA,
TwCA SUP, TwCLC 1, TwCWr,
WebE&AL, WhDW, WhE&EA, WhThe,
WhoLA, WhoTwCL, WorAl

Galvin, Brendan 1938- *BioIn 12, ConAu 1NR,*
−45, DcLB 5[port], DrAP 75,
DrAP&F 83, DrAS 74E, −78E, −82E,
IntWWP 77

Gambaccini, Peter 1950- *ConAu 105*

Gammage, Allen Z 1917- *AmM&WS 73S,*
−78S, ConAu 5R, −11NR, IntAu&W 76,
WhoWest 76, −78

Gammage, William Leonard 1942-
ConAu 10NR, −57

Gammond, Peter 1925- *ConAu 81,*
IntAu&W 77, WhoMus 72

Gamoran, Mamie G 1900- *ConAu 3NR, −5R,*
ForWC 70, IntAu&W 76, −77, −82,
WhoAmW 74, −68, −70, −72

Gamow, George 1904-1968 *AmAu&B, AsBiEn,*
BiESc, BioIn 1, −2, −4, −8, ConAu 102,
−93, CurBio 51, −68, DcScB, EncSF,
InSci, McGMS 80[port], ObitOF 79,
REnAL, ScF&FL 1, TwCA SUP,
WebAB, −79, WhAm 5, WhE&EA,
WorAl

Gann, Ernest Kellogg 1910- *AmAu&B,*
AmNov, AuNews 1, BioIn 2, −3, −4, −7, −8,
−9, −10, −11, −12, BlueB 76, ConAu 1R,
−1NR, ConLC 23[port], DcLEL 1940,
LinLib L, NewYTBS 81[port], Novels,
TwCWr, WhoAm 74, −76, −78, −80, −82,
WhoPNW, WhoWest 74, WorAl, WorAu,
WrDr 76, −80, −82, −84

Gannett, Lewis Stiles 1891-1966 *AmAu&B,*
BioIn 1, −4, −7, ChhPo, ConAu 89,
CurBio 41, −66, REnAL, TwCA,
TwCA SUP, WhAm 4, −4A

Gannon, Robert Haines 1931- *BioIn 11,*
ConAu 4NR, −9R, SmATA 8

Ganz, David 1951?- *ConAu 105, DrAS 82F*

Garagiola, Joe 1926- *BioNews 74, CelR 73,*
CurBio 76, LesBEnT, NewYTET,
WhoAm 74, −76, −78, −80, −82, WhoE 74

Garbedian, H Gordon 1905- *WhE&EA*

Garbo, Norman 1919- *ConAu 9NR, −17R,*
EncSF, ScF&FL 1, −2, WhoAm 74, −76,
−78, −80, −82, WhoE 74, −75

Garcia, Ann O'Neal 1939- *ConAu 108*

Gard, Wayne 1899- *AmAu&B, AnMV 1926,*
BioIn 9, ConAu 1R, REnAW, TexWr,
WhJnl, WhNAA

Gardam, Jane 1928- *AuBYP SUP,*
ConAu 2NR, −49, DcLB 14[port],
SmATA 28, TwCCW 78, −83, Who 82,
−83, WrDr 80, −82, −84

Garden, Nancy 1938- *AuBYP SUP, BioIn 11,*
ConAu 33R, DrAP&F 83, SmATA 12,
WrDr 76, −80, −82, −84

Garden, Robert Hal 1937- *ConAu 69*

Gardner, Brian 1931- *Au&Wr 6, ChhPo S2,*
ConAu 13R, IntAu&W 82, WrDr 76, −80,
−82, −84

Gardner, Erle Stanley 1889-1970 *AmAu&B,*
BioIn 1, −2, −4, −5, −6, −7, −8, −9, −10, −11,
−12, CmCal, ConAu 5R, −25R, CorpD,
CurBio 44, −70, EncMys, EvLB, FilmgC,
LinLib L, −S, LongCTC, MnBBF,
NewYTBE 70, Novels, ObitOF 79,
ObitT 1961, OxAmL, PenC AM, REn,
REnAL, TwCA, TwCA SUP,
TwCCr&M 80, TwCWr, WebAB, −79,
WhAm 6, WhE&EA, WhNAA, WorAl

Gardner, Gerald 1929- *ConAu 1R, −5NR*

Gardner, Herb 1934- *BiE&WWA, BioIn 6,*
NatPD 81[port], NotNAT

Gardner, John 1933-1982 *AnObit 1982[port],*
AuBYP SUP, AuNews 1, BioIn 7, −10,
−11, −12, ConAu 107, −65, ConLC 2, −3,
−5, −7, −8, −10, −18, ConNov 76, −82,
CurBio 78, −82N, DcLB Y82A[port], −2,
DcLEL 1940, DrAF 76, EncSF,
ModAL SUP, NewYTBS 82[port], Novels,
RAdv 1, ScF&FL 1, SmATA 31N,
WhoAm 74, −76, −78, −80, −82,
WorAu 1970, WrDr 76, −80, −82

Gardner, Joseph Lawrence 1933- *ConAu 29R,*
WhoAm 76, −78, −80, −82, WhoE 75

Gardner, Leonard 1934?- *BioIn 8, DrAF 76*

Gardner, Martin 1914- *AmAu&B,*
AuBYP SUP, BioIn 6, −10, −12, ChhPo,
−S1, −S2, −S3, ConAu 73, EncSF,
SmATA 16, WhoE 74

Gardner, Richard A 1931- *AuBYP SUP,*
BiDrAPA 77, ConAu 33R, SmATA 13,
WhoAm 74, −76, −78, −80, −82, WhoE 77,
WhoWor 78, WrDr 76, −80, −82, −84

Gardner, Richard M 1931- *AmAu&B, BioIn 8,*
ConAu 10NR, −21R, DrAP&F 83,
SmATA 24[port], WrDr 76, −80, −82

Gardner, Richard M *see also* Cummings, Richard

Gardner, Robert 1911- *AmBench 79,*
ConAu 61, WhoAmL 78, WhoGov 75

Gardner, Robert 1929- *AuBYP SUP*

Gardner, Sheldon 1934- *ConAu 104,*
SmATA 33[port]

Gardner, William Earl 1928- *ConAu 3NR, −5R,*
LEduc 74, WhoAm 78, −80, −82,
WhoMW 76, −78, −80, −82

Gardonyi, Geza 1863-1922 *BioIn 1, CasWL,*
ClDMEL, PenC EUR

Garfield, Brian 1939- *BioIn 10, ConAu 1R,*
−6NR, IntAu&W 76, −77, −82, Novels,
TwCCr&M 80, WhoAm 74, −76, −78, −80,
−82, WhoSpyF, WrDr 76, −80, −82, −84

Garfield, Leon 1921- *Au&Wr 6, AuBYP SUP,*
BioIn 8, −9, −10, ConAu 17R, ConLC 12,
FourBJA, PiP, ScF&FL 1, −2, SenS,

SmATA 1, –32[port], TwCCW 78, –83,
Who 82, –83, WhoChL, WrDr 76, –80,
–82, –84

Garfunkel, Art 1941?- BiDAmM, BioIn 7, –8,
–10, –11, –12, CelR 73, CurBio 74,
EncPR&S, –77, IntMPA 82, –84,
NewYTBS 82[port], RkOn 78, –84,
RolSEnR 83, WhoAm 74, –76, –78, –80,
–82, WhoRocM 82, WorAl

Garlan, Patricia Wallace 1926- WhoAm 74,
WhoAmW 74

Garland, Hamlin 1860-1940 AmAu&B, AmBi,
AmLY, ApCAB SUP, ApCAB X, AtlBL,
BbD, BiD&SB, BiDPara, BioIn 1, –2, –3,
–4, –5, –6, –8, –9, –10, –11, –12, CasWL,
Chambr 3, ChhPo, CnDAL, ConAmA,
ConAmL, ConAu 104, CurBio 40,
CyWA, DcAmAu, DcAmB S2, DcAmSR,
DcBiA, DcLB 12[port], DcLEL, DcNAA,
EncAAH, EncO&P 78, EvLB, LinLib L,
–S, LongCTC, ModAL, NatCAB 8,
NotNAT B, Novels, OxAmL, OxCan,
OxEng, PenC AM, RAdv 1, REn,
REnAL, REnAW, ScF&FL 1, Str&VC,
TwCA, TwCA SUP, TwCBDA,
TwCLC 3, WebAB, –79, WebE&AL,
WhAm 1, WhLit, WhNAA, WisWr,
WorAl

Garner, Alan 1934- Au&Wr 6, BioIn 8, –9,
–10, –11, –12, BrCA, CasWL, ChhPo S1,
–S3, ConAu 73, ConLC 17, ConSFA,
EncSF, IntAu&W 76, –77, –82, Novels,
PiP, ScF&FL 1, SenS, SmATA 18,
TelT, ThrBJA, TwCCW 78, –83, Who 82,
–83, WhoChL, WrDr 76, –80, –82, –84

Garner, Claud Wilton 1891- ConAu 9R

Garnett, Emmeline AuBYP SUP

Garnett, Henry 1905- Au&Wr 6

Garraty, John Arthur 1920- BioIn 10,
ConAu 1R, –2NR, DcLB 17[port],
DrAS 74H, –78H, –82H, SmATA 23,
WhoAm 74, –76, –78, –80, WhoWor 74

Garreau, Joel 1948- ConAu 101

Garrett, Charles 1925?-1977 BioIn 11,
ConAu 73, DrAS 74H, NewYTBS 77

Garrett, Randall 1927- ConSFA, EncSF,
ScF&FL 1, ThrBJA, WhoSciF, WrDr 84

Garrigue, Sheila 1931- AuBYP SUP,
BioIn 12, ConAu 69, SmATA 21[port]

Garrison, Webb B 1919- ConAu 1R, –2NR,
SmATA 25[port]

Garrow, David J 1953- ConAu 93

Garry, Charles R 1909- BioIn 8, –10, –11,
CivR 74, ConAu 73, MugS, WhoAm 74,
–76, –78

Garson, Barbara 1941- AmAu&B, BioIn 7,
ConAu 33R, NatPD, –81[port],
WhoAm 74, –76, WhoAmW 74, –68, –70,
–72

Garst, Doris 1894?- BioIn 1, –2, –7, –9,
ConAu 1R, ForWC 70, SmATA 1

Garst, Doris see also Garst, Shannon

Garst, Shannon 1894?- AuBYP, BioIn 2, –7,
–9, ConAu X, CurBio 47, InWom,
JBA 51, SmATA 1

Garst, Shannon see also Garst, Doris

Garstang, James Gordon 1927- ConAu 13R

Garve, Andrew 1908- BioIn 10, ConAu X,
EncMys, Novels, TwCCr&M 80, WorAu,
WrDr 80, –82, –84

Garve, Andrew see also Winterton, Paul

Garvin, Charles David 1929- ConAu 6NR, –57,
WhoAm 80, WhoMW 78

Garvin, Philip 1947- ConAu 73

Gascoigne, Bamber 1935- ConAu 10NR, –25R,
IntAu&W 76, –77, –82, Who 82, –83,
WhoThe 15, –16, –81, WrDr 76, –80, –82,
–84

Gaskell, Elizabeth Cleghorn 1810-1865 Alli,
Alli SUP, AtlBL, BbD, BiD&SB,
BioIn 1, –2, –3, –4, –5, –7, –8, –9, –10, –11,
–12, BrAu 19, BrWr 5, CasWL, CelCen,
ChhPo S3, CrtT 3, CyWA, DcBiA,
DcBiPP, DcEnA, DcEuL, DcLB 21[port],
DcLEL, EvLB, HsB&A, InWom,
IntDcWB, LinLib L, –S, LongCEL,
McGEWB, MouLC 3, NewC, OxEng,
PenC ENG, RAdv 1, REn, WebE&AL,
WhDW, WhoHr&F, WorAl

Gaskell, Thomas F 1916- ConAu 17R,
IntAu&W 76

Gaskin, Catherine 1929- AmAu&B,
Au&Wr 6, BioIn 4, ConAu 10NR, –65,
DcLEL 1940, IntAu&W 76, –77, –82,
Novels, TwCCr&M 80, TwCWr, Who 74,
–82, –83, WhoAmW 61, WhoWor 78,
WrDr 76, –80, –82, –84

Gass, William H 1924- AmAu&B, Au&Wr 6,
BioIn 7, –8, –10, –11, –12, ConAu 17R,
ConLC 1, –2, –8, –11, –15, ConNov 72, –76,
–82, DcLB 2, DcLEL 1940, DrAF 76,
DrAP&F 83, DrAS 74P, –78P, –82P,
EncWL, –2, IntAu&W 76, –77, –82,
ModAL SUP, Novels, PenC AM,
RAdv 1, WhoAm 74, –76, –78, –80, –82,
WorAu, WrDr 76, –80, –82, –84

Gassner, John 1903-1967 AmAu&B,
BiE&WWA, BioIn 1, –3, –7, –8,
ConAu 1R, –3NR, –25R, CurBio 47, –67,
EncWT, NotNAT B, ObitOF 79,
REnAL, WhAm 4, WhNAA, WhThe

Gaston, Paul M 1928- DrAS 74H, –78H, –82H

Gat, Dimitri V 1936- BiDrLUS 70,
ConAu 29R, ScF&FL 1, –2, WhoLibS 66

Gately, George 1928- WhoAm 82, WorECar

Gates, David 1940- EncPR&S, –77, IlEncRk,
RkOn 78, –84, WhoRocM 82, WorAl

Gates, Doris 1901- AnCL, Au&ICB, AuBYP,
BioIn 1, –2, –8, –9, ConAu 1R, –1NR,
DcLB 22[port], JBA 51, SmATA 1,
–34[port], TwCCW 78, –83,
WhoAmW 58, –61, –64, WrDr 80, –82, –84

Gathorne-Hardy, Jonathan 1933- Au&Wr 6,
ConAu 104, IntAu&W 76, –82,

SmATA 26, TwCCW 78, WrDr 76, –80, –82, –84

Gatland, Kenneth William 1924- *Au&Wr 6, WrDr 76, –80, –82, –84*

Gauch, Patricia Lee 1934- *ChhPo S3, ConAu 9NR, –57, SmATA 26[port]*

Gaul, Albro T *AuBYP, BioIn 7*

Gault, William Campbell 1910- *AuBYP, BioIn 5, –7, –11, ConAu 1NR, –49, EncMys, SmATA 8, TwCCr&M 80, WrDr 82, –84*

Gay, John 1685-1732 *Alli, AtlBL, Baker 78, BiD&SB, BioIn 1, –2, –3, –5, –6, –7, –9, –10, –12, BrAu, BrWr 3, CarSB, CasWL, Chambr 2, ChhPo, –S1, –S2, –S3, CnE&AP, CnThe, CrtT 2, –4, CyWA, DcBiPP, DcEnA, –AP, DcEnL, DcEuL, DcLEL, EncWT, EvLB, LinLib L, –S, LongCEL, McGEWB, McGEWD, –84[port], MouLC 2, NewC, NewEOp 71, NotNAT A, –B, OxEng, OxMus, OxThe, PenC ENG, PIP&P, –A, REn, REnWD, WebE&AL, WhDW, WorAl*

Gay, Kathlyn 1930- *AuBYP SUP, BioIn 11, ConAu 8NR, –21R, SmATA 9, WhoAmW 74, –75, WrDr 76, –80, –82, –84*

Gay, Peter 1923- *AmAu&B, BioIn 11, BlueB 76, ConAu 13R, DrAS 74H, –78H, –82H, WhoAm 74, –76, –78, –80, –82, WhoE 74, WhoWor 74, WrDr 80, –82, –84*

Gayle, Addison, Jr. 1932- *BioIn 11, BlkAWP, BroadAu, ConAu 25R, InB&W 80, IntAu&W 77, LivgBAA, SelBAA, WhoBlA 77, –80*

Gaylin, Willard 1925- *AmM&WS 76P, –79P, –82P, BiDrAPA 77, ConAu 21R, IntAu&W 77, WhoAm 74, –76, –78, –80, –82, WhoE 74, –75, WrDr 76, –80, –82, –84*

Geary, Efton F 1940- *BlkAWP*

Gedge, Pauline Alice 1945- *WhoAm 80, –82*

Geduld, Harry M 1931- *ConAu 5NR, –9R, DrAS 74E, –78E, –82E*

Gee, Maurice 1931- *ConAu 97, ConNov 76, –82, TwCCW 83, WrDr 76, –80, –82, –84*

Gehrig, Eleanor 1905- *BioIn 10, WhoAmW 58*

Geisinger, David L 1938- *ConAu 110*

Geismar, Maxwell 1909-1979 *Au&Wr 6, BioIn 1, –4, –8, –12, ConAu 1R, –104, ConLCrt, –82, IntAu&W 76, –77, NewYTBS 79, RAdv 1, REnAL, TwCA SUP, WhAm 7, WhoAm 74, –76, –78, WhoE 74, WhoWor 74, WhoWorJ 72, –78, WrDr 76, –80*

Gelatt, Roland 1920- *ConAu 13R, WhoAm 74, –76, –78, –80, WhoE 74, –75, –77, WhoWor 74*

Gelderman, Carol Wettlaufer 1935- *ConAu 105, DrAS 74E, –78E, –82E*

Gelinas, Paul J 1911- *BioIn 11, ConAu 41R, IntAu&W 76, SmATA 10, WhoE 77, –79*

Geller, Allen 1941- *ConAu 25R*

Geller, Uri 1946- *BioIn 10, –11, BioNews 74, ConAu 69, CurBio 78, EncO&P 78, IntAu&W 82, UFOEn, WorAl*

Gelman, Steve 1934- *AuBYP SUP, BioIn 9, ConAu 25R, SmATA 3, WhoE 74*

Gemme, Leila Boyle 1942- *ConAu 81*

Gennaro, Joseph Francis 1924- *AmM&WS 73P, –76P, –79P, –82P, ConAu 101*

Genovese, Eugene D 1930- *AmAu&B, BioIn 11, BlueB 76, ConAu 10NR, –69, DcLB 17[port], DrAS 74H, –78H, –82H, PolProf J, WhoAm 74, –76, –78, –80, –82, WhoEc, WorAu 1970*

Gensler, Kinereth *IntWWP 82*

Gentry, Byron B 1913- *ConAu 13R, WhoGov 77, –75*

Gentry, Curt 1931- *ConAu 5NR, –9R, EncSF, IntAu&W 77, ScF&FL 1, –2, WrDr 84*

Georgakas, Dan 1938- *ConAu 1NR, –45, DrAP 75, DrAP&F 83, IntWWP 77, –82, MichAu 80*

George, Barbara Crutchfield 1935- *AmM&WS 73S, WhoAmW 77*

George, Frank Honywill 1921- *Au&Wr 6*

George, Jean Craighead 1919- *AmAu&B, AmWomWr, AnCL, Au&Wr 6, AuBYP, BioIn 5, –6, –7, –9, –10, –12, ChlLR 1, ConAu 5R, IlsCB 1946, IntAu&W 76, –77, MorBMP, MorJA, NinCLC 1966, SmATA 2, TwCCW 78, –83, WhoAm 82, WhoAmW 58, –61, WrDr 80, –82, –84*

George, John Lothar 1916- *AmAu&B, AmM&WS 73P, –76P, –79P, –82P, AnCL, AuBYP, BiDLA, BioIn 7, –9, BkCL, ConAu 5R, SmATA 2*

George, Peter 1924-1966 *BioIn 7, ConAu 25R, EncSF, ObitOF 79, ScF&FL 1, WhoSciF*

Geras, Adele 1944- *ConAu 97, SmATA 23*

Gerassi, John 1931- *AuBYP SUP, ConAu 8NR*

Gerber, Dan 1940- *ConAu 33R, DrAF 76, DrAP 75, DrAP&F 83, IntWWP 77X, –82X, MichAu 80*

Gerber, Merrill Joan 1938- *ConAu 10NR, DrAP&F 83, IntAu&W 76, –77*

Gerber, William 1908- *ConAu 37R, DrAS 74P, –78P, –82P, WhoAm 74, –76, –78, –80, –82, WhoAmJ 80, WhoWorJ 72, –78, WrDr 76, –80, –82, –84*

Gerlach, Larry Reuben 1941- *ConAu 109, DrAS 74H, –78H, –82H*

German, Herb 1911- *ConAu X*

German, Herb *see also* Germar, William H

Germar, William H 1911- *ConAu 21R*

Germond, Jack 1928- *BioIn 11, ConAu 108*

Geronimo 1829-1909 *AmBi, ApCAB, BioIn 1, –2, –3, –4, –5, –8, –9, –10, –11, –12, DcAmB, EncAB-H, FilmgC, HarEnUS[port], McGEWB, NatCAB 23, OxAmH, REn,*

REnAL; REnAW, WebAB, –79, WebAMB, WhDW, WhAm HSA, –4, WorAl

Gerrold, David 1944- *BioIn 12, ConAu 85, –93, DcLB 8[port], EncSF, ScF&FL 1, –2, WhoSciF, WrDr 84*

Gersh, Harry 1912- *BioIn 11, ConAu 1R, –1NR, NewYTBS 76, –77, WhoWorJ 72, –78*

Gerson, Corinne 1927- *ConAu 93, DrAP&F 83, SmATA 37*

Gerson, Noel Bertram 1914- *AmAu&B, Au&Wr 6, AuBYP, BioIn 8, ConAu 81, IntAu&W 76, ScF&FL 1, SmATA 22[port], WhoAm 74, –76, –78, –80, –82, WhoE 74, –75, –77, –79, –81, –83, WhoWor 74, –76, –78, –80, –82, WrDr 76, –80, –82, –84*

Gesch, Roy 1920- *ConAu 21R, IntAu&W 77, WrDr 76, –80, –82, –84*

Gessner, Lynne 1919- *ConAu 10NR, –25R, IntAu&W 77, SmATA 16, WrDr 76, –80, –82, –84*

Geyer, Georgie Anne 1935- *BioIn 7, –9, ConAu 29R, ForWC 70, IntAu&W 77, –82, WhoAm 74, –76, –78, –80, –82, WhoAmW 74, –68, –70, –72, –75, –77, –79, –81, –83, WhoMW 74, –76, WhoWor 74, –76*

Giannetti, Louis D 1937- *ConAu 33R, DrAS 82E*

Gibb, Barry 1946- *BioIn 12, CurBio 81[port], WhoAm 80, –82, WhoRocM 82*

Gibb, Barry see also Bee Gees, The

Gibb, Jocelyn Easton 1907- *Au&Wr 6, ChhPo S1, IntAu&W 76, –77*

Gibb, Maurice 1949- *WhoAm 80, –82, WhoRocM 82*

Gibb, Maurice see also Bee Gees, The

Gibb, Robin 1949- *WhoAm 80, –82, WhoRocM 82*

Gibb, Robin see also Bee Gees, The

Gibbons, Faye 1938- *ConAu 109*

Gibbons, Reginald *DrAP&F 83*

Gibbs, Alonzo 1915- *AuBYP, BioIn 8, –10, ConAu 5R, –5NR, IntAu&W 77, –82, SmATA 5, WhoE 83, WrDr 76, –80, –82, –84*

Giblin, James C 1933- *ConAu 106, SmATA 33[port], WhoLibI 82*

Gibran, Kahlil 1883-1931 *AmAu&B, BioIn 1, –2, –3, –4, –5, –7, –9, –10, CasWL, ChhPo S1, –S3, ConAu 104, DcNAA, EncO&P 78, LinLib L, ScF&FL 1, TwCA, TwCA SUP, TwCLC 1, –9[port], WorAl*

Gibson, Althea 1927- *BioIn 4, –5, –6, –7, –8, –9, –10, –11, –12, CurBio 57, Ebony 1, GoodHs, HerW, InB&W 80, InWom, IntDcWB, LibW, NegAl 76, –83, NewYTBS 80, WebAB, –79, WhoAm 74, –76, –78, –80, –82, WhoAmW 74, –66, –68,*

–70, –72, –83, WhoBlA 75, –77, –80, WorAl

Gibson, Charles E 1916- *Au&Wr 6, ConAu 5R, IntAu&W 76, –77, WrDr 76, –80, –82, –84*

Gibson, Donald B 1933- *ConAu 25R, DrAS 74E, –78E, –82E*

Gibson, Evan Keith 1909- *ConAu 105, DrAS 74E, –78E, –82E*

Gibson, Gwen 1927- *ForWC 70, WhoAmW 58, –61, –66*

Gibson, Karon Rose 1946- *ConAu 105, WhoAmW 77, –81*

Gibson, Margaret 1948- *ConAu 103, Po&Wr 77*

Gibson, Robert 1935- *BioIn 7, –8, –9, –10, –11, CurBio 68, InB&W 80, WhoAm 74, –76, –82, WhoBlA 75, –77, –80, WhoCtE 79, WhoProB 73*

Gibson, Walker 1919- *AmAu&B, ChhPo S3, ConAu 1R, –1NR, DrAS 74E, –78E, –82E, LinLib L*

Gibson, Walter B 1897- *BioIn 7, ConAu 108, –110, EncMys, ScF&FL 1, TwCCr&M 80, WhJnl, WhNAA, WrDr 82, –84*

Gibson, William 1914- *BiE&WWA, BioIn 3, –4, –5, –10, –12, ChhPo S2, CnMD, ConAu 9R, –9NR, ConDr 73, –77, –82, ConLC 23[port], CurBio 83[port], DcLB 7[port], DcLEL 1940, EncWT, IntAu&W 77, McGEWD, –84, ModAL, ModWD, NatPD, –81[port], NotNAT, –A, PenC AM, PIP&P, REnAL, WhoAm 74, –76, –78, –80, –82, WhoE 74, WhoThe 15, –16, –81, WhoWor 74, WorAu, WrDr 76, –80, –82, –84*

Gidley, M 1941- *ConAu 102*

Gielgud, Sir John 1904- *BiDFilm, BiE&WWA, BioIn 1, –2, –3, –4, –5, –6, –7, –9, –10, –11, –12, BlueB 76, CelR 73, CnThe, CurBio 47, EncWT, FamA&A, Film 2, FilmgC, IntMPA 77, –75, –76, –78, –79, –81, –82, –84, IntWW 74, –75, –76, –77, –78, –79, –80, –81, –82, –83, MotPP, MovMk, NewC, NewYTBE 70, NewYTBS 79, –80[port], NotNAT, –A, OxFilm, OxThe, PIP&P, REn, WhDW, Who 74, –82, –83, WhoHol A, WhoPolA, WhoThe 15, –16, –81, WorAl, WorEFlm, WrDr 80, –82, –84*

Gies, Frances 1915- *ConAu 9NR, –25R, WhoAmW 74, –75*

Gies, Joseph 1916- *ConAu 5R, –9NR*

Giff, Patricia Reilly 1935- *ConAu 101, SmATA 33[port]*

Gifford, Denis 1927- *ConAu 101, IntAu&W 82, ScF&FL 1, –2, WhoArt 80, –82, WhoWor 78, WorECar A, WrDr 76, –80, –82, –84*

Gifford, Frank 1930- *BioIn 4, –5, –6, –7, –8, –9, –11, CelR 73, ConAu 109, CurBio 64,*

Gimpel, Jean 1918- *ConAu 69*

Ginns, Patsy M 1937- *ConAu 69*

Ginsberg, Allen 1926- *AmAu&B, AuNews 1, BioIn 7, -8, -9, -10, -11, -12, BioNews 74, BlueB 76, CasWL, CelR 73, CmCal, ConAu 1R, -2NR, ConLC 1, -2, -3, -4, -6, -13, ConP 70, -75, -80, CroCAP, CurBio 70, DcLB 5[port], -16[port], DcLEL 1940, DrAP 75, DrAP&F 83, EncAB-H, EncWL, -2, IntAu&W 77, -82, IntWW 74, -75, -76, -77, -78, -79, -80, -81, -82, -83, IntWWP 77, -82, LinLib L, -S, LongCTC, MakMC, McGEWB, ModAL, ModAL SUP, MugS, NewYTBE 72, OxAmL, PenC AM, PlP&P A, PolProf E, PolProf J, RAdv 1, REn, REnAL, TwCWr, WebAB, -79, WebE&AL, WhDW, WhoAm 74, -76, -78, -80, -82, WhoAmJ 80, WhoE 79, WhoRocM 82, WhoTwCL, WhoWest 82, WhoWor 74, -78, -80, -82, WhoWorJ 72, -78, WorAu, WrDr 76, -80, -82, -84*

Ginsburg, Mirra 1919- *AuBYP SUP, BioIn 10, ConAu 11NR, -17R, ConSFA, EncSF, IntAu&W 77, -82, ScF&FL 1, -2, SmATA 6, WhoAmW 74, -75, -77*

Ginzburg, Eugenia 1936-1977 *BioIn 12, NewYTBS 81[port]*

Ginzburg, Natalia 1916- *BioIn 10, CasWL, ConAu 85, ConLC 5, -11, DcItL, EncWL, -2, EncWT, IntAu&W 77, IntDcWB, IntWW 74, -75, -76, -77, -78, -79, -80, -81, -82, -83, McGEWD 84, ModRL, WhoWor 74, WorAu*

Giovanni, Nikki 1943- *AmWomWr, AuBYP SUP, AuNews 1, BioIn 9, -10, -12, BioNews 75, BlkAWP, BroadAu, CelR 73, ChlLR 6[port], ChhPo S2, CivR 74, ConAu 29R, ConLC 2, -4, -19, ConP 75, -80, CroCAP, CurBio 73, DcLB 5[port], DcLEL 1940, DrAP 75, DrAP&F 83, Ebony 1, InB&W 80, IntWWP 77, LivgBAA, NegAl 76[port], -83[port], RAdv 1, SelBAA, SmATA 24[port], TwCCW 78, WhoAm 74, -76, -78, -80, -82, WhoAmW 81, WhoBlA 75, -77, -80, WorAu 1970, WrDr 76, -80, -82, -84*

Gipe, George 1933- *ConAu 77*

Gipson, Fred 1908-1973 *ConAu 3NR, CurBio 57, NewYTBE 73, ObitOF 79, REnAW, TwCCW 83*

Gipson, Frederick Benjamin 1908-1973 *AmAu&B, AuBYP, BioIn 4, -5, -8, -9, -10, -12, ConAu 1R, -45, CurBio 57, NewYTBE 73, SmATA 2, -24N, ThrBJA, TwCCW 78*

Girion, Barbara 1937- *ConAu 85, SmATA 26[port], WhoAmW 81, -83*

Gish, Lillian 1896?- *BiDFilm, BiE&WWA, BioIn 2, -3, -4, -5, -6, -8, -9, -10, -11, -12, BlueB 76, CelR 73, CmMov, CurBio 44,* -78, FamA&A, Film 1, -2, FilmgC, GoodHs, InWom, IntDcWB, IntMPA 77, -75, -76, -78, -79, -81, -82, -84, IntWW 74, -75, -76, -77, -78, -79, -80, -81, -82, -83, LibW, MotPP, MovMk, NewYTBS 80[port], -82[port], NotNAT, -A, OxFilm, PlP&P, REn, ThFT, TwYS, WebAB, -79, Who 74, -82, -83, WhoAm 74, -76, -78, -80, -82, WhoAmW 74, -58, -61, -64, -66, -68, -70, -72, -83, WhoHol A, WhoThe 15, -16, -81, WhoWor 74, WomWMM, WorAl, WorEFlm, WrDr 80, -82, -84*

Gittell, Marilyn 1931- *AmM&WS 73S, ConAu 9NR, -21R, LEduc 74, WhoAmW 74, -83*

Gittelson, Celia *BioIn 12, ConAu 105*

Gladych, B Michael 1910- *ConAu 5R*

Glanville, Brian 1931- *Au&Wr 6, AuBYP SUP, BioIn 6, -10, BlueB 76, ConAu 3NR, -5R, ConLC 6, ConNov 72, -76, -82, DcLB 15[port], DcLEL 1940, IntAu&W 76, -77, -82, NewC, Novels, Who 74, -82, -83, WhoWor 76, WorAu, WrDr 76, -80, -82, -84*

Glaser, Dianne E 1937- *ConAu 77, SmATA 31*

Glaskin, G M 1923- *ConAu 5NR, EncSF, IntAu&W 77, -82, WrDr 80, -82, -84*

Glass, Frankcina 1955?- *BioIn 11, InB&W 80*

Glass, Malcolm 1936- *ConAu 104, DrAP 75, Po&Wr 77*

Glazer, Tom 1914- *AmSCAP 66, AuBYP SUP, BioIn 11, ConAu 8NR, -61, EncFCWM 69, RkOn 74, SmATA 9*

Gleasner, Diana 1936- *ConAu 65, SmATA 29[port]*

Gleason, Judith 1929- *BioIn 8, ConAu 9NR, -61, DrAP&F 83, SmATA 24*

Gleason, Ralph J 1917-1975 *BioIn 5, -10, CmCal, ConAu 61, -65, EncJzS 70, MugS, NewYTBS 75, ObitOF 79, WhAm 6, WhoAm 74, WhoWest 74*

Gleaves, Suzanne 1904- *ConAu 9R, WhoAmW 61, -64*

Gleazer, Edmund John, Jr. 1916- *BioIn 7, WhoAm 74, -76, -78, -80, -82, WhoS&SW 75, -76*

Glenn, Harold T 1910- *ConAu 5R, -5NR*

Glenn, Jerome Clayton 1945- *Future, WhoWor 82*

Glimcher, Arnold B 1938- *BioIn 10, ConAu 81, IntAu&W 82, WhoAmA 73, -76, -78, -80, -82*

Glines, Carroll Vane, Jr. 1920- *BioIn 12, ConAu 1R, -2NR, SmATA 19, WhoAm 76, -78, -80, -82, WhoE 79, -81, WhoS&SW 76, WhoWor 80, -82*

Gloag, Julian 1930- *AmAu&B, AuNews 1, BioIn 10, ConAu 10NR, -65, ConNov 72, -76, -82, DrAF 76, DrAP&F 83, IntAu&W 76, -77, -82, WhoWor 80,*

WrDr 80, –82, –84

Globe, Leah Ain 1900- *ConAu 107,
WhoWorJ 72, –78*

Glubok, Shirley 1933- *AuBYP, BioIn 8, –9,
–10, ChlLR 1, ConAu 4NR, –5R,
ForWC 70, MorBMP, SmATA 6,
ThrBJA, WhoAmW 74, –64, –66, –68, –70,
–72, –75, –77, WhoE 74, WrDr 80, –82,
–84*

Gluck, Herb 1925- *ConAu 2NR, –45*

Gluck, Louise 1943- *BioIn 10, –12,
ConAu 33R, ConLC 7, –22, ConP 70, –75,
–80, CroCAP, DcLB 5[port],
DcLEL 1940, DrAP 75, DrAP&F 83,
IntWWP 77, –82, WhoAm 76, –78, –80,
–82, WhoAmW 83, WorAu 1970,
WrDr 76, –80, –82, –84*

Glyn, Caroline 1947- *BioIn 7, ConAu 5NR,
–9R, DcLEL 1940, IntAu&W 77, –82,
WhoAmW 74, –68, –70, –72*

Gnaegy, Charles 1938- *ConAu 89*

Godden, Rumer 1907- *AnCL, ASpks,
Au&Wr 6, AuBYP, BioIn 2, –4, –6, –7, –8,
–9, –10, –11, BlueB 76, ChhPo, –S1, –S2,
ConAu 4NR, –5R, ConNov 72, –76, –82,
CurBio 76, DcLEL, FamMS, FilmgC,
InWom, IntAu&W 76, –77X, –82,
IntWW 74, –75, –76, –77, –78, –79, –80, –81,
–82, –83, IntWWP 77X, –82X, LongCTC,
ModBrL, MorJA, NewC, Novels, PiP,
RAdv 1, REn, ScF&FL 1, –2, SmATA 3,
–36, TwCA, TwCA SUP, TwCCW 78,
–83, TwCWr, WhE&EA, Who 74, –82,
–83, WhoAmW 74, –70, –70A, –72, –75,
WhoChL, WhoWor 74, –76, –78, WrDr 76,
–80, –82, –84*

Godey, John 1912- *AuNews 1, BioIn 9, –10,
ConAu X, EncMys, Novels,
TwCCr&M 80, WrDr 82, –84*

Godfrey, Arthur 1903-1983 *AmPS A, –B,
AmSCAP 66, BiDAmM, BioIn 1, –2, –3,
–4, –5, –6, –8, –9, –10, BioNews 75,
BlueB 76, CelR 73, CmpEPM,
CurBio 48, –83N, IntMPA 77, –75, –76,
–78, –79, –81, –82, LesBEnT[port],
NewYTBS 83[port], NewYTET, WebAB,
–79, WhoAm 74, –76, –78, –80, –82,
WhoHol A, WorAl*

Godwin, Gail 1937- *AmWomWr, BioIn 12,
ConAu 29R, ConLC 5, –8, –22[port],
ConNov 82, DcLB 6[port], DrAF 76,
DrAP&F 83, WhoAm 80, –82,
WhoAmW 75, –83, WrDr 82, –84*

Godwin, Parke 1816-1904 *Alli, Alli SUP,
AmAu, AmAu&B, AmBi, ApCAB, BbD,
BiD&SB, BioIn 1, –2, –12, CyAL 2,
DcAmAu, DcAmB, DcBiPP, DcEnL,
DcLB 3, DcNAA, Drake, HarEnUS,
NatCAB 11, –35, OxAmH, OxAmL,
REnAL, TwCBDA, WhAm 1*

Goertzel, Victor 1914- *AmM&WS 73S,
WhoWest 78*

Goettel, Elinor 1930- *BioIn 11, ConAu 29R,
SmATA 12, WhoAmW 75, WrDr 76, –80,
–82, –84*

Goetz, Delia 1898- *AuBYP, BioIn 2, –7,
ConAu 73, CurBio 49, InWom,
SmATA 22*

Goffstein, M B 1940- *ChlLR 3, ConAu 9NR,
–21R, FourBJA, IlsCB 1967, SmATA 8*

Goffstein, Marilyn Brooke 1940- *AuBYP SUP,
BioIn 11, –12, WhoAmW 74, –75, –77*

Goggan, John Patrick 1905- *PenC AM*

Goggan, John Patrick *see also* Patrick, John

Gogol, Nikolai V 1809-1852 *AtlBL, BbD,
BiD&SB, BioIn 1, –2, –3, –4, –5, –6, –7, –8,
–9, –10, –12, CasWL, CnThe, CyWA,
DcAmSR, DcBiA, DcBiPP, DcEuL,
DcRusL, Dis&D, EncWT, EuAu,
EvEuW, LinLib L, McGEWB, NewC,
NewEOp 71, NotNAT A, –B, OxEng,
OxThe, PenC EUR, PIP&P, RComWL,
REn, REnWD, WhDW, WhoHr&F,
WorAl*

Gohman, Fred Joseph 1918- *ConAu 5R*

Goins, Ellen H 1927- *ConAu 33R*

Goitein, S D 1900- *ConAu 8NR, –61*

Golan, Aviezer 1922- *ConAu 104*

Gold, Andrew 1951?- *BioIn 11, IlEncRk,
RkOn 78, WhoRocM 82*

Gold, Herbert 1924- *AmAu&B, BioIn 3, –4,
–6, –7, –8, –9, –10, CmCal, ConAu 9R,
ConLC 4, –7, –14, ConNov 72, –76, –82,
CurBio 55, DcLB Y81A[port], –2,
DcLEL 1940, DrAF 76, DrAP&F 83,
IntAu&W 76, –77, MichAu 80, ModAL,
Novels, OxAmL, PenC AM, RAdv 1,
REnAL, TwCWr, WhoAm 74, –76, –78,
–80, –82, WhoAmJ 80, WhoWor 74,
WhoWorJ 72, –78, WorAu, WrDr 76, –80,
–82, –84*

Gold, Phyllis 1941- *BioIn 12, ConAu 57,
SmATA 21, WhoAmW 77*

Gold, Phyllis *see also* Goldberg, Phyllis

Gold, Robert S 1924- *ConAu 53, DrAS 74E,
–78E, –82E, IntAu&W 77, –82*

Gold, Sharlya *BioIn 11, ConAu 8NR, –61,
SmATA 9*

Goldberg, George 1935- *ConAu 69*

Goldberg, Herbert S 1926- *AmM&WS 73P,
–76P, –79P, –82P, ConAu 5R, Dun&B 79,
SmATA 25[port]*

Goldberg, Phyllis 1941- *ConAu 57*

Goldberg, Phyllis *see also* Gold, Phyllis

Goldberger, Judith M 1948- *WhoLibI 82*

Golden, Harry 1902?-1981 *AmAu&B,
AnObit 1981[port], BioIn 5, –6, –7, –8, –10,
–12, CelR 73, ConAu 1R, –2NR, –104,
CurBio 59, –81N, DcAmSR, EncSoH,
NewYTBS 81[port], PenC AM, RAdv 1,
REnAL, WhoAm 74, –76, –78, –80,
WhoAmJ 80, WhoS&SW 73, –75,
WhoWor 74, –76, WhoWorJ 72, –78,
WorAl, WorAu*

Golden, Jeffrey 1950- *BioIn 9, ConAu 33R*
Goldenson, Daniel R 1944- *ConAu 25R, WhoE 74, -75, -77*
Goldenthal, Allan Benarria 1920- *ConAu 17R*
Goldfarb, Ronald L 1933- *BlueB 76, ConAu 9NR, -21R, IntAu&W 76, WhoAm 74, -76, -78, -80, -82, WhoAmJ 80, WhoAmL 78, -79, WhoS&SW 73, WrDr 76, -80, -82, -84*
Goldfrank, Helen Colodny 1912- *AuBYP, BioIn 10, ConAu 1R, -3NR, ForWC 70, SmATA 6, WhoE 83*
Goldfrank, Helen Colodny *see also* Kay, Helen
Goldin, Augusta 1906- *ConAu 7NR, -17R, ForWC 70, LEduc 74, SmATA 13, WhoAmW 74, -75, -83, WrDr 76, -80, -82, -84*
Goldin, Stephen 1947- *ConAu 77, DrAP&F 83, ScF&FL 1, -2, WrDr 84*
Golding, Morton J 1925- *ConAu 21R, ScF&FL 1, -2*
Golding, William 1911- *BioIn 6, -7, -8, -9, -10, -11, -12, BlueB 76, CasWL, CnMWL, ConAu 5R, ConLC 1, -2, -3, -8, -10, -17, -27[port], ConNov 72, -76, -82, CurBio 64, DcLB 15[port], DcLEL 1940, EncSF, EncWL, -2[port], IntAu&W 76, -77, IntWW 74, -75, -76, -77, -78, -79, -80, -81, -82, -83, LinLib L, LongCEL, LongCTC, MakMC, ModBrL, ModBrL SUP, ModWD, NewC, NewYTBS 83[port], Novels, PenC ENG, RAdv 1, REn, ScF&FL 1, -2, TwCWr, WebE&AL, WhDW, WhE&EA, Who 74, -82, WhoAm 80, -82, WhoHr&F, WhoTwCL, WhoWor 74, -78, -80, -82, WorAl, WorAu, WrDr 76, -80, -82, -84*
Goldman, Albert 1927- *AmAu&B, BioIn 12, ConAu 9NR, -17R, DrAS 74E, -78E, -82E, NewYTBS 81[port], WhoE 74, -75*
Goldman, Edward A 1873-1946 *BioIn 1, -2, WhAm 2, WhNAA*
Goldman, James 1927- *AmAu&B, BiE&WWA, BioIn 10, -12, BlueB 76, ConAu 1NR, -45, ConDr 73, -77, -82, FilmgC, McGEWD, -84, NatPD 81[port], NotNAT, WhoAm 74, -76, -78, -80, -82, WhoE 74, WhoThe 81, WhoWor 74, WrDr 76, -80, -82, -84*
Goldman, Peter L 1933- *ConAu 8NR, -21R*
Goldman, William 1931- *AmAu&B, BiE&WWA, BioIn 12, BioNews 75, BlueB 76, ConAu 9R, ConDr 73, -77A, -82A, ConLC 1, ConNov 72, -76, -82, DcLEL 1940, DrAF 76, DrAP&F 83, FilmgC, IntAu&W 76, IntMPA 78, -79, -81, -82, -84, LinLib L, NotNAT, Novels[port], PenC AM, ScF&FL 1, -2, WebE&AL, WhoAm 74, -76, -78, -80, -82, WhoE 74, WhoWor 74, WorAu 1970, WrDr 76, -80, -82, -84*
Goldner, Orville 1906- *ConAu 53*

Goldreich, Gloria *DrAP&F 83*
Goldsmith, Donald 1943- *ConAu 77*
Goldsmith, Maurice 1913- *Au&Wr 6, WhoWor 76, WhoWorJ 78*
Goldsmith, Oliver 1728?-1774 *Alli, AtlBL, BbD, BiD&SB, BioIn 1, -2, -3, -4, -5, -6, -7, -8, -9, -10, -11, -12, BrAu, BrWr 3, CarSB, CasWL, Chambr 2, ChhPo, -S1, -S2, -S3, CnE&AP, CnThe, CrtT 2, -4, CyEd, CyWA, DcBiA, DcBiPP, DcEnA, -AP, DcEnL, DcEuL, DcIrB, DcIrL, DcIrW 1, DcLEL, Dis&D, EncWT, EvLB, HsB&A, InSci, LinLib L, -S, LongCEL, McGEWB, McGEWD, -84[port], MouLC 2, NewC, NewEOp 71, NotNAT A, -B, Novels, OxEng, OxMus, OxThe, PenC ENG, PIP&P, PoIre, RAdv 1, REn, REnWD, SmATA 26[port], WebE&AL, WhDW, WorAl*
Goldsmith, Ruth *WhoAmP 83*
Goldstein, Lisa 1953- *ConAu 108*
Goldstein, Philip 1910- *AuBYP SUP, ConAu 53, SmATA 23[port]*
Goldstein, Richard 1944- *BioIn 7, -10, -11, ConAu 25R, MugS*
Goldstein, Ruth Tessler 1924- *ConAu 69, WhoAmW 79, -81*
Goldston, Robert Conroy 1927- *AmAu&B, Au&Wr 6, AuBYP SUP, BioIn 10, ConAu 17R, FourBJA, ScF&FL 1, -2, SmATA 6, WhoAm 74, -76, -78, -80, -82*
Golenbock, Peter 1946- *BioIn 12, ConAu 8NR, -57, NewYTBS 80[port]*
Goll, Reinhold W 1897- *AuBYP, BioIn 8, ConAu 5R, ScF&FL 1, -2, SmATA 26[port], WrDr 76, -80, -82, -84*
Gollomb, Joseph 1881-1950 *AmAu&B, AnCL, AuBYP, BioIn 2, -4, -7, JBA 34, -51, ObitOF 79, REnAL, TwCA, TwCA SUP, WhAm 3, WhE&EA*
Gombrich, Sir Ernst 1909- *BioIn 10, BlueB 76, ConAu 53, DcLEL 1940, IntAu&W 77, -82, IntWW 74, -75, -76, -77, -78, -79, -80, -81, -82, -83, Who 74, -82, -83, WhoArt 80, -82, WhoWor 74, -76, -78, WorAu, WrDr 76, -80, -82, -84*
Gonzales, Rodolfo 1928?- *BioIn 9, -10, ChiSch, CivR 74*
Gonzalez, Gloria 1940- *ConAu 65, NatPD, -81[port], SmATA 23[port], WhoAmW 79*
Gonzalez, Nancie L S 1929- *AmM&WS 73S, -76P, ConAu 103, FifIDA, WhoAm 74, -76, -78, -80, -82, WhoAmW 74, -72, -75, -77*
Goodall, Jane 1934- *BioIn 12, ConAu X, -2NR, CurBio 67, InWom, IntDcWB*
Goodall, Jane *see also* VanLawick-Goodall, Jane
Goodavage, Joseph F 1925- *ConAu 25R*
Goode, Ruth 1905- *ConAu 77*
Goode, Stephen 1943- *ConAu 105*

Gooderham, Kent *OxCan SUP*

Goodfellow, Thomas Mackey 1907- *BioIn 4, EncAB 31, WhoAm 74, –76, WhoF&I 74, WhoS&SW 73*

Goodfield, June *WhoAm 74, WhoAmW 74*

Goodhart, Robert Stanley 1909- *AmM&WS 73P, –76P, –79P, –82P, BioIn 1, ConAu 89, WhoAm 74, –76, –78, –80*

Goodman, Elaine 1930- *AuBYP SUP, BioIn 11, ConAu 37R, SmATA 9*

Goodman, Ellen Holtz 1941- *BioIn 12, ConAu 104, WhoAm 78, –80, –82, WhoAmW 74, –75, –77, –81, –83, WhoE 83*

Goodman, George Jerome Waldo 1930- *AmAu&B, BioIn 8, –12, ConAu 21R, NewYTBS 81[port], WhoAm 74, –76, –78, –80, –82*

Goodman, Linda 1925- *CelR 73, ConAu 89, WhoAm 74, –76, –78, –80, –82, WhoAmW 74, –72*

Goodman, Nathan Gerson 1899-1953 *AmAu&B, BioIn 3, –4, NatCAB 40, REnAL, WhAm 3*

Goodman, Roger B 1919- *ConAu 9NR, –21R, WrDr 76, –80, –82, –84*

Goodman, Saul 1919- *ConAu 103*

Goodman, Walter 1927- *AuBYP SUP, BioIn 11, ConAu 7NR, –9R, SmATA 9, WhoAm 74, –76, –78, –80, –82, WhoAmJ 80, WhoE 74*

Goodrich, Frances 1891?- *AmAu&B, BiE&WWA, BioIn 4, –11, CmMov, CurBio 56, DcLB 26[port], FilmgC, InWom, McGEWD, –84, NotNAT, WhoAm 74, –76, –78, –80, –82, WomWMM, WorEFlm*

Goodrich, L Carrington 1894- *ConAu 2NR, –5R*

Goodrich, Norma Lorre 1917- *ConAu 53, DrAS 78F, –82F, IntAu&W 77, WhoAm 74, –76, –78, –80, –82*

Goodrum, John Cornelius 1918- *WhoF&I 74, –75*

Goodwin, Harold Leland 1914- *ConAu 1R, –2NR, ScF&FL 1, SmATA 13, WhoE 75, –77, –79, WhoGov 77, –72, –75, WhoS&SW 75*

Goodyear, Robert Arthur Hanson 1877?-1948 *BioIn 8, MnBBF, WhE&EA, WhLit, WhoChL, WhoLA*

Gordimer, Nadine 1923- *AfSS 78, –79, –80, –81, –82, Au&Wr 6, BioIn 3, –5, –7, –9, –10, –11, –12, CasWL, ConAu 3NR, –5R, ConLC 3, –5, –7, –10, –18, ConNov 72, –76, –82, CurBio 59, –80[port], DcLEL 1940, EncSoA, EncWL 2, InWom, IntAu&W 76, –77, –82, IntDcWB, IntWW 74, –75, –76, –77, –78, –79, –80, –81, –82, –83, ModCmwL, NewC, NewYTBS 81[port], Novels, PenC ENG, TwCWr, Who 74, –82, –83, WhoAmW 70, –72, WhoTwCL, WhoWor 74, –76, –78,*

–82, WorAu, WrDr 76, –80, –82, –84

Gordon, Barbara 1913- *ConAu 89, Who 74*

Gordon, Caroline 1895-1981 *AmAu&B, AmNov, AmWomWr, AmWr, AnObit 1981, BioIn 2, –3, –4, –5, –7, –8, –9, –12, CasWL, CathA 1952, ConAu 103, ConAu P-1, ConLC 6, –13, ConNov 72, –76, CyWA, DcLB Y81A[port], –4, –9[port], DrAF 76, EncWL 2, InWom, IntAu&W 76, –77, ModAL SUP, NewYTBS 81[port], Novels, OxAmL, PenC AM, RAdv 1, REn, REnAL, ScF&FL 1, TwCA, TwCA SUP, WhAm 7, WhE&EA, WhoAm 74, –76, –78, WhoAmW 74, –70, –72, WrDr 76, –80, –82*

Gordon, Charles William 1860-1937 *BiD&SB, BioIn 1, –2, –11, CanNov, CanWr, Chambr 3, ConAu 109, CreCan 1, DcLEL, DcNAA, EvLB, LinLib L, –S, LongCTC, LuthC 75, MacDCB 78, NewC, OxAmL, OxCan, REnAL, TwCA, TwCA SUP, WhLit, WhNAA*

Gordon, Charles William *see also* Connor, Ralph

Gordon, Donald 1924- *ConAu X, DrRegL 75, WrDr 76, –82, –84*

Gordon, Donald *see also* Payne, Donald Gordon

Gordon, Ethel Edison 1915- *ConAu 53, WrDr 76, –80, –82, –84*

Gordon, George N 1926- *ConAu 1R, –5NR, IntAu&W 76, –77, WrDr 76, –80, –82, –84*

Gordon, Gordon 1912- *Au&Wr 6, AuBYP SUP, BioIn 7, –8, ConAu 5R, –7NR, EncMys, IndAu 1917*

Gordon, John 1925- *BioIn 10, ConAu 103, –11NR, –25R, ScF&FL 1, –2, SmATA 6, TwCCW 78, –83, WhoWor 76, WrDr 76, –80, –82, –84*

Gordon, John Steele 1944- *ConAu 57*

Gordon, Linda 1940- *ConAu 10NR, –65, DrAS 78H, –82H*

Gordon, Mildred 1912-1979 *Au&Wr 6, AuBYP SUP, BioIn 7, –8, –11, ConAu 5R, –7NR, –85, EncMys, IntAu&W 76, SmATA 24N, TwCCr&M 80, WhoAmW 74, –75*

Gordon, Sol 1923- *AmM&WS 73S, –78S, AuBYP SUP, BioIn 11, ConAu 4NR, –53, ConLC 26[port], IntAu&W 77, LEduc 74, SmATA 11, WhoE 83*

Gordon, Suzanne 1945- *ConAu 4NR, –49*

Goreau, Laurraine Roberta 1918- *ForWC 70, WhoAmW 58, –61, –64, –66, –75, –77, WhoS&SW 76*

Gorenstein, Shirley 1928- *ConAu 73, FifIDA, WhoAm 82, WhoAmW 75, –81, WomPO 78*

Gores, Joe 1931- *ConAu X, Novels, TwCCr&M 80, WrDr 82, –84*

Gores, Joseph N 1931- *AmCath 80, Au&Wr 6, ConAu 10NR, –25R, WhoAm 74, –76, –78, –80, –82,*

WhoWor 80, –82

Gorey, Edward 1925- *BioIn 5, –8, –10, –11, –12, ChhPo, –S1, –S3, ConAu 5R, –9NR, Conv 1, CurBio 76, FourBJA, IlsBYP, IlsCB 1957, –1967, NewYTBE 73, ScF&FL 1, –2, SmATA 27, –29[port], WhoAm 78, –80, –82, WhoGrA 82[port], WrDr 80, –82, –84*

Gorham, Charles Orson 1911-1975 *AmAu&B, AmNov, BioIn 2, –10, ConAu 1R, –6NR, –61, SmATA 36*

Gorky, Maxim 1868-1936 *AtlBL, BiD&SB, BioIn 1, –2, –3, –4, –5, –6, –7, –8, –9, –10, –11, –12, CasWL, CIDMEL, CnMD, CnMWL, CnThe, ConAu X, CyWA, DcRusL, EncWL, –2[port], EncWT, EvEuW, FilmgC, LinLib L, –S, MakMC, McGEWB, McGEWD, –84[port], ModSL 1, ModWD, NewEOp 71, OxEng, OxFilm, OxThe, PenC EUR, RComWL, REn, REnWD, TwCA, TwCA SUP, TwCLC 8[port], TwCWr, WhDW, WhLit, WhoTwCL, WorAl*

Gorman, Tom 1919- *BioIn 12*

Gossett, Margaret *AuBYP, BioIn 8*

Gostelow, Mary 1943- *ConAu 8NR, –61*

Goswami, Amit 1936- *AmM&WS 73P, –76P, –79P, –82P, WhoAtom 77*

Gotlieb, Phyllis 1926- *Au&Wr 6, CanWW 79, –80, –81, –83, CanWr, ConAu 7NR, –13R, ConLC 18, ConP 70, –75, –80, ConSFA, CreCan 2, DcLEL 1940, EncSF, IntAu&W 76, –82, IntWWP 77, –82, OxCan, OxCan SUP, ScF&FL 1, –2, WhoAm 76, –78, –80, –82, WrDr 76, –80, –82, –84*

Gots, Ronald E 1943- *ConAu 65*

Gottesman, Ronald 1933- *ConAu 33R, DrAS 74E, –78E, –82E*

Gottschalk, Alfred 1930- *DrAS 82P, LEduc 74, WhoAm 74, –76, –78, –80, –82, WhoAmJ 80, WhoMW 80, –82, WhoRel 75, –77, WhoWor 74, –80, –82, WhoWorJ 72, –78*

Gottschalk, Elin Toona 1937- *ConAu 81*

Goudge, Elizabeth 1900-1984 *Au&Wr 6, AuBYP, BioIn 1, –2, –3, –4, –8, –9, –10, BlueB 76, ChhPo, ConAu 5R, –5NR, CurBio 40, InWom, IntAu&W 76, –77, LongCTC, NewC, REn, ScF&FL 1, –1A, –2, SmATA 2, ThrBJA, TwCA, TwCA SUP, TwCCW 78, –83, TwCWr, WhE&EA, Who 74, –82, –83, WhoAmW 74, –68, –70, –72, –75, WhoChL, WrDr 76, –80, –82, –84*

Goulart, Ron 1933- *BioIn 8, –10, ConAu 7NR, –25R, ConSFA, EncSF, IntAu&W 82, ScF&FL 1, –2, SmATA 6, TwCCr&M 80, WhoSciF, WrDr 82, –84*

Goulart, Ron *see also* Robeson, Kenneth

Gould, Jean Rosalind 1919?- *AuBYP, BioIn 7, –11, ConAu 3NR, –5R, IntAu&W 77, –82,*

OhA&B, SmATA 11, WhoAm 74, –76, –78, –80, –82, WhoAmW 74, –61, –64, WhoE 74, WrDr 76, –80, –82, –84

Gould, Joan 1927- *ConAu 107*

Gould, John 1908- *AmAu&B, BioIn 1, –4, –11, ChhPo S2, ConAu 65, REnAL, TwCA SUP, WhoAm 74, –76, –78, –80*

Gould, John A 1944- *ConAu 57*

Gould, Lilian 1920- *ConAu 2NR, –49, SmATA 6*

Gould, Stephen Jay 1941- *AmM&WS 73P, –76P, –79P, BioIn 11, –12, ConAu 10NR, –77, NewYTBS 83[port], WhoAm 78, –80*

Goulding, Ray 1922- *BioIn 3, –4, –5, –9, –10, CelR 73, ConAu 85, CurBio 57, WorAl*

Gove, Philip Babcock 1902-1972 *BioIn 6, –9, –10, ConAu 37R, ConAu P-1, CurBio 62, –73N, EncSF, LinLib L, NewYTBE 72, ScF&FL 1, –2, WhAm 5*

Graber, Richard 1927- *ConAu 85, SmATA 26[port]*

Graedon, Joe 1945- *ConAu 77*

Graff, S Stewart 1908- *AuBYP, ConAu 49, SmATA 9*

Graffman, Gary 1928- *Baker 78, BioIn 4, –7, –8, –9, –11, –12, BlueB 76, CurBio 70, IntWW 74, –75, –76, –77, –78, –79, –80, –81, –82, –83, IntWWM 77, MusSN, NewYTBE 72, –73, NewYTBS 81[port], WhoAm 74, –78, –80, –82, WhoAmM 83, WhoWor 74*

Graham, Ada 1931- *BioIn 11, ConAu 4NR, –29R, IntAu&W 77, –82, SmATA 11, WhoAmW 75, –77, WomPO 78, WrDr 76, –80, –82, –84*

Graham, Billy 1918- *BioIn 11, –12, BioNews 74, BlueB 76, CelR 73, ChhPo S1, ConAu X, CurBio 51, –73, EncSoB SUP, IntWW 74, –75, –76, –77, –78, –79, –80, –81, –82, –83, LinLib L, McGEWB, OxAmH, PolProf E, PolProf K, PolProf NF, WebAB, –79, Who 74, –82, –83, WhoAm 74, –76, –78, WhoRocM 82, WrDr 80, –82, –84*

Graham, Billy *see also* Graham, William Franklin

Graham, Brenda Knight 1942- *ConAu 103, SmATA 32[port]*

Graham, Frank, Jr. 1925- *AuBYP, BioIn 8, –11, ConAu 4NR, –9R, IntAu&W 76, SmATA 11, WhoE 74, –75, WrDr 76, –80, –82, –84*

Graham, Lorenz B 1902- *AuBYP SUP, BioIn 9, –10, BlkAWP, ConAu 9R, InB&W 80, IntAu&W 77, LivgBAA, MorBMP, REnAL, SelBAA, SmATA 2, ThrBJA, TwCCW 78, –83, WhoBlA 75, –77, –80, WrDr 80, –82*

Graham, Robin Lee 1949?- *BioIn 8, –10, ConAu 49, SmATA 7*

Graham, Shirley 1907?-1977 *AmAu&B, AmWomWr, AuBYP, BioIn 1, –4, –6, –8, –11, –12, BkCL, BlkAWP, ConAu X, –77,*

*CurBio 46, –77N, InB&W 80, InWom,
LivgBAA, MorJA, NegAl 76, –83,
SelBAA, SmATA X, Str&VC,
TwCA SUP, WhAm 7, WhoAm 74, –76,
WhoAmW 74, –58, –61, –64, –70, –72,
WhoBlA 75, –77*
Graham, Shirley *see also* DuBois, Shirley Graham
Graham, William Franklin 1918- *AmAu&B,
BioIn 2, –3, –4, –5, –6, –7, –8, –9, –10, –11,
–12, ChhPo S1, ConAu 9R, CurBio 51,
–73, DcAmSR, EncAAH, EncAB-H,
IntAu&W 77, IntWW 74, –75, –76, –77,
–78, –79, –83, LinLib S, WebAB,
Who 74, –83, WhoAm 74, –76, –78, –80,
WhoRel 75, –77, WhoWor 76, –78*
Graham, William Franklin *see also* Graham, Billy
Graham, Winston 1909?- *Au&Wr 6, BioIn 4,
ConAu 2NR, –49, ConLC 23[port],
ConNov 72, –76, –82, CurBio 55,
IntAu&W 76, –77, Novels, TwCCr&M 80,
TwCWr, WhE&EA, Who 74, –82, –83,
WrDr 76, –80, –82, –84*
Grahame, Kenneth 1859-1932 *AnCL, AtlBL,
AuBYP, BioIn 1, –2, –3, –5, –6, –7, –8, –9,
–11, –12, BkCL, CarSB, CasWL,
Chambr 3, ChlLR 5[port], ChhPo, –S1,
–S3, CnMWL, ConAu 108, CyWA,
DcLEL, EvLB, FamSYP, JBA 34,
LinLib L, LongCTC, ModBrL, NewC,
OxEng, PenC ENG, REn, ScF&FL 1A,
Str&VC, TwCA, TwCA SUP,
TwCCW 78, –83, TwCWr, WhDW,
WhLit, WhoChL, WorAl, YABC 1*
Gramet, Charles *AuBYP, BioIn 8,
ConAu 1R*
Granbeck, Marilyn 1927- *ConAu 77*
Granger, Peg 1925-1977 *AuBYP SUP*
Grant, Bruce 1893-1977 *AuBYP, BioIn 2, –7,
–10, –11, ConAu 1R, –6NR, –69,
SmATA 25N, –5*
Grant, Charles L 1942- *ConAu 85, EncSF,
WrDr 84*
Grant, Cynthia D 1950- *ConAu 104,
DrAP&F 83, SmATA 33[port]*
Grant, David 1942- *ConAu X, WrDr 84*
Grant, David *see also* Thomas, Craig
Grant, Joan 1907- *Au&Wr 6, BioIn 4, –8,
ConAu X, EncO&P 78, ScF&FL 1, –2,
TwCWr, WhE&EA, Who 74, –82, –83,
WhoHr&F*
Grant, Joan *see also* Kelsey, Joan Marshall
Grant, John 1933- *ConAu 77*
Grant, Madeleine Parker 1895- *AuBYP,
BioIn 8, ConAu 73, WhoAmW 58*
Grant, Michael 1914- *Au&Wr 6, BlueB 76,
ConAu 1R, –4NR, Who 74, –82, –83,
WrDr 76, –80, –82, –84*
Grant, Neil 1938- *BioIn 12, ConAu 33R,
SmATA 14, WrDr 76, –80, –82, –84*
Grant, Zalin 1941- *ConAu 73*
Grass, Gunter 1927- *BioIn 6, –7, –8, –9, –10,
–11, –12, CasWL, CelR 73, CnMD,*

*ConAu 13R, ConLC 1, –2, –4, –6, –11, –15,
–22[port], CroCD, CurBio 64, –83[port],
EncWL, –2[port], EncWT, EvEuW,
IntAu&W 76, –77, IntWW 74, –75, –76,
–77, –78, –79, –80, –81, –82, –83,
IntWWP 77, LinLib L, –S, MakMC,
McGEWB, McGEWD, –84[port], ModGL,
ModWD, Novels[port], OxGer,
PenC EUR, PrintW 83[port], REnWD,
TwCWr, WhDW, Who 74, –82, –83,
WhoWor 74, –78, –80, –82, WorAl,
WorAu*
Grau, Shirley Ann 1929- *AmAu&B,
AmWomWr, Au&Wr 6, AuNews 2,
BioIn 3, –5, –8, –9, –10, –11, –12, BlueB 76,
ConAu 1R, –89, ConLC 4, –9, ConNov 72,
–76, –82, CurBio 59, DcLB 2,
DcLEL 1940, DrAF 76, DrAP&F 83,
ForWC 70, InWom, IntAu&W 76, –77,
LibW, LinLib L, ModAL, Novels,
OxAmL, PenC AM, REn, REnAL,
WhoAm 74, –76, –78, –80, –82,
WhoAmW 74, –58, –61, –64, –66, –66A, –68,
–70, –72, –75, –77, –83, WhoE 74,
WhoWor 74, WorAl, WorAu, WrDr 76,
–80, –82, –84*
Graves, Charles Parlin 1911-1972 *AuBYP,
BioIn 8, –9, ConAu 4NR, –5R, –37R,
SmATA 4*
Graves, Charles Parlin *see also* Parlin, John
Graves, Charles Patrick Ranke 1899- *Au&Wr 6,
BioIn 2, WhE&EA*
Graves, John 1920- *ConAu 1R, –9NR, –13R,
DcLB Y83B[port]*
Graves, Robert 1895- *AnCL, Au&Wr 6,
AuBYP, BioIn 1, –2, –4, –5, –6, –7, –8, –9,
–10, –11, –12, BlueB 76, CasWL, ChhPo,
–S1, –S2, –S3, CnE&AP, CnMWL,
ConAu 5R, –5NR, ConLC 1, –2, –6, –11,
ConLCrt, –82, ConNov 72, –76, –82,
ConP 70, –75, –80, CurBio 78, CyWA,
DcLB 20[port], DcLEL, EncSF, EncWL,
–2[port], EvLB, IntAu&W 76, –82,
IntWW 74, –75, –76, –77, –78, –79, –80, –81,
–82, –83, IntWWP 77, LinLib L, –S,
LongCEL, LongCTC, MakMC,
McGEWB, ModBrL, ModBrL SUP,
NewC, Novels[port], OxEng, PenC ENG,
RAdv 1, REn, ScF&FL 1, –2, TwCA,
TwCA SUP, TwCWr, WebE&AL,
WhDW, WhE&EA, WhLit, Who 74, –82,
–83, WhoTwCL, WhoWor 74, –76, –78,
–82, WorAl, WrDr 76, –80, –82, –84*
Graves, Susan B 1933- *ConAu 41R*
Gray, Bettyanne 1934- *ConAu 81*
Gray, Charles A 1938- *AmM&WS 73P, –79P,
–82P, ConAu 17R, WrDr 76*
Gray, Elizabeth Janet 1902- *AmAu&B, AnCL,
AuBYP, BioIn 1, –2, –3, –4, –5, –7, –10, –11,
ConAu X, InWom, JBA 34, –51,
Newb 1922, SmATA 6, TwCCW 83,
WrDr 82, –84*

Gray, Elizabeth Janet *see also* Vining, Elizabeth
   Gray
Gray, Genevieve S 1920-   *BioIn 9, ConAu 33R,
   SmATA 4*
Gray, Lee Learner 1924-   *AuBYP SUP,
   ConAu 73*
Gray, Michael 1946-   *IntAu&W 76,
   WhoWest 84*
Gray, Nicholas Stuart 1922-1981
   *AnObit 1981[port], AuBYP SUP, BioIn 9,
   –10, ConAu 103, –11NR, –21R,
   IntAu&W 76, –77, PiP, ScF&FL 1, –2,
   SmATA 27N, –4, TwCCW 78, –83,
   WhoThe 15, –16, –81, WrDr 76, –80, –82*
Gray, Ronald 1919-   *ConAu 7NR, –17R*
Gray, Simon 1936-   *Au&Wr 6, AuNews 1,
   BioIn 10, –11, –12, BioNews 74, CnThe,
   ConAu 21R, ConDr 73, –77, –82,
   ConLC 9, –14, ConNov 72, –76, –82,
   CreCan 2, CurBio 83[port],
   DcLB 13[port], DcLEL 1940, EncWT,
   IntAu&W 76, –77, IntWW 81, –82, –83,
   McGEWD 84, NotNAT, OxCan,
   OxCan SUP, PlP&P A, Who 74, –82, –83,
   WhoEc, WhoThe 15, –16, –81, WrDr 76,
   –80, –82, –84*
Gray, Vanessa   *ConAu X*
Gray, William R 1946-   *ConAu 97,
   IntAu&W 82*
Grayson, Melvin Jay 1924-   *ConAu 45,
   WhoF&I 74, –75, –77, –81, –83,
   WhoWor 82*
Greaves, Griselda   *ChhPo S2*
Greaves, Margaret 1914-   *Au&Wr 6,
   AuBYP SUP, BioIn 10, ConAu 25R,
   SmATA 7, TwCCW 78, –83, WrDr 76,
   –80, –82, –84*
Greeley, Andrew M 1928-   *AmCath 80,
   AmM&WS 73S, –78S, BioIn 9, –10, –11,
   –12, BlueB 76, ConAu 5R, –7NR,
   CurBio 72, LEduc 74,
   NewYTBS 81[port], –82[port], WhoAm 74,
   –76, –78, –80, –82, WhoRel 77, WrDr 80,
   –82, –84*
Green, Constance McLaughlin 1897-1975
   *AmAu&B, BioIn 6, –10, –12, ConAu 9R,
   –61, CurBio 63, DrAS 74H, EncAAH,
   ForWC 70, LinLib L, NewYTBS 75,
   NotAW MOD, ObitOF 79, OxAmL,
   WhAm 6, WhoAm 74, –76, WhoAmW 74,
   –70, –72, WhoWor 74, WrDr 76, –80, –82*
Green, Fitzhugh 1888-1947   *AmAu&B, BioIn 2,
   CarSB, DcNAA, NatCAB 36,
   ScF&FL 1, WhAm 2, WhNAA*
Green, Fitzhugh 1917-   *ConAu 77, WhoAm 74,
   –76, –78, –80, WhoGov 77, –72, –75,
   WhoWor 74, –76, –78, –80, –82*
Green, Gerald 1922-   *AmAu&B, ASpks,
   BioIn 4, –6, –8, –9, –10, –11, ConAu 8NR,
   –13R, WhoAm 74, –76, –78, –80, –82,
   WhoWor 74, WorAu, WrDr 80, –82, –84*
Green, Hannah 1932-   *BioIn 12, DrAF 76,*

SmATA X
Green, Hannah *see also* Greenberg, Joanne
Green, Margaret Murphy 1926-   *AuBYP,
   BioIn 8, ConAu 1R, –1NR, ForWC 70,
   WhoAmW 75*
Green, Mark J 1945-   *BioIn 10, –12,
   ConAu 41R, NewYTBS 80[port],
   WhoAm 80, –82*
Green, Martyn 1899-1975   *BiE&WWA,
   BioIn 1, –2, –3, –5, –10, ConAu 57,
   CurBio 50, –75N, –76, FilmgC,
   NewYTBS 75, NotNAT A, –B,
   ObitOF 79, ObitT 1971, WhScrn 2,
   WhoHol C, WhoThe 15, –16*
Green, Paul 1894-1981   *AmAu&B,
   AmSCAP 66, AnObit 1981[port],
   Au&Wr 6, AuNews 1, BiE&WWA,
   BioIn 2, –3, –4, –5, –8, –9, –10, –12,
   BlueB 76, CnDAL, CnMD, CnThe,
   ConAmA, ConAmL, ConAu 3NR, –5R,
   –103, ConDr 73, –77, –82,
   ConLC 25[port], DcLB Y81A[port],
   –7[port], –9[port], DcLEL, EncWL,
   EncWT, IntAu&W 76, –77, –82,
   IntWW 74, –75, –76, –77, –78, –79, –80, –81,
   –81N, LongCTC, McGEWD, –84,
   ModAL, ModWD, NewYTBS 81[port],
   NotNAT, –A, OxAmL, OxThe,
   PenC AM, PlP&P, REn, REnAL,
   REnWD, TwCA, TwCA SUP, WebAB,
   –79, WebE&AL, WhAm 7, WhE&EA,
   WhLit, WhNAA, Who 74, –82N,
   WhoAm 74, –76, –78, –80, WhoThe 15, –16,
   –81, WhoWor 74, WrDr 76, –80, –82, –84*
Green, Peter   *ConAu X*
Green, Peter Morris 1924-   *Au&Wr 6, ChhPo,
   –S3, ConAu 4NR, –5R, ConNov 72, –76,
   DcLEL 1940, DrAS 78F, –82F,
   IntAu&W 76, –77, –82, Who 74, –82, –83,
   WrDr 76, –80, –82, –84*
Green, Phyllis 1932-   *BioIn 12, ConAu 1NR,
   –45, MichAu 80, SmATA 20*
Green, Roger Curtis 1932-   *AmM&WS 73S,
   –76P, ConAu 45, FifIDA*
Green, Roger Lancelyn 1918-   *Au&Wr 6,
   AuBYP, BioIn 8, –9, ChhPo, –S1, –S2, –S3,
   ConAu 1R, –2NR, IntAu&W 76, –77,
   ScF&FL 1, –2, SmATA 2, ThrBJA,
   TwCCW 78, –83, WhE&EA, Who 82, –83,
   WhoChL, WrDr 80, –82, –84*
Green, Roland 1944-   *ConAu 77,
   IntAu&W 77, ScF&FL 1, –2*
Green, Timothy 1936-   *Au&Wr 6,
   ConAu 5NR, –49, WrDr 76, –80, –82, –84*
Greenbank, Anthony Hunt 1933-   *ConAu 4NR,
   –49*
Greenberg, Alvin 1932-   *ConAu 33R, DrAF 76,
   DrAP 75, DrAP&F 83, DrAS 74E, –78E,
   –82E, IntWWP 77, –82, WrDr 76, –80,
   –82, –84*
Greenberg, Eliezer 1896?-1977   *BioIn 11, –12,
   CasWL, ConAu 69, NewYTBS 77,*

WhoWorJ 72

Greenberg, Harvey R 1935- *BiDrAPA 77,
BioIn 10, ConAu 33R, SmATA 5*

Greenberg, Joanne 1932- *AmAu&B,
AmWomWr, BioIn 12, ConAu 5R,
ConLC 7, DrAF 76, DrAP&F 83,
SmATA 25[port], WhoAm 74, -76, -78,
-80, -82, WhoAmJ 80, WhoAmW 74, -68,
-70, -72, WrDr 80, -82, -84*

Greenberg, Joanne *see also* Green, Hannah

Greenberg, Martin Harry 1941-
*AmM&WS 73S, BiDrAPA 77, ConAu 49,
EncSF, IntAu&W 77, ScF&FL 1, -2*

Greenberg, Saul Norman 1923- *WhoE 74*

Greenberg, Sylvia S *AmM&WS 73P*

Greene, A C 1923- *ConAu 37R, IntAu&W 77,
WhoAm 74, -76, -78, -80, -82, WrDr 76,
-80, -82, -84*

Greene, Bette 1934- *AuBYP SUP, BioIn 11,
ChlLR 2, ConAu 4NR, -53, DrAP&F 83,
SmATA 8, TwCCW 78, -83, WhoAm 78,
-80, -82, WhoAmJ 80, WrDr 76, -80, -82,
-84*

Greene, Bob 1946?- *BioIn 10, ConAu X*

Greene, Constance C 1924- *AuBYP SUP,
BioIn 11, -12, ConAu 8NR, -61, FourBJA,
SmATA 11, TwCCW 78, -83, WrDr 80,
-82, -84*

Greene, Felix 1909- *Au&Wr 6, ConAu 1R,
-6NR, Who 82, -83*

Greene, Graham 1904- *Au&Wr 6,
AuBYP SUP, AuNews 2, BiE&WWA,
BioIn 1, -2, -3, -4, -5, -6, -7, -8, -9, -10,
-11, -12, BioNews 74, BlueB 76, CasWL,
CathA 1930, CelR 73, ChhPo S2,
CnMD, CnMWL, CnThe, ConAu 13R,
ConDr 73, -77, -82, ConLC 1, -3, -6, -9,
-14, -18, -27[port], ConNov 72, -76, -82,
CorpD, CroCD, CurBio 69, CyWA,
DcLB 13[port], -15[port], EncMys,
EncWL, -2[port], EncWT, FilmgC,
IntAu&W 76, -77, IntWW 74, -75, -76,
-77, -78, -79, -80, -81, -82, -83, LinLib L,
-S, LongCTC, MakMC, McGEWB,
McGEWD, -84, ModBrL, ModBrL SUP,
ModWD, NewC, NewYTBE 71,
NotNAT, -A, Novels[port], OxEng,
OxFilm, OxThe, PenC ENG, PIP&P,
RAdv 1, REn, ScF&FL 1, -2,
SmATA 20, TwCA, TwCA SUP,
TwCCW 78, TwCCr&M 80, TwCWr,
WebE&AL, WhDW, WhE&EA, Who 74,
-82, -83, WhoAm 80, -82, WhoChL,
WhoFr 79, WhoSpyF, WhoThe 15, -16,
-81, WhoTwCL, WhoWor 74, -76, -78,
-80, -82, WorAl, WorEFlm, WrDr 76,
-80, -82, -84*

Greene, Howard Rodger 1937- *ConAu 61,
WhoE 77, -79, -81*

Greene, Sir Hugh 1910- *BioIn 6, -7, BlueB 76,
ConAu 102, CurBio 63, IntAu&W 77,
-82, IntWW 74, -75, -76, -77, -78, -79,*

*-80, -81, -82, -83, IntYB 78, -79, -80, -81,
-82, WhE&EA, Who 74, -82, -83,
WhoAm 74, -76, -78, WhoWor 74, -76,
-78, WrDr 82, -84*

Greene, Laura 1935- *ConAu 107*

Greenebaum, Louise G 1919- *ConAu 69,
WomPO 76*

Greenfeld, Howard *AuBYP SUP, BioIn 10,
-12, ConAu 81, SmATA 19*

Greenfeld, Josh 1927?- *BioIn 12*

Greenfield, Eloise 1929- *BioIn 10, -12,
BlkAWP, ChlLR 4[port], ConAu 1NR,
-49, InB&W 80, IntAu&W 77, -82,
LivgBAA, SelBAA, SmATA 19,
TwCCW 83, WhoAm 78, -80, -82,
WhoBlA 77, -80, WrDr 76, -80, -82, -84*

Greenfield, Jeff 1943- *BioIn 8, -10,
ConAu 37R*

Greenleaf, Barbara Kaye 1942- *BioIn 10,
ConAu 29R, SmATA 6, WhoAmW 75,
-77, -79*

Greenspan, Bud 1926?- *BioIn 10, ConAu 103,
LesBEnT, WhoAm 76, -78*

Greenwald, Jerry 1923- *ConAu 57*

Greenwald, Sheila 1934- *BioIn 8, -11, ChhPo,
ConAu X, IlsBYP, IlsCB 1957,
SmATA 8, WhoAmA 78, -80, -82,
WhoAmW 75*

Greenway, James Cowan, Jr. 1903- *WhoAm 74*

Greer, Germaine 1939- *ASpks, AuNews 1,
BioIn 9, -10, -11, -12, BioNews 75,
BlueB 76, CelR 73, ConAu 81,
CurBio 71, DcLEL 1940, IntAu&W 76,
-77, IntDcWB, IntWW 74, -75, -76, -77,
-78, -79, -80, -81, -82, -83, MakMC,
NewYTBE 71, Who 82, -83, WhoAm 78,
-80, -82, WhoAmW 74, -75, -77, -81, -83,
WhoWor 74, -76, -78, WrDr 76, -80, -82,
-84*

Greet, W Cabell *ConAu 37R, NewYTBE 72*

Gregg, Charles T 1927- *AmM&WS 73P, -76P,
-79P, -82P, ConAu 81*

Gregg, James R 1914- *AmM&WS 73P, -76P,
-79P, -82P, ConAu 21R*

Gregor, Arthur 1923- *ConAu 11NR, -25R,
ConLC 9, ConP 70, -75, -80, DrAP 75,
DrAP&F 83, IntAu&W 76, -77,
IntWWP 77, LinLib L, SmATA 36,
WhoAm 74, -76, -78, -80, -82,
WhoAmJ 80, WhoE 83, WrDr 76, -80,
-82, -84*

Gregorian, Joyce Ballou 1946- *ConAu 107,
SmATA 30[port]*

Gregory, Diana 1933- *ConAu 97*

Gregory, Dick 1932- *AmAu&B, BioIn 5, -6,
-7, -8, -9, -10, -11, -12, BioNews 74,
BlueB 76, CelR 73, CivR 74, CivRSt,
ConAu 7NR, -45, CurBio 62, DrBlPA,
Ebony 1, LivgBAA, NegAl 76[port],
-83[port], NotNAT A, PolProf J,
UFOEn, WhoAm 74, -76, -78, -80, -82,
WhoAmP 73, -75, -77, -79, -81, -83,*

WhoBlA 75, –77, WhoHol A, WorAl,
WrDr 76, –80, –82, –84
Gregory, Horace 1898-1982 *AmAu&B,*
AnObit 1982[port], BioIn 4, –5, –9, –12,
BlueB 76, ChhPo, –S1, –S2, CnDAL,
ConAmA, ConAu 3NR, –5R, –106,
ConP 70, –75, –80, DcLEL, DrAP 75,
IntAu&W 77, IntWW 74, –75, –76, –77,
–78, –79, –80, –81, –82, –83N, IntWWP 77,
LinLib L, ModAL, NewYTBS 82,
OxAmL, PenC AM, RAdv 1, REn,
REnAL, SixAP, TwCA, TwCA SUP,
WhoAm 74, –76, –78, –80, –82, WhoE 74,
WhoWor 74, WrDr 76, –80, –82
Gregory, Stephen 1942- *ConAu X*
Gregory, Stephen *see also* Penzler, Otto M
Greiner, James Duane 1933- *WhoWest 76, –78*
Gresham, William Lindsay 1909-1962
AmAu&B, BioIn 1, –2, –4, –6,
TwCA SUP
Grey, Beryl 1927- *Au&Wr 6, BioIn 1, –2, –3,*
–4, –5, –7, –11, –12, BlueB 76, ConAu 109,
InWom, IntAu&W 76, –77, –82, IntDcWB,
IntWW 74, –75, –76, –77, –78, –79, –80, –81,
–82, –83, WhThe, Who 74, –82, –83,
WhoWor 74, –76, –78, –80, –82, WrDr 76,
–80, –82, –84
Grey, Elizabeth 1917- *Au&Wr 6, AuBYP,*
BioIn 8, ConAu X
Grey, Elizabeth *see also* Hogg, Beth
Grey, Ian 1918- *Au&Wr 6, ConAu 2NR, –5R,*
IntAu&W 76, –77, –82, WhoWor 76,
WrDr 76, –80, –82, –84
Grey, Jerry 1926- *AmM&WS 73P, –79P, –82P,*
BioIn 11, ConAu 5NR, –53, IntWWE,
SmATA 11, WhoAm 74, –76, –78, –80, –82,
WhoE 74, –83, WhoTech 82, WhoWor 74,
WrDr 82, –84
Grey, Zane 1872?-1939 *AmAu&B, AmBi,*
ArizL, BioIn 1, –2, –3, –4, –5, –6, –7, –8, –9,
–10, –11, –12, CmCal, ConAu 104,
DcAmB S2, DcLB 9[port], DcLEL,
DcNAA, EncAAH, EvLB, FilmgC,
LinLib L, LongCTC, MnBBF,
Novels[port], OhA&B, OxAmL,
PenC AM, REn, REnAL, REnAW,
TwCA, TwCA SUP, TwCLC 6[port],
TwCWr, WebAB, –79, WebE&AL,
WhAm 1, WhE&EA, WhLit, WhNAA,
WorAl
Grice, Frederick 1910- *Au&Wr 6, BioIn 10,*
ConAu 3NR, –9R, IntAu&W 77, –82,
SmATA 6, TwCCW 78, –83, WrDr 76,
–80, –82, –84
Gridley, Marion Eleanor 1906-1974
AuBYP SUP, BioIn 2, ConAu 103, –45,
ForWC 70, SmATA 26N, –35, WhAm 6,
WhoAmW 68, –70, –75
Grierson, John 1909-1977 *BioIn 11, ConAu 69,*
ConAu P-2, IntAu&W 77, NewYTBS 77,
WhE&EA, WrDr 76
Griffin, Alice 1924- *DrAS 74E, –78E, –82E*

Griffin, Donald 1915- *AmM&WS 73P, –76P,*
–79P, –82P, BlueB 76, ConAu 37R,
IntAu&W 77, –82, IntWW 74, –75, –76,
–77, –78, –79, –80, –81, –82, –83,
WhoAm 74, –80, –82, WhoE 83, WrDr 76,
–80, –82, –84
Griffin, John Howard 1920-1980 *AmAu&B,*
AmCath 80, AnObit 1980[port],
Au&Wr 6, AuNews 1, BioIn 3, –4, –5, –6,
–9, –10, –11, –12, BlueB 76, ConAu 1R,
–2NR, –101, CurBio 60, –80N,
IntAu&W 76, LinLib L, –S,
NewYTBS 80, Novels, WhAm 7,
WhoAm 74, –76, –78, –80, WhoRel 75, –77,
WhoWor 74, WorAu, WrDr 76, –80, –82
Griffin, John Q 1948- *ConAu 77*
Griffin, Judith Berry *AuBYP SUP, BlkAWP,*
ConAu 108, SmATA 34[port]
Griffin, Susan 1943- *AmWomWr, BioIn 12,*
ConAu 3NR, –49, DrAF 76, DrAP 75,
DrAP&F 83, IntAu&W 77, –82,
IntWWP 77, –82, NatPD, –81[port]
Griffith, A Kinney 1897- *ConAu 1R, WhNAA*
Griffith, Field *AuBYP SUP*
Griffiths, G D 1910-1973 *ConAu P-2,*
SmATA 20N, TwCCW 78, –83
Griffiths, Gordon Douglas 1910-1973 *Au&Wr 6,*
BioIn 12
Griffiths, Helen 1939- *AuBYP SUP,*
ConAu 7NR, –17R, FourBJA,
IntAu&W 82, SmATA 5, TwCCW 78,
–83, WrDr 80, –82, –84
Griffiths, John C 1934- *ConAu 108, Who 83*
Grigson, Geoffrey 1905- *Au&Wr 6, AuBYP,*
BioIn 2, –4, –8, BlueB 76, ChhPo, –S1,
–S2, ConAu 25R, ConLC 7, ConP 70,
–75, –80, DcLEL, EvLB, IntAu&W 76,
–77, IntWW 74, –75, –76, –77, –78, –79,
–80, –81, –82, –83, IntWWP 77, –82,
LongCTC, ModBrL, ModBrL SUP,
NewC, PenC ENG, REn, TwCA SUP,
WhE&EA, Who 74, –82, –83, WhoTwCL,
WhoWor 74, –78, WrDr 76, –80, –82, –84
Grigson, Jane 1928- *ConAu 1NR, –49,*
IntAu&W 77, –82, Who 82, –83,
WrDr 80, –82, –84
Grimm, Jakob Ludwig Karl 1785-1863 *AnCL,*
AtlBL, AuBYP, BbD, BiD&SB, BioIn 1,
–3, –6, –7, –8, –9, –12, CarSB, CasWL,
ChhPo, –S3, DcEuL, EuAu, EvEuW,
FamSYP, FilmgC, LinLib L, –S,
McGEWB, NewC, NewEOp 71, OxEng,
OxGer, PenC EUR, REn, Str&VC,
WhoChL
Grimm, Wilhelm Karl 1786-1859 *AnCL, AtlBL,*
AuBYP, BiD&SB, BioIn 1, –3, –6, –7, –8,
–9, –12, CarSB, CasWL, ChhPo, –S2, –S3,
DcBiPP, DcEuL, Dis&D, EuAu, EvEuW,
FamSYP, FilmgC, LinLib L, McGEWB,
OxEng, OxGer, PenC EUR, REn,
SmATA 22[port], Str&VC, WhDW,
WorAl

Grimm, William Carey 1907- *BioIn 12,*
ConAu 49, SmATA 14

Grinnell, George Bird 1849-1938 *AmAu&B,*
AmBi, AmLY, BbD, BiD&SB, BioIn 2,
-4, -9, -12, CarSB, DcAmAu, DcAmB S2,
DcNAA, EncAAH, JBA 34, -51,
NatCAB 13, -30, OxAmL, REnAL,
REnAW, SmATA 16, Str&VC,
TwCBDA, WebAB, -79, WhAm 1,
WhLit, WhNAA

Grinspoon, Lester 1928- *AmM&WS 79P, -82P,*
BiDrAPA 77, ConAu 81, WhoE 81

Gripe, Maria 1923- *AuBYP SUP, BioIn 9,*
ChlLR 5[port], ConAu 29R,
IntAu&W 76, -77, -82, ScF&FL 1,
SmATA 2, ThrBJA, TwCCW 78B, -83B

Grissom, Virgil Ivan 1926-1967 *BioIn 5, -6, -7,*
-8, -9, -10, -12, CurBio 65, -67, WhAm 4,
WorAl

Griswold, Wesley S 1909- *ConAu 1R*

Groch, Judith 1929- *AuBYP, BioIn 8,*
ConAu 9R, SmATA 25[port],
WhoAmW 74, -72, -75

Grohskopf, Bernice 1921- *AuBYP SUP,*
BioIn 10, ChhPo, -S3, ConAu 3NR, -5R,
DrAP&F 83, ForWC 70, IntAu&W 76,
-77, -82, SmATA 7, WrDr 76, -80, -82,
-84

Gropman, Donald S 1936- *ConAu 101*

Groseclose, Elgin 1899-1983 *AmAu&B,*
AmM&WS 73S, -78S, AmNov, BioIn 2,
BlueB 76, ConAu 109, ConAu P-2,
IntAu&W 76, -77, -82, NewYTBS 83,
WhoAm 74, -76, -78, -80, -82,
WhoCon 73, WhoRel 75, -77,
WhoWor 74, -80, -82, WrDr 76, -80, -82,
-84

Gross, Joel 1949?- *BioIn 9, ConAu 29R,*
WrDr 76, -80, -82, -84

Gross, Leonard 1922- *WhoWest 84*

Gross, Milton 1911?-1973 *BioIn 6, -9,*
ConAu 41R

Gross, Nathalie Friedland 1919- *WhoAdv 72,*
WhoAmW 72

Gross, Samuel Harry 1933- *ConAu 45*

Grosser, Morton 1931- *ConAu 97, ScF&FL 1*

Grosswirth, Marvin 1931- *ConAu 33R,*
WhoWorJ 72, -78

Groussard, Serge 1921- *ConAu 108,*
IntAu&W 76, -77, IntWW 74, -75, -76,
-77, -78, -79, -80, -81, -82, -83, REn,
WhoFr 79, WhoWor 74, -76, -78

Grove, Fred 1913- *ConAu 1R, -2NR,*
IntAu&W 76, -77, -82, WrDr 84

Groves, Ernest Rutherford 1877-1946 *AmAu&B,*
BioIn 1, CurBio 43, -46, DcNAA,
WhAm 2, WhNAA

Grubb, Davis 1919-1980 *AmAu&B, Au&Wr 6,*
BioIn 6, -12, ConAu 1R, -4NR, -101,
DcLB 6, NewYTBS 80[port], ScF&FL 2,
WhoHr&F

Gruber, Gary R 1940- *AmM&WS 76P, -79P,*

ConAu 9NR, -53

Gruber, Ruth *BioIn 1, -2, ConAu 25R,*
ForWC 70, WhoAmW 58, -61, -64, -66,
WhoWorJ 72, -78

Gruber, Terry 1953- *ConAu 97*

Gruen, John 1926- *BioIn 8, -9, ConAmC,*
ConAu 8NR, -17R, WhoAmA 76, -78, -80,
-82

Grumbach, Doris 1918- *AmWomWr, BioIn 12,*
ConAu 5R, -9NR, ConLC 13, -22[port],
DrAP&F 83, DrAS 74E, -78E, -82E,
ForWC 70, WhoAm 78, -80, -82,
WrDr 84

Grun, Max Von Der 1926- *BioIn 12, OxGer*

Grund, Josef Carl 1920- *ConAu 73*

Grzimek, Bernhard 1906?- *BioIn 9, -10,*
CurBio 73, IntAu&W 77

Guard, David 1934- *ConAu 77*

Guareschi, Giovanni 1908-1968 *BioIn 2, -3, -4,*
-7, -8, -9, CathA 1952, ConAu 105, -25R,
EncWL, FilmgC, ModRL, ObitOF 79,
ScF&FL 1, TwCA SUP, TwCWr,
WhDW, WhAm 5, WorECar

Guerber, Helene Adeline 1859-1929 *AmLY,*
BiD&SB, DcAmAu, DcNAA, HarEnUS,
WhAm 1, WhNAA, WomWWA 14

Guess, Edward Preston 1925- *ConAu 73*

Guest, Judith 1936- *BioIn 10, -11, -12,*
ConAu 77, ConLC 8, DrAP&F 83,
MichAu 80, WhoAm 78, -80, -82,
WrDr 80, -82, -84

Guffy, Ossie 1931- *BioIn 9, InB&W 80*

Gugliotta, Bobette 1918- *BioIn 10,*
ConAu 41R, SmATA 7

Guild, Nicholas M 1944- *ConAu 93*

Guillaume, Alfred 1888- *ConAu P-1,*
WhE&EA, WhLit, WhoLA

Guillaumin, Emile 1873-1951 *BioIn 2, -3,*
OxFr

Guillen, Jorge 1893- *BioIn 1, -4, -8, -10, -11,*
-12, CasWL, ClDMEL, CnMWL,
ConAu 89, ConLC 11, DcSpL, EncWL,
-2[port], EvEuW, LinLib L, MakMC,
ModRL, OxSpan, PenC EUR, REn,
TwCWr, WhoTwCL, WorAu

Guillen, Nicolas 1902- *EncWL 2, IntWW 83*

Guillot, Rene 1900-1969 *AuBYP, BioIn 6, -7,*
-8, -10, -11, ConAu 49, MorJA,
ScF&FL 1, -2, SmATA 7, TwCCW 78B,
-83B, WhoChL

Guisewite, Cathy Lee 1950- *BioIn 11,*
WhoAm 80, -82, WhoAmW 81

Gulick, Bill 1916- *ConAu X*

Gulick, Bill see also Gulick, Grover C

Gulick, Grover C 1916- *ConAu 33R,*
WhoPNW

Gulik, Robert Hans Van 1910-1967 *BioIn 8,*
ConAu X, CorpD

Gulik, Robert Hans Van see also Van Gulik,
Robert H

Gummere, Richard M, Jr. 1912- *ConAu 45*

Gunderson, Keith 1935- *ConAu 33R,*

DrAP 75, DrAP&F 83, DrAS 74P, –78P,
–82P, WhoAm 74
Gunn, James E 1923- BioIn 12, ConAu 5NR,
–9R, ConSFA, DcLB 8[port], DrAF 76,
DrAP&F 83, EncSF, IntAu&W 76, –82,
ScF&FL 1, –2, SmATA 35, WhoSciF,
WrDr 76, –80, –82, –84
Gunn, Thom 1929- AmAu&B, Au&Wr 6,
BioIn 10, –12, BlueB 76, CasWL, ChhPo,
–S1, –S2, CnE&AP, ConAu 9NR, –17R,
ConLC 3, –6, –18, ConP 70, –75, –80,
DrAP 75, DrAP&F 83, IntAu&W 77,
–82, IntWW 74, –75, –76, –77, –78, –79,
–80, –81, –82, –83, IntWWP 82X,
LinLib L, LongCTC, ModBrL,
ModBrL SUP, NewC, PenC ENG,
RAdv 1, REn, TwCWr, WebE&AL,
WhoAm 74, –76, –78, –80, –82, WhoTwCL,
WorAu, WrDr 76, –80, –82, –84
Gunston, Bill 1927- Au&Wr 6, BioIn 11,
ConAu X, –49, IntAu&W 76, –77, –82,
SmATA X, WrDr 76, –80, –82, –84
Gunston, Bill see also Gunston, William Tudor
Gunston, David Au&Wr 6, IntAu&W 76
Gunston, William Tudor 1927- AuBYP SUP,
BioIn 11, ConAu 3NR, –49, SmATA 9,
WrDr 76, –80
Gunston, William Tudor see also Gunston, Bill
Gunther, John 1901-1970 AmAu&B, AmNov,
AuBYP, BioIn 1, –2, –3, –4, –5, –6, –7, –8,
–9, ConAu 9R, –25R, CurBio 41, –61, –70,
DcAmDH, EvLB, LinLib L, –S,
LongCTC, NewYTBE 70, ObitOF 79,
ObitT 1961, OxAmL, PenC AM, REn,
REnAL, ScF&FL 1, –2, SmATA 2,
TwCA, TwCA SUP, WebAB, –79,
WhAm 6, WorAl
Gurko, Leo 1914- BioIn 9, –11, ConAu 5R,
–5NR, DrAS 74E, –78E, –82E, SmATA 9,
ThrBJA, WhoAm 74, –76
Gurko, Miriam BioIn 9, –11, ConAu 1R,
SmATA 9, ThrBJA, WrDr 76, –80, –82,
–84
Gurney, A R, Jr. 1930- ConAu 77, ConDr 77,
–82, DrAP&F 83, NatPD, –81[port],
NewYTBS 82[port], ScF&FL 1,
WhoThe 81, WrDr 80, –82, –84
Gurney, Gene 1924- ConAu 5R, –9NR
Gustafson, Elton T AuBYP, BioIn 8
Gutcheon, Beth R 1945- BioIn 12,
ConAu 2NR, –49
Gutheim, Frederick 1908- AmAu&B, BioIn 11,
ConAu 9NR, –21R, WhoAm 74, –76, –78,
–80, –82
Guthrie, A B, Jr. 1901- CmMov, ConAu 57,
ConLC 23[port], ConNov 82, CurBio 50,
DcLB 6, DrAP&F 83, IntAu&W 76, –77,
Novels, REnAW, WrDr 76, –80, –82, –84
Guthrie, Alfred Bertram, Jr. 1901- AmAu&B,
AmNov, BioIn 2, –4, –5, –7, –8, –10,
CnDAL, ConAu 57, ConNov 72, –76,
CyWA, DcLEL, –1940, DrAF 76,

IndAu 1917, ModAL, OxAmL, REnAL,
TwCA SUP, WhoAm 74, –76, –78, –80,
–82, WhoPNW, WhoWest 74, –76,
WhoWor 74, WrDr 76
Guthrie, Anne 1890-1979 AuBYP, BioIn 7,
ConAu 5R, SmATA 28, WhoAmW 61,
–64
Guthrie, Arlo 1947- AmAu&B, BiDAmM,
BioIn 7, –8, –9, –11, –12, CelR 73,
CurBio 82[port], EncFCWM 69, IlEncRk,
RkOn 78, WhoAm 74, –76, –78, –80, –82,
WhoHol A, WhoRocM 82, WorAl
Guthrie, Sir Tyrone 1900-1971 BiE&WWA,
BioIn 3, –4, –5, –6, –8, –9, –10, –11, –12,
CnThe, ConAu 29R, CreCan 1,
CurBio 54, –71, –71N, DcIrB, EncWT,
LinLib S, NewC, NewYTBE 71,
NotNAT A, –B, ObitOF 79, ObitT 1971,
OxThe, PIP&P, WhThe, WhoHol B,
WhoThe 15, WorAl
Guthrie, Woody 1912-1967 AmAu&B,
Baker 78, BioIn 6, –7, –8, –9, –10, –11, –12,
CmpEPM, ConAu X, CurBio 63, –67,
EncFCWM 69, IlEncRk, ObitOF 79,
REnAW, RolSEnR 83, WebAB, –79,
WhAm 4, WhoRocM 82, WorAl
Gutman, Bill AuBYP SUP
Gutman, Herbert George 1928- ConAu 65,
DrAS 74H, –78H, –82H, WhoAm 80, –82
Gutman, Judith Mara 1928- ConAu 21R,
WhoAmW 74, –75, –83, WrDr 76, –80, –82,
–84
Gutnik, Martin J 1942- ConAu 3NR, –49
Gutteridge, Lindsay 1923- ConAu 49, EncSF,
ScF&FL 1, –2, WrDr 80, –82, –84
Guy, David 1948- ConAu 105
Guy, Rosa 1928- BioIn 12, BlkAWP,
ConAu 17R, ConLC 26[port], InB&W 80,
SelBAA, SmATA 14, TwCCW 78, –83,
WrDr 80, –82, –84
Gzowski, Peter 1934- ConAu 106

H

Haar, Jaap Ter 1922- *BioIn 10, FourBJA*
Haar, Jaap Ter *see also* Ter Haar, Jaap
Haas, Gerda 1922- *ConAu 110*
Haas, Kenneth B, Sr. 1898- *ConAu 6NR, -57*
Habberton, William 1899- *AuBYP, BioIn 8*
Habel, Norman C 1932- *ConAu 17R,*
  DrAS 74P
Habeler, Peter 1942- *BioIn 11, -12*
Habenstreit, Barbara 1937- *AuBYP SUP,*
  BioIn 10, ConAu 29R, SmATA 5
Haber, Eitan 1940- *ConAu 104*
Haber, Louis 1910- *BioIn 11, ConAu 29R,*
  SmATA 12, WhoE 75
Habig, Marion Alphonse 1901- *AmCath 80,*
  BioIn 1, BkC 2, CathA 1930, ConAu 5R,
  -5NR, DrAS 74H, -78H, -82H,
  IntAu&W 77, WhoRel 75, -77, WrDr 76,
  -80, -82, -84
Hacker, Frederick J 1914- *BiDrAPA 77,*
  ConAu 104
Hackett, Albert 1900- *AmAu&B, AuBYP,*
  BiE&WWA, BioIn 4, -8, -11, CmMov,
  CurBio 56, DcLB 26[port], Film 1, -2,
  FilmgC, ModWD, NotNAT, OxAmL,
  REnAL, TwYS, WhoAm 74, -76, -78,
  WorEFlm
Hadas, Moses 1900-1966 *AmAu&B, BioIn 5,*
  -7, -9, -10, ConAu 1R, -6NR, -25R,
  CurBio 60, -66, LinLib L, NatCAB 52,
  ObitOF 79, PenC AM, REnAL,
  WhAm 4, WorAu
Haddix, Cecille 1937- *ConAu X*
Haddix, Cecille *see also* Haddix-Kontos, Cecille P
Haddix-Kontos, Cecille P 1937- *ConAu 69*
Hader, Berta 1890?-1976 *AmAu&B, AmPB,*
  Au&ICB, AuBYP, BioIn 1, -2, -4, -5, -7,
  -8, -10, -12, BkP, Cald 1938, ConAu 65,
  -73, ConICB, IlsBYP, IlsCB 1744, -1946,
  -1957, -1967, InWom, JBA 34, -51,
  ScF&FL 1, SmATA 16, Str&VC,
  TwCCW 78, -83, WhAm 6, -7, WhE&EA,
  WhoAm 74, WhoAmW 74, -58, -64, -66,
  -68, -70, -72
Hader, Elmer Stanley 1889-1973 *AmAu&B,*
  AmPB, Au&ICB, AuBYP, BioIn 1, -2, -4,
  -5, -7, -8, -12, BkP, Cald 1938,
  ConAu 73, ConICB, IlsBYP, IlsCB 1744,
  -1946, -1957, -1967, JBA 34, -51,

  ScF&FL 1, SmATA 16, Str&VC,
  TwCCW 78, -83, WhAm 7, WhE&EA,
  WhoAm 74, WhoAmA 73, -76, -78N,
  -80N, -82N
Hagberg, David J 1942- *ConAu 106*
Hageman, Howard Garberich 1921- *ConAu 1R,*
  -5NR, DrAS 74P, -78P, -82P,
  WhoAm 74, -76, -78, -80, -82, WhoRel 75,
  WhoWor 78
Haggard, Sir Henry Rider 1856-1925 *Alli SUP,*
  BbD, BiD&SB, BioIn 1, -2, -3, -5, -7, -8,
  -11, -12, Chambr 3, ConAu 108, CyWA,
  DcBiA, DcEnA AP, DcEuL, DcLEL,
  EncSF, EncSoA, EvLB, FilmgC,
  LinLib L, -S, LongCTC, MnBBF,
  ModBrL, NewC, Novels, OxEng,
  PenC ENG, REn, ScF&FL 1,
  SmATA 16, TelT, TwCA, TwCA SUP,
  TwCLC 11[port], WebE&AL, WhLit,
  WhoBW&I A, WhoChL, WhoHr&F
Haggerty, James Joseph 1920- *BioIn 10,*
  ConAu 41R, IntAu&W 77, SmATA 5,
  WhoE 79, -81, -83, WhoS&SW 73, -75,
  -76
Hagon, Priscilla 1915- *ConAu X,*
  IntAu&W 76X, -77X, -82X, SmATA X,
  -5, TwCCW 83, WrDr 76, -80, -82, -84
Hagon, Priscilla *see also* Allan, Mabel Esther
Haher, Heinz 1913- *AuBYP, CurBio 52*
Haher, Louis 1910- *ConAu 29R, SmATA 12*
Hahn, Emily 1905- *AmAu&B, AmWomWr,*
  AuBYP, BioIn 1, -2, -3, -4, -7, -8, -9, -11,
  -12, ConAu 1R, -1NR, CurBio 42,
  InWom, LongCTC, REnAL, SmATA 3,
  TwCA SUP, WhNAA, WhoAm 74, -76,
  -78, -80, -82, WhoAmW 74, -58, -64, -66,
  -68, -70, -72, -75, -77, -83, WhoE 74,
  WhoWor 74, -76, WrDr 80, -82, -84
Hahn, James 1947- *BioIn 11, ConAu 2NR,*
  -49, SmATA 9
Hahn, Lynn 1949- *BioIn 11, ConAu 2NR,*
  -49, SmATA 9
Haig-Brown, Roderick Langmere 1908-1976
  Au&Wr 6, BioIn 1, -2, -6, -11, -12,
  CanNov, CanWW 70, CanWr, CasWL,
  ConAu 4NR, -5R, -69, ConLC 21[port],
  CreCan 1, CurBio 50, IntAu&W 76, -77,
  OxCan, REnAL, SmATA 12,

TwCCW 78, –83, WhAm 7, WhoAm 74, –76, WhoCan 73, –75, WhoWest 74, –76, WrDr 76

Hailey, Arthur 1920- *AmAu&B, Au&Wr 6, AuNews 2, BioIn 7, –9, –10, –11, BlueB 76, CanWW 70, –83, CanWr, ConAu 1R, –2NR, ConLC 5, ConNov 72, –76, –82, CreCan 2, CurBio 72, DcLB Y82B[port], DcLEL 1940, EncSF, IntAu&W 76, IntWW 74, –75, –76, –77, –78, –79, –80, –81, –82, –83, LinLib L, NewYTBS 79, Novels[port], OxCan, Who 82, –83, WhoAm 76, –78, –80, –82, WhoE 74, WhoWor 74, –76, –78, –80, –82, WorAl, WorAu 1970, WrDr 76, –80, –82, –84*

Haines, Charles 1928- *AuBYP SUP, ConAu 41R, DrAS 74E, –78E, –82E, IntAu&W 77, –82*

Haines, Gail Kay 1943- *AuBYP SUP, BioIn 11, ConAu 37R, SmATA 11, WhoAmW 83, WrDr 76, –80, –82, –84*

Haining, Peter 1940- *BioIn 12, ConAu 1NR, –45, ConSFA, EncO&P 80, EncSF, IntAu&W 76, –77, –82, ScF&FL 1, –2, SmATA 14, WhoHr&F, WhoSciF, WhoWor 76, WrDr 76, –80, –82, –84*

Halacy, D S, Jr. 1919- *ConAu 9NR, EncSF, ScF&FL 1, –2, SmATA 36*

Halacy, Daniel Stephen, Jr. 1919- *AuBYP, BioIn 8, ConAu 5R*

Halberstam, David 1934- *AmAu&B, BioIn 9, –10, –11, –12, BlueB 76, CelR 73, ConAu 10NR, –69, CurBio 73, DcLEL 1940, NewYTBS 79, PolProf K, WhoAm 74, –76, –78, –80, –82, WhoWor 74, WorAu 1970, WrDr 76, –80, –82, –84*

Halcomb, Ruth 1936- *ConAu 97*

Haldeman, Joe 1943- *BioIn 12, ConAu 6NR, –53, DcLB 8[port], DrAP&F 83, EncSF, IntAu&W 82, ScF&FL 1, –2, WhoAm 78, –80, –82, WrDr 80, –82, –84*

Haldeman, Linda 1935- *ConAu 85*

Hale, Arlene 1924- *AuBYP, BioIn 8, ConAu 1R, –1NR, WhoAmW 74, –66, –68, –70, –72, –75, –77*

Hale, Edward Everett 1822-1909 *Alli, Alli SUP, AmAu, AmAu&B, AmBi, ApCAB, BbD, BiDAmM, BiD&SB, BioIn 1, –2, –3, –4, –5, –7, –9, –12, CarSB, Chambr 3, ChhPo, –S1, –S2, –S3, CnDAL, CyAL 2, CyWA, DcAmAu, DcAmB, DcBiPP, DcEnL, DcLB 1, DcLEL, DcNAA, Drake, EncSF, EvLB, HarEnUS[port], JBA 34, LinLib L, –S, LuthC 75, McGEWB, NatCAB 1, OxAmH, OxAmL, PenC AM, REn, REnAL, ScF&FL 1, SmATA 16, TwCBDA, WebAB, –79, WhAm 1*

Hale, Janet Campbell 1947- *AuBYP SUP, ChhPo, ConAu 49, DrAF 76*

Hale, John Rigby 1923- *Au&Wr 6, ConAu 102, IntAu&W 76, –77, IntWW 75, –76, –77, –78, –79, –80, –81, –82, –83, Who 82, –83*

Hale, Nancy 1908- *AmAu&B, AmWomWr, Au&Wr 6, BioIn 1, –2, –4, –7, –8, –12, ConAu 5R, ConNov 72, –76, –82, DcLB Y80B[port], DrAF 76, DrAP&F 83, InWom, IntAu&W 76, –77, –82, LinLib L, OxAmL, REn, REnAL, SmATA 31[port], TwCA SUP, WhoAm 74, –76, –78, –80, –82, WhoAmW 74, –58, –61, –64, –66, –68, –70, –72, WhoS&SW 73, WhoWor 74, –76, WrDr 76, –80, –82, –84*

Hale, William Harlan 1910-1974 *AmAu&B, BioIn 1, –10, –12, ConAu 49, –93, NatCAB 58[port], REnAL, WhAm 6, WhoAm 74, WhoE 74*

Haley, Alex 1921- *ASpks, BioIn 7, –9, –11, ConAu 77, ConLC 8, –12, CurBio 77, Ebony 1, LivgBAA, NegAl 83, SelBAA, WhoAm 76, –78, –80, –82, WhoWest 74, WhoWor 74, –78, WorAl, WrDr 80, –82, –84*

Haley, Neale *ConAu 41R*

Hall, Adam 1920- *ConAu X, DcLEL 1940, EncMys, IntAu&W 76X, –77X, Novels, SmATA X, TwCCr&M 80, Who 82, –83, WrDr 76, –80, –82, –84*

Hall, Adam *see also* Trevor, Elleston

Hall, Adele 1910- *AuBYP, BioIn 10, ConAu 1R, SmATA 7, WhoAmW 64*

Hall, Carolyn Vosburg 1927- *AuBYP SUP, ChhPo, ConAu 61, MichAu 80*

Hall, Daryl 1948?- *BioIn 11, –12, WhoAm 82*

Hall, Daryl *see also* Hall & Oates

Hall, Donald 1928- *AmAu&B, AuBYP, BioIn 6, –8, –10, –12, ChhPo, –S1, CnE&AP, ConAu 2NR, –5R, ConLC 1, ConP 70, –75, –80, DcLB 5[port], DcLEL 1940, DrAF 76, DrAP 75, DrAP&F 83, NewYTBS 83[port], OxAmL, PenC AM, RAdv 1, REn, REnAL, SmATA 23[port], WhoAm 74, –76, –78, –80, –82, WorAu, WrDr 76, –80, –82, –84*

Hall, Douglas Kent 1938- *BioIn 9, ConAu 33R*

Hall, Edward Twitchell 1914- *AmAu&B, AmM&WS 73S, –76P, ConAu 65, FifIDA, WhoAm 74, –76, –78, –80, –82*

Hall, Elizabeth 1929- *AuBYP SUP, ConAu 65, WhoAm 76, –78, WhoAmW 79, –81*

Hall, Elvajean 1910- *AuBYP, BiDrLUS 70, BioIn 7, –10, ConAu 8NR, –13R, DrLC 69, ForWC 70, SmATA 6, WhoAmW 74, –66, –68, –70, –72, –75, –77, –79, –81, –83, WhoE 74, –75, –77, WhoLibS 55, –66, WhoS&SW 78, –80, –82*

Hall, Gordon Langley 1923?- *Au&Wr 6,*

AuBYP, BioIn 8, –11, ConAu X, –1R

Hall, Gordon Langley see also Simmons, Dawn Langley

Hall, Grover C, Jr. 1915-1971 BioIn 9, NewYTBE 71, WhAm 5

Hall, James Norman 1887-1951 AmAu&B, AmNov, AuBYP, BioIn 1, –2, –3, –4, –5, –7, –8, –9, –12, CyWA, DcAmB S5, DcLEL, JBA 34, LinLib L, –S, MnBBF, ObitOF 79, OxAmL, PenC AM, REn, REnAL, SmATA 21[port], TwCA, TwCA SUP, WhAm 3, WhLit, WhNAA, WorAl

Hall, Lynn 1937- AuBYP SUP, BioIn 9, ConAu 9NR, –21R, SmATA 2, TwCCW 83, WrDr 84

Hall, Malcolm 1945- AuBYP SUP, BioIn 10, ConAu 4NR, –49, SmATA 7

Hall, Marjory 1908- AuBYP, BioIn 4, –8, ConAu X, CurBio 57, ForWC 70, InWom, IntAu&W 77X, –82X, SmATA X, WhoAmW 74, –58, –61, –64, –66, –68, –70, –72, –75, –77, WhoE 74, WrDr 76, –80, –82, –84

Hall, Marjory see also Yeakley, Marjory Hall

Hall, Nancy Lee 1923- ConAu 57, WhoWest 78

Hall, Oakley 1920- CmCal, ConAu 3NR, –9R, WrDr 84

Hall, Robert Anderson, Jr. 1911- AmAu&B, BioIn 11, ConAu 5NR, –13R, DrAS 74F, –78F, –82F, WhoAm 74, –76, –78, –80, –82, WhoWor 78, –80, –82

Hall, Roger 1919- Au&Wr 6, ConAu 29R

Hall & Oates RkOn 84, RolSEnR 83

Hall-Quest, Olga 1899- Au&Wr 6, AuBYP, BioIn 8, –11, ConAu 5R, ForWC 70, SmATA 11, WhoAm 74, –76, –78, WhoAmW 74

Hallahan, William H ConAu 109

Haller, John Samuel, Jr. 1940- IntAu&W 82, WhoMW 78

Hallet, Jean-Pierre 1927- BioIn 9, ConAu 17R, IntAu&W 76, WhoWest 74, –76, –78, WhoWor 74, –76

Halliburton, Richard 1900-1939 AmAu&B, AmBi, BioIn 2, –5, –6, –7, CnDAL, DcNAA, EvLB, LinLib L, –S, NatCAB 35, OxAmL, REnAL, TwCA, TwCA SUP, WhAm 1, –1C, WhE&EA, WhNAA

Halliburton, Warren J 1924- BioIn 12, ConAu 33R, LivgBAA, SelBAA, SmATA 19

Halliday, Ernest Milton 1913- ConAu 1R

Halliday, Frank Ernest 1903-1982 Au&Wr 6, BioIn 5, ConAu 1R, –2NR, –106, IntAu&W 77, –82, Who 74, –82, –83N

Halliday, William Ross 1926- ConAu 49, IntAu&W 82, WhoAm 82, WhoGov 77, WhoPNW, WhoWest 74, –76, –78, –80, –82, –84, WhoWor 82

Hallman, Ruth 1929- ConAu 85, SmATA 28

Hallstead, William Finn, III 1924- AuBYP SUP, BioIn 11, ConAu 5R, –6NR, SmATA 11, WhoE 74, –75, –77, –79

Halmi, Robert 1924- WhoAm 82

Halsell, Grace 1923- AuBYP, AuNews 1, BioIn 8, –10, ConAu 21R, SmATA 13, WhoAmW 74, –72, –75

Halter, Jon C 1941- AuBYP SUP, ConAu 61, SmATA 22[port]

Hamalian, Leo 1920- ConAu 2NR, –5R, DrAS 74E, –78E, –82E, WhoE 75

Hamblin, Dora Jane 1920- AuBYP, BioIn 6, ConAu 37R, ForWC 70, SmATA 36, WhoAmW 74, –64, –66, –68, –70, –72

Hamerstrom, Frances 1907- AmM&WS 79P, –82P, BioIn 12, ConAu 69, SmATA 24[port]

Hamill, Pete 1935- BioIn 8, CelR 73, ConAu 25R, ConLC 10, IntMPA 77, –75, –76, –78, –79, –81, –82, –84, WomWMM

Hamilton, Clive 1898-1963 BioIn 1, –3, –4, –6, –7, –8, –9, –10, –11, –12, ConAu X, CurBio 44, –64, EvLB, LongCTC, NewC, SmATA X, TwCA SUP

Hamilton, Clive see also Lewis, C S

Hamilton, Dorothy 1906-1983 BioIn 11, ConAu 110, –33R, SmATA 12, –35N, WhoAmW 75, –77, –79, WomPO 76

Hamilton, Edith 1867-1963 AmAu&B, AmWomWr, AnCL, BioIn 3, –4, –5, –6, –7, –8, –9, –11, –12, ConAu 77, CurBio 63, DcAmB S7, EncAB-H, HerW, InWom, IntDcWB, LibW, LinLib L, –S, NatCAB 52, NotAW MOD, ObitOF 79, REn, REnAL, SmATA 20, TwCA, TwCA SUP, WebAB, –79, WhAm 4, WhNAA, WhoAmW 58, –64

Hamilton, Edmond 1904-1977 AmAu&B, BioIn 7, –11, –12, ConAu 1R, –3NR, ConLC 1, ConSFA, DcLB 8[port], EncSF, LinLib L, OhA&B, ScF&FL 1, –2, WhoSciF

Hamilton, Eleanor 1909- AmM&WS 73S, –78S, ConAu 1R, –2NR, WhoAmW 58, –61, –64, –81, –83

Hamilton, Franklin W 1923- ConAu 33R, DrAS 74E, –78E, –82E, MichAu 80, WrDr 76, –80, –82, –84

Hamilton, Gail AuBYP SUP, ConAu X, DrAP&F 83, IntAu&W 82X

Hamilton, Gail see also Corcoran, Barbara

Hamilton, Virginia 1936- AmWomWr, Au&ICB, AuBYP, AuNews 1, BioIn 9, –10, –11, –12, BlkAWP, ChlLR 1, ChhPo S2, ConAu 25R, ConLC 26[port], FourBJA, InB&W 80, MorBMP, NinCLC 1966, SelBAA, SmATA 4, TwCCW 78, –83, WhoAm 76, –78, –80, –82, WhoAmW 74, –77, –81, –83, WrDr 80, –82, –84

Hamilton-Paterson, James Lee 1908-
  AuBYP SUP, WhE&EA
Hamley, Dennis 1935- *ConAu 11NR, –57,*
  ScF&FL 1A
Hamlisch, Marvin 1944?- *AmSCAP 66,*
  Baker 78, BioIn 10, –11, –12, BioNews 74,
  CurBio 76, IntMPA 78, –79, –81, –82, –84,
  RkOn 78, –84, WhoAm 78, –80, –82,
  WhoThe 81
Hamm, Jack 1916- *BioIn 2, ConAu 5R,*
  –9NR
Hammer, Richard 1928- *BioIn 10,*
  ConAu 11NR, –25R, SmATA 6
Hammett, Dashiell 1894-1961 *AuNews 1,*
  BioIn 2, –4, –6, –7, –8, –10, –11, –12,
  CasWL, CmCal, CmMov, CnDAL,
  CnMWL, ConAu 81, ConLC 3, –5, –10,
  –19, CorpD, CyWA, DcFM, EncAB-H,
  EncMys, FilmgC, LinLib L, LongCTC,
  ModAL, ModAL SUP, Novels[port],
  ObitOF 79, ObitT 1961, OxAmL, OxEng,
  OxFilm, PenC AM, PolProf T, REn,
  REnAL, ScF&FL 1, TwCA, TwCA SUP,
  TwCCr&M 80, TwCWr, WebAB, –79,
  WebE&AL, WhoTwCL, WorAl,
  WorEFlm
Hammond, Cleon E 1908- *AmSCAP 66*
Hammond Innes, Ralph 1913- *Au&Wr 6,*
  AuBYP, BioIn 3, –4, –5, –8, –10, BlueB 76,
  ConAu 4NR, –5R, CurBio 54,
  IntAu&W 76, –77, –82, IntWW 76, –77,
  –78, –79, –80, –81, –82, –83, LongCTC,
  Who 74, –82, –83, WhoWor 74, –76, –78,
  WrDr 76, –80, –82, –84
Hammond Innes, Ralph *see also* Innes, Hammond
Hammonds, Michael 1942- *ConAu 45*
Hamner, Earl, Jr. 1923- *AuNews 2, BioIn 10,*
  –11, ConAu 73, ConLC 12,
  DcLB 6[port], LesBEnT, NewYTET,
  WhoAm 76, –78, –80, –82
Hamori, Laszlo Dezso 1911- *ConAu 9R*
Hampden, John 1898-1974 *Au&Wr 6,*
  ConAu 109, ScF&FL 1, WhE&EA,
  Who 74
Hample, Stoo 1926- *ChhPo*
Hampshire, Susan 1938?- *BioIn 8, –9, –10, –12,*
  CelR 73, CurBio 74, FilmgC,
  IntMPA 77, –75, –76, –78, –79, –81, –82, –84,
  IntWW 82, –83, NewYTBE 70, Who 82,
  –83, WhoAm 74, –76, –78, –80, –82,
  WhoAmW 74, –83, WhoHol A,
  WhoThe 15, –16, –81, WhoWor 78,
  WorAl
Hampson, Alfred Leete 1889?-1952 *BioIn 2, –3,*
  ChhPo
Hamre, Leif 1914- *Au&Wr 6, BioIn 10,*
  ConAu 4NR, –5R, FourBJA,
  IntAu&W 76, –82, SmATA 5,
  TwCCW 78B, –83B, WrDr 76, –80, –82,
  –84
Hanaburgh, David Henry 1910- *WhoCon 73,*
  WhoE 77

Hanckel, Frances Stuart 1944- *BiDrAPH 79*
Hancock, Carla *ConAu 89*
Hancock, Lyn 1938- *BioIn 9, ConAu 77*
Hancock, Niel Anderson 1941- *ConAu 97*
Hancock, Ralph Lowell 1903- *AmAu&B,*
  Au&Wr 6, ConAu P-1, IndAu 1917,
  IntAu&W 76, –77, WhoAm 74, –76, –78,
  –80, –82
Hand, Jackson 1913- *ConAu 10NR, –61*
Hanenkrat, Frank Thomas 1939- *ConAu 93,*
  DrAS 74E, –78E, –82E
Hanes, Frank Borden 1920- *AmAu&B,*
  BioIn 3, –4, ConAu 1R, DrAP&F 83,
  WhoAm 76, –78, –80, –82, WhoS&SW 73,
  –75, –76, WhoWor 82, WrDr 76, –80, –82,
  –84
Haney, Lynn 1941- *ConAu 1NR, –49,*
  SmATA 23[port]
Hanff, Helene *BioIn 11, –12, ConAu 3NR,*
  –5R, IntAu&W 76, NewYTBS 82[port],
  SmATA 11
Hanley, Hope Anthony 1926- *ConAu 5NR,*
  –9R
Hanlon, Emily 1945- *BioIn 12, DrAP&F 83,*
  SmATA 15
Hanna, Mary Carr 1905- *ConAu 45,*
  DrAP&F 83
Hannam, Charles Lewis 1925- *ConAu 11NR,*
  –61, IntAu&W 77, WrDr 76, –80, –82,
  –84
Hannay, Allen 1946- *ConAu 109*
Hannay, Margaret Patterson 1944- *ConAu 104,*
  DrAS 78E, –82E
Hannum, Alberta Pierson 1906- *AmAu&B,*
  AmNov, BioIn 2, –3, ConAu 65, InWom,
  OhA&B, WhE&EA, WhoAm 74, –76,
  WhoAmW 61, –77, –79, –81
Hannum, Sara *AuBYP, BioIn 8, ChhPo S1*
Hano, Arnold 1922- *AuBYP, BioIn 8, –11,*
  ConAu 5NR, –9R, SmATA 12,
  WhoWest 74, –76, –82
Hanrahan, John David 1938- *ConAu 77,*
  IntAu&W 82
Hansberry, Lorraine 1930-1965 *AmAu&B,*
  AmWomWr, AuNews 2, BiE&WWA,
  BioIn 5, –6, –7, –8, –9, –10, –12, BlkAWP,
  CasWL, CnMD SUP, ConAu 109, –25R,
  ConDr 77F, –82E, ConLC 17, CroCD,
  DcAmB S7, DcLB 7[port], DcLEL 1940,
  DrBlPA, EncWL 2, EncWT, GoodHs,
  InB&W 80, InWom, IntDcWB, LibW,
  LinLib L, McGEWD, –84, ModAL SUP,
  ModBlW, ModWD, NatCAB 60,
  NegAl 76[port], –83[port], NotAW MOD,
  NotNAT B, ObitOF 79, PIP&P, –A,
  REnAL, SelBAA, WhAm 4,
  WhoAmW 64, WorAl, WorAu
Hansen, Caryl 1929- *ConAu 108*
Hansen, Harry 1884-1977 *AmAu&B, AuBYP,*
  BioIn 1, –4, –8, –11, ConAu 69, –73,
  CurBio 42, LinLib L, –S, NewYTBS 77,
  REnAL, TwCA, TwCA SUP, WhAm 7,

Who 74, WhoAm 74, –76, –78
Hansen, Joseph 1923- *ConAu 29R,
DrAP&F 83, IntAu&W 77, –82, Novels,
TwCCr&M 80, WrDr 82, –84*
Hanser, Richard F 1909-1981 *AuBYP SUP,
BioIn 12, ConAu 5R, –8NR, –105,
NewYTBS 81, SmATA 13, WhoAm 74,
–76, –78, –80, –82, WhoWor 74, –76*
Hapgood, Charles Hutchins 1904- *Au&Wr 6,
ConAu 17R*
Haq, Mahbub Ul 1934- *ConAu 13R,
WhoUN 75*
Harbaugh, William Henry 1920- *ConAu 1R,
DrAS 74H, –78H, –82H, WhoAm 74, –76,
–78, –80, –82*
Harbin, Robert 1909- *Au&Wr 6*
Harbin, Robert *see also* Williams, Ned
Hardin, Tim 1940?-1980 *AnObit 1980,
BioIn 12, ConAu 102, EncPR&S, –77,
NewYTBS 80[port], RolSEnR 83,
WhoRocM 82*
Harding, Lee 1937- *ConAu 106, EncSF,
IntAu&W 77, –82, SmATA 31, –32,
WrDr 84*
Harding, Vincent 1931- *BlkAWP, CivR 74,
Ebony 1, InB&W 80, LivgBAA, SelBAA,
WhoAm 74, –76, –78, WhoBlA 75, –77, –80*
Harding, Walter 1917- *ChhPo S1, ConAu 1R,
–1NR, DrAS 74E, –78E, –82E,
IntAu&W 76, –77, WhoE 75, –77,
WrDr 76, –80, –82, –84*
Hardwick, Elizabeth 1916- *AmAu&B,
AmWomWr, BioIn 3, –4, –5, –8, –9, –10,
–11, –12, BlueB 76, ConAu 3NR, –5R,
ConLC 13, ConNov 82, CurBio 81[port],
DcLB 6[port], IntAu&W 76, –77, Novels,
WhoAm 74, –76, –78, –80, –82,
WhoAmW 74, –66, –68, –70, –72, WorAu,
WrDr 76, –80, –82, –84*
Hardwick, Mollie *Au&Wr 6, ConAu 2NR,
–49, IntAu&W 76, –77, –82, Novels,
Who 82, –83, WrDr 76, –80, –82, –84*
Hardy, David A 1936- *ConAu 8NR, –61,
IntAu&W 77, –82, SmATA 9*
Hardy, Thomas 1840-1928 *Alli SUP, AnCL,
AtlBL, BbD, BiD&SB, BioIn 1, –2, –3, –4,
–5, –6, –7, –8, –9, –10, –11, –12, BrAu 19,
BrWr 6, CasWL, CelCen, Chambr 3,
ChhPo, –S1, –S2, –S3, CnE&AP, CnMWL,
ConAu 104, CrtT 3, –4, CyWA, DcBiA,
DcEnA, –AP, DcEnL, DcEuL,
DcLB 18[port], –19[port], DcLEL, Dis&D,
EncWL, –2[port], EvLB, FilmgC,
LinLib L, –S, LongCEL, LongCTC,
McGEWB, ModBrL, ModBrL SUP,
ModWD, NewC, NewEOp 71,
Novels[port], OxEng, OxMus, PenC ENG,
RAdv 1, RComWL, REn,
SmATA 25[port], TwCLC 4[port],
–10[port], TwCWr, WebE&AL, WhDW,
WhE&EA, WhLit, WhoChL, WhoLA,
WhoTwCL, WorAl*

Hardy, William M 1922- *ConAu 1R, –2NR*
Hark, Mildred 1908- *BioIn 2, –11, ConAu X,
SmATA X*
Hark, Mildred *see also* McQueen, Mildred Hark
Harker, Herbert *OxCan SUP*
Harker, Ronald 1909- *ConAu 77*
Harkins, Philip 1912- *AuBYP, BioIn 6, –7,
–10, ConAu 29R, MorJA, ScF&FL 1, –2,
SmATA 6*
Harlan, Elizabeth 1945- *SmATA 35*
Harley, Timothy *Alli SUP*
Harlow, Alvin Fay 1875-1963 *AmAu&B,
AuBYP, BioIn 6, –8, ObitOF 79,
WhAm 4, WhNAA*
Harman, Carter 1918- *Baker 78, BioIn 3,
ConAmC, DcCM*
Harmelink, Barbara *BioIn 11, ConAu 61,
SmATA 9*
Harmon, Margaret 1906- *BioIn 12, ConAu 69,
SmATA 20*
Harnan, Terry 1920- *BioIn 11, ConAu 45,
IntAu&W 77X, –82X, SmATA 12*
Harness, Charles L 1915- *BioIn 12, ConSFA,
DcLB 8, EncSF, Novels, ScF&FL 1, –2,
WhoSciF, WrDr 84*
Harnett, Cynthia 1893-1981 *Au&Wr 6,
AuBYP, BioIn 2, –5, –7, –8, –9, –10,
ConAu P-1, IlsCB 1946, IntAu&W 76,
SmATA 32N, –5, ThrBJA, TwCCW 78,
–83, WhoChL, WrDr 76, –80, –82*
Harnishfeger, Lloyd *ScF&FL 1*
Harper, Elaine *ConAu X*
Harragan, Betty Lehan 1921?- *ConAu 77,
ForWC 70, WhoAmW 75, –77, –79*
Harrah, Michael William 1941- *WhoWest 78,
–80*
Harrer, Heinrich 1912- *Au&Wr 6, BioIn 3,
–5, –7, –8, –12, ConAu 7NR, –17R,
CurBio 54, InSci, IntAu&W 77, –82,
LinLib L, Who 74, –82, –83*
Harribance, Sean 1939- *BioIn 10, –11,
BioNews 74*
Harries, Joan 1922- *ConAu 107*
Harrington, John F, Jr. 1942- *DrAS 74E, –78E,
–82E*
Harrington, Joyce 1930?- *TwCCr&M 80*
Harrington, Lyn 1911- *AuBYP, BioIn 7, –10,
CaW, ConAu X, –5R, IntAu&W 76,
OxCan, OxCan SUP, Profile, SmATA 5*
Harrington, Michael 1928- *AmAu&B, BioIn 8,
–11, CelR 73, ConAu 17R,
ConIsC 1[port], CurBio 69, LinLib L,
NewYTBE 72, OxCan, PolProf J,
PolProf K, WhoAm 74, –76, –78, –80, –82,
WorAl, WrDr 80, –82, –84*
Harris, Christie 1907- *AuBYP SUP, BioIn 10,
CaW, ConAu 5R, –6NR, ConLC 12,
FourBJA, IntAu&W 77, OxCan SUP,
Profile, ScF&FL 1, –2, SmATA 6,
TwCCW 78, –83, WhoAm 82, WrDr 80,
–82, –84*
Harris, David 1946- *BioIn 11, –12, ConAu 69*

Harris, Del 1937- *ConAu 8NR, WhoS&SW 82*

Harris, George Lawrence 1910- *AmM&WS 73S, –76P*

Harris, Janet 1932-1979 *AuBYP SUP, BioIn 9, –12, ConAu 33R, –93, SmATA 23N, –4*

Harris, Joel Chandler 1848-1908 *Alli SUP, AmAu, AmAu&B, AmBi, AnCL, ApCAB, ApCAB X, AtlBL, AuBYP, BbD, BiD&SB, BiDSA, BioIn 1, –2, –3, –4, –5, –6, –7, –8, –10, –11, –12, CarSB, CasWL, Chambr 3, ChhPo, –S1, –S2, –S3, CnDAL, ConAu 104, CyWA, DcAmAu, DcAmB, DcAmSR, DcBiA, DcCathB, DcEnA AP, DcLB 11[port], –23[port], DcLEL, DcNAA, EncAAH, EncAB-H, EncSoH, EvLB, FamAYP, HarEnUS, JBA 34, LinLib L, –S, McGEWB, NatCAB 1, Novels, OxAmL, OxEng, PenC AM, RAdv 1, REn, REnAL, Str&VC, TwCBDA, TwCCW 78A, –83A, TwCLC 2, WebAB, –79, WebE&AL, WhDW, WhAm 1, WhLit, WhoChL, WorAl, YABC 1*

Harris, John *AuBYP SUP*

Harris, John 1916- *Au&Wr 6, ConAu 93, IntAu&W 82, ScF&FL 1, WhoS&SW 78, WrDr 76, –80, –82, –84*

Harris, John *see also* Hebden, Mark

Harris, John *see also* Hennessy, Max

Harris, John Beynon 1903-1969 *BioIn 7, –8, –10, –12, ConAu 102, –89, ConLC 19, ConSFA, EncSF, MnBBF, ObitOF 79, ScF&FL 1, WorAu*

Harris, John Beynon *see also* Wyndham, John

Harris, Julie 1925- *AuBYP SUP, BiDFilm, BiE&WWA, BioIn 2, –3, –4, –5, –6, –7, –9, –10, –11, BioNews 74, CelR 73, CnThe, ConAu 103, CurBio 56, –77, EncWT, FilmgC, GoodHs, InWom, IntMPA 77, –75, –76, –78, –79, –81, –82, –84, IntWW 79, –80, –81, –82, –83, MotPP, MovMk, NotNAT, OxFilm, PIP&P A, WhoAm 74, –76, –78, –80, –82, WhoAmW 74, –58, –64, –66, –68, –70, –72, –75, –81, –83, WhoHol A, WhoThe 15, –16, –81, WhoWor 74, WorAl*

Harris, Lavinia *ConAu X, SmATA X*

Harris, Lavinia *see also* Johnston, Norma

Harris, MacDonald 1921- *BioIn 12, ConAu X, ConLC 9, WrDr 80, –82, –84*

Harris, MacDonald *see also* Heiney, Donald William

Harris, Marilyn 1931- *ConAu X, WrDr 84*

Harris, Marilyn *see also* Springer, Marilyn Harris

Harris, Mark 1922- *AmAu&B, Au&Wr 6, BioIn 5, –7, –8, –10, –12, ConAu 2NR, –5R, ConLC 19, ConNov 72, –76, –82, CurBio 59, DcLB Y80A[port], –2, DcLEL 1940, DrAF 76, DrAP&F 83,*

DrAS 74E, –78E, –82E, IntAu&W 76, –77, –82, OxAmL, RAdv 1, WhoAm 74, –76, –78, –80, –82, WhoAmJ 80, WhoWor 74, WorAu 1970, WrDr 76, –80, –82, –84

Harris, Mark Jonathan 1941- *ConAu 104, SmATA 32[port]*

Harris, Neil 1938- *DrAS 74H, –78H, –82H*

Harris, Patricia *ConAu 57*

Harris, Ricky 1922- *ConAu 103*

Harris, Rosemary 1923- *Au&Wr 6, AuBYP SUP, BioIn 9, ConAu 33R, CurBio 67, FourBJA, IntAu&W 76, –77, –82, NewYTBS 76, ScF&FL 1, –2, SmATA 4, TwCCW 78, –83, TwCCr&M 80, Who 74, –82, –83, WrDr 76, –80, –82, –84*

Harris, Sydney Justin 1917- *AmAu&B, BioIn 3, ConAmTC, ConAu 11NR, –61, WhoAm 74, –76, –78, –80, –82, WhoMW 74*

Harris, William H 1944- *DrAS 82H*

Harrison, Barbara Grizzuti 1934- *ConAu 77, WhoAm 82*

Harrison, C William 1913- *AuBYP, BioIn 8, ConAu 107, IndAu 1917, SmATA 35*

Harrison, Deloris 1938- *BioIn 11, ConAu 61, InB&W 80, SmATA 9*

Harrison, Elizabeth Cavanna 1909- *ForWC 70, WrDr 76, –80, –82, –84*

Harrison, Elizabeth Cavanna *see also* Cavanna, Betty

Harrison, George 1943- *Baker 78, BioIn 6, –7, –8, –9, –10, –11, –12, BlueB 76, CelR 73, CurBio 66, EncPR&S, –77, IlEncRk, IntWW 74, –75, –76, –77, –78, –79, –80, –81, –82, –83, IntWWM 77, MotPP, RkOn 78, –84, RolSEnR 83, WhoAm 80, –82, WhoHol A, WhoRocM 82, WhoWor 74, –78, –80, –82, WorAl*

Harrison, George *see also* Beatles, The

Harrison, George Russell 1898-1979 *AmM&WS 73P, –76P, –79P, BioIn 2, –3, –4, –12, ConAu 17R, ConAu P-2, McGMS 80[port], NewYTBS 79, WhAm 7*

Harrison, Hank 1940- *ConAu 41R, IntAu&W 76, WhoWest 76, –78, –80, –82*

Harrison, Harry 1925- *AuBYP SUP, BioIn 9, –11, –12, ConAu 1R, –5NR, ConSFA, DcLB 8[port], EncSF, IntAu&W 76, LinLib L, Novels, ScF&FL 1, –2, SmATA 4, WhoSciF, WrDr 76, –80, –82, –84*

Harrison, Jim 1937- *AmAu&B, ConAu X, ConLC 6, –14, ConP 70, –75, –80, DcLB Y82B[port], DrAF 76, DrAP 75, IntWWP 77X, MichAu 80, RAdv 1, WhoAm 76, –78, –80, WorAu 1970, WrDr 76, –80, –82, –84*

Harrison, William 1933- *BioIn 9, ConAu 9NR, –17R, DrAF 76, DrAS 74E, –78E, –82E, ScF&FL 1, –2, WhoAm 76,*

–78, –80, –82

Harrison, William C 1919- *ConAu 25R*

Harry, Debbie 1946?- *CurBio 81[port], NewYTBS 79*

Harsanyi, Zsolt 1887-1943 *CurBio 44, ObitOF 79, PenC EUR*

Hart, Bruce 1938- *AmSCAP 66, BioIn 12, ConAu 107*

Hart, Carole 1943?- *BioIn 12, ConAu 107*

Hart, Carolyn Gimpel 1936- *ConAu 13R, ForWC 70*

Hart, John 1948- *ConAu 11NR, –65, IntWWP 82*

Hart, John Lewis 1931- *AmAu&B, BioIn 4, –5, –10, BlueB 76, ConAu 4NR, –49, WhoAm 74, –76, –78, –80, –82, WhoAmA 76, –78, –80, –82*

Hart, John Lewis *see also* Hart, Johnny

Hart, Johnny 1931- *ArtCS, AuNews 1, BioNews 74, ConAu X, –49, IntAu&W 77, WorECom*

Hart, Johnny *see also* Hart, John Lewis

Hart, Kitty *BioIn 12*

Hart, Moss 1904-1961 *AmAu&B, BiDAmM, BioIn 1, –2, –4, –5, –6, –7, –12, CasWL, CnDAL, CnMD, CnThe, ConAu 109, –89, CurBio 40, –60, –62, DcAmB S7, DcLB 7[port], EncMT, EncWT, FilmgC, LongCTC, McGEWD, –84[port], ModWD, NatCAB 46, NewCBMT, NotNAT A, –B, ObitOF 79, ObitT 1961, OxAmL, OxThe, PenC AM, PIP&P, REn, REnAL, REnWD, TwCA, TwCA SUP, WebAB, –79, WebE&AL, WhAm 4, WhThe, WorAl, WorEFlm*

Harte, Bret 1836?-1902 *AmAu, AmAu&B, AtlBL, AuBYP, BiD&SB, BioIn 1, –3, –4, –5, –6, –7, –8, –9, –10, –11, –12, CasWL, CmCal, CnDAL, ConAu 104, CrtT 3, –4, CyWA, DcAmAu, DcAmB, DcAmSR, DcLB 12[port], DcNAA, EncAAH, LinLib L, Novels[port], OxAmH, OxAmL, PenC AM, RAdv 1, REn, REnAL, REnAW, SmATA 26[port], TwCBDA, TwCLC 1, WebAB, –79, WebE&AL, WhDW, WhAm 1, WorAl*

Hartley, Fred Allan, III 1953- *ConAu 106*

Hartley, L P 1895-1972 *ChhPo S3, ConAu 37R, ConLC 22[port], DcLB 15[port], EncSF, EncWL 2, LongCEL, Novels, ObitOF 79, ObitT 1971, ScF&FL 1, –2, WhoHr&F*

Hartley, Leslie Poles 1895-1972 *Au&Wr 6, BioIn 4, –6, –7, –9, –10, –11, CasWL, ConAu 37R, –45, ConLC 2, ConNov 72, –76, DcLEL, EncWL, EvLB, IntAu&W 76, –77, LongCTC, ModBrL, ModBrL SUP, NewC, PenC ENG, RAdv 1, REn, TwCA SUP, TwCWr, WebE&AL, WhAm 5, WhE&EA, WhoTwCL*

Hartman, Evert 1937- *SmATA 35,*

TwCCW 83B

Hartman, Gertrude 1876-1955 *AmAu&B, BioIn 2, –3, –4, JBA 51, ObitOF 79, WhAm 3*

Hartman, Jane E 1928- *ConAu 105*

Hartog, Jan De 1914- *BioIn 2, –3, –4, –7, –8, CasWL, EncWL, EncWT, IntAu&W 77, IntWW 74, –75, –76, –77, –78, –79, –80, –81, –82, –83, TwCA SUP*

Harvey, Harriet 1924- *ConAu 109*

Harvey, Virginia I 1917- *ConAu 57*

Harwood, Ronald 1934- *Au&Wr 6, BioIn 12, ConAu 1R, –4NR, ConDr 82, DcLB 13[port], IntAu&W 76, IntMPA 77, –75, –76, –78, –79, –81, –82, –84, NewYTBS 81[port], Novels, Who 82, –83, WhoThe 81, WhoWor 76, –78, WrDr 76, –80, –82, –84*

Hasek, Jaroslav 1883-1923 *BioIn 1, –10, –11, –12, CasWL, ClDMEL, ConAu 104, EncWL, –2[port], EncWT, EvEuW, LongCTC, MakMC, ModSL 2, Novels, PenC EUR, REn, TwCA, TwCA SUP, TwCLC 4[port], TwCWr, WhDW, WhoTwCL, WorAl*

Haskell, Molly *WomWMM*

Haskins, James 1941- *AuBYP SUP, BioIn 11, ChlLR 3, ConAu 33R, DrAS 82E, InB&W 80, IntAu&W 77, NegAl 76, SelBAA, SmATA 9, WhoE 75*

Haskins, Jim 1941- *AuBYP SUP, ChlLR 3, ConAu X, LivgBAA, SmATA X, WrDr 76, –80, –82, –84*

Haslam, Gerald William 1937- *ConAu 11NR, –29R, DrAS 74E, –78E, –82E, IntAu&W 82, Po&Wr 77, WhoWest 80, –82, –84, WrDr 76, –80, –82, –84*

Hasler, Joan 1931- *ConAu 29R, SmATA 28*

Hass, Hans 1919- *Au&Wr 6, BioIn 4, –11, ConAu 108, CurBio 55, InSci*

Hassler, Jon 1933- *BioIn 12, ConAu 73, SmATA 19*

Hastings, Max 1945- *ConAu 81, IntAu&W 82, WhoWor 80*

Haston, Dougal 1940-1977 *BioIn 11, ConAu 105, WrDr 76*

Haswell, Chetwynd John Drake 1919- *ConAu 41R, IntAu&W 76, –82, WrDr 76, –80, –82, –84*

Haswell, Chetwynd John Drake *see also* Haswell, Jock

Haswell, Jock 1919- *Au&Wr 6, ConAu X, IntAu&W 76X, –82X, WrDr 76, –80, –82, –84*

Haswell, Jock *see also* Haswell, Chetwynd John Drake

Hatch, Alden 1898-1975 *AmAu&B, Au&Wr 6, AuBYP, BioIn 8, –10, ConAu 57, –65, NewYTBS 75, ObitOF 79, WhAm 6, WhoAm 74*

Hathaway, Donny 1945?-1979 *BiDAfM, BioIn 11, EncPR&S 77, InB&W 80,*

NewYTBS 79, RkOn 78, –84,
RolSEnR 83, WhoBlA 77
Hathaway, Nancy 1946- *ConAu 108*
Haugaard, Erik Christian 1923- *AuBYP,*
BioIn 8, –9, –12, ConAu 3NR, –5R,
IntAu&W 76, –77, –82, SmATA 4,
ThrBJA, TwCCW 78, –83, WhoWor 76,
WrDr 76, –80, –82, –84
Haupt, Enid Annenberg 1906- *BioIn 5,*
ForWC 70, InWom, NewYTBE 70,
NewYTBS 82, WhoAmW 74, –64, –66, –68,
–70, –72, –75
Hauser, Thomas 1946- *ConAu 85*
Hausman, Gerald 1945- *ConAu 2NR, –45,*
DrAP 75, IntWWP 82, SmATA 13
Hautzig, Deborah 1956- *ConAu 89,*
SmATA 31[port]
Hautzig, Esther 1930- *AuBYP, BioIn 8, –9,*
–10, –11, ConAu 1R, –5NR, ForWC 70,
HerW, IntAu&W 77, –82, MorBMP,
SmATA 4, ThrBJA, WhoAmW 83,
WrDr 76, –80, –82, –84
Havens, Richie 1941- *BioIn 8, –9, DrBlPA,*
EncPR&S, –77, IlEncRk, InB&W 80,
RkOn 78, –84, RolSEnR 83,
WhoRocM 82
Haverstock, Mary Sayre 1932- *AuBYP SUP,*
ConAu 81, WhoAmW 75
Haviaras, Stratis 1935- *ConAu X,*
DrAP&F 83, Po&Wr 77, WrDr 82, –84
Havighurst, Walter 1901- *AmAu&B, AmNov,*
Au&Wr 6, AuBYP, BioIn 2, –4, –6, –7, –9,
CnDAL, ConAu 1R, –1NR, DrAS 74E,
–78E, –82E, IntAu&W 76, –77,
MichAu 80, MorJA, OhA&B, OxAmL,
REnAL, SmATA 1, TwCA SUP,
WhE&EA, WhoAm 74, –76, WhoWor 78,
WrDr 76, –80, –82, –84
Havrevold, Finn 1905- *AuBYP SUP,*
ConAu 109, IntAu&W 77, IntWW 74,
–75, –76, –77, –78, –79, –80, –81, –82, –83,
WhoWor 74, –76, –78
Hawes, Charles Boardman 1889-1923 *AmAu&B,*
AuBYP, BioIn 4, –7, DcAmB, DcNAA,
JBA 34, Newb 1922, REnAL, TwCA,
TwCCW 83
Hawes, Evelyn Johnson *AuNews 1, BioIn 10,*
ConAu 13R, ForWC 70, IntAu&W 82,
WhoAmW 74, –70, –72, –75, –77, –79, –81
Hawes, Gene R 1922- *ConAu 3NR, –5R*
Hawkes, Jacquetta 1910- *Au&Wr 6, BioIn 3,*
–4, BlueB 76, ConAu 69, EncSF,
IntAu&W 76, –77, –82, IntWW 74, –75,
–76, –77, –78, –79, –80, –81, –82, –83,
LongCTC, REn, ScF&FL 1, TwCA SUP,
Who 74, –82, –83, WhoWor 74, –76, –78,
WrDr 76, –80, –82, –84
Hawkes, Terence 1932- *ConAu 17R*
Hawkesworth, Eric 1921- *AuBYP SUP,*
ConAu 29R, SmATA 13, WrDr 76, –80,
–82, –84
Hawkins, Sir Anthony Hope 1863-1933 *BbD,*

BiD&SB, BioIn 2, –4, –5, –8, –12,
Chambr 3, DcEnA AP, DcLEL, EvLB,
LinLib L, –S, LongCTC, NewC,
NotNAT B, OxEng, REn, TelT, TwCA,
TwCA SUP, WhoChL
Hawkins, Sir Anthony Hope *see also* Hope,
Anthony
Hawkins, Arthur 1903- *BioIn 12,*
ConAu 8NR, –21R, IlsBYP, SmATA 19,
WhE&EA
Hawkins, Gerald Stanley 1928-
AmM&WS 73P, BiESc, ConAu 17R,
DrRegL 75, WhoE 74, WhoGov 77,
WhoWor 74, WrDr 76, –80, –82, –84
Hawkins, Jim 1944- *ConAu 73*
Hawthorne, Nathaniel 1804-1864 *Alli,*
Alli SUP, AmAu, AmAu&B, AmBi,
AmWr, ApCAB, AtlBL, AuBYP SUP,
BbD, BiAUS, BiD&SB, BioIn 1, –2, –3,
–4, –5, –6, –7, –8, –9, –10, –11, –12, CarSB,
CasWL, CelCen, Chambr 3, ChhPo S1,
–S2, –S3, CnDAL, CrtT 3, –4, CyAL 2,
CyWA, DcAmAu, DcAmB, DcAmSR,
DcBiA, DcBiPP, DcEnA, –AP, DcEnL,
DcLB 1, DcLEL, DcNAA, Dis&D,
Drake, EncAAH, EncAB-H, EncSF,
EvLB, FamAYP, FilmgC, HarEnUS[port],
LinLib L, –S, LuthC 75, McGEWB,
MouLC 3, NatCAB 3, NewEOp 71,
Novels[port], OxAmH, OxAmL, OxEng,
PenC AM, RAdv 1, RComWL, REn,
REnAL, ScF&FL 1, Str&VC, TwCBDA,
WebAB, –79, WebE&AL, WhDW,
WhAm HS, WhoChL, WhoHr&F,
WorAl, YABC 2
Hay, John 1915- *AmAu&B, ConAu 9NR, –65,*
EncSF, IntWWP 77, –82, SmATA 13,
WhoAm 74, –76, –78, –80, –82
Hayakawa, S I 1906- *AlmAP 78, –80,*
–82[port], CelR 73, CmCal, CurBio 59,
–77, LinLib L, WhoWest 74, –76, –78, –80,
–82, WrDr 80, –82, –84
Hayakawa, Samuel Ichiye 1906- *AmAu&B,*
AmM&WS 73S, –78S, BiDAmEd,
BioIn 3, –4, –5, –8, –9, –10, –11, BlueB 76,
CngDr 77, –79, –81, ConAu 13R,
DrAS 74F, –78F, –82F, IntAu&W 77,
IntWW 74, –75, –76, –77, –78, –79, –80, –81,
–82, –83, IntYB 78, –79, –80, –81, –82,
LEduc 74, REn, REnAL, TwCA SUP,
WebAB, –79, WhoAm 74, –76, –78, –80,
–82, WhoAmP 77, –79, –81, –83,
WhoGov 77, WhoWor 78, –80, –82,
WorAl, WrDr 76
Haycraft, Howard 1905- *AmAu&B, AuBYP,*
BiDrLUS 70, BioIn 3, –7, –8, –9, –10,
ConAu 21R, CurBio 41, –54, EncMys,
IntAu&W 76, –77, IntWW 74, –75, –76,
–77, –78, –79, –80, –81, –82, –83, IntYB 78,
–79, –80, –81, –82, REnAL, SmATA 6,
WhoAm 74, –76, –78, –80, WhoLibl 82,
WhoLibS 55, –66

Haycraft, Molly 1911- *BioIn 10, ConAu 13R, SmATA 6*

Hayden, Melissa 1923?- *BioIn 3, –4, –6, –7, –9, –10, –11, CanWW 70, –79, –80, –81, –83, CurBio 55, InWom, LibW, NewYTBE 73, WhoAm 74, –76, –78, WhoAmW 74, –58, –61, –64, –66, –70, –72, –75, WhoHol A, WhoWor 74, –76, WorAl*

Hayden, Robert C, Jr. 1937- *ConAu 69, SelBAA, SmATA 28, WrDr 76, –80, –82, –84*

Hayden, Robert E 1913-1980 *AmAu&B, AnObit 1980, AuBYP SUP, BioIn 4, –10, –11, –12, BlkAWP, BroadAu[port], ChhPo S1, –S2, –S3, ConAu 69, –97, ConLC 5, –9, –14, ConP 70, –75, –80, Conv 1, CroCAP, DcLB 5[port], DcLEL 1940, DrAP 75, InB&W 80, LinLib L, LivgBAA, ModBlW, NegAl 76, –83, NewYTBS 80[port], SelBAA, SmATA 19, –26N, WhAm 7, WhoAm 76, –80, WorAu 1970, WrDr 76, –80, –82*

Hayden, Torey L 1951- *ConAu 103*

Hayes, Billy *AmSCAP 66, ConAu 97, NewYTBE 73*

Hayes, Carlton Joseph Huntley 1882-1964 *AmAu&B, AmLY, BiDAmEd, BioIn 1, –2, –4, –7, –11, –12, CathA 1930, ConAu 1R, –3NR, CurBio 42, –64, DcAmB S7, LongCTC, REnAL, SmATA 11, TwCA SUP, WhAm 4, WhNAA*

Hayes, Elvin 1945- *BioIn 7, –8, –9, –11, –12, InB&W 80, WhoAm 78, –80, –82, WhoBbl 73, WhoBlA 75, –77, –80, WorAl*

Hayes, Sheila 1937- *ConAu 106*

Haykal, Muhammad Husayn 1888-1956 *DcOrL 3*

Hayman, LeRoy 1916- *AuBYP SUP, ConAu 85*

Haynes, Betsy 1937- *ConAu 8NR, –57, SmATA 37*

Haynes, James 1932- *ConAu 110*

Hays, Hoffman Reynolds 1904-1980 *AmAu&B, BioIn 4, –12, ConP 70, –75, DrAP 75, TwCA SUP, WhoE 75, –77, –79, WrDr 76*

Hays, James D 1933- *AmM&WS 73P, –76P, –79P, –82P, BiESc, WhoAm 78, –80, –82*

Hays, Wilma Pitchford 1909- *AuBYP, BioIn 8, –9, ConAu 1R, –5NR, ForWC 70, IntAu&W 77, SmATA 1, –28[port], ThrBJA, WhoAmW 74, –58, –61, –75, WrDr 76, –80, –82, –84*

Hayward, Charles Harold 1898- *Au&Wr 6, ConAu 7NR, –9R, WhE&EA*

Haywood, Charles 1904- *Baker 78, BlueB 76, ConAu 1R, DrAS 74H, –78H, –82H, IntAu&W 76, –77, IntWWM 77, OxCan, WhoAm 74, –76, –78, –80, –82, WhoAmJ 80, WhoAmM 83, WhoWor 74, WhoWorJ 72, –78, WrDr 76, –80, –82, –84*

Hazelton, Elizabeth Baldwin *AuBYP SUP*

Hazen, Barbara Shook 1930- *ConAu 105, SmATA 27[port]*

Hazo, Samuel 1928- *ConAu 5R, –8NR, ConP 70, –75, –80, DrAP 75, DrAP&F 83, DrAS 74E, –78E, –82E, IntWWP 77, –82, WhoAm 76, –78, –80, WhoE 75, WrDr 82, –84*

Hazzard, Shirley 1931- *AmAu&B, Au&Wr 6, BioIn 12, ConAu 4NR, –9R, ConLC 18, ConNov 72, –76, –82, DcLB Y82B[port], DcLEL 1940, DrAF 76, DrAP&F 83, IntAu&W 76, –82, NewYTBS 76, –80[port], –82[port], Novels, WhoAm 74, –76, –78, –80, –82, WhoAmW 74, –70, –72, –75, –83, WorAu 1970, WrDr 76, –80, –82, –84*

Head, Ann 1915- *ConAu X*

Head, Ann *see also* Morse, Anne Christensen

Head, Bessie 1937- *AfSS 79, –80, –81, –82, AfrA, ConAu 29R, ConLC 25[port], ConNov 72, –76, –82, DcLEL 1940, IntAu&W 76, –77, –82, WrDr 76, –80, –82, –84*

Headington, Christopher 1930- *AuBYP SUP, Baker 78, ConAu 106, IntWW 78, –79, –80, –81, –82, –83, IntWWM 77, WhoMus 72, WrDr 76, –80, –82, –84*

Headley, Elizabeth 1909- *AuBYP, BioIn 2, –6, –7, –9, ConAu X, MorJA, SmATA X, –1, TwCCW 83, WrDr 80*

Headley, Elizabeth *see also* Cavanna, Betty

Headstrom, Richard 1902- *AuBYP, ConAu 1R, –2NR, –77, SmATA 8, WrDr 82, –84*

Heal, Edith 1903- *BioIn 10, ConAu 1R, –2NR, SmATA 7, WhoAmW 58, –61, –64, –66, –68, –70, –72, WhoE 74*

Heal, Edith *see also* Berrien, Edith Heal

Healey, Larry 1927- *ConAu 101*

Healey, Robert C 1921- *ConAu 61*

Healy, John D 1921- *ConAu 93*

Heaney, Seamus 1939- *BioIn 10, –12, ChhPo S2, ConAu 85, ConLC 5, –7, –14, –25[port], ConP 70, –75, –80, CurBio 82[port], DcIrL, DcLEL 1940, EncWL 2, IntWWP 77, ModBrL SUP, NewYTBS 83[port], Who 82, –83, WhoWor 80, –82, WorAu 1970, WrDr 76, –80, –82, –84*

Heaps, Willard A 1908?- *AuBYP, BioIn 8, ConAu 85, SmATA 26[port], WhoLibS 55, –66*

Hearn, Lafcadio 1850-1904 *Alli SUP, AmAu, AmAu&B, AmBi, AnCL, AtlBL, BbD, BiD&SB, BiDSA, BioIn 1, –2, –3, –4, –5, –6, –8, –9, –10, –11, –12, CasWL, Chambr 3, ChhPo, –S3, CnDAL, ConAu 105, CrtT 3, CyWA, DcAmAu, DcAmB, DcBiA, DcEuL, DcLB 12[port], DcLEL, DcNAA, Dis&D, EncAB-H, EncO&P 78, EvLB, LinLib L, –S,*

McGEWB, ModAL, NatCAB 1, NewC,
Novels, OhA&B, OxAmH, OxAmL,
OxEng, PenC AM, –ENG, PoIre,
RAdv 1, REn, REnAL, ScF&FL 1,
TwCLC 9[port], WebAB, –79, WhAm 1,
WhLit, WhoHr&F

Hearne, John 1926- *ConNov 82, Novels,*
WrDr 82

Hearon, Shelby 1931- *AuNews 2, BioIn 11,*
–12, ConAu 25R, DrAP&F 83,
WhoS&SW 73, –75, –76

Hearst, James 1900- *BioIn 12, ChhPo,*
ConAu 85, DrAP 75

Heath, Monroe 1899-1966 *AmAu&B,*
ConAu P-1

Heatter, Maida *NewYTBS 81[port]*

Heaven, Constance 1911- *ConAu 2NR, –49,*
IntAu&W 77, SmATA 7, WhoWor 76,
WrDr 76, –80, –82, –84

Heaven, Constance *see also* Fecher, Constance

Hebblethwaite, Peter 1930- *WhoWor 80,*
WrDr 82

Hebden, Mark *ConAu X, IntAu&W 82X,*
WrDr 76, –80, –82, –84

Hebden, Mark *see also* Harris, John

Hebert, Ernest 1941- *ConAu 102*

Hechler, Ken 1914- *AmAu&B, BiDrAC,*
BioIn 5, CngDr 74, ConAu 109,
NewYTBS 75, WhoAm 74, –76, –78,
WhoAmP 73, –75, –77, –79, –81, –83,
WhoE 75, WhoGov 77, –72, –75

Hecht, Anthony 1923- *ConAu 6NR,*
ConLC 19, ConP 80, DcLB 5[port],
DrAS 82E, IntWW 80, –81, –82,
WhoAm 82, WrDr 82

Heck, Bessie Holland 1911- *ConAu 5R,*
ForWC 70, SmATA 26[port]

Heckel, Inge 1940- *WhoAm 82*

Hedges, Elaine R 1927- *ConAu 7NR,*
DrAS 82E

Heer, Friedrich 1916- *OxGer*

Heffron, Dorris 1944- *ConAu 49, WrDr 80,*
–82, –84

Hefley, James C 1930- *ConAu 7NR, –13R*

Hegarty, Walter 1922- *ConAu 65, WrDr 80,*
–82, –84

Hegner, Robert William 1880-1942 *BioIn 2,*
NatCAB 36, WhAm 2, WhNAA

Heide, Florence Parry 1919- *AuBYP SUP,*
ChhPo S1, –S2, ConAu 93, FourBJA,
SmATA 32[port], TwCCW 83

Heidish, Marcy 1947- *ConAu 101,*
DcLB Y82B[port]

Heilbroner, Robert L 1919- *AmAu&B,*
AmEA 74, BioIn 9, –10, ConAu 1R,
–4NR, CurBio 75, Future, IntWW 79,
–80, –81, –82, –83, WhoAm 74, –76, –78,
–80, –82, WhoE 74, –75, –83, WhoEc,
WrDr 80, –82, –84

Heilbrun, Carolyn G 1926- *AmWomWr,*
BioIn 12, ConAu 1NR, –45, ConLC 25,
DrAS 74E, –78E, –82E, TwCCr&M 80,

WrDr 82, –84

Heilbrun, Carolyn G *see also* Cross, Amanda

Heilman, Grant 1919- *ConAu 53*

Heiman, Grover 1920- *ConAu 5R, –6NR,*
IntAu&W 76, –77, WhoAm 82

Hein, Piet 1905- *BioIn 1, –7, CasWL,*
ConAu 4NR, –49, IntAu&W 77,
PenC EUR, WhoWor 74, –76

Heiney, Donald William 1921- *ConAu 1R,*
–3NR, ConLC 9, DrAS 74E, –78E, –82E

Heiney, Donald William *see also* Harris,
MacDonald

Heinlein, Robert A 1907- *AmAu&B,*
Au&Wr 6, AuBYP, BioIn 3, –4, –6, –7,
–10, –11, –12, ConAu 1R, –1NR,
ConLC 1, –3, –8, –14, –26[port],
ConNov 72, –76, –82, ConSFA, CurBio 55,
DcLB 8[port], DrAF 76, EncSF, InSci,
IntAu&W 76, LinLib L, MorJA,
NewYTBS 80[port], Novels, PenC AM,
REnAL, ScF&FL 1, –2, SmATA 9,
TwCA SUP, TwCCW 78, –83, TwCWr,
WebAB, –79, WebE&AL, WhoAm 74,
–76, –78, –80, –82, WhoSciF, WhoWor 76,
–78, –80, –82, WorAl, WrDr 76, –80, –82,
–84

Heintze, Carl 1922- *ConAu 57,*
SmATA 26[port]

Heinz, Hans Joachim 1904- *WhoAm 74, –76,*
–78

Heinz, W C 1915- *ConAu 4NR, –5R,*
SmATA 26[port], WhoE 83, WrDr 76,
–80, –82, –84

Heiser, Victor George 1873-1972 *AmAu&B,*
BioIn 1, –2, –3, –9, ConAu 33R,
CurBio 42, –72, –72N, InSci,
NewYTBE 72, WhAm 5, WhNAA

Heizer, Robert Fleming 1915-1979
AmM&WS 73S, –76P, BioIn 12,
ConAu 102, NewYTBS 79, OxCan SUP,
WhAm 7, WhoAm 74, –76, –78,
WhoWor 74, –76

Helfman, Elizabeth S 1911- *AuBYP, BioIn 8,*
–9, ConAu 5R, –5NR, ForWC 70,
SmATA 3, WhoE 83, WrDr 76, –80, –82,
–84

Helias, Pierre Jakez 1914- *BioIn 11,*
WhoFr 79

Heller, David 1922-1968 *BioIn 8, ConAu P-1*

Heller, Deane 1924- *ConAu 9R, ForWC 70*

Heller, Joseph 1923- *AmAu&B, AuNews 1,*
BioIn 8, –9, –10, –11, –12, BioNews 74,
BlueB 76, CasWL, ConAu 5R, –8NR,
ConDr 73, –77, –82, ConLC 1, –3, –5, –8,
–11, ConNov 72, –76, –82, CurBio 73,
DcLB Y80A[port], –2, DcLEL 1940,
DrAF 76, DrAP&F 83, EncWL 2,
IntAu&W 76, IntWW 83, LinLib L,
ModAL, ModAL SUP, NewYTBS 79,
NotNAT, Novels[port], OxAmL,
PenC AM, RAdv 1, TwCWr, WebE&AL,
WhoAm 74, –76, –78, –80, –82, WhoTwCL,

WorAl, WorAu, WrDr 76, –80, –82, –84
Heller, Peter 1920- *ConAu 41R, DrAS 74F,
–78F, –82F, WhoAm 74, –76, –78*
Hellman, Hal 1927- *ConAu X, Future,
IntAu&W 77X, –82X, SmATA 4,
WrDr 76, –80, –82, –84*
Hellman, Hal *see also* Hellman, Harold
Hellman, Harold 1927- *AuBYP SUP, BioIn 9,
ConAu 10NR, –25R, IntAu&W 77, –82,
SmATA 4*
Hellman, Harold *see also* Hellman, Hal
Hellman, Lillian 1905?-1984 *AmAu&B,
AmWomWr, AmWr SUP, Au&Wr 6,
AuNews 1, –2, BiE&WWA, BioIn 1, –2,
–4, –5, –7, –8, –9, –10, –11, –12, BioNews 74,
BlueB 76, CasWL, CelR 73, CnDAL,
CnMD, CnThe, ConAu 13R, ConDr 73,
–77, –82, ConLC 2, –4, –8, –14, –18,
CroCD, CurBio 41, –60, CyWA, DcFM,
DcLB 7[port], EncAB-H, EncSoH,
EncWL, –2, EncWT, FilmgC, ForWC 70,
GoodHs, InWom, IntAu&W 76, –77,
IntDcWB, IntMPA 77, –75, –76, –78, –79,
–81, –82, –84, IntWW 74, –75, –76, –77,
–78, –79, –80, –81, –82, –83, LibW,
LinLib L, LongCTC, McGEWB,
McGEWD, –84[port], ModAL,
ModAL SUP, ModWD, NatPD, –81[port],
NewYTBS 73, NewYTBS 75, NotNAT,
–A, OxAmL, OxFilm, OxThe, PenC AM,
PIP&P, PolProf T, REn, REnAL,
REnWD, TwCA, TwCA SUP, WebAB,
–79, WebE&AL, WhE&EA, Who 74,
–82, –83, WhoAm 74, –76, –78, –80, –82,
WhoAmJ 80, WhoAmW 74, –58, –61, –64,
–66, –68, –70, –72, –79, –81, –83, WhoE 74,
WhoThe 15, –16, –81, WhoTwCL,
WhoWor 74, –76, –78, –80, –82,
WhoWorJ 72, –78, WomWMM, WorAl,
WorEFlm, WrDr 76, –80, –82, –84*
Helm, June 1924- *AmM&WS 73S, FifIDA,
WhoAmW 66, –68, –72, WhoMW 74*
Helm, Thomas 1919- *ConAu 5R,
WhoS&SW 73*
Helprin, Mark 1947- *BioIn 12, ConAu 81,
ConLC 7, –10, –22[port], WhoAm 82*
Hemery, David 1944- *BioIn 9, –11,
WhoTr&F 73*
Hemingway, Ernest 1899?-1961 *AmAu&B,
AmNov, AmWr, ArizL, AuNews 2,
BioIn 1, –2, –3, –4, –5, –6, –7, –8, –9, –10,
–11, –12, CasWL, Chambr 3, ChhPo S1,
–S2, –S3, CnDAL, CnMD, CnMWL,
ConAmA, ConAmL, ConAu 77,
ConLC 1, –3, –8, –10, –13, –19, CyWA,
DcAmB S7, DcLB DS1[port], –Y81A[port],
–4, –9[port], DcLEL, EncAB-H, EncWL,
–2[port], EvLB, FilmgC, LinLib L, –S,
LongCTC, MakMC, McGEWB,
MichAu 80, ModAL, ModAL SUP,
ModWD, NatCAB 57,
NewYTBS 81[port], NotNAT B,*

*Novels[port], ObitOF 79, ObitT 1961,
OxAmH, OxAmL, OxEng, OxFilm,
PenC AM, RAdv 1, RComWL, REn,
REnAL, TwCA, TwCA SUP, TwCWr,
WebAB, –79, WebE&AL, WhDW,
WhAm 4, WhE&EA, WhFla, WhoTwCL,
WorAl, WorEFlm*
Hemingway, Gregory H 1931?- *BioIn 10, –12,
NewYTBS 76*
Hemingway, Joan 1950?- *BioIn 10*
Hemming, Roy 1928- *BioIn 11, ConAu 61,
SmATA 11, WhoAm 78, –80, –82,
WhoE 74*
Hemphill, Paul 1936?- *AuBYP SUP,
AuNews 2, BioIn 9, –10, –11, ConAu 49,
WrDr 76, –80, –82, –84*
Henderson, Bill 1941- *ConAu 33R,
Po&Wr 77, ScF&FL 1*
Henderson, Harold Gould 1889-1974 *BioIn 10,
ChhPo, –S1, ConAu 53, DrAS 74F, –78F,
WhAm 6*
Henderson, Richard 1924- *ConAu 5NR, –13R,
IntAu&W 77, WrDr 76, –80, –82, –84*
Henderson, Robert 1906- *ConAu 106,
WhoE 75*
Henderson, Zenna 1917- *AmWomWr,
BioIn 10, –12, ConAu 1R, –1NR, ConSFA,
DcLB 8[port], EncSF, ForWC 70,
ScF&FL 1, –2, SmATA 5, WhoSciF,
WrDr 84*
Hendin, David 1945- *ConAu 41R,
IntAu&W 76, –77, WhoAm 74, –76, –78,
–80, –82, WorAl*
Hendrich, Paula Griffith 1928- *ConAu 1R,
–1NR*
Hendry, James Findlay 1912- *ChhPo S1, –S2,
–S3, ConAu 29R, DrAS 74F,
IntAu&W 77, –82, PenC ENG,
WhE&EA, WhoCan 73, WhoWor 78,
WrDr 76, –80, –82, –84*
Henissart, Paul 1923- *ConAu 29R,
IntAu&W 77, WhoSpyF, WrDr 76, –80,
–82, –84*
Henkle, Henrietta 1909-1983 *AmAu&B,
BioIn 1, –2, –10, ConAu 69, CurBio 46,
InWom, OhA&B*
Henkle, Henrietta *see also* Buckmaster, Henrietta
Henkle, Henrietta *see also* Stephens, Henrietta
Henkle
Henle, Faye d1972 *BioIn 9, ConAu 37R,
NewYTBE 72*
Henley, Don 1946- *WhoRocM 82*
Henley, Don *see also* Eagles, The
Hennessy, Max *ConAu X, IntAu&W 82X,
WrDr 80, –82, –84*
Hennessy, Max *see also* Harris, John
Henri, Adrian 1932- *ConAu 25R, ConP 70,
–75, –80, DcLEL 1940, IntWWP 77, –82,
Who 82, –83, WhoArt 80, –82,
WhoWor 80, WrDr 76, –80, –82, –84*
Henri, Florette 1908- *AmAu&B, ConAu 73*
Henry, Marguerite 1902- *AmAu&B,*

AmWomWr, Au&ICB, Au&Wr 6,
AuBYP, BioIn 1, -2, -3, -4, -7, -8, -11, -12,
BkCL, ChlLR 4[port], ConAu 9NR, -17R,
CurBio 47, DcLB 22[port], FamMS,
InWom, IntAu&W 77, -82, JBA 51,
LinLib L, Newb 1922, SmATA 11,
TwCCW 78, -83, WhoAm 74, -76, -78,
-80, -82, WhoAmW 74, -58, -61, -66, -70,
-72, -75, -77, WhoWor 74, -76, WrDr 76,
-80, -82, -84

Henry, O 1862-1910 *AmAu&B, AmBi, AtlBL,*
BiDSA, BioIn 1, -2, -3, -4, -5, -6, -7, -8,
-9, -10, -12, CasWL, Chambr 3, ChhPo,
CnDAL, ConAu X, CyWA, DcAmB,
DcAmSR, DcLEL, DcNAA, Dis&D,
EncMys, EncWL, EvLB, FilmgC,
LinLib LP, LongCTC, McGEWB,
ModAL, Novels, OxAmL, OxEng,
PenC AM, RAdv 1, REn, REnAL,
TwCA, TwCA SUP, TwCLC 1, TwCWr,
WebAB, -79, WebE&AL, WhDW,
WhAm 1, WhoTwCL, WorAl, YABC X

Henry, O *see also* Porter, William Sydney

Henry, Oliver *ConAu X, YABC X*

Henry, Oliver *see also* Porter, William Sydney

Henry, Robert Selph 1889-1970 *BioIn 10,*
ConAu 1R, -103, DcLB 17[port],
NatCAB 55, NewYTBE 70, ObitOF 79,
WhAm 5, WhNAA

Henry, Will 1912- *AmAu&B, AuBYP SUP,*
ConAu X, WrDr 84

Hentoff, Nat 1925- *AuBYP, ChlLR 1,*
ChhPo S2, ConAu 1R, -5NR,
ConLC 26[port], IntAu&W 77, LinLib L,
REnAL, SmATA 27, ThrBJA,
TwCCW 78, -83, WrDr 76, -80, -82, -84

Hentoff, Nathan Irving 1925- *AmAu&B,*
BioIn 7, -8, -9, WhoAm 74, -76, -78, -80,
-82, WhoE 74, WhoWor 74

Henwood, James N J 1932- *ConAu 29R,*
DrAS 74H, -78H, -82H

Hepler, Loren George 1928- *AmM&WS 73P,*
-76P, -79P, -82P

Herald, Kathleen *ConAu X, -69, ThrBJA,*
TwCCW 83

Herald, Kathleen *see also* Peyton, Kathleen
Wendy

Herber, Harold L 1929- *ConAu 108,*
DrAS 74E, -78E, -82E

Herbert, Frank 1920- *AmAu&B, BioIn 10,*
-11, -12, ConAu 5NR, -53, ConLC 12,
-23[port], ConSFA, DcLB 8[port],
EncSF, IntAu&W 77, MnBBF,
NewYTBS 81[port], Novels, ScF&FL 1,
-2, SmATA 37, -9, WhoAm 74, -76, -78,
-80, -82, WhoSciF, WorAl, WorAu 1970,
WrDr 76, -80, -82, -84

Herbert, Wally 1934- *ConAu X, SmATA X,*
WhoWor 74, -76

Herbert, Wally *see also* Herbert, Walter William

Herbert, Walter William 1934- *ConAu 69,*
SmATA 23, Who 74, -82, -83

Herbert, Walter William *see also* Herbert, Wally

Herda, D J 1946?- *IntAu&W 76,*
WhoMW 76

Herge 1907-1983 *ChlLR 6[port], ConAu X,*
IntAu&W 77X, -82X, SmATA X,
WorECom

Herge *see also* Remi, Georges

Herkimer, L R 1925?- *ConAu 110*

Herlihy, James Leo 1927- *AmAu&B,*
Au&Wr 6, BiE&WWA, BioIn 6, -7, -10,
BlueB 76, CelR 73, ConAu 1R, -2NR,
ConDr 73, -77, -82, ConLC 6,
ConNov 72, -76, -82, CurBio 61,
DcLEL 1940, DrAF 76, DrAP&F 83,
IntAu&W 76, -77, LinLib L, NotNAT,
Novels, WhoAm 74, -76, -78, -80, -82,
WhoE 74, -75, WhoWor 74, -76, -78, -80,
WorAl, WorAu, WrDr 76, -80, -82, -84

Herlin, Hans 1925- *ConAu 77*

Herman, Ben 1927- *ConAu 104*

Herman, Charlotte 1937- *BioIn 12,*
ConAu 41R, SmATA 20

Herman, Lewis 1905- *BiE&WWA,*
WhoAmL 78, -79

Hermanns, William 1895- *BioIn 9,*
ConAu 37R, WrDr 76

Hermes, Patricia 1936- *ConAu 104,*
SmATA 31[port]

Herndon, James Emmett 1925- *ConAu 89,*
WhoBlA 75, -77, -80, WhoRel 77

Herold, Jean Christopher 1919-1964 *AmAu&B,*
BioIn 5, -7, ConAu P-1, CurBio 59, -65,
WhAm 4

Herrick, Robert 1591-1674 *Alli, AnCL,*
AtlBL, BbD, BiD&SB, BioIn 1, -2, -3, -4,
-5, -6, -7, -10, -12, BrAu, BrWr 2,
CasWL, Chambr 1, ChhPo, -S1, -S2,
CnE&AP, CroE&S, CrtT 1, -4, CyWA,
DcBiPP, DcEnA, DcEnL, DcEuL,
DcLEL, Dis&D, EvLB, LinLib L, -S,
LongCEL, LongCTC, McGEWB,
MouLC 1, NewC, OxEng, OxMus,
PenC ENG, RAdv 1, REn, WebE&AL,
WhDW, WorAl

Herring, Reuben 1922- *ConAu 7NR, -17R*

Herring, Robert H 1938- *ConAu 105*

Herriot, James 1916- *BioIn 9, -10, -11, -12,*
ConAu X, ConLC 12, IntAu&W 76, -77,
IntWW 82, -83, Who 82, -83, WorAl,
WrDr 76, -80, -82, -84

Herriot, James *see also* Wight, James Alfred

Herrmanns, Ralph 1933- *AuBYP SUP,*
BioIn 11, ConAu 3NR, -9R,
IntAu&W 77, -82, SmATA 11, WrDr 76,
-80, -82, -84

Herron, Edward A 1912- *BioIn 9, ConAu 5R,*
SmATA 4

Hersey, John Richard 1914- *AmAu&B,*
AmNov, BioIn 1, -2, -4, -5, -7, -8, -9, -10,
-12, BlueB 76, CasWL, CelR 73,
ChhPo S3, CnDAL, ConAu 17R,
ConLC 1, -2, -7, -9, ConNov 72, -76, -82,

*CurBio 44, CyWA, DcLB 6[port],
DcLEL 1940, DrAF 76, DrAP&F 83,
DrAS 74E, −78E, −82E, EncSF,
IntAu&W 76, −77, −82, IntWW 74, −75,
−76, −77, −78, −79, −80, −81, −82, −83,
LinLib L, −S, LongCTC, ModAL, Novels,
OxAmL, PenC AM, RAdv 1, REn,
REnAL, ScF&FL 1, −2, SmATA 25[port],
TwCA SUP, WebAB, −79, Who 74, −82,
−83, WhoAm 74, −76, −78, −80, −82,
WhoE 74, WhoWor 74, −76, −78, −80, −82,
WorAl, WrDr 76, −80, −82, −84*

Hersh, Seymour M 1936?- *AmAu&B,
AuNews 1, −1, BioIn 8, −9, −10, −11,
ConAu 73, WhoAm 74, −76, −78, −80, −82,
WhoS&SW 73, −75*

Hershey, Edward Norman 1944- *WhoE 79, −81,
−83*

Herst, Herman, Jr. 1909- *BioIn 5, −9,
ConAu 1R, −2NR, WhoS&SW 76, −78*

Herz, Peggy 1936- *ConAu 37R*

Herz, Peggy see also Hudson, Peggy

Herzberg, Max J 1886-1958 *AmAu&B,
REnAL, WhAm 3, WhNAA*

Herzberg, Max John 1886-1958 *BioIn 4*

Herzog, Arthur, III 1927- *ConAu 9NR, −17R,
EncSF, IntAu&W 77, ScF&FL 1, −2,
WhoAm 76, −78, −80, −82, WhoE 74,
WrDr 76, −80, −82, −84*

Herzog, Maurice 1919- *BioIn 3, −5, −9,
CurBio 53, InSci, IntWW 74, −75, −76,
−77, −78, −79, −80, −81, −82, −83, WhoFr 79,
WhoWor 74, −76, −78*

Hesse, Hermann 1877-1962 *AtlBL, BioIn 1, −2,
−3, −4, −5, −6, −7, −8, −9, −10, −11, −12,
CasWL, CIDMEL, ConAu P-2, ConLC 1,
−2, −3, −6, −11, −17, −25[port], CurBio 62,
CyWA, EncO&P 78, EncSF, EncWL,
−2[port], EvEuW, LinLib L, −S, MakMC,
McGEWB, ModGL, Novels[port],
ObitOF 79, ObitT 1961, OxGer,
PenC EUR, RComWL, REn, ScF&FL 1,
TwCA, TwCA SUP, TwCWr, WhDW,
WhAm 4, WhoTwCL, WorAl*

Hettlinger, Richard F 1920- *ConAu 7NR,
−17R, DrAS 74P, −78P, −82P*

Heuer, Kenneth John 1927- *ConAu 110,
WhoAm 76, −78, −80, −82*

Heuman, William 1912-1971 *AuBYP, BioIn 7,
−8, −12, ConAu 5R, −7NR,
SmATA 21[port], WrDr 84*

Heward, William L 1949- *ConAu 4NR, −53,
MichAu 80*

Hewes, Agnes Danforth 1874-1963 *AmAu&B,
AuBYP, BioIn 2, −8, JBA 34, −51,
SmATA 35, WhoAmW 58, −61*

Hewes, Henry 1917- *AmAu&B, BiE&WWA,
ConAmTC, ConAu 13R, NotNAT,
OxThe, WhoAm 74, −76, −78, −80, −82,
WhoThe 15, −16, −81, WhoWor 74, −76*

Hewitt, Geof 1943- *ConAu 33R, ConP 70,
−75, −80, DrAP 75, DrAP&F 83,*

WrDr 76, −80, −82, −84

Hey, Nigel 1936- *BioIn 12, ConAu 33R,
IntAu&W 76, SmATA 20, WhoWor 78,
WrDr 76, −80, −82, −84*

Heyer, Georgette 1902-1974 *Au&Wr 6,
BioIn 4, −10, ConAu 49, −93, CorpD,
DcLEL, EncMys, LongCTC, NewC,
NewYTBS 74, Novels, ObitOF 79,
ObitT 1971, REn, TwCA, TwCA SUP,
TwCCr&M 80, TwCWr, WhAm 6,
WhE&EA, WhLit, Who 74, WhoAm 74,
WhoAmW 66, −72, WhoWor 74, WorAl*

Heyerdahl, Thor 1914- *Au&Wr 6, BioIn 1, −2,
−3, −4, −5, −6, −8, −9, −10, −11, −12, CelR 73,
ConAu 5R, −5NR, ConLC 26[port],
CurBio 47, −72, InSci, IntAu&W 76, −77,
−82, IntWW 74, −75, −76, −77, −78, −79,
−80, −81, −82, −83, LinLib L, −S,
LongCTC, OxShips, SmATA 2,
TwCA SUP, TwCWr, UFOEn, WhDW,
Who 74, −82, −83, WhoAm 80, −82,
WhoWor 74, −76, −78, −82, WorAl,
WrDr 76, −80, −82, −84*

Heyman, Abigail 1942- *ConAu 57, ConPhot,
WrDr 76, −80, −82, −84*

Heyn, Ernest V 1904- *WhoAm 74, −76, −78,
−80, −82, WhoWor 78*

Hibbert, Christopher 1924- *Au&Wr 6,
BioIn 9, BlueB 76, ConAu 1R, −2NR,
IntAu&W 76, −77, −82, LongCTC, OxCan,
SmATA 4, Who 74, −82, −83,
WhoWor 76, −80, WrDr 76, −80, −82, −84*

Hibbert, Eleanor 1906- *BioIn 7, −9, −10, −11,
ConAu 9NR, −17R, ConLC 7, EncMys,
IntAu&W 76, −77, NewYTBS 77,
SmATA 2, Who 74, −82, −83, WorAu,
WrDr 76, −80, −82, −84*

Hibbert, Eleanor see also Carr, Philippa

Hibbert, Eleanor see also Holt, Victoria

Hibbert, Eleanor see also Plaidy, Jean

Hickel, Walter Joseph 1919- *AmCath 80,
BiDrGov, BiDrUSE, BioIn 8, −9, −10, −11,
−12, BlueB 76, ConAu 41R,
CurBio 69, IntAu&W 77, IntWW 74, −75,
−76, −77, −78, −79, −80, −81, −82, −83,
PolProf NF, WhoAm 74, −76, −78, −80, −82,
WhoAmP 73, −75, −77, −79, −81, −83,
WhoWor 74, −76, −78*

Hicken, Victor 1921- *ConAu 21R, DrAS 74H,
−78H, −82H, WhoAm 74, −76, −78, −80, −82,
WrDr 76, −80, −82, −84*

Hickman, Janet 1940- *BioIn 11,
ConAu 10NR, −65, SmATA 12*

Hickok, Lorena A 1892?-1968 *AuBYP,
BioIn 7, −8, −10, −12, ConAu 73, InWom,
NotAW MOD, SmATA 20*

Hicks, Clifford B 1920- *AmAu&B, AuBYP,
ConAu 9NR, ScF&FL 1, −2, WhoAm 80*

Hicks, Granville 1901-1982 *AmAu&B,
AmNov, AnObit 1982[port], BioIn 1, −2,
−4, −6, −7, −12, CnDAL, ConAmA,
ConAu 9R, −107, ConLCrt, −82,*

ConNov 72, –76, –82, CurBio 42, –82N,
DcLEL, IntAu&W 76, –77, IntWW 74,
–75, –76, –77, –78, –79, –80, –81, –82, –83N,
NewYTBS 82[port], OxAmL, PenC AM,
RAdv 1, REn, REnAL, ScF&FL 1,
TwCA, TwCA SUP, WhLit, WhoAm 74,
–76, –78, WhoWor 74, –76, –78, WrDr 76,
–80, –82

Hiebert, Ray Eldon 1932- AmAu&B,
ConAu 7NR, –17R, DrAS 74E, –78E,
SmATA 13, WhoAm 74, –76, –78, –80, –82,
WhoCon 73, WhoE 74, –75, –77, –79, –81,
–83, WhoPubR 72, –76, WhoWor 82

Higbee, Kenneth Leo 1941- AmM&WS 73S,
–78S, ConAu 101, WhoWest 78

Higdon, Hal 1931- AuBYP SUP, BioIn 9, –12,
ConAu 3NR, –9R, ScF&FL 1, –2,
SmATA 4, WrDr 76, –80, –82, –84

Higgins, Colin 1941- ConAu 33R,
DcLB 26[port], IntMPA 79, –81, –82, –84,
WhoAm 82, WrDr 76, –80

Higgins, George V 1939- BioIn 9, –10, –12,
ConAu 77, ConLC 4, –7, –10, –18,
ConNov 76, –82, DcLB Y81A[port], –2,
DrAF 76, DrAP&F 83, IntAu&W 77,
Novels, TwCCr&M 80, WhoAm 76, –78,
–80, –82, WorAl, WrDr 76, –80, –82, –84

Higgins, Jack 1929- BioIn 12,
NewYTBS 80[port], TwCCr&M 80,
Who 82, –83, WhoAm 78, –80, –82,
WhoWor 78, –80, –82, WorAl, WrDr 76,
–80, –82, –84

Higgins, Jack see also Patterson, Henry

Higgins, Marguerite 1920-1966 AmAu&B,
AmWomWr, BioIn 2, –3, –4, –5, –7, –8, –9,
–12, ConAu 5R, –25R, CurBio 51, –66,
DcAmDH, GoodHs, InWom,
NotAW MOD, ObitOF 79, WhAm 4,
WhoAmW 58, –64, –66

Higgins, Reynold Alleyne 1916- ConAu 25R,
IntAu&W 76, Who 74, –82, –83,
WrDr 76, –80, –82, –84

Higginson, Thomas Wentworth 1823-1911 Alli,
Alli SUP, AmAu, AmAu&B, AmBi,
ApCAB, BbD, BiDAmM, BiD&SB,
BioIn 3, –5, –6, –8, –9, CasWL, Chambr 3,
ChhPo, –S1, –S2, CnDAL, CyAL 2,
DcAmAu, DcAmB, DcAmSR, DcLB 1,
DcLEL, DcNAA, Drake, HarEnUS[port],
LinLib L, –S, McGEWB, NatCAB 1,
OxAmL, REn, REnAL, TwCBDA,
WebAB, –79, WhAm 1

Higham, Charles 1931- Au&Wr 6,
ConAu 33R, ConP 70, –75, –80,
DcLEL 1940, IntWWP 77, ScF&FL 1, –2,
WrDr 76, –80, –82, –84

Highsmith, Patricia 1921- AmWomWr,
Au&Wr 6, BioIn 10, –12, BioNews 74,
BlueB 76, ConAu 1R, –1NR, ConLC 2,
–4, –14, ConNov 72, –76, –82, EncMys,
IntAu&W 76, –77, –82, IntWW 82, –83,
Novels[port], TwCCr&M 80, Who 74, –82,

–83, WhoAmW 75, WhoHr&F,
WhoTwCL, WhoWor 76, WorAl, WorAu,
WrDr 76, –80, –82, –84

Hightower, Florence 1916-1981 Au&Wr 6,
AuBYP, BioIn 7, –9, –12, ConAu 1R,
–103, SmATA 27N, –4, ThrBJA,
TwCCW 78, –83, WhoAmW 74, –72, –75

Highwater, Jamake 1942- BioIn 11, –12,
ConAu 10NR, –65, ConLC 12,
DrAP&F 83, IntAu&W 77, NatPD,
SmATA 30, –32[port], TwCCW 83,
WhoAm 80, –82, WhoAmA 78, –80, –82,
WhoE 79, –81, –83, WhoWor 80,
WrDr 84

Highwater, Jamake see also Marks, J

Hilberry, Conrad Arthur 1928- ConAu 10NR,
–25R, DrAP 75, DrAP&F 83,
DrAS 74E, –78E, –82E, IntAu&W 77, –82,
IntWWP 77, –82, MichAu 80, WrDr 76,
–80, –82, –84

Hildick, E W 1925- AuBYP SUP, BioIn 8, –9,
ConAu X, FourBJA, SmATA 2,
TwCCW 78, –83, WhoChL, WrDr 80, –82,
–84

Hildick, Edmund Wallace 1925- Au&Wr 6,
ConAu 25R, IntAu&W 76, SmATA 2,
TwCCr&M 80

Hill, Dave 1936- ConAu X

Hill, Donna Marie BiDrLUS 70, ConAu 7NR,
–13R, DrAP&F 83, SmATA 24[port],
WhoAmW 77, –83, WhoLibS 55, –66

Hill, Douglas 1935- Au&Wr 6, BioIn 10,
ConAu 4NR, –53, ConP 70, ConSFA,
IntAu&W 76, IntWWP 77, OxCan SUP,
ScF&FL 1, –2, WrDr 76, –80, –82, –84

Hill, Frank Ernest 1888-1969? AmAu&B,
AuBYP, BioIn 4, –8, ChhPo, ConAu 73,
MedHR, REnAL, TwCA, TwCA SUP,
WhAm 5

Hill, Helen M 1915- ChhPo S3, ConAu 57,
SmATA 27

Hill, Janet AuBYP SUP

Hill, Margaret 1915- AuBYP, BioIn 1, –8,
ConAu 1R, –1NR, SmATA 36

Hill, Phyllis Malie Sites 1923- BiDrLUS 70,
WhoAmW 74, –68, –70, –72, –75, –77, –79,
–83

Hill, Ruth Livingston 1898- BioIn 11,
ConAu X, SmATA X

Hill, Ruth Livingston see also Munce, Ruth Hill

Hillary, Sir Edmund 1919- AsBiEn, ASpks,
Au&Wr 6, BioIn 3, –4, –5, –6, –7, –8, –9,
–10, –11, –12, BlueB 76, CurBio 54,
FarE&A 78, –79, –80, –81, IntAu&W 77,
IntWW 74, –75, –76, –77, –78, –79, –80, –81,
–82, –83, LinLib L, –S, LongCTC,
NewYTBE 70, WhDW, Who 74, –82, –83,
WhoWor 74, –82, WorAl, WrDr 76, –80,
–82, –84

Hillcourt, William 1900- AmAu&B, AuBYP,
BioIn 7, ConAu 93, SmATA 27,
WhoAm 74, –76, –78, –80, –82

Hiller, Carl E *AuBYP SUP*
Hillerman, Tony 1925- *BioIn 8, –10, –12, ConAu 29R, SmATA 6, TwCCr&M 80, WrDr 82, –84*
Hilliard, Robert L 1925- *ConAu 107, DrAS 74E, –78E, –82E, WhoGov 77, –72, –75*
Hillman, Howard 1934- *ConAu 41R*
Hillman, May *AuBYP, BioIn 8*
Hillocks, George, Jr. 1934- *ConAu 53, LEduc 74*
Hills, C A R 1955- *ConAu 106*
Hilton, James 1900-1954 *Alli SUP, BioIn 1, –2, –3, –4, –5, ChhPo S1, ConAu 108, CurBio 42, –55, CyWA, DcLEL, EncMys, EncSF, EvLB, FilmgC, LongCTC, MnBBF, ModBrL, NewC, NotNAT B, Novels, ObitOF 79, ObitT 1951, PenC ENG, REn, REnAL, ScF&FL 1, SmATA 34[port], TwCA, TwCA SUP, TwCCr&M 80, TwCWr, WhAm 3, WhE&EA, WhLit, WhoBW&I A, WorAl*
Hilton, Ralph 1907- *BioIn 11, ConAu 29R, SmATA 8, WhoS&SW 76, –78, –80, –82*
Hilton, Suzanne 1922- *AuBYP SUP, BioIn 9, ConAu 29R, IntAu&W 77, SmATA 4, WhoAmW 75, WrDr 76, –80, –82, –84*
Himes, Chester 1909- *AmAu&B, AmNov, BioIn 1, –2, –5, –9, –10, –11, –12, BlkAWP, ConAu 25R, ConLC 2, –4, –7, –18, ConNov 72, –76, –82, DcLB 2, DcLEL 1940, DrAF 76, DrAP&F 83, EncWL, –2, InB&W 80, IntAu&W 76, –77, –82, LinLib L, LivgBAA, ModAL, ModAL SUP, ModBlW, NegAl 76[port], –83, Novels, OhA&B, PenC AM, RAdv 1, SelBAA, TwCCr&M 80, WebE&AL, WhoAm 74, –76, –78, –80, –82, WhoBlA 75, –77, –80, WorAu, WrDr 76, –80, –82, –84*
Hinckley, Helen 1903- *AuBYP, BioIn 8, ConAu X, IntAu&W 76X, –77X, –82X, SmATA X, WrDr 76, –80, –82, –84*
Hinckley, Helen *see also* Jones, Helen Hinckley
Hindley, Geoffrey 1935- *Au&Wr 6, ConAu 109*
Hine, Al 1915- *AuBYP, BioIn 8, –9, ChhPo, –S1, ConAu 1R, –2NR, ScF&FL 1, –2, ThrBJA*
Hine, Virginia H 1920- *ConAu 97*
Hines, Barry 1939- *ConAu 102, IntAu&W 76, –77, –82, Novels, WhoWor 76, WrDr 76, –80, –82, –84*
Hingley, Ronald 1920- *Au&Wr 6, ConAu 5R, EncSF, IntAu&W 77, ScF&FL 1, –2*
Hinkemeyer, Michael T 1940- *ConAu 11NR, –69, DrAP&F 83*
Hinton, Nigel 1941- *ConAu 85*
Hinton, Phyllis 1900- *Au&Wr 6, IntAu&W 76, –77, WhE&EA*
Hinton, S E 1950- *AuBYP SUP, BioIn 8, –12, ChlLR 3, ConAu 81, FourBJA,*

SmATA 19, TwCCW 78, –83, WhoAm 82, WrDr 80, –82, –84
Hinton, Susie E 1950- *BioIn 8, –12*
Hintz, Martin 1945- *ConAu 65*
Hintze, Naomi 1909- *BioIn 8, ConAu 1NR, –45, ScF&FL 1, –2, WrDr 76, –80, –82, –84*
Hipple, Theodore W 1935- *ConAu 10NR, –65*
Hiraoka, Kimitake 1925-1970 *BioIn 7, –8, –9, –10, –12, ConAu 29R, –97, ConLC 9, WorAu*
Hiraoka, Kimitake *see also* Mishima, Yukio
Hirsch, Edward 1950- *ConAu 104, DrAS 82E*
Hirsch, Phil 1926- *ConAu 102, –97, SmATA 35*
Hirsch, S Carl 1913- *AnCL, AuBYP SUP, BioIn 9, ConAu 2NR, –5R, IntAu&W 76, –77, SmATA 2, ThrBJA, WrDr 76, –80, –82, –84*
Hirschfeld, Burt 1923- *AuBYP SUP, ScF&FL 1*
Hirshberg, Albert Simon 1909-1973 *AuBYP, BioIn 7, –9, ConAu 1R, –41R, WhAm 6, WhoE 74*
Hirst, Stephen Michael 1939- *ConAu 53*
Hitchcock, Alfred 1899-1980
  AnObit 1980[port], Au&Wr 6, BiDFilm, BioIn 1, –2, –3, –4, –5, –6, –7, –8, –9, –10, –11, –12, BioNews 74, BlueB 76, CelR 73, CmCal, CmMov, ConAu 97, ConLC 16, CurBio 41, –60, –80N, DcFM, EncMys, Film 2, FilmgC, IntAu&W 77, IntMPA 77, –75, –76, –78, –79, IntWW 74, –75, –76, –77, –78, –79, –80, LesBEnT, LinLib S, MakMC, McGEWB, MovMk, NewC, NewYTBE 72, NewYTBS 74, –80[port], NewYTET, OxAmH, OxFilm, REnAL, ScF&FL 1, SmATA 24N, –27[port], WebAB, –79, WhDW, WhAm 7, Who 74, WhoAm 74, –76, –78, –80, WhoHr&F, WhoWest 74, –76, WhoWor 74, –78, WorAl, WorEFlm
Hitchcock, Henry-Russell 1903- *BioIn 3, –6, –9, –12, DcD&D, IntAu&W 77, –82, IntWW 74, –75, –76, –77, –78, –79, –80, –81, –82, –83, Who 74, –82, –83, WhoAm 74, –76, –78, –80, –82, WhoAmA 73, –76, –78, –80, –82, WhoWor 74, WrDr 82, –84*
Hitchcock, Susan Tyler 1950- *ConAu 102*
Hitching, Francis 1933- *ConAu 103*
Hjortsberg, William 1941- *BioIn 8, ConAu 33R, DrAP&F 83, EncSF, IntAu&W 77, –82, ScF&FL 1, –2, WhoAm 80, –82, WrDr 76, –80, –82, –84*
Hoag, Edwin 1926- *AuBYP, BioIn 8, ConAu 13R, WrDr 82, –84*
Hoagland, Edward 1932- *AmAu&B, BioIn 9, –10, –12, ConAu 1R, –2NR, ConNov 72, –76, –82, CurBio 82[port], DcLB 6[port], DrAF 76, DrAP&F 83, IntAu&W 76, –77, NewYTBS 81[port], REnAL, WhoE 74, –75, –77, WorAu 1970,*

WrDr 76, -80, -82, -84

Hoagland, Mahlon Bush 1921- *AmM&WS 73P, -76P, -79P, -82P, AsBiEn, BiESc, ConAu 85, McGMS 80[port], WhoAm 74, -76, -78, -80, -82, WhoAtom 77, WhoE 83, WhoTech 82*

Hoare, Robert J 1921-1975 *Alli, Au&Wr 6, BiDLA, ConAu 6NR, -9R, IntAu&W 76, WrDr 76*

Hoban, Lillian 1925- *AmPB, AuBYP, BioIn 8, -9, -12, ChhPo S1, ConAu 69, IlsCB 1957, -1967, SmATA 22[port], ThrBJA*

Hoban, Russell 1925- *AuBYP, BioIn 6, -8, -9, -10, -12, ChlLR 3, ChhPo S1, -S2, ConAu 5R, ConLC 7, -25[port], IlrAm G, Novels, ScF&FL 1, -1A, -2, SmATA 1, ThrBJA, TwCCW 78, -83, Who 82, -83, WhoAm 82, WrDr 76, -80, -82, -84*

Hobart, Lois *AuBYP, BioIn 6, -7, -10, ConAu 5R, ForWC 70, MinnWr, SmATA 7, WhoAmW 58, WrDr 76, -80, -82, -84*

Hobsbawm, E J 1917- *IntAu&W 76, -77, WorAu 1970*

Hobsbawm, Eric J 1917- *Au&Wr 6, ConAu 3NR, -5R, Who 74, -82, -83, WhoWor 82, WrDr 76, -80, -82, -84*

Hobson, Burton 1933- *ConAu 2NR, -5R, SmATA 28, WhoAm 74, -76, -78, -80, -82, WhoE 75, -77*

Hobson, Julius W 1922?-1977 *AuBYP SUP, BioIn 7, -8, -9, -11, CivR 74, ConAu 102, InB&W 80, LivgBAA, NewYTBS 77, ObitOF 79*

Hobson, Laura 1900- *AmAu&B, AmNov, AmWomWr, Au&Wr 6, BioIn 1, -2, -3, -4, -6, -12, ConAu 17R, ConLC 7, -25[port], ConNov 72, -76, -82, CurBio 47, DcLEL 1940, InWom, IntAu&W 76, -77, REn, REnAL, TwCA SUP, WhoAm 74, -76, -78, -80, -82, WhoAmW 74, -58, -61, -64, -66, -68, -70, -72, -75, -77, -83, WrDr 76, -80, -82, -84*

Hochstein, Rolaine *ConAu 45, DrAP&F 83, Po&Wr 77*

Hodge, Jane Aiken 1917- *Au&Wr 6, AuBYP, BioIn 8, ConAu 3NR, -5R, IntAu&W 76, -77, -82, Novels, WhoWor 76, WrDr 76, -80, -82, -84*

Hodge, Paul William 1934- *AmM&WS 73P, -76P, -79P, -82P, BioIn 11, ConAu 33R, IntAu&W 77, -82, WhoAm 74, -76, -78, -80, -82, WhoTech 82, WhoWest 76, WrDr 76, -80, -82, -84*

Hodgell, P C 1951- *ConAu 109*

Hodges, C Walter 1909- *BioIn 1, ConAu 5NR, -13R, IlsCB 1967, IntAu&W 77, -82, SmATA 2, TwCCW 78, -83, Who 82, -83, WrDr 80, -82, -84*

Hodges, Cyril Walter 1909- *AnCL, Au&Wr 6, AuBYP, BioIn 4, -5, -7, -8, -9, -12, ChhPo S2, IlsCB 1744, -1946, -1957, SmATA 2, ThrBJA, Who 74, WhoArt 80, -82, WhoChL*

Hodges, Gil 1924-1972 *ConAu 109, CurBio 62, -72, -72N, NewYTBE 72, ObitOF 79, WorAl*

Hodges, Gilbert Ray 1924-1972 *BioIn 2, -3, -4, -5, -6, -7, -8, -9, -10, WhAm 5, WhoProB 73*

Hodges, Hollis *DrAP&F 83*

Hodges, Margaret 1911- *AuBYP SUP, BiDrLUS 70, BioIn 9, ConAu 1R, -2NR, DrAS 74E, -78E, -82E, ForWC 70, FourBJA, IndAu 1917, IntAu&W 77, -82, SmATA 1, -33[port], WhoAm 74, -76, -78, -80, -82, WhoAmW 74, -58, -61, -72, -75, -77, -83, WhoLibS 66, WrDr 76, -80, -82, -84*

Hoehling, Adolph A *ConAu 1R*

Hoehling, Mary 1914- *AuBYP, BioIn 7, ConAu 93*

Hoexter, Corinne 1927- *BioIn 10, ConAu 49, SmATA 6, WhoAmW 77, -79, WhoE 79, -81, -83*

Hoff, Rhoda *ChhPo S1*

Hoff, Syd 1912- *AmAu&B, Au&Wr 6, AuBYP, ChhPo S1, ConAu 4NR, -5R, IlsCB 1957, -1967, SmATA 9, ThrBJA, TwCCW 78, -83, WhoAm 74, -76, -78, -82, WhoWor 74, WhoWorJ 72, -78, WorECar, WrDr 80, -82, -84*

Hoff, Sydney 1912- *AuBYP, BioIn 7, -8, -9, -11*

Hoffer, Eric 1902-1983 *BioIn 2, -4, -6, -7, -8, -10, -11, CelR 73, CmCal, ConAu 109, -13R, ConIsC 2[port], CurBio 65, -83N, LinLib L, NewYTBS 83[port], PolProf J, RAdv 1, WebAB, -79, WhoAm 74, -76, -78, -80, -82, WorAl, WorAu, WrDr 76, -80, -82, -84*

Hoffer, William 1943- *ConAu 65*

Hoffman, Alice 1952- *ConAu 77*

Hoffman, Edwin D *ConAu 101*

Hoffman, Elizabeth 1921- *BiDrLUS 70, ConAu 77, WhoAmW 74, -70, -72, -75, -77, -79, WhoE 74, -75*

Hoffman, Lee 1932- *ConAu 25R, ConSFA, EncSF, ScF&FL 1, -2, WrDr 84*

Hoffman, Marshall 1942- *ConAu 106*

Hoffman, Nancy Jo 1942- *ConAu 107*

Hoffman, Paul 1934- *ConAu 1NR, -45*

Hoffmann, Banesh 1906- *AmM&WS 73P, -79P, -82P, BioIn 10, ConAu 3NR, -5R, IntAu&W 77, WhoAmJ 80, WhoWorJ 72, -78, WrDr 76, -80, -82, -84*

Hoffmann, Margaret Jones 1910- *AuBYP, BioIn 5, -7, ConAu 2NR, -5R*

Hoffmann, Margaret Jones *see also* Hoffmann, Peggy

Hoffmann, Peggy 1910- *AuBYP, ConAmC,*

ConAu X, ForWC 70, WrDr 76, –80, –82, –84

Hoffmann, Peggy *see also* Hoffmann, Margaret Jones

Hofstadter, Richard 1916-1970 *AmAu&B, BioIn 4, –8, –9, –10, –11, ConAu 1R, –4NR, –29R, CurBio 56, –70, DcLB 17[port], EncAAH, EncAB-H, IntEnSS 79, NewYTBE 70, ObitOF 79, OxAmL, PenC AM, PolProf E, REn, REnAL, WebAB, –79, WhAm 5, WorAl, WorAu*

Hogan, Bernice Harris 1929- *BioIn 11, ChhPo, ConAu 7NR, –13R, ForWC 70, SmATA 12*

Hogan, Desmond 1950?- *ConAu 102, DcIrL, DcLB 14[port]*

Hogan, James Philip 1915- *WhoRel 75, –77*

Hogan, Ray 1908- *ConAu 9R, WrDr 84*

Hogarth, Grace 1905- *Au&Wr 6, BlueB 76, ConAu 89, IntAu&W 76, –77, TwCCW 78, –83, WhoAm 78, –80, –82, WhoAmW 74, –72, –75, –77, WrDr 80, –82, –84*

Hogben, Lancelot 1895-1975 *BioIn 1, –2, –4, –5, –10, –11, –12, BlueB 76N, Chambr 3, ConAu 61, –73, CurBio 41, EvLB, InSci, IntWW 74, –75, –76N, LinLib L, –S, LongCTC, NewC, NewYTBS 75, ObitT 1971, TwCA, TwCA SUP, WhAm 6, –7, WhE&EA, Who 74*

Hogg, Beth 1917- *AuBYP, BioIn 8, ConAu X, –5R*

Hogg, Beth *see also* Grey, Elizabeth

Hogg, Garry 1902-1976 *Au&Wr 6, BioIn 8, –9, ConAu 10NR, –21R, IntAu&W 76, SmATA 2, WhoChL, WrDr 76*

Hogner, Dorothy Childs 1904- *AmAu&B, AuBYP, BioIn 2, –7, –9, ConAu 33R, IntAu&W 77, JBA 51, OxCan, SmATA 4, WhNAA, WhoAmW 58, –81, WrDr 76, –80, –82, –84*

Hogrefe, Pearl d1977 *ConAu P-1, DrAS 74E, WhAm 7, WhoAm 74, –76, –78, WhoAmW 74, –58, –64, –66, –68, –70*

Hoig, Stan 1924- *ConAu 1R, –1NR*

Hoke, Helen 1903- *AuBYP, BioIn 2, –8, –12, ConAu 73, ScF&FL 1, SmATA 15, WhoAmW 58*

Hoke, John Lindsay 1925- *BioIn 10, ConAu 41R, SmATA 7*

Holbrook, Hal 1925- *BiE&WWA, BioIn 5, –6, –7, –10, BioNews 74, CelR 73, CurBio 61, FilmgC, IntMPA 77, –75, –76, –78, –79, –81, –82, –84, MotPP, NewYTBE 73, NotNAT, WhoAm 74, –76, –78, –80, –82, WhoHol A, WhoThe 15, –16, –81, WorAl*

Holbrook, Sabra 1912- *BioIn 1, ConAu X, CurBio 48, InWom, WhoAmW 58, –61, –64, –66*

Holbrook, Sabra *see also* Erickson, Sabra Rollins

Holden, William Curry 1896?- *AmAu&B, AmM&WS 73S, Au&Wr 6, TexWr, WhNAA*

Holder, William G 1937- *AuBYP SUP, ConAu 10NR, –25R*

Holding, James 1907- *AuBYP, BioIn 8, –9, ConAu 25R, SmATA 3, TwCCr&M 80*

Holdstock, Robert 1948- *EncSF, IntAu&W 82, WrDr 84*

Holland, Barbara A 1925- *ConAu 57, DrAP 75, DrAP&F 83, IntAu&W 76, –77, IntWWP 77, –82*

Holland, Cecelia 1943- *ASpks, BioIn 7, –8, –9, –11, ConAu 9NR, –17R, DrAF 76, DrAP&F 83, EncSF, WhoAm 74, –76, –78, WhoAmW 74, WrDr 76, –80, –82, –84*

Holland, Isabelle 1920- *AuBYP SUP, BioIn 11, ConAu 10NR, –21R, ConLC 21[port], IntAu&W 82, SmATA 8, TwCCW 78, –83, WhoAmW 58, –66, WrDr 80, –82, –84*

Holland, John Lewis 1919- *AmM&WS 73S, –78S, BioIn 12, ConAu 25R, LEduc 74, SmATA 20*

Holland, Robert 1940- *ConAu 33R*

Hollander, John 1929- *AmAu&B, AuBYP, BioIn 8, –10, –12, ChhPo, –S1, ConAu 1R, –1NR, ConLC 2, –5, –8, –14, ConP 70, –75, –80, DcLB 5[port], DcLEL 1940, DrAP 75, DrAP&F 83, DrAS 74E, –78E, –82E, IntAu&W 77, –82, IntWW 78, –79, –80, –81, –82, –83, IntWWP 77, –82, LinLib L, OxAmL, PenC AM, REnAL, SmATA 13, WhoAm 74, –76, –78, –80, –82, WhoE 74, WhoTwCL, WorAu, WrDr 76, –80, –82, –84*

Hollander, Phyllis 1928- *AuBYP SUP, ConAu 97*

Hollander, Zander 1923- *AuBYP SUP, ConAu 65*

Hollon, William Eugene 1913- *AmAu&B, AuNews 1, ConAu 1R, DrAS 74H, –78H, –82H, EncAAH, REnAW, WhoAm 74, –76, –78, –80, –82*

Hollow, John Walter 1939- *DrAS 74E, –78E, –82E*

Holly, Buddy 1936?-1959 *AmPS A, BioIn 9, –10, –11, –12, EncPR&S, –77, IlEncRk, RkOn 74, –82, RkOneH, RolSEnR 83, WorAl*

Holm, Anne 1922- *AnCL, BioIn 9, ConAu 17R, FourBJA, ScF&FL 1A, SmATA 1, TwCCW 78B, –83B*

Holman, Felice 1919- *AuBYP, BioIn 8, –10, ChhPo S2, –S3, ConAu 3NR, –5R, FourBJA, IntAu&W 77, –82, ScF&FL 1, SmATA 7, TwCCW 78, –83, WhoAmW 75, –77, –83, WrDr 76, –80, –82, –84*

Holme, Bryan 1913- *AuBYP, BioIn 8, –9, ConAu 103, SmATA 26[port], WhoE 75*

Holmes, Burnham 1942- *ConAu 97*
Holmes, David Charles 1919- *ConAu 9R,*
WhoE 83
Holmes, Marjorie 1910- *AmAu&B, AmNov,*
Au&Wr 6, AuBYP, AuNews 1, BioIn 2,
-8, -10, ConAu 1R, -5NR, ForWC 70,
InWom, IntAu&W 76, -77, WhoAm 78,
-80, -82, WhoAmW 74, -58, -61, -72, -75,
-77, -79, WrDr 76, -80, -82, -84
Holmes, Martin 1905- *Au&Wr 6,*
ConAu 1NR, -49, MnBBF, WrDr 80, -82,
-84
Holmes, Oliver Wendell 1809-1894 *Alli,*
Alli SUP, AmAu, AmAu&B, AmBi,
AmWr SUP, ApCAB, AsBiEn, AtlBL,
BbD, BiDAmM, BiD&SB, BiESc,
BiHiMed, BioIn 1, -2, -3, -4, -5, -6, -7, -8,
-9, -10, -11, -12, CasWL, CelCen,
Chambr 3, ChhPo, -S1, -S2, -S3, CnDAL,
CrtT 3, -4, CyAL 2, CyWA, DcAmAu,
DcAmB, DcAmMeB, DcAmSR, DcBiA,
DcBiPP, DcEnA, DcEnL, DcLB 1,
DcLEL, DcNAA, Dis&D, Drake,
EncAB-H, EvLB, HarEnUS, InSci,
LinLib L, -S, McGEWB, MouLC 4,
NatCAB 2, Novels, OxAmH, OxAmL,
OxEng, PenC AM, PoChrch, RAdv 1,
REn, REnAL, ScF&FL 1,
SmATA 34[port], Str&VC, TwCBDA,
WebAB, -79, WebE&AL, WhDW,
WhAm HS, WorAl
Holmes, W J 1900- *ConAu 29R*
Holst, Imogen 1907- *Baker 78, IntWWM 77,*
OxMus, Who 82, -83
Holt, John Caldwell 1923- *AmAu&B, BioIn 8,*
-11, -12, ConAu 69, ConIsC 2[port],
CurBio 81[port], WhoAm 82
Holt, John Robert 1926- *ConAu 11NR, -25R,*
ScF&FL 1
Holt, Michael 1929- *Au&Wr 6, ConAu 5NR,*
-53, IntAu&W 76, -77, SmATA 13,
WrDr 76, -80, -82, -84
Holt, Rackham 1899-1963 *BioIn 6, CurBio 44,*
InWom, SmATA X, WhAm 4
Holt, Victoria 1906- *AmAu&B, Au&Wr 6,*
BioIn 7, -9, -10, -11, ConAu X, CorpD,
EncMys, IntAu&W 77X, NewYTBS 77,
Novels, SmATA 2, Who 74, -82, -83,
WhoAm 74, -76, -78, -80, -82,
WhoAmW 74, -72, -75, -77, -79, -81, -83,
WorAl, WorAu, WrDr 76, -80, -82, -84
Holt, Victoria see also Hibbert, Eleanor
Holton, Leonard 1915- *AuBYP, ConAu X,*
EncMys, IntAu&W 76X, -77X, -82X,
SmATA 2, TwCCr&M 80, WorAu,
WrDr 80, -82, -84
Holton, Leonard see also Wibberley, Leonard
Holtzman, Jerome 1926- *ConAu 4NR, -53,*
WhoAm 80, -82
Holz, Loretta 1943- *BioIn 12, ConAu 65,*
SmATA 17
Holzer, Hans 1920- *AmSCAP 66, BiDPara,*

ConAu 7NR, -13R, EncO&P 78,
ScF&FL 1, -2, WhoAm 74, -76, -78, -80,
-82, WhoE 74, WhoWor 82
Holzman, Red 1920- *ConAu X, WorAl*
Homze, Alma C 1932- *BioIn 12, ConAu 29R,*
SmATA 17
Hong, Edna H 1913- *ConAu 9NR, -21R,*
WhoAmW 74, -75, -77
Honig, Donald 1931- *BioIn 12, ConAu 9NR,*
-17R, DrAF 76, DrAP&F 83,
IntAu&W 77, SmATA 18
Honig, Edwin 1919- *AmAu&B, Au&Wr 6,*
BiE&WWA, BioIn 10, -12, BlueB 76,
ConAu 4NR, -5R, ConP 70, -75, -80,
DcLB 5[port], DrAP 75, DrAP&F 83,
DrAS 74E, -78E, -82E, IntAu&W 76, -82,
IntWWP 77, -82, LinLib L, NotNAT,
WhoAm 74, -76, -78, -80, -82,
WhoAmJ 80, WhoWor 74, -76,
WhoWorJ 72, -78, WorAu, WrDr 76, -80,
-82, -84
Honness, Elizabeth H 1904- *AuBYP, BioIn 7,*
-9, ConAu 25R, SmATA 2,
WhoAmW 74
Honour, Alan Edward 1918- *Au&Wr 6*
Hoobler, Dorothy *ConAu 11NR, -69,*
SmATA 28[port]
Hoobler, Thomas *ConAu 11NR, -69,*
SmATA 28[port]
Hood, Hugh 1928- *Au&Wr 6, CanWW 70,*
-79, -80, -81, -83, CanWr, CasWL,
ConAu 1NR, -49, ConLC 15, ConNov 72,
-76, -82, CreCan 1, DcLEL 1940,
IntAu&W 76, -77, -82, OxCan,
OxCan SUP, WrDr 76, -80, -82, -84
Hook, Diana Ffarington 1918- *ConAu 61*
Hook, Donald Dwight 1928- *ConAu 4NR, -53,*
DrAS 74F, -78F, -82F
Hooke, Nina Warner 1907- *ConAu 73*
Hooker, Richard *BioIn 10, ConAu X*
Hooks, William H 1921- *BioIn 12, ConAu 81,*
SmATA 16
Hooper, Meredith Jean 1939- *ConAu 106,*
IntAu&W 76, -77, SmATA 28[port],
WrDr 76, -80, -82, -84
Hooper, Walter 1931- *ChhPo S1, -S2,*
ConAu 7NR, -17R
Hoopes, Ned E 1932- *BioIn 12, ConAu 17R,*
DrAS 74E, -78E, -82E, ScF&FL 1, -2,
SmATA 21[port], WrDr 76, -80, -82, -84
Hoopes, Roy 1922- *AuBYP SUP, BioIn 11,*
ConAu 21R, SmATA 11
Hoover, F Louis 1913- *AmArch 70,*
ConAu 41R
Hoover, H M 1935- *ConAu 105, ScF&FL 1,*
SmATA 33
Hoover, Helen 1910- *Au&Wr 6, BioIn 9, -11,*
ConAu 21R, ForWC 70, IntAu&W 76,
-77, -82, SmATA 12, WhoAm 74, -76,
-78, -80, -82, WhoAmW 74, -66, -68, -70,
-72, -75, -77, -79, WhoE 74, -75, -77,
WhoWest 78, -80, -82, WhoWor 80,

WrDr 76, -80, -82, -84

Hoover, J Edgar 1895-1972 AmArch 70,
AmAu&B, ConAu 1R, -2NR, -33R,
CurBio 40, -50, -72, -72N, EncAB 5[port],
EncE 75, HisEWW, LinLib S, McGEWB,
NewYTBE 72, ObitOF 79, ObitT 1971,
PolProf E, PolProf J, PolProf K,
PolProf NF, PolProf T, REnAL,
WhAm 5, WhScrn 2, WorAl

Hoover, John Page 1910- AmM&WS 73S,
BioIn 2, ConAu 53, WhoAm 74, -76, -78

Hope, Anthony 1863-1933 BiD&SB, BioIn 2,
-4, -5, -8, -12, Chambr 3, CyWA, DcBiA,
DcEnA AP, DcLEL, EvLB, FilmgC,
LinLib LP, -S, LongCTC, ModBrL,
NewC, NotNAT B, Novels, OxEng,
PenC ENG, REn, TwCA, TwCA SUP,
TwCWr, WhLit, WhThe, WhoChL

Hope, Anthony see also Hawkins, Sir Anthony
Hope

Hope, Christopher 1944- ConAu 106

Hope, Laura Lee 1893?-1982 BioIn 10,
ConAu X, -17R, REnAL, SmATA X, -1,
WebAB, -79, WhoChL

Hope, Laura Lee see also Adams, Harriet S

Hope-Simpson, Jacynth 1930- Au&Wr 6,
BioIn 11, ConAu 7NR, -13R,
IntAu&W 76, -82, SmATA 12,
TwCCW 78, -83, WhoWor 76, WrDr 76,
-80, -82, -84

Hopf, Alice L 1904- AuBYP SUP, BioIn 10,
ConAu 9NR, -17R, ForWC 70,
IntAu&W 76, -77, -82, MichAu 80,
SmATA 5, WhoAmW 74, -72, -75, -77

Hopf, Alice L see also Lightner, A M

Hopke, William E 1918- ConAu 21R

Hopkins, Jerry 1935- ConAu 25R, LinLib L

Hopkins, Joseph G E 1909- AmCath 80,
BioIn 11, ConAu 1R, -5NR, DrAS 74H,
-78H, -82H, SmATA 11, WhoAm 74, -76,
-78

Hopkins, Lee Bennett 1938- AuBYP SUP,
BioIn 9, ChhPo S1, -S2, ConAu 25R,
IntAu&W 82, SmATA 3, WhoBlA 75,
-77, -80, WhoE 74, -75, WrDr 76, -80,
-82, -84

Hopkins, Pauline Elizabeth 1859-1930
AmWomWr, BioIn 12, BlkAWP,
InB&W 80

Hoppe, Joanne 1932- ConAu 81

Horan, James D 1914-1981 AmAu&B,
AnObit 1981, BioIn 12, ConAu 9NR,
-105, -13R, NewYTBS 81, WhoAm 74,
-76, -78, -80, WhoE 74, -75, -77, -79, -81,
WrDr 80, -82

Horgan, Paul 1903- AmAu&B, AmCath 80,
AmNov, Au&Wr 6, AuBYP, BioIn 1, -2,
-3, -4, -5, -6, -7, -8, -9, -10, BlueB 76,
CathA 1930, ChhPo, CnDAL,
ConAu 9NR, -13R, ConLC 9,
ConNov 72, -76, -82, CurBio 71, DcLEL,
DrAF 76, DrAP&F 83, DrAS 74H, -78H,

-82H, IlsCB 1744, IntAu&W 76, -77, -82,
Novels, OxAmL, REnAL, REnAW,
ScF&FL 1, -2, SmATA 13, TwCA SUP,
WhE&EA, WhNAA, WhoAm 74, -76,
-78, -80, -82, WhoE 74, WhoGov 72,
WhoWor 74, -78, -80, -82, WrDr 76, -80,
-82, -84

Horman, Richard Eliot 1945- ConAu 29R,
WhoE 75, -77, -83, WhoGov 77, -75

Horn, Daniel 1916- WhoAm 74, -76, -78,
WhoGov 77, -72, -75

Horn, Daniel 1934- ConAu 21R

Horn, George F 1917- ConAu 5R, -8NR

Hornby, Leslie 1949- ConAu 103, CurBio 68,
GoodHs, InWom, NewYTBE 71, -72,
WhoAm 74, WhoAmW 74

Hornby, Leslie see also Twiggy

Horne, Alistair 1925- Au&Wr 6, ConAu 5R,
-9NR, IntAu&W 76, -82, OxCan,
Who 74, -82, -83, WhoWor 74, -76,
WrDr 76, -80, -82, -84

Horner, Dave 1934- BioIn 11, ConAu 17R,
SmATA 12

Horner, Joyce Mary 1903-1980 BioIn 12,
DrAS 74E, WhoAmW 70

Horney, Karen 1885-1952 AmAu&B,
AmWomWr, BioIn 3, -4, -7, -10, -11, -12,
CurBio 41, -53, DcAmB 55, EncTR,
GoodHs, GuPsyc[port], InSci, InWom,
IntDcWB, LibW, McGEWB, NamesHP,
NewYTBE 73, NotAW MOD, ObitOF 79,
TwCA SUP, WhDW, WhAm 3, WorAl

Hornik, Edith Lynn 1930- ConAu X, -61

Hornsby, Alton, Jr. 1940- ConAu 37R,
DrAS 74H, -78H, -82H, LivgBAA,
WhoBlA 75, -77, -80, WhoS&SW 76, -78,
WrDr 76, -80, -82, -84

Hornung, Clarence Pearson 1899- ConAu 9NR,
-17R, WhoAmA 73, -76, -78, -80, -82

Hornung, Ernest William 1866-1921 BbD,
BiD&SB, BioIn 1, -2, Chambr 3, CorpD,
DcLEL, EncMys, EvLB, LongCTC,
MnBBF, NewC, REn, TwCA,
TwCA SUP, TwCWr, WhLit

Horowitz, Edward 1904- ConAu 1R, -4NR,
WhoWorJ 72, -78

Horowitz, Israel Albert 1907-1973 ConAu 41R,
GolEC

Horton, Louise 1916- ConAu 2NR, -49

Horvath, Joan 1944- BioIn 10, ConAu 81,
WomWMM A

Horwitz, Elinor Lander AuBYP SUP,
SmATA 33

Horwitz, Sylvia L 1911- ConAu 61

Hosford, Jessie 1892- BioIn 10, ConAu 41R,
SmATA 5

Hoskins, Robert 1933- ConAu 29R, EncSF,
ScF&FL 1, -2, WrDr 84

Hosley, Richard 1921- ConAu 5R, -8NR,
DrAS 74E, -78E, -82E

Hosokawa, Bill 1915- ConAu X

Hosokawa, William K 1915- ConAu 11NR,

*ConAu 9R, ConLC 15, ConP 70, –75, –80,
DcLEL 1940, DrAP 75, DrAP&F 83,
ForWC 70, IntAu&W 76, –77, –82,
IntWWP 77, –82, PenC AM, REnAL,
SmATA 5, WhoAm 74, –76, –78, –80, –82,
WhoAmW 58, –61, –83, WorAu, WrDr 76,
–80, –82, –84*

Howland, Bette 1937- *ConAu 85*

Hoxie, Ralph Gordon 1919- *DrAS 74H, –78H,
–82H, WhoAm 74, –76, –78, –80, –82,
WhoE 74, –75, –77, –79, –81, –83,
WhoWor 80, –82*

Hoyle, Fred 1915- *AsBiEn, Au&Wr 6,
BiESc, BioIn 4, –5, –6, –10, –12, BlueB 76,
ConAu 3NR, –5R, ConNov 72, ConSFA,
CurBio 60, DcLEL 1940, EncSF, InSci,
IntAu&W 76, –77, IntWW 74, –75, –76,
–77, –78, –79, –80, –81, –82, –83, LinLib L,
McGMS 80[port], Novels, ScF&FL 1, –2,
TwCWr, Who 74, –82, –83, WhoSciF,
WhoWor 74, –76, –78, –82, WorAu,
WrDr 76, –80, –82, –84*

Hoyle, Geoffrey 1942- *Au&Wr 6, BioIn 12,
ConAu 6NR, –53, ConSFA, EncSF,
IntAu&W 77, –82, Novels, ScF&FL 1, –2,
SmATA 18, WhoWor 76, WrDr 76, –80,
–82, –84*

Hoyt, Edwin Palmer, Jr. 1923- *AuBYP,
BioIn 2, –8, ConAu 1R, –1NR,
DrAP&F 83, SmATA 28*

Hoyt, Murray 1904- *ConAu 9R,
IntAu&W 76, –77, –82*

Hoyt, Olga 1922- *AuBYP SUP, BioIn 12,
ConAu 25R, SmATA 16, WhoAmW 74,
–75, –79*

Hsu, Kai-Yu 1922- *ConAu 21R, DrAS 74F,
–78F, –82F, WrDr 76, –80, –82, –84*

Hu, Chang-Tu 1921- *DrAS 74H, –78H, –82H,
LEduc 74*

Huberman, Edward 1910- *ConAu 13R,
DrAS 74E, –78E, –82E, WhoE 75*

Huberman, Elizabeth 1915- *ConAu 13R,
DrAS 74E, –78E, –82E*

Hubler, H Clark 1910- *AmM&WS 73P,
WhoMW 74, –76*

Hubler, Richard G 1912- *AmAu&B, AmNov,
BioIn 2, BlueB 76, ConAu 1R, –2NR,
DrAP&F 83, DrAS 74E, –78E,
IntAu&W 76, –77, –82, WhoWest 74, –76,
–78, WrDr 76, –80, –82, –84*

Huckaby, Elizabeth 1905- *ConAu 106*

Huckaby, Gerald 1933- *ConAu 33R*

Huddy, Delia 1934- *ConAu 25R*

Hudson, Geoffrey 1903-1974 *BioIn 10,
ConAu 49, WhLit*

Hudson, Gossie Harold 1930- *ConAu 93,
DrAS 74H, WhoBlA 75, –77, –80*

Hudson, James A 1924- *ConAu 33R,
WhoE 75, WrDr 76, –80, –82, –84*

Hudson, Lois Phillips 1927- *ConAu 1R,
ForWC 70, WhoAmW 74, –66, –68, –70,
–72*

Hudson, Peggy 1936- *ConAu X, ForWC 70*

Hudson, Peggy *see also* Herz, Peggy

Hudson, William Henry 1841-1922 *Alli SUP,
AnCL, AtlBL, BioIn 1, –2, –3, –5, –6, –8,
–9, –12, CarSB, CasWL, Chambr 3,
ChhPo S1, –S2, –S3, CyWA, DcBiA,
DcEuL, DcLEL, Dis&D, EncSF, EvLB,
InSci, LinLib S, LongCTC, ModBrL,
NewC, OxEng, OxSpan, PenC ENG,
RAdv 1, REn, SmATA 35, TwCA,
TwCA SUP, TwCWr, WebE&AL,
WhDW*

Huff, Darrell 1913- *ConAu 1R, –5NR*

Huff, Tom E 1937?- *AuNews 2, BioIn 11*

Huffaker, Clair 1927?- *CmMov, FilmgC,
WhoAm 74, WorEFlm, WrDr 84*

Huffard, Grace Thompson 1892- *ChhPo,
ConAu P-1, IndAu 1917, WhoAmW 68*

Huggett, Frank Edward 1924- *Au&Wr 6,
ConAu 3NR, –9R, IntAu&W 77, –82,
WhoWor 76, WrDr 76, –80, –82, –84*

Huggins, Nathan Irvin 1927- *ConAu 29R,
DrAS 74H, –78H, –82H, InB&W 80,
LivgBAA, WhoAm 74, –78, –80, –82,
WhoBlA 77, –80, WhoE 74*

Hughes, Dean 1943- *ConAu 106,
SmATA 33[port]*

Hughes, Erica 1931- *ConAu 109*

Hughes, Langston 1902-1967 *AmAu&B,
AmSCAP 66, AmWr SUP, AnCL,
AuBYP, BiDAfM, BiDAmM,
BiE&WWA, BioIn 1, –2, –3, –4, –5, –6, –7,
–8, –9, –10, –11, –12, BkCL, BlkAWP,
BroadAu, ChhPo, CnDAL, CnMD,
ConAmA, ConAu 1R, –1NR, –25R,
ConLC 1, –5, –10, –15, ConP 75, CroCD,
CurBio 40, –67, DcLB 4, –7[port],
DrBlPA, EncJzS 70, EncWL, –2, EncWT,
FourBJA, LinLib L, –S, LongCTC,
McGEWB, McGEWD, –84, ModAL,
ModAL SUP, ModBlW, ModWD,
NegAl 76[port], –83[port], NotNAT A, –B,
Novels, ObitOF 79, ObitT 1961, OxAmL,
PenC AM, RAdv 1, REn, REnAL,
SixAP, SmATA 33[port], –4, Str&VC,
TwCA, TwCA SUP, WebAB, –79,
WebE&AL, WhDW, WhAm 4,
WhE&EA, WhoTwCL, WorAl*

Hughes, Mary Gray 1930- *ConAu 61*

Hughes, Mary Louise 1910- *ConAu 29R*

Hughes, Monica 1925- *BioIn 12, ConAu 77,
SmATA 15, WrDr 84*

Hughes, Pennethorne 1907-1967 *ChhPo S3,
ConAu P-2*

Hughes, Richard 1900-1976 *Alli, Alli SUP,
Au&Wr 6, BioIn 4, –5, –6, –7, –8, –9, –10,
–11, CasWL, ChhPo, –S2, ConAu 4NR,
–5R, –65, ConLC 1, –11, ConNov 72, –76,
CyWA, DcLB 15[port], DcLEL, EncWL,
–2, EvLB, IntAu&W 76, IntWW 74, –75,
–76, –77N, IntWWP 77, LongCTC,
ModBrL, ModBrL SUP, NewC,*

NewYTBS 76, Novels, ObitOF 79,
OxEng, PenC ENG, RAdv 1, REn,
ScF&FL 1, SmATA 25N, –8, TwCA,
TwCA SUP, TwCCW 78, –83, TwCWr,
WhAm 7, WhE&EA, Who 74, WhoChL,
WhoLA, WhoTwCL, WhoWor 74,
WrDr 76
Hughes, Riley 1914?-1981 *AmCath 80,*
BioIn 3, –4, BkC 5, ConAu 103, –107
Hughes, Ted 1930- *AuBYP SUP, BioIn 7, –9,*
–10, –11, –12, BlueB 76, CasWL,
ChlLR 3, ChhPo, –S1, –S2, –S3, CnE&AP,
ConAu 1R, –1NR, ConLC 2, –4, –9, –14,
ConP 70, –75, –80, CurBio 79,
DcLEL 1940, EncSF, EncWL, –2[port],
IntAu&W 76, –77, IntWW 74, –75, –76,
–77, –78, –79, –80, –81, –82, –83,
IntWWP 77, LinLib L, LongCEL,
LongCTC, MakMC, ModBrL,
ModBrL SUP, NewC, PenC ENG,
RAdv 1, SmATA 27, TwCCW 78, –83,
TwCWr, WebE&AL, WhDW, Who 74,
–82, –83, WhoAm 82, WhoTwCL,
WhoWor 74, –76, –78, –82, WorAl,
WorAu, WrDr 76, –80, –82, –84
Hughes, Terry A 1933- *ConAu 65*
Hughes, Thomas 1822-1896 *Alli SUP, BbD,*
BiD&SB, BioIn 3, –4, –5, –6, –8, –9, –12,
BrAu 19, CarSB, CasWL, CelCen,
ChhPo S3, CyEd, CyWA, DcBiA,
DcBiPP, DcEnA, DcEnL, DcEuL,
DcLB 18[port], DcLEL, EvLB, JBA 34,
LinLib L, –S, LuthC 75, MnBBF,
MouLC 4, NewC, Novels, OxEng,
PenC ENG, REn, SmATA 31[port],
TelT, TwCCW 83A, WhoBW&I A,
WhoChL, WorAl
Hughes, Zach 1928- *IntAu&W 77X,*
ScF&FL 1, –2, WrDr 76, –80, –82, –84
Hugo, Richard 1923-1982 *AnObit 1982[port],*
BioIn 12, ConAu 3NR, –108, –49,
ConLC 6, –18, ConP 70, –75, –80,
DcLB 5[port], DcLEL 1940, DrAP 75,
IntWWP 77, NewYTBS 82, WhoAm 76,
–78, –80, –82, WhoPNW, WrDr 76, –80,
–82, –84
Hugo, Victor Marie 1802-1885 *AtlBL, BbD,*
BiD&SB, BioIn 1, –2, –3, –4, –5, –6, –7, –8,
–9, –10, –11, –12, CasWL, CelCen, ChhPo,
–S1, –S2, –S3, CnThe, CyWA, DcBiA,
DcBiPP, DcEnL, DcEuL, Dis&D,
EncMys, EncO&P 78, EncWT, EuAu,
EvEuW, HsB&A, LinLib L, –S,
McGEWB, McGEWD, –84[port], MnBBF,
NewC, NewEOp 71, NotNAT A, –B,
Novels[port], OxEng, OxFr, OxMus,
OxThe, PenC EUR, RComWL, REn,
REnWD, ScF&FL 1, WhDW, WorAl
Hulke, Malcolm 1924- *Au&Wr 6, ConAu 81,*
IntAu&W 76, –77, ScF&FL 1, –2,
WrDr 76, –80
Hull, Bobby 1939- *BioIn 7, –8, –9, –10, –11,*

–12, CelR 73, CurBio 66, NewYTBE 73,
NewYTBS 78, –80[port], WorAl
Hull, Bobby *see also* Hull, Robert Marvin
Hull, Denison Bingham 1897- *ConAu 37R,*
IntAu&W 76, WhoAm 74, –76,
WhoWor 76
Hull, E Mayne 1905-1975 *ConSFA,*
ScF&FL 1, –2, WhoSciF
Hull, Eleanor 1913- *BioIn 12, ConAu 4NR,*
–9R, ForWC 70, IntAu&W 77,
SmATA 21[port], WhoAmW 58, –61, –75,
–77, WrDr 76, –80, –82, –84
Hull, Gloria T 1944- *ConAu 108, WhoBlA 75,*
–77, –80
Hull, Jesse Redding 1932- *ConAu X*
Hull, Jessie Redding 1932- *ConAu 109*
Hull, Robert Marvin 1939- *BioIn 10, –11, –12,*
CanWW 81, –83, WhoAm 74, –76, –78,
–80, –82, WhoHcky 73, WhoMW 74
Hull, Robert Marvin *see also* Hull, Bobby
Hulme, Kathryn 1900-1981 *AmAu&B,*
AmWomWr, BioIn 4, –6, –8, –12, BkC 5,
ConAu 104, ConAu P-1,
NewYTBS 81[port], WhoAm 74,
WhoAmW 74, –58, –61, –64, –66, –68, –70,
–72, –75, –77, WhoWor 74
Hulme, William Edward 1920- *ConAu 5NR,*
–13R, DrAS 74P, –78P, –82P
Hulteng, John L 1921- *BioIn 2, BlueB 76,*
ConAu 33R, DrAS 74E, –78E, –82E,
WhoAm 74, –76, –78, –80, –82, WrDr 80,
–82, –84
Hume, Ruth 1922-1980 *AuBYP, BioIn 8,*
ConAu 97, SmATA 22N, –26
Humphrey, William 1924- *AmAu&B, BioIn 4,*
–7, –8, –10, –11, ConAu 77, ConNov 72,
–76, –82, DcLB 6, DcLEL 1940,
DrAF 76, IntAu&W 76, Novels,
PenC AM, REnAL, WhoAm 74, WorAu,
WrDr 76, –80, –82, –84
Hunt, Bernice Kohn 1920- *IntAu&W 77,*
WhoAmW 83, WhoE 81, –83, WrDr 76,
–80, –82, –84
Hunt, Douglas 1918- *ConAu 13R*
Hunt, Irene 1907- *AmWomWr, AuBYP,*
BioIn 7, –8, –9, –10, –12, ChlLR 1,
ConAu 8NR, –17R, MorBMP,
NewbC 1966, SmATA 2, ThrBJA,
TwCCW 78, –83, WhoAm 74,
WhoAmW 74, –70, –72, WrDr 80, –82, –84
Hunt, Kari 1920- *AuBYP, ConAu 41R,*
WhoAmA 73, –76, –78, –80, –82
Hunt, M 1920- *Au&Wr 6, ConAu 5R,*
SmATA 22, WhoE 81, –83
Hunt, Mabel Leigh 1892-1971 *AmAu&B,*
AmWomWr, AuBYP, BioIn 2, –3, –7, –9,
–12, ConAu 106, ConAu P-1, CurBio 51,
InWom, IndAu 1917, JBA 51, SmATA 1,
–26N, TwCCW 78, –83, WhAm 5,
WhoAmW 58, –61, –64, –66, –68, –70
Hunter, Beatrice Trum 1918- *ConAu 7NR,*
–17R, ForWC 70, WhoAmW 74, –75, –77

Hunter, David E 1943- *AmM&WS 73S, –76P, FifIDA*

Hunter, Evan 1926- *AmAu&B, AmSCAP 66, Au&Wr 6, AuBYP, BioIn 4, –5, –8, –10, –12, BlueB 76, ConAu 5R, –5NR, ConLC 11, ConNov 72, –76, –82, CurBio 56, DcLB Y82B[port], DcLEL 1940, DrAF 76, DrAP&F 83, EncMys, EncSF, FilmgC, IntAu&W 76, –77, IntWW 74, –75, –76, –77, –78, –79, –80, –81, –82, –83, Novels, PenC AM, REn, REnAL, ScF&FL 1, –2, SmATA 25[port], TwCCr&M 80, Who 82, –83, WhoAm 74, –76, –78, –80, –82, WhoE 74, WhoTwCL, WhoWor 74, WorAl, WorAu, WorEFlm, WrDr 76, –80, –82, –84*

Hunter, Hilda 1921?- *Au&Wr 6, AuBYP SUP, BioIn 10, ConAu 49, SmATA 7, WhoMus 72*

Hunter, Jim 1939- *Au&Wr 6, ConAu 7NR, –9R, ConNov 72, –76, DcLB 14[port], DcLEL 1940, IntAu&W 76, –77, NewYTBS 74, ScF&FL 1, –2, WrDr 76, –80, –82, –84*

Hunter, Kristin 1931- *Au&ICB, AuBYP, AuNews 1, BioIn 10, –11, BlkAWP, ChlLR 3, ConAu 13R, ConNov 72, –76, –82, DrAF 76, DrAP&F 83, ForWC 70, FourBJA, InB&W 80, IntAu&W 76, –77, LinLib L, LivgBAA, SelBAA, SmATA 12, TwCCW 78, –83, WhoAm 74, –76, –78, –80, –82, WhoAmW 74, –68, –70, –72, –75, WhoBlA 75, –77, –80, WrDr 76, –80, –82, –84*

Hunter, Mollie 1922- *AuBYP, BioIn 9, –11, –12, ConAu X, ConLC 21[port], IntAu&W 77X, ScF&FL 1, –2, SmATA 2, ThrBJA, TwCCW 78, –83, WrDr 76, –80, –82, –84*

Hunter, Mollie *see also* McIlwraith, Maureen Mollie Hunt

Hunter, Norman 1899- *Au&Wr 6, BioIn 8, ChhPo S2, ConAu 93, EncSF, IntAu&W 76, –77, –82, SmATA 26[port], TwCCW 78, –83, WhE&EA, WhLit, WhoChL, WrDr 76, –80, –82, –84*

Hunter, Sam 1923- *ConAu 8NR, –13R, WhoAm 74, –76, –78, –80, –82, WhoAmA 73, –76, –78, –80, –82, WhoE 74, WhoWor 74, –76*

Huntsberry, William E 1916- *BioIn 10, ConAu 1R, –2NR, DrAS 74E, –78E, –82E, SmATA 5*

Hurley, F Jack 1940- *ConAu 45*

Hurley, Leslie J 1911- *AuBYP, ConAu 49*

Hurlimann, Bettina 1909-1983 *BioIn 9, ChhPo S1, ConAu X, SmATA 34N, ThrBJA*

Hurwitz, Howard Lawrence 1916- *ConAu 37R, DrAS 74H, –78H, –82H, NewYTBS 76*

Hurwood, Bernhardt J 1926- *BioIn 11, ConAu 25R, ScF&FL 1, –2, SmATA 12*

Huston, John 1906- *BiDFilm, BioIn 1, –2, –3, –4, –5, –6, –7, –8, –9, –10, –11, –12, BlueB 76, CelR 73, CmMov, ConAu 73, ConDr 73, –77A, –82A, ConLC 20, CurBio 81[port], DcFM, DcLB 26[port], FilmgC, IntAu&W 77, IntMPA 77, –78, –79, –81, –82, –84, IntWW 74, –75, –76, –77, –78, –79, –80, –81, –82, –83, MovMk, OxFilm, REnAL, WebAB, –79, Who 74, –82, –83, WhoAm 74, –76, –78, –80, –82, WhoHol A, WhoWor 74, WorAl, WorEFlm*

Hutchins, Francis Gilman 1939- *AmM&WS 73S, –78S, ConAu 21R, IntAu&W 77, –82, WrDr 76, –80, –82, –84*

Hutchins, Francis Gilman *see also* Madison, Frank

Hutchins, Ross Elliott 1906- *AuBYP, BioIn 8, –9, ConAu 5NR, –9R, SmATA 4, ThrBJA, WhoAm 74, –76, –78, –80*

Hutchinson, Mary Jane 1924- *ConAu 106*

Hutchinson, Ray Coryton 1907-1975 *Au&Wr 6, BioIn 4, –12, ConAu 1R, –3NR, –61, ConNov 72, –76, CurBio 40, IntAu&W 76, IntWW 74, –75, –75N, LongCTC, ModBrL, NewC, REn, TwCA, TwCA SUP, TwCWr, WhAm 6, WhE&EA, Who 74, WhoWor 74*

Hutchison, Chester Smith 1902- *AmM&WS 73P, ConAu P-2, WhoMW 74, –76*

Huthmacher, J Joseph 1929- *BioIn 10, ConAu 21R, DrAS 74H, –78H, –82H, SmATA 5, WhoAm 78, WrDr 76, –80, –82, –84*

Hutto, Nelson 1904- *BioIn 12, ConAu P-1, SmATA 20*

Hutton, Richard 1949- *ConAu 109*

Huxley, Aldous 1894-1963 *AmAu&B, AtlBL, BiDPara, BioIn 1, –2, –3, –4, –5, –6, –7, –8, –9, –10, –11, –12, CasWL, Chambr 3, ChhPo, –S1, –S2, CmCal, CnMD, CnMWL, ConAu 85, ConLC 1, –3, –4, –5, –8, –11, –18, CyWA, DcAmB S7, DcLEL, Dis&D, EncO&P 78, EncSF, EncWL, –2[port], EvLB, IlEncMy[port], LinLib L, –S, LongCEL, LongCTC, MakMC, McGEWB, ModBrL, ModBrL SUP, ModWD, NewC, NotNAT B, Novels[port], ObitOF 79, ObitT 1961, OxEng, PenC ENG, RAdv 1, REn, ScF&FL 1, TwCA, TwCA SUP, TwCWr, WebE&AL, WhDW, WhAm 4, WhE&EA, WhLit, WhoSciF, WhoTwCL, WorAl*

Huxley, Elspeth 1907- *Au&Wr 6, BioIn 5, –8, –10, –11, BlueB 76, ConAu 77, DcLEL, EncMys, IntAu&W 76, –77, –82, IntWW 74, –75, –76, –77, –78, –79, –80, –81, –82, –83, LongCTC, TwCCr&M 80,*

TwCWr, WhE&EA, Who 74, –82, –83,
WhoAmW 74, –66, –68, –72, WhoWor 74,
–76, –78, WorAu, WrDr 76, –80, –82, –84

Huxley, Sir Julian 1887-1975 *Au&Wr 6,*
BiESc, BioIn 1, –3, –4, –5, –6, –9, –10, –11,
–12, BlueB 76N, Chambr 3,
ConAu 7NR, –9R, –57, CurBio 42, –63,
–75N, DcLEL, EvLB, InSci, IntWW 74,
–75N, LinLib L, –S, LongCTC,
McGMS 80[port], NewC, NewYTBS 75,
NinCLC 1956, ObitOF 79, ObitT 1971,
OxEng, OxFilm, PenC ENG, REn,
TwCA, TwCA SUP, TwCWr, WhDW,
WhAm 6, WhE&EA, Who 74, WhoLA,
WhoUN 75, WhoWor 74

Huyck, Willard 1945?- *BioIn 10, IntMPA 81,*
–82, –84, WomWMM

Huygen, Wil 1922- *ConAu 81*

Huynh, Quang Nhuong 1946- *ConAu 107*

Hwang, David H 1957?- *BioIn 12,*
NatPD 81[port], NewYTBS 81

Hyatt, Richard Herschel 1944- *ConAu 101*

Hyde, Dayton O 1925- *AuBYP SUP,*
BioIn 11, ConAu 25R, IntAu&W 77, –82,
MichAu 80, SmATA 9, WhoAm 74, –76,
–78, –80, –82, WrDr 76, –80, –82, –84

Hyde, George E 1882- *ConAu 5R*

Hyde, H Montgomery 1907- *BlueB 76,*
Who 74, –82, –83, WrDr 80, –82, –84

Hyde, Margaret Oldroyd 1917- *AuBYP,*
BioIn 8, –9, ConAu 1R, –1NR,
ConLC 21[port], SmATA 1, ThrBJA,
WhoAmW 58, –61

Hyde, Michael 1908- *Au&Wr 6,*
IntAu&W 76, –77, WrDr 76, –80, –82, –84

Hylander, Clarence John 1897-1964 *AmAu&B,*
AuBYP, BioIn 7, –9, –10, ConAu 5R,
NatCAB 53, SmATA 7

Hyman, Dick 1904- *ConAu 7NR, –17R*

Hynd, Alan 1904?-1974 *BioIn 10, ConAu 45*

Hyndman, Jane Andrews 1912-1978 *AuBYP,*
BioIn 6, –9, –11, ConAu X, –5NR, –89,
SmATA 1, –23N

Hyndman, Jane Andrews *see also* Wyndham, Lee

Hynek, Joseph Allen 1910- *AmM&WS 73P,*
–76P, –79P, –82P, BioIn 7, CurBio 68,
EncO&P 78S1, WhoAm 74, WhoWor 74

I

Ian, Janis 1951- *BiDAmM, BioIn 7, –8, –10, –11, ChhPo, –S2, ConAu 105, ConLC 21[port], EncPR&S, –77, GoodHs, IlEncRk, NewYTBS 77, RkOn 78, –84, RolSEnR 83, WhoAm 76, –78, –80, –82, WhoAmW 74, –68, –70, –72, –81, WhoRocM 82, WorAl*

Iannuzzi, John N 1935- *ConAu 93, TwCCr&M 80, WhoAmL 78, –79, WrDr 82, –84*

Ibarruri, Dolores 1895- *BioIn 6, –7, –8, –11, CurBio 67, InWom, IntDcWB[port], NewYTBS 77, –83[port], WhDW*

Ibsen, Henrik 1828-1906 *AtlBL, BbD, BiD&SB, BioIn 1, –2, –3, –4, –5, –6, –7, –8, –9, –10, –11, –12, CasWL, CelCen, ChhPo S3, CIDMEL, CnMD, CnThe, ConAu 104, CyWA, DcAmSR, DcEuL, Dis&D, EncWL, EncWT, EuAu, EvEuW, LinLib L, –S, LongCEL, LongCTC, McGEWB, McGEWD, –84[port], NewC, NewEOp 71, NotNAT A, –B, OxEng, OxGer, OxMus, OxThe, PenC EUR, RComWL, REn, REnWD, TwCLC 2, –8[port], WhDW, WhLit, WorAl*

Icenhower, Joseph Bryan 1913- *AuBYP, BioIn 8, ConAu 5R, –5NR*

Idyll, Clarence Purvis 1916- *AmM&WS 73P, –76P, –79P, –82P, Au&Wr 6, ConAu 9R, WhoS&SW 73*

Ilowite, Sheldon A 1931- *ConAu 106, SmATA 27[port]*

Immel, Mary Blair 1930- *AuBYP, ConAu 6NR, –13R, ForWC 70, SmATA 28[port], WhoAmW 77, –79, WrDr 76, –80, –82, –84*

Ind, Allison 1903-1974 *ConAu P-1*

Ing, Dean 1931- *ConAu 106*

Ingalls, Robert Paul 1941- *ConAu 107, –110, DrAS 78H, –82H*

Ingraham, Leonard W 1913- *BioIn 9, ConAu 25R, SmATA 4*

Ingram, Tom 1924- *ChhPo, ConAu X, –49, ScF&FL 1*

Innes, Hammond 1913- *AmAu&B, BioIn 3, –4, –5, –8, –10, ConAu X, ConNov 72, –76, –82, CurBio 54, IntWW 74, –75, –76, –77, –78, –79, –80, –81, –82, –83, LinLib L,*

LongCTC, Novels, REn, TwCCr&M 80, TwCWr, Who 74, –82, –83, WorAu, WrDr 76, –80, –82, –84

Innes, Hammond *see also* Hammond Innes, Ralph

Innes, Jean 1932- *ConAu X, IntAu&W 82X, WrDr 76, –80, –82, –84*

Inouye, Daniel Ken 1924- *AlmAP 78, –80, –82[port], –84[port], BiDrAC, BioIn 5, –6, –8, –9, –10, –11, –12, BlueB 76, CelR 73, CngDr 74, –77, –79, –81, –83, ConAu 25R, CurBio 60, IntWW 74, –75, –76, –77, –78, –79, –80, –81, –82, –83, IntYB 80, –81, –82, PolProf J, PolProf NF, WhoAm 74, –76, –78, –80, –82, WhoAmL 78, –79, WhoAmP 73, –75, –77, –79, –81, –83, WhoGov 77, –72, –75, WhoWest 74, –76, –78, –80, –82, –84, WhoWor 74, –76, –78, –80, –82, WorAl*

Ionesco, Eugene 1912- *BiE&WWA, BioIn 5, –6, –7, –8, –9, –10, –11, –12, CasWL, CelR 73, CnMD, CnMWL, CnThe, ConAu 9R, ConLC 1, –4, –6, –9, –11, –15, CroCD, CurBio 59, EncWL, –2[port], EncWT, EvEuW, IntAu&W 76, –77, –82, IntWW 74, –75, –76, –77, –78, –79, –80, –81, –82, –83, LinLib L, LongCTC, MakMC, McGEWB, McGEWD, –84[port], ModFrL, ModRL, ModWD, NewYTBE 70, NotNAT, –A, OxThe, PenC EUR, PIP&P, RComWL, REn, REnWD, ScF&FL 1, –2, SmATA 7, TwCWr, WhDW, Who 74, –82, WhoAm 74, –76, –78, –80, –82, WhoFr 79, WhoThe 15, –16, –81, WhoTwCL, WhoWor 74, –78, –82, WorAl, WorAu*

Ipcar, Dahlov 1917- *AuBYP, BioIn 5, –8, –9, –12, BkP, ChhPo S1, –S2, ConAu 9NR, –17R, IlsCB 1946, –1957, –1967, IntAu&W 77, –82, ScF&FL 1, –2, SmATA 1, ThrBJA, WhoAm 80, –82, WhoAmA 76, –78, –80, –82, WhoAmW 74, –58, –61, –75, –77*

Ipsen, D C 1921- *ConAu 33R, IntAu&W 77, –82, WhoWest 78, –80, –82, WrDr 76, –80, –82, –84*

Ireland, David 1927- *ConAu 25R, ConNov 76, –82, IntAu&W 77, WrDr 76, –80, –82,*

–84

Ireson, Barbara 1927- *Au&Wr 6, ChhPo, –S1, –S3, ConAu 5R, ScF&FL 1, –2*

Irving, Clifford 1930- *Au&Wr 6, AuNews 1, BioIn 9, –10, –11, BioNews 74, ConAu 1R, –2NR, DrInf[port], NewYTBE 72, WrDr 76, –80, –82, –84*

Irving, Washington 1783-1859 *Alli, AmAu, AmAu&B, AmBi, AmWr, ApCAB, AtlBL, BbD, BiAUS, BiD&SB, BioIn 1, –2, –3, –4, –5, –6, –7, –8, –9, –10, –11, –12, CarSB, CasWL, CelCen, Chambr 3, ChhPo, –S2, –S3, CnDAL, CrtT 3, –4, CyAL 1, CyWA, DcAmAu, DcAmB, DcAmDH, DcBiA, DcBiPP, DcEnA, DcEnL, DcLB 3, –11[port], DcLEL, DcNAA, DcSpL, Dis&D, Drake, EncAAH, EncAB-H, EvLB, FamAYP, HarEnUS[port], LinLib L, –S, McGEWB, MouLC 3, NatCAB 3, NewEOp 71, NewYHSD 57, NotNAT B, Novels[port], OxAmH, OxAmL, OxCan, OxEng, OxSpan, OxThe, PenC AM, PIP&P, RAdv 1, REn, REnAL, REnAW, ScF&FL 1, TwCBDA, WebAB, –79, WebE&AL, WhDW, WhAm HS, WhoChL, WhoHr&F, WisWr, WorAl, YABC 2*

Irwin, Constance Frick 1913- *BioIn 10, ConAu 1R, –5NR, ForWC 70, IndAu 1917, IntAu&W 77, –82, SmATA 6, WhoAmW 58, –61, –64, –68, –83, WhoLibS 66, WrDr 76, –80, –82, –84*

Irwin, Constance Frick *see also* Frick, Constance

Irwin, Hadley *ConAu X*

Irwin, Keith Gordon 1885-1964 *BioIn 11, ConAu 5R, SmATA 11*

Irwin, Vera Rushforth 1913- *ConAu 33R, DrAS 74E, –78E, WhoAmW 75, –77*

Isaacs, Neil D 1931- *ConAu 5R, –9NR, ConSFA, DrAS 74E, –78E, –82E, ScF&FL 1, –2*

Isenberg, Irwin M 1931-1979 *ConAu 11NR, –17R*

Ish-Kishor, Judith 1892-1972 *BioIn 11, ConAu 1R, –103, SmATA 11, WhoAmW 66*

Ish-Kishor, Sulamith 1897?-1977 *BioIn 8, –11, –12, ConAu 69, –73, NewYTBS 77, ScF&FL 1, SmATA 17, TwCCW 78, –83*

Isherwood, Christopher 1904- *AmAu&B, Au&Wr 6, BioIn 1, –2, –3, –4, –7, –8, –9, –10, –11, –12, BlueB 76, CasWL, CelR 73, CmCal, CnMD, CnMWL, ConAu 13R, ConDr 73, –77, –82, ConLC 1, –9, –11, –14, ConNov 72, –76, –82, CurBio 72, DcLB 15[port], DcLEL, DrAF 76, DrAP&F 83, EncWL, –2, EncWT, EvLB, IntAu&W 77, IntWW 74, –75, –76, –77, –78, –79, –80, –81, –82, –83, IntWWP 77, LinLib L, LongCTC, MakMC, McGEWD, –84, ModBrL,*

ModBrL SUP, ModWD, NewC, NewYTBE 72, –73, NewYTBS 79, Novels[port], OxAmL, OxEng, PenC ENG, PIP&P, RAdv 1, REn, REnAL, TwCA, TwCA SUP, TwCWr, WebE&AL, WhDW, WhE&EA, WhThe, Who 74, –82, –83, WhoAm 74, –76, –78, –80, –82, WhoTwCL, WhoWor 74, –76, –78, WorAl, WrDr 76, –80, –82, –84

Ishigo, Estelle 1899- *ConAu 61*

Ishmole, Jack 1924- *ConAu 49*

Iskander, Fazil 1929- *ConAu 102, IntWW 79, –80, –81, –82, –83, WhoSocC 78*

Issawi, Charles 1916- *AmEA 74, AmM&WS 73S, –78S, Au&Wr 6, ConAu 4NR, –5R, IntAu&W 76, MidE 78, –79, –80, –81, –82, WhoAm 74, –76, –78, –80, –82, WhoArab 81, WhoE 74, –83, WhoWor 80*

Issler, Anne Roller 1892- *ConAu 49, IndAu 1917, IntAu&W 76, WrDr 76*

Iverson, Lucille K 1925- *ConAu 61, DrAP 75*

Izenberg, Jerry *AuBYP SUP*

J

Jablonski, Edward 1922- *AuBYP, ConAu 1R, -2NR, WhoAm 78, -80, -82, WhoE 75, -77*

Jacker, Corinne 1933- *AuBYP, ConAu 17R, ForWC 70, NatPD, -81[port], WhoAm 80, -82, WhoAmW 74, -68, -70, -72, -75, -79, -81, -83, WhoThe 81, WrDr 76, -80, -82, -84*

Jacks, Oliver *ConAu X, -69, IntAu&W 77X, -82X, TwCCr&M 80, WhoSpyF, WrDr 82, -84*

Jackson, Anne 1924?- *BioIn 6, -8, -12, ConAu X, CurBio 80[port], FilmgC, InWom, MotPP, MovMk, NotNAT, WhoAm 80, -82, WhoAmW 72, -75, WhoHol A, WhoThe 15, -16, -81, WorAl*

Jackson, Basil 1920- *ConAu 8NR, -57*

Jackson, C Paul 1902- *AuBYP, ConAu 5R, -6NR, MichAu 80, SmATA 6*

Jackson, C Paul *see also* Jackson, O B

Jackson, C Paul *see also* Paulson, Jack

Jackson, Caary Paul 1902- *AuBYP, BioIn 7, -10, ConAu X, -5R, SmATA 6*

Jackson, Donald Dale 1935- *ConAu 1NR, -49, WhoE 77*

Jackson, Helen Hunt 1830?-1885 *Alli SUP, AmAu, AmAu&B, AmBi, AmWom, AmWomWr, ApCAB, BbD, BiD&SB, BioIn 1, -2, -8, -10, -11, -12, CarSB, CasWL, ChhPo, -S1, -S2, CmCal, CnDAL, DcAmB, DcAmSR, DcBiA, DcLEL, DcNAA, EncAAH, EncAB-H, EvLB, HarEnUS, InWom, IntDcWB, JBA 34, LibW, LinLib L, -S, McGEWB, MouLC 4, NatCAB 1, NotAW, OxAmH, OxAmL, REn, REnAL, REnAW, Str&VC, TwCBDA, WebAB, -79, WhAm HS, WorAl*

Jackson, Jacqueline 1928- *AuBYP SUP, BioIn 12, ConAu 45, DrAS 74E, -78E, -82E, FourBJA, WhoAm 74, -76, -78, -80, -82*

Jackson, Jesse 1908-1983 *AuBYP, BioIn 8, -9, -11, BlkAWP, ConAu 109, -25R, ConLC 12, InB&W 80, LinLib L, LivgBAA, OhA&B, SelBAA, SmATA 2, -29[port], TwCCW 78, -83, WrDr 80, -82, -84*

Jackson, Joe 1955- *NewRR 83, RolSEnR 83, WhoRocM 82*

Jackson, Joseph Henry 1894-1955 *AmAu&B, BioIn 3, -4, CmCal, DcAmB S5, REnAL, TwCA, TwCA SUP, WhAm 2, -3, WhNAA*

Jackson, Livia E Bitton *BioIn 12*

Jackson, Livia Elvira Bitton *DrAS 78H*

Jackson, Mahalia 1911-1972 *Baker 78, BiDAfM, BiDAmM, BioIn 3, -4, -5, -6, -7, -8, -9, -10, -11, -12, CmpEPM, ConAu 33R, CurBio 57, -72, -72N, DrBlPA, EncJzS 70, GoodHs, HerW, InB&W 80, InWom, IntDcWB, LibW, LinLib S, NegAl 76[port], -83, NewYTBE 72, NotAW MOD, ObitOF 79, ObitT 1971, WebAB, -79, WhAm 5, WhScrn 2, WhoAmW 58, -64, -66, -68, -70, -72, WhoHol B, WorAl*

Jackson, O B 1902- *AuBYP, BioIn 8, -10, ConAu X, SmATA 6*

Jackson, O B *see also* Jackson, C Paul

Jackson, Robert 1911- *Au&Wr 6, ConAu 9R*

Jackson, Robert Blake 1926- *AuBYP, BioIn 7, -11, ConAu 5R, SmATA 8, WhoLibS 55, -66*

Jackson, Shirley 1919-1965 *AmAu&B, AmNov, AmWomWr, BioIn 1, -2, -3, -4, -6, -7, -8, -9, -10, -12, ConAu 1R, -4NR, -25R, ConLC 11, ConNov 76, -82A, DcAmB S7, DcLB 6[port], DcLEL 1940, EncSF, InWom, LongCTC, ModAL, Novels, ObitOF 79, OxAmL, PenC AM, RAdv 1, REn, REnAL, ScF&FL 1, -2, SmATA 2, TwCA SUP, TwCCr&M 80, WhAm 4, WhoAmW 58, -64, -66, WhoHr&F, WorAl*

Jacob, Piers Anthony 1934- *BioIn 12, ConAu 21R, ScF&FL 1, WhoAm 82, WrDr 76, -80*

Jacob, Piers Anthony *see also* Anthony, Piers

Jacobs, David Michael 1942- *ConAu 57*

Jacobs, Francine 1935- *ConAu 1NR, -49*

Jacobs, Frank 1929- *AuBYP, BioIn 8, ConAu 6NR, -13R, SmATA 30[port], WrDr 76, -80, -82, -84*

Jacobs, Helen Hull 1908- *AmAu&B, Au&Wr 6, AuBYP, BioIn 1, -7, -8, -9,*

*–11, –12, CmCal, ConAu 9R, GoodHs,
InWom, IntAu&W 76, –77, –82,
SmATA 12, WhE&EA, WhoAm 74, –76,
–78, –80, –82, WhoAmW 74, –58, –64, –66,
–68, –70, –72, WorAl, WrDr 76, –80, –82,
–84*

Jacobs, Jane 1916- *AmAu&B, AmWomWr,
BioIn 6, –8, –10, –11, –12, ConAu 21R,
CurBio 77, DcLEL 1940, PolProf K,
WhoAm 74, –76, –78, –80, –82,
WhoAmW 74, –66, –68, –70, –72, –79,
WhoWor 74, –76*

Jacobs, Jim 1942- *ConAu 97, ConDr 77D,
–82D, ConLC 12, NatPD, –81[port],
WhoAm 76, –78, –80, –82, WhoMW 74,
–76*

Jacobs, John Kedzie 1918- *ConAu 21R,
WhoAm 74, –76, WhoS&SW 73*

Jacobs, Karen Folger 1940- *AmM&WS 78S*

Jacobs, Lewis 1906- *ConAu 77, OxFilm*

Jacobs, Linda C 1943- *BioIn 12, ConAu 29R,
SmATA 21[port]*

Jacobs, Lou, Jr. 1921- *AuBYP SUP, BioIn 9,
–11, ConAu 9NR, –21R, IntAu&W 76,
–77, SmATA 2, WhoWest 74, –76, –78*

Jacobs, Paul 1918-1978 *AmAu&B, BioIn 7, –9,
–10, –11, BioNews 74, ConAu 13R, –73,
IntAu&W 76, NewYTBS 74, –78,
ObitOF 79, WhAm 7, WhoAm 74, –76,
–78, WhoWest 74, –76, –78, WhoWor 74*

Jacobs, Susan 1940- *ConAu X, SmATA 30*

Jacobs, W W 1863-1943 *Novels, ObitOF 79,
WhoHr&F*

Jacobs, William Jay 1933- *ConAu 7NR, –57,
LEduc 74, SmATA 28[port]*

Jacobson, Dan 1929- *AfSS 78, –79, –80, –81,
–82, Au&Wr 6, BioIn 10, CasWL,
ConAu 1R, –2NR, ConLC 4, –14,
ConNov 72, –76, –82, DcLB 14[port],
DcLEL 1940, IntAu&W 76, –77, –82,
IntWW 77, –78, –79, –80, –81, –82, –83,
ModBrL SUP, ModCmwL, NewC,
Novels, PenC ENG, ScF&FL 1, –2,
TwCWr, WebE&AL, WhoAm 74, –76,
–78, –80, –82, WhoWor 74, –78, WorAu,
WrDr 76, –80, –82, –84*

Jacobson, Daniel 1923- *AmM&WS 73S, –76P,
AuBYP SUP, BioIn 11, ConAu 53,
MichAu 80, SmATA 12, WhoMW 78*

Jacobson, Morris K 1906- *BioIn 12,
ConAu 3NR, –45, IntAu&W 77,
SmATA 21[port]*

Jacoby, Susan *ConAu 108*

Jaffe, Bernard 1896- *ConAu 5R, REnAL,
WhoWorJ 72*

Jaffe, Leonard 1926- *WhoGov 72, –75,
WhoWorJ 72, –78*

Jaffe, Rona 1932?- *AmAu&B, AuNews 1,
BioIn 5, –9, –10, –12, BioNews 75,
ConAu 73, InWom, NewYTBS 79,
Novels, WhoAm 80, –82, WhoAmW 81,
–83, WhoWorJ 72, WrDr 76, –80, –82,*

–84

Jaffee, Al 1921- *SmATA 37*

Jagendorf, Moritz 1888-1981 *AnObit 1981,
AnCL, AuBYP, BioIn 3, –6, –8, –9, –12,
ConAu 5R, –102, CurBio 52,
IntAu&W 77, –82, MorJA, NewYTBS 81,
SmATA 2, –24N, WhNAA, WhoAm 78,
–80, WrDr 76, –80, –82*

Jagger, Mick 1939?- *BioIn 7, –8, –9, –10, –11,
–12, BioNews 75, BlueB 76, CelR 73,
ConLC 17, CurBio 72, FilmgC,
IntMPA 84, IntWW 77, –78, –79, –80, –81,
–82, –83, NewYTBS 83[port], WhoAm 74,
–76, –78, –80, –82, WhoHol A,
WhoRocM 82, WorAl*

Jagger, Mick *see also* Rolling Stones, The

Jahn, Mike 1943?- *BioIn 8, ConAu X, –49,
SmATA X*

Jakes, John 1932- *AuBYP SUP, BioIn 11,
ConAu 10NR, –57, ConSFA,
DcLB Y83B[port], EncSF, IntAu&W 82,
OxCan SUP, ScF&FL 1, –2, WhoAm 78,
–80, –82, WhoHr&F, WrDr 82, –84*

James, Bessie Rowland 1895-1974 *AmAu&B,
BioIn 10, ConAu 107, WhNAA*

James, Edward T 1917- *ConAu 33R,
DrAS 74H, –78H, –82H*

James, Henry 1843-1916 *Alli SUP, AmAu,
AmAu&B, AmBi, AmWr, ApCAB,
AtlBL, BbD, BiD&SB, BioIn 1, –2, –3, –4,
–5, –6, –7, –8, –9, –10, –11, –12, BrWr 6,
CasWL, CelCen, CnDAL, CnMD,
CnMWL, CnThe, ConAu 104, CrtT 3, –4,
CyWA, DcAmAu, DcAmB, DcBiA,
DcEnA, –AP, DcEnL, DcEuL,
DcLB 12[port], DcLEL, DcNAA, Dis&D,
EncAB-H, EncWL, –2[port], EncWT,
EvLB, HarEnUS, LinLib L, –S,
LongCEL, LongCTC, McGEWB,
McGEWD, –84[port], ModAL,
ModAL SUP, ModBrL, ModBrL SUP,
ModWD, NatCAB 1, NewC,
NewEOp 71, NotNAT B, Novels[port],
OxAmH, OxAmL, OxEng, OxThe,
PenC AM, –ENG, RAdv 1, RComWL,
REn, REnAL, REnWD, ScF&FL 1,
TwCBDA, TwCLC 2, –11[port], TwCWr,
WebAB, –79, WebE&AL, WhDW,
WhAm HSA, –1, –4A, WhLit, WhoHr&F,
WhoTwCL, WorAl*

James, Janet Wilson 1918- *DrAS 74H, –78H,
–82H, WhoAmW 74, –58, –61, –64, –66,
–68, –70, –72, –75, –77*

James, John *ConAu 45*

James, Marquis 1891-1955 *AmAu&B, BioIn 1,
–2, –4, –6, DcAmB S5, LinLib L, –S,
NatCAB 44, OxAmL, REnAL, TwCA,
TwCA SUP, WhAm 3, WhE&EA,
WhNAA*

James, Michael 1922?-1981 *BioIn 12,
ConAu 104, NewYTBS 81*

James, Naomi 1949- *BioIn 12, ConAu 102,*

Who 82, –83

James, P D 1920- *ASpks, BioIn 10, –11, –12, ConAu 21R, ConLC 18, CurBio 80[port], EncMys, NewYTBS 80[port], Novels, TwCCr&M 80, WorAl, WrDr 80, –82*

James, Rick 1952- *BioIn 12, NewRR 83, RolSEnR 83*

James, Will 1892-1942 *ArtsAmW, AuBYP, BioIn 1, –2, –3, –4, –7, –8, –12, CurBio 42, DcAmB S3, DcNAA, IlBEAAW, JBA 34, –51, LinLib L, NatCAB 35, Newb 1922, OxAmL, REnAL, REnAW, SmATA 19, TwCA, TwCA SUP, TwCCW 78, –83, WhAm 2, WhNAA*

Janes, Edward C 1908- *AuBYP, BioIn 8, ConAu 93, SmATA 25[port]*

Janeway, Elizabeth 1913- *AmAu&B, AmNov, AmWomWr, Au&Wr 6, AuBYP, AuNews 1, BioIn 2, –3, –4, –8, –9, –10, –12, ChhPo, ConAu 2NR, –45, CurBio 44, DcLEL 1940, DrAF 76, InWom, IntAu&W 76, IntWW 80, –81, –82, –83, NewYTBS 79, REnAL, SmATA 19, TwCA SUP, WhoAm 74, –76, –78, –80, –82, WhoAmW 74, –58, –64, –66, –68, –72, –75, –77, –79, –81, –83, WhoE 74, WhoWor 74, –76, –78*

Janovy, John, Jr. 1937- *AmM&WS 82P, BioIn 12, ConAu 97*

Janowitz, Tama 1957- *BioIn 12, ConAu 106, DrAP&F 83*

Janson, Dora Jane 1916- *AuBYP, BioIn 8, ConAu 106, SmATA 31[port]*

Janson, H W 1913-1982 *ConAu 4NR, –107, NewYTBS 82[port]*

Janson, Horst Woldemar 1913- *AuBYP, BioIn 8, –10, –11, ConAu 1R, DrAS 74H, –78H, –82H, SmATA 9, WhoAm 74, –76, –78, –80, WhoAmA 73, –76, –78, –80, –82, WhoArt 80, –82, WhoWor 74, –76, WrDr 76, –80, –82*

Jansson, Tove 1914- *Au&Wr 6, BioIn 6, –8, –9, –12, ChlLR 2, ConAu 17R, EncWL 2, IlsCB 1957, –1967, IntAu&W 76, –77, –82, SmATA 3, ThrBJA, TwCCW 78B, –83B, WhoChL, WhoWor 78, –80, –82, WorECom*

Jantzen, Steven L 1941- *ConAu 77*

Jardine, Alan 1942- *BioIn 11, –12*

Jardine, Alan *see also* Beach Boys, The

Jares, Joe 1937- *ConAu 33R, WrDr 76, –80, –82, –84*

Jarman, Thomas Leckie 1907- *Au&Wr 6, ConAu 4NR, –5R, IntAu&W 76, –77, –82, WhE&EA, WrDr 76, –80, –82, –84*

Jarrell, Randall 1914-1965 *AmAu&B, AmWr, AnCL, AuBYP, BioIn 3, –4, –5, –7, –8, –9, –10, –11, –12, CasWL, ChlLR 6[port], ChhPo, –S1, –S3, CnDAL, CnE&AP, ConAu 5R, –6NR, –25R, ConLC 1, –2, –6, –9, –13, ConLCrt, –82, ConP 75, –80A, CroCAP, DcAmB S7, DcLEL 1940,*

EncWL, –2, LinLib L, ModAL, ModAL SUP, Novels, ObitOF 79, OxAmL, PenC AM, RAdv 1, REn, REnAL, ScF&FL 1, –2, SixAP, SmATA 7, ThrBJA, TwCA SUP, TwCCW 78, –83, TwCWr, WebAB, –79, WebE&AL, WhAm 4, WhoAmA 78N, –80N, –82N, WhoTwCL, WorAl

Jaspersohn, William 1947- *ConAu 102*

Jastrow, Robert 1925- *AmM&WS 73P, –76P, –79P, –82P, BioIn 9, –10, BlueB 76, ConAu 21R, CurBio 73, IntAu&W 77, –82, IntWW 74, –75, –76, –77, –78, –79N, –80, –81, –82, –83, WhoAm 74, –76, –78, –80, –82, WhoGov 77, –72, –75, WhoWor 74, WrDr 76, –80, –82, –84*

Jauss, Anne Marie 1907- *AuBYP, BioIn 5, –8, –10, –11, ConAu 1R, –4NR, ForWC 70, FourBJA, IlsCB 1946, –1957, –1967, SmATA 10, WhoAmA 73, –76, –78, –80, –82, WhoAmW 58, WrDr 76, –80, –82, –84*

Jaworski, Irene D *AuBYP, BioIn 8*

Jay, Ruth I Johnson 1920- *ConAu X*

Jayne, Caroline Furness 1873-1909 *WhAm 1*

Jayne, Mitchell F *ScF&FL 1*

Jeffers, Harry Paul 1934- *AuBYP*

Jefferson Airplane *BiDAmM, CelR 73, EncPR&S, –77, IlEncRk, MugS, RkOn 78, –84, RkOneH, RolSEnR 83, WhoRocM 82*

Jefferson Airplane *see also* Balin, Marty

Jefferson Airplane *see also* Casady, Jack

Jefferson Airplane *see also* Dryden, Spencer

Jefferson Airplane *see also* Kaukonen, Jorma

Jefferson Airplane *see also* Slick, Grace

Jefferson Starship *RkOn 78, WhoRocM 82*

Jefferson Starship *see also* Jefferson Airplane

Jeffery, Gordon 1918- *Au&Wr 6*

Jeffreys-Jones, Rhodri 1942- *ConAu 77*

Jeffries, Roderic 1926- *Au&Wr 6, AuBYP, BioIn 8, –9, ConAu 9NR, –17R, EncMys, SmATA 4, TwCCr&M 80, WrDr 82, –84*

Jeffries, Roderic *see also* Ashford, Jeffrey

Jenkins, Alan C 1912?- *Au&Wr 6, IntAu&W 76, –77, –82, MnBBF*

Jenkins, Elizabeth 1905?- *BioIn 5, –10, ConAu 73, DcLEL, InWom, IntWW 80, –81, –82, –83, Who 82, –83, WorAu, WrDr 82, –84*

Jenkins, Geoffrey 1920- *Au&Wr 6, EncSoA, ScF&FL 1, –2*

Jenkins, Jerry B 1949- *ConAu 5NR, –49, WhoAm 80, –82*

Jenkins, Marie Magdalen 1909- *AmM&WS 73P, –76P, –79P, –82P, AuBYP SUP, BioIn 10, ConAu 41R, SmATA 7, WhoAmW 74, –70, –72, –75*

Jenkins, Peter 1951- *ConAu 89*

Jenkins, Robin 1912- *CasWL, ConAu 1NR, ConNov 72, –76, –82, DcLB 14[port], WorAu, WrDr 76, –80, –82, –84*

Jenner, Bruce 1949- *BioIn 11, -12,*
ConAu 110, CurBio 77, NewYTBS 76,
-77, -78, WhoAm 78, -80, -82, WorAl
Jenner, Chrystie 1950- *BioIn 11, -12,*
ConAu 77
Jenness, Aylette 1934- *ConAu 25R*
Jenness, Diamond 1886-1969 *BioIn 5, -6, -9,*
MacDCB 78, OxCan, WhLit
Jennings, Gary 1928- *AuBYP, BioIn 8, -11,*
-12, ConAu 5R, -9NR, IntAu&W 76, -77,
-82, SmATA 9
Jennings, Michael 1931- *ConAu 69, WhoE 79*
Jennings, William Dale 1917- *ConAu 25R,*
WhoAm 76, -78, -80
Jennison, Keith Warren 1911- *AmAu&B,*
AuBYP, BioIn 3, -4, -8, -12, ConAu 73,
SmATA 14
Jensen, Gordon D 1926- *AmM&WS 73P, -76P,*
-79P, BiDrAPA 77, ConAu 106
Jensen, Joan Maria 1934- *DrAS 74H, -78H,*
-82H
Jensen, Oliver 1914- *ConAu 25R, DrAS 74H,*
-78H, -82H, St&PR 75, WhoAm 74, -76,
-78, -80, -82, WhoE 74, WhoWor 74, -76
Jeppson, Janet O 1926- *BiDrAPA 77,*
ConAu 49, WhoAmW 70, WhoE 81, -83,
WrDr 76, -82
Jerome, Jerome Klapka 1859-1927 *Alli SUP,*
BbD, BiD&SB, BioIn 2, -5, -10, -12,
CasWL, Chambr 3, CyWA, DcBiA,
DcEnA AP, DcLB 10[port], DcLEL,
EncWT, EvLB, LinLib L, -S, LongCTC,
McGEWD, -84[port], MnBBF, ModBrL,
ModWD, NewC, NotNAT A, -B, Novels,
OxEng, OxThe, PenC ENG, REn,
ScF&FL 1, TwCA, TwCWr, WhDW,
WhLit, WhThe, WhoBW&I A,
WhoStg 1908
Jerome, John 1932- *ConAu 2NR, -45,*
IntAu&W 76
Jerome, Judson 1927- *BioIn 7, ConAu 4NR,*
-9R, ConP 70, -75, -80, DrAF 76,
DrAP 75, DrAP&F 83, DrAS 74E,
IntAu&W 82, IntWWP 77,
WhoS&SW 75, WrDr 76, -80, -82, -84
Jespersen, James 1934- *AmM&WS 79P, -82P,*
ConAu 103
Jessel, Camilla 1937- *ConAu 104,*
IntAu&W 77, SmATA 29[port],
WhoWor 82
Jeune, Paul 1950- *ConAu 101*
Jewett, Sarah Orne 1849-1909 *Alli SUP,*
AmAu, AmAu&B, AmBi, AmWom,
AmWomWr, AmWr, ApCAB, AtlBL,
AuBYP, BbD, BiD&SB, BioIn 1, -2, -3,
-4, -5, -6, -7, -8, -9, -11, -12, CarSB,
CasWL, Chambr 3, ChhPo, -S1, -S2,
CnDAL, ConAu 108, CrtT 3, -4, CyWA,
DcAmAu, DcAmB, DcBiA,
DcLB 12[port], DcLEL, DcNAA, Dis&D,
EncAAH, EvLB, HarEnUS, InWom,
IntDcWB, JBA 34, LibW, LinLib L, -S,

McGEWB, ModAL, NatCAB 1, NotAW,
Novels, OxAmL, OxEng, PenC AM,
RAdv 1, REn, REnAL, SmATA 15,
TwCBDA, TwCLC 1, WebAB, -79,
WebE&AL, WhAm 1, WhLit, WorAl
Jhabvala, Ruth Prawer 1927- *Au&Wr 6,*
BioIn 10, -11, -12, ConAu 1R, ConLC 4,
-8, ConNov 72, -76, -82, CurBio 77,
DcLEL 1940, DrAP&F 83, EncWL 2,
IntAu&W 76, -82, IntWW 77, -78, -79,
-80, -81, -82, -83, ModCmwL, NewC,
NewYTBE 73, NewYTBS 76, -83[port],
Novels, TwCWr, Who 82, -83, WorAu,
WrDr 76
Jiminez, Janey 1953- *ConAu 77*
Jinks, William Howard, Jr. 1938- *ConAu 41R*
Joel, Billy 1949- *BioIn 10, -11, -12,*
BioNews 74, ConAu X, ConLC 26[port],
CurBio 79, RkOn 78, -84, RolSEnR 83,
WhoAm 80, -82, WhoRocM 82,
WhoWor 80, -82, WorAl
Joffe, Joyce 1940- *Au&Wr 6, ConAu 77*
Johannesson, Olof 1908- *ConAu X, EncSF,*
ScF&FL 1, -2
Johannesson, Olof *see also* Alfven, Hannes Olof
Geosta
Johannis, Theodore B, Jr. 1914-
AmM&WS 73S, ConAu 33R
Johanson, Donald C 1943- *BioIn 12,*
ConAu 107, ConIsC 1[port],
NewYTBS 79, WhoAm 82, WhoMW 76,
-78
John, Elton 1947- *Baker 78, BioIn 9, -10, -11,*
-12, BioNews 74, CelR 73, CurBio 75,
EncPR&S, -77, IllEncRk, IntWW 77, -78,
-79, -80, -81, -82, -83, NewYTBE 71,
NewYTBS 74, RkOn 78, -84, RkOneH,
RolSEnR 83, Who 83, WhoAm 76, -78,
-80, -82, WhoHol A, WhoRocM 82,
WhoWor 74, -76, -78, -80, -82, WorAl
John, Otto 1909- *BioIn 3, -4, -5, -6, -9,*
EncE 75
Johnsgard, Paul A 1931- *AmM&WS 73P,*
-76P, -79P, -82P, ConAu 1NR, -49,
IntAu&W 77, -82, WhoMW 76,
WrDr 76, -80, -82, -84
Johnson, A 1921- *ConAu X*
Johnson, A *see also* Johnson, Annabel Jones
Johnson, A E *ConAu X, IntAu&W 76X,*
SmATA 2, WrDr 80, -84
Johnson, A E *see also* Johnson, Annabel Jones
Johnson, A E *see also* Johnson, Edgar Raymond
Johnson, Alvin Saunders 1874-1971 *AmAu&B,*
BiDAmEd, BioIn 1, -2, -3, -4, -7, -9,
ConAu 29R, CurBio 42, -71, -71N,
DcAmLiB, DcAmSR, EncAB-H,
McGEWB, NewYTBE 71, ObitOF 79,
REnAL, TwCA SUP, WebAB, -79,
WhAm 5
Johnson, Annabel Jones 1921- *AmAu&B,*
AuBYP, BioIn 4, -8, -9, ConAu 9R,
SmATA 2, ThrBJA, TwCCW 83

Johnson, Annabel Jones *see also* Johnson, A E
Johnson, Audrey P 1915- *ConAu 93*
Johnson, Bruce *see* Beach Boys, The
Johnson, Charlene 1935- *ConAu X*
Johnson, Charlene *see also* Crawford, Char
Johnson, Clive 1930- *ConAu 29R*
Johnson, Curt 1928- *ConAu 33R*
Johnson, Dorothy Marie 1905- *Au&Wr 6,*
BioIn 10, ConAu 5R, ForWC 70,
SmATA 6, WhoAmW 58, –61, –64, –66,
–68, WhoPNW, WrDr 84
Johnson, Edgar Raymond 1912- *BioIn 9,*
ConAu 9R, SmATA 2, ThrBJA,
TwCCW 78, –83
Johnson, Edgar Raymond *see also* Johnson, A E
Johnson, Eric W 1918- *AuBYP SUP,*
BioIn 11, ConAu 5R, LEduc 74,
SmATA 8, WhoE 75, –77, WrDr 76, –84
Johnson, Frederick 1932- *BioIn 11, ConAu 73*
Johnson, Gaylord 1884- *BioIn 10, ConAu P-1,*
SmATA 7
Johnson, George 1917- *ConAu 5R,*
IndAu 1917, WhoAdv 72, WhoF&I 75,
–77, –79
Johnson, Gerald White 1890-1980 *AmAu&B,*
AnObit 1980[port], AnCL, AuBYP,
BioIn 2, –3, –4, –7, –9, –12, CnDAL,
ConAu 85, –97, EncSoH,
NewYTBS 80[port], OxAmL, REnAL,
SmATA 19, –28N, ThrBJA, TwCA SUP,
WhAm 7, WhJnl, WhNAA, WhoAm 74,
–76, –78, –80, WhoWor 74
Johnson, J Rosamond 1873-1954 *AmSCAP 66,*
Baker 78, BiDAfM, CmpEPM,
NotNAT B, ObitOF 79, WhFla,
WhoColR, –A
Johnson, James E 1927- *ConAu 77,*
DrAS 74H, –78H, –82H
Johnson, James Ralph 1922- *AuBYP, BioIn 8,*
–9, ConAu 1R, –2NR, IntAu&W 76, –77,
–82, SmATA 1, WhoAmA 76, –78, –80,
–82, WhoWest 78, WrDr 76, –80, –82, –84
Johnson, James Ross, Jr. 1931- *AmArch 70*
Johnson, James Rosser 1916- *ConAu 9R,*
DrAS 74H, –78H, –82H, WhoAm 76, –78,
–80, –82
Johnson, James Weldon 1871-1938 *AmAu&B,*
AmBi, AmSCAP 66, AnCL, AnMV 1926,
Baker 78, BiDAfM, BiDAmM, BioIn 1,
–2, –4, –6, –7, –8, –9, –10, –12, BlkAWP,
CasWL, ChhPo, –S1, –S2, –S3, ConAmA,
ConAmL, ConAu 104, DcAmB S2,
DcAmSR, DcLEL, DcNAA, DrBlPA,
EncAB-H, EncSoH, EncWL 2, FourBJA,
InB&W 80, LinLib L, McGEWB,
ModAL SUP, ModBlW, NegAl 76, –83,
OxAmH, OxAmL, PenC AM, RAdv 1,
REn, REnAL, SelBAA, SixAP,
SmATA X, TwCA, TwCA SUP,
TwCLC 3, WebAB, –79, WebE&AL,
WhAm 1, WhAmP, WhFla, WhLit,
WhNAA, WhoColR A

Johnson, James William 1871-1938
SmATA 31[port]
Johnson, James William *see also* Johnson, James
Weldon
Johnson, Joy Duvall 1932- *ConAu 110,*
WhoAmW 77, –79
Johnson, Lois W 1936- *ConAu 6NR, –57,*
SmATA 22[port]
Johnson, Margaret 1926- *ConAu 37R*
Johnson, Natalie 1934- *SmATA X*
Johnson, Natalie *see also* Robison, Nancy L
Johnson, Nicholas 1934- *AmAu&B, BioIn 8,*
–9, –10, BlueB 76, CelR 73, ConAu 29R,
CurBio 68, NewYTBE 71, NewYTET,
WhoAm 74, –76, –78, –80, –82, WhoGov 72,
WhoS&SW 73, WhoWor 74, –76,
WrDr 76, –80, –82, –84
Johnson, Nora 1933- *Au&Wr 6, ConAu 106*
Johnson, Richard C 1919- *ConAu 33R*
Johnson, Ruth I 1920- *ConAu X*
Johnson, Ruth I *see also* Jay, Ruth I Johnson
Johnson, Samuel 1709-1784 *Alli, AtlBL, BbD,*
BiD&SB, BioIn 1, –2, –3, –4, –5, –6, –7, –8,
–9, –10, –11, –12, BrAu, BrWr 3, CasWL,
ChhPo, –S1, –S2, –S3, CnE&AP, CrtT 2,
–4, CyEd, CyWA, DcBiA, DcBiPP,
DcEnA, –AP, DcEnL, DcEuL, DcLEL,
Dis&D, EncSF, EvLB, LinLib L, –S,
LongCEL, LuthC 75, McGEWB,
MouLC 2, NewC, NinCLC 1956,
NotNAT B, OxAmL, OxEng, OxMus,
OxThe, PenC ENG, PIP&P, RComWL,
REn, WebE&AL, WhDW, WorAl
Johnson, Stanley 1940- *ConAu 21R,*
IntAu&W 77, ScF&FL 1, –2, Who 83
Johnson, Virginia Weisel 1910- *ConAu 17R,*
WhoAmW 70, WhoPNW
Johnson, Wendell Stacy 1927- *ConAu 1R,*
DrAS 74E, –78E, –82E, IntAu&W 76, –77,
–82, WrDr 76, –80, –82, –84
Johnson, William Oscar 1894-1960 *BioIn 5*
Johnson, William Weber 1909- *AmAu&B,*
AuBYP, BioIn 8, –10, ConAu 17R,
IntAu&W 77, –82, SmATA 7,
WhoAm 74, –76, WhoWest 74, –76, –78,
WrDr 76, –80, –82, –84
Johnson, Winifred 1905- *ConAu 5R,*
ForWC 70, WhoAmW 68, –68A
Johnston, Jennifer 1930- *ConAu 85, ConLC 7,*
DcIrL, DcLB 14[port], Novels, Who 82,
–83
Johnston, Johanna 1914?-1982 *AuBYP,*
BioIn 8, –11, ConAu 7NR, –108, –57,
FourBJA, SmATA 12, –33N
Johnston, Lynn 1947?- *BioIn 12, ConAu 110*
Johnston, Mary 1870-1936 *AmAu&B, AmBi,*
AmWomWr, BbD, BiD&SB, BiDSA,
BioIn 4, –5, –6, –8, –12, Chambr 3, ChhPo,
CnDAL, ConAmL, ConAu 109, CyWA,
DcAmAu, DcAmB S2, DcBiA,
DcEnA AP, DcLB 9[port], DcNAA,
EncSoH, InWom, LibW, LongCTC,

NatCAB 10, NotAW, OxAmL, REn, REnAL, ScF&FL 1, TwCA, TwCBDA, WhAm 1, WomWWA 14

Johnston, Norma *ConAu 105, SmATA 29[port], WrDr 84*

Johnston, Ronald 1926- *Au&Wr 6, ConAu 13R, IntAu&W 76, WrDr 76, -80, -82, -84*

Johnston, William Denis 1901- *DcIrW 1, -2, DcLEL, IntAu&W 76, -77, IntWW 74, -76, -77, -78, -79, -80, -82, -83, Who 74, -82, -83, WhoWor 76, WrDr 76*

Johnstone, Iain 1943- *ConAu 108*

Jones, Adrienne 1915- *BioIn 10, ConAu 33R, IntAu&W 77, -82, ScF&FL 1, -2, SmATA 7, WhoAmW 75, -77, -79, WrDr 76, -80, -82, -84*

Jones, Betty Millsaps 1940- *ConAu 109*

Jones, Brian 1942?-1969 *BioIn 8, -12, ObitOF 79, WhAm 5, WhScrn 2, WhoRocM 82*

Jones, Brian *see also* Rolling Stones, The

Jones, David 1895-1974 *CasWL, CnE&AP, CnMWL, ConAu 9R, -53, ConLC 2, -4, -7, -13, ConP 70, -75, DcLB 20[port], EncWL 2, IntWWP 77, LongCTC, McGDA, ModBrL, ModBrL SUP, NewC, ObitOF 79, ObitT 1971, OxEng, PenC ENG, PhDcTCA 77, RAdv 1, REn, TwCWr, WhAm 6, Who 74, WhoTwCL, WorAu*

Jones, David Robert 1947- *ConAu 103*

Jones, Diana Wynne 1934- *Au&Wr 6, BioIn 11, ConAu 4NR, -49, ConLC 26[port], IntAu&W 76, -77, ScF&FL 1, SmATA 9, TwCCW 78, -83, WrDr 76, -80, -82, -84*

Jones, Dorothy H *ConAu 9R, ForWC 70*

Jones, Douglas C 1924- *BioIn 11, ConAu 21R, WrDr 80, -84*

Jones, Emrys 1920- *Au&Wr 6, BlueB 76, ConAu 17R, IntAu&W 76, -82, Who 74, -82, -83, WrDr 76, -80, -82, -84*

Jones, Evan 1915- *AmAu&B, Au&Wr 6, BioIn 9, ConAu 6NR, -9R, IntAu&W 76, SmATA 9, -3*

Jones, Everett L 1915- *ConAu 13R, DrAS 74E, -78E, -82E*

Jones, Gayl 1949- *AmWomWr, BioIn 11, -12, BlkAWP, ConAu 77, ConLC 6, -9, DrAF 76, DrAP&F 83, IntAu&W 77, -82, SelBAA*

Jones, Glyn 1905- *Au&Wr 6, BioIn 10, BlueB 76, CnMWL, ConAu 3NR, -9R, ConNov 72, -76, -82, ConP 70, -75, -80, DcLB 15[port], IntAu&W 76, -77, -82, IntWWP 77, ModBrL, WorAu, WrDr 76, -80, -82, -84*

Jones, Helen Hinckley 1903- *AuBYP, ChhPo S2, ConAu 5R, -5NR, IntAu&W 76, -77, -82, SmATA 26[port],*

WhoAmW 75, WrDr 76, -82, -84

Jones, Helen Hinckley *see also* Hinckley, Helen

Jones, Hettie 1934- *AuBYP SUP, ConAu 81, SmATA 27*

Jones, Holway Roy 1922- *BiDrLUS 70, WhoLibI 82, WhoLibS 55, -66, WhoWest 74, -76, -78*

Jones, James 1921-1977 *AmAu&B, AuNews 1, -2, BioIn 2, -3, -4, -7, -8, -9, -10, -11, -12, BioNews 74, CasWL, CelR 73, ConAu 1R, -6NR, -69, ConLC 1, -3, -10, ConNov 72, -76, -82A, DcLB 2, DrAF 76, EncWL, -2, IntWW 74, -77N, LinLib L, ModAL, ModAL SUP, NewYTBS 77, Novels, ObitOF 79, OxAmL, PenC AM, RAdv 1, REn, REnAL, TwCA SUP, TwCWr, WebE&AL, WhAm 7, Who 74, WhoAm 74, WhoE 74, WhoWor 74, WorAl, WrDr 76*

Jones, Katharine MacBeth 1900- *ConAu 5R, WhoAmW 58, -61, -64, -66*

Jones, LeRoi 1934- *BiDAfM, BioIn 7, -8, -9, -10, -11, -12, BlueB 76, BroadAu, CasWL, CelR 73, ConAu 21R, ConDr 73, -77, -82, ConLC 1, -2, -10, -14, ConNov 72, -76, -82, ConP 70, -75, -80, CroCAP, CroCD, DcLEL 1940, DrAP&F 83, DrBlPA, EncWL, EncWT, IntWW 75, -76, -77, -78, -79, -80, -81, -82, -83, LinLib L, LivgBAA, McGEWD, ModAL, ModAL SUP, ModWD, MugS, NotNAT, Novels, OxAmL, PenC AM, PIP&P A, RAdv 1, RComWL, SelBAA, WebAB, -79, WebE&AL, WhoAm 74, -76, -78, -80, -82, WhoBlA 77, -80, WhoTwCL, WhoWor 74, -76, -78, WorAu, WrDr 76, -80, -82, -84*

Jones, LeRoi *see also* Baraka, Amiri

Jones, Mary Brush 1925- *ConAu 25R*

Jones, McClure *SmATA 34[port]*

Jones, Peter 1921- *ConAu 5R*

Jones, Peter Austin 1929- *ConAu 4NR, -53, WrDr 76, -80, -82, -84*

Jones, Peter D'Alroy 1931- *ConAu 3NR, -5R, DrAS 74H, -78H, -82H, WhoAm 74, -76, -78, -80, -82*

Jones, Peter Gaylord 1929- *ConAu 73*

Jones, R Ben 1933- *ConAu 108, -25R, IntAu&W 82*

Jones, Raymond F 1915- *ConAu 106, ConSFA, ScF&FL 1, WhoSciF, WrDr 84*

Jones, Rebecca C 1947- *ConAu 106, SmATA 33[port]*

Jones, Ron 1941- *BioIn 12*

Jones, Thelma Hamilton *ChhPo S2*

Jones, Thomas Laird 1930- *WhoRel 75, -77*

Jones, Tristan 1924- *BioIn 12, ConAu 73, WrDr 84*

Jones, Weyman B 1928- *AuBYP, BioIn 8, -9,*

ConAu 17R, Dun&B 79, FourBJA,
ODwPR 79, SmATA 4, WhoE 83,
WhoPubR 72, –76

Joos, Martin 1907-1979 BioIn 12, ConAu P-1,
DrAS 74F, WhoAm 74

Joplin, Janis 1943-1970 Baker 78, BiDAmM,
BioIn 8, –9, –10, –11, –12, BioNews 74,
BluesWW, CurBio 70, EncPR&S, –77S,
GoodHs, IlEncRk, IntDcWB,
NewYTBE 70, NotAW MOD, ObitOF 79,
RkOn 78, –84, RkOneH, RolSEnR 83,
WhAm 5, WhScrn 2, WhoHol B,
WhoRocM 82, WorAl

Jordan, Archibald Campbell 1906-1968 AfrA,
PenC CL

Jordan, Grace Edgington ConAu 1R,
ForWC 70, WhoAmW 74, –68, –70, –72,
–75, WhoPNW, WhoS&SW 73

Jordan, Hope D 1905- BioIn 12, ConAu 77,
SmATA 15

Jordan, June 1936- AuBYP SUP, BioIn 9,
–12, BlkAWP, ChhPo S1, –S2,
ConAu 33R, ConLC 5, –11, –23[port],
ConP 80, DrAF 76, DrAP 75,
DrAP&F 83, FourBJA, InB&W 80,
IntAu&W 77, IntWWP 77, –82, LinLib L,
LivgBAA, NegAl 83, SelBAA, SmATA 4,
TwCCW 78, –83, WhoAmW 75, –77,
WhoBlA 77, –80, WrDr 76, –80, –82, –84

Jordan, Pat 1941?- BioIn 9, –10, –12,
ConAu 33R

Jordan, Ruth 1926- ConAu 7NR, –57,
IntAu&W 77, –82, WrDr 76, –80, –82, –84

Jorgenson, Ivar AuBYP, ConAu X,
DcLEL 1940, EncSF, ScF&FL 1,
SmATA X, ThrBJA, WorAu 1970

Jorgenson, Ivar see also Silverberg, Robert

Joseph, Alexander 1907-1976 AmM&WS 73P,
–76P, –79P, AuBYP, BioIn 8, –11,
ConAu 13R, NewYTBS 76

Joseph, James Herz 1924- ConAu 1R, –2NR,
IndAu 1917

Joseph, Joan 1937?- ConAu 25R,
SmATA 34[port], WhoAmW 74, –75, –77,
–79, –81, WhoE 75

Joseph, Joseph M 1903-1979 ConAu 5R,
SmATA 22[port]

Joseph, Marie ConAu 109

Joseph, Stephen M 1938- ConAu 25R,
DrAF 76, WhoE 75, WrDr 76, –80, –82,
–84

Josephson, Hannah 1900-1976 BioIn 11,
ConAu 69, ConAu P-2, NewYTBS 76,
WhoAmW 68

Josephy, Alvin M, Jr. 1915- ConAu 8NR, –17R,
OxCan SUP, St&PR 75, WhoAm 74, –76,
–78, –80, –82, WhoE 74, WrDr 76, –80,
–82, –84

Joslin, Sesyle 1929- Au&Wr 6, AuBYP,
BioIn 8, –9, ConAu X, SmATA 2,
ThrBJA, TwCCW 78, WrDr 80, –82, –84

Joyce, James 1882-1941 AtlBL, AuBYP SUP,

BioIn 1, –2, –3, –4, –5, –6, –7, –8, –9, –10,
–11, –12, CasWL, Chambr 3, ChhPo, –S1,
CnMD, CnMWL, ConAu 104, CurBio 41,
CyWA, DcIrB, DcIrL, DcIrW 1,
DcLB 10[port], –19[port], DcLEL, Dis&D,
EncWL, –2[port], EncWT, EvLB,
LinLib L, –S, LongCEL, LongCTC,
MakMC, McGEWB, McGEWD, –84[port],
ModBrL, ModBrL SUP, ModWD, NewC,
NotNAT B, Novels[port], ObitOF 79,
OxEng, PenC ENG, PoIre, RAdv 1,
RComWL, REn, TwCA, TwCA SUP,
TwCLC 3, –8[port], TwCWr, WebE&AL,
WhDW, WhE&EA, WhoHol A,
WhoTwCL, WorAl

Joyce, James Avery 1902- Au&Wr 6, BioIn 5,
–11, CurBio 59, IntAu&W 76, –77, –82,
WhoAm 74, –76, –82, WhoWor 74, –78,
–80, –82

Judd, Denis 1938- ConAu 25R, IntAu&W 76,
–77, –82, SmATA 33[port], WhoWor 76,
WrDr 76, –80, –82, –84

Judd, Frances K ConAu P-2, SmATA 1

Judson, Clara 1879-1960 AmAu&B, Au&ICB,
AuBYP, BioIn 1, –2, –3, –5, –7, CarSB,
CurBio 48, InWom, IndAu 1816, JBA 51,
LinLib L, OxCan, SmATA 27, WhAm 4,
WhE&EA, WhJnl, WhLit, WhNAA,
WhoAmW 58

Judson, Harry Pratt 1849-1927 Alli SUP,
AmAu&B, BiDAmEd, BiD&SB, DcAmB,
DcNAA, HarEnUS, LinLib L,
NatCAB 11, –20, TwCBDA, WhAm 1

Judson, William ConAu X

Judson, William see also Corley, Edwin

Judy, Stephen N 1942- ConAu 89, DrAS 82E

Judy, Susan J 1944- ConAu 107

Jungk, Robert 1913- Au&Wr 6, BioIn 3,
ConAu 85, Future, IntAu&W 76,
WhoWor 74

Jurgensen, Barbara 1928- ConAu 17R,
ForWC 70, IntAu&W 76, –82,
WhoAmW 75, WrDr 76, –80, –82, –84

Just, Ward 1935- ConAu 25R, ConLC 4,
–27[port], DrAF 76, WhoAm 74, –76, –78,
–80, –82

K

Kadesch, Robert R 1922- *AmM&WS 73P,*
–76P, –79P, –82P, AuBYP SUP,
ConAu 57, SmATA 31, WhoAm 74, –76,
–78, –80, WhoTech 82

Kael, Pauline 1919- *AmAu&B, AmWomWr,*
Au&Wr 6, BioIn 7, –8, –9, –10, –12,
BlueB 76, CelR 73, CmCal, ConAu 6NR,
–45, CurBio 74, ForWC 70,
IntAu&W 76, –77, –82, IntMPA 77, –75,
–76, –78, –79, –81, –82, –84, LibW, OxFilm,
WhoAm 74, –76, –78, –80, –82,
WhoAmW 74, –68A, –70, –72, –75, –77, –81,
–83, WomWMM, WorAu 1970,
WrDr 76, –80, –82, –84

Kafka, Franz 1883-1924 *AtlBL, BioIn 1, –2,*
–3, –4, –5, –6, –7, –8, –9, –10, –11, –12,
CasWL, ClDMEL, CnMD, CnMWL,
ConAu 105, CyWA, Dis&D, EncSF,
EncWL, –2[port], EncWT, EvEuW,
LinLib L, –S, LongCTC, MakMC,
McGEWB, ModGL, NewEOp 71,
Novels[port], OxEng, OxGer, PenC EUR,
RComWL, REn, ScF&FL 1, TwCA,
TwCA SUP, TwCLC 2, –6[port], TwCWr,
WhDW, WhoHr&F, WhoTwCL, WorAl

Kagan, Norman 1931- *AmM&WS 73S,*
LEduc 74

Kahn, Albert E 1912?-1979 *BioIn 12,*
ConAu 89, NewYTBS 79, WhoWest 78

Kahn, E J, Jr. 1916- *AmArch 70, ConAu 65,*
WhoWorJ 72, –78

Kahn, Ely Jacques, Jr. 1916- *AmAu&B,*
Au&Wr 6, BioIn 2, –4, –11, TwCA SUP,
WhoAm 74, –76, –78, –80, –82,
WhoAmJ 80, WhoE 74

Kahn, James 1947- *ConAu 109*

Kahn, Joan 1914- *AuBYP SUP, BioIn 3, –8,*
ConAu 77, ScF&FL 1, WhoAmW 58,
–68

Kahn, Kathy 1945- *BioIn 10, ConAu 41R,*
WhoAm 76

Kahn, Margaret 1949- *ConAu 101*

Kahn, Roger 1927- *AuBYP, BioIn 4, –8, –9,*
–10, –11, –12, ConAu 25R, Conv 3,
SmATA 37, WhoE 77

Kain, John F 1935- *AmEA 74,*
AmM&WS 73S, –78S, ConAu 29R,
IndAu 1917, IntAu&W 77, WhoAm 74,

–76, –78, –80, –82, WhoE 74, WhoEc,
WrDr 76, –80, –82, –84

Kains, Maurice Grenville 1868-1946 *BioIn 1, –2,*
ChhPo, DcNAA, NatCAB 36,
ObitOF 79, WhAm 2, WhLit, WhNAA

Kaiser, Robert Greeley 1943- *ConAu 65,*
WhoAm 76, –78, –80, –82

Kalb, Bernard 1932?- *ASpks, BioIn 12,*
ConAu 109, LesBEnT

Kalb, Jonah 1926- *AuBYP SUP, ConAu 4NR,*
–53, SmATA 23

Kalb, Marvin 1930- *AmAu&B, ASpks,*
ConAu 5R, IntMPA 77, –75, –76, –78, –79,
–81, –82, –84, LesBEnT, WhoAm 74, –76,
–78, –82, WhoS&SW 73, WhoWor 74

Kalb, S William 1897- *ConAu 33R,*
WhoWorJ 72, –78

Kallen, Lucille *ConAu 97, WomWMM*

Kals, W S 1910- *ConAu 45*

Kalter, Joanmarie 1951- *ConAu 102*

Kaminsky, Stuart M 1934- *ConAu 73,*
DrAS 78E, –82E

Kamm, Josephine 1905?- *Au&Wr 6,*
ConAu 5NR, –9R, IntAu&W 76, –77, –82,
SmATA 24[port], TwCCW 78, –83,
WhE&EA, WhoWor 80, WrDr 76, –80,
–82, –84

Kane, Robert S 1925- *ConAu 7NR, –9R*

Kanin, Garson 1912- *AmAu&B, AmSCAP 66,*
AuNews 1, BiDFilm, BiE&WWA,
BioIn 1, –3, –8, –9, –10, –11, –12,
BioNews 75, BlueB 76, CelR 73, CmMov,
CnMD, CnThe, ConAu 5R, –7NR,
ConDr 73, –77, –82, ConLC 22[port],
CurBio 41, –52, DcFM, DcLB 7[port],
EncWT, FilmgC, IntAu&W 76, –77, –82,
IntMPA 77, –75, –76, –78, –79, –81, –82, –84,
IntWW 82, –83, McGEWD 84, ModWD,
MovMk, NatPD, –81[port],
NewYTBS 80[port], NotNAT, –A,
OxAmL, OxFilm, PenC AM, REnAL,
WhoAm 74, –76, –78, –80, –82, WhoThe 15,
–16, –81, WhoWor 74, WorAl, WorAu,
WorEFlm, WrDr 76, –80, –82, –84

Kantner, Paul 1941?- *BioIn 9, –12,*
WhoAm 80, –82

Kantor, MacKinlay 1904-1977 *AmAu&B,*

*AmNov, ASpks, AuBYP, BioIn 1, –2, –3,
–4, –7, –8, –9, –10, –11, –12, ChhPo S1,
CnDAL, ConAmA, ConAu 61, –73,
ConLC 7, ConNov 72, –76, ConSFA,
DcLB 9[port], DcLEL, EncMys, EncSF,
FilmgC, IntAu&W 76, –77, LinLib L, –S,
ModAL, NewYTBS 77, Novels,
ObitOF 79, OxAmL, PenC AM, REn,
REnAL, ScF&FL 1, –2, TwCA,
TwCA SUP, TwCWr, WhAm 7,
WhoAm 74, –76, –78, WrDr 76*

Kaplan, Albert A *AuBYP, BioIn 8*

Kaplan, Anne Bernays 1930- *ConAu 1R, –5NR,
SmATA 32[port]*

Kaplan, Anne Bernays *see also* Bernays, Anne

Kaplan, Helen Singer 1929- *AmM&WS 73P,
–76P, –79P, –82P, AuNews 1,
BiDrAPA 77, BioIn 10, –12, ConAu 102,
WhoAm 78, –80, –82, WhoAmJ 80,
WhoAmW 74, –68, –70, –72, –75, –77, –81,
–83*

Kaplan, Janice Ellen 1955- *WhoAmW 79, –81*

Kaplan, Justin 1925- *AmAu&B, Au&Wr 6,
AuNews 1, BioIn 10, –12, BioNews 74,
ConAu 8NR, –17R, DrAS 74E, –78E, –82E,
IntAu&W 76, WhoAm 74, –76, –78, –80,
–82, WhoAmJ 80, WhoE 74,
WorAu 1970, WrDr 76, –80, –82, –84*

Kaplan, Philip 1916- *ConAu 13R, St&PR 75*

Kaplan, Richard 1929- *ConAu 73,
WhoAm 74, –76*

Kapp, Colin 1928?- *ConSFA, EncSF,
ScF&FL 1, WhoSciF, WrDr 84*

Kardish, Laurence 1945- *CanWW 70, –79, –80,
–81, –83, ConAu 49*

Karen, Ruth 1922- *AuBYP, BioIn 8, –11,
ConAu 11NR, –17R, SmATA 9,
WhoAmW 74, –75, –83, WrDr 76, –80, –82,
–84*

Kark, Nina Mary 1925- *AuBYP SUP,
BioIn 9, –10, –11, ConAu 8NR, –17R,
SmATA 4, Who 74, –82, –83,
WhoAmW 74, –75*

Kark, Nina Mary *see also* Bawden, Nina

Karl, Frederick R 1927- *Au&Wr 6, BioIn 11,
ConAu 3NR, –5R, DrAS 74E, –78E, –82E*

Karl, Jean E 1927- *AuBYP SUP, BioIn 11,
ChhPo S1, ConAu 29R, ForWC 70,
SmATA 34[port], WhoAm 76, –78, –80,
–82, WhoAmW 74, –72, –75*

Karlin, Muriel Schoenbrun *ConAu 85,
WhoAmJ 80, WhoAmW 74, –72, –77, –79,
WhoE 75, –77, –79, –81*

Karp, Abraham J 1921- *ConAu 3NR, –5R,
DrAS 74H, –78H, –82H, IntAu&W 77,
–82, WhoAm 74, –76, –78, –80, –82,
WhoAmJ 80, WhoWorJ 72, –78,
WrDr 76, –80, –82, –84*

Karp, David 1922- *AmAu&B, Au&Wr 6,
BioIn 4, BlueB 76, ConAu 1R, –1NR,
ConNov 72, –76, –82, CurBio 57,
DcLEL 1940, EncSF, IntAu&W 76, –77,*

*–82, IntWW 74, –75, –76, –77, –78, –79,
–80, –81, –82, –83, ScF&FL 1, –2,
Who 74, –82, –83, WhoAm 74, –76, –78,
–80, –82, WhoAmJ 80, WrDr 76, –80, –82,
–84*

Karp, Walter *AuBYP SUP*

Karpf, Holly W 1946- *ConAu 37R*

Karr, Phyllis Ann 1944- *ConAu 101*

Karras, Alex 1935- *BioIn 7, –9, –10, –11, –12,
BioNews 74, ConAu 107, IntMPA 84,
WhoAm 74, –76, –78, –80, –82, WhoHol A,
WorAl*

Karst, Gene 1906- *WhoProB 73*

Kastner, Erich 1899-1974 *AuBYP, BioIn 1, –5,
–6, –7, –8, –9, –10, –12, CasWL,
ChlLR 4[port], ClDMEL, CnMD,
CurBio 64, –74, –74N, EncWL, –2,
EncWT, EvEuW, IntAu&W 76,
IntWW 74, LinLib L, ModGL, ModWD,
ObitT 1971, OxGer, PenC EUR,
SmATA 14, ThrBJA, TwCW 78B, –83B,
WhDW, WhAm 6, WhE&EA, Who 74,
WhoChL, WhoWor 74, WorAu*

Kastner, Jonathan 1937- *ConAu 25R*

Kastner, Marianna 1940- *ConAu 25R*

Kath, Terry 1945?-1978 *BioIn 11, BioNews 74,
WhAm 7, WhoAm 76, –78, WhoRocM 82*

Kath, Terry *see also* Chicago

Katz, Fred 1938- *ConAu 49, SmATA 6*

Katz, Gloria 1943?- *BioIn 10, ConAu 107,
IntMPA 81, –82, –84, WomWMM*

Katz, Jacqueline Hunt *AuBYP SUP*

Katz, Jane 1934- *ConAu 85,
SmATA 33[port]*

Katz, Naomi Corrine *TexWr*

Katz, William Loren 1927- *AuBYP SUP,
BioIn 11, BlueB 76, ConAu 9NR, –21R,
IntAu&W 76, –77, SmATA 13,
WhoAm 74, –76, –78, –80, –82, WhoE 74,
WrDr 80, –82, –84*

Katzman, David Manners 1941- *ConAu 5NR,
–53, DrAS 74H, –78H, –82H*

Kauffmann, Stanley 1916- *Au&Wr 6, BioIn 2,
–7, –10, –12, BlueB 76, ConAmTC,
ConAu 5R, –6NR, LongCTC, Novels,
PenC AM, WhoAm 74, –76, –78, –80, –82,
WhoE 74, WhoWor 74, –76, WorAu,
WrDr 76, –80, –82, –84*

Kaufman, Bel *AmAu&B, BioIn 7, –12,
BlueB 76, ConAu 13R, DrAF 76,
DrAP&F 83, ForWC 70, IntAu&W 82,
WhoAm 74, –76, –78, –80, –82,
WhoAmJ 80, WhoAmW 74, –66, –68, –72,
–75, –81, –83, WhoE 74, WhoWor 74,
WrDr 76, –80, –82, –84*

Kaufman, Mervyn D 1932- *BioIn 9,
ConAu 5R, SmATA 4, WhoAm 82*

Kaufmann, Helen L 1887- *AuBYP SUP,
Baker 78, ConAu 5R, –7NR,
IntWWM 77, WhE&EA, WhoAmW 61,
–64, WhoMus 72*

Kaufmann, John 1931- *BioIn 8, –12,*

ConAu 81, IlsBYP, IlsCB 1957, –1967, SmATA 18

Kaufmann, Walter 1921-1980 *AmAu&B, AnObit 1980, BioIn 6, ConAu 1R, –1NR, –101, DcLEL 1940, DrAS 74P, –78P, IntAu&W 76, –77, –82, IntWWP 77, –82, WhAm 7, WhoAm 74, –76, –78, –80, WhoAmJ 80, WhoE 74, –75, –77, –79, WhoWor 74, –76, WrDr 76, –80, –82*

Kaufmann, Walter 1933- *ConAu 61*

Kaukonen, Jorma 1941?- *BioIn 9, –12, WhoRocM 82*

Kaukonen, Jorma *see also* Jefferson Airplane

Kaula, Edna Mason 1906- *AuBYP, BioIn 8, –11, ConAu 5R, SmATA 13*

Kavaler, Lucy 1929?- *AuBYP, BioIn 8, ConAu 7NR, –57, IntAu&W 77, SmATA 23[port], WhoAmW 74, –72, –75, WhoE 75, –77*

Kawabata, Yasunari 1899-1972 *BiDJaL, BioIn 8, –9, –10, –12, CasWL, CnMWL, ConAu 33R, –93, ConLC 2, –5, –9, –18, CurBio 69, –72, –72N, DcOrL 1, EncWL, –2[port], LinLib L, MakMC, McGEWB, NewYTBE 72, Novels, ObitOF 79, PenC CL, RComWL, REn, WhDW, WhAm 5, WhoTwCL, WorAl, WorAu*

Kay, Helen 1912- *AuBYP, BioIn 7, –10, ConAu X, ForWC 70, SmATA 6, WhoAmW 66, –68, –75, –77*

Kay, Helen *see also* Goldfrank, Helen Colodny

Kay, Mara *BioIn 11, ConAu 2NR, –5R, ForWC 70, IntAu&W 76, –77, –82, SmATA 13, WhoAmW 68, WrDr 76, –80, –82, –84*

Kay, Terry 1918- *ConAu X*

Kay, Terry Winter 1938- *ConAu 110*

Kaye, Geraldine 1925- *Au&Wr 6, BioIn 11, ConAu 7NR, –13R, IntAu&W 76, –77, –82, SmATA 10, TwCCW 78, –83, WhoWor 76, –80, WrDr 76, –80, –82, –84*

Kaye, M M 1908?- *ConAu 89, NewYTBS 78, Novels, WrDr 82*

Kaye, Marvin 1938- *ConAu 5NR, –53, DrAP&F 83, IntAu&W 77, WrDr 76, –80, –82, –84*

Kayira, Legson Didimu 1940?- *AfrA, Au&Wr 6, BioIn 9, ConAu 17R, DcLEL 1940, InB&W 80, IntAu&W 76, RGAfL*

Kazan, Elia 1909- *ASpks, BiDFilm, BiE&WWA, BioIn 1, –2, –3, –4, –5, –6, –7, –8, –9, –10, –11, –12, BlueB 76, CelR 73, CnThe, ConAu 21R, ConLC 6, –16, CurBio 48, –72, DcFM, EncWT, FilmgC, IntAu&W 77, IntMPA 77, –75, –76, –78, –79, –81, –82, –84, IntWW 74, –75, –76, –77, –78, –79, –80, –81, –82, –83, MovMk, NewYTBE 72, NotNAT, –A, Novels, OxAmL, OxFilm, OxThe, PIP&P, PolProf T, REnAL, WebAB, –79, WhThe, Who 74, –82, –83, WhoAm 74, –76, –78,*

–80, –82, WhoE 74, WhoHol A, WhoThe 15, WhoWor 74, –78, –80, –82, WorAl, WorEFlm, WrDr 76, –80, –82, –84

Kazimiroff, Theodore L 1941- *ConAu 109*

Kazin, Alfred 1915- *AmAu&B, Au&Wr 6, BioIn 2, –4, –6, –7, –9, –11, BlueB 76, CasWL, CelR 73, ConAu 1R, –1NR, ConLCrt, –82, CurBio 66, DcLEL 1940, DrAS 74E, –78E, –82E, IntAu&W 76, –77, IntWW 74, –75, –76, –77, –78, –79, –80, –81, –82, –83, LinLib L, OxAmL, PenC AM, RAdv 1, REn, REnAL, TwCA SUP, WhoAm 74, –76, –78, –80, –82, WhoAmJ 80, WhoWor 74, WhoWorJ 72, –78, WorAl, WrDr 80, –82, –84*

Keane, Bil 1922- *BioIn 9, ConAu 33R, SmATA 4, WhoAm 78, –80, –82, WhoAmA 73, –76, –78, –80, –82, WhoWest 76, –78*

Keane, John 1945?- *BioIn 11*

Kearns, Martha 1945- *ConAu 57, WhoAmW 77, –79*

Keating, Bern 1915- *BioIn 11, ConAu X, SmATA X, WrDr 76, –80, –82, –84*

Keating, Bern *see also* Keating, Leo Bernard

Keating, H R F 1926- *ConAu 33R, Novels, TwCCr&M 80, WhoSpyF, WorAu 1970, WrDr 80, –82, –84*

Keating, Lawrence A 1903-1966 *AuBYP, BioIn 7, ConAu 5R, SmATA 23*

Keating, Leo Bernard 1915- *BioIn 11, ConAu 29R, SmATA 10*

Keating, Leo Bernard *see also* Keating, Bern

Keats, Ezra Jack 1916-1983 *AmPB, Au&ICB, AuBYP, AuNews 1, BioIn 5, –6, –7, –8, –9, –10, –12, BioNews 74, BkP, ChlLR 1, ChhPo S1, –S2, ConAu 109, –77, IlsBYP, IlsCB 1946, –1957, –1967, LinLib L, MorJA, NewYTBS 83, NinCLC 1956, NewbC 1956, SmATA 14, –34N, TwCCW 78, –83, WhoAm 74, –76, –78, –80, –82, WhoAmA 76, –78, –80, –82, WrDr 76, –80, –82, –84*

Keats, John 1795-1821 *Alli, AnCL, AtlBL, BiD&SB, BiHiMed, BioIn 1, –2, –3, –4, –5, –6, –7, –8, –9, –10, –11, –12, BrAu 19, BrWr 4, CasWL, CelCen, Chambr 3, ChhPo, –S1, –S2, –S3, CnE&AP, CrtT 2, –4, CyWA, DcBiPP, DcEnA, DcEnL, DcEuL, DcLEL, Dis&D, EvLB, LinLib L, –S, LongCEL, McGEWB, MouLC 2, NewC, OxEng, PenC ENG, RAdv 1, RComWL, REn, Str&VC, WebE&AL, WhDW, WorAl*

Keefe, John Edwin 1942- *ConAu 107, DrAS 74F*

Keegan, Marcia 1943- *AmAu&B, BioIn 11, ConAu 49, IntAu&W 77, SmATA 9, WhoAmW 75, –77, –79, WhoE 77, –79*

Keene, Carolyn *AmAu&B, BioIn 9, –10, –11, –12, ConAu X, EncMys, SmATA X, WebAB, –79*

Keene, Carolyn *see also* Adams, Harriet S
Keene, Carolyn *see also* Stratemeyer, Edward L
Keene, Donald 1922- *AmAu&B, BiE&WWA, BioIn 12, ConAu 1R, –5NR, DrAS 74F, –78F, –82F, NotNAT, WhoAm 74, –76*
Keese, Parton 1926- *ConAu 109*
Keil, Sally VanWagenen 1946- *ConAu 89*
Keillor, Garrison 1942- *BioIn 12, DrAP 75, DrAP&F 83, WhoMW 76*
Keith, Agnes Newton 1901- *AmAu&B, AmWomWr, Au&Wr 6, BioIn 1, –2, –4, –12, CanWW 70, –79, –80, –81, ConAu 17R, IntAu&W 76, –77, –82, LinLib L, REnAL, TwCA SUP, WhoAmW 74, –58, –70, –72, WrDr 76, –80, –82, –84*
Keith, Harold 1903- *AmAu&B, AuBYP, BioIn 4, –5, –6, –7, –9, –10, ConAu 2NR, –5R, CurBio 58, LinLib L, MorBMP, MorJA, NinCLC 1956, SmATA 2, TwCCW 78, –83, WhNAA, WrDr 80, –82, –84*
Keith, Sam 1921- *ConAu 65*
Keith-Lucas, Alan 1910- *ConAu 2NR, –5R, WhoAm 74, –76, –78, –80*
Keithley, George 1935- *ConAu 37R, DrAF 76, DrAP 75, DrAS 74E, –78E, –82E, IntWWP 77, –82, WhoAm 74, –76, –78, –80, –82, WhoWest 74, –76*
Kelder, Diane M 1934- *ConAu 25R, WhoAm 80, WhoAmA 76, –78, –80, –82*
Kelen, Emery 1896-1978 *AuBYP SUP, BioIn 1, –11, ConAu 9R, –103, IlsCB 1744, SmATA 13, –26N*
Keller, Allan 1904- *ConAu 29R*
Keller, Beverly L *AuBYP SUP, BioIn 11, ConAu 1NR, SmATA 13*
Keller, Charles 1942- *AuBYP SUP, BioIn 11, ConAu 2NR, –49, SmATA 8*
Keller, Helen 1880-1968 *AmAu&B, AmWomWr, ApCAB X, BiDSA, BioIn 1, –2, –3, –4, –5, –6, –7, –8, –9, –10, –11, –12, ChhPo S1, –S3, ConAu 101, –89, CurBio 42, –68, DcLEL, Dis&D, EncAB 6, EncSoH, GoodHs, HarEnUS, HerW, InWom, IntDcWB[port], LibW, LinLib L, –S, LongCTC, LuthC 75, McGEWB, NatCAB 15, –57, NotAW MOD, ObitOF 79, ObitT 1961, OxAmH, OxAmL, REn, REnAL, WebAB, –79, WhDW, WhAm 5, WhE&EA, WhNAA, WhoAmW 58, –61, –64, –66, –68, WhoHol B, WomWWA 14, WorAl*
Kelley, Leo P 1928- *ConAu 107, ConSFA, EncSF, ScF&FL 1, –2, SmATA 31, –32[port], WrDr 84*
Kellogg, Marjorie 1922- *AmAu&B, BioIn 8, ConAu 81, ConLC 2, WomWMM*
Kelly, Eric Philbrook 1884-1960 *AmAu&B, AnCL, AuBYP, BioIn 2, –4, –5, –6, –7, –11, ConAu 93, JBA 34, –51, NatCAB 44,*

Newb 1922, REnAL, TwCCW 78, –83, WhAm 3, WhNAA, YABC 1
Kelly, Frank K 1914- *BioIn 1, –3, ConAu 1R, –1NR, WhoSciF*
Kelly, Gary F 1943- *ConAu 89*
Kelly, Karen 1938- *ForWC 70*
Kelly, Robert 1935- *Au&Wr 6, BioIn 10, –12, ConAu 17R, ConP 70, –75, –80, ConSFA, CroCAP, DcLB 5, DrAF 76, DrAP 75, EncSF, IntWWP 77, LinLib L, PenC AM, ScF&FL 1, –2, WhoAm 76, –78, –80, –82, WrDr 76, –80, –82, –84*
Kelly, Walt 1913-1973 *AmAu&B, AmSCAP 66, ArtCS, BioIn 1, –2, –3, –4, –6, –10, –12, CelR 73, ConAu 45, –73, CurBio 56, –73, –73N, IlsBYP, LinLib L, NewYTBE 73, ObitOF 79, REnAL, SmATA 18, WhAm 6, WhoAm 74, WorECom*
Kelsey, Joan Marshall 1907- *ConAu 5R*
Kelsey, Joan Marshall *see also* Grant, Joan
Kelty, Jean McClure 1926- *DrAS 74E, –78E, –82E, WhoAmW 66, –68, WhoMW 74, –76*
Kemal, Yashar 1922?- *BioIn 10, ConAu 89, ConLC 14, IntWW 74, –75, –76, –77, –78, –79, –80, –81, –82, –83, TwCWr, WhoWor 74, WorAu*
Kemelman, Harry 1908- *AmAu&B, ASpks, AuNews 1, BioIn 10, –11, ConAu 6NR, –9R, ConLC 2, DcLEL 1940, EncMys, IntAu&W 76, –77, –82, Novels, TwCCr&M 80, WhoAm 74, –76, –78, –80, –82, WhoWorJ 72, –78, WorAl, WorAu 1970, WrDr 76, –80, –82, –84*
Kemp, Gene 1926- *ConAu 69, IntAu&W 82, SmATA 25[port], TwCCW 83, WrDr 76, –80, –82, –84*
Kemp, Lysander 1920- *AmAu&B, ConAu 1NR, –45, WhoAm 76, –78, WhoS&SW 73, –75, –76*
Kemperman, Steve 1955- *ConAu 108*
Kendall, Carol 1917- *AuBYP, BioIn 7, –9, –11, ConAu 5R, –7NR, ForWC 70, IntAu&W 76, –77, –82, OhA&B, ScF&FL 1, –2, SmATA 1, ThrBJA, TwCCW 78, –83, WhoAmW 68, WrDr 80, –82, –84*
Kendall, Lace *AmAu&B, ConAu X, IntWWP 77, SmATA 3, ThrBJA, WhoAm 74, –76, –78, WrDr 82, –84*
Kendall, Lace *see also* Stoutenburg, Adrien
Keneally, Thomas 1935- *ASpks, BioIn 9, –10, –11, BlueB 76, CasWL, ConAu 10NR, –85, ConLC 5, –8, –10, –14, –19, –27[port], ConNov 72, –76, –82, DcLEL 1940, FarE&A 78, –79, –80, –81, IntAu&W 76, –77, IntWW 78, –79, –80, –81, –82, –83, ModCmwL, Novels, ScF&FL 1, Who 82, –83, WhoWor 78, –82, WorAu 1970, WrDr 76, –80, –82, –84*
Keniston, Kenneth 1930- *AmAu&B, BioIn 9,*

ConAu 25R, WhoAm 74, -76, -78, -80, -82

Kennedy, David Michael 1941- ConAu 29R, DrAS 74H, -78H, IntAu&W 77, -82, WhoAm 82, WrDr 76, -80, -82

Kennedy, John F 1917-1963 AmAu&B, AnCL, BiDrAC, BiDrUSE, BioIn 1, -2, -3, -4, -5, -6, -7, -8, -9, -10, -11, -12, ChhPo, ConAu 1R, -1NR, CurBio 50, -61, -64, DcAmB S7, DcAmSR, DcPol, EncAAH, EncAB-H, EncSoH, LinLib L, -S, MakMC, McGEWB, NatCAB 52, NewYTBE 72, ObitOF 79, ObitT 1961, OxAmH, OxAmL, PolProf E, PolProf K, REn, REnAL, SmATA 11, WebAB, -79, WhDW, WhAm 4, WhAmP, WorAl

Kennedy, Ludovic 1919- Au&Wr 6, BioIn 3, ConAu 65, IntAu&W 77, IntWW 78, -79, -80, -81, -82, -83, Who 74, -82, -83, WrDr 76, -80, -82, -84

Kennedy, Malcolm Duncan 1895- ConAu 9R, IntAu&W 76, -77, WrDr 76, -80, -82, -84

Kennedy, Michael 1926- ConAu 5NR, -13R, IntAu&W 77, IntWWM 77, Who 74, -82, -83, WhoMus 72, WhoWor 76, WrDr 76, -80, -82, -84

Kennedy, Richard 1932- ConAu 7NR, SmATA 22, WhoAm 82

Kennedy, Robert Francis 1925-1968 AmAu&B, BiDrAC, BiDrUSE, BioIn 4, -5, -6, -7, -8, -9, -10, -11, -12, ConAu 1R, -1NR, CurBio 58, -68, DcPol, EncAB-H, McGEWB, ObitOF 79, WebAB, -79, WhAm 5, WhAmP, WorAl

Kennedy, Theodore R 1936- ConAu 105, WhoBlA 80

Kennel, Arthur John 1929- WhoMW 80, -82

Kenner, Hugh 1923- BiE&WWA, BlueB 76, ConAu 21R, ConLCrt, -82, DrAS 74E, -78E, -82E, WorAu, WrDr 80, -82, -84

Kennerly, Karen 1940- ConAu 33R

Kenny, Kathryn ConAu X, IntAu&W 76X

Kenny, Kathryn see also Sanderlin, Owenita

Kenrick, Tony 1935- Au&Wr 6, BioIn 9, ConAu 104, TwCCr&M 80, WrDr 82, -84

Kent, Alexander 1924- Au&Wr 6, ConAu X, DcLEL 1940, IntAu&W 76, -76X, -77, -77X, Novels, SmATA X, WrDr 76, -80, -82, -84

Kent, Alexander see also Reeman, Douglas Edward

Kent, Deborah Ann 1948- ConAu 103

Kenworthy, Leonard Stout 1912- BioIn 10, -11, ConAu 1R, -1NR, IndAu 1917, SmATA 6

Kenyon, Karen 1938- ConAu 106

Kenyon, Raymond G 1922- AuBYP, BioIn 7

Keppel, Charlotte WrDr 84

Ker Wilson, Barbara 1929- Au&Wr 6, BioIn 12, ConAu 5R, -7NR, FourBJA, SmATA 20

Ker Wilson, Barbara see also Wilson, Barbara Ker

Kerber, Linda Kaufman 1940- DrAS 74H, -78H, -82H, WhoAmW 77, WhoMW 82

Kern, Gregory 1919- ConAu X, EncSF, ScF&FL 1, WrDr 84

Kern, Gregory see also Tubb, E C

Kern, Louis J 1909- St&PR 75

Kernan, Alvin Bernard 1923- ConAu 49, DrAS 74E, -78E, -82E, LEduc 74, WhoAm 74, -76, 78, -80, -82, WhoE 74

Kerouac, Jack 1922-1969 AmAu&B, AuNews 1, BioIn 4, -5, -7, -8, -9, -10, -11, -12, BioNews 75, CasWL, CmCal, CnMWL, ConAu X, ConLC 1, -2, -3, -5, -14, ConNov 76, -82A, ConP 70, CurBio 59, -69, DcLB DS3[port], -2, -16[port], DcLEL 1940, EncAB-H, EncWL, -2, LinLib L, LongCTC, MakMC, ModAL, ModAL SUP, NewYTBS 79, Novels[port], ObitOF 79, ObitT 1961, OxAmL, PenC AM, PolProf E, RAdv 1, REn, REnAL, TwCWr, WebAB, -79, WebE&AL, WhDW, WhAm 5, WhoHol B, WhoTwCL, WorAl, WorAu

Kerouac, Jack see also Kerouac, Jean-Louis Lebrid De

Kerouac, Jean-Louis Lebrid De 1922-1969 AuNews 1, ConAu 5R, -25R

Kerouac, Jean-Louis Lebrid De see also Kerouac, Jack

Kerouac, John 1922-1969 ConAu X

Kerouac, John see also Kerouac, Jack

Kerr, Jean 1923- AmAu&B, AmCath 80, AmSCAP 66, AmWomWr, BiE&WWA, BioIn 4, -5, -6, -10, -12, BlueB 76, CelR 73, ConAu 5R, -7NR, ConLC 22[port], CurBio 58, DcLEL 1940, InWom, IntAu&W 77, IntWW 74, -75, -76, -77, -78, -79, -80, -81, -82, -83, LibW, McGEWD 84, NatPD 81[port], NewYTBE 73, NewYTBS 80, NotNAT, OxAmL, WhoAm 74, -76, -78, -80, -82, WhoAmW 74, -64, -66, -68, -70, -72, -81, -83, WhoThe 15, -16, -81, WhoWor 74, -78, -80, -82, WorAl, WorAu, WrDr 76, -80, -82, -84

Kerr, Jessica 1901- AuBYP SUP, BioIn 11, ConAu P-2, SmATA 13

Kerr, Judith 1923- AuBYP SUP, ConAu 93, SmATA 24[port], TwCCW 78, -83, WrDr 80, -82, -84

Kerr, M E 1927?- AuBYP SUP, BioIn 10, -12, ConAu X, ConLC 12, FourBJA, SmATA X, TwCCW 78, -83, WrDr 80, -82, -84

Kerr, M E see also Meaker, Marijane

Kerry, Lois 1954- ConAu X, IntAu&W 82X, SmATA 1

Kerry, Lois see also Arquette, Lois S

Kesey, Ken 1935- AmAu&B, BioIn 8, -10,

–11, –12, CasWL, CmCal, ConAu 1R,
ConLC 1, –3, –6, –11, ConNov 72, –76, –82,
CurBio 76, DcLB 2, –16[port],
DcLEL 1940, DrAF 76, DrAP&F 83,
EncWL, –2, IntAu&W 76, –77, –82,
LinLib L, MakMC, ModAL SUP, MugS,
Novels, PenC AM, RAdv 1, REnAW,
WebE&AL, WhoAm 74, –76, –78, –80, –82,
WhoTwCL, WorAl, WorAu 1970,
WrDr 76, –80, –82, –84

Kesselman, Judi R 1934- *ConAu X, –61*

Kesselman-Turkel, Judi 1934- *ConAu X*

Kessner, Lawrence 1957- *ConAu 109*

Kessner, Thomas 1946- *ConAu 11NR, –69,*
DrAS 78H, –82H

Kesteven, G R *BioIn 12, ConAu X, –69,*
SmATA X

Ketcham, Hank 1920- *ArtCS, BioIn 3, –4, –5,*
–11, ConAu X, CurBio 56, LinLib L,
SmATA X, WhoAmA 82

Ketchum, Richard M 1922- *BioIn 10, –11,*
ConAu 25R, WhoAm 74, –76, –78, –80,
–82, WhoWor 74, WrDr 76, –80, –82, –84

Kett, Joseph Francis 1938- *ConAu 25R,*
DrAS 74H, –78H, –82H

Kettelkamp, Larry Dale 1933- *AuBYP,*
BioIn 8, –9, –12, ConAu 29R, ConLC 12,
IlsCB 1957, –1967, IntAu&W 77, –82,
SmATA 2, ThrBJA, WrDr 76, –80, –82,
–84

Kevles, Bettyann 1938- *ConAu 11NR, –69,*
SmATA 23[port]

Key, Alexander 1904-1979 *AuBYP, BioIn 8,*
–11, –12, ConAu 5R, –6NR, –89,
IntAu&W 77, ScF&FL 1, –2,
SmATA 23N, –8, WrDr 76, –80

Key, Mary Ritchie 1924- *ConAu 1NR, –45,*
DrAS 74F, –78F, –82F, FifIDA,
IntAu&W 76, –77, WhoAm 82,
WhoAmW 77, –79, –81, –83, WhoWest 80,
–82, –84, WhoWor 82

Keyes, Daniel 1927- *BioIn 7, ConAu 10NR,*
–17R, ConSFA, DrAP&F 83, DrAS 74E,
–78E, –82E, EncSF, Novels, ScF&FL 1,
–2, SmATA 37, WhoAm 82, WhoHol A,
WhoSciF, WrDr 76, –80, –82, –84

Keyes, Fenton 1915- *AmM&WS 73S, –78S,*
ConAu 107, SmATA 34[port],
WhoAm 74, –76, –78, –80, –82

Keyes, Frances Parkinson 1885-1970 *AmAu&B,*
AmNov, AmWomWr, BiCAW, BioIn 1,
–2, –3, –4, –5, –7, –9, –12, BkC 5,
CathA 1930, CelR 73, ConAu 5R,
–7NR, –25R, EvLB, InWom, LongCTC,
Novels, ObitOF 79, ObitT 1961,
PenC AM, REn, TwCA, TwCA SUP,
TwCWr, WhAm 5, WhNAA,
WhoAmW 58, –64, –66, –68, –70, –72

Keyes, Ralph 1945- *ConAu 3NR, –49*

Khan, Ismith 1925- *BioIn 9, ConNov 82,*
WrDr 84

Khayyam, Omar 1050?-1125? *BbD, BiD&SB,*

BioIn 4, –5, –8, –9, –10, ChhPo S1, –S2,
DcOrL 3, InSci, NewC

Kherdian, David 1931- *BioIn 12, ChhPo S3,*
ConAu 21R, ConLC 6, –9, DrAP 75,
DrAP&F 83, IntAu&W 76, –77,
IntWWP 77, SmATA 16, WhoAm 82,
WrDr 76, –80, –82, –84

Kidd, Virginia 1921- *ConAu 10NR, –65,*
DrAP&F 83, IntAu&W 77, –82,
ScF&FL 1, –2

Kiddell, John 1922- *Alli, Au&Wr 6, BioIn 9,*
ConAu 29R, SmATA 3

Kidder, Rushworth M 1944- *ConAu 77,*
DrAS 74E, –78E, –82E

Kidder, Tracy 1945- *BioIn 12, ConAu 109,*
NewYTBS 81[port]

Kiefer, Irene 1926- *BioIn 12, ConAu 11NR,*
–69, SmATA 21[port]

Kiefer, Warren 1929?- *ConAu 77,*
IntAu&W 77, WrDr 76, –80, –82, –84

Kienzle, William X 1928- *BioIn 12,*
ConAu 9NR, –93, ConLC 25[port]

Kieran, John 1892-1981 *AmAu&B,*
AuBYP SUP, BioIn 1, –2, –3, –4, –5, –7, –8,
–9, –12, CathA 1930, ChhPo S1, –S3,
ConAu 101, –105, CurBio 82N,
NewYTBS 81[port], REn, REnAL,
WhoAm 74, –76, –78, WhoE 74

Kiesel, Stanley 1925- *ConAu 104, DrAP 75,*
SmATA 35

Kiev, Ari 1933- *BiDrAPA 77, BlueB 76,*
ConAu 3NR, –9R, IntMed 80,
WhoCon 73, WhoE 74, –75, –77, –79,
WrDr 76, –80, –82, –84

Kilby, Clyde Samuel 1902- *BioIn 11,*
ChhPo S1, ConAu 9NR, –13R,
DrAS 74E, –78E, –82E

Kilgore, Al 1927- *WhoAm 74, –76,*
WhoAmA 76, –78, –82

Kilgore, Kathleen 1946- *ConAu 109*

Killens, John Oliver 1916- *BlkAWP,*
ConAu 77, ConLC 10, ConNov 72, –76,
–82, DrAF 76, DrAP&F 83, DrBlPA,
InB&W 80, IntAu&W 76, –77, LivgBAA,
ModBlW, NegAl 76[port], –83[port],
PenC AM, SelBAA, WhoAm 74, –76,
WhoBlA 75, –77, –80, WhoE 74,
WorAu 1970, WrDr 76, –80, –82, –84

Killilea, Marie 1913- *BioIn 9, ConAu 5R,*
IntAu&W 76, SmATA 2, WhoAmW 61,
WhoE 74

Killough, Lee 1942- *ConAu 89, WrDr 84*

Killy, Jean-Claude 1943- *BioIn 7, –8, –9, –10,*
–12, BioNews 74, CelR 73, CurBio 68,
WhoFr 79, WhoHol A, WhoWor 74, –76,
WorAl

Kim, Richard E 1932- *BioIn 6, –9, –12,*
ConAu 5R, ConNov 72, –76, –82,
DcLEL 1940, DrAF 76, DrAP&F 83,
IntAu&W 76, –77, WhoAm 74, –76, –78,
–80, –82, WhoE 74, WhoWor 74,
WrDr 76, –80, –82, –84

Kim, Yong-Ik 1920- *ConAu 17R*
Kimball, Dean 1912- *AuBYP SUP, ConAu 69*
Kimbrell, Grady 1933- *ConAu 33R*
Kimbrough, Emily 1899- *AmAu&B,*
  AmWomWr, Au&Wr 6, BioIn 1, -2, -3,
  -4, -9, -10, -12, BlueB 76, ConAu 17R,
  CurBio 44, InWom, IndAu 1917,
  OxAmL, REnAL, SmATA 2,
  WhoAm 74, -76, -78, -80, -82,
  WhoAmW 74, -58, -61, -64, -66, -68, -70,
  -72, -83, WhoWor 74, -76, WorAu,
  WrDr 76, -80, -82, -84
Kimmel, Eric A 1946- *BioIn 11, ConAu 3NR,*
  -49, IntAu&W 77, SmATA 13,
  WrDr 76, -80, -82, -84
Kinder, Gary 1946- *ConAu 109*
King, B B 1925- *BiDAfM, BioIn 8, -9, -10,*
  -11, -12, BioNews 74, BluesWW,
  CurBio 70, DrBlPA, Ebony 1, EncJzS 70,
  IlEncJ, NegAl 76[port], -83[port],
  RkOn 74, WhoAm 74, -76, -78, -80, -82,
  WhoBlA 75, -77, -80, WhoRocM 82,
  WorAl
King, Billie Jean 1943- *BioIn 7, -8, -9, -10, -11,*
  -12, BioNews 74, CelR 73, CmCal,
  ConAu 10NR, -53, CurBio 67, GoodHs,
  HerW, InWom, IntDcWB, IntWW 76,
  -77, -78, -79, -80, -81, -82, -83, LibW,
  NewYTBE 70, NewYTBS 74, -75, -76,
  -77, -80[port], -82[port], -83[port],
  SmATA 12, WhDW, Who 82, -83,
  WhoAm 74, -76, -78, -80, -82,
  WhoAmW 79, -81, -83, WhoWor 78,
  WorAl, WrDr 80, -82, -84
King, C Daly 1895-1963 *TwCCr&M 80,*
  WhE&EA
King, Carole 1941?- *BiDAmM, BioIn 9, -10,*
  -12, CelR 73, CurBio 74, EncPR&S 77,
  GoodHs, NewYTBE 70, RkOn 74, -82,
  RolSEnR 83, WhoAm 74, -76, -78, -80,
  -82, WhoAmW 74, -75, -81,
  WhoRocM 82, WorAl
King, Charles 1844-1933 *Alli, Alli SUP,*
  AmAu&B, AmBi, AmLY, ApCAB,
  ArizL, BiD&SB, BioIn 5, -8, CarSB,
  DcAmAu, DcNAA, HarEnUS,
  NatCAB 5, -25, OxAmL, TwCBDA,
  WhAm 1, WhNAA, WisWr
King, Charles Lester 1922- *ConAu 57,*
  DrAS 74F, -78F, -82F
King, Clarence 1842-1901 *Alli SUP, AmAu,*
  AmAu&B, AmBi, ApCAB, BiDAmS,
  BiD&SB, BioIn 1, -2, -4, -5, -8, -10, -12,
  CmCal, ConAu 110, DcAmAu, DcAmB,
  DcLB 12[port], DcNAA, DcScB,
  EncAAH, HarEnUS, InSci, LinLib L, -S,
  McGEWB, NatCAB 13, NewYTBS 74,
  OxAmH, OxAmL, REn, REnAL,
  TwCBDA, WebAB, -79, WhDW,
  WhAm 1
King, Clarence 1884?-1974 *BioIn 10,*
  ConAu 53

King, Clive 1924- *ConAu 104, SmATA 28,*
  TwCCW 78, -83, WrDr 82, -84
King, Coretta 1927- *Au&Wr 6, BiDAfM,*
  BioIn 7, -8, -9, -10, -11, -12, BlueB 76,
  CelR 73, CivR 74, CivRSt, ConAu 29R,
  CurBio 69, Ebony 1, GoodHs, HerW,
  InB&W 80, IntAu&W 77, IntDcWB,
  IntWW 83, LivgBAA, NegAl 76[port],
  -83[port], NewYTBE 72, PolProf J,
  SelBAA, WhoAm 74, -76, -78, -80, -82,
  WhoAmW 74, -70, -70A, -72, -75, -77, -79,
  -81, -83, WhoBlA 75, -77, -80,
  WhoRel 77, WhoS&SW 73, -75, -76,
  WhoWor 74, -76, WorAl
King, Cynthia 1925- *BioIn 10, ConAu 29R,*
  DrAP&F 83, MichAu 80, ScF&FL 1A,
  SmATA 7, WrDr 76, -80, -82, -84
King, Marian *AmAu&B, Au&Wr 6,*
  ConAu 2NR, -5R, ForWC 70,
  SmATA 23[port], WhoAm 74, -76, -78,
  -80, -82, WhoAmW 74, -58, -64, -66, -68,
  -70, -72, -77, -79, -81, WhoE 83,
  WhoS&SW 73, WrDr 76, -80, -82, -84
King, Martin Luther, Jr. 1929-1968 *AmAu&B,*
  BioIn 4, -5, -6, -7, -8, -9, -10, -11, -12,
  BlkAWP, CivRSt, ConAu P-2, CurBio 57,
  -65, -68, DcAmReB, DcAmSR, DcPol,
  EncAB-H, EncSoH, InB&W 80,
  LinLib L, -S, LuthC 75, MakMC,
  McGEWB, NatCAB 54, NegAl 76[port],
  -83[port], NewYTBS 74, ObitOF 79,
  ObitT 1961, OxAmH, OxAmL,
  PolProf E, PolProf J, PolProf K, REnAL,
  SelBAA, SmATA 14, WebAB, -79,
  WhDW, WhAm 4A, WhAmP, WorAl
King, Mary Louise 1911- *ConAu 21R*
King, Stephen 1947?- *BioIn 11, -12,*
  ConAu 1NR, -61, ConLC 12, -26[port],
  CurBio 81[port], DcLB Y80B[port],
  EncSF, NewYTBS 79, -81[port], Novels,
  ScF&FL 1, -2, SmATA 9, WhoAm 78,
  -80, -82, WhoHr&F, WrDr 82, -84
King, Woodie, Jr. 1937- *BlkAWP, ConAu 103,*
  DrBlPA, InB&W 80, LivgBAA, SelBAA,
  WhoAm 74, -76, -78, -80, -82, WhoBlA 75,
  -77, -80, WhoThe 81
King-Hall, Stephen 1893-1966 *BioIn 3, -7,*
  ChhPo S2, ConAu 5R, LongCTC,
  ScF&FL 1, -2, WhE&EA, WhLit,
  WhThe, WhoLA
Kingman, Lee 1919-1978 *AuBYP, BioIn 1, -6,*
  -8, -9, ChhPo, -S1, ConAu X, -5R,
  ConLC 17, ForWC 70, MorJA,
  ScF&FL 1, SmATA 1, TwCCW 78, -83,
  WhoAmW 58, -61, -64, WrDr 76, -80, -82,
  -84
Kingman, Russ 1917- *ConAu 101*
Kingsley, Charles 1819-1875 *Alli, Alli SUP,*
  AnCL, AtlBL, AuBYP, BbD, BiD&SB,
  BioIn 1, -2, -3, -4, -5, -6, -8, -9, -10, -11,
  -12, Br&AmS, BrAu 19, CarSB,
  CasWL, CelCen, Chambr 3, ChhPo, -S1,

–S2, –S3, CrtT 3, CyEd, CyWA,
DcAmSR, DcBiA, DcBiPP, DcBrBI,
DcEnA, DcEnL, DcEuL, DcLB 21[port],
DcLEL, Dis&D, EvLB, FamPYP,
JBA 34, LinLib L, LongCEL, LuthC 75,
McGEWB, MouLC 3, NewC, Novels,
OxEng, PenC ENG, RAdv 1, REn, TelT,
TwCCW 83A, WebE&AL, WhDW,
WhoChL, YABC 2
Kingston, Maxine 1940- *AmWomWr,*
BioIn 11, –12, ConAu 69, ConLC 12, –19,
DcLB Y80B[port], NewYTBS 77,
–80[port], WhoAm 78, –80, –82,
WhoAmW 83, WrDr 80, –82, –84
Kinkead, Eugene 1906- *ConAu 1R, –1NR*
Kinnell, Galway 1927- *AmAu&B, BioIn 6,*
–10, –12, ConAu 9R, –10NR, ConLC 1,
–2, –3, –5, –13, ConP 70, –75, –80,
CroCAP, DcLB 5[port], DcLEL 1940,
DrAF 76, DrAP 75, DrAP&F 83,
EncWL 2, IntAu&W 82, IntWW 77, –78,
–79, –80, –81, –82, –83, IntWWP 77, –82,
LinLib L, ModAL SUP, OxAmL,
PenC AM, RAdv 1, WhoAm 74, –76, –78,
–80, –82, WhoTwCL, WhoWor 74,
WorAu, WrDr 76, –80, –82, –84
Kinross, Lord Patrick 1904-1976 *Au&Wr 6,*
ConAu 9R, –65
Kinsella, W P 1935- *BioIn 12, ConAu 97,*
ConLC 27[port], WrDr 82, –84
Kinter, Judith 1928- *ConAu 109*
Kipling, Rudyard 1865-1936 *Alli SUP, AnCL,*
ApCAB SUP, AtlBL, AuBYP, BbD,
BiD&SB, BioIn 1, –2, –3, –4, –5, –6, –7, –8,
–9, –10, –11, –12, BrWr 6, CarSB,
CasWL, Chambr 3, ChhPo, –S1, –S2, –S3,
CmCal, CnE&AP, CnMWL, ConAu 105,
CrtT 3, –4, CyWA, DcAmAu, DcBiA,
DcBrBI, DcEnA, –AP, DcEuL, DcInB,
DcLB 19[port], DcLEL, Dis&D, EncSF,
EncWL, –2, EvLB, FamAYP, FamSYP,
FilmgC, JBA 34, LinLib L, LongCEL,
LongCTC, MnBBF, ModBrL,
ModBrL SUP, NewC, Novels[port],
OxAmL, OxCan, OxEng, OxMus,
PenC ENG, RAdv 1, RComWL, REn,
ScF&FL 1, Str&VC, TelT, TwCA,
TwCA SUP, TwCCW 78, –83,
TwCLC 8[port], TwCWr, WebE&AL,
WhDW, WhE&EA, WhLit,
WhoBW&I A, WhoChL, WhoHr&F,
WhoLA, WhoTwCL, WorAl, YABC 2
Kipnis, Claude 1938-1981 *AnObit 1981,*
BioIn 12, ConAu 103, –107,
NewYTBS 81, WhoAm 78, –80
Kirk, Rhina *AuBYP SUP*
Kirk, Richard 1931- *ConAu 13R*
Kirk, Robert Warren 1922- *AmM&WS 73P,*
–76P, –79P, –82P
Kirk, Ruth 1925- *AuBYP, BioIn 8, –10,*
ConAu 9NR, –13R, ForWC 70,
SmATA 5, WhoAmW 75, WhoPNW

Kirkham, George L 1941- *BioIn 11,*
ConAu 77, WrDr 80, –82, –84
Kirkup, James 1918?- *AntBDN Q, Au&Wr 6,*
BioIn 4, –5, –8, –10, –11, BlueB 76, ChhPo,
–S2, –S3, ConAu 1R, –2NR, ConLC 1,
ConP 70, –75, –80, DcLEL 1940,
FarE&A 78, –79, –80, –81, IntAu&W 76,
–77, –82, IntWW 74, –75, –76, –77, –78,
–79, –80, –81, –82, –83, IntWWP 77, –82,
LongCTC, NewC, PenC ENG, REn,
SmATA 12, Who 74, –82, –83,
WhoWor 74, –78, –82, WorAu, WrDr 76,
–80, –82, –84
Kirkwood, James 1930- *Au&Wr 6, AuNews 2,*
BioIn 11, ConAu 1R, –6NR, ConLC 9,
NatPD, –81[port], NewYTBS 82[port],
WhoAm 76, –78, –80, –82, WhoThe 81,
WrDr 80, –82, –84
Kirst, Hans Hellmut 1914- *ASpks, BioIn 6, –8,*
–10, –11, CasWL, ConAu 104, EncSF,
IntAu&W 76, –77, IntWW 74, –75, –76,
–77, –78, –79, –80, –81, –82, –83, ModGL,
ScF&FL 1, TwCCr&M 80B, TwCWr,
WhoWor 74, –82, WorAu
Kirwan, Molly Morrow 1906- *Au&Wr 6,*
ConAu P-1
Kis, Danilo 1935- *CasWL, ConAu 109,*
IntAu&W 76, WhoSocC 78
Kishon, Ephraim 1924- *Au&Wr 6,*
ConAu 2NR, –49, IntAu&W 77, –82,
McGEWD 84, REnWD, WhoWor 76,
WhoWorJ 78
Kissin, Eva H 1923- *BioIn 11, ConAu 29R,*
SmATA 10
Kister, Kenneth F 1935- *BiDrLUS 70,*
ConAu 25R, WhoLibI 82, WhoLibS 66
Kitman, Marvin 1929- *AmAu&B, BioIn 7, –8,*
ConAu 101, ScF&FL 1, WhoAm 74, –76,
–78, –80
Kitson, Harry Dexter 1886-1959 *BiDAmEd,*
BioIn 1, –2, –5, –9, CurBio 51, –59, InSci,
IndAu 1816, NatCAB 52, ObitOF 79,
WhAm 3, WhNAA
Kittredge, William 1932- *DrAF 76,*
DrAS 78E, –82E
Kjelgaard, James Arthur 1910-1959 *AuBYP,*
BioIn 2, –3, –5, –7, –12, ConAu 109,
SmATA 17, Str&VC, TwCCW 78
Kjelgaard, Jim 1910-1959 *ConAu X, JBA 51,*
ScF&FL 1, SmATA X, Str&VC,
TwCCW 83
Klagsbrun, Francine Lifton *ConAu 21R,*
ForWC 70, SmATA 36, WhoAmW 68,
–70, –75, –77, –79, –81
Klamkin, Lynn 1950- *ConAu 45*
Klaperman, Libby Mindlin 1921-1982 *BioIn 12,*
ConAu 9R, –107, SmATA 31N, –33
Klass, Morton 1927- *AmM&WS 73S, –76P,*
AuBYP SUP, BioIn 11, ConAu 1R,
–5NR, FifIDA, SmATA 11
Klass, Philip J 1919?- *BioIn 12, ConAu 25R,*
IntAu&W 76, LElec, ScF&FL 1,

UFOEn[port], WhoEng 80,
WhoS&SW 73, -75, -76, WhoTech 82,
WhoWorJ 72, -78, WrDr 84

Klass, Sheila Solomon 1927- ConAu 37R,
DrAP&F 83, IntAu&W 77,
WhoAmW 83, WrDr 76, -80, -82, -84

Klaw, Spencer 1920- ConAu 25R, WhoAm 82

Klebanow, Diana 1935- DrAS 74H

Klein, Aaron E 1930- AmBench 79,
AuBYP SUP, ConAu 25R, SmATA 28

Klein, Dave 1940- ConAu 89

Klein, David 1919- AmM&WS 73S, -78S,
AuBYP, BioIn 8, -9, ConAu 1R, -1NR,
IntWW 83

Klein, Deana Tarson 1925- AmM&WS 73P,
-76P, -79P

Klein, Elizabeth 1939- ConAu 110,
IntWWP 77, -77X, Po&Wr 77

Klein, Gerard 1937- ConAu 49, EncSF,
ScF&FL 1, -2

Klein, H Arthur AuBYP, BioIn 11,
ConAu 13R, SmATA 8

Klein, Joe 1946- ConAu X

Klein, Mina Cooper 1906- BioIn 11,
ConAu 37R, IntAu&W 77, -82,
SmATA 8

Klein, Norma 1938- AuBYP SUP, BioIn 10,
ChlLR 2, ConAu 41R, DrAF 76,
DrAP&F 83, IntAu&W 77, SmATA 7,
TwCCW 78, -83, WhoAmW 83,
WrDr 82, -84

Klein, Richard M 1923- AmM&WS 73P, -76P,
-79P, -82P, ConAu 108

Kleinfield, Sonny 1950- BioIn 12, ConAu 97,
WhoAm 82

Klever, Anita AuBYP SUP

Kline, Morris 1908- AmM&WS 73P, -76P,
-79P, -82P, ConAu 2NR, -5R,
IntAu&W 77, -82, WhoAm 74, -76, -78,
WhoAmJ 80, WrDr 76, -80, -82, -84

Kline, Nancy Meadors 1946- ConAu 57

Kline, Peter 1936- ConAu 25R, WhoE 75,
WrDr 76, -80, -82, -84

Klinkowitz, Jerome 1943- ConAu 1NR, -45,
DrAS 78E, -82E

Kloepfer, Marguerite 1916- ConAu 97,
IntAu&W 82

Klots, Alexander Barrett 1903-
AmM&WS 73P, ConAu 107

Kluckhohn, Clyde 1905-1960 AmAu&B,
BioIn 1, -2, -3, -4, -5, -6, CurBio 51, -60,
DcSoc, InSci, McGEWB, NamesHP,
ObitOF 79, REnAL, REnAW,
TwCA SUP, WhAm 4

Kluge, P F 1942- ConAu 73

Kluger, Ruth 1914?-1980 AnObit 1981,
BioIn 10, ConAu 108

Knebel, Fletcher 1911- AmAu&B, Au&Wr 6,
AuNews 1, BioIn 7, -10, -12, BioNews 75,
ConAu 1R, -1NR, ConLC 14,
ConNov 72, -76, -82, DcLEL 1940,
DrAP&F 83, EncSF, IntAu&W 76, -77,

-82, NewYTBS 74, ScF&FL 1, -2,
SmATA 36, WhoAm 74, -76, -78, -80, -82,
WhoE 74, WhoWor 74, WrDr 76, -80,
-82, -84

Knight, Alanna ConAu 81, IntAu&W 76, -77,
-82, WhoWor 80

Knight, Arthur 1916- BioIn 9, ConAu 41R,
IntMPA 77, -75, -76, -78, -79, -81,
-82, -84, OxFilm, WhoAm 74, -76, -78,
-80, -82

Knight, Bernard 1931- Au&Wr 6,
ConAu 2NR, -49, IntAu&W 76,
IntMed 80, WrDr 76, -80, -82, -84

Knight, Charles Robert 1874-1953 BioIn 1, -3,
-4, -5, -12, IlsCB 1946, NatCAB 39,
NewYHSD 57, WhAm 3

Knight, Charles W 1891- ConAu P-1

Knight, Damon 1922- BioIn 10, -11, -12,
ConAu 3NR, -49, ConSFA, DcLB 8[port],
EncSF, IntAu&W 76, LinLib L, Novels,
ScF&FL 1, -2, SmATA 9, WhoSciF,
WorAu, WrDr 76, -80, -82

Knight, David C 1925- AuBYP, BioIn 8, -12,
ConAu 73, SmATA 14

Knight, Eric 1897-1943 AuBYP, BioIn 1, -3,
-4, -5, -7, -8, -12, CnDAL, CurBio 42,
-43, CyWA, FourBJA, NatCAB 40,
REn, REnAL, ScF&FL 1, SmATA 18,
TwCA, TwCA SUP, TwCCW 83,
WhAm 2, WhoChL, WorAl

Knight, Franklin W 1942- ConAu 101,
DrAS 82H, IntAu&W 82

Knight, Harold V 1907- ConAu 21R

Knight, Ruth Adams 1898-1974 AuBYP,
BioIn 3, -4, -6, -8, ConAu 5R, -49,
CurBio 43, -55, ForWC 70, InWom,
MorJA, OhA&B, SmATA 20N,
WhoAmW 58, -61

Knoke, Heinz 1921- BioIn 4

Knott, Will C 1927- ConAu X

Knowles, Anne 1933- ConAu 102, SmATA 37,
WrDr 80, -82, -84

Knowles, John 1926- AmAu&B, Au&Wr 6,
BioIn 7, -10, -11, BlueB 76, CasWL,
ConAu 17R, ConLC 1, -4, -10, -26[port],
ConNov 72, -76, -82, DcLB 6,
DcLEL 1940, DrAF 76, IntAu&W 76,
-77, -82, LinLib L, Novels, RAdv 1,
SmATA 8, WhoAm 74, -76, -78, -80, -82,
WhoWor 74, WorAl, WorAu, WrDr 76,
-80, -82, -84

Knowlton, William H 1927- ConAu 17R,
IntAu&W 77, WrDr 76, -80, -82, -84

Knox, Calvin M 1935- AuBYP, ConAu X,
DcLEL 1940, EncSF, ScF&FL 1,
SmATA X, ThrBJA, WorAu 1970,
WrDr 84

Knox, Calvin M see also Silverberg, Robert

Knox, Donald E 1936- ConAu 45

Knox-Johnston, Robin 1939- Au&Wr 6,
BioIn 8, ConAu 29R, IntAu&W 76, -77,
-82, Who 82, -83, WhoWor 76, -78,

WrDr 76, –80, –82, –84

Knudson, R R 1932- *BioIn 10, ConAu X, SmATA 7*

Knudson, Rozanne Ruth 1932- *BioIn 10, ConAu 33R, ForWC 70, SmATA 7, WhoAmW 74, WrDr 76, –80, –82, –84*

Kobryn, A P 1949- *ConAu 93*

Koch, Claude F 1918- *AmCath 80, BioIn 3, CathA 1952, ConAu 9R, DrAP&F 83, DrAS 74E, –78E, –82E, IntAu&W 76, –77, –82, WrDr 76, –80, –82, –84*

Koch, Eric 1919- *ConAu 69, OxCan, OxCan SUP, ScF&FL 1, WhoE 79*

Koch, Howard 1902- *AmAu&B, ConAu 73, ConDr 73, –77A, –82A, DcLB 26[port], FilmgC, IntMPA 77, –75, –76, –78, –79, –81, –82, –84, WorEFlm*

Koch, Kenneth 1925- *AmAu&B, BioIn 10, –11, –12, BlueB 76, ChhPo S1, –S2, –S3, ConAu 1R, –6NR, ConDr 73, –77, –82, ConLC 5, –8, ConP 70, –75, –80, CroCAP, CurBio 78, DcLB 5[port], DcLEL 1940, DrAF 76, DrAP 75, DrAP&F 83, DrAS 74E, –78E, –82E, IntAu&W 77, IntWWP 77, LinLib L, McGEWD 84, NewYTBE 70, PenC AM, RAdv 1, WebE&AL, WhoAm 74, –76, –78, –80, –82, WhoWor 74, –76, WorAu, WrDr 76, –80, –82, –84*

Kochan, Lionel 1922- *Au&Wr 6, ConAu 105*

Kocher, Paul H 1907- *AmCath 80, ConAu 65, DrAS 74E, –78E, –82E, ScF&FL 1, WhoAm 74, –76, –78, –80, –82*

Koehn, Ilse *BioIn 11, ConAu X, SmATA X*

Koenig, Laird *BlkAWP, ConAu 29R*

Koenig, Laird Philip 1927- *WhoAm 74*

Koenig, Walter 1936- *ConAu 104*

Koestler, Arthur 1905-1983 *ASpks, Au&Wr 6, BioIn 1, –2, –3, –4, –5, –6, –7, –8, –9, –10, –11, –12, BlueB 76, CasWL, CnMWL, ConAu 1R, –1NR, –109, ConLC 1, –3, –6, –8, –15, ConNov 72, –76, –82, CurBio 43, –62, –83N, CyWA, DcAmSR, DcLB Y83N[port], EncSF, EncWL, –2, IntAu&W 76, –77, –82, IntWW 74, –75, –76, –77, –78, –79, –80, –81, –82, –83N, LinLib L, –S, LongCTC, MakMC, ModBrL, NewC, NewYTBE 70, NewYTBS 83[port], Novels[port], OxEng, PenC ENG, REn, ScF&FL 1, TwCA SUP, TwCWr, WebE&AL, WhDW, WhE&EA, Who 74, –82, –83, WhoTwCL, WhoWor 74, –76, –78, –82, WhoWorJ 72, –78, WorAl, WrDr 76, –80, –82, –84*

Koff, Richard Myram 1926- *ConAu 89, WhoAm 74, –76, –78, –80, –82, WrDr 82, –84*

Kohl, Herbert 1937- *AmAu&B, BioIn 10, –11, ConAu 65, NewYTBE 73, WhoAmP 75, –77, –79*

Kohn, Bernice 1920- *AuBYP, BioIn 8, –9,*

ConAu 9R, IntAu&W 77X, SmATA 4, WrDr 76

Kohout, Pavel 1928- *BioIn 9, –11, –12, ConAu 3NR, –45, ConLC 13, EncWT, IntAu&W 82, McGEWD 84, NewYTBS 79, WhoSocC 78*

Kolbas, Grace Holden 1914- *ConAu 93, IntAu&W 82*

Komisar, Lucy 1942- *AuBYP SUP, BioIn 11, ConAu 33R, ForWC 70, SmATA 9, WrDr 76, –80, –82, –84*

Komroff, Manuel 1890-1974 *AmAu&B, AmNov, AuBYP, BioIn 2, –3, –4, –7, –9, –10, –12, CnDAL, ConAu 1R, –4NR, –53, DcLB 4, NewYTBS 74, ObitOF 79, OxAmL, REnAL, ScF&FL 1, –2, SmATA 2, –20N, TwCA, TwCA SUP, WhAm 6, WhE&EA, WhoAm 74, WhoWor 74, WrDr 76*

Konecky, Edith 1922- *ConAu 69*

Konigsberg, Hans 1921- *AmAu&B, Au&Wr 6, ConAu 1R, SmATA 5, WhoWor 74, WorAu, WrDr 76, –80, –82, –84*

Konigsberger, Hans *see also* Koningsberger, Hans

Konigsburg, E L 1930- *AmWomWr, ConAu 21R, ScF&FL 1, TwCCW 83, WrDr 80, –82, –84*

Konigsburg, Elaine L 1930- *AnCL, Au&ICB, AuBYP, BioIn 8, –9, –10, –12, ChlLR 1, ConAu 21R, MorBMP, NewbC 1966, SmATA 4, ThrBJA, TwCCW 78, WhoAm 74, –76, –78, –80, –82, WhoAmW 74, –72, WrDr 76*

Koningsberger, Hans 1921- *AmAu&B, Au&Wr 6, BioIn 10, BlueB 76, ConAu 1R, –2NR, DrAP&F 83, SmATA 5, WhoWor 74, WorAu*

Koningsberger, Hans *see also* Konigsberger, Hans

Konvitz, Jeffrey 1944- *BioIn 10, ConAu 7NR, –53, ScF&FL 1, –2, WrDr 80, –82, –84*

Konwicki, Tadeusz 1926- *BioIn 10, –12, ConAu 101, ConLC 8, DcFM, EncWL 2, IntWW 76, –77, –78, –79, –80, –81, –82, –83, OxFilm, WhoSocC 78, WhoWor 74, –82*

Koob, Theodora 1918- *AuBYP, ConAu 5R, SmATA 23[port]*

Kopal, Zdenek 1914- *AmM&WS 73P, –76P, –79P, –82P, BioIn 2, –8, BlueB 76, ConAu 93, CurBio 69, IntAu&W 77, Who 74, –82, –83, WhoWor 74, WrDr 80, –82, –84*

Kopit, Arthur 1937- *AmAu&B, AuNews 1, BiE&WWA, BioIn 9, –10, –12, CasWL, ConAu 81, ConDr 73, –77, –82, ConLC 1, –18, CroCD, CurBio 72, DcLB 7[port], DcLEL 1940, EncWT, LinLib L, McGEWD, –84, NatPD, –81[port], NotNAT, OxAmL, PenC AM, REn, WebE&AL, WhoAm 74, –76, –78, –80, –82, WhoThe 15, –16, –81, WorAu, WrDr 76, –80, –82, –84*

Kopper, Philip 1937- *ConAu 97*

Koppett, Leonard 1923- *ConAu 11NR, –25R, WhoAm 80, –82, WhoE 74, –75, WhoWorJ 72, –78*

Korchnoi, Viktor 1931- *BioIn 10, –11, –12, GolEC*

Koren, Edward 1935- *BioIn 10, –12, ConAu 11NR, –25R, SmATA 5, WhoAm 80, –82, WhoAmA 76, –78, –80, –82, WhoE 74, WhoGrA 82[port], WorECar*

Korinetz, Yuri 1923- *BioIn 11, ChlLR 4[port], ConAu 11NR, –61, SmATA 9, TwCCW 78B, –83B*

Kornbluth, C M 1923-1958 *ConAu 105, DcLB 8[port], EncSF, ScF&FL 1, TwCLC 8[port], WhoSciF, WorAl*

Kornbluth, Cyril M 1923-1958 *BioIn 4, –10, –12, LinLib L, Novels, ObitOF 79, WorAu*

Kornfeld, Anita Clay 1928- *BioIn 12, ConAu 97, DrAP&F 83*

Korschunow, Irina 1925- *IntAu&W 77, –82*

Kosinski, Jerzy 1933- *AmAu&B, ASpks, BioIn 7, –9, –10, –11, –12, ConAu 9NR, –17R, ConLC 1, –2, –3, –6, –10, –15, ConNov 72, –76, –82, CurBio 74, DcLB Y82A[port], –2, DcLEL 1940, DrAF 76, DrAP&F 83, EncSF, EncWL, –2, IntAu&W 76, ModAL SUP, NewYTBS 79, –82[port], RAdv 1, Who 82, –83, WhoAm 74, –76, –78, –80, –82, WhoE 74, –75, –77, –79, –81, –83, WhoWor 74, –76, –78, –80, –82, WorAl, WorAu, WrDr 76, –80, –82, –84*

Kostelanetz, Richard 1940- *AmAu&B, BioIn 12, BlueB 76, ConAu 13R, ConP 75, –80, DrAF 76, DrAP 75, DrAP&F 83, DrAS 74H, –78E, –82E, Future, IntAu&W 76, –77, –82, IntWWP 77, –82, WhoAm 74, –76, –78, –80, –82, WhoWor 78, –82, WrDr 76, –80, –82, –84*

Kotzwinkle, William 1938- *ChlLR 6[port], ConAu 3NR, –45, ConLC 5, –14, EncSF, SmATA 24[port], WhoAm 82*

Koufax, Sandy 1935- *BioIn 12, CelR 73, CmCal, ConAu X, CurBio 64, NewYTBS 80[port], WorAl*

Koufax, Sanford 1935- *BioIn 4, –5, –6, –7, –8, –9, –10, –11, ConAu 89, WebAB, –79, WhoAm 74, –76, WhoProB 73*

Kouwenhoven, John A 1909- *AmAu&B, BioIn 3, –9, ConAu 1R, DrAS 74E, –78E, –82E, IntAu&W 77, WhoAm 74, –76, –78, –80, –82, WhoAmA 73, –76, –78, –80, –82, WrDr 76, –80, –82, –84*

Kovic, Ron 1946- *BioIn 11*

Kowet, Don 1937- *AuBYP SUP, ConAu 10NR, –57*

Kozelka, Paul 1909- *BiE&WWA, ConAu P-2, NotNAT*

Kozol, Jonathan 1936- *AmAu&B, BioIn 5, –8,*

–9, –10, CelR 73, ConAu 61, ConLC 17, WhoAm 74, –76, –78, –80, –82

Kraft, Ken 1907- *ConAu 1R, –1NR*

Kraft, Stephanie 1944- *ConAu 105*

Kramer, Aaron 1921- *ConAu 21R, DrAP 75, DrAP&F 83, DrAS 74E, –78E, –82E, IntAu&W 77, –82, IntWWP 77, –82, WhoAm 76, –78, –80, –82, WhoE 74, –75, –77, –79, WhoWorJ 72, –78, WrDr 76, –80, –82, –84*

Kramer, Daniel Caleb 1934- *AmM&WS 73S, –78S, ConAu 53, WhoAmL 78, –79*

Kramer, Jane 1938- *ConAu 102, WhoAm 82*

Kramer, Mark 1944- *ConAu 97*

Kramer, Paul 1914- *ConAu 21R*

Kramer, Samuel Noah 1897- *AmAu&B, ConAu 9R, DrAS 74H, WhoWorJ 72, –78*

Kramer, William A 1941- *WhoAmL 79*

Kramer, William Joseph 1939- *WhoAmL 78, –79, –83*

Krantz, Hazel 1920- *BioIn 11, ConAu 1NR, ForWC 70, IntAu&W 77, SmATA 12, WhoAmW 75, WrDr 76, –80, –82, –84*

Kraske, Robert *SmATA 36*

Krauss, Robert G 1924- *ConAu 1R*

Krementz, Jill 1940- *AuNews 1, –2, BioIn 8, –10, –11, –12, BioNews 75, ChlLR 5[port], ConAu 41R, NewYTBS 82[port], SmATA 17, WhoAm 74, –76, –78, –80, –82, WhoAmW 74, –70, –72, –83*

Krensky, Stephen 1953- *ConAu 73*

Krents, Harold 1944- *BioIn 8, –9, ConAu 37R, WhoAmL 78, –79*

Krepps, Robert Wilson 1919-1980 *Au&Wr 6, ConAu 1R, –1NR, IntAu&W 76, WhoE 74*

Krevitsky, Nathan I 1914- *ConAu 9R*

Krevitsky, Nathan I *see also* Krevitsky, Nik

Krevitsky, Nik 1914- *BioIn 7, ConAu X*

Krevitsky, Nik *see also* Krevitsky, Nathan I

Kriegel, Leonard 1933- *BioIn 16, ConAu 33R, DrAP&F 83, DrAS 74E, –78E, –82E, IntAu&W 77, –82, WhoE 74, –75, WrDr 76, –80, –82, –84*

Kristofferson, Kris 1936- *BioIn 9, –10, –11, –12, BioNews 74, CelR 73, ConAu 104, ConLC 26[port], CurBio 74, EncPR&S, –77, IlEncRk, IntMPA 78, –79, –81, –82, –84, MovMk, NewYTBE 70, RkOn 78, –84, RolSEnR 83, WhoAm 76, –78, –80, –82, WhoHol A, WhoRocM 82, WorAl*

Kroeber, A L 1876-1960 *ConAu 110, CurBio 58, –60*

Kroeber, Theodora 1897-1979 *AmAu&B, AmWomWr, BioIn 9, –12, ConAu 5R, –5NR, –89, ForWC 70, SmATA 1, WhoAmW 64, WrDr 76*

Kroetsch, Robert 1927- *Au&Wr 6, BioIn 7, –12, CaW, CanWW 70, –79, –80, –81, –83, ConAu 8NR, –17R, ConLC 5, –23[port], ConNov 76, –82, DcLEL 1940, DrAS 74E,*

-78E, -82E, IntAu&W 82, OxCan SUP, WrDr 76, -80, -82, -84

Kroll, Steven 1941- *BioIn 12, ConAu 9NR, -65, SmATA 19*

Kronenberger, Louis 1904-1980 *AmAu&B, AnObit 1980, Au&Wr 6, BiE&WWA, BioIn 2, -3, -4, -5, -9, -12, ChhPo, ConAu 1R, -2NR, -97, CurBio 44, -80N, DrAS 74E, -78E, LinLib L, -S, NewYTBS 80[port], NotNAT, OhA&B, OxAmL, REnAL, TwCA SUP, WhAm 7, WhE&EA, WhoAm 74, -76, -78, -80, WhoThe 15, -16, -81N, WhoWor 74, WhoWorJ 72, WrDr 76, -80*

Kropp, Paul 1948- *SmATA 34*

Krosney, Mary Stewart 1939- *ConAu 17R*

Kruger, Rayne *Au&Wr 6, ConAu 5R*

Kruif, Paul De 1890-1971 *CurBio 42, -63, NewYTBE 71*

Kruif, Paul De *see also* DeKruif, Paul

Krumgold, Joseph 1908-1980 *AnObit 1980, AuBYP, BioIn 3, -4, -5, -6, -7, -8, -9, -12, ConAu 7NR, -9R, -101, ConLC 12, EncMys, FamMS, LinLib L, MorJA, Newb 1922, NinCLC 1956, SmATA 1, -23N, TwCCW 78, -83, WhAm 7, WrDr 80*

Krusch, Werner E 1927- *AuBYP, BioIn 7, ConAu 5R*

Krutch, Joseph Wood 1893-1970 *AmAu&B, Au&Wr 6, BiE&WWA, BioIn 1, -3, -4, -5, -6, -8, -9, -12, BlueB 76N, CnDAL, ConAmA, ConAmL, ConAu 1R, -4NR, -25R, ConLC 24[port], CurBio 59, -70, DcLEL, EncAAH, EncWT, EvLB, InSci, LinLib L, NewYTBE 70, NotNAT B, ObitOF 79, OxAmL, OxThe, PenC AM, REn, REnAL, TwCA, TwCA SUP, WebAB, -79, WhAm 5, WhJnl, WhNAA, WhThe*

Krythe, Maymie Richardson *ConAu 17R, WhoAmW 58, -61, -64, -66*

Kubie, Nora 1899- *AuBYP, BioIn 8, ConAu 5R, WhoAmW 74, -58, -61, -72*

Kubler-Ross, Elisabeth 1926- *AmWomWr, BioIn 12, ConIsC 2[port], CurBio 80[port], EncO&P 80, WhoAm 82, WorAl*

Kublin, Hyman 1919- *AuBYP SUP, ConAu 9R, DrAS 74H, -78H, -82H, WhoE 75, WhoWorJ 72, -78*

Kubrick, Stanley 1928- *BiDFilm, BioIn 4, -5, -6, -7, -9, -10, -11, -12, BlueB 76, CelR 73, ConAu 81, ConDr 73, -77A, -82A, ConLC 16, CurBio 63, -70, DcFM, DcLB 26[port], EncSF, FilmgC, IntAu&W 76, -77, IntMPA 77, -75, -76, -78, -79, -81, -82, -84, IntWW 74, -75, -76, -77, -78, -79, -80, -81, -82, -83, MovMk, NewYTBE 72, OxFilm, WebAB, -79, Who 74, -82, -83, WhoAm 74, -76, -78, -80, -82, WhoAmJ 80, WhoSciF,*

WhoWor 74, -76, -78, -80, -82, WhoWorJ 78, WomWMM, WorAl, WorEFlm, WrDr 80, -82, -84

Kugelmass, Joseph Alvin 1910-1972 *AmAu&B, AuBYP, BioIn 8, -9, ConAu 5R, -33R, WhNAA, WhoAm 74, -76*

Kuhn, Ferdinand 1905-1978 *AmAu&B, BioIn 11, ConAu 5R, -57, -81, CurBio 74, IntWW 74, -75, -76, -77, -78, -79N, WhAm 7, WhE&EA, WhoAm 74, -76, -78*

Kuhns, William 1943- *ConAu 21R, DrAF 76, IntAu&W 76*

Kullman, Harry 1919-1982 *Au&Wr 6, ConAu 93, SmATA 35*

Kulski, Julian 1929- *AmArch 70, AmM&WS 73S, ConAu 21R, WhoAm 80, -82, WhoF&I 74, WhoS&SW 73, WhoWor 80*

Kumin, Maxine 1925- *AmAu&B, AmWomWr, AnCL, AuBYP, AuNews 2, BioIn 8, -10, -11, -12, ChhPo S1, ConAu 1R, -1NR, ConLC 5, -13, ConP 75, -80, DcLB 5[port], DrAF 76, DrAP 75, DrAP&F 83, ForWC 70, IntAu&W 77, IntWWP 77, SmATA 12, WhoAm 74, -76, -78, -80, -82, WhoAmW 74, -58, -61, -68A, -70, -72, -75, -77, -81, -83, WorAl, WorAu 1970, WrDr 76, -80, -82, -84*

Kundera, Milan 1929- *BioIn 10, -11, -12, CasWL, ConAu 85, ConLC 4, -9, -19, CurBio 83[port], EncWL 2, IntAu&W 76, -77, IntWW 74, -75, -76, -77, -78, -79, -80, -81, -82, -83, IntWWP 77, McGEWD 84, ModSL 2, NewYTBS 82[port], PenC EUR, WhoFr 79, WhoSocC 78, WorAu 1970*

Kunen, James Simon 1948- *BioIn 8, ConAu 25R, WhoE 74, -75*

Kuniczak, W S 1930- *BioIn 12, ConAu 85*

Kunitz, Stanley 1905- *AmAu&B, BioIn 5, -8, -10, -12, BlueB 76, CnE&AP, ConAu 41R, ConLC 6, -11, -14, ConP 70, -75, -80, CurBio 43, -59, DrAP 75, DrAP&F 83, DrAS 74E, -78E, -82E, IntAu&W 76, -77, IntWW 74, -75, -76, -77, -78, -79, -80, -81, -82, -83, IntWWP 77, LinLib L, ModAL, ModAL SUP, OxAmL, PenC AM, RAdv 1, REn, REnAL, WebE&AL, WhoAm 74, -76, -78, -80, -82, WhoTwCL, WhoWor 74, WhoWorJ 72, -78, WorAl, WorAu, WrDr 76, -80, -82, -84*

Kuper, Jack 1932- *BioIn 12, ConAu 21R*

Kupfer, Fern 1946- *ConAu 106*

Kupferberg, Herbert 1918- *BioIn 12, ConAu 29R, SmATA 19, WhoAmJ 80, WhoE 75, WhoWorJ 72, -78, WrDr 76, -80, -82, -84*

Kupferberg, Tuli 1923- *AmAu&B, BioIn 10, -11, ConAu X, DcLB 16[port], MugS, WhoRocM 82*

Kuralt, Charles 1934- *BioIn 10, –11, –12, ConAu 89, CurBio 81[port], IntMPA 82, –84, LesBEnT[port], WhoAm 74, –76, –78, –80, –82*

Kurland, Gerald 1942- *BioIn 11, ConAu 41R, DrAS 74H, –78H, –82H, SmATA 13, WhoS&SW 80*

Kurland, Michael 1938- *ConAu 11NR, –61, ConSFA, DrAP&F 83, EncSF, ScF&FL 1, –2, WrDr 84*

Kursh, Harry 1919- *ConAu 9R, WhoE 75*

Kurten, Bjorn 1924- *ConAu 25R, FifIDA, WrDr 76, –80, –82, –84*

Kurtz, Edwin Bernard, Jr. 1926- *AmM&WS 73P, –76P, –79P, –82P*

Kurtz, Katherine 1944- *ConAu 29R, EncSF, ScF&FL 1, –2, WhoHr&F, WrDr 76, –80, –82, –84*

Kurzman, Dan 1927?- *ConAu 69, IntAu&W 76, WhoE 83, WrDr 80, –82, –84*

Kusche, Larry 1940- *ConAu X*

Kusche, Lawrence David 1940- *BioIn 10, –11, ConAu 5NR, –53, EncO&P 78*

Kushner, Harold S 1935- *ConAu 107, WhoAmJ 80, WrDr 84*

Kuslan, Louis Isaac 1922- *AmM&WS 73P, –76P, –79P, –82P, ConAu 1NR, –45, LEduc 74, WhoAm 74, –76, –78, –80, –82*

Kusnick, Barry A 1910- *ConAu 53*

Kutner, Luis 1908- *ConAu 109, WhoAm 74, –76, WhoAmL 79*

Kuttner, Henry 1914?-1958 *AmAu&B, BioIn 4, –7, –12, ConAu 107, DcLB 8[port], EncMys, EncSF, LinLib L, Novels, ObitOF 79, ScF&FL 1, –2, TwCLC 10[port], WhoHr&F, WhoSciF*

Kwolek, Constance 1933- *ConAu X, WrDr 76, –80, –82*

Kwolek, Constance *see also* Porcari, Constance Kwolek

Kyle, David A 1912?- *EncSF*

Kyle, Duncan 1930- *ConAu X, –65, IntAu&W 76, –77X, –82X, Novels, WrDr 76, –80, –82, –84*

Kyle, Elisabeth d1982 *AuBYP, BioIn 6, –7, –8, –9, BlueB 76, ConAu X, IntAu&W 76, –77, MorJA, SmATA 3, TwCCW 78, –83, WhE&EA, Who 74, –82, –83N, WhoChL, WrDr 76, –80, –82*

Kyle, Elisabeth *see also* Dunlop, Agnes M R

L

LaBastille, Anne 1938- *BioIn 10, -11, -12,*
ConAu 8NR, -57, NewYTBS 77,
WhoAmW 77, -79, -81, -83
Lacaze, Andre 1918- *WhoFr 79*
Lacey, Robert 1944- *Au&Wr 6, BioIn 12,*
ConAu 33R, WhoWor 76, WrDr 76, -80,
-82, -84
Lackmann, Ron 1934- *ConAu 29R*
LaCroix, Mary 1937- *ConAu 106*
Lacy, Dan 1914- *BiDrLUS 70, BioIn 2, -3, -7,*
-11, ConAu 37R, CurBio 54, Dun&B 79,
ODwPR 79, St&PR 75, WhoAm 74, -76,
-78, -80, -82, WhoF&I 74, WhoLibI 82,
WhoLibS 55
Lacy, Leslie Alexander 1937- *BioIn 8, -10,*
ConAu 33R, InB&W 80, LivgBAA,
SelBAA, SmATA 6, WhoBlA 77, -80
Ladd, Veronica *ConAu X*
Lader, Lawrence 1919- *AmAu&B, BioIn 10,*
ConAu 1R, -2NR, SmATA 6,
WhoAm 74, -76, -78, -80, -82, WhoE 74
LaFarge, Oliver 1901-1963 *AmAu&B, AmNov,*
AuBYP, BioIn 2, -3, -4, -5, -6, -7, -8, -9,
-12, CnDAL, ConAmA, ConAu 81,
CurBio 53, -63, DcAmB S7,
DcLB 9[port], DcLEL, InSci, LongCTC,
Novels, ObitOF 79, OxAmH, OxAmL,
PenC AM, REn, REnAL, REnAW,
SmATA 19, TwCA, TwCA SUP,
WhAm 4, WhE&EA, WhNAA, WorAl
Laffin, John 1922- *Au&Wr 6, AuBYP,*
ConAu 7NR, -53, IntAu&W 76, -77, -82,
SmATA 31[port], WhoWor 74, -76, -78,
-80, -82, WrDr 76, -80, -82, -84
LaFountaine, George 1934- *ConAu 7NR, -57,*
WrDr 76, -80, -82, -84
Lagerkvist, Par 1891-1974 *BioIn 1, -2, -3, -4,*
-5, -8, -9, -10, -11, CasWL, CIDMEL,
CnMD, CnThe, ConAu 49, ConLC 7,
-10, -13, CurBio 52, -74N, CyWA,
EncWL, -2[port], EncWT, EvEuW,
IntWW 74, LinLib L, McGEWB,
McGEWD, -84[port], ModWD,
NewYTBS 74, Novels, ObitOF 79,
ObitT 1971, OxThe, PenC EUR, REn,
REnWD, ScF&FL 1, TwCA SUP,
TwCWr, WhDW, WhAm 6, WhE&EA,
Who 74, WhoTwCL, WhoWor 74,

WorAl
Lahue, Kalton C 1934- *ConAu 7NR, -13R*
Laing, Frederick 1905- *BioIn 4, ConAu 105*
Laing, Martha *ConAu X*
Laird, Carobeth 1895-1983 *BioIn 11,*
ConAu 8NR, -110, -61, DcLB Y82B[port]
Laird, Charlton G 1901- *ConAu 13R, WhJnl*
Laird, Jean E 1930- *AmCath 80,*
ConAu 6NR, -9R, ForWC 70,
WhoAmW 74, -68, -70, -72, -75, -77, -79,
-81, -83, WhoMW 74, -76, -78
Laitin, Ken 1963- *ConAu 102*
Laitin, Steve 1965- *ConAu 102*
Lake, David J 1929- *ConAu 10NR, -65,*
EncSF, WrDr 84
Laklan, Carli 1907- *AuBYP SUP, BioIn 10,*
ConAu 1NR, ForWC 70, IntAu&W 77,
SmATA 5
Laklan, Carli *see also* Clarke, John
Laliberte, Norman 1925- *AmAu&B, BioIn 8,*
ConAu 104, WhoAm 74, -76,
WhoAmA 73, -76, -78, -80
Lally, John Ronald 1939- *LEduc 74*
LaMare, Walter De 1873-1956 *JBA 51,*
ScF&FL 1, TwCA, TwCA SUP
LaMare, Walter De *see also* DeLaMare, Walter
Lamb, Beatrice Pitney 1904- *BioIn 12,*
ConAu 5R, IntAu&W 76,
SmATA 21[port], WhoAmW 61, -64, -66,
-68, -70
Lamb, Charles 1775-1834 *Alli, AtlBL, BbD,*
BiD&SB, BiDLA, BioIn 1, -2, -3, -4, -5,
-6, -7, -8, -9, -10, -11, -12, BrAu 19,
BrWr 4, CarSB, CasWL, CelCen,
Chambr 3, ChhPo, -S1, -S2, -S3, CrtT 2,
CyWA, DcBiPP, DcEnA, DcEnL,
DcEuL, DcInB, DcLEL, Dis&D, EvLB,
LinLib L, -S, LongCEL, McGEWB,
MouLC 3, NewC, NotNAT B, OxEng,
OxMus, OxThe, PenC ENG, RAdv 1,
RComWL, REn, SmATA 17, TelT,
WebE&AL, WhDW, WhoChL,
WhoHol A, WorAl
Lamb, Eleanor 1917- *ConAu 69*
Lamb, G F *ConAu 4NR, -53*
Lamb, G F *see also* Lamb, Geoffrey Frederick
Lamb, Geoffrey Frederick *Au&Wr 6,*
AuBYP SUP, BioIn 11, ConAu 53,

IntAu&W 76, –77, –82, SmATA 10,
WrDr 76, –80, –82, –84
Lamb, Geoffrey Frederick *see also* Balaam
Lamb, Geoffrey Frederick *see also* Lamb, G F
Lamb, Harold 1892-1962 *AmAu&B, AuBYP,*
BioIn 1, –2, –3, –4, –6, –7, –9, ChhPo S2,
ConAu 101, –89, JBA 34, –51,
NatCAB 52, ObitOF 79, OxAmL, REn,
REnAL, ScF&FL 1, TwCA, TwCA SUP,
WhAm 4, WhE&EA, WhNAA
Lamb, Hugh 1946- *ConAu 1NR, –49,*
ScF&FL 1, –2, WhoHr&F
Lamb, Mary Ann 1764-1847 *Alli, BioIn 1, –2,*
–6, –8, –9, –10, –11, –12, CarSB, ChhPo,
–S2, –S3, DcEnA, DcEnL, DcLEL,
Dis&D, NewC, OxEng, SmATA 17,
TelT, WhoChL
Lamb, Ruth Stanton *ConAu 45, DrAS 74F,*
–78F, –82F, WhoAmW 74, –68, –70, –72,
–75, –77
Lambdin, William 1936- *ConAu 102*
Lambert, Gavin 1924- *BioIn 11, ConAu 1R,*
–1NR, DcLEL 1940, FilmgC,
IntAu&W 77, –82, TwCWr, WhoWor 76,
WorEFlm, WrDr 76, –80, –82, –84
Lambert, Janet 1894-1973 *AuBYP, BioIn 3, –7,*
–9, ConAu 41R, CurBio 54, InWom,
IndAu 1917, REnAL, SmATA 25[port],
ThrBJA, WhoAmW 58, –61
Lamburn, John Battersby Crompton 1893-
ConAu P-1, ScF&FL 1
Lame Deer 1895?-1976 *BioIn 9, –11,*
ConAu 69
Lamm, Robert 1945- *BioNews 74,*
WhoAm 76, –78, –80, –82, WhoRocM 82
Lamm, Robert *see also* Chicago
L'Amour, Louis 1908- *AuNews 1, –2,*
BioIn 10, –11, 12, CmCal, ConAu 1R,
–3NR, ConLC 25[port], CurBio 80[port],
DcLB Y80B[port], NewYTBS 81[port],
Novels, REnAW, WhoAm 74, –76, –78,
–80, –82, WhoWest 76, –78, –80, –82,
WhoWor 76, –78, WrDr 76, –80, –82, –84
Lampedusa, Giuseppe 1896-1957 *BioIn 5, –6,*
–10, CasWL, EncWL, –2, EvEuW,
ModRL, Novels, PenC EUR, REn,
TwCWr, WhDW, WhoTwCL, WorAl,
WorAu
Lampell, Millard 1919- *AmAu&B, AmNov,*
BiE&WWA, BioIn 1, –2, ConAu 9R,
EncFCWM 69, NotNAT, PIP&P,
REnAL, WhoAm 74
Lampman, Evelyn 1907-1980 *AnObit 1980,*
AuBYP, BioIn 6, –7, –9, –12, ConAu 101,
–11NR, –13R, MorJA, NewYTBS 80,
ScF&FL 1, –1A, –2, SmATA 23N, –4,
TwCCW 78, –83, WhoAmW 74, –58, –61,
–64, –66, –68, –70, –72, –75, –77, WhoPNW,
WrDr 80, –82
Lamprey, Louise 1869-1951 *AmAu&B,*
BioIn 2, –12, CarSB, ChhPo, JBA 34,
–51, REnAL, WhAm 3, WhE&EA,

WhLit, WhNAA, YABC 2
Lamson, Peggy 1912- *ConAu 25R, OhA&B*
Lancaster, Bruce 1896-1963 *AmAu&B,*
AmNov, BioIn 1, –2, –4, –6, –7, –11,
ConAu P-1, NatCAB 48, ObitOF 79,
SmATA 9, TwCA, TwCA SUP,
WhAm 4, WhE&EA
Lancaster, Richard *ConAu 21R*
Lancour, Gene *ConAu X, EncSF,*
ScF&FL 1
Land, Barbara 1923- *BioIn 12, ConAu 81,*
IntAu&W 76, –77, –82, SmATA 16,
WhoAmW 61
Landau, Elaine 1948- *AuBYP SUP, BioIn 11,*
ConAu 5NR, –53, IntAu&W 77,
SmATA 10, WhoAmW 77, –79, –81
Landau, Lev Davidovich 1908-1968 *AsBiEn,*
BiESc, BioIn 5, –6, –7, –8, –11, –12,
CurBio 63, –68, DcScB, McGEWB,
McGMS 80[port], ObitOF 79,
ObitT 1961, WhDW, WhAm 5, WorAl
Lande, Nathaniel 1939- *BioIn 11, ConAu 104*
Landeck, Beatrice 1904- *AuBYP, BioIn 7, –12,*
ConAu 73, LEduc 74, SmATA 15
Landers, Gunnard W 1944- *ConAu 93*
Landis, Paul H 1901- *AmM&WS 73S,*
ConAu 5R, –5NR, IntAu&W 76, –77,
WhE&EA
Landon, Margaret 1903- *AmAu&B,*
AmWomWr, BioIn 4, –12, ConAu 13R,
ConAu P-1, CurBio 45, ForWC 70,
InWom, PIP&P, TwCA SUP,
WhoAmW 58
Landorf, Joyce *AuNews 1, BioIn 9, –10*
Landry, Lionel 1919- *WhoAm 74, –76, –78, –80,*
–82
Landsburg, Alan 1933- *BioIn 12, ConAu 103,*
IntMPA 77, –75, –76, –78, –79, –81, –82, –84,
NewYTET, WhoWest 76, –78
Lane, Arthur 1945- *WhoAmL 83,*
WhoReal 83
Lane, Burton 1912- *AmPS, AmSCAP 66,*
BiDAmM, BiE&WWA, BioIn 5, –6, –7, –8,
–9, –10, –12, CmpEPM, CurBio 67,
EncMT, NewCBMT, NotNAT, PIP&P,
WhoAm 74, –76, –78, –80, –82, WhoThe 15,
–16, –81
Lane, Carolyn 1926- *AuBYP SUP, BioIn 11,*
ConAu 29R, SmATA 10, WhoAmW 75,
–77, –79, WhoE 77, –79, –81, WrDr 76,
–80, –82, –84
Lane, Peter 1925- *Au&Wr 6*
Lane, Rose Wilder 1886-1968 *AmAu&B,*
AmWomWr, AuBYP SUP, BioIn 4, –8,
–10, –12, ConAu 102, InWom,
NatCAB 54, NotAW MOD, REnAL,
SmATA 28, –29[port], TwCA,
TwCA SUP, WhAm 5, WhNAA,
WhoAmW 58A
Lane, Rose Wilder *see also* Wilder, Rose
Lang, Daniel 1915-1981 *AmAu&B,*
AnObit 1981, BioIn 12, ConAu 4NR, –5R,

-105, NewYTBS 81[port], WhoAm 74,
-76, -78, -80, WhoAmJ 80
Lang, H Jack 1904- BioIn 5, WhoAm 74, -76,
-78, -80, -82
Lang, Paul Henry 1901- AmAu&B, Baker 78,
ConAu 103, IntWW 74, -75, -76,
IntWWM 77, OxMus, REnAL,
WhoMus 72
Lang, Robert 1912- BiDrLUS 70,
ConAu 41R, DrAS 74H, -78H,
WhoLibS 55, -66
Lange, Oliver 1927- ConAu 103, EncSF,
ScF&FL 1
Lange, Suzanne 1945- BioIn 10, ConAu 29R,
SmATA 5
Langland, Joseph 1917- ConAu 5R, -8NR,
ConP 70, -75, -80, DrAP 75, DrAS 74E,
-78E, -82E, IntWWP 77, -82, LinLib L,
PenC AM, WhoAm 78, -80, -82,
WrDr 76, -80, -82, -84
Langley, Bob 1936?- ConAu 85, WrDr 80,
-82, -84
Langone, John 1929- ConAu 1NR, -49
Langton, Jane 1922- AuBYP, BioIn 9,
ConAu 1R, -1NR, ForWC 70,
ScF&FL 1A, SmATA 3, TwCCW 78,
-83, WhoAmW 83, WrDr 76, -80, -82,
-84
Lanham, Urless Norton 1918- AmM&WS 73P,
-76P, -79P, -82P, WhoAm 82,
WhoWest 74, -76, -78, -80
Lanier, Sidney 1842-1881 Alli SUP, AmAu,
AmAu&B, AmBi, AmWr SUP, ApCAB,
AtlBL, Baker 78, BbD, BiDAmM,
BiD&SB, BiDSA, BioIn 1, -2, -3, -4, -5,
-6, -8, -9, -10, -11, -12, CarSB, CasWL,
Chambr 3, ChhPo, -S1, -S2, -S3, CnDAL,
CnE&AP, CrtT 3, -4, CyWA, DcAmAu,
DcAmB, DcEnA AP, DcLEL, DcNAA,
DrAS 78E, -82E, Dis&D, EncAAH,
EncSoH, EvLB, HarEnUS, LinLib L, -S,
McGEWB, MouLC 3, NatCAB 2,
OxAmL, OxEng, PenC AM, RAdv 1,
REn, REnAL, SmATA 18, TwCBDA,
WebAB, -79, WebE&AL, WhAm HS,
WhFla, WorAl
Lanier, Sterling E 1927- AuBYP, EncSF,
ScF&FL 1, -2, WhoHr&F, WrDr 84
Lansing, Alfred 1921-1975 BioIn 10,
ConAu 13R, -61, SmATA 35
Lansing, Elizabeth 1911- AuBYP, ConAu 5R
Lao She 1899-1966 CasWL, DcOrL 1,
EncWL, PenC CL
Lapage, Geoffrey 1888-1971 Au&Wr 6,
BioIn 9, ConAu P-1, WhE&EA
Lapierre, Dominique 1931- BioIn 9, -12,
CelR 73, ConAu 69, NewYTBS 80[port],
WhoAm 76, -78, -80, -82, WhoFr 79,
WhoWor 74, -76
Lapp, Ralph Eugene 1917- AmAu&B,
AmM&WS 73P, BioIn 3, -4, ConAu 81,
CurBio 55, InSci, WhoAm 74, -76,

WhoWor 74
Lappe, Frances Moore 1944- ConAu 37R,
IntAu&W 82, WhoAmW 83, WrDr 76,
-80, -82, -84
Laqueur, Walter 1921- AmAu&B, BlueB 76,
ConAu 5R, IntAu&W 77, IntWW 75,
-76, -77, -78, -79, -80, -81, -82, -83,
Who 74, -82, -83, WhoAm 74, -76, -78,
-80, -82, WhoAmJ 80, WhoWor 74, -78,
-80, -82, WhoWorJ 72, -78, WrDr 76,
-80, -82, -84
LaRamee, Louise De 1839-1908 BiD&SB,
BrAu 19, DcEnA, JBA 34
LaRamee, Louise De see also DeLaRamee,
Louise
Lardner, Rex 1881-1941 AmAu&B,
AuBYP SUP, ObitOF 79, REnAL
Lardner, Ring 1885-1933 AmAu&B, AmBi,
AmSCAP 66, AmWr, AtlBL, BioIn 1, -3,
-4, -5, -6, -7, -9, -10, -11, -12, CasWL,
CnDAL, CnMWL, ConAmA, ConAmL,
ConAu 104, CyWA, DcLB 11[port],
-25[port], DcLEL, EncWL, EncWT,
LinLib L, LongCTC, ModAL,
ModAL SUP, NatCAB 32, NotNAT B,
Novels, OxAmL, PenC AM, RAdv 1,
REn, REnAL, TwCA, TwCA SUP,
TwCLC 2, TwCWr, WebAB, -79,
WebE&AL, WhAm 1, WhNAA,
WhoTwCL, WorAl
Largo, Michael 1950- ConAu 73
Larkin, Rochelle 1935- ConAu 33R,
IntAu&W 77, WrDr 76, -80, -82, -84
Larrabee, Harold A 1894-1979 AmAu&B,
AuBYP, BioIn 1, -8, -11, ConAu 85,
ConAu P-1, NewYTBS 79, WhAm 7,
WhoAm 74, -76
Larrick, Nancy 1910- AuBYP, BioIn 7, -9,
-10, ChhPo, -S1, -S2, -S3, ConAu 1R,
-1NR, LEduc 74, MorBMP, SmATA 4,
WhoAmW 74, -58, -61, -64, -66, -68, -72,
-75, -77, -79, -81, WrDr 76, -80, -82, -84
Larsen, Carl 1934- BioIn 12, ConAu 77,
DrAF 76, DrAP 75, NatPD
Larsen, Egon 1904- Au&Wr 6, BioIn 12,
ConAu 3NR, -9R, IntAu&W 76, -77, -82,
ScF&FL 1, -2, SmATA 14, WrDr 76,
-80, -82, -84
Larson, Charles R 1938- BioIn 11,
ConAu 4NR, -53, DrAS 78E, -82E,
IntAu&W 77
Larson, E Richard 1944- ConAu 105
Larson, George C 1942- ConAu 9NR, -65
Larson, Peggy 1931- ConAu 81
Larson, Rodger 1934?- BioIn 8
Larue, Gerald A 1916- ConAu 21R,
DrAS 74P, -78P, WhoRel 75, -77
Lash, Joseph P 1909- BioIn 9, -11,
ConAu 17R, CurBio 72, WhoAm 74, -76,
-78, -80, -82, WhoE 74, WorAu 1970,
WrDr 80, -82, -84
Laski, Marghanita 1915- Au&Wr 6, BioIn 2,

*-4, ConAu 105, CurBio 51, DcLEL 1940,
EncSF, InWom, IntAu&W 76, -77,
LongCTC, ModBrL, REn, ScF&FL 1,
TwCA SUP, WhE&EA, Who 74, -82, -83,
WrDr 82, -84*

Lasky, Kathryn 1944- *BioIn 11,
ConAu 11NR, -69, SmATA 13*

Lasky, Victor 1918- *AmAu&B, AuNews 1,
BioIn 8, -10, BioNews 75, BlueB 76,
CelR 73, ConAu 5R, -10NR, WhoAm 74,
-76, -78, -80, -82, WhoAmJ 80, WhoE 74,
WhoWorJ 72, -78, WrDr 76, -80, -82, -84*

Lass, Abraham H 1907- *BioIn 2, -11,
ConAu 9R, NewYTBE 71*

Lassiter, Barbara B 1934- *NewYTBE 71,
WhoAmW 70, -72*

Lasson, Kenneth 1943- *ConAu 33R,
IntAu&W 77, WrDr 76, -80, -82, -84*

Lasson, Robert 1922- *AuBYP, BioIn 8*

Latham, Aaron 1943- *BioIn 11, ConAu 33R*

Latham, Frank B 1910- *AuBYP SUP,
BioIn 10, ConAu 49, SmATA 6*

Latham, Jean Lee 1902- *AmAu&B,
AmWomWr, Au&Wr 6, AuBYP,
AuNews 1, BioIn 4, -6, -7, -8, -9, -10, -12,
ConAu 5R, -7NR, ConLC 12, CurBio 56,
InWom, LinLib L, MorBMP, MorJA,
SmATA 2, Str&VC, TwCCW 78, -83,
WhoAm 74, -76, -78, -80, -82,
WhoAmW 74, -58, -64, -66, -68, -70, -72,
WrDr 80, -82, -84*

Latourette, Kenneth Scott 1884-1968 *AmAu&B,
BioIn 3, -4, -6, -8, ConAu P-2, CurBio 53,
-69, DcAmReB, EncSoB SUP, LinLib L,
LuthC 75, OhA&B, TwCA SUP,
WhE&EA, WhNAA*

Lattimore, Eleanor 1904- *AmAu&B, AuBYP,
BioIn 1, -2, -5, 7, -8, -10, ConAu 6NR,
-9R, IlsCB 1744, -1946, -1957, InWom,
JBA 34, -51, LinLib L, SmATA 5, -7,
TwCCW 78, -83, WhoAmW 58, -61,
WrDr 80, -82, -84*

Lattimore, Owen 1900- *AmAu&B,
AmM&WS 73S, BioIn 1, -2, -3, -4, -5, -6,
-7, -9, -11, BlueB 76, ConAu 97,
CurBio 45, -64, IntWW 74, -75, -76, -77,
-78, -79, -80, -81, -82, -83, OxAmL,
PolProf T, REnAL, TwCA SUP,
WhE&EA, Who 74, -82, -83, WhoAm 74,
-76, -78, -80, -82, WhoWor 74*

Lattimore, Richmond 1906- *AmAu&B,
BiE&WWA, BioIn 4, -6, BlueB 76,
ConAu 1NR, ConLC 3, ConP 70, -75,
-80, DrAP&F 83, DrAS 74F,
IntAu&W 77, -82, IntWWP 77, LinLib L,
ModAL, ModAL SUP, NotNAT,
OxAmL, RAdv 1, REnAL, TwCA SUP,
WhoAm 74, -76, WhoE 83, WhoWor 74,
WrDr 76, -80, -82, -84*

Lauber, Patricia 1924- *AuBYP, BioIn 7, -9,
ConAu 6NR, -9R, ForWC 70, SmATA 1,
-33[port], ThrBJA, WhoAmW 58*

Laubin, Gladys *BioIn 1, -6, WhoAmW 77,
-79*

Laufe, Abe 1906- *ConAu 17R, DrAS 74E,
-78E*

Laumer, Keith 1925- *AmAu&B, BioIn 12,
ConAu 7NR, -9R, ConSFA,
DcLB 8[port], EncSF, ScF&FL 1, -2,
WhoSciF, WrDr 84*

Laure, Ettagale 1940- *ConAu 103*

Laure, Jason 1940- *ConAu 104*

Laurence, David Herbert 1885-1930 *MakMC*

Laurence, Margaret 1926- *Au&Wr 6, BioIn 8,
-10, -11, -12, BlueB 76, CaW,
CanWW 70, -79, -80, -81, -83, CanWr,
ConAu 5R, ConLC 3, -6, -13, ConNov 72,
-76, -82, CreCan 1, EncWL 2,
IntAu&W 76, -77, ModCmwL, Novels,
OxCan, OxCan SUP, WhoAmW 68, -70,
-83, WhoWor 74, WorAu 1970,
WrDr 76, -80, -82, -84*

Laurents, Arthur 1918?- *AmAu&B,
BiE&WWA, BioIn 4, -9, -10, -12,
BlueB 76, CnMD, ConAu 8NR, -13R,
ConDr 73, -77, -82, DcLB 26[port],
DcLEL 1940, EncMT, EncWT, FilmgC,
IntAu&W 76, IntMPA 77, -75, -76, -78,
-79, -81, -82, McGEWD, -84[port],
ModWD, NewCBMT, NotNAT, OxAmL,
PenC AM, PIP&P, REnAL, TwCA SUP,
WhoAm 74, -76, -78, -80, -82, WhoE 74,
WhoThe 15, -16, -81, WhoWor 74, -76,
WrDr 76, -80, -82, -84*

Laurie, Rona *ConAu 85, IntAu&W 77,
WhoWor 78, WrDr 76, -80, -82, -84*

Lauritzen, Jonreed 1902- *BioIn 3, -11,
ConAu 5R, CurBio 52, SmATA 13,
WrDr 76, -80, -82, -84*

Laury, Jean Ray 1928- *ConAu 77,
WhoAmA 73, -76, -78, -80, WhoAmW 74,
-72, -75*

Lavender, David 1910- *AuBYP, BioIn 8, -11,
CmCal, ConAu 1R, -2NR, REnAW*

Laver, James 1899-1975 *Au&Wr 6,
BiE&WWA, BioIn 4, -6, -10, BlueB 76N,
ChhPo S3, ConAu 1R, -3NR, -57, EvLB,
IntWW 74, -75, -75N, LongCTC,
ModBrL, NewC, NewYTBS 75,
NotNAT A, ObitOF 79, ObitT 1971,
OxThe, PenC ENG, ScF&FL 1, -2,
TwCA, TwCA SUP, WhE&EA, WhLit,
WhThe, Who 74, WhoWor 74, -76,
WorFshn*

Lavine, Sigmund Arnold 1908- *AuBYP,
BioIn 7, -9, ConAu 1R, -4NR, SmATA 3,
WhoE 75, -77, WrDr 76, -80, -82, -84*

Law, Janice *ConAu X, -65*

Lawick-Goodall, Jane Van 1934- *BioIn 8, -9,
-10, -11, -12, CurBio 67*

Lawler, Donald L 1935- *ConAu 105,
DrAS 82E*

Lawrence, D H 1885-1930 *AtlBL, CnE&AP,
CnMWL, CnThe, ConAu 104, CyWA,*

DcLB 10[port], –19[port], EncWL 2[port],
FilmgC, LongCTC, McGEWD 84,
ModBrL, ModBrL SUP, ModWD, NewC,
NotNAT B, Novels[port], OxAmL,
PenC ENG, RAdv 1, RComWL, REn,
REnAL, ScF&FL 1, TwCLC 2, –9[port],
TwCWr, WebE&AL, WhThe, WhoTwCL,
WorAl

Lawrence, David Herbert 1885-1930 *BioIn 1, –2,*
–3, –4, –5, –6, –7, –8, –9, –10, –11, –12,
CasWL, Chambr 3, ChhPo, –S1, –S3,
CnMD, DcLEL, Dis&D, EncWL,
EncWT, EvLB, LinLib L, –S, LongCEL,
McGEWB, OxEng, TwCA, TwCA SUP,
WhDW, WhLit

Lawrence, Jerome 1915- *AmAu&B,*
AmSCAP 66, BiE&WWA, BioIn 10,
BlueB 76, ConAu 41R, ConDr 73, –77,
–82, EncMT, IntAu&W 76, –77,
LinLib L, ModWD, NatPD 81[port],
NotNAT, OhA&B, WhoAm 74, –76, –78,
–80, –82, WhoAmJ 80, WhoThe 15, –16,
–81, WhoWest 84, WhoWor 74,
WhoWorJ 72, –78, WrDr 76, –80, –82, –84

Lawrence, Jim *BioIn 8*

Lawrence, Louise 1943- *ConAu 97, EncSF,*
ScF&FL 1, –2, TwCCW 83

Lawrence, Louise DeKiriline 1894-
AmM&WS 73P, –76P, –79P, –82P,
BioIn 11, ConAu 25R, SmATA 13,
WrDr 76, –80

Lawrence, Mildred 1907- *AuBYP, BioIn 3, –6,*
–8, –9, ConAu 1R, –5NR, CurBio 53,
ForWC 70, InWom, MichAu 80, MorJA,
SmATA 3, TwCCW 78, WhoAmW 74,
–58, –61, –64, –66, –68, –70, –72, –75

Lawrence, R D 1921- *BioIn 12, ConAu 11NR,*
–65

Lawson, Donald E 1917- *AuBYP, BioIn 7, –11,*
ConAu 1R, –2NR, IntAu&W 76,
LEduc 74, SmATA 9, WhoAm 74, –76,
–78, –80, –82, WhoMW 74, –76, –78, –80,
–82

Lawson, Donna Roberta 1937- *ConAu 41R*

Lawson, Marion 1896- *ConAu P-1,*
SmATA 22, WhoAmW 75

Lawson, Robert 1892-1957 *Alli, Alli SUP,*
AmAu&B, AmPB, AnCL, Au&ICB,
AuBYP, BioIn 1, –2, –3, –4, –5, –7, –8, –10,
–12, BkCL, Cald 1938, ChlLR 2, ChhPo,
–S2, –S3, CurBio 41, –57, DcAmB S6,
DcLB 22[port], FamAIYP, ForIl,
IlBEAAW, IlsBYP, IlsCB 1744, –1946,
JBA 51, LinLib L, Newb 1922,
ObitOF 79, ScF&FL 1, Str&VC,
TwCCW 78, –83, WhAm 3,
WhoAmA 80N, –82N, YABC 2

Lawson, Ted 1917- *BioIn 12, CurBio 43,*
InSci

Lawton, George 1900-1957 *BiDPara, BioIn 1,*
–4, EncO&P 78

Laycock, George 1921- *AuBYP, BioIn 8, –10,*

ConAu 4NR, –5R, SmATA 5,
WhoMW 74, –76

Laye, Camara 1928-1980 *AfrA,*
AnObit 1980[port], BioIn 3, –7, –8, –9, –10,
–12, CasWL, ConAu 85, –97, ConLC 4,
EncWL, LongCTC, McGEWB, Novels,
PenC CL, RGAfL, TwCWr, WhoTwCL,
WorAu

Layton, Irving 1912- *Au&Wr 6, BioIn 9, –10,*
–12, CanWW 70, –79, –80, –81, –83,
CanWr, CasWL, ConAu 1R, –2NR,
ConLC 2, –15, ConP 70, –75, –80,
CreCan 2, DcLEL, –1940, EncWL 2,
IntWWP 77, ModCmwL, OxCan,
OxCan SUP, PenC ENG, REnAL,
WebE&AL, WhoAm 74, –76, –78,
WhoWorJ 72, –78, WorAu, WrDr 76, –80,
–82, –84

LaZebnik, Edith 1897- *ConAu 85*

Leach, MacEdward 1896-1967 *BioIn 7, –8,*
ChhPo S1, WhAm 4

Leach, Maria 1892-1977 *AuBYP, BioIn 8, –11,*
ChhPo S2, ConAu 53, –69, FourBJA,
IntAu&W 77, SmATA 28, WhoAmW 58,
–61, –64

Leacroft, Helen 1919- *Au&Wr 6, BioIn 10,*
ConAu 2NR, –5R, SmATA 6

Leadon, Bernie *WhoRocM 82*

Leadon, Bernie *see also* Eagles, The

Leahy, Syrell Rogovin 1935- *BioIn 10,*
ConAu 57

Leakey, Louis 1903-1972 *Au&Wr 6, BiESc,*
BioIn 6, –7, –8, –9, –10, –11, ConAu 37R,
–97, CurBio 66, –72, –72N, DcScB,
LinLib L, –S, McGEWB, NewYTBE 72,
ObitOF 79, ObitT 1971, WhDW,
WhAm 5, WhE&EA, WorAl

Leakey, Mary Douglas 1913- *AfSS 81, –82,*
BioIn 6, –10, –11, –12, ConAu 97, FifIDA,
IntDcWB, IntWW 77, –78, –79, –80, –81,
–82, –83, NewYTBS 80[port], Who 74,
–82, –83, WhoAm 82, WhoWor 78, –80,
–82, WorAl

Leakey, Richard E 1944- *AfSS 78, –79, –80,*
–81, –82, BioIn 8, –9, –10, –11, –12,
ConAu 93, CurBio 76, IntWW 74, –75,
–76, –77, –78, –79, –80, –81, –82, –83,
NewYTBS 79, Who 82, –83, WhoAm 82,
WhoWor 78, –82, WorAl

Lear, Norman 1922- *BioIn 9, –10, –11, –12,*
BioNews 74, ConAu 73, ConLC 12,
CurBio 74, IntMPA 78, –79, –81, –82, –84,
LesBEnT[port], WhoAm 74, –76, –78, –80,
–82, WhoWest 84, WhoWor 80, –82,
WorAl

Leary, Lewis 1906- *AmAu&B, Au&Wr 6,*
CnDAL, ConAu 1R, –4NR, DcLEL 1940,
DrAS 74E, –78E, –82E, REnAL,
WhoAm 74, –76, –78, –80, –82, WrDr 80,
–82, –84

Leary, Paris 1931- *ConAu 17R, ConP 70,*
DcLEL 1940

Leeming, Joseph 1897-1968 *AuBYP, BioIn 2, –7, ConAu 73, JBA 51, SmATA 26[port]*

Leeson, Robert 1928- *ConAu 105, TwCCW 78, –83, WrDr 80, –82, –84*

Leete, Harley 1918- *St&PR 75, WhoAdv 72*

Leeuw, Adele De 1899- *JBA 51, WhNAA*

Leeuw, Adele De *see also* DeLeeuw, Adele Louise

LeFanu, Joseph Sheridan 1814-1873 *Alli SUP, AtlBL, BbD, BiD&SB, BioIn 2, –5, –9, –12, BrAu 19, CasWL, Chambr 3, ChhPo, CyWA, DcEnA, DcEnL, DcEuL, DcIrB, DcIrL, DcIrW 1, DcLB 21[port], DcLEL, Dis&D, EncMys, EvLB, HsB&A, LinLib L, NewC, OxEng, PenC ENG, PoIre, REn, WorAl*

Lefebure, Molly *Au&Wr 6, AuBYP SUP, ConAu 57, WrDr 76, –80, –82, –84*

Leffland, Ella 1931- *ConAu 29R, ConLC 19, WhoAmW 74, –75*

LeFlore, Ron 1952?- *BioIn 10, –11, –12, InB&W 80, NewYTBS 80, –83[port], WorAl*

LeGuin, Ursula K 1929- *AmWomWr, Au&Wr 6, AuBYP SUP, AuNews 1, BioIn 9, –10, –12, BioNews 74, ChlLR 3, ConAu 9NR, –21R, ConLC 8, –13, –22[port], ConNov 76, –82, ConSFA, CurBio 83[port], DcLB 8[port], DrAF 76, DrAP&F 83, EncSF, FourBJA, IntAu&W 77, Novels, ScF&FL 1, –2, SmATA 4, TwCCW 78, –83, WhoAm 74, –76, –78, –80, –82, WhoAmW 74, –81, –83, WhoSciF, WorAl, WorAu 1970, WrDr 76, –80, –82, –84*

Legum, Colin 1919- *Au&Wr 6, BioIn 11, ConAu 1R, –4NR, IntAu&W 76, –77, –82, SmATA 10, WhoWor 78, –80, –82, WrDr 76, –80, –82, –84*

Lehane, Brendan 1936- *ConAu 10NR, –21R*

Lehman, Emil 1907- *WhoAmJ 80, WhoRel 75, –77, WhoWorJ 78*

Lehman, Ernest 1920- *BioIn 7, –8, FilmgC, IntMPA 77, –75, –76, –78, –79, –81, –82, –84, WhoAm 74, –76, –78, –80, –82, WorEFlm*

Lehmann, Johannes 1929- *ConAu 37R, IntAu&W 77*

Lehmann, John 1907- *Au&Wr 6, BioIn 4, –5, –7, –8, –12, BlueB 76, CasWL, ConAu 8NR, –9R, ConP 70, –75, –80, DcLEL, EvLB, IntAu&W 76, –77, –82, IntWW 74, –75, –76, –77, –78, –79, –80, –81, –82, –83, IntWWP 77, LongCTC, ModBrL, NewC, OxEng, PenC ENG, REn, TwCA, TwCA SUP, TwCWr, WebE&AL, WhE&EA, Who 74, –82, –83, WhoWor 74, –76, –78, –82, WrDr 76, –80, –82, –84*

Lehmann, Linda 1906- *ConAu 85*

Lehmberg, Paul 1946- *ConAu 102*

Lehrman, Robert L 1921- *ConAu 5R, –7NR*

Leib, Amos Patten 1917- *ConAu 45,*

DrAS 74E

Leiber, Fritz 1910- *AmAu&B, BioIn 7, –12, ConAu 2NR, –45, ConLC 25[port], ConNov 76, –82, ConSFA, DcLB 8[port], DrAF 76, DrAP&F 83, EncSF, LinLib L, Novels, ScF&FL 1, –2, WhoAm 82, WhoHr&F, WhoSciF, WrDr 76, –80, –82, –84*

Leiber, Justin Fritz 1938- *ConAu 97, DrAS 74P, –78P, –82P*

Leicht, Kathleen F 1930- *WhoAmW 66*

Leigh, Roberta *WrDr 84*

Leighton, Frances Spatz *BioIn 8, –12, ConAu 81, ForWC 70, ScF&FL 1, WhoAm 82, WhoAmW 66, –68, –70, –72, WhoWor 82*

Leighton, Margaret 1896- *AmAu&B, Au&Wr 6, AuBYP, BioIn 3, –6, –8, –9, ConAu 9R, InWom, MorJA, OhA&B, SmATA 1, Str&VC, WhE&EA, WhoAm 74, –76, –78, –80, WhoAmW 74, –58, –61, –64, –66, –68, –70, –72, –83, WrDr 76, –80, –82, –84*

Leinwand, Gerald 1921- *ConAu 5R, –9NR, WhoAm 80, –82*

Leitch, Patricia 1933- *BioIn 11, ConAu 9NR, –61, ScF&FL 1A, SmATA 11*

Lekachman, Robert 1920- *AmAu&B, AmEA 74, AmM&WS 73S, –78S, BioIn 11, ConAu 106, WhoAm 74, –76, –78, –80, –82, WhoEc, WhoWor 74*

Leland, Charles Godfrey 1824-1903 *Alli, Alli SUP, AmAu, AmAu&B, AmBi, ApCAB, BbD, BiD&SB, BioIn 5, –6, –8, –9, CasWL, CelCen, Chambr 3, ChhPo, –S1, –S2, –S3, CyAL 2, CyEd, DcAmAu, DcAmB, DcBiPP, DcEnA, –AP, DcEnL, DcLB 11[port], DcNAA, Drake, EncO&P 78, EvLB, HarEnUS, LinLib L, NatCAB 5, OxAmL, OxEng, PenC AM, REn, ScF&FL 1, TwCBDA, WhAm 1*

Lem, Stanislaw 1921- *BioIn 11, –12, ConAu 105, ConLC 8, –15, EncSF, IntAu&W 82, NewYTBS 83[port], Novels, ScF&FL 1, WhoSciF, WhoSocC 78, WorAl, WorAu 1970*

Lemarchand, Elizabeth 1906- *Au&Wr 6, ConAu 10NR, –25R, IntAu&W 77, –82, TwCCr&M 80, WrDr 76, –80, –82, –84*

LeMay, Alan 1899-1964 *AmAu&B, CmMov, EncAB 36[port], FilmgC, IndAu 1917, NotNAT B, WhAm 4, WhE&EA, WhNAA*

Lembeck, Ruth 1919- *ConAu 105*

LeMond, Alan 1938- *ConAu 9NR, –61, WhoAm 74, –76, –78, –80, –82, WrDr 80, –82, –84*

Lenard, Alexander 1910-1972 *BioIn 5, –6, –9, –12, ConAu 4NR, –5R, –89, SmATA 21N*

Lenburg, Greg 1956- *ConAu 105*

Lenburg, Jeff 1956- *ConAu 104*

L'Engle, Madeleine 1918- *AmAu&B, AmNov,*

AmWomWr, AuBYP, AuNews 2,
BioIn 2, -6, -7, -9, -10, -11, -12, BlueB 76,
ChlLR 1, ChhPo, -S1, -S3, ConAu 1R,
-3NR, ConLC 12, ForWC 70, InWom,
IntAu&W 77, LinLib L, MorBMP,
MorJA, PiP, ScF&FL 1, -2, SenS,
NewbC 1956, SmATA 1, -27[port],
TwCCW 78, -83, WhoAm 74, -76, -78,
-80, -82, WhoAmW 74, -64, -66, -68, -70,
-72, -75, -77, -79, -81, -83, WhoE 74,
WhoWor 82, WrDr 76, -80, -82, -84

Lengyel, Cornel Adam 1915- *ConAu 1R, -1NR,*
DrAF 76, DrAP 75, DrAP&F 83,
DrAS 78E, -82E, IntAu&W 76,
IntWWP 77, -82, SmATA 27,
WhoAm 74, -76, -78, -80, -82,
WhoWest 76, WhoWor 76, WrDr 76, -80,
-82, -84

Lengyel, Emil 1895- *AmAu&B,*
AmM&WS 73S, BioIn 4, -9,
ConAu 3NR, -9R, CurBio 42, DrAS 74H,
-78H, -82H, REnAL, SmATA 3, TwCA,
TwCA SUP, WhE&EA, WhNAA,
WhoAm 74, -76, -78, WhoWor 74

Lennon, John 1940-1980 *AnObit 1980[port],*
Au&Wr 6, Baker 78, BioIn 6, -7, -8, -9,
-10, -11, -12, BlueB 76, CelR 73,
ConAu 102, ConLC 12, CurBio 65, -81N,
DcLEL 1940, EncPR&S, -77, IlEncRk,
IntWW 74, -75, -76, -77, -78, -79, -80,
-81N, IntWWP 77, LinLib L, McGEWB,
MotPP, NewYTBS 80[port], RkOn 78,
-84, RolSEnR 83, WhAm 7, WhoAm 80,
WhoHol A, WhoRocM 82, WhoWor 74,
-76, -78, -80, WorAl, WrDr 76, -80, -82

Lennon, John *see also* Beatles, The

Lens, Sidney 1912- *AuBYP, BioIn 7, -11,*
ConAu 1R, -1NR, SmATA 13,
WhoAm 74, -76, -78, -80, -82,
WhoWor 74

Lenski, Lois 1893-1974 *AmAu&B, AmPB,*
AmWomWr, Au&ICB, Au&Wr 6,
AuBYP, BioIn 1, -2, -3, -4, -5, -7, -8, -9,
-10, -11, -12, BkCL, BkP, CarSB,
ChhPo, -S1, -S2, ConAu 53, ConAu P-1,
ConICB, DcLB 22[port], FamAIYP,
HerW, IlsCB 1744, -1946, -1957, -1967,
InWom, JBA 34, -51, LinLib L,
NewYTBS 74, Newb 1922, OhA&B,
REnAL, SmATA 1, -26[port],
TwCCW 78, -83, WhAm 6, WhE&EA,
WhNAA, Who 74, WhoAm 74,
WhoAmA 73, -76, -78N, -80N, -82N,
WhoAmW 74, -58, -61, -64, -66, -68, -70,
-72

Lent, Henry Bolles 1901-1973 *AuBYP, BioIn 1,*
-2, -7, -12, ConAu 73, JBA 51,
SmATA 17, Str&VC

Leon-Portilla, Miguel 1926- *ChiSch,*
ConAu 11NR, -21R, FifIDA, IntWW 74,
-75, -76, -77, -78, -79, -80, -81, -82, -83,
OxSpan, WhoS&SW 73, -75, -76, -78,

WhoWor 74, -76, -78, -80, -82

Leonard, Constance 1923- *ConAu 49,*
WrDr 76, -80, -82, -84

Leonard, Hugh 1926- *BioIn 10, -12,*
ConAu X, ConDr 73, -77, -82, ConLC 19,
CroCD, CurBio 83[port], DcIrL,
DcLB 13[port], IntAu&W 76, -82X,
IntWW 79, -80, -81, -82, -83, Who 74,
-82, -83, WhoAm 80, -82, WhoThe 15,
-16, -81, WhoWor 82, WorAu 1970,
WrDr 76, -80, -82, -84

Leonard, Jonathan Norton 1903-1975 *BioIn 10,*
ConAu 57, -61, NewYTBS 75,
SmATA 36, WhAm 6, WhoAm 74

Leontief, Wassily 1906- *AmEA 74,*
AmM&WS 73S, -78S, BioIn 7, -8, -10,
-11, -12, BlueB 76, ConAu P-1,
CurBio 67, IntAu&W 76, -77, -82,
IntEnSS 79, IntWW 74, -75, -76, -77, -78,
-79, -80, -81, -82, -83, IntYB 78, -79, -80,
-81, -82, NewYTBE 73, WebAB, -79,
Who 82, -83, WhoAm 74, -76, -78, -80,
-82, WhoE 74, -77, -79, -81, -83, WhoEc,
WhoF&I 83, WhoWor 74, -76, -78, -80,
-82, WorAl

Lerman, Rhoda 1936- *AmWomWr, BioIn 10,*
-12, ConAu 49, DrAP&F 83, ScF&FL 1,
-2, WrDr 80, -82, -84

Lerner, Aaron Bunsen 1920- *AmM&WS 73P,*
-76P, -79P, -82P, ConAu 108, IntMed 80,
SmATA 35, WhoAm 74, -76, -78, -80

Lerner, Alan Jay 1913- *AmAu&B, AmPS,*
AmSCAP 66, BiDAmM, BiE&WWA,
BioIn 4, -5, -6, -7, -9, -10, -11, -12,
BlueB 76, CelR 73, CmMov, CmpEPM,
ConAu 77, ConDr 73, -77D, -82D,
CurBio 58, EncMT, EncWT, FilmgC,
IntAu&W 76, -77, IntMPA 77, -75, -76,
-78, -79, -81, -82, -84, IntWW 74, -75,
-76, -77, -78, -79, -80, -81, -82, -83,
ModWD, NewCBMT, NotNAT, OxAmL,
OxFilm, PIP&P, REnAL, Who 74, -82,
-83, WhoAm 74, -76, -78, -80, -82,
WhoThe 15, -16, -81, WhoWor 74, -78,
-80, -82, WorAl, WorEFlm

Lerner, Gerda 1920- *AmWomWr, BioIn 11,*
-12, ConAu 25R, DrAS 74H, -78H, -82H,
WhoAm 74, -76, -82, WhoAmW 74, -72,
-75, -77, -83, WhoMW 82

Lerner, Max 1902- *AmAu&B,*
AmM&WS 73S, Au&Wr 6, AuNews 1,
BioIn 4, -5, -7, -10, -11, BioNews 74,
BlueB 76, CelR 73, ConAu 13R,
CurBio 42, IntAu&W 76, -77, -82,
IntWW 74, -75, -76, -77, -78, -79, -80, -81,
-82, -83, IntYB 78, -79, -80, -81, -82,
OxAmL, PenC AM, PolProf T, REnAL,
TwCA, TwCA SUP, Who 74, -82, -83,
WhoAm 74, -76, -78, -80, -82, WhoE 74,
-81, -83, WhoWor 74, -78, -80, -82,
WhoWorJ 72, -78, WorAl, WrDr 76, -80,
-82, -84

LeRoy, Gen *SmATA 36*

Lerrigo, Marion Olive 1896-1968 *BioIn 8,*
ConAu 109, SmATA 29N, WhAm 5,
WhoAmW 58, –61, –64, –68, –70

LeShan, Eda J 1922- *AuBYP SUP, BioIn 12,*
ChlLR 6[port], ConAu 13R,
IntAu&W 76, –77, –82, NewYTBE 73,
SmATA 21[port], WhoAmW 58, –61, –64,
–66, WrDr 76, –80, –82, –84

LeShan, Lawrence L 1920- *ConAu 17R,*
EncO&P 78, –81, WhoAm 78, –80, –82

Leslie, Clare Walker 1947- *ConAu 108*

Leslie, Robert Franklin 1911- *Au&Wr 6,*
BioIn 10, ConAu 49, IntAu&W 77,
SmATA 7, WrDr 76, –80, –82, –84

Leslie-Melville, Betty 1929- *BioIn 10,*
ConAu 81

Lessing, Doris 1919- *ASpks, Au&Wr 6,*
BioIn 5, –6, –7, –8, –9, –10, –11, –12,
BlueB 76, CnMD, ConAu 9R, ConDr 73,
–77, –82, ConLC 1, –2, –3, –6, –10, –15,
–22[port], ConNov 72, –76, –82, CroCD,
CurBio 76, DcLB 15[port], DcLEL 1940,
DrAF 76, DrAP&F 83, EncSF, EncWL,
–2[port], EncWT, GoodHs, InWom,
IntAu&W 76, –77, IntDcWB, IntWW 74,
–75, –76, –77, –78, –79, –80, –81, –82, –83,
LongCEL, LongCTC, ModBrL,
ModBrL SUP, ModCmwL, ModWD,
NewC, NewYTBS 80[port], –82[port],
Novels[port], PenC ENG, RAdv 1, REn,
ScF&FL 1, –2, TwCWr, WebE&AL,
WhDW, Who 74, –82, –83, WhoAm 80,
–82, WhoAmW 74, –68, –70, –72,
WhoTwCL, WhoWor 74, –76, –78, –80, –82,
WorAl, WorAu, WrDr 76, –80, –82, –84

Lester, Julius 1939- *AmAu&B, Au&ICB,*
AuBYP, BiDAfM, BioIn 11, BlkAWP,
ChlLR 2, CivR 74, ConAu 8NR, –17R,
FourBJA, InB&W 80, LivgBAA,
NegAl 76[port], –83[port], SelBAA,
SmATA 12, TwCCW 83, WhoAm 74,
–76, –78, –80, –82, WhoBlA 75, –77, –80,
WhoE 75, –77

LeSueur, Meridel 1900- *AmWomWr, BioIn 6,*
–10, –12, ConAu 2NR, –49, MinnWr,
MorJA, SmATA 6

Leuchtenburg, William Edward 1922-
AmAu&B, BlueB 76, ConAu 5R,
DrAS 74H, –78H, –82H, WhoAm 74, –76,
–78, –80, –82, WhoWor 74, –76, –78, –80,
–82

Leutscher, Alfred 1913- *Au&Wr 6,*
ConAu 73, SmATA 23[port]

Levenkron, Steven 1941- *ConAu 109*

Levenson, Dorothy 1927- *ConAu 9R*

Levenson, Jordan 1936- *ConAu 7NR, –57*

Levenson, Sam 1911-1980 *AnObit 1980[port],*
AuNews 1, BioNews 74, CelR 73,
ConAu 101, –65, CurBio 59, –80N,
IntMPA 77, –75, –76, –78, –79,
NewYTBS 80[port], WhoAmJ 80,

WhoWorJ 78, WorAl

Levenson, Samuel 1911-1980 *BioIn 2, –3, –4, –5,*
–7, –10, –11, –12, WhAm 7, WhoAm 74,
–76, –78, –80

Levertov, Denise 1923- *AmAu&B,*
AmWomWr, BioIn 8, –9, –10, 12,
BlueB 76, ConAu 1R, –3NR, ConLC 1,
–2, –3, –5, –8, –15, ConP 70, –75, –80,
CroCAP, DcLB 5[port], DcLEL 1940,
DrAP 75, DrAP&F 83, EncWL 2, LibW,
LinLib L, ModAL, ModAL SUP,
ModBrL, NewC, OxAmL, PenC AM,
RAdv 1, REn, REnAL, WebE&AL,
WhoAm 74, –76, –78, –80, WhoAmW 74,
–66, –68, –70, –72, –81, –83, WhoE 74,
WhoTwCL, WhoWor 74, WorAl, WorAu,
WrDr 76, –80, –82, –84

Levi, Herbert W 1921- *AmM&WS 73P, –76P,*
–79P, –82P, WhoAm 74, –76, –78, –80, –82,
WhoAmJ 80, WhoE 74, WhoWorJ 72,
–78

Levi, Peter 1931- *Au&Wr 6, BioIn 10, –12,*
ChhPo, ConAu 5R, ConP 70, –80,
DcLEL 1940, IntAu&W 77, –82,
IntWWP 77, NewC, Who 82, –83,
WorAu, WrDr 76, –80, –82, –84

Levin, Betty 1927- *BioIn 12, ConAu 9NR,*
–65, SmATA 19, TwCCW 83

Levin, Harry 1912- *AmAu&B, Au&Wr 6,*
BioIn 4, BlueB 76, ConAu 1R, –2NR,
ConLCrt, –82, DcLEL, DrAS 74E, –78E,
–82E, IntAu&W 77, IntWW 74, –75, –76,
–77, –78, –79, –80, –81, –82, –83, LinLib L,
PenC AM, RAdv 1, REnAL,
TwCA SUP, WhoAm 74, –76, –78, –80,
–82, WhoE 81, –83, WrDr 76, –80, –82,
–84

Levin, Ira 1929- *AmAu&B, AmSCAP 66,*
ASpks, Au&Wr 6, BiE&WWA, BioIn 7,
–11, ConAu 21R, ConLC 3, –6,
ConNov 72, –76, –82, EncMys, EncSF,
IntAu&W 77, NatPD 81[port], NotNAT,
Novels[port], ScF&FL 1, –2,
TwCCr&M 80, WhoAm 78, –80, –82,
WhoThe 81, WorAl, WorAu 1970,
WrDr 76, –80, –82, –84

Levin, Jane Whitbread 1914- *ConAu 106*

Levin, Jenifer 1955- *ConAu 108*

Levin, Marcia 1918- *AuBYP, BioIn 8, –11,*
ConAu 13R, ForWC 70, SmATA 13

Levin, Meyer 1905-1981 *AmAu&B, AmNov,*
AnObit 1981[port], Au&Wr 6, AuNews 1,
BiE&WWA, BioIn 2, –4, –7, –10, –12,
BioNews 74, CelR 73, CnMD,
ConAu 9R, –104, ConLC 7, ConNov 72,
–76, –82, CurBio 40, –81N, DcAmSR,
DcLB Y81A[port], –9[port], DcLEL,
IntAu&W 76, –77, –82, ModAL,
NewYTBS 81[port], NotNAT, Novels,
OxAmL, PenC AM, REn, REnAL,
ScF&FL 1, –2, SmATA 21[port], –27N,
TwCA, TwCA SUP, WhoAm 74, –76, –78,

–80, WhoWorJ 72, –78, WorAl, WrDr 76, –80, –82

Levine, Betty K 1933- *ConAu 93, WhoAmW 77, –79*

Levine, David 1926- *BioIn 8, –9, –10, –11, –12, CurBio 73, IlsCB 1957, SmATA 35, WhoAm 78, –80, –82, WhoAmA 76, –78, –80, –82, WhoGrA 82[port], WorECar*

Levine, Israel E 1923- *AuBYP, BioIn 11, ConAu 1R, IntAu&W 77, –82, SmATA 12, WhoAmJ 80, WhoWorJ 72, –78, WrDr 76, –80, –82, –84*

Levine, Robert Erwin 1930- *WhoS&SW 73, –75, –76*

Levine, Sol 1914- *ConAu 9R, WhoWorJ 72, –78*

Levinger, Elma 1887-1958 *AmAu&B, AuBYP, BioIn 4, –7, OhA&B, REnAL, WhAm 3, WhNAA*

Levinson, Nancy Smiler 1938- *ConAu 107, SmATA 33[port]*

Levison, Andrew 1948- *ConAu 93, WrDr 76, –80, –82, –84*

Levitan, Sar A 1914- *AmEA 74, AmM&WS 73S, –78S, ConAu 3NR, –9R, WhoAm 76, –78, –80, –82, WhoAmJ 80, WhoEc, WhoS&SW 73*

Levitin, Sonia 1934- *AuBYP SUP, BioIn 9, ConAu 29R, ConLC 17, SmATA 4, WhoAmW 74, –72*

Levitt, I M 1908- *ConAu 45*

Levitt, I M *see also* Levitt, Israel Monroe

Levitt, Israel Monroe 1908- *AmM&WS 73P, –76P, –79P, –82P, WhoAm 74, –76, –78, –80, –82, WhoTech 82*

Levitt, Israel Monroe *see also* Levitt, I M

Levitt, Leonard 1941- *ConAu 104*

Levoy, Myron *AuBYP SUP, ConAu 93, SmATA 37*

Levy, Elizabeth 1942- *AuBYP SUP, ConAu 77, IntAu&W 82, SmATA 31[port]*

Levy, Owen *DrAP&F 83*

Lewellen, John Bryan 1910-1956 *AuBYP, BioIn 4, –6, –7, EncAB 31[port], IndAu 1917, MorJA, ObitOF 79*

Lewin, Michael Z 1942- *ConAu 73, TwCCr&M 80, WrDr 76, –80, –82, –84*

Lewis, Alfred Henry 1858?-1914 *AmAu&B, AmBi, AtlBL, AuBYP, BiD&SB, BioIn 12, Chambr 3, CnDAL, DcAmAu, DcAmB, DcLB 25[port], DcLEL, DcNAA, EncMys, NatCAB 25, OhA&B, OxAmL, REnAL, WhAm 1*

Lewis, Anthony 1927- *BioIn 3, –4, –7, –9, BlueB 76, ConAu 9R, CurBio 55, SmATA 27[port], Who 74, –83, WhoAm 74, –76, –78, –80, –82, WorAl*

Lewis, C Day 1904-1972 *NewYTBE 72*

Lewis, C Day *see also* Day-Lewis, Cecil

Lewis, C Day *see also* Lewis, Cecil Day

Lewis, C S 1898-1963 *AnCL, ChlLR 3,*

ConAu 81, ConLC 1, –3, –6, –14, –27[port], ConLCrt, –82, DcLB 15[port], EncSF, EncWL 2, LinLib L, LongCTC, ModBrL, ModBrL SUP, MorJA, NewC, Novels, ObitT 1961, PenC ENG, RAdv 1, REn, ScF&FL 1, SmATA 13, TwCCW 78, –83, TwCWr, WebE&AL, WhoSciF, WorAl

Lewis, C S *see also* Hamilton, Clive

Lewis, C S *see also* Lewis, Clive Staples

Lewis, Cecil Day 1904-1972 *BioIn 2, –3, –4, –5, –6, –8, –9, –10, –12, CasWL, Chambr 3, ChhPo, ConAu X, ConLC 1, CurBio 40, –69, CyWA, DcLEL, EncMys, EvLB, LongCEL, LongCTC, McGEWB, ModBrL, NewC, ObitT 1971, OxEng, PenC ENG, REn, TwCWr, WhE&EA, WhoChL, WorAl*

Lewis, Cecil Day *see also* Day-Lewis, Cecil

Lewis, Clive Staples 1898-1963 *Au&ICB, AuBYP, BioIn 1, –3, –4, –6, –7, –8, –9, –10, –11, –12, CasWL, ChhPo S1, –S2, CurBio 44, –64, DcIrB, DcIrW 2, DcLEL, EncWL, EvLB, LongCEL, LuthC 75, MakMC, OxEng, TelT, TwCA SUP, WhDW, WhAm 4, WhE&EA, WhoChL*

Lewis, Clive Staples *see also* Lewis, C S

Lewis, David 1922- *AmArch 70, ConArch, ConAu 41R, WhoAm 74, –76, –82*

Lewis, Elizabeth 1892-1958 *AmAu&B, AmWomWr, AuBYP, BioIn 2, –4, –5, –7, –12, ChhPo S1, JBA 34, –51, Newb 1922, ObitOF 79, TwCCW 83, WhAm 3, WhE&EA, YABC 2*

Lewis, Gogo *ScF&FL 1*

Lewis, Janet 1899- *AmAu&B, AmNov, AmSCAP 66, AmWomWr, Au&Wr 6, BioIn 2, –4, –10, –12, ChhPo, –S1, CnDAL, ConAu X, ConNov 72, –76, –82, DrAP&F 83, ForWC 70, InWom, IntAu&W 76, –77, IntWWP 77, –82, –82X, OxAmL, TwCA SUP, WhE&EA, WhoAm 74, –76, –78, WhoAmW 74, –58, –68, –70, –72, WrDr 76, –80, –82, –84*

Lewis, Mary 1907- *ConAu 77*

Lewis, Mildred D 1912- *AuBYP, BioIn 7, ConAu 13R*

Lewis, Naomi *AuBYP SUP, ForWC 70*

Lewis, Norman *Au&Wr 6, IntAu&W 82, TwCWr, Who 82, –83, WorAu*

Lewis, Oscar 1914-1970 *AmAu&B, BioIn 8, –9, –10, ConAu 29R, ConAu P-1, CurBio 68, –71, –71N, IntEnSS 79, LinLib L, NewYTBE 70, ObitOF 79, WhDW, WhAm 5, WorAl, WorAu*

Lewis, Richard 1935- *AuBYP, BioIn 8, –9, BkP, ChhPo S1, ConAu 5NR, –9R, DrAP 75, OxCan SUP, SmATA 3*

Lewis, Richard Stanley 1916- *ConAu 9NR, –57, WhoAm 74, –76, –78, –80, –82*

Lewis, Roy 1933- *Au&Wr 6, ConAu 105, IntAu&W 82X, TwCCr&M 80, WrDr 82, –84*

Lewis, Sinclair 1885-1951 *AmAu&B, AmNov, AmWr, AtlBL, BioIn 1, -2, -3, -4, -5, -6, -7, -8, -9, -10, -11, -12, Chambr 3, ChhPo, CnDAL, CnMD, CnMWL, ConAmA, ConAmL, ConAu 104, CyWA, DcAmB S5, DcAmSR, DcLB DS1[port], -9[port], DcLEL, Dis&D, EncAAH, EncSF, EncWL, -2[port], FilmgC, LinLib L, -S, LongCTC, MakMC, McGEWB, ModAL, ModAL SUP, ModWD, NatCAB 57, NotNAT B, Novels[port], ObitOF 79, ObitT 1951, OxAmH, OxAmL, OxEng, PenC AM, RAdv 1, RComWL, REn, REnAL, ScF&FL 1, TwCA, TwCA SUP, TwCLC 3, -4[port], TwCWr, WebAB, -79, WebE&AL, WhDW, WhAm 3, WhE&EA, WhLit, WhNAA, WhoTwCL, WorAl*

Lewiton, Mina 1904-1970 *AuBYP, BioIn 6, -8, -9, ConAu 29R, ConAu P-2, MorJA, SmATA 2*

Lewty, Marjorie 1906- *Au&Wr 6, ConAu P-1, IntAu&W 76, WrDr 76, -80, -82, -84*

Lexau, Joan M *AuBYP, BioIn 8, -9, BkP, ConAu 11NR, -17R, SmATA 1, -36, TwCCW 83, WrDr 80, -82, -84*

Lexau, Joan M *see also* Nodset, Joan L

Ley, Willy 1906-1969 *AmAu&B, AsBiEn, Au&Wr 6, AuBYP, BioIn 2, -3, -4, -7, -8, -9, ConAu 9R, -25R, CurBio 41, -53, -69, EncSF, InSci, LinLib L, ObitOF 79, REnAL, SmATA 2, ThrBJA, TwCA SUP, WhAm 5, WhoSciF, WorAl*

Leydet, Francois Guillaume 1927- *ConAu 9R, WhoWest 76, -78, -80, -82, -84*

Leyland, Malcolm Rex 1944- *Au&Wr 6*

Lias, Godfrey *ConAu 5R, WhE&EA*

Libbey, Elizabeth 1947- *ConAu 110*

Libby, Bill 1927- *ConAu X, SmATA 5, WrDr 76, -80, -82, -84*

Libby, William M 1927- *AuBYP SUP, BioIn 10, ConAu 10NR, -25R, SmATA 5*

Lichello, Robert 1926- *AuBYP, BioIn 7, ConAu 13R, WhoE 75, -77, -79, -81*

Lichtenberg, Jacqueline 1942- *ConAu 73, ScF&FL 1, WrDr 76, -80, -82, -84*

Lichtenstein, Grace 1941- *ConAu 2NR, -49, ForWC 70, WhoAmW 75*

Liddell Hart, Basil Henry 1895-1970 *BioIn 3, -4, -7, -8, -9, ConAu 103, -89, CurBio 40, -70, DcLEL, EvLB, HisEWW, LinLib L, -S, LongCTC, NewC, TwCA, TwCA SUP, WhE&EA, WhWW-II, WhoMilH 76*

Liddy, G Gordon 1930- *CurBio 80[port], WorAl*

Lieberman, E James 1934- *BiDrAPA 77, BiDrAPH 79, ConAu 45*

Lieberman, Edwin James 1934- *AmM&WS 73S, -76P, -79P, -82P*

Lieberman, Jethro K 1943- *ConAu 10NR,*

-21R, WhoAmL 79, -83, WhoE 75, -77, WhoS&SW 73

Lieberman, Mark 1942- *ConAu 29R*

Lieberman, Nancy 1958- *BioIn 11, -12, NewYTBS 80, -82[port]*

Lieberman, Robert 1941- *ConAu 10NR*

Liebers, Arthur 1913- *BioIn 11, ConAu 3NR, -5R, SmATA 12, WrDr 76, -80, -82, -84*

Liebman, Arthur 1926- *ConAu 6NR, -57*

Lief, Philip 1947- *ConAu 107*

Lifshin, Lyn 1942?- *ConAu 8NR, -33R, ConP 75, -80, DrAP 75, DrAP&F 83, IntAu&W 82, WrDr 76, -80, -82, -84*

Lifton, Betty Jean 1926- *AuBYP, BioIn 8, -9, -10, ConAu 5R, ForWC 70, SmATA 6, ThrBJA, TwCCW 78, -83, WrDr 80, -82, -84*

Lifton, Robert Jay 1926- *AmAu&B, AmM&WS 73S, -76P, -79P, -82P, BiDrAPA 77, BioIn 8, -10, BlueB 76, ConAu 17R, CurBio 73, WhoAm 74, -76, -78, -80, -82, WhoAmJ 80, WorAu 1970, WrDr 80, -82, -84*

Liggett, Clayton Eugene 1930- *ConAu 29R, IntAu&W 76, WhoWest 74, -76, -78, -80*

Light, Ivan 1941- *ConAu 73, WhoWest 84*

Lightfoot, Gordon 1938?- *AmSCAP 66, BioIn 8, -10, -11, -12, BioNews 74, CanWW 81, -83, ConAu 109, ConLC 26[port], CreCan 2, CurBio 78, EncPR&S, -77, IlEncRk, RkOn 78, -84, RolSEnR 83, WhoAm 78, -80, -82, WhoRocM 82, WorAl*

Lightner, A M *AuBYP SUP, BioIn 10, ConAu X, IntAu&W 76X, -77X, -82X, MichAu 80, SmATA 5*

Lightner, A M *see also* Hopf, Alice L

Lightner, Robert P 1931- *ConAu 1NR, -49, DrAS 74P, -78P, -82P, WhoRel 77*

Lilienfeld, Robert Henry 1927- *ConAu 1R, -1NR*

Lilienthal, David 1896?-1953 *BioIn 3*

Lilienthal, David E 1899-1981 *AmAu&B, AnObit 1981[port], BiDAmBL 83, BioIn 1, -2, -5, -7, -8, -9, -10, -11, -12, BlueB 76, CelR 73, ConAu 3NR, -5R, -102, CurBio 44, -81N, DcAmSR, EncAB-H, IntWW 74, -75, -76, -77, -78, -79, -80, -81N, IntYB 78, -79, -80, -81, LinLib S, McGEWB, NewYTBS 81[port], PolProf T, WebAB, -79, WhAm 7, Who 74, -82N, WhoAm 74, -76, -78, -80, WhoWor 74, WhoWorJ 72, -78*

Lillington, Kenneth James 1916- *Au&Wr 6, ConAu 3NR, -5R, WrDr 76, -80, -82, -84*

Liman, Ellen 1936- *AuBYP SUP, ConAu 61, SmATA 22*

Limburg, Peter R 1929- *BioIn 11, ConAu 33R, IntAu&W 77, -82, SmATA 13, WhoE 75, WrDr 76, -80, -82, -84*

Lincoln, Abraham 1809-1865 *AmAu&B, AmBi, ApCAB, AtlBL, BbD, BiAUS, BiD&SB,*

BiDSA, BiDrAC, BiDrUSE, BioIn 1, –2, –3, –4, –5, –6, –7, –8, –9, –10, –11, –12, CelCen, Chambr 3, ChhPo S2, –S3, CivWDc, CyAG, CyWA, DcAmAu, DcAmB, DcAmReB, DcAmSR, DcBiPP, DcLEL, DcNAA, Dis&D, Drake, EncAAH, EncAB-H, EncO&P 78, EncSoH, EvLB, FilmgC, HarEnUS[port], LinLib L, McGEWB, NatCAB 2, OxAmH, OxAmL, OxEng, OxFilm, PenC AM, RComWL, REn, REnAL, REnAW, TwCBDA, WebAB, –79, WebE&AL, WhDW, WhAm HS, WhAmP, WorAl

Lincoln, C Eric 1924- *AmAu&B, AmM&WS 73S, –78S, CivR 74, ConAu 1R, –1NR, DrAS 74P, –78P, –82P, Ebony 1, IntAu&W 82, LivgBAA, SmATA 5, WhoAm 74, –76, –78, –80, –82, WhoBlA 77, –80, WhoRel 75, –77, WhoWor 74, WrDr 76, –80, –82, –84*

Lind, Levi Robert 1906- *ConAu 5R, DrAS 74F, –78F, –82F, IntAu&W 76, WhoAm 74, –76, –78, –80, –82, WrDr 76, –80, –82, –84*

Lindberg, Richard 1953- *ConAu 110*

Lindbergh, Anne Morrow 1906- *AmAu&B, AmWomWr, AnCL, BioIn 4, –5, –6, –8, –9, –10, –11, –12 , CelR 73, ChhPo, ConAu 17R, CurBio 76, GoodHs, InSci, InWom, IntAu&W 76, –77, –82, LibW, LinLib L, –S, LongCTC, NewYTBS 80[port], OxAmH, OxAmL, REn, REnAL, SmATA 33[port], TwCA, TwCA SUP, Who 74, –82, –83, WhoAm 74, –76, –78, –80, –82, WhoAmW 74, –58, –61, –64, –66, –68, –70, –72, –75, –77, –79, –81, –83, WhoWor 74, WrDr 76, –80, –82, –84*

Lindbergh, Charles A 1902-1974 *AmAu&B, AsBiEn, BioIn 1, –2, –3, –4, –5, –6, –7, –8, –9, –10, –11, –12, BioNews 74, BlueB 76N, CelR 73, ConAu 53, –93, CurBio 41, –54, –74, –74N, DcAmSR, EncAB-H, InSci, IntWW 74, –75N, LinLib L, –S, McGEWB, MedHR, NatCAB 60, NewYTBE 71, NewYTBS 74, ObitOF 79, ObitT 1971, OxAmH, OxAmL, REn, REnAL, SmATA 33[port], WebAB, –79, WebAMB, WhDW, WhAm 6, WhNAA, Who 74, WhoAm 74, WhoWor 74, WorAl*

Lindblom, Steven 1946- *ConAu 106*

Linden, Catherine 1939- *ConAu 110*

Lindenmeyer, Otto J 1936- *ConAu 77*

Linderman, Frank Bird 1868?-1938 *AmAu&B, BioIn 2, –4, –8, DcNAA, JBA 34, –51, NatCAB 40, OhA&B, OxAmL, REnAL, WhAm 1, WhNAA*

Lindop, Edmund 1925- *AuBYP SUP, BioIn 10, ConAu 2NR, –5R, SmATA 5*

Lindquist, Willis 1908- *AuBYP, BioIn 6, –8, –12, ConAu 73, MorJA, SmATA 20*

Lindsay, Jeanne Warren 1929- *ConAu 106*

Lindsay, Merrill K 1915- *ConAu 73*

Lindsay, Rachel *WrDr 84*

Lindsey, Robert 1935- *ConAu 97*

Line, Les 1935- *ConAu 73, SmATA 27[port]*

Lines, Kathleen *AuBYP SUP, ChhPo, –S1*

Lineweaver, Thomas H, III 1926- *ConAu 73*

Lingard, Joan 1932- *Au&Wr 6, AuBYP SUP, BioIn 11, ConAu 41R, IntAu&W 82, SmATA 8, TwCCW 78, –83, WrDr 76, –80, –82, –84*

Lingeman, Richard R 1931- *ConAu 11NR, –17R, IndAu 1917, WhoAm 80, –82*

Lingenfelter, Mary Rebecca 1893-1953 *BioIn 3, WhAm 3*

Linington, Elizabeth 1921- *AmWomWr, Au&Wr 6, ConAu 1R, –1NR, EncMys, Novels, TwCCr&M 80, WrDr 82, –84*

Linn, Charles F 1930- *AuBYP SUP, ConAu 85*

Linneman, Robert E 1928- *AmM&WS 73S, –78S, ConAu 29R, WhoE 74, –75*

Linton, Ralph 1893-1953 *AmAu&B, BioIn 3, –4, –5, –9, DcAmB S5, InSci, McGEWB, NamesHP, ObitOF 79, TwCA SUP, WebAB, –79, WhAm 3, WhE&EA, WhNAA*

Lipman, David 1931- *AuBYP SUP, BioIn 12, ConAu 21R, IntAu&W 77, SmATA 21[port], WhoAm 74, –76, –78, –80, –82, WhoAmJ 80, WhoMW 74, –76, WhoWor 78, WrDr 76, –80, –82, –84*

Lipman, Jean 1909- *ConAu 10NR, –21R, ForWC 70, WhoAmA 73, –76, –78, –82*

Lipp, Frederick J 1916- *BioIn 7, ConAu 106*

Lippard, Lucy Rowland 1937- *ConAu 25R, IntAu&W 76, –77, –82, WhoAmA 73, –76, –78, –80, –82, WhoAmW 74, –75*

Lippincott, David M 1925- *AmSCAP 66, ConAu 9NR, –61*

Lippincott, Joseph Wharton 1887-1976 *AmAu&B, AuBYP, BioIn 1, –3, –4, –6, –7, –11, –12, ConAu 69, –73, CurBio 55, –77, –77N, MorJA, NewYTBS 76, ObitOF 79, REnAL, SmATA 17, TwCCW 78, –83, WhAm 7, WhE&EA, WhLit, WhNAA*

Lippincott, Sarah Lee 1920- *AmM&WS 73P, –76P, –79P, –82P, ConAu 17R, ForWC 70, SmATA 22[port], WhoAm 78, –80, –82, WhoAmW 74, –75, –77, WhoTech 82*

Lipscomb, James 1926- *ConAu 85*

Lipsyte, Robert 1938- *AuBYP SUP, BioIn 10, ConAu 8NR, –17R, ConLC 21[port], IntAu&W 77, SmATA 5*

Lipton, James 1926- *AmSCAP 66*

Lisca, Peter 1925- *ConAu 37R, DrAS 74E, –78E, –82E, IntAu&W 82*

Lisker, Sonia O 1933- *AuBYP SUP, ConAu 2NR, –49*

Liss, Howard 1922- *AuBYP, BioIn 8, –9,*

ConAu 25R, SmATA 4

List, Albert, Jr. 1928- AmM&WS 82P

List, Ilka 1935- BioIn 10, ConAu 37R, ForWC 70, SmATA 6, WrDr 80, -82, -84

Liston, Robert A 1927- AuBYP, BioIn 8, -10, ConAu 17R, SmATA 5

Litowinsky, Olga 1936- ConAu 81, SmATA 26[port]

Littell, Robert 1896-1963 AmAu&B, BioIn 6, -8, ConAu 93, NatCAB 50, NotNAT B, WhAm 4, WhJnl, WhNAA, WhThe

Littell, Robert 1937- AuBYP SUP

Little, Charles Eugene 1931- WhoAm 74, -76

Little, Jean 1932- AuBYP, BioIn 8, -9, -10, -12, CaW, ChlLR 4[port], ChhPo S2, ConAu 21R, FourBJA, OxCan SUP, Profile, SmATA 2, TwCCW 78, -83, WrDr 80, -82, -84

Little, Lessie Jones 1906- ConAu 101

Little, Malcolm 1925-1965 AmAu&B, BioIn 9, -10, -11, -12, BlkAWP, InB&W 80, ObitOF 79, SelBAA, WebAB 79

Little, Malcolm see also Malcolm X

Little, Sara Pamela 1919- WhoAmW 75, -77, WhoRel 75, -77

Little, Stuart W 1921- BiE&WWA, ConAu 1NR, -45, NotNAT, WhoE 75, -77, WrDr 76, -80, -82, -84

Little, Thomas Russell 1911- Au&Wr 6, ConAu 13R, IntAu&W 76

Littledale, Freya 1929- ConAu 10NR, -21R, IntAu&W 76, -77, -82, ScF&FL 1, -2, SmATA 2, WhoAmW 74, -68, -72, -75, -77, -81, -83, WhoE 75, -77, -81, -83, WrDr 76, -80, -82, -84

Litwack, Leon F 1929- ConAu 1R, -1NR, DrAS 74H, -78H, -82H, WhoAm 82, WrDr 82, -84

Lively, Penelope 1933- Au&Wr 6, AuBYP SUP, BioIn 10, -11, ChhPo S2, ConAu 41R, DcLB 14[port], FourBJA, IntAu&W 77, -82, Novels, ScF&FL 1, -2, SmATA 7, TwCCW 78, -83, Who 82, -83, WrDr 76, -80, -82, -84

Liversidge, Douglas 1913- BioIn 11, ConAu P-1, IntAu&W 76, -77, -82, SmATA 8

Liversidge, Douglas see also Liversidge, Henry Douglas

Liversidge, Henry Douglas 1913- Au&Wr 6, BioIn 11, WhE&EA, WrDr 76, -80, -82, -84

Liversidge, Henry Douglas see also Liversidge, Douglas

Livingston, James T 1931- DrAS 74E, -78E, -82E

Livingston, Myra Cohn 1926- AmAu&B, AmWomWr, AnCL, AuBYP SUP, BioIn 10, -12, BkCL, BkP, ChhPo, -S1, -S2, -S3, ConAu 1R, -1NR, FourBJA, IntAu&W 76, -77, -82, IntWWP 77, -82, SmATA 5, TwCCW 78, -83, WhoAm 82,

WhoAmW 75, -77, -83, WhoWor 82, WrDr 80, -82, -84

Livsey, Clara G 1924- BiDrAPA 77, ConAu 107

Llewellyn, Edward 1917- ConAu X

Llewellyn, Richard 1906-1983 BioIn 2, 4, -5, -11, ConAu X, ConLC 7, CurBio 40, CyWA, DcLB 15[port], DcLEL, EvLB, IntAu&W 82X, LongCTC, NewC, NewYTBS 83[port], Novels, RAdv 1, REn, SmATA X, TwCA, TwCA SUP, TwCWr, Who 74, -82, -83, WhoWor 74, WorAl, WrDr 76, -80, -82, -84

Llewellyn, Richard see also Llewellyn Lloyd, Richard D V

Llewellyn Lloyd, Richard D V 1906-1983 ConAu 7NR, -53, CurBio 40, SmATA 11, -37N, TwCA, TwCA SUP

Llewellyn Lloyd, Richard D V see also Llewellyn, Richard

Lloyd, Alan C 1915- ConAu 1R, -1NR, LEduc 74, WhoE 75, -77

Lloyd, Chris Evert BioIn 12, NewYTBS 80[port]

Llywelyn, Morgan 1937- ConAu 81

Lo, Ruth Earnshaw 1910- BioIn 12, ConAu 106

Lobb, Charlotte 1935- ConAu 65

Lobenz, Norman Mitchell 1919- AmAu&B, ConAu 9R, SmATA 6

Lobley, Robert John 1934- Au&Wr 6, ConAu 29R, WrDr 76, -80, -82

Locke, Charles O 1896?-1977 BioIn 11, ConAu 69, NewYTBS 77

Lockerbie, Jeanette W Honeyman ConAu 9R

Lockley, Ronald Mathias 1903- Au&Wr 6, BioIn 12, ConAu 5NR, -9R, IntAu&W 76, -77, ScF&FL 1, -2, WhE&EA, Who 74, -82, -83, WhoWor 76, WrDr 76, -80, -82, -84

Lockwood, Charles Andrews 1890-1967 AmAu&B, BioIn 1, -2, -7, -9, ConAu 1R, EncAB 38[port], NatCAB 53, ObitOF 79, OxShips, WhAm 4

Lockwood, Douglas 1918- ConAu 21R, WhoWor 74, -78

Lockwood, Lee 1932- ASpks, BioIn 7, -11, ConAu 37R, WhoAm 74, -76, -78, -80, WhoBlA 75, -77, -80

Loeb, Robert H, Jr. 1917- BioIn 12, ConAu 29R, SmATA 21[port]

Loebl, Suzanne AuBYP SUP, ConAu 69, WhoAm 76, -78, -80, WhoAmW 74, -70, -72, -75, WhoE 74

Loeper, John J 1929- BioIn 11, ConAu 29R, IntAu&W 77, -82, SmATA 10, WhoE 75, WrDr 76, -80, -82, -84

Loescher, Ann Dull 1942- BioIn 12, ConAu 9NR, -61, SmATA 20

Loescher, Gil 1945- BioIn 12, ConAu 9NR, -61, SmATA 20

Loftis, Anne 1922- ConAu 45

Lofts, Norah 1904-1983 *Au&Wr 6,*
AuBYP SUP, AuNews 2, BioIn 3, -4, -9,
-10, -11, ConAu 5R, -6NR, -110,
IntAu&W 76, -77, -82, LinLib L,
LongCTC, Novels, ScF&FL 1, -2,
SmATA 36N, -8, TwCA, TwCA SUP,
TwCCr&M 80, WhE&EA, WhNAA,
Who 74, -82, -83, WhoAm 74,
WhoAmW 74, -64, -66, -68, -70, -72, -75,
WhoWor 76, WrDr 76, -80, -82, -84

Logan, Rayford W 1897-1982 *AmAu&B,*
BioIn 5, -9, ConAu 1R, -1NR, -108,
DrAS 74H, -78H, InB&W 80, NegAl 76,
-83, NewYTBS 82, SelBAA, WhoAm 74,
-76, -78, -80, -82, WhoBlA 75,
WhoWor 74, -76, -78, -80, -82

Loggins, Kenny 1947- *BioIn 11, -12,*
WhoAm 80, -82, WhoRocM 82, WorAl

Loggins, Kenny *see also* Loggins & Messina

Loggins & Messina *EncPR&S, -77, IlEncRk,*
RkOn 78, -84

Loggins & Messina *see also* Loggins, Kenny

Loggins & Messina *see also* Messina, Jim

Logsdon, Richard H 1912- *AuBYP,*
BiDrLUS 70, BioIn 1, -8, ConAu 2NR,
-5R, DrLC 69, WhoAm 74, -76, -78, -80,
-82, WhoLibI 82, WhoLibS 55, -66,
WhoWor 80, -82

Loh, Jules 1931- *ConAu 33R*

Loken, Newton 1919- *ConAu 1R,*
SmATA 26[port]

Lolli, Giorgio 1905-1979 *BioIn 11, -12,*
ConAu 1R, -2NR, -85

Lomas, Steve *BioIn 10, ConAu X,*
SmATA 6

Lomas, Steve *see also* Brennan, Joseph Lomas

Lomask, Milton 1909- *AuBYP, BioIn 8, -12,*
BkC 6, ConAu 1R, -1NR, DrAS 74H,
SmATA 20, WhoS&SW 76, -78, -80, -82

Lomax, Alan 1915- *AmAu&B, Au&Wr 6,*
Baker 78, BiDAmM, BioIn 2, -4, -5,
BlueB 76, ConAu 1R, -1NR, CurBio 41,
EncFCWM 69, IntWW 74, -75, -76, -77,
-78, -79, -80, -81, -82, -83, LinLib L,
REnAL, TexWr, TwCA SUP, WebAB,
-79, WhoAm 74, -76, WhoWor 74

Lomax, Bliss *ConAu X, OhA&B*

Lomax, Bliss *see also* Drago, Harry Sinclair

Lomax, John Avery 1867?-1948 *AmAu&B,*
Baker 78, BiDAmM, BiDSA, BioIn 1, -2,
-3, -4, -5, ChhPo, -S3, CnDAL,
DcAmB S4, DcNAA, EncFCWM 69,
LinLib L, NatCAB 38, ObitOF 79,
OxAmL, OxMus, REn, REnAL,
REnAW, Str&VC, TexWr, TwCA SUP,
WebAB, -79, WhAm 2, WhNAA

Lomax, Louis E 1922-1970 *AmAu&B, BioIn 5,*
-7, -8, -9, ConAu P-2, InB&W 80,
NewYTBE 70, SelBAA, WhAm 5,
WhScrn 2

Lombardi, Vince 1913-1970 *CurBio 63, -70,*
NewYTBE 70, ObitOF 79, WorAl

Lombardi, Vincent Thomas 1913-1970 *BioIn 6,*
-8, -9, -10, -11, -12, WebAB, -79,
WhAm 5, WhoFtbl 74

London, Jack 1876-1916 *AmAu&B, AmBi,*
AmWr, ApCAB X, AtlBL, AuBYP,
AuNews 2, BiD&SB, BioIn 1, -2, -3, -4,
-5, -6, -7, -8, -9, -10, -11, -12, CarSB,
CasWL, Chambr 3, CmCal, CnDAL,
ConAmL, ConAu X, CyWA, DcAmAu,
DcAmB, DcAmSR, DcBiA, DcLB 8[port],
-12[port], DcLEL, DcNAA, Dis&D,
EncAB-H, EncMys, EncSF, EncWL, -2,
FamAYP, FilmgC, JBA 34, LinLib L, -S,
LongCTC, MakMC, McGEWB, MnBBF,
ModAL, ModAL SUP, NatCAB 13, -57,
NotNAT B, Novels[port], OxAmH,
OxAmL, OxCan, OxEng, PenC AM,
RAdv 1, RComWL, REn, REnAL,
ScF&FL 1, SmATA 18, Str&VC, TwCA,
TwCA SUP, TwCLC 9[port], TwCWr,
WebAB, -79, WebE&AL, WhDW,
WhAm 1, WhoBW&I A, WhoHr&F,
WhoRocM 82, WhoTwCL, WorAl

London, Mel 1923- *ConAu 107*

Long, Judy 1953- *ConAu X, -65, SmATA X*

Longfellow, Henry Wadsworth 1807-1882 *Alli,*
Alli SUP, AmAu, AmAu&B, AmBi,
AmWr, AnCL, ApCAB, AtlBL, AuBYP,
BbD, BiDAmM, BiD&SB, BioIn 1, -2, -3,
-4, -5, -6, -7, -8, -9, -10, -11, -12, CasWL,
CelCen, Chambr 3, ChhPo, -S1, -S2, -S3,
CnDAL, CnE&AP, CrtT 3, CyAL 2,
CyEd, CyWA, DcAmAu, DcAmB,
DcAmSR, DcBiA, DcBiPP, DcEnA,
DcEnL, DcLB 1, DcLEL, DcNAA,
DcSpL, Drake, EncAAH, EncAB-H,
EvLB, FamAYP, FamPYP,
HarEnUS[port], LinLib L, -S, LuthC 75,
McGEWB, MouLC 4, NatCAB 2,
NewEOp 71, OxAmH, OxAmL, OxEng,
OxSpan, PenC AM, RAdv 1, RComWL,
REn, REnAL, SmATA 19, Str&VC,
TwCBDA, WebAB, -79, WebE&AL,
WhDW, WhAm HS, WorAl

Longford, Elizabeth 1906- *Au&Wr 6,*
BlueB 76, ConAu 5R, DcLEL 1940,
IntAu&W 76, -77, -82, IntWW 77, -81,
Who 74, -82, -83, WhoAmW 74, -70, -72,
WhoWor 74, -76, -78, WrDr 76, -80, -82,
-84

Longland, Jean R 1913- *BiDrLUS 70,*
ConAu 10NR, -21R, IntWWP 77, -82,
WhoAm 82, WhoAmW 58, -68,
WhoLibI 82, WhoLibS 55, -66

Longo, Lucas 1919- *ConAu 25R, WrDr 76,*
-80, -82, -84

Longstreet, Stephen 1907- *AmAu&B,*
BiE&WWA, BioIn 4, ConAu 7NR, -9R,
ConDr 73, -77D, -82D, FilmgC,
IntMPA 77, -75, -76, -78, -79, -81, -82, -84,
NotNAT, Novels, REnAL, TwCA SUP,
WhoAm 74, -76, -78, -80, -82,

WhoAmA 73, –76, –78, –80, –82,
WhoWorJ 72, –78, WrDr 76, –80, –82, –84

Longstreth, Thomas Morris 1886-1975
AmAu&B, Au&Wr 6, AuBYP, BioIn 2,
–6, –7, ConAu 5R, CurBio 50, MorJA,
OxCan, WhAm 7, WhoAm 74, –76

Longsworth, Polly 1933- *AuBYP, BioIn 8,*
ConAu 106, SmATA 28[port]

Longyear, Barry B 1942- *ConAu 102,*
IntAu&W 82

Loomis, Frederic Brewster 1873-1937 *AmLY,*
DcNAA, NatCAB 30, WhAm 1,
WhNAA

Loomis, Robert D *AuBYP, BioIn 7, –10, –11,*
ConAu 17R, SmATA 5

Lopez, Barry 1945- *ConAu 7NR, –65,*
DrAP&F 83

Lopez Y Fuentes, Gregorio 1897?-1966 *BioIn 7,*
CasWL, DcSpL, EncLatA, EncWL 2,
OxSpan, PenC AM, REn

Lorayne, Harry 1926- *ConAu 41R,*
IntAu&W 76, –77

Lord, Athena V 1932- *ConAu 109,*
WomPO 78

Lord, Bette Bao 1938- *BioIn 12, ConAu 107,*
ConLC 23[port], NewYTBS 81[port],
WhoAmW 83

Lord, Gabrielle 1946- *ConAu 106*

Lord, Walter 1917- *AmAu&B, AmSCAP 66,*
BioIn 5, –9, –10, ConAu 1R, –5NR,
CurBio 72, IntAu&W 76, –77, –82,
REnAL, SmATA 3, WhoAm 74, –76, –78,
–80, –82, WorAu, WrDr 80, –82, –84

Lorenz, Ellen Jane 1907- *AmSCAP 66,*
ConAmC, InWom, IntWWM 77,
WhoAmM 83, WhoAmW 58, –61, –64, –66,
WhoMus 72

Lorenz, Konrad 1903- *AmAu&B, BiESc,*
BioIn 2, –3, –4, –8, –10, –11, –12,
ConAu 61, CurBio 55, –77, EncTR, InSci,
IntAu&W 77, IntEnSS 79, IntWW 74,
–75, –76, –77, –78, –79, –80, –81, –82, –83,
LinLib L, MakMC, McGMS 80[port],
NewYTBE 73, WhDW, Who 74, –82, –83,
WhoWor 76, –78, –80, –82, WorAl,
WorAu 1970

Lorenzo, Carol Lee 1939- *ConAu 53*

Lorimer, Lawrence T 1941- *ConAu 6NR, –57*

Lorrah, Jean *ConAu 103, DrAS 74E, –78E,*
–82E

Lortz, Richard 1930-1980 *ConAu 102, –57*

Lose, M Phyllis 1925- *BioIn 12, ConAu 101*

Lossing, Benson John 1813-1891 *Alli,*
Alli SUP, AmAu, AmAu&B, BbD,
BiD&SB, ChhPo, CyAL 2, DcAmAu,
DcNAA, EarABI, EarABI SUP

Lott, Milton 1919- *BioIn 3, ConAu 17R,*
WhoPNW, WrDr 84

Lottman, Eileen 1927- *ConAu 57,*
IntAu&W 76, WhoAmW 68

Lotz, Wolfgang 1921- *BioIn 7, –9*

Loughnane, Lee 1946- *BioNews 74,*

WhoAm 78, –80, –82, WhoRocM 82,
WhoWor 80

Loughnane, Lee *see also* Chicago

Louis, Joe 1914-1981 *AnObit 1981[port],*
BioIn 1, –2, –3, –4, –5, –6, –7, –8, –9, –10,
–11, –12, CelR 73, ConAu X, CurBio 40,
–81N, Ebony 1, EncAB-H, InB&W 80,
McGEWB, NegAl 76, –83, NewYTBS 79,
–81[port], OxAmH, WebAB, –79, WhDW,
WhAm 7, WhoAm 74, –76, –78, –80,
WhoBlA 75, –77, –80, WhoBox 74, WorAl

Louis, Murray 1926- *BioIn 8, –9, –11,*
CurBio 68, WhoAm 78, –80, –82,
WhoE 83

Louria, Donald B 1928- *AmM&WS 73P, –76P,*
–79P, –82P, BiDrACP 79, ConAu 107,
IntMed 80, WhoAm 82, WhoE 75

Louthworth, John 1904- *WrDr 80*

Love, Edmund 1912- *AmAu&B, BioIn 7,*
ConAu X, –4NR, NewYTBE 73,
ScF&FL 1, –2

Love, Mike 1941- *BioIn 11, –12,*
WhoRocM 82

Love, Mike *see also* Beach Boys, The

Love, Sandra 1940- *ConAu 11NR, –69,*
SmATA 26[port]

Lovejoy, Bahija F 1914- *AuBYP, BioIn 8,*
ConAu 5R

Lovejoy, Clarence Earle 1894-1974 *AmAu&B,*
Au&Wr 6, BioIn 6, –10, ConAu 5R, –45,
NewYTBS 74, WhAm 6, WhJnl,
WhNAA

Lovejoy, Jack 1931- *WhoAmP 73*

Lovelace, Delos Wheeler 1894-1967 *AmAu&B,*
AuBYP, BioIn 4, –6, –7, –10, ConAu 5R,
–25R, MinnWr, ScF&FL 1, –2,
SmATA 7, TwCA, TwCA SUP,
WhAm 4, WhE&EA, WhNAA

Lovelace, Maud 1892-1980 *AmAu&B,*
Au&Wr 6, AuBYP, BioIn 2, –4, –5, –6, –7,
–9, –11, ConAu 5R, –104, JBA 51,
MinnWr, REnAL, SmATA, –23N,
TwCA, TwCA SUP, TwCCW 83,
WhE&EA, WhNAA, WhoAmW 74, –58,
–61, –64, –66, –68, –70, –72

Lovell, Alfred Charles Bernard 1913- *AsBiEn,*
BioIn 2, –5, DcLEL 1940, IntAu&W 77,
McGEWB, Who 82, –83, WorAl

Lovell, Alfred Charles Bernard *see also* Lovell,
Bernard

Lovell, Bernard 1913- *Au&Wr 6, BiESc,*
BioIn 7, BlueB 76, ConAu 6NR, –13R,
CurBio 59, InSci, IntAu&W 82,
IntWW 74, –75, –76, –77, –78, –79, –80, –81,
–82, –83, IntYB 78, –80, –81, –82,
LinLib L, –S, McGMS 80[port], WhDW,
Who 74, WhoPubR 76, WhoWor 74, –76,
–78, –82, WrDr 76, –80, –82, –84

Lovell, Bernard *see also* Lovell, Alfred Charles
Bernard

Lovesey, Peter 1936- *Au&Wr 6, ConAu 41R,*
EncMys, IntAu&W 77, –82, Novels,

TwCCr&M 80, WrDr 76, –80, –82, –84

Lovett, Margaret 1915- *Au&Wr 6, ConAu 61, ScF&FL 1, SmATA 22[port], WrDr 76, –80, –82, –84*

Low, Alice 1926- *AuBYP SUP, BioIn 11, ConAu 8NR, –61, SmATA 11*

Lowell, Robert 1917-1977 *Alli, AmAu&B, AmWr, BioIn 1, –3, –4, –5, –6, –7, –8, –9, –10, –11, –12, BlueB 76, CelR 73, ChhPo, –S3, CnDAL, CnE&AP, CnMWL, CnThe, ConAu 9R, –73, ConDr 77, ConLC 1, –2, –3, –4, –5, –8, –9, –11, –15, ConP 70, –75, –80A, CroCAP, CroCD, CurBio 47, –72, –77, –77N, DcLB 5[port], DcLEL 1940, DrAP 75, EncAB-H, EncWL, –2[port], EncWT, EvLB, IntAu&W 76, –77, IntWW 74, –75, –76, –77, –78N, IntWWP 77, LinLib L, MakMC, McGEWB, ModAL, ModAL SUP, ModWD, NewYTBS 77, NotNAT, ObitOF 79, OxAmL, PenC AM, PolProf J, RAdv 1, RComWL, REn, REnAL, ScF&FL 1, TwCA SUP, TwCWr, WebAB, –79, WebE&AL, WhDW, WhAm 7, Who 74, WhoAm 74, –76, –78, WhoTwCL, WhoWor 74, WorAl, WrDr 76*

Lowenfels, Walter 1897-1976 *AmAu&B, AuBYP SUP, BioIn 11, –12, BlueB 76, ConAu 1R, –3NR, –65, ConP 70, –75, DcLB 4, DrAP 75, IntAu&W 76, IntWWP 77, NewYTBS 76, PenC AM, RAdv 1, WhAm 7, WhoAm 76, WrDr 76*

Lowery, Bruce Arlie 1931- *BioIn 5, ConAu 1R, –1NR, DrAF 76, WhoAm 74, –76, –78, –80, –82, WhoE 74*

Lowery, Mike *DrAP&F 83*

Lownsbery, Eloise 1888- *BioIn 1, –2, CurBio 47, InWom, JBA 51*

Lowrey, Janette Sebring 1892- *AmAu&B, AuBYP, BioIn 1, –7, ChhPo, ConAu 13R, TexWr, WhoAmW 58, –61*

Lowry, Bates 1923- *BioIn 7, –8, BlueB 76, ConAu 1R, –1NR, DrAS 74H, –78H, –82H, IntWW 74, –75, –76, –77, –78, –79, –80, –81, –82, –83, WhoAm 74, –76, –78, –80, –82, WhoAmA 73, –76, –78, –80, –82*

Lowry, Beverly 1938- *ConAu 101, DrAP&F 83*

Lowry, Goodrich 1912- *BioIn 7*

Lowry, Lois 1937- *AuBYP SUP, ChlLR 6[port], ConAu 69, SmATA 23[port]*

Lowry, Peter 1953- *AuBYP SUP, BioIn 10, ConAu 49, SmATA 7*

Lozier, Herbert 1915- *ConAu 49, SmATA 26*

Luard, Nicholas 1937- *ConAu 85, IntAu&W 76, Novels, WhoSpyF*

Lubin, Leonard B *IlsCB 1967, SmATA 37*

Lubowe, Irwin I 1905- *ConAu 53*

Lucas, Alec 1913- *CanWW 70, –79, –80, –81,*

–83, ConAu 101, DrAS 74E, –78E, –82E, OxCan, OxCan SUP, WhoCan 82

Lucas, George 1944?- *BiDrACP 79, BioIn 9, –10, –11, –12, ConAu 77, ConLC 16, CurBio 78, DcVicP, EncSF, IntMPA 77, –75, –76, –78, –79, –81, –82, –84, IntWW 82, –83, MovMk, NewYTBE 73, NewYTBS 81[port], WhoAm 78, –80, –82, WrDr 80, –82, –84*

Luce, Clare Boothe 1903- *AmAu&B, AmCath 80, AmPolW 80, –80A, –80C, AmWomWr, Au&Wr 6, BiDrAC, BioIn 1, –2, –3, –4, –5, –9, –10, –11, –12, BlueB 76, CathA 1930, CelR 73, ConAu 45, CurBio 42, –53, GoodHs, InWom, IntAu&W 76, –77, IntWW 74, –75, –76, –77, –83, IntYB 78, –79, –80, –81, –82, LibW, LinLib L, –S, McGEWD, NewYTBS 79, –81[port], –82[port], NotNAT, –A, OxAmL, PolProf E, PolProf T, REn, REnAL, TwCA SUP, UFOEn, WebAB, –79, WhE&EA, WhoAm 74, –76, –78, –80, –82, WhoAmP 73, –75, –77, –79, –81, –83, WhoAmW 64, –66, –68, –70, –75, –77, –79, –81, –83, WhoWor 74, –78, –80, –82, WomWMM, WorAl, WrDr 80, –82, –84*

Luce, William 1931- *AmSCAP 66, ConAu 11NR, –65*

Luciano, Ron 1937- *BioIn 10, –11, –12, NewYTBS 77, –79*

Lucie-Smith, Edward 1933- *BioIn 8, –9, –10, BlueB 76, ChhPo, –S1, –S2, –S3, ConAu 7NR, –13R, ConP 70, –75, –80, EncSF, IntAu&W 77, –82, IntWWP 77, LinLib L, Who 74, –82, –83, WorAu, WrDr 76, –80, –82, –84*

Ludlum, Robert 1927- *BiE&WWA, BioIn 11, –12, ConAu 33R, ConLC 22[port], CurBio 82[port], DcLB Y82B[port], IntAu&W 76, NotNAT, Novels[port], TwCCr&M 80, WhoAm 78, –80, –82, WhoE 75, WorAl, WrDr 76, –80, –82, –84*

Ludlum, Robert *see also* Ryder, Jonathan

Ludwig, Charles Shelton 1918- *ConAu 5NR, –9R, WhoRel 75, –77*

Ludwig, Emil 1881-1948 *BioIn 1, –2, –4, EncTR, EvEuW, LinLib L, –S, LongCTC, NotNAT B, ObitOF 79, OxGer, TwCA, TwCA SUP, WhAm 2, WhE&EA, WhLit, WhoLA*

Lueders, Edward 1923- *AuBYP SUP, BioIn 12, ChhPo S1, ConAu 5NR, –13R, DrAP 75, DrAP&F 83, DrAS 74E, –78E, –82E, SmATA 14, WhoAm 74, –76, –78, –80, –82*

Luehrmann, Arthur Willett, Jr. 1931- *AmM&WS 73P, –76P, –79P, –82P, BioIn 9*

Luger, Harriett M 1914- *ConAu 1NR, –45, SmATA 23[port]*

Luis, Earlene W 1929- *BioIn 11, ConAu 61, SmATA 11*

Lukas, J Anthony 1933- *AmAu&B,*
AuBYP SUP, BioIn 9, –10, –11, BlueB 76,
ConAu 2NR, –49, WhoAm 74, –76, –78,
–80, –82

Luke, Mary M 1919- *ConAu 21R,*
WhoAmW 75

Luke, Thomas 1946- *ConAu X, WrDr 84*

Luke, Thomas *see also* Masterton, Graham

Lum, Peter 1911- *AnCL, AuBYP, BioIn 7,*
–8, –10, ConAu X, IntAu&W 76X, –77X,
–82X, SmATA 6, WrDr 76, –80, –82, –84

Lum, Peter *see also* Crowe, Bettina Lum

Lund, Doris Herold 1919- *BioIn 11,*
ChhPo S2, ConAu 17R, ForWC 70,
IndAu 1917, IntAu&W 77, SmATA 12

Lundquist, James Carl 1941- *ConAu 65,*
DrAS 74E, –78E, –82E

Lundwall, Sam J 1941- *ConAu 1NR, –49,*
EncSF, Novels, ScF&FL 1, –2, WhoSciF

Lunn, Janet 1928- *BioIn 9, –10, CaW,*
ConAu 33R, OxCan SUP, ScF&FL 1,
SmATA 4, WhoAmW 75

Lupoff, Richard A 1935- *ConAu 9NR, –21R,*
ConSFA, EncSF, ScF&FL 1, –2,
WhoSciF, WrDr 84

Lurie, Alison 1926- *BioIn 10, –12, BlueB 76,*
ConAu 1R, –2NR, ConLC 4, –5, –18,
ConNov 72, –76, –82, DcLB 2, DrAF 76,
DrAP&F 83, DrAS 82E, IntAu&W 76,
–77, –82, NewYTBS 82[port],
Novels[port], WhoAm 78, –80, –82,
WhoAmW 83, WorAu 1970, WrDr 76,
–80, –82, –84

Lustbader, Eric Van 1946- *BioIn 12,*
ConAu 85, NewYTBS 80[port]

Lustgarten, Karen 1944- *ConAu 85*

Lustig, Arnost 1926- *BioIn 11, CasWL,*
ConAu 69, EncWL 2, IntAu&W 76, –77,
–82, IntWW 74, –75, –76, –77, –78, –79,
–80, –81, –82, –83, ModSL 2, TwCWr,
WhoWor 74

Luszki, Walter A 1914- *AmM&WS 73S, –78S,*
WhoS&SW 82

Lutyens, Mary 1908- *Au&Wr 6, BioIn 5,*
ConAu 25R, IntAu&W 76, –77, –82,
WhE&EA, Who 74, –82, –83,
WhoWor 74, –76, WrDr 76, –80, –82, –84

Lutz, Frank Eugene 1879-1943 *BioIn 5, –7, –9,*
CurBio 44, DcAmB S3, DcNAA, InSci,
NatCAB 42, ObitOF 79, WhAm 2

Lutz, John 1939- *ConAu 9NR, –65,*
TwCCr&M 80, WrDr 82, –84

Lutzker, Edythe 1904- *AmM&WS 76P, –79P,*
–82P, BioIn 10, ConAu 37R, DrAS 74H,
–78H, –82H, IntAu&W 77, –82,
SmATA 5, WhoAmW 77, –79, –81, –83,
WrDr 76, –80, –82, –84

Lux, Donald Gregory 1924- *LEduc 74*

Lyall, Gavin 1932- *Au&Wr 6, BioIn 7,*
ConAu 4NR, –9R, DcLEL 1940, EncMys,
IntAu&W 76, –77, Novels, TwCCr&M 80,
Who 74, –82, –83, WrDr 76, –80, –82, –84

Lydecker, Beatrice 1938- *ConAu 106*

Lydon, Michael 1942- *BioIn 10, –11,*
ConAu 85, MugS, SmATA 11

Lyle, Katie Letcher 1938- *BioIn 11,*
ConAu 49, DrAP&F 83, SmATA 8

Lynds, Dennis 1924- *Au&Wr 6, ConAu 1R,*
–6NR, DrAP&F 83, EncMys, ScF&FL 1,
SmATA 37, TwCCr&M 80, WrDr 82,
–84

Lynds, Dennis *see also* Arden, William

Lynds, Dennis *see also* Collins, Michael

Lynn, Elizabeth A 1946- *BrAu 19, ConAu 81*

Lynn, Loretta 1932?- *BiDAmM, BioIn 9, –10,*
–11, –12, BioNews 74, CelR 73,
ConAu 81, CurBio 73, EncFCWM 69,
GoodHs, IntDcWB, NewYTBE 72,
RolSEnR 83, WhoAm 74, –76, –78, –80,
–82, WhoAmW 79, –81, –83, WorAl

Lynne, James Broom 1920- *BioIn 10,*
ConAu 77, ConDr 73, WrDr 76, –80, –82,
–84

Lynton, Harriet Ronken 1920- *ConAu 73*

Lyon, Eugene 1929?- *BioIn 10, –11,*
ConAu 106

Lyon, Lyman R 1907- *BioIn 11, –12,*
ConAu X, EncSF, SmATA X

Lyon, Lyman R *see also* DeCamp, L Sprague

Lyons, Augusta Wallace *ConAu 85,*
WhoAmW 74, –72, –75

Lyons, Barbara 1912- *ConAu 93*

Lyons, Dorothy Marawee 1907- *AmAu&B,*
BioIn 9, ConAu 1R, ForWC 70,
IntAu&W 82, SmATA 3, WhoAmW 64,
–66, –68, WrDr 76, –80, –82, –84

Lytle, Ruby 1917- *ConAu P-1, ForWC 70*

Lyttelton, Humphrey 1921- *BioIn 3, –5, –10,*
CmpEPM, EncJzS 70, IlEncJ,
IntAu&W 77, IntWW 74, –75, –76, –77,
–78, –79, –80, –81, –82, –83, Who 82, –83,
WhoMus 72

Lyttle, Richard B 1927- *AuBYP SUP,*
ConAu 33R, SmATA 23[port]

Lytton, Baron Edward G E Lytton Bulwer
1803-1873 *Alli, Alli SUP, BiD&SB,*
BioIn 1, –2, –5, –9, –10, –11, –12, BrAu 19,
CasWL, CelCen, ChhPo, –S2, DcEnA,
DcEuL, DcLEL, EvLB, HsB&A,
LinLib L, –S, LongCEL, MnBBF, NewC,
OxEng, OxThe, PenC ENG, REn,
ScF&FL 1, SmATA 23[port], TelT

M

Maas, Peter 1929- *AmAu&B, AmCath 80,
BioIn 10, BioNews 74, ConAu 93,
LinLib L, WhoAm 74, –76, –78, –80, –82,
WrDr 76, –80, –82, –84*

MacArthur, D Wilson 1903- *ConAu 5NR, –9R,
WhLit*

MacArthur, D Wilson *see also* Wilson, David

Macaulay, David A 1946- *AuBYP SUP,
BioIn 11, –12, ChlLR 3, ConAu 5NR, –53,
IlsCB 1967, SmATA 27, WhoAm 82,
WhoAmA 80, –82, WhoE 79, –81, –83,
WrDr 76, –80, –82, –84*

MacBeth, George 1932- *AuBYP SUP,
BioIn 8, –9, –10, ChhPo S2, ConAu 25R,
ConLC 2, –5, –9, ConP 70, –75, –80,
DcLEL 1940, DrAP&F 83, IntAu&W 76,
–77, –82, IntWWP 77, ModBrL SUP,
RAdv 1, SmATA 4, Who 74, –82, –83,
WhoWor 76, WorAu, WrDr 76, –80, –82,
–84*

MacClintock, Dorcas 1932- *AuBYP SUP,
BioIn 11, ConAu 6NR, –57, SmATA 8,
WhoAmA 78, –80, –82*

MacCloskey, Monro 1902- *ConAu 5NR, –9R*

MacCracken, Mary 1926- *ConAu 49,
WrDr 80, –82, –84*

MacDonald, Bernice 1930- *BiDrLUS 70,
WhoLibS 55*

MacDonald, Donald 1900- *Au&Wr 6*

MacDonald, George 1824-1905 *Alli, Alli SUP,
AuBYP, BbD, BiD&SB, BioIn 1, –3, –4,
–6, –7, –8, –9, –10, –11, –12, BrAu 19,
CarSB, CasWL, Chambr 3, ChhPo, –S1,
–S2, –S3, ConAu 106, DcBiA, DcBiPP,
DcEnA, –AP, DcEnL, DcEuL,
DcLB 18[port], DcLEL, EncSF, EvLB,
FamSYP, JBA 34, LongCTC, NewC,
Novels, OxEng, PenC ENG, REn,
ScF&FL 1, –1A, SmATA 33[port], TelT,
TwCCW 78A, –83A, TwCLC 9[port],
WebE&AL, WhoChL, WhoHr&F*

MacDonald, John D 1916- *AmAu&B, ASpks,
BioIn 3, –5, –7, –9, –10, –11, –12,
ConAu 1R, –1NR, ConLC 3, –27[port],
CorpD, DcLB 8[port], EncMys, EncSF,
IntAu&W 82, Novels, ScF&FL 1, –2,
TwCCr&M 80, WhoAm 74, –76, –78, –80,
–82, WhoSpyF, WorAl, WorAu,*

WrDr 76, –80, –82, –84

MacDonald, Philip 1896?- *AmAu&B, BioIn 4,
ConAu 81, EncMys, EvLB, IntMPA 77,
–75, –76, –78, –79, –84, LongCTC, NewC,
TwCA, TwCA SUP, TwCCr&M 80,
WhE&EA, WhLit*

Macdonald, Ross 1915-1983 *ASpks, BioIn 11,
–12, BlueB 76, CmCal, ConAu X,
ConLC 1, –2, –3, –14, ConNov 72, –76, –82,
CorpD, CurBio 53, –79, –83N,
DcLEL 1940, DrAP&F 83, EncMys,
IntAu&W 76X, IntWW 81, –82, –83,
LinLib L, ModAL, ModAL SUP,
NewYTBS 83[port], Novels,
TwCCr&M 80, WhoAm 76, WorAl,
WorAu, WrDr 76, –80, –82, –84*

Macdonald, Ross *see also* Millar, Kenneth

Macdonald, Shelagh 1937- *ConAu 97,
SmATA 25[port], WrDr 76, –80, –82, –84*

Mace, Elisabeth 1933- *ConAu 77,
SmATA 27[port], WrDr 80, –82, –84*

MacFall, Russell P 1903-1983 *ChhPo S2,
ConAu 110, ConAu P-1, IndAu 1917*

MacGowan, Kenneth 1888-1963 *AmAu&B,
BioIn 6, –12, ConAu 93, EncWT, FilmgC,
LinLib L, –S, NotNAT B, OxFilm,
OxThe, PIP&P, REnAL, WhAm 4,
WhE&EA, WhNAA, WhThe, WorEFlm*

MacGregor-Hastie, Roy 1929- *AuBYP,
BioIn 7, –8, –9, ConAu 1R, –2NR,
IntAu&W 76, –77, IntWWP 77,
SmATA 3, WhoWor 78, –80, –82,
WrDr 76, –80, –82, –84*

Macgregor-Morris, Pamela 1925- *ConAu 29R*

Mach, Elyse Janet *WhoAmM 83*

Machado, Antonio 1875-1939 *BioIn 10,
ClDMEL, CnMWL, ConAu 104,
EncWL 2, McGEWD, –84[port], ModRL,
PenC EUR, REn, TwCLC 3, TwCWr,
WhDW, WhoTwCL, WorAu*

Machetanz, Sara 1918- *ConAu 1R,
ForWC 70, WhoAmW 58, –61, –70, –72*

Machiavelli, Niccolo 1469-1527 *AtlBL,
BiD&SB, BioIn 1, –3, –4, –5, –6, –7, –8, –9,
–10, –11, –12, CasWL, CnThe, CyWA,
DcAmSR, DcCathB, DcEuL, DcItL,
Dis&D, EncWT, EuAu, EvEuW,
LinLib L, –S, LongCEL, LuthC 75,*

*McGEWB, McGEWD, –84[port], NewC,
NewEOp 71, NotNAT B, OxEng, OxThe,
PenC EUR, PIP&P, RComWL, REn,
REnWD, WhDW, WorAl*

Machlis, Joseph 1906- *Au&Wr 6, Baker 78,
ConAu 1R, –2NR, IntAu&W 76,
NewYTBS 82[port], WhoAmM 83*

Machorton, Ian 1923- *BioIn 7, ConAu 8NR,
–17R, IntAu&W 77, –82*

MacInnes, Helen 1907- *AmAu&B, ASpks,
Au&Wr 6, BioIn 1, –2, –4, –8, –10, –11,
–12, BlueB 76, ConAu 1R, –1NR,
ConLC 27[port], ConNov 72, –76, CorpD,
CurBio 67, EncMys, ForWC 70, InWom,
IntAu&W 76, –77, –82, IntWW 74, –75,
–76, –77, –78, –79, –80, –81, –82, –83, LibW,
LinLib L, NewC, NewYTBS 78, Novels,
REnAL, SmATA 22[port], TwCA SUP,
TwCCr&M 80, WhE&EA, Who 74, –82,
–83, WhoAm 74, –76, –78, –80, –82,
WhoAmW 74, –58, –64, –66, –68, –70, –72,
–83, WhoE 74, WhoSpyF, WhoWor 78,
–80, –82, WorAl, WrDr 76, –80, –82, –84*

MacIntyre, Donald George 1904- *Au&Wr 6,
ConAu 5R, WrDr 76, –82, –84*

Mack, John Edward 1929- *BiDrAPA 77,
ConAu 106, LEduc 74, WhoAm 78, –80,
–82, WhoE 79, –81, –83*

Mack Smith, Denis 1920- *Au&Wr 6,
ConAu 21R, IntAu&W 77, Who 74, –82,
–83, WrDr 80, –82, –84*

Mackal, Roy Paul 1925- *AmM&WS 73P, –76P,
–79P, BioIn 12, ConAu 73, WhoAm 74,
–76, –78, –80, WhoWor 74*

Mackay, David *AuBYP SUP, ChhPo S1*

MacKaye, Percy 1875-1956 *AmAu&B,
AnMV 1926, ApCAB X, BioIn 1, –2, –4,
–12, Chambr 3, ChhPo, –S1, –S2, –S3,
CnDAL, CnMD, CnThe, ConAmA,
ConAmL, DcAmB S6, DcLEL, EncWT,
LinLib L, –S, McGEWD, –84[port],
ModAL, ModWD, NatCAB 14,
NotNAT B, ObitOF 79, OxAmL, OxThe,
PIP&P, REn, REnAL, REnWD,
SmATA 32[port], Str&VC, TwCA,
TwCA SUP, WhAm 3, WhLit, WhNAA,
WhThe, WhoStg 1908*

MacKellar, William 1914- *AuBYP, BioIn 7,
–9, ConAu 33R, ScF&FL 1, SmATA 4*

Macken, Walter 1915-1967 *AuBYP SUP,
BioIn 2, –4, –7, –10, CnMD, ConAu 25R,
ConAu P-1, DcIrB, DcIrL, DcIrW 1,
DcLB 13[port], NotNAT B, ObitOF 79,
SmATA 36, TwCCW 78, –83, WhAm 4,
WhScrn 2, WhoHol B, WorAu*

MacKenzie, Christine Butchart 1917-
ConAu 13R

MacKenzie, Midge *BioIn 10, WomWMM B*

MacKenzie, Rachel 1909-1980 *BioIn 12,
ConAu 102, –97, NewYTBS 80[port]*

Mackey, Mary 1945- *ConAu 77, DrAS 74E,
–78E, –82E*

MacKinnon, John 1947- *ConAu 103,
WrDr 76, –80, –82, –84*

Mackler, Bernard 1934- *AmM&WS 73S,
ConAu 21R, LEduc 74, WhoE 77*

MacLaine, Shirley 1934- *AmWomWr,
BiDFilm, BioIn 3, –4, –5, –6, –7, –8, –9, –10,
–11, –12, BlueB 76, CelR 73, ConAu X,
CurBio 59, –78, FilmgC, ForWC 70,
GoodHs, HerW, InWom, IntAu&W 77,
IntMPA 77, –75, –76, –78, –79, –81, –82, –84,
IntWW 74, –75, –76, –77, –78, –79, –80, –81,
–82, –83, MotPP, MovMk, NewYTBE 71,
OxFilm, WhoAm 74, –76, –78, –80, –82,
WhoAmW 74, –61, –64, –66, –68, –70, –72,
–79, –81, –83, WhoHol A, WhoWor 74,
WomWMM, WorAl, WorEFlm, WrDr 80,
–82, –84*

MacLean, Alistair 1922- *AuBYP SUP,
BioIn 9, –10, BlueB 76, ConAu 57,
ConLC 3, –13, DcLEL 1940, FilmgC,
IntAu&W 76, –77, IntWW 74, –75, –76,
–77, –78, –79, –80, –81, –82, –83,
Novels[port], SmATA 23[port],
TwCCr&M 80, Who 74, –82, –83,
WhoAm 78, –80, –82, WhoSpyF,
WhoWor 76, –80, –82, WorAl, WorAu,
WrDr 76, –80, –82, –84*

Maclean, Charles 1946- *ConAu 109*

Maclean, Sir Fitzroy 1911- *Au&Wr 6,
BioIn 2, –8, –12, BlueB 76, ConAu 29R,
IntAu&W 77, –82, IntWW 74, –75, –76,
–77, –78, –79, –80, –81, –82, –83, IntYB 78,
–79, –80, –81, –82, WhWW-II, Who 74,
WhoWor 74, –78, –80, –82, WrDr 76, –80,
–82, –84*

MacLean, Katherine 1925- *BioIn 12,
ConAu 33R, ConSFA, DcLB 8, EncSF,
IntAu&W 76, ScF&FL 1, –2, WhoSciF,
WrDr 76, –80, –82, –84*

Maclean, Norman Fitzroy 1902- *BioIn 11, –12,
ConAu 102, DrAS 74E, –78E, –82E,
WhoAm 74*

MacLeish, Archibald 1892-1982 *AmAu&B,
AmSCAP 66, AmWr, AnObit 1982[port],
BiDAmM, BiE&WWA, BioIn 1, –2, –3, –4,
–5, –7, –8, –9, –10, –11, –12, CasWL,
CelR 73, ChhPo S1, –S2, –S3,
CnDAL, CnE&AP, CnMD, CnMWL,
CnThe, ConAmA, ConAmL, ConAu 9R,
–106, ConDr 73, –77, –82, ConLC 3, –8,
–14, ConP 70, –75, –80, CroCD,
CurBio 40, –59, –82N, CyWA, DcAmDH,
DcAmSR, DcLB Y82A[port], –4, –7[port],
DcLEL, DrAP 75, EncWL, –2, EncWT,
EvLB, IntAu&W 76, –77, –82, IntWW 74,
–75, –76, –77, –78, –79, –80, –81, –82, –82N,
IntWWP 77, –82, LinLib L, LongCTC,
McGEWB, McGEWD, –84, ModAL,
ModAL SUP, ModWD,
NewYTBS 82[port], NotNAT, OxAmL,
OxEng, OxThe, PenC AM, PIP&P,
RAdv 1, REn, REnAL, SixAP, TwCA,*

TwCA SUP, TwCWr, WebAB, –79, WebE&AL, WhDW, WhNAA, Who 74, –82, –83N, WhoAm 74, –76, –78, –80, –82, WhoThe 15, –16, –81, WhoWor 74, –78, –80, WorAl, WrDr 76, –80, –82

MacLennan, Hugh 1907- *Au&Wr 6, BioIn 1, –3, –4, –9, –10, –11, –12, BlueB 76, CaW, CanNov, CanWW 70, –79, –80, –81, –83, CanWr, CasWL, ConAu 5R, ConLC 2, –14, ConNov 72, –76, –82, CreCan 2, CurBio 46, EncWL, –2, IntAu&W 76, –77, –82, IntWW 77, –78, –79, –80, –81, –82, –83, LinLib L, LongCTC, McGEWB, ModCmwL, NewC, Novels, OxAmL, OxCan, OxCan SUP, PenC ENG, RAdv 1, REn, REnAL, TwCA SUP, TwCWr, WebE&AL, WhDW, WhE&EA, Who 74, –82, –83, WhoAm 74, –76, –78, –80, –82, WhoCan 73, –77, WhoWor 74, WrDr 76, –80, –82, –84*

MacLennan, Hugh *see also* MacLennan, John Hugh

MacLennan, John Hugh 1907- *CreCan 2, DcLEL 1940*

MacLennan, John Hugh *see also* MacLennan, Hugh

MacLeod, Charlotte 1922- *ConAu 21R, SmATA 28[port], WrDr 84*

MacLeod, Ellen Jane 1916- *Au&Wr 6, BioIn 12, ConAu 3NR, –5R, IntAu&W 76, –77, –82, SmATA 14, WrDr 76, –80, –82, –84*

MacLeod, Ellen Jane *see also* Anderson, Ella

MacLeod, Jean Sutherland 1908- *Au&Wr 6, ConAu 3NR, –9R, IntAu&W 76, –77, –82, WrDr 84*

MacLeod, Mary d1914 *ChhPo, –S2, –S3, WhLit*

MacManus, Yvonne 1931- *ConAu 11NR, –25R, IntAu&W 77, –82, WhoAm 76, –78, –80, –82, WhoCon 73*

Macnamara, Ellen 1924- *ConAu 103, WrDr 76, –80, –82, –84*

MacPeek, Walter G 1902-1973 *AuBYP SUP, BioIn 9, ConAu 41R, ConAu P-2, SmATA 25N, –4, WhNAA*

MacPherson, Margaret 1908- *AuBYP, BioIn 7, –11, BrCA, ConAu 49, FourBJA, SmATA 9, TwCCW 78, –83, WrDr 80, –82, –84*

MacQuitty, William *ConAu 7NR, –17R, FilmgC, IntMPA 77, –75, –76, –78, –79, –81, –82, –84*

Macrorie, Ken 1918- *ConAu 65*

MacShane, Frank 1927- *ConAu 3NR, –9R, DrAS 74E, –78E, –82E, IntAu&W 77, –82, WrDr 76, –80, –82, –84*

Macvey, John W 1923- *ConAu 7NR, –17R, IntAu&W 77, –82, ScF&FL 1A, WhoWor 76, WrDr 76, –80, –82, –84*

Madden, David 1933- *BioIn 10, ConAu 1R, –4NR, ConLC 5, –15, ConNov 76, –82,*

DcLB 6[port], DrAF 76, DrAP 75, DrAS 78E, –82E, IntAu&W 76, –77, –82, IntWWP 77, –82, LinLib L, WhoAm 76, –78, –80, –82, WrDr 76, –80, –82, –84

Maddock, Reginald 1912- *Au&Wr 6, AuBYP SUP, BioIn 12, ConAu 81, ScF&FL 1, SmATA 15, TwCCW 78*

Maddox, John Royden 1925- *BioIn 12, Who 74, –82, –83, WhoWor 74, –76, –80*

Maddux, Rachel 1912- *BioIn 11, ConAu 1R, –5NR, DrAP&F 83, EncSF, ForWC 70, ScF&FL 1, –2*

Madgett, Naomi Long 1923- *BlkAWP, BroadAu[port], ChhPo, ConAu 33R, DrAP 75, DrAP&F 83, InB&W 80, IntWWP 77, –82, LivgBAA, MichAu 80, SelBAA, WhoAm 78, –80, –82, WhoAmW 75, –77, –79, –81, WhoBlA 75, –77, –80, WrDr 76, –80, –82, –84*

Madison, Arnold 1937- *AuBYP SUP, BioIn 10, ConAu 9NR, –21R, SmATA 6*

Madison, Frank *ConAu X, IntAu&W 77X, –82X, WrDr 76, –80, –82, –84*

Madison, Frank *see also* Hutchins, Francis Gilman

Madison, Winifred *BioIn 10, ConAu 37R, SmATA 5*

Madlee, Dorothy 1917-1980 *AuBYP SUP, ConAu 10NR, –17R, ForWC 70*

Madruga, Lenor 1942- *BioIn 12, ConAu 102*

Maeterlinck, Maurice 1862-1949 *AtlBL, BbD, BiD&SB, BioIn 1, –2, –3, –4, –5, –6, –8, –9, –10, –11, –12, CasWL, ChhPo, ClDMEL, CnMD, CnThe, ConAu 104, CyWA, Dis&D, EncO&P 78, EncWL, –2[port], EncWT, EvEuW, LinLib L, –S, LongCTC, McGEWB, McGEWD, –84[port], ModFrL, ModRL, ModWD, NewC, NewEOp 71, NotNAT A, –B, ObitOF 79, OxEng, OxFr, OxThe, PenC EUR, PIP&P, RComWL, REn, REnWD, TwCA, TwCA SUP, TwCLC 3, TwCWr, WhDW, WhAm 2, WhE&EA, WhLit, WhThe, WhoLA, WhoTwCL, WorAl*

Maffei, Paolo 1926- *ConAu 108*

Magary, Alan 1944- *ConAu 8NR, –61*

Magary, Kerstin Fraser 1947- *ConAu 61*

Maggin, Elliot S 1950- *ConAu 102*

Magnusson, Magnus 1929- *BioIn 12, ConAu 105, IntAu&W 76, –77, –82, Who 82, –83, WhoWor 80, –82, WrDr 80, –82, –84*

Magruder, Jeb Stuart 1934- *BioIn 9, –10, –11, –12, ConAu 101, NewYTBE 73, PolProf NF, WhoAm 74, –76, WorAl*

Magubane, Peter 1932- *ConPhot, InB&W 80*

Mahlmann, Lewis *AuBYP SUP*

Mahoney, Irene 1921- *ConAu 61, DrAS 74E, –78E, –82E*

Mahony, Elizabeth Winthrop 1948- *BioIn 11,*

ConAu 41R, SmATA 8

Mahony, Elizabeth Winthrop *see also* Winthrop, Elizabeth

Mahovlich, Frank 1938- *BioIn 6, –8, –9, WhoHcky 73*

Maier, Paul Luther 1930- *ConAu 2NR, –5R, DrAS 74H, –78H, –82H, IntAu&W 76, –77, –82, WhoAm 82, WhoMW 74, –76, –78, –82, WrDr 76, –80, –82, –84*

Mailer, Norman 1923- *AmAu&B, AmNov, AmWr, ASpks, Au&Wr 6, AuNews 2, BioIn 1, –2, –4, –5, –6, –7, –8, –9, –10, –11, –12, BioNews 74, BlueB 76, CasWL, CelR 73, CnDAL, ConAu 9R, ConLC 1, –2, –3, –4, –5, –8, –11, –14, ConNov 72, –76, –82, CurBio 48, –70, DcLB DS3[port], –Y80A[port], –Y83A[port], –2, –16[port], DcLEL 1940, DrAF 76, DrAP&F 83, EncAB-H, EncWL, –2[port], FilmgC, IntAu&W 76, –77, IntWW 74, –75, –76, –77, –78, –79, –80, –81, –82, –83, IntWWP 77, LinLib L, –S, LongCTC, MakMC, McGEWB, ModAL, ModAL SUP, NewYTBS 82[port], Novels[port], OxAmL, OxFilm, PenC AM, PolProf J, PolProf K, PolProf NF, RAdv 1, REn, REnAL, TwCA SUP, TwCWr, WebAB, –79, WebE&AL, WhDW, Who 74, –82, –83, WhoAm 74, –76, –78, –80, –82, WhoAmJ 80, WhoE 74, WhoHol A, WhoTwCL, WhoWor 74, –78, WhoWorJ 72, –78, WorAl, WorEFlm, WrDr 76, –80, –82, –84*

Maiorano, Robert 1947- *BioIn 9, –12*

Majerus, Janet 1936- *ConAu 65*

Major, Clarence 1936- *BlkAWP, BroadAu[port], ConAu 21R, ConLC 3, –19, ConNov 82, ConP 75, –80, DrAF 76, DrAP 75, DrAP&F 83, DrAS 78E, –82E, InB&W 80, IntAu&W 82, IntWWP 77, –82, LinLib L, LivgBAA, NegAl 76, –83, SelBAA, WhoAm 76, –78, WhoBlA 75, –77, –80, WhoE 75, WorAu 1970, WrDr 76, –80, –82, –84*

Major, Kevin 1949- *ConAu 97, ConLC 26[port], SmATA 32[port], TwCCW 83, WhoAm 82*

Makeba, Miriam 1932- *AmSCAP 66, Baker 78, BiDAfM, BioIn 5, –6, –7, –8, –9, –11, ConAu 104, CurBio 65, DrBlPA, EncFCWM 69, InB&W 80, InWom, WhoBlA 75, –77, –80, WhoE 74, WorAl*

Malamud, Bernard 1914- *AmAu&B, AmWr SUP, Au&Wr 6, BioIn 5, –6, –7, –8, –9, –10, –11, –12, BlueB 76, CasWL, CelR 73, CnMWL, ConAu 5R, ConLC 1, –2, –3, –5, –8, –9, –11, –18, –27[port], ConNov 72, –76, –82, CurBio 58, –78, DcLB Y80A[port], –2, DcLEL 1940, DrAF 76, DrAP&F 83, EncWL, –2[port], IntAu&W 76, –77, –82, IntWW 74, –75,*

–76, –77, –78, –79, –80, –81, –82, –83, LinLib L, –S, ModAL, ModAL SUP, NewYTBS 80[port], –83[port], Novels[port], OxAmL, PenC AM, RAdv 1, REn, REnAL, TwCWr, WebAB, –79, WebE&AL, WhDW, Who 74, –82, –83, WhoAm 74, –76, –78, –80, –82, WhoE 74, WhoTwCL, WhoWor 78, –80, –82, WhoWorJ 72, –78, WorAl, WorAu, WrDr 76, –80, –82, –84

Malcolm X 1925-1965 *AmAu&B, BioIn 6, –7, –8, –9, –10, –11, –12, BlkAWP, CivRSt, DcAmB S7, DcAmReB, DcPol, EncAB-H, LinLib L, –S, LuthC 75, MakMC, McGEWB, NegAl 76[port], –83[port], ObitOF 79, WebAB, –79, WhAm 4, WhAmP, WorAl*

Malcolm X *see also* Little, Malcolm

Malcolmson, Anne 1910- *AnCL, AuBYP, BioIn 6, –8, –9, ChhPo S2, ConAu X, MorJA, SmATA 1*

Malcolmson, Anne *see also* VonStorch, Anne B

Male, David Arthur 1928- *ConAu 57*

Maling, Arthur 1923- *ConAu 3NR, –49, TwCCr&M 80, WrDr 82, –84*

Mallan, Lloyd 1914- *ConAu 5R*

Mallinson, Jeremy 1937- *ConAu 6NR, –57, IntAu&W 77, WrDr 76, –80, –82, –84*

Malo, John W 1911- *BioIn 9, ConAu 33R, SmATA 4*

Malocsay, Zoltan 1946- *ConAu 81*

Malone, Bill Charles 1934- *ConAu 65, DrAS 74H, –78H, –82H*

Malone, Dorothy 1925?- *BiDFilm, BioIn 10, –12, FilmgC, HolP 40, IntMPA 77, –75, –76, –78, –79, –81, –82, –84, MotPP, MovMk, WhoAm 74, WhoHol A, WorAl, WorEFlm*

Malone, Ruth 1918- *ConAu 93*

Malory, Sir Thomas 1410?-1471? *Alli, AnCL, AtlBL, BbD, BiD&SB, BioIn 2, –3, –4, –5, –6, –7, –9, –10, –11, –12, BrAu, CarSB, CasWL, Chambr 1, CrtT 1, –4, CyWA, DcBiPP, DcCathB, DcEnA, DcEnL, DcEuL, DcLEL, EvLB, LongCEL, MouLC 1, NewC, OxEng, PenC ENG, RAdv 1, RComWL, REn, SmATA 33, WebE&AL, WorAl*

Malraux, Andre 1901-1976 *Au&Wr 6, BioIn 1, –2, –3, –4, –5, –6, –7, –8, –9, –10, –11, –12, CasWL, ClDMEL, CnMD, CnMWL, ConAu 21R, –69, ConAu P-2, ConLC 1, –4, –9, –13, –15, CurBio 59, –77, –77N, CyWA, DcFM, DcPol, EncWL, –2[port], EncWT, EvEuW, HisEWW, IntAu&W 76, –77, IntWW 74, –75, –76, –77N, LinLib L, –S, LongCTC, MakMC, McGDA, McGEWB, ModFrL, ModRL, NewYTBE 72, NewYTBS 76, Novels[port], ObitOF 79, OxEng, OxFilm, OxFr, PenC EUR, REn, TwCA, TwCA SUP, TwCWr, WhDW, WhAm 7,*

Who 74, WhoAmA 78N, -80N, -82N, WhoTwCL, WhoWor 74, -76, WorAl, WorEFlm

Maltin, Leonard 1950- *ConAu 29R, WhoE 75*

Maltz, Maxwell 1899-1975 *BioIn 3, -4, -8, -10, ConAu 57, -65, WhoAm 74, -76, -78, -80, -82, WhoWor 78, -80, -82*

Malvern, Gladys d1962 *AmAu&B, AuBYP, BioIn 2, -3, -6, -7, ConAu 73, JBA 51, SmATA 23[port]*

Malzberg, Barry N 1939- *AuBYP SUP, BioIn 12, ConAu 61, ConLC 7, DcLB 8[port], EncSF, Novels, ScF&FL 1, -2, WhoE 77, WhoSciF, WrDr 84*

Manchel, Frank 1935- *AuBYP SUP, BioIn 11, ConAu 37R, DrAS 74E, -78E, -82E, IntAu&W 82, ScF&FL 1, -2, SmATA 10, WhoE 75, WrDr 76, -80, -82, -84*

Manchester, Harland 1898-1977 *BioIn 11, -12, ConAu 1R, -73, NatCAB 60[port], NewYTBS 77*

Manchester, Melissa 1951- *BioIn 10, -12, IlEncRk, RkOn 78, -84, RolSEnR 83, WhoAm 78, -80, -82, WhoAmW 81, -83, WhoRocM 82*

Manchester, William 1922- *AmAu&B, ASpks, Au&Wr 6, AuNews 1, BioIn 2, -7, -8, -9, -10, -11, -12, BlueB 76, CelR 73, ConAu 1R, -3NR, CurBio 67, DcLEL 1940, IntAu&W 76, -77, -82, IntWW 74, -75, -76, -77, -78, -79, -80, -81, -82, -83, LinLib L, Who 74, -82, -83, WhoAm 74, -76, -78, -80, -82, WhoE 74, WhoWor 74, -76, -78, -80, -82, WorAl, WorAu, WrDr 76, -80, -82, -84*

Mandel, Leon 1928- *ConAu 77, WhoWest 82, -84*

Mandel, Morris 1911- *ConAu 5R, -6NR*

Mandel, Sally Elizabeth 1944- *ConAu 102*

Mandino, Og 1923- *BioIn 10, ConAu 103, WhoAm 74, -76, -78, -80, -82, WhoWor 82*

Manes, Stephen 1949- *ConAu 97, DrAP&F 83*

Manfred, Frederick 1912- *AmAu&B, Au&Wr 6, BioIn 4, -6, -7, -10, -11, ConAu 5NR, -9R, ConNov 72, -76, -82, DcLB 6, DrAF 76, DrAP&F 83, IntAu&W 76, -77, -82, MinnWr, OxAmL, REnAL, REnAW, SmATA 30[port], TwCA SUP, WhoAm 74, -76, -78, -80, -82, WrDr 76, -80, -82, -84*

Mangione, Jerre 1909- *AmAu&B, AmNov, BioIn 1, -2, -10, -11, ConAu 13R, ConNov 72, -76, -82, CurBio 43, DrAF 76, DrAP&F 83, DrAS 74E, -78E, -82E, IntAu&W 76, REnAL, SmATA 6, WhoAm 74, -76, -78, -80, -82, WrDr 76, -80, -82, -84*

Manilow, Barry 1946- *BioIn 10, -11, -12, CurBio 78, EncPR&S 77S, IlEncRk,*

RkOn 78, -84, RolSEnR 83, WhoAm 76, -82, WhoRocM 82, WorAl

Mankiewicz, Herman J 1897-1953 *BioIn 3, -9, -11, DcAmB S5, DcFM, DcLB 26[port], FilmgC, NotNAT B, ObitOF 79, OxFilm, WhAm 3, WorEFlm*

Mankowitz, Wolf 1924- *Au&Wr 6, BioIn 4, -5, -6, -8, -10, -12, BlueB 76, ConAu 5R, -5NR, ConDr 73, -77, -82, ConNov 72, -76, -82, CurBio 56, DcLB 15[port], DcLEL 1940, FilmgC, IntAu&W 76, -77, -82, IntMPA 77, -75, -76, -78, -79, -81, -82, -84, IntWW 74, -75, -76, -77, -78, -79, -80, -81, -82, -83, LongCTC, NewC, NewYTBS 80[port], NotNAT, Novels, REn, ScF&FL 1, TwCWr, Who 74, -82, -83, WhoThe 15, -16, -81, WhoWor 74, -78, -82, WorAu, WrDr 76, -80, -82, -84*

Manley, Seon *AuBYP SUP, BioIn 12, ChlLR 3, ConAu 85, ScF&FL 1, SmATA 15*

Mann, Klaus 1906-1949 *BioIn 1, -2, -4, -11, ClDMEL, EncTR, EncWL, EncWT, LongCTC, ModGL, ObitOF 79, OxGer, ScF&FL 1, TwCA, TwCA SUP, WhAm 3, WhE&EA, WhoLA*

Mann, Marty 1904-1980 *BiDrAPA 77, BioIn 1, -2, -3, -6, -9, -12, ConAu 101, -103, CurBio 80N, InWom, NewYTBS 80[port], WhAm 7, WhoAm 74, -76, -78, -80, WhoAmW 74, -58, -61, -64, -66, -68, -70, -72, -75, -77*

Mann, Peggy *AmSCAP 66, BioIn 3, -10, CmpEPM, ConAu 10NR, -25R, DrAP&F 83, IntAu&W 77, -82, SmATA 6, WrDr 76, -80, -82, -84*

Mann, Thomas 1875-1955 *AtlBL, BioIn 1, -2, -3, -4, -5, -6, -7, -8, -9, -10, -11, -12, CasWL, ClDMEL, CmCal, CnMWL, ConAu 104, CurBio 42, -55, CyWA, Dis&D, EncTR, EncWL, -2[port], EncWT, EvEuW, LinLib L, -S, LongCTC, MakMC, McGEWB, ModGL, NewEOp 71, Novels[port], ObitOF 79, ObitT 1951, OxEng, OxGer, OxMus, PenC EUR, RComWL, REn, REnAL, ScF&FL 1, TwCA, TwCA SUP, TwCLC 2, -8[port], TwCWr, WhDW, WhAm 3, WhoTwCL, WorAl*

Mannes, Marya 1904- *AmAu&B, AmWomWr, BioIn 5, -6, -7, -9, -10, CelR 73, ConAu 1R, -3NR, ConSFA, CurBio 59, DcLEL 1940, DrAF 76, DrAP&F 83, EncSF, ForWC 70, InWom, IntAu&W 76, -77, -82, LibW, NewYTBE 71, ScF&FL 1, -2, WhoAmW 74, -61, -66, -68, -70, -72, -75, WorAu, WrDr 76, -80, -82, -84*

Manning, Rosemary 1911- *Au&Wr 6, AuBYP, BioIn 8, -10, -11, ConAu 1R, -1NR, DcLEL 1940, IntAu&W 76, -77, -82, SmATA 10, TwCCW 78, -83, WorAu,*

WrDr 76, –80, –82, –84

Manning, Rosemary *see also* Voyle, Mary

Manning-Sanders, Ruth 1895- *AuBYP SUP,*
BioIn 9, –12, ChhPo, ConAu 73,
SmATA 15, ThrBJA, TwCCW 78, –83,
WhE&EA, WrDr 80, –82, –84

Mannix, Daniel P *AuBYP SUP*

Manry, Robert 1918-1971 *BioIn 7, –8, –9,*
ConAu 29R, ConAu P-2, ObitOF 79

Mansfield, Katherine 1888-1923 *AtlBL,*
BioIn 1, –2, –3, –4, –5, –6, –7, –8, –9, –10,
–11, –12, CasWL, Chambr 3, ChhPo S1,
CnMWL, ConAu X, CyWA, DcLEL,
Dis&D, EncWL, –2, EvLB, InWom,
IntDcWB, LinLib L, LongCEL,
LongCTC, MakMC, ModBrL,
ModBrL SUP, ModCmwL, NewC,
Novels, OxEng, PenC ENG, RAdv 1,
REn, TwCA, TwCA SUP, TwCLC 2,
–8[port], TwCWr, WebE&AL, WhDW,
WhoTwCL, WorAl

Mantle, Mickey 1931- *BioIn 2, –3, –4, –5, –6,*
–7, –8, –9, –10, –11, –12, BioNews 74,
ConAu 89, CurBio 53, NewYTBS 74,
–81[port], WebAB, –79, WhoAm 74, –76,
–78, –80, –82, WhoProB 73, WorAl

Manton, Jo 1919- *AuBYP, ConAu X,*
SmATA 3

Manvell, Roger 1909- *Au&Wr 6, ConAu 1R,*
–6NR, EncSF, FilmgC, IntAu&W 76,
–77, –82, IntMPA 77, –75, –78, –79, –81,
–82, –84, OxFilm, ScF&FL 1, –2,
Who 74, –82, –83, WrDr 76, –80, –82, –84

Mao, Tse-Tung 1893-1976 *BioIn 1, –2, –3, –4,*
–5, –6, –7, –8, –9, –10, –11, –12, ConAu 69,
–73, CurBio 43, –62, –76N, DcOrL 1,
DcPol, HisEWW, IntWW 74, –75, –76,
–77N, LinLib L, –S, MakMC, McGEWB,
NewYTBE 70, –72, NewYTBS 76,
ObitOF 79, OxEng, REn, WhDW,
WhAm 6, –7, WhWW-II, WhoMilH 76,
WhoPRCh 81A, WhoSocC 78,
WhoWor 76, WorAl

Marangell, Virginia J 1924- *ConAu 93,*
IntAu&W 82

Marasco, Robert 1936?- *BioIn 8, NotNAT,*
WhoThe 15, –16, –81

March, William 1893-1954 *AmAu&B, BioIn 2,*
–3, –4, –5, –12, CnDAL, ConAmA,
ConAu X, DcAmB S5, DcLB 9[port],
LongCTC, ModAL, ObitOF 79, OxAmL,
REn, REnAL, TwCA SUP

March, William *see also* Campbell, William
Edward March

Marchand, Leslie A 1900- *ConAu 65,*
DrAS 74E, –78E, –82E, WhoAm 74, –76,
–78, –80, –82, WrDr 80, –82, –84

Marchant, Rex Alan 1933- *Au&Wr 6,*
ConAu 13R, WrDr 76, –80, –82, –84

Marckwardt, Albert H 1903-1975 *BioIn 10, –12,*
BlueB 76, ConAu 1R, –4NR, –61,
DrAS 74E, NewYTBS 75, USBiR 74,

WhAm 6, WhoAm 74

Marcus, Joe 1933- *ConAu 65*

Marcus, Rebecca B 1907- *AuBYP, BioIn 7,*
–11, ConAu 1R, –1NR, –5R, SmATA 9,
WrDr 76, –80, –82, –84

Mare, Walter DeLa 1873-1956 *Chambr 3,*
JBA 34, –51, ObitT 1951, TwCA,
TwCA SUP

Mare, Walter DeLa *see also* DeLaMare, Walter

Marek, George R 1902- *ASpks, AuBYP SUP,*
BioIn 4, –5, –10, –11, ConAu 1NR, –49,
St&PR 75, WhoAm 74, –76, –78, –80, –82,
WhoF&I 74

Marek, Kurt W 1915-1972 *AmAu&B,*
Au&Wr 6, BioIn 3, –4, –9, –10,
ConAu 33R, ConAu P-2, CurBio 57, –72,
–72N, NewYTBE 72, ObitOF 79,
REnAL, WhAm 5, WorAu

Marek, Kurt W *see also* Ceram, C W

Marger, Mary Ann 1934- *ConAu 93*

Margolies, Marjorie Sue 1942- *BioIn 10,*
ConAu 65, WhoAmW 79, –81

Margolis, Richard J 1929- *AuBYP SUP,*
BioIn 9, ChhPo S1, ConAu 29R,
SmATA 4, WhoE 75, WhoWorJ 72, –78

Marine, Gene 1926- *ConAu 65, WhoAm 74,*
–76, –78, –80, –82

Mark, Herman F 1895- *AmM&WS 73P, –76P,*
–79P, –82P, BioIn 1, –3, –5, –6, –7, –10, –12,
CurBio 61, InSci, IntWW 74, –75, –76,
–77, –78, –79, –80, –81, –82, –83,
McGMS 80[port], WhoAm 74, –76, –78,
–80

Mark, Jan 1943- *ConAu 93, IntAu&W 82,*
SmATA 22[port], TwCCW 83, WrDr 80,
–82, –84

Mark Twain 1835-1910 *CmCal, CyAL 2,*
EncO&P 78, EncSoH, HarEnUS,
PseudAu, Str&VC

Mark Twain *see also* Clemens, Samuel Langhorne

Markandaya, Kamala 1924- *Au&Wr 6,*
BioIn 6, –10, CasWL, ConAu X, –77,
ConLC 8, ConNov 72, –76, –82, DcOrL 2,
EncWL 2, IntAu&W 76, ModCmwL,
REn, WebE&AL, WhoWor 74, WorAu,
WrDr 76, –80, –82, –84

Markandaya, Kamala *see also* Taylor, Kamala
Purnaiya

Marks, Geoffrey 1906- *AuBYP SUP,*
ConAu 33R

Marks, J 1942- *ConAu X, DrAP&F 83,*
IntAu&W 77X, SmATA X

Marks, J *see also* Highwater, Jamake

Marks, James Macdonald 1921- *AuBYP SUP,*
BioIn 11, ConAu 61, IntAu&W 77, –82,
SmATA 13, WrDr 76, –80, –82, –84

Marks, Mickey Klar 1914- *AuBYP, BioIn 7,*
–8, –11, ConAu 1R, –6NR, SmATA 12

Markstein, George 1928- *Novels*

Markus, Julia 1939- *ConAu 105,*
DrAP&F 83, WrDr 84

Marley, Bob 1945-1981 *AnObit 1981[port],*

Baker 78, BioIn 10, –11, –12, ConAu X, ConLC 17, EncPR&S 77S, NewYTBS 77, –81[port], RkOn 84, RolSEnR 83, WhoRocM 82, WorAl

Marlow, David 1943- ConAu 107, WrDr 80, –82, –84

Marlowe, Christopher 1564-1593 Alli, AtlBL, BiD&SB, BioIn 1, –2, –3, –4, –5, –6, –7, –8, –9, –10, –11, –12, BrAu, BrWr 1, CasWL, Chambr 1, ChhPo, –S1, CnE&AP, CnThe, CroE&S, CrtT 1, –4, CyWA, DcBiPP, DcEnA, DcEnL, DcEuL, DcLEL, Dis&D, EncE 75, EncWT, EvLB, LinLib L, –S, LongCEL, McGEWB, McGEWD, –84[port], MouLC 1, NewC, NewEOp 71, NotNAT A, –B, OxEng, OxThe, PenC ENG, PlP&P, RComWL, REn, REnWD, WebE&AL, WhDW, WorAl

Marney, Dean 1952- ConAu 110

Marquand, J P 1893-1960 CurBio 42, –60, EncWL 2, LinLib L, ObitOF 79, WorAl

Marquand, John Phillips 1893-1960 AmAu&B, AmNov, AmWr, BioIn 1, –2, –3, –4, –5, –6, –7, –8, –9, –12, CasWL, CnDAL, ConAu 85, ConLC 2, –10, CyWA, DcAmB S6, DcLB 9[port], DcLEL, DrAF 76, EncMys, EncWL, EvLB, FilmgC, LinLib S, LongCTC, ModAL, NatCAB 47, Novels, OxAmL, PenC AM, RAdv 1, REn, REnAL, TwCA, TwCA SUP, TwCCr&M 80, TwCWr, WebAB, –79, WebE&AL, WhAm 4

Marquardt, Dorothy 1921- BiDrLUS 70, ConAu 13R, ForWC 70, WhoAmW 75, WhoLibS 66

Marquis, Arnold ConAu 57, WhoWest 78, –80, –82

Marquis, Don 1878-1937 AmAu&B, AmBi, AmLY, BiD&SB, BiDSA, BioIn 1, –4, –5, –6, –8, –10, –12, CnDAL, CnE&AP, ConAmA, ConAmL, ConAu 104, DcAmB S2, DcLB 11[port], –25[port], DcNAA, LinLib L, LongCTC, ModAL, NatCAB 30, NotNAT A, Novels, OxAmL, PenC AM, RAdv 1, REn, REnAL, ScF&FL 1, Str&VC, TwCA, TwCA SUP, TwCLC 7[port], TwCWr, WhAm 1, WhNAA, WhThe

Marrin, Albert 1936- ConAu 49

Marriott, Alice Lee 1910- AmAu&B, AnCL, AuBYP, BioIn 2, –7, –8, ConAu 57, CurBio 50, InSci, InWom, SmATA 31[port]

Marsh, Dave 1950- ConAu 97

Marsh, John 1907- Au&Wr 6, ConAu P-1, IntAu&W 76, –77, –82, ScF&FL 1, –2, WhE&EA, WhoAmL 78, –79, WhoE 74, –75, –77, WhoGov 77, –75, WrDr 76, –80, –82

Marsh, Ngaio 1899-1982 AnObit 1982[port], Au&Wr 6, AuBYP, BioIn 1, –4, –5, –7, –8,

–11, –12, BlueB 76, ConAu 6NR, –9R, ConLC 7, ConNov 72, –76, –82, CorpD, DcLEL, EncMys, EvLB, FarE&A 78, –79, –80, –81, InWom, IntAu&W 76, IntWW 74, –75, –76, –77, –78, –79, –80, –81, –82N, LongCTC, NewC, NewYTBS 82[port], Novels, OxEng, REn, TwCA, TwCA SUP, TwCCr&M 80, TwCWr, WhE&EA, Who 74, –82, –83N, WhoAmW 70, –72, –75, WhoWor 74, –82, WorAl, WrDr 76, –80, –82

Marshall, Alan 1902- Au&Wr 6, BioIn 6, –9, –12, ConAu 85, IntAu&W 76, –77, WhoWor 78, –80, –82

Marshall, Anthony Dryden 1924- BioIn 12, ConAu 29R, SmATA 18, WhoAm 74, –76, –78, WhoAmP 73, –75, –77, –79, WhoGov 77, –72, –75, WhoWor 74, –76

Marshall, Catherine 1914-1983 AmWomWr, AuBYP, BioIn 3, –4, –5, –7, –9, –11, –12, ConAu 8NR, –109, –17R, CurBio 55, –83N, LinLib L, –S, NewYTBS 83, SmATA 2, –34N, WorAl, WrDr 76, –80, –82, –84

Marshall, Edison 1894-1967 AmAu&B, AmNov, BioIn 1, –2, –3, –4, –8, ConAu 29R, ConAu P-1, EncSF, IndAu 1917, ObitOF 79, REnAL, ScF&FL 1, –2, TwCA SUP, WhAm 4, WhE&EA, WhLit, WhoHr&F

Marshall, James 1942- AuBYP SUP, BioIn 10, –12, ConAu 41R, FourBJA, IlsCB 1967, SmATA 6, TwCCW 83, WhoAm 76, –78, –80, –82

Marshall, James Vance 1887-1964 ConAu X, ConAu P-1, WrDr 76

Marshall, James Vance 1924- ConAu X, IntAu&W 76X, –77X, –82X, WrDr 82, –84

Marshall, James Vance see also Doone, Jice

Marshall, James Vance see also Payne, Donald

Marshall, John 1922- Au&Wr 6, ConAu 89, IntAu&W 77, WrDr 76, –80, –82, –84

Marshall, Mel 1912- ConAu 29R, IntAu&W 82

Marshall, Norman 1901-1980 BlueB 76, CnThe, ConAu 108, Who 74, WhoThe 15, –16, –81, WrDr 76, –80, –82, –84

Marshall, Paule 1929- AmAu&B, AmWomWr, BlkAWP, ConAu 77, ConLC 27[port], ConNov 72, –76, –82, DrAF 76, InB&W 80, IntAu&W 76, –77, LivgBAA, NegAl 76, –83, NewYTBS 83[port], SelBAA, WhoAmW 66, –68, –70, –72, WorAu 1970, WrDr 76, –80, –82, –84

Marshall, S L A 1900-1977 ConAu 73, –81, CurBio 53, –78, –78N, NewYTBS 77, ObitOF 79, SmATA 21[port]

Marshall, Samuel Lyman Atwood 1900-1977 AmAu&B, AuBYP, BioIn 3, –5, –8, –10, –11, –12, CurBio 53, WhAm 7, WhoAm 74, –76, –78, WorAu

Marshall, Shirley E 1925- *ChhPo S2,*
ConAu 21R, WhoAmW 74,
WomPO 76, –78
Martin, Albert *ConAu X*
Martin, Alfred 1916- *DrAS 74P, –78P,*
LEduc 74
Martin, Alfred Manuel 1928- *BioIn 3, –4, –5,*
–7, –8, –9, –10, –11, ConAu 108,
NewYTBS 77, WhoAm 74, –76, –78, –80,
–82, WhoProB 73
Martin, Alfred Manuel *see also* Martin, Billy
Martin, Billy 1928- *BioIn 3, –4, –5, –7, –8, –10,*
–11, –12, CmCal, ConAu X, CurBio 76,
NewYTBE 72, –73, NewYTBS 74, –75,
–77, –83[port], WorAl
Martin, Billy *see also* Martin, Alfred Manuel
Martin, Calvin 1948- *DrAS 78H, –82H*
Martin, David C 1943- *ConAu 102,*
WhoAm 82
Martin, Don 1931- *ConAu 101, WhoAm 82,*
WorECar
Martin, Donald Franklin 1944- *ConAu 65*
Martin, Dorothy 1921- *ConAu 6NR, –57*
Martin, George R R 1948- *ConAu 81, EncSF,*
WrDr 84
Martin, George Raymond Richard 1948-
WhoAm 78, –80, –82
Martin, Graham Dunstan 1932- *ConAu 106,*
IntAu&W 77, –82
Martin, John Bartlow 1915- *AmAu&B,*
Au&Wr 6, BioIn 3, –4, –7, –11, BlueB 76,
ConAu 8NR, –13R, CurBio 56,
IntAu&W 76, IntWW 74, OhA&B,
PolProf K, WhoAm 78, –80, –82
Martin, Malachi 1921- *ASpks, AuNews 1,*
BioIn 10, –11, BioNews 75, ConAu 81
Martin, Patricia Miles 1899- *AuBYP, BioIn 7,*
–9, ConAu 1R, –2NR, ForWC 70,
IntAu&W 77, SmATA 1, TwCCW 78,
–83, WhoAmW 74, –66, –68, –70, –72, –75,
WrDr 76, –80, –82, –84
Martin, Patricia Miles *see also* Miles, Miska
Martin, Ralph G 1920- *AmAu&B, ASpks,*
AuBYP, BioIn 8, –10, –11, BlueB 76,
ConAu 5R, IntAu&W 76, –77,
WhoAm 74, –76, –78, –80, –82, WhoE 74,
WhoWor 80, WrDr 76, –80, –82, –84
Martin, Robert Allen 1930- *ConAu 110,*
DrAS 78E, –82E
Martin, Vicky *BioIn 12, ConAu X,*
IntAu&W 77X, SmATA X
Martin, Vicky *see also* Storey, Victoria Carolyn
Martin, William G *AuBYP SUP*
Martindale, Andrew Henry Robert 1932-
Au&Wr 6, WrDr 76, –80, –82, –84
Martine-Barnes, Adrienne 1942- *ConAu 110*
Martinez, Al 1929- *ConAu 57*
Martini, Teri 1930- *AuBYP, BioIn 7, –9,*
ConAu 2NR, –5R, ForWC 70,
IntAu&W 76, SmATA 3, WhoAmW 74,
–66, –72, –75, WrDr 76, –80, –82, –84
Martins, Peter 1946- *BioIn 8, –10, –11, –12,*

CurBio 78, NewYTBS 75, –76, –79,
–80[port], –83[port], WhoAm 78, –80, –82
Marton, Kati Ilona 1947- *WhoAm 80*
Martyn, Norma Sydney 1927- *Au&Wr 6*
Martz, William J 1928- *ConAu 9NR, –21R,*
DrAS 74E, –78E, –82E
Marx, Groucho 1890?-1977 *AmAu&B,*
AmPS B, BiE&WWA, BioIn 1, –2, –3, –4,
–5, –6, –7, –9, –10, –11, –12, BioNews 74,
BlueB 76, CelR 73, CmCal, ConAu X,
–73, –81, CurBio 48, –73, –77, –77N,
DcFM, EncMT, FamA&A, Film 2,
IntAu&W 77, IntMPA 77, –75, –76,
IntWW 74, –75, –76, –77, –78N, LesBEnT,
MGM, MotPP, MovMk, NewYTBE 70,
–72, NewYTBS 77, NewYTET,
ObitOF 79, OxFilm, WebAB, –79,
WhDW, WhoHol A, WhoThe 81N,
WhoWor 74
Marx, Robert F 1936- *AuBYP, ConAu 6NR,*
–9R, SmATA 24[port]
Marx, Samuel 1902- *ConAu 103, IntMPA 81,*
–82, –84
Marx, Wesley 1934- *ConAu 21R,*
IntAu&W 77, –82, WhoAm 74, –76, –78,
–80, –82
Marzan, Julio 1946- *DrAP 75, IntWWP 77*
Marzani, Carl 1912- *Au&Wr 6, BioIn 1, –11,*
ConAu 61, SmATA 12, WrDr 76, –80,
–82
Marzollo, Jean 1942- *ChhPo S3, ConAu 81,*
SmATA 29[port]
Mascaro, Juan *WhE&EA*
Masefield, John 1878-1967 *AnCL, AuBYP,*
BioIn 1, –2, –3, –4, –5, –6, –7, –8, –9, –10,
–11, –12, Br&AmS, CasWL, Chambr 3,
ChhPo, –S1, –S2, –S3, CnE&AP, CnMD,
CnMWL, ConAu 25R, ConAu P-2,
ConLC 11, DcLB 10[port], –19[port],
DcLEL, EncWL, –2, EvLB, LinLib L, –S,
LongCEL, LongCTC, McGEWD,
–84[port], MnBBF, ModBrL,
ModBrL SUP, ModWD, NewC,
NotNAT B, Novels, ObitOF 79,
ObitT 1961, OxEng, OxShips, OxThe,
PenC ENG, PIP&P, RAdv 1, REn,
ScF&FL 1, SmATA 19, Str&VC, TelT,
TwCA, TwCA SUP, TwCCW 78, –83,
TwCWr, WebE&AL, WhDW, WhAm 4,
WhE&EA, WhLit, WhThe,
WhoBW&I A, WhoChL, WhoTwCL,
WorAl
Maslach, Christina 1946- *AmM&WS 73S,*
–78S, WhoAmW 83, WhoWest 84
Mason, A E W 1865-1948 *Novels, ScF&FL 1,*
TwCCr&M 80, WhoSpyF
Mason, Alpheus Thomas 1899- *AmAu&B,*
AmM&WS 73S, –78S, BlueB 76,
ConAu 1R, IntAu&W 77, –82, IntYB 78,
–79, –80, –81, –82, REnAL, WhoAm 76,
–78, –80, –82, WhoE 74, WhoWor 74
Mason, Douglas R 1918- *Au&Wr 6,*

ConAu 1NR, –49, ConSFA, EncSF, IntAu&W 76, –77, –82, ScF&FL 1, –2, WhoSciF, WhoWor 78, WrDr 76, –80, –82, –84

Mason, F VanWyck 1901-1978 *AmAu&B, AmNov, Au&Wr 6, AuBYP, BioIn 11, BlueB 76, ConAu 5R, –8NR, –81, LinLib L, –S, ObitOF 79, REnAL, SmATA 26N, –3, TwCCr&M 80, WhE&EA, WhoSpyF, WhoWor 74*

Mason, F VanWyck *see also* Coffin, Geoffrey

Mason, F VanWyck *see also* Mason, Francis VanWyck

Mason, F VanWyck *see also* Mason, Frank W

Mason, F VanWyck *see also* Mason, VanWyck

Mason, F VanWyck *see also* Weaver, Ward

Mason, Francis Scarlett, Jr. 1921- *WhoAm 82, WhoAmA 80, –82, WhoE 74, –75, –77, –79, –81, –83, WhoF&I 75, WhoWor 82*

Mason, Francis VanWyck 1901-1978 *BioIn 9, –11, WhAm 7, WhoAm 74, –76, –78*

Mason, Francis VanWyck *see also* Mason, F VanWyck

Mason, Frank W 1901-1978 *AuBYP, BioIn 1, –2, –7, –9, ConAu X, SmATA X, WhoSpyF*

Mason, Frank W *see also* Mason, F VanWyck

Mason, Herbert Molloy, Jr. 1927- *ConAu 6NR, –13R, WrDr 80, –82, –84*

Mason, Miriam Evangeline 1900-1973 *AmAu&B, AuBYP, BioIn 6, –7, –9, ConAu 1R, –103, IndAu 1917, MorJA, SmATA 2, –26N, WhAm 6, WhoAmW 74, –58, –70, –72*

Mason, Philip 1906- *Au&Wr 6, BlueB 76, ChhPo S3, ConAu 3NR, –9R, IntAu&W 76, –77, –82, IntWW 74, –75, –76, –77, –78, –79, –80, –81, –82, –83, WhE&EA, Who 74, –82, –83, WhoWor 74, –78, WrDr 76, –80, –82, –84*

Mason, VanWyck 1901-1978 *ConAu X, EncMys, ScF&FL 1, WhoAm 74, –76, –78*

Mason, VanWyck *see also* Mason, F VanWyck

Mason, Zane Allen 1919- *DrAS 74H, –78H, –82H*

Masselink, Ben 1919- *ConAu 17R*

Masselman, George 1897-1971 *BioIn 12, ConAu 9R, SmATA 19*

Massie, Robert K 1929- *ASpks, BioIn 8, –10, –11, –12, ConAu 77, NewYTBS 80[port], WhoAm 76, –78, –80, –82*

Mast, Gerald J 1940- *ConAu 69, DrAS 74E, –78E, –82E*

Masterman-Smith, Virginia 1937- *ConAu 110*

Masteroff, Joe 1919- *AmAu&B, BiE&WWA, ConDr 73, –77D, –82D, NotNAT, WhoAm 74, –76, –78, –80, –82*

Masters, Edgar Lee 1869?-1950 *AmAu&B, AmLY, AmWr SUP, AtlBL, BioIn 1, –2, –3, –4, –5, –6, –8, –9, –10, –11, –12, CasWL, Chambr 3, ChhPo, –S1, –S2, –S3, CnDAL, CnE&AP, CnMWL, ConAmA, ConAmL,*

ConAu 104, CyWA, DcAmB S4, DcLEL, EncAAH, EncWL, –2, EvLB, LinLib L, –S, LongCTC, McGEWB, ModAL, NatCAB 37, ObitOF 79, OxAmL, OxEng, PenC AM, RAdv 1, REn, REnAL, SixAP, TwCA, TwCA SUP, TwCLC 2, TwCWr, WebAB, –79, WebE&AL, WhDW, WhAm 2, –2A, WhoTwCL, WorAl

Masters, Kelly Ray 1897- *Au&Wr 6, AuBYP, BioIn 3, –7, –9, ConAu 1R, CurBio 53, SmATA 3*

Masters, Kelly Ray *see also* Ball, Zachary

Masters, Nicholas A 1929- *AmM&WS 73S, ConAu 13R*

Masterton, Graham 1946- *ConAu 105, IntAu&W 77, WrDr 80, –82, –84*

Maston, T B 1897- *ConAu 2NR, –5R*

Maston, Thomas Bufford 1897- *AmAu&B, Au&Wr 6, ConAu 5R, IntAu&W 77, –82, WhoAm 74, –76, WrDr 76, –80, –82, –84*

Matchette, Katharine E 1941- *ConAu 53*

Mather, Anne *WrDr 84*

Matheson, Richard 1926- *BioIn 12, CmMov, ConAu 97, ConSFA, DcLB 8[port], EncSF, FilmgC, NewYTET, Novels, ScF&FL 1, –2, WhoHr&F, WhoSciF, WorEFlm, WrDr 84*

Mathews, Mitford McLeod, Sr. 1891- *AmAu&B*

Mathewson, Christopher 1880-1925 *BioIn 1, –2, –3, –4, –5, –6, –7, –8, –9, –10, –11, –12, DcAmB, DcNAA, Dis&D, WebAB, –79, WhAm HSA, –4, WhoProB 73*

Mathewson, Christopher *see also* Mathewson, Christy

Mathewson, Christy 1880-1925 *OxAmH, WhScrn 2, WorAl*

Mathewson, Christy *see also* Mathewson, Christopher

Mathiessen, Peter 1927- *IntAu&W 76*

Mathis, Sharon Bell 1937- *AuBYP SUP, BioIn 10, BlkAWP, ChlLR 3, ConAu 41R, DrAF 76, DrAP 75, DrAP&F 83, FourBJA, InB&W 80, LivgBAA, SelBAA, SmATA 7, TwCCW 78, –83, WhoAm 74, –76, –78, –80, –82, WhoAmW 74, WhoBlA 75, –77, –80, WrDr 76, –80, –82, –84*

Matson, Emerson N 1926- *BioIn 11, ConAu 45, IntAu&W 76, SmATA 12, WhoAdv 80, WrDr 76, –80, –82, –84*

Matthew, Eunice Sophia 1916- *AuBYP, BioIn 8, WhoAmW 66, –68*

Matthews, Herbert Lionel 1900-1977 *AmAu&B, Au&Wr 6, AuBYP, BioIn 1, –4, –8, –9, –10, –11, BlueB 76, ConAu 1R, –2NR, –73, CurBio 43, –77, –77N, IntAu&W 77, IntWW 74, –75, –76, –77, –78N, ObitOF 79, REnAL, WhAm 7, WhoAm 74, –76, –78, WhoWor 74, WrDr 80, –82, –84*

Matthews, L Harrison 1901- *WrDr 82*
Matthews, Patricia 1927- *BioIn 11,*
ConAu 9NR, –29R, –69, SmATA 28[port],
WhoAmW 79, WrDr 84
Matthews, Patricia *see also* Brisco, Patty
Matthews, William 1942- *BioIn 12, ConP 80,*
DcLB 5[port], IntAu&W 82, IntWWP 82,
WrDr 82, –84
Matthews, William Henry, III 1919-
AmM&WS 82P, AuBYP SUP,
ConAu 9R, SmATA 28
Matthiessen, Peter 1927- *AmAu&B,*
Au&Wr 6, BioIn 6, –9, –10, BlueB 76,
ConAu 9R, ConLC 5, –7, –11, ConNov 72,
–76, –82, CurBio 75, DcLB 6[port],
DcLEL 1940, DrAF 76, IntAu&W 77,
SmATA 27[port], WhoAm 74, –76, –78,
–80, –82, WhoWor 74, WorAu, WrDr 76,
–80, –82, –84
Maugham, Robert Cecil Romer 1916-1981 *Alli,*
BioIn 4, –9, –10, –12, BlueB 76,
ConAu 9R, –103, DcLEL 1940,
NewYTBS 81, TwCA SUP, Who 74
Maugham, Robert Cecil Romer *see also*
Maugham, Robin
Maugham, Robin 1916-1981 *AnObit 1981[port],*
Au&Wr 6, BioIn 4, –9, –10, –12,
BlueB 76, ConAu X, ConNov 72, –76,
DcLEL 1940, IntAu&W 76, –77, –82,
LongCTC, NewC, NewYTBS 81, Novels,
REn, ScF&FL 1, –2, TwCCr&M 80,
WorAu 1970, WrDr 76, –80, –82
Maugham, Robin *see also* Maugham, Robert
Cecil Romer
Maugham, W Somerset 1874-1965 *BrWr 6,*
ConAu 25R, ConLC 11, –15,
DcLB 10[port], EncE 75, EncWL 2,
FilmgC, LinLib L, McGEWD 84[port],
Novels[port], ObitOF 79, ScF&FL 1, –2,
TwCCr&M 80, WhAm 4, WhScrn 2,
WhoSpyF, WorAl
Maugham, William Somerset 1874-1965 *Alli,*
AtlBL, BiE&WWA, BiHiMed, BioIn 1,
–2, –3, –4, –5, –6, –7, –8, –9, –10, –11, –12,
CasWL, Chambr 3, CnMD, CnMWL,
CnThe, ConAu 5R, ConLC 1, CyWA,
DcBiA, DcLEL, Dis&D, EncMys,
EncWL, EncWT, EvLB, FilmgC,
LinLib S, LongCEL, LongCTC, MakMC,
McGEWB, McGEWD, ModBrL,
ModBrL SUP, ModWD, NewC,
NotNAT A, –B, OxEng, OxThe,
PenC ENG, PIP&P, RAdv 1, REn,
REnWD, TwCA, TwCA SUP, TwCWr,
WebE&AL, WhE&EA, WhLit,
WhScrn 2, WhThe, WhoTwCL
Mauldin, Bill 1921- *BioIn 7, –9, –10, –11,*
CelR 73, CurBio 45, –64, OxAmL,
REnAL, WhoAmA 73, –76, –78, –80, –82,
WhoHol A
Mauldin, Bill *see also* Mauldin, William H
Mauldin, William H 1921- *AmAu&B, BioIn 1,*

–2, –3, –4, –5, –6, –7, –9, –10, –11,
CurBio 45, –64, TwCA SUP, WebAB, –79,
WebAMB, WhoAm 76, –78, –80, –82,
WhoMW 74, –76, –78, –80, –82,
WhoWor 74, –76, WorECar
Mauldin, William H *see also* Mauldin, Bill
Maule, Hamilton Bee 1915- *AuBYP, BioIn 7,*
–9, –10, ConAu 1R, –3NR, WhoAm 74,
–76, –78, –80, –82
Maule, Hamilton Bee *see also* Maule, Tex
Maule, Henry Ramsay 1915- *Au&Wr 6,*
IntAu&W 77
Maule, Tex 1915- *BioIn 7, –9, –10, ConAu X*
Maule, Tex *see also* Maule, Hamilton Bee
Maupassant, Guy De 1850-1893 *AtlBL,*
BiD&SB, BioIn 1, –2, –3, –4, –5, –7, –8, –9,
–10, –12, CIDMEL, CyWA, DcEuL,
Dis&D, EncWT, EuAu, LinLib L,
NewC, NewEOp 71, Novels[port], OxEng,
OxFr, PenC EUR, RComWL, REn,
ScF&FL 1, WhDW, WhoHr&F, WorAl
Maupassant, Guy De *see also* DeMaupassant,
Guy
Maureen, Sister Mary 1924- *ConAu 21R*
Maurier, Daphne Du 1907- *CurBio 40,*
InWom, LongCTC, ScF&FL 1, TwCA,
TwCA SUP, WhLit
Maurier, Daphne Du *see also* DuMaurier,
Daphne
Maxey, Dale 1927- *ChhPo S1, IlsCB 1957,*
WhoRel 75
Maxon, Anne 1892-1974 *BioIn 2, –5, –7, –9,*
ConAu X, SmATA X
Maxon, Anne *see also* Best, Allena Champlin
Maxwell, Ann 1944- *ConAu 105*
Maxwell, Edith 1923- *AuBYP SUP, BioIn 10,*
ConAu 49, IntAu&W 77, SmATA 7,
WhoAmW 77
Maxwell, Gavin 1914-1969 *AuBYP, BioIn 7,*
–8, –9, –10, ConAu 5R, –25R,
DcLEL 1940, LongCTC, NewC,
ObitOF 79, TwCWr, WhAm 5, WorAu
Maxwell, William 1908- *AmAu&B, AmNov,*
AuBYP, BioIn 2, –4, –7, –12, ConAu 93,
ConLC 19, ConNov 72, –76, –82,
DcLB Y80B, IntAu&W 76, –77, OxAmL,
REn, TwCA SUP, WhoAm 74, –76, –78,
–80, –82, WhoWor 74, WrDr 76, –80, –82,
–84
May, Charles Paul 1920- *AuBYP, BioIn 7, –8,*
–9, ConAu 1R, –5NR, IntAu&W 76, –77,
–82, SmATA 4
May, Julian 1931- *AuBYP, BioIn 11,*
ConAu 1R, –6NR, SmATA 11
May, Rollo 1909- *AmAu&B, BioIn 8, –9, –10,*
BioNews 74, CelR 73, CurBio 73,
NewYTBE 71, WhoAm 74, –76, –78, –80,
–82, WhoE 74
May, Wynne *IntAu&W 82X, WrDr 84*
Mayall, R Newton 1904- *ConAu P-1*
Maybury, Anne *WrDr 84*

Mayer, Albert Ignatius, Jr. 1906-1960
  ConAu 109, OhA&B, SmATA 29N
Mayer, Debby 1946- *ConAu X, DrAP&F 83*
Mayer, Jean 1920- *AmM&WS 73P, -76P,
  -79P, -82P, BioIn 8, -9, -10, -11, -12,
  CurBio 70, IntMed 80, NewYTBS 76,
  WhoAm 74, -76, -78, -80, -82,
  WhoAmP 73, -75, -77, -79, -81, -83,
  WhoAmW 70, WhoE 74, WhoWor 74,
  -76*
Mayer, Joseph 1887-1975 *AmM&WS 73S,
  WhAm 6, WhE&EA, WhNAA,
  WhoAm 74*
Mayer, Marianna 1945- *BioIn 12, ConAu 93,
  FourBJA, SmATA 32[port]*
Mayer, Martin Prager 1928- *AmAu&B,
  Au&Wr 6, BioIn 3, -6, -8, -10,
  ConAu 5R, IntAu&W 76, -77,
  WhoAm 74, -76, -78, -80, -82, WorAu*
Mayer, Mercer 1943- *BioIn 12, ChhPo S3,
  ConAu 85, FourBJA, IlsBYP, IlsCB 1967,
  SmATA 16, -32[port]*
Mayerson, Charlotte Leon *ConAu 13R,
  ForWC 70, SmATA 36, WhoAmW 68*
Mayerson, Evelyn Wilde 1935- *ConAu 101*
Mayhar, Ardath 1930- *ConAu 103,
  IntWWP 77, WrDr 76*
Maynard, Joyce 1953- *BioIn 9, -10,
  ConLC 23[port], NewYTBE 72*
Maynard, Olga 1920- *WhoAmW 77, -79, -81*
Maynard, Richard Allen 1942- *ConAu 33R*
Mayne, William 1928- *AnCL, AuBYP,
  BioIn 6, -7, -8, -9, -10, ConAu 9R,
  ConLC 12, DcLEL 1940, IntAu&W 82,
  ScF&FL 1, -2, SenS, SmATA 6,
  ThrBJA, TwCCW 78, -83, Who 82, -83,
  WhoAm 74, -76, -78, -80, -82, WhoChL,
  WhoWor 74, WrDr 76, -80, -82, -84*
Mayo, Margaret 1935- *ConAu 107*
Mays, Buddy 1943- *ConAu 73*
Mays, Lucinda L 1924- *ConAu 101*
Mays, Victor 1927- *BioIn 10, ConAu 25R,
  FourBJA, SmATA 5,
  WhoAmA 78, -80, -82*
Mays, Willie 1931- *BioIn 2, -3, -4, -5, -6, -7,
  -8, -9, -10, -11, -12, BioNews 74,
  BlkAWP, CelR 73, CmCal, ConAu 105,
  CurBio 55, -66, Ebony 1, LinLib S,
  NegAl 76[port], -83[port], NewYTBE 70,
  -73, NewYTBS 74, -79, WebAB, -79,
  WhoAm 74, -76, -78, -80, WhoBlA 75, -77,
  -80, WhoProB 73, WorAl*
Mazer, Harry 1925- *ConAu 97,
  SmATA 31[port]*
Mazer, Norma Fox 1931- *ConAu 69,
  ConLC 26[port], DrAP&F 83,
  SmATA 24[port]*
Mazo, Joseph H 1938- *ConAu 69*
Mazzeo, Henry *ScF&FL 1*
McAleavy, Henry 1912-1968 *ConAu P-2*
McBain, Gordon D, III 1946- *ConAu 106*

McBain, William Norseworthy 1918-
  AmM&WS 73S, -78S
McBeath, Marcia 1925- *WhoAmW 72,
  WhoWest 78*
McBride, Chris 1941?- *BioIn 11, ConAu 81*
McBurney, Laressa Cox 1883- *IntWWP 77,
  WhNAA*
McCabe, John C, III 1920- *ConAu 1R, -1NR,
  DrAS 74E, -78E, -82E, IntAu&W 76, -77,
  -82, WhoAm 74, -76, -78, -80, -82,
  WhoMW 74, -76, -78, WhoWor 78,
  WrDr 76, -80, -82, -84*
McCabe, Joseph E 1912- *BlueB 76,
  ConAu 17R, IntAu&W 76, -77,
  LEduc 74, WhoAm 74, -76, -78,
  WhoMW 74, -76, -78*
McCaffrey, Anne 1926- *AmWomWr,
  AuNews 2, BioIn 10, -11, -12,
  ConAu 25R, ConLC 17, ConSFA,
  DcLB 8[port], EncSF, IntAu&W 77, -82,
  LinLib L, ScF&FL 1, -2, SmATA 8,
  WhoAm 74, -76, -78, -80, -82,
  WhoAmW 74, WhoSciF, WrDr 76, -80,
  -82, -84*
McCague, James 1909-1977 *ConAu 1R, -2NR*
McCaleb, Walter Flavius 1873-1967 *AmAu&B,
  ConAu P-1, OhA&B, TexWr, WhAm 5,
  WhE&EA*
McCall, Dan Elliott 1940- *BioIn 8, -10,
  DrAF 76, DrAS 74E*
McCall, Daniel Francis 1918- *AmM&WS 73S,
  -76P, ConAu 17R, FifIDA*
McCall, Virginia Nielsen 1909- *AuBYP SUP,
  BioIn 11, ConAu 1R, -1NR, ForWC 70,
  SmATA 13, WhoAmW 74, -68, -70, -72,
  -75*
McCallum, John D 1924- *ConAu 4NR, -53,
  IntAu&W 77*
McCammon, Robert R 1952- *ConAu 81*
McCannon, Dindga *AfroAA*
McCarry, Charles 1930- *ConAu 103,
  DrAP&F 83, Novels, TwCCr&M 80,
  WhoSpyF, WrDr 80, -82, -84*
McCarter, Neely Dixon 1929- *ConAu 109,
  WhoRel 75, -77*
McCarthy, Agnes 1933- *BioIn 9, ConAu 5R,
  -17R, SmATA 10, -4, WhoAmW 74, -68,
  -75, -77*
McCarthy, Eugene J 1916- *AmAu&B,
  AmCath 80, BiDrAC, BioIn 3, -4, -5, -6,
  -8, -9, -10, -11, -12, BlueB 76, ConAu 1R,
  -2NR, CurBio 55, DcPol, EncAB-H,
  IntAu&W 77, IntWW 74, -75, -76, -77,
  -78, -79, -80, -81, -82, -83, IntYB 78, -79,
  -80, -81, -82, McGEWB, MinnWr,
  NewYTBE 71, PolProf E, PolProf J,
  PolProf K, PolProf NF, WebAB, -79,
  Who 74, -82, -83, WhoAm 74, -76, -78,
  -80, -82, WhoAmP 73, -75, -77, -79, -81,
  -83, WhoWor 74, -78, -80, -82, WorAl,
  WrDr 76, -80, -82, -84*
McCarthy, Joe 1915-1980 *ConAu X, -1R, -97*

McCarthy, Mary 1912- *AmAu&B,*
AmWomWr, AmWr, ASpks, Au&Wr 6,
BiE&WWA, BioIn 3, -4, -6, -7, -8, -9, -10,
-11, -12, BlueB 76, CasWL, CelR 73,
ConAu 5R, ConLC 1, -3, -5, -14, -24[port],
ConLCrt, -82, ConNov 72, -76, -82,
CurBio 55, -69, DcLB Y81A[port], -2,
DcLEL 1940, DrAF 76, DrAP&F 83,
EncWL, -2, GoodHs, InWom,
IntAu&W 76, -77, -82, IntDcWB,
IntWW 74, -75, -76, -77, -78, -79, -80, -81,
-82, -83, LibW, LongCTC, MakMC,
ModAL, ModAL SUP, NewYTBS 79,
NotNAT, Novels[port], OxAmL,
PenC AM, PolProf J, RAdv 1, REn,
REnAL, TwCA SUP, TwCWr, WebAB,
-79, WebE&AL, Who 74, -82, -83,
WhoAm 74, -76, -78, -80, -82,
WhoAmW 74, -58, -64, -66, -68, -70, -72,
WhoTwCL, WhoWor 74, -80, -82, WorAl,
WrDr 76, -80, -82, -84

McCartney, Linda 1941?- *BioIn 9, -10, -11,*
WhoRocM 82

McCartney, Paul 1942- *BioIn 6, -7, -8, -9, -10,*
-11, -12, BioNews 74, BlueB 76,
CelR 73, CurBio 66, EncPR&S, -77,
IlEncRk, IntWW 74, -75, -76, -77, -78,
-79, -80, -81, -82, -83, IntWWM 77,
MotPP, RkOn 78, -84, RolSEnR 83,
Who 82, -83, WhoHol A, WhoRocM 82,
WhoWor 78, -80, -82, WorAl

McCartney, Paul *see also* Beatles, The

McCartney, Paul *see also* Wings

McCaslin, Nellie 1914- *ConAu 33R,*
DrAS 74E, -78E, -82E, IntAu&W 77, -82,
SmATA 12, WhoAmW 74, -70, -72, -75,
-77, WrDr 76, -80, -82, -84

McClary, Jane Stevenson 1919- *ConAu 1R,*
-1NR, ForWC 70, WhoAmW 66, -68,
-75, -77

McClary, Jane Stevenson *see also* McIlvaine,
Jane

McClean, Don 1945- *EncPR&S, IlEncRk*

McClendon, Sarah 1910?- *BioIn 4, -6, -10, -11,*
-12, CelR 73, ConAu 73, InWom,
WhoAm 76, -78, -80, -82, WhoAmW 79,
-81, -83

McClory, Robert Joseph 1932- *ConAu 77*

McCloskey, William B, Jr. 1928- *ConAu 101*

McClung, Robert M 1916- *AuBYP,*
AuNews 2, BioIn 6, -7, -8, -9, -11, -12,
ConAu 6NR, -13R, IlsCB 1957, -1967,
MorJA, SmATA 2, WhoE 75, -77,
WrDr 76, -80, -82, -84

McClure, Arthur F, II 1936- *ConAu 10NR,*
-65, DrAS 74H, -78H, -82H

McConnell, Frank DeMay 1942- *ConAu 104,*
DrAS 74E, -78E, -82E

McConnell, James Douglas R 1915-
ConAu 6NR, -9R, EncMys, WrDr 76

McConnell, James Douglas R *see also*
Rutherford, Douglas

McCord, David 1897- *AmAu&B, AnCL,*
BioIn 6, -9, -11, -12, BkCL, BkP, ChhPo,
-S1, -S2, -S3, ConAu 73, OxAmL,
REnAL, SmATA 18, Str&VC, ThrBJA,
TwCCW 78, -83, WhE&EA, WhNAA,
WhoAm 74, -76, -78, -80, -82,
WhoWor 74, -76, -78, -80, -82, WrDr 80,
-82, -84

McCord, Jean 1924- *ConAu 49,*
SmATA 34[port]

McCormick, Donald 1911- *BioIn 12,*
ConAu 9R, -73, IntAu&W 76X, -77X,
-82X, SmATA 14, WrDr 76, -80, -82,
-84

McCormick, Jack 1929-1979 *AmM&WS 73P,*
-76P, -79P, ConAu 5NR, -9R, -85,
IndAu 1917, WrDr 76, -80, -82, -84

McCormick, Mona *ConAu 77, WhoLibI 82*

McCoy, Iola Fuller 1906- *BiDrLUS 70,*
ConAu 13R, InWom, MichAu 80,
SmATA 3

McCoy, Iola Fuller *see also* Fuller, Iola

McCoy, Jerome J 1917- *AuBYP, BioIn 8, -11,*
ConAu 6NR, -13R, SmATA 8

McCoy, Kathy 1945- *ConAu X*

McCracken, Harold 1894- *AmAu&B, AuBYP,*
BioIn 2, -7, -8, ConAu 107, CurBio 49,
JBA 51, WhoAm 74, -76, -78, -80, -82,
WhoAmA 73, -76, -78, -80, -82,
WhoWest 76, WhoWor 78

McCrackin, Mark 1949- *ConAu 107*

McCready, Albert Lee 1918- *WhoAm 74, -76,*
-78, -80, -82, WhoWest 82

McCullers, Carson 1917-1967 *AmAu&B,*
AmNov, AmWomWr, AmWr,
BiE&WWA, BioIn 2, -4, -5, -6, -7, -8, -9,
-10, -11, -12, CasWL, CnDAL, CnMD,
CnMWL, ConAu 5R, -25R, ConLC 1, -4,
-10, -12, ConNov 76, -82A, CurBio 40,
-67, CyWA, DcLB 2, -7[port],
DcLEL 1940, EncSoH, EncWL, -2,
EncWT, FilmgC, GoodHs, InWom,
IntDcWB, LibW, LinLib L, LongCTC,
McGEWD, -84[port], ModAL,
ModAL SUP, ModWD, NotAW MOD,
NotNAT B, Novels[port], ObitOF 79,
ObitT 1961, OxAmL, PenC AM, PIP&P,
RAdv 1, REn, REnAL, SmATA 27[port],
TwCA, TwCA SUP, TwCWr, WebAB,
-79, WebE&AL, WhDW, WhAm 4,
WhoAmW 64, -66, -68, -70, WhoTwCL,
WorAl

McCullough, Colleen 1937?- *BioIn 11, -12,*
ConAu 81, ConLC 27[port],
CurBio 82[port], NewYTBS 81[port],
WorAl

McCullough, David 1933- *BioIn 11, -12,*
ConAu 2NR, -49, NewYTBS 77,
WhoAm 80, -82, WhoE 81

McCullough, David William 1945-
WhoAmA 78, -80, -82

McDermott, Gerald 1941- *AuNews 2,*

BioIn 10, –11, –12, ConAu 85, IlsBYP, IlsCB 1967, NewbC 1966, SmATA 16, WhoAm 76, –78, WhoAmA 80, –82

McDonagh, Don 1932- *ConAu 1NR, –49, IntAu&W 77X, –82X*

McDonald, Elvin 1937- *ConAu 5R, –8NR*

McDonald, Forrest 1927- *AuBYP SUP, ConAu 5NR, –9R, DcLB 17[port], DrAS 74H, –78H, –82H, IntAu&W 77, –82, WrDr 76, –80, –82, –84*

McDonald, Gerald D 1905-1970 *BiDrLUS 70, BioIn 1, –6, –8, –9, ChhPo, ConAu P-1, OhA&B, SmATA 3, WhoLibS 55, –66*

McDonald, Gregory 1937- *BlueB 76, ConAu 3NR, –5R, TwCCr&M 80, WhoAm 82, WrDr 82, –84*

McDonald, Lucile Saunders 1898- *AuBYP, BioIn 7, –10, –11, ConAu 1R, –4NR, ForWC 70, InWom, IntAu&W 76, –77, –82, SmATA 10, WhoAmW 74, –58, –61, –64, –66, –68, –70, –72, –75, –77, –79, –81, WhoPNW*

McDonnell, Virginia Bleecker 1917- *AuBYP SUP, ConAu 8NR, –21R, IntAu&W 76, WhoAmW 75, –77, –79, –81, –83, WhoE 75, –77, –79, –83*

McDougald, Gilbert James 1928- *BioIn 2, –3, –4, –5, St&PR 75, WhoProB 73*

McDowell, Bart 1923- *ConAu 25R*

McDowell, Margaret B 1923- *ConAu 69*

McDowell, Michael 1950- *ConAu 93, WrDr 84*

McElfresh, Adeline 1918- *ConAu 1R, WhoAmW 58, –61, WrDr 84*

McEntee, Howard Garrett 1905- *AuBYP SUP*

McFadden, Dorothy Loa 1902- *AuBYP, BioIn 8, ConAu 17R, InWom, WhoAmW 58, –61*

McFall, Christie 1918- *BioIn 11, ConAu 5R, SmATA 12*

McFarland, Kenton D 1920- *AuBYP SUP, BioIn 11, ConAu 61, ODwPR 79, SmATA 11*

McFarlane, Milton *BlkAWP*

McGahern, John 1934- *Au&Wr 6, ConAu 17R, ConLC 5, –9, ConNov 72, –76, –82, DcIrL, DcLB 14[port], DcLEL 1940, IntAu&W 76, –77, –82, ModBrL SUP, Who 82, –83, WrDr 76, –80, –82, –84*

McGarrity, Mark 1943- *ConAu 1NR, –45*

McGee, Dorothy Horton 1913- *AuBYP, BioIn 7, WhoAmW 74, –58, –61, –64, –66, –68, –70, –72, –75, –77, –79, –81, –83, WhoE 74, –75, –77, –79, –81, –83*

McGill, Ormond 1913- *ConAu 2NR, –49*

McGinley, Phyllis 1905-1978 *AmAu&B, AmCath 80, AmWomWr, Au&Wr 6, AuBYP, BioIn 1, –2, –3, –4, –5, –6, –7, –8, –9, –10, –11, BlueB 76, BkP, CelR 73, ChhPo, –S1, –S2, –S3, CnE&AP, CnMWL, ConAu 9R, –77, ConLC 14, ConP 70, –75,*

CurBio 41, –61, –78, –78N, DcLB 11[port], EvLB, InWom, IntAu&W 77, IntWW 74, –75, –76, –77, –78N, IntWWP 77, JBA 51, LibW, LinLib L, LongCTC, ModAL, NewYTBS 78, ObitOF 79, OxAmL, PenC AM, RAdv 1, REn, REnAL, SmATA 2, –24N, TwCA SUP, TwCCW 78, –83, TwCWr, WhAm 7, WhoAm 74, –76, –78, WhoAmW 74, –58, –61, –64, –66, –68, –70, –72, –75, –77, WhoTwCL, WhoWor 74, WorAl, WrDr 76

McGinnis, Duane 1938- *ConAu 41R*

McGinnis, Duane *see also* Niatum, Duane

McGinniss, Joe 1942- *AmAu&B, AuNews 2, BioIn 9, –12, ConAu 25R, NewYTBS 80[port], WhoAm 82, WrDr 76, –80, –82, –84*

McGivern, Maureen Daly 1921- *ConAu 9R*

McGivern, Maureen Daly *see also* Daly, Maureen

McGivern, William P 1922?-1982 *AmAu&B, AnObit 1982[port], BioIn 10, –11, ConAu 7NR, –108, –49, EncMys, EncSF, LinLib L, NewYTBS 82, Novels, TwCCr&M 80, WhoAm 80, –82, WhoWor 80, –82, WorAu, WrDr 82*

McGough, Elizabeth 1934- *ConAu 107, SmATA 33[port]*

McGovern, Ann *AuBYP, BioIn 7, –9, –11, BkP, ConAu 2NR, –49, FourBJA, IntAu&W 77, –82, SmATA 8*

McGowen, Thomas 1927- *AuBYP SUP, BioIn 9, ConAu 8NR, –21R, SmATA 2*

McGowen, Tom 1927- *ConAu X, ScF&FL 1, –2, SmATA 2*

McGrady, Mike 1933- *BioIn 10, ConAu 2NR, –49, SmATA 6*

McGraw, Eloise Jarvis 1915- *AmAu&B, AuBYP, BioIn 3, –4, –6, –7, –9, ConAu 4NR, –5R, CurBio 55, InWom, IntAu&W 82, MorJA, SmATA 1, TwCCW 78, –83, WhoAmW 58, –61, WhoPNW, WrDr 80, –82, –84*

McGraw, Tug 1944- *BioIn 10, –12, NewYTBE 70, –72, –73, NewYTBS 76, –80[port], WorAl*

McGregor, Craig 1933- *Au&Wr 6, BioIn 11, ConAu 21R, SmATA 8*

McGuire, Edna 1899- *AuBYP, BioIn 8, –11, ConAu 2NR, –5R, SmATA 13*

McHale, Tom 1941-1982 *AuNews 1, BioIn 10, –11, –12, ConAu 106, –77, ConLC 3, –5, ConNov 72, –76, –82, DrAF 76, IntAu&W 76, –77, WrDr 76, –80, –82*

McHargue, Georgess 1941- *AuBYP SUP, BioIn 9, ChlLR 2, ConAu 25R, ScF&FL 1, –1A, –2, SmATA 4*

McHargue, Georgess *see also* Chase, Alice Elizabeth

McIlvaine, Jane 1919- *AuBYP, BioIn 7, ConAu X*

McIlvaine, Jane *see also* McClary, Jane
Stevenson
McIlwraith, Maureen Mollie Hunter 1922-
*Au&Wr 6, BioIn 9, -11, -12, ConAu 29R,
IntAu&W 77, ScF&FL 1, SmATA 2,
ThrBJA, WrDr 76, -80*
McIlwraith, Maureen Mollie Hunter *see also*
Hunter, Moll
McInerny, Ralph Matthew 1929- *AmCath 80,
ConAu 21R, DrAS 74P, -78P, -82P,
WhoAm 76, -78, -80, -82, WhoWor 82,
WrDr 76, -80, -82, -84*
McIntosh, Clarence Fredric 1922- *DrAS 74H,
-78H, -82H*
McIntyre, Vonda N 1948- *ConAu 81,
ConLC 18, EncSF, IntAu&W 82,
WhoAm 80, -82, WhoSciF, WrDr 84*
McKay, Claude 1890-1948 *AmAu&B, BioIn 1,
-2, -4, -6, -7, -8, -9, -10, -11, -12,
BlkAWP, BroadAu, CasWL, CathA 1930,
ChhPo S2, ConAmA, ConAu 104,
DcAfL, DcAmB S4, DcCathB, DcLB 4,
DcLEL, DcNAA, EncWL 2, InB&W 80,
LinLib L, McGEWB, ModBlW,
NegAl 76, -83, Novels, ObitOF 79,
OxAmL, REn, REnAL, SelBAA, TwCA,
TwCA SUP, TwCLC 7[port], WebAB,
-79, WebE&AL, WhAm 2, -5*
McKay, Don *BioIn 1*
McKay, Don 1932- *ConAu 33R*
McKay, Ernest A 1918- *ConAu 21R,
DrAS 74H, -78H, -82H, WhoE 74*
McKay, Robert W 1921- *AuBYP SUP,
BioIn 12, ConAu 10NR, -13R,
SmATA 15*
McKee, Alexander 1918- *Au&Wr 6,
ConAu 9R, -11NR*
McKendrick, Melveena 1941- *ConAu 93,
WhoWor 78*
McKenna, Richard 1913-1964 *BioIn 7,
ConAu 5R, EncSF, ObitOF 79,
ScF&FL 1, -2, WhoSciF*
McKenney, Kenneth 1929- *Au&Wr 6,
ConAu 69, WhoWor 76, WrDr 76, -80,
-82, -84*
McKenney, Ruth 1911-1972 *AmAu&B,
AmWomWr, BioIn 1, -2, -3, -4, -9,
ConAu 37R, -93, CurBio 42, -72, -72N,
InWom, LongCTC, NewYTBE 72,
NotNAT B, ObitOF 79, OhA&B,
OxAmL, REn, REnAL, TwCA,
TwCA SUP, WhAm 5, WhoAmW 61,
-64, -66, -68, -70, -72*
McKern, Sharon S 1941- *ConAu 37R*
McKillip, Patricia A 1948- *AuBYP SUP,
ConAu 4NR, -49, EncSF, ScF&FL 1, -2,
SmATA 30[port]*
McKinley, Robin 1952- *ConAu 107,
SmATA 32*
McKinney, Roland Joseph 1898- *AuBYP,
BioIn 7*
McKown, Harry Charles 1892-1963 *BiDAmEd,

BioIn 6, -9, NatCAB 52, ObitOF 79,
WhAm 4, WhE&EA*
McKown, Robin 1907?-1976 *Au&Wr 6,
AuBYP, BioIn 7, -9, -10, ConAu 1R,
-1NR, InWom, SmATA 6, ThrBJA,
WhoE 75*
McKuen, Rod 1933- *AmAu&B, AmSCAP 66,
AuNews 1, Baker 78, BiDAmM, BioIn 8,
-9, -10, -11, BioNews 74, BlueB 76,
CelR 73, CmCal, ConAmC, ConAu 41R,
ConLC 1, -3, ConP 70, CurBio 70,
EncFCWM 69, IntAu&W 77, -82,
IntWW 74, -75, -76, -77, -78, -79, -80, -81,
-82, -83, IntWWP 77, LinLib L,
NewYTBE 71, WebAB, -79, Who 82, -83,
WhoAm 74, -76, -78, -80, -82, WhoE 74,
WhoHol A, WhoWest 74, -76, -78,
WhoWor 78, WorAl, WrDr 76, -80, -82,
-84*
McLanathan, Richard 1916- *AuBYP SUP,
ConAu 81, IntAu&W 82, WhoAm 74,
-76, -78, -80, -82, WhoAmA 73, -76, -78,
-80, -82, WhoWor 74, -76, -78*
McLaughlin, Lorrie Bell 1924-1971 *ConAu 5R,
-5NR, TwCCW 78*
McLaughlin, Terence Patrick 1928- *Au&Wr 6,
ConAu 33R, IntAu&W 82, WrDr 76, -80,
-82, -84*
McLean, Allan Campbell 1922- *Au&Wr 6,
BioIn 11, BrCA, ConAu 1R, -4NR,
FourBJA, IntAu&W 77, TwCCW 78, -83,
WrDr 76, -80, -82, -84*
McLean, Don 1945- *AmCath 80, BiDAmM,
BioIn 9, -10, -12, CurBio 73,
EncPR&S 77, NewYTBE 72, RkOn 78,
-84, RolSEnR 83, WhoAm 74, -76, -78,
-80, -82, WhoRocM 82, WorAl*
McLean, Kathryn 1909-1966 *AmWomWr,
BioIn 2, -7, -11, ConAu 25R, ConAu P-2,
SmATA 9*
McLean, Kathryn *see also* Forbes, Kathryn
McLean, Susan 1937- *ConAu 106*
McLeave, Hugh George 1923- *ConAu 5R,
-6NR*
McLeish, Kenneth 1940- *ConAu 29R,
IntAu&W 77, -82, SmATA 35, WrDr 76,
-80, -82, -84*
McLellan, David 1940- *Au&Wr 6,
ConAu 33R, IntAu&W 82, Who 82, -83,
WrDr 76, -80, -82, -84*
McLintock, Gordon 1903- *BioIn 3, CurBio 53,
NewYTBE 70, WhoE 74*
McLoughlin, John C 1949- *ConAu 108*
McLuhan, Herbert Marshall 1911-1980 *BioIn 7,
-8, -9, -10, -11, -12, CasWL,
DcLEL 1940, DrAS 74E, -78E, -82E,
Future, IntWW 74, -75, MakMC,
PenC AM, WhAm 7, WhoAm 74, -76,
-78, -80, WhoCan 77, -80, -82,
WhoWor 74, -78, WorAl*
McLuhan, Herbert Marshall *see also* McLuhan,
Marshall

McLuhan, Marshall 1911-1980 *AmAu&B,
AnObit 1980[port], BlueB 76,
CanWW 70, -79, -80, CanWr, CelR 73,
ConAu 9R, -102, CurBio 67, -81N,
IntAu&W 77, -82, IntWW 76, -77, -78,
-79, -80, -81N, LesBEnT, LinLib L,
MugS, NewC, NewYTBS 81[port],
NewYTET, OxCan, OxCan SUP,
Who 74, -82N, WhoTwCL, WorAu,
WrDr 76, -80, -82*

McLuhan, Marshall *see also* McLuhan, Herbert
Marshall

McManus, Patrick 1933- *ConAu 105*

McMillen, Wheeler 1893- *AmAu&B, AuBYP,
BioIn 2, -7, ConAu 33R, OhA&B,
WhNAA, WhoAm 74, -76, -78, -80, -82,
WhoS&SW 73*

McMillin, Laurence, Jr. 1923- *ConAu 33R,
WhoWest 76, -78, -80*

McMullan, Frank 1907- *Au&Wr 6,
BiE&WWA, ConAu 5R, NotNAT*

McMurry, Linda O 1945- *ConAu 106*

McMurtrey, Martin A 1921- *BioIn 12,
ConAu 69, SmATA 21*

McMurtry, Larry 1936- *AmAu&B,
AuNews 2, BioIn 12, ConAu 5R,
ConLC 2, -3, -7, -11, -27[port],
ConNov 76, -82, DcLB Y80A[port], -2,
DrAF 76, DrAP&F 83, EncWL,
REnAW, WrDr 76, -80, -82, -84*

McMurty, Larry 1936- *DcLB Y80A[port]*

McNab, Tom *ConAu X*

McNair, Kate 1911- *AuBYP SUP, BioIn 9,
ConAu 17R, IndAu 1917, SmATA 3,
WrDr 76, -80, -82, -84*

McNally, Raymond T 1931- *ConAu 37R,
DrAS 74H, -78H, -82H, ScF&FL 1, -2*

McNally, Robert 1946- *ConAu 107*

McNamara, Robert Strange 1916-
*BiDAmBL 83, BiDrUSE, BioIn 5, -6, -7,
-8, -9, -10, -11, -12, BlueB 76, CelR 73,
CurBio 61, DcPol, EncAB-H, IntWW 74,
-75, -76, -77, -78, -79, -80, -81, -82, -83,
IntYB 78, -79, -80, -81, -82, LinLib S,
NewYTBE 73, NewYTBS 75, PolProf J,
PolProf K, PolProf NF, St&PR 75,
Ward 77G, WebAMB, WhDW, Who 74,
-82, -83, WhoAm 74, -76, -78, -80, -82,
WhoF&I 74, -79, -81, WhoGov 77, -72,
-75, WhoUN 75, WhoWor 74, -76, -78,
-80, -82, WorAl, WrDr 80, -82, -84*

McNamee, James Owen 1904- *Au&Wr 6,
AuBYP, BioIn 8, ConAu 5R*

McNeer, May Yonge 1902- *AmAu&B,
AuBYP, BioIn 2, -7, -9, -10, BkCL, BkP,
ConAu 2NR, -5R, JBA 34, -51,
ScF&FL 1, -2, SmATA 1, Str&VC*

McNeill, Janet 1907- *Au&Wr 6,
AuBYP SUP, BioIn 9, ChhPo S3,
ConAu X, -9R, DcIrL, DcIrW 1,
FourBJA, IntAu&W 76X, -77X, -82X,
ScF&FL 1A, SmATA 1, TwCCW 78,*

-83, WrDr 76, -80, -82, -84

McNeill, William Hardy 1917- *BioIn 6,
BlueB 76, ConAu 2NR, -5R, DrAS 74H,
-78H, -82H, IntAu&W 76, WhoAm 74,
-76, -78, -80, -82, WhoWor 74, WrDr 76,
-80, -82, -84*

McNeish, James 1931- *ConAu 69,
ConNov 82, IntAu&W 76, -77, LElec,
WrDr 76, -80, -82, -84*

McNickle, D'Arcy 1904-1977 *AmM&WS 73S,
BioIn 9, -12, ConAu 5NR, -9R, -85,
ConIsC 1[port], IntAu&W 77,
SmATA 22N, WhoPNW, WrDr 76, -80*

McNulty, Faith 1918- *BioIn 11, -12,
ConAu 1NR, -49, SmATA 12,
WhoAmW 75, WrDr 76, -80, -82, -84*

McPhee, John Angus 1931- *BioIn 10, -11, -12,
ConAu 65, CurBio 82[port], WhoAm 78,
-80, -82, WhoWor 80, WorAu 1970*

McPherson, James Alan 1943- *AmAu&B,
BioIn 12, BlkAWP, ConAu 25R,
ConLC 19, ConNov 82, DrAF 76,
InB&W 80, LivgBAA, NegAl 83[port],
SelBAA, WhoAm 74, -76, -80, -82,
WhoBlA 77, -80, WhoE 83, WrDr 84*

McPherson, James Munro 1936- *BioIn 12,
ConAu 9R, DrAS 74H, -78H, -82H,
IntAu&W 82, SmATA 16, WhoAm 74,
-76, -78, -80, -82, WrDr 76, -80, -82, -84*

McQueen, Ian 1930- *ConAu 104,
IntAu&W 77, WrDr 76, -80, -82*

McQueen, Mildred Hark 1908- *BioIn 11,
ConAu P-1, SmATA 12*

McQueen, Mildred Hark *see also* Hark, Mildred

McQuigg, R Bruce 1927- *ConAu 17R*

McShane, Mark 1929?- *Au&Wr 6,
ConAu 7NR, -17R, ScF&FL 1,
TwCCr&M 80, WrDr 76, -80, -82, -84*

McSherry, Frank D, Jr. 1927- *ConAu 107*

McSweeny, William Francis 1929- *Dun&B 79,
WhoAm 82, WhoE 79, -81, -83,
WhoF&I 75, -77, -79, -81, -83,
WhoWor 78*

McTaggart, Lynne Ann 1951- *WhoAm 78, -80*

McVey, Ruth T 1930- *AmM&WS 73S, -78S,
ConAu 109*

McVie, Christine Perfect 1943- *WhoAm 78,
-80, -82, WhoAmW 81, WhoRocM 82*

McVie, Christine Perfect *see also* Fleetwood
Mac

McVie, John 1946- *WhoAm 78, -80, -82,
WhoRocM 82*

McVie, John *see also* Fleetwood Mac

McWhirter, A Ross 1925-1975 *ConAu 17R, -61,
SmATA 31N*

McWhirter, Millie *BioIn 8, ForWC 70*

McWhirter, Norris Dewar 1925- *Au&Wr 6,
BioIn 8, -12, ConAu 13R, CurBio 79,
IntWW 81, -82, -83, Who 82, -83, WorAl*

McWhirter, Ross 1925-1975 *BioIn 8, -10,
ObitT 1971, WorAl*

McWilliams, Carey 1905-1980 *AmAu&B,*

AnObit 1980, BioIn 4, -8, -10, -12,
CelR 73, ChiSch, CmCal, ConAu 2NR,
-101, -45, CurBio 43, -80N,
NewYTBS 80[port], OxAmL, REnAL,
TwCA SUP, WhAm 7, WhoAm 74, -76,
-78, -80, WhoE 75, -77, WhoWor 74

Mead, Margaret 1901-1978 AmAu&B,
AmM&WS 73S, -76P, -79P, AmWomWr,
Au&Wr 6, AuBYP, AuNews 1, BioIn 2,
-3, -4, -5, -6, -7, -8, -9, -10, -11, -12,
BioNews 74, BlueB 76, CelR 73,
ConAu 1R, -4NR, -81, ConIsC 1[port],
CurBio 40, -51, -79N, DcLEL, EncAB-H,
EvLB, FifIDA, ForWC 70, GoodHs,
HerW, InSci, InWom, IntAu&W 77,
IntDcWB, IntEnSS 79, IntWW 74, -75,
-76, -77, -78, -79N, LibW, LinLib L, -S,
LongCTC, MakMC, McGEWB,
McGMS 80[port], NewYTBE 70, -72,
NewYTBS 78, ObitOF 79, OxAmL,
PenC AM, REn, REnAL, SmATA 20N,
TwCA, TwCA SUP, WebAB, -79,
WhDW, WhAm 7, WhNAA, Who 74,
WhoAm 74, -76, -78, WhoAmW 74, -58,
-61, -64, -66, -68, -70, -72, -79,
WhoWor 74, -76, -78, WorAl, WrDr 76

Mead, Robert Douglas 1928-1983 ConAu 110,
-41R, IntAu&W 82

Mead, Russell 1935- BioIn 11, ConAu 9R,
IntAu&W 76, -82X, SmATA 10,
WhoE 75, -77, -79, -83, WrDr 76, -80, -82,
-84

Meade, Ellen 1936- BioIn 10, ConAu 41R,
SmATA 5

Meade, Marion 1934- ConAu 1NR, -49,
SmATA 23[port]

Meader, Stephen Warren 1892-1977 AmAu&B,
AuBYP, BioIn 2, -3, -7, -9, ConAu 5R,
JBA 34, -51, LinLib L, REnAL,
SmATA 1, TwCCW 78, -83, WhAm 7,
WhE&EA, WhoAm 74, -76, -78,
WrDr 80

Meaker, Marijane 1927?- BioIn 12,
ConAu 107, SmATA 20, WhoAm 82,
WrDr 80, -82, -84

Meaker, Marijane see also Kerr, M E

Means, Florence Crannell 1891-1980 AmAu&B,
AmWomWr, AuBYP, BioIn 1, -2, -7, -9,
-12, BkCL, ConAu 1R, -103, ForWC 70,
IntAu&W 76, -77, -82, JBA 34, -51,
LinLib L, SmATA 1, -25N, TwCCW 78,
-83, WhAm 7, WhE&EA, WhNAA,
WhoAm 74, -76, -78, -80, WhoAmW 74,
-58, -61, -64, -66, -68, -70, -72, -75, -77,
WhoWest 76, -78, WrDr 80, -82

Mearian, Judy Frank 1936- ConAu 101

Mebane, Mary E 1933- BioIn 12, BlkAWP,
ConAu 73, DrAP&F 83, DrAS 74E, -78E

Mech, L David 1937- ConAu 33R,
IntAu&W 77, -82, WrDr 76, -80, -82, -84

Medary, Marjorie 1890- BioIn 2, -12,
ConAu 73, JBA 51, SmATA 14,

WhoAmW 58, -61

Medearis, Mary 1915- BioIn 10, ConAu 69,
SmATA 5

Medoff, Mark 1940- AuNews 1, BioIn 10,
-12, ConAu 5NR, -53, ConDr 77, -82,
ConLC 6, -23[port], DcLB 7[port],
IntAu&W 77, -82, NatPD, -81[port],
NotNAT, WhoAm 80, -82, WhoThe 81,
WrDr 80, -82, -84

Medved, Harry 1961?- ConAu 93

Medved, Michael 1948- ConAu 11NR, -65

Medvedev, Roy Alexandrovich 1925- BioIn 8,
-10, -11, ConAu 81, IntWW 75, -76, -77,
-78, -79, -80, -81, -82, -83, NewYTBS 79,
WhoSocC 78, WrDr 80, -82, -84

Mee, Charles L, Jr. 1938- BiE&WWA,
BioIn 11, -12, ConAu 3NR, -45,
SmATA 8

Meed, Vladka 1921- WhoAmJ 80

Meehan, James Robert 1904- WhoAm 74

Meek, Jacklyn O'Hanlon 1933- ConAu 77,
SmATA 34

Meek, Jay 1937- ConAu 107, DrAP 75,
DrAP&F 83, IntWWP 77

Meeker, Joseph W 1932- ConAu 49

Meeker, Oden 1918?-1976 AuBYP, BioIn 8,
-10, -12, ConAu 65, -73, NewYTBS 76,
SmATA 14

Meeropol, Michael 1943- AmEA 74, BioIn 10,
BioNews 74

Meeropol, Robert 1947?- BioIn 10,
BioNews 74

Meggs, Brown 1930- ConAu 7NR, -61,
TwCCr&M 80, WhoAm 76, -78, -80, -82,
WrDr 82, -84

Meglin, Nick 1935- ConAu 69

Mehdevi, Anne Sinclair 1918?- AmAu&B,
AuBYP, BioIn 8, -10, -11, ConAu 5R,
FourBJA, SmATA 8, WorAu

Mehta, Ved Parkash 1934- Au&Wr 6,
BioIn 4, -6, -9, -10, -11, -12, ConAu 1R,
-2NR, CurBio 75, DcLEL 1940,
IntAu&W 76, -77, -82, LinLib L,
NewYTBE 72, NewYTBS 78, Who 74,
-82, -83, WhoWor 74, -76, WorAu,
WrDr 76, -80, -82, -84

Meier, August 1923- ConAu 3NR, -9R,
DrAS 74H, -78H, -82H, WhoAm 74, -76,
-78, -80, -82, WhoBlA 75, -77, -80,
WhoMW 74, -76, -78

Meier, Matt S 1917- ConAu 41R

Meigs, Cornelia Lynde 1884-1973 AmAu&B,
AmWomWr, AnCL, AuBYP, BioIn 1, -2,
-4, -7, -10, ChhPo, ConAu 9R, -45,
ForWC 70, JBA 34, -51, NewYTBE 73,
Newb 1922, REnAL, SmATA 6,
Str&VC, TwCCW 78, -83, WhAm 6, -7,
WhoAmW 58, -61, -64, -66, -68, -70, -72

Meilach, Dona Zweigoron 1926- AuBYP SUP,
ConAu 5NR, -9R, ForWC 70,
SmATA 34[port], WhoAmA 78,
WhoAmW 68, -70, WhoWest 80, -82

Meinke, Peter 1932- *BioIn 12, ConAu 25R, DcLB 5[port], DrAP 75, DrAP&F 83, IntAu&W 77, –82, IntWWP 77, –82, WhoFla, WrDr 76, –80, –82, –84*

Meir, Golda 1898-1978 *BioIn 4, –8, –9, –10, –11, –12, CelR 73, ConAu 81, –89, CurBio 70, –79N, DcPol, GoodHs, HerW, InWom, IntDcWB, IntWW 74, –75, –76, –77, –78, –79N, IntYB 78, –79, LinLib S, McGEWB, MidE 78, NewYTBS 74, –78, WhDW, WhAm 7, Who 74, WhoAmW 74, –66, –68, –70, –72, –75, WhoGov 72, WhoWor 74, WhoWorJ 72, –78, WorAl*

Meisner, Maurice 1931- *ConAu 21R, DrAS 74H, –78H, –82H*

Meisner, Randy 1946?- *BioIn 12, WhoRocM 82*

Meisner, Randy *see also* Eagles, The

Meissner, Hans-Otto 1909- *ConAu 2NR, –49*

Melchior, Ib 1917- *ConAu 2NR, –45, DrAP&F 83, FilmgC, IntAu&W 76, IntMPA 77, –75, –76, –78, –79, –81, –82, –84, WhoWest 76, –78, –80, –82, WrDr 80, –82, –84*

Melick, Arden D 1940- *ConAu 106, ODwPR 79*

Mellers, Wilfrid Howard 1914- *Au&Wr 6, Baker 78, BioIn 6, BlueB 76, ConAu 4NR, –5R, CurBio 62, DcCM, IntAu&W 77, –82, IntWWM 77, OxMus, Who 74, –82, –83, WhoMus 72, WhoWor 74, WrDr 76, –80, –82, –84*

Mellersh, Harold Edward Leslie 1897- *Au&Wr 6, BioIn 11, ConAu 53, SmATA 10, WrDr 76*

Mellin, Jeanne 1929- *AuBYP, BioIn 7, ConAu 49*

Mellow, James Robert 1926- *BlueB 76, ConAu 105, WhoAm 74, –76, –78, –80, –82, WhoAmA 73*

Melton, David 1934- *AuBYP SUP, ConAu 69, WrDr 80, –82, –84*

Meltzer, David 1937- *BioIn 8, ConAu 6NR, –9R, ConP 70, –75, –80, ConSFA, DcLB 16[port], DcLEL 1940, DrAF 76, DrAP 75, EncSF, IntWWP 77, PenC AM, ScF&FL 1, –2, WhoAm 76, –78, –80, –82, WhoAmJ 80, WrDr 76, –80, –82, –84*

Meltzer, Milton 1915- *AuBYP SUP, BioIn 9, –10, ConAu 13R, ConLC 26[port], DrAS 74H, –78H, –82H, MorBMP, SmATA 1, ThrBJA, WhoAm 74, –76, –78, –80, –82*

Meltzoff, Nancy 1952- *ConAu 93*

Meluch, R M 1956- *ConAu 109*

Melville, Anne *ConAu X, IntAu&W 82X, SmATA X, WrDr 80, –82, –84*

Melville, Fred J 1882- *WhE&EA, WhLit*

Melville, Herman 1819-1891 *Alli, Alli SUP, AmAu, AmAu&B, AmBi, AmWr,*

ApCAB, AtlBL, BbD, BiD&SB, BioIn 1, –2, –3, –4, –5, –6, –7, –8, –9, –10, –11, –12, CasWL, Chambr 3, ChhPo, –S2, CnDAL, CnE&AP, CrtT 3, –4, CyAL 2, CyWA, DcAmAu, DcAmB, DcBiA, DcEnA, DcEnL, DcLB 3, DcLEL, DcNAA, Dis&D, Drake, EncAB-H, EncSF, EvLB, InSci, LinLib L, –S, LuthC 75, McGEWB, MouLC 4, NatCAB 4, NewEOp 71, Novels[port], OxAmH, OxAmL, OxEng, OxShips, PenC AM, RAdv 1, RComWL, REn, REnAL, TwCBDA, WebAB, –79, WebE&AL, WhDW, WhAm HS, WorAl

Melville, Jennie *ConAu X, IntAu&W 77X, Novels, TwCCr&M 80, WrDr 82, –84*

Melville, Jennie *see also* Butler, Gwendoline

Melvin, A Gordon 1894- *ConAu 9R, IntAu&W 77, WhoE 79, –81, –83, WrDr 80, –82, –84*

Melvin, Arthur Gordon 1894- *Au&Wr 6, ConAu 9R, WrDr 76*

Melwood, Mary *BioIn 12, ConAu X, SmATA X, TwCCW 78, –83, WrDr 82, –84*

Mendelsohn, Felix, Jr. 1906- *ConAu 29R, EncSF, ScF&FL 1, –2*

Mendelson, Lee 1933- *ConAu 33R, NewYTET, WhoAm 78, –80, –82, WrDr 76, –80, –82, –84*

Mendes, Helen Althia Davenport 1935- *WhoAmW 74, –72, –75, –77, –79, –81, WhoBlA 77, –80*

Mendonca, Susan 1950- *ConAu 102*

Mendoza, George 1934- *AuBYP SUP, BioIn 9, –11, ConAu 73, ThrBJA*

Menen, Aubrey 1912- *BioIn 3, –4, –5, –9, BlueB 76, ConAu 1R, –2NR, ConNov 72, –76, –82, EncWL, IntAu&W 76, –77, IntWW 74, –75, –76, –77, –78, –79, –80, –81, –82, –83, LinLib L, LongCTC, ModBrL, ModCmwL, NewC, REn, ScF&FL 1, –2, TwCA SUP, WhoAm 74, –76, –78, –80, –82, WhoWor 74, –76, –78, WrDr 76, –80, –82, –84*

Meng, Heinz Karl 1924- *AmM&WS 73P, –76P, –79P, –82P, BioIn 11, ConAu 69, SmATA 13*

Menke, Frank Grant 1885-1954 *BioIn 1, –3, ObitOF 79, OhA&B*

Menon, Bhaskar 1934- *St&PR 75, WhoF&I 75, –77*

Menuhin, Yehudi 1916- *Baker 78, BiDAmM, BioIn 1, –2, –3, –4, –5, –6, –7, –8, –9, –10, –11, –12, BlueB 76, CelR 73, CmCal, ConAu 2NR, –45, CurBio 41, –73, IntWW 74, –75, –76, –77, –78, –79, –80, –81, –82, –83, IntWWM 77, LinLib S, MusSN, NewYTBS 76, –81[port], OxMus, WebAB, –79, Who 74, –82, –83, WhoAm 74, –76, –78, –80, –82, WhoAmJ 80, WhoAmM 83, WhoFr 79,*

WhoHol A, WhoMus 72, WhoWor 74,
–78, –80, –82, WhoWorJ 78, WorAl,
WrDr 80, –82, –84

Menville, Douglas 1935- ConAu 57, EncSF,
IntAu&W 77, ScF&FL 2, WhoWest 78

Menzel, Donald Howard 1901-1976
AmM&WS 73P, –76P, AsBiEn, BiESc,
BioIn 3, –4, –11, –12, BlueB 76,
ConAu 69, ConAu P-2, CurBio 56, –77,
–77N, InSci, IntAu&W 77, IntWW 74,
–75, –76, –77N, McGMS 80[port],
NatCAB 59[port], NewYTBE 70,
NewYTBS 76, ObitOF 79, UFOEn,
WhAm 7, WhoAm 74, –76, WrDr 80

Mercatante, Anthony Stephen 1940-
ConAu 41R, IntAu&W 76, –82

Mercer, Charles 1917- AmAu&B,
AuBYP SUP, BioIn 12, ConAu 1R,
–2NR, SmATA 16, WhoAm 74, –76, –78,
–80, –82, WhoE 74

Mercier, Vivian H 1919- ConAu 81,
DrAS 74E, –78E, –82E, WhoWest 78

Meredith, Don 1938- ConAu 102,
DrAP&F 83, NewYTBS 77, NewYTET,
WhoAm 76, –78, –80, –82, WorAl

Meredith, Richard C 1937- ConAu 85, EncSF,
ScF&FL 1

Meredith, Scott 1923- AmAu&B, BioIn 10,
ConAu 3NR, –9R, WhoAm 74, –76, –78,
–80, –82, WhoE 74, –75, –77, –79, –81,
WrDr 76, –80, –82, –84

Meriwether, Louise 1923- BlkAWP,
ConAu 77, DrAF 76, DrAP&F 83,
Ebony 1, InB&W 80, LivgBAA, SelBAA,
SmATA 31, WhoBlA 75, –77, –80

Merle, Robert 1908- Au&Wr 6, ConAu 93,
EncSF, IntAu&W 76, –77, ScF&FL 1,
Who 74, –82, –83, WhoFr 79

Merne, Oscar James 1943- ConAu 102,
IntAu&W 77, WrDr 76, –80, –82, –84

Merriam, Eve 1916- AmAu&B, AuBYP,
BioIn 1, –8, –9, –12, BkP, ChhPo, –S1, –S2,
–S3, ConAu 5R, DrAP 75, DrAP&F 83,
ForWC 70, SmATA 3, ThrBJA,
TwCCW 78, –83, WhoAm 74, –76, –78,
–80, –82, WhoAmW 74, –66, –68, –70, –72,
–75, –77, –81, WhoE 74, WrDr 80, –82,
–84

Merril, Judith 1923- AmWomWr, BioIn 10,
–12, CaW, ConAu 13R, ConSFA,
EncSF, IntAu&W 76, –77, LinLib L,
Novels, ScF&FL 1, –2, WhoAmW 58, –61,
WhoSciF, WorAu, WrDr 84

Merrill, John Nigel 1943- Au&Wr 6,
IntAu&W 76, –77, WrDr 76, –80

Merritt, A 1884-1943 EncSF, ScF&FL 1,
WhoHr&F

Mersand, Joseph 1907- AmAu&B, ConAu 1R,
–1NR, DrAS 74E, –78E, WhNAA,
WhoE 74, –75, –77, –79, –81, WhoWorJ 78

Merton, Thomas 1915-1968 AmAu&B,
BioIn 1, –2, –3, –4, –5, –8, –9, –10, –11, –12,

CathA 1930, ConAu 5R, –25R, ConLC 1,
–3, –11, DcAmReB, DcLB Y81B[port],
IlEncMy, LinLib L, –S, LongCTC,
MakMC, ModAL, ObitOF 79, OxAmL,
PenC AM, REnAL, TwCA SUP,
WebAB, –79, WhAm 5

Mertz, Barbara Gross 1927- Au&Wr 6,
BioIn 11, ConAu 11NR, –21R,
DrAS 74H, ScF&FL 1, TwCCr&M 80,
WrDr 76, –80, –82, –84

Mertz, Barbara Gross see also Michaels, Barbara

Mertz, Barbara Gross see also Peters, Elizabeth

Merwin, W S 1927- BioIn 11, BlueB 76,
ConLC 8, –13, –18, ConP 80,
DcLB 5[port], DrAP&F 83, EncWL 2,
IntAu&W 77, WhoWor 74, WrDr 80, –82,
–84

Merwin, William Stanley 1927- AmAu&B,
BioIn 8, –10, –12, CasWL, ChhPo S2,
CnE&AP, ConAu 13R, ConLC 1, –2, –3,
–5, ConP 70, –75, CroCAP, DcLEL 1940,
DrAF 76, DrAP 75, IntWWP 77,
ModAL, ModAL SUP, OxAmL,
PenC AM, RAdv 1, WebE&AL,
WhoAm 74, –76, –78, –80, –82, WhoE 74,
WhoTwCL, WorAu, WrDr 76

Meserole, Harrison Talbot 1921- DrAS 74E,
–78E, –82E

Messer, Ronald Keith 1942- ConAu 57

Messina, Jim 1947- WhoRocM 82, WorAl

Messina, Jim see also Loggins & Messina

Messner, Reinhold 1944- BioIn 11, ConAu 81,
CurBio 80[port], IntAu&W 77, –82

Metcalf, George R 1914- ConAu 25R

Metcalf, Harlan Goldsbury 1899- WhoE 77,
–79, –81

Metos, Thomas H 1932- ConAu 93,
LEduc 74, SmATA 37

Metzger, Norman 1924- ConAu 9NR, –53

Metzker, Isaac 1901- ConAu 45, WhoAmJ 80,
WhoWorJ 72, –78

Metzler, Paul 1914- ConAu 6NR, –57

Mewshaw, Michael 1943- BioIn 9, –12,
ConAu 7NR, –53, ConLC 9,
DcLB Y80B[port], IntAu&W 82,
WrDr 76, –80, –82, –84

Meyer, Alfred W 1927- DrAS 82P

Meyer, Carolyn 1935- AuBYP SUP, BioIn 11,
ConAu 2NR, –49, SmATA 9

Meyer, Edith Patterson 1895- AuBYP,
BioIn 1, –8, –10, ConAu 1R, –1NR,
SmATA 5, WhoAmW 58, –61, –64, –75,
–77, –79

Meyer, Howard N 1914- BioIn 10,
ConAu 13R, WhoAmJ 80, WhoAmL 78,
–79, WhoE 75, WhoWorJ 72, –78

Meyer, Jerome Sydney 1895-1975 Au&Wr 6,
AuBYP, BioIn 7, –9, –10, BlueB 76,
ConAu 1R, –4NR, –57, SmATA 25N, –3,
WhoWorJ 72

Meyer, Karl Ernest 1928- AmAu&B, BioIn 10,
–11, ConAu 1R, –1NR, WhoAm 80, –82,

WhoWor 74

Meyer, Milton W 1923- DrAS 74H, –78H, –82H

Meyer, Nicholas 1945- BioIn 10, –11, –12, ConAu 7NR, –49, IntAu&W 76, –77, NewYTBS 82[port], TwCCr&M 80, WhoAm 76, –78, –80, –82, WrDr 76, –80, –82, –84

Meyer, Susan E 1940- ConAu 2NR, –45, IntAu&W 77, WhoAm 74, –76, –78, –80, –82, WhoAmA 76, –78, –80, –82

Meyers, Jeffrey 1939- ConAu 73, DrAS 78E, –82E, WrDr 84

Mezey, Robert 1935- AmAu&B, BioIn 10, ConAu 7NR, –57, ConP 70, –75, –80, CroCAP, DrAP 75, DrAP&F 83, DrAS 74E, –78E, –82E, IntWWP 77, –82, PenC AM, SmATA 33, WorAu 1970, WrDr 76, –80, –82, –84

Michaels, Barbara 1927- BioIn 11, ConAu X, ScF&FL 1, –1A, –2, TwCCr&M 80, WrDr 76, –80, –82, –84

Michaels, Barbara see also Mertz, Barbara Gross

Michaels, Kristin WrDr 80, –82, –84

Michaels, Leonard 1933- BioIn 12, ConAu 61, ConLC 6, –25[port], ConNov 82, DrAF 76, DrAS 74E, –78E, –82E, NewYTBS 81[port], WhoAm 76, –78, –80, –82, WrDr 82, –84

Michell, John 1933- ConAu 107

Michelmore, Peter 1930- ConAu 5R, –7NR

Michener, James Albert 1907- AmAu&B, AmNov, Au&Wr 6, AuNews 1, BioIn 1, –2, –3, –4, –5, –6, –7, –8, –9, –10, –11, –12, BioNews 74, BlueB 76, CelR 73, ConAu 5R, ConLC 1, –5, –11, ConNov 72, –76, –82, Conv 3, CurBio 48, –75, DcLB 6[port], DcLEL, –1940, FilmgC, IntAu&W 76, –77, IntWW 74, –75, –76, –77, –78, –79, –80, –81, –82, –83, LinLib L, –S, LongCTC, ModAL, NewYTBE 72, NewYTBS 78, –82, Novels[port], OxAmL, PenC AM, PIP&P, RAdv 1, REnAL, TwCA SUP, WebAB, –79, Who 74, –82, –83, WhoAm 74, –76, –78, –80, –82, WhoWor 74, –78, WorAl, WrDr 76, –80, –82, –84

Michie, Allan Andrew 1915-1973 AuBYP, BioIn 8, –10, –12, ConAu 45, CurBio 42, –52, –74, –74N, NatCAB 58[port], NewYTBE 73, WhE&EA

Micoleau, Tyler IlsBYP

Middlebrook, Diane W 1939- ConAu 81, DrAS 74E, –78E, –82E

Middlekauff, Robert Lawrence 1929- DrAS 74H, –78H, –82H, WhoAm 74, –76, –78

Middleton, Robert Gordon 1908- WhoWest 76, –78, –80, –82, –84

Miers, Earl Schenck 1910-1972 AmAu&B, AuBYP, BioIn 1, –2, –5, –7, –8, –9, –10, ChhPo S2, ConAu 1R, –2NR, –37R,

CurBio 49, –67, –73, –73N, NewYTBE 72, REnAL, SmATA 1, –26N, ThrBJA, WhAm 5, –7, WhoAm 74, –76

Miesel, Sandra 1941- IntAu&W 82, ScF&FL 1, –2

Mihaly, Mary E 1950- ConAu 97, IntAu&W 82

Miklowitz, Gloria D 1927- AuBYP SUP, BioIn 9, ConAu 10NR, –25R, IntAu&W 82, SmATA 4, WhoAmW 79, –81, WrDr 76, –80, –82, –84

Milam, James Robert 1922- AmM&WS 73S, –78S, WhoWest 76, –78

Milcsik, Margie 1950- ConAu 110

Mild, Warren Paul 1922- ConAu 8NR, –21R, DrAS 74E, –78E, –82E, WhoRel 75

Mileck, Joseph 1922- ConAu 107, DrAS 74F, –78F, –82F

Miles, Sir Bernard 1907- BioIn 5, CnThe, EncWT, FilmgC, IntMPA 77, –75, –76, –78, –79, IntWW 74, –75, –76, –77, –78, –79, –80, –81, OxThe, PIP&P, Who 74, WhoAmP 75, WhoHol A, WhoThe 15, –16, –81

Miles, Betty 1928- AuBYP, BioIn 8, –11, ConAu 1R, –5NR, ForWC 70, SmATA 8, WhoAmW 66, –68, –70, WomWMM B, WrDr 76, –80, –82, –84

Miles, Miska 1899- AuBYP, ChhPo S2, ConAu X, FourBJA, IntAu&W 77X, SmATA 1, TwCCW 78, –83, WrDr 76, –80, –82, –84

Miles, Miska see also Martin, Patricia Miles

Miles, Patricia 1930- AuBYP SUP, ConAu 11NR, –69, SmATA 29[port]

Milford, Nancy 1938- ConAu 29R, DrAS 78E, WrDr 76, –80, –82, –84

Milgram, Gail Gleason 1942- ConAu 29R, IntAu&W 76, WhoAmW 75, –77, –79, –83, WrDr 76, –80, –82, –84

Millar, Barbara F 1924- BioIn 11, ConAu 25R, SmATA 12, WhoAmW 74

Millar, Jeff 1942- BioIn 10, ConAu 11NR, –69

Millar, Kenneth 1915-1983 AmAu&B, AmNov, Au&Wr 6, BioIn 2, –3, –5, –8, –9, –10, –11, –12, BlueB 76, ConAu 9R, –110, ConLC 14, CurBio 53, –79, –83N, DcLB Y83N[port], –2, DcLEL 1940, EncMys, IntAu&W 76, IntWW 81, –82, –83, Po&Wr 77, TwCCr&M 80, WhoAm 74, –76, –78, –80, –82, WhoWest 76, –78, WhoWor 74, WorAu, WrDr 76, –80, –82, –84

Millar, Kenneth see also Macdonald, Ross

Millar, Margaret Ellis 1915- AmAu&B, AmNov, Au&Wr 6, BioIn 1, –2, –5, –9, –10, –12, CanWW 70, –79, –80, –81, –83, ConAu 13R, ConNov 76, –82, CurBio 46, EncMys, InWom, IntAu&W 76, Novels, REnAL, TwCCr&M 80, WhoAm 74, –76, –78, –80, –82, WhoAmW 64, –66, –68, –70,

–72, WhoWest 76, –78, WhoWor 74, –76, WorAu, WrDr 76, –80, –82, –84

Millar, Ronald 1919- *BioIn 10, ConAu 73, ConDr 73, –77, –82, DcLEL 1940, IntAu&W 77, –82, Who 82, –83, WhoThe 15, –16, –81, WrDr 76, –80, –82, –84*

Millard, Charles Warren, III 1932- *WhoAm 80, WhoAmA 76, –78, –80, –82, WhoE 79, –83*

Millard, Reed *AuBYP SUP*

Millay, Edna St. Vincent 1892-1950 *AmAu&B, AmSCAP 66, AmWomWr, AmWr, ApCAB X, AtlBL, BioIn 1, –2, –3, –4, –5, –6, –8, –9, –10, –11, –12, CasWL, Chambr 3, ChhPo, –S1, –S2, –S3, CnDAL, CnE&AP, CnMD, CnMWL, ConAmA, ConAmL, ConAu 104, CyWA, DcAmB S4, DcLEL, EncWL, –2, EvLB, GoodHs, HerW, InWom, IntDcWB, LibW, LinLib L, –S, LongCTC, McGEWB, McGEWD, –84, ModAL, ModWD, NatCAB 38, NotAW, NotNAT B, OxAmL, OxEng, PenC AM, RAdv 1, REn, REnAL, SixAP, Str&VC, TwCA, TwCA SUP, TwCLC 3, –4[port], TwCWr, WebAB, –79, WhDW, WhAm 3, WhNAA, WorAl*

Miller, Albert G 1905-1982 *BioIn 11, –12, ConAu 1R, –1NR, –107, NewYTBS 82, SmATA 31N*

Miller, Alice Duer 1874-1942 *AmAu&B, AmWomWr, ChhPo, –S1, CurBio 41, –42, DcAmAu, DcNAA, InWom, LibW, LongCTC, NotAW, NotNAT B, ObitOF 79, REn, REnAL, TwCA, TwCA SUP, WhAm 2, WhLit, WhNAA, WhoHol B, WomWWA 14*

Miller, Alice Patricia McCarthy *Au&Wr 6, ConAu 9R, –29R, ForWC 70, SmATA 22[port], WhoAmW 74, –66, –68, –70, –72, –75, –77, WhoE 74*

Miller, Arthur 1915- *AmAu&B, AmNov, AmWr, Au&Wr 6, AuNews 1, BiE&WWA, BioIn 1, –2, –4, –5, –7, –8, –9, –10, –11, –12, BioNews 74, BlueB 76, CasWL, CelR 73, CnDAL, CnMD, CnMWL, CnThe, ConAu 1R, –2NR, ConDr 73, –77, –82, ConLC 1, –2, –6, –10, –15, –26[port], CroCD, CurBio 47, –73, CyWA, DcFM, DcLB 7[port], DcLEL 1940, DrAF 76, EncAB-H, EncWL, –2[port], EncWT, FilmgC, IntAu&W 76, –77, IntMPA 84, IntWW 74, –75, –76, –77, –78, –79, –80, –81, –82, –83, LinLib L, –S, LongCTC, MakMC, McGEWB, McGEWD, –84[port], ModAL, ModAL SUP, ModWD, NatPD, –81[port], NewEOp 71, NewYTBE 72, NewYTBS 80[port], NotNAT, –A, OxAmL, OxEng, OxFilm, OxThe, PenC AM, PIP&P, PolProf E, PolProf T, RComWL, REn, REnAL, REnWD,*

TwCA SUP, TwCWr, WebAB, –79, WebE&AL, WhDW, Who 74, –82, –83, WhoAm 74, –76, –78, –80, –82, WhoAmJ 80, WhoThe 15, –16, –81, WhoTwCL, WhoWor 74, –78, –80, –82, WhoWorJ 72, –78, WorAl, WorEFlm, WrDr 76, –80, –82, –84

Miller, Arthur Raphael 1934- *BioIn 12, WhoAm 74, –76, –78, –82, WhoAmL 83*

Miller, Casey 1919- *ConAu 69*

Miller, Charles A 1937- *ConAu 29R, WrDr 76, –80, –82, –84*

Miller, David William 1940- *ConAu 49, DrAS 74H, –78H, –82H, WhoMW 74*

Miller, Douglas T 1937- *ConAu 21R, DrAS 74H, –78H, IntAu&W 77, WrDr 76, –80, –84*

Miller, Edwin Haviland 1918- *ConAu 110, DrAS 74E, –78E, –82E*

Miller, Eugene 1925- *ConAu 101, Dun&B 79, ODwPR 79, SmATA 33[port], St&PR 75, WhoAm 74, –76, –78, –80, –82, WhoF&I 74, –75, –77, –79, –81, –83, WhoMW 74, –76, –78, –80, –82, WhoPubR 72, –76*

Miller, Floyd C 1912- *ConAu 1R, –2NR, IndAu 1917*

Miller, Helen Knapp 1899- *AuBYP*

Miller, Helen Knapp *see also* Miller, Helen Markley

Miller, Helen Markley 1899- *AmAu&B, AuBYP, BioIn 7, –10, ConAu 1R, –2NR, SmATA 5*

Miller, Isabel *ConAu 49, MichAu 80*

Miller, Jason 1939?- *AuNews 1, BioIn 9, –10, CelR 73, ConAu 73, ConDr 73, –77, –82, ConLC 2, CurBio 74, DcLB 7[port], NotNAT, PIP&P A, WhoAm 74, –76, –78, –80, –82, WhoThe 16, –81, WorAl, WorAu 1970, WrDr 76, –80, –82*

Miller, Jean Baker 1927- *BiDrAPA 77*

Miller, Jonathan 1934- *BiE&WWA, BioIn 6, –7, –9, –11, BlueB 76, ConAu 110, EncWT, FilmgC, IntWW 74, –75, –76, –77, –78, –79, –80, –81, –82, –83, NewYTBS 82[port], NotNAT, Who 74, –82, –83, WhoHol A, WhoOp 76, WhoThe 15, –16, –81, WorAl, WrDr 80, –82, –84*

Miller, Katherine *AuBYP, BioIn 8*

Miller, Lillian Beresnack 1923- *ConAu 9NR, –21R, DrAS 74H, –78H, –82H, WhoGov 75*

Miller, Mara 1944- *ConAu 97*

Miller, Margaret J 1911- *Au&Wr 6, ConAu X, IntAu&W 76X, –77X*

Miller, Margaret J *see also* Dale, Margaret J Miller

Miller, Mary Beth 1942- *BioIn 11, ConAu 61, SmATA 9*

Miller, May *BlkAWP, DrAP 75, DrAP&F 83, InB&W 80, SelBAA*

Minton, Sherman Anthony 1919-
  AmM&WS 73P, -76P, -79P, -82P,
  ConAu 45, *IndAu* 1917
Mintz, Lorelie Miller *AuBYP SUP*
Mintz, Morton Abner 1922- *ConAu* 13R,
  WhoAm 74, -76, -78, -80, -82,
  WhoAmJ 80, *WhoS&SW* 73, -75, -76
Mintz, Thomas 1931- *ConAu* 108
Mirvish, Robert Franklin 1921- *AmAu&B,*
  Au&Wr 6, *BioIn* 3, -4, -6, *CanWW* 70,
  -79, -80, -81, -83, *ConAu* 1R, *CurBio* 57,
  WhoAm 74, -76, -78, -80, -82,
  WhoWor 74, -76, *WrDr* 76, -80, -82, -84
Mishima, Yukio 1925-1970 *Au&Wr* 6,
  BiDJaL, BioIn 2, -5, -7, -8, -9, -10, -12,
  CasWL, CnMD, ConAu X, -29R,
  ConLC 2, -4, -6, -9, -27[port], *DcOrL* 1,
  EncWL, -2[port], *EncWT, LinLib* L,
  ModWD, NewYTBE 70, *Novels[port],*
  ObitOF 79, *PenC CL, RComWL, REn,*
  WhDW, WhAm 5, *WhScrn,* -2,
  WhoTwCL, WorAl, WorAu
Mishima, Yukio *see also* Hiraoka, Kimitake
Mitchell, Don 1947- *ConAu* 33R,
  DrAP&F 83
Mitchell, Gladys 1901-1983 *Au&Wr* 6,
  BioIn 5, *ConAu* 9R, -9NR, -110, *EncMys,*
  IntAu&W 76, -77, -82, *LongCTC, Novels,*
  SmATA 35N, *TwCCr&M* 80, *WhE&EA,*
  Who 74, -82, -83, *WrDr* 76, -80, -82, -84
Mitchell, Jerry 1905?-1972 *BioIn* 9,
  ConAu 33R
Mitchell, Joni 1943- *BioIn* 8, -9, -10, -11,
  BioNews 74, *CanWW* 81, *CelR* 73,
  ConLC 12, *CurBio* 76, *EncPR&S* 77,
  GoodHs, RkOn 78, -84, *RolSEnR* 83,
  WhoAm 74, -76, -78, -80, -82,
  WhoAmW 70, -72, -75, -77, -79, -81,
  WorAl
Mitchell, Joseph Brady 1915- *ConAu* 9R,
  DcLEL 1940, *WhoS&SW* 73, -75, -76, -78,
  -80, -82
Mitchell, Joyce Slayton 1933- *ConAu* 65,
  WhoAmW 72
Mitchell, Margaret 1900-1949 *AmAu&B,*
  AmWomWr, BioIn 1, -2, -3, -4, -5, -6, -7,
  -8, -10, -11, *CasWL, Chambr* 3, *CnDAL,*
  CyWA, DcAmB S4, *DcLB* 9[port],
  DcLEL, DcNAA, EvLB, FilmgC,
  GoodHs, InWom, LibW, LinLib L, -S,
  LongCTC, ModAL, NatCAB 38, *NotAW,*
  Novels[port], ObitOF 79, *OxAmL,*
  PenC AM, REn, REnAL, TwCA,
  TwCA SUP, TwCWr, WebAB, -79,
  WebE&AL, WhAm 2, *WhNAA, WorAl*
Mitchell, William Ormond 1914- *BioIn* 3,
  CaW, CanWW 70, -79, -80, -81, -83,
  CanWr, CasWL, ConAu 77, *ConNov* 72,
  -76, *CreCan* 1, *DcLEL* 1940, *OxCan,*
  TwCWr, WrDr 76
Mitchison, Naomi 1897-1964 *Au&Wr* 6,
  BioIn 4, -8, -10, -12, *BlueB* 76, *CasWL,*

Chambr 3, *ChhPo,* -S2, -S3, *ConAu* 77,
  ConNov 72, -76, -82, *ConSFA, DcLEL,*
  EncSF, EvLB, InWom, IntAu&W 76, -77,
  -82, *IntWW* 74, -75, -76, -77, -78, -79,
  -80, -81, -82, -83, *LongCTC, ModBrL,*
  NewC, Novels, PenC ENG, REn,
  ScF&FL 1, -2, *SmATA* 24[port], *TwCA,*
  TwCA SUP, TwCCW 78, -83, *WhE&EA,*
  Who 74, -82, -83, *WhoChL, WhoLA,*
  WhoSciF, WhoWor 74, *WrDr* 76, -80,
  -82, -84
Mitford, Jessica 1917- *AmAu&B, AmWomWr,*
  ASpks, BioIn 8, -9, -10, -11, -12,
  BlueB 76, *ConAu* 1R, -1NR, *CurBio* 74,
  IntAu&W 76, -77, *IntDcWB, IntWW* 74,
  -75, -76, -77, -78, -79, -80, -81, -82, -83,
  NewC, NewYTBS 77, *Who* 82, -83,
  WhoAm 76, -78, -80, -82, *WhoAmW* 74,
  -66, -68, -70, -72, -75, -83, *WhoWor* 74,
  -76, -78, *WorAu, WrDr* 76, -80, -82, -84
Mitgang, Herbert 1920- *AmAu&B, BioIn* 11,
  -12, *ConAu* 4NR, -9R, *IntAu&W* 76, -77,
  ScF&FL 1, -2, *WhoAm* 74, -76, -78, -80,
  -82, *WhoAmJ* 80, *WhoE* 74,
  WhoWor 74, -80, *WhoWorJ* 72, *WrDr* 76,
  -80, -82, -84
Mitton, Jacqueline 1948- *ConAu* 97
Mitton, Simon 1946- *ConAu* 97
Mizener, Arthur 1907- *AmAu&B, BioIn* 2, -4,
  BlueB 76, *ConAu* 5R, -5NR, *DrAS* 74E,
  -78E, -82E, *IntAu&W* 76, -77, -82,
  IntWW 74, -75, -76, -77, -78, -79, -80, -81,
  -82, -83, *REnAL, TwCA SUP,*
  WhoAm 74, -76, -78, -80, *WhoE* 74,
  WhoWor 74, *WrDr* 76, -80, -82, -84
Mizner, Elizabeth Howard 1907- *AuBYP,*
  BioIn 2, *ConAu* 13R, *CurBio* 51, *InWom,*
  IntAu&W 76, -77, -82, *SmATA* 27[port],
  WhoAmW 68, -70
Mizner, Elizabeth Howard *see also* Howard,
  Elizabeth
Mizumura, Kazue *AmPB, BioIn* 8, -9, -12,
  ChhPo S2, *ConAu* 85, *IlsBYP,*
  IlsCB 1957, -1967, *SmATA* 18, *ThrBJA*
Moche, Dinah L 1936- *ConAu* 89
Moe, Barbara 1937- *BioIn* 12, *ConAu* 69,
  SmATA 20
Moeri, Louise 1924- *ConAu* 9NR, -65,
  SmATA 24[port]
Moffat, Gwen 1924- *Au&Wr* 6,
  ConAu 10NR, -13R, *TwCCr&M* 80,
  WrDr 82, -84
Moffat, Mary Jane 1933- *ConAu* 97
Mohr, Nicholasa 1935- *AfroAA, AuBYP SUP,*
  BioIn 11, *ConAu* 1NR, -49, *IntAu&W* 77,
  SmATA 8
Mojtabai, A G 1938- *AmWomWr, ConAu* 85,
  ConLC 5, -9, -15
Moldafsky, Annie 1930- *ConAu* 61,
  WhoAmW 79, -81
Molden, Fritz P 1924- *BioIn* 11, -12,
  IntYB 78, -79, -80, -81, -82, *WhoWor* 74,

–76

Moliere 1622-1673 *AtIBL, BbD, BiD&SB, CasWL, ChhPo, CnThe, CyWA, DcCathB, DcEnL, DcEuL, Dis&D, EncWT, EuAu, EvEuW, LinLib L, –S, LongCEL, McGEWB, McGEWD, –84[port], NewC, NewEOp 71, NotNAT A, –B, OxEng, OxFr, OxMus, OxThe, PenC EUR, PIP&P, –A, RComWL, REn, REnWD, WorAl*

Molloy, Anne Stearns 1907- *AuBYP, BioIn 7, ConAu 13R, ForWC 70, SmATA 32[port], WhoAmW 58*

Molloy, Paul 1920- *BioIn 6, –10, ChhPo S2, ConAu 1R, SmATA 5, WhoAm 74, –76, WhoMW 74*

Momaday, N Scott 1934- *AmAu&B, BioIn 9, –10, –11, –12, ChhPo S1, CmCal, ConAu 25R, ConLC 2, –19, ConNov 76, –82, CurBio 75, DrAF 76, DrAP&F 83, REnAW, SmATA 30, WrDr 76, –80, –82, –84*

Momaday, Navarre Scott 1934- *BioIn 9, –10, –11, –12, DrAS 74E, –78E, –82E, WhoAm 74, –76, –78, –80, –82*

Momiyama, Nanae 1919?- *WhoAmA 76, –78, –80, –82, WhoAmW 75, –77, –79, –83*

Monaco, James 1942- *ConAu 69*

Monaghan, Patricia 1946- *ConAu 107, DrAP&F 83*

Mondale, Joan Adams 1930- *BioIn 10, –11, –12, ConAu 41R, CurBio 80[port], NewYTBS 76, –78, WhoAm 78, –80, –82, WhoAmA 78, –80, –82, WhoAmW 68, –70, –72, –77, –79, –81, WhoE 77, –79, –81, –83*

Mondey, David 1917- *ConAu 93*

Monjo, F N 1924-1978 *AuBYP SUP, ChlLR 2, ConAu 81, SmATA 16, TwCCW 83, WrDr 80*

Monjo, Ferdinand Nicholas 1924-1978 *BioIn 11, –12, ChlLR 2, TwCCW 78*

Monsarrat, Nicholas 1910-1979 *Au&Wr 6, BioIn 1, –2, –4, –7, –9, –12, BlueB 76, CanWW 70, –79, CanWr, ConAu 1R, –3NR, ConNov 72, –76, ConSFA, CurBio 50, –79N, DcLB 15[port], DcLEL, EncSF, EvLB, IntAu&W 76, –77, IntWW 74, –75, –76, –77, –78, –79, LinLib L, LongCTC, ModBrL, NewYTBS 79, Novels, REn, ScF&FL 1, TwCA SUP, TwCWr, WhAm 7, WhE&EA, Who 74, WhoWor 74, –76, –78, WrDr 76, –80*

Montagu, Ashley 1905- *AmAu&B, AmM&WS 73S, –76P, –79P, Au&Wr 6, BioIn 3, –4, –7, –8, –11, BlueB 76, CelR 73, ConAu 5R, –5NR, FifIDA, IntEnSS 79, TwCA SUP, WebAB, –79, Who 74, –82, –83, WhoAm 74, –76, –78, –80, –82, WhoAmJ 80, WhoE 74, WhoWor 76, WhoWorJ 72, –78, WorAl, WrDr 80, –82, –84*

Montagu, Ewen Edward Samuel 1901- *Au&Wr 6, BioIn 3, –4, –8, –11, BlueB 76, ConAu 77, CurBio 56, IntAu&W 76, –77, –82, Who 74, –82, –83, WhoWor 76, WhoWorJ 72, –78, WrDr 76, –80, –82, –84*

Monteleone, Thomas F 1946- *ConAu 109, EncSF, IntAu&W 82, WrDr 84*

Montgomerie, Norah Mary 1913- *AuBYP, BioIn 5, –7, –8, ChhPo, –S1, –S2, ConAu 105, IlsCB 1946, –1957, SmATA 26*

Montgomerie, William 1904- *Au&Wr 6, ChhPo, ConP 70, IntAu&W 76, –77, –82, IntWWP 77*

Montgomery, Elizabeth Rider 1902- *AuBYP, BioIn 2, –3, –7, –9, ChhPo S1, –S2, –S3, ConAu 1R, –3NR, CurBio 52, ForWC 70, InWom, IntAu&W 76, –77, –82, SmATA 3, –34[port], WhoAmW 74, –58, –61, –64, –68, –70, –72, –75, –77, –79, –81, WhoPNW, WhoThe 15, –16, –81*

Montgomery, L M 1874-1942 *ConAu 108, CurBio 42, ObitOF 79, TwCCW 83*

Montgomery, Lucy Maud 1874-1942 *BioIn 1, –3, –4, –6, –7, –10, –11, –12, CanWr, CarSB, CasWL, Chambr 3, ChhPo, –S1, –S2, –S3, CreCan 2, DcLEL, DcNAA, EvLB, InWom, JBA 34, LinLib L, LongCTC, MacDCB 78, OxAmL, OxCan, REn, REnAL, TwCA, TwCCW 78, TwCWr, WhNAA, YABC 1*

Montgomery, Robert Bruce 1921- *BioIn 1, –2, –10, CurBio 49, ScF&FL 1, WhoWest 76, –78, WorAu*

Montgomery, Robert Bruce *see also* Crispin, Edmund

Montgomery, Ruth Shick 1912- *AmWomWr, AuNews 1, BioIn 1, –4, –9, –10, ConAu 1R, –2NR, CurBio 57, ForWC 70, InWom, IntAu&W 76, –77, –82, WhoAm 74, –76, –78, –80, –82, WhoAmW 74, –58, –61, –64, –66, –68, –70, –72, –75, –77, WhoWor 74, –76, WrDr 76, –80, –82, –84*

Montgomery, Rutherford George 1894- *AmAu&B, AuBYP, BioIn 6, –7, –9, ConAu 9R, MorJA, ScF&FL 1, –2, SmATA 3, TwCCW 78, –83, WhNAA, WhoAm 74, –76, –78, WrDr 76, –80, –82, –84*

Montross, Lynn 1895-1961 *AmAu&B, BioIn 5, ObitOF 79, WhE&EA, WhNAA*

Moody, Anne 1940- *BioIn 8, –9, –11, ConAu 65, HerW, InB&W 80, IntAu&W 77, LivgBAA, SelBAA*

Moody, Ralph 1898- *AuBYP, BioIn 2, –3, –4, –6, –7, –8, –9, –12, ConAu P-1, CurBio 55, SmATA 1, WhoAm 74, –76, –78*

Moody, Raymond Avery, Jr. 1944- *ConAu 93, WhoAm 78, –80, –82*

Moon, Keith 1947-1978 *BioIn 11, –12, ObitOF 79, WhoRocM 82*

Moon, Keith *see also* Who, The
Mooney, Michael Macdonald 1930- *ConAu 65,*
DrAP&F 83, WrDr 82, –84
Moorcock, Michael 1939- *BioIn 12,*
ConAu 2NR, –45, ConLC 5, –27[port],
ConSFA, DcLB 14[port], EncSF,
IntAu&W 76, –77, LinLib L, MnBBF,
Novels, ScF&FL 1, –2, WhoHr&F,
WhoSciF, WrDr 76, –80, –82, –84
Moore, Barbara 1934- *ConAu 53,*
WhoAmW 74, WrDr 76, –80, –82, –84
Moore, Bob 1948- *ConAu 61*
Moore, Brian 1921- *ASpks, Au&Wr 6,*
BioIn 6, –8, –9, –10, –11, –12, BlueB 76,
CaW, CanWW 70, –79, –80, –81, –83,
CanWr, CasWL, ConAu 1R, –1NR,
ConLC 1, –3, –5, –7, –8, –19, ConNov 72,
–76, –82, CreCan 2, DcIrL, DcIrW 1,
DcLEL 1940, DrAF 76, DrInf, EncSF,
EncWL 2, IntAu&W 76, –77, –82,
IntWW 76, –77, –78, –79, –80, –81, –82, –83,
ModBrL SUP, NewC, Novels, OxCan,
OxCan SUP, PenC ENG, RAdv 1, REn,
REnAL, ScF&FL 1, –2, TwCWr,
WebE&AL, Who 74, –82, –83,
WhoAm 78, –80, –82, WhoE 75, WorAl,
WorAu, WrDr 76, –80, –82, –84
Moore, C L 1911-1958 *ConAu 104, ConSFA,*
EncSF, Novels, ScF&FL 1, –2,
WhoHr&F, WhoSciF
Moore, Carman Leroy 1936- *Baker 78,*
BiDAfM, BioIn 10, ConAmC, ConAu 61,
DrBIPA, InB&W 80, IntAu&W 77, –82,
LivgBAA, WhoAm 76, –78, –80, –82,
WhoAmM 83, WhoBlA 75, –77, –80,
WhoE 75, WrDr 76, –80, –82, –84
Moore, Frank Gardner 1865-1955 *BioIn 4,*
NatCAB 61[port], WhAm 3, WhNAA
Moore, Gaylen *WomWMM B*
Moore, Honor 1945- *ConAu 85, DrAP 75,*
DrAP&F 83, IntWWP 77, NatPD,
–81[port]
Moore, Janet Gaylord 1905- *BioIn 12,*
ConAu 77, IlsBYP, SmATA 18,
WhoAmW 58, –61
Moore, John A 1915- *AmM&WS 73P, –76P,*
–79P, –82P, Au&Wr 6, BioIn 11,
BlueB 76, ConAu 45, IntAu&W 82,
IntWW 74, –75, –76, –77, –78, –79, –80, –81,
–82, –83, McGMS 80[port], WhoAm 74,
–76, –78, –80, –82, WrDr 76, –80, –82, –84
Moore, John Newton 1920- *AmM&WS 73P,*
WhoAm 82, WhoMW 76, –78, –80
Moore, Kenny 1943- *BioIn 9, –12, ConAu X*
Moore, Lilian 1917-1967 *AuBYP, BioIn 7, –8,*
BkP, ChhPo S1, –S3, ConAu 1R, –2NR,
–103, FourBJA, ObitOF 79, WhAm 4,
WhoAmW 58, –61, –64, –66, –68, –70,
WhoLibS 55
Moore, Marianne Craig 1887-1972 *AmAu&B,*
AmWomWr, AmWr, AnCL, AnMV 1926,
BioIn 1, –2, –3, –4, –5, –6, –7, –8, –9, –10,

–11, –12, CasWL, ChhPo S2, CnDAL,
CnE&AP, CnMWL, ConAmA, ConAmL,
ConAu 1R, –3NR, –33R, ConLC 1, –2, –4,
–8, –10, –13, –19, ConP 70, CurBio 52,
–68, –72, –72N, DcLEL, EncAB-H,
EncWL, –2, EvLB, ForWC 70, GoodHs,
InWom, IntDcWB, IntWWP 77, LibW,
LinLib L, –S, LongCTC, MakMC,
McGEWB, ModAL, ModAL SUP,
NatCAB 57, NewYTBE 72,
NotAW MOD, ObitOF 79, ObitT 1971,
OxAmL, OxEng, PenC AM, RAdv 1,
REn, REnAL, SixAP, SmATA 20,
TwCA, TwCA SUP, TwCWr, WebAB,
–79, WebE&AL, WhDW, WhAm 5,
WhE&EA, WhoAmW 58, –61, –64, –66,
–68, –70, –72, WhoTwCL, WorAl
Moore, Patrick 1923- *Au&Wr 6, AuBYP,*
BioIn 7, BlueB 76, ConAu 8NR, –13R,
DcLEL 1940, EncSF, FourBJA,
IntAu&W 77, –82, ScF&FL 1, –2,
Who 74, WhoSciF, WhoWor 76,
WrDr 76, –80, –82, –84
Moore, Robert Lowell, Jr. 1925- *AmAu&B,*
AuNews 1, BioIn 10, ConAu 13R,
WhoAm 74, –76, –78, –80, –82
Moore, Robert Lowell, Jr. *see also* Moore, Robin
Moore, Robin 1925- *ArtCS, AuNews 1,*
BioIn 10, BioNews 74, CelR 73,
ConAu X, WorAl
Moore, Robin *see also* Moore, Robert Lowell, Jr.
Moore, Ruth 1908- *AmAu&B, Au&Wr 6,*
ConAu 1R, –6NR, CurBio 54,
IntAu&W 76, SmATA 23, WhoAm 74,
–76, –78, –80, –82, WhoAmW 74, –58, –64,
–66, –68, –70, –72
Moore, Ruth Nulton 1923- *ConAu 81,*
IntAu&W 82
Moore, S E *ConAu 2NR, –49, SmATA 23*
Moore, Silas *ScF&FL 1*
Moore, Susanna 1948- *ConAu 109*
Moorehead, Alan 1910-1983 *Au&Wr 6,*
BioIn 4, –6, –9, BlueB 76, ConAu 5R,
–6NR, –110, DcLEL 1940, FarE&A 78,
–79, –80, –81, IntAu&W 76, –77,
IntWW 74, –75, –76, –77, –78, –79, –80, –81,
–82, –83, LongCTC, NewC,
NewYTBS 83[port], REn, TwCA SUP,
WhE&EA, Who 74, –82, –83,
WhoWor 74, WrDr 76, –80, –82, –84
Moorehead, Caroline 1944- *ConAu 101,*
WrDr 82, –84
Moorhouse, Geoffrey 1931- *BioIn 10,*
ConAu 25R, IntAu&W 76, –77, –82,
Who 82, –83, WrDr 76, –80, –82, –84
Mooser, Stephen 1941- *ConAu 89,*
SmATA 28[port]
Moquin, Wayne 1930- *ChiSch, ConAu 33R*
Mora, Joseph Jacinto 1876-1947 *ArtsAmW,*
BioIn 1, ChhPo, DcNAA, IIBEAAW,
WhAm 2
Moraes, Frank 1907-1974 *BioIn 4, –10,*

*ConAu 49, ConAu P-1, CurBio 57, –74,
–74N, NewYTBS 74, ObitOF 79,
WhE&EA, WhoWor 74*

Moray Williams, Ursula 1911- *FourBJA,
IntAu&W 76, TwCCW 83, WhE&EA,
WrDr 76, –80, –82, –84*

Moray Williams, Ursula *see also* Williams,
Ursula Moray

More, Sir Thomas 1478-1535 *Alli, AtlBL,
BbD, BiDAmS, BiD&SB, BioIn 1, –2, –3,
–4, –5, –6, –7, –8, –9, –10, –11, –12, BrAu,
CasWL, Chambr 1, ChhPo, –S2, CroE&S,
CrtT 1, –4, CyEd, CyWA, DcAmSR,
DcBiPP, DcCathB, DcEnA, DcEnL,
DcEuL, DcLEL, Dis&D, EncSF,
EncUrb[port], EvLB, LinLib L, –S,
LongCEL, LuthC 75, McGEWB,
MouLC 1, NewC, OxEng, OxLaw,
PenC ENG, RAdv 1, REn, WebE&AL,
WhDW, WorAl*

Morehead, Albert Hodges 1909-1966 *AmAu&B,
AmSCAP 66, BioIn 3, –4, –7, ConAu P-1,
CurBio 55, –66, ObitOF 79, WhAm 4*

Morell, David Louis 1939- *WhoE 77, –79*

Morey, Walt 1907- *Au&Wr 6, AuBYP,
BioIn 8, –9, ConAu 29R, SmATA 3,
ThrBJA, TwCCW 78, –83, WrDr 80, –82,
–84*

Morey, Walter Nelson 1907- *WhoAm 74, –76,
–78, –80, –82, WhoPNW*

Morgan, Alfred Powell 1889-1972 *AuBYP,
BioIn 6, –7, –9, ConAu 107, MorJA,
SmATA 33[port], WhAm 5, WhNAA*

Morgan, Alison Mary 1930- *ConAu 1NR, –49,
SmATA 30[port], TwCCW 78, –83,
WrDr 76, –80, –82, –84*

Morgan, Bryan Stanford 1923-1976 *Au&Wr 6,
AuBYP SUP, ConAu 5R, –8NR, –9NR,
IntAu&W 76, –77, WhoWor 76, WrDr 76,
–80*

Morgan, Charles, Jr. 1930- *BioIn 6, –8, –11,
–12, CivR 74, ConAu 17R, WhoAm 80,
–82, WhoS&SW 73, –75, –76*

Morgan, Clifford Thomas 1915-1976
*AmM&WS 73P, BioIn 10, –11,
ConAu 1R, –4NR, –65, WhAm 6, –7,
WhoAm 74, –76*

Morgan, Edmund Sears 1916-1966 *AmAu&B,
Au&Wr 6, BlueB 76, ConAu 4NR, –9R,
DcLB 17[port], DrAS 74H, –78H, –82H,
WhoAm 74, –76, –78, –80, –82*

Morgan, Elizabeth 1947- *ConAu 108,
WhoAm 82, WhoE 83, WhoS&SW 80*

Morgan, Fred Troy 1926- *ConAu 89*

Morgan, Frederick 1922- *BioIn 10,
ConAu 17R, ConLC 23[port], ConP 75,
–80, DrAP 75, DrAP&F 83, IntWWP 77,
–82, WhoF&I 74, –75, WrDr 76, –80, –82,
–84*

Morgan, Geoffrey 1916- *AuBYP SUP,
ConAu 21R, MnBBF*

Morgan, Gwyneth *ConAu X*

Morgan, James 1861-1955 *Alli, Alli SUP,
AmAu&B, BioIn 3, –4, ObitOF 79,
WhAm 3, WhNAA*

Morgan, Joe Leonard 1943- *BioIn 10, –11, –12,
WhoAm 74, –78, –80, –82, WhoBlA 77, –80,
WhoProB 73, WorAl*

Morgan, Lael 1936- *ConAu 5NR, –53,
WrDr 76, –80, –82, –84*

Morgan, Murray 1916- *AmAu&B, AmNov,
BioIn 2, ConAmTC, ConAu 107,
WhoPNW*

Morgan, Roberta 1953- *ConAu 93,
IntAu&W 82*

Morgan, Robin 1941- *BioIn 1, ConAu 69,
ConLC 2, WhoAmW 79, –81, –83,
WhoHol A*

Morgan, Speer 1946- *ConAu 97, DrAP&F 83*

Morgan, Ted 1932- *BioIn 11, –12,
ConAu 3NR*

Morgan, Ted *see also* DeGramont, Sanche

Morgan-Grenville, Gerard Wyndham 1931-
*ConAu 57, IntAu&W 77, WrDr 76, –80,
–82, –84*

Morgenroth, Barbara *SmATA 36*

Morgenthau, Hans Joachim 1904-1980
*AmAu&B, AmM&WS 73S, –78S,
AnObit 1980[port], BioIn 4, –6, –11, –12,
ConAu 9R, –101, CurBio 63, –80N,
IntEnSS 79, NewYTBS 80, PolProf J,
TwCA SUP, WhAm 7, WhoAm 74, –76,
–78, –80, WhoAmJ 80, WhoWor 74,
WhoWorJ 72, –78*

Moriarty, Florence Jarman *ConAu 104,
WhoAm 74, WhoAmW 74, –64, –66, –68,
–70, –72, –75, –79, –81, –83, WhoE 74*

Morice, Anne 1918- *ConAu X, IntAu&W 76,
TwCCr&M 80, WrDr 82, –84*

Morison, Samuel Eliot 1887-1976 *AmAu&B,
AmWr SUP, ASpks, Au&Wr 6, AuBYP,
BioIn 2, –3, –4, –5, –6, –7, –8, –10, –11, –12,
BlueB 76, CelR 73, ConAu 1R, –4NR,
–65, CurBio 51, –62, –76, –76N,
DcLB 17[port], DcLEL, DrAS 74H,
EncAB-H, IntAu&W 76, –77, IntWW 74,
–75, –76, –77N, LinLib L, –S, LongCTC,
McGEWB, NatCAB 61, NewYTBE 71,
NewYTBS 76, ObitOF 79, OxAmH,
OxAmL, OxCan SUP, OxShips,
PenC AM, REn, REnAL, TwCA SUP,
WebAB, –79, WebAMB, WhAm 6, –7,
WhLit, Who 74, WhoAm 74, –76,
WhoWor 74, WorAl, WrDr 76*

Morman, Jean Mary 1925- *ConAu 61*

Morowitz, Harold Joseph 1927-
*AmM&WS 73P, –76P, –79P, –82P,
ConAu 104, WhoAm 74, –76, –78, –80, –82,
WhoTech 82, WhoWorJ 72, –78,
WrDr 84*

Morrell, David 1943- *ConAu 7NR, –57,
IntAu&W 76, –77, –82, Novels,
WhoMW 78*

Morressy, John 1930- *AuBYP SUP, BioIn 7,*

ConAu 8NR, -21R, DrAF 76, EncSF,
IntAu&W 77, ScF&FL 1, -2,
SmATA 23[port], WrDr 76, -80, -82, -84
Morris, Aldyth Vernon 1901- ConAu 29R,
NatPD, -81[port], WhoAmW 58, -61, -75,
-77
Morris, Desmond 1928- Au&Wr 6, BioIn 6,
-8, -10, -11, -12, BlueB 76, CelR 73,
ConAu 2NR, -45, CurBio 74,
DcLEL 1940, IntAu&W 76, -77, -82,
IntWW 74, -75, -76, -77, -78, -79, -80, -81,
-82, -83, LinLib L, SmATA 14, Who 74,
-82, -83, WhoAm 74, -76, -78, -80, -82,
WhoWor 74, -76, -78, -82, WrDr 76, -80,
-82, -84
Morris, Edita 1902- AmAu&B, AmNov,
Au&Wr 6, BioIn 2, -12, ConAu 1R,
-1NR, InWom, WhE&EA
Morris, Edmund 1940- ConAu 89,
WhoAm 82, WrDr 82, -84
Morris, Harry 1924- ChhPo S2, ConAu 9R,
DrAP 75, DrAP&F 83, DrAS 74E, -78E,
-82E, WrDr 76, -80, -82, -84
Morris, Ivan 1925-1976 Au&Wr 6, BioIn 11,
ConAu 9R, -11NR, -65, DrAS 74H,
NewYTBS 76, WhAm 7, WhoE 74,
WorAu 1970
Morris, James 1926- Au&Wr 6, BioIn 10,
-11, ConAu X, -1R, CurBio 64,
DcLEL 1940, IntAu&W 76X, -77X, -82X,
IntWW 74, -75, -76, -77, -78, -79, -80, -81,
-82, -83, NewYTBS 74, Who 74, -82, -83,
WhoWor 74, WorAu, WrDr 82, -84
Morris, James see also Morris, Jan
Morris, Jan 1926- ASpks, BioIn 10, -11,
BlueB 76, ConAu 1NR, -53,
IntAu&W 76, -77, -82, IntWW 74, -75,
-76, -77, -78, -79, -80, -81, -82, -83,
NewYTBS 74, Who 74, -82, -83,
WrDr 76, -80, -82, -84
Morris, Jan see also Morris, James
Morris, Jeannie 1935?- BioIn 9, -10
Morris, Mary Elizabeth 1913- ConAu 53,
WhoAm 74, -76, -78, -80, -82,
WhoAmW 74
Morris, Michelle 1941- ConAu 108
Morris, Norval 1923- BlueB 76, ConAu 37R,
DrAS 74P, -78P, -82P, WhoAm 76, -78,
-80, -82, WhoAmL 78, -79, -83,
WhoWor 74, -76
Morris, Richard 1939- ConAu 1NR, -45,
DrAP 75
Morris, Richard Brandon 1904- AmAu&B,
AuBYP, BioIn 7, ConAu 2NR, -49,
DcLB 17[port], DrAS 74H, -78H, -82H,
WhoAm 74, -76, -78, -80, -82
Morris, Richard Knowles 1915-
AmM&WS 73S, -76P, ConAu 21R,
LEduc 74, WhoE 74
Morris, Taylor 1923- ConAu 103
Morris, Terry Lesser 1914- ConAu 9R,
WhoAmW 74, -72, -75, -77, WhoE 74, -75,

-77, -79
Morris, William 1913- AmAu&B, BlueB 76,
ConAu 17R, LinLib L, SmATA 29[port],
WhoAm 74, -76, -78, -80, -82
Morris, Willie 1934- ASpks, AuBYP SUP,
AuNews 2, BioIn 7, -8, -9, -10, -11, -12,
BlueB 76, CelR 73, ConAu 17R,
CurBio 76, DcLB Y80B[port], DrAF 76,
IntAu&W 77, IntWW 74, -75, -76, -77,
-78, -79, -83, WhoAm 74, -76, -78, -80,
-82, WhoE 74, WhoWor 74, WorAl,
WrDr 80, -82, -84
Morris, Wright 1910- AmAu&B, AmNov,
AmWr, Au&Wr 6, BioIn 1, -2, -4, -7, -8,
-9, -10, -12, BlueB 76, CasWL, CmCal,
ConAu 9R, ConLC 1, -3, -7, -18,
ConNov 72, -76, -82, ConPhot,
CurBio 82[port], DcLB Y81A[port], -2,
DcLEL 1940, DrAF 76, EncWL, -2,
IntAu&W 76, -77, -82, ModAL,
ModAL SUP, NewYTBS 82[port],
Novels[port], OxAmL, PenC AM,
RAdv 1, REn, REnAL, TwCA SUP,
TwCWr, WebE&AL, WhoAm 74, -76,
-78, -80, -82, WhoTwCL, WhoWest 76,
WhoWor 74, WrDr 76, -80, -82, -84
Morrison, Carl V 1908- BiDrAPA 77,
ConAu 93
Morrison, Dorothy Nafus ConAu 8NR, -61,
SmATA 29[port]
Morrison, Lillian 1917- AnCL, BiDrLUS 70,
BioIn 2, -9, BkP, ChhPo, -S1, -S2, -S3,
ConAu 7NR, -9R, DrAP 75, DrAP&F 83,
SmATA 3, WhoAmW 58, WhoLibI 82,
WhoLibS 55, -66
Morrison, Lucile Phillips 1896- SmATA 17,
WhNAA, WhoAmW 74, -58, -61, -64, -66,
-68, -70, -72, -75, -77, -79, -81, -83,
WhoWest 74, -76, -78, -80, -82, -84
Morrison, Sean ChhPo S1
Morrison, Toni 1931- AmWomWr, BioIn 11,
-12, BlkAWP, ConAu 29R, ConLC 4,
-10, -22[port], ConNov 82, CurBio 79,
DcLB Y81A[port], -6[port], DrAF 76,
EncWL 2, InB&W 80, IntDcWB,
LivgBAA, ModBlW, NegAl 83[port],
NewYTBS 77, -79, -81[port], SelBAA,
WrDr 84
Morrison, Van 1945- BioIn 11, -12,
ConLC 21[port], EncPR&S 77, RkOn 78,
-84, RolSEnR 83, WhoRocM 82
Morriss, James E 1932- AuBYP SUP,
BioIn 11, ConAu 57, SmATA 8,
WhoE 77
Morrow, Charlotte ConAu X
Morrow, Charlotte see also Kirwan, Molly
Morrow
Morrow, Honore Willsie 1880-1940 AmAu&B,
AmWomWr, CurBio 40, DcNAA,
InWom, NatCAB 29, OxAmL, REnAL,
TwCA, WhAm 1, WisWr
Morrow, James 1947- ConAu 108

Morse, Anne Christensen 1915- *ConAu 1R*

Morse, Carol 1908- *ConAu X, CurBio 57, InWom, SmATA X, WrDr 76, -80, -82, -84*

Morse, Carol *see also* Yeakley, Marjory Hall

Morse, David 1940- *ChhPo S2, ConAu 37R*

Morse, Flo 1921- *ConAu 106, SmATA 30[port]*

Mortimer, John Clifford 1923- *Au&Wr 6, BioIn 10, BlueB 76, CnMD, CnThe, ConAu 13R, ConDr 73, -77, -82, CroCD, CurBio 83[port], DcLB 13[port], DcLEL 1940, EncWT, FilmgC, IntAu&W 76, -77, IntWW 81, -82, -83, LongCTC, McGEWD, -84, ModWD, NewC, Novels, REnWD, TwCWr, Who 74, -82, -83, WhoThe 15, -16, -81, WhoWor 74, WorAu, WrDr 76, -80, -82, -84*

Mortimer, Penelope 1918- *Au&Wr 6, BioIn 10, -12, BlueB 76, ConAu 57, ConLC 5, ConNov 72, -76, -82, DcLEL 1940, IntAu&W 76, -77, Novels, PenC ENG, TwCWr, Who 74, -82, -83, WhoAmW 74, -68, -70, -72, WhoWor 74, WorAu, WrDr 76, -80, -82, -84*

Morton, Alexander C 1936- *ConAu 25R*

Morton, Frederic 1924- *AmAu&B, AmNov, Au&Wr 6, BioIn 2, -10, ConAu 1R, -3NR, ModAL, WhoAm 74, -76, -78, -80, -82, WorAu*

Morton, Miriam 1918- *AuBYP SUP, BioIn 11, ChhPo, -S1, -S2, ConAu 2NR, -49, IntAu&W 76, SmATA 9, WhoAmW 77, -79, -81, -83*

Moscati, Sabatino 1922- *Au&Wr 6, ConAu 77, IntAu&W 76, -77, -82, WhoWor 78*

Moseley, Elizabeth Robards *ForWC 70, WhoAmW 66, -68, -70*

Moser, Don 1932- *ConAu 106, SmATA X*

Mosesson, Gloria Rubin 1924- *ConAu 41R, ForWC 70, SmATA 24[port], WhoAmW 58, -61, -64, -66, -68, -70, -72, -75, -77, WhoWorJ 72, -78*

Moskin, Marietta D 1928- *ConAu 73, SmATA 23[port]*

Moskowitz, Sam 1920- *ConAu 4NR, -5R, ConSFA, EncSF, IntAu&W 77, -82, LinLib L, ScF&FL 1, -2, WhoAm 76, -78, -80, -82, WhoHr&F, WhoSciF, WhoWor 78, -80, -82*

Mosley, Leonard 1913- *Au&Wr 6, ConAu 108, -109, IntAu&W 76, WrDr 76, -80, -82, -84*

Moss, Howard 1922- *AmAu&B, Au&Wr 6, BioIn 10, -12, ChhPo S3, ConAu 1R, -1NR, ConLC 7, -14, ConP 70, -75, -80, CroCAP, DcLB 5[port], DcLEL 1940, DrAP 75, DrAP&F 83, Dun&B 79, IntAu&W 76, -77, -82, IntWWP 77, -82, LElec, LinLib L, PenC AM, RAdv 1,*

WhoAm 74, -76, -78, -80, -82, WhoS&SW 75, -76, -78, WhoWest 82, -84, WhoWor 74, WorAu, WrDr 76, -80, -82, -84

Moss, Norman Bernard 1928- *BiDrAPA 77, ConAu 49, WhoAm 76, -78, -80, -82*

Mostert, Noel 1929- *ConAu 105, IntAu&W 82, WrDr 76, -80, -82, -84*

Mothner, Ira S 1932- *ConAu 21R, WhoE 74*

Motta, Dick 1931- *BioIn 9, -10, -11, WhoBbl 73*

Motz, Lloyd 1910- *AmM&WS 73P, -76P, -79P, -82P, BioIn 12, ConAu 4NR, -9R, IntAu&W 77, -82, SmATA 20, WhoAm 74, -76, -78, -80, -82, WhoAmJ 80, WhoWorJ 72, -78*

Mountfort, Guy Reginald 1905- *ConAu 17R, Who 74, -82, -83, WhoWor 76*

Moussard, Jacqueline 1924- *ConAu 8NR, -61, SmATA 24[port]*

Mowat, Farley 1921- *AmAu&B, Au&Wr 6, AuBYP, BioIn 2, -4, -5, -7, -9, -10, -11, -12, BlueB 76, CaW, CanWW 70, -79, -80, -81, -83, CanWr, CasWL, ConAu 1R, -4NR, ConLC 26[port], CreCan 2, DcLEL 1940, IntAu&W 76, -77, -82, IntWW 74, -75, -76, -77, -78, -79, -80, -81, -82, -83, LinLib L, OxCan, OxCan SUP, SmATA 3, ThrBJA, TwCCW 78, -83, WhoAm 74, -76, -78, -80, -82, WhoCan 73, -75, -77, -80, -82, WhoE 74, WhoWor 82, WorAu, WrDr 76, -80, -82, -84*

Mowry, George Edwin 1909- *AmAu&B, ConAu 1R, DrAS 74H, -78H, -82H, WhoAm 74, -76, -78, -80, -82, WhoWor 80, -82*

Moyers, Bill D 1934- *AuNews 1, BioIn 6, -7, -8, -9, -10, -11, -12, BlueB 76, ConAu 61, CurBio 66, -76, IntAu&W 77, IntWW 74, -75, -76, -77, -78, -79, -80, -81, -82, -83, NewYTET, PolProf J, Who 74, -82, -83, WhoAm 74, -76, -78, -80, -82, WhoAmP 73, WhoWor 74, -78, -80, -82, WorAl*

Moyes, Patricia 1923- *Au&Wr 6, BiE&WWA, ConAu 17R, EncMys, Novels, TwCCr&M 80, WrDr 76, -80, -82, -84*

Moynihan, Daniel Patrick 1927- *AlmAP 78, -80, -82[port], -84[port], AmAu&B, AmCath 80, AmM&WS 73S, BioIn 7, -8, -9, -10, -11, -12, BlueB 76, CelR 73, CngDr 77, -79, -81, -83, ConAu 5R, CurBio 68, DcAmDH, DcLEL 1940, IntWW 74, -75, -76, -77, -78, -79, -80, -81, -82, -83, IntYB 78, -79, -80, -81, -82, LinLib S, NewYTBS 74, -75, -76, -79, PolProf J, PolProf NF, USBiR 74, Who 83, WhoAm 74, -76, -78, -80, -82, WhoAmP 73, -75, -77, -79, -81, -83, WhoE 74, -77, -79, -81, -83, WhoGov 77,*

*-72, WhoWor 74, -76, -78, -80, -82,
WorAl, WrDr 80, -82, -84*
Mphahlele, Ezekiel 1919- *AfSS 78, -79, -80,
-81, -82, AfrA, BioIn 7, -8, -9, -11,
CasWL, ConAu 81, ConLC 25[port],
ConNov 72, -76, -82, DcLEL 1940,
DrAF 76, DrAP&F 83, EncWL, -2,
InB&W 80, IntAu&W 76, -77,
IntWW 74, -75, -76, -77, -78, -79, -80, -81,
-82, -83, LongCTC, ModBlW,
ModCmwL, Novels, PenC CL, -ENG,
RGAfL, TwCWr, WhoTwCL,
WhoWor 74, WorAu 1970, WrDr 76, -80,
-82, -84*
Mueller, Amelia 1911- *ConAu 57*
Mueller, Charles S 1929- *ConAu 5NR, -13R*
Mueller, Lisel 1924- *ConAu 93, ConLC 13,
DrAP 75, DrAP&F 83*
Muenchen, Al 1917- *ConAu 49, IlrAm F*
Muhammad Ali 1942- *CelR 73, CivR 74,
WebAB*
Muhammad Ali *see also* Ali, Muhammad
Muhlhausen, John Prague 1940- *ConAu 61,
WhoF&I 83*
Muir, Jean 1906-1973 *ConAu 29R, -41R,
ConAu P-2, ForWC 70, WhoAmW 74,
-66, -68, -70, -72, WorFshn*
Muir, John 1838-1914 *AmAu&B, AmBi,
ApCAB SUP, ApCAB X, BiDAmS,
BiD&SB, BioIn 1, -2, -3, -4, -5, -6, -7, -8,
-9, -10, -11, -12, CmCal, DcAmAu,
DcAmB, DcLEL, DcNAA, EncAAH,
EvLB, HarEnUS[port], InSci, JBA 34,
LinLib L, -S, McGEWB, NatCAB 9,
OxAmH, OxAmL, REn, REnAL,
REnAW, TwCA, TwCA SUP, TwCBDA,
WebAB, -79, WhAm 1, WisWr, WorAl*
Muirden, James 1942- *Au&Wr 6, ScF&FL 1*
Mukerji, Dhan Gopal 1890-1936 *AnCL,
AuBYP, BioIn 4, -7, BkCL, JBA 34,
LongCTC, Newb 1922, TwCA,
TwCCW 78, -83, WhAm 1*
Mulac, Margaret Elizabeth 1912- *ConAu 2NR,
-5R, ForWC 70, WhoAmW 74, -66, -68,
-72, -75, -77, -79*
Mulholland, Jim 1949- *ConAu 61*
Mulholland, John 1898-1970 *AmAu&B,
BioIn 3, -8, ConAu 5R, -89, REnAL,
WhAm 5, WhNAA*
Muller, Charles G 1897- *ConAu 1R, -2NR,
IntAu&W 77, -82, WhNAA, WrDr 76,
-80, -82, -84*
Muller, Marcia 1944- *ConAu 81*
Munce, Ruth Hill 1898- *BioIn 11, ConAu P-1,
SmATA 12*
Muncy, Raymond Lee 1928- *ConAu 49*
Mungo, Raymond 1946- *BioIn 9, -10,
ConAu 2NR, -49*
Munro, Alice 1931- *AuNews 2, BioIn 11,
CaW, CanWW 70, -79, -80, -81, -83,
ConAu 33R, -33R, ConLC 6, -10, -19,
ConNov 72, -76, -82, CreCan 1,*

*DcLEL 1940, IntAu&W 76, -77, OxCan,
OxCan SUP, SmATA 29[port],
WhoAm 80, -82, WhoAmW 83, WrDr 76,
-80, -82, -84*
Munro, Eleanor C 1928- *AuBYP, BioIn 7,
ConAu 1R, SmATA 37, WhoAmA 82,
WhoAmW 81, -83*
Munro, George Colin 1907- *AmM&WS 73P*
Munro, Hector Hugh 1870-1916 *Alli SUP,
AtlBL, BioIn 1, -5, -9, -10, -12, CasWL,
ChhPo, ConAu 104, DcLEL, EncSF,
EvLB, LongCTC, ModBrL, NewC,
Novels, OxEng, PenC ENG, RAdv 1,
REn, ScF&FL 1, TwCA, TwCA SUP,
TwCLC 3, WhoHr&F, WorAl*
Munro, Hector Hugh *see also* Saki
Munshower, Suzanne 1945- *ConAu 97*
Munson, Kenneth George 1929- *IntAu&W 77,
-82*
Munson, Thurman 1947-1979 *BioIn 11, -12,
ConAu 108, -89, CurBio 77, -79N,
NewYTBS 75, -79, WhoAm 78,
WhoBlA 77, WhoProB 73, WorAl*
Muntz, Hope 1907-1981 *BioIn 2,
IntAu&W 76, -77, -82, Who 74, -82N*
Munves, James 1922- *ConAu 3NR, -5R,
SmATA 30*
Munz, Peter 1921- *ConAu 13R, IntAu&W 77,
-82, WrDr 76, -80, -82, -84*
Munzer, Martha E 1899- *AuBYP SUP,
BioIn 9, ConAu 1R, -4NR, IntAu&W 77,
-82, SmATA 4, WrDr 76, -80, -82, -84*
Murari, Timeri N 1941- *ConAu 102,
IntAu&W 76, WhoWor 78*
Murchie, Guy 1907- *AmAu&B, BioIn 3,
ConAu 1R, IntAu&W 77, LinLib L,
WhE&EA, WhoAm 74, -76, -78, -80, -82,
WrDr 76, -80, -82, -84*
Murdoch, Iris 1919- *BioIn 3, -4, -5, -7, -8, -10,
-11, -12, BlueB 76, CasWL,
ConAu 8NR, -13R, ConDr 73, -77, -82,
ConLC 1, -2, -3, -4, -6, -8, -11, -15,
-22[port], ConNov 72, -76, -82,
CurBio 58, -80[port], DcIrW 1,
DcLB 14[port], EncWL, -2[port], InWom,
IntDcWB, IntWW 74, -75, -76, -77, -78,
-79, -80, -81, -82, -83, LinLib L,
LongCEL, LongCTC, ModBrL,
ModBrL SUP, NewC, Novels[port],
PenC ENG, PIP&P, RAdv 1, REn,
TwCWr, WebE&AL, Who 74, -82, -83,
WhoAm 80, -82, WhoAmW 74, -66, -68,
-70, -72, WhoTwCL, WhoWor 74, -76,
-78, -80, -82, WorAl, WorAu, WrDr 76,
-80, -82, -84*
Muro, Diane P 1940- *BioIn 11, ConAu 65*
Murphy, Arthur William 1922- *WhoAm 74,
-76, -78, -80, -82, WhoAtom 77*
Murphy, Barbara Beasley 1933- *BioIn 10,
ConAu 41R, DrAP&F 83, SmATA 5*
Murphy, Beatrice M 1908- *BlkAWP,
BroadAu[port], ConAu 9NR, -53,*

InB&W 80, LivgBAA, SelBAA,
WhoBlA 75, –77, –80
Murphy, Brian 1931- ConAu 21R
Murphy, E Jefferson 1926- AuBYP SUP,
BioIn 9, ConAu 25R, LEduc 74,
SmATA 4, WrDr 76, –80, –82, –84
Murphy, E Jefferson see also Murphy, Pat
Murphy, James Francis 1908- WhoMW 74
Murphy, Jim 1947- SmATA 32, –37
Murphy, Pat 1926- BioIn 9, ConAu X,
SmATA 4
Murphy, Pat see also Murphy, E Jefferson
Murphy, Patrick T 1939- ConAu 108,
WhoAmL 79
Murphy, Robert William 1902-1971 AuBYP,
BioIn 8, –9, –11, ConAu 29R, ConAu P-1,
ObitOF 79, SmATA 10
Murphy, Sharon Margaret 1940- ConAu 77,
WhoAmW 75, –77, –83
Murphy, Shirley Rousseau 1928- ConAu 21R,
SmATA 36, WhoAmW 74, –75, –77, –79,
WrDr 76, –80, –82, –84
Murray, Albert 1916- BioIn 9, BlkAWP,
ConAu 49, InB&W 80, LivgBAA,
NegAl 83, SelBAA, WhoAm 74, –76, –78,
WhoBlA 75, –77, –80, WrDr 76, –80, –82,
–84
Murray, Donald M 1924- AmAu&B, AuBYP,
ConAu 1R, WhoAm 74, –76, –78
Murray, Jim 1919- BioIn 10, –11, ConAu 65,
IntAu&W 76
Murray, John 1923- ConAu 4NR, –5R
Murray, Marian BioIn 10, ConAu 41R,
SmATA 5
Murray, Michael V 1906- ConAu 5R
Murray, Michael William 1932- WhoMW 80,
–82
Murray, Michele 1933-1974 AuBYP SUP,
BioIn 10, ConAu 49, NewYTBS 74,
ObitOF 79, SmATA 7
Murray, Pauli 1910- AmWomWr, BioIn 9,
–11, –12, BlkAWP, Ebony 1, InB&W 80,
NewYTBS 74, SelBAA, WhoAm 76, –78,
–82, WhoAmW 58, –61, –64, –66, –72, –77,
WhoBlA 75, –77, –80
Murray, Robert Keith 1922- ConAu 53,
DrAS 74H, –78H, –82H, IndAu 1917,
WhoAm 74, –76, –78, –80, –82
Murrell, Elsie Kathleen Seth-Smith 1883-
ConAu P-1
Murrow, Edward Roscoe 1908-1965 BioIn 1, –2,
–3, –4, –5, –6, –7, –8, –9, –10, –11, –12,
ConAu 103, –89, CurBio 42, –53, –65,
DcAmB S7, DcAmDH, EncAB-H,
LesBEnT[port], LinLib L, –S, McGEWB,
NatCAB 52, NewYTET, ObitOF 79,
PolProf E, PolProf K, REnAL, WebAB,
–79, WhDW, WhAm 4, WhScrn, –2,
WhoHol B
Musciano, Walter A AuBYP, BioIn 7
Musgrave, Florence 1902- AuBYP, BioIn 7, –9,
ConAu P-1, SmATA 3

Myers, Alpha Blanche 1912- BiDrLUS 70,
WhoAmW 75, –77, WhoLibS 55, –66
Myers, Arthur 1922- ConAu 7NR, –17R
Myers, Bernard Samuel 1908- Au&Wr 6,
ConAu 65, IntAu&W 76, –77,
WhoAm 76, –78, –80, –82, WhoE 75,
WhoWorJ 72, –78
Myers, Elisabeth Perkins 1918- AuBYP SUP,
ConAu 5R, ForWC 70, SmATA 36,
WhoAmW 74, WrDr 76
Myers, Gail Eldridge 1923- ConAu 1NR, –49,
DrAS 74E, –78E, –82E, LEduc 74,
WhoAm 78, –80, –82, WhoS&SW 82
Myers, John Myers 1906- AmAu&B, AmNov,
BioIn 2, –4, ConAu 1R, –1NR,
ScF&FL 1, –2, TwCA SUP, WrDr 84
Myers, Robert Manson 1921- BioIn 9,
ConAu 37R, DrAS 78E, –82E,
IntAu&W 76, –77, –82, NewYTBE 72,
WhoAm 74, –76, –78, –80, –82, WrDr 76,
–80, –82, –84
Myers, Walter Dean 1937- AuBYP SUP,
BlkAWP, ChlLR 4[port], ConAu 33R,
LivgBAA, SelBAA, SmATA 27,
WhoAm 76
Myrdal, Alva 1902- BioIn 2, –12, ConAu 69,
Future, InWom, IntDcWB, IntWW 74,
–75, –76, –77, –78, –79, –80, –81, –82, –83,
IntYB 78, –80, –81, –82, NewYTBS 82,
Who 74, –82, –83, WhoAmW 74, –68, –70,
–72, WhoWor 74, –76, –78, –80, –82
Myres, Sandra Lynn 1933- ConAu 33R,
DrAS 74H, –78H, –82H, WhoAmW 75,
–77
Myron, Robert 1926- AuBYP SUP,
ConAu 13R, DrAS 74H, –78H, –82H
Myrus, Donald 1927- AuBYP, BioIn 8,
ConAu 1R, –4NR, SmATA 23[port]

N

Nabokov, Peter 1940- *ConAu 9NR, –21R*
Nabokov, Vladimir 1899-1977 *AmAu&B,
AmNov,· AmWr, Au&Wr 6, BioIn 1, –2,
–4, –5, –6, –7, –8, –9, –10, –11, –12,
BlueB 76, CasWL, CelR 73, ClDMEL,
CnMWL, ConAu 5R, –69, ConLC 1, –2,
–3, –6, –8, –11, –15, –23[port], ConNov 72,
–76, ConP 75, CurBio 66, –77, –77N,
DcLB DS3[port], –Y80A[port], –2, DcLEL,
DcRusL, DrAF 76, EncSF, EncWL,
–2[port], EvEuW, IntAu&W 76, –77,
IntWW 74, –75, –76, –77, –78N,
IntWWP 77, –82, LinLib L, LongCTC,
MakMC, McGEWB, ModAL,
ModAL SUP, ModSL 1, NewYTBE 71,
–72, NewYTBS 77, Novels, ObitOF 79,
OxAmL, OxEng, PenC AM, RComWL,
REn, REnAL, ScF&FL 1, –2,
TwCA SUP, TwCWr, WebAB, –79,
WebE&AL, WhDW, WhAm 7, Who 74,
WhoAm 74, –76, –78, WhoTwCL,
WhoWor 74, WorAl, WrDr 76*
Nader, Ralph 1934- *AmAu&B, BioIn 7, –8,
–9, –10, –11, –12, BlueB 76, CelR 73,
ConAu 77, CurBio 68, EncAB-H,
IntAu&W 77, IntWW 74, –75, –76, –77,
–78, –79, –80, –81, –82, –83, LinLib L, –S,
MakMC, McGEWB, MugS,
NewYTBS 76, PolProf J, PolProf NF,
WebAB, –79, WhDW, Who 74, –82, –83,
WhoAm 74, –76, –78, –80, –82,
WhoAmL 78, –79, WhoWor 74, –78,
WorAl, WrDr 82, –84*
Naether, Carl 1892- *ConAu 25R, WhLit*
Nagel, Shirley 1922- *ConAu 93*
Nagenda, Musa *ConAu X*
Naha, Ed 1950- *ConAu 109*
Naipaul, Shiva 1945- *ConNov 82, Novels,
WrDr 82*
Naipaul, V S 1932- *BlueB 76, ConAu 1R,
–1NR, ConLC 4, –7, –9, –13, –18,
ConNov 82, CurBio 77, EncWL 2[port],
IntAu&W 82, IntWW 74, –75, –76, –77,
–78, –79, –80, –81, –82, –83, LinLib L,
ModCmwL, NewYTBS 80[port],
Novels[port], WhoWor 74, –76, –78, –80,
–82, WorAl, WrDr 80, –82, –84*
Naismith, James 1861-1939 *BioIn 1, –3, –4, –5,*

–9, –10, *DcAmB S2, NatCAB 33,
WebAB, –79, WhAm 1, WhoBbl 73,
WorAl*
Najafi, Najmeh *BioIn 6, –7, ConAu 25R,
InWom*
Nalty, Bernard Charles 1931- *ConAu 102,
DrAS 74H, –78H, –82H*
Namath, Joe 1943- *BioIn 7, –8, –9, –10, –11,
–12, BioNews 74, BlueB 76, CelR 73,
ConAu X, CurBio 66, FilmgC,
IntMPA 84, NewYTBE 70, –71, –72, –73,
NewYTBS 74, –75, –81[port], WhoAm 74,
–76, WhoFtbl 74, WhoHol A, WorAl*
Namioka, Lensey 1929- *ConAu 11NR, –69,
SmATA 27[port]*
Napier, John Russell 1917- *FifIDA, WrDr 84*
Narayan, R K 1906- *BioIn 1, ConAu 81,
ConLC 7, ConNov 82, EncWL 2,
LinLib L, McGEWB, ModCmwL, Novels,
Who 74, –82, –83, WrDr 80, –82, –84*
Narayan, Rasipuram Krishnaswami 1906-
*Au&W 6, BioIn 4, –6, –7, –9, –10, –11,
–12, CasWL, ConNov 72, –76, DcLEL,
DcOrL 2, EncWL, FarE&A 78, –79, –80,
–81, IntAu&W 76, –77, IntWW 74, –75,
–76, –77, –78, –79, –80, –81, –82, –83,
LongCTC, NewC, PenC ENG, REn,
TwCA SUP, WebE&AL, WhDW,
WhoWor 74, WrDr 76*
Naremore, James 1941- *ConAu 11NR, –69*
Narramore, Clyde Maurice 1916- *WhoAm 78*
Nasaw, Jonathan Lewis 1947- *ConAu 61*
Nash, Graham 1942- *BioIn 11, –12, IlEncRk,
RkOn 78, WhoAm 78, –80, –82,
WhoRocM 82, WorAl*
Nash, Graham *see also* Crosby, Stills, Nash &
Young
Nash, Jay Robert, III 1937- *ConAu 21R,
WhoAm 76, –78, –80, –82, WhoMW 82*
Nash, Ogden 1902-1971 *AmAu&B,
AmSCAP 66, AnCL, Au&Wr 6, AuBYP,
BiE&WWA, BioIn 1, –2, –3, –4, –5, –6, –7,
–8, –9, –10, –12, BkCL, CasWL, ChhPo,
–S1, –S2, –S3, CnDAL, CnE&AP,
CnMWL, ConAmA, ConAu 29R,
ConAu P-1, ConLC 23[port], ConP 70,
CurBio 41, –71, –71N, DcLB 11[port],
DcLEL, EncMT, EncWL, FourBJA,*

LinLib L, LongCTC, ModAL,
NewYTBE 71, NotNAT B, ObitOF 79,
ObitT 1971, OxAmL, PenC AM,
RAdv 1, REn, REnAL, SmATA 2,
TwCA, TwCA SUP, TwCWr, WebAB,
−79, WebE&AL, WhDW, WhAm 5,
WhoTwCL, WorAl

Naske, Claus-Michael 1935- *ConAu 77,*
DrAS 74H, −78H, −82H

Nathan, Robert 1894- *AmAu&B, AmNov,*
AmSCAP 66, Au&Wr 6, BioIn 1, −2, −4,
−5, −6, −8, −10, −12, BlueB 76, ChhPo, −S1,
−S3, CnDAL, ConAmA, ConAmC A,
ConAmL, ConAu 13R, −13R, ConNov 72,
−76, −82, DcInB, DcLB 9[port], EncSF,
IntAu&W 76, −77, −82, IntWW 74, −75,
−76, −77, −78, −79, −80, −81, −82, −83,
LinLib L, LongCTC, OxAmL, REn,
REnAL, ScF&FL 1, −2, SmATA 6,
TwCA, TwCA SUP, WhE&EA,
WhoAm 74, −76, −78, WhoAmJ 80,
WhoWest 74, WhoWorJ 72, −78,
WrDr 76, −80, −82, −84

Navarra, John Gabriel 1927- *AmM&WS 73P,*
−76P, −79P, −82P, AuBYP SUP, BioIn 5,
−11, ConAu 41R, IntAu&W 76, −77,
SmATA 8, WhoE 74

Navasky, Victor Saul 1932- *BioIn 12,*
ConAu 10NR, −21R, ScF&FL 1, −2,
WhoAm 80, −82, WhoE 74

Naylor, Gloria 1950- *ConAu 107,*
DrAP&F 83

Naylor, Penelope 1941- *BioIn 11, ConAu 37R,*
IlsBYP, SmATA 10

Naylor, Phyllis Reynolds 1933- *AuBYP SUP,*
BioIn 11, ConAu 8NR, −21R,
DrAP&F 83, IndAu 1917, IntAu&W 77,
−82, SmATA 12, WhoAmW 74, −75,
WrDr 76, −80, −82, −84

Neal, Harry Edward 1906- *AuBYP, BioIn 7,*
−10, ConAu 2NR, −5R, IntAu&W 76, −77,
−82, SmATA 5, WhoAm 76, −78, −80, −82,
WrDr 76, −80, −82, −84

Neame, Alan John 1924- *Au&Wr 6,*
ConAu 1R, −2NR, ConP 70, WrDr 76,
−80, −82, −84

Nebrensky, Alex *ConAu X*

Nee, Brett DeBary 1943- *ConAu 101*

Nee, Kay Bonner *BioIn 11, ConAu 2NR, −49,*
DrRegL 75, SmATA 10, WhoAmP 73,
WhoAmW 77, WhoF&I 83, WhoMW 80,
−82

Needleman, Jacob 1934- *BioIn 10,*
ConAu 29R, DrAS 74P, −78P, −82P,
SmATA 6, WhoRel 75, −77

Neels, Betty *WrDr 84*

Neely, Henry Mason 1942- *WhoBlA 75, −77,*
−80, WhoGov 77, −75

Neeper, Cary *BioIn 10, ConAu 57*

Nef, Evelyn Stefansson 1913- *ConAu 49,*
WhoAm 76, −78, −80, −82, WhoAmW 74,
−72, −75, −77

Nef, Evelyn Stefansson *see also* Stefansson,
Evelyn Bair

Neff, H Richard 1933- *ConAu 33R,*
WhoRel 77, WrDr 76, −80

Neft, David S 1937- *AmM&WS 73S,*
ConAu 41R

Neider, Charles 1915- *AmAu&B, BioIn 7, −10,*
ConAu 17R, WhoWest 80

Neiderman, Andrew 1940- *BioIn 9,*
ConAu 33R, DrAP&F 83

Neier, Aryeh 1937- *BioIn 10, −11, ConAu 57,*
CurBio 78, WhoAm 74, −76, −78, −80, −82

Neigoff, Mike 1920- *BioIn 11, ConAu 2NR,*
−5R, SmATA 13

Neihardt, John Gneisenau 1881-1973 *AmAu&B,*
AmLY, AnMV 1926, BioIn 3, −4, −11, −12,
ChhPo, −S2, −S3, CnDAL, ConAmA,
ConAmL, ConAu P-1, DcLB 9[port],
IntAu&W 76, −77, IntWW 74, −75, −76N,
IntWWP 77, LinLib L, −S, OxAmL, REn,
REnAL, REnAW, TwCA, TwCA SUP,
WebAB, −79, WhAm 6, WhLit,
WhoMW 74

Neil, Randy *ConAu X*

Neilan, Sarah *ConAu 69, WrDr 80, −82, −84*

Neill, A S 1883-1973 *ConAu 101, CurBio 61,*
−73, −73N, NewYTBE 73, ObitOF 79,
ObitT 1971, ScF&FL 1

Neill, Alexander Sutherland 1883-1973 *BioIn 1,*
−5, −6, −8, −9, −10, −12, ConAu 45, EvLB,
LongCTC, McGEWB, WhDW, WhAm 6,
WhE&EA, WhoWor 74

Neimark, Anne E 1935- *BioIn 9, ConAu 29R,*
SmATA 4, WhoAmW 75

Neimark, Paul G 1934- *AuBYP SUP,*
SmATA 37

Nelson, Carl Ellis 1916- *LEduc 74,*
WhoAm 74

Nelson, Cordner 1918- *ConAu 29R,*
IntAu&W 76, SmATA 29, WhoWest 78,
−80, −82, WrDr 76, −80, −82, −84

Nelson, Edna *BioIn 6, ConAu 5R,*
ForWC 70, MinnWr

Nelson, Eugene Clifford 1911- *ConAu 13R,*
DrAS 74P, −78P, WhoRel 77

Nelson, George 1908- *BioIn 12, ConArch,*
ConAu 81, DcD&D, DrRegL 75,
WhoAm 82

Nelson, Kent 1943- *ConAu 77, DrAP&F 83*

Nelson, Marg 1899- *AuBYP, ConAu 1R,*
−2NR

Nelson, Mary Carroll 1929- *ConAu 1NR, −49,*
SmATA 23[port], WhoAmA 78, −80, −82,
WhoAmW 79, WhoWest 80, −82, −84

Nelson, Ray Faraday 1931- *ConAu 69,*
DrAP&F 83, WrDr 84

Nelson, Richard K 1941- *ConAu 29R*

Nelson, Roy Paul 1923- *ConAu 7NR, −17R,*
DrAS 74E, −78E, −82E, WhoWest 74, −76,
−78, WrDr 76, −80, −82, −84

Nelson, Russell Sage, Jr. 1927- *DrAS 74H,*
−78H, −82H

Nelson, Shirley *DrAP&F 83*
Nelson, Walter Henry 1928- *AmAu&B,
ConAu 7NR, –13R, WhoAm 74, –76, –78,
–80, –82, WhoWor 78, –80, –82*
Nelson, Willie 1933- *BiDAmM, BioIn 11, –12,
ConAu 107, ConLC 17, CurBio 79,
EncFCWM 69, IntMPA 84,
NewYTBS 78, RolSEnR 83, WhoAm 78,
–80, –82, WhoRocM 82*
Nemerov, Howard 1920- *AmAu&B, AmWr,
Au&Wr 6, BioIn 4, –5, –7, –8, –10, –12,
BlueB 76, CasWL, ChhPo S1, CnE&AP,
ConAu 1R, –1NR, ConLC 2, –6, –9,
ConNov 72, –76, –82, ConP 70, –75, –80,
CroCAP, CurBio 64, DcLB Y83A,
–5[port], –6[port], DcLEL 1940, DrAF 76,
DrAP 75, DrAP&F 83, EncWL 2,
IntAu&W 76, –82, IntWW 74, –75, –76,
–77, –78, –79, –80, –81, –82, –83,
IntWWP 77, –82, LinLib L, ModAL,
ModAL SUP, Novels, OxAmL,
PenC AM, RAdv 1, REn, REnAL,
TwCA SUP, WhoAm 74, –76, –78, –80,
–82, WhoTwCL, WhoWor 74, –80, –82,
WhoWorJ 72, –78, WorAl, WrDr 76, –80,
–82, –84*
Nemiroff, Robert *AuNews 2, ConDr 77D,
–82D, NotNAT*
Neruda, Pablo 1904-1973 *BioIn 2, –4, –7, –8, –9,
–10, –11, –12, CasWL, CelR 73, CnMWL,
ConAu 45, ConAu P-2, ConLC 1, –2, –5,
–7, –9, CurBio 70, –73, –73N, DcSpL,
EncLatA, EncWL, –2[port], LinLib L, –S,
MakMC, ModLAL, NewYTBE 71, –73,
ObitOF 79, ObitT 1971, OxSpan,
PenC AM, REn, TwCA SUP, TwCWr,
WhDW, WhAm 6, WhoTwCL,
WhoWor 74, –78, WorAl*
Neruda, Pablo *see also* Reyes Y Basoalto,
Ricardo E Neft
Nesbitt, Cathleen 1888-1982 *AnObit 1982[port],
BiE&WWA, BioIn 4, –10, –11,
ConAu 107, CurBio 56, –82N, FilmgC,
MovMk, NewYTBS 82[port], NotNAT,
–A, Who 74, –82, WhoHol A,
WhoThe 15, –16, –81*
Ness, Evaline 1911- *AuBYP, BioIn 4, –6, –7,
–8, –9, BkP, ChlLR 6[port], ChhPo, –S1,
–S2, –S3, ConAu 5R, –5NR, IlsBYP,
IlsCB 1957, –1967, NewbC 1966,
SmATA 1, –26[port], ThrBJA,
TwCCW 78, –83, WhoAm 74, –76, –78,
–80, –82, WhoAmA 76, –78, –80, –82,
WhoAmW 74, –66, –68, –70, –72, –75,
WrDr 80, –82, –84*
Nestor, William P 1947- *ConAu 109*
Nettinga, James Zwemer 1912- *WhoRel 75*
Neufeld, John 1938- *AuBYP, BioIn 10,
ConAu 11NR, –25R, ConLC 17,
ScF&FL 1, –2, SmATA 6*
Nevell, Richard 1947- *ConAu 102*
Neville, Emily Cheney 1919- *AmWomWr,*

*AuBYP, BioIn 6, –7, –9, –10, BkCL,
ConAu 3NR, –5R, ConLC 12, ForWC 70,
LinLib L, MorBMP, NinCLC 1956,
SmATA 1, –1, ThrBJA, TwCCW 78, –83,
WhoAm 74, –76, –78, –80, –82,
WhoAmW 74, –66, –68, –70, –72, –75,
WrDr 80, –82, –84*
Nevins, Albert J 1915- *AmCath 80, AuBYP,
BioIn 3, –7, –12, BkC 6, CathA 1952,
ConAu 5R, –5NR, SmATA 20,
WhoAm 74, –76, –78, –80, –82, WhoRel 75,
–77, WhoWor 78*
Newbery, John 1713-1767 *Alli, BioIn 3, –4, –7,
–8, –9, –11, –12, BrAu, ChhPo, –S1,
DcLEL, LinLib L, NewC, REn, REnAL,
SmATA 20, WhoChL*
Newby, Eric 1919- *Au&Wr 6, BioIn 6, –8, –9,
ConAu 5R, IntAu&W 76, –77, –82,
Who 74, –82, –83, WrDr 76, –80, –82, –84*
Newby, P H 1918- *BlueB 76, ConAu 5R,
ConLC 13, ConNov 82, CurBio 53,
DcLB 15[port], LinLib L, Novels,
ScF&FL 1, –2, WrDr 80, –82, –84*
Newby, Percy Howard 1918- *Au&Wr 6,
BioIn 3, –4, –9, –10, CasWL, ConAu 5R,
ConLC 2, ConNov 72, –76, DcLEL 1940,
IntAu&W 76, –77, –82, IntWW 74, –75,
–76, LongCTC, ModBrL, ModBrL SUP,
NewC, RAdv 1, REn, TwCA SUP,
TwCWr, WebE&AL, WhoWor 74, –78,
–80, –82, WrDr 76*
Newcomb, Covelle 1908- *AmAu&B, AuBYP,
BioIn 1, –2, –7, BkC 1, CathA 1930,
ConAu P-2, JBA 51*
Newcomb, Kerry 1946- *ConAu 10NR, –65*
Newcombe, Jack *AuBYP, BioIn 12,
SmATA 33*
Newell, Hope 1896-1965 *AmAu&B, AuBYP,
BioIn 6, –7, ConAu 73, LinLib L,
MorJA, SmATA 24[port]*
Newell, Peter 1862-1924 *AmAu&B, AmBi,
CarSB, ChhPo, –S2, –S3, DcAmAu,
DcAmB, DcNAA, NatCAB 20, OxAmL,
TwCBDA, WhAm 1, WorECar*
Newhall, Beaumont 1908- *BioIn 11,
ConAu 9R, DcCAr 81, WhoAm 76, –78,
–80, –82, WhoAmA 73, –76, –78, –80, –82,
WhoWor 80, –82*
Newlon, Clarke 1905?-1982 *AuBYP SUP,
BioIn 10, ConAu 10NR, –108, –49,
IntAu&W 76, SmATA 33N, –6*
Newman, Andrea 1938- *Au&Wr 6, ConAu 73,
IntAu&W 77, –82, Novels, WrDr 76, –80,
–82, –84*
Newman, Bernard 1897-1968 *AuBYP SUP,
BioIn 5, –8, ConAu 25R, –97, ConSFA,
CurBio 59, –68, EncSF, LongCTC,
ScF&FL 1, TwCCr&M 80, WhAm 5,
WhE&EA, WhoSpyF*
Newman, Daisy 1904- *AuBYP SUP,
ConAu 37R, IntAu&W 76,
SmATA 27[port], WhoAmW 58, –61, –66,*

WrDr 76, -80, -82, -84

Newman, Edwin 1919- *BioIn 7, -8, -10, -11, BioNews 74, CelR 73, ChhPo S3, ConAu 5NR, -69, ConLC 14, CurBio 67, IntAu&W 82, IntMPA 78, -79, -81, -82, IntWW 77, -78, -79, -80, -81, -82, -83, NewYTET, WhoAm 74, -76, -78, -80, -82, WhoE 74, -75, WorAl*

Newman, Gerald 1931- *Dun&B 79, WhoAm 74, -76, -78, -80, -82, WhoAmJ 80, WhoF&I 74, -77, -79*

Newman, James Roy 1907-1966 *AmAu&B, BioIn 1, -4, -7, -9, WhAm 4*

Newman, Lee Scott 1953- *ConAu 65*

Newman, Randy 1943- *BiDAmM, BioIn 9, -10, -11, -12, CurBio 82[port], EncPR&S, -77, IlEncRk, NewYTBE 71, -72, RkOn 78, -84, RolSEnR 83, WhoAm 78, -80, -82, WhoRocM 82, WorAl*

Newman, Robert 1909- *AuBYP, BioIn 8, -9, ConAu 1R, -4NR, ScF&FL 1, -2, SmATA 4, TwCCW 83*

Newman, Sharan 1949- *ConAu 106*

Newman, Shirlee Petkin 1924- *AuBYP SUP, BioIn 11, ConAu 5R, ForWC 70, SmATA 10, WhoAmW 74, -66, -68, -72, -75, -77, WhoE 74*

Newman, Stephen Aaron 1946- *ConAu 97, WhoAmL 78, -79*

Newman, Thelma R 1925-1978 *BioIn 11, ConAu 7NR, -13R, -81, ForWC 70, LEduc 74*

Newman, William S 1912- *Baker 78, BlueB 76, ConAmC, ConAu 1R, -3NR, DrAS 74H, -78H, -82H, WhoAm 74, -76, -78, -80, -82, WhoAmM 83, WhoMus 72, WhoWor 74, WrDr 76, -80, -82, -84*

Newton, Huey P 1942- *BioIn 8, 9, -10, -11, -12, CelR 73, CivR 74, CivRSt, CmCal, CurBio 73, Ebony 1, LivgBAA, MugS, NegAl 76[port], -83[port], NewYTBE 70, PolProf J, SelBAA, WhoBlA 75, -77, -80*

Newton, Suzanne 1936- *AuBYP SUP, BioIn 10, ConAu 41R, IntAu&W 77, SmATA 5, WrDr 76, -80, -82, -84*

Ney, John 1923- *AuBYP SUP, SmATA 33*

Nguyen-Dinh-Hoa 1924- *ConAu 21R*

Nguyen-Du 1765-1820 *CasWL, DcOrL 2, PenC CL*

Niatum, Duane 1938- *ConAu X, DrAP 75, DrAP&F 83, IntWWP 77*

Niatum, Duane *see also* McGinnis, Duane

Niccacci, Rufino *BioIn 7*

Nicholas, A X 1943- *BlkAWP*

Nicholls, Peter 1939- *ConAu 105, EncSF, WhoSciF*

Nichols, John 1940- *BioIn 7, -12, ConAu 6NR, -9R, DcLB Y82B[port], WrDr 84*

Nichols, Nell Beaubien *AuBYP SUP, WhoAmW 58, -61, -64*

Nichols, Ruth 1948- *Au&Wr 6, AuBYP SUP,*

BioIn 10, -12, ConAu 25R, FourBJA, IntAu&W 76, OxCan SUP, Profile, ScF&FL 1, -2, SmATA 15, TwCCW 78, -83, WrDr 80, -82, -84

Nicholson, Margaret Beda 1924- *Au&Wr 6, ConAu 5R, IntAu&W 76, WrDr 76, -82, -84*

Nickelsburg, Janet 1893- *BioIn 11, ConAu 65, SmATA 11*

Nickson, Hilda 1912- *IntAu&W 76, -77*

Nicole, Christopher 1930- *Au&Wr 6, BioIn 10, ConAu 13R, ConNov 72, -76, -82, DcLEL 1940, IntAu&W 76, -77, -82, SmATA 5, TwCCr&M 80, WhoSpyF, WhoWor 76, -78, -80, WrDr 76, -80, -82, -84*

Niebling, Richard F *ChhPo S1, WhoAmP 75, -77*

Nieburg, Herbert Alan 1946- *WhoE 79, -81*

Niehuis, Charles C *AuBYP, BioIn 7*

Nielsen, Virginia 1909- *ConAu X, SmATA X*

Nielsen, Virginia *see also* McCall, Virginia Nielsen

Nierenberg, Gerard I 1923- *BioIn 12, ConAu 25R, -61, IntAu&W 77, WhoAmL 78, -79, WhoE 74, WrDr 76, -80, -82, -84*

Nies, Judith 1941- *ConAu 77, WhoAmW 75*

Niggli, Josefina 1910- *BioIn 12, ChiSch, ConAu P-2, DcLB Y80B[port], DrAS 74E, -78E, NatPD*

Niggli, Josephina 1910- *AmAu&B, AmNov, AmWomWr, BioIn 1, -2, -3, CurBio 49, InWom*

Nilsson, Harry 1941- *BiDAmM, BioIn 9, EncPR&S, -77, IlEncRk, RkOn 84, RolSEnR 83, WhoAm 74, -76, -78, -80, -82, WhoHol A, WhoRocM 82, WorAl*

Nilsson, Lennart 1922- *ConPhot*

Nisenson, Samuel 1905?-1968 *BioIn 8, IlsBYP*

Nissenson, Hugh 1933- *BioIn 10, ConAu 17R, ConLC 4, -9, DrAF 76, WhoAmJ 80, WhoWorJ 72, -78, WrDr 76, -80, -82, -84*

Niven, David 1910-1983 *Alli, ASpks, BioIn 4, -5, -7, -8, -9, -10, -11, BlueB 76, CelR 73, ConAu 110, -77, CurBio 57, -83N, FilmgC, IntAu&W 76, -77, IntMPA 77, -75, -76, -78, -79, -81, -82, IntWW 74, -75, -76, -77, -78, -79, -80, -81, -82, -83, MotPP, MovMk, NewYTBS 83[port], OxFilm, Who 74, -82, WhoAm 74, -76, -78, -80, -82, WhoHol A, WhoWor 74, WorAl, WorEFlm, WrDr 76, -80, -82, -84*

Niven, Larry *DrAF 76, WhoAm 74*

Niven, Larry 1938- *BioIn 12, ConAu X, ConLC 8, ConSFA, DcLB 8[port], EncSF, IntAu&W 82, Novels, ScF&FL 1, -2, WhoSciF, WrDr 80, -82, -84*

Niven, Larry *see also* Niven, Laurence VanCott

Niven, Laurence VanCott 1938- *BioIn 12, ConAu 21R, WhoAm 76, -78, -80, -82*

Niven, Laurence VanCott *see also* Niven, Larry

Niven, Laurence VonCott 1938- *WorAl*

Nixon, Joan Lowery 1927- *AuBYP SUP, BioIn 11, ConAu 7NR, –9R, IntAu&W 76, SmATA 8*

Nixon, Richard Milhous 1913- *AmAu&B, BiDrAC, BiDrUSE, BioIn 1, –2, –3, –4, –5, –6, –7, –8, –9, –10, –11, –12, BioNews 74, BlueB 76, CelR 73, CmCal, CngDr 74, ConAu 73, CurBio 48, –58, –69, DcAmSR, DcPol, EncAAH, EncAB-H, EncSoH, IntWW 74, –75, –76, –77, –78, –79, –80, –81, –82, –83, IntYB 78, –79, –80, –81, –82, LinLib L, –S, McGEWB, NewYTBE 71, –72, –73, NewYTBS 74, –75, PolProf E, PolProf J, PolProf K, PolProf NF, PolProf T, WebAB, –79, WhDW, Who 74, –82, –83, WhoAm 74, –76, –78, –80, –82, WhoAmP 73, –75, –77, –79, –81, –83, WhoE 74, –81, –83, WhoGov 77, –72, –75, WhoS&SW 73, WhoWest 74, –76, –78, WhoWor 74, –78, –80, –82, WorAl, WrDr 80, –82, –84*

Nizer, Louis 1902- *AmSCAP 66, BiE&WWA, BioIn 4, –6, –9, –11, CelR 73, ConAu 53, CurBio 55, IntMPA 77, –75, –76, –78, –79, –81, –82, –84, LinLib L, NewYTBE 71, NewYTBS 77, NotNAT, St&PR 75, WebAB, –79, WhoAm 74, –76, –78, –80, –82, WhoAmJ 80, WhoAmL 78, –79, WhoE 74, WhoWor 74, –76, WhoWorJ 72, –78, WorAl, WrDr 76, –80, –82, –84*

Nketia, J H Kwabena 1921- *ConAu 7NR, –X, InB&W 80, IntAu&W 76, WhoAmM 83*

Noad, Frederick 1929- *ConAu 4NR, –9R*

Nobile, Philip 1941- *WhoE 74, –75, –77*

Noble, Iris 1922- *AuBYP, BioIn 7, –10, ConAu 1R, –2NR, SmATA 5, WhoAmW 66*

Noble, Jeanne Laveta 1926- *BioIn 6, InB&W 80, InWom, LivgBAA, NegAl 76[port], –83[port], WhoAmW 58, –68, –70*

Noble, Mark d1827 *Alli, BiDLA, DcEnL*

Nodset, Joan L *AuBYP, BioIn 8, –9, ConAu X, SmATA 1, TwCCW 83, WrDr 80, –82, –84*

Nodset, Joan L *see also* Lexau, Joan M

Noel, Ruth 1947- *ConAu 69*

Noel Hume, Ivor 1927- *Au&Wr 6, BlueB 76, ConAu 13R, DrAS 82H, IntAu&W 76, –77, WhoAm 74, –76, –78, –80, –82, WhoWor 74, –76, –80, –82, WrDr 76, –80, –82, –84*

Nolan, Dennis 1945- *SmATA 34*

Nolan, Jeannette Covert 1897?-1974 *AmAu&B, Au&Wr 6, AuBYP, BioIn 2, –7, –9, ConAu 4NR, –5R, –53, ForWC 70, IndAu 1917, IntAu&W 76, JBA 51, SmATA 2, –27N, WhAm 6, WhE&EA, WhoAm 74, WhoAmW 74, –58, –61, –64, –66, –68, –70, –72, –75*

Nolan, Paul Thomas 1919- *ConAu 2NR, –5R, DrAS 74E, –74P, –78E, –78P, –82E, WhoAm 74, –76, –78, –80, –82, WhoS&SW 73, –75, –76, WrDr 76, –80, –82, –84*

Nolan, William F 1928- *BioIn 9, –12, ConAu 1R, –1NR, ConSFA, DcLB 8[port], EncMys, EncSF, IntAu&W 76, ScF&FL 1, –2, SmATA 28, St&PR 75, TwCCr&M 80, WhoAm 80, –82, WhoSciF, WhoWest 74, WrDr 76, –80, –82, –84*

Nolen, Barbara 1902- *ChhPo S2, ConAu 104, WhoAmW 74, –66, –68, –70, –72, –75, –77, WhoE 74, –75, –77*

Noonan, Michael John 1921- *Au&Wr 6, ConAu 21R, IntAu&W 76, WrDr 76, –80, –82, –84*

Nordberg, Robert B 1921- *ConAu 13R, LEduc 74*

Nordhoff, Charles Bernard 1887-1947 *AmAu&B, AmNov, AuBYP, BioIn 1, –2, –4, –5, –7, –8, –12, CnDAL, ConAu 108, CyWA, DcAmB S5, DcLB 9[port], DcLEL, DcNAA, JBA 34, LinLib L, LongCTC, MnBBF, Novels, ObitOF 79, OxAmL, PenC AM, REn, REnAL, SmATA 23[port], TwCA, TwCA SUP, WhAm 2, WorAl*

Noren, Catherine 1938- *ConAu 65, WhoAmW 79, –81*

Norfleet, Barbara Pugh 1926- *AmM&WS 78S, ConAu 107, WhoAmA 78, –80, –82*

Norman, Charles 1904- *AmAu&B, AuBYP, BioIn 4, –7, ChhPo S2, ConAu 107, REnAL, TwCA SUP, WhoAm 74, –76*

Norman, James 1912- *ConAu X, DrAP&F 83, ScF&FL 1, SmATA X, TwCCr&M 80, WhE&EA, WrDr 82, –84*

Norman, James *see also* Schmidt, James Norman

Norman, John 1931- *ConAu X, WrDr 84*

Norman, Lilith 1927- *ConAu 1NR, –45, TwCCW 78, –83, WrDr 80, –82, –84*

Norris, Frank 1870-1902 *AmAu&B, AmBi, AmWr, AtlBL, BbD, BiD&SB, BioIn 1, –2, –3, –4, –5, –6, –8, –9, –10, –11, –12, CasWL, Chambr 3, CmCal, CnDAL, CrtT 3, –4, CyWA, DcAmAu, DcAmB, DcBiA, DcLB 12[port], DcLEL, DcNAA, EncAAH, EvLB, LinLib L, LongCTC, ModAL, NatCAB 14, –15, Novels, OxAmH, OxAmL, OxEng, PenC AM, RAdv 1, REn, REnAL, REnAW, ScF&FL 1, TwCA, TwCA SUP, TwCBDA, TwCWr, WebAB, –79, WebE&AL, WhDW, WhAm 1, WhoHr&F, WorAl*

Norris, Kenneth Stafford 1924- *AmM&WS 73P, –76P, –79P, –82P, ConAu 77, WhoOcn 78, WhoWest 80, –82, –84*

Norris, Louanne 1930- *ConAu 53*

Norris, Marianna *AuBYP SUP*

North, Andrew 1912- *AmAu&B, ConAu X, CurBio 57, EncSF, IntAu&W 77X, ScF&FL 1, SmATA 1, TwCCW 83, WorAu, WrDr 84*

North, Andrew *see also* Norton, Alice Mary

North, Joan Marian 1920- *Au&Wr 6, AuBYP SUP, BioIn 12, ConAu 13R, IntAu&W 76, –77, ScF&FL 1, –2, SmATA 16, WhoAmW 70, WrDr 76, –80, –82, –84*

North, Sterling 1906-1974 *AmAu&B, AmNov, Au&Wr 6, AuBYP, BioIn 2, –4, –6, –7, –9, –10, BlueB 76N, ConAu 5R, –53, CurBio 43, –75, –75N, LinLib L, –S, NewYTBS 74, REnAL, ScF&FL 1, –2, SmATA 1, ThrBJA, TwCA, TwCA SUP, TwCCW 78, –83, WhAm 6, WhE&EA, WhoAm 74, WhoE 74*

North, Wheeler James 1922- *AmM&WS 73P, –76P, –79P, –82P, ConAu 101, WhoAm 76, –78, –80, –82, WhoOcn 78, WhoWest 74, –76, –78*

Norton, Alden H 1903- *ConAu 101, ConSFA, ScF&FL 1, –2, WhoSciF*

Norton, Alice Mary 1912- *AmAu&B, AuBYP, BioIn 4, –6, –9, –10, –12, ConAu 1R, –2NR, CurBio 57, OhA&B, SmATA 1*

Norton, Alice Mary *see also* North, Andrew

Norton, Alice Mary *see also* Norton, Andre

Norton, Andre 1912- *AuBYP, BioIn 4, –6, –9, –10, –12, ConAu X, ConLC 12, ConSFA, CurBio 57, DcLB 8, EncSF, InWom, IntAu&W 76, –77, LinLib L, MorJA, Novels, OhA&B, ScF&FL 1, –2, SenS, SmATA 1, TwCCW 78, –83, WhoAm 80, –82, WhoAmW 58, –61, WhoHr&F, WhoSciF, WorAu, WrDr 76, –80, –82, –84*

Norton, Andre *see also* Norton, Alice Mary

Norton, Browning *ConAu X, SmATA X*

Norton, Browning *see* Norton, Frank R B

Norton, Frank R B 1909- *BioIn 11, ConAu 61, SmATA 10*

Norton, Joseph Louis 1918- *AmM&WS 73S, –78S, ConAu 29R, LEduc 74, WhoE 75*

Norton, Mary 1903- *AnCL, Au&ICB, Au&Wr 6, AuBYP, BioIn 5, –6, –8, –9, –12, BkCL, CasWL, ChlLR 6[port], ConAu 97, ScF&FL 1, SmATA 18, ThrBJA, TwCCW 78, –83, WrDr 76, –80, –82, –84*

Norton, Olive 1913- *Au&Wr 6, ConAu 9R, WrDr 84*

Norvil, Manning *ConAu X*

Norway, Kate 1913- *ConAu X, WrDr 84*

Norway, Kate *see also* Norton, Olive

Norwood, Warren *DrAP&F 83*

Noshpitz, Joseph Dove 1922- *AmM&WS 73S, –76P, –79P, –82P, BiDrAPA 77, WhoAm 82*

Nostlinger, Christine 1936- *SmATA 37,*

TwCCW 78B, –83B

Nourse, Alan E 1928- *Au&Wr 6, AuBYP, BioIn 7, –12, ConAu 1R, –3NR, ConSFA, DcLB 8[port], EncSF, LinLib L, ScF&FL 1, –2, WhoPNW, WhoSciF, WrDr 84*

Nourse, James G 1947- *ConAu 105*

Novack, George 1905- *BlueB 76, ConAu 49, IntAu&W 77, WhoAm 74, –76, –78, –80, –82, WhoWor 74, WrDr 80, –82, –84*

Noverr, Douglas Arthur 1942- *ConAu 102, DrAS 78E, –82E*

Noyes, Nell Braly 1921- *ConAu 37R, IntAu&W 77, WrDr 76, –80*

Nugilak *OxCan SUP*

Null, Gary 1945- *ConAu 65*

Nunn, William Curtis 1908- *ConAu 1NR, –1R, DrAS 74H, –78H, –82H, IntAu&W 76, –82, WrDr 76, –80, –82, –84*

Nunn, William Curtis *see also* Curtis, Will

Nunn, William Curtis *see also* Twist, Ananias

Nurnberg, Maxwell 1897- *ChhPo S2, ConAu 2NR, –5R, SmATA 27*

Nutt, Grady 1934- *ConAu 97*

Nuttall, Kenneth 1907- *ConAu 17R, IntAu&W 76, WrDr 76*

Nyad, Diana 1949?- *BioIn 9, –10, –11, –12, CurBio 79, NewYTBS 78*

Nye, Naomi Shihab *DrAP&F 83*

Nye, Robert 1939- *Au&Wr 6, BioIn 10, ConAu 33R, ConLC 13, ConNov 72, –76, –82, ConP 70, –75, –80, DcLB 14[port], IntAu&W 76, –82, IntWWP 77, –82, Novels, SmATA 6, TwCCW 78, –83, Who 82, –83, WhoWor 76, WorAu 1970, WrDr 76, –80, –82, –84*

Nye, Russel Blaine 1913- *AmAu&B, Au&Wr 6, BioIn 4, BlueB 76, ConAu 1R, –4NR, CurBio 45, DrAS 74E, –78E, –82E, MichAu 80, OxAmL, REnAL, TwCA SUP, WhoAm 74, –76, –78, –80, –82, WrDr 76, –80, –82, –84*

Nyro, Laura 1947- *BiDAmM, BioIn 8, –9, –10, CelR 73, ConLC 17, EncPR&S, –77, IlEncRk, NewYTBS 76, RkOn 78, –84, RolSEnR 83, WhoAm 74, –76, –78, –80, –82, WhoAmW 74, –70, –72, –81, WorAl*

O

Oakes, Vanya 1909-1983 *BiDrLUS 70,*
BioIn 7, –10, ConAu 33R, SmATA 37N,
–6, WhoAmW 74, –70, –72, WhoWest 74,
–76
Oakes, Vanya *see also* Oakes, Virginia
Oakes, Virginia 1909- *AuBYP, BioIn 7, –10,*
WhE&EA
Oakes, Virginia *see also* Oakes, Vanya
Oakley, Ann 1944- *ConAu 6NR, –57,*
IntAu&W 77, IntDcWB, WrDr 76, –80,
–82, –84
Oakley, Mary Ann Bryant 1940- *ConAu 45,*
IntAu&W 76, WhoAmW 77, –79
Oaks, Dallin Harris 1932- *BlueB 76,*
ConAu 25R, DrAS 74P, –78P, –82P,
IntAu&W 77, LEduc 74, WhoAm 74, –76,
–78, –80, –82, WhoAmL 79, –83,
WhoRel 75, –77, WhoWest 74, –76, –78,
–80, –82, –84, WrDr 76, –80, –82, –84
Oates, John 1948- *BioIn 11, –12, WhoAm 80,*
–82, WhoRocM 82
Oates, John *see also* Hall & Oates
Oates, Joyce Carol 1938- *AmAu&B,*
AmWomWr, AuNews 1, BioIn 8, –9, –10,
–11, –12, BioNews 74, BlueB 76,
CelR 73, ChhPo S3, ConAu 5R,
ConLC 1, –2, –3, –6, –9, –11, –15, –19,
ConNov 72, –76, –82, CurBio 70,
DcLB Y81A[port], –2, –5[port],
DcLEL 1940, DrAF 76, DrAP&F 83,
EncWL, –2, ForWC 70, IntAu&W 76,
–77, –82, IntDcWB, LibW, LinLib L,
ModAL SUP, NewYTBS 80[port],
–82[port], Novels, Po&Wr 77, RAdv 1,
WhoAm 74, –76, –78, –80, –82,
WhoAmW 74, –70, –72, –81, –83,
WhoWor 74, –80, –82, WorAl,
WorAu 1970, WrDr 76, –80, –82, –84
Oates, Stephen Baery 1936- *ConAu 4NR, –9R,*
DrAS 74H, –78H, –82H, IntAu&W 77,
–82, WhoAm 74, –76, –78, –80, –82,
WrDr 76, –80, –82, –84
Oatley, Keith 1939- *ConAu 45*
O'Ballance, Edgar 1918- *ConAu 5R, –7NR,*
IntAu&W 76, –77, –82, WrDr 76, –80, –82,
–84
Oberg, James Edward 1944- *ConAu 108,*
UFOEn[port]

O'Brien, Andrew William 1910- *ConAu 25R*
O'Brien, Andrew William *see also* O'Brien, Andy
O'Brien, Andy 1910- *Au&Wr 6, ConAu X,*
WrDr 76, –80, –82, –84
O'Brien, Andy *see also* O'Brien, Andrew William
O'Brien, Esse Forrester 1895?-1975 *ConAu 61,*
ForWC 70, SmATA 30N, TexWr
O'Brien, Jack 1898-1938 *LinLib L, MorJA*
O'Brien, Jack *see also* O'Brien, John Sherman
O'Brien, John Sherman 1898-1938 *AuBYP,*
BioIn 1, –6, –7, DcNAA
O'Brien, John Sherman *see also* O'Brien, Jack
O'Brien, Justin 1906-1968 *Au&Wr 6, BioIn 1,*
–3, –8, ConAu 5R, –5NR, NotNAT B,
WhAm 5
O'Brien, Robert C 1918-1973 *AuBYP SUP,*
BioIn 9, ChlLR 2, ConAu X, EncSF,
FourBJA, NinCLC 1966, ScF&FL 1,
SmATA X, TwCCW 78, –83
O'Brien, Robert C *see also* Conly, Robert L
O'Brien, Tim 1946- *BioIn 12, ConAu 85,*
ConLC 7, –19, DcLB Y80B[port]
Obukhova, Lydia *ScF&FL 1*
O'Casey, Sean 1880?-1964 *AtlBL, BiE&WWA,*
BioIn 1, –2, –3, –4, –5, –6, –7, –8, –9, –10,
–11, –12, CasWL, Chambr 3, CnMD,
CnMWL, CnThe, ConAu 89, ConLC 1,
–5, –9, –11, –15, CroCD, CurBio 62, –64,
CyWA, DclrB, DclrL, DclrW 1, –2,
DcLB 10[port], DcLEL, EncWL, –2[port],
EncWT, EvLB, FilmgC, LinLib L, –S,
LongCEL, LongCTC, MakMC,
McGEWB, McGEWD, –84[port], ModBrL,
ModBrL SUP, ModWD, NewC,
NewYTBE 72, NotNAT A, –B,
ObitOF 79, ObitT 1961, OxEng, OxThe,
PenC ENG, PIP&P, RComWL, REn,
REnWD, TwCA, TwCA SUP, TwCWr,
WebE&AL, WhDW, WhAm 4,
WhE&EA, WhThe, WhoTwCL, WorAl
Ochs, Phil 1940-1976 *AmSCAP 66, BioIn 8,*
–10, –11, ConAu 65, ConLC 17,
EncFCWM 69, NewYTBE 71,
NewYTBS 76, ObitOF 79, RolSEnR 83,
WhAm 7, WhoRocM 82
O'Connell, Desmond Henry 1906-1973 *WhAm 5,*
WhoF&I 74
O'Connell, Margaret F 1935-1977 *BioIn 11,*

235

ConAu 73, NewYTBS 77, SmATA 30N
O'Connor, Dick 1930- *ConAu 97*
O'Connor, Edwin 1918-1968 *AmAu&B,*
BioIn 4, -5, -6, -7, -8, -10, ConAu 25R,
-93, ConLC 14, CurBio 63, -68,
DcLEL 1940, LinLib L, ModAL,
NotNAT B, Novels, ObitOF 79, OxAmL,
PenC AM, REnAL, WhAm 5, WorAl,
WorAu
O'Connor, Flannery 1925-1964 *AmAu&B,*
AmWomWr, AmWr, BioIn 2, -3, -4, -5,
-6, -7, -8, -9, -10, -11, -12, ConAu 1R,
-3NR, ConLC 1, -2, -3, -6, -10, -13, -15,
-21[port], ConNov 76, -82A, CurBio 58,
-65, DcLB Y80A[port], -2, DcLEL 1940,
EncWL, -2[port], InWom, IntDcWB,
LibW, LinLib L, ModAL, ModAL SUP,
NatCAB 55, NotAW MOD, Novels,
ObitOF 79, OxAmL, PenC AM, RAdv 1,
REn, REnAL, TwCWr, WebE&AL,
WhAm 4, WhoAmW 58, -61, -64, -66,
WhoTwCL, WorAl, WorAu
O'Connor, Frank 1903-1966 *AmAu&B, AtlBL,*
BioIn 2, -3, -4, -5, -7, -8, -11, -12, CasWL,
CnMD, ConAu X, ConLC 14, -23[port],
DcIrB, DcIrL, DcIrW 1, -2, -3, DcLEL,
EncWL 2, EvLB, LinLib L, LongCEL,
LongCTC, ModBrL, ModBrL SUP,
NewC, NotNAT B, Novels, ObitOF 79,
ObitT 1961, OxEng, PenC ENG,
RAdv 1, REn, TwCA SUP, WhDW,
WhAm 4, WhE&EA
O'Connor, Karen 1938- *SmATA 34[port]*
O'Connor, Karen *see also* Sweeney, Karen
O'Connor
O'Connor, Patrick 1915-1983 *AuBYP, BbtC,*
ConAu X, EncMys, IntAu&W 76X, -77X,
-82X, TwCCW 83, WrDr 80, -82, -84
O'Connor, Patrick *see also* Wibberley, Leonard
O'Connor, Richard 1915-1975 *AmAu&B,*
AuBYP SUP, BioIn 10, -12, ConAu 57,
-61, IndAu 1917, NewYTBS 75,
ObitOF 79, SmATA 21N, TwCCr&M 80,
WhAm 6, WhoAm 74, WhoE 74
O'Connor, Rod 1934- *AmM&WS 73P, -76P,*
-79P, -82P, WhoAm 74, -76, -78, -80, -82,
WhoTech 82
O'Daniel, Janet 1921- *ConAu 29R,*
SmATA 24[port], WrDr 76, -80, -82, -84
O'Dell, Scott 1903?- *AmAu&B, AmNov,*
AnCL, Au&ICB, AuBYP, BioIn 1, -2, -5,
-6, -7, -9, -10, -11, BkCL, ChlLR 1,
ConAu 61, LinLib L, MorJA,
NinCLC 1956, PiP, SenS, SmATA 12,
Str&VC, TwCCW 78, -83, WhoAm 74,
-76, -78, -80, -82, WhoWor 74, -78,
WrDr 80, -82, -84
O'Donnell, Jim *ConAu X*
O'Donnell, Kevin, Jr. 1950- *ConAu 106*
O'Donnell, Lillian 1926- *AmWomWr,*
ConAu 3NR, -5R, TwCCr&M 80,
WhoAmW 68, -70, WrDr 82, -84

O'Donoghue, Bryan 1921- *ConAu 77*
O'Faolain, Sean 1900- *BioIn 1, -3, -4, -5, -6,*
-7, -8, -11, BlueB 76, CasWL,
CathA 1930, ConAu 61, ConLC 1, -7,
-14, ConNov 72, -76, -82, CyWA, DcIrL,
DcIrW 1, -2, DcLB 15[port], DcLEL,
EncWL, EvLB, IntAu&W 76, -77,
IntWW 74, -75, -76, -77, -78, -79, -80, -81,
-82, -83, LinLib L, LongCEL, LongCTC,
ModBrL, ModBrL SUP, NewC, Novels,
PenC ENG, RAdv 1, REn, TwCA,
TwCA SUP, TwCWr, WhE&EA, WhLit,
Who 74, -82, -83, WhoAm 74,
WhoWor 74, -76, -78, WorAl, WrDr 76,
-80, -82, -84
Ofek, Uriel 1926- *ConAu 101, SmATA 36,*
WhoWorJ 72, -78
Offit, Sidney 1928- *AuBYP SUP, BioIn 11,*
ConAu 1R, -1NR, DrAF 76, SmATA 10,
WhoAm 74, -76, -78, -80, -82, WhoE 74,
-75, -77, WrDr 76, -80, -82, -84
Offutt, Andrew J 1934- *ConAu 41R, EncSF,*
ScF&FL 1, -2, WrDr 84
O'Flaherty, Liam 1896- *Au&Wr 6, BioIn 4,*
-5, -9, -10, -11, CasWL, Chambr 3,
ConAu 101, ConLC 5, ConNov 72, -76,
-82, CyWA, DcIrL, DcIrW 1, -3,
DcLEL, EncWL, EvLB, IntAu&W 76,
-77, -82, IntWW 74, -75, -76, -77, -78,
-79, -80, -81, -82, -83, LinLib L,
LongCEL, LongCTC, ModBrL,
ModBrL SUP, NewC, Novels, OxEng,
PenC ENG, REn, TwCA, TwCA SUP,
TwCWr, WhDW, WhE&EA, Who 74,
-82, -83, WhoWor 74, WorAl, WrDr 76,
-80, -82, -84
Ogan, George F 1912- *AuBYP SUP, BioIn 11,*
ConAu 4NR, -9R, SmATA 13
Ogan, Margaret E 1923-1979 *AuBYP SUP,*
BioIn 11, ConAu 4NR, -9R, SmATA 13
Ogburn, Charlton, Jr. 1911- *AmAu&B,*
Au&Wr 6, BioIn 9, ConAu 3NR, -5R,
IntAu&W 82, SmATA 3, WhoAm 74,
-76, -78, -80, -82, WhoS&SW 73,
WrDr 80, -82, -84
Ogg, Oscar 1908-1971 *BioIn 9, ConAu 33R,*
ConAu P-1, LinLib L, NewYTBE 71,
WhoAmA 78N, -80N, -82N, WhoGrA
Ogilvie, Elisabeth 1917- *AmAu&B, AmNov,*
AuBYP, BioIn 2, -4, -5, -8, ConAu 103,
CurBio 51, InWom, SmATA 29,
TwCA SUP, WhoAmW 74, -58, -61, -64,
-66, -68, -70, -72, -75, -77, WhoE 74,
WrDr 84
Ogle, James Lawrence 1911- *ConAu 5R*
Ogle, Jim *ConAu X*
Ogle, Jim *see also* Ogle, James Lawrence
Oglesby, Carl 1935- *BioIn 11, PolProf J,*
WhoAm 74
O'Hanlon, Jacklyn *ConAu X, SmATA X*
O'Hanlon, Jacklyn *see also* Meek, Jacklyn
O'Hanlon

O'Hara, Mary 1885-1980 *AmAu&B, AmNov, AnObit 1980[port], BioIn 1, -2, -3, -4, -7, -9, -12, CathA 1952, ConAu X, CurBio 44, -81N, InWom, LinLib L, REn, REnAL, SmATA X, -2, TwCA SUP, TwCCW 78, -83, WhAm 7, WhoAm 74, -76, -78, -80, WhoAmW 74, -58, -61, -66, -68, -70, -72, WorAl, WrDr 80, -82*

O'Hara, Mary *see also* Alsop, Mary O'Hara

O'Kane, Dick *AuBYP SUP*

O'Keeffe, Georgia 1887- *ArtsAmW, BioIn 1, -2, -4, -5, -6, -7, -8, -9, -10, -11, -12, BnEnAmA, CelR 73, ConArt 83, ConAu 110, CurBio 41, -64, DcAmArt, DcCAA 71, -77, DcCAr 81, EncAB-H, GoodHs, IntDcWB, LibW, LinLib S, McGDA, McGEWB, OxArt, OxTwCA, PhDcTCA 77, REn, WebAB, -79, Who 74, -82, -83, WhoAm 74, -76, -78, -80, -82, WhoAmA 73, -76, -80, -82, WhoAmW 74, -58, -64, -66, -68, -70, -83, WhoWest 74, WomArt, -A, WorAl*

Okimoto, Jean Davies 1942- *ConAu 97, SmATA 34[port]*

Okrent, Daniel 1948- *ConAu 105, WhoAm 74, -76*

Okun, Lawrence E 1929- *ConAu 101*

Okun, Milton 1923?- *AmSCAP 66, EncFCWM 69, WhoE 79, -81*

Olander, Joseph D *ScF&FL 1*

Olcheski, Bill 1925- *ConAu 8NR, -61*

Olcott, Henry Steel 1832-1907 *Alli, Alli SUP, AmAu&B, AmBi, BiDPara, BioIn 4, -8, -9, DcAmB, DcAmReB, DcNAA, EncO&P 78, NatCAB 8, OhA&B, WhAm 1, WorAl*

Oldham, Mary 1944- *ConAu 109*

O'Leary, Liam 1910- *ConAu 109, DcIrW 2, IntAu&W 77, WrDr 76, -80, -82, -84*

Oleksy, Walter 1930- *ConAu 1NR, -45, SmATA 33[port]*

Olesker, J Bradford *BioIn 10*

Olesky, Walter 1930- *SmATA X*

Olesky, Walter *see also* Oleksy, Walter

Olfson, Lewy 1937- *ConAu 93, NatPD*

Oliver, Carl Russell 1941- *ConAu 106*

Oliver, Jane 1903-1970 *Au&Wr 6, AuBYP, BioIn 8, ChhPo, ConAu X*

Oliver, Jane *see also* Rees, Helen Christina Easson

Oliver, Mary 1935- *BioIn 12, ChhPo S2, ConAu 9NR, -21R, ConLC 19, DcLB 5, IntAu&W 77, -82, IntWWP 77, WhoAm 74, -76, -78, -80, -82, WhoAmW 83, WrDr 76, -80, -82, -84*

Oliver, Roland 1923- *Au&Wr 6, BlueB 76, ConAu 73, IntAu&W 76, -77, -82, IntWW 74, -75, -76, -77, -78, -79, -80, -81, -82, -83, Who 74, -82, -83, WhoWor 78, WrDr 76, -80, -82, -84*

Olney, Ross Robert 1929- *AuBYP, BioIn 11,*

ConAu 7NR, -13R, IntAu&W 77, -82, ScF&FL 1, -2, SmATA 13, WhoWest 76, -78, WrDr 76, -80, -82, -84

Olsen, Alfa-Betty 1947- *ConAu 103*

Olsen, Eugene E 1936- *ConAu 33R*

Olsen, Jack 1925- *ConAu X, WhoAm 74, -76, -78, -80, -82, WhoWor 82*

Olsen, Jack *see also* Olsen, John Edward

Olsen, John Edward 1925- *ConAu 9NR, -17R, IndAu 1917*

Olsen, John Edward *see also* Olsen, Jack

Olsen, Theodore Victor 1932- *ConAu 1R, WrDr 76*

Olsen, Viggo Norskov 1916- *ConAu 53, DrAS 74P, -78P, -82P, WhoAm 82, WhoRel 75, WhoWest 82, -84*

Olson, David F 1938- *ConAu 49*

Olson, Eric 1944- *ConAu 53*

Olson, Eugene E 1936- *ConAu 33R, ScF&FL 1, UFOEn*

Olson, Eugene E *see also* Steiger, Brad

Olson, Gene 1922- *AuBYP, BioIn 7, ConAu 106, SmATA 32[port]*

Olson, McKinley C 1931- *WrDr 82*

Olson, Sigurd F 1899-1982 *AmM&WS 73P, BioIn 6, -7, -8, -12, BlueB 76, ConAu 1R, -1NR, -105, IntAu&W 77, MinnWr, NewYTBS 82[port], OxCan, WhoAm 74, -76, -78, WhoMW 74, -76, WrDr 80, -82, -84*

Olson, Toby 1937- *ConAu 9NR, -65, ConP 80, DrAP&F 83, WrDr 82, -84*

O'Meara, Walter Andrew 1897- *AmAu&B, Au&Wr 6, BioIn 1, -4, -5, -6, -10, ConAu 13R, CurBio 58, MinnWr, ScF&FL 1, -2, WhoAm 74, -76*

Oneal, Zibby *ConAu X, SmATA X*

O'Neil, Robert M 1934- *BioIn 12, ConAu 106, DrAS 82P, WhoAm 82*

O'Neil, Terry 1949- *ConAu 61*

O'Neill, David P 1918- *ConAu 17R*

O'Neill, Eugene 1888-1953 *AmAu&B, AmWr, ApCAB X, AtlBL, AuNews 1, BioIn 1, -2, -3, -4, -5, -6, -7, -8, -9, -10, -11, -12, BioNews 74, Chambr 3, CmCal, CnDAL, CnMD, CnMWL, CnThe, ConAmA, ConAmL, ConAu 110, CroCD, CyWA, DcAmB S5, DcLB 7[port], DcLEL, Dis&D, EncAB-H, EncWL, -2[port], EncWT, EvLB, FilmgC, LinLib L, -S, LongCTC, MakMC, McGEWB, McGEWD, -84[port], ModAL, ModAL SUP, ModWD, NatCAB 55, NewEOp 71, NotNAT A, -B, ObitOF 79, ObitT 1951, OxAmH, OxAmL, OxEng, OxThe, PenC AM, PIP&P, -A, RComWL, REn, REnAL, REnWD, TwCA, TwCA SUP, TwCLC 1, -6[port], TwCWr, WebAB, -79, WebE&AL, WhDW, WhAm 3, WhE&EA, WhThe, WhoTwCL, WorAl*

O'Neill, Gerard Kitchen 1927- *AmM&WS 76P,*

−79P, BioIn 11, −12, ConAu 93,
CurBio 79, Future, IntAu&W 82,
WhoAm 74, −76, −78, −80, −82,
WhoWor 80, −82

O'Neill, William Lawrence 1935- *ConAu 21R,*
DcLEL 1940, DrAS 74H, −78H, −82H,
IntAu&W 77, −82, WhoAm 80, −82,
WhoE 79, −81, −83, WrDr 76, −80, −82, −84

Onoda, Hiroo 1922- *BioIn 10, ConAu 108,*
NewYTBS 74

Opdyke, John Baker 1878-1956 *AmAu&B,*
ObitOF 79

Opie, Iona 1923- *AnCL, Au&Wr 6, BioIn 9,*
ChhPo, −S1, −S2, −S3, ConAu 61,
IntAu&W 76, −77, −82, SmATA 3,
Who 82, −83, WrDr 76, −80, −82, −84

Opie, Peter 1918-1982 *AnObit 1982, AnCL,*
Au&Wr 6, BioIn 9, ChhPo S3,
ConAu 2NR, −5R, −106, IntAu&W 76, −77,
−82, SmATA 28N, −3, Who 82, −83N,
WhoWor 78, WrDr 76, −80, −82

Oppenheim, A Leo 1904-1974 *ConAu 49*

Oppenheim, Shulamith 1930- *ConAu 73*

Oppenheimer, Joan L 1925- *ConAu 37R,*
IntAu&W 82, SmATA 28[port]

Orbach, Susie 1946- *ConAu 85*

Orben, Robert 1927- *BioIn 9, −10, −12,*
ConAu 81, NewYTET, WhoAm 82,
WhoS&SW 80, −82

Orczy, Baroness Emmuska 1865-1947 *AuBYP,*
BioIn 1, −4, −5, −8, ConAu X, DcLEL,
EncMys, EvLB, InWom, LongCTC,
NewC, NotNAT B, REn, TelT, TwCA,
TwCA SUP, TwCWr, WhThe, WhoLA

Ordish, George 1908?- *Au&Wr 6,*
ConAu 9NR, −61, IntAu&W 76, −77,
WrDr 76, −80, −82, −84

Ordway, Frederick Ira, III 1927-
AmM&WS 73P, −79P, BioIn 12,
BlueB 76, ConAu 5R, −5NR, WhoAm 74,
−76, −78, −80, −82, WhoWor 74, WrDr 80,
−82, −84

Orgel, Doris 1929- *AuBYP, AuNews 1,*
BioIn 8, −10, ChhPo S3, ConAu 2NR, −45,
FourBJA, SmATA 7, TwCCW 78, −83,
WrDr 84

Orkin, Ruth 1921- *ConPhot, WhoAmA 82*

Orlob, Helen Seaburg 1908- *AuBYP SUP,*
ConAu 5R, WhoPNW

Ormond, Clyde 1906- *ConAu 9R*

O'Rourke, Frank 1916- *AmAu&B, ScF&FL 1,*
WrDr 84

O'Rourke, William 1945- *ConAu 1NR, −45,*
DrAF 76, WhoAm 76, −78, −80, −82,
WhoE 75, WrDr 76, −80, −82, −84

Orr, Bobby 1948- *BioIn 7, −8, −9, −10, −11, −12,*
CelR 73, CurBio 69, NewYTBE 71,
WorAl

Orr, Jack *AuBYP SUP, ChhPo*

Orr, Robert Thomas 1908- *AmM&WS 73P,*
−76P, −79P, −82P, ConAu 33R,
WhoAm 74, −76, −78, −80, −82,

WhoWest 74, −76

Orrmont, Arthur 1922- *AuBYP SUP,*
ConAu 1R, −4NR, WhoCon 73, WhoE 77,
−79

Ortego, Philip D 1926- *DrAF 76, DrAP 75,*
DrAP&F 83, DrAS 74E

Ortiz, Simon J 1941- *ConP 80, DrAP 75,*
DrAP&F 83, WrDr 82, −84

Ortiz, Victoria 1942- *ConAu 107*

Ortzen, Leonard Edwin 1912- *Au&Wr 6,*
IntAu&W 76, WhoWor 76

Orwell, George 1903-1950 *AtlBL, BioIn 1, −2,*
−3, −4, −5, −6, −7, −8, −9, −10, −11, −12,
CasWL, CnMWL, ConAu X, CyWA,
DcAmSR, DcLB 15[port], DcLEL,
EncSF, EncWL, −2[port], EvLB,
LinLib L, −LP, LongCEL, LongCTC,
MakMC, McGEWB, ModBrL,
ModBrL SUP, NewC, NewYTBE 72,
Novels[port], ObitOF 79, OxEng,
PenC ENG, RAdv 1, REn, ScF&FL 1,
SmATA X, TwCA, TwCA SUP,
TwCLC 2, −6[port], TwCWr, WebE&AL,
WhDW, WhAm 4, WhoSciF, WhoTwCL,
WorAl

Osborne, Adam 1939- *AmM&WS 73P,*
BioIn 12, ConAu 109, LElec

Osborne, Charles 1927- *ConAu 13R, ConP 70,*
DcLEL 1940, IntAu&W 76, −77, −82,
IntWWM 77, IntWWP 77, −82, Who 82,
−83, WhoMus 72, WrDr 76, −80, −82, −84

Osborne, David 1935- *AuBYP, ConAu X,*
SmATA X, ThrBJA, WrDr 84

Osborne, David *see also* Silverberg, Robert

Osborne, John Franklin 1907-1981 *AnObit 1981,*
BioIn 8, −9, −12, ConAu 10NR, −108, −61,
NewYTBS 81[port], WhAm 7,
WhoAm 74, −76, −78, −80

Osborne, John James 1929- *Au&Wr 6,*
BiE&WWA, BioIn 4, −5, −6, −7, −8, −9, −10,
−11, −12, BlueB 76, CasWL, CelR 73,
CnMD, CnMWL, CnThe, ConAu 13R,
ConDr 73, −77, −82, ConLC 1, −2, −5, −11,
CroCD, DcLB 13[port], DcLEL 1940,
EncWL, −2[port], EncWT, FilmgC,
IntAu&W 76, −77, −82, IntMPA 77, −75,
−76, −78, −79, −81, −82, −84, IntWW 74,
−75, −76, −77, −78, −79, −80, −81, −82, −83,
LinLib L, LongCEL, LongCTC, MakMC,
McGEWB, McGEWD, −84[port], ModBrL,
ModBrL SUP, ModWD, NewC, NotNAT,
−A, OxEng, OxFilm, OxThe, PenC ENG,
PIP&P, RComWL, REn, REnWD,
TwCWr, WebE&AL, WhDW, Who 74,
−83, WhoAm 74, −76, −78, −80, −82,
WhoHol A, WhoThe 15, −16, −81,
WhoTwCL, WhoWor 74, −76, −78, −80, −82,
WorAl, WorAu, WorEFlm, WrDr 76, −80,
−82, −84

Osgood, Charles 1933- *BioIn 12, ConAu X,*
WhoAm 80, −82

Osgood, William E 1926- *AuBYP,*

BiDrLUS 70, ConAu 33R, SmATA 37, WhoLibS 55, –66

Osis, Karlis 1917- *AmM&WS 73S, –78S, BiDPara, ConAu 85, EncO&P 78, WhoE 81, –83*

Osmond, Marie 1959- *BioIn 11, –12, IntMPA 79, –81, –82, –84, WhoAm 78, –80, –82, WorAl*

Otis, Raymond 1900-1938 *AmAu&B, DcNAA*

Ott, Virginia 1917- *ConAu 77*

Ottley, Reginald *Au&Wr 6, AuBYP SUP, ConAu 93, FourBJA, SmATA 26[port], TwCCW 78, WrDr 80, –82, –84*

Otto, James Howard 1912?-1972 *IndAu 1917*

Oughton, Frederick 1923- *Au&Wr 6, ConAu 1R*

Ouida 1839-1908 *BbD, BiD&SB, BioIn 1, –2, –3, –4, –5, –11, –12, BrAu 19, CasWL, CelCen, Chambr 3, CyWA, DcBiA, DcEnA, –AP, DcEnL, DcEuL, DcLB 18[port], DcLEL, EvLB, HsB&A, InWom, IntDcWB, JBA 34, LinLib LP, –S, LongCTC, NewC, Novels, OxEng, PenC ENG, PseudAu, SmATA X, TelT, WhLit*

Ouida *see also* DeLaRamee, Louise

Oursler, Fulton 1893-1952 *AmAu&B, AuBYP, BioIn 1, –2, –3, –4, –6, –7, –8, CathA 1930, ConAu 108, CurBio 42, –52, DcAmB S5, DcCathB, DcSpL, NatCAB 45, NotNAT B, REn, REnAL, ScF&FL 1, TwCA SUP, TwCCr&M 80, WhAm 3, WhNAA*

Outlar, Jesse 1923- *WhoS&SW 73*

Overholser, Stephen 1944- *ConAu 97, WhoAm 78, –80*

Overstreet, Harry Allen 1875-1970 *AmAu&B, BioIn 2, –3, –4, –9, –10, ConAu 29R, ConAu P-1, CurBio 50, –70, NatCAB 55, NewYTBE 70, ObitOF 79, REnAL, TwCA, TwCA SUP, WhAm 5, WhNAA*

Overton, Jenny 1942- *Au&Wr 6, ConAu 57, IntAu&W 77, SmATA 36, TwCCW 78, –83, WrDr 76, –80, –82, –84*

Ovington, Ray *AuBYP, BioIn 8*

Owen, Betty Meek 1913- *ForWC 70*

Owen, Guy 1925-1981 *AnObit 1981, BioIn 12, ConAu 1R, –3NR, –104, ConNov 76, –82, DcLB 5[port], DrAF 76, DrAP 75, DrAS 74E, –78E, –82E, IntAu&W 82, WhoAm 82, WhoS&SW 73, –80, WrDr 76, –80, –82, –84*

Owen, Wilfred 1912- *AmM&WS 73S, ConAu 37R*

Owens, Bill 1938- *ConAu 73, ConPhot*

Owens, Jesse 1913-1980 *AnObit 1980[port], BioIn 3, –4, –5, –6, –7, –8, –9, –10, –11, –12, BioNews 74, ConAu 110, CurBio 56, –80N, Ebony 1, LinLib S, McGEWB, NegAl 76, –83, NewYTBS 80[port], SelBAA, St&PR 75, WebAB, –79, WhDW, WhAm 7, WhoAm 76, –78, –80,*

WhoBlA 75, –77, WorAl

Oz, Amos 1939- *ASpks, BioIn 9, –10, –11, CasWL, ConAu 53, ConLC 5, –8, –11, –27[port], CurBio 83[port], EncWL 2, IntAu&W 77, –82, Novels, WhoWorJ 72, –78, WorAu 1970, WrDr 76, –80, –82, –84*

P

Pace, Mildred Mastin 1907- *AuBYP SUP*,
ConAu 5R, –5NR, SmATA 29
Pack, Robert 1929- *AmAu&B*, *AuBYP*,
*BioIn 8, –10, –12, ChhPo, ConAu 1R,
–3NR, ConLC 13, ConP 70, –75, –80,
DcLB 5[port], DrAP 75, IntWWP 77,
LinLib L, PenC AM, REnAL,
WhoAm 82, WorAu, WrDr 76, –80, –82,
–84*
Packard, Jerrold M 1943- *ConAu 106*
Packard, Vance 1914- *AmAu&B, ASpks,
AuNews 1, BioIn 4, –5, –6, –7, –8, –10, –11,
BioNews 74, BlueB 76, CelR 73,
ConAu 7NR, –9R, CurBio 58,
DcLEL 1940, IntAu&W 76, –77, –82,
IntWW 74, –75, –76, –77, –78, –79, –80, –81,
–82, –83, LinLib L, –S, LongCTC,
PolProf E, REnAL, Who 74, –82, –83,
WhoAm 74, –76, –78, –80, –82, WhoE 74,
WhoWor 74, –78, –80, –82, WorAl,
WorAu, WrDr 76, –80, –82, –84*
Packer, Joy 1905-1977 *Au&Wr 6, AuBYP,
BioIn 2, –8, –10, ConAu 1R, –3NR,
DcLEL 1940, EncSoA, IntAu&W 76, –77,
TwCWr, Who 74, WrDr 76*
Paddock, Paul 1907-1975 *BioIn 10, ConAu 61,
ConAu P-2, NewYTBS 75*
Paddock, William 1921- *AmM&WS 73P,
ConAu 21R, Future*
Padovano, Anthony John 1933- *DcCAA 71,
–77, DcCAr 81, WhoAm 78, –80,
WhoAmA 73, –76, –78, –80, –82, WhoE 75,
–77*
Padover, Saul K 1905-1981 *AmAu&B,
AmM&WS 73S, –78S, AnObit 1981[port],
BioIn 3, –12, ConAu 2NR, –103, –49,
CurBio 52, –81N, IntAu&W 77,
NewYTBS 81[port], REnAL, WhAm 7,
WhE&EA, WhNAA, WhoAm 74, –76,
–78, –80, WhoWor 74, WhoWorJ 72, –78*
Page, Bruce 1936- *IntWW 80, –81, –82, –83,
Who 82, –83*
Page, Gerald W 1939- *ConAu 93, WhoHr&F*
Page, Lou Williams 1912- *AuBYP, ConAu 5R,
–5NR*
Page, Thomas 1942- *ConAu 81, EncSF,
ScF&FL 1, –2*
Page, Thornton Leigh 1913- *AmM&WS 73P,*

*–76P, –79P, –82P, ConAu 2NR, –5R,
UFOEn, WhoAm 74, –76, –78, –80, –82,
WhoS&SW 73, WhoWor 74*
Pagels, Elaine Hiesey 1943- *ConAu 2NR, –45,
DrAS 74P, –78P, –82P, WhoAm 80, –82,
WhoAmW 77, –79, –81, –83, WhoRel 75,
–77*
Pagnol, Marcel 1895-1974 *BiE&WWA,
BioIn 1, –4, –5, –6, –9, –10, –11, –12,
CasWL, CIDMEL, CnMD, ConAu 49,
CurBio 56, –74, –74N, DcFM, EncWL, –2,
EncWT, EvEuW, FilmgC, IntAu&W 76,
–77, McGEWD, –84[port], ModFrL,
ModWD, MovMk, NewYTBS 74,
NotNAT A, –B, ObitOF 79, ObitT 1971,
OxFilm, OxFr, PenC EUR, REn,
TwCWr, WhAm 6, WhThe, Who 74,
WhoWor 74, WorAu, WorEFlm*
Paige, Harry W 1922- *SmATA 35*
Paine, Albert Bigelow 1861-1937 *AmAu&B,
AmBi, AuBYP SUP, BiD&SB, BioIn 4,
CarSB, ChhPo, –S1, –S2, CnDAL,
ConAu 108, DcAmAu, DcAmB S2,
DcNAA, JBA 34, LinLib L, NatCAB 13,
–28, OxAmL, REn, REnAL, ScF&FL 1,
TwCA, TwCBDA, WhAm 1, WhNAA*
Paine, Lauran 1916- *Au&Wr 6, ConAu 7NR,
–45, IntAu&W 76, ScF&FL 1, –2*
Paine, Roberta M 1925- *AuBYP SUP,
BioIn 11, ConAu 33R, SmATA 13,
WhoAmW 75, –77, –79*
Painter, Charlotte 1926- *BioIn 10, ConAu 1R,
–3NR, DrAF 76, WhoAmW 75,
WrDr 82, –84*
Painter, Nell Irvin 1942- *DrAS 82H,
InB&W 80, WhoBlA 80*
Paisley, Tom 1932- *BioIn 11, ChlLR 3,
ConAu 61, SmATA X*
Paisley, Tom *see also* Bethancourt, T Ernesto
Palder, Edward L 1922- *BioIn 10, SmATA 5*
Paley, Alan L 1943- *ConAu 69*
Paley, Grace 1922- *AmAu&B, AmWomWr,
AuNews 1, BioIn 5, –8, –9, –10, –11,
BioNews 74, ConAu 25R, ConLC 4, –6,
ConNov 76, –82, DcLEL 1940, DrAF 76,
WhoAm 76, –78, –80, –82, WhoAmW 74,
–70, –72, –81, –83, WorAu 1970, WrDr 76,
–80, –82, –84*

Palgrave, Francis Turner 1824-1897 *Alli,*
Alli SUP, BiD&SB, BioIn 2, –6, –9,
BrAu 19, CasWL, CelCen, Chambr 3,
ChhPo, –S1, –S2, –S3, DcBiPP, DcEnA,
–AP, DcEnL, DcEuL, DcLEL, EvLB,
NewC, OxEng, PenC ENG, REn,
WebE&AL

Palin, Michael 1943- *BioIn 10, –11,*
ConAu 107, ConLC 21[port]

Pall, Ellen Jane 1952- *ConAu 93*

Pallas, Norvin 1918- *ConAu 1R, –3NR,*
SmATA 23[port], WrDr 76, –80, –82, –84

Pallenberg, Corrado 1912- *ConAu 13R*

Palmer, Bernard 1914- *ConAu 7NR, –57,*
ScF&FL 1, –2, SmATA 26[port]

Palmer, Joan Lilian 1934- *IntAu&W 76, –77*

Palmer, Lilli 1914- *BioIn 2, –9, –10, –11,*
ConAu X, CurBio 51, FilmgC, InWom,
IntMPA 77, –75, –76, –78, –79, –81, –82, –84,
IntWW 83, MotPP, MovMk, NotNAT A,
OxFilm, WhoAm 74, –76, –78, –80, –82,
WhoAmW 74, –58, –64, –66, –68, –70, –72,
–83, WhoHol A, WhoThe 15, –16, –81,
WhoWor 74, –76, WorAl, WorEFlm

Palmer, Robert Franklin, Jr. 1945- *WhoAm 82*

Palmer, Robin 1911- *AuBYP, BioIn 7,*
ConAu 109

Palmer, Roy 1932- *ConAu 8NR, –61*

Panati, Charles 1943- *ConAu 81*

Panella, Vincent 1939- *ConAu 97*

Panger, Daniel 1926- *ConAu 93*

Pankow, James 1947- *WhoAm 76, –78, –80,*
–82, WhoRocM 82

Pankow, James *see also* Chicago

Panov, Valery 1938?- *BioIn 10, –11, –12,*
BioNews 74, ConAu 102, CurBio 74,
WhoAm 82

Panshin, Alexei 1940- *BioIn 12, ConAu 57,*
ConSFA, DcLB 8[port], EncSF,
ScF&FL 1, –2, WhoAm 74, –76, –78, –80,
–82, WhoSciF, WrDr 84

Panter, Carol 1936- *AuBYP SUP, BioIn 11,*
ConAu 49, SmATA 9

Panzarella, Andrew 1940- *ConAu 25R*

Papanek, Ernst 1900-1973 *BioIn 10,*
ConAu 1R, –4NR, WhAm 6, WhoE 74

Paperny, Myra 1932- *ConAu 69, SmATA 33,*
WhoAm 78

Pappas, Lou Seibert 1930- *ConAu 8NR, –61*

Paradis, Adrian Alexis 1912- *AuBYP, BioIn 6,*
–7, –9, ConAu 1R, –3NR, IntAu&W 77,
MorJA, SmATA 1, WhoPubR 72, –76,
WrDr 76, –80, –82, –84

Parazaider, Walt 1948- *BioNews 74*

Parazaider, Walt *see also* Chicago

Paredes, Americo 1915- *ChiSch, ConAu 37R,*
DrAS 74E, –78E, –82E, IntAu&W 77, –82,
WhoAm 82

Parent, Gail 1940- *BioIn 10, –11, –12,*
ConAu 101, WomWMM

Parenteau, Shirley Laurolyn 1935- *ConAu 85,*
WhoAmW 75, –77

Parenti, Michael 1933- *ConAu 73*

Pares, Marion Stapylton 1914- *Au&Wr 6,*
ConAu 17R, IntAu&W 76, –82

Pares, Marion Stapylton *see also* Campbell,
Judith

Paretti, Sandra *Au&Wr 6, ConAu 7NR, –53*

Pargeter, Edith Mary 1913- *Au&Wr 6,*
BlueB 76, ConAu 1R, –4NR,
IntAu&W 76, –77, –82, LongCTC, Novels,
ScF&FL 1, –1A, –2, TwCCr&M 80,
WhE&EA, Who 74, –82, –83,
WhoWor 76, WorAu, WrDr 76, –80, –82,
–84

Pargeter, Edith Mary *see also* Peters, Ellis

Paris, Jeanne 1918- *ConAu 1R, WhoAm 74,*
–76, WhoAmW 74, –72, –79, WhoE 74

Parisi, Joseph 1944- *ConAu 93, DrAS 78E,*
–82E

Park, Brad 1948- *BioIn 9, –10, –11,*
CurBio 76, WorAl

Park, Ruth 1920?- *Au&Wr 6, BioIn 3, –6,*
CathA 1952, ConAu 105, InWom,
SingR 2, SmATA 25, TwCCW 78, –83,
TwCWr, WrDr 80, –82, –84

Parker, Brant Julian 1920- *WhoAm 78, –80,*
–82, WorECom

Parker, Dorothy 1893-1967 *AmAu&B,*
AmSCAP 66, AmWomWr, BiE&WWA,
BioIn 1, –4, –6, –7, –8, –9, –10, –12, CasWL,
ChhPo, –S2, –S3, CnDAL, CnE&AP,
ConAmA, ConAu 25R, ConAu P-2,
ConLC 15, DcLB 11[port], DcLEL,
DrAS 74E, –78E, –82E, EvLB, GoodHs,
InWom, IntDcWB, LibW, LinLib L,
LongCTC, McGEWB, ModAL,
NotAW MOD, NotNAT A, –B,
Novels[port], ObitOF 79, ObitT 1961,
OxAmL, PenC AM, RAdv 1, REn,
REnAL, TwCA, TwCA SUP, TwCWr,
WebAB, –79, WhDW, WhAm 4,
WhoAmW 58, –61, –64, –66, –68, WorAl

Parker, Elinor Milnor 1906- *BioIn 9, ChhPo,*
–S3, ConAu 1R, –3NR, SmATA 3,
WhoAm 74, –76, –78, –80, WhoAmW 58,
–61, –79, –81, –83

Parker, Geoffrey 1933- *ConAu 49*

Parker, James *ConAu X*

Parker, James *see also* Newby, Eric

Parker, John 1923- *BiDrLUS 70, ConAu 5R,*
–5NR, DrAS 74H, –78H, –82H,
WhoLibS 55, –66

Parker, Richard 1915- *AuBYP, BioIn 8, –12,*
ConAu 73, ScF&FL 1, SmATA 14,
TwCCW 78, –83, WrDr 76, –80, –82, –84

Parker, Robert B 1932- *ConAu 1NR, –49,*
ConLC 27[port], TwCCr&M 80,
WhoAm 80, –82, WrDr 82, –84

Parker, Rowland 1912- *ConAu 10NR, –65*

Parker, W H 1912- *ConAu 33R, WrDr 76,*
–80, –82, –84

Parker, Watson 1924- *ConAu 106,*
DrAS 74H, –78H, –82H, EncAAH

Parkes, Sir Alan Sterling 1900- *Au&Wr 6,*
BlueB 76, IntAu&W 76, –77, IntWW 74,
–75, –76, –77, –78, –79, –80, –81, –82, –83,
WhE&EA, Who 74, –82, –83,
WhoWor 74

Parkinson, Cyril Northcote 1909- *Au&Wr 6,*
BioIn 4, –5, –6, –7, –10, –11, –12, BlueB 76,
ConAu 5R, –5NR, CurBio 60,
IntAu&W 76, –77, –82, IntWW 74, –75,
–76, –77, –78, –79, –80, –81, –82, –83,
LinLib L, –S, LongCTC, NewYTBE 71,
RAdv 1, WhE&EA, Who 74, –82, –83,
WhoAm 74, –76, –78, –80, –82,
WhoWor 74, –76, –78, WorAu, WrDr 76,
–80, –82, –84

Parkinson, Ethelyn Minerva 1906-
AuBYP SUP, BioIn 11, ConAu 1NR, –49,
ScF&FL 1, SmATA 11, WhoAm 74, –76,
–78, –80, –82, WhoAmW 74

Parkman, Francis 1823-1893 *Alli, Alli SUP,*
AmAu, AmAu&B, AmBi, ApCAB,
AtlBL, BbD, BbtC, BiD&SB, BioIn 1,
–2, –3, –4, –5, –6, –7, –8, –9, –10, –11,
CasWL, CyAL 2, CyWA, DcAmAu,
DcAmB, DcLB 1, DcLEL, DcNAA,
Dis&D, Drake, EncAAH, EncAB-H,
EvLB, HarEnUS[port], LinLib L, –S,
McGEWB, MouLC 4, NatCAB 1,
OxAmH, OxAmL, OxCan, OxEng,
PenC AM, REn, REnAL, REnAW,
TwCBDA, WebAB, –79, WebE&AL,
WhDW, WhAm HS

Parks, Edd Winfield 1906-1968 *AmAu&B,*
BioIn 7, –10, –11, ConAu 5R, NatCAB 54,
SmATA 10, WhAm 5

Parks, Gordon 1912- *AfroAA, AmAu&B,*
AuNews 2, BiDAfM, BioIn 3, –4, –6, –7,
–8, –9, –10, –11, –12, BlueB 76, BlkAWP,
CelR 73, ConAu 41R, ConLC 1, –16,
ConPhot, CurBio 68, DrBlPA, Ebony 1,
FilmgC, InB&W 80, IntMPA 77, –75, –76,
–78, –79, –81, –82, –84, LinLib L,
LivgBAA, NegAl 76[port], SelBAA,
SmATA 8, WhoAm 74, –76, –78, –80, –82,
WhoBlA 75, –77, –80, WhoE 74,
WhoWor 74, –82, WrDr 76, –80, –82, –84

Parlett, David 1939- *ConAu 103*

Parlin, John 1911-1972 *AuBYP, BioIn 8, –9,*
ConAu X, SmATA 4

Parlin, John *see also* Graves, Charles Parlin

Parmer, Jess Norman 1925- *BlueB 76,*
ConAu 5R, DrAS 74H, IndAu 1917,
WhoAm 74, –76, –78, –80, –82

Parmet, Herbert S 1929- *ConAu 11NR, –21R,*
DrAS 74H, –78H, –82H, WhoE 74,
WrDr 76, –80, –82, –84

Parrinder, Geoffrey 1910- *Who 74, –82, –83*

Parrish, John A 1939- *ConAu 37R*

Parry, Ellwood C, III 1941- *ConAu 93,*
DrAS 78H, –82H, WhoAmA 78, –80, –82,
WrDr 76, –80, –82, –84

Parry, John Horace 1914-1982 *AmAu&B,*

BlueB 76, ConAu 5R, –6NR, DrAS 74H,
–78H, –82H, IntAu&W 77, IntWW 74,
–75, –76, –77, –78, –79, –80, –81, –82, –83N,
NewYTBS 82, Who 74, –82, –83N,
WhoAm 78, –80, –82, WhoWor 74,
WrDr 82

Parry, Michel 1947- *ScF&FL 1, –2,*
WhoHr&F

Pascal, Francine 1938- *SmATA 37*

Paschal, Nancy 1900- *AuBYP, BioIn 7, –11,*
ConAu X, ForWC 70, SmATA X

Paschal, Nancy *see also* Trotter, Grace V

Pasinetti, Pier-Maria 1913- *BioIn 5, ModRL,*
TwCWr, WhoAm 74, –76, –78, –80, –82,
WhoWor 76, –78, –80, –82

Passos, John Dos 1896-1970 *BioIn 1, –2, –10,*
CurBio 40, –70, PenC AM, TwCA,
TwCA SUP, WhLit

Passos, John Dos *see also* DosPassos, John

Passwater, Richard Albert 1937- *ConAu 97,*
WhoE 77, –79, –81, –83

Pastan, Linda 1932- *BioIn 12, ConAu 61,*
ConLC 27[port], ConP 80, DcLB 5[port],
DrAP 75, IntAu&W 76, WrDr 82, –84

Pasternak, Boris 1890-1960 *AtlBL, BioIn 1, –2,*
–4, –5, –6, –7, –8, –9, –10, –11, –12, CasWL,
ChhPo S1, CIDMEL, CnMWL, ConLC 7,
–10, –18, CurBio 59, –60, DcAmSR,
DcRusL, EncWL 2[port], EvEuW,
LinLib L, –S, LongCTC, MakMC,
McGEWB, ModSL 1, Novels[port],
ObitOF 79, ObitT 1951, OxEng,
PenC EUR, RComWL, REn,
TwCA SUP, TwCWr, WhDW, WhAm 4,
WhoTwCL, WorAl

Patchett, Mary Elwyn 1897- *Au&Wr 6,*
AuBYP, BioIn 8, ConAu 3NR, –5R,
IntAu&W 76, –77, –82, SingR 1,
TwCCW 78, –83, WrDr 76, –80, –82, –84

Pate, Billie 1932- *ConAu 61*

Patent, Dorothy Hinshaw 1940- *AuBYP SUP,*
ConAu 9NR, –61, SmATA 22[port]

Paterson, Katherine 1932- *AuBYP SUP,*
AuBYP SUPA, BioIn 11, –12,
ConAu 21R, ConLC 12, SmATA 13,
TwCCW 83, WhoAm 78, –80, –82,
WhoAmW 81, WrDr 84

Paton, Alan Stewart 1903- *AfSS 78, –79, –80,*
–81, –82, Au&Wr 6, AuBYP, BioIn 2, –3,
–4, –5, –7, –8, –11, –12, BlueB 76, CasWL,
ConAu P-1, ConLC 4, –10, –25[port],
ConNov 72, –76, –82, CurBio 52, CyWA,
DcAmSR, DcLEL 1940, EncSoA,
EncWL, –2, IntAu&W 76, –77, –82,
IntWW 74, –75, –76, –77, –78, –79, –80, –81,
–82, –83, LinLib L, –S, LongCTC,
McGEWB, ModCmwL, NewC,
Novels[port], PenC ENG, PlP&P, REn,
SmATA 11, TwCA SUP, TwCWr,
WebE&AL, WhDW, Who 74, –82, –83,
WhoTwCL, WhoWor 74, WorAl,
WrDr 76, –80, –82, –84

Paton Walsh, Gillian 1937?- *Au&Wr 6,*
BioIn 9, IntAu&W 77, SmATA 4,
WhoAmW 74
Paton Walsh, Gillian *see also* Paton Walsh, Jill
Paton Walsh, Gillian *see also* Walsh, Gillian
Paton
Paton Walsh, Gillian *see also* Walsh, Jill Paton
Paton Walsh, Jill 1937?- *BioIn 9, SmATA 4,*
TwCCW 78, -83, WrDr 76, -80, -82, -84
Paton Walsh, Jill *see also* Paton Walsh, Gillian
Patrick, John 1905- *AmAu&B, BiE&WWA,*
BioIn 3, -4, -10, -12, BlueB 76,
ConAu 89, ConDr 73, -77, DcLEL 1940,
EncWT, IntAu&W 76, -77, IntWW 74,
-75, -76, -77, -78, -79, -80, -81, -82, -83,
McGEWD, MnBBF, ModWD, NotNAT,
OxAmL, PenC AM, REn, REnAL,
TwCA SUP, WhoAm 74, -76, -78, -80,
-82, WhoThe 15, -16, WhoWor 74, -80,
-82, WorAl, WrDr 76, -80
Patrick, John *see also* Goggan, John Patrick
Patrick, Ted 1930?- *BioIn 10, -11, -12,*
InB&W 80
Patten, Brian 1946- *BioIn 10, ChhPo S3,*
ConAu 25R, ConP 70, -75, -80,
IntAu&W 76, -77, -82, IntWWP 77, -82,
LinLib L, SmATA 29, TwCCW 78, -83,
Who 82, -83, WrDr 76, -80, -82, -84
Patten, Lewis Byford 1915-1981 *AnObit 1981,*
BioIn 12, ConAu 103, -25R, WhAm 7,
WhoAm 74, -76, -78, -80, WhoWest 74,
-76, -78, WhoWor 76
Patterson, Charles Darold 1928- *BiDrLUS 70,*
WhoAm 82, WhoLibI 82, WhoLibS 66,
WhoS&SW 76, -78, -80, -82
Patterson, Emma L 1904- *ConAu P-2,*
WhoLibS 55
Patterson, Floyd 1935- *BioIn 3, -4, -5, -6, -7,*
-8, -9, -10, -11, CurBio 60, InB&W 80,
NewYTBE 70, -72, WhoBox 74, WorAl
Patterson, Freeman Wilford 1937- *CanWW 81,*
-83
Patterson, Harry 1929- *Au&Wr 6, BioIn 12,*
ConAu X, Who 82, -83, WrDr 76, -80,
-82, -84
Patterson, Harry *see also* Patterson, Henry
Patterson, Henry 1929- *ConAu 13R,*
TwCCr&M 80, WrDr 76, -80, -82, -84
Patterson, Henry *see also* Higgins, Jack
Patterson, Henry *see also* Patterson, Harry
Patterson, Lillie G *AuBYP, BioIn 7, -12,*
ConAu 73, InB&W 80, SmATA 14
Patterson, Lindsay Waldorf 1942- *BlkAWP,*
ConAu 77, InB&W 80, LivgBAA,
WhoBlA 77, -80
Patton, Frances Gray 1906- *AmAu&B,*
AmWomWr, Au&Wr 6, BioIn 3, -4, -5,
CnDAL, ConAu 101, ConNov 72, -76,
CurBio 55, InWom, REnAL, WrDr 76,
-80, -82, -84
Patton, George Smith 1885-1945 *BioIn 1, -2, -3,*
-4, -5, -6, -7, -8, -9, -10, -11, -12,

DcAmB S3, EncAB-H, HisEWW,
McGEWB, NatCAB 37, ObitOF 79,
OxAmH, REnAL, WebAB, -79,
WebAMB, WhDW, WhAm 2, WhWW-II,
WhoMilH 76, WorAl
Patton, Oliver Beirne 1920- *ConAu 81,*
IntAu&W 82, WhoGov 75
Paul, Aileen 1917- *AuBYP SUP, BioIn 11,*
ConAu 41R, IntAu&W 76, SmATA 12,
WhoWest 82
Paul, Charlotte 1916- *Au&Wr 6, ConAu 5R,*
-7NR, ForWC 70, WhoAmW 61
Pauli, Hertha Ernestine 1909-1973 *AmAu&B,*
AuBYP, BioIn 1, -4, -7, -9, BkC 5,
CathA 1930, ConAu 1R, -2NR, -41R,
ForWC 70, NewYTBE 73, SmATA 26N,
-3, WhAm 5, WhoAmW 74, -58, -61, -64,
-68, -70, -72, WhoE 74
Pauline, Lawrence Joseph 1932- *LEduc 74,*
WhoE 75, -77
Paulsen, Gary 1939- *ConAu 73, Po&Wr 77,*
SmATA 22[port]
Paulson, Jack 1902- *BioIn 7, -10, ConAu X,*
MichAu 80, SmATA 6
Paulson, Jack *see also* Jackson, C Paul
Paulsson, Bjoern 1932- *ConAu 61*
Paustovsky, Konstantin 1892-1968 *CasWL,*
ConAu 25R, -93, EncWL 2, ObitOF 79,
ObitT 1961, PenC EUR, TwCWr,
WhDW, WhAm 5, WorAu
Pavarotti, Luciano 1935- *BiDamM, BioIn 8,*
-9, -10, -11, -12, CurBio 73, IntWW 79,
-80, -81, -82, -83, MusSN, NewEOp 71,
NewYTBS 76, -80[port], WhoAm 74, -76,
-78, -80, -82, WhoAmM 83, WhoMus 72,
WhoOp 76, WhoWor 78, -80, -82, WorAl
Pavletich, Aida *ConAu 101*
Pawley, Martin Edward 1938- *ConAu 101,*
WrDr 76, -80, -82, -84
Pawlicki, T B 1930- *ConAu 109*
Paxton, Tom 1937- *BiDamM, BioIn 8,*
ConAu X, CurBio 82[port],
EncFCWM 69, RolSEnR 83, WhoAm 74,
-76, -82
Payne, Donald Gordon 1924- *Au&Wr 6,*
ConAu 9NR, -13R, IntAu&W 76, -77, -82,
ScF&FL 1, -2, SmATA 37, WhoWor 76,
WrDr 76, -80, -82, -84
Payne, Donald Gordon *see also* Cameron, Ian
Payne, Donald Gordon *see also* Gordon, Donald
Payne, Donald Gordon *see also* Marshall, James
Vance
Payne, Robert 1911-1969 *AmAu&B,*
Au&Wr 6, BioIn 4, -5, -6, -7, -8, -9, -11,
ConAu 25R, CurBio 47, ScF&FL 1, -2,
WhoE 74, WhoWor 74, -76
Paz, Octavio 1914- *BioIn 6, -9, -10, -12,*
CasWL, CnMWL, ConAu 73, ConLC 3,
-4, -6, -10, -19, CurBio 74, DcCLAA,
EncLatA, EncWL, -2[port], IntAu&W 76,
-77, IntWW 74, -75, -76, -77, -78, -79,
-80, -81, -82, -83, IntWWP 77, LinLib L,

*ModLAL, OxSpan, PenC AM, TwCWr,
Who 74, –82, –83, WhoAm 74, –76, –78,
WhoTwCL, WhoWor 74, –78, –80, –82,
WorAl, WorAu*

Peake, Lilian 1924- *IntAu&W 76, –77X, –82X,
WrDr 84*

Pearce, Mary E 1932- *ConAu 69,
IntAu&W 77, WrDr 76, –80, –82, –84*

Pearce, Philippa 1920- *AuBYP, ConAu X,
–5R, ConLC 21[port], SenS, SmATA 1,
ThrBJA, Who 82, –83*

Pearcy, George Etzel 1905-1980
*AmM&WS 73S, ConAu 1R, –3NR,
IndAu 1917, WhAm 7, WhoAm 74, –76,
–78*

Peare, Catherine Owens 1911- *Au&Wr 6,
AuBYP, BioIn 5, –6, –7, –11, ConAu 5R,
CurBio 59, InWom, MorJA, SmATA 9,
WhoAmW 58, –61, –64*

Pearl, Jack 1923- *ConAu X*

Pearl, Jack *see also* Pearl, Jacques Bain

Pearl, Jacques Bain 1923- *ConAu 5R*

Pearl, Richard Maxwell 1913-1980
*AmM&WS 73P, –76P, –79P, AuBYP,
BioIn 7, –12, ConAu 3NR, –9R, WhAm 7,
WhoAm 76, –78, –80, WhoWor 80*

Pearlman, Moshe 1911- *ConAu X, –5R,
IntAu&W 76, WhoWor 74, –76,
WhoWorJ 72, WrDr 76, –80, –82, –84*

Pearsall, Ronald 1927- *ChhPo S2,
ConAu 21R, IntAu&W 77, WhoWor 76,
WrDr 76, –80, –82, –84*

Pearson, Norman Holmes 1909-1975 *AmAu&B,
BioIn 10, ConAu 61, ConAu P-1,
DrAS 74E, NewYTBS 75, WhAm 6,
WhoAm 74, –76, WhoGov 72, –75,
WhoWor 74, WrDr 76*

Peary, Danny *ConAu X*

Pease, Howard 1894-1974 *AmAu&B, AuBYP,
BioIn 1, –2, –7, –9, –10, ConAu 5R, –106,
JBA 34, –51, REnAL, SmATA 2, –25N,
TwCCW 78, –83, WhoAm 74, –76*

Peattie, Donald Culross 1898-1964 *AmAu&B,
AuBYP, BioIn 2, –3, –4, –7, ConAmA,
ConAu 102, CurBio 40, –65, DcAmB S7,
DcLEL, InSci, LinLib L, MnBBF,
OxAmL, REnAL, TwCA, TwCA SUP,
WhAm 4, WhE&EA, WhNAA*

Peavy, Linda 1943- *ConAu 109*

Peccei, Aurelio 1908- *BioIn 12, Future,
IntWW 74, –75, –76, –77, –78, –79, –80, –81,
–82, –83, WhoWor 74*

Peck, Anne Merriman 1884- *AmAu&B,
AuBYP, BioIn 1, –2, –5, –8, –12, ChhPo,
–S1, ConAu 77, IlsCB 1744, –1946,
InWom, JBA 34, –51, SmATA 18*

Peck, Ira 1922- *ConAu 77*

Peck, Ralph H *ConAu 69*

Peck, Richard 1934- *BioIn 12, ChhPo S2,
ConAu 85, ConLC 21[port], DrAF 76,
DrAP 75, IntAu&W 82, SmATA 18,
TwCCW 78, –83, WhoAm 80, –82,*

WrDr 80, –82, –84

Peck, Richard E 1936- *ConAu 81, DrAS 74E,
–78E, –82E, EncSF*

Peck, Robert Newton 1928- *AuBYP SUP,
BioIn 12, ConAu 1R, –81, ConLC 17,
SmATA 21[port], TwCCW 78, –83,
WrDr 80, –82, –84*

Pedersen, Elsa Kienitz 1915- *AuBYP, BioIn 8,
ConAu 1R, –2NR, ForWC 70*

Peek, Dan *WhoRocM 82*

Peek, Dan *see also* America

Peek, Walter W 1922- *ConAu 45*

Peekner, Ray *WrDr 82, –84*

Pei, Mario Andrew 1901-1978 *AmAu&B,
AmCath 80, BioIn 3, –4, –8, –9, –11, –12,
ConAu 5R, –5NR, –77, CurBio 68, –78,
–78N, DrAS 74F, LinLib L,
NatCAB 60[port], ObitOF 79, REnAL,
ScF&FL 1, –2, TwCA SUP, WhAm 7,
WhoAm 74, –76, –78, WhoWor 74,
WrDr 76*

Peirce, Neal R 1932- *ConAu 25R,
WhoAm 76, –78, –80, –82, WhoS&SW 73,
WhoWor 80, –82, WrDr 80, –82, –84*

Peissel, Michel 1937- *ConAu 25R*

Pelissier, Roger 1924-1972 *ConAu 37R,
ConAu P-2*

Pell, Arthur Robert 1920- *ConAu 11NR, –29R,
WhoAm 74, –76, –78, –80, –82, WhoE 74,
WhoF&I 74, –75*

Pell, Derek 1947- *ConAu 77, IntAu&W 82,
IntWWP 82, WhoE 81*

Pell, Eve 1937- *ConAu 33R*

Pelletier, Jean 1935- *AmCath 80, CanWW 83,
WhoAm 80, –82, WhoE 81, –83,
WhoFr 79, WhoWor 82*

Pelta, Kathy 1928- *BioIn 12, ConAu 85,
SmATA 18*

Peltier, Leslie Copus 1900-1980
*AmM&WS 73P, –76P, –79P, BioIn 1, –2,
–7, –11, –12, ConAu 17R, SmATA 13*

Pelton, Robert W 1934- *ConAu 29R*

Penfield, Thomas 1903- *ConAu 5R*

Penner, Dick 1936- *DrAS 82E*

Pennington, Howard 1923- *ConAu 49*

Penrod, James Wilford 1934- *WhoAm 82,
WhoWest 80*

Penzler, Otto M 1942- *ConAu 81,
IntAu&W 76, –77*

Penzler, Otto M *see also* Adler, Irene

Pepe, Phil 1935- *ConAu 25R, SmATA 20*

Peper, George Frederick 1950- *ConAu 108,
WhoAm 80, –82, WhoE 83*

Peple, Edward Henry 1869-1924 *AmAu&B,
DcNAA, ScF&FL 1, WhAm 1*

Percival, John 1927- *ConAu 33R*

Percy, Walker 1916- *AmAu&B, AmCath 80,
BioIn 9, –10, –11, –12, ConAu 1R, –1NR,
ConLC 2, –3, –6, –8, –14, –18, ConNov 72,
–76, –82, CurBio 76, DcLB Y80A[port],
–2, DcLEL 1940, DrAF 76, DrAP&F 83,
EncSoH, EncWL, –2, IntAu&W 76, –77,*

LinLib L, ModAL, ModAL SUP,
NewYTBS 80[port], Novels, OxAmL,
RAdv 1, ScF&FL 1, –2, WebE&AL,
WhoAm 74, –76, –78, –80, –82,
WhoS&SW 73, –75, WhoWor 74, WorAl,
WorAu, WrDr 76, –80, –82, –84
Perelman, S J 1904-1979 *AmAu&B,*
Au&Wr 6, AuNews 1, –2, BiE&WWA,
BioNews 75, BlueB 76, CelR 73, CnDAL,
ConAu 73, –89, ConDr 73, –77, ConLC 3,
–5, –9, –15, –23[port], CurBio 71, –80N,
DcLB 11[port], DcLEL, FilmgC,
LongCTC, McGEWD, –84, NewYTBE 70,
–72, NewYTBS 79, NotNAT, Novels,
OxAmL, PenC AM, RAdv 1, REn,
REnAL, TwCA, TwCA SUP, WebE&AL,
Who 74, WorAl, WrDr 76, –80
Perelman, Sidney Joseph 1904-1979 *BioIn 3, –4,*
–5, –6, –7, –8, –9, –10, –11, –12,
IntAu&W 76, –77, IntWW 74, –75, –76,
–77, –78, –79, WebAB, –79, WhDW,
WhAm 7, WhoAm 74, –76, –78, –80,
WhoWor 74, –78, WorECar
Peretz, Don 1922- *AmM&WS 73S, –78S,*
ConAu 4NR, –9R, IntAu&W 77, –82,
WhoAmJ 80, WhoWorJ 72, –78
Perez, Norah A *OxCan SUP*
Perkins, Charles Elliott 1881-1943 *NatCAB 32,*
WhAm 2
Perkins, Edwin Judson 1939- *ConAu 106,*
DrAS 74H, –78H, –82H
Perkins, Marlin 1905- *BioIn 3, –7, –12,*
ConAu 103, LinLib L, –S,
SmATA 21[port], WebAB, –79,
WhoAm 74, –76, –78, –80
Perl, Lila *AuBYP, BioIn 8, –10, ConAu 33R,*
SmATA 6
Perl, Teri 1926- *ConAu 93*
Perlman, Anne S *DrAP&F 83*
Pernoud, Regine 1909- *ConAu 102*
Perrault, Charles 1628-1703 *DcBiPP, Novels,*
SmATA 25[port]
Perrett, Geoffrey 1940- *ConAu 4NR, –53*
Perrin, Blanche Chenery 1894?-1973 *BioIn 9,*
–10, ConAu 5R, –41R
Perrin, Noel 1927- *AmAu&B, Au&Wr 6,*
ConAu 13R, DrAS 74E, –78E, –82E,
IntAu&W 76, –77, WhoE 75
Perry, George 1935- *BiDBrA, ConAu 103,*
IntAu&W 77, –82, WrDr 76, –80, –82
Perry, Jim 1942- *ConAu 53*
Perry, Richard 1909- *ConAu 41R, WhE&EA*
Persico, Joseph E 1930- *ConAu 93,*
IntAu&W 82, WrDr 80, –82, –84
Perske, Robert 1927- *ConAu 106*
Pesek, Ludek 1919- *ConAu 29R, ScF&FL 1,*
–2
Peter, Laurence Johnston 1919-
AmM&WS 73S, Au&Wr 6, BioIn 8, –10,
ConAu 17R, IntAu&W 76, –77, –82,
LEduc 74, WhoAm 74, –76, –78, –80, –82,
WrDr 80, –82, –84

Peters, Charles 1926- *DcAfL, WhoAm 82*
Peters, Daniel 1948- *ConAu 85*
Peters, Donald Leslie 1925- *ConAu 21R,*
IntAu&W 76, –77, WhoWest 74, –76
Peters, Elizabeth 1927- *ConAu X, –57,*
TwCCr&M 80, WrDr 76, –82, –84
Peters, Elizabeth *see also* Mertz, Barbara Gross
Peters, Ellis 1913- *ConAu X, IntAu&W 76X,*
–77X, –82X, Novels, TwCCr&M 80,
Who 82, –83, WorAu, WrDr 76, –80, –82,
–84
Peters, Ellis *see also* Pargeter, Edith Mary
Peters, Ken 1929- *ConAu 17R*
Peters, Margaret Evelyn 1936- *ConAu 53*
Peters, Mike 1943- *ConAu X, WorECar*
Peters, S H 1862-1910 *ConAu X, YABC X*
Peters, S H *see also* Porter, William Sydney
Peterson, Harold Leslie 1922-1978 *BioIn 2, –11,*
ConAu 1R, –4NR, DrAS 74H, EncAAH,
SmATA 8, WhoS&SW 76, WrDr 76
Peterson, Levi S 1933- *ConAu 109,*
DrAS 74E, –78E, –82E
Peterson, Ottis 1907- *ConAu 21R*
Peterson, P J *WhoOcn 78*
Peterson, Robert W 1925?- *ConAu 33R,*
WhoAmP 83
Peterson, Roger Tory 1908- *AmAu&B,*
AmM&WS 76P, –79P, –82P, BioIn 4, –5,
–6, –7, –8, –10, –11, –12, BlueB 76,
CelR 73, ConAu 1R, –1NR, CurBio 59,
InSci, IntAu&W 77, –82, IntWW 74, –75,
–76, –77, –78, –79, –80, –81, –82, –83,
LinLib L, NewYTBS 74, –80[port],
REnAL, TwCA SUP, WebAB, –79,
WhoAm 74, –76, –78, –80, –82,
WhoAmA 76, –78, –80, –82, WhoWor 74
Petesch, Natalie L M *ConAu 6NR, –57,*
DrAF 76, DrAP&F 83
Petrakis, Harry Mark 1923- *AmAu&B,*
BioIn 10, ConAu 4NR, –9R, ConLC 3,
ConNov 72, –76, –82, DrAF 76,
DrAP&F 83, IntAu&W 76, –77, –82,
WhoAm 74, –76, –78, –80, –82,
WhoWor 74, WrDr 76, –80, –82, –84
Petrosky, Anthony *DrAP&F 83*
Petrovskaya, Kyra 1918- *BioIn 5, –11,*
ConAu X, –1R, SmATA 8
Petrovskaya, Kyra *see also* Wayne, Kyra
Petrovskaya
Petry, Ann 1908?- *AmAu&B, AmNov,*
AmWomWr, AnCL, AuBYP, BioIn 1, –2,
–3, –4, –6, –7, –9, –10, BlkAWP,
ConAu 4NR, –5R, ConLC 1, –7, –18,
ConNov 72, –76, –82, CurBio 46,
DcLEL 1940, DrAP 75, DrAP&F 83,
InB&W 80, InWom, IntAu&W 76, –82,
LinLib L, LivgBAA, NegAl 76, –83, REn,
REnAL, SelBAA, SmATA 5, ThrBJA,
TwCA SUP, TwCCW 78, –83,
WhoAmW 74, –58, –70, –72, WhoBlA 77,
–80, WrDr 76, –80, –82, –84
Pettersson, Allan 1911-1980 *AnObit 1980,*

Au & Wr 6, BioIn 2, –4, –6, –7, –8, –9, –10,
–11, ConAu 1R, –4NR, –25R, CurBio 57,
–69, DcAmReB, EncO&P 78, LinLib L,
–S, LuthC 75, NatCAB 56, ObitOF 79,
PolProf J, PolProf K, WhAm 5, WorAl

Pilarski, Laura P 1926- *AmCath 80, BioIn 11,*
ConAu 29R, IntAu&W 77, SmATA 13,
WhoAmW 75, –77, –79, WrDr 76, –80, –82,
–84

Pilat, Oliver 1903- *AmAu&B, ConAu 5R,*
WhoAm 76, –78, –80, –82, WhoE 74, –75,
–77, –79, –81, –83, WhoWor 80, –82

Pilcer, Sonia 1949- *ConAu 89*

Pilcher, Rosamunde 1924- *Au&Wr 6,*
ConAu 57, IntAu&W 76, –77, –82,
WrDr 76, –80, –82, –84

Pilgrim, Anne 1915- *AuBYP, BioIn 10,*
ConAu X, IntAu&W 76X, –77X, –82X,
SmATA X, –5, WrDr 76, –80, –82, –84

Pilgrim, Anne *see also* Allan, Mabel Esther

Pilkington, Roger Windle 1915- *Au&Wr 6,*
AuBYP, BioIn 7, –11, ConAu 1R, –5NR,
IntAu&W 77, –82, ScF&FL 1,
SmATA 10, Who 74, –82, –83,
WhoWor 80, WrDr 76, –80, –82, –84

Pincher, Chapman 1914- *BlueB 76, ConSFA,*
EncSF, IntAu&W 76, –77, –82,
ScF&FL 1, –2, Who 74, –82, –83,
WhoSpyF, WrDr 80, –82, –84

Pinchot, Ann 1910?- *AmAu&B, AmNov,*
BioIn 2, ConAu 1R, –4NR, InWom,
IntAu&W 77, WhoAmW 75, WrDr 76,
–80, –82, –84

Pincus, Edward R 1938- *ConAu 33R,*
WrDr 76, –80, –82, –84

Pines, Maya *Au&Wr 6, ConAu 13R,*
IntAu&W 76, WrDr 76, –80, –82, –84

Pinkerton, Kathrene Sutherland 1887-1967
AuBYP, BioIn 1, –3, –7, –8, ConAu 1R,
–103, CurBio 40, –67, InWom,
SmATA 26N, WhAm 4A, WhE&EA,
WhoAmW 58

Pinkerton, Todd 1917- *ConAu 69*

Pinkham, Mary Ellen 1946?- *BioIn 12,*
ConAu 101, NewYTBS 81[port],
WhoAm 82, WhoWor 82

Pinkwater, Daniel Manus 1941- *BioIn 11,*
ChlLR 4[port], ConAu 29R,
IntAu&W 77, –77X, WhoE 77

Pinney, Roy 1911- *ConAu 5R, –6NR*

Pinson, William M, Jr. 1934- *ConAu 9NR,*
–17R, DrAS 74P, –78P, –82P,
IntAu&W 77, WhoAm 82, WhoRel 75,
–77, WhoS&SW 73, WhoWor 82,
WrDr 76, –80, –82, –84

Pinter, Harold 1930- *Au&Wr 6, BiE&WWA,*
BioIn 6, –7, –8, –9, –10, –11, –12, BlueB 76,
CasWL, CelR 73, CnMD, CnThe,
ConAu 5R, ConDr 73, –77, –82, ConLC 1,
–3, –6, –9, –11, –15, –27[port], ConP 70,
CroCD, CurBio 63, DcFM,
DcLB 13[port], DcLEL 1940, EncWL,

–2[port], EncWT, FilmgC, IntAu&W 76,
–77, IntMPA 84, IntWW 74, –75, –76,
–77, –78, –79, –80, –81, –82, –83,
IntWWP 77, LinLib L, LongCEL,
LongCTC, MakMC, McGEWB,
McGEWD, –84, ModBrL, ModBrL SUP,
ModWD, NewC, NewYTBE 71,
NewYTBS 79, NotNAT, OxFilm, OxThe,
PenC ENG, PIP&P, RComWL, REn,
REnWD, TwCWr, WebE&AL, WhDW,
Who 74, –82, –83, WhoAm 80, –82,
WhoThe 15, –16, –81, WhoTwCL,
WhoWor 74, –78, –80, –82, WorAl,
WorAu, WorEFlm, WrDr 76, –80, –82,
–84

Piper, H Beam 1904-1964 *BioIn 12,*
ConAu 110, DcLB 8[port], EncSF,
ScF&FL 1, WhoSciF

Piper, Roger 1909- *ConAu X, SmATA X*

Piper, Roger *see also* Fisher, John

Piro, Richard 1934- *BioIn 10, ConAu 49,*
SmATA 7

Pirsig, Robert M 1928- *BioIn 10, ConAu 53,*
ConLC 4, –6, IntAu&W 77,
NewYTBS 74, WhoAm 76, –78, –80, –82

Piserchia, Doris 1928- *ConAu 107, EncSF,*
ScF&FL 1, –2, WrDr 84

Pitcher, Robert Walter 1918- *AmM&WS 73S,*
–78S, ConAu 29R, LEduc 74,
WhoMW 74, –76, –78

Pitkin, Dorothy 1898?-1972 *BioIn 9,*
ConAu 37R

Pitkin, Thomas Monroe 1901- *ConAu 17R,*
DrAS 74H, –78H

Pitrone, Jean Maddern 1920- *AuBYP SUP,*
BioIn 9, ConAu 8NR, –17R, ForWC 70,
SmATA 4, WhoAmW 74, –75, –83,
WrDr 76, –80, –82, –84

Pitt, Valerie Joan 1925- *ConAu 5R*

Pizer, Vernon 1918- *AuBYP, BioIn 7, –12,*
ConAu 1R, –4NR, SmATA 21[port],
WrDr 76, –80, –82, –84

Place, Marian Templeton 1910- *AuBYP,*
BioIn 7, ConAu 1R, –5NR, IndAu 1917,
ScF&FL 1, SmATA 3, WhoAmW 74,
–72, WhoPNW

Place, Marian Templeton *see also* White, Dale

Place, Marian Templeton *see also* Whitinger, R
D

Plagemann, Bentz 1913- *AmAu&B, AmNov,*
AuBYP SUP, BioIn 2, –3, ConAu 1R,
–4NR, WrDr 84

Plaidy, Jean 1906- *Au&Wr 6, BioIn 7, –9,*
–10, –11, ConAu X, ConLC 7,
IntAu&W 77X, NewYTBS 77,
Novels[port], SmATA 2, TwCWr,
Who 74, –82, –83, WorAu, WrDr 76, –80,
–82, –84

Plaidy, Jean *see also* Hibbert, Eleanor

Plain, Belva 1918?- *ConAu 81, WrDr 80, –82,*
–84

Plante, David 1940- *Au&Wr 6, ConAu 37R,*

ConLC 7, –23[port], ConNov 76, –82,
DcLB Y83B[port], IntAu&W 76, –77, –82,
Novels, WhoWor 76, WrDr 76, –80, –82,
–84

Plate, Robert 1918- AuBYP, BioIn 7,
ConAu 17R, WrDr 76, –80, –82, –84

Plate, Thomas 1944- ConAu 69

Plath, Sylvia 1932-1963 AmAu&B,
AmWomWr, AmWr SUP, AuBYP SUP,
BioIn 7, –8, –9, –10, –11, –12, CasWL,
ChhPo S1, ConAu P-2, ConLC 1, –2, –3,
–5, –9, –11, –14, –17, ConP 75, –80A,
CroCAP, DcAmB S7, DcLB 5, –6[port],
DcLEL 1940, EncWL, –2, GoodHs,
IntDcWB, LibW, LinLib L, LongCEL,
LongCTC, MakMC, ModAL SUP,
NewYTBS 74, NotAW MOD, Novels,
OxAmL, PenC AM, RAdv 1, TwCWr,
WebE&AL, WhDW, WhAm 4,
WhoAmW 61, WhoTwCL, WorAl,
WorAu

Platt, Charles Michael 1949- WhoAm 74, –76,
–78, –80, –82

Platt, Colin 1934- WrDr 84

Platt, Kin 1911- AuBYP SUP, BioIn 8, –12,
ConAu 11NR, –17R, ConLC 26[port],
ScF&FL 1, SmATA 21[port],
WhoAm 74

Platt, Rutherford 1894-1975 BioIn 10,
ConAu 61, NewYTBS 75, OhA&B,
WhAm 6

Player, Gary 1935- BioIn 5, –6, –7, –8, –9, –10,
–11, –12, BioNews 74, CelR 73,
ConAu 101, CurBio 61, EncSoA,
IntWW 76, –77, –78, –79, –80, –81, –82, –83,
NewYTBS 74, –78, Who 82, –83,
WhoAm 74, –76, –78, –80, –82, WhoGolf,
WhoWor 74, –78, –80, –82, WorAl

Playfair, Guy Lyon 1935- ConAu 106

Pleasants, Henry 1910- AmAu&B,
ConAu 107, IntAu&W 77, –82,
WhoAm 78, –80, –82, WrDr 76, –80, –82,
–84

Plimpton, George 1927- AuNews 1, BioIn 4,
–6, –7, –8, –9, –10, –11, –12, BlueB 76,
CelR 73, ConAu 21R, CurBio 69,
LinLib L, NewYTBE 70, SmATA 10,
WebAB, –79, WhoAm 74, –76, –78, –80,
–82, WhoHol A, WhoWor 74, WrDr 80,
–82, –84

Plotz, Helen Ratnoff 1913- ChhPo, –S1,
ConAu 8NR, –9R, WhoAmW 72

Plowden, Alison 1931- ConAu 33R, WrDr 76,
–80, –82, –84

Plowden, David 1932- BioIn 11, ConAu 33R,
ConPhot

Plowman, Edward E 1931- ConAu 37R,
WhoRel 75, –77, WrDr 76, –80, –82, –84

Plowman, Stephanie 1922- BioIn 10,
ConAu 5NR, –53, SmATA 6,
TwCCW 78, –83, WrDr 76, –80, –82, –84

Plumb, John Harold 1911- Au&Wr 6,

BioIn 10, ConAu 5R, DcLEL 1940,
IntAu&W 77, –82, IntWW 74, –75, –76,
–77, –78, –79, –80, –81, –82, –83, LongCTC,
Who 74, –82, –83, WhoWor 82, WorAu,
WrDr 76, –80, –82, –84

Plummer, Beverly J 1918- ConAu 29R,
WhoAmW 75, WrDr 76, –80, –82, –84

Plumpp, Sterling Dominic 1940- BlkAWP,
BroadAu, ConAu 5R, DrAP 75,
DrAP&F 83, InB&W 80, IntAu&W 76,
SelBAA, WhoBlA 77, –80

Plunkett, Jim 1947- BioIn 9, –10, –11, –12,
CelR 73, CmCal, CurBio 71, –82[port],
NewYTBE 70, –71, NewYTBS 81[port],
WhoAm 74, WhoFtbl 74

Poe, Charlsie 1909- ConAu P-2

Poe, Edgar Allan 1809-1849 Alli, AmAu,
AmAu&B, AmBi, AmWr, AnCL,
ApCAB, AtlBL, BbD, BiD&SB, BiDSA,
BioIn 1, –2, –3, –4, –5, –6, –7, –8, –9, –10,
–11, –12, CasWL, CelCen, Chambr 3,
ChhPo, –S1, –S2, –S3, CnDAL, CnE&AP,
CrtT 3, –4, CyAL 2, CyWA, DcAmAu,
DcAmB, DcBiA, DcBiPP, DcEnA,
DcEnL, DcLB 3, DcLEL, DcNAA,
Dis&D, Drake, EncAB-H, EncMys,
EncO&P 78, EncSF, EncSoH, EvLB,
FilmgC, HarEnUS, LinLib L, –S,
McGEWB, MnBBF, MouLC 3,
NatCAB 1, NewEOp 71, NotNAT B,
Novels[port], OxAmH, OxAmL, OxEng,
PenC AM, RAdv 1, RComWL, REn,
REnAL, ScF&FL 1, SmATA 23[port],
Str&VC, TwCBDA, TwCCr&M 80A,
WebAB, –79, WebE&AL, WhDW,
WhAm HS, WhoHr&F, WhoSciF,
WhoSpyF, WorAl

Pohl, Frederik 1919- AmAu&B, BioIn 10, –11,
–12, ConAu 11NR, –61, ConLC 18,
ConNov 72, –76, –82, ConSFA,
DcLB 8[port], DrAF 76, DrAP&F 83,
EncSF, Future, IntAu&W 76, –77, –82,
LinLib L, Novels, PenC AM, ScF&FL 1,
–2, SmATA 24, WhoAm 74, –76, –78, –80,
WhoSciF, WorAl, WorAu, WrDr 76, –80,
–82, –84

Pohlmann, Lillian 1902- AuBYP, BioIn 8, –11,
ConAu 9R, ForWC 70, SmATA 11, –8,
WrDr 76, –80, –82, –84

Pointer, Larry 1940- ConAu 101

Poirier, Richard 1925- AmAu&B, BlueB 76,
ConAu 1R, –3NR, ConLCrt, –82,
DcLEL 1940, DrAS 74E, –78E, –82E,
WhoAm 74, –76, –78, –80, –82, WhoE 74,
WorAu 1970, WrDr 76, –80, –82, –84

Poitier, Sidney 1924?- BiDFilm, BiE&WWA,
BioIn 4, –5, –6, –7, –8, –9, –10, –11, –12,
BioNews 74, BlueB 76, CelR 73,
CivR 74, ConLC 26[port], CurBio 59,
DrBlPA, Ebony 1, FilmgC, InB&W 80,
IntMPA 77, –75, –76, –78, –79, –81, –82, –84,
IntWW 74, –75, –76, –77, –78, –79, –80, –81,

-82, -83, LinLib S, MotPP, MovMk,
NegAl 76[port], -83[port], NotNAT,
OxFilm, Who 74, -82, -83, WhoAm 74,
-76, -78, -80, -82, WhoBlA 75, -77, -80,
WhoHol A, WhoThe 15, -16, -81,
WhoWor 74, -78, WorAl

Polatnick, Florence 1923- *BioIn 10,*
ConAu 29R, SmATA 5

Polenberg, Richard 1937- *ConAu 21R,*
DrAS 74H, -78H, -82H, WhoAm 74, -76,
-78, -80, WhoAmJ 80, WhoE 74,
WrDr 82, -84

Polgreen, John *IlsBYP*

Polk, Dora 1923- *ConAu 49*

Pollack, Peter 1911-1978 *BioIn 11, ConAu 77,*
-81, WhoAmA 73, -76, -78, -80N, -82N

Polland, Madeleine A 1918- *AuBYP, BioIn 7,*
-9, -10, ConAu 3NR, -5R, SmATA 6,
ThrBJA, TwCCW 78, -83, WrDr 80, -82,
-84

Pollard, Jack 1926- *ConAu 29R*

Pollock, Bruce 1945- *ConAu 7NR, -57*

Pollowitz, Melinda 1944- *ConAu 77,*
SmATA 26[port]

Polmar, Norman 1938- *Au&Wr 6, ConAu 49,*
IntAu&W 77

Polner, Murray 1928- *ConAu 5NR, -13R*

Polvay, Marina 1928- *BioIn 12, IntAu&W 82,*
WhoAmW 83

Pomerance, Bernard 1940- *ConAu 101,*
ConDr 82, ConLC 13, WrDr 84

Pomeroy, Earl 1915- *AmAu&B, CmCal,*
ConAu 17R, DrAS 74H, -78H, -82H,
REnAW, WhoAm 74, -76, -78, -80, -82,
WhoAmP 81, WhoPNW

Pomeroy, Pete 1925- *AuBYP SUP, ConAu X,*
SmATA X

Pomeroy, Pete *see also* Roth, Arthur J

Pomeroy, Wardell Baxter 1913-
AmM&WS 73S, -78S, BioIn 10,
ConAu 1R, -1NR, CurBio 74,
IndAu 1917, WhoAm 74, -76, -78, -80,
-82

Pond, John Hamilton 1923- *WhoF&I 74, -75,*
-77

Ponsot, Marie B 1922- *ConAu 9R,*
DrAP&F 83, ForWC 70, WhoAmW 70

Poole, Frederick King 1934- *BioIn 9,*
ConAu 25R

Poole, Gary Thomas 1931- *ConAu 107,*
WhoAm 74, WhoF&I 74

Poole, Gray Johnson 1906- *AuBYP,*
AuBYP SUP, BioIn 7, -9, ConAu 5R,
-6NR, IntAu&W 76, SmATA 1

Poole, Josephine 1933- *Au&Wr 6, BioIn 10,*
ConAu 10NR, -21R, ConLC 17,
IntAu&W 76, -77, ScF&FL 1, -2,
SmATA 5, TwCCW 78, -83, WrDr 76,
-80, -82, -84

Poole, Lynn 1910-1969 *AmAu&B, AuBYP,*
AuBYP SUP, BioIn 3, -6, -7, -8, -9,

ConAu 5R, CurBio 54, -69, MorJA,
SmATA 1, WhAm 5

Poole, Victoria 1927- *ConAu 102*

Poortvliet, Rien 1933?- *BioIn 12, SmATA 37*

Pope, Clifford Hillhouse 1899-1974 *AmAu&B,*
AmM&WS 73P, Au&Wr 6, AuBYP,
BioIn 7, ConAu 1R, -103, WhAm 6,
WhoAm 74

Pope, Dudley Bernard Egerton 1925-
Au&Wr 6, BioIn 10, ConAu 2NR, -5R,
DcLEL 1940, IntAu&W 76, -77, -82,
Who 74, -82, -83, WhoE 74, WhoWor 74,
WorAu, WrDr 76, -80, -82, -84

Pope, Elizabeth Marie 1917- *AuBYP SUP,*
ConAu 49, DrAS 74E, -78E, -82E,
ScF&FL 1A, SmATA 36, WhoAmW 58,
-68, -70

Pope-Hennessy, John 1913- *BioIn 12,*
IntWW 83, Who 83, WhoWor 82,
WrDr 84

Popham, Estelle L 1906- *ConAu 1R, -5NR,*
ForWC 70, WhoAm 74, WhoAmW 74,
-66, -68, -70, -72

Popkin, Henry 1924- *DrAS 74E, -78E, -82E*

Popkin, Zelda 1898-1983 *AmAu&B, AmNov,*
BioIn 2, -4, ConAu 109, -25R, CurBio 51,
-83N, InWom, NewYTBS 83,
TwCCr&M 80, WhoAmJ 80,
WhoWorJ 72, -78, WrDr 76, -80, -82, -84

Porcari, Constance Kwolek 1933- *ConAu 33R*

Porcari, Constance Kwolek *see also* Kwolek,
Constance

Porges, Paul Peter 1927- *WorECar*

Porter, Eliot Furness 1901- *BioIn 7, -8, -10,*
-11, -12, ConAu 5R, ConPhot,
CurBio 76, LinLib L, WhoAm 74, -76,
-78, -80, -82, WhoAmA 76, -78, -80, -82

Porter, Jack Nusan 1944- *AmM&WS 73S,*
-78S, ConAu 41R, IntAu&W 82,
WhoE 79, -81

Porter, Katherine Anne 1890-1980 *AmAu&B,*
AmWomWr, AmWr, AnObit 1980[port],
AuNews 2, BioIn 1, -3, -4, -5, -6, -7, -8,
-9, -10, -11, -12, BlueB 76, CasWL,
CelR 73, -73, CnDAL, CnMWL,
ConAmA, ConAu 1R, -1NR, -101,
ConLC 1, -3, -7, -10, -13, -15, -27[port],
ConNov 72, -76, CurBio 40, -63, -80N,
CyWA, DcLB Y80A[port], -4, DcLEL,
DrAF 76, EncSoH, EncWL, -2[port],
EvLB, ForWC 70, GoodHs, InWom,
IntAu&W 76, -77, IntDcWB, IntWW 74,
-75, -76, -77, -78, -79, -80, -81N, LibW,
LinLib L, -S, LongCTC, MakMC,
McGEWB, ModAL, ModAL SUP,
NewYTBE 70, NewYTBS 80[port],
Novels[port], OxAmL, OxEng, PenC AM,
RAdv 1, REn, REnAL, SmATA 23N,
TwCA, TwCA SUP, TwCWr, WebAB,
-79, WebE&AL, WhDW, WhAm 7,
WhE&EA, Who 74, WhoAm 74, -76, -78,
-80, WhoAmW 74, -58, -61, -64, -66, -68,

*-70, -72, -75, -77, -79, -81, WhoE 74,
WhoTwCL, WhoWor 74, -78, WorAl,
WrDr 76, -80*
Porter, Sheena 1935- *BioIn 7, -9, ConAu 81,
IntAu&W 82, SmATA 24[port], ThrBJA,
TwCCW 78, -83, WrDr 80, -82, -84*
Porter, William Sydney 1862-1910 *AmAu&B,
AmBi, AtlBL, AuBYP SUP, BioIn 1, -2,
-3, -4, -5, -6, -7, -8, -9, -10, -11, -12,
CasWL, CnDAL, ConAu 104, DcAmB,
DcLB 12[port], DcLEL, DcNAA, Dis&D,
EncMys, EncSoH, EvLB, LinLib L, -S,
LongCTC, NatCAB 15, OhA&B,
OxAmL, OxEng, PenC AM, REn,
REnAL, TwCA SUP, WebAB,
-79, WebE&AL, YABC 2*
Porter, William Sydney *see also* Henry, O
Porter, William Sydney *see also* Henry, Oliver
Porter, William Sydney *see also* Peters, S H
Portis, Charles 1933- *AmAu&B, ConAu 1NR,
-45, DcLB 6, WrDr 84*
Portisch, Hugo 1927- *ConAu 21R,
WhoWor 74, -76*
Posell, Elsa Z *AuBYP SUP, BioIn 9,
ConAu 1R, -4NR, SmATA 3,
WhoAmW 74, -66, -72, WhoLibS 66*
Post, Elizabeth Lindley 1920- *BioIn 12,
ConAu 49, WhoAm 76, -78, -80, -82,
WhoAmW 74, -72, -75*
Post, Robert Charles 1937- *DrAS 82H*
Potok, Chaim 1929- *AmAu&B, ASpks,
Au&Wr 6, AuNews 1, -2, BioIn 7, -10,
-11, BioNews 74, ConAu 17R, ConLC 2,
-7, -14, -26[port], CurBio 83[port],
DrAF 76, DrAP&F 83, IntAu&W 76,
-77, LinLib L, Novels, SmATA 33[port],
WhoAm 74, -76, -78, -80, -82,
WhoAmJ 80, WhoE 74, WhoWor 74,
WhoWorJ 72, -78, WorAl, WrDr 76, -80,
-82, -84*
Potter, David Morris 1910-1971 *AmAu&B,
BioIn 5, -8, -9, -10, ConAu 108,
DcLB 17[port], EncAB-H, EncSoH,
NewYTBE 71, WhAm 5, WorAu 1970*
Potter, Marian 1915- *BioIn 11, ConAu 1NR,
-49, SmATA 9, WhoAmW 77, -79, -81*
Potter, Robert Ducharme 1905-1978
*AmM&WS 73P, AuBYP, BioIn 7, -11,
ConAu 77, NewYTBS 78, WhoE 74*
Potter, Simeon 1898-1976 *Au&Wr 6,
BlueB 76, ConAu 4NR, -5R,
IntAu&W 76, -77, Who 74, WrDr 76*
Pough, Frederick Harvey 1906-
*AmM&WS 73P, -76P, -79P, -82P, AuBYP,
BioIn 2, -7, ConAu 81, WhoAm 74, -76,
-78, -80, -82, WhoTech 82, WhoWest 82*
Pough, Richard Hooper 1904- *AmM&WS 73P,
-76P, -79P, -82P, BioIn 1, -9, WhoAm 74,
-76, -78, -80, -82*
Pound, Ezra 1885-1972 *AmAu&B, AmLY,
AmWr, Au&Wr 6, BioIn 1, -2, -3, -4, -5,
-6, -7, -8, -9, -10, -11, -12, CasWL,*

*Chambr 3, ChhPo, CnDAL, CnE&AP,
CnMD, CnMWL, ConAmA, ConAmL,
ConAu 5R, -37R, ConLC 1, -2, -3, -4, -5,
-7, -10, -13, -18, ConLCrt, -82, ConP 70,
CurBio 42, -63, -72, -72N, CyWA,
DcAmSR, DcCM, DcLB 4, DcLEL,
EncAB-H, EncWL, -2[port], EncWT,
EvLB, LinLib L, -S, LongCEL,
LongCTC, MakMC, McGEWB, ModAL,
ModAL SUP, NewYTBE 72, ObitOF 79,
ObitT 1971, OxAmH, OxAmL, OxEng,
PenC AM, RAdv 1, RComWL, REn,
REnAL, SixAP, TwCA, TwCA SUP,
TwCWr, WebAB, WebE&AL, WhDW,
WhAm 5, -7, WhE&EA, WhLit,
WhoTwCL, WorAl*
Pournelle, Jerry 1933- *AmM&WS 73S,
ConAu 77, DrAF 76, DrAP&F 83,
EncSF, Novels, ScF&FL 1, -2,
SmATA 26[port], WhoWest 74, -76, -78,
WrDr 84*
Poverman, C E *DrAP&F 83, Po&Wr 77*
Powell, John Roland 1889- *ConAu P-1*
Powell, Lawrence Clark 1906- *AmAu&B,
AmEA 74, BiDAmEd, BiDrLUS 70,
BioIn 2, -3, -5, -7, -8, -10, ChhPo, -S3,
CmCal, ConAu 8NR, -21R, CurBio 60,
LinLib L, WhoAm 74, -76, WhoLibI 82,
WhoLibS 55, -66, WorAu*
Powell, Richard Pitts 1908- *AmAu&B,
Au&Wr 6, BioIn 5, -6, -10, ConAu 1R,
WhoAm 74, -76, -78, -80, -82,
WhoWor 78, -80, -82, WorAu*
Powell, Shirley 1931- *ConAu 106,
DrAP&F 83*
Power, Phyllis M *SingR 1*
Powers, Bill 1931- *ConAu 77, SmATA 31*
Powers, David Francis 1911- *BioIn 6, -11,
PolProf K*
Powers, David Guy 1911-1967 *BioIn 8,
ConAu P-2, EncAB 40[port]*
Powers, J F 1917- *ConAu 2NR, ConLC 8,
ConNov 82, IntAu&W 76, -77, Novels,
WrDr 80, -82, -84*
Powers, James Farl 1917- *AmAu&B,
AmCath 80, Au&Wr 6, BioIn 3, -4, -6,
-8, -12, CathA 1952, ConAu 1R,
ConLC 1, -4, ConNov 72, -76, DrAF 76,
ModAL, OxAmL, RAdv 1, REnAL,
TwCA SUP, WebE&AL, WhoAm 74, -76,
-78, -80, -82, WhoTwCL, WrDr 76*
Powers, John James 1945- *ConAu 69*
Powers, John James *see also* Powers, John R
Powers, John R 1945- *ConAu X, -69,
DrAS 78E, WhoAm 82*
Powers, John R *see also* Powers, John James
Powers, Robert M 1942- *ConAu 77,
IntAu&W 82, WrDr 82, -84*
Powers, Thomas Moore 1940- *ConAu 37R,
WhoAm 74, -76, -78, -80, -82, WhoE 74,
-75, -77*
Powers, William K 1934- *ConAu 25R,*

OxCan SUP

Powledge, Fred 1935- *ConAu 9NR, –21R, SmATA 37, WhoE 74, WrDr 76, –80, –82, –84*

Powlis, LaVerne *InB&W 80*

Pownall, Eve *SingR 1*

Poyer, Joe 1939- *ConAu X, –49, ConSFA, EncSF, MichAu 80, Novels, ScF&FL 1, –2, WhoSpyF, WrDr 76, –80, –82, –84*

Poynter, Margaret 1927- *ConAu 93, SmATA 27[port]*

Prabhavananda, Swami 1893-1976 *ConAu 8NR, –65*

Prago, Albert 1911- *ChiSch, ConAu 29R, IntAu&W 77, –82*

Prange, Gordon William 1910-1980 *BioIn 12, ConAu 97, DrAS 74H, –78H, NewYTBS 80*

Prather, Alfred Val Jean 1926- *WhoAmL 78, –79*

Prather, Hugh 1938- *BioIn 11, ConAu 2NR, –45, NewYTBS 77, ScF&FL 1, –2*

Pratt, Fletcher 1897-1956 *AmAu&B, AuBYP, BioIn 1, –2, –4, –6, –7, CurBio 42, –56, EncSF, NatCAB 46, ObitOF 79, REnAL, ScF&FL 1, –2, TwCA SUP, WhAm 3, WhE&EA, WhNAA, WhoHr&F, WhoSciF*

Pratt, John 1931- *Au&Wr 6, ConAu 1R, –1NR, IntAu&W 76*

Pratt, William Crouch, Jr. 1927- *ConAu 6NR, –13R, DrAS 74E, –78E, –82E, IntWWP 77, –82, WhoAm 80, –82, WhoMW 78, –80, –82, WhoWor 80, –82*

Presberg, Miriam Goldstein 1919-1978 *ConAu 1R, –3NR, ForWC 70, WhoAmW 70, WhoWorJ 72, –78, WrDr 76, –80, –82, –84*

Presberg, Miriam Goldstein *see also* Gilbert, Miriam

Prescott, Gerald Webber 1899- *AmM&WS 73P, –76P, –79P, Au&Wr 6, WrDr 76*

Prescott, Orville 1906- *AmAu&B, ASpks, AuBYP, BioIn 4, –8, –11, ConAu 41R, CurBio 57, LinLib L, –S, REnAL, WhoAm 74, –76, –78, –80, –82*

Prescott, Peter Sherwin 1935- *BioIn 9, –10, ConAu 37R, WhoAm 76, –78, –80, –82, WhoE 75, –77, WhoWor 78*

Prescott, William Hickling 1796-1859 *Alli, AmArch 70, AmAu, AmAu&B, AmBi, ApCAB, AtlBL, BbD, BiD&SB, BioIn 1, –3, –4, –5, –6, –7, –8, –9, –11, CelCen, Chambr 3, CyAL 1, CyWA, DcAmAu, DcAmB, DcBiPP, DcEnA, DcEnL, DcLB 1, DcLEL, DcNAA, DcSpL, Drake, EncAAH, EncLatA, EvLB, HarEnUS[port], LinLib L, –S, McGEWB, NatCAB 6, OxAmH, OxAmL, OxEng, OxSpan, PenC AM, REn, REnAL, TwCBDA, WebAB, –79, WhDW,*

WhAm HS

Prestidge, Pauline 1922- *ConAu 103*

Preston, Don Alan 1930- *BioIn 12, WhoAm 76, –78, –80, –82*

Preston, Edward 1925- *ConAu X*

Preston, Edward *see also* Guess, Edward Preston

Preston, Edward Francis 1919- *WhoAm 74, –76, –78, –80, WhoGov 77, –72, –75*

Preston, Richard Joseph, Jr. 1905- *AmM&WS 73P, –76P, –79P, WhoAm 74, –76, –78*

Preussler, Otfried 1923- *AuBYP, BioIn 8, ConAu 77, ConLC 17, FourBJA, IntAu&W 76, –77, ScF&FL 1, SmATA 24[port], TwCCW 78B, –83B*

Previn, Dory 1925?- *AmSCAP 66, BioIn 9, –10, –11, –12, CurBio 75, GoodHs, NewYTBE 70, WhoAm 76, –78, –80, –82, WhoAmW 74, –72, –75*

Prewitt, Cheryl 1957- *BioIn 12*

Price, Christine 1928-1980 *Au&Wr 6, AuBYP, BioIn 5, –6, –7, –8, –9, –12, ChhPo S1, –S3, ConAu 4NR, –5R, –93, IlsCB 1946, –1957, –1967, IntAu&W 76, –77, MorJA, SmATA 23N, –3, WhoAmW 74, –58, –61, –64, –66, –68, –70, –72, –75, –77, WrDr 76, –80*

Price, Eugenia 1916- *AmAu&B, BioIn 4, –5, –12, ConAu 2NR, –5R, WhoAmW 74, –68, –70, –72, WhoS&SW 73, –75*

Price, George 1901- *AmAu&B, BioIn 1, ConAu 103, WhoAm 74, –76, –78, –80, –82, WhoAmA 73, –76, –78, –80, –82, WhoWor 74, WorECar*

Price, Jonathan Reeve 1941- *ConAu 3NR, –45, DrAP 75, DrAP&F 83, WhoE 75, WhoWest 84*

Price, Nelson Lynn 1931- *ConAu 8NR, –61, WhoRel 75, –77*

Price, Raymond Kissam, Jr. 1930- *BioIn 8, –11, –12, BlueB 76, ConAu 105, WhoAm 74, –76, –78, –80, WhoGov 72, –75, WhoS&SW 73*

Price, Reynolds 1933- *AmAu&B, BioIn 6, –8, –10, –11, ConAu 1R, –1NR, ConLC 3, –6, –13, ConNov 72, –76, –82, DcLB 2, DrAF 76, DrAP&F 83, Novels, PenC AM, RAdv 1, WhoAm 74, –76, –78, –80, –82, WhoWor 74, WorAu, WrDr 76, –80, –82, –84*

Price, Richard 1949- *BioIn 10, –12, ConAu 3NR, –49, ConLC 6, –12, DcLB Y81B[port], DrAF 76, DrAP&F 83, NewYTBS 81[port], WhoAm 76, –78, –80, –82, WhoAmJ 80*

Price, Steven D 1940- *ConAu 1NR, –49*

Price, Susan 1955- *ConAu 105, SmATA 25, TwCCW 78, –83, WrDr 76, –80, –82, –84*

Price, Willard 1887- *AmAu&B, Au&Wr 6, AuBYP, BioIn 2, –8, BlueB 76, ConAu 1R, –1NR, IntAu&W 76, –77, IntWW 74, –75, –76, –77, –78, –79, –80, –81,*

WhoWor 78, WrDr 76, –80, –82, –84

Pyle, Ernie 1900-1945 *AmAu&B, BioIn 1, –2, CurBio 41, –45, LinLib L, NatCAB 33, OxAmL, REn, REnAL, WorAl*

Pyle, Howard 1853-1911 *Alli SUP, AmAu, AmAu&B, AmBi, AnCL, AntBDN B, ApCAB, AuBYP, BbD, BiD&SB, BioIn 1, –2, –3, –5, –7, –8, –10, –12, CarSB, ChhPo, –S1, –S2, –S3, ConAu 109, DcAmAu, DcAmB, DcBrBI, DcLEL, DcNAA, DrRegL 75, FamSYP, HarEnUS, IlBEAAW, IlrAm A, IlsBYP, JBA 34, LinLib L, –S, NatCAB 9, –29, OxAmL, REnAL, ScF&FL 1, SmATA 16, TwCBDA, TwCCW 78A, –83A, WebAB, –79, WhAm 1, WhoChL*

Pynchon, Thomas 1937- *AmAu&B, BioIn 6, –8, –9, –10, –12, BlueB 76, CasWL, ConAu 13R, ConLC 2, –3, –6, –9, –11, –18, ConNov 72, –76, –82, DcLB 2, DcLEL 1940, DrAF 76, DrAP&F 83, EncSF, EncWL, –2, IntAu&W 76, –77, MakMC, ModAL, ModAL SUP, Novels, PenC AM, RAdv 1, WebE&AL, WhoAm 74, –76, –78, –80, –82, WorAl, WorAu, WrDr 76, –80, –82, –84*

Q

Queen, Ellery 1905-1971 *AmAu&B, ASpks,*
AuBYP, BioIn 2, -3, -4, -8, -9, -10, -11,
-12, CelR 73, ConAu X, ConLC 3, -11,
CorpD, CurBio 40, DcLEL, EncMys,
EvLB, IntAu&W 76X, -77X, IntWW 74,
-75, -76, -77, -78, -79, -80, -81, -82,
LinLib LP, LongCTC, Novels[port],
OxAmL, PenC AM, REn, REnAL,
ScF&FL 1, SmATA 3, TwCA,
TwCA SUP, TwCCr&M 80, TwCWr,
WebAB, -79, Who 74, -82, WorAl,
WrDr 76, -80, -82, -84
Queen, Ellery *see also* Dannay, Frederic
Queen, Ellery *see also* Lee, Manfred B
Queneau, Raymond 1903-1976 *Au&Wr 6,*
BioIn 4, -7, -9, -11, -12, CasWL,
CnMWL, ConAu 69, -77, ConLC 2, -5,
-10, DcFM, EncSF, EncWL, -2, EvEuW,
IntWW 74, -75, -76, -77N, LinLib L,
MakMC, ModFrL, ModRL,
NewYTBS 76, Novels, OxFilm, OxFr,
PenC EUR, REn, TwCA SUP, TwCWr,
WhE&EA, WhoTwCL, WhoWor 74, -76,
WorEFlm
Quennell, Charles Henry Bourne 1872-1935
BioIn 6, DcBrBI, LongCTC, MorJA,
TwCA, TwCA SUP, WhE&EA
Quennell, Marjorie 1884-1972 *BioIn 4, -6,*
ConAu 73, DcBrA 1, DcLEL, EvLB,
JBA 34, LinLib L, LongCTC, MorJA,
SmATA 29[port], TwCA, TwCA SUP,
WhE&EA
Quentin, Dorothy 1911- *WhE&EA*
Quentin, Patrick 1912- *AmAu&B, Au&Wr 6,*
BioIn 10, BlueB 76, ConAu X, EncMys,
IntAu&W 76X, TwCCr&M 80, WorAu,
WrDr 80, -82, -84
Quilici, Folco 1930- *ConAu 105, DcFM,*
WhoWor 82, WorEFlm
Quiller-Couch, Sir Arthur Thomas 1863-1944
BbD, BiD&SB, BioIn 1, -4, -5, -12,
CasWL, Chambr 3, ChhPo, -S1, -S2, -S3,
CurBio 44, DcBiA, DcEnA, -AP, DcLEL,
EvLB, JBA 34, LinLib L, LongCTC,
MnBBF, ModBrL, NewC, Novels,
ObitOF 79, OxEng, PenC ENG, RAdv 1,
REn, TwCA, TwCA SUP, TwCWr,
WhAm 2, WhE&EA, WhLit, WhoHr&F

Quimby, Myrtle 1891- *ConAu P-2*
Quin-Harkin, Janet 1941- *BioIn 12,*
ConAu 81, IntAu&W 82, SmATA 18
Quinlan, Joseph *BioIn 11, -12*
Quinlan, Julia *BioIn 11, -12*
Quinn, David Beers 1909- *Au&Wr 6,*
BlueB 76, ConAu 77, DrAS 78H, -82H,
IntAu&W 82, OxCan, OxCan SUP,
Who 74, -82, -83, WhoAm 74, -76, -78,
WrDr 80, -82, -84
Quintero, Jose 1924- *BiDrAPA 77,*
BiE&WWA, BioIn 3, -4, -5, -9, -10, -11,
CnThe, CurBio 54, EncWT,
NewYTBS 74, -77, NotNAT, -A, PIP&P,
-A, WhDW, WhoAm 74, -76, -78, -80,
-82, WhoE 74, WhoThe 15, -16, -81,
WhoWor 74
Quirk, Randolph 1920- *BioIn 12, BlueB 76,*
ConAu 2NR, -5R, IntAu&W 82,
IntWW 82, -83, WhoWor 76, WrDr 76,
-80, -82, -84

R

Raab, Robert Allen 1924- *ConAu 29R*
Rabalais, Maria 1921- *ConAu 61*
Raban, Jonathan 1942- *ConAu 61, ConDr 73, -77B, -82B, IntAu&W 77, WrDr 76, -80, -82, -84*
Rabe, Berniece 1928- *BioIn 10, ConAu 1NR, -49, IntAu&W 82, SmATA 7, WrDr 80, -82, -84*
Rabinovitz, Rubin 1938- *ConAu 21R, DrAS 74E, -78E, -82E, WrDr 76, -80, -82, -84*
Rabinow, Paul 1944- *BioIn 11, ConAu 61*
Rabinowich, Ellen 1946- *ConAu 106, SmATA 29[port]*
Rabkin, Brenda 1945- *ConAu 101*
Rabkin, Eric S 1946- *ConAu 4NR, -49, DrAS 74E, -78E, -82E, EncSF, WhoMW 78*
Rachleff, Owen Spencer 1934- *ConAu 21R, WhoAm 76, -78, -80, -82, WhoE 74, -75, -77*
Rachlin, Carol King 1919- *AmM&WS 73S, -76P, ConAu 57, FifIDA, WhoAmW 74, -66, -68, -70, -72, -75*
Rachlin, Harvey 1951- *ConAu 107, WhoE 79, -81, -83*
Rachlin, Nahid *ConAu 81, DrAP&F 83*
Radice, Betty 1912- *Au&Wr 6, ConAu 25R, IntAu&W 76, -77, -82, WhoWor 76, WrDr 76, -80, -82, -84*
Radin, Paul 1883-1959 *BioIn 5, DcAmB S6, IntMPA 77, -76, -78, -79, -81, -82, -84, McGEWB, OxCan, WebAB, -79, WhAm 3*
Radley, Gail 1951- *ConAu 89, SmATA 25[port]*
Radley, Sheila *WrDr 84*
Rado, James 1932?- *ConAu 105, ConDr 73, -77D, -82D, ConLC 17, EncMT, NotNAT, PIP&P*
Raeburn, John Hay 1941- *ConAu 57, DrAS 74E, -78E, -82E*
Raeburn, Michael 1940- *ConAu 107*
Ragni, Gerome 1942- *ConAu 105, ConDr 73, -77D, -82D, ConLC 17, EncMT, NotNAT, PIP&P*
Ragosta, Millie J 1931- *ConAu 73*
Rahn, Joan Elma 1929- *AmM&WS 73P, -76P,*

-79P, -82P, ConAu 37R, SmATA 27[port]
Raht, John Milton 1928- *WhoF&I 81, -83, WhoWest 78, -80, -82, WhoWor 82*
Raiff, Stan 1930- *BioIn 11, ConAu 61, SmATA 11*
Raines, Howell 1943- *ConAu 73*
Rainwater, Clarence Elmer 1884-1925? *DcNAA, NatCAB 21, WhAm 1*
Ralbovsky, Martin Paul 1942- *ConAu 49*
Ramati, Alexander 1921- *Au&Wr 6, ConAu 7NR, -13R*
Ramee, Louise DeLa 1839-1908 *BiD&SB, BioIn 1, -2, -3, -11, BrAu 19, Chambr 3, DcEuL, EvLB, HsB&A, JBA 34, LinLib L, -S*
Ramee, Louise DeLa *see also* DeLaRamee, Louise
Rampa, T Lopsang 1911?- *EncO&P 78*
Rampo, Edogawa 1894- *ScF&FL 1*
Ramsay, William M 1922- *ConAu 13R, WhoS&SW 75, -76*
Ramsey, Jarold 1937- *ConAu 33R, DrAP 75, DrAP&F 83, DrAS 74E, -78E, -82E, IntWWP 77, -82, WhoE 75, -77, WrDr 76, -80, -82, -84*
Rand, Ayn 1905-1982 *AmAu&B, AmNov, AmWomWr, AnObit 1982[port], BioIn 2, -4, -5, -6, -7, -8, -10, -11, -12, CasWL, CelR 73, ConAu 105, -13R, ConLC 3, ConNov 72, -76, -82, CurBio 82[port], EncSF, ForWC 70, InWom, IntAu&W 76, -77, LibW, NewYTBS 82[port], Novels, OxAmL, PenC AM, PolProf E, REn, REnAL, ScF&FL 1, -2, TwCA SUP, WebAB, -79, WebE&AL, WhoAm 74, -76, -78, -80, -82, WhoAmW 74, -58, -66, -68, -70, -72, -75, -77, -81, -83, WhoSciF, WhoTwCL, WorAl, WrDr 76, -80, -82*
Rand, Suzanne 1950- *BioIn 12*
Randall, Dudley 1914- *BiDrLUS 70, BioIn 10, BlkAWP, BroadAu[port], ConAu 25R, ConLC 1, ConP 70, -75, -80, DcLEL 1940, DrAP 75, DrAP&F 83, Ebony 1, InB&W 80, IntAu&W 82, IntWWP 82, LinLib L, LivgBAA, MichAu 80, SelBAA, WhoAm 76, -78,*

*WhoBlA 75, –77, –80, WhoF&I 75,
WhoLibS 55, –66, WhoMW 74, –76, –78,
WrDr 76, –80, –82, –84*

Randall, Florence Engel 1917- *AuBYP SUP,
BioIn 10, BlkAWP, ConAu 41R,
IntAu&W 76, –77, ScF&FL 1, –2,
SmATA 5, WhoAmW 77, –79, –81,
WrDr 84*

Randall, Janet *AuBYP, BioIn 7, –9,
ConAu X, IntAu&W 76X, –77X, –82X,
PoIre, SmATA 3, WrDr 76, –80, –82, –84*

Randall, Janet *see also* Young, Janet Randall

Randall, Janet *see also* Young, Robert W

Randall, Marta 1948- *WrDr 84*

Randall, Robert *AuBYP, ConAu X, OxCan,
SmATA X, ThrBJA, WrDr 84*

Randall, Robert *see also* Silverberg, Robert

Randall, Rona *Au&Wr 6, IntAu&W 76,
–76X, –77, WrDr 76, –80, –82, –84*

Randall, Ruth Elaine Painter 1892-1971
*AmAu&B, AmWomWr, Au&Wr 6,
AuBYP, BioIn 4, –7, –8, –9, ConAu 1R,
–103, CurBio 57, InWom, SmATA 3,
WhAm 5, WhoAmW 58, –64, –66, –68, –70,
–72*

Randi, James 1928?- *BioIn 12, EncO&P 81*

Randolph, David 1914- *AmAu&B, BioIn 10,
IntWWM 77, WhoAm 74, –76, –78, –80,
–82, WhoE 83, WhoWor 74*

Ranelagh, John *Who 83*

Raphael, Bertram 1936- *AmM&WS 73P, –76P,
–79P, ConAu 97, WhoWest 74, –76, –78*

Raphael, Chaim 1908- *BioIn 6, ConAu 85,
CurBio 63, Who 74, –82, –83*

Raphael, Rick 1919- *ConAu 10NR, –21R,
ConSFA, DrRegL 75, EncSF, ScF&FL 1,
–2, WhoMW 76, –78, –80, –82, WrDr 84*

Rapoport, Roger 1946- *ConAu 33R, WrDr 76,
–80, –82, –84*

Rapp, Joel *AuNews 1, BioIn 10*

Rappoport, Ken 1935- *ConAu 4NR, –53*

Rasch, Sunna Cooper 1925- *ConAu 105,
WhoAmW 70, WhoE 74*

Rashke, Richard L 1936- *ConAu 107*

Rashkis, Harold A 1920- *BiDrAPA 77*

Raskin, Edith Lefkowitz 1908- *AuBYP SUP,
BioIn 11, ConAu 3NR, –9R, ForWC 70,
SmATA 9*

Raskin, Ellen 1928-1984 *ALA 80, AmPB,
BioIn 8, –9, –10, –12, BkP, ChlLR 1,
ChhPo, –S1, –S2, ConAu 21R,
IlsBYP, IlsCB 1957, –1967, IntAu&W 76,
SmATA 2, ThrBJA, TwCCW 78, –83,
WhoAm 80, –82, WhoAmA 80, –82,
WrDr 80, –82, –84*

Rathbone, Julian 1935- *ConAu 101,
IntAu&W 82, TwCCr&M 80, WrDr 80,
–82, –84*

Rather, Dan 1931- *AuNews 1, BioIn 10, –11,
–12, BioNews 74, ConAu 9NR, –53,
CurBio 75, IntMPA 79, –81, –82, –84,
IntWW 83, LesBEnT[port], NewYTET,*

PolProf NF, WhoAm 76, –78, –80, –82

Rau, Margaret 1913- *BioIn 11, ConAu 8NR,
–61, IntAu&W 82, SmATA 9*

Rauch, Constance 1937- *BioIn 10, ConAu 57*

Raucher, Herman 1928- *BioIn 11,
ConAu 29R, Novels, ScF&FL 1, –2,
SmATA 8, WhoAm 80, –82, WhoE 77,
–79, –81, –83, WrDr 76, –80, –82, –84*

Ravielli, Anthony 1916- *Au&Wr 6, AuBYP,
BioIn 5, –7, –8, –9, ConAu 11NR, –29R,
IlsCB 1946, –1957, –1967, SmATA 3,
ThrBJA, WhoE 74*

Ravin, Neil 1947- *ConAu 105*

Rawlings, Marjorie Kinnan 1896-1953
*AmAu&B, AmNov, AmWomWr, BioIn 1,
–2, –3, –4, –5, –7, –8, –9, –10, –11, –12,
CnDAL, ConAu 104, CurBio 42, –54,
CyWA, DcAmB S5, DcLB 9[port],
–22[port], DcLEL, EvLB, InWom, LibW,
LinLib L, LongCTC, ModAL,
NotAW MOD, Novels, ObitOF 79,
OxAmL, PenC AM, REn, REnAL,
ThrBJA, TwCA, TwCA SUP,
TwCCW 78, –83, TwCLC 4[port],
TwCWr, WhAm 3, WhFla, YABC 1*

Rawls, Wilson 1913?- *AuBYP SUP,
AuNews 1, BioNews 74, ConAu 1R,
–5NR, IntAu&W 76, –77X, –82X,
SmATA 22[port]*

Ray, John 1929- *Au&Wr 6, ConAu 11NR,
–25R*

Ray, Karen 1956- *ConAu 108*

Ray, Mary Eva Pedder 1932- *Au&Wr 6,
BioIn 9, ConAu 29R, IntAu&W 76, –77,
–82, SmATA 2, TwCCW 78, –83,
WrDr 76, –80, –82, –84*

Ray, N L 1918- *ConAu 109*

Ray, Trevor 1934- *ConAu 107*

Ray, Willis Eugene 1929- *LEduc 74*

Rayner, Claire 1931- *Au&Wr 6, ConAu 21R,
IntAu&W 76, Novels, ScF&FL 1, –2,
WhoAmW 74, WrDr 76, –80, –82, –84*

Rayner, Mary 1933- *BioIn 12, ConAu 69,
SmATA 22[port], TwCCW 83*

Rayner, William 1929- *Au&Wr 6, ConAu 77,
SmATA 36, TwCCW 78, WrDr 80, –82,
–84*

Raynes, John 1929- *ArtCS, BioIn 6, IlsBYP*

Rayson, Steven 1932- *ConAu 106,
SmATA 30[port], WrDr 76, –80, –82, –84*

Read, Miss *BioIn 5, –10, Novels*

Read, Anthony 1935- *ConAu 107*

Read, Bill 1917- *ConAu 13R, DrAS 74E,
–78E*

Read, Elfreida 1920- *Au&Wr 6,
AuBYP SUP, BioIn 9, ConAu 9NR,
–21R, IntAu&W 76, –77, SmATA 2,
WrDr 76, –80, –82, –84*

Read, Sir Herbert 1893-1968 *BioIn 1, –3, –4, –6,
–7, –8, –9, –10, –12, CasWL, ChhPo, –S1,
CnE&AP, ConAu 25R, –85, ConLC 4,
CurBio 62, –68, DcLB 20[port], DcLEL,*

EncSF, EncWL, EvLB, LinLib L,
LongCTC, McGDA, ModBrL,
ModBrL SUP, NewC, ObitOF 79,
ObitT 1961, OxEng, OxTwCA,
PenC ENG, RAdv 1, REn, ScF&FL 1,
TwCA, TwCA SUP, TwCWr, WhDW,
WhAm 5, WhE&EA, WhLit, WhoBbl 73,
WhoLA, WhoTwCL

Read, Piers Paul 1941- *Au&Wr 6, BioIn 10,*
-12, ConAu 21R, ConDr 73, -77B,
ConLC 4, -10, -25[port], ConNov 76, -82,
DcLB 14[port], DcLEL 1940,
IntAu&W 76, -77, -82, Novels[port],
SmATA 21[port], Who 74, -82, -83,
WhoAm 82, WorAu 1970, WrDr 76, -80,
-82, -84

Reader, Dennis Joel 1939- *ConAu 106,*
DrAP&F 83, DrAS 74E, -78E, -82E

Reagan, Ronald 1911- *BiDAmLL, BiDFilm,*
BiDrGov, BioIn 2, -3, -7, -8, -9, -10, -11,
-12, BioNews 74, BlueB 76, CelR 73,
CmCal, CngDr 81, -83, ConAu 85,
CurBio 49, -67, -82[port], DcPol,
EncAB-H, FilmgC, IntMPA 77, -75, -76,
-78, -79, -81, -82, -84, IntWW 74, -75,
-76, -77, -78, -79, -80, -81, -82, -83,
IntYB 78, -79, -80, -81, -82, LesBEnT,
LinLib S, MotPP, MovMk,
NewYTBE 70, NewYTBS 74, -79,
-80[port], NewYTET, OxFilm, PolProf J,
PolProf NF, Who 82, -83, WhoAm 74,
-76, -78, -80, -82, WhoAmP 73, -75, -77,
-79, -81, -83, WhoE 81, -83, WhoGov 77,
-72, -75, WhoHol A, WhoWest 74, -76,
WhoWor 74, -76, -78, -80, -82, WorAl,
WorEFlm

Reasoner, Harry 1923- *AmAu&B, AuNews 1,*
BioIn 7, -8, -10, -11, -12, BioNews 75,
CelR 73, CurBio 66, IntMPA 77, -75, -76,
-78, -79, -81, -82, -84, LesBEnT[port],
NewYTET, WhoAm 74, -76, -78, -80, -82,
WhoE 74, -75, WorAl

Reck, David 1935- *ConAmC, ConAu 73,*
DcCM

Red Fox, William 1871?-1976 *BioIn 10,*
ConAu 65, NewYTBS 76

Reddick, Lawrence Dunbar 1910- *AmAu&B,*
BioIn 5, -9, ConAu 61, DrAS 74H, -78H,
-82H, Ebony 1, InB&W 80, WhoBlA 75,
-77, -80

Reddy, T J 1945- *BlkAWP, ConAu 45,*
DrAP 75, DrAP&F 83

Redgate, John *ConAu X*

Redmond, Eugene B 1937- *BlkAWP,*
ConAu 25R, DrAP 75, DrAP&F 83,
DrAS 74E, -78E, -82E, InB&W 80,
IntWWP 77, LivgBAA, SelBAA,
WhoWest 76, -78, -80, WrDr 76, -80, -82,
-84

Reed, A W 1908-1979 *ConAu 4NR, -9R,*
WrDr 76, -80

Reed, Alexander Wyclif 1908-1979 *Au&Wr 6,*

ConAu 9R, IntAu&W 76, -77, -82,
WhE&EA, WrDr 76

Reed, Barry Clement 1927- *ConAu 29R*

Reed, Graham Frederick 1923- *CanWW 83,*
WhoCan 82

Reed, Gwendolyn E 1932- *AuBYP, BioIn 8,*
-10, -12, ChhPo S1, ConAu 25R,
SmATA 21, -7, WhoAmW 74, -75

Reed, Ishmael 1938- *AmAu&B, BioIn 10, -11,*
-12, BlkAWP, BroadAu[port],
ConAu 21R, ConLC 2, -3, -5, -6, -13,
ConNov 72, -76, -82, ConP 70, -75, -80,
Conv 3, DcLB 2, -5[port], DcLEL 1940,
DrAF 76, DrAP 75, DrAP&F 83,
InB&W 80, IntAu&W 76, -77,
IntWWP 77, LivgBAA, ModAL SUP,
ModBlW, NegAl 76[port], -83, Novels,
SelBAA, TwCCr&M 80, WhoAm 74, -76,
-78, -80, -82, WorAu 1970, WrDr 76, -80,
-82, -84

Reed, J D 1940- *BioIn 10, ConAu 33R,*
DrAP 75, WhoPubR 76

Reed, John 1887-1920 *AmAu&B, AmLY,*
BioIn 1, -3, -4, -5, -6, -7, -8, -10, -11, -12,
ConAu 106, DcAmB, DcAmSR, DcNAA,
EncAB-H, LongCTC, McGEWB, ModAL,
NatCAB 19, OxAmH, OxAmL,
PenC AM, REn, REnAL, TwCA,
TwCA SUP, TwCLC 9[port], WebAB,
-79, WhAm 1, -4A, WorAl

Reed, Kenneth Terrence 1937- *ConAu 73,*
DrAS 74E, -78E, -82E

Reed, Kit 1932- *AmAu&B, Au&Wr 6,*
ConAu X, DrAP&F 83, EncSF,
IntAu&W 76, ScF&FL 1, -2,
SmATA 34[port], WhoAm 74, -76, -78,
-80, -82, WhoAmW 74, -70, -72,
WrDr 76, -80, -82, -84

Reed, Lou 1940?- *BioIn 10, -11, -12,*
ConLC 21[port], EncPR&S, -77, MugS,
RkOn 78, -84, RolSEnR 83,
WhoRocM 82, WorAl

Reed, Rex 1938?- *AuNews 1, BioIn 8, -9, -10,*
CelR 73, ConAmTC, ConAu 9NR, -53,
CurBio 72, NewYTBE 72, WhoAm 76,
-78, -80, -82, WhoE 74, -75, -77,
WhoHol A, WorAl, WrDr 76, -80, -82,
-84

Reed, W Maxwell 1871-1962 *JBA 51,*
WhE&EA

Reed, William Leonard 1910- *Baker 78,*
IntWWM 77, WhoMus 72, WhoWor 76

Reed, Willis 1942- *BioIn 7, -8, -9, -10, -11,*
-12, ConAu 104, CurBio 73, InB&W 80,
NegAl 76[port], -83, NewYTBE 70,
NewYTBS 74, -77, -82[port], St&PR 75,
WhoAm 74, -78, -80, WhoBbl 73,
WhoBlA 75, -77, -80, WorAl

Reeder, Red, Colonel 1902- *AuBYP, BioIn 9,*
ConAu X

Reeder, Red, Colonel *see also* Reeder, Russell P,
Jr.

Reeder, Russell P, Jr. 1902- *AuBYP, BioIn 7, –9, ConAu 1R, –5NR, SmATA 4*
Reeder, Russell P, Jr. *see also* Reeder, Red, Colonel
Reeman, Douglas Edward 1924- *Au&Wr 6, ConAu 1R, –3NR, DcLEL 1940, IntAu&W 76, –76X, –77, –77X, Novels, SmATA 28, WrDr 76, –80, –82, –84*
Reeman, Douglas Edward *see also* Kent, Alexander
Rees, Barbara 1934- *ConAu 9NR, –53, IntAu&W 77, –82, WrDr 76, –80, –82, –84*
Rees, David 1928- *Au&Wr 6, ConAu 9R, –11NR, IntAu&W 76, –77*
Rees, Helen Christina Easson 1903-1970 *AuBYP, BioIn 8, ConAu 5R, –89, ScF&FL 1*
Rees, Helen Christina Easson *see also* Oliver, Jane
Rees, Lucy 1943- *ConAu 107*
Reese, Terence 1913- *ConAu 109, IntAu&W 77, Who 74, –83*
Reeves, Bruce Douglas 1940?- *ConAu 11NR, –21R*
Reeves, James 1909-1978 *AnCL, Au&Wr 6, AuBYP, BioIn 7, –8, –9, –10, –12, BlueB 76, BkCL, ChhPo, –S1, –S2, –S3, ConAu 5R, ConP 70, –75, DcLEL 1940, IntAu&W 76, –77, IntWWP 77, PenC ENG, ScF&FL 1, –2, SmATA 15, ThrBJA, TwCCW 78, –83, Who 74, WhoChL, WhoTwCL, WorAu, WrDr 76*
Reeves, Marjorie Ethel 1905- *Au&Wr 6, ConAu 13R, IntAu&W 76, –77, –82, WhE&EA, Who 74, –82, –83, WhoWor 78, WrDr 76, –80, –82, –84*
Regehr, Lydia 1903- *ConAu 45*
Reginald, R 1948- *ConAu X, –57, ScF&FL 1, –2*
Reichert, Richard *AmCath 80*
Reichler, Joseph Lawrence 1918- *ConAu 103*
Reid, George Kell 1918- *AmM&WS 73P, –76P, –79P, –82P*
Reid, Henrietta *WrDr 84*
Reid, Jan 1945- *ConAu 61*
Reid, Patrick Robert 1910- *Au&Wr 6, IntAu&W 77, –82, IntYB 78, –79, –80, –81, –82, Who 74, –82, –83*
Reinfeld, Fred 1910-1964 *AuBYP, BioIn 6, –7, –9, ConAu P-1, GolEC, ObitOF 79, SmATA 3*
Reinfeld, Fred *see also* Young, Edward
Reingold, Carmel Berman *AuBYP SUP*
Reinsmith, Richard *ConAu X*
Reischauer, Edwin Oldfather 1910- *AmAu&B, BioIn 5, –6, –7, –10, –11, BioNews 74, BlueB 76, ConAu 17R, CurBio 62, DcAmDH, DcLEL 1940, DrAS 74H, –78H, –82H, IntAu&W 76, –77, –82, IntWW 74, –75, –76, –77, –78, –79, –80, –81, –82, –83, IntYB 78, –79, –80, –81, –82, LinLib L, PolProf J, PolProf K,*

WhoAm 74, –76, –78, –80, –82, WhoE 74, WhoWor 74, –78, –80, –82, WrDr 76, –80, –82, –84
Reiss, David S 1953- *ConAu 108*
Reiss, James *DrAP&F 83*
Reiss, Johanna 1929?- *AuBYP SUP, BioIn 10, –11, ConAu 85, TwCCW 78B*
Reit, Seymour 1918- *AuBYP SUP, BioIn 12, ConAu 93, SmATA 21[port]*
Remarque, Erich Maria 1898-1970 *AmAu&B, BioIn 1, –3, –4, –5, –9, CasWL, CIDMEL, ConAu 29R, –77, ConLC 21[port], CyWA, Dis&D, EncTR, EncWL, EvEuW, FilmgC, LinLib L, –S, LongCTC, McGEWB, ModGL, NewYTBE 70, NotNAT B, Novels, ObitOF 79, ObitT 1961, OxEng, OxGer, PenC EUR, REn, REnAL, TwCA, TwCA SUP, TwCWr, WhDW, WhAm 5, WhE&EA, WhScrn 2, WhoTwCL, WorAl*
Rembar, Charles 1915- *Au&Wr 6, ConAu 25R, WhoAm 74, –76, –78, –80, –82, WhoAmL 83, WrDr 76, –80, –82, –84*
Remi, Georges 1907-1983 *BioIn 11, ConAu 109, –69, IntAu&W 77, –82, NewYTBS 83, SmATA 13, –32, –32N, WorECom*
Remi, Georges *see also* Herge
Remington, Frederic 1861-1909 *AmAu, AmAu&B, AmBi, ApCAB X, ArtsAmW, AtlBL, BioIn 1, –2, –3, –4, –5, –6, –7, –8, –9, –10, –11, –12, CnDAL, ConAu 108, DcAmArt, DcAmAu, DcAmB, DcLB 12[port], DcLEL, DcNAA, EncAAH, EncAB-H, IlBEAAW, IlrAm A, LinLib L, –S, McGDA, McGEWB, NatCAB 7, –22, OxAmH, OxAmL, REn, REnAL, REnAW, WebAB, –79, WhAm 1, WhoAmP 79, –83, WhoFtbl 74, WorAl*
Remini, Robert Vincent 1921- *ConAu 3NR, –9R, DrAS 74H, –78H, –82H, IntAu&W 76, –77, WhoAm 74, –76, –78, –80, –82*
Renard, Jules 1864-1910 *BioIn 1, –7, CasWL, CIDMEL, CnMD, Dis&D, EncWL, EuAu, EvEuW, McGEWD, –84, ModWD, NotNAT B, OxFr, PenC EUR*
Renault, Mary 1905-1983 *Au&Wr 6, AuBYP, BioIn 5, –6, –8, –9, –10, –11, BlueB 76, ConAu X, ConLC 3, –11, –17, ConNov 72, –76, –82, CurBio 59, DcLB Y83N[port], EncSoA, InWom, IntAu&W 76, –77, IntWW 74, –75, –76, –77, –78, –79, –80, –81, –82, –83, LinLib L, –LP, LongCTC, ModBrL SUP, ModCmwL, NewC, NewYTBS 79, –83[port], Novels[port], RAdv 1, REn, SmATA X, TwCWr, Who 74, –82, –83, WhoAmW 66, –68, –70, –72, WhoWor 74, –76, –78, WorAl, WorAu, WrDr 76, –80, –82, –84*
Renault, Mary *see also* Challans, Mary

Rendell, Joan *Au&Wr 6, ConAu 7NR, –61, IntAu&W 76, –77, SmATA 28[port], WrDr 76, –80, –82, –84*

Rendell, Ruth 1930- *BioIn 12, ConAu 109, Novels, TwCCr&M 80, WrDr 82, –84*

Rendina, Laura Cooper 1902- *AuBYP, BioIn 6, –7, –11, ConAu 9R, MorJA, SmATA 10*

Rendon, Armando B 1939- *ChiSch, ConAu 37R, DrAP 75, DrAP&F 83, WrDr 76, –80, –82, –84*

Renich, Jill 1916- *ConAu 25R, MichAu 80, WhoAmW 74, –75*

Rennert, Vincent P 1928- *ODwPR 79, WhoPubR 76*

Reno, Marie R *ConAu 10NR, –65*

Rentzel, T Lance 1943- *WhoFtbl 74*

Renvoize, Jean 1930- *Au&Wr 6, BioIn 10, ConAu 41R, IntAu&W 76, SmATA 5*

Resnick, Michael D 1942- *ConAu 107, ConSFA, EncSF, ScF&FL 1, –2*

Resnick, Mike 1942- *ConAu X*

Resnick, Seymour 1920- *AuBYP, BioIn 8, ConAu 73, DrAS 74F, –78F, –82F, SmATA 23*

Rethi, Lili 1894?-1969 *BioIn 8, IlsBYP*

Rettig, Jack Louis 1925- *AmM&WS 73S, –78S, ConAu 57, WhoCon 73*

Reuben, David 1933- *Au&Wr 6, AuNews 1, BioIn 9, –10, BioNews 74, CelR 73, ConAu 41R, WhoAm 76, –78, –80, –82, WhoWest 74, WorAl, WrDr 76, –80, –82, –84*

Reuter, Carol 1931- *BioIn 9, ConAu 21R, SmATA 2*

Revson, Peter 1939-1974 *BioIn 9, –10, –12, BioNews 74, CelR 73, ObitOF 79, ObitT 1971*

Rexroth, Kenneth 1905-1982 *AmAu&B, AnObit 1982[port], BioIn 4, –7, –8, –9, –10, –12, BlueB 76, CelR 73, ChhPo, –S3, CmCal, CnE&AP, ConAu 5R, –107, ConDr 73, –77, –82, ConLC 1, –2, –6, –11, –22[port], ConP 70, –75, –80, CurBio 81[port], –82N, DcLB Y82A[port], –16[port], DcLEL 1940, DrAP 75, EncWL, IndAu 1917, IntAu&W 76, –77, IntWW 74, –75, –76, –77, –78, –79, –80, –81, –82, –83N, IntWWP 77, LinLib 1, ModAL, ModAL SUP, NewYTBS 82, OxAmL, PenC AM, RAdv 1, REn, REnAL, TwCA SUP, WebE&AL, WhoAm 74, –76, –78, –80, –82, WhoTwCL, WhoWest 74, WhoWor 74, WrDr 76, –80, –82*

Rey, H A 1898-1977 *ChlLR 5[port], ChsFB A, ConAu 6NR, –73, DcLB 22[port], IlsCB 1967, SmATA 26[port], TwCCW 83, WhoAmA 73, –76, –78, –80, –82N, WhoFr 79N*

Rey, Hans Augusto 1898-1977 *AmPB, Au&ICB, AuBYP, BioIn 1, –2, –5, –7, –8, –9, –10, –11, –12, BkP, ChsFB A,*

ConAu 5R, FamAIYP, IlsCB 1744, –1946, –1957, JBA 51, SmATA 1, TwCCW 78, WhoAmA 73

Rey, Lester Del 1915- *ScF&FL 1, ThrBJA*

Rey, Lester Del *see also* DelRey, Lester

Reyes Y Basoalto, Ricardo E Neftali 1904-1973 *ConAu X, ConLC 9*

Reyes Y Basoalto, Ricardo E Neftali *see also* Neruda, Pablo

Reynolds, Charles O 1921- *ConAu 9R*

Reynolds, Dallas McCord 1917- *BioIn 12, ConAu 5R, –9NR, ScF&FL 1*

Reynolds, Dallas McCord *see also* Reynolds, Mack

Reynolds, David K 1940- *ConAu 9NR, –65*

Reynolds, Mack 1917- *AuBYP SUP, BioIn 12, ConAu X, ConSFA, DcLB 8[port], EncSF, IntAu&W 76X, Novels, ScF&FL 1, –2, WhoSciF, WrDr 84*

Reynolds, Mack *see also* Reynolds, Dallas McCord

Reynolds, Marjorie Harris 1903- *AuBYP, ConAu 5R, WhoAmW 66*

Reynolds, Moira Davison 1915- *ConAu 105*

Reynolds, Pamela 1923?- *ConAu 103, ScF&FL 1, –2, SmATA 34[port]*

Reynolds, Quentin 1902?-1965 *AmAu&B, AuBYP, BioIn 2, –3, –4, –6, –7, –8, –9, BlueB 76, ConAu 73, CurBio 41, –65, DcAmB S7, IntWW 74, –75, –76, –77, –78, –79, LongCTC, ObitOF 79, ObitT 1961, REnAL, St&PR 75, TwCA SUP, WhAm 4, WhE&EA, WhScrn 2, WhoAm 74, –76, –78, WhoF&I 74, –75, WhoWest 74, –76, –78*

Rezmerski, John Calvin 1942- *ConAu 29R, DrAP 75, DrAP&F 83, IntWWP 77, WhoMW 74, –76*

Rhinehart, Luke *BioIn 9*

Rhodehamel, Josephine DeWitt 1901- *ConAu 61, WhoLibS 55, WhoWest 78*

Rhodes, Eugene Manlove 1869-1934 *AmAu&B, AmBi, AmLY, BioIn 1, –2, –3, –4, –6, –8, –11, CmCal, DcAmB S1, DcLEL, DcNAA, EncAAH, NatCAB 45, OxAmL, REnAL, REnAW, TwCA, TwCA SUP, WhAm 1, WhNAA*

Rhodes, Evan H 1929- *ConAu 10NR, –57*

Rhodes, John J 1916- *AlmAP 78, –80, –82[port], BiDrAC, BioIn 9, –10, –11, –12, BioNews 74, BlueB 76, CngDr 74, –77, –79, –81, ConAu 103, CurBio 76, IntWW 75, –76, –77, –78, –79, –80, –81, –82, –83, NewYTBE 72, –73, NewYTBS 76, –80[port], PolProf J, PolProf K, PolProf NF, WhoAm 74, –76, –78, –80, –82, WhoAmP 73, –75, –77, –79, –81, –83, WhoGov 77, –72, –75, WhoWest 74, –76, –78, –80, –82, WorAl*

Ribner, Irving 1921-1972 *BiE&WWA, BioIn 9, ConAu 1R, –3NR, –37R, NewYTBE 72, NotNAT B, WhAm 5*

Ricci, Larry J 1948- *ConAu 109*
Ricciardi, Lorenzo 1930- *ConAu 109*
Ricciuti, Edward R 1938- *BioIn 11,*
ConAu 41R, IntAu&W 76, –77,
SmATA 10
Rice, Anne 1941- *ConAu 65, WrDr 80, –82,*
–84
Rice, Edward E 1918- *AuBYP SUP,*
ConAu 1NR, –49
Rice, Eve 1951- *AuBYP SUP, BioIn 12,*
ConAu 4NR, –53, IlsCB 1967,
SmATA 34[port]
Rice, Tamara *AuBYP SUP*
Rice, Tim 1944- *BioIn 9, ConAu 103,*
ConDr 73, –77D, –82D, ConLC 21[port],
IntWW 80, –81, –82, –83, LinLib L,
NewYTBE 71, WhoRocM 82,
WhoThe 16, –81
Rich, Adrienne 1929- *AmWomWr,*
AmWr SUP, BioIn 9, –10, –11, –12,
ChhPo S3, ConAu 9R, ConLC 3, –6, –7,
–11, –18, ConP 70, –75, –80, CroCAP,
CurBio 76, DcLB 5[port], DcLEL 1940,
DrAP 75, DrAP&F 83, IntDcWB,
IntWWP 77, LinLib L, ModAL,
ModAL SUP, OxAmL, PenC AM,
RAdv 1, WhoAm 76, –78, –80, –82,
WhoAmW 58, –81, –83, WorAu, WrDr 76,
–80, –82, –84
Rich, Josephine 1912- *AuBYP, BioIn 7, –11,*
ConAu 5R, SmATA 10
Rich, Louise Dickinson 1903- *AmAu&B,*
AmWomWr, AuBYP, BioIn 1, –2, –3, –4,
–7, ConAu 73, CurBio 43, InWom,
REnAL, TwCA SUP, WhoAmW 58, –61,
–64, –66, –68, –70, –72
Rich, Norman 1921- *ConAu 45, DrAS 74H,*
–78H, –82H
Richard, Adrienne 1921- *AuBYP SUP,*
BioIn 10, ConAu 29R, SmATA 5,
WhoAmW 75, WrDr 76, –80, –82, –84
Richard, Keith 1943- *BioIn 8, –10, –11, –12,*
CelR 73, ConAu X, ConLC 17,
WhoAm 74, –76, –78, –80, –82
Richard, Keith *see also* Rolling Stones, The
Richards, Arlene Kramer 1935- *ConAu 11NR,*
–65, LEduc 74, WhoAmW 74, –75, –83
Richards, David Adams 1950- *CaW,*
ConAu 93
Richards, Larry 1931- *ConArch A, ConAu X*
Richards, Larry *see also* Richards, Lawrence O
Richards, Lawrence O 1931- *ConAu 29R,*
WhoRel 75, WhoWest 74, –76
Richards, Lawrence O *see also* Richards, Larry
Richards, Stanley 1918-1980 *BiDrLUS 70,*
BioIn 12, ConAu 101, –25R,
IntAu&W 76, –77, –82, IntMPA 77, –75,
–76, –78, –79, –81, OxCan, WhoE 74,
WhoLibS 66
Richardson, Ben *AfroAA, WhoAmP 83*
Richardson, Frank Howard 1882-1970
AmAu&B, AuBYP SUP, BioIn 9,

ConAu 104, SmATA 27N, WhAm 6,
WhE&EA, WhLit, WhNAA
Richardson, Grace Lee 1916- *ConAu X,*
IntAu&W 77X, SmATA 8
Richardson, Grace Lee *see also* Dickson, Naida
Richardson, Harry W 1938- *ConAu 29R,*
WrDr 80, –82, –84
Richardson, Henry Handel 1870-1946 *BioIn 1,*
–2, –3, –4, –5, –6, –8, –9, –10, –12, CasWL,
ConAu X, CurBio 46, CyWA, DcLEL,
EncWL, EvLB, IntDcWB, LinLib LP,
LongCTC, McGEWB, ModCmwL, NewC,
Novels, OxEng, PenC ENG, REn,
TwCA, TwCA SUP, TwCLC 4[port],
TwCWr, WebE&AL, WhE&EA, WhLit,
WhoTwCL
Richardson, Henry Vokes-Mackey 1923-
ConAu 25R, WhoPNW, WhoWest 74,
–76, –78, –80, WrDr 82, –84
Richardson, Jack 1935- *AmAu&B,*
BiE&WWA, BioIn 10, –12, CnMD,
CnThe, ConAu 5R, ConDr 73, –77, –82,
CroCD, DcLB 7[port], DcLEL 1940,
McGEWD, –84, ModWD, NotNAT,
PenC AM, PIP&P, REnAL, REnWD,
WorAu, WrDr 76, –80, –82, –84
Richardson, Joanna *Au&Wr 6, BlueB 76,*
ConAu 10NR, –13R, IntAu&W 76, –77,
–82, Who 74, –82, –83, WhoWor 78,
WrDr 76, –80, –82, –84
Richardson, John Adkins 1929- *ConAu 57,*
WhoAmA 82, WhoMW 78, –80, –82
Richardson, Robert S 1902- *BioIn 8, –11,*
ConAu 49, IntAu&W 77, –82, ScF&FL 1,
–2, SmATA 8, WrDr 84
Richason, Benjamin 1922- *AmM&WS 73P,*
–76P, BioIn 11, ConAu 41R, WhoAm 74
Richelson, Geraldine 1922- *ConAu 106,*
SmATA 29
Richie, Donald 1924- *ConAu 8NR, –17R*
Richler, Mordecai 1931- *Au&Wr 6,*
AuNews 1, BioIn 9, –10, –11, –12,
BioNews 75, BlueB 76, CaW,
CanWW 70, –79, –80, –81, –83, CanWr,
CasWL, ConAu 65, ConLC 3, –5, –9, –13,
–18, ConNov 72, –76, –82, CreCan 1,
CurBio 75, DcLEL 1940, EncWL,
IntAu&W 76, –77, IntWW 74, –75, –76,
–77, –78, –79, –80, –81, –82, –83,
ModCmwL, NewYTBS 80[port], –83[port],
Novels, OxCan, OxCan SUP, PenC ENG,
REnAL, SmATA 27, TwCWr,
WebE&AL, Who 74, –82, –83,
WhoAm 76, –78, –80, –82, WhoTwCL,
WhoWor 74, –78, –80, –82, WorAl,
WorAu, WrDr 76, –80, –82, –84
Richmond, Julius B 1916- *AmM&WS 76P,*
–79P, –82P, AuBYP SUP, ConAu 29R,
WhoAm 74, –76, –78, –80, –82,
WhoAmP 81, WhoE 74
Richmond, Leonard *WhE&EA*
Richoux, Pat 1927- *BioIn 10, ConAu 25R*

Richoux, Pat *see also* Richoux, Patricia
Richoux, Patricia 1927- *SmATA* 7
Richoux, Patricia *see* Richoux, Pat
Richter, Conrad 1890-1968 *AmAu&B*, *AmNov*,
    AuBYP SUP, *BioIn* 1, *-2*, *-3*, *-4*, *-5*, *-7*, *-8*,
    -9, *-12*, *CnDAL*, *ConAu* 5R, *-25R*,
    CurBio 51, *-68*, *CyWA*, *DcLB* 9[port],
    DcLEL, *LinLib L*, *McGEWB*, *ModAL*,
    Novels, *ObitOF* 79, *OxAmL*, *PenC AM*,
    RAdv 1, *REn*, *REnAL*, *REnAW*,
    ScF&FL 1, *SmATA* 3, *TwCA*,
    TwCA SUP, *WhAm* 5, *WhE&EA*,
    WhNAA
Richter, Ed *AuBYP SUP*
Richter, Hans Peter 1925- *BioIn* 9, *-10*,
    ConAu 2NR, *-45*, *FourBJA*,
    IntAu&W 76, *-77*, *-82*, *SmATA* 6,
    TwCCW 78B, *-83B*, *WhoWor* 78
Rickenbacker, Edward Vernon 1890-1973
    AmAu&B, *ApCAB X*, *BiDAmBL* 83,
    BioIn 1, *-2*, *-3*, *-5*, *-6*, *-7*, *-8*, *-9*, *-10*, *-11*,
    -12, *CelR* 73, *ConAu* 101, *-41R*,
    CurBio 40, *-52*, *-73*, *-73N*, *InSci*,
    LinLib L, *-S*, *MedHR*, *NewYTBE* 73,
    ObitOF 79, *OhA&B*, *WebAB*, *-79*,
    WebAMB, *WhAm* 5, *WhoMilH* 76,
    WorAl
Rickett, Frances 1921- *ConAu* 107
Rickey, Don, Jr. 1925- *ConAu* 5R, *-9NR*
Riddell, Charlotte Eliza Lawson 1832?-1906
    Alli SUP, *BbD*, *BiD&SB*, *CelCen*,
    DcEnL, *DcIrW* 1, *InWom*, *NewC*
Rider, John R 1923- *ConAu* 25R, *DrAS* 74E,
    -78E, *-82E*, *WhoMW* 74, *-76*
Ridge, Martin 1923- *DrAS* 74H, *-78H*, *-82H*,
    EncAAH, *WhoAm* 78, *-80*, *-82*
Ridgeway, James Fowler 1936- *AmAu&B*,
    BioIn 7, *ConAu* 106, *WhoAm* 74, *-76*,
    -78, *-80*, *-82*
Ridgeway, Rick 1949?- *BioIn* 12, *ConAu* 93
Ridgway, John 1938- *BioIn* 12, *ConAu* 25R,
    IntAu&W 77, *-82*, *WrDr* 76, *-80*, *-82*, *-84*
Ridle, Julia Brown 1923- *ConAu* 1R
Ridley, Anthony 1933- *Au&Wr* 6,
    ConAu 107, *IntAu&W* 77, *-82*, *WrDr* 76,
    -80, *-82*, *-84*
Riedman, Sarah Regal 1902- *AuBYP*, *BioIn* 8,
    -9, *ConAu* 1R, *-1NR*, *ForWC* 70,
    SmATA 1, *WhoAmW* 58, *-61*, *-64*
Rienow, Leona Train *AuBYP*, *BioIn* 8,
    ScF&FL 1, *WhoAmW* 74, *-70*, *-72*, *-75*,
    -77, *WhoE* 74
Rienow, Robert 1909- *AmM&WS* 73S, *-78S*,
    ConAu 21R, *ScF&FL* 1, *-2*
Rieseberg, Harry E 1892- *BioIn* 9, *ConAu* 5R
Riesenberg, Felix 1879-1939 *AmAu&B*, *AmLY*,
    DcNAA, *NatCAB* 29, *OxAmL*, *REnAL*,
    TwCA, *WhAm* 1, *WhNAA*
Riesenberg, Felix, Jr. 1913-1962 *AuBYP*,
    BioIn 4, *-7*, *ConAu* 101, *CurBio* 57,
    SmATA 23
Riesman, David 1909- *AmAu&B*,

AmM&WS 73S, *-78S*, *Au&Wr* 6,
    BiDAmEd, *BioIn* 3, *-4*, *-5*, *-12*, *BlueB* 76,
    ConAu 5R, *CurBio* 55, *DcLEL* 1940,
    EncAB-H, *IntAu&W* 76, *IntWW* 74, *-75*,
    -76, *-77*, *-78*, *-79*, *-80*, *-81*, *-82*, *-83*,
    LinLib L, *NewYTBS* 80[port], *PenC AM*,
    REnAL, *TwCA SUP*, *WebAB*, *-79*,
    WhoAm 74, *-76*, *-78*, *-80*, *WhoE* 74,
    WhoWor 74, *-78*, *-80*, *-82*, *WhoWorJ* 72,
    -78, *WrDr* 80, *-82*, *-84*
Riessen, Clare 1941- *AuBYP SUP*
Riessen, Clare *see also* Riessen, Martin Clare
Riessen, Martin Clare 1941- *ConAu* 41R
Riessen, Martin Clare *see also* Riessen, Clare
Riker, Tom L 1936- *ConAu* 104
Rikhoff, Jean 1928- *AuBYP SUP*, *BioIn* 11,
    ConAu 61, *DrAP&F* 83, *IntAu&W* 82,
    SmATA 9
Riley, James Whitcomb 1849-1916 *Alli SUP*,
    AmAu, *AmAu&B*, *AmBi*, *AmSCAP* 66,
    ApCAB, *ApCAB X*, *BbD*, *BiD&SB*,
    BioIn 1, *-2*, *-3*, *-4*, *-5*, *-6*, *-7*, *-8*, *-9*, *-10*,
    -11, *-12*, *BlkAWP*, *CarSB*, *CasWL*,
    Chambr 3, *ChrP*, *ChhPo*, *-S1*, *-S2*, *-S3*,
    CnDAL, *DcAmAu*, *DcAmB*, *DcEnA AP*,
    DcLEL, *DcNAA*, *EncAAH*, *EvLB*,
    IndAu 1816, *JBA* 34, *LinLib L*, *-S*,
    LongCTC, *McGEWB*, *NatCAB* 6,
    OxAmL, *PenC AM*, *RAdv* 1, *REn*,
    REnAL, *SmATA* 17, *Str&VC*, *TwCBDA*,
    WebAB, *-79*, *WhAm* 1, *WhFla*, *WhLit*,
    WorAl
Riley, Jocelyn *DrAP&F* 83
Rilke, Rainer Maria 1875-1926 *AtlBL*, *BioIn* 1,
    -2, *-3*, *-4*, *-5*, *-6*, *-7*, *-8*, *-9*, *-10*, *-11*, *-12*,
    CasWL, *ChhPo S3*, *ClDMEL*, *CnMWL*,
    ConAu 104, *CyWA*, *Dis&D*, *EncWL*,
    EvEuW, *IlEncMy*, *LinLib L*, *-S*,
    LongCTC, *LuthC* 75, *MakMC*,
    McGEWB, *ModGL*, *OxEng*, *PenC EUR*,
    RComWL, *REn*, *TwCA*, *TwCA SUP*,
    TwCLC 1, *-6*[port], *TwCWr*, *WhDW*,
    WhAm 4A, *WhoTwCL*, *WorAl*
Rimland, Ingrid 1936- *ConAu* 61
Rinehart, Mary Roberts 1876-1958 *AmAu&B*,
    AmNov, *AmWomWr*, *ApCAB X*,
    BioIn 1, *-2*, *-3*, *-4*, *-5*, *-11*, *-12*, *ConAmL*,
    ConAu 108, *CorpD*, *DcAmB S6*, *DcBiA*,
    DcLEL, *EncAB* 2, *EncMys*, *EvLB*,
    InWom, *LibW*, *LinLib L*, *-S*, *LongCTC*,
    ModWD, *NotAW MOD*, *NotNAT B*,
    Novels, *ObitOF* 79, *ObitT* 1951, *OxAmL*,
    PenC AM, *REn*, *REnAL*, *TwCA*,
    TwCA SUP, *TwCCr&M* 80, *TwCWr*,
    WebAB, *-79*, *WhAm* 3, *WhLit*, *WhNAA*,
    WhThe, *WomWWA* 14, *WorAl*
Rink, Paul 1912- *AuBYP*, *BioIn* 7
Rinker, Rosalind Beatrice 1906- *ConAu* 5R,
    -5NR
Rinkoff, Barbara Jean 1923-1975 *AuBYP*,
    BioIn 8, *-9*, *-10*, *ConAu* 57, *ConAu* P-2,
    IntAu&W 76, *MorBMP*, *SmATA* 27N, *-4*,

WhAm 6, WhoAmW 75, WrDr 76

Rintels, David W 1938?- ConAu 73, LesBEnT,
  NewYTET, WhoAm 78, -80, -82

Riordan, James 1936- ConAu 11NR, -69,
  SmATA 28[port], WrDr 82, -84

Rios, Tere 1917- BioIn 9, ConAu X,
  ForWC 70, ScF&FL 1, -2, SmATA 2

Rios, Tere see also Versace, Marie Teresa Rios

Ripley, Dillon 1913- ConAu 73, Who 83

Ripley, Dillon see also Ripley, Sidney Dillon

Ripley, Elizabeth 1906-1969 AuBYP, BioIn 4,
  -5, -7, -8, -10, ChhPo S2, ConAu 1R,
  -3NR, CurBio 58, InWom, SmATA 5

Ripley, S Dillon 1913- AmM&WS 73P,
  BlueB 76, CelR 73, CurBio 66,
  IntAu&W 76, -77, -82, IntWW 74, -75,
  -76, -77, -78, -79, -80, -81, -82, -83,
  WhoGov 77, -72, -75, WhoS&SW 73, -75,
  -76

Ripley, Sidney Dillon 1913- AmM&WS 76P,
  -79P, -82P, BioIn 2, -7, -9, -10, -11,
  Who 83, WhoAm 74, -76, -78, -80, -82,
  WhoE 79, -81, WhoWor 74

Ripley, Sidney Dillon see also Ripley, Dillon

Rischin, Moses 1925- ConAu 3NR, -9R,
  DrAS 74H, -78H, -82H, IntAu&W 77,
  WhoRel 75, -77, WhoWorJ 78, WrDr 76,
  -80, -82, -84

Riser, Wayne H 1909- AmM&WS 73P, -76P,
  -79P, BioIn 4, ConAu P-1

Ritch, Ocee 1922- WhoWest 74, -76, -78, -80

Ritchie, Barbara Gibbons 1943- AuBYP,
  BiDrLUS 70, BioIn 8, -12, ConAu 73,
  SmATA 14

Rittenhouse, Mignon 1904- ConAu 41R,
  WhoAmW 74, -58, -61, -64, -66, -68, -70,
  -72, -75, -77, -79, -81

Ritter, Lawrence S 1922- AmEA 74,
  AmM&WS 73S, -78S, ConAu 21R,
  WhoAm 74, -76, WhoE 74

Rivera, Edith AuBYP SUP

Rivera, Edward DrAP&F 83

Rivera, Feliciano 1932- ChiSch, ConAu 45,
  DrAS 74H, -78H, -82H, IntAu&W 76

Rivera, Geraldo 1943- AuBYP SUP, BioIn 9,
  -10, -12, BioNews 74, CelR 73,
  ConAu 108, CurBio 75, IntMPA 78, -79,
  -81, -82, -84, LesBEnT[port],
  NewYTBE 71, NewYTET, SmATA 28,
  WhoAm 78, -80, -82

Rivers, Caryl 1937- BioIn 10, ConAu 4NR,
  -49

Rivers-Coffey, Rachel 1943- ConAu 73

Riviere, Bill 1916- ConAu X

Riviere, Bill see also Riviere, William Alexander

Riviere, William Alexander 1916- ConAu 5R,
  -8NR

Roach, Marilynne K 1946- BioIn 11,
  ConAu 57, SmATA 9

Robbins, Chandler S 1918- AmM&WS 73P,
  -76P, -79P, -82P, WhoE 83

Robbins, Harold 1912?- AmAu&B, AmNov,

BioIn 8, -9, -10, -12, CelR 73, ConAu 73,
  ConLC 5, CurBio 70, FilmgC,
  IntAu&W 76, -77, IntWW 74, -75, -76,
  -77, -78, -79, -80, -81, -82, -83,
  Novels[port], TwCWr, Who 74, -82, -83,
  WhoAm 74, -76, -78, -80, -82,
  WhoWor 78, -80, -82, WorAl, WrDr 76,
  -80, -82, -84

Robbins, Tom 1936- BioIn 9, -11, -12,
  ConAu X, ConLC 9, ConNov 82,
  DcLB Y80B[port], NewYTBS 80[port],
  WhoAm 82, WrDr 82, -84

Roberts, Cecil 1892-1976 Au&Wr 6, BioIn 3,
  -4, -7, -8, -9, -10, -11, ChhPo, -S1, -S2,
  ConAu 69, ConAu P-2, DcLEL,
  IntAu&W 76, IntMed 80, LongCTC,
  NewC, ScF&FL 1, -2, TwCA,
  TwCA SUP, WhAm 7, WhE&EA,
  WhLit, WhNAA, Who 74, WrDr 76

Roberts, Charles G D 1860-1943 ApCAB,
  ApCAB SUP, ConAu 105, EncSF,
  NatCAB 11, ScF&FL 1, SmATA 29,
  TwCCW 78, -83, TwCLC 8[port],
  WhAm 3, WhE&EA

Roberts, Sir Charles G D 1860-1943 Alli SUP,
  BbD, BiD&SB, BioIn 1, -4, -5, -9, -10,
  CanNov, CanWr, Chambr 3, ChhPo, -S1,
  -S2, -S3, ConAmL, CreCan 2,
  CurBio 44, DcAmAu, DcBiA, DcNAA,
  EvLB, JBA 34, LinLib L, -S, LongCTC,
  MacDCB 78, ObitOF 79, OxAmL,
  OxCan, OxEng, PenC ENG, REn,
  REnAL, TwCA, TwCA SUP, WebE&AL,
  WhAm 3, WhE&EA, WhLit

Roberts, David S 1943- ConAu 33R

Roberts, Elliott B 1899- ConAu 1R, WrDr 76,
  -80, -82, -84

Roberts, Eric 1914- Au&Wr 6, ConAu 5R,
  IntAu&W 76, WrDr 76, -80, -82, -84

Roberts, Jane 1929- AmWomWr, ConAu 41R,
  ConSFA, EncSF, ScF&FL 1, -2,
  WrDr 80, -82, -84

Roberts, John G 1913- ConAu 49,
  SmATA 27[port]

Roberts, Keith 1935- ConAu 25R, ConLC 14,
  ConSFA, EncSF, Novels, ScF&FL 1, -2,
  WhoSciF, WrDr 76, -80, -82, -84

Roberts, Kenneth Lewis 1885-1957 AmAu&B,
  AmNov, BioIn 1, -2, -4, -5, -7, -12,
  CasWL, CnDAL, ConAmA, ConAu 109,
  DcAmAu, DcAmB S6, DcLB 9[port],
  DcLEL, EvLB, LinLib L, -S, LongCTC,
  ModAL, NatCAB 48, Novels, ObitOF 79,
  ObitT 1951, OxAmL, OxCan, PenC AM,
  REn, REnAL, TwCA, TwCA SUP,
  TwCWr, WhAm 3, WhE&EA, WhLit,
  WhNAA, WorAl

Roberts, Lawrence WrDr 82

Roberts, Nancy Correll 1924- AuBYP SUP,
  ConAu 6NR, -9R, ForWC 70,
  SmATA 28, WhoAmW 74, -68, -70, -72,
  -75, -77

Roberts, Thom 1940- *ConAu 81*
Roberts, Willo Davis 1928- *BioIn 12,
ConAu 3NR, –49, MichAu 80,
SmATA 21[port], WrDr 76, –80, –82, –84*
Robertson, Charles Patrick 1919- *WhoLib 54*
Robertson, Don 1929- *BioIn 11, ConAu 7NR,
–9R, SmATA 8*
Robertson, Dougal 1924- *BioIn 10, ConAu 61*
Robertson, James Oliver 1932- *ConAu 106,
DrAS 74H, –78H, –82H*
Robertson, Keith 1914- *Au&Wr 6, AuBYP,
BioIn 6, –7, –9, –10, ConAu 9R, MorBMP,
MorJA, SmATA 1, TwCCW 78, –83,
WhoRocM 82, WrDr 80, –82, –84*
Robertson, Martin *ConAu X*
Robertson, Mary Elsie 1937- *ConAu 81,
DrAP&F 83*
Robeson, Kenneth 1933- *ConAu X,
TwCCr&M 80, WrDr 82, –84*
Robeson, Kenneth *see also* Goulart, Ron
Robichaud, Beryl 1919- *Dun&B 79,
ForWC 70, St&PR 75, WhoAm 74, –76,
–78, –82, WhoAmW 74, –70, –72, –75, –77,
WhoF&I 74, –75, –77*
Robins, Denise 1897- *BioIn 7, ConAu 10NR,
–65, IntAu&W 76, –77, –82, Novels,
WhE&EA, Who 74, –82, –83, WrDr 76,
–80, –82, –84*
Robins, Elizabeth 1862?-1952 *AmAu&B,
AmWomWr, BbD, BioIn 2, –4, –11, –12,
CnDAL, InWom, LongCTC, NotNAT A,
–B, ObitOF 79, ObitT 1951, OhA&B,
OxAmL, OxThe, REn, REnAL, TwCA,
TwCA SUP, WhThe*
Robinson, Alice M 1920-1983 *ConAu 108, –109,
WhoAmW 74, –75, –77*
Robinson, Barbara Webb 1927- *AuBYP,
BioIn 8, –11, ConAu 1R, SmATA 8,
WhoAmW 64*
Robinson, Bill *ConAu X*
Robinson, Chaille Howard Payne *ConAu 13R,
WhoAmW 58*
Robinson, Charles 1931- *BioIn 10, –12,
ConAu 49, IlsBYP, IlsCB 1967,
SmATA 6, WhoBW&I 1*
Robinson, Charles Alexander, Jr. 1900-1965
*AmAu&B, AuBYP, BioIn 1, –3, –7,
ConAu 1R, SmATA 36, WhAm 4,
WhE&EA*
Robinson, David A 1925- *ConAu 17R,
WhoTech 82*
Robinson, Derek 1932- *AmEA 74, BioIn 10,
BlueB 76, ConAu 77, IntAu&W 82,
Who 74, –82, WrDr 76, –80, –82*
Robinson, Donald 1913- *ConAu 25R,
IntAu&W 77*
Robinson, Frank 1935- *BioIn 6, –7, –8, –9, –10,
–11, –12, BioNews 74, CelR 73, CmCal,
CurBio 71, InB&W 80, NewYTBS 74,
–75, WhoAm 74, –76, –78, –80, –82,
WhoBlA 75, –77, –80, WhoProB 73,
WhoWest 84, WorAl*

Robinson, Frank M 1926- *ConAu 3NR, –49,
EncSF, ScF&FL 1, –2, WhoSciF,
WrDr 84*
Robinson, Jerry 1922- *IlsBYP, SmATA 34*
Robinson, Joan G 1910- *Au&Wr 6,
AuBYP SUP, BioIn 8, 9, –10, ConAu 5R,
–5NR, IntAu&W 77, –77X, –82, –82X,
SmATA 7, TwCCW 78, –83, WhoChL,
WrDr 80, –82, –84*
Robinson, Kathleen *ConAu X*
Robinson, Kathleen *see also* Robinson, Chaille
Howard Payne
Robinson, Logan G 1949- *BioIn 12,
ConAu 108*
Robinson, Mabel Louise 1874-1962 *AmAu&B,
AmNov, BioIn 1, –2, –6, –7,
DcLB 22[port], InWom, JBA 51,
NatCAB 47, WhAm 4, WhE&EA,
WhLit, WhNAA, WhoAmW 58*
Robinson, Margaret A 1937- *ConAu 107,
DrAP&F 83*
Robinson, Margaret King 1906- *WhoAmP 83*
Robinson, Marilynne 1944- *ConLC 25[port]*
Robinson, Nancy K 1942- *ConAu 106,
SmATA 31, –32[port]*
Robinson, Ray 1920- *AuBYP, BioIn 7,
ConAu 77, SmATA 23*
Robinson, Richard 1945- *BioIn 10, ConAu 57,
MugS*
Robinson, Sondra Till 1931- *ConAu 7NR, –53*
Robinson, Spider 1948- *ConAu 11NR, –65,
EncSF, IntAu&W 82, WrDr 84*
Robinson, Stuart 1936- *BiE&WWA*
Robinson, Veronica 1926- *AuBYP SUP,
ConAu 105, SmATA 30[port]*
Robinson, Willard B 1935- *AmArch 70,
ConAu 57*
Robison, Nancy L 1934- *ConAu 93*
Robotham, John Stanley 1924- *BiDrLUS 70,
WhoLibS 55, –66*
Robottom, John 1934- *Au&Wr 6, BioIn 10,
ConAu 29R, IntAu&W 76, SmATA 7,
WrDr 76, –80, –82, –84*
Robson, Ernest *DrAP&F 83*
Robson, Lucia St. Clair 1942- *ConAu 108*
Rock, Gail *AuBYP SUP, SmATA 32*
Rockne, Knute Kenneth 1888-1931 *AmBi,
BioIn 1, –2, –3, –4, –5, –6, –7, –8, –9, –10,
–11, –12, DcAmB, DcCathB, IndAu 1917,
McGEWB, NatCAB 25, OxAmH,
WebAB, –79, WhAm 1, WhoFtbl 74,
WorAl*
Rockowitz, Murray 1920- *ConAu 25R,
WhoE 74*
Rocks, Lawrence 1933- *AmM&WS 73P, –76P,
–79P, –82P, ConAu 85, WhoE 81, –83,
WhoTech 82*
Rockwell, Anne 1934- *BioIn 12, ChhPo S3,
ConAu 21R, IlsBYP, IlsCB 1967,
SmATA 33[port]*
Rockwell, Frederick Frye 1884-1976 *BioIn 10,
ConAu 49, NatCAB 61[port],*

NewYTBS 76, WhAm 7

Rockwell, Norman 1894-1978 *BioIn 1, −2, −3, −4, −5, −6, −7, −9, −10, −11, −12, BlueB 76, CelR 73, ChhPo S2, ConAu 81, −89, CurBio 45, −79N, ForII, IlBEAAW, IlrAm C, IlsBYP, IlsCB 1744, LinLib S, NewYTBE 71, NewYTBS 78, ObitOF 79, PrintW 83, REn, REnAL, SmATA 23[port], WebAB, −79, WhAm 7, WhoAm 74, −76, −78, WhoAmA 73, −76, −78, −80N, −82N, WhoGrA, WhoWor 74, WorAl, WorECar*

Rockwell, Thomas 1933- *BioIn 10, ChlLR 6[port], ChhPo S1, ConAu 29R, IntAu&W 77, SmATA 7, WrDr 76, −80, −82, −84*

Rockwood, Joyce 1947- *ConAu 6NR, −57*

Rockwood, Louis G 1925- *ConAu 45, WhoMW 76*

Roddenberry, Gene 1921- *ConAu X, ConLC 17, ConSFA, FilmgC, IntMPA 84, LesBEnT, NewYTET, ScF&FL 1, −2, WhoSciF*

Roderus, Frank 1942- *ConAu 89*

Rodgers, Bill 1947- *BioIn 11, −12, CurBio 82[port], NewYTBS 81[port], WorAl*

Rodgers, Mary 1931- *AmSCAP 66, AuBYP SUP, BiE&WWA, BioIn 5, −11, ConAmC, ConAu 8NR, −49, ConLC 12, EncMT, InWom, IntAu&W 77, NewCBMT, NotNAT, ScF&FL 1, −2, SmATA 8, TwCCW 78, −83, WhoAm 78, −80, −82, WhoAmW 74, −61, −70, −72, −75, WrDr 80, −82, −84*

Rodinson, Maxime 1915- *ConAu 4NR, −53, FifIDA, WhoFr 79*

Rodman, Bella 1903- *AuBYP SUP, ConAu P-2*

Rodman, Maia 1927- *ConAu X, DrAP&F 83, ForWC 70, SmATA X, −1, TwCCW 83*

Rodman, Maia *see also* Wojciechowska, Maia

Rodman, Selden 1909- *AmAu&B, AuBYP SUP, BioIn 4, −11, ChhPo, −S1, ConAu 5R, −5NR, LinLib L, OxAmL, REn, REnAL, SmATA 9, TwCA SUP, WhoAm 74, −76, −78, WhoAmA 73, −76, −78, −80, −82, WhoWor 74*

Rodowsky, Colby 1932- *BioIn 12, ConAu 69, SmATA 21*

Rodriguez, Richard 1944- *ConAu 110*

Roesch, Roberta F 1919- *ConAu 2NR, −5R, IntAu&W 76, −82, WhoAmW 68, −70*

Roethke, Theodore 1908-1963 *AmAu&B, AmWr, AnCL, AtlBL, BioIn 3, −4, −6, −7, −8, −9, −10, −11, −12, CasWL, ChhPo, −S1, −S2, −S3, CnDAL, CnE&AP, ConAu 81, ConLC 1, −3, −8, −11, −19, ConP 75, −80A, CroCAP, DcAmB S7, DcLB 5, DcLEL 1940, EncWL, LinLib L, LongCTC, MakMC, McGEWB, MichAu 80, ModAL, ModAL SUP,*

ObitOF 79, ObitT 1961, OxAmL, PenC AM, RAdv 1, REn, REnAL, TwCA SUP, TwCWr, WebAB, −79, WebE&AL, WhDW, WhAm 4, WhoPNW, WhoTwCL, WorAl

Rofes, Eric Edward 1954- *ConAu 106*

Rogers, Barbara Radcliffe 1939- *WhoAmP 73, −75, −77, −79, −81, −83*

Rogers, Dale Evans 1912- *AmAu&B, BioIn 3, −4, −9, −10, −12, ConAu 103, CurBio 56, InWom, WhoAm 76, −78, −80, −82*

Rogers, Frances 1888-1974 *BioIn 11, ConAu 5R, MichAu 80, SmATA 10*

Rogers, Isabel Wood 1924- *DrAS 74P, −78P, −82P, WhoRel 75, −77*

Rogers, James Tracy 1921- *ConAu 45, WhoAmP 73, WhoE 75, −77*

Rogers, Julia Ellen 1866- *AmAu&B, WhAm 4, WomWWA 14*

Rogers, Katharine M 1932- *AmWomWr, ConAu 8NR, −21R, DrAS 74E, −78E, −82E, WhoAmW 74, −70, −75, −79, −81, −83, WrDr 76, −80, −84*

Rogers, Kenny 1938?- *BioIn 11, −12, ConAu X, CurBio 81[port], RkOn 78, WorAl*

Rogers, Michael 1950- *ConAu 1NR, −49, DrAF 76, ScF&FL 1, −2*

Rogers, Pamela 1927- *AuBYP SUP, BioIn 11, ConAu 4NR, −49, SmATA 9, WrDr 80, −82, −84*

Rogers, Thomas 1927- *BioIn 8, ConAu 89, IntAu&W 82, WhoAm 74, −76, −78, WhoE 75, −77, WrDr 76, −80, −82, −84*

Rogers, W G 1896-1978 *ConAu 77, SmATA 23[port]*

Rogers, William Garland 1896-1978 *AmAu&B, AuBYP, BioIn 1, −8, −11, ConAu 9R, IntAu&W 77, NewYTBS 78, WrDr 76*

Rohmer, Sax 1883-1959 *BioIn 1, −4, −5, −6, −9, ConAu X, CorpD, EncMys, EncO&P 78, EncSF, EvLB, LinLib LP, LongCTC, MnBBF, NewC, NotNAT B, Novels, ObitOF 79, ObitT 1951, PenC ENG, ScF&FL 1, TwCA, TwCA SUP, TwCCr&M 80, TwCWr, WhE&EA, WhLit, WhThe, WhoBW&I A, WhoHr&F, WhoLA, WhoSpyF, WorAl*

Rohmer, Sax *see also* Ward, Arthur Sarsfield

Roland, Albert 1925- *BioIn 11, ConAu 61, SmATA 11, USBiR 74, WhoGov 77*

Roll, Winifred 1909- *BioIn 10, ConAu 49, SmATA 6*

Rolling Stones, The *CelR 73, EncPR&S, −77, IlEncRk, MakMC, RkOn 78, −84, RkOneH, RolSEnR 83*

Rolling Stones, The *see also* Jagger, Mick

Rolling Stones, The *see also* Jones, Brian

Rolling Stones, The *see also* Richard, Keith

Rolling Stones, The *see also* Taylor, Mick

Rolling Stones, The *see also* Watts, Charles

Rolling Stones, The *see also* Wyman, Bill

Rollins, Charlemae Hill 1897-1979
ALA 80N[port], AuBYP, BioIn 2, -3, -7,
BlkAWP, ChhPo S1, ConAu 9R, -104,
ForWC 70, InB&W 80, LivgBAA,
MorBMP, SelBAA, SmATA 26N, -3,
WhAm 7, WhoAm 76, WhoAmW 58, -61,
-64, -66, -68, -70, WhoLibS 55
Rollins, Ellen Chapman Hobbs 1831-1881
Alli SUP, ApCAB, DcAmAu, DcNAA
Rollins, Ellen Chapman Hobbs see also Arr, E H
Rolston, Holmes, III 1932- *DrAS 74P, -78P,*
-82P, WhoWest 82
Rolvaag, O E 1876-1931 *DcLB 9[port], WorAl*
Rome, Margaret *WrDr 84*
Romulo, Carlos P 1899- *AmAu&B, BiDrAC,*
BioIn 1, -2, -3, -4, -5, -6, -8, -10,
CathA 1930, ConAu 10NR, -13R,
CurBio 43, -57, FarE&A 78, -79, -80, -81,
IntAu&W 77, -82, IntWW 74, -75, -76,
-77, -78, -79, -80, -81, -82, -83, IntYB 78,
-79, -80, -81, -82, LinLib L, -S,
McGEWB, WhE&EA, WhNAA,
WhoUN 75, WhoWor 74, -76, -78, -80,
-82
Ronan, Colin Alistair 1920- *Au&Wr 6,*
ConAu 5R, -6NR, IntAu&W 76, -77, -82,
WhoWor 76, WrDr 76, -80, -82, -84
Ronan, Margaret 1918- *ConAu 102,*
WhoAmW 66
Ronning, Chester A 1894- *CanWW 70*
Rood, Robert Thomas 1942- *AmM&WS 73P,*
-76P, -79P, -82P, ConAu 107
Rood, Ronald 1920- *BioIn 11, ConAu 9NR,*
-21R, SmATA 12
Rooke, Patrick John 1925- *Au&Wr 6*
Rooney, Andrew Aitkin 1919- *BioIn 12,*
ConAu 5R, -9NR, LesBEnT, NewYTET,
WhoAm 74, -76, -78, -80, -82
Rooney, James R 1927- *AmM&WS 73P, -76P,*
ConAu 61
Roos, Ann *AuBYP, BioIn 6, -7, MorJA*
Roosevelt, Eleanor 1884-1962 *AmAu&B,*
AmWomWr, AuBYP, BioIn 1, -2, -3, -4,
-5, -6, -7, -8, -9, -10, -11, -12, BioNews 74,
ConAu 89, CurBio 40, -49, -63,
DcAmB S7, GoodHs, HerW, InWom,
IntDcWB, LibW, LinLib L, LongCTC,
NatCAB 57, ObitOF 79, ObitT 1961,
OxAmH, OxAmL, PolProf E, PolProf K,
PolProf T, REn, REnAL, WebAB, -79,
WhWW-II
Roosevelt, James 1907- *BiDrAC, BioIn 1, -2,*
-3, -7, -8, -11, ConAu 69, PolProf T,
WhoAm 74, -76, -78, -80, -82,
WhoAmP 73, WhoWor 80
Root, Vernon Metcalf 1923- *DrAS 74E, -78E,*
-82P, WhoS&SW 75, -76
Root, William Pitt 1941- *ConAu 25R,*
ConP 70, -75, -80, DrAP 75, DrAP&F 83,
IntWWP 77, WhoAm 76, -78, -80, -82,
WrDr 76, -80, -82, -84
Roots, Clive George 1935- *WhoAm 82,*

WhoMW 78, -80
Roper, Laura Wood 1911- *ConAu 57,*
IntAu&W 77, SmATA 34[port],
WhoAm 76, -78, WhoAmW 58, WrDr 76,
-80, -82, -84
Roper, Laura Wood see also Wood, Laura N
Rosa, Joseph G 1932- *ConAu 13R,*
IntAu&W 76
Rose, Al 1916- *ConAu 97, IntAu&W 82,*
WrDr 76, -80, -82, -84
Rose, Anne *BioIn 11, ConAu 2NR, -49,*
SmATA 8
Rose, Mark Allen 1939- *ConAu 10NR, -25R,*
DrAS 78E, -82E, WhoAm 76, -78, -80,
-82, WhoAmJ 80
Rose, Mary 1929- *AmM&WS 73P, -79P*
Rose, Phyllis Davidoff 1942- *DrAS 74E, -78E,*
-82E
Roseboro, John 1933- *BioIn 7, -11,*
ConAu 102, InB&W 80, WhoAm 74,
WhoBlA 75, -77, -80, WhoProB 73
Rosen, Charles 1927- *Baker 78, BioIn 3, -9,*
-10, -11, IntWW 74, -75, -76, -77, -78,
-79, -80, -81, -82, -83, IntWWM 77,
Who 82, -83, WhoAm 74, -76, -78, -80,
-82, WhoAmM 83
Rosen, Kenneth Mark 1938- *DrAS 74E, -78E,*
-82E
Rosen, Lillian 1928- *ConAu 108*
Rosen, Sidney 1916- *AmM&WS 73P, -76P,*
-79P, -82P, BioIn 9, ConAu 9R,
IntAu&W 76, -77, -82, LEduc 74,
SmATA 1, WrDr 76, -80, -82
Rosen, Stephen 1934- *AmM&WS 73P, -76P,*
-79P, -82P, ConAu 65, Future
Rosen, Winifred 1943- *BioIn 11, ConAu 29R,*
SmATA 8
Rosenberg, Arthur D 1939- *AmEA 74,*
ConAu 61
Rosenberg, David A 1940- *ConAu 93*
Rosenberg, Ethel 1915-1953 *BioIn 9, -12,*
ConAu 29R, IntDcWB, SmATA 3,
WhoAmW 77
Rosenberg, Ethel see also Clifford, Eth
Rosenberg, Jessie 1941- *ConAu 21R*
Rosenberg, Philip 1942- *ConAu 103*
Rosenblatt, Roger Alan 1945- *BiDrAPH 79*
Rosenbloom, Joseph 1928- *BioIn 12,*
ConAu 6NR, -57, DrAS 82H,
SmATA 21[port], WhoWorJ 78,
WrDr 82, -84
Rosenblum, Davida 1927- *ConAu 93*
Rosenblum, Mort 1943- *ConAu 73*
Rosenburg, John M 1918- *AuBYP, BioIn 7,*
-10, ConAu 21R, SmATA 6
Rosenfeld, Albert 1920- *ConAu 11NR, -65,*
Future
Rosenfeld, Sam 1920- *AuBYP SUP,*
ConAu 9R
Rosenheim, Lucille 1902- *BioIn 2*
Rosenstiel, Annette 1911- *AmM&WS 73S,*
WhoAmW 58, -61, -64

Rosenstone, Robert Allan 1936- *ConAu 29R, DrAS 74H, –78H, –82H, IntAu&W 82*

Rosenthal, Abraham Michael 1922-1982 *AmAu&B, BioIn 5, –6, –7, –10, –11, –12, ConAu 21R, IntWW 74, –75, –76, –77, –78, –79, –80, –81, –82, –83, NewYTBS 83, WhoAm 74, –76, –78, –80, –82, WhoE 74, –83, WhoF&I 74, WhoWor 78*

Rosenthal, Harold 1914- *BioIn 2, WhoAmJ 80, WhoWorJ 78*

Rosenthal, M L 1917- *BlueB 76, ConAu 1R, –4NR, ConP 70, –75, –80, DcLB 5[port], DrAP 75, DrAP&F 83, WorAu, WrDr 76, –80, –82, –84*

Rosenthal, Macha Louis 1917- *BioIn 10, –12, DrAS 74E, –78E, –82E, IntAu&W 77, IntWWP 77, –82, WhoAm 74, –76, –78, –80, –82, WhoWorJ 72, –78*

Rosenthal, Sylvia 1911- *ConAu 109*

Rosmond, Babette 1921?- *AmAu&B, AmNov, BioIn 2, ConAu 5R, –6NR, ForWC 70, InWom, WhoAmW 74, –64, –66, –68, –72, –75, –77, WhoE 74, –75, –77*

Rosner, Stanley 1928- *AmM&WS 73S, ConAu 41R*

Ross, Al 1911- *WorECar*

Ross, Anne 1925- *Au&Wr 6*

Ross, Dana *WrDr 82*

Ross, Frances Aileen 1909- *ConAu P-1*

Ross, Frank, Jr. 1914- *AuBYP SUP, ChhPo S1, ConAu 93, SmATA 28[port]*

Ross, George E 1931- *ConAu X*

Ross, George E *see also* Morgan-Grenville, Gerard Wyndha

Ross, Ishbel 1897-1975 *AmAu&B, AmNov, ASpks, BioIn 2, –10, –11, ConAu 61, –93, ForWC 70, InWom, NewYTBS 75, WhoAmW 58A, –61, –70*

Ross, Leonard Q 1908- *AmAu&B, BioIn 4, –5, –8, ConAu X, CurBio 42, IntAu&W 76X, –77X, –82X, LongCTC, OxAmL, PenC AM, REnAL, TwCA, TwCA SUP, Who 74, –82, –83, WrDr 76, –80, –82, –84*

Ross, Leonard Q *see also* Rosten, Leo Calvin

Ross, Nancy Wilson 1907- *AmAu&B, AmNov, BioIn 1, –2, –3, –4, CurBio 52, DrAP&F 83, InWom, Po&Wr 77, TwCA SUP, WhE&EA, WhoAm 74, –78, –80, –82, WhoAmW 74, –58, –64, –66, –68, –70, –72*

Ross, Patricia Fent 1899- *AnCL, AuBYP, BioIn 8*

Ross, Sinclair 1908- *BioIn 1, –11, CaW, CanWW 80, CanWr, CasWL, ConAu 73, ConLC 13, ConNov 72, –76, –82, CreCan 2, DcLEL 1940, IntAu&W 76, –77, OxCan, OxCan SUP, TwCWr, WebE&AL, WrDr 76, –80, –82, –84*

Ross, Tony 1938- *BioIn 12, ConAu 77, IntAu&W 82, SmATA 17*

Rossel, Seymour 1945- *ConAu 5NR, –53,*

IntAu&W 77, SmATA 28, WhoWorJ 78, WrDr 76, –80, –82, –84

Rossi, Alfred 1935- *ConAu 29R, DrAS 74E, –78E, –82E*

Rossi, Alice S 1922- *AmM&WS 73S, –78S, ConAu 1NR, –45, WhoAm 74, –76, –78, –80, WhoAmW 66, –79, –81*

Rossiter, Clinton 1917-1970 *AmAu&B, BioIn 6, –7, –8, –9, –11, ConAu 25R, CurBio 67, –70, NewYTBE 70, ObitOF 79, PolProf E, WhAm 5*

Rossman, Parker 1919- *ConAu 69*

Rossner, Judith 1935- *AuNews 2, BioIn 10, –11, –12, ConAu 17R, ConLC 6, –9, DcLB 6, DrAF 76, DrAP&F 83, Novels, WhoAm 76, –78, –80, –82, WhoAmW 79, –81, –83, WorAl, WrDr 76, –80, –82, –84*

Rostand, Edmond 1868-1918 *AtlBL, BiD&SB, BioIn 1, –5, –11, CasWL, CIDMEL, CnMD, CnThe, ConAu 104, CyWA, Dis&D, EncWL, EncWT, EvEuW, LinLib L, –S, LongCTC, McGEWD, –84[port], ModFrL, ModRL, ModWD, NewC, NotNAT B, OxEng, OxFr, OxThe, PenC EUR, REn, REnWD, TwCA, TwCA SUP, TwCLC 6[port], WhDW, WhLit, WhThe, WorAl*

Rosten, Leo Calvin 1908- *AmAu&B, Au&Wr 6, BioIn 4, –5, –8, BlueB 76, ConAu 5R, –6NR, ConNov 72, –76, –82, CurBio 42, DcLB 11[port], IntAu&W 76, –77, –82, LinLib L, OxAmL, PenC AM, REn, REnAL, TwCA, TwCA SUP, WhNAA, Who 74, –82, –83, WhoAm 74, –76, –78, –80, –82, WhoAmJ 80, WhoWor 74, WhoWorJ 72, –78, WrDr 76, –80, –82, –84*

Rosten, Leo Calvin *see also* Ross, Leonard Q

Rote, Kyle 1950?- *BioIn 10, –11, –12, BioNews 74, NewYTBS 74*

Roth, Arnold 1929- *AuBYP SUP, BioIn 12, ConAu 21R, IlsBYP, SmATA 21[port], WhoE 74, –75, –77, WorECar*

Roth, Arthur 1920- *ConAu 1R*

Roth, Arthur J 1925- *AuBYP SUP, ConAu 7NR, –53, DrAF 76, ScF&FL 1, SmATA 28*

Roth, Arthur J *see also* Pomeroy, Pete

Roth, Bernhard A *AuBYP SUP*

Roth, Charles 1939- *AmM&WS 73P, –76P, –79P, –82P*

Roth, David 1940- *SmATA 36*

Roth, Henry 1906- *AmAu&B, BioIn 7, –10, –12, BlueB 76, CasWL, ConAu P-1, ConLC 2, –6, –11, ConNov 72, –76, –82, EncWL, IntAu&W 76, –77, ModAL, Novels, PenC AM, RAdv 1, WebE&AL, WhoAm 74, –76, –78, –80, –82, WhoTwCL, WhoWor 74, WorAu, WrDr 76, –80, –82, –84*

Roth, June 1926- *ConAu 5NR, –9R, ForWC 70, IntAu&W 76, –77, –82,*

WhoAm 80, –82, WhoAmW 74, –68, –72, –75, –79, –81, –83, WhoE 74, –79, –81, –83, WhoWor 80, WrDr 76, –80, –82, –84

Roth, Philip 1933- *AmAu&B, BioIn 5, –7, –8, –9, –10, –11, BlueB 76, CasWL, CelR 73, ConAu 1R, –1NR, ConLC 1, –2, –3, –4, –6, –9, –15, –22[port], ConNov 72, –76, –82, CurBio 70, DcLB Y82A[port], –2, DcLEL 1940, DrAF 76, DrAP&F 83, EncSF, EncWL, IntAu&W 76, –77, –82, IntWW 74, –75, –76, –77, –78, –79, –80, –81, –82, –83, LinLib L, ModAL, ModAL SUP, NewYTBE 71, NewYTBS 81[port], Novels, OxAmL, PenC AM, RAdv 1, REn, REnAL, ScF&FL 1, –2, TwCWr, WebAB, –79, WebE&AL, WhoAm 74, –76, –78, –80, –82, WhoAmJ 80, WhoTwCL, WhoWor 74, –76, –78, –80, –82, WhoWorJ 78, WorAl, WorAu, WrDr 76, –80, –82, –84*

Roth, Richard, Jr. 1933- *AmArch 70, WhoReal 83*

Rothberg, Abraham 1922- *AmAu&B, ConAu 33R, ScF&FL 1, –2, WhoAm 74, –76, –78, –80, –82, WhoAmJ 80*

Rothchild, Sylvia 1923- *ConAu 77, ForWC 70, WhoAmJ 80, WhoAmW 58, –61, –68, WhoWorJ 72, –78*

Rothenberg, Jerome 1931- *BioIn 10, –12, ConAu 1NR, –45, ConLC 6, ConP 70, –75, –80, CroCAP, DcLB 5[port], DcLEL 1940, DrAP 75, DrAP&F 83, IntAu&W 77, –82, IntWWP 77, PenC AM, RAdv 1, WhoAm 76, –78, –80, –82, WorAu 1970, WrDr 76, –80, –82, –84*

Rothenstein, Michael 1908- *ConArt, DcBrA 1, Who 74, –82, –83, WhoArt 80, –82*

Rothkopf, Carol Z 1929- *BioIn 9, ConAu 25R, SmATA 4, WhoAmW 74, –75*

Rothman, Milton A 1919- *AmM&WS 73P, –76P, –79P, –82P, ConAu 41R*

Rotman, Morris Bernard 1918- *ODwPR 79, WhoAm 74, –76, –78, –80, –82, WhoCon 73, WhoF&I 79, –81, –83, WhoPubR 72, –76*

Rotsler, William 1926- *ConAu 4NR, –53, EncSF, IntAu&W 82, ScF&FL 1, –2, WrDr 84*

Roueche, Berton 1911- *AmAu&B, Au&Wr 6, BioIn 5, ConAu 1R, –1NR, CurBio 59, DrAF 76, DrAP&F 83, IntAu&W 76, REnAL, ScF&FL 1, –2, SmATA 28[port], WhoAm 74, –76, –78, –80, –82, WhoWor 74, –76*

Roughead, William 1870-1952 *BioIn 2, –3, –4, LongCTC, NewC, REn, TwCA, TwCA SUP, WhE&EA, WhoLA*

Rounds, David 1930-1983 *NewYTBS 83[port], NotNAT, WhoAm 82, WhoHol A*

Rounds, Glen H 1906- *AuBYP, BioIn 1, –2, –3, –5, –7, –8, –10, –11, –12, ChhPo S1, –S2, ConAu 7NR, –53, IlsCB 1744, –1946,*

–1957, –1967, JBA 51, REnAL, SmATA 8, TwCCW 78, –83, WrDr 80, –82, –84

Rourke, Constance Mayfield 1885-1941 *AmAu&B, AmWomWr, AnCL, BioIn 1, –6, –11, –12, CnDAL, ConAmA, ConAu 107, CurBio 41, DcAmB S3, DcNAA, InWom, LibW, ModAL, MorJA, NatCAB 32, NotAW, OhA&B, OxAmL, PenC AM, REn, REnAL, TwCA, TwCA SUP, TwCLC 12[port], WhAm 1, YABC 1*

Rouse, Parke Shepherd, Jr. 1915- *ConAu 17R, IntAu&W 77, –82, WhoGov 77, –75, WhoS&SW 73, WrDr 76, –80, –82, –84*

Rouse, William Henry Denham 1863-1950 *BioIn 2, –5, DcInB, WhE&EA, WhLit, WhoLA*

Rover, Constance Mary 1910- *ConAu 21R, WrDr 76, –80, –82, –84*

Rovin, Jeff 1951- *ConAu 77*

Rowe, Jack Field 1927- *Dun&B 79, WhoAm 74, –76, –78, –80, –82, WhoEng 80, WhoF&I 74, –77, WhoTech 82*

Rowe, Jeanne A 1938- *ConAu 29R*

Rowe, Terry *AuNews 2, BioIn 11*

Rowell, Galen 1940- *ConAu 65*

Rowes, Barbara Gail *ConAu 101*

Rowland-Entwistle, Theodore 1925- *IntAu&W 76, –77, IntWWM 77, SmATA 31[port]*

Rowlands, John *IntAu&W 82*

Rowling, Marjorie Alice 1900- *Au&Wr 6, ConAu 5R, IntAu&W 77, WrDr 76, –80, –82, –84*

Rowse, Alfred Leslie 1903- *Au&Wr 6, BioIn 2, –4, –6, –7, –11, –12, BlueB 76, ChhPo, –S1, ConAu 1R, –1NR, ConP 70, –75, –80, CurBio 79, IntAu&W 76, –77, –82, IntWW 74, –75, –76, –77, –78, –79, –80, –81, –82, –83, IntWWP 77, –82, LinLib L, LongCTC, ModBrL, NewC, TwCA SUP, WhE&EA, Who 74, –82, –83, WhoWor 74, –76, –78, WrDr 76, –80, –82, –84*

Rowsome, Frank, Jr. 1914-1983 *AmAu&B, ChhPo S3, SmATA 36, WhoGov 77, –75, WhoS&SW 73*

Roy, Cal *ChhPo*

Royce, Kenneth 1920- *Au&Wr 6, ConAu 13R, IntAu&W 77X, –82X, TwCCr&M 80, WhoSpyF, WrDr 76, –80, –82, –84*

Rozin, Skip 1941- *ConAu 89*

Ruark, Robert 1915-1965 *AmAu&B, BioIn 1, –2, –3, –4, –5, –6, –7, ConAu 25R, ConAu P-2, DcAmB S7, LinLib L, LongCTC, ObitOF 79, REn, REnAL, WhAm 4, WhScrn 2, WorAl*

Rubens, Bernice 1927?- *Au&Wr 6,
ConAu 25R, ConLC 19, ConNov 72, -76,
-82, DcLB 14[port], DcLEL 1940,
IntAu&W 76, -77, Novels, Who 82, -83,
WhoAmW 74, WrDr 76, -80, -82, -84*

Rubens, Peter Paul 1577-1640 *AtlBL, BioIn 1,
-2, -3, -4, -5, -6, -7, -8, -9, -10, -11, -12,
ChhPo, DcBiPP, DcCathB, Dis&D,
LinLib S, LuthC 75, McGDA,
McGEWB, NewC, OxArt, REn, WhDW,
WorAl*

Rubenstein, Joshua 1949- *ConAu 103*

Rubin, Arnold P 1946- *ConAu 69, WhoE 79,
-81*

Rubin, Barry 1950- *ConAu 108, DrAS 82H*

Rubin, Charles J 1950- *ConAu 101*

Rubin, Jerry 1938- *AmAu&B, BioIn 8, -10,
-11, -12, ConAu 69, MugS,
NewYTBS 76, PolProf J*

Rubin, Jonathan 1940?- *BioIn 10*

Rubin, Louis D, Jr. 1923- *ChhPo S1, -S3,
ConAu 1R, -6NR, DrAS 74E, -78E, -82E,
WhoAm 74, -76, -78, -80, -82*

Rubin, Michael 1935- *ConAu 1R, -1NR*

Rubin, Robert Jay 1932- *AmM&WS 73P, -76P,
-79P*

Rubinstein, Morton Karl 1930- *WhoWest 74,
-76*

Rubinstein, Robert E 1943- *ConAu 106*

Rublowsky, John M 1928- *AuBYP SUP,
ConAu 17R, WhoE 74*

Ruby, Kathryn 1947- *ConAu 65, DrAP 75,
DrAP&F 83, IntWWP 82*

Ruby, Lois 1942- *ConAu 97, SmATA 34, -35,
WhoLibI 82*

Ruchlis, Hyman 1913- *AuBYP, BioIn 7, -9,
ConAu 1R, -2NR, SmATA 3*

Ruckman, Ivy 1931- *SmATA 37*

Rudley, Stephen 1946- *ConAu 106,
SmATA 30*

Rudloe, Jack 1943- *ConAu 97*

Rudolph, Wilma 1940- *BioIn 5, -6, -7, -8, -9,
-10, -11, -12, CurBio 61, GoodHs, HerW,
InB&W 80, InWom, IntDcWB, LibW,
LinLib S, NegAl 76[port], -83[port],
WhoBlA 77, -80, WhoTr&F 73, WorAl*

Rudwick, Elliott 1927- *AmM&WS 78S,
DrAS 74H*

Rue, Leonard Lee, III 1926- *AuBYP SUP,
BioIn 12, ConAu 1R, -1NR,
IntAu&W 76, -77, -82, WrDr 76, -80, -82,
-84*

Ruesch, Hans 1913- *Au&Wr 6, BioIn 5,
ConAu 13R*

Ruffell, Ann 1941- *ConAu 107,
SmATA 30[port]*

Ruggles, Eleanor 1916- *AmAu&B, Au&Wr 6,
BioIn 3, -4, ConAu 5R, ForWC 70,
REnAL, TwCA SUP, WhoAm 74, -76,
-78, WhoAmW 74, -58, -61, -64, -66, -68,
-70, -72*

Rugoff, Milton 1913- *ConAu 21R, DrAS 74E,*

-78E, -82E, SmATA 30[port],
WhoAm 76, -78, -80, -82*

Ruhen, Olaf 1911- *Au&Wr 6, BioIn 6, -12,
ConAu 1R, -5NR, IntAu&W 76, -77, -82,
SingR 2, SmATA 17, WhoWor 76,
WrDr 76, -80, -82, -84*

Ruiz, Ramon Eduardo 1921- *ChiSch,
ConAu 11NR, -25R, DrAS 74H, -78H,
-82H, WhoAm 74, -76, -78, -80, -82*

Rukeyser, Muriel 1913-1980 *AmAu&B,
AmWomWr, AnObit 1980[port], AuBYP,
BioIn 4, -7, -8, -10, -11, -12, BlueB 76,
CasWL, ChhPo, -S1, CnDAL, ConAu 5R,
-93, ConLC 6, -10, -15, -27[port],
ConP 70, -75, -80, CurBio 43, -80N,
DcLEL, DrAP 75, DrAS 74E, -78E,
ForWC 70, InWom, IntDcWB,
IntWW 78, -79, IntWWP 77, -82, LibW,
LinLib L, ModAL, ModAL SUP,
NewYTBS 80[port], OxAmL, PenC AM,
RAdv 1, REn, REnAL, SixAP,
SmATA 22N, TwCA, TwCA SUP,
TwCWr, WebE&AL, WhAm 7,
WhoAm 74, -76, -78, -80, WhoAmW 74,
-58, -61, -64, -66, -68, -70, -72, -83,
WhoWor 74, -76, WorAl, WrDr 76, -80*

Rulfo, Juan 1918- *BioIn 7, CasWL,
ConAu 85, ConLC 8, DcCLAA,
EncLatA, EncWL, ModLAL, Novels,
OxSpan, PenC AM, TwCWr,
WhoS&SW 73, WorAu 1970*

Rundgren, Todd 1948- *BioIn 11, -12,
EncPR&S, -77, IlEncRk, RkOn 78, -84,
RolSEnR 83, WhoAm 80, -82,
WhoRocM 82, WorAl*

Runyon, Catherine 1947- *ConAu 61*

Runyon, Damon 1884?-1946 *AmAu&B,
BioIn 1, -2, -3, -4, -5, -7, -11, -12, CasWL,
CnDAL, CnMWL, ConAu 107,
CurBio 47, DcAmB S4, DcLB 11[port],
DcLEL, DcNAA, EncMys, Film 2,
FilmgC, LinLib L, LongCTC, ModAL,
ModWD, NatCAB 39, NotNAT A, -B,
Novels[port], ObitOF 79, OxAmL,
PenC AM, PIP&P, REn, REnAL,
TwCA, TwCA SUP, TwCLC 10[port],
TwCWr, WebAB, -79, WebE&AL,
WhDW, WhAm 2, WhScrn 2,
WhoHol B, WorAl*

Runyon, Richard Porter 1925- *AmM&WS 73S,
-78S, ConAu 3NR, -45, WhoWest 82,
-84*

Rus, Vladimir 1931- *ConAu 17R,
IntAu&W 77*

Rush, Anne Kent 1945- *ConAu 8NR, -61,
WhoAmW 83*

Rushdie, Salman 1947- *ConAu 108,
ConLC 23[port], EncSF, IntWW 82, -83,
WrDr 84*

Rushforth, Peter 1945- *ConAu 101,
ConLC 19*

Rushing, Jane Gilmore 1925- *ConAu 49,*

WhoAm 78, -80, -82, WrDr 84
Rushmore, Robert 1926- *BioIn 11,*
ConAu 25R, DrAF 76, DrAP&F 83,
IntAu&W 77, SmATA 8
Rushton, William Faulkner 1947- *ConAu 101*
Rusk, Howard A 1901- *AmM&WS 73P, -76P,*
-79P, BioIn 1, -2, -3, -5, -7, -8, -9, -10,
CelR 73, ConAu 103, CurBio 46, -67,
InSci, WhoAm 74, -76, -78, -80, -82,
WhoWor 74
Ruskin, Ariane 1935- *AuBYP, BioIn 8, -10,*
ConAu 13R, SmATA 7
Russ, Joanna 1937- *AmWomWr, Au&Wr 6,*
ConAu 11NR, -25R, ConLC 15, ConSFA,
DcLB 8[port], EncSF, IntAu&W 76,
ScF&FL 1, -2, WhoAm 74, -76, -78, -80,
-82, WhoAmW 74, -75, WhoSciF,
WrDr 76, -80, -82, -84
Russ, Lavinia 1904- *AuBYP SUP, BioIn 9,*
ConAu 25R
Russ, Martin 1931- *BioIn 4, ConAu 106*
Russell, Andrew J 1830-1902 *DcAmArt*
Russell, Andy 1915- *BioIn 9, ConAu 10NR,*
-21R, WhoHol A
Russell, Bertrand 1872-1970 *AsBiEn, AtlBL,*
BiEsc, BioIn 1, -2, -3, -4, -5, -6, -7, -8, -9,
-10, -11, -12, CasWL, Chambr 3,
ConAu 25R, ConAu P-1, CurBio 40, -51,
-70, DcAmSR, DcLEL, DcScB, EncSF,
EvLB, IlEncMy[port], InSci, IntEnSS 79,
LinLib L, -S, LongCEL, LongCTC,
LuthC 75, MakMC, McGEWB, ModBrL,
NewC, NewYTBE 70, ObitOF 79,
OxEng, PenC ENG, REn, ScF&FL 1, -2,
TwCA, TwCA SUP, TwCWr,
WebE&AL, WhDW, WhAm 5,
WhE&EA, WhLit, WhoLA, WorAl
Russell, Bill 1934- *BioIn 10, -11, -12,*
CelR 73, CmCal, ConAu X, NegAl 76,
-83, NewYTBE 73, WhoAm 74, -76, -80,
-82, WhoBbl 73, WhoBlA 75, -77, -80,
WhoRocM 82, WorAl
Russell, Cazzie 1944- *BioIn 7, -8, -12,*
InB&W 80, NewYTBE 70,
NewYTBS 80[port], WhoBbl 73,
WhoBlA 75, -77, -80
Russell, Franklin Alexander 1926- *AmAu&B,*
Au&Wr 6, AuBYP, BioIn 11,
ConAu 11NR, -17R, OxCan, SmATA 11,
WhoAm 74, -76, -78, -80, -82, WrDr 76,
-80, -82, -84
Russell, Helen Ross 1915- *AmM&WS 73P,*
-76P, -79P, -82P, BioIn 11, ConAu 33R,
SmATA 8, WhoAmW 61, -64, -66, -75,
WrDr 76, -80, -82
Russell, Howard S 1887-1980 *ConAu 105*
Russell, Jeffrey Burton 1934- *ConAu 11NR,*
-25R, DrAS 74H, -78H, -82H,
IntAu&W 76, WhoAm 80, -82,
WhoWest 74, -76, -78, -80, -82,
WhoWor 82
Russell, John 1919- *Au&Wr 6, ConAu 13R,*

IntAu&W 77, Who 74, -82, -83,
WhoAm 78, -80, -82, WhoArt 80, -82,
WhoE 75
Russell, Mark 1932- *BioIn 8, -11, -12,*
ConAu 108, CurBio 81[port], Who 83,
WhoAm 80, -82
Russell, Robert William 1923?- *ConAu 1R,*
DrAS 74E, -78E, -82E, WhoF&I 74, -75,
WhoMW 74, -76
Russell, Ross 1909- *ConAu 1R*
Rust, Claude 1916- *ConAu 109*
Ruth, Babe 1895-1948 *BioIn 1, -2, -3, -4, -5,*
-6, -7, -8, -9, -10, -11, -12, BioNews 74,
CurBio 44, -48, Film 2, OxAmH,
WhDW, WhScrn, -2, WhoHol B
Ruth, Babe *see also* Ruth, George Herman
Ruth, George Herman 1895-1948 *BioIn 1, -2,*
-3, -4, -5, -6, -7, -8, -9, -10, -11, -12,
CurBio 44, -48, DcAmB S4, DcCathB,
EncAB-H, LinLib S, McGEWB,
NewYTBE 73, ObitOF 79, WebAB, -79,
WhAm 2, WhoProB 73, WorAl
Ruth, George Herman *see* Ruth, Babe
Ruth, Rod 1912- *BioIn 11, EncSF, IlsBYP,*
SmATA 9
Rutherford, Douglas 1915- *Au&Wr 6,*
ConAu X, TwCCr&M 80, WrDr 76, -80,
-82, -84
Rutherford, Douglas *see also* McConnell, James
Douglas R
Rutman, Leo 1935?- *ConAu 45, NatPD,*
-81[port], WhoE 75, -77
Rutsala, Vern 1934- *AmAu&B, ConAu 6NR,*
-9R, ConP 70, -75, -80, DcLEL 1940,
DrAP 75, DrAP&F 83, IntWWP 77, -82,
LinLib L, WrDr 76, -80
Rutstrum, Calvin 1895-1982 *BioIn 6, -12,*
ConAu 1R, -1NR, -106, IndAu 1917,
IntAu&W 77, MinnWr
Ruxton, George Frederick Augustus 1820-1848
Alli, ApCAB, ArtsAmW, BioIn 2, -7, -10,
-12, Drake, OxAmH, OxAmL, REnAL
Ryan, Alan 1940- *ConAu 29R, WrDr 80, -82,*
-84
Ryan, Betsy 1943- *ConAu X, SmATA X*
Ryan, Betsy *see also* Ryan, Elizabeth
Ryan, Bob 1946- *ConAu 4NR, -49*
Ryan, Cornelius 1920-1974 *BioIn 2, -7, -10,*
-11, -12, CelR 73, ConAu 53, -69,
ConLC 7, DcIrB, DcIrW 2,
IntAu&W 76, NewYTBS 74, -79,
ObitOF 79, WhAm 6, Who 74,
WhoAm 74, WhoE 74, WhoWor 74,
WorAl, WorAu 1970
Ryan, Desmond 1893-1964 *DcIrB, DcIrW 2,*
WhE&EA
Ryan, Elizabeth 1943- *ConAu 7NR, -61,*
SmATA 30[port]
Ryan, Nolan 1947- *BioIn 8, -9, -10, -11, -12,*
CmCal, CurBio 70, NewYTBE 70, -73,
NewYTBS 83[port], WhoAm 74, -76, -78,
-80, -82, WorAl

Ryback, Eric 1952- *ConAu 37R*

Ryckmans, Pierre 1891-1959 *BioIn 1, –2, –5,
–11, ObitOF 79, WhAm 3*

Rydberg, Ernest E 1901- *BioIn 12,
ConAu 13R, SmATA 21[port]*

Rydberg, Ernie 1901- *WrDr 76, –80, –82, –84*

Rydberg, Lou 1908- *ConAu 69, SmATA 27*

Rydell, Wendy 1927- *BioIn 9, ConAu 33R,
IntAu&W 82, SmATA 4, WhoAmW 75,
–77, –79, WrDr 76, –80, –82, –84*

Ryden, Hope *BioIn 10, –11, –12, ConAu 33R,
ForWC 70, SmATA 8, WhoAmW 74, –64,
–66, –68, –72, WhoE 74, WomWMM A,
–B*

Ryder, Jonathan 1927- *ConAu X, WrDr 76,
–80, –82, –84*

Ryder, Jonathan *see also* Ludlum, Robert

S

Sabatier, Robert 1923?- *ConAu 102,*
IntAu&W 76, -77, IntWW 74, -75, -76,
-77, -78, -79, -80, -81, -82, -83, WhoFr 79,
WhoWor 82

Sabatini, Rafael 1875-1950 *BioIn 2, -4, -11,*
DcBiA, DcLEL, EvLB, FilmgC,
LongCTC, MnBBF, NewC, NotNAT B,
ObitOF 79, REn, TwCA, TwCA SUP,
TwCWr, WhAm 2, WhE&EA, WhLit,
WhThe, WhoSpyF

Saberhagen, Fred 1930- *BioIn 12,*
ConAu 7NR, -57, ConSFA, DcLB 8[port],
EncSF, ScF&FL 1, -2, SmATA 37,
WhoSciF, WrDr 84

Sabin, Francene *ConAu 11NR, -69,*
SmATA 27

Sabin, Louis 1930- *ConAu 11NR, -69,*
SmATA 27

Sachar, Howard Morley 1928- *ConAu 5R,*
-6NR, DrAS 78H, -82H, WhoAm 80, -82,
WhoAmJ 80, WhoE 79, -81, -83,
WhoWorJ 72, -78

Sachar, Louis 1954- *ConAu 81*

Sachs, Marilyn Stickle 1927- *AmWomWr,*
BioIn 9, ChlLR 2, ConAu 17R, FourBJA,
IntAu&W 77, -82, SmATA 3,
TwCCW 78, -83, WhoAmW 75,
WrDr 76, -80, -82, -84

Sack, John 1930- *BioIn 7, ConAu 21R,*
WhoE 74

Sackett, Susan 1943- *ConAu 106*

Sackler, Howard 1929-1982 *AnObit 1982,*
BioIn 10, -12, ChhPo S2, ConAu 108, -61,
ConDr 73, -77, -82, ConLC 14,
DcLB 7[port], McGEWD, -83, NatPD 81,
NewYTBS 82[port], NotNAT, PIP&P,
WhoAm 74, -76, -78, -80, -82, WorAl,
WrDr 76, -80, -82

Sackson, Sid 1920- *BioIn 12, ConAu 69,*
SmATA 16

Sadat, Anwar 1918-1981 *AnObit 1981[port],*
BioIn 9, -10, -11, -12, BioNews 75,
ConAu 101, -104, CurBio 71, -81N,
IntYB 78, -79, -80, -81, LinLib S,
NewYTBE 70, -72, NewYTBS 81[port],
WhDW, WhoGov 72, WhoWor 74, -76,
-78, -80, WorAl

Sadoul, Georges 1904-1967 *OxFilm*

Saffell, David C 1941- *ConAu 11NR, -61*

Safire, William 1929- *BioIn 8, -9, -10, -11,*
-12, ConAu 17R, ConLC 10, CurBio 73,
NewYTBE 73, PolProf NF, WhoAm 74,
-76, -78, -80, -82, WhoE 79, -81, -83,
WhoGov 72, WhoS&SW 73, WorAl

Sagan, Carl 1934- *AmM&WS 73P, -76P, -79P,*
-82P, AsBiEn, BiESc, BioIn 6, -8, -10,
-11, -12, BlueB 76, ConAu 11NR, -25R,
ConIsC 2[port], CurBio 70, EncSF,
IntAu&W 76, IntWW 76, -77, -78, -79,
-80, -81, -82, -83, NewYTBS 79, UFOEn,
WhoAm 74, -76, -78, -80, -82, WhoE 74,
-75, -77, -79, -81, -83, WhoWor 78, -80,
-82, WorAl, WrDr 76, -80, -82, -84

Sagarin, Edward 1913- *AmM&WS 73S, -78S,*
ConAu 4NR, -5R

Sager, Carole Bayer 1945?- *BioIn 11, -12,*
RolSEnR 83, WhoAm 80, -82,
WhoRocM 82

Saggs, Henry 1920- *ConAu 5R, IntAu&W 82,*
WrDr 76, -80, -82, -84

Sagnier, Thierry 1946- *ConAu 53*

Sahakian, William S 1921- *AmM&WS 73S,*
-78S, BlueB 76, ConAu 8NR, -17R,
DrAS 74P, -78P, -82P, IntAu&W 77, -82,
WhoAm 74, -76, -78, -80, -82,
WhoWor 74, -76, -82, WrDr 76, -80, -82,
-84

Sahgal, Nayantara 1927- *BioIn 3, -6,*
ConAu 9R, -11NR, ConNov 72, -76, -82,
FarE&A 78, IntAu&W 76, -77, -82,
IntWW 75, -76, -77, -78, -79, -80, -81, -82,
-83, WhoWor 74, -76, -78, WrDr 76, -80,
-82, -84

Sailor, Charles 1947- *ConAu 97*

Saint, Dora Jessie 1913- *Au&Wr 6, BioIn 5,*
-10, -11, ConAu 7NR, -13R,
IntAu&W 76, -77, -82, SmATA 10,
WhoWor 78, WorAu, WrDr 76, -80, -82,
-84

St. Aubyn, Giles 1925- *Au&Wr 6,*
ConAu 4NR, -5R, IntAu&W 77, -82,
WhoWor 76, WrDr 76, -80, -82, -84

St. Clair, David 1932- *ConAu 33R,*
EncO&P 80, WhoWest 76

Saint-Exupery, Antoine De 1900-1944 *AnCL,*
AtlBL, BioIn 1, -2, -3, -4, -5, -7, -9, -10,

ObitOF 79, REnAL, ScF&FL 1, TwCA SUP, WhAm 5, WhoWorJ 72
Samuels, Charles 1902-1982 *BioIn 11, –12, ConAu 1R, –5NR, –106, SmATA 12*
Samuels, Charles Thomas 1936-1974 *ConAu 41R, –49*
Samuels, Gertrude *AuBYP, BioIn 7, –12, ConAu 6NR, –9R, ForWC 70, NatPD, –81[port], SmATA 17, WhoAmW 58, –61, –64, –66, –75, –77, –79, –81, WhoWorJ 72, –78*
Samuelson, Paul Anthony 1915- *AmAu&B, AmM&WS 73S, –78S, BioIn 5, –7, –9, –11, –12, BlueB 76, CelR 73, ConAu 5R, CurBio 65, EncAB-H, IndAu 1917, IntAu&W 77, –82, IntWW 74, –75, –76, –77, –78, –79, –80, –81, –82, –83, McGEWB, NewYTBE 70, –71, PolProf J, PolProf K, PolProf NF, WebAB, –79, Who 74, –82, –83, WhoAm 74, –76, –78, –80, –82, WhoE 74, –77, –79, –81, –83, WhoEc, WhoF&I 79, –81, –83, WhoWor 74, –78, –80, –82, WorAl, WrDr 76, –80, –82, –84*
Sanborn, Duane 1914- *AuBYP, ConAu 1R, –1NR, WhoAmW 64, –66, –68*
Sanborn, Duane *see also* Bradley, Duane
Sanborn, Margaret 1915- *ConAu 4NR, –53, WrDr 76, –80, –82, –84*
Sancha, Sheila 1924- *ConAu 11NR, –69*
Sanchez, Thomas 1943?- *BioIn 9, ConAu 2NR, –45, DrAF 76*
Sand, George 1804-1876 *AtlBL, BbD, BiD&SB, BioIn 1, –2, –3, –4, –5, –6, –7, –8, –9, –10, –11, –12, CasWL, CelCen, CyWA, DcAmSR, DcBiA, DcEnL, DcEuL, Dis&D, EuAu, EvEuW, GoodHs, IntDcWB[port], LinLib L, –LP, –S, McGEWB, NotNAT B, Novels[port], OxEng, OxFr, PenC EUR, RComWL, REn, ScF&FL 1, WhDW, WorAl*
Sand, George X *AuBYP SUP, ConAu 13R*
Sandburg, Carl 1878-1967 *AmAu&B, AmSCAP 66, AmWr, AnCL, ApCAB X, AtlBL, AuBYP, BiDAmM, BioIn 1, –2, –3, –4, –5, –6, –7, –8, –9, –10, –11, –12, CasWL, Chambr 3, ChhPo, –S1, –S2, –S3, CnDAL, CnE&AP, CnMWL, ConAmA, ConAmL, ConAu 5R, –25R, ConLC 1, –4, –10, –15, CurBio 40, –63, –67, CyWA, DcLB 17[port], DcLEL, EncAAH, EncAB-H, EncFCWM 69, EncWL, EvLB, FamPYP, LinLib L, –S, LongCTC, MakMC, McGEWB, ModAL, ModAL SUP, ObitOF 79, ObitT 1961, OxAmH, OxAmL, OxEng, OxMus, PenC AM, RAdv 1, REn, REnAL, SixAP, SmATA 8, Str&VC, TwCA, TwCA SUP, TwCWr, WebAB, –79, WebE&AL, WhDW, WhAm 4, WhE&EA, WhoTwCL, WisWr, WorAl*
Sande, Theodore Anton 1933- *AmArch 70, ConAu 65, WhoAm 82, WhoE 74*

Sanderlin, George 1915- *BioIn 9, ConAu 13R, DrAS 74E, –78E, –82E, IntAu&W 76, –77, –82, SmATA 4, WrDr 76, –80, –82, –84*
Sanderlin, Owenita 1916- *BioIn 11, ConAu 7NR, –17R, SmATA 11, WhoAmW 83, WhoWest 84, WrDr 76, –80, –82, –84*
Sanders, Dennis 1949- *ConAu 108*
Sanders, Lawrence 1920- *ASpks, BioIn 8, –11, –12, ConAu 81, EncSF, IntAu&W 76, –77, NewYTBS 80[port], Novels, TwCCr&M 80, WhoAm 80, –82, WorAl, WrDr 82, –84*
Sanders, Leonard 1929- *ConAu 9R, ScF&FL 1, WhoAm 74, –76, –78, –80*
Sanders, Marion K 1905-1977 *BioIn 11, ConAu 33R, –73, ForWC 70, NewYTBS 77, WhoAmW 58, –61*
Sanders, Thomas E 1926- *BioIn 10, ConAu 21R, NewYTBE 73, ScF&FL 1, –2*
Sanders, William B 1944- *ConAu 10NR, –65*
Sanderson, Derek 1946- *BioIn 9, –10, –11, CurBio 75, NewYTBE 70, –72, –73, NewYTBS 74, –78, –83[port], WhoAm 76, –78, WhoHcky 73*
Sanderson, Ivan T 1911-1973 *AmAu&B, AmM&WS 73P, –76P, AuBYP, BioIn 1, –4, –5, –7, –9, –10, –11, ConAu 37R, –41R, EncO&P 78S1, EncSF, IlsCB 1744, –1946, InSci, LinLib L, NatCAB 57, NewYTBE 73, REnAL, ScF&FL 1, SmATA 6, TwCA, TwCA SUP, UFOEn[port]*
Sandman, Peter Mark 1945- *AmM&WS 73S, –78S, ConAu 25R, IntAu&W 77, WrDr 76, –80, –82, –84*
Sandoz, Mari 1901-1966 *AmAu&B, AmWomWr, AuBYP, BioIn 3, –4, –5, –7, –9, –10, –12, CnDAL, ConAu 1R, –25R, DcLB 9[port], EncAAH, InWom, LinLib L, NotAW MOD, ObitOF 79, OxAmL, REn, REnAL, REnAW, SmATA 5, ThrBJA, TwCA, TwCA SUP, WhAm 4, WhNAA, WhoAmW 58*
Sands, Bill *AmAu&B*
Sands, Leo George 1912- *ConAu 17R, WhoAm 76, –78, –80*
Sandved, Kjell *BioIn 12*
Sanford, Agnes Mary White 1898- *ConAu 17R, WhoAmW 58, –61*
Sanger, Margaret 1883-1966 *AmAu&B, AmWomWr, BioIn 2, –3, –4, –7, –8, –9, –10, –11, –12, ConAu 89, CurBio 44, –66, DcAmSR, EncAB-H, InWom, IntDcWB, LibW, LinLib L, –S, LongCTC, LuthC 75, McGEWB, NatCAB 52, NotAW MOD, ObitOF 79, ObitT 1961, OxAmL, WebAB, –79, WhAm 4, WorAl*
Sanger, Marjory Bartlett 1920- *AuBYP SUP, BioIn 11, ConAu 37R, SmATA 8,*

WrDr 76, –80, –82, –84

Santalo, Lois *AuBYP, BioIn 8*

Santee, Ross 1888?-1965 *AmAu&B, ArizL, ArtsAmW, BioIn 2, –3, –4, –7, –8, ConAu 108, IlBEAAW, ObitOF 79, REnAL, REnAW, TwCA SUP*

Santesson, Hans Stefan 1914?-1975 *BioIn 10, ConAu 57, –93, ConSFA, EncSF, ScF&FL 1, –2, SmATA 30N*

Santoli, Al 1949- *ConAu 105*

Santos, Bienvenido N 1911- *ConAu 101, ConLC 22[port], ConP 70, DrAP&F 83*

Sargent, Pamela 1948- *BioIn 12, ConAu 8NR, –61, DcLB 8, DrAF 76, DrAP&F 83, EncSF, ScF&FL 2, SmATA 29, WrDr 84*

Sargent, Sarah 1937- *ConAu 106*

Sargent, Shirley 1927- *AuBYP, BioIn 7, –11, ConAu 1R, –2NR, ForWC 70, SmATA 11*

Sargent, William 1946- *ConAu 106*

Sarnoff, Jane 1937- *AuBYP SUP, BioIn 11, ConAu 9NR, –53, SmATA 10*

Sarnoff, Paul 1918- *ConAu 2NR, –5R, NewYTBS 80[port]*

Saroyan, Aram 1943- *AmAu&B, ConAu 21R, ConP 70, –75, –80, DcLEL 1940, IntWWP 77, WrDr 76, –80, –82, –84*

Saroyan, William 1908-1981 *AmAu&B, AmNov, AnObit 1981[port], Au&Wr 6, BiE&WWA, BioIn 1, –2, –3, –4, –5, –6, –7, –8, –9, –10, –11, –12, BlueB 76, CasWL, CelR 73, CmCal, CnDAL, CnMD, CnMWL, CnThe, ConAmA, ConAu 5R, –103, ConDr 73, –77, ConLC 1, –8, –10, ConNov 72, –76, CurBio 40, –72, –81N, CyWA, DcLB Y81A[port], –7[port], –9[port], DcLEL, DrAF 76, EncWL, EncWT, EvLB, FilmgC, IntAu&W 76, –77, IntWW 74, –75, –77, –78, –79, –80, –81, –81N, LinLib L, –S, LongCTC, McGEWB, McGEWD, –84, ModAL, ModAL SUP, ModWD, NewYTBE 72, NewYTBS 75, –79, –81[port], NotNAT, –A, Novels, OxAmL, OxThe, PenC AM, PIP&P, RAdv 1, REn, REnAL, REnWD, SmATA 23[port], –24N, TwCA, TwCA SUP, TwCWr, WebAB, –79, WebE&AL, WhAm 7, WhE&EA, Who 74, –82N, WhoAm 74, –76, –78, –80, WhoThe 15, –16, –81, WhoTwCL, WhoWor 74, WorAl, WrDr 76, –80, –82*

Sarris, Andrew 1928- *AmAu&B, BioIn 9, –10, ConAu 21R, OxFilm, WhoAm 76, –78, –80, –82, WhoE 74, –75, WhoWor 78*

Sarton, May 1912- *AmAu&B, AmWomWr, BioIn 4, –5, –8, –10, –11, –12, BlueB 76, ConAu 1R, –1NR, ConLC 4, –14, ConNov 72, –76, –82, ConP 70, –75, –80, CurBio 82[port], DcLB Y81B[port], DrAF 76, DrAP 75, DrAP&F 83, DrAS 74E, –78E, –82E, IntAu&W 76, –77,*

IntWWP 77, ModAL, ModAL SUP, NewYTBS 83[port], Novels, OxAmL, PenC AM, RAdv 1, REnAL, ScF&FL 1, SmATA 36, TwCA SUP, WhoAm 74, –76, –78, –80, –82, WhoAmW 58, –64, –66, –68, –70, –72, –81, –83, WhoWor 74, WrDr 76, –80, –82, –84

Sartre, Jean-Paul 1905-1980 *AnObit 1980[port], –1981, Au&Wr 6, BiE&WWA, BioIn 1, –2, –3, –4, –5, –6, –7, –8, –9, –10, –11, –12, CasWL, CelR 73, CIDMEL, CnMD, CnMWL, CnThe, ConAu 9R, –97, ConLC 1, –4, –7, –9, –13, –18, –24[port], CroCD, CurBio 47, –71, –80N, CyWA, EncWL, EncWT, EvEuW, FilmgC, IntAu&W 76, –77, IntWW 74, –75, –76, –77, –78, –79, LinLib L, –S, LongCTC, LuthC 75, MakMC, McGEWB, McGEWD, –84[port], ModFrL, ModRL, ModWD, NewYTBE 71, NewYTBS 80[port], NotNAT, –A, Novels, OxEng, OxFr, OxThe, PenC EUR, PIP&P, RComWL, REn, REnWD, ScF&FL 1, –2, TwCA SUP, TwCWr, WhDW, WhAm 7, Who 74, WhoFr 79, WhoThe 15, –16, –81, –81N, WhoTwCL, WhoWor 74, –78, WorAl*

Satchidananda, Swami 1914- *WhoRel 77*

Satterfield, Archie 1933- *BioIn 12, ConAu 57*

Sattler, Helen Roney 1921- *AuBYP SUP, BioIn 9, ConAu 33R, SmATA 4*

Sauer, Julia 1891-1983 *BioIn 6, ConAu 81, MorJA, ScF&FL 1, SmATA 32[port], –36N, TwCCW 83, WhoLibS 55*

Saul, John 1942- *ConAu 81, WhoAm 82*

Saunders, Blanche 1906-1964 *Au&Wr 6, AuBYP, BioIn 2, –7, ConAu P-1*

Saunders, Keith 1910- *BioIn 11, ConAu 57, SmATA 12*

Saunders, Rubie Agnes 1929- *BioIn 12, ConAu 49, ForWC 70, SmATA 21, WhoAm 78, –80, –82, WhoAmW 74, –68, –75, –79, –81*

Savage, Elizabeth 1918- *AmAu&B, AmWomWr, ConAu 1R, –1NR*

Savage, Katharine 1905- *Au&Wr 6, ConAu 13R, FourBJA*

Savage, William Woodrow, Jr. 1943- *ConAu 57, DrAS 74H, –78H, –82H*

Savitch, Jessica 1947?-1983 *BioIn 11, –12, ConAu 108, –110, CurBio 83[port], ForWC 70, LesBEnT, NewYTBS 83[port], WhoAm 80, –82, WhoAmW 83*

Savitt, Sam 1917- *AuBYP, BioIn 7, –11, ChhPo S3, ConAu 1R, –1NR, IlBEAAW, IntAu&W 77, SmATA 8, WhoAmA 78, –80, –82, WhoAmJ 80, WhoE 77, –79, WrDr 76, –80, –82, –84*

Savitz, Harriet May 1933- *AuBYP SUP, BioIn 10, ConAu 41R, SmATA 5, WhoAmW 79, –81, –83, WhoE 83*

Sawkins, Raymond 1923- *Au&Wr 6,*

ConAu 103

Sawkins, Raymond see also Forbes, Colin

Sawyer, Ruth 1880-1970 AmAu&B, AmLY, AmWomWr, AnCL, AuBYP, BioIn 2, –4, –6, –7, –8, –9, –11, –12, BkCL, CarSB, ChhPo, ConAu 73, DcLB 22[port], HerW, JBA 51, Newb 1922, NotAW MOD, SmATA 17, TwCA, TwCA SUP, TwCCW 78, –83, WhAm 5, WhE&EA, WhNAA, WhoAmW 58, –70, –72

Saxon, James Anthony 1912- WhoWest 74, –76, –78, –80, –82

Saxton, Mark 1914- AmAu&B, AmNov, BioIn 2, ConAu 93, WhoAm 76, –78, –80, –82, WhoWor 80

Say, Allen 1937- ConAu 29R, SmATA 28[port]

Sayer, Leo 1948?- BioIn 11, RkOn 78, WhoRocM 82

Sayers, Charles Marshall 1892-1957 AuBYP, BioIn 1

Sayers, Dorothy Leigh 1893-1957 BioIn 2, –4, –8, –10, –11, –12, CasWL, Chambr 3, CnMD, ConAu 104, CorpD, DcLB 10[port], DcLEL, EncMys, EncWL, EvLB, InWom, IntDcWB[port], LinLib L, –LP, –S, LongCTC, ModBrL, ModBrL SUP, ModWD, NewC, NotNAT B, Novels[port], ObitOF 79, ObitT 1951, OxEng, PenC ENG, REn, ScF&FL 1, TwCA, TwCA SUP, TwCCr&M 80, TwCLC 2, TwCWr, WhAm 3, WhE&EA, WhLit, WhThe, WhoHr&F, WorAl

Sayers, Gale 1943- BioIn 7, –8, –9, –10, –12, ConAu 73, Ebony 1, InB&W 80, NegAl 76, –83, NewYTBE 70, –72, WhoAm 74, –76, –78, –80, –82, WhoFtbl 74, WorAl

Sayre, Anne 1923?- ConAu 61, WhoE 79

Sayre, Joel 1900-1979 AmAu&B, AmNov, BioIn 2, –12, ConAu 89, NewYTBS 79

Scaduto, Anthony ConAu 104

Scagnetti, Jack 1924- AuBYP SUP, BioIn 10, ConAu 4NR, –49, MichAu 80, SmATA 7

Scalzo, Joe 1941- ConAu 49

Scanlon, Marion Stephany d1977 BioIn 6, –11, ConAu 5R, ForWC 70, MichAu 80, MinnWr, SmATA 11, WhoAmW 58, –61, –64, –66, WrDr 76, –80

Scarf, Maggie 1932- BioIn 10, –12, ConAu 29R, NewYTBS 80[port], SmATA 5, WhoAmW 75, WrDr 84

Scarne, John 1903- BioIn 1, –4, –7, CelR 73, IntAu&W 76, WhoAm 76, –78, –80, –82

Scarry, Richard 1919- AuBYP, BioIn 8, –9, –10, –12, ChlLR 3, ConAu 17R, FamAIYP, IlsCB 1957, –1967, IntAu&W 77, –82, NewYTBS 76, –80[port], PiP, SmATA 2, –35, ThrBJA, TwCCW 78, –83, WhoAm 78, –80, –82,

WrDr 76, –80, –82, –84

Schaap, Dick 1934- ConAu X

Schaap, Richard 1934- AmAu&B, BioIn 8, ConAu 5NR, –9R, WhoE 74

Schaefer, Jack Warner 1907- AmAu&B, Au&Wr 6, AuBYP, BioIn 5, –8, –9, –11, ConAu 17R, ConAu P-1, IntMPA 77, –75, –76, –78, –79, –81, –82, –84, OhA&B, REnAW, ScF&FL 1, SmATA 3, ThrBJA, TwCCW 78, –83, WhoAm 74, –76, –78, –80, –82, WhoWest 74

Schaefer, Vincent Joseph 1906- AmM&WS 73P, –76P, –79P, AsBiEn, BiESc, BioIn 1, –2, –5, CurBio 48, InSci, McGMS 80[port], WhoAm 74, –76, –78, –80, –82, WhoTech 82

Schafer, William John 1937- ConAu 49, DrAS 74E, –78E, –82E

Schaff, Louise E AuBYP SUP

Schaffer, Ulrich 1942- ConAu 69

Schaffner, Nicholas 1953- ConAu 85

Schaller, George B 1933- AuBYP SUP, BioIn 12, ConAu 5R, –9NR, FifIDA, SmATA 30

Schapira, Joel Richard 1949- WhoS&SW 76

Scharfenberg, Doris 1925- ConAu 108

Schary, Dore 1905-1980 AmAu&B, AnObit 1980[port], BiDFilm, BiE&WWA, BioIn 1, –2, –3, –4, –5, –6, –9, –10, –12, BlueB 76, ConAu 1R, –1NR, –101, ConDr 73, –77, CurBio 48, –80N, DcFM, FilmgC, IntAu&W 76, IntMPA 77, –75, –76, –78, –79, –81, –82, LinLib L, –S, MGM A, ModWD, NatPD, NewYTBE 70, NewYTBS 80[port], NotNAT, OxFilm, REnAL, WhAm 7, WhoAm 74, –76, –78, –80, WhoAmJ 80, WhoE 74, –75, –77, –79, –81, WhoThe 15, –16, –81, WhoWor 74, –76, –78, –80, WhoWorJ 72, –78, WorAl, WorAu, WorEFlm, WrDr 76, –80

Schatt, Stanley 1943- ConAu 69

Schechter, Betty 1921- AuBYP, BioIn 8, –10, ConAu 5R, FourBJA, SmATA 5

Schechter, William 1934- ConAu 21R, ODwPR 79, WhoPubR 76

Scheffer, Victor B 1906- BioIn 10, ConAu 11NR, –29R, SmATA 6, WhoAm 74, –76, WrDr 80, –82, –84

Scheinfeld, Amram 1897-1979 Au&Wr 6, BioIn 12, ConAu 17R, –89, NewYTBS 79, WhoWorJ 72, –78

Schell, Jessie DrAF 76, DrAP&F 83

Schell, Jonathan 1943?- BioIn 12, ConAu 73, WrDr 84

Schell, Orville H 1940- AuBYP SUP, BioIn 11, –12, ConAu 25R, SmATA 10, WrDr 84

Schellie, Don 1932- ConAu 101, SmATA 29[port]

Schemm, Mildred Walker 1905- BioIn 12, ConAu 1R, –1NR, DrAS 74E, InWom,

WhE&EA, WhLit, WhoLA

Schollander, Don 1946- *CmCal, CurBio 65*

Scholz, Jackson Volney 1897- *AuBYP, BioIn 6, –8, ConAu 5R, MorJA, WhoTr&F 73*

Schonborg, Virginia 1913- *ConAu 77*

Schoor, Gene 1921- *AuBYP, BioIn 7, –9, ConAu 29R, SmATA 3*

Schotter, Roni *DrAP&F 83*

Schowalter, John E 1936- *ConAu 109*

Schraff, Anne E 1939- *AuBYP SUP, ConAu 1NR, –49, SmATA 27[port]*

Schram, Martin Jay 1942- *ConAu 69, WhoAm 76, –78, –80, –82*

Schrank, Jeffrey 1944- *ConAu 29R, IntAu&W 77, WrDr 76, –80, –82, –84*

Schreiber, Flora Rheta 1918- *AuNews 1, BioIn 10, –11, BioNews 74, BlueB 76, ConAu 11NR, –53, DrAS 74E, –78E, –82E, ForWC 70, WhoAm 78, –80, –82, WhoAmW 74, –58, –61, –64, –66, –68, –70, –72, –75, –77, –79, –81, WhoE 77, –79, WhoWor 80, WhoWorJ 72, –78*

Schroeder, Henry Alfred 1906-1975 *AmM&WS 73P, –76P, BioIn 10, ConAu P-2, NewYTBS 75, WhAm 6, WhoE 74, –75*

Schroeder, Paul Clemens 1938- *AmM&WS 73P, –76P, –79P, –82P*

Schrotenboer, Kathryn 1952?- *BioIn 12*

Schueler, Donald G 1929- *ConAu 106, DrAS 74E, –78E, –82E*

Schulberg, Budd 1914- *AmAu&B, AmNov, AmSCAP 66, BiE&WWA, BioIn 1, –2, –3, –4, –7, –10, –12, BlueB 76, CelR 73, CmCal, CnDAL, ConAu 25R, ConDr 73, –77D, –82D, ConLC 7, ConNov 72, –76, –82, CurBio 41, –51, DcFM, DcLB Y81A[port], –6[port], –26[port], DcLEL 1940, DrAF 76, DrAP&F 83, FilmgC, IntAu&W 76, –77, IntMPA 77, –75, –76, –78, –79, –81, –82, –84, IntWW 74, –75, –76, –77, –78, –79, –80, –81, –82, –83, LinLib L, LongCTC, ModAL, NewYTBE 72, NotNAT, Novels, OxAmL, OxFilm, PenC AM, REn, REnAL, TwCA SUP, WebE&AL, WhE&EA, WhoAm 74, –76, –78, –80, –82, WhoWor 74, WorEFlm, WrDr 76, –80, –82, –84*

Schulian, John Nielsen 1945- *WhoAm 82*

Schulke, Flip Phelps Graeme 1930- *ConAu 105, WhoS&SW 73*

Schulman, Grace *ConAu 65, DrAP 75, DrAP&F 83, DrAS 74E, –78E, –82E, IntAu&W 82, IntWWP 77, –82, WhoAmW 75 , –77*

Schulman, L M 1934- *ConAu 33R, ScF&FL 1, –2, SmATA 13*

Schulman, Paul 1948- *WhoAdv 80*

Schulte, Elaine L 1934- *ConAu 73,*

SmATA 36

Schultes, Richard Evans 1915- *AmM&WS 73P, –76P, –79P, –82P, BioIn 12, ConAu 108, WhoAm 74, –76, –78, –80, –82, WhoRel 75, –77*

Schultz, Barbara 1923- *ConAu 21R*

Schultz, Duane P 1934- *AmM&WS 73S, ConAu 29R*

Schultz, John 1932- *ConAu 41R, DrAP&F 83, WhoAm 74, –76*

Schultz, Pearle Henriksen 1918- *BioIn 12, ConAu 1NR, –49, SmATA 21[port]*

Schulz, Charles Monroe 1922- *AmAu&B, ArtCS, AuBYP, BioIn 4, –5, –6, –7, –8, –9, –10, –11, –12, CelR 73, CmCal, ConAu 6NR, –9R, ConLC 12, CurBio 60, IntWW 78, –79, –80, –81, –82, –83, LesBEnT, LinLib L, MinnWr, NewYTET, SmATA 10, ThrBJA, WebAB, –79, WhoAm 74, –76, –78, –80, –82, WhoAmA 73, –76, –78, –80, –82, WhoWor 74, WorAl, WorECom, WrDr 76, –80, –82, –84*

Schulz, David A 1933- *AmM&WS 73S, –78S, ConAu 29R, WhoE 74, –75, –77*

Schur, Edwin Michael 1930- *ConAu 7NR, –13R, WhoE 77, –83*

Schuster, Edgar Howard 1930- *DrAS 74E*

Schutz, Susan Polis 1944- *ConAu 105*

Schuyler, Pamela R 1948- *ConAu 106, SmATA 30[port]*

Schwab, Gustav Benjamin 1792-1850 *BiD&SB, BioIn 7, CasWL, DcEuL, EuAu, OxGer, REn*

Schwartz, Alvin 1927- *AuBYP SUP, BioIn 9, ChlLR 3, ConAu 7NR, –13R, SmATA 4, WhoE 75, –77*

Schwartz, Bernard 1923- *BioIn 4, –10, –11, DrAS 74P, –78P, –82P, PolProf E, WhoAm 74, –76, –78, –80, –82, WhoAmL 78, –79, –83*

Schwartz, Charles Walsh 1914- *AuBYP, BioIn 7, –11, ConAu 13R, –73, SmATA 8*

Schwartz, Delmore 1913-1966 *AmAu&B, AtlBL, BioIn 4, –5, –7, –8, –10, –11, –12, CasWL, CnDAL, CnE&AP, CnMWL, ConAu 25R, ConAu P-2, ConLC 2, –4, –10, ConLCrt, –82, ConP 75, –80A, CurBio 60, –66, EncWL, LinLib L, ModAL, ModAL SUP, ObitOF 79, OxAmL, PenC AM, RAdv 1, REn, REnAL, SixAP, TwCA, TwCA SUP, TwCWr, WebE&AL, WhAm 4, WhoTwCL, WorAl*

Schwartz, Elliott S 1936- *Baker 78, CpmDNM 81, –82, ConAmC, ConAu 13R, IntAu&W 77, –82, WhoAmM 83, WhoE 75, –77, WrDr 76, –80, –82*

Schwartz, George 1908-1974 *BioIn 6, –10, ConAu 104*

Schwartz, Howard 1945- *ConAu 49, DrAF 76, DrAP 75*

Seals & Crofts *EncPR&S, –77, IlEncRk, RkOn 78, –84, RolSEnR 83*

Seals & Crofts SA Crofts, Dash

Sealts, Merton M, Jr. 1915- *ConAu 13R, DrAS 74E, –78E, –82E, WhoAm 74, –76, –78, WrDr 76, –80, –82, –84*

Searight, Mary W 1918- *BioIn 12, ConAu 29R, SmATA 17, WhoAmW 75, –77, –79, WhoWest 78, –80, –82*

Searle, Ronald 1920- *Au&Wr 6, BioIn 1, –2, –4, –5, –6, –12, BlueB 76, ChhPo S2, ConAu 9R, DcBrA 1, DcLEL 1940, IlsBYP, IlsCB 1946, IntWW 74, –75, –76, –77, –78, –79, –80, –81, –82, –83, NewC, OxTwCA, WhDW, Who 74, –82, –83, WhoAm 74, –76, –78, –80, –82, WhoArt 80, –82, WhoGrA, –82[port], WhoWor 74, –82, WorECar, WrDr 76, –80, –82, –84*

Searls, Hank 1922- *BioIn 11, ConAu X, EncSF, ScF&FL 1, –2, WrDr 84*

Searls, Hank *see also* Searls, Henry Hunt, Jr.

Searls, Henry Hunt, Jr. 1922- *Au&Wr 6, ConAu 13R*

Searls, Henry Hunt, Jr. *see also* Searls, Hank

Sears, Paul Bigelow 1891- *AmAu&B, BiESc, BioIn 3, –4, –5, –7, BlueB 76, ConAu 17R, CurBio 60, InSci, IntWW 74, –75, –76, –77, –78, –79, –80, –81, –82, –83, McGMS 80[port], OhA&B, WhoAm 74, –76, –78, –80*

Sears, Stephen W 1932- *BioIn 9, ConAu 33R, SmATA 4*

Sebastian, Lee 1935- *ConAu X, DcLEL 1940, SmATA X, ThrBJA, WorAu 1970, WrDr 84*

Sebastian, Lee *see also* Silverberg, Robert

Sebestyen, Ouida 1924- *ConAu 107, WrDr 82, –84*

Sebrell, William Henry 1901- *AmM&WS 76P, –79P, BiDrAPH 79, BioIn 2, –3, InSci, WhoAm 74, –76, –78, –80, –82, WhoWor 74*

Sechan, Edmond 1919- *DcFM, WhoFr 79, WorEFlm*

Sechrist, Elizabeth Hough 1903- *AmAu&B, AuBYP, BioIn 7, –9, ChhPo, ConAu 5R, ScF&FL 1, –2, SmATA 2, WhE&EA, WhoAm 74, –76, –78, WhoAmW 74, –58, –64, –66, –68, –70, –72, –75, –77, –79*

Sedaka, Neil 1939- *AmPS B, BioIn 6, –10, –11, –12, ConAu 103, CurBio 78, EncPR&S, –77, IlEncRk, RkOn 74, –78, –82, –84, RolSEnR 83, WhoAm 78, –80, –82, WhoRocM 82, WorAl*

Sedgwick, John 1813-1864 *AmBi, ApCAB, BioIn 1, –7, –12, CivWDc, DcAmB, Drake, HarEnUS[port], NatCAB 4, TwCBDA, WebAMB, WhAm HS*

Seed, Suzanne Liddell 1940- *AuBYP SUP, WhoAmA 82, WhoAmW 77, –79, –81*

Seeger, Elizabeth 1889?-1973 *BioIn 10, –12, ConAu 45, SmATA 20N*

Seeger, Pete 1919- *Baker 78, BioIn 12, BioNews 74, BlueB 76, CelR 73, CmpEPM, ConAu 69, CurBio 63, EncAAH, EncFCWM 69, SmATA 13, WebAB, –79, WhoAm 74, –76, –78, –80, –82, WhoHol A, WhoRocM 82, WhoWor 74, WorAl*

Seegers, Kathleen Walker 1915- *ConAu 21R*

Seelye, John 1931- *ConAu 97, ConLC 7, DrAS 74E, –78E, –82E, WrDr 84*

Seeman, Bernard 1911- *Au&Wr 6, ConAu 21R, WhoE 74, –75, –77, –79, –81, –83, WhoF&I 74, –75, –77, –79, –81, –83, WhoWor 82*

Seeman, Ernest Albright 1887- *ConAu 85*

Sefton, Catherine 1941- *TwCCW 83*

Segal, Abraham 1910?-1977 *BioIn 11, ConAu 69*

Segal, Erich 1937- *AmAu&B, AmSCAP 66, ASpks, BioIn 8, –9, –10, –11, –12, BlueB 76, CelR 73, ConAu 25R, ConLC 3, –10, CurBio 71, DrAS 74F, –78F, –82F, IntAu&W 76, –82, LinLib L, NewYTBE 71, Novels, WhoAm 74, –76, –78, –80, –82, WhoE 74, WhoHol A, WhoWor 80, –82, WhoWorJ 72, –78, WorAl, WrDr 76, –80, –82, –84*

Segal, Julius 1924- *AmM&WS 73S*

Segal, Lore 1928- *AmAu&B, AuBYP SUP, BioIn 9, ConAu 5NR, –13R, DrAF 76, DrAP&F 83, FourBJA, IntAu&W 76, –77, –82, SmATA 4, WhoAm 74, –76, –78, –80, –82, WhoAmJ 80, WhoAmW 66, –70, –72, WrDr 76, –80, –82, –84*

Segal, Marilyn Mailman 1927- *AmM&WS 78S, ConAu 8NR, –17R, ForWC 70, WhoAmW 74, WhoFla, WhoS&SW 82*

Seger, Bob 1945?- *BioIn 11, –12, RkOn 78, –84, RolSEnR 83, WhoAm 78, –80, –82, WhoRocM 82*

Segovia, Andres 1894- *Baker 78, BioIn 1, –2, –3, –4, –5, –6, –7, –10, –11, –12, CelR 73, CurBio 48, –64, IntWW 74, –75, –76, –77, –78, –79, –80, –81, –82, –83, IntWWM 77, MusSN, NewYTBE 73, NewYTBS 77, OxMus, WhDW, Who 74, –82, –83, WhoAm 76, –78, –80, –82, WhoMus 72, WhoWor 74, –78, –80, –82, WorAl*

Segre, Emilio 1905- *BiESc, BioIn 12, IntWW 83, Who 83, WhoTech 82, WhoWest 84, WhoWor 82, WrDr 84*

Seide, Diane 1930- *ConAu 73*

Seidman, Laurence 1925- *BioIn 12, ConAu 77, SmATA 15*

Seifert, Shirley L 1889?-1971 *AmAu&B, AmNov, Au&Wr 6, BioIn 2, –9, ConAu 1R, –2NR, –33R, CurBio 51, ForWC 70, InWom, NewYTBE 71, WhNAA, WhoAmW 58, –61, –70, –72*

Selden, George 1929- *AuBYP, BioIn 8, –9, –10, ConAu X, FourBJA, MorBMP,*

ScF&FL 1, –2, SmATA 4, TwCCW 78,
–83, WrDr 80, –82, –84
Selden, Neil 1931- *ConAu 106, NatPD,*
–81[port]
Selden, Samuel 1899-1979 *AuBYP,*
BiE&WWA, BioIn 7, ConAu 1R, –3NR,
DrAS 74E, NotNAT, WhoAm 74
Self, Margaret Cabell 1902- *AmAu&B,*
AuBYP, BioIn 7, ConAu 3NR, –5R,
IntAu&W 76, –77, –82, OhA&B,
SmATA 24[port], WhoAm 74, –76, –78,
–80, –82, WhoAmW 74, –58, –64, –66, –68,
–70, –72, WhoS&SW 73, –75, –76,
WrDr 76, –80, –82, –84
Seligson, Tom 1946- *ConAu 33R*
Selinko, Annemarie 1914- *Au&Wr 6, BioIn 3,*
–4, CurBio 55, InWom
Sellers, Cleveland 1944?- *BioIn 9*
Selsam, Millicent Ellis 1912- *AmPB, AnCL,*
AuBYP, BioIn 6, –7, –9, BkP, ChlLR 1,
ConAu 5NR, –9R, IntAu&W 76, –77,
MorJA, SmATA 1, –29[port],
WhoAmW 58, –61, –64
Selvin, David F 1913- *ConAu 25R*
Selzer, Richard 1928- *ConAu 65*
Sen, Sudhir 1906- *ConAu 33R*
Senger, Valentin 1918- *BioIn 12*
Senior, Clarence 1903-1974 *AmAu&B,*
AmM&WS 73S, BioIn 6, –10, ConAu 53,
–65, CurBio 61, –74N, NewYTBS 74,
WhAm 6, WhoAm 74
Senn, Steve 1950- *ConAu 105*
Sennett, Richard 1943- *BioIn 11, ConAu 73,*
IntAu&W 82, WhoAm 82, WrDr 82, –84
Serafini, Anthony Louis 1943- *WhoE 81, –83*
Seraphine, Dan 1948- *BioNews 74*
Seraphine, Dan *see also* Chicago
Seredy, Kate 1899?-1975 *AmWomWr, AnCL,*
Au&ICB, AuBYP, BioIn 1, –2, –4, –5, –7,
–8, –9, –10, BkCL, ChhPo, ConAu 5R,
–57, CurBio 40, –75, –75N,
DcLB 22[port], IlsCB 1744, –1946,
InWom, JBA 51, LinLib L, Newb 1922,
SmATA 1, –24N, Str&VC, TwCCW 78,
–83, WhoAmA 73, WhoAmW 58, –61
Sergio, Lisa 1905- *ConAu 61, CurBio 44,*
InWom, WhoAmW 58, –75
Serif, Med 1924- *ConAu 17R, ODwPR 79,*
WhoPubR 72, –76
Serling, Robert 1918- *ConAu 1NR, –45,*
WhoE 74, WrDr 76, –80, –82, –84
Serling, Rod 1924-1975 *AmAu&B, AuNews 1,*
BioIn 4, –5, –6, –7, –10, CelR 73,
ConAu 57, –65, ConDr 73, CurBio 59,
–75, –75N, DcLB 26[port], EncO&P 80,
EncSF, FilmgC, IntMPA 75, –76,
LesBEnT[port], LinLib L, NewYTBS 75,
NewYTET, ObitOF 79, REnAL,
ScF&FL 1, WhAm 6, WhScrn 2,
WhoAm 74, WhoSciF, WhoWor 74,
WorAl, WorEFlm
Seroff, Victor I 1902-1979 *Au&Wr 6,*

Baker 78, BioIn 11, ConAu 25R, –85,
SmATA 12, –26N, WhoMus 72
Serraillier, Ian 1912- *Au&Wr 6, BioIn 9,*
ChlLR 2, ChhPo, –S1, –S2, ConAu 1R,
–1NR, IntWWP 77, –77X, LinLib L,
SmATA 1, ThrBJA, TwCCW 78, –83,
WhE&EA, WrDr 76, –80, –82, –84
Service, Robert William 1874-1958
AuBYP SUP, BioIn 1, –2, –3, –4, –5, –11,
–12, CanNov, CanWr, CasWL,
Chambr 3, ChhPo, –S1, –S2, –S3, CnDAL,
CnE&AP, CreCan 1, DcAmB S6,
DcLEL, EncSF, EvLB, LinLib L, –S,
LongCTC, MacDCB 78, NewC,
ObitOF 79, ObitT 1951, OxAmL, OxCan,
PenC ENG, REn, REnAL, ScF&FL 1,
SmATA 20, TwCA, TwCA SUP,
TwCWr, WebE&AL, WhDW, WhAm 3,
WhE&EA, WhLit, WhNAA, WhoLA,
WorAl
Seth, Ronald 1911- *Au&Wr 6, AuBYP,*
ConAu 106, EncE 75, WhoSpyF
Seth-Smith, Elsie K 1883- *ConAu X*
Seth-Smith, Elsie K *see also* Murrell, Elsie
Kathleen Seth Smith
Seton, Anya 1916- *AmAu&B, AmNov,*
AmWomWr, Au&Wr 6, BioIn 2, –3, –4,
–6, –9, ConAu 17R, CurBio 53, InWom,
IntAu&W 76, –77, –82, LongCTC, Novels,
OxAmL, PenC AM, REn, REnAL,
ScF&FL 1, –2, SmATA 3, TwCA SUP,
WhE&EA, Who 74, –82, –83, WhoAm 74,
–76, –78, –80, –82, WhoAmW 58, –58A,
–61, –64, –66, –68, –70, –72, –83,
WhoWor 74, –76, WorAl, WrDr 76, –80,
–82, –84
Settel, Gertrude S 1919- *ConAu 17R*
Settel, Trudy S 1919- *ConAu X*
Settle, Mary Lee 1918- *BioIn 3, –5, –7, –10,*
–12, ConAu 89, ConLC 19, CurBio 59,
DcLB 6[port], DrAP&F 83, InWom,
NewYTBS 80[port], Po&Wr 77,
WhoAm 80, –82, WhoAmW 81, –83,
WorAu
Settle, William Anderson, Jr. 1915- *DrAS 74H,*
–78H, –82H, WhoAm 74
Seuling, Barbara 1937- *BioIn 11,*
ConAu 8NR, –61, SmATA 10
Sevareid, Eric 1912- *AmAu&B, AuNews 1,*
BioIn 4, –5, –7, –8, –10, –11, –12,
BioNews 74, CelR 73, ConAu 69,
CurBio 42, –66, IntMPA 77, –75, –76, –78,
–79, –81, –82, –84, IntWW 74, –75, –76,
–77, –78, –79, –80, LesBEnT[port],
LinLib L, –S, NewYTBS 79, NewYTET,
WhoWor 74, WorAl
Severin, Timothy 1940- *Au&Wr 6,*
ConAu 10NR, –21R, IntAu&W 77,
–82, Who 82, –83, WrDr 76, –80, –82, –84
Severn, Bill 1914- *AuBYP, ConAu X,*
SmATA 1
Severn, Bill *see also* Severn, William Irving

Severn, David 1918- *AuBYP, BioIn 7, -12, BlueB 76, ConAu X, IntAu&W 76X, -77X, -82X, ScF&FL 1, -2, SmATA X, TwCCW 78, -83, Who 74, -82, -83, WrDr 76, -80, -82, -84*

Severn, David *see also* Unwin, David Storr

Severn, William Irving 1914- *BioIn 7, -9, ConAu 1R, -1NR, SmATA 1*

Severn, William Irving *see also* Severn, Bill

Severson, John H 1933- *BioIn 7, ConAu 13R*

Seward, Desmond 1935- *IntAu&W 77*

Sexton, Anne Harvey 1928-1974 *AmAu&B, AmWomWr, BioIn 7, -9, -10, -11, -12, BlueB 76N, CasWL, ChhPo S1, ConAu 1R, -3NR, -53, ConLC 2, -4, -6, -8, -10, -15, ConP 70, -75, -80A, CroCAP, DcLB 5[port], DcLEL 1940, DrAS 74E, -78E, -82E, ForWC 70, GoodHs, IntAu&W 76, IntDcWB, LibW, LinLib L, MakMC, ModAL, ModAL SUP, NewYTBS 74, NotAW MOD, ObitOF 79, PenC AM, RAdv 1, SmATA 10, WebE&AL, WhAm 6, WhoAm 74, WhoAmW 74, -68, -70, -72, -75, WhoE 74, WhoTwCL, WorAl, WorAu*

Sexton, Linda Gray 1953- *WrDr 84*

Seymour, Gerald 1941- *ConAu 101, Novels, WrDr 80, -82, -84*

Seymour, Miranda Jane 1948- *ConAu X, WrDr 80, -84*

Seymour-Smith, Martin 1928- *Au&Wr 6, ChhPo S2, ConAu 5R, ConP 70, -75, -80, DcLEL 1940, IntAu&W 77, -82, IntWWP 77, WhoWor 76, WorAu 1970, WrDr 76, -80, -82, -84*

Sgroi, Peter Philip 1936- *ConAu 57*

Sgroi, Suzanne M 1943- *ConAu 108, WhoAmW 77*

Shaara, Michael Joseph, Jr. 1929- *AuNews 1, BioIn 8, -10, ConAu 102, ConLC 15, DcLB Y83B[port], DrAS 74E, -78E, -82E, WhoAm 76, -78, -80, -82, WhoS&SW 78, -80, -82, WrDr 76, -80, -82, -84*

Shaff, Albert L 1937- *ConAu 29R*

Shaffer, Anthony 1926- *ConAu 110, WrDr 84*

Shaffer, Peter 1926- *Au&Wr 6, BiE&WWA, BioIn 7, -8, -9, -10, -11, -12, BlueB 76, CnMD, CnThe, ConAu 25R, ConDr 73, -77, -82, ConLC 5, -14, -18, CroCD, CurBio 67, DcLB 13[port], DcLEL 1940, EncMys, EncWT, IntAu&W 76, -77, IntWW 74, -75, -76, -77, -78, -79, -80, -81, -82, -83, McGEWD, -84, ModBrL SUP, ModWD, NewC, NewYTBS 75, NotNAT, PenC ENG, PIP&P, -A, REnWD, TwCCr&M 80, TwCWr, Who 74, -82, -83, WhoThe 15, -16, -81, WhoWor 74, -76, -78, -82, WorAl, WorAu, WrDr 76, -80, -82, -84*

Shah, Diane K 1945- *ConAu 73*

Shah, Idries 1924- *BioIn 10, -12, BlueB 76,*

ConAu 7NR, -17R, CurBio 76, EncO&P 78S1, IntAu&W 76, -77, -82, IntWWP 77, -82, IntYB 78, -79, -80, -81, -82, MakMC, MidE 78, -79, -80, -81, -82, WhoAm 76, -78, WhoRel 77, WhoWor 74, -76, WrDr 76, -80, -82, -84

Shah, Krishna Bhogilal 1938- *ConAu 17R, WhoE 74, -75*

Shahn, Ben 1898-1969 *AtlBL, BioIn 1, -2, -3, -4, -5, -6, -7, -8, -9, -10, -12, BnEnAmA, ChhPo S1, ConArt, -83, ConAu 89, ConPhot, CurBio 54, -69, DcAmArt, DcCAA 71, -77, EncAB-H, IlsCB 1957, -1967, McGDA, McGEWB, ObitOF 79, ObitT 1961, OxAmL, OxArt, OxTwCA, PhDcTCA 77, PrintW 83, REn, SmATA 21N, WhAm 5, WhoAmA 78N, -80N, -82N, WhoGrA, WorAl*

Shakespeare, William 1564-1616 *Alli, AnCL, AtlBL, BbD, BiD&SB, BioIn 1, -2, -3, -4, -5, -6, -7, -8, -9, -10, -11, -12, BrAu, BrWr 1, CarSB, CasWL, Chambr 1, -2, -3, ChhPo, -S1, -S2, -S3, CnE&AP, CnThe, CroE&S, CrtT 1, -4, CyWA, DcBiPP, DcEnA, -AP, DcEnL, DcEuL, DcLEL, Dis&D, EncWT, EvLB, FamAYP, FilmgC, LinLib L, -S, LongCEL, LuthC 75, McGEWB, McGEWD, -84[port], MouLC 1, NewC, NewEOp 71, NotNAT A, -B, OxEng, OxFilm, OxFr, OxGer, OxMus, OxThe, PenC ENG, PIP&P, -A, RComWL, REn, REnWD, WebE&AL, WhDW, WorAl*

Shange, Ntozake 1948- *BioIn 11, -12, ConAu 85, ConDr 82, ConLC 8, -25[port], CurBio 78, DrAP&F 83, DrBlPA, InB&W 80, NatPD, -81[port], NegAl 83, NewYTBS 76, -77, Po&Wr 77, SelBAA, WhoAm 80, -82, WhoAmW 83, WhoBlA 77, -80, WhoThe 81, WrDr 84*

Shankar, Ravi 1920- *AuBYP SUP, Baker 78, BioIn 6, -7, -8, -9, -11, CelR 73, CurBio 68, FarE&A 78, -79, -80, -81, IntWW 74, -75, -76, -77, -78, -79, -80, -81, -82, -83, IntWWM 77, WhoHol A, WhoMus 72, WhoRocM 82, WhoWor 74, WorAl, WorEFlm*

Shanks, Ann Zane Kushner *BioIn 11, ConAu 53, SmATA 10, WhoAm 78, -80, -82, WhoAmW 74, -70, -72, -75, -77, -79, WomWMM B*

Shannon, Doris 1924- *ConAu 8NR, -61, ScF&FL 1, -2, WrDr 80, -82, -84*

Shapiro, Fred C 1931- *ConAu 17R*

Shapiro, Harry L 1902- *AmAu&B, AmM&WS 73S, -76P, -79P, -82P, BioIn 3, -5, -12, BlueB 76, ConAu 49, CurBio 52, FifIDA, InSci, IntAu&W 77, -82, IntWW 74, -75, -76, -77, -78, -79, -80, -81, -82, -83, WhoAm 74, -76, -78, -80, WhoAmJ 80, WhoWor 74, WhoWorJ 72, WrDr 80, -82, -84*

Shapiro, Irwin 1911-1981 *AuBYP, BioIn 2, –7, ChhPo S1, ConAu 81, JBA 51, SmATA 32[port]*

Shapiro, James E 1946- *ConAu 108*

Shapiro, Karl Jay 1913- *AmAu&B, AnCL, BioIn 1, –4, –5, –7, –8, –10, –11, –12, BlueB 76, CasWL, CelR 73, ChhPo, –S2, –S3, CnDAL, CnE&AP, ConAu 1R, –1NR, ConLC 4, –8, –15, ConLCrt, –82, ConP 70, –75, –80, CroCAP, CurBio 44, DcLEL, DrAF 76, DrAP 75, DrAP&F 83, DrAS 74E, –78E, –82E, EncWL, EvLB, IntAu&W 77, IntWW 74, –75, –76, –77, –78, –79, –80, –81, –82, –83, IntWWP 77, LinLib L, ModAL, ModAL SUP, OxAmL, PenC AM, RAdv 1, REn, REnAL, SixAP, TwCA SUP, TwCWr, WebAB, –79, WebE&AL, WhE&EA, WhoAm 74, –76, –78, –80, –82, WhoTwCL, WhoWest 74, WhoWor 74, WhoWorJ 72, –78, WorAl, WrDr 76, –80, –82, –84*

Shapiro, Milton 1926- *AuBYP, BioIn 7, ConAu 81, SmATA 32[port], WhoAm 74, –76, –78, –80, –82*

Shapiro, Rebecca *AuBYP, BioIn 8*

Shapiro, Stanley 1937- *WhoF&I 83, WhoTech 82*

Shapley, Harlow 1885-1972 *AmAu&B, AmM&WS 73P, –76P, AsBiEn, BiESc, BioIn 1, –3, –4, –7, –9, –10, –11, ConAu 37R, CurBio 41, –52, –72, –72N, DcScB, EncAB-H, InSci, LinLib L, –S, McGEWB, McGMS 80[port], NewYTBE 72, ObitOF 79, OxAmH, REnAL, TwCA, TwCA SUP, WebAB, –79, WhDW, WhAm 5*

Sharmat, Marjorie Weinman 1928- *AuBYP SUP, BioIn 9, ConAu 25R, IntAu&W 76, –77, –82, SmATA 33[port], –4, TwCCW 78, –83, WhoAmW 74, –75, WrDr 76, –80, –82, –84*

Sharp, Harold S 1909- *BiDrLUS 70, ConAu 3NR, –9R, IntAu&W 76, –77, –82, WhoLibS 66*

Sharp, Margery 1905- *Au&Wr 6, AuBYP, BioIn 1, –2, –4, –8, –9, BlueB 76, ConAu 21R, ConNov 72, –76, –82, DcLEL, EvLB, IntAu&W 76, –77, IntWW 74, –75, –76, –77, –78, –79, –80, –81, –82, –83, LongCTC, NewC, RAdv 1, REn, ScF&FL 1, –2, SmATA 1, –29[port], ThrBJA, TwCA, TwCA SUP, TwCCW 78, –83, WhLit, WhThe, Who 74, –82, –83, WhoAmW 74, –68, –70, –72, WhoWor 74, –76, –78, WrDr 76, –80, –82, –84*

Sharp, Marilyn 1941?- *BioIn 11*

Sharpe, Mitchell R 1924- *Au&Wr 6, BioIn 11, ConAu 29R, SmATA 12, WhoS&SW 75, –76, WrDr 76, –80, –82, –84*

Sharpe, Roger Carter 1948- *ConAu 93*

Shattuck, Roger Whitney 1923- *AmAu&B, Au&Wr 6, BioIn 10, BlueB 76, ConAu 5R, –7NR, DrAP 75, DrAP&F 83, DrAS 74F, –78F, –82F, IntAu&W 76, –77, –82, IntWWP 77, –82, WhoAm 74, –76, –78, –80, –82, WorAu, WrDr 76, –80, –82, –84*

Shavelson, Melville 1917- *CmMov, ConAu 4NR, –53, FilmgC, IntMPA 77, –75, –76, –78, –79, –81, –82, –84, WhoAm 74, –76, –78, –80, –82, WorEFlm*

Shaw, Arnold 1909- *AmSCAP 66, AuBYP SUP, Baker 78, BioIn 3, –9, CpmDNM 82, ConAmC, ConAu 1R, –1NR, ScF&FL 1, SmATA 4, Who 74, –82, –83, WhoAm 74, –76, –78, –80, –82, WhoAmM 83, WhoE 74, WhoWor 78*

Shaw, Bob 1931- *ConAu 1NR, –49, ConSFA, EncSF, IntAu&W 77, –82, Novels, ScF&FL 1, –2, WhoSciF, WrDr 76, –80, –82, –84*

Shaw, David 1943- *ConAu 49*

Shaw, George Bernard 1856-1950 *Alli SUP, AtlBL, Baker 78, BiD&SB, BioIn 1, –2, –3, –4, –5, –6, –7, –8, –9, –10, –11, –12, BrWr 6, CasWL, Chambr 3, ChhPo, –S2, –S3, CnMD, CnMWL, CnThe, ConAu 104, DcAmSR, DcBiA, DcEnA AP, DcIrB, DcIrW 1, –2, DcLEL, Dis&D, EncSF, EncWL, EncWT, EvLB, Film 2, LinLib L, –S, LongCEL, LuthC 75, MakMC, McGEWB, McGEWD, –84[port], ModBrL, ModBrL SUP, ModWD, NewC, NotNAT, –B, Novels, ObitOF 79, OxEng, OxMus, OxThe, PenC ENG, PIP&P, RComWL, REn, REnWD, ScF&FL 1, TwCA, TwCA SUP, TwCLC 3, TwCWr, WebE&AL, WhDW, WhAm 3, WhE&EA, WhLit, WhScrn 2, WhoStg 1906, –1908, WhoTwCL, WorAl*

Shaw, Irwin 1913- *AmAu&B, AmNov, Au&Wr 6, AuNews 1, BiE&WWA, BioIn 1, –2, –4, –5, –6, –7, –8, –10, –12, BlueB 76, CelR 73, CnDAL, CnMD, CnThe, ConAu 13R, ConDr 73, –77, –82, ConLC 7, –23[port], ConNov 72, –76, –82, CurBio 42, DcLB 6[port], DcLEL, DrAF 76, DrAP&F 83, EncWL, EncWT, FilmgC, IntAu&W 76, –77, –82, IntWW 74, –75, –76, –77, –78, –79, –80, –81, –82, –83, LinLib L, LongCTC, McGEWD, –84, ModAL, ModWD, NewYTBS 80[port], –83[port], NotNAT, Novels[port], OxAmL, PenC AM, PIP&P, RAdv 1, REn, REnAL, TwCA, TwCA SUP, TwCWr, Who 74, –82, –83, WhoAm 74, –76, –78, –80, –82, WhoThe 15, –16, –81, WhoTwCL, WhoWor 74, –78, –80, –82, WorAl, WorEFlm, WrDr 76, –80, –82, –84*

Shaw, Peter 1936- *ConAu 9NR, –65,*

DrAS 74E, –78E, –82E

Shaw, Richard 1923- *BioIn 11, ChhPo S2, –S3, ConAu 37R, DrAP 75, SmATA 12, WrDr 76, –80, –82, –84*

Shaw, Robert 1927-1978 *AuNews 1, BiDrAPA 77, BiE&WWA, BioIn 4, –6, –7, –8, –9, –10, –11, BlueB 76, CelR 73, ConAu 1R, –4NR, –81, ConDr 73, –77, ConLC 5, ConNov 72, –76, CroCD, CurBio 49, –66, –68, –78, –78N, DcLB 13[port], –14[port], DcLEL 1940, EncWT, FilmgC, IntAu&W 76, –77, IntMPA 77, –75, McGEWD, MovMk, NewYTBE 70, –72, NewYTBS 78, –80[port], NotNAT, ObitOF 79, PIP&P, –A, TwCWr, WhAm 7, Who 74, WhoAdv 72, WhoAm 76, –78, –82, WhoHol A, WhoS&SW 80, –82, WhoThe 15, –16, –81N, WhoWor 74, WorAl, WorAu, WrDr 76*

Shaw, Robert Byers 1916- *AmM&WS 73S, –78S, ConAu 37R, DrAS 74H, –78H, –82H*

Shay, Arthur 1922- *BioIn 9, ConAu 33R, SmATA 4, WhoAm 74, –76, –78, WhoMW 74, –76*

Shcharansky, Avital 1951?- *BioIn 12*

Shea, Michael *EncSF, ScF&FL 1*

Shearer, John 1947- *SmATA 27*

Sheats, Mary Boney 1918- *ConAu 13R, DrAS 74P, –78P, –82P*

Sheats, Mary Boney *see also* Boney, Mary Lily

Shebar, Sharon Sigmond 1945- *ConAu 103, SmATA 36, WhoE 83*

Sheckley, Robert 1928- *BioIn 12, ConAu 1R, –2NR, ConSFA, DcLB 8[port], EncSF, IntAu&W 77, Novels, ScF&FL 1, –2, WhoSciF, WrDr 84*

Shecter, Ben 1935- *AuBYP, BioIn 8, –12, ChhPo S1, ConAu 81, IlsCB 1957, –1967, ScF&FL 1, SmATA 16, ThrBJA, WrDr 76, –80, –82, –84*

Shedd, Charlie W 1915- *BioIn 10, –12, ConAu 17R*

Shedley, Ethan I *ConAu X*

Sheean, Vincent 1899-1975 *AmAu&B, AmNov, AuBYP SUP, BioIn 1, –2, –3, –4, –5, –10, CnDAL, ConAmA, ConAu 61, CurBio 41, –75, –75N, IntAu&W 76, –77, LinLib L, NewYTBS 74, –75, ObitOF 79, OxAmL, REn, REnAL, ScF&FL 1, –2, TwCA, TwCA SUP*

Sheed, Wilfrid 1930- *AmCath 80, BioIn 8, –10, –11, –12, ConAu 65, ConLC 2, –4, –10, ConNov 72, –76, –82, CurBio 81[port], DcLB 6[port], DrAF 76, DrAP&F 83, IntAu&W 76, ModAL SUP, NewC, WhoAm 74, –76, –78, –80, –82, WorAu, WrDr 76, –80, –82, –84*

Sheehan, Susan 1937- *Au&Wr 6, ConAu 21R, WhoAmW 74, –75, –77, –81, –83, WrDr 76, –80, –82, –84*

Shefter, Harry 1910- *ConAu 9R*

Sheldon, Alice Hastings 1915- *BioIn 12, ConAu 108, WrDr 84*

Sheldon, Alice Hastings *see also* Tiptree, James, Jr.

Sheldon, Mary 1955?- *BioIn 12*

Sheldon, Walter J 1917- *AuBYP, AuNews 1, BioIn 10, ConAu 10NR, –25R*

Shellabarger, Samuel 1888-1954 *AmAu&B, AmNov, BioIn 1, –2, –3, –4, –7, CnDAL, CurBio 45, –54, DcAmB S5, NatCAB 40, –47, ObitOF 79, OhA&B, REn, REnAL, TwCA SUP, WhAm 3*

Shelley, Mary Wollstonecraft 1797-1851 *Alli, AtlBL, BbD, BiD&SB, BioIn 1, –2, –3, –4, –5, –7, –8, –9, –10, –11, –12, BrAu 19, CasWL, Chambr 3, ChhPo, –S1, –S3, CrtT 4, CyWA, DcBiA, DcBiPP, DcEnA, DcEnL, DcEuL, DcLEL, EncMys, EncSF, EvLB, FilmgC, HerW, InWom, IntDcWB, LinLib L, –S, MouLC 3, NewC, Novels[port], OxEng, PenC ENG, RAdv 1, REn, ScF&FL 1, SmATA 29[port], WebE&AL, WhDW, WhoHr&F, WhoSciF, WorAl*

Shelley, Percy Bysshe 1792-1822 *Alli, AtlBL, BbD, BiD&SB, BioIn 1, –2, –3, –4, –5, –6, –7, –8, –9, –10, –11, –12, BrAu 19, BrWr 4, CasWL, CelCen, Chambr 3, ChhPo, –S1, –S2, –S3, CnE&AP, CnThe, CrtT 2, –4, CyWA, DcBiPP, DcEnA, DcEnL, DcEuL, DcLEL, Dis&D, EncWT, EvLB, IlEncMy, LinLib L, –S, LongCEL, McGEWB, McGEWD, –84[port], MouLC 2, NewC, NotNAT B, OxThe, PenC ENG, RAdv 1, RComWL, REn, REnWD, ScF&FL 1, WebE&AL, WhDW, WorAl*

Shelnutt, Eve *DrAP&F 83*

Shelton, William Roy 1919- *AuBYP SUP, AuNews 1, BiDrAPA 77, BioIn 2, –10, ConAu 5R, –11NR, IntAu&W 76, –77, –82, ScF&FL 1, –2, SmATA 5, WhoS&SW 76, –78*

Shen, Ts'ung-Wen 1902?- *BioIn 9, CasWL, DcOrL 1*

Shenton, Edward 1895- *AmAu&B, BioIn 1, –2, –5, IlrAm E, IlsBYP, IlsCB 1744, –1946*

Shenton, James Patrick 1925- *AmAu&B, BlueB 76, ConAu 2NR, –5R, DrAS 74H, –78H, –82H, WhoAm 74, –76, –78, –80, –82, WrDr 80, –82, –84*

Shepard, Sam 1942?- *BioIn 10, –11, –12, BioNews 74, ConAu 69, ConDr 73, –77, –82, ConLC 4, –6, –17, CroCD, CurBio 79, DcLB 7[port], DcLEL 1940, EncWT, IntMPA 81, –82, –84, McGEWD 84, ModAL SUP, NatPD, –81[port], NewYTBS 80[port], NotNAT, PIP&P, WhoAm 74, –76, –78, –80, –82,*

WhoRocM 82, WhoThe 16, –81,
WorAu 1970, WrDr 76, –80, –82, –84

Shepard, Thomas Rockwell, Jr. 1918-
ConAu 105, St&PR 75, WhoAdv 72,
WhoAm 74, –76, –78, –80, –82, WhoE 74,
–75, –77, –79, –81, WhoF&I 74, –75, –77,
–79, –81

Shephard, Esther 1891-1975 *BioIn 1, –10,*
ConAu 57, ConAu P-2, DrAS 74E,
SmATA 26N, –5, WhoAmW 58

Shepherd, Walter Bradley 1904- *Au&Wr 6,*
ConAu 105, WhE&EA

Shepherd, William Robert 1871-1934 *DcAmAu,*
DcAmB S1, DcNAA, HarEnUS,
WhAm 1

Sheppard, Harold L 1922- *AmM&WS 73S,*
ConAu 1NR, –45, IntAu&W 76,
WhoS&SW 76

Sherburne, Zoa 1912- *AuBYP, BioIn 8, –9,*
ConAu 1R, –3NR, EncSF, ForWC 70,
FourBJA, ScF&FL 1, –2, SmATA 3,
WhoAmW 66, –68, –70, –72, WhoPNW

Sheridan, Richard Brinsley 1751-1816 *Alli,*
AtlBL, BbD, BiD&SB, BiDLA, BioIn 1,
–2, –3, –4, –5, –6, –7, –8, –9, –10, –11, –12,
BrAu, BrWr 3, CasWL, CelCen,
Chambr 2, ChhPo, CnThe, CrtT 2, –4,
CyWA, DcBiPP, DcEnA, DcEnL,
DcEuL, DcInB, DcIrB, DcIrL, DcIrW 1,
DcLEL, EncWT, EvLB, LinLib L, –S,
LongCEL, McGEWB, McGEWD,
–84[port], MouLC 2, NewC,
NewEOp 71, NotNAT A, –B, OxEng,
OxThe, PenC ENG, PIP&P, PoIre, REn,
REnWD, WebE&AL, WhDW, WorAl

Sherlock, John 1932- *ConAu 3NR, –9R,*
IntAu&W 77

Sherlock, Philip Manderson 1902- *AnCL,*
Au&Wr 6, AuBYP, BioIn 7, –9,
BlueB 76, ConAu 5R, –6NR, ConP 70,
DcAfL, IntAu&W 77, Who 74, –82, –83,
WhoWor 74, –76, WrDr 80, –82, –84

Sherman, D R 1934- *ConAu 8NR, –13R,*
SmATA 29

Sherman, Diane 1928- *BioIn 11, ConAu 5NR,*
–9R, SmATA 12

Sherman, Roger 1930- *AmEA 74,*
ConAu 37R, DrAS 74E, –78E,
IntAu&W 77, –82, WrDr 76, –80, –84

Sherriff, Robert Cedric 1896-1975 *Au&Wr 6,*
BiE&WWA, BioIn 2, –4, –5, –8, –10,
Chambr 3, CnMD, CnThe, ConAu 61,
ConDr 73, CroCD, CyWA, DcLEL,
EncWT, EvLB, IntAu&W 76,
IntMPA 75, IntWW 74, –75, –76N,
LongCTC, McGEWD, ModBrL, ModWD,
NewC, NewYTBS 75, NotNAT A, –B,
OxEng, OxThe, PenC ENG, REn,
TwCA, TwCA SUP, TwCWr, WhE&EA,
WhThe, Who 74, WhoThe 15,
WhoWor 74

Sherrill, Elizabeth 1928- *ConAu 110*

Sherrod, Jane *ConAu X, SmATA 4*

Sherwin, Judith Johnson 1936- *ConAu 25R,*
ConLC 7, –15, ConP 75, –80,
DcLEL 1940, DrAF 76, DrAP 75,
DrAP&F 83, IntAu&W 76, –77, –82,
IntWWP 77, –82, WhoAm 76, –78, –80,
–82, WhoAmW 79, –81, –83, WrDr 76,
–80, –82, –84

Sherwin, Martin Jay 1937- *ConAu 110,*
DrAS 74H, –78H

Sherwood, Debbie *ConAu 25R, WhoAmW 74,*
–75, WrDr 76, –80, –82, –84

Sherwood, Robert Emmett 1896-1955 *AmAu&B,*
BioIn 1, –2, –4, –5, –6, –7, –9, –12, CasWL,
CnDAL, CnMD, CnThe, ConAmA,
ConAu 104, CurBio 40, –56, CyWA,
DcAmB S5, DcLB 7[port], –26[port],
DcLEL, EncWL, EncWT, EvLB, FilmgC,
LinLib L, –S, LongCTC, McGEWB,
McGEWD, –84[port], ModAL, ModWD,
NotNAT A, –B, ObitOF 79, ObitT 1951,
OxAmL, OxThe, PenC AM, PIP&P,
REn, REnAL, REnWD, TwCA SUP,
TwCLC 3, TwCWr, WebAB, –79,
WebE&AL, WhAm 3, WhE&EA,
WhThe, WorAl

Shevey, Sandra *WomWMM B*

Shikes, Ralph Edmund 1912- *ConAu 29R,*
IntAu&W 77, –82, WrDr 76, –80, –82, –84

Shimer, Dorothy Blair 1911- *ConAu 45,*
DrAS 74E, –78E, –82E, WhoAmW 74, –68,
–70, –75, –77, –79, WomPO 76

Shipler, David Karr 1942- *ConAu 103,*
WhoAm 76, –78, –80, –82

Shipley, Joseph Twaddell 1893- *AmAu&B,*
AnMV 1926, BioIn 2, BlueB 76, ChhPo,
–S1, ConAmTC, ConAu 9NR, –13R,
IntAu&W 76, –82, NotNAT, REnAL,
WhJnl, WhNAA, WhoAm 74, –76, –78,
–80, –82, WhoThe 15, –16, –81, WrDr 76,
–80, –82, –84

Shippen, Katherine Binney 1892-1980 *AnCL,*
AuBYP, BioIn 2, –3, –6, –7, –9, –12,
ConAu 5R, –93, CurBio 54, InWom,
IntAu&W 76, MorJA, SmATA 1, –23N,
Str&VC

Shirer, William Lawrence 1904- *AmAu&B,*
Au&Wr 6, AuBYP, BioIn 1, –2, –3, –4, –6,
–7, –8, –11, –12, BlueB 76, ConAu 7NR,
–9R, CurBio 41, –62, DcLB 4, EncTR,
IntAu&W 76, –77, –82, IntWW 74, –75,
–76, –77, –78, –79, –80, –81, –82, –83,
LinLib L, NewYTBS 82[port], OxAmL,
REn, REnAL, TwCA SUP, WebAB, –79,
WhE&EA, Who 74, –82, –83, WhoAm 74,
–76, –78, –80, –82, WhoWor 74, –78,
WorAl, WrDr 76, –80, –82, –84

Shirreffs, Gordon Donald 1914- *AuBYP,*
BioIn 7, –11, ConAu 6NR, –13R,
IntAu&W 76, SmATA 11, WrDr 76, –80,
–82, –84

Shirts, Morris A 1922- *ConAu 73, LEduc 74*

Shockley, Robert Joseph 1921- *LEduc 74*

Sholokhov, Mikhail Aleksandrovich 1905-1984
*AuBYP SUP, BioIn 1, –4, –5, –6, –7, –9,
–10, –11, –12, CasWL, ClDMEL,
CnMWL, ConAu 101, ConLC 7, –15,
CurBio 42, –60, CyWA, DcRusL, EncWL,
EvEuW, IntAu&W 76, –77, IntWW 74,
–75, –76, –77, –78, –79, –80, –81, –82, –83,
LinLib L, –S, LongCTC, MakMC,
McGEWB, ModSL 1, Novels,
PenC EUR, REn, SmATA 36N, TwCA,
TwCA SUP, TwCWr, Who 74, –82, –83,
WhoSocC 78, WhoTwCL, WhoWor 74,
–82, WorAl*

Shook, Robert L 1938- *ConAu 8NR, –61*

Shore, Jane 1947- *ConAu 77, DrAP 75,
DrAP&F 83, Po&Wr 77*

Shorris, Earl 1936- *ConAu 10NR, –65*

Short, Lester LeRoy, Jr. 1933- *AmM&WS 73P,
–76P, –79P, –82P, WhoE 75*

Short, Robert Lester 1932- *ConAu 77,
WhoMW 74, –76*

Shostak, Stanley 1938- *AmM&WS 73P, –76P,
–79P, –82P*

Shotwell, Louisa Rossiter 1902- *AuBYP SUP,
BioIn 3, –9, –10, ConAu 1R, –4NR,
MorBMP, SmATA 3, ThrBJA,
TwCCW 78, –83, WhoAmW 58,
WrDr 76, –80, –82, –84*

Shoumatoff, Alex 1946- *ConAu 9NR, –53*

Shrader, Robert Louis 1913- *WhoWest 74, –76*

Shreve, Susan E 1952- *ConAmC*

Shreve, Susan Richards 1939- *ConAu 5NR,
–49, ConLC 23[port], DrAP&F 83,
WrDr 76, –80, –82, –84*

Shriver, Donald Woods, Jr. 1927- *ConAu 1NR,
–45, DrAS 74P, –78P, –82P, WhoAm 80,
–82, WhoE 81, –83, WhoRel 75*

Shroyer, Frederick Benjamin 1916- *AmAu&B,
ConAu 13R, DrAS 74E, –78E, –82E,
IndAu 1917, WhoAm 74, –76, –78, –80,
–82, WhoWest 74, –76, WhoWor 78, –80,
–82*

Shu, Ch'ing-Ch'un 1898?-1966 *BioIn 10,
ConAu 109, CurBio 45, DcOrL 1,
PenC CL*

Shulman, Alix Kates 1932- *BioIn 10,
ConAu 29R, ConLC 2, –10, DrAF 76,
DrAP&F 83, SmATA 7, WhoAmW 74,
–75*

Shulman, Arthur 1927- *WhoAm 74, –76, –78,
–80, –82*

Shultz, Gladys Denny 1895- *ConAu 49,
WhoAmW 58, –61, WhoWest 78, –80*

Shuman, James B 1932- *ConAu 61*

Shura, Mary Francis 1923- *BioIn 9, –10, –12,
ConAu X, ForWC 70, IntAu&W 77X,
–82X, SmATA 6, ThrBJA, WrDr 76, –80,
–82, –84*

Shura, Mary Francis *see also* Craig, Mary
Francis

Shurkin, Joel N 1938- *ConAu 69*

Shute, Nevil 1899-1960 *BioIn 3, –4, –5, –7,
ConAu X, CurBio 42, –60, DcLEL,
EncSF, EvLB, FilmgC, InSci, LinLib LP,
LongCTC, ModBrL, NewC, Novels,
ObitOF 79, ObitT 1951, PenC ENG,
REn, ScF&FL 1, TwCA, TwCA SUP,
TwCCr&M 80, TwCWr, WhAm 3, –4,
WhoTwCL, WorAl*

Shuttle, Penelope 1947- *ConAu 93, ConP 80,
DcLB 14[port], Who 82, WrDr 82*

Shuttlesworth, Dorothy Edwards 1907- *AuBYP,
BioIn 7, –9, ConAu 1R, –4NR, ForWC 70,
SmATA 3, WhoAmW 58, –61*

Shuy, Roger W 1931- *ConAu 61, DrAS 74F,
–78F, –82F*

Shwartz, Susan Martha 1949- *ConAu 109*

Shyer, Marlene Fanta *BioIn 11,
ConAu 11NR, –69, SmATA 13,
WhoAmW 81*

Sibley, Mulford Quickert 1912-
*AmM&WS 73S, –78S, ConAu 5R, –6NR,
DrAS 74H, –78H, –82H, IntAu&W 76,
WhoMW 76*

Siddons, Anne Rivers *ConAu 101*

Siebert, Richard W 1912- *WhoProB 73*

Siedel, James Meredith 1937- *ConAu 25R,
WhoMW 74, –76, –78*

Siegal, Aranka 1930- *SmATA 37*

Siegal, Mordecai 1934- *ConAu 102*

Siegel, Beatrice *ConAu 101, SmATA 36*

Siegel, Benjamin 1914- *ConAu 1R, –4NR,
WhoE 75, –77, WrDr 76, –80, –82, –84*

Siegel, Dorothy Schainman 1932- *ConAu 9R,
ForWC 70, WhoAmW 72*

Siegel, Marcia B 1932- *ConAu 69*

Siegel, Maxwell E 1933- *BioIn 8, ConAu 101*

Siegel, Richard Lewis 1940- *AmM&WS 73S,
–78S, ConAu 73, WhoWest 84*

Siegel, Robert 1939- *BioIn 12, ConAu 5NR,
DrAP&F 83, DrAS 74E, –78E, –82E*

Siegelman, Jim *ConAu X*

Siegmeister, Elie 1909- *AmAu&B,
AmSCAP 66, Au&Wr 6, AuBYP,
Baker 78, BiDAmM, BiE&WWA,
BioIn 1, –2, –7, –8, –9, –11, BlueB 76,
CompSN SUP, ConAmC, ConAu 1R,
–1NR, DcCM, IntWWM 77, NotNAT,
OxMus, WhoAm 74, –76, –78, –80, –82,
WhoAmJ 80, WhoAmM 83, WhoE 83,
WhoMus 72, WhoWorJ 72, WrDr 76, –80,
–82, –84*

Sienkiewicz, Henryk 1846-1916 *AtlBL, BbD,
BiD&SB, BioIn 1, –5, –7, –8, –9, CasWL,
ClDMEL, CmCal, ConAu 104, CyWA,
DcBiA, DcCathB, DcEuL, EncWL,
EuAu, EvEuW, LinLib L, –S, LongCTC,
McGEWB, ModSL 2, NotNAT A, –B,
Novels, PenC EUR, REn, WhDW,
WhLit, WorAl*

Sievers, Harry J 1920-1977 *BioIn 11,
ConAu 25R, –73, DrAS 74H, LEduc 74,
NewYTBS 77, WhAm 7, WhoAm 74, –76,*

DrAS 74P, –78P, –82P, WhoRel 75, –77

Simon, Anne W 1914- *ConAu 105,*
WhoAmW 74, –68, –70, –72, –75, –79, –81

Simon, Carly 1945- *BiDAmM, BioIn 9, –10,*
–11, –12, CelR 73, ConAu 105,
ConLC 26[port], CurBio 76, EncPR&S,
–77, GoodHs, HerW, IlEncRk,
NewYTBS 74, –77, RkOn 78, –84,
RolSEnR 83, WhoAm 74, –76, –78, –80,
–82, WhoAmW 81, –83, WhoRocM 82,
WorAl

Simon, Charlie May 1897-1977 *AmAu&B,*
AuBYP, BioIn 1, –2, –3, –7, –9, –11, –12,
ConAu X, CurBio 46, InWom, JBA 51,
NatCAB 60[port], SmATA 3, WhE&EA,
WhoAm 74, –76, –78, WhoAmW 74, –58,
–64, –66, –68, –70, –72, WhoWor 76

Simon, Charlie May *see also* Fletcher, Charlie
May Hogue

Simon, Edith 1917- *Au&Wr 6, BioIn 3, –10,*
ConAu 13R, CurBio 54, InWom,
IntAu&W 76X, ScF&FL 1, –2, WorAu,
WrDr 76, –80, –82, –84

Simon, George Thomas 1912- *BioIn 8,*
ConAu 25R, IntAu&W 77, –82,
WhoAm 74, –76, –78, –80, –82

Simon, Hilda Rita 1921- *AuBYP, BioIn 8,*
ConAu 77, FourBJA, IlsCB 1957, –1967,
SmATA 28

Simon, Howard 1903-1979 *BioIn 1, –5, –6, –8,*
–9, –12, ChhPo, ConAu 33R, –89, IlsBYP,
IlsCB 1744, –1946, –1957, –1967, MorJA,
NewYTBS 79, SmATA 21N, –32[port],
WhoAmA 73, –76, –78, –80N, –82N

Simon, John 1925- *BiE&WWA, BioIn 10, –11,*
ConAmTC, ConAu 21R, NotNAT,
WhoAm 76, –78, –80, –82, WhoThe 15, –16,
WorAu

Simon, Kate Grobsmith *BioIn 6, –12,*
WhoAmW 74, –66, –68, –70, –72, WhoE 74

Simon, Neil 1927- *AmAu&B, AuNews 1,*
BiE&WWA, BioIn 6, –7, –8, –9, –10, –11,
–12, BlueB 76, CelR 73, CnThe,
ConAu 21R, ConDr 73, –77, –82,
ConLC 6, –11, CroCD, CurBio 68,
DcLB 7[port], EncMT, EncWT, FilmgC,
IntAu&W 76, –77, IntMPA 77, –75, –76,
–78, –79, –81, –82, –84, IntWW 74, –75,
–76, –77, –78, –79, –80, –81, –82, –83,
LesBEnT[port], LinLib L, McGEWD,
–84[port], ModAL, ModWD,
NatPD 81[port], NewCBMT,
NewYTBE 70, –71, NewYTBS 75, –78,
–81[port], –83[port], NewYTET, NotNAT,
PIP&P, –A, WebAB, –79, Who 74, –82,
–83, WhoAm 74, –76, –78, –80, –82,
WhoAmJ 80, WhoThe 15, –16, –81,
WhoWor 74, –78, WorAl, WorAu,
WrDr 76, –80, –82, –84

Simon, Paul 1941?- *BiDAmM, BioIn 7, –8, –9,*
–10, –11, –12, BlueB 76, CelR 73,
ConLC 17, CurBio 75, EncPR&S, –77,

IlEncRk, NewYTBE 72,
NewYTBS 82[port], RkOn 84, RkOneH,
RolSEnR 83, WhoAm 74, –76, –78, –80,
–82, WhoRocM 82, WhoWor 74, WorAl

Simon, Seymour 1931- *AuBYP SUP, BioIn 9,*
ConAu 11NR, –25R, SmATA 4,
WrDr 76, –80, –82, –84

Simpson, Colin 1908- *Au&Wr 6, BioIn 6, –12,*
ConAu 5NR, –53, IntAu&W 76, –77, –82,
SmATA 14, WrDr 76, –80, –82, –84

Simpson, Eileen B *BioIn 11, –12*

Simpson, George Eaton 1904- *AmM&WS 73S,*
–78S, BioIn 5, ConAu 77, FifIDA,
WhoAm 74, –76

Simpson, George Gaylord 1902- *AmAu&B,*
AmM&WS 73P, –76P, –79P, –82P,
Au&Wr 6, BiESc, BioIn 1, –3, –4, –7, –11,
BlueB 76, ConAu P-1, CurBio 64,
FifIDA, IntWW 74, –75, –76, –77, –78, –79,
–80, –81, –82, –83, McGMS 80[port],
TwCA SUP, WebAB, –79, WhoAm 74,
–76, –78, –80, –82, WhoWor 74, –78, –82

Simpson, Howard N *BiDrACP 79*

Simpson, Jacqueline Mary 1930- *Au&Wr 6,*
ConAu 5NR, –13R, IntAu&W 76, –77, –82,
WhoWor 78, WrDr 76, –80, –82, –84

Simpson, Louis Aston Marantz 1923- *BioIn 7,*
–8, –9, –10, –12, BlueB 76, ChhPo, –S1,
–S3, CnE&AP, ConAu 1R, ConLC 4, –7,
–9, ConP 70, –75, –80, CroCAP,
CurBio 64, DcAfL, DcLB 5[port],
DcLEL 1940, DrAF 76, DrAP 75,
DrAP&F 83, DrAS 82E, IntWW 79, –80,
–81, –82, –83, IntWWP 77, –82, LinLib L,
ModAL, ModAL SUP,
NewYTBS 82[port], OxAmL, PenC AM,
RAdv 1, REn, REnAL, WebE&AL,
WhoAm 74, –76, –78, –80, –82, WhoE 74,
WhoTwCL, WhoWor 74, WorAl, WorAu,
WrDr 76, –80, –82, –84

Simpson, O J 1947- *BioIn 12, CelR 73,*
CmCal, ConAu 103, CurBio 69, DrBlPA,
IntMPA 84, NegAl 76, –83,
NewYTBE 70, –73, NewYTBS 75, –76,
WhoAm 76, –78, –80, –82, WhoHol A,
WorAl

Simpson, O J *see also* Simpson, Orenthal James

Simpson, Orenthal James 1947- *BioIn 8, –9,*
–10, –11, –12, InB&W 80, WhoAm 74,
WhoBlA 77, –80, WhoFtbl 74

Simpson, Orenthal James *see also* Simpson, O J

Simpson, William Hood 1888-1980 *BioIn 1, –3,*
–12, HisEWW, WebAMB

Sims, Edward Howell 1923- *AmAu&B,*
Au&Wr 6, ConAu 1R, –6NR,
WhoAm 74, –76, –78, –80, –82,
WhoWor 74, –76

Sims, Naomi 1949- *BioIn 8, –9, –10, –12,*
ConAu 69, Ebony 1, InB&W 80,
NegAl 76[port], –83[port], WhoAm 76,
–78, –80, –82, WhoBlA 75, –77, –80

Sims, Patsy 1938- *ConAu 110, WhoAmW 74,*

–72, –75

Sinclair, Andrew 1935- *Au&Wr 6, BioIn 10, ConAu 9R, ConLC 2, –14, ConNov 72, –76, –82, DcLB 14[port], DcLEL 1940, IntAu&W 76, –77, –82, IntMPA 77, –75, –76, –78, –79, –81, –82, –84, NewC, Novels, RAdv 1, ScF&FL 1, –2, Who 74, –82, –83, WhoWor 78, WorAu, WrDr 76, –80, –82, –84*

Sinclair, Harold Augustus 1907-1966 *AmAu&B, AmNov, BioIn 2, –4, –7, –9, ConAu 5R, ObitOF 79, REnAL, TwCA, TwCA SUP, WhAm 4, WhE&EA*

Sinclair, Upton 1878-1968 *AmAu&B, AmNov, ApCAB X, AuBYP, BiDPara, BioIn 1, –2, –4, –5, –6, –8, –9, –10, –11, –12, CasWL, Chambr 3, ChhPo S1, CmCal, CnDAL, ConAmA, ConAmL, ConAu 5R, –7NR, –25R, ConLC 1, –11, –15, CurBio 62, –69, CyWA, DcAmAu, DcAmSR, DcLB 9[port], DcLEL, EncAAH, EncAB-H, EncO&P 78, EncSF, EncWL, EvLB, LinLib L, –S, LongCTC, McGEWB, ModAL, NatCAB 14, Novels, ObitOF 79, ObitT 1961, OxAmH, OxAmL, OxEng, OxFilm, PenC AM, RAdv 1, REn, REnAL, ScF&FL 1, –2, SmATA 9, TwCA, TwCA SUP, TwCWr, WebAB, –79, WebE&AL, WhDW, WhE&EA, WhLit, WhNAA, WhoTwCL, WorAl, WorEFlm*

Singer, B *AmM&WS 79P, –82P*

Singer, David L 1937- *ConAu 73, WhoCon 73*

Singer, Isaac Bashevis 1904- *AmAu&B, AmWr, AnCL, ASpks, Au&Wr 6, AuBYP, AuNews 1, –2, BioIn 6, –7, –8, –9, –10, –11, –12, BlueB 76, CasWL, CelR 73, ChlLR 1, ChhPo S3, ConAu 1R, –1NR, ConLC 1, –3, –6, –9, –11, –15, –23[port], ConNov 72, –76, –82, CurBio 69, DcLB 6[port], DrAF 76, EncWL, IntAu&W 76, –77, IntWW 74, –75, –76, –77, –78, –79, –80, –81, –82, –83, LinLib L, –S, McGEWB, ModAL SUP, MorBMP, NewYTBE 70, –72, NewYTBS 75, –78, –79, Novels[port], PenC AM, ScF&FL 1, –2, SmATA 27[port], –3, ThrBJA, TwCCW 78, –83, TwCWr, WebAB, –79, WebE&AL, Who 82, –83, WhoAm 74, –76, –78, –80, –82, WhoAmJ 80, WhoE 74, –79, –81, –83, WhoTwCL, WhoWor 74, –78, –80, –82, WorAl, WorAu, WrDr 76, –80, –82, –84*

Singer, Isaac Merritt 1811-1875 *AmBi, ApCAB, BioIn 2, –5, –6, –7, –9, –11, DcAmB, NatCAB 5, –30, TwCBDA, WebAB, WhDW, WhAm HS*

Singer, Joy Daniels 1928- *ConAu 29R, WhoAmW 83, WhoE 81, –83*

Singer, Kurt Deutsch 1911- *AmAu&B, Au&Wr 6, BioIn 3, ConAu 2NR, –49,*

CurBio 54, ScF&FL 1, –2, WhoAm 74, –76, –78, –80, –82, WhoHr&F, WhoWest 74, –76, –78, WhoWor 74, –76

Singer, Marilyn Phyllis 1931- *WhoAmJ 80, WhoE 79, –81*

Singer, Peter 1946- *ConAu 8NR, –57, WrDr 84*

Singer, Samuel L 1911- *ConAu 65, IntWWM 77, WhoAm 74, –76, –78, –80, –82, WhoAmJ 80*

Singh, Arjan 1919- *ConAu 49, FarE&A 78, –79, IntAu&W 76, IntWW 74, –75, –76, –77, –78, –79, –80, –81, –82, –83, WhoWor 74, –78*

Sirof, Harriet 1930- *ConAu 104, SmATA 37*

Sisson, Rosemary Anne 1923- *Au&Wr 6, BioIn 11, ConAu 13R, SmATA 11, WhoWor 76, WrDr 76, –80, –82, –84*

Sive, Helen R 1951- *ConAu 107, SmATA 30[port]*

Sjowall, Maj 1935- *BioIn 9, –10, ConAu X, ConLC 7, EncMys, NewYTBE 71, Novels, WorAl, WorAu 1970*

Skagen, Kiki 1943- *ConAu 37R*

Skaggs, Calvin Lee 1937- *DrAS 74E, –78E*

Skarda, Patricia Lyn 1946- *ConAu 106, DrAS 74E, –78E, –82E*

Skelton, Geoffrey 1916- *Au&Wr 6, ConAu 1NR, –49, IntAu&W 77, –82, WhoMus 72, WrDr 76, –80, –82, –84*

Skinner, B F 1904- *BlueB 76, CelR 73, ConIsC 2[port], CurBio 64, –79, EncSF, Future, GuPsyc[port], IntEnSS 79, WorAl, WorAu 1970, WrDr 80, –82, –84*

Skinner, Burrhus Frederic 1904- *AmAu&B, AmM&WS 73S, –78S, Au&Wr 6, BiDAmEd, BioIn 1, –6, –7, –8, –9, –10, –11, –12, ConAu 9R, EncAB-H, IntWW 74, –75, –76, –77, –78, –79, –80, –81, –82, –83, MakMC, McGEWB, McGMS 80[port], WebAB, –79, WhDW, Who 82, –83, WhoAm 74, –76, –78, –80, –82, WhoWor 74, WrDr 76*

Skinner, Cornelia Otis 1901-1979 *AmAu&B, AmWomWr, Au&Wr 6, BiE&WWA, BioIn 1, –2, –3, –4, –5, –7, –9, –12, BlueB 76, CelR 73, ChhPo, ConAu 17R, –89, CurBio 42, –64, –79N, DcLEL, EncWT, EvLB, FilmgC, InWom, IntAu&W 76, –77, IntWW 74, –75, –76, –77, –78, –79N, LinLib L, LongCTC, NewYTBS 79, NotNAT, –A, OxAmL, OxThe, PenC AM, REn, REnAL, SmATA 2, TwCA SUP, TwCWr, Who 74, WhoAm 74, –76, –78, WhoAmW 74, –58, –61, –64, –66, –68, –70, –72, WhoHol A, WhoThe 15, –16, –81N, WhoWor 74, –78, –80, WorAl, WrDr 76, –80*

Skinner, Elliott Percival 1924- *AmM&WS 73S, –76P, ConAu 13R, FifIDA, InB&W 80, NegAl 76, –83, WhoBlA 77, –80*

Skinner, June 1922- *Au&Wr 6, ConAu 1R, –5R, ScF&FL 1, WrDr 84*

Skinner, Quentin 1940- *Who 82, –83, WrDr 82, –84*

Skjei, Eric William 1947- *ConAu 97*

Sklar, Morty 1935- *ConAu 77, DrAP&F 83, IntWWP 77, –82, Po&Wr 77*

Sklar, Robert Anthony 1936- *AmAu&B, ConAu 8NR, –21R, DrAS 74H, –78E, –82E, WhoAm 74, –76, –78, –80, –82, WhoWor 74, WrDr 76, –80, –82, –84*

Sklare, Arnold Beryl 1924- *ConAu 17R, DrAS 74E, –78E, –82E*

Skolnik, Peter L 1944- *ConAu 57*

Skornia, Harry Jay 1910- *ConAu P-2, IntAu&W 77, –82, WhoAm 74, –76, –78, –80, WhoWor 74, –76, WrDr 76, –80, –82, –84*

Skoyles, John 1949- *ConAu 104, DrAP&F 83, IntWWP 82, Po&Wr 77*

Skulicz, Matthew V 1944- *ConAu 37R*

Skurzynski, Gloria 1930- *BioIn 11, ConAu 33R, SmATA 8*

Skutch, Alexander F 1904- *BioIn 9, –11, –12, ConAu 33R, IntAu&W 77, –82, WrDr 76, –80, –82, –84*

Slade, Afton 1919- *ConAu 89*

Slade, Jack *IntAu&W 77X*

Slade, Richard 1910-1971 *Au&Wr 6, BioIn 11, ConAu 21R, ConAu P-2, SmATA 9*

Sladek, John T 1937- *ConAu 25R, ConSFA, EncSF, ScF&FL 1, –2, WhoSciF, WrDr 84*

Slater, Jim 1929- *BioIn 9, BlueB 76, SmATA 34*

Slater, Joy 1954?- *BioIn 12*

Slaughter, Frank Gill 1908- *AmAu&B, AmNov, Au&Wr 6, AuNews 2, BioIn 1, –2, –3, –4, –5, –7, –10, –11, ConAu 5R, –5NR, CurBio 42, InSci, IntAu&W 76, –77, –82, LongCTC, Novels, PenC AM, REnAL, ScF&FL 1, –2, TwCA SUP, Who 74, –82, –83, WhoAm 74, –76, –78, –80, –82, WhoWor 74, –76, WrDr 76, –80, –82, –84*

Slaughter, Jean *AuBYP SUP, ConAu X, SmATA X*

Slaughter, Jean see also Doty, Jean Slaughter

Sleator, William 1945- *BioIn 9, ConAu 29R, ScF&FL 1, –2, SmATA 3*

Slesar, Henry 1927- *ConAu 1R, –1NR, EncSF, TwCCr&M 80, WhoSciF, WrDr 76, –80, –82, –84*

Slick, Grace 1939?- *BiDAmM, BioIn 8, –9, –10, –11, –12, CelR 73, CurBio 82[port], GoodHs, IntDcWB, WhoAm 74, –76, –78, –80, –82, WhoAmW 74, –70, –72, –79, –81, –83, WhoRocM 82, WorAl*

Slick, Grace see also Jefferson Airplane

Sliwa, Curtis 1954?- *BioIn 12, CurBio 83[port]*

Sloan, Irving J 1924- *ConAu 7NR, –17R*

Sloane, Eric 1910- *AmAu&B, ConAu 108, CurBio 72, IlBEAAW, IlsCB 1957, WhoAm 74, –76, –78, WhoAmA 73, –76, –78, –80, –82*

Sloane, Eugene A 1926- *ConAu 65*

Sloane, William Milligan, III 1906-1974 *AmAu&B, ConAu 53, WhAm 6, WhE&EA*

Slobodkin, Florence Gersh 1905- *BioIn 10, ConAu 1R, SmATA 5*

Slobodkin, Louis 1903-1975 *AmAu&B, AuBYP, BioIn 1, –2, –4, –5, –7, –8, –9, –10, BkCL, BkP, Cald 1938, ChhPo, ConAu 13R, –57, CurBio 57, –75, –75N, IlsBYP, IlsCB 1744, –1946, –1957, –1967, JBA 51, NewYTBS 75, ObitOF 79, REnAL, ScF&FL 1, –2, SmATA 1, –26[port], TwCCW 78, –83, WhAm 6, WhoAm 74, WhoAmA 73, –76N, –78N, –80N, –82N, WhoWorJ 72, –78*

Slocombe, Lorna Lowry 1914- *WhoAmW 58, –61, –64, –66, –68, –70*

Slote, Alfred 1926- *AuBYP SUP, BioIn 11, ChlLR 4[port], SmATA 8*

Small, Alice Jean 1918- *WhoAmW 74, –75, –77, –79, –81, WhoWest 74, –76, –78*

Small, David 1937- *ConAu 108*

Smaridge, Norah 1903- *AuBYP, BioIn 8, –10, ConAu 37R, SmATA 6*

Smart, Ninian 1927- *Au&Wr 6, ConAu 29R, DrAS 78P, –82P, Who 74, –82, –83, WrDr 76, –80, –82, –84*

Smedley, Agnes 1894?-1950 *AmAu&B, AmWomWr, BioIn 2, –4, –10, –12, CurBio 44, –50, DcAmB S4, InWom, IntDcWB, LibW, NotAW, ObitOF 79, TwCA, TwCA SUP, WhAm 3*

Smith, Agnes *AuBYP, BioIn 7, WhoAm 74, –76, –78, –80, –82, WhoAmW 74, –64, –66, –68*

Smith, Anne Warren 1938- *SmATA 34*

Smith, Anthony 1938- *ConAu 10NR, –53, Who 82*

Smith, Beatrice S *BioIn 11, ConAu 10NR, –57, SmATA 12*

Smith, Betty 1896-1972 *AmAu&B, AmNov, AmWomWr, CnDAL, ConAu 5R, –33R, ConLC 19, CurBio 43, –72, CyWA, DcLB Y82B[port], DcLEL 1940, LongCTC, NewYTBE 72, NotNAT B, ObitOF 79, OxAmL, PenC AM, REn, REnAL, SmATA 6, TwCA SUP, WhAm 5, WhE&EA, WhoAmW 61, –66, –68, –70, –72*

Smith, Bradley 1910- *BioIn 7, ConAu 2NR, –5R*

Smith, Charles Merrill *BioIn 10, –11*

Smith, Clark Ashton 1893-1961 *BioIn 12, ChhPo, –S1, CmCal, EncSF, ScF&FL 1, WhNAA, WhoHr&F*

Smith, Cordelia Titcomb 1902- *BiDrLUS 70,*

ConAu P-1, ConSFA, ScF&FL 1, –2, WhoLibS 55, –66

Smith, Curt 1951- *ConAu 81*

Smith, Datus Clifford, Jr. 1907- *AuBYP SUP, BioIn 7, –11, BlueB 76, ConAu 11NR, ConAu P-1, SmATA 13, WhoAm 74, –76, –78, –80, –82, WhoWor 74*

Smith, Dave 1942- *ConAu X, ConLC 22[port], ConP 80, DcLB 5[port], DrAP&F 83, DrRegL 75, WrDr 82, –84*

Smith, Dave *see also* Smith, David Jeddie

Smith, David Bruce 1923- *WhoS&SW 82*

Smith, David Jeddie 1942- *BioIn 12, ConAu 1NR, –49, DrAF 76, DrAP 75*

Smith, David Jeddie *see also* Smith, Dave

Smith, Dennis 1940- *BioIn 12, ConAu 10NR, –61, DrAP&F 83, WhoAm 82, WhoE 79, WrDr 80, –82, –84*

Smith, Dinitia *DrAP&F 83*

Smith, Dodie 1896- *Au&Wr 6, BiE&WWA, BioIn 12, Chambr 3, ConAu 33R, ConDr 77, –82, DcLB 10[port], DcLEL, IntAu&W 82, IntWW 77, –78, –79, –80, –81, –82, –83, LongCTC, McGEWD, –84, NewC, NotNAT, PIP&P, REn, ScF&FL 1, SmATA 4, TwCCW 83, WhE&EA, Who 74, –82, –83, WhoThe 15, –16, –81, WhoWor 74, –76, –78, WorAu, WrDr 76, –82, –84*

Smith, Doris Buchanan 1934- *AuBYP SUP, ConAu 11NR, –69, SmATA 28[port]*

Smith, E E 1890-1965 *DcLB 8[port], EncSF, Novels, ScF&FL 1, WhoSciF*

Smith, Edward Elmer 1890-1965 *BioIn 12*

Smith, Eleanor Touhey 1910- *BiDrLUS 70, ConAu 25R, ForWC 70, WhoAmW 74, –64, –66, –68, –70, –72, –75, –77, WhoLibI 82, WhoLibS 55, –66*

Smith, Elsdon Coles 1903- *AmAu&B, ConAu 1R, –6NR, DrAS 74E, –78F, –82F, IntAu&W 77, –82, IntYB 78, –79, –80, –81, –82, WhoAm 74, –76, –78, –80, WrDr 76, –80, –82, –84*

Smith, Emma 1923- *AuBYP, BioIn 8, ConAu 73, ConNov 72, –76, –82, DcLEL 1940, IntAu&W 76, –77, –82, LongCTC, SmATA 36, TwCCW 78, –83, Who 74, –82, –83, WrDr 76, –80, –82, –84*

Smith, Ethel Sabin 1887- *ConAu P-1, IntAu&W 77, WhoAmW 58, WrDr 76, –80, –82, –84*

Smith, Frank Kingston 1919- *BioIn 5, –10, ConAu 102*

Smith, Gary Milton 1943- *ConAu 97*

Smith, Gary Richard 1932- *BioIn 12, ConAu 69, SmATA 14*

Smith, George O 1911-1981 *BioIn 12, ConAu 103, –97, DcLB 8[port], EncSF, NewYTBS 81, ScF&FL 1, –2, WhoSciF, WrDr 84*

Smith, Grahame J C 1942- *AmM&WS 73P, –76P, –79P, –82P*

Smith, Harry Allen 1907-1976 *AmAu&B, BioIn 1, –3, –4, –6, –10, –11, –12, ChhPo, TwCA SUP, WhE&EA*

Smith, Hedrick 1933- *BlueB 76, ConAu 11NR, –65, IntAu&W 82, WhoAm 76, –78, –80, –82, WhoS&SW 73, WorAl, WrDr 80, –82, –84*

Smith, Henry Nash 1906- *AmAu&B, BlueB 76, ConAu 1R, –2NR, DrAS 74E, –78E, –82E, IntAu&W 77, –82, IntWW 74, –75, –76, –77, –78, –79, –80, –81, –82, –83, REnAL, REnAW, WhoAm 74, –76, –78*

Smith, Howard E, Jr. 1927- *ConAu 25R, SmATA 12, WrDr 76, –80, –82, –84*

Smith, Joan 1938- *WrDr 84*

Smith, Joseph Burkholder 1921- *BioIn 12, ConAu 65, WhoS&SW 80, –82*

Smith, Kay Nolte 1932- *ConAu 101*

Smith, Ken 1902- *ConAu 1NR, –45*

Smith, Lacey Baldwin 1922- *AmAu&B, ConAu 5R, –6NR, DrAS 74H, –78H, –82H, WhoAm 74, –76, –78, –80, –82, WrDr 76, –80, –82, –84*

Smith, LeRoi 1934- *AuBYP SUP, ConAu 29R, WhoAm 82, WhoWest 74*

Smith, Lillian Eugenia 1897-1966 *AmAu&B, AmNov, AmWomWr, BioIn 2, –3, –4, –6, –7, –8, –9, –12, CnDAL, ConAu 25R, ConAu P-2, CurBio 44, –66, DcAmSR, EncSoH, InWom, LinLib L, LongCTC, NotAW MOD, ObitOF 79, OxAmL, REn, REnAL, TwCA SUP, WhAm 4, WhE&EA, WhoAmW 58, –64, –66*

Smith, Lou 1918- *ConAu 73*

Smith, Michael Townsend 1935- *BioIn 10, ConAu 11NR, –21R, ConDr 73, –77, –82, WhoAm 74, –76, –78, –80, –82, WrDr 76, –80, –82, –84*

Smith, Nancy Covert 1935- *BioIn 11, ConAu 10NR, –57, SmATA 12*

Smith, Norman F 1920- *BioIn 10, ConAu 29R, SmATA 5*

Smith, Norman Lewis 1941- *ConAu 77, WhoE 81, –83*

Smith, Page 1917- *AmAu&B, ConAu 1R, –2NR, DrAS 74H, –78H, –82H, WhoAm 74, WrDr 80, –82, –84*

Smith, Patrick John 1932- *ConAu 41R, IntWWM 77, WhoAmM 83*

Smith, Patti 1946?- *BioIn 10, –11, –12, ConAu 93, ConLC 12, EncPR&S 77S, NewRR 83, RolSEnR 83, WhoRocM 82, WorAl*

Smith, Pauline C 1908- *ConAu 29R, SmATA 27[port]*

Smith, Red 1905-1982 *AnObit 1982[port], BioIn 1, –2, –3, –4, –5, –6, –10, –11, –12, CelR 73, ConAu X, –77, CurBio 59, –82N, NewYTBS 82[port], REnAL, WebAB, –79, WhoAm 76, –78, –80, –82*

Smith, Red *see also* Smith, Walter Wellesley

LinLib L, ModAL SUP, MugS,
PenC AM, RAdv 1, REn, REnAL,
WebE&AL, WhoAm 74, –76, –78, –80, –82,
WhoE 74, –77, –79, WhoWor 74, WorAu,
WrDr 76, –80, –82, –84

Snyder, Gerald S 1933- *ConAu 61,*
SmATA 34

Snyder, Jerome 1916-1976 *ConAu 65, IlsBYP,*
IlsCB 1957, WhoGrA

Snyder, Louis L 1907- *AuBYP, BioIn 8,*
BlueB 76, ConAu 1R, –2NR, DrAS 74H,
–78H, –82H, IntAu&W 76, –77,
WhoAm 74, –76, –78, WhoE 74,
WhoWor 74, –76, WrDr 76, –80, –82, –84

Snyder, Zilpha Keatley 1927- *AmWomWr,*
AuBYP, BioIn 8, –9, –10, ConAu 9R,
ConLC 17, MorBMP, ScF&FL 1, –1A, –2,
SmATA 1, –28[port], ThrBJA,
TwCCW 78, –83, WhoAm 82, WrDr 80,
–82, –84

Sobel, Robert 1931- *AmArch 70, ConAu 5R,*
–8NR, DrAS 74H, –78H, –82H,
ScF&FL 1, –2

Sobol, Donald J 1924- *AuBYP, BioIn 8, –9,*
ChlLR 4[port], ConAu 1R, –1NR,
FourBJA, SmATA 1, –31[port],
TwCCW 78, –83, WhoAm 78, –80, –82,
WhoAmJ 80, WhoWor 80, –82, WrDr 84

Sobol, Harriet Langsam 1936- *ConAu 8NR,*
–61, SmATA 34

Sobol, Rose 1931- *ConAu 101*

Sohn, David A 1929- *ConAu 6NR, –9R,*
IndAu 1917, ScF&FL 1, –2, WhoMW 74,
–76

Sokolov, Sasha 1944?- *BioIn 11, ConAu X,*
–73

Solberg, Carl 1915- *ConAu 73*

Solbert, Romaine G 1925- *BioIn 9, –12,*
ConAu 29R, SmATA 2

Solbert, Romaine G *see also* Solbert, Ronni G

Solbert, Ronni G 1925- *BioIn 5, –8, –12,*
ChhPo S2, –S3, ConAu X, IlsBYP,
IlsCB 1946, –1957, –1967, SmATA 2

Solbert, Ronni G *see also* Solbert, Romaine G

Solensten, John M 1929- *ConAu 110,*
DrAS 74E

Solomon, Louis 1910?-1981 *AuBYP, BioIn 8,*
–12

Solzhenitsyn, Aleksandr Isayevich 1918-
AuNews 1, BioIn 7, –8, –9, –10, –11, –12,
BioNews 74, CasWL, ConAu 25R, –69,
ConLC 1, –2, –4, –7, –9, –10, –18, –26[port],
DcPol, EncWL, IntAu&W 76, –77,
IntWW 74, –75, –76, –77, –78, –79, –80, –81,
–82, –83, IntYB 78, –79, –80, –81, –82,
LinLib L, –S, MakMC, McGEWB,
ModSL 1, NewYTBE 70, –72,
NewYTBS 74, –80[port], Novels[port],
PenC EUR, RComWL, REn, TwCWr,
WhDW, Who 74, –82, –83, WhoAm 76,
–78, –80, –82, WhoTwCL, WhoWor 74,
–78, –80, –82, WorAl, WorAu

Somer, John Laddie 1936- *ConAu 37R,*
DrAS 78E, –82E

Somerlott, Robert 1928- *ConAu 105,*
ScF&FL 1A

Somerville, Lee 1915- *ConAu 69*

Somma, Robert 1944- *BioIn 10, MugS*

Sommer, Elyse 1929- *AuBYP SUP, BioIn 10,*
ConAu 2NR, –49, SmATA 7

Sommer, Scott 1951- *ConAu 106,*
ConLC 25[port]

Sommerfelt, Aimee 1892- *AuBYP,*
ConAu 37R, SmATA 5, ThrBJA,
TwCCW 78B, –83B

Sonnabend, Roger P 1925- *BioIn 8,*
St&PR 75, WhoAm 74, –76, –78, –80,
WhoAmJ 80, WhoE 74, WhoWorJ 72,
–78

Sootin, Harry *AuBYP, BioIn 7*

Soper, Tony 1939- *ConAu 105, WrDr 80, –82,*
–84

Sorel, Julia *ConAu X*

Sorell, Walter 1905- *ConAu 21R, WhoE 74*

Sorensen, Theodore Chaikin 1928- *AmAu&B,*
BioIn 5, –6, –7, –8, –11, BlueB 76,
ConAu 2NR, –45, CurBio 61,
IntAu&W 77, IntWW 74, –75, –76, –77,
–78, –79, –80, –81, –82, –83, PolProf K,
WhoAm 74, –76, –78, –80, –82,
WhoAmP 73, –75, –77, –79, –81, –83,
WhoWor 74, –78

Sorensen, Virginia 1912- *AmAu&B, AmNov,*
Au&Wr 6, AuBYP, BioIn 2, –4, –6, –7, –9,
–10, ConAu 13R, CurBio 50, InWom,
MorBMP, MorJA, NewbC 1956,
SmATA 2, TwCA SUP, TwCCW 78, –83,
WhoAm 74, –76, –78, –80, –82,
WhoAmW 58, –72, WhoWor 74,
WrDr 76, –80, –82, –84

Sorrentino, Gilbert 1929- *BioIn 7, –12,*
ConAu 77, ConLC 3, –7, –14, –22[port],
ConNov 82, ConP 70, –75, –80,
DcLB Y80B[port], –5[port], DrAF 76,
DrAP 75, DrAP&F 83, IntAu&W 77,
IntWWP 77, PenC AM, RAdv 1,
WhoAm 80, –82, WrDr 76, –80, –82, –84

Sorrentino, Joseph N 1937- *ConAu 3NR, –49,*
SmATA 6

Soto, Gary 1952- *ChiSch, DrAP 75,*
DrAP&F 83

Soto, Pedro Juan 1928- *BioIn 12, DcCLAA,*
EncWL, ModLAL, PueRA

Soule, Gardner Bosworth 1913- *AuBYP SUP,*
BioIn 12, ConAu 2NR, –5R, SmATA 14,
WhoAm 74, –76, –78, –80, –82,
WhoWor 78

South, Joe 1942?- *BioIn 8, EncPR&S, –77,*
IlEncRk, RkOn 74, –82, RolSEnR 83,
WhoRocM 82

South, Malcolm Hudson 1937- *ConAu 107,*
DrAS 74E, –78E, –82E

South, Wesley W 1919- *WhoBlA 77, –80*

Southall, Ivan 1921- *Au&Wr 6, AuBYP,*

*Chambr 3, ChhPo, –S2, –S3, CnE&AP,
CnMD, CnMWL, ConAu 9R, ConLC 1,
–2, –5, –10, ConLCrt, –82, ConP 70, –75,
–80, CurBio 40, –77, CyWA,
DcLB 20[port], DcLEL, EncWL, EvLB,
IntAu&W 76, –77, IntWW 74, –75, –76,
–77, –78, –79, –80, –81, –82, –83,
IntWWP 77, LinLib L, –S, LongCEL,
LongCTC, MakMC, ModBrL,
ModBrL SUP, ModWD, NewC, OxEng,
PenC ENG, RAdv 1, REn, TwCA,
TwCA SUP, TwCWr, WebE&AL,
WhDW, WhE&EA, Who 74, –82, –83,
WhoAm 76, WhoTwCL, WhoWor 74, –78,
–80, –82, WorAl, WrDr 76, –80, –82, –84*

Sperber, Murray A 1940- *ConAu 61*

Sperry, Armstrong W 1897-1976 *AmPB, AnCL,
AuBYP, BioIn 1, –2, –4, –5, –7, –9, –10,
ConAu 107, ConAu P-1, CurBio 41,
IlsCB 1744, –1946, JBA 51, LinLib L,
Newb 1922, SmATA 1, –27N, Str&VC,
TwCCW 78, –83*

Spicer, Dorothy Gladys d1975 *AuBYP,
BioIn 8, ConAu 1R, –4NR, ForWC 70,
SmATA 32, WhoAmW 58, –61, –64*

Spicer, Keith 1934- *CanWW 79, –80, –81, –83*

Spielberg, Steven 1947- *BioIn 10, –11, –12,
ConAu 77, ConLC 20, CurBio 78,
FilmgC, IntMPA 77, –75, –76, –78, –79, –81,
–82, –84, IntWW 83, NewYTBS 82[port],
SmATA 32[port], WhoAm 78, –80, –82*

Spies, Werner 1937- *ConAu 37R*

Spinner, Stephanie 1943- *ChhPo S2,
ConAu 45*

Spinrad, Norman 1940- *Au&Wr 6, BioIn 12,
ConAu 37R, ConSFA, DcLB 8[port],
DrAF 76, EncSF, IntAu&W 76, Novels,
ScF&FL 1, –2, WhoSciF, WhoWest 76,
WrDr 76, –80, –82, –84*

Spires, Elizabeth 1952- *ConAu 106,
DrAP&F 83*

Splaver, Sarah 1921- *AuBYP SUP, ConAu 85,
SmATA 28, WhoAmJ 80, WhoAmW 74,
–58, –61, –64, –66, –68, –70, –72, –75, –77,
–79, –81, WhoE 74, –75, –77, –79, –81,
WhoWorJ 72, –78*

Spock, Benjamin 1903- *AmAu&B, Au&Wr 6,
AuNews 1, BioIn 3, –4, –5, –6, –7, –8, –9,
–10, –11, –12, BioNews 74, BlueB 76,
CelR 73, ConAu 21R, CurBio 56, –69,
EncAB-H, InSci, IntWW 74, –75, –76, –77,
–78, –79, –80, –81, –82, –83, LinLib L,
MakMC, MugS, NewYTBE 72,
PolProf J, PolProf NF, REnAL, WebAB,
–79, Who 74, –82, –83, WhoAm 74, –76,
–78, –80, –82, WhoAmP 73, –75, –77, –79,
–81, –83, WhoWor 74, –78, WorAl,
WrDr 76, –80, –82, –84*

Sprague, Gretchen 1926- *AuBYP, BioIn 8,
ConAu 13R, SmATA 27[port]*

Sprague, Ken 1945- *ConAu 108*

Sprague, Marshall 1909- *ConAu 1R, –1NR,*

DrAS 74H, –78H, –82H, OhA&B

Sprague, Rosemary 1922?- *AmWomWr,
AuBYP, BioIn 8, ConAu 17R,
DrAS 74E, –78E, –82E, OhA&B,
WhoAmW 74, –68, –72*

Spring, Norma 1917- *ConAu 61*

Springer, Marilyn Harris 1931- *ConAu 9NR,
–21R*

Springer, Marilyn Harris *see also* Harris, Marilyn

Springer, Nancy 1948- *ConAu 101,
DrAP&F 83*

Springfield, Rick 1949- *BioIn 12, RkOn 78,
–84, RolSEnR 83, WhoRocM 82*

Springsteen, Bruce 1949- *BioIn 10, –11, –12,
BioNews 74, ConLC 17, CurBio 78,
EncPR&S 77S, IntWW 82, –83, RkOn 78,
–84, RolSEnR 83, WhoAm 80, –82,
WhoRocM 82, WorAl*

Springstubb, Tricia 1950- *ConAu 105,
DrAP&F 83*

Sprunt, Alexander, Jr. 1898-1973 *BioIn 1, –9,
ConAu 37R, EncAB 21, WhAm 5*

Spyker, John Howland 1918- *ConAu 101*

Spykman, Elizabeth Choate 1896-1965 *BioIn 6,
–7, –11, MorJA, SmATA 10,
TwCCW 78*

Squire, Elizabeth 1919- *ConAu 13R*

Squires, Radcliffe 1917- *ConAu 1R, –6NR,
ConP 70, –75, –80, DrAP 75, DrAS 74E,
–78E, –82E, IntWWP 77, WrDr 76, –80,
–82, –84*

Stableford, Brian M 1948- *ConAu 57, EncSF,
IntAu&W 82, Novels, ScF&FL 1, –2,
WhoSciF, WrDr 76, –80, –82, –84*

Stachow, Hasso G 1924- *ConAu 109*

Stafford, Jean 1915-1979 *AmAu&B, AmNov,
AmWomWr, BioIn 2, –3, –4, –7, –11, –12,
BlueB 76, CnDAL, ConAu 1R, –3NR, –85,
ConLC 4, –7, –19, ConNov 72, –76,
CurBio 51, –79N, DcLB 2, DcLEL 1940,
DrAF 76, EncWL, InWom,
IntAu&W 76, –77, LinLib L, ModAL,
NewYTBS 79, Novels, OxAmL,
PenC AM, RAdv 1, REn, REnAL,
SmATA 22N, TwCA SUP, WhAm 7,
WhoAm 74, –76, –78, WhoAmW 74, –58,
–64, –66, –68, –70, –72, WhoE 74,
WhoTwCL, WhoWor 74, WorAl,
WrDr 76, –80*

Stafford, Kim R 1949- *ConAu 69,
DrAP&F 83, IntWWP 77*

Stafford, William Edgar 1914- *AmAu&B,
BioIn 8, –10, –11, –12, BlueB 76, ChhPo,
–S1, –S3, ConAu 5R, –5NR, ConLC 4, –7,
ConP 70, –75, –80, CroCAP,
DcLB 5[port], DcLEL 1940, DrAP 75,
DrAP&F 83, DrAS 74E, –78E, –82E,
IntWWP 77, LinLib L, ModAL SUP,
OxAmL, PenC AM, RAdv 1,
WhoAm 74, –76, –78, –80, –82, WhoPNW,
WorAu, WrDr 76, –80, –82, –84*

Stahl, Ben 1910- *BioIn 1, –2, –7, –8, –10, –11,*

−12, ConAu 29R, IlsCB 1967,
ScF&FL 1, −2, WhoAm 74, −76, −78, −80,
−82, WhoAmA 73, −76, −78, −80, −82,
WhoS&SW 73, −75, −76, WhoWor 80, −82
Staicar, Tom *ConAu X*
Stall, Sylvanus 1847-1915 *Alli SUP, ApCAB,*
DcAmAu, DcNAA, LuthC 75, WhAm 1
Stallman, Robert Wooster 1911-1982 *AmAu&B,*
Au&Wr 6, ConAu 1R, −3NR, DrAS 74E,
−78E, −82E, NewYTBS 82, REnAL,
WhoAm 74, −76, −78, −80, −82, WhoE 74
Stallone, Sylvester 1946- *BioIn 11, −12,*
ConAu 77, CurBio 77, IntMPA 78, −79,
−81, −82, −84, NewYTBS 76, WhoAm 78,
−80, −82, WorAl
Stallworth, Anne Nall 1935- *ConAu 85,*
IntAu&W 82
Stalvey, Lois Mark 1925- *BioIn 9, −10, −12,*
ConAu 29R, WhoAmW 75, WrDr 76, −80,
−82, −84
Stamaty, Mark Alan 1947- *BioIn 11, −12,*
ConAu 61, IlsCB 1967, SmATA 12,
WhoGrA 82[port]
Stamberg, Susan 1938- *BioIn 10, −12,*
ConAu 103
Stambler, Irwin 1924- *AuBYP, BioIn 8, −10,*
ConAu 2NR, −5R, IntAu&W 76,
SmATA 5, WrDr 76, −80, −82, −84
Stampp, Kenneth M 1912- *AmAu&B,*
ConAu 13R, DcLB 17[port], DrAS 74H,
−78H, −82H, IntAu&W 77, −82,
WhoAm 74, −76, −78, −80, −82,
WhoWor 74, WrDr 76, −80, −82, −84
Stanbury, David 1933- *Au&Wr 6,*
ConAu 104
Standen, Michael Fred George 1937-
WhoWor 76
Standing Bear, Luther 1868-1947 *AmAu&B,*
DcNAA, REnAL, WhNAA
Standish, Carole *IntAu&W 82X*
Stands-In-Timber, John 1884-1967 *BioIn 8, −9*
Stanek, Carolyn 1951- *ConAu 107*
Stanford, Barbara 1943- *ConAu 37R,*
IntAu&W 77, LEduc 74, WrDr 76, −80,
−82, −84
Stanford, Derek 1918- *Au&Wr 6, ChhPo S2,*
ConAu 9R, ConP 70, DcLEL 1940,
IntAu&W 77, IntWWP 77, −82, ModBrL,
NewC, WrDr 82, −84
Stanford, Don 1918- *ConAu 53*
Stanford, Gene 1944- *ConAu 37R, LEduc 74*
Stankevich, Boris 1928- *BioIn 9, ConAu 21R,*
SmATA 2
Stanley, Sir Henry Morton 1841-1904 *Alli SUP,*
AmAu&B, AmBi, ApCAB, BbD,
BiD&SB, BioIn 1, −2, −3, −4, −5, −6, −7, −8,
−9, −10, −11, −12, BrAu 19, CarSB,
CelCen, Chambr 3, DcAmAu, DcAmB,
DcBiPP, DcBrBI, DcEnA, −AP, EvLB,
HarEnUS[port], LinLib L, −S, LuthC 75,
McGEWB, NatCAB 4, OxAmH, OxAmL,
OxEng, REn, REnAL, WebAB, −79,

WhDW, WhAm 1, WorAl
Stansbury, Donald Lloyd 1929- *ConAu 37R,*
WhoWest 76, −78, −80, −82
Stanton, Stephen Sadler 1915- *DrAS 74E,*
−78E, −82E
Stapledon, Olaf 1886-1950 *DcLB 15[port],*
EncSF, Novels, ScF&FL 1, −2, WhoSciF
Stapler, Harry Bascom 1919- *ConAu 61,*
WhoMW 74, −76, −78, −80, −82
Starbird, Kaye 1916- *AuBYP, BioIn 10,*
ChhPo, −S1, −S3, ConAu 17R, SmATA 6
Starkey, Marion L 1901- *BioIn 11,*
ConAu 1R, −1NR, ForWC 70,
SmATA 13, −8, WhoAmW 58, −61, −64,
WrDr 76, −80, −82, −84
Starr, Bart 1934- *BioIn 7, −8, −9, −10, −11, −12,*
BioNews 75, CurBio 68,
NewYTBS 81[port], WorAl
Starr, Bart *see also* Starr, Byran B
Starr, Byran B 1934- *WhoFtbl 74*
Starr, Byran B *see also* Starr, Bart
Starr, Ringo 1940- *Baker 78, BioIn 6, −7, −8,*
−9, −10, −11, −12, BlueB 76, CelR 73,
CurBio 65, EncPR&S, −77, IlEncRk,
IntWW 74, −75, −76, −77, −78, −79, −80, −81,
−82, −83, MotPP, RkOn 78, −84,
RolSEnR 83, WhoAm 78, −80, −82,
WhoHol A, WhoRocM 82, WhoWor 74,
−78, −80, −82, WorAl
Starr, Ringo *see also* Beatles, The
Stasheff, Christopher 1944- *ConAu 10NR, −65,*
EncSF, ScF&FL 1, WhoE 79
Stasheff, Edward 1909- *BiE&WWA,*
ConAu 5R, DrAS 74E, −78E, −82E,
WhoAm 76, −78
Statler, Oliver 1915- *Au&Wr 6, ConAu 5R,*
WrDr 76, −80, −82, −84
Staubach, Roger 1942- *BioIn 6, −9, −10, −11,*
−12, CelR 73, ConAu 104, CurBio 72,
NewYTBE 71, −72, WhoAm 74, −76, −78,
−80, −82, WhoFtbl 74, WorAl
Stead, Christina 1902-1983 *Au&Wr 6,*
BioIn 1, −4, −8, −9, −10, −11, CasWL,
ConAu 109, −13R, ConLC 2, −5, −8,
ConNov 72, −76, −82, DcLEL, EvLB,
FarE&A 78, −79, −80, −81, InWom,
IntAu&W 76, −77, IntDcWB, IntWW 77,
−78, −79, −80, −81, −82, −83N, LongCTC,
ModCmwL, NewYTBS 83, Novels,
RAdv 1, ScF&FL 1, −2, TwCA,
TwCA SUP, TwCWr, WhE&EA,
Who 74, −82, −83, WhoAmW 74, −68, −70,
−72, −75, −77, WhoTwCL, WhoWor 74,
−76, WorAl, WrDr 76, −80, −82, −84
Stearn, Jess *ConAu 97, WrDr 76, −80, −82,*
−84
Stearns, Marshall 1908-1966 *BioIn 7, −8,*
ConAu 110, WhAm 4
Stearns, Monroe 1913- *AuBYP SUP,*
BioIn 10, ConAu 2NR, −5R,
IntAu&W 76, SmATA 5, WrDr 76, −80,
−82, −84

Stearns, Pamela Fujimoto 1935- *ConAu 65*
Stedman, Raymond W 1930- *DrAS 74E, -78E, -82E*
Stedwell, Paki 1945- *ConAu 103*
Steegmuller, Francis 1906- *AmAu&B, Au&Wr 6, BioIn 2, -4, -12, ChhPo, ConAu 2NR, -49, ConNov 72, -76, DrAP&F 83, IntAu&W 76, -77, -82, NewYTBS 80[port], REnAL, ScF&FL 1, TwCA SUP, WhE&EA, Who 74, -82, -83, WhoAm 74, -76, -78, -80, -82, WrDr 76, -80, -82, -84*
Steel, Danielle 1947- *BioIn 11, ConAu 81, IntAu&W 82, WhoAmW 81, -83, WrDr 84*
Steele, George Peabody 1924- *ConAu 1R, WhoF&I 79, -81, -83, WhoWor 80, -82, WrDr 82, -84*
Steele, Mary Quintard 1922- *AuBYP, BioIn 8, -9, -11, ConAu 1R, -6NR, ScF&FL 1, -2, SmATA 3, ThrBJA, TwCCW 78, -83, WrDr 76, -80, -82, -84*
Steele, Mary Quintard *see also* Gage, Wilson
Steele, Phillip W 1934- *ConAu 61*
Steele, William Owen 1917-1979 *AmAu&B, Au&Wr 6, AuBYP, BioIn 6, -8, -9, -12, BlueB 76, BkCL, ConAu 1R, -2NR, -5R, IntAu&W 77, LinLib L, MorJA, SmATA 1, -27N, TwCCW 78, -83, WhAm 7, WhoAm 74, -76, -78, WrDr 76, -80*
Steelman, Robert J 1914- *ConAu 11NR, -69, WrDr 84*
Stefansson, Evelyn Baird 1913- *AuBYP, BioIn 8, ConAu 49, WhoAmW 61, -64*
Stefansson, Evelyn Baird *see also* Nef, Evelyn Stefansson
Stefansson, Thorsteinn 1912- *ConAu 77, IntAu&W 77, -82, WhoWor 80*
Steffan, Alice Jack Kennedy 1907- *ConAu 5R, WhoAmW 68, WhoPNW*
Steffan, Jack 1907- *ConAu X*
Steffan, Jack *see also* Steffan, Alice Kennedy
Steffens, Lincoln 1866-1936 *AmAu&B, AmBi, BioIn 1, -2, -3, -4, -5, -6, -8, -9, -10, -11, -12, CmCal, DcAmB S2, DcAmSR, LinLib L, LongCTC, McGEWB, ModAL, NatCAB 14, OxAmH, OxAmL, PenC AM, REn, REnAL, REnAW, TwCA, TwCA SUP, WebAB, -79, WebE&AL, WhAm 1, WorAl*
Stefferud, Alfred 1903- *AuBYP, BioIn 8, ConAu P-1, IntYB 78, -79, -80, -81, WhoAm 74, -76, -78, WhoE 74, -75*
Stegner, Wallace Earle 1909- *AmAu&B, AmNov, Au&Wr 6, AuNews 1, BioIn 2, -3, -4, -9, -10, -11, -12, BlueB 76, CmCal, CnDAL, ConAu 1R, -1NR, ConLC 9, ConNov 72, -76, -82, CurBio 77, DcLB 9[port], DrAF 76, DrAP&F 83, DrAS 74E, -78E, -82E, IntAu&W 76, -77, LinLib L, ModAL, Novels, OxAmL,*

OxCan, PenC AM, RAdv 1, REn, REnAL, REnAW, TwCA, TwCA SUP, WhE&EA, WhNAA, WhoAm 74, -76, -78, -80, -82, WhoWest 74, -76, WrDr 76, -80, -82, -84
Steiger, Brad 1936- *ConAu X, EncO&P 78S1, ScF&FL 1, -2, UFOEn[port]*
Steiger, Brad *see also* Olsen, Eugene E
Stein, Aaron Marc 1906- *ConAu 6NR, -9R, EncMys, IntAu&W 77, -82, Novels, TwCCr&M 80, WhoAm 82, WrDr 82, -84*
Stein, Joseph 1912- *BiE&WWA, ConAu 13R, ConDr 73, -82D, EncMT, NatPD, -81[port], NewCBMT, NotNAT, WhoAm 82, WhoThe 16, -81*
Stein, Meyer Lewis 1920- *AmM&WS 73S, AuBYP, BioIn 8, -10, ConAu 17R, DrAS 74E, -78E, -82E, IntAu&W 76, SmATA 6, WhoE 74*
Stein, R Conrad 1937- *ConAu 41R, SmATA 31*
Stein, Sol 1926- *AmEA 74, AuNews 1, BioIn 8, -10, -12, BioNews 74, ConAu 2NR, -49, IntAu&W 76, -77, -82, NewYTBS 80[port], WhoAm 74, -76, -78, -80, -82, WrDr 76, -80, -82, -84*
Stein, Stanley J 1920- *ConAu 108, DrAS 74H, -78H, -82H*
Steinbeck, John 1902-1968 *AmAu&B, AmNov, AmWr, AuBYP SUP, BiE&WWA, BioIn 1, -2, -3, -4, -5, -6, -7, -8, -9, -10, -11, -12, CasWL, CmCal, CnDAL, CnMD, CnMWL, CnThe, ConAmA, ConAu 1R, -1NR, -25R, ConLC 1, -5, -9, -13, -21[port], CurBio 40, -63, -69, CyWA, DcAmSR, DcLB DS2[port], -7[port], -9[port], DcLEL, EncAAH, EncAB-H, EncWL, EncWT, EvLB, FilmgC, LinLib L, -S, LongCTC, MakMC, McGEWB, McGEWD, -84[port], ModAL, ModWD, NatCAB 61[port], NotNAT B, Novels[port], ObitOF 79, ObitT 1961, OxAmH, OxAmL, OxEng, OxFilm, OxThe, PenC AM, RAdv 1, RComWL, REn, REnAL, REnAW, ScF&FL 1, -2, SmATA 9, TwCA, TwCA SUP, TwCWr, WebAB, -79, WebE&AL, WhDW, WhAm 5, WhThe, WhoTwCL, WorAl*
Steinberg, Alfred 1917- *AuBYP, BioIn 8, -11, ConAu 5R, -9NR, SmATA 9*
Steinberg, David Joel 1937- *AmEA 74, ConAu 25R, DrAS 74H, -78H, -82H*
Steinberg, Rafael Mark 1927- *ConAu 9NR, -61, WhoAm 74, -76, -78, -80, -82, WhoAmJ 80, WhoE 74*
Steinberg, Saul 1914- *AmAu&B, BioIn 1, -2, -3, -4, -5, -7, -8, -9, -11, -12, CelR 73, ConArt, -83, ConAu 89, CurBio 57, DcAmArt, DcCAA 71, -77, IntWW 74, -75, -76, -77, -78, -79, -80, -81, -82, -83,*

LinLib L, McGDA, OxAmL, OxTwCA,
PhDcTCA 77, REn, WebAB, -79,
WhoAm 74, -76, -78, -80, -82,
WhoAmA 78, -80, -82, WhoGrA,
WhoWor 74, WorECar

Steinbrunner, Chris 1933- ConAu 1NR, -45,
ScF&FL 1, -2

Steiner, George 1929- BioIn 8, -10, -11,
BlueB 76, ConAu 73, ConLC 24[port],
ConLCrt, -82, CurBio 83[port],
DcLEL 1940, EncWL, IntAu&W 76, -77,
-82, IntWW 74, -75, -76, -77, -78, -79,
-80, -81, -82, -83, ModBrL SUP, RAdv 1,
REnAL, Who 74, -82, -83, WhoAm 74,
-76, -78, WhoWor 74, -76, -78, WorAu,
WrDr 76, -80, -82, -84

Steiner, Stan 1925- ChiSch, ChhPo S1,
ConAu 1NR, -45, IntAu&W 77,
SmATA 14, WhoAm 74, -76, -78, -80, -82,
WrDr 80, -82, -84

Steiner, Stanley 1925- AmAu&B, BioIn 12,
ConAu 45

Steinhauer, Harry 1905- ConAu 1R, -1NR,
DrAS 74F, -78F, -82F, WhoAm 74

Steinmark, Fred 1948?-1971 BioIn 9, -12,
NewYTBE 71

Steinmark, Freddie J 1948?-1971 ObitOF 79,
WhoFtbl 74

Steneman, Shep 1945- ConAu 107

Stensland, Anna Lee 1922- DrAS 74E, -78E,
-82E, WhoAm 80, WhoAmW 79, -81

Stephens, Eve ConAu X

Stephens, Eve see also Ward-Thomas, Evelyn
Bridget

Stephens, Henrietta Henkle 1909-1983
ConAu 6NR, -9R, -109, ScF&FL 1

Stephens, Henrietta Henkle see also Buckmaster,
Henrietta

Stephens, James 1882-1950 AnCL,
AuBYP SUP, BioIn 1, -2, -3, -4, -5, -6, -7,
-10, -11, -12, CarSB, CasWL, Chambr 3,
ChhPo, -S1, -S2, -S3, CnE&AP,
ConAu 104, CyWA, DcIrL, DcIrW 1,
DcLB 19[port], DcLEL, EncWL, EvLB,
LinLib L, LongCTC, McGEWB,
ModBrL, ModBrL SUP, NewC, Novels,
OxEng, PenC ENG, PoIre, RAdv 1,
REn, ScF&FL 1, Str&VC, TwCA,
TwCA SUP, TwCLC 4[port], TwCWr,
WhDW, WhAm 3

Stephens, Mary Jo 1935- BioIn 11,
ConAu 37R, SmATA 8

Stephens, Peggy AuBYP SUP

Stephens, William M 1925- AuBYP SUP,
BioIn 12, ConAu 57, SmATA 21[port]

Stephenson, Andrew M 1946- WrDr 84

Stephenson, Ralph 1910- Au&Wr 6,
ConAu 17R, IntAu&W 77, WhoWor 76,
WrDr 76, -80, -82, -84

Steptoe, John Lewis 1950- AfroAA, BioIn 8,
-11, -12, BlkAWP, ChlLR 2,
ConAu 3NR, -49, FourBJA, IlsBYP,

IlsCB 1967, InB&W 80, LivgBAA,
SelBAA, SmATA 8, TwCCW 78, -83,
WhoAm 74, -76, WrDr 80, -82, -84

Sterling, Claire 1920?- ConIsC 2[port],
NewYTBS 81[port]

Sterling, Dorothy 1913- AuBYP, BioIn 5, -8,
-9, -10, BkCL, ChlLR 1, ConAu 5NR,
-9R, ForWC 70, MorBMP, SmATA 1,
ThrBJA

Sterling, Philip 1907- BioIn 11, ConAu 49,
SmATA 8

Stern, Ellen Norman 1927- ConAu 37R,
SmATA 26[port], WrDr 76, -80, -82, -84

Stern, Geraldine 1907- ConAu 101

Stern, Harold Phillip 1922-1977 BioIn 11,
ConAu 69, DrAS 74H, NewYTBS 77,
WhAm 7, WhoAmA 73, -76, -78N, -80N,
-82N, WhoGov 77, -75

Stern, Jane 1946- ConAu 10NR, -61

Stern, Michael 1910- ConAu P-2,
IntAu&W 76, -77, -82, WhoWor 76, -78,
-80, -82, WhoWorJ 72, -78

Stern, Philip VanDoren 1900- AmAu&B,
AmNov, Au&Wr 6, AuBYP SUP,
BioIn 2, -4, -11, ConAu 5R, -6NR,
DrAS 74H, -78H, REnAL, ScF&FL 1, -2,
SmATA 13, TwCA SUP, WhE&EA,
WhNAA, WhoAm 74, -76, -78, -80, -82

Stern, Richard Martin 1915- AmAu&B,
Au&Wr 6, BioIn 1, BlueB 76,
ConAu 1R, -2NR, TwCCr&M 80,
WhoAm 74, -76, -78, -80, -82, WrDr 76,
-80, -82, -84

Stern, Susan 1943-1976 BioIn 10, -11,
ConAu 65, NewYTBS 76, ObitOF 79

Sterne, Emma Gelders 1894-1971 AmAu&B,
BioIn 4, -6, -10, ConAu R, -5NR,
MorJA, SmATA 6, TwCA, TwCA SUP,
WhoAmW 58, -64, -66, -68, -70, -72

Stetson, Erlene ConAu 108

Steurt, Marjorie Rankin 1888- BioIn 11,
ConAu 13R, SmATA 10, WrDr 76, -80

Stevens, Cat 1948- BiDAmM, BioIn 9, -10,
-12, BioNews 74, ConAu X, EncPR&S,
-77, IlEncRk, NewYTBE 71, RkOn 78,
-84, RolSEnR 83, WhoAm 74, -76, -78,
-80, -82, WhoRocM 82, WorAl

Stevens, Franklin 1933- BioIn 10, ConAu 29R,
SmATA 6

Stevens, Gwendolyn 1944- ConAu 104,
SmATA 33[port], WhoAmW 83

Stevens, Leonard A 1920- ConAu 17R

Stevens, Patricia Bunning 1931- ConAu 53,
SmATA 27

Stevens, William 1925- AmAu&B,
ConAu 21R

Stevens, William Oliver 1878-1955 AmAu&B,
AmLY, AuBYP, BiDPara, BioIn 3, -8,
ChhPo, EncAB 26, EncO&P 78,
WhAm 3, WhE&EA, WhNAA

Stevenson, Anne IntAu&W 76, WrDr 84

Stevenson, Burton Egbert 1872-1962 AmAu&B,

BiD&SB, BioIn 4, –6, ChhPo, –S2, –S3,
ConAu 102, –89, DcAmAu, DcAmLiB,
EvLB, NatCAB 13, ObitOF 79, OhA&B,
REn, REnAL, ScF&FL 1, SmATA 25,
TwCA, TwCA SUP, WhAm 4, WhJnl,
WhNAA

Stevenson, David Lloyd 1910-1975 ConAu 57,
ConAu P-2, WhAm 6

Stevenson, E Robert 1882-1978 WhAm 7,
WhJnl

Stevenson, Gloria 1945- ConAu 61

Stevenson, Janet 1913- AuBYP SUP,
BioIn 11, ConAu 13R, ForWC 70,
SmATA 8, WhoAmW 61, –66, –68, –70

Stevenson, Robert Louis 1850-1894 Alli SUP,
AnCL, ApCAB SUP, AtlBL, AuBYP,
BbD, BiD&SB, BioIn 1, –2, –3, –4, –5, –6,
–7, –8, –9, –10, –11, –12, BrAu 19, BrWr 5,
CarSB, CasWL, Chambr 3, ChrP,
ChhPo, –S1, –S2, –S3, CmCal, CrtT 3,
CyWA, DcBiA, DcBrBI, DcEnA, –AP,
DcEuL, DcLB 18[port], DcLEL, Dis&D,
EncMys, EncSF, EvLB, FamAYP,
FamPYP, FilmgC, JBA 34, LinLib L,
McGEWB, MnBBF, MouLC 4, NewC,
Novels[port], OxAmL, OxEng, OxMus,
PenC ENG, RAdv 1, REn, REnAL,
ScF&FL 1, –1A, Str&VC, TelT,
TwCCW 78A, –83A, WebE&AL, WhDW,
WhoBW&I A, WhoChL, WhoHr&F,
YABC 2

Stevenson, Robert Murrell 1916- DrAS 78H,
–82H, IntAu&W 77, –82, IntWWM 77,
WhoAm 74, –76, –78, –80, –82, WhoRel 75,
–77, WhoWest 82, WhoWor 76, –78, –80

Stevenson, William 1924?- BioIn 12,
ConAu 13R, TwCCW 78, WhoAm 78,
WrDr 80, –84

Stewart, A C AuBYP SUP, ConAu 77,
SmATA 15, TwCCW 78, –83, WrDr 84

Stewart, Allan 1939- ConAu 1R

Stewart, Desmond 1924-1981 AmAu&B,
Au&Wr 6, ConAu 104, –37R,
DcLEL 1940, IntAu&W 76, –77, –82,
Who 74, –82N

Stewart, Donald Ogden 1894-1980 AmAu&B,
AnObit 1980[port], BiE&WWA, BioIn 4,
–10, –12, CarSB, ConAu 101, –81,
Conv 1, CurBio 41, –80N, DcLB 4,
–11[port], –26[port], DcLEL, FilmgC,
NotNAT, OhA&B, OxAmL, PenC AM,
REnAL, TwCA, TwCA SUP, WhAm 7,
WhJnl, WhNAA, WhThe, WhoAm 74,
WorEFlm

Stewart, Fred Mustard 1936- BioIn 8, –12,
ConAu 37R, NewYTBS 81[port],
ScF&FL 1, –2, WhoE 75, –77, WrDr 76,
–80, –82, –84

Stewart, George Rippey 1895-1980 AmAu&B,
AmNov, AnObit 1981, Au&Wr 6,
BioIn 1, –2, –4, –9, –12, CmCal, CnDAL,
ConAu 1R, –3NR, –101, CurBio 42, –80N,

DcLB 8[port], EncSF, IntAu&W 77,
NewYTBS 80, OxAmL, REnAL,
ScF&FL 1, –2, SmATA 23N, –3,
TwCA SUP, WhAm 7, WhE&EA,
WhNAA, WhoAm 74, WrDr 76, –80

Stewart, Harold Frederick 1916- ConAu 69,
ConP 70, –75, –80, DcLEL 1940,
IntAu&W 76, –82, IntWWP 77, –82,
TwCWr, WrDr 76, –80, –82, –84

Stewart, J I M 1906- ConAu 85, ConLC 7,
–14, ConNov 82, Novels, TwCCr&M 80,
WrDr 80, –82, –84

Stewart, Jackie 1939?- BioIn 7, –8, –9, –10, –11,
–12, Who 74, –82, –83, WorAl

Stewart, John Craig 1915- BioIn 2, DrAS 74E,
–78E, –82E, WhoS&SW 73, –75, –76

Stewart, John William 1920- BioIn 12,
ConAu 33R, SmATA 14

Stewart, Marjabelle 1930?- BioIn 12

Stewart, Mary 1916- Au&Wr 6, BioIn 5, –8,
–9, –10, –11, –12, ConAu 1R, –1NR,
ConLC 7, CorpD, DcLEL 1940, EncMys,
IntAu&W 76, –77, –82, LongCTC,
NewYTBS 79, Novels[port], PoIre,
ScF&FL 1, –2, SmATA 12,
TwCCr&M 80, TwCWr, Who 74, –82,
–83, WhoAm 74, –76, –78, –80, –82,
WhoAmW 74, –70, –72, –75, –77,
WhoWor 74, –76, WorAl, WorAu,
WrDr 76, –80, –82, –84

Stewart, Ora Pate 1910- ForWC 70,
IntAu&W 76, –77, –82, IntWWP 77, –82,
WhoAmW 74, –61, –66, –68, –70, –72,
WhoWest 74

Stewart, Ramona 1922- ASpks, ConAu 1R,
–6NR, ForWC 70, ScF&FL 1, –2

Stewart, Rod 1945- BioIn 10, –11, –12,
CurBio 79, EncPR&S, –77, IlEncRk,
RkOn 78, –84, RkOneH, RolSEnR 83,
WhoRocM 82, WorAl

Stickgold, Bob 1945- ConAu 104

Stiles, Martha Bennett BioIn 10, ConAu 37R,
DrAP&F 83, IntAu&W 82, MichAu 80,
SmATA 6, WhoAmW 75

Still, C Henry 1920- ConAu 9R, WhoWest 74,
–76, –78

Stilley, Frank 1918- ConAu 61,
SmATA 29[port]

Stillman, Myra Stephens 1915- AuBYP,
BioIn 8, ConAu 5R, –6NR, ForWC 70

Stillman, Richard Joseph 1917- ConAu 37R,
IntAu&W 77, –82, WrDr 76, –80, –82

Stills, Stephen 1945- EncPR&S, –77, IlEncRk,
WhoRocM 82, WorAl

Stills, Stephen see also Crosby, Stills, Nash &
Young

Stine, G Harry 1928- ConAu 9NR, –65,
EncSF, ScF&FL 1, WrDr 84

Stine, George Harry 1928- AuBYP, BioIn 8,
–11, SmATA 10, WhoAm 82,
WhoWest 80, –82

Stine, George Harry see also Correy, Lee

Stine, Jovial Bob *ConAu X, SmATA X*
Stinetorf, Louise A 1900- *BioIn 11,*
ConAu 9R, ForWC 70, SmATA 10
Stinson, Robert William 1941- *DrAS 74H,*
–78H, –82H
Stirling, Jessica *ConAu X, WrDr 76, –80, –82,*
–84
Stirling, Nora B 1900- *AuBYP, BioIn 8, –9,*
ConAu 3NR, –5R, SmATA 3, WrDr 76,
–80, –82, –84
Stobbs, William 1914- *ArtCS, BioIn 5, –6, –8,*
–9, –12, ChhPo, –S2, ConAu 81, IlsBYP,
IlsCB 1946, –1957, –1967, SmATA 17,
ThrBJA, WhoChL
Stockton, Frank R 1834-1902 *Alli, AmAu,*
AmAu&B, AuBYP, BbD, BiD&SB,
BioIn 1, –5, –6, –8, –12, CarSB, CnDAL,
ConAu X, CyAL 2, DcAmB, DcLEL,
EncMys, EncSF, EvLB, FamSYP,
JBA 34, LinLib L, OxAmL, OxEng,
RAdv 1, REn, ScF&FL 1, SmATA 32,
TwCCW 78A, –83A, WebAB, –79
Stoddard, Edward G 1923- *AuBYP, BioIn 8,*
–11, ConAu 9R, SmATA 10, WhoE 75,
–77
Stoddard, Hope 1900- *AuBYP, BioIn 8, –10,*
ConAu 49, SmATA 6
Stoddard, Sandol 1927- *BioIn 12,*
ConAu 8NR, FourBJA, SmATA X
Stoddard, Sandol *see also* Warburg, Sandol
Stoddard
Stohlman, Martha Lou Lemmon 1913-
ConAu 65
Stoiko, Michael 1919- *BioIn 12, ConAu 9R,*
SmATA 14
Stokely, Wilma Dykeman 1920- *ConAu 1R*
Stokely, Wilma Dykeman *see also* Dykeman,
Wilma
Stoker, Bram 1847-1912 *Alli SUP, BioIn 5, –6,*
–8, –10, –11, –12, ConAu X, CyWA,
DcIrL, DcLEL, EncMys, EncO&P 78,
EncSF, EvLB, FilmgC, LongCTC,
NotNAT B, Novels, PenC ENG, REn,
ScF&FL 1, SmATA X, TwCA,
TwCA SUP, TwCCr&M 80,
TwCLC 8[port], WhDW, WhLit,
WhoChL, WhoHr&F, WorAl
Stokes, Geoffrey 1940- *ConAu 69*
Stokesbury, James Lawton 1934- *ConAu 93,*
DrAS 74H, –78H, –82H
Stokley, James 1900- *AmAu&B, WhJnl,*
WhoAm 74, –76, –78
Stolz, Mary Slattery 1920- *AmAu&B,*
Au&Wr 6, AuBYP, AuNews 1, BioIn 3,
–6, –7, –10, –11, BioNews 74, ConAu 5R,
ConLC 12, CurBio 53, ForWC 70,
InWom, MorBMP, MorJA, REnAL,
SmATA 10, TwCCW 78, –83,
WhoAm 74, –76, –78, –80, –82,
WhoAmW 74, –58, –61, –64, –66, –68, –70,
–72, WrDr 80, –82, –84
Stolzenberg, Mark 1950- *ConAu 102*

Stone, A Harris *AuBYP SUP*
Stone, George Kenneth *AuBYP, BioIn 8*
Stone, Irving 1903- *AmAu&B, AmNov,*
Au&Wr 6, AuNews 1, BioIn 2, –4, –5, –6,
–7, –8, –9, –10, –12, BlueB 76, CelR 73,
CmCal, ConAu 1R, –1NR, ConLC 7,
ConNov 72, –76, –82, CurBio 67,
DrAS 74E, –78E, –82E, IntAu&W 76, –77,
IntWW 74, –75, –76, –77, –78, –79, –80, –81,
–82, –83, LinLib L, LongCTC,
NewYTBS 80[port], Novels, PenC AM,
REn, REnAL, SmATA 3, TwCA,
TwCA SUP, TwCWr, WhE&EA,
WhNAA, WhoAm 74, –76, –78, –80, –82,
WhoAmJ 80, WhoWor 74, –78,
WhoWorJ 72, –78, WorAl, WrDr 76, –80,
–82, –84
Stone, Josephine Rector 1936- *ConAu X,*
SmATA X
Stone, Josephine Rector *see also* Dixon, Jeanne
Stone, Peter Bennet 1933- *WhoUN 75,*
WhoWor 80
Stone, Peter H 1930- *AmAu&B, ConAu 7NR,*
–9R, ConDr 73, –82D, IntAu&W 76, –82,
IntMPA 81, –82, –84, WhoAm 74, –76, –78,
–80, –82, WhoThe 15, –81
Stone, Ralph A 1934- *ConAu 37R, WrDr 76,*
–80, –82, –84
Stone, Robert Anthony 1937- *BioIn 12,*
ConLC 23[port], DrAP&F 83,
WhoAm 76, –78, –80, –82
Stone, Scott Clinton Stuart 1932- *ConAu 25R,*
WhoAm 74, –76, –78, –80, WhoWor 80
Stonehouse, Bernard 1926- *Au&Wr 6,*
BioIn 11, ConAu 2NR, –49, IntAu&W 77,
–82, SmATA 13, WrDr 76, –80, –82, –84
Stoppard, Tom 1937- *Au&Wr 6, BioIn 8, –9,*
–10, –11, –12, BlueB 76, CnThe,
ConAu 81, ConDr 73, –77, –82, ConLC 1,
–3, –4, –5, –8, –15, CroCD, CurBio 74,
DcLB 13[port], DcLEL 1940, EncWL,
EncWT, IntAu&W 76, IntWW 74, –75,
–76, –77, –78, –79, –80, –81, –82, –83,
MakMC, McGEWD, –84[port],
ModBrL SUP, ModWD, NewYTBE 72,
NewYTBS 74, NotNAT, PIP&P A,
WebE&AL, Who 74, –82, –83,
WhoAm 80, –82, WhoThe 15, –16, –81,
WhoTwCL, WhoWor 82, WorAl,
WorAu 1970, WrDr 76, –80, –82, –84
Storer, Doug 1899- *ConAu 57*
Storey, David Malcolm 1933- *BioIn 12,*
ConDr 73, –82, ConLC 2, –4, –5,
ConNov 72, –76, –82, DcLB 13[port],
–14[port], DcLEL 1940, IntWW 77, –78,
–79, –80, –81, –82, –83, LongCTC,
McGEWD 84, ModBrL SUP, NewC,
Novels, TwCWr, Who 74, –82, –83,
WhoThe 81, WhoWor 74, –76, –78, –80,
–82, WorAu, WrDr 76, –82, –84
Storey, Margaret 1926- *BioIn 11,*
ConAu 1NR, –49, ScF&FL 1, SmATA 9,

TwCCW 78, –83, WrDr 80, –82, –84

Storey, Robert Gerald 1893-1981 *BioIn 2, –3, –4, –5, –7, BlueB 76, CurBio 53, IntWW 74, –75, –76, –77, –78, –79, –80, –81N, WhAm 7, WhoAm 74, –76, –78, –80, WhoS&SW 73, WhoWor 74, –76, –78*

Storey, Victoria Carolyn 1945- *BioIn 12, ConAu 33R, IntAu&W 77, SmATA 16*

Storme, Peter *AuBYP SUP, BioIn 2, –4, –11, ConAu X, SmATA X*

Storme, Peter *see also* Stern, Philip VanDoren

Storr, Catherine 1913- *Au&Wr 6, AuBYP SUP, BioIn 11, ConAu 13R, EncSF, SmATA 9, TwCCW 78, –83, WrDr 76, –80, –82, –84*

Storr, Catherine *see also* Adler, Irene

Story, Ronald Dean 1946- *ConAu 11NR, –65, UFOEn, WhoWest 80, –82*

Stott, William Merrell 1940- *ConAu 61, DrAS 74E, –78E, –82E*

Stout, Rex Todhunter 1886-1975 *AmAu&B, AuNews 2, BioIn 1, –2, –3, –4, –5, –7, –8, –9, –10, –11, –12, BlueB 76N, CasWL, CelR 73, ConAu 61, ConLC 3, ConNov 76, CorpD, CurBio 46, –76, –76N, EncMys, EncSF, EvLB, IndAu 1917, LinLib L, LongCTC, NatCAB 59[port], NewYTBE 71, NewYTBS 75, Novels[port], ObitOF 79, ObitT 1971, OxAmL, PenC AM, REn, REnAL, ScF&FL 1, –2, TwCA, TwCA SUP, TwCCr&M 80, TwCWr, WhAm 6, –7, WhoAm 74, –76, WorAl*

Stoutenburg, Adrien 1916- *AmAu&B, Au&Wr 6, AuBYP, BioIn 6, –8, –9, ChhPo S2, ConAu 5R, ConP 70, –75, –80, DrAP 75, ForWC 70, IntWWP 77, MinnWr, ScF&FL 1, –2, SmATA 3, ThrBJA, WhoAm 74, –76, –78, –80, –82, WhoAmW 74, –68, –70, –72, WhoWest 74, WrDr 76, –80, –82, –84*

Stowe, Harriet Beecher 1811-1896 *Alli, Alli SUP, AmAu, AmAu&B, AmBi, AmWom, AmWomWr, AmWr SUP, ApCAB, AtlBL, AuBYP SUP, BbD, BiDAmM, BiD&SB, BioIn 1, –2, –3, –4, –5, –6, –7, –8, –9, –10, –11, –12, CarSB, CasWL, CelCen, Chambr 3, ChhPo, –S1, –S2, CivWDc, CnDAL, CrtT 3, –4, CyAL 2, CyWA, DcAmAu, DcAmB, DcAmReB, DcAmSR, DcBiA, DcBiPP, DcEnA, DcEnL, DcLB 1, –12[port], DcLEL, DcNAA, Drake, EncAAH, EncAB-H, EvLB, FilmgC, GoodHs, HarEnUS[port], HerW, InWom, IntDcWB, JBA 34, LibW, LinLib L, –S, McGEWB, MouLC 4, NatCAB 1, NotAW, NotNAT B, Novels, OhA&B, OxAmH, OxAmL, OxEng, PenC AM, PIP&P, RAdv 1, REn, REnAL,*

TwCBDA, WebAB, –79, WebE&AL, WhDW, WhAm HS, WhAmP, WhFla, WhoChL, WorAl, YABC 1

Strachan, Margaret Pitcairn 1908- *BioIn 12, ConAu 5R, SmATA 14, WhoPNW, WrDr 76, –80, –82, –84*

Strachey, Lytton 1880-1932 *AtlBL, BioIn 1, –2, –3, –4, –8, –9, –10, –12, CnMWL, ConAu 110, CyWA, LinLib L, LongCTC, ModBrL, NewC, PenC ENG, REn, TwCA, TwCA SUP, TwCLC 12[port], TwCWr, WebE&AL, WhDW, WhoTwCL, WorAl*

Straight, Michael 1916- *AmAu&B, BioIn 1, –10, –11, ConAu 5R, –7NR, ConNov 72, –76, CurBio 44, IntAu&W 76, –77, WhoAmA 73, –76, –78, WhoGov 77, –72, –75, WrDr 76, –80, –82, –84*

Strain, Frances Bruce 1892-1975 *AmAu&B, ConAu P-2, OhA&B, WhE&EA, WhoAmW 58, –64*

Strait, Raymond 1924- *ConAu 4NR, –53, IntAu&W 77, –82*

Strang, Ruth 1895-1971 *BiDAmEd, BioIn 5, –9, –12, ConAu 1R, –2NR, CurBio 60, –71, –71N, NewYTBE 71, NotAW MOD, WhoAmW 58, –61, –64, –66, –68, –70, –72*

Stranger, Joyce *BioIn 12, ConAu X, IntAu&W 77, SmATA X, TwCCW 78, –83, WrDr 80, –82, –84*

Stranger, Joyce *see also* Wilson, Joyce M

Strasberg, Lee 1901-1982 *AnObit 1982[port], BiE&WWA, BioIn 5, –6, –10, –11, –12, BlueB 76, CelR 73, CnThe, ConAu 106, –13R, CurBio 60, –82N, EncWT, FilmgC, IntMPA 81, –82, IntWW 74, –75, –76, –77, –78, –79, –80, –81, –82N, NewYTBS 75, –82[port], NotNAT, PIP&P, WhoAm 74, –76, –78, –80, WhoE 77, –79, –81, WhoHol A, WhoThe 15, –16, –81, WhoWor 74, WorAl*

Strasser, Todd 1950?- *BioIn 11*

Stratemeyer, Edward L 1862-1930 *AmAu&B, ApCAB X, BiD&SB, BioIn 9, –11, CarSB, ConAu P-2, DcAmAu, DcAmB, DcNAA, EncMys, HarEnUS, HsB&A, NatCAB 16, –32, OxAmL, REn, REnAL, SmATA 1, TwCBDA, WebAB, –79, WhAm 1, WorAl*

Stratemeyer, Edward L *see also* Appleton, Victor

Stratemeyer, Edward L *see also* Dixon, Franklin W

Stratemeyer, Edward L *see also* Keene, Carolyn

Stratemeyer, Edward L *see also* West, Jerry

Straub, Peter 1943- *BioIn 12, ConAu 85, WrDr 80, –82, –84*

Streatfeild, Noel 1895?- *AuBYP, BioIn 2, –3, –6, –7, –8, –9, –12, ChhPo S2, ConAu 81, ConLC 21[port], IntAu&W 76, –77, JBA 51, LongCTC, SmATA 20, TelT, TwCCW 78, –83, WhE&EA, Who 74, –82, –83, WhoChL, WrDr 76, –80, –82, –84*

Street, Alicia 1911- *ConAu 5R*
Street, James 1903-1954 *AmAu&B, AmNov, BioIn 1, -2, -3, -4, -5, CnDAL, CurBio 46, -54, NatCAB 42, ObitOF 79, REnAL, TwCA SUP, WhAm 3*
Street, Thomas Watson 1916- *WhoAm 74, -76, -78, WhoRel 75, -77*
Streeter, Floyd Benjamin 1888- *WhNAA*
Stren, Patti 1949- *ChlLR 5[port]*
Streshinsky, Shirley G 1934- *ConAu 85*
Strete, Craig *EncSF, WrDr 84*
Stretton, Barbara 1936- *SmATA 35*
Stricker, George 1936- *AmM&WS 73S, -78S, ConAu 37R*
Strieber, Whitley 1945- *ConAu 81*
Stromberg, Roland N 1916- *ConAu 6NR, DrAS 82H, WhoAm 82*
Strong, Charles *AuBYP, ConAu X, SmATA X*
Strong, Charles *see also* Epstein, Beryl Williams
Strong, Charles *see also* Epstein, Samuel
Strother, Elsie 1912- *ConAu 11NR, -65*
Stroup, Herbert Hewitt 1916- *AmAu&B, AmM&WS 73S, -78S, BlueB 76, ConAu 13R, WhoAm 74, -76, -78, -80, -82, WrDr 76, -80, -82, -84*
Strousse, Flora G 1897?-1974 *BioIn 10, ConAu 49*
Struble, Mitch 1945- *ConAu 93*
Strugatski, Arkadi 1925- *Novels, ScF&FL 1, WhoSciF*
Strugatski, Boris 1931?- *EncSF, WhoSciF*
Strunk, William 1869-1946 *BioIn 1, -10, ChhPo S3, DcNAA, WhAm 2*
Strutton, Bill 1918- *Au&Wr 6, ScF&FL 1, WrDr 76, -80, -82, -84*
Strutton, Bill *see also* Strutton, William Harold
Strutton, William Harold 1918- *ConAu 77, IntAu&W 76, -77*
Strutton, William Harold *see also* Strutton, Bill
Stryk, Lucien 1924- *BioIn 10, ConAu 10NR, -13R, ConP 70, -75, -80, DrAP 75, DrAP&F 83, IntWWP 77, WrDr 76, -80, -82, -84*
Stuart, Colin 1910- *BioIn 8, ConAu 104*
Stuart, George E *AuBYP SUP*
Stuart, Granville 1834-1918 *AmAu&B, BioIn 6, -7, -9, -11, DcAmB, DcNAA, NatCAB 12, REnAW*
Stuart, Jesse 1907-1984 *AmAu&B, AmNov, Au&Wr 6, AuBYP SUP, BioIn 1, -2, -3, -4, -5, -6, -8, -9, -10, -11, -12, BlueB 76, ChhPo, -S1, ConAu 5R, ConLC 1, -8, -11, -14, ConNov 72, -76, -82, CurBio 40, CyWA, DcLB 9[port], IntAu&W 76, -77, IntWW 74, -75, -76, -77, -78, -79, -80, -81, -82, -83, IntWWP 77, LinLib L, -S, OxAmL, RAdv 1, REn, REnAL, SixAP, SmATA 2, -36N, TwCA SUP, TwCWr, WhoAm 74, -76, -78, -80, -82, WhoS&SW 73, -75, -76, WhoWor 74, -78, WrDr 76, -80, -82, -84*

Stubenrauch, Robert *AuBYP SUP*
Sturgeon, Theodore 1918- *AmAu&B, BioIn 7, -10, -12, ConAu 81, ConLC 22[port], ConSFA, DcLB 8[port], DrAF 76, DrAP&F 83, EncSF, LinLib L, Novels, PenC AM, REnAL, ScF&FL 1, -2, WhoAm 74, -76, -78, -80, -82, WhoHr&F, WhoSciF, WorAl, WorAu, WrDr 84*
Sturges, Patricia P 1930- *ConAu 69*
Sturtzel, Howard A 1894- *BioIn 6, -9, ConAu 1R, -6NR, SmATA 1*
Sturtzel, Jane Levington 1903- *BioIn 9, ConAu 1R, -6NR, MichAu 80, SmATA 1*
Sturtzel, Jane Levington *see also* Annixter, Jane
Styles, Frank Showell 1908- *BioIn 11, ConAu 1R, IntAu&W 82, SmATA 10, Who 82, -83, WrDr 82, -84*
Styron, Rose 1928- *ConAu 17R*
Styron, William 1925- *AmAu&B, AmWr, Au&Wr 6, BioIn 2, -4, -6, -8, -9, -10, -11, -12, BlueB 76, CasWL, CelR 73, ConAu 5R, -6NR, ConLC 1, -3, -5, -11, -15, ConNov 72, -76, -82, Conv 3, CurBio 68, DcLB Y80A[port], -2, DcLEL 1940, DrAF 76, DrAP&F 83, EncSoH, EncWL, IntAu&W 76, -77, -82, IntWW 74, -75, -76, -77, -78, -79, -80, -81, -82, -83, LinLib L, ModAL, ModAL SUP, NewYTBS 79, Novels, OxAmL, PenC AM, RAdv 1, REn, REnAL, TwCWr, WebE&AL, WhoAm 74, -76, -78, -80, -82, WhoE 74, WhoTwCL, WhoWor 74, WorAl, WorAu, WrDr 76, -80, -82, -84*
Sudbery, Rodie 1943- *ConAu 104, IntAu&W 77, ScF&FL 1, TwCCW 78, -83, WrDr 76, -80, -82, -84*
Suddaby, Donald 1900-1964 *BioIn 8, EncSF, LongCTC, ScF&FL 1, TwCCW 78, -83, WhoChL*
Sugar, Bert Randolph 1937- *ConAu 9NR, -65, WhoAm 76, -78, -80, -82*
Sugarman, Daniel A 1931- *AmM&WS 73S, ConAu 21R*
Sugarman, Tracy 1921- *ConAu 21R, IlrAm F, SmATA 37*
Suggs, Robert Carl 1932- *AuBYP, BioIn 6, -8, ConAu 9R*
Sugimoto, Etsu 1874-1950 *BioIn 2, -4, -6, InWom, JBA 34, TwCA, TwCA SUP*
Suhl, Yuri 1908- *AuBYP SUP, BioIn 11, ChlLR 2, ConAu 2NR, -45, IntAu&W 76, SmATA 8, WhoWorJ 72, -78*
Suid, Murray 1942- *ConAu 97, SmATA 27[port]*
Sulkin, Sidney 1918- *ConAu 2NR, -5R, DrAP&F 83, Po&Wr 77, WhoAm 78, -80, -82, WhoAmJ 80*
Sullivan, George Edward 1927- *AuBYP, BioIn 8, -9, -12, ConAu 13R, IntAu&W 76, SmATA 4, WrDr 76, -80,*

–82, –84

Sullivan, Gerard 1927- *WhoMW 78, –80, –82*

Sullivan, Mary W 1907- *BioIn 11, ConAu 73, SmATA 13, WhoAmW 81, –83*

Sullivan, Michael 1916- *ConAu 3NR, –5R, DrAS 74H, –78H, –82H, Who 74, –82, –83, WhoAm 74, –76, –78, –80, –82, WhoWor 74, WrDr 76, –80, –82, –84*

Sullivan, Navin 1929- *Au&Wr 6, ConAu 5R*

Sullivan, Tom 1947- *BioIn 10, –11, –12, ConAu X, IntAu&W 82X, SmATA X*

Sullivan, Walter Seager 1918- *AmAu&B, AmM&WS 73P, –76P, –79P, –82P, BioIn 6, –10, –12, BlueB 76, ConAu 1R, –2NR, CurBio 80[port], IntAu&W 76, –77, –82, IntWW 74, –75, –76, –77, –78, –79, –80, –81, –82, –83, WhoAm 74, –76, –78, –80, –82, WhoWor 74, WrDr 76, –80, –82, –84*

Sullivan, William Healy 1922- *BioIn 9, –11, –12, CurBio 79, IntWW 74, –75, –76, –77, –78, –79, –80, –81, –82, –83, MidE 78, –79, –80, –81, NewYTBE 73, NewYTBS 79, PolProf J, PolProf K, USBiR 74, WhoAm 76, –78, WhoAmP 77, –79, WhoGov 77, –72, –75, WhoWor 74, –76, –78*

Sully, Francois 1927-1971 *AuBYP SUP, BioIn 9, ConAu 29R, ConAu P-2*

Sully, Nina 1948- *ConAu 110*

Sulzberger, C L 1912- *BlueB 76, CelR 73, ConAu 7NR, –53, CurBio 44, PolProf E, ScF&FL 1, –2, WrDr 80, –82, –84*

Sulzberger, Cyrus Leo 1912- *Au&Wr 6, BioIn 3, –4, –7, –8, –9, –10, –11, ConAu 53, IntAu&W 76, –77, IntWW 74, –75, –76, –77, –78, –79, –80, –81, –82, –83, REnAL, WhoAm 74, –76, –78, –80, –82, WhoWor 74*

Summerlin, Sam 1928- *ConAu 45, WhoAm 74, –76, –78, –80, WhoE 74, –75*

Summers, Clyde Wilson 1918- *BlueB 76, ConAu 109, DrAS 74P, –78P, –82P, WhoAm 74, –76, –78, –80, –82, WhoAmL 83*

Summers, Ian 1939- *ConAu 105*

Summers, James L 1910- *AuBYP, BioIn 6, –8, ConAu 13R, MorJA, SmATA 28*

Sundell, Abner *AuBYP SUP*

Sung, Betty Lee 1924- *AmM&WS 78S, ConAu 10NR, –25R, SmATA 26[port]*

Supree, Burton 1941- *ConAu 65*

Surge, Frank 1931- *BioIn 11, ConAu 69, SmATA 13*

Surkin, Marvin 1938- *ConAu 61*

Suskind, Richard 1925- *ConAu 9NR, –13R*

Sussman, Aaron 1903- *WhoAm 74, –76, –78, –80, –82, WhoWor 80, –82*

Sussman, Barry 1934- *BioIn 9, ConAu 53, IntAu&W 77, WhoAm 74, –76, –78, –80, –82, WhoAmJ 80, WrDr 76, –80, –82, –84*

Sussman, Cornelia Silver 1914- *ConAu 5R, InWom, WhoAmW 68*

Sussman, Irving 1908- *AmM&WS 73P, –76P, –79P, –82P, IntAu&W 82, WhoAm 74*

Sutcliff, Rosemary 1920- *Au&Wr 6, AuBYP, BioIn 5, –6, –7, –8, –10, –11, BlueB 76, BrCA, CasWL, ChlLR 1, ChhPo, ConAu 5R, ConLC 26[port], DcBrA 1, DcLEL 1940, HerW, IntAu&W 77, –82, LinLib L, MorJA, PiP, ScF&FL 1, –2, SenS, SmATA 6, TelT, TwCCW 78, –83, Who 74, –82, –83, WhoAmW 74, –66, –68, –72, WhoChL, WhoWor 74, –76, WrDr 76, –80, –82, –84*

Sutherland, Audrey Margaret 1940- *WhoLib 72*

Sutton, Ann 1923- *AuBYP, BioIn 8, ConAu 5R, –10NR, SmATA 31[port]*

Sutton, Caroline 1953- *ConAu 106*

Sutton, Jean 1916?- *AuBYP SUP, ConSFA, EncSF, ScF&FL 1, –2, WrDr 84*

Sutton, Jeff 1913-1979 *AuBYP SUP, ConAu X, ConSFA, EncSF, ScF&FL 1, –2, WhoSciF*

Sutton, Jefferson H 1913-1979 *ConAu 10NR, –21R*

Sutton, Margaret 1903- *AuBYP, BioIn 8, –9, ConAu 1R, ForWC 70, IntAu&W 77, SmATA 1, WhoAmW 58, –61*

Sutton, Myron Daniel 1925- *AuBYP, BioIn 8, ConAu 107, SmATA 31[port]*

Svenson, Andrew E 1910-1975 *BioIn 9, –10, ConAu 5R, –61, NewYTBS 75, ObitOF 79, SmATA 2, –26N, WhoE 74*

Svenson, Andrew E *see also* Dixon, Franklin W

Svenson, Andrew E *see also* West, Jerry

Swados, Elizabeth 1951- *BioIn 11, –12, ConAu 97, ConLC 12, CurBio 79, NewYTBS 77, –78, WhoAm 78, –80, –82, WhoAmW 81, WhoThe 81*

Swados, Harvey 1920-1972 *AmAu&B, AuBYP SUP, BioIn 5, –6, –9, –10, ConAu 5R, –6NR, –37R, ConLC 5, ConNov 72, DcLB 2, DcLEL 1940, IntAu&W 76, LinLib L, ModAL, NewYTBE 72, Novels, OxAmL, PenC AM, REnAL, WhAm 5, WorAu*

Swain, Roger 1949- *ConAu 102*

Swallow, Norman 1921- *Au&Wr 6, ConAu 21R, IntAu&W 77, IntMPA 77, –75, –76, –78, –79, –81, –82, –84, WrDr 76, –80, –82, –84*

Swanberg, William Andrew 1907- *Au&Wr 6, BioIn 6, –10, ConAu 5R, DcLEL 1940, MinnWr, WhoAm 74, –76, –78, –80, –82, WorAu, WrDr 76, –80*

Swann, Thomas Burnett 1928-1976 *ChhPo S1, ConAu 4NR, –5R, ConSFA, EncSF, ScF&FL 1, –2, WhoHr&F*

Swansea, Charleen 1932- *BioIn 11, ConAu 103, DrAP&F 83*

Swarthout, Glendon 1918- *AuBYP, BioIn 4, –11, ConAu 1R, –1NR, ConNov 72, –76, –82, DcLEL 1940, DrAP&F 83, FourBJA, IntAu&W 76, –77, MichAu 80,*

Novels, SmATA 26[port], WhoAm 80, –82, WhoWest 74, –76, –78, WrDr 76, –80, –82, –84

Swarthout, Kathryn 1919- *AuBYP, BioIn 10, ConAu 41R, FourBJA, MichAu 80, SmATA 7*

Sweeney, James B 1910- *BioIn 12, ConAu 29R, SmATA 21[port], WhoS&SW 75*

Sweeney, Karen O'Connor 1938- *ConAu 89, SmATA X*

Sweeney, Karen O'Connor *see also* O'Connor, Karen

Sweet, Jeffrey 1950- *ConAu 81, NatPD, –81[port], WhoMW 82*

Sweetkind, Morris 1898- *ChhPo S1, ConAu 13R, DrAS 74E*

Swenson, May 1919- *AmAu&B, AmWomWr, AnCL, AuBYP SUP, BioIn 8, –9, –10, –12, ChhPo S1, –S2, ConAu 5R, ConLC 4, –14, ConP 70, –75, –80, CroCAP, DcLB 5[port], DcLEL 1940, DrAP 75, DrAP&F 83, IntWWP 77, –82, PenC AM, RAdv 1, SmATA 15, WhoAm 74, –76, –78, –80, –82, WhoAmW 74, –68, –70, –72, –75, –77, –81, WhoWor 74, WorAu, WrDr 76, –80, –82, –84*

Swezey, Kenneth M 1905?-1972 *BioIn 9, ConAu 33R*

Swift, Benjamin *ConAu X*

Swift, Clive 1936- *WhoHol A, WhoThe 15, –16, –81*

Swift, Hildegarde Hoyt 1890?-1977 *AuBYP, BioIn 2, –7, –11, –12, ChhPo S2, ConAu 69, JBA 51, NewYTBS 77, SmATA 20N, WhoAmW 58, –61, –64, –66, –68*

Swift, Jonathan 1667-1745 *Alli, AtlBL, BbD, BiD&SB, BioIn 1, –2, –3, –4, –5, –6, –7, –8, –9, –10, –11, –12, BrAu, BrWr 3, CarSB, CasWL, Chambr 2, ChhPo, –S1, –S3, CnE&AP, CrtT 2, –4, CyWA, DcBiA, DcBiPP, DcEnA, –AP, DcEnL, DcEuL, DcIrB, DcIrL, DcIrW 1, –2, DcLEL, Dis&D, EncSF, EvLB, HsB&A, LinLib L, –S, LongCEL, LuthC 75, McGEWB, MouLC 2, NewC, Novels[port], OxEng, OxMus, PenC ENG, PoIre, RAdv 1, RComWL, REn, ScF&FL 1, SmATA 19, UFOEn, WebE&AL, WhDW, WhoChL, WorAl*

Swift, Kate 1923- *ConAu 69*

Swiger, Elinor Porter 1927- *AuBYP SUP, BioIn 11, ConAu 37R, SmATA 8, WhoAmL 79, –83, WhoAmW 75, –77, –79*

Swinburne, Laurence 1924- *BioIn 11, ConAu 61, SmATA 9, WhoE 79*

Swindell, Larry 1929- *ConAu 25R*

Swindells, Robert E 1939- *ConAu 97, SmATA 34*

Swindler, William Finley 1913- *Au&Wr 6, ConAu 13R, DrAS 74P, –78P, –82P,*

WhoAm 74, –76, –78, –80, –82, WhoAmL 78, WrDr 76, –80, –82, –84

Swinford, Betty 1927- *ConAu 5R, –7NR, ForWC 70, IndAu 1917*

Switzer, Ellen 1923- *ConAu 2NR, –45*

Swortzell, Lowell Stanley 1930- *ConAu 1NR, –49, DrAS 74E, –78E, –82E, LEduc 74*

Sydenham, Michael John 1923- *Au&Wr 6, ConAu 17R, DrAS 74H, –78H, –82H, WrDr 76, –80, –82, –84*

Sykes, Pamela 1927- *Au&Wr 6, AuBYP SUP, ScF&FL 1*

Sylvander, Carolyn Wedin 1939- *DrAS 78E, –82E, WhoAmW 83*

Syme, Ronald 1913- *Au&Wr 6, AuBYP, BioIn 9, ConAu 6NR, –9R, MorJA, SmATA 2, TwCCW 78*

Symonds, Pamela 1916- *Au&Wr 6, WrDr 76, –80, –82, –84*

Symons, Geraldine 1909- *ConAu 85, SmATA 33[port], TwCCW 78, –83, WrDr 76, –80, –82, –84*

Symons, Julian Gustave 1912- *Au&Wr 6, BioIn 4, –9, BlueB 76, ConAu 3NR, –49, ConLC 2, –14, ConNov 72, –76, –82, ConP 70, –80, DcLEL 1940, EncMys, IntAu&W 76, –77, LongCTC, ModBrL, Novels, TwCA SUP, TwCCr&M 80, WhE&EA, Who 74, –82, –83, WhoAm 82, WhoSpyF, WorAl, WrDr 76, –80, –82, –84*

Synge, John Millington 1871-1909 *AtlBL, BioIn 1, –3, –4, –5, –6, –7, –8, –9, –10, –11, –12, CasWL, Chambr 3, ChhPo S1, CnMD, CnMWL, CnThe, CyWA, DcEuL, DcIrB, DcIrL, DcIrW 1, DcLB 10[port], –19[port], DcLEL, Dis&D, EncWL, EncWT, EvLB, LinLib L, –S, LongCEL, LongCTC, McGEWD, –84[port], ModBrL, ModBrL SUP, ModWD, NewC, NewEOp 71, NotNAT A, –B, OxEng, OxThe, PenC ENG, PIP&P, PoIre, RComWL, REn, REnWD, TwCA, TwCLC 6[port], TwCWr, WebE&AL, WhDW, WhoTwCL, WorAl*

Synge, Ursula 1930- *BioIn 11, ConAu 1NR, –49, IntAu&W 77, SmATA 9, WrDr 76, –80, –82, –84*

Syrett, Netta d1943 *ChhPo S2, DcBrBI, ScF&FL 1, WhE&EA, WhLit*

Szasz, Suzanne 1919- *AuBYP, BioIn 8, –11, ConAu 3NR, –5R, SmATA 13, WhoAmW 68, –70*

Szulc, Tad 1926- *AmAu&B, BioIn 10, ConAu 4NR, –9R, IntAu&W 76, SmATA 26[port], WhoAm 74, –76, –78, –80, –82, WhoWor 74, –80, WrDr 76, –80, –82, –84*

Szydlowski, Mary Vigliante 1946- *ConAu 104, DrAP&F 83*

T

Taaffe, James Griffith 1932- *ConAu 17R,*
DrAS 74E, –78E, –82E, LEduc 74,
WhoAm 74, –76, –78, –80, –82
Taber, Anthony Scott 1944- *ConAu 105*
Tagliavia, Sheila 1936- *ConAu 104*
Tait, Dorothy 1902?-1972 *BioIn 9,*
ConAu 33R, ObitOF 79
Tait, Dorothy *see also* Fairbairn, Ann
Takashima, Shizuye 1928- *BioIn 11,*
ConAu 45, CreCan 2, HerW,
IntAu&W 77, OxCan SUP, SmATA 13,
WhoAmA 78, –80, –82
Talbert, William Franklin 1918- *Au&Wr 6,*
BioIn 3, –4, –5, CurBio 57
Talbot, Charlene Joy 1924?- *AuBYP SUP,*
BioIn 11, ConAu 8NR, –17R, ForWC 70,
SmATA 10, WrDr 76, –80, –82, –84
Talbot, Toby 1928- *AuBYP SUP, BioIn 12,*
ConAu 21R, SmATA 14, WomWMM B
Talbot Rice, Tamara 1904- *IntAu&W 77, –82*
Talbott, Strobe 1946- *AuNews 1, BioIn 10,*
ConAu 93, WhoAm 78, –80, –82
Tall, Stephen 1908- *WrDr 84*
Tallcott, Emogene *BioIn 11, ConAu 29R,*
SmATA 10
Talmadge, Marian *AuBYP, BioIn 8, –12,*
SmATA 14
Tamarin, Alfred H 1913-1980 *BioIn 10, –11,*
–12, ConAu 4NR, –102, –29R,
IntMPA 77, –75, –76, –78, –79, MorBMP,
NewYTBS 80, SmATA 13, WrDr 80, –82,
–84
Tames, Richard Lawrence 1946- *Au&Wr 6,*
ConAu 103, WrDr 76, –80, –82, –84
Tanizaki, Jun'ichiro 1886-1965 *BiDJaL,*
BioIn 10, –12, CasWL, CnMWL,
ConAu 25R, –93, ConLC 8, –14, DcOrL 1,
EncWL, LinLib L, MakMC, McGEWB,
Novels, ObitOF 79, PenC CL, REn,
WhAm 4, WhoTwCL, WorAu
Tannehill, Ivan Ray 1890-1959 *AuBYP,*
BioIn 8, OhA&B
Tannen, Mary 1943- *ConAu 105, SmATA 37*
Tannenbaum, Beulah Goldstein 1916- *AuBYP,*
BioIn 9, ConAu 5R, –7NR, ForWC 70,
SmATA 3, WhoAmW 68
Tannenbaum, Frank 1893-1969 *AmAu&B,*
BioIn 2, –8, ConAu 9R, IntEnSS 79,

ObitOF 79, WhNAA
Tanner, Chuck 1930- *WhoAm 74, –76,*
WhoE 79, –81, –83
Tanner, Edward Everett, III 1921-1976
AmAu&B, BioIn 4, –5, –6, –7, –10, –11,
ConAu 69, –73, CurBio 59, –77, –77N,
WhAm 7, WhoAm 74, –76, WorAu,
WrDr 76
Tanner, Edward Everett, III *see also* Dennis,
Patrick
Tanner, Helen Hornbeck 1916- *ConAu 61,*
DrAS 74H, –78H, –82H, WhoAmW 68,
–70, –72, –83
Tanner, Louise S 1922- *AuBYP SUP,*
BioIn 11, ConAu 69, SmATA 9
Tapley, Caroline 1934- *AuBYP SUP,*
ConAu 97
Tappan, Eva March 1854-1930 *AmAu&B,*
AmLY, AmWomWr, BiDAmEd,
BiD&SB, CarSB, ChhPo, –S1, DcAmAu,
DcAmB, DcNAA, JBA 34, NatCAB 22,
NotAW, REnAL, TwCA, TwCBDA,
WhAm 1, WhNAA, WomWWA 14
Tardieu, Jean 1903- *BioIn 10, CnMD, CnThe,*
EncWL, EncWT, IntAu&W 76, –77,
IntWW 74, –75, –76, –77, –78, –79, –80, –81,
–82, –83, McGEWD, –84, ModFrL,
ModWD, PenC EUR, REn, REnWD,
WhoFr 79, WhoWor 74, –76, –78, WorAu
Targan, Barry 1932- *ConAu 73, DrAF 76,*
DrAP 75, DrAP&F 83
Tarkenton, Fran 1940- *BioIn 12, CelR 73,*
ConAu 103, CurBio 69, NewYTBE 71,
–72, WorAl
Tarkenton, Fran *see also* Tarkenton, Francis
Asbury
Tarkenton, Francis Asbury 1940- *BioIn 6, –7,*
–8, –9, –10, –11, NewYTBE 70,
WhoAm 74, –76, –78, –80, –82,
WhoFtbl 74
Tarkenton, Francis Asbury *see also* Tarkenton,
Fran
Tarkington, Booth 1869-1946 *AmAu&B,*
ApCAB X, AtlBL, BioIn 1, –2, –3, –4, –5,
–6, –8, –10, –11, –12, CarSB, ChhPo S2,
CnDAL, ConAmA, ConAmL, ConAu 110,
CurBio 46, CyWA, DcAmAu,
DcAmB S4, DcLB 9[port], DcLEL,

307

ConAu 85, ConLC 21[port], InB&W 80, SmATA 15, TwCCW 83

Taylor, Paula 1942- *SmATA 33*

Taylor, Peter Hillsman 1917- *AmAu&B, BioIn 3, –4, –8, –9, BlueB 76, ConAu 9NR, –13R, ConLC 1, –4, –18, ConNov 72, –76, –82, DcLB Y81B[port], DcLEL 1940, DrAF 76, DrAP&F 83, IntAu&W 76, –77, ModAL, ModAL SUP, Novels, OhA&B, PenC AM, REnAL, TwCA SUP, WhoAm 74, –76, –78, –80, WrDr 76, –80, –82, –84*

Taylor, Robert Lewis 1912- *AmAu&B, Au&Wr 6, BioIn 1, –2, –5, –7, –8, –10, –11, BlueB 76, ConAu 1R, –3NR, ConLC 14, ConNov 72, –76, CurBio 59, EncSF, IntAu&W 76, –77, OxAmL, REnAL, ScF&FL 1, –2, SmATA 10, WhoAm 74, –76, –78, –80, –82, WhoE 74, –75, –77, WhoWor 74, –76, –78, –80, –82, WorAu, WrDr 76, –80, –82, –84*

Taylor, Sydney 1904?-1978 *AuBYP, BioIn 6, –8, –9, –10, –11, BkCL, ConAu 4NR, –5R, –77, IntAu&W 76, –77, MorBMP, MorJA, NewYTBS 78, SmATA 1, –26N, –28[port], TwCCW 78, –83, WrDr 76*

Taylor, Theodore 1921?- *AuBYP SUP, BioIn 10, ConAu 9NR, –21R, FourBJA, IntAu&W 77, SmATA 5, TwCCW 78, –83, WhoAm 74, –76, –78, –80, –82, WrDr 76, –80, –84*

Tchekhov, Anton Pavlovich 1860-1904 *CasWL, DcEuL, LongCTC, OxEng*

Tchekhov, Anton Pavlovich *see also* Chekhov, Anton Pavlovich

Teague, Bob 1929- *BlkAWP, ConAu X, DrBIPA, LivgBAA, NegAl 76, –83[port], SelBAA, SmATA X, WhoAmP 83*

Teague, Robert 1929- *AuBYP SUP, BioIn 8, ConAu 106, InB&W 80, SmATA 31, –32[port], WhoBlA 75, –77, –80*

Teale, Edwin Way 1899-1980 *AmAu&B, AnObit 1980[port], Au&Wr 6, AuBYP, BioIn 1, –2, –3, –4, –5, –6, –7, –8, –9, –10, –12, ConAu 1R, –2NR, –102, CurBio 61, –81N, InSci, LinLib L, –S, NewYTBS 80[port], REnAL, SmATA 25N, –7, Str&VC, ThrBJA, TwCA SUP, WhAm 7, WhNAA, WhoAm 74, –76, –78, –80, WhoWor 74, WrDr 76, –80, –82, –84*

Tebbel, John 1912- *AmAu&B, BioIn 3, ConAu 85, CurBio 53, DrAS 74E, –78E, –82E, SmATA 26[port], WhoAm 74, –76, –78, –80, –82*

Tec, Nechama 1931- *ConAu 9R, WhoAmW 68, –70, –72, –75*

Techter, David 1932- *BiDPara, EncO&P 78*

Tedeschi, Frank P 1938- *WhoEng 80*

Tedlock, Dennis 1939- *DrAS 82P, FifIDA*

Tegner, Bruce 1928- *ConAu 8NR, –61, IntAu&W 76*

Teissier DuCros, Janet 1906- *ConAu P-2, WrDr 76, –82*

Teleki, Geza 1943- *ConAu 3NR, –49*

Telemaque, Eleanor Wong 1934- *ConAu 104, DrAP&F 83*

Temkin, Sara Anne 1912?- *AuBYP, BiDrLUS 70, BioIn 8, ConAu 1R, ForWC 70, SmATA 26[port], WhoAmW 66, WhoLibI 82, WhoLibS 66*

TenBoom, Corrie 1892-1983 *BioIn 10, –11, –12, ConAu 109*

Tene, Benjamin 1914- *IntWWP 77, –82, WhoWorJ 72, –78*

Tennenbaum, Silvia 1928- *BioIn 11, ConAu 77, DrAP&F 83*

Tennissen, Anthony Cornelius 1920- *AmM&WS 73P, –76P, –79P, –82P*

Tennyson, Alfred 1809-1892 *Alli, Alli SUP, AnCL, AtlBL, AuBYP, BbD, BiD&SB, BioIn 1, –2, –3, –4, –5, –6, –7, –8, –9, –10, –11, –12, BrAu 19, BrWr 4, CasWL, CelCen, Chambr 3, ChhPo, –S1, –S2, –S3, CnE&AP, CnThe, CrtT 3, –4, CyWA, DcBiPP, DcEnA, –AP, DcEnL, DcEuL, DcLEL, Dis&D, EvLB, IlEncMy, LinLib L, –S, LongCEL, LuthC 75, McGEWB, McGEWD, MouLC 4, NewC, NewEOp 71, NotNAT B, OxEng, OxMus, OxThe, PenC ENG, PoLE, RAdv 1, RComWL, REn, REnWD, Str&VC, WebE&AL, WhDW, WorAl*

Tepper, Terri P 1942- *ConAu 107*

Ter Haar, Jaap 1922- *ConAu 37R, IntAu&W 76, SmATA 6*

Ter Haar, Jaap *see also* Haar, Jaap Ter

Terhune, Albert Payson 1872-1942 *AmAu&B, AmLY, AuBYP, BiD&SB, BioIn 2, –5, –7, –8, –9, –11, –12, ChhPo, CnDAL, CurBio 42, DcAmAu, DcAmB S3, DcLB 9[port], DcNAA, EvLB, JBA 34, LinLib L, NatCAB 10, –34, ObitOF 79, OxAmL, REnAL, SmATA 15, TwCA, TwCA SUP, TwCBDA, TwCCW 83, WebAB, –79, WhAm 2, WhLit, WhNAA, WorAl*

Terkel, Studs 1912- *AmAu&B, AuNews 1, BioIn 7, –10, –11, –12, ConAu 57, CurBio 74, IntWW 83, LinLib L, WhoAm 74, –76, –78, –80, –82, WhoMW 74, –76, –80, –82, WorAl, WrDr 76, –80, –82, –84*

Terlouw, Jan 1931- *ConAu 108, SmATA 30[port], WhoWor 82*

Terman, Douglas *BioIn 12*

Terraine, John Alfred 1921- *Au&Wr 6, ConAu 5R, IntAu&W 76, –77, IntWW 77, –78, –79, –80, –81, –82, –83, Who 74, –82, –83, WrDr 76, –80, –82, –84*

Terrell, Donna McManus 1908- *ConAu 57*

Terrell, John Upton 1900- *AmAu&B, AmNov, AuBYP, BioIn 2, –8, ConAu 29R, OxCan SUP, WhoWest 74*

Terrell, Robert L 1943- *BlkAWP, ConAu 41R, WhoBlA 75, –77, –80*

Terres, John Kenneth 1905- *AmAu&B, AmM&WS 73P, –76P, –79P, Au&Wr 6, BioIn 5, ConAu 5R, –5NR, WhoAm 74, –76, –78, –80, –82, WhoWor 78*

Terrien, Samuel 1911- *ConAu 81, DrAS 74P, –78P, –82P, WhoAm 74, –76, –78*

Terrill, Ross Gladwin 1938- *AmM&WS 73S, –78S, BioIn 9, ConAu 25R, IntAu&W 77, –82, WhoAm 74, –76, –78, –80, –82, WhoWor 82*

Terrill, Tom E 1935- *ConAu 41R, DrAS 74H, –78H, –82H*

Terris, Susan 1937- *AuBYP SUP, BioIn 9, ConAu 29R, DrAP&F 83, IntAu&W 76, –77, –82, SmATA 3, WhoAmW 75, WrDr 76, –80, –82, –84*

Terry, Luther Leonidas 1911- *AmM&WS 73P, –76P, –79P, –82P, BiDrACP 79, BiDrAPH 79, BioIn 5, –11, BlueB 76, ConAu P-2, CurBio 61, InSci, IntWW 74, –75, –76, –77, –78, –79, –80, –81, –82, –83, PolProf J, PolProf K, SmATA 11, WhoAm 74, –76, –78, –80, –82, WhoWor 82*

Terry, Walter 1913-1982 *AmAu&B, AnObit 1982[port], AuBYP, BioIn 8, –12, ConAu 10NR, –107, –21R, NewYTBS 82[port], SmATA 14, WhoAm 74, –76, –78, –80, –82*

Terzian, James P 1915- *AuBYP SUP, BioIn 12, ConAu 13R, SmATA 14*

Tesich, Steve 1943?- *ConAu 105, ConDr 82, DcLB Y83B[port], IntMPA 82, –84, NatPD 81, NewYTBS 80[port], –82[port], WhoAm 82, WrDr 84*

Tevis, Walter 1928- *ConSFA, DrAP&F 83, EncSF, NewYTBS 83[port], ScF&FL 1, WrDr 84*

Tey, Josephine 1897?-1952 *BioIn 2, –3, –4, –12, ConAu X, CorpD, DcLEL, EncMys, EvLB, LongCTC, NewC, Novels, ObitOF 79, ObitT 1951, PenC ENG, REn, TwCA SUP, TwCCr&M 80, TwCWr, WorAl*

Thacher, Alida McKay 1951- *ConAu 11NR, –69*

Thackeray, William Makepeace 1811-1863 *Alli, ArtsNiC, AtlBL, BbD, BiD&SB, BioIn 1, –2, –3, –4, –5, –6, –7, –8, –9, –10, –11, –12, BrAu 19, BrWr 5, CarSB, CasWL, CelCen, Chambr 3, ChhPo, –S1, –S2, –S3, CrtT 3, –4, CyWA, DcBiA, DcBiPP, DcBrBI, DcBrWA, DcEnA, –AP, DcEnL, DcEuL, DcInB, DcLB 21[port], DcLEL, Dis&D, EvLB, FamSYP, HsB&A, LinLib L, –S, LongCEL, McGEWB, MouLC 3, NewC, Novels[port], OxAmL, OxEng, PenC ENG, RAdv 1, RComWL, REn, ScF&FL 1, –1A, SmATA 23[port], TelT, WebE&AL, WhDW, WhoChL,*

WorAl

Thaler, Susan 1939- *ConAu 21R*

Thane, Adele 1904- *AuBYP SUP, BiE&WWA, ConAu 25R*

Thane, Elswyth 1900- *AmAu&B, AmNov, AmWomWr, Au&Wr 6, BioIn 2, –11, ConAu 5R, ForWC 70, InWom, REnAL, ScF&FL 1, –2, SmATA 32[port], WhE&EA, WhThe, WhoAm 74, –76, –78, WhoAmW 74, –58, –64, –66, –68, –70, –72, WhoE 74, WrDr 84*

Tharp, Louise Hall 1898- *AmAu&B, Au&Wr 6, AuBYP, BioIn 2, –3, –4, –6, –8, –9, –10, ChhPo, ConAu 1R, CurBio 55, ForWC 70, InWom, MorJA, RAdv 1, SmATA 3, WhoAm 74, –76, –78, WhoAmW 58, –64, –66, –68, –70, –72, WorAu*

Thayer, Charles Wheeler 1910-1969 *BioIn 2, –4, –8, –11, ConAu 1R, –103, NatCAB 56, ObitOF 79, WhAm 5*

Thayer, James Stewart 1949- *ConAu 73*

Thayer, Marjorie *BioIn 4*

Theroux, Paul 1941- *Au&Wr 6, BioIn 11, –12, ConAu 33R, ConLC 5, –8, –11, –15, ConNov 72, –76, –82, ConP 70, CurBio 78, DcLB 2, DrAF 76, DrAP&F 83, IntAu&W 76, –77, –82, NewYTBS 76, –78, Novels[port], Who 82, –83, WhoAm 78, –80, –82, WhoE 74, WorAl, WorAu 1970, WrDr 76, –80, –82, –84*

Thiele, Colin 1920- *Au&Wr 6, BioIn 12, ConAu 29R, ConLC 17, ConP 70, –75, DcLEL 1940, IntWWP 77, SingR 1, SmATA 14, TwCCW 78, –83, WrDr 76, –80, –82, –84*

Thom, James Alexander 1933- *BioIn 12, ConAu 77, DrAP&F 83, WhoMW 80, –82*

Thom, Robert 1929-1979 *BioIn 11, –12, ConAu 21R, –85, NewYTBS 79, ScF&FL 1, –2*

Thomas, Arline 1913- *ConAu 49, NewYTBE 71*

Thomas, Benjamin Platt 1902-1956 *AuBYP, BioIn 3, –4, –7, –8, NatCAB 47, ObitOF 79, WhAm 3*

Thomas, Bill 1934- *ConAu 8NR, –61, IntAu&W 82, WhoMW 78, –80*

Thomas, Bob 1922- *BioIn 10, ConAu X*

Thomas, Craig 1942- *ConAu 108, EncSF, Novels, WrDr 84*

Thomas, Craig *see also* Grant, David

Thomas, Denis 1922- *Au&Wr 6, ConAu 77, IntAu&W 77, –82, WhoWor 76, WrDr 76, –80, –82, –84*

Thomas, Dian 1945- *ConAu 10NR, –65, WhoWest 84*

Thomas, Elizabeth Marshall 1931- *Au&Wr 6, ConAu 17R*

Thomas, Estelle Webb 1899- *ArizL, ConAu 21R, IntAu&W 77, WrDr 76, –80,*

–84

Thomas, Gordon 1933- *ConAu 9R,
IntAu&W 76, –77, –82, WhoWor 78,
WrDr 82, –84*

Thomas, Hugh Swynnerton 1931- *Au&Wr 6,
BioIn 10, ConAu 5NR, –9R, DcLEL 1940,
IntAu&W 76, –77, –82, IntWW 80, –81,
NewC, Who 74, WhoWor 76, WorAu,
WrDr 80, –82, –84*

Thomas, J C *ConAu 57*

Thomas, John 1890- *ConAu 49, IntAu&W 77*

Thomas, Joyce Carol 1938- *DrAP&F 83,
WhoBlA 75, –77, –80*

Thomas, Kurt 1956- *BioIn 11, –12,
NewYTBS 80[port], WorAl*

Thomas, Lewis 1913- *AmM&WS 73P, –76P,
–79P, –82P, BioIn 10, –12, ConAu 85,
CurBio 75, IntMed 80, IntWW 77, –78,
–79, –80, –81, –82, –83, LEduc 74,
WhoAm 74, –76, –78, –80, –82, WhoE 74,
WhoWor 78, –80, –82, WrDr 82, –84*

Thomas, Liz 1952- *ConAu X*

Thomas, Lowell 1892-1981 *AmAu&B,
AnObit 1981[port], Au&Wr 6, AuBYP,
AuNews 1, –2, BioIn 1, –2, –3, –4, –5, –7,
–8, –10, –11, –12, BioNews 74, CelR 73,
ConAu 3NR, –104, –45, CurBio 40, –52,
–81N, FilmgC, IntAu&W 77,
IntMPA 77, –75, –76, –78, –79, –81, –82,
JBA 34, LesBEnT[port], LinLib L, –S,
MnBBF, NewYTBE 70,
NewYTBS 81[port], NewYTET, OhA&B,
OxCan, REnAL, TwCA, TwCA SUP,
WebAB, –79, WhE&EA, WhJnl,
WhNAA, Who 74, –82N, WhoAm 74, –76,
–78, –80, WhoAmP 81, WhoHol A,
WorAl, WrDr 80, –82*

Thomas, Piri 1928- *AmAu&B, BioIn 7, –8, –9,
–10, ConAu 73, ConLC 17, DrAF 76,
DrAP 75, DrAP&F 83, IntAu&W 77,
WhoE 74, WrDr 76, –80, –82, –84*

Thomas, Ross Elmore 1926- *Au&Wr 6,
ConAu 33R, EncMys, Novels,
TwCCr&M 80, WhoAm 74, –76, –78, –80,
–82, WhoS&SW 73, WrDr 76, –80, –82,
–84*

Thomas, Ross Elmore *see also* Bleeck, Oliver

Thomas, Tony 1927- *WhoHol A*

Thompson, Arthur Leonard Bell 1917-1975
BioIn 10, ConAu 53, –61

Thompson, Arthur Leonard Bell *see also* Clifford,
Francis

Thompson, Don 1935- *ConAu 53*

Thompson, Gene 1924- *ConAu 103, –104*

Thompson, Hunter S 1939?- *BioIn 7, –9, –11,
–12, ConAu 17R, ConLC 9, –17,
CurBio 81[port], IntAu&W 76, –77, –82,
NewYTBS 79, WhoAm 76, –78, –80, –82,
WhoE 74*

Thompson, Jean *DrAP&F 83*

Thompson, Kay 1912- *AmAu&B, BioIn 12,
CelR 73, ChhPo, ConAu 85, CurBio 59,*

*FourBJA, SmATA 16, WhoAm 74, –76,
WhoAmW 74, –61, –64, –66, –68, –70, –72,
WorAl*

Thompson, Lawrance Roger 1906-1973
*AmAu&B, Au&Wr 6, BioIn 9, ChhPo,
ConAu 5R, –10NR, –41R, NewYTBE 73,
ObitOF 79, WhAm 5*

Thompson, Paul Devries 1939- *AmM&WS 73P,
–79P, –82P*

Thompson, Robert Grainger Ker 1916- *BioIn 8,
BlueB 76, Who 74, –82, –83, WhoWor 74,
–76*

Thompson, Steven Lynn 1948- *WhoE 83*

Thompson, Stith 1885-1976 *AmAu&B, AnCL,
Au&Wr 6, BioIn 10, –11, –12, ConAu 5R,
–5NR, –61, FifIDA, IndAu 1917,
NewYTBS 76, OxCan, SmATA 20N,
WhAm 6*

Thompson, Thomas 1933?-1982 *BioIn 12,
ConAu 108, IntAu&W 82, WrDr 82*

Thompson, William E, Jr. 1923- *ConAu 13R*

Thomson, Arthur 1861-1933 *InSci, LongCTC,
WhE&EA*

Thomson, Betty Flanders 1913-
*AmM&WS 73P, –76P, Au&Wr 6,
ConAu 9R, WhoAmW 74, –68, –72, –75,
WhoE 74*

Thomson, David 1914- *Au&Wr 6, BioIn 10,
–11, ConAu 107, WrDr 76, –80, –82, –84*

Thomson, June 1930- *ConAu 81,
IntAu&W 82, TwCCr&M 80, WrDr 82,
–84*

Thorburn, David 1940- *Alli, ConAu 7NR, –53*

Thoreau, Henry David 1817-1862 *Alli, AmAu,
AmAu&B, AmBi, AmWr, AnCL,
ApCAB, AtlBL, BbD, BbtC, BiD&SB,
BioIn 1, –2, –3, –4, –5, –6, –7, –8, –9, –10,
–11, –12, CasWL, CelCen, Chambr 3,
ChhPo, CnDAL, CnE&AP, CrtT 3, –4,
CyAL 2, CyWA, DcAmAu, DcAmB,
DcAmSR, DcEnA, DcLB 1, DcLEL,
DcNAA, Dis&D, Drake, EncAAH,
EncAB-H, EvLB, HarEnUS[port],
IlEncMy, InSci, LinLib L, –S, McGEWB,
MouLC 3, NatCAB 2, OxAmH, OxAmL,
OxCan, OxEng, PenC AM, RAdv 1,
RComWL, REn, REnAL, REnAW,
TwCBDA, WebAB, –79, WebE&AL,
WhDW, WhAm HS, WorAl*

Thorn, John 1947- *ConAu 97*

Thorndike, Joseph J 1913- *St&PR 75,
WhoAm 74, –76, –78, –80, –82, WrDr 80,
–82, –84*

Thorne, Ian *ConAu X, SmATA X*

Thorne, Ian *see also* May, Julian

Thorvall, Kerstin 1925- *BioIn 11, ConAu 17R,
SmATA 13*

Thorwald, Juergen 1916- *ConAu 1NR, –49,
WhoWor 74, –76*

Thrapp, Dan Lincoln 1913- *ConAu 4NR, –9R*

Thrasher, Crystal 1921- *ConAu 8NR, –61,
SmATA 27[port]*

Throckmorton, Peter 1928- *AuBYP, BioIn 8,
–9, ConAu 17R, WhoWor 76*

Thum, Gladys 1920- *ConAu 41R,
SmATA 26[port]*

Thum, Marcella *AuBYP SUP, BioIn 9,
ConAu 6NR, –9R, IntAu&W 77,
SmATA 28[port], –3, WhoAmW 75,
WrDr 76, –80, –82, –84*

Thurber, James 1894-1961 *AmAu&B,
AmWr SUP, AnCL, AtlBL, AuBYP,
BioIn 1, –2, –3, –4, –5, –6, –7, –8, –9, –10,
–11, –12, BkCL, CasWL, CnDAL,
CnMWL, ConAmA, ConAu 73,
ConLC 5, –11, –25[port], CurBio 40, –60,
–62, CyWA, DcAmB S7, DcLB 4,
–11[port], –22[port], DcLEL, EncWL,
EvLB, FilmgC, LinLib L, –S, LongCTC,
McGEWB, McGEWD, –84[port], ModAL,
MorJA, NatCAB 57, NotNAT A, –B,
Novels, ObitOF 79, ObitT 1961, OhA&B,
OxAmL, OxEng, PenC AM, RAdv 1,
REn, REnAL, ScF&FL 1, SmATA 13,
TwCA, TwCA SUP, TwCCW 78, –83,
TwCWr, WebAB, –79, WebE&AL,
WhDW, WhAm 4, WhoGrA, WhoTwCL,
WorAl, WorECar*

Thurman, Howard 1899?-1981
*AnObit 1981[port], BioIn 3, –4, –5, –7, –8,
–11, –12, BlueB 76, BlkAWP, CmCal,
ConAu 103, –97, CurBio 55, –81N,
Ebony 1, InB&W 80, LinLib L, –S,
LivgBAA, NegAl 76, –83,
NewYTBS 81[port], SelBAA, WhAm 7,
WhoAm 74, –76, –78, WhoBlA 75, –77, –80,
WhoRel 77*

Thurman, Judith 1946- *ChhPo S3,
ConAu 1NR, –49, DrAP 75, DrAP&F 83,
SmATA 33*

Thurman, Wallace 1902-1934 *AmAu&B,
BioIn 10, BlkAWP, ConAu 104, DrBlPA,
InB&W 80, ModBlW, NegAl 76, –83,
REnAL, SelBAA, TwCLC 6[port]*

Thurston, David 1818?- *DcCanB 11*

Thurston, Robert 1936- *ConAu 85, WrDr 84*

Thwaite, Anthony 1930- *Au&Wr 6, BioIn 8,
ChhPo S1, ConAu 5R, ConP 70, –75, –80,
DcLEL 1940, IntAu&W 76, –77, –82,
IntWWP 77, NewC, Who 74, –82, –83,
WorAu 1970, WrDr 76, –80, –82, –84*

Tibbets, Albert B 1888- *AuBYP SUP,
ConAu 5R*

Tibbets, Paul 1915- *BioIn 10, –11, –12,
WhWW-II*

Tibble, Anne 1912-1980 *Au&Wr 6, BioIn 12,
ChhPo S2, ConAu 9R, –10NR, –102,
IntAu&W 76, –77, –82, WrDr 80*

Tibbles, Thomas Henry 1838-1928 *Alli SUP,
AmAu, DcAmB, DcNAA, HarEnUS,
NatCAB 21, OhA&B, WhAm 1*

Tiger, Lionel 1937- *AmM&WS 73S, –76P,
–79P, –82P, BioIn 10, –11, –12, BlueB 76,
CanWW 70, –79, –80, –81, –83,*

Tigue, Ethel Erkkila 1916?- *BioIn 6,
ConAu 21R, IntAu&W 76, MinnWr,
WhoAmW 74, –75*

Tilley, Patrick 1928- *ConAu 106, EncSF*

Timerman, Jacobo 1923- *BioIn 11, –12,
ConAu 109, CurBio 81[port],
NewYTBS 79*

Tinkle, Lon 1906-1980 *AmAu&B, ConAu 104,
SmATA 36, WhoS&SW 73, –75, –76*

Tinkleman, Murray 1933- *SmATA 12*

Tinnin, David Bruce 1930- *ConAu 49,
WhoAm 74, –76, –78, WhoE 74,
WhoWor 74, –76, –78, WrDr 80, –82, –84*

Tipton, James 1942- *ConAu 8NR, –57,
DrAF 76, DrAP 75, IntWWP 77, –82,
MichAu 80*

Tiptree, James, Jr. 1915- *BioIn 12, ConAu X,
DcLB 8, EncSF, Novels, ScF&FL 1, –2,
WhoSciF, WrDr 84*

Tiptree, James, Jr. *see also* Sheldon, Alice
Hastings

Tirro, Frank Pascale 1935- *ConAmC,
ConAu 81, DrAS 78H, –82H,
WhoAmM 83*

Titcomb, Margaret 1891- *ConAu 5R, –5NR,
ForWC 70, WhoAmW 58, –61, –64, –66,
–68, WhoLibS 55*

Titler, Dale Milton 1926- *AuBYP SUP,
ConAu 81, SmATA 28, –35*

Tobin, Richard Lardner 1910- *AmAu&B,
BioIn 1, –5, ConAu 1R, –1NR, CurBio 44,
St&PR 75, WhoAm 74, –76, –78*

Tocqueville, Alexis, Comte De 1805-1859 *AmBi,
ApCAB, AtlBL, BbD, BiD&SB, BioIn 1,
–2, –4, –5, –6, –7, –8, –10, –11, –12, CasWL,
CelCen, CnDAL, CyAG, DcAmSR,
DcBiPP, DcEuL, Drake, EuAu,
HarEnUS, LinLib L, –S, McGEWB,
NewC, OxAmH, OxAmL, OxEng, OxFr,
PenC AM, REn, REnAL, REnAW,
WhDW, WhAm HS, WorAl*

Tocqueville, Alexis, Comte De *see also*
DeTocqueville, Alexis

Tod, Osma Gallinger 1898-1982? *ConAu 108,
ConAu P-1, WhoAmA 80, –82*

Todd, Alden 1918- *ConAu 1R, –6NR,
DrAS 74H, –78H, –82H, IntAu&W 77,
WhoE 74, –75, WhoF&I 79*

Todd, Anne Ophelia *AuBYP, BioIn 10, –12,
ConAu X, SmATA 7*

Todd, Anne Ophelia *see also* Dowden, Anne
Ophelia Todd

Todd, Karen Iris Rohne Pritchett 1936-
*AmM&WS 73S, –78S, LEduc 74,
WhoAmW 74, –72, –75*

Toepfer, Ray Grant 1923- *ConAu 21R*

Toffler, Alvin 1928- *AmAu&B, BioIn 10, –12,
ConAu 13R, ConIsC 1[port], CurBio 75,*

DcLEL 1940, EncSF, Future,
NewYTBS 80, WhoAm 74, –76, –78, –80,
–82, WhoE 75, WrDr 76, –80, –82, –84
Tolan, Stephanie S 1942- ConAu 77,
DrAP&F 83, Po&Wr 77
Toland, John Willard 1912- Au&Wr 6,
BioIn 10, ConAu 1R, –6NR, LinLib L,
WhoAm 74, –76, –78, –80, –82,
WhoWor 80, –82, WorAu, WrDr 76, –82,
–84
Tolchin, Martin 1928- WhoE 74, –75
Toliver, Raymond Frederick 1914- ConAu 17R,
IntAu&W 76, –77, WhoWest 74, –76, –78,
–80, –82, WrDr 76, –80, –82, –84
Tolkien, J R R 1892-1973 CelR 73,
ConAu P-2, ConLC 8, –12, CurBio 57,
–67, –73, –73N, DcLB 15[port], EncSF,
LinLib L, –S, NewYTBE 73, Novels[port],
ObitOF 79, ObitT 1971, ScF&FL 1, –2,
SmATA 24N, –32[port], TwCCW 83,
WhoHr&F, WorAl
Tolkien, John Ronald Reuel 1892-1973 AnCL,
Au&Wr 6, AuBYP, AuNews 1, BioIn 3,
–4, –6, –7, –8, –9, –10, –11, –12, CasWL,
CelR 73, ChhPo, –S1, –S2, –S3, CnMWL,
ConAu 45, ConAu P-2, ConLC 1, –2, –3,
ConNov 72, –76, CurBio 57, –67, –73,
DcLEL, EncWL, LongCTC, MakMC,
ModBrL, ModBrL SUP, MorJA, NewC,
OxEng, PenC ENG, RAdv 1, REn,
SmATA 2, TelT, TwCCW 78, TwCWr,
WebE&AL, WhDW, WhAm 6, WhLit,
WhoChL, WhoTwCL, WhoWor 74,
WorAu
Toll, Robert Charles 1938- ConAu 53,
WrDr 76, –80, –82, –84
Tolstoy, Leo Nikolayevich 1828-1910 AtlBL,
BbD, BiD&SB, BioIn 1, –2, –3, –4, –5, –6,
–7, –8, –9, –10, –11, –12, CasWL, CelCen,
ClDMEL, CnMD, CnThe, ConAu 104,
CyWA, DcAmSR, DcBiA, DcEuL,
DcRusL, DrAP 75, Dis&D, EncWT,
EuAu, EvEuW, FilmgC, LinLib S,
LongCEL, LongCTC, LuthC 75,
McGEWB, McGEWD, –84[port],
ModSL 1, ModWD, NewEOp 71,
NotNAT B, Novels, OxEng, OxThe,
PenC EUR, PIP&P, RComWL, REn,
REnWD, SmATA 26[port],
TwCLC 4[port], –11[port], WhDW,
WorAl
Toma, David 1934?- BioIn 9, –10, –12
Tomalin, Nicholas 1931-1973 Au&Wr 6,
BioIn 10, ConAu 45, ObitT 1971
Tombaugh, Clyde William 1906-
AmM&WS 73P, AsBiEn, BiESc, BioIn 4,
–6, –10, –12, BlueB 76, InSci, IntWW 74,
–75, –76, –77, –78, –79, –80, –81, –82, –83,
UFOEn, WhDW, WhoAm 74, –76,
WhoWest 74, –76, –78, WhoWor 74
Tomerlin, John 1930- AuBYP SUP
Tomkins, Calvin 1925- BioIn 2, ConAu 8NR,

–13R, WhoAmA 78, –80, –82, WrDr 76,
–80, –82, –84
Tomlinson, Gerald 1933- ConAu 85
Tompkins, Peter 1919- ConAu 9R
Tonkin, Peter 1950- ConAu 101
Toole, John Kennedy 1937-1969 BioIn 12,
ConAu 104, ConLC 19,
DcLB Y81B[port]
Toperoff, Sam 1933- BioIn 8, ConAu 45
Toppin, Edgar Allan 1928- ConAu 21R,
DrAS 74H, –78H, –82H, InB&W 80,
LivgBAA, SelBAA, WhoBlA 75, –77, –80
Torbado, Jesus 1943- BioIn 12, IntAu&W 76,
–77, –82
Torbet, Laura 1942- ConAu 69,
WhoAmW 81, –83
Torgoff, Martin 1952- ConAu 109
Torok, Lou 1927- BioIn 10, ConAu 49
Torrey, Volta Wray 1905- ConAu 69,
WhoAm 74, –76, WhoGov 72, –75,
WhoWor 74
Tosches, Nick 1949- ConAu 81
Toth, Susan Erickson Allen 1940- ConAu 105,
DrAS 74E, –78E, –82E
Tournier, Michel 1924- BioIn 10,
ConAu 3NR, –49, ConLC 6, –23[port],
EncWL, IntAu&W 76, –77, –82,
IntWW 74, –75, –76, –77, –78, –79, –80, –81,
–82, –83, ModFrL, SmATA 23[port],
TwCCW 78B, –83B, WhoFr 79
Touster, Irwin AuBYP SUP
Tovey, Doreen Evelyn 1918- Au&Wr 6,
ConAu 104
Towne, Mary AuBYP SUP, ConAu X,
SmATA X
Townsend, Doris Ann McFerran 1914-
ConAu 103, ForWC 70, WhoAmW 74,
–66, –68, –70, –72, –75, WhoE 74, –75
Townsend, Janet 1925- AuBYP SUP,
ConAu 107
Townsend, John Rowe 1922- Au&Wr 6,
AuBYP SUP, ChlLR 2, ChhPo S2, –S3,
ConAu 37R, DcLEL 1940, FourBJA,
IntAu&W 76, –77, –82, PiP, SmATA 4,
TwCCW 78, –83, WhoWor 74, –76,
WrDr 76, –80, –82, –84
Townshend, Peter 1945- ConAu 107,
ConLC 17, CurBio 83[port], WhoAm 80,
–82
Townshend, Peter see also Who, The
Tracey, Hugh 1903-1977 ConAu 77,
ConAu P-2, OxMus
Trachtenberg, Alan 1932- DrAS 74E, –78E,
–82E, WhoAm 80, WhoE 79, –81
Trachtenberg, Marvin L 1939- ConAu 65,
DrAS 74H, –78H, –82H, WhoAm 80, –82,
WhoE 79, –81
Trahey, Jane 1923- BioIn 8, ConAu 17R,
ForWC 70, SmATA 36, WhoAdv 72,
WhoAmW 74, –58, –61, –64, –66, –68, –70,
–72, –75, –79, –81, WhoE 74, WhoF&I 74
Transtromer, Tomas 1931- BioIn 9, CasWL,

IntWWP 77, WorAu 1970

Trapp, Maria Augusta Von 1905- *AmAu&B,*
BioIn 3, –6, –7, –8, –9, –10, –12,
CathA 1952, CurBio 68, GoodHs,
InWom, SmATA 16, WhoAm 74, –76, –78,
–80, –82, WhoAmW 74, –58, –61, –64, –66,
–68, –70, –72, WhoE 74, WhoWor 74, –76,
WorAl

Traven, B 1890?-1969 *AmAu&B, BioIn 1, –2,*
–4, –5, –6, –7, –8, –9, –11, –12, ConAu 25R,
ConAu P-2, ConLC 8, –11, DcLB 9[port],
EncWL, ObitOF 79, OxAmL, OxGer,
REnAL, ScF&FL 1, TwCA, TwCA SUP,
WebE&AL, WhAm 5

Treadgold, Mary 1910- *Au&Wr 6, BioIn 8,*
ConAu 13R, IntAu&W 76, TwCCW 78,
–83, WhoChL, WrDr 76, –80, –82, –84

Trease, Geoffrey 1909- *AuBYP, BioIn 6, –7,*
–8, –9, –10, ConAu 5R, –7NR, DcLEL,
MnBBF, MorJA, SmATA 2, TelT,
TwCCW 78, –83, Who 74, –82, –83,
WhoBW&I A, WhoChL, WrDr 76, –80,
–82, –84

Treat, Roger L 1905- *AuBYP, BioIn 7*

Treece, Henry 1911?-1966 *AuBYP, BioIn 4,*
–6, –7, –8, –9, CathA 1930, ConAu 1R,
–6NR, –25R, DcLEL, EvLB,
LongCTC, ModBrL, MorJA, NewC,
ObitOF 79, PenC ENG, REn,
ScF&FL 1, –2, SmATA 2, TwCA SUP,
TwCCW 78, –83, TwCWr, WhoChL

Trefil, James S 1938- *AmM&WS 73P, –76P,*
–79P, –82P, ConAu 101, WhoTech 82

Tregaskis, Richard 1916-1973 *AmAu&B,*
Au&Wr 6, AuBYP, BioIn 7, –9, –10, –12,
BlueB 76, ConAu 1R, –2NR, –45,
CurBio 73, –73N, NatCAB 59[port],
NewYTBE 73, ObitOF 79, SmATA 26N,
–3, WebAMB, WhAm 6, WhoAm 74,
WhoWor 74

Tregear, Thomas R 1897- *ConAu 21R,*
WrDr 76, –80, –82, –84

Trelease, Allen William 1928- *AuBYP SUP,*
ConAu 108, DrAS 74H, –78H, –82H,
WhoAm 74, –76, –78, –80, –82

Tretyak, Vladislav 1952- *BioIn 11*

Trevanian 1925?- *ConAu 108, NewYTBS 79,*
Novels, TwCCr&M 80, WhoAm 82,
WhoSpyF, WrDr 82, –84

Trever, John Cecil 1915- *BioIn 1, ConAu 17R,*
DrAS 74P, –78P, –82P, IntAu&W 77, –82,
WrDr 76, –80, –82, –84

Treves, Ralph 1906- *ConAu 13R, WrDr 76,*
–80, –82, –84

Trevino, Elizabeth B De 1904- *AuBYP,*
BioIn 7, –8, –9, –10, –11, ConAu 9NR,
–17R, NinCLC 1966, ScF&FL 1, –2,
SmATA 1, –29[port], ThrBJA,
WhoAm 74, –76, –78, –80, –82,
WhoAmW 74, –70, –72, WhoS&SW 73,
–75, –76

Trevino, Elizabeth B De *see also* DeTrevino,
Elizabeth B

Trevor, Elleston 1920- *Au&Wr 6, ConAu 5R,*
DcLEL 1940, EncMys, EncSF,
IntAu&W 76, –77, MnBBF, Novels,
ScF&FL 1, –2, SmATA 28[port],
TwCCW 78, TwCCr&M 80, Who 74, –82,
–83, WhoAm 74, –76, –78, –80, –82,
WhoWor 74, –82, WrDr 76, –80, –82, –84

Trevor, Meriol 1919- *Au&Wr 6, BioIn 11,*
ConAu 1R, –1NR, IntAu&W 76, –77, –82,
IntWWP 77, –82, ScF&FL 1, –2,
SmATA 10, TwCCW 78, –83, Who 74,
–82, –83, WhoAmW 74, –68, –70, –72, –75,
WhoWor 74, –76, WrDr 76, –80, –82, –84

Trevor, William 1928- *Alli, BioIn 10,*
BlueB 76, ConAu X, ConDr 73, –77, –82,
ConLC 7, –9, –14, –25[port], ConNov 72,
–76, –82, DcIrL, DcIrW 1,
DcLB 14[port], DcLEL 1940,
IntAu&W 76, –77, –82, IntWW 81, –82,
–83, ModBrL SUP, NewC, Novels,
TwCWr, Who 74, –82, –83, WhoWor 74,
–76, WorAu, WrDr 76, –80, –82, –84

Trew, Antony 1906- *ConAu 2NR, –45,*
EncSoA, ScF&FL 1, –2, WhoSpyF,
WrDr 80, –82, –84

Tripp, Eleanor B 1936- *BioIn 9, ConAu 29R,*
SmATA 4

Trivelpiece, Laurel *DrAP&F 83*

Trogdon, William Oren 1920- *AmM&WS 73P,*
–76P, –79P, –82P, LEduc 74, WhoAm 76,
–78, –80, –82, WhoS&SW 73, –76

Troise, Joe 1942- *ConAu 103*

Trojanski, John 1943- *ConAu 45*

Troop, Elizabeth 1931- *Au&Wr 6,*
ConDr 82B, DcLB 14[port]

Tropp, Martin 1945- *ConAu 65*

Trotsky, Leon 1879-1940 *BioIn 1, –2, –3, –4, –5,*
–6, –7, –8, –9, –10, –11, –12, CasWL,
CurBio 40, DcAmSR, DcRusL, Film 1,
HisEWW, LinLib L, –S, LongCTC,
MakMC, McGEWB, REn, WhScrn 2,
WhoHol B, WorAl

Trotter, Grace V 1900- *AuBYP, BioIn 7, –11,*
ConAu 1R, –1NR, SmATA 10

Trotter, Grace V *see also* Paschal, Nancy

Troy, Simon *TwCCr&M 80*

Truax, Carol 1900- *ConAu 5R*

Trudeau, G B 1948- *ConAu 81*

Trudeau, Garry B 1948- *AuNews 2, ConAu X,*
ConLC 12, CurBio 75, SmATA 35,
WhoAm 78, –80, –82, WorECom,
WrDr 76, –80, –82, –84

Truman, Harry S 1884-1972 *AmAu&B,*
Au&Wr 6, BiDrAC, BiDrUSE, BioIn 1,
–2, –3, –4, –5, –6, –7, –8, –9, –10, –11, –12,
ConAu 106, –37R, CurBio 42, –45, –73N,
DcAmSR, DcPol, EncAAH, EncAB-H,
EncSoH, HisEWW, LinLib L, –S,
McGEWB, NatCAB 57, NewYTBE 70,
–72, ObitOF 79, ObitT 1971, OxAmH,

OxAmL, PolProf E, PolProf J, PolProf K, PolProf T, REn, REnAL, UFOEn, WebAB, –79, WhDW, WhAm 5, WhAmP, WhWW-II, WhoGov 72, WorAl

Truman, Margaret 1924- *BioIn 12, BioNews 74, CelR 73, ConAu 105, CurBio 50, InWom, NewYTBS 80[port], WhoAm 74, –78, –80, –82*

Trumbo, Dalton 1905-1976 *AmAu&B, ASpks, BioIn 2, –4, –5, –9, –11, CmCal, ConAu 10NR, –21R, –69, ConDr 73, –77A, ConLC 19, ConNov 72, –76, CurBio 41, –76, –76N, DcFM, DcLB 26[port], FilmgC, IntAu&W 76, –77, IntMPA 75, –76, NewYTBE 70, NewYTBS 76, Novels, ObitOF 79, OxFilm, PolProf T, REnAL, ScF&FL 1, –2, TwCA, TwCA SUP, WhAm 7, WhE&EA, WhoAm 74, –76, –78, WhoThe 81N, WhoWor 76, WorEFlm, WrDr 76*

Trumbull, Robert 1912- *AmAu&B, ConAu 5NR, –9R, WhoAm 74, –76, –78, –80, –82, WhoWor 74, –76, –78, –80*

Trump, Fred 1924- *ConAu 13R*

Trupin, James E 1940- *ConAu 37R*

Truss, Jan 1925- *ConAu 102, SmATA 35, TwCCW 83*

Tryon, Thomas 1926- *Alli, ASpks, AuNews 1, BioIn 10, –11, BioNews 75, CelR 73, ConAu 29R, ConLC 3, –11, Conv 1, CurBio 77, IntAu&W 76, –77, Novels, ScF&FL 1, –2, WhoAm 74, –76, –78, –80, –82, WorAl, WrDr 76, –80, –82, –84*

Tubb, E C 1919- *ConAu 101, ConSFA, EncSF, MnBBF, ScF&FL 1, –2, WhoSciF, WrDr 84*

Tubb, E C *see also* Kern, Gregory

Tuchman, Barbara Wertheim 1912- *AmAu&B, AmWomWr, Au&Wr 6, BioIn 6, –10, –11, –12, BlueB 76, CelR 73, ConAu 1R, –3NR, ConIsC 1[port], CurBio 63, DrAS 74H, –78H, –82H, InWom, IntAu&W 76, –77, IntWW 74, –75, –76, –77, –78, –79, –80, –81, –82, –83, LibW, LinLib L, NewYTBS 78, –79, OxAmL, WhoAm 74, –76, –78, –80, –82, WhoAmJ 80, WhoAmW 74, –58, –61, –64, –66, –68, –70, –72, –75, –77, –81, –83, WhoE 74, WhoWor 74, –78, –80, –82, WhoWorJ 72, –78, WorAl, WorAu, WrDr 76, –80, –82, –84*

Tucker, Glenn 1892-1976 *AmAu&B, BioIn 11, ConAu 5R, –69, IndAu 1917, IntAu&W 76, WhAm 7, WhoAm 74, –76*

Tucker, Wilson 1914- *ConAu 17R, ConSFA, IntAu&W 76, ScF&FL 1, –2, WhoSciF, WrDr 84*

Tuffs, Jack Elsden 1922- *Au&Wr 6, ConAu 5R, WrDr 76*

Tully, Andrew Frederick, Jr. 1914- *AmAu&B, ConAu 17R, IntAu&W 76, WhoAm 74,*

–76, –78, –80, –82, WrDr 76, –80, –82, –84

Tunis, Edwin 1897-1973 *AuBYP, BioIn 5, –6, –8, –9, –10, ChlLR 2, ConAu 5R, –7NR, –45, IlsCB 1946, –1957, –1967, MorJA, SmATA 1, –24N, –28[port], WhoAmA 73, –76N, –78N, –80N, –82N*

Tunis, John R 1889-1975 *Au&ICB, AuBYP, BioIn 4, –6, –7, –8, –10, –12, ConAu 57, –61, ConLC 12, DcLB 22[port], LinLib L, MorJA, NatCAB 58[port], NewYTBS 75, ObitOF 79, REnAL, SmATA 30, –37, TwCA, TwCA SUP, TwCCW 78, –83*

Tunley, Roul 1912- *AmAu&B, ConAu 13R, WhoAm 74, –76, –78, –80, –82, WrDr 76, –80, –82, –84*

Tunnard, Christopher 1910-1979 *AmAu&B, BioIn 5, –11, –12, ConAu 5R, –6NR, –85, CurBio 59, –79N, NewYTBS 79, WhAm 7, WhoAm 74, –76, –78, WhoWor 74*

Turgenev, Ivan S 1818-1883 *AtlBL, BbD, BiD&SB, BioIn 1, –2, –3, –4, –5, –6, –7, –8, –9, –10, –11, –12, CasWL, ClDMEL, CnThe, CyWA, DcBiA, DcEuL, DcRusL, Dis&D, EncWT, EuAu, EvEuW, LinLib L, McGEWB, McGEWD, –84[port], NewC, NewEOp 71, NotNAT A, –B, Novels[port], OxEng, PenC EUR, PlP&P, RComWL, REn, REnWD, ScF&FL 1, WhDW, WhoHr&F, WorAl*

Turki, Fawaz 1940- *ConAu 41R*

Turnage, Anne Shaw 1927- *ConAu 77*

Turnage, Mac N 1927- *ConAu 77*

Turnbull, Agnes 1888-1982 *AmAu&B, AmNov, AmWomWr, AnObit 1982[port], Au&Wr 6, AuBYP, BioIn 2, –4, –5, –7, –12, ConAu 1R, –2NR, –105, InWom, NewYTBS 82, REnAL, SmATA 14, TwCA, TwCA SUP, WhE&EA, WhNAA, WhoAm 74, –76, –78, –80, –82, WhoAmW 74, –58, –61, –64, –66, –68, –70, –72*

Turnbull, Andrew 1921-1970 *BioIn 8, –10, ChhPo S2, ConAu 1R, –3NR, –25R, DcLEL 1940, DrAS 74H, –78H, NatCAB 55, NewYTBE 70, ObitOF 79, WhAm 5*

Turnbull, Ann 1943- *BioIn 12, ConAu 65, NewYTBS 76, SmATA 18*

Turnbull, Bob 1936- *BioIn 10, ConAu 37R*

Turnbull, Colin M 1924- *AmM&WS 73S, –76P, ASpks, AuNews 1, BioIn 7, –9, –10, –11, –12, ConAu 1R, –3NR, CurBio 80[port], WhoAm 82, WorAu 1970*

Turner, Alice K 1940- *BioIn 11, ConAu 53, SmATA 10, WhoAm 76, –78, –80, –82*

Turner, Ann W 1945- *BioIn 12, ConAu 69, SmATA 14*

Turner, Darwin T 1931- *BlkAWP, ConAu 11NR, –21R, DrAS 74E, –78E,*

–82E, InB&W 80, LinLib L, LivgBAA,
SelBAA, WhoAm 74, –76, –78, –80, –82,
WhoBlA 75, –77, –80, WhoWor 78,
WrDr 76, –80, –82, –84

Turner, Frederick W, III 1937- ConAu 37R,
DrAS 74E

Turner, George Eugene 1925- ConAu 5NR, –53,
WhoS&SW 76, –78

Turner, Kay 1932- ConAu 69

Turner, Kermit 1936- ConAu 104,
DrAP&F 83

Turner, Philip 1925- Au&Wr 6, BioIn 7, –11,
ConAu 11NR, –25R, FourBJA,
IntAu&W 77, –82, SmATA 11,
TwCCW 78, –83, WrDr 80, –82, –84

Turner, Philip see also Chance, Stephen

Turner, Richard E 1920- BioIn 8, ConAu 29R

Turner, Susan 1952- ConAu 106

Turner, William Oliver 1914- Au&Wr 6,
AuNews 1, BioIn 10, BioNews 74,
ConAu 1R, –3NR, IntAu&W 76, –77, –82,
WrDr 76

Turngren, Ellen d1964 AuBYP, BioIn 6, –7,
–9, ConAu 5R, MinnWr, SmATA 3

Tusiani, Joseph 1924- AmAu&B, AmCath 80,
AuBYP, BioIn 8, BkC 6, ChhPo S2,
ConAu 5NR, –9R, DrAS 74F, –82F,
IntAu&W 76, –77, –82, IntWWP 77,
ScF&FL 1, –2, WhoAm 74, –76, –78, –80,
–82

Tuska, Jon 1942- ConAu 73

Tute, Warren 1914- Au&Wr 6, ConAu 1R,
–1NR, IntAu&W 77, –82, Novels,
Who 82, –83, WhoWor 76, –78, WrDr 76,
–80, –82, –84

Tutko, Thomas Arthur 1931- AmM&WS 73S,
–78S, ConAu 69, WhoWest 76

Tutu, Desmond Mpilo 1931- AfSS 80, –81, –82,
BioIn 12, IntWW 81, –82, –83,
NewYTBS 82[port], Who 82, –83

Tuve, George L 1896-1980 AmM&WS 73P,
–79P, BioIn 4, –8, –12, WhoEng 80

Twain, Mark 1835-1910 Alli, Alli SUP,
AmAu, AmAu&B, AmBi, AmWr, AtlBL,
AuBYP, BiD&SB, BiDPara, BiDSA,
BioIn 1, –2, –3, –4, –5, –6, –7, –8, –9, –10,
–11, –12, CasWL, CelCen, Chambr 3,
CmCal, CnDAL, ConAu X, CrtT 3, –4,
CyWA, DcAmAu, DcAmB, DcAmSR,
DcBiPP, DcEnA, –AP, DcEnL,
DcLB 11[port], DcLEL, DcNAA, Dis&D,
EncAAH, EncAB-H, EncMys, EncSF,
EncSoA, EncSoH, EncWL, EvLB,
FamAYP, FilmgC, HarEnUS, JBA 34,
LinLib LP, –S, McGEWB, ModAL,
ModAL SUP, NotNAT B, Novels[port],
OxAmH, OxAmL, OxEng, OxMus,
PenC AM, RAdv 1, RComWL, REn,
REnAL, REnAW, ScF&FL 1,
TwCCW 78A, –83A, TwCLC 6[port],
–12[port], WebAB, –79, WebE&AL,
WhDW, WhLit, WhoChL, WhoTwCL,

WorAl, YABC X

Twain, Mark see also Clemens, Samuel
Langhorne

Tweedie, Michael Willmer Forbes 1907-
Au&Wr 6

Tweton, D Jerome 1933- DrAS 74H, –78H,
–82H

Twichell, Chase DrAP&F 83

Twiggy 1949- BioIn 7, –8, –9, –10, –11, –12,
CelR 73, ConAu X, CurBio 68, FilmgC,
GoodHs, InWom, IntMPA 77, –75, –76,
–78, –79, –81, –82, –84, NewYTBS 83[port],
WhoAm 74, –76, –78, –80, WhoHol A,
WorAl

Twiggy see also Hornby, Leslie

Twist, Ananias ConAu X, IntAu&W 76X,
–82X, WrDr 76, –80, –82, –84

Twist, Ananias see also Nunn, William Curtis

Twombly, Wells 1935-1977 BioIn 11,
ConAu 41R, –69, NewYTBS 77,
WhAm 7, WhoAm 76, WhoWest 74, –76

Twyman, Gib 1943- ConAu X

Tyler, Anne 1941- AmWomWr, BioIn 10, –11,
–12, ConAu 9R, ConLC 7, –11, –18,
ConNov 72, –76, –82, CurBio 81[port],
DcLB Y82A[port], –6, DcLEL 1940,
DrAF 76, DrAP&F 83, IntAu&W 76,
–77, NewYTBS 77, SmATA 7,
WhoAm 76, –78, –80, –82, WhoAmW 74,
–68, –70, –72, –75, –79, –81, –83, WhoE 74,
–75, –77, WorAu 1970, WrDr 76, –80, –82,
–84

Tyler, Hamilton A 1917- ConAu 5NR, –9R

Tyler-Whittle, Michael 1927- Au&Wr 6,
ConAu 4NR, –5R, IntAu&W 77,
WrDr 76, –80, –82, –84

Tyll, Al AuBYP SUP

Tynan, Kathleen 1940- BioIn 8, –11,
ConAu 97, IntAu&W 82

Tynan, Kenneth 1927-1980 AnObit 1980[port],
BiE&WWA, BioIn 3, –5, –6, –7, –8, –9, –10,
–11, –12, BlueB 76, ConAu 101, –13R,
CroCD, CurBio 63, –80N, DcLEL 1940,
EncWT, IntAu&W 76, –77, IntWW 74,
–75, –76, –77, –78, –79, –80, –81N,
LinLib L, LongCTC, ModBrL, NewC,
NewYTBS 80[port], NotNAT,
PenC ENG, WhAm 7, Who 74,
WhoThe 15, –16, –81, –81N, WhoWor 74,
–78, –80, WorAu, WrDr 76, –80

U

Uchida, Yoshiko 1921- *AuBYP, BioIn 6, –7, BkCL, ChlLR 6[port], ConAu 6NR, –13R, DrAP&F 83, MorJA, SmATA 1, TwCCW 78, –83, WrDr 80, –82, –84*

Udall, Stewart 1920- *AmAu&B, BiDrAC, BiDrUSE, BioIn 5, –6, –7, –8, –9, –10, –11, –12, BlueB 76, ConAu 69, CurBio 61, EncAAH, IntWW 74, –75, –76, –77, –78, –79, –80, –81, –82, –83, IntYB 78, –79, –80, –81, –82, LinLib L, –S, PolProf J, PolProf K, REnAW, WhoAm 74, –76, –78, –80, –82, WhoWor 78, WorAl, WrDr 80, –82, –84*

Uden, Grant 1910- *AuBYP SUP, ConAu 102, FourBJA, SmATA 26*

Uggams, Leslie 1943- *BiDAfM, BiDAmM, BioIn 6, –7, –8, –11, CelR 73, CurBio 67, DrBlPA, Ebony 1, EncMT, FilmgC, InB&W 80, InWom, IntMPA 77, –75, –76, –78, –79, –81, –82, –84, NegAl 76[port], –83[port], NotNAT, WhoAm 74, –76, –78, –80, –82, WhoAmW 74, –68, –70, –75, –81, –83, WhoBlA 75, –77, –80, WhoHol A, WorAl*

Uhlman, Fred 1901- *BioIn 2, –5, ConAu 105, DcBrA 1, WhoArt 80, –82*

Uhnak, Dorothy 1933?- *AmWomWr, AuNews 1, BioIn 9, –10, –12, ConAu 81, EncMys, NewYTBE 71, NewYTBS 81[port], Novels, TwCCr&M 80, WhoAmW 74, –72, WorAl, WrDr 76, –80, –82, –84*

Ulam, S M 1909- *ConAu 61*

Ulanoff, Stanley M 1922- *AmM&WS 73S, –78S, ConAu 7NR, –17R, IntAu&W 77, –82, WhoE 74, –75, –77, WhoPubR 76*

Ullman, James Ramsey 1907-1971 *AmAu&B, Au&Wr 6, AuBYP, BioIn 1, –2, –4, –7, –9, –10, –11, ConAu 1R, –3NR, –29R, CurBio 45, –71, –71N, FourBJA, LinLib L, LongCTC, NatCAB 56, NewYTBE 71, ObitOF 79, REn, REnAL, ScF&FL 1, –2, SmATA 7, TwCA SUP, WhAm 5, WhNAA*

Ullman, Michael 1945- *ConAu 103*

Ullman, Montague 1916- *AmM&WS 73S, –76P, –79P, BiDPara, BiDrAPA 77, ConAu 41R, EncO&P 78*

Ullmann, Liv 1938?- *BiDFilm, BioIn 9, –10, –11, –12, BioNews 74, CelR 73, ConAu 102, CurBio 73, GoodHs, IntDcWB, IntMPA 77, –75, –76, –78, –79, –81, –84, IntWW 75, –76, –77, –78, –79, –80, –81, –82, –83, MovMk, NewYTBE 72, NewYTBS 77, –82[port], PIP&P A, Who 82, –83, WhoAm 76, –78, –80, –82, WhoAmW 83, WhoHol A, WorAl*

Ullyot, Joan 1940- *ConAu 73*

Ulyatt, Kenneth 1920- *BioIn 12, ConAu 8NR, –61, SmATA 14*

Underhill, Miriam E 1898?-1976 *BioIn 10, ConAu 61, IntDcWB, NewYTBS 76*

Underhill, Ruth Murray 1884- *AmAu&B, Au&Wr 6, BioIn 3, –7, BlueB 76, ConAu 1R, –3NR, CurBio 54, FifIDA, InSci, InWom, IntAu&W 77, OxCan SUP, WhAm 7, WhoAm 76, WhoAmW 58, –61, –64, –66, –68, –70, –72, WhoWor 78, WrDr 76, –80*

Underwood, John Weeden 1932- *ConAu 17R*

Undset, Sigrid 1882-1949 *AtlBL, AuBYP, BioIn 1, –2, –3, –4, –5, –7, –8, –9, –10, –11, –12, CasWL, CathA 1930, ClDMEL, ConAu 104, CurBio 40, –49, CyWA, DcCathB, EncWL, EvEuW, GoodHs, InWom, LinLib L, –S, LongCTC, McGEWB, Novels, ObitOF 79, OxEng, PenC EUR, REn, TwCA, TwCA SUP, TwCLC 3, TwCWr, WhAm 2, WhE&EA, WorAl*

Ungar, Sanford J 1945- *ConAu 37R, WrDr 76, –80, –82, –84*

Unitas, John 1933- *BioIn 5, –6, –7, –8, –9, –10, –11, –12, CelR 73, CurBio 62, NewYTBS 74, WebAB, –79, WhoAm 74, –76, –78, –80, –82, WhoFtbl 74, WorAl*

Unitas, Johnny 1933- *BioNews 74, NewYTBE 71*

Unkelbach, Kurt 1913- *AuBYP SUP, BioIn 9, ConAu 8NR, –21R, SmATA 4*

Unsworth, Walt 1928- *ConAu X, SmATA 4*

Unterecker, John 1922- *AmAu&B, Au&Wr 6, AuBYP, ConAu 17R, DrAP 75, DrAP&F 83, DrAS 74E, –78E, –82E, IntAu&W 77, –82, IntWWP 77, –82, WhoAm 74, –76, –78, –80, –82, WrDr 76,*

–80, –82, –84

Untermeyer, Louis 1885-1977 *AmAu&B,*
AmLY, AnCL, AnMV 1926, ApCAB X,
Au&Wr 6, AuBYP, BioIn 1, –4, –5, –6, –7,
–8, –9, –11, BlueB 76, CelR 73,
Chambr 3, ChhPo, –S1, –S2, –S3, CnDAL,
ConAmA, ConAmL, ConAu 5R, –73,
ConP 70, –75, CurBio 67, –78, –78N,
DcLEL, EvLB, IntAu&W 76, –77,
IntWW 74, –75, –76, –77, –78N,
IntWWP 77, –82, LinLib L, –S, LongCTC,
NewYTBS 75, –77, ObitOF 79, OxAmL,
REn, REnAL, ScF&FL 1, –2, SmATA 2,
–26N, TwCA, TwCA SUP, TwCWr,
WhAm 7, WhNAA, Who 74,
WhoAm 74, –76, WhoWorJ 72, –78,
WorAl, WrDr 76

Unwin, David Storr 1918- *Au&Wr 6, AuBYP,*
BioIn 7, –12, BlueB 76, ConAu 6NR, –9R,
IntAu&W 76, –77, –82, ScF&FL 1,
SmATA 14, Who 74, –82, –83, WrDr 76,
–80, –82, –84

Unwin, David Storr *see also* Severn, David

Upchurch, Boyd 1919- *BioIn 8, –12,*
ConAu 25R, ScF&FL 1, WrDr 76, –80,
–82, –84

Upchurch, Boyd *see also* Boyd, John

Upchurch, Michael Vincent *DrAP&F 83*

Updike, John 1932- *AmAu&B, AmWr,*
AnCL, Au&Wr 6, AuBYP, BioIn 5, –6,
–7, –8, –9, –10, –11, –12, BlueB 76, CasWL,
CelR 73, ChhPo, –S3, ConAu 1R, –4NR,
ConLC 1, –2, –3, –5, –7, –9, –13, –15,
–23[port], ConNov 72, –76, –82, ConP 70,
–75, –80, CurBio 66, DcLB DS3[port],
–Y80A[port], –Y82A[port], –2, –5[port],
DcLEL 1940, DrAF 76, DrAP&F 83,
EncAB-H, EncWL, IntAu&W 76, –77,
IntWW 74, –75, –76, –77, –78, –79, –80, –81,
–82, –83, IntWWP 77, LinLib L, –S,
MakMC, ModAL, ModAL SUP,
NewYTBS 78, Novels[port], OxAmL,
PenC AM, RAdv 1, REn, REnAL,
ScF&FL 1, –2, TwCWr, WebAB, –79,
WebE&AL, Who 74, –82, –83,
WhoAm 74, –76, –78, –80, –82, WhoTwCL,
WhoWor 74, –78, –80, –82, WorAl,
WorAu, WrDr 76, –80, –82, –84

Upfield, Arthur W 1888-1964 *BioIn 1, –4, –6,*
–7, –11, CorpD, CurBio 48, –64, EncMys,
LongCTC, Novels, ObitOF 79,
TwCA SUP, TwCCr&M 80

Uphaus, Suzanne Henning 1942- *DrAS 78E,*
–82E

Upton, Monroe 1898- *ConAu P-2*

Urdang, Constance 1922- *ConAu 9NR, –21R,*
ConP 70, –75, –80, DrAF 76, DrAP 75,
DrAP&F 83, IntWWP 77, –82, LinLib L,
WhoAmW 74, –75, WrDr 76, –80, –82, –84

Urdang, Laurence 1927- *ConAu 89,*
WhoAm 82, WhoLibS 66

Uris, Leon 1924- *AmAu&B, ASpks,*

Au&Wr 6, AuNews 1, –2, BioIn 3, –5,
–10, –11, –12, BlueB 76, CelR 73,
ConAu 1R, –1NR, ConLC 7, ConNov 72,
–76, –82, CurBio 59, –79, DcLEL 1940,
IntAu&W 76, –77, IntWW 74, –75, –76,
–77, –78, –79, –80, –81, –82, –83, LinLib L,
Novels, REn, REnAL, TwCWr, WebAB,
–79, WhoAm 74, –76, –78, –80, –82,
WhoAmJ 80, WhoSpyF, WhoWor 74, –78,
WorAl, WorAu, WrDr 76, –80, –82, –84

Urwin, George Glencarin 1916- *Au&Wr 6*

Usher, Shaun 1937- *ConAu 77*

Uslan, Michael E 1951- *IntMPA 84*

Uston, Ken 1935- *BioIn 12, ConAu 108*

Utley, Robert M 1929- *ConAu 2NR, –5R,*
DrAS 74H, –78H, –82H, IntAu&W 76,
–77, REnAW, WhoGov 77, –75,
WrDr 76, –80, –82, –84

Uttley, Alice Jane 1884-1976 *BioIn 9,*
ConAu 7NR, –53, –65, SmATA 26N, –3

Uttley, Alice Jane *see also* Uttley, Alison

Uttley, Alison 1884-1976 *Au&Wr 6, AuBYP,*
BioIn 3, –8, –10, –12, ChhPo, ConAu X,
–65, DcLEL, IntAu&W 76, LongCTC,
ScF&FL 1, SmATA X, –3, TelT,
TwCCW 78, –83, WhE&EA, Who 74,
WhoChL, WrDr 76

Uttley, Alison *see also* Uttley, Alice Jane

V

Vaeth, Joseph Gordon 1921- *BioIn 12,*
ConAu 5R, SmATA 17, WhoAm 74, -76,
-78, -80, -82, WhoGov 72, -75,
WhoS&SW 73, WhoWor 74
Vaizey, John 1929- *Au&Wr 6, BioIn 6, -7,*
-10, ConAu 4NR, -5R, CurBio 64,
DcLEL 1940, IntAu&W 77, -82,
IntWW 74, -75, -76, -77, -78, -79, -80, -81,
Who 74, WhoWor 74, WrDr 76, -80, -82,
-84
Vaizey, Marina 1938- *IntAu&W 82,*
WhoArt 80, -82
Valdes, Joan 1931- *ConAu 49*
Valdez, Luis 1940- *BioIn 10, -12, ChiSch,*
ConAu 101, ConDr 82, WhoThe 81,
WrDr 84
Valencak, Hannelore *IntAu&W 77X, -82X*
Valens, Evans G 1920- *AuBYP, BioIn 7, -9,*
ChhPo S2, ConAu 3NR, -5R, -81,
SmATA 1, WhoAm 80, -82, WhoWest 76,
-78
Valenti, Jack 1921- *BioIn 6, -7, -8, -10, -11,*
BlueB 76, BusPN, CelR 73, ConAu 73,
CurBio 68, DrRegL 75, FilmgC,
IntMPA 77, -75, -76, -78, -79, -81, -82, -84,
IntWW 74, -75, -76, -77, -78, -79, -80, -81,
-82, -83, LesBEnT, NewYTBS 82[port],
NewYTET, PolProf J, WhoAm 76, -78,
-80, -82, WhoGov 72, -75, WhoLab 76,
WhoS&SW 73, WhoWor 74, -78, -80, -82,
WorAl
Valentine, James Cheyne 1935- *ConAu 45*
Valentine, James Cheyne *see also* Valentine, Tom
Valentine, Tom 1935- *ConAu X*
Valentine, Tom *see also* Valentine, James Cheyne
Valeriani, Richard Gerard 1932- *ConAu 65,*
WhoAm 74, -76, -78, -80, -82,
WhoS&SW 73
Valette, Jean-Paul 1937- *DrAS 74F, -78F,*
-82F
Valgardson, W D 1939- *CaW, ConAu 41R,*
DrAP&F 83
Valin, Jonathan Louis 1948- *ConAu 101*
Vallee, Jacques F 1939- *ConAu 10NR, -17R,*
Future, UFOEn[port]
VanAtta, Winfred 1910- *ConAu 1R, -1NR,*
IntAu&W 76
VanBrunt, H L 1936- *ConAu 49, DrAP 75,*

DrAP&F 83, WhoE 77, -79
VanBuren, Abigail 1918- *AmAu&B, BioIn 4,*
-5, -8, -12, CelR 73, ConAu X,
CurBio 60, ForWC 70, GoodHs, InWom,
LibW, WhoAm 74, -76, -78, -80, -82,
WhoAmJ 80, WhoAmW 74, -58, -61, -64,
-66, -68, -70, -72, -75, -77, -79, -81, -83,
WorAl
Vance, Jack 1916?- *AmAu&B, BioIn 12,*
ConAu X, ConSFA, DcLB 8, EncSF,
IntAu&W 77, Novels, ScF&FL 1, -2,
WhoHr&F, WhoSciF, WrDr 76, -80, -82,
-84
Vance, Jack *see also* Vance, John Holbrook
Vance, John Holbrook 1916?- *BioIn 12,*
ConAu 29R, EncMys, LinLib L,
TwCCr&M 80, WhoAm 82, WrDr 82,
-84
Vance, John Holbrook *see also* Vance, Jack
Vandenberg, Philipp 1941- *ConAu 8NR, -61*
VanDerPost, Laurens 1906- *Au&Wr 6,*
BioIn 4, -8, -9, -10, BlueB 76, CasWL,
ConAu 5R, ConLC 5, ConNov 72, -76,
-82, DcLEL, EncSoA, IntAu&W 76, -77,
-82, IntWW 74, -75, -76, -77, -78, -79,
-80, -81, -82, -83, LinLib L, LongCTC,
ModCmwL, Novels, PenC ENG, REn,
TwCWr, Who 74, -82, -83, WhoAm 74,
-76, -78, WhoWor 74, -76, -78, WorAu,
WrDr 76, -80, -82, -84
VanDersal, William Richard 1907-
AmM&WS 73P, -76P, -79P, ConAu 77,
IntAu&W 82, WhoGov 72
VanDerVeer, Judy 1912-1982 *BioIn 9, ChhPo,*
-S1, ConAu 108, -33R, SmATA 33N, -4,
WhNAA
Vandervelde, Marjorie 1908- *ConAu 10NR,*
-21R
VanDeWater, Frederic F 1890-1968 *AmNov,*
BioIn 2, -4, -8, ConAu 110, REnAL,
TwCA SUP, WhAm 5, WhNAA
VanDeWetering, Janwillem 1931- *ConAu 4NR,*
-49, Novels, TwCCr&M 80B
Vandivert, Rita 1905- *BioIn 12, ConAu 5R,*
-6NR, SmATA 21[port], WhoAmW 74,
-68, -70, -72, -75, WhoE 74, -75
VanDoren, Mark 1894-1972 *AmAu&B,*
Au&Wr 6, BiDAmEd, BiE&WWA,

*BioIn 1, –3, –4, –5, –7, –8, –9, –10, –12,
CasWL, ChhPo, –S1, –S2, –S3, CnDAL,
CnE&AP, ConAmA, ConAu 1R, –3NR,
–37R, ConLC 6, –10, ConNov 72,
ConP 70, CurBio 40, –73, –73N, DcLEL,
EvLB, IntAu&W 76, –77, LinLib L,
LongCTC, ModAL, ModAL SUP,
NewYTBE 72, Novels, ObitOF 79,
OxAmL, PenC AM, RAdv 1, REn,
REnAL, ScF&FL 1, –2, SixAP, TwCA,
TwCA SUP, TwCWr, WebAB, –79,
WhAm 5, WhE&EA, WhNAA, WorAl*

VanDuyn, Janet 1910- *BioIn 12, ConAu 69,
SmATA 18*

VanDuyn, Mona 1921- *AmAu&B, BioIn 12,
ConAu 7NR, –9R, ConLC 3, –7, ConP 70,
–75, –80, DcLB 5[port], DrAP 75,
DrAP&F 83, IntWWP 77X, WhoAm 76,
–78, –80, –82, WorAu 1970, WrDr 76, –80,
–82, –84*

VanDyke, Henry 1852-1933 *Alli SUP,
AmAu&B, AmBi, ApCAB, ApCAB X,
BbD, BiDAmM, BiD&SB, BioIn 1, –2, –5,
–6, –11, Chambr 3, ChhPo, –S1, –S2, –S3,
ConAmL, DcAmAu, DcAmB, DcAmReB,
DcNAA, EvLB, HarEnUS, JBA 34,
LinLib L, –S, LongCTC, NatCAB 7, –25,
REnAL, ScF&FL 1, Str&VC, TwCA,
TwCA SUP, TwCBDA, WhAm 1, WhLit,
WhNAA*

VanDyke, Henry *see also* Dyke, Henry Van

VanEvery, Dale 1896-1976 *AmAu&B, AmNov,
BioIn 2, –4, ConAu 1R, –3NR, REnAW,
WhAm 7, WhoAm 74, –76*

VanGelder, Richard G 1928- *AmM&WS 73P,
–76P, –79P, –82P, AuBYP SUP,
ConAu 73, WhoAm 74, –76, –78, –80, –82,
WhoWor 74*

VanGulik, Robert H 1910-1967 *Au&Wr 6,
ConAu 1R, –3NR, –25R, EncMys,
ObitOF 79, TwCCr&M 80B*

VanGulik, Robert H *see also* Gulik, Robert Hans
Van

VanIterson, S R *ConAu 102,
SmATA 26[port]*

VanLawick, Hugo 1937- *AuBYP SUP,
ConAu 85, IntAu&W 77, WrDr 76, –80,
–82, –84*

VanLawick-Goodall, Jane 1934- *ASpks,
BioIn 8, –9, –10, –11, –12, ConAu X, –45,
CurBio 67, InWom, LinLib L*

VanLawick-Goodall, Jane *see also* Goodall, Jane

VanLeeuwen, Jean 1937- *BioIn 10,
ConAu 11NR, –25R, SmATA 6,
WhoAmW 74, –75*

VanLhin, Erik 1915- *ConAu X, EncSF,
ScF&FL 1, SmATA X*

VanLhin, Erik *see also* DelRey, Lester

VanLoon, Hendrik Willem 1882-1944 *AmAu&B,
AnCL, AuBYP, BioIn 1, –2, –3, –4, –7, –8,
–9, –12, ChhPo S2, ConAmA, ConAmL,
CurBio 44, DcAmB S3, DcLEL, DcNAA,*

*JBA 34, LinLib L, –S, LongCTC,
NatCAB 33, Newb 1922, ObitOF 79,
OxAmL, REn, REnAL, ScF&FL 1,
SmATA 18, TwCA, TwCA SUP,
WhAm 2, WhLit, WhNAA*

VanLustbader, Eric *EncSF*

VanNess, Bethann Faris 1902- *WhoAmW 66,
–70, –72*

VanOrden, M D 1921- *AuBYP SUP,
ConAu 37R, SmATA 4, WhoOcn 78*

VanOver, Raymond 1934- *IntAu&W 76, –77,
–82*

VanRensselaer, Alexander 1892-1962 *AuBYP,
BioIn 6, –8, –12, ConAu 73, EncAB 33,
SmATA 14*

VanRjndt, Philippe 1950- *BioIn 11, ConAu 65,
WrDr 80, –82, –84*

VanScyoc, Sydney J 1939- *ConAu 89, EncSF,
ScF&FL 1, –2, WrDr 84*

VanSteenwyk, Elizabeth Ann 1928-
*AuBYP SUP, ConAu 101,
SmATA 34[port]*

VanTuyl, Barbara 1940- *BioIn 11, ConAu 53,
SmATA 11*

VanVogt, A E 1912- *ConAu 21R,
ConSFA, DcLB 8[port], EncSF,
IntAu&W 76, –77, LinLib L, Novels,
ScF&FL 1, –2, SmATA 14, WhoSciF,
WrDr 84*

VanVogt, Alfred Elton 1912- *AmAu&B,
AmNov, Au&Wr 6, BioIn 2, –4, –7, –10,
–12, CanWW 70, –79, –80, –81, –83,
CnMWL, ConAu 21R, ConLC 1,
IntAu&W 82, REnAL, TwCA SUP,
WhoAm 82, WhoWest 78, –80, –82,
WorAl*

VanVoris, Jacqueline 1922- *ConAu 57*

VanWormer, Joe 1913- *ConAu X,
IntAu&W 77X, SmATA 35*

Vardaman, James M 1921- *ConAu 104*

Varley, H Paul 1931- *ConAu 77*

Varley, John 1947- *ConAu 69,
DcLB Y81B[port], EncSF, WhoAm 80,
–82, WrDr 84*

Vasquez, Richard *BioIn 8, ChiSch, DrAF 76,
DrAP&F 83*

Vaughan, Harold Cecil 1923- *BioIn 12,
ConAu 29R, SmATA 14, WhoE 75*

Vaughn, Ruth 1935- *BioIn 12, ConAu 41R,
IntAu&W 76, –77, SmATA 14,
WhoAmW 77, WhoS&SW 78*

Vecsey, George 1939- *BioIn 11,
ConAu 10NR, –61, SmATA 9*

Veder, Bob 1940- *ConAu 104*

Veglahn, Nancy 1937- *AuBYP, BioIn 8, –10,
ConAu 7NR, –17R, SmATA 5*

Velie, Lester 1907- *BioIn 1, ConAu P-2,
WhoAm 74, –76, –78, –80, –82*

Vendler, Helen Hennessy 1933- *AmWomWr,
ConAu 41R, DrAS 74E, –78E, –82E,
IntAu&W 77, WhoAm 74, –76, –78, –80,
–82, WhoAmW 83, WrDr 82, –84*

Venturo, Betty Lou Baker 1928- *AuBYP, ConAu 1R, ThrBJA*

Venturo, Betty Lou Baker *see also* Baker, Betty

Verdick, Mary 1923- *ConAu 1R, –4NR*

Vergara, William C 1923- *AmM&WS 73P, –79P, –82P, ConAu 1R, WhoE 77, –79, WhoTech 82*

Vermes, Hal G d1965 *AuBYP, BioIn 7*

Verne, Jules 1828-1905 *AtlBL, AuBYP, BbD, BiD&SB, BioIn 1, –2, –3, –4, –5, –6, –7, –8, –9, –10, –11, –12, CarSB, CasWL, CelCen, ConAu 110, CyWA, DcBiA, DcBiPP, DcCathB, DcEnL, DcEuL, Dis&D, EncSF, EuAu, EvEuW, FilmgC, JBA 34, –51, LinLib L, –LP, –S, LongCEL, LongCTC, McGEWB, MnBBF, NewC, Novels, OxEng, OxFr, OxShips, PenC EUR, REn, ScF&FL 1, SmATA 21[port], TwCLC 6[port], WhDW, WhoBW&1 A, WhoChL, WhoSciF, WorAl*

Vernon, Louise A 1914- *BioIn 12, ConAu 53, SmATA 14*

Versace, Marie Teresa Rios 1917- *ConAu 17R, SmATA 2*

Versace, Marie Teresa Rios *see also* Rios, Tere

Veryan, Patricia 1923- *WrDr 84*

Vestal, Stanley 1887-1957 *AmAu&B, BioIn 4, CnDAL, OxAmL, REn, REnAL, REnAW, TwCA, TwCA SUP, WhE&EA, WhNAA*

Vestal, Stanley *see also* Campbell, Walter Stanley

Vickers, Roy 1888?-1965 *Au&Wr 6, EncMys, MnBBF, TwCCr&M 80, WhE&EA*

Victor, Joan Berg 1937- *BioIn 8, ConAu 105, IlsBYP, IlsCB 1957, –1967, SmATA 30[port]*

Vidal, Gore 1925- *AmAu&B, AmNov, ASpks, AuNews 1, BiE&WWA, BioIn 2, –3, –4, –5, –6, –7, –8, –9, –10, –11, –12, BioNews 74, BlueB 76, CasWL, CelR 73, CnMD, ConAu 5R, ConDr 73, –77, –82, ConLC 2, –4, –6, –8, –10, –22[port], ConNov 72, –76, –82, CroCD, CurBio 65, –83[port], DcLB 6[port], DcLEL 1940, DrAF 76, DrAP&F 83, EncMys, EncSF, EncWL, EncWT, IntAu&W 76, –77, IntWW 74, –75, –76, –77, –78, –79, –80, –81, –82, –83, LinLib L, LongCTC, MakMC, McGEWD, –84, ModWD, NatPD 81[port], NewYTBS 76, NotNAT, –A, Novels[port], OxAmL, PenC AM, RAdv 1, REn, REnAL, ScF&FL 1, –2, TwCA SUP, TwCCr&M 80, TwCWr, WebAB, –79, WebE&AL, Who 74, –82, –83, WhoAm 74, –76, –78, –80, –82, WhoSpyF, WhoThe 15, –16, –81, WhoTwCL, WhoWor 74, WorAl, WorEFlm, WrDr 76, –80, –82, –84*

Viertel, Joseph 1915- *BioIn 3, ConAu 13R, DrAP&F 83, IntAu&W 77, St&PR 75,*

WhoS&SW 75, –76, WrDr 76, –80, –82, –84

Villarreal, Jose Antonio 1924- *ChiSch*

Villas Boas, Claudio 1916- *IntWW 74, –75, –76, –77, –78, –79, –80, –81, –82, –83*

Villas Boas, Orlando 1914- *IntWW 74, –75, –76, –77, –78, –79, –80, –81, –82, –83*

Villet, Barbara 1931- *ConAu 85*

Villiard, Paul 1910-1974 *AuBYP SUP, BioIn 10, –12, ConAu 10NR, –53, ConAu P-2, SmATA 20N*

Villiers, Alan John 1903-1982 *Au&Wr 6, AuBYP, BioIn 1, –4, –7, –10, –11, BlueB 76, ConAu 1R, –1NR, DcLEL, EvLB, IntAu&W 76, –77, IntWW 74, –75, –76, –77, –78, –79, –80, –81, –82N, LinLib L, LongCTC, OxShips, SingR 1, SmATA 10, TwCA, TwCA SUP, TwCWr, WhE&EA, WhNAA, Who 74, –82, –83N, WhoAm 74, WhoWor 74, –76, –78, WhDr 80, –82*

Vine, Louis L 1922- *ConAu 1R, –3NR, IntAu&W 77*

Vinge, Joan D 1948- *ConAu 93, EncSF, SmATA 36, WrDr 84*

Vining, Elizabeth Gray 1902- *AmAu&B, AmWomWr, AuBYP, BioIn 1, –2, –3, –4, –5, –7, –10, –11, ConAu 5R, –7NR, InWom, IntAu&W 76, JBA 51, SmATA 6, TwCCW 78, –83, WhoAm 74, –76, –78, –80, –82, WhoAmW 74, –58, –68, –70, –72, –75, WrDr 80, –82, –84*

Vining, Elizabeth Gray *see also* Gray, Elizabeth Janet

Vinson, Kathryn 1911- *BioIn 12, ConAu 5R, IntAu&W 77X, SmATA 21[port], WrDr 76, –80, –82, –84*

Viola, Herman J 1938- *AmM&WS 73S, –76P, ConAu 8NR, –61, DrAS 74H, –78H, –82H, IntAu&W 82, WhoAm 74, –76, –78, –80, –82, WhoGov 77, WhoLibI 82*

Viorst, Milton 1930- *BioIn 12, ConAu 9R, WhoAm 74, –76, –78, –80, –82, WhoS&SW 73, –75, –76, WrDr 82, –84*

Vipont, Charles 1902- *ConAu X, IntAu&W 76X, –77X, –82X, WhoChL, WrDr 76, –80, –82, –84*

Vipont, Charles *see also* Foulds, Elfrida Vipont

Vipont, Elfrida 1902- *Au&Wr 6, BioIn 2, –8, ChhPo S1, ConAu X, IntAu&W 76X, –77X, –82X, TwCCW 78, –83, WhoChL, WrDr 76, –80, –82, –84*

Vipont, Elfrida *see also* Foulds, Elfrida Vipont

Virgines, George E 1920- *ConAu 25R*

Viscardi, Henry 1912- *BioIn 2, –3, –7, –9, ConAu 5R, –5NR, CurBio 54, –66, NewYTBE 72, WhoAm 74, –76, –78, –80, WhoE 74*

Viscott, David S 1938- *AuNews 1, BiDrAPA 77, BioIn 9, –10, ConAu 29R, IntAu&W 76, –77, WrDr 76, –80, –82, –84*

Vizenor, Gerald 1934- *BioIn 12, ConAu 5NR,*

–13R, DrAP 75, DrAP&F 83,
IntWWP 77

Vlahos, Olivia 1924- *ConAu 21R,*
SmATA 31[port]

Vliet, R G 1929- *ConAu 37R,*
ConLC 22[port], ConP 75, –80, DrAF 76,
DrAP 75, DrAP&F 83, WrDr 76, –80,
–82, –84

Voelker, John Donaldson 1903- *AmAu&B,*
BioIn 4, –5, –10, BlueB 76, ConAu 1R,
IntAu&W 76X, –77X, MichAu 80,
WhoAm 74, –76, –78, WorAu, WrDr 76,
–80, –82, –84

Vogel, Ezra F 1930- *AmM&WS 73S, –78S,*
ConAu 13R, WhoAm 74, –76, –78, –80,
–82

Vogel, John H 1950- *BioIn 12, ConAu 77,*
SmATA 18

Vogelman, Joyce 1936- *ConAu 106*

Vogelsang, Arthur 1942- *ConAu 49, DrAP 75,*
DrAP&F 83

Vogelsinger, Hubert 1938- *ConAu 25R,*
WhoE 74, –75, –77

Voight, Virginia Frances 1909- *AuBYP,*
BioIn 6, –8, –11, ConAu 2NR, –5R,
MorJA, SmATA 8

Voigt, Cynthia 1942- *ConAu 106, SmATA 33*

Voinovich, Vladimir 1932?- *BioIn 10, –11,*
ConAu 81, ConLC 10, IntWW 83,
NewYTBS 77, TwCWr

Volpe, Edmond L 1922- *BlueB 76, ConAu 1R,*
–1NR, DrAS 74E, –78E, –82E, LEduc 74,
WhoAm 74, –76, –78, –80, –82, WhoE 83,
WrDr 76, –80, –82, –84

Voltaire 1694-1778 *AsBiEn, AtlBL, CasWL,*
CnThe, DcEnL, DcEuL, Dis&D, EncSF,
EncWT, EvEuW, LinLib LP, LongCEL,
LuthC 75, McGEWB, McGEWD,
–84[port], NamesHP, NewC,
NewEOp 71, Novels, OxEng, OxMus,
OxThe, PenC EUR, RComWL, REn,
REnWD, ScF&FL 1

Voltaire, Francois-Marie Arouet De 1694-1778
BbD, BiD&SB, BioIn 1, –2, –3, –4, –5, –6,
–7, –8, –9, –10, –11, –12, CyEd, CyWA,
DcBiA, DcBiPP, DcScB, EuAu, InSci,
NotNAT B, OxCan, OxFr, OxGer,
WhDW, WorAl

VonAlmedingen, Martha Edith *ConAu X,*
SmATA 3

VonAlmedingen, Martha Edith *see also*
Almedingen, E M

VonBraun, Wernher 1912-1977 *AmAu&B,*
AmM&WS 73P, –76P, –79P, BiESc,
BioIn 2, –3, –4, –5, –6, –7, –8, –9, –10, –11,
–12, BlueB 76, CelR 73, ConAu 5R,
–9NR, –69, CurBio 52, –77N, InSci,
LinLib S, McGEWB, McGMS 80[port],
ObitOF 79, PolProf E, PolProf K,
ScF&FL 1, –2, WebAB, –79, WhAm 7,
Who 74, WhoAm 74, –76, WhoS&SW 73,
WhoWor 74, WrDr 76

VonBraun, Wernher *see also* Braun, Wernher
Von

VonDaeniken, Erich 1935- *AuNews 1,*
BioNews 75, ConAu 37R

VonDaeniken, Erich *see also* VonDaniken, Erich

VonDamm, Helene A 1938- *WhoAm 82,*
WhoAmP 81, –83, WhoAmW 83

VonDaniken, Erich 1935- *AuBYP SUP,*
AuNews 1, BioIn 10, –11, –12,
BioNews 75, ConAu X, CurBio 76,
EncO&P 78S1, EncSF, IntAu&W 77,
UFOEn[port], WhoSciF, WhoWor 82,
WorAl

VonDaniken, Erich *see also* VonDaeniken, Erich

VonFrisch, Karl 1886-1982 *AnObit 1982[port],*
Au&Wr 6, ConAu 107, CurBio 74,
WhAm 7, Who 82, –83N, WhoAm 76,
–78, –80, –82, WhoWor 74, –76, –78, –80,
–82

VonFrisch, Otto 1929- *ConAu 101*

VonHagen, Victor Wolfgang 1908- *AmAu&B,*
Au&Wr 6, AuBYP, BioIn 3, –4, –5, –8,
ConAu 105, CurBio 42, IntAu&W 77,
REnAL, SmATA 29[port], TwCA SUP,
WhE&EA, Who 74, –82, –83, WhoAm 74,
–76, –78, WhoWor 74, WrDr 76, –80, –82,
–84

VonHoffman, Nicholas 1929- *AmAu&B,*
BioIn 8, –10, CelR 73, ConAu 81,
IntAu&W 82, WhoAm 74, –76, –78, –80,
–82, WhoS&SW 73, –75, –76

Vonnegut, Kurt, Jr. 1922- *AmAu&B, ASpks,*
Au&Wr 6, AuNews 1, BioIn 2, –8, –9,
–10, –11, –12, BlueB 76, CasWL,
CelR 73, ConAu 1R, –1NR, ConDr 77,
–82, ConLC 1, –2, –3, –4, –5, –8, –12,
–22[port], ConNov 72, –76, –82, ConSFA,
CurBio 70, DcLB DS3[port], –Y80A[port],
–2, –8[port], DcLEL 1940, DrAF 76,
DrAP&F 83, EncAB-H, EncSF, EncWL,
IndAu 1917, IntAu&W 76, –77,
IntWW 74, –75, –76, –77, –78, –79, –80, –81,
–82, –83, LinLib L, –S, MakMC,
ModAL SUP, MugS, NatPD, –81[port],
NewYTBE 70, –71, Novels, PenC AM,
RAdv 1, ScF&FL 1, –2, WebAB, –79,
WebE&AL, Who 83, WhoAm 74, –76,
–78, –80, –82, WhoSciF, WhoSpyF,
WhoTwCL, WhoWor 74, –76, –78, –80, –82,
WorAl, WorAu, WrDr 76, –80, –82, –84

Vonnegut, Mark 1947- *AuNews 2, BioIn 10,*
–11, –12, ConAu 65

VonStaden, Wendelgard 1925- *BioIn 12,*
ConAu 110

VonStorch, Anne B 1910- *BioIn 9,*
ConAu 29R, ConAu P-2, SmATA 1

VonStorch, Anne B *see also* Malcolmson, Anne

Vorwald, Alan *AuBYP, BioIn 8*

Voss, Carl Hermann 1910- *AmAu&B,*
BlueB 76, ConAu 10NR, –21R,
IntAu&W 76, –77, –82, WhoAm 74, –76,
–78, –80, –82, WhoWor 80

Voss, Carroll A Schell 1899-   *ForWC 70,*
   WhoAmW 74, –66, –68, –70, –72,
   WhoMW 74
Voyle, Mary   *AuBYP, BioIn 11, ConAu X,*
   DcLEL 1940, IntAu&W 76X, –77X, –82X,
   SmATA X, WorAu
Voyle, Mary *see also* Manning, Rosemary
Vreeland, Herbert Harold, III 1920-
   AmM&WS 73S, –76P
Vrettos, Theodore 1919-   *ConAu 13R*
Vroman, Mary Elizabeth 1923-1967 *BioIn 7,*
   BlkAWP, ConAu 109, DcAfL,
   InB&W 80, SelBAA

W

Wade, Graham 1940- *ConAu 107*

Wade, Henry William Rawson 1918- *BlucB 76, ConAu 109, Who 74, -82, -83, WhoWor 80, WrDr 80, -82, -84*

Wade, Henry William Rawson *see also* Wade, William

Wade, Nicholas 1942- *ConAu 77*

Wade, William 1918- *ConAu 1R, -4NR*

Wade, William *see also* Wade, Henry William Rawson

Wade, Wyn Craig 1944- *ConAu 103*

Wagenheim, Kal 1935- *BioIn 12, ConAu 29R, SmATA 21*

Wagenknecht, Edward 1900- *AmAu&B, BioIn 4, BlueB 76, ConAu 1R, -6NR, DrAS 74E, -78E, -82E, IntAu&W 76, -77, -82, REn, REnAL, ScF&FL 1, -2, TwCA SUP, WhE&EA, WhoAm 74, -76, -78, -80, -82, WrDr 76, -80, -82, -84*

Wagenvoord, James 1937- *ConAu 41R*

Wagner, Frederick 1928- *AuBYP, BioIn 7, ConAu 5R*

Wagner, Sharon 1936- *BioIn 9, ConAu 10NR, -25R, IntAu&W 77, ScF&FL 1, -2, SmATA 4, WhoAmW 74, -75, WrDr 76, -80, -82, -84*

Wagoner, David 1926- *AmAu&B, BioIn 3, -10, -12, ConAu 1R, -2NR, ConLC 3, -5, -15, ConNov 72, -76, -82, ConP 70, -75, -80, CroCAP, DcLB 5, DcLEL 1940, DrAF 76, DrAP 75, DrAP&F 83, DrAS 74E, -78E, -82E, IntAu&W 76, -77, IntWWP 77, LinLib L, SmATA 14, WhoAm 76, -78, -80, -82, WhoPNW, WhoWor 78, WorAu, WrDr 76, -80, -82, -84*

Wahl, Jan 1933- *AuBYP, BioIn 8, -9, ConAu 25R, SmATA 2, -34[port], ThrBJA, TwCCW 78, -83, WhoAm 82, WrDr 80, -82, -84*

Wahloo, Per 1926-1975 *BioIn 9, -10, ConAu 57, -61, ConLC 7, EncMys, EncSF, LinLib L, NewYTBE 71, NewYTBS 75, Novels, ObitOF 79, TwCCr&M 80B, WorAl, WorAu 1970*

Wain, John 1925- *Au&Wr 6, BioIn 3, -4, -5, -6, -8, -9, -10, BlueB 76, CasWL, ConAu 5R, ConLC 2, -11, -15, ConLCrt,*

-82, ConNov 72, -76, -82, ConP 70, -75, -80, DcLB 15[port], DcLEL 1940, EncWL, IntAu&W 76, -77, IntWW 74, -75, -76, -77, -78, -79, -80, -81, -82, -83, IntWWP 77, LongCEL, LongCTC, ModBrL, ModBrL SUP, NewC, Novels, PenC ENG, RAdv 1, REn, TwCWr, Who 74, -82, -83, WhoTwCL, WhoWor 74, WorAu, WrDr 76, -80, -82, -84

Wainwright, Gordon Ray 1937- *Au&Wr 6, IntAu&W 76, -77, WhoWor 78, WrDr 76, -80, -82, -84*

Waite, Helen Elmira 1903-1967 *BioIn 7, ConAu 1R*

Waitley, Douglas 1927- *ConAu 9NR, -21R, SmATA 30[port]*

Wakefield, Dan 1932- *AmAu&B, ASpks, BioIn 9, -10, -11, BlueB 76, ConAu 21R, ConLC 7, DcLEL 1940, DrAF 76, DrAP&F 83, IndAu 1917, WhoAm 74, -76, -78, -80, -82, WrDr 80, -82, -84*

Wakefield, H Russell 1888-1964 *Novels, ScF&FL 1, -2, WhoHr&F*

Wakin, Edward 1927- *ConAu 2NR, -5R, SmATA 37, WhoE 74*

Wakoski, Diane 1937- *AmWomWr, BioIn 10, -11, -12, ConAu 9NR, -13R, ConLC 2, -4, -7, -9, -11, ConP 70, -75, -80, CroCAP, DcLB 5[port], DcLEL 1940, DrAP 75, DrAP&F 83, IntWWP 77, ModAL SUP, PenC AM, RAdv 1, WhoAm 80, -82, WorAu 1970, WrDr 76, -80, -82, -84*

Walcott, Derek 1930- *BioIn 9, -10, -11, -12, CasWL, ConAu 89, ConDr 73, -77, -82, ConLC 2, -4, -9, -14, -25[port], ConP 70, -75, -80, DcAfL, DcLB Y81B[port], DcLEL 1940, DrAP 75, DrAP&F 83, DrBlPA, InB&W 80, IntWWP 77, LongCTC, ModBlW, ModCmwL, NewYTBS 79, -82[port], PenC ENG, PIP&P A, WebE&AL, WhDW, WhoWor 82, WorAu, WrDr 82, -84*

Walden, Amelia Elizabeth 1909- *AuBYP, BioIn 4, -6, -7, -9, ConAu 1R, -2NR, CurBio 56, ForWC 70, InWom, IntAu&W 82, MorJA, SmATA 3,*

*WhoAm 74, –76, –78, –80, –82,
WhoAmW 74, –58, –61, –64, –68, –70, –72,
–75, –77, –83, WhoE 74, –77, WhoWor 74,
–76, –78, –80, –82, WrDr 76, –80, –82, –84*
Walden, Daniel 1922- *ConAu 25R,
DrAS 74E, –78E, –82E*
Waldo, Anna Lee 1925- *BioIn 11, –12,
ConAu 85, NewYTBS 79*
Waldo, Myra *BioIn 12, ConAu 93,
ForWC 70, WhoAmW 58, –61*
Waldron, Ann 1924- *BioIn 12, ConAu 7NR,
–13R, SmATA 16, WhoAm 74, –76*
Waldrop, W Earl 1910- *ConAu 5R*
Waley, Arthur 1889-1966 *BioIn 4, –7, –8, –9,
–12, CasWL, ChhPo, –S1, –S2, –S3,
CnE&AP, CnMWL, ConAu 25R, –85,
DcLEL, EvLB, LongCTC, MakMC,
NewC, ObitT 1961, OxEng, PenC ENG,
REn, TwCA, TwCA SUP, TwCWr,
WhDW, WhE&EA*
Walker, Alice 1944- *AmWomWr, ASpks,
BioIn 11, BlkAWP, BroadAu,
ConAu 9NR, –37R, ConLC 5, –6, –9, –19,
–27[port], DcLB 6[port], DrAF 76,
DrAP 75, DrAP&F 83, InB&W 80,
IntAu&W 82, IntDcWB, LivgBAA,
ModBlW, NegAl 76, –83,
NewYTBS 83[port], SmATA 31[port],
WhoAm 74, –76, –78, WhoAmW 74, –72,
WhoBlA 75, –77, –80, WomPO 76, –78*
Walker, Barbara 1921- *AuBYP SUP, BioIn 9,
ConAu 33R, SmATA 4*
Walker, Braz 1934- *ConAu 69*
Walker, David 1911- *BioIn 6, –10, –11,
CanWW 70, –79, –80, –81, –83, CanWr,
CasWL, ConAu 1R, –1NR, ConLC 14,
ConNov 72, –76, DcLEL 1940, EncSF,
IntAu&W 76, –77, –82, LongCTC, OxCan,
OxCan SUP, Profile, REnAL, ScF&FL 1,
–2, SmATA 8, TwCCW 78, –83, Who 74,
–82, –83, WhoAm 76, –78, –80, –82,
WhoCan 73, –75, –77, –80[port], –82[port],
WhoWor 80, WorAu, WrDr 76, –80, –82,
–84*
Walker, Diana 1925- *AuBYP SUP, BioIn 11,
ConAu 4NR, –49, SmATA 9*
Walker, Greta 1927- *ConAu 77*
Walker, Irma Ruth 1921- *ConAu 5R, –6NR*
Walker, Kathrine Sorley *AuBYP, BioIn 8*
Walker, Louise Jean 1891-1976 *ConAu 110,
DrAS 74E, MichAu 80, SmATA 35N,
WhoAmW 68*
Walker, Margaret 1915- *AmWomWr, BioIn 7,
–8, –9, –10, BlkAWP, BroadAu,
ChhPo S1, –S2, ConAu 73, ConLC 1, –6,
ConNov 72, –76, –82, ConP 70, –75, –80,
CroCAP, CurBio 43, DrAF 76, EncSoH,
InWom, IntAu&W 76, –77, LivgBAA,
ModBlW, NegAl 76, –83, WhoAm 74, –76,
–78, WhoAmW 74, –58, –61, –68A, –72,
WhoBlA 75, –77, –80, WrDr 76, –80, –82,
–84*

Walker, Mary Alexander 1927- *ConAu 104,
DrAP&F 83*
Walker, Mildred 1905- *AmAu&B, AmNov,
Au&Wr 6, BioIn 1, –2, –4, ConAu X,
CurBio 47, InB&W 80, InWom,
MichAu 80, REnAL, SmATA X,
TwCA SUP, WhoAm 74, –76,
WhoAmW 74, –58, –64, –66, –68, –70, –72,
–75, WrDr 76, –80, –82, –84*
Walker, Mildred *see also* Schemm, Mildred
Walker
Walker, Mort 1923- *BioIn 2, –8, –11,
ConAu 3NR, –49, LinLib L, SmATA 8,
WhoAm 74, –76, –78, –80, –82,
WhoAmA 73, –76, –78, –80, –82, WhoE 74,
WhoWor 74*
Walker, Richard Louis 1922- *AmM&WS 73S,
–78S, ConAu 7NR, –9R, IntAu&W 77,
–82, WhoAm 74, –76, –78, –80, –82,
WhoWor 82*
Walker, Robert Harris 1924- *ConAu 7NR,
–13R, DrAS 74E, –78E, –82H,
WhoAm 80, –82, WhoE 79*
Walker, Robert Wayne 1948- *ConAu 93,
IntAu&W 82*
Wall, Leonard Wong 1941- *AmM&WS 79P*
Wallace, Amy 1955- *BioIn 11, –12, ConAu 81*
Wallace, Barbara Brooks 1922- *BioIn 9,
ConAu 11NR, –29R, IntAu&W 76, –77,
SmATA 4, WhoAmW 77, –79, –81,
WrDr 76, –80, –82, –84*
Wallace, Bill *ConAu X*
Wallace, Bill *see also* Wallace, William N
Wallace, David Rains 1945- *ConAu 81*
Wallace, Edgar 1875-1932 *BioIn 2, –7, –8, –10,
CasWL, DcLEL, EncMys, EncSF,
EncSoA, EncWT, EvLB, FilmgC,
LongCTC, MnBBF, ModBrL, NewC,
NotNAT A, –B, Novels[port], OxEng,
OxThe, PenC ENG, REn, ScF&FL 1,
TwCA, TwCA SUP, TwCCr&M 80,
TwCWr, WhThe, WhoBW&I A,
WhoSpyF, WhoTwCL, WorAl*
Wallace, Ian 1912- *ConAu X, ConSFA,
IntAu&W 82X, WrDr 84*
Wallace, Irving 1916- *AmAu&B, ASpks,
Au&Wr 6, AuNews 1, BioIn 6, –8, –9,
–10, –11, –12, BioNews 74, BlueB 76,
CelR 73, ConAu 1R, –1NR, ConLC 7,
–13, CurBio 79, DcLEL 1940,
IntAu&W 76, IntMPA 77, –75, –76, –78,
–79, –81, –82, –84, Novels, TwCWr,
Who 74, –82, –83, WhoAm 74, –76, –78,
–80, –82, WorAl, WrDr 76, –80, –82, –84*
Wallace, Lew 1827-1905 *AmBi, ApCAB X,
BioIn 1, LinLib L, Novels, OxAmH,
WorAl*
Wallace, Lewis 1827-1905 *Alli SUP, AmAu,
AmAu&B, AmBi, ApCAB, ArtsAmW,
BbD, BiD&SB, BioIn 2, –3, –5, –6, –7, –12,
CarSB, CasWL, Chambr 3, ChhPo, –S3,
CivWDc, CnDAL, CyWA, DcAmAu,*

DcAmB, DcAmDH, DcBiA, DcEnA AP,
DcLEL, DcNAA, Drake, EncAB-H,
EvLB, HarEnUS[port], IlBEAAW,
IndAu 1816, JBA 34, LinLib S,
McGEWB, NatCAB 4, NewYHSD 57,
NotNAT B, OxAmL, PenC AM,
RAdv 1, REn, REnAL, TwCBDA,
WebAB, -79, WebAMB, WhAm 1

Wallace, May Nickerson 1902- AuBYP,
BioIn 7, ScF&FL 1, WhoAmW 58, -61

Wallace, Robert 1932- AmAu&B,
ConAu 10NR, -13R, DrAP 75,
DrAP&F 83, DrAS 74E, SmATA 37,
WhoAm 74, -76, -80, -82

Wallace, William N 1924- ConAu 13R,
MnBBF

Wallach, Anne Tolstoi 1929?- BioIn 12

Wallechinsky, David 1948- BioIn 12,
ConAu 61, WhoAm 78, -80

Wallenstein, Barry 1940- ConAu 11NR, -45,
DrAP 75, DrAP&F 83, DrAS 78E, -82E,
IntWWP 77

Waller, Irene Ellen 1928- ConAu 109,
IntAu&W 77, -82, NewYTBE 70,
WhoAmW 72, WrDr 76, -80, -82, -84

Waller, Leslie 1923- AmAu&B, AmNov,
Au&Wr 6, AuBYP SUP, BioIn 2, -6, -12,
ConAu 1R, -2NR, ScF&FL 1, -1A,
SmATA 20, WrDr 84

Wallerstein, James S 1910- ScF&FL 1

Walley, David Gordon 1945- ConAu 41R,
IntAu&W 77

Wallhauser, Henry T 1930- ConAu 29R,
DrRegL 75

Wallig, Gaird 1942- ConAu 106

Walsh, Chad 1914- AmAu&B, Au&Wr 6,
BioIn 2, -4, -6, -10, ConAu 1R, -6NR,
ConP 70, -75, -80, CurBio 62, DrAP 75,
DrAP&F 83, DrAS 74E, -78E, -82E,
IntWWP 77, ScF&FL 1, -2, WhoAm 74,
-76, -78, WorAu, WrDr 76, -80, -82, -84

Walsh, Gillian Paton 1937?- BioIn 9,
ConAu 37R

Walsh, Gillian Paton see also Paton Walsh,
Gillian

Walsh, Jill Paton 1937?- AuBYP SUP,
ChlLR 2, ConAu X, FourBJA,
SmATA 4, TwCCW 83

Walsh, Jill Paton see also Paton Walsh, Gillian

Walsh, John 1927- ConAu 17R

Walsh, Raoul 1892?-1980 AnObit 1980[port],
BiDFilm, BioIn 7, -9, -10, -11, -12,
CmMov, ConAu 102, DcFM, Film 1, -2,
FilmgC, IntMPA 77, -75, -76, -78, -79, -81,
MovMk, NewYTBS 74, -81[port], OxFilm,
TwYS A, WhoHol A, WorEFlm,
WrDr 76, -80

Walsh, Richard John 1886-1960 AmAu&B,
AuBYP, BioIn 1, -5, -7, ObitOF 79,
WhAm 4

Walsh, William Bertalan 1920- AmCath 80,
AuBYP SUP, BioIn 6, ConAu 4NR, -49,

CurBio 62, WhoAm 74, -76, -78, -80, -82,
WhoWor 76, -78, -80

Waltari, Mika 1908-1979 Au&Wr 6, BioIn 2,
-4, -12, CasWL, ConAu 9R, -89,
CurBio 50, -79N, DcLEL 1940, EncWL,
IntAu&W 76, -77, IntWW 74, -75, -76,
-77, -78, -79, LinLib L, NewYTBS 79,
PenC EUR, REn, ScF&FL 1,
TwCA SUP, WhE&EA, Who 74,
WhoWor 74, -76

Walter, Elizabeth ScF&FL 1, -2, WhoHr&F,
WrDr 76, -80, -82, -84

Walter, Mildred Pitts AuBYP SUP

Walters, Hugh 1910- AuBYP, BioIn 8,
ConAu X, ConSFA, EncSF, ScF&FL 1,
-2, SmATA X, WrDr 84

Waltner, Elma 1912- AuBYP, BioIn 7,
ConAu 17R, ForWC 70

Waltner, Willard AuBYP, BioIn 7

Walton, Bryce 1918- ConAu 21R, EncSF,
ScF&FL 1, -2, WhoSciF

Walton, Ed 1931- ConAu 105

Walton, Evangeline 1907- AmWomWr,
ScF&FL 1, WhoAmW 58, -61, -64, -66,
WhoHr&F

Walton, Richard J 1928- BioIn 9, ConAu 25R,
IntAu&W 76, -77, OxCan SUP,
SmATA 4, WrDr 76, -80, -82, -84

Walworth, Nancy Z 1917- BioIn 12,
ConAu 3NR, -5R, SmATA 14,
WomPO 76

Wambaugh, Joseph 1937- ASpks, AuNews 1,
BioIn 9, -10, -11, -12, BioNews 74,
ConAu 33R, ConLC 3, -18,
CurBio 80[port], DcLB Y83A[port],
-6[port], NewYTBE 73, Novels,
TwCCr&M 80, WhoAm 74, -76, -78, -80,
-82, WorAl, WorAu 1970, WrDr 76, -80,
-82, -84

Wand, John William Charles 1885- Au&Wr 6,
BioIn 7, BlueB 76, IntWW 74, -75,
WhE&EA, Who 74

Wangerin, Walter, Jr. 1944- ConAu 108,
SmATA 37

Warburg, Sandol Stoddard 1927- AuBYP,
BioIn 8, -12, BkP, ChhPo S1, ConAu X,
-5R, ForWC 70, ScF&FL 1, -2,
SmATA 14, WhoAmW 68, -70

Warburg, Sandol Stoddard see also Stoddard,
Sandol

Ward, Arthur Sarsfield 1883-1959 BioIn 6, -9,
ConAu 108, EncMys, EncO&P 78, EvLB,
LongCTC, MnBBF, ObitOF 79,
ObitT 1951, PenC ENG, ScF&FL 1,
WhoBW&I A

Ward, Arthur Sarsfield see also Rohmer, Sax

Ward, Bill G 1929- WhoBW&I I

Ward, Bill G see also Ward, William G

Ward, Don 1911- ConAu 17R, ScF&FL 1

Ward, Herman M 1914- ChhPo, ConAu 2NR,
-5R, -9R, DrAS 74E, -78E, -82E

Ward, Hiley Henry 1929- Au&Wr 6,

ConAu 1R, –2NR, IndAu 1917,
WhoAm 74, –76, –78, –80, –82,
WhoMW 74, –76

Ward, Lynd 1905- *AmAu&B, Au&ICB,*
AuBYP, BioIn 1, –2, –3, –4, –5, –6, –7, –8,
–9, –10, –12, BkP, Cald 1938, ChhPo, –S2,
–S3, ConAu 17R, ConICB,
DcLB 22[port], FourBJA, IlrAm E,
IlsBYP, IlsCB 1744, –1946, –1957, –1967,
JBA 34, –51, LinLib L, McGDA,
ScF&FL 1, –2, SmATA 2, –36, Str&VC,
WhoAm 74, –76, –78, –80, WhoAmA 73,
–76, –78, –80, –82, WrDr 76, –80, –82, –84

Ward, Peter 1914- *WhoAmL 78*

Ward, Ritchie R 1906- *ConAu 29R,*
IntAu&W 77, WhoWest 74, –76, –78,
WrDr 76, –80, –82, –84

Ward, William G 1929- *ConAu 21R,*
WhoMW 74, –76, –78, –80

Ward, William G *see also* Ward, Bill G

Ward-Thomas, Evelyn Bridget 1928- *Au&Wr 6,*
ConAu 5NR, –9R, WhoSpyF, WrDr 82,
–84

Ward-Thomas, Evelyn Bridget *see also* Anthony,
Evelyn

Ware, Leon 1909-1976 *AuBYP, BioIn 7, –9,*
ConAu 1R, –2NR, SmATA 4

Warner, Gary 1936- *ConAu 21R*

Warner, Lucille Schulberg *ConAu 11NR, –69,*
SmATA 30[port]

Warner, Marina 1946- *ConAu 65,*
IntAu&W 82, WrDr 80, –82, –84

Warner, Matt 1922- *AuBYP SUP, ConAu X,*
WrDr 80, –82, –84

Warner, Matt *see also* Fichter, George S

Warner, Oliver 1903-1976 *Au&Wr 6,*
ConAu 1R, –3NR, –69, DcLEL 1940,
IntAu&W 77, LongCTC, OxCan SUP,
SmATA 29, WhLit, Who 74

Warner, Rex 1905- *BioIn 1, –4, –7, –8,*
BlueB 76, ChhPo, –S1, ConAu 89,
ConNov 72, –76, –82, ConP 70, –75, –80,
DcLB 15[port], DcLEL, EncSF,
IntAu&W 76, –77, IntWW 74, –75, –76,
–77, –78, –79, –80, –81, –82, –83,
IntWWP 77, LongCTC, ModBrL, NewC,
Novels, PenC ENG, REn, ScF&FL 1,
TwCA, TwCA SUP, TwCWr,
WebE&AL, WhE&EA, Who 74, –82, –83,
WhoAm 74, –76, WhoWor 74, WrDr 76,
–80, –82, –84

Warner, Sylvia Townsend 1893-1978 *Baker 78,*
BioIn 4, –11, –12, BlueB 76, Chambr 3,
ChhPo S1, –S2, –S3, ConAu 61, –77,
ConLC 7, –19, ConNov 72, –76, DcLEL,
EvLB, InWom, IntAu&W 76, –77,
LongCTC, ModBrL, ModBrL SUP,
NewC, Novels, PenC ENG, RAdv 1,
REn, ScF&FL 1, –2, TwCA, TwCA SUP,
TwCWr, WhE&EA, Who 74,
WhoAmW 74, –68, –70, –72, WhoTwCL,
WhoWor 74, –76, WrDr 76

Warner, Wayne E 1933- *ConAu 3NR, –49,*
WhoRel 77

Warren, Fred Franklin 1922- *AuBYP SUP,*
WhoBlA 77, –80

Warren, Mary Phraner 1929- *AuBYP SUP,*
BioIn 11, ConAu 5NR, –53, SmATA 10

Warren, Patricia Nell 1936- *ConAu 1NR,*
WhoAmW 75

Warren, Robert Penn 1905- *AmAu&B,*
AmNov, AmWr, Au&Wr 6, AuNews 1,
BioIn 2, –3, –4, –5, –6, –7, –8, –9, –10, –11,
–12, BlueB 76, CasWL, ChhPo S3,
CnDAL, CnE&AP, CnMD, ConAmA,
ConAu 10NR, –13R, ConLC 1, –4, –6, –8,
–10, –13, –18, ConLCrt, –82, ConNov 72,
–76, –82, ConP 70, –75, –80, Conv 1,
CurBio 70, CyWA, DcLB Y80A[port], –2,
DcLEL, DrAF 76, DrAP 75,
DrAP&F 83, EncSoH, EncWL, EvLB,
FilmgC, IntAu&W 76, –77, –82,
IntWW 74, –75, –76, –77, –78, –79, –80, –81,
–82, –83, IntWWP 77, –82, LinLib L, –S,
LongCTC, McGEWB, ModAL,
ModAL SUP, ModWD, Novels, OxAmL,
PenC AM, RAdv 1, RComWL, REn,
REnAL, SixAP, TwCA, TwCA SUP,
WebAB, –79, WebE&AL, WhDW,
WhE&EA, WhNAA, Who 74, –82, –83,
WhoAm 74, –76, –78, –80, –82, WhoTwCL,
WhoWor 74, –80, –82, WorAl, WrDr 76,
–80, –82, –84

Warrick, Patricia Scott 1925- *ConAu 8NR,*
–61, DrAS 82E, ScF&FL 1, –2,
SmATA 35, WhoMW 78, –80, –82

Warshofsky, Fred 1931- *ConAu 9R,*
SmATA 24[port], WhoE 74

Warth, Robert Douglas 1921- *ConAu 9R,*
DrAS 74H, –78H, –82H, IntAu&W 76,
WhoAm 74, –76, –78, –80, –82

Wartski, Maureen 1940- *ConAu 89,*
SmATA 37

Warwick, Dolores 1936- *ConAu X*

Warwick, Dolores *see also* Frese, Dolores
Warwick

Washburn, Dorothy K 1945- *ConAu 106*

Washburn, Mark 1948- *ConAu 77*

Washington, Booker T 1856-1915 *AmAu&B,*
AmBi, ApCAB, ApCAB X, BiDAmEd,
BiD&SB, BiDSA, BioIn 1, –2, –3, –4, –5,
–6, –7, –8, –9, –10, –11, –12, BlkAWP,
CasWL, Chambr 3, CyAG, DcAmAu,
DcAmB, DcAmReB, DcAmSR, DcLEL,
DcNAA, EncAAH, EncAB-H, EncSoH,
HarEnUS, InB&W 80, LinLib L, –S,
LongCTC, LuthC 75, McGEWB,
NatCAB 7, NegAl 76, –83, OxAmH,
OxAmL, OxEng, PenC AM, REn,
REnAL, SelBAA, SmATA 28[port],
TwCBDA, TwCLC 10[port], WebAB, –79,
WebE&AL, WhAm 1, WhoColR, WorAl

Waskow, Arthur I 1933- *ConAu 4NR, –5R,*
DrAS 74H, –78H, –82P, Future,

WhoAm 74, –76, –78, –80, –82

Wason, Betty 1912- *ConAu X, CurBio 43,*
InWom, WhoAmW 64, –66, –68, –70, –72

Wasserman, Dale 1917- *AmAu&B, BiDAmM,*
BiE&WWA, BlueB 76, ConAu 49,
ConDr 73, –77D, –82D, EncMT,
IntMPA 77, –75, –76, –78, –79, –81, –82, –84,
NatPD 81[port], NewYTET, NotNAT,
WhoAm 74, –76, –78, –80, –82, WrDr 76,
–80, –82, –84

Wassmer, Arthur C 1947- *ConAu 103,*
WhoWest 82

Waters, Frank 1902- *AmAu&B, AmNov,*
BioIn 2, –9, –10, –12, CnDAL,
ConAu 3NR, –5R, DrAF 76, DrAP&F 83,
IntAu&W 76, –77, –82, REnAW,
WhNAA, WhoAm 74, –76, –78,
WhoWest 74, –76, WrDr 84

Waters, John F 1930- *AuBYP SUP, BioIn 9,*
ConAu 37R, IntAu&W 77, –82,
SmATA 4, WhoE 75, –77, WrDr 76, –80,
–82, –84

Watkins, Peter 1934- *ConAu 109*

Watkins, William Jon 1942- *BioIn 9,*
ConAu 41R, DrAP&F 83, EncSF,
IntAu&W 76, Po&Wr 77, ScF&FL 1, –2,
WrDr 84

Watson, Aldren Auld 1917- *BioIn 1, –5, –8, –12,*
ChhPo, –S2, –S3, ConAu 4NR, –81, ForIl,
IlsBYP, IlsCB 1744, –1946, –1957, –1967,
SmATA 36, WhoAmA 73, –76, –78, –80,
–82

Watson, Andrew Samuel 1920-
AmM&WS 73S, –76P, –79P, –82P,
BiDrAPA 77, ConAu 45, DrAS 74P, –78P,
–82P, WhoAmL 83, WhoMW 80, –82

Watson, Bryan 1942- *BioIn 7, WhoHcky 73*

Watson, Clyde 1947- *AuBYP SUP, BioIn 10,*
ChlLR 3, ChhPo S2, ConAu 4NR, –49,
DrRegL 75, FourBJA, SmATA 5,
TwCCW 78, –83, WrDr 76, –80, –82, –84

Watson, Colin 1920-1983 *Au&Wr 6,*
ConAu 1R, –2NR, –108, EncMys,
IntAu&W 76, Novels, TwCCr&M 80,
WrDr 82, –84

Watson, Ian 1943- *ConAu 61, EncSF,*
IntAu&W 82, Novels, ScF&FL 1, –2,
WhoSciF, WrDr 84

Watson, James Dewey 1928- *AmAu&B,*
AmM&WS 73P, –76P, –79P, –82P, AsBiEn,
BiESc, BioIn 5, –6, –7, –8, –9, –12,
BlueB 76, ConAu 25R, CurBio 63,
EncAB-H, IntWW 74, –75, –76, –77, –78,
–79, –80, –81, –82, –83, MakMC,
McGEWB, McGMS 80[port],
NewYTBE 70, NewYTBS 80[port],
WebAB, –79, Who 74, –82, –83,
WhoAm 74, –76, –78, –80, –82, WhoE 81,
–83, WhoWor 74, –76, –78, –80, –82,
WorAl

Watson, Jane Werner 1915- *AuBYP SUP,*
BioIn 9, ConAu 5R, –8NR, SmATA 3,

WhoAmW 58, –61, –64, –68, –70

Watson, Lyall 1939- *ConAu 8NR, –57,*
DcCAr 81, EncO&P 78S1, WrDr 76, –80,
–82, –84

Watson, Paul 1951?- *BioIn 12*

Watson, Sally 1924- *AuBYP SUP, BioIn 9,*
ConAu 3NR, –5R, FourBJA,
IntAu&W 77, –82, SmATA 3

Watson, Simon *EncSF*

Watson, Tom 1949- *BioIn 10, –11, –12,*
CurBio 79, NewYTBS 79, –80, –82[port],
WorAl

Watt, Thomas 1935- *Alli, BioIn 9,*
ConAu 37R, SmATA 4, WhoE 79

Watt-Evans, Lawrence 1954- *ConAu X*

Wattenberg, Ben J 1933- *BioIn 8, BlueB 76,*
ConAu 57, WhoAm 76, –78, –80, –82,
WrDr 80, –82, –84

Watts, Alan 1915-1973 *AmAu&B, BioIn 5, –6,*
–7, –9, –10, –11, –12, CelR 73,
ConAu 41R, –45, CurBio 62, –74, –74N,
DcLB 16[port], EncO&P 81, LinLib L,
MugS, NewYTBE 73, ObitOF 79,
WebAB, –79, WhAm 6, WhoAm 74,
WhoWor 74, WomWMM, WorAl,
WorAu

Watts, Charles 1941- *BioIn 12, WhoAm 80,*
–82

Watts, Charles *see also* Rolling Stones, The

Watzlawick, Paul 1921- *ConAu 4NR, –9R,*
WhoWest 82

Waugh, Carol-Lynn Roessel 1947- *ConAu 107*

Waugh, Evelyn 1903-1966 *AtlBL, BioIn 1, –2,*
–3, –4, –5, –6, –7, –8, –9, –10, –11, –12,
CasWL, CathA 1930, CmCal, CnMWL,
ConAu 25R, –85, ConLC 1, –3, –8, –13,
–19, –27[port], CyWA, DcLB 15[port],
DcLEL, EncSF, EncWL, EvLB,
LinLib L, –S, LongCEL, LongCTC,
MakMC, McGEWB, ModBrL,
ModBrL SUP, NewC, NewYTBE 73,
Novels[port], ObitOF 79, ObitT 1961,
OxEng, PenC ENG, RAdv 1, REn,
ScF&FL 1, TwCA, TwCA SUP, TwCWr,
WebE&AL, WhDW, WhAm 4,
WhE&EA, WhoTwCL, WomWMM,
WorAl

Waugh, Hillary 1920- *Au&Wr 6, ConAu 1R,*
–2NR, EncMys, Novels, TwCCr&M 80,
WrDr 82, –84

Way, Margaret *WrDr 84*

Way, Peter 1936- *IntAu&W 76, ScF&FL 1,*
WrDr 80, –82, –84

Wayne, Kyra Petrovskaya 1918- *BioIn 11,*
ConAu X, –4NR, SmATA 8,
WhoAmW 66, –68, –70, –72, WhoWest 76,
–78, –80, –82

Wayne, Kyra Petrovskaya *see also* Petrovskaya,
Kyra

Weale, Anne 1929- *Au&Wr 6, IntAu&W 76,*
–77

Weales, Gerald 1925- *AmAu&B, BiE&WWA,*

BioIn 11, ConAmTC, ConAu 3NR, –5R, DrAS 74E, –78E, –82E, IndAu 1917, SmATA 11, WrDr 80, –82, –84

Weaver, Earl S 1930- *BioIn 10, –12, CurBio 83[port], WhoAm 74, –76, –78, –80, –82, WhoE 81, WhoProB 73, WorAl*

Weaver, Robert Glenn 1920- *DrAS 74E, –78E, –82E, IlsBYP*

Weaver, Ward *AmNov X, AuBYP, BioIn 1, –2, –9, ConAu X, SmATA X, WhoSpyF*

Weaver, Ward *see also* Mason, F VanWyck

Webb, Charles 1939- *BioIn 8, ConAu 25R, ConLC 7, DcLEL 1940, IntAu&W 76, –77, WhoAm 74, –76, –78, WrDr 76, –80, –82, –84*

Webb, Christopher 1915-1983 *ConAu X, EncMys, IntAu&W 76X, –77X, –82X, ScF&FL 1, SmATA 2, TwCCW 83, WrDr 80, –82, –84*

Webb, Christopher *see also* Wibberley, Leonard

Webb, Jean Francis 1910- *ConAu 5R, –6NR, IntAu&W 77, ScF&FL 1, –2, SmATA 35, WrDr 76, –80, –82, –84*

Webb, Jimmy 1946- *BioIn 8, –9, –11, WhoAm 74, –76, –78, –80, WhoRocM 82*

Webb, Nancy 1915- *ConAu 1R, ForWC 70*

Webb, Robert N 1906- *AuBYP, BioIn 8*

Webb, Sharon *DrAP&F 83*

Webb, Walter Prescott 1888-1963 *AmAu&B, BioIn 3, –4, –5, –6, –7, –8, –9, –10, –11, DcAmB S7, DcLB 17[port], EncAAH, EncAB 36[port], NatCAB 51, ObitOF 79, OxAmL, REnAL, REnAW, TexWr, WhAm 4, WhE&EA*

Webb, William 1919- *Alli, BiDLA, BioIn 3, ConAu 25R*

Webber, Andrew Lloyd 1948- *BioIn 9, –12, ConLC 21, LinLib L, NewYTBE 71, WhoAm 82*

Weber, Bruce 1942- *ConAu 97*

Weber, Dick 1929- *BioIn 6, –7, –8, –9, –10, CurBio 70, WhoWor 74, –76*

Weber, Eric 1942- *BioIn 12, ConAu 101*

Weber, Lenora Mattingly 1895-1971 *AmAu&B, AuBYP, BioIn 2, –9, BkC 3, ConAu 29R, ConAu P-1, ConLC 12, MorJA, SmATA 2, –26N, WhoAmW 58, –61*

Weber, William John 1927- *BioIn 12, ConAu 69, SmATA 14*

Webster, Jean 1876-1916 *AmAu&B, AmWomWr, BioIn 8, –12, CarSB, ChhPo, –S3, CnDAL, DcAmB, DcNAA, EvLB, JBA 34, LibW, LongCTC, NotAW, NotNAT B, OxAmL, REn, REnAL, SmATA X, TwCA, TwCCW 83, TwCWr, WhAm 1, WhoChL, WomWWA 14*

Wechsberg, Joseph 1907-1983 *AmAu&B, Au&Wr 6, BioIn 1, –3, –4, –9, –10, –12, BlueB 76, ConAu 105, –109, CurBio 55, –83N, NewYTBS 83, OxAmL, REnAL, WhE&EA, WhoAm 74, –76, –78, –80, –82, WhoMus 72, WhoWor 74, –76, WrDr 80,*

–82, –84

Wechsler, James 1915-1983 *AmAu&B, BioIn 1, –3, –6, –9, –11, BlueB 76, CelR 73, ConAu 101, –110, IntWW 74, –75, –76, NewYTBS 83[port], PolProf T, WhoAm 82, WhoE 74, WhoWor 74, WhoWorJ 72, –78*

Wechter, Nell Wise 1913- *BioIn 5, ConAu 57, ScF&FL 1, –2, WhoAmW 77, –79, –81, WhoS&SW 78*

Wedel, Leonard E 1909- *ConAu 21R*

Wedgwood, Cicely Veronica 1910- *BioIn 4, DcLEL, IntAu&W 76, –77, IntWW 74, –75, –78, –83, LongCTC, ModBrL, REn, WhE&EA, Who 74, –82, –83, WhoAm 74, WhoAmW 68, –70, –72, WhoWor 74, –76, –78, WrDr 76*

Weekley, Ernest 1865-1954 *BioIn 4, DcLEL, EvLB, LongCTC, ObitT 1951, REn, TwCA, TwCA SUP, WhE&EA, WhLit*

Weesner, Theodore 1935- *ConAu 105, MichAu 80*

Wegner, Fritz 1924- *BioIn 5, –12, ChhPo S2, IlsBYP, IlsCB 1946, –1967, SmATA 20, WhoArt 80, –82*

Wehen, Joy DeWeese 1926?- *AuBYP, BioIn 8, ConAu 3NR, –5R, WrDr 76, –80, –82, –84*

Weider, Joe *BioIn 8*

Weidman, John 1946- *ConAu 109, NatPD, –81[port]*

Weil, Gordon Lee 1937- *BioIn 9, ConAu 73, WhoAmP 75, –77, –79, –83, WhoE 83*

Weilerstein, Sadie Rose 1894- *BioIn 9, ConAu 5R, SmATA 3, WhoAmW 66, –68, WhoWorJ 72*

Weiman, Eiveen 1925- *ConAu 108*

Weinbaum, Eleanor Perlstein *IntAu&W 76, –77, –82, IntWWP 77, –82, WhoAmW 77, –79, –81, –83, WhoS&SW 80, –82*

Weinbaum, Stanley G 1902-1935 *BioIn 7, –10, –12, ConAu 110, DcLB 8[port], DcNAA, EncSF, ScF&FL 1, WhoSciF, WorAu*

Weinberg, Larry *WhoAmP 77, –79, –81*

Weingartner, Charles 1922- *BioIn 10, ConAu 49, DrAS 74E, –78E, –82E, Future, LEduc 74, SmATA 5*

Weingast, David E 1912- *AuBYP, BioIn 8, ConAu 5R*

Weinstein, Grace W 1935- *ConAu 10NR, –61, ForWC 70, WhoAmW 81, –83*

Weinstein, Howard 1954- *ConAu 107*

Weinstein, Nathan Wallenstein 1903?-1940 *ConAu 104, LongCTC, ScF&FL 1, TwCA, TwCA SUP, WebAB, –79*

Weinstein, Nathan Wallenstein *see also* West, Nathanael

Weinstein, Robert A 1914- *ConAu 29R, WhoWest 80, –82*

Weir, LaVada *BioIn 9, ConAu 9NR, –21R, SmATA 2, WrDr 76, –80, –82, –84*

Weir, Rosemary 1905- *Au&Wr 6, AuBYP, BioIn 8, –12, ConAu 10NR, –13R,*

SmATA 21[port], *TwCCW 78*, *-83*, *WrDr 80*, *-82*, *-84*

Weisberger, Bernard A 1922- *BioIn 12*, *ConAu 5R*, *-7NR*, *DrAS 74H*, *-78H*, *-82H*, *SmATA 21[port]*

Weisenfeld, Murray 1923- *ConAu 104*

Weisman, John 1942- *ConAu 1NR*, *-45*

Weiss, Ann E 1943- *ConAu 1NR*, *-11NR*, *-45*, *SmATA 30*

Weiss, Carol *AuBYP SUP*

Weiss, Ehrich *DcAmB*, *DcNAA*, *WebAB*, *-79*, *WhDW*

Weiss, Harvey 1922- *AuBYP*, *BioIn 5*, *-8*, *-9*, *ChlLR 4[port]*, *ConAu 5R*, *-6NR*, *IlsCB 1946*, *-1957*, *-1967*, *SmATA 1*, *-27[port]*, *ThrBJA*, *WhoAmA 73*, *-76*, *-78*, *-80*, *-82*, *WhoE 75*, *-77*

Weiss, Karl 1926- *OxGer*, *WhoAm 74*

Weiss, Louise 1893-1983 *BioIn 10*, *ConAu 109*, *NewYTBS 83*, *WhoFr 79*, *WhoWor 78*, *-80*, *-82*

Weiss, Malcolm E 1928- *BioIn 9*, *ConAu 11NR*, *-25R*, *SmATA 3*, *WhoE 74*, *-75*, *-77*

Weiss, Morton Jerome 1926- *ConAu 9NR*, *-17R*

Weiss, Morton Jerry 1926- *ConAu X*, *DrAS 74E*, *-78E*, *-82E*

Weiss, Peter 1916-1982 *AnObit 1982[port]*, *AuBYP SUP*, *BioIn 7*, *-8*, *-10*, *-12*, *CasWL*, *CnThe*, *ConAu 3NR*, *-106*, *-45*, *ConLC 3*, *-15*, *CroCD*, *CurBio 68*, *-82N*, *EncWL*, *EncWT*, *IntAu&W 76*, *-77*, *IntWW 74*, *-75*, *-76*, *-77*, *-78*, *-79*, *-80*, *-81*, *-82*, *-82N*, *LinLib L*, *McGEWD*, *-84[port]*, *ModGL*, *ModWD*, *NewYTBS 82[port]*, *NotNAT*, *-A*, *OxFilm*, *OxGer*, *PenC EUR*, *PIP&P*, *-A*, *REnWD*, *TwCWr*, *Who 74*, *-82*, *-83N*, *WhoF&I 83*, *WhoThe 15*, *-16*, *-81*, *WhoWor 74*, *WorAl*, *WorAu*, *WorEFlm*

Weiss, Peter 1925- *WhoAmP 73*

Weissler, Paul W 1936- *Ward 77F*

Weissman, Dick 1935- *ConAu X*

Weitz, Joseph Leonard 1922- *AmM&WS 73P*, *-76P*, *-79P*, *-82P*

Weitzman, David 1898- *IntYB 78*, *-79*, *-80*, *-81*, *-82*, *Who 74*, *-82*, *-83*

Welburn, Ron 1944- *BlkAWP*, *ConAu 1NR*, *-45*, *DrAF 76*, *DrAP 75*, *DrAP&F 83*, *IntAu&W 77*, *-82*, *IntWWP 77*, *-82*

Welch, Bob 1946- *BioIn 11*, *NewYTBS 80[port]*, *RkOn 78*, *WhoRocM 82*

Welch, Bob *see also* Fleetwood Mac

Welch, James 1940- *BioIn 10*, *-12*, *ConAu 85*, *ConLC 6*, *-14*, *ConP 75*, *-80*, *DrAP 75*, *WrDr 76*, *-80*, *-82*, *-84*

Welch, Lew 1926-1971 *BioIn 12*, *ConP 70*, *DcLB 16[port]*

Welch, Mary Scott 1914?- *ConAu 104*, *IntAu&W 76*, *-77*, *-82*, *WhoAmW 74*, *-72*,

-75, *-77*, *-83*, *WhoE 79*, *-81*, *-83*

Welch, Ronald 1909-1982 *BioIn 8*, *-9*, *ConAu X*, *IntAu&W 77X*, *SmATA 3*, *TwCCW 78*, *-83*, *WhoChL*, *WrDr 82*

Welch, Ronald *see also* Felton, Ronald Oliver

Weld, Philip Saltonstall 1914- *WhoAm 74*, *-76*, *-78*

Weldon, Fay 1931?- *Au&Wr 6*, *BioIn 9*, *ConAu 21R*, *ConDr 73*, *-77C*, *-82C*, *ConLC 6*, *-9*, *-11*, *-19*, *ConNov 82*, *DcLB 14[port]*, *IntAu&W 77*, *IntWW 83*, *Novels*, *Who 82*, *-83*, *WrDr 76*, *-80*, *-82*, *-84*

Wellard, James Howard 1909- *Au&Wr 6*, *BioIn 2*, *ConAu 3NR*, *-5R*, *IntAu&W 76*, *-77*, *-82*, *ScF&FL 1*, *-2*, *WrDr 76*, *-80*, *-82*, *-84*

Welles, Orson 1915- *AmAu&B*, *BiDFilm*, *BiE&WWA*, *BioIn 1*, *-2*, *-3*, *-4*, *-5*, *-6*, *-7*, *-8*, *-9*, *-10*, *-11*, *-12*, *BlueB 76*, *CelR 73*, *CmCal*, *CmMov*, *CnThe*, *ConAu 93*, *ConDr 73*, *-77A*, *-82A*, *ConLC 20*, *CurBio 41*, *-65*, *DcAmSR*, *DcFM*, *EncAB-H*, *EncMT*, *EncWT*, *FamA&A*, *FilmgC*, *IntMPA 77*, *-75*, *-76*, *-78*, *-79*, *-81*, *-82*, *-84*, *IntWW 74*, *-75*, *-76*, *-77*, *-78*, *-79*, *-80*, *-81*, *-82*, *-83*, *LinLib L*, *-S*, *MotPP*, *MovMk*, *NewYTBE 72*, *NotNAT*, *-A*, *OxAmH*, *OxFilm*, *OxThe*, *PIP&P*, *REn*, *REnAL*, *ScF&FL 1*, *UFOEn*, *WebAB*, *-79*, *WhDW*, *WhThe*, *Who 74*, *-82*, *-83*, *WhoAm 74*, *-76*, *-78*, *-80*, *-82*, *WhoHol A*, *WhoThe 15*, *WhoWor 74*, *WorAl*, *WorEFlm*, *WrDr 80*, *-82*, *-84*

Wellman, Henry Q 1945- *ConAu 37R*

Wellman, Manly Wade 1903- *AuBYP*, *BioIn 3*, *-4*, *-5*, *-6*, *-8*, *-10*, *ConAu 1R*, *-6NR*, *ConSFA*, *CurBio 55*, *EncMys*, *EncSF*, *MorJA*, *ScF&FL 1*, *-2*, *SmATA 6*, *WhoHr&F*, *WhoSciF*, *WrDr 84*

Wellman, Paul 1928- *CurBio 49*, *WhoE 75*, *WhoEng 80*

Wellman, Paul Iselin 1898-1966 *AmAu&B*, *AmNov*, *Au&Wr 6*, *AuBYP*, *BioIn 1*, *-2*, *-4*, *-7*, *-8*, *-9*, *ConAu 1R*, *-25R*, *ObitOF 79*, *REn*, *REnAL*, *REnAW*, *SmATA 3*, *TwCA SUP*, *WhAm 4*, *WhE&EA*

Wells, Evelyn *ConAu 53*, *WhoAmW 58*, *-61*, *-64*, *-66*, *-68*, *-70*, *-72*

Wells, H G 1866-1946 *AtlBL*, *BbD*, *BiD&SB*, *BrWr 6*, *CnMWL*, *ConAu 110*, *CyWA*, *EncMys*, *EncSF*, *EncUrb*, *FilmgC*, *LinLib L*, *LongCTC*, *ModBrL*, *ModBrL SUP*, *NewC*, *Novels[port]*, *PenC ENG*, *PIP&P*, *RAdv 1*, *RComWL*, *REn*, *ScF&FL 1*, *SmATA 20*, *TwCLC 6[port]*, *-12[port]*, *TwCWr*, *WebE&AL*, *WhScrn*, *-2*, *WhoHol B*, *WhoHr&F*, *WhoSciF*, *WhoTwCL*, *WorAl*

Wells, H G *see also* Wells, Herbert George

Wells, Helen 1910?- *AuBYP, BioIn 2, –8, –9, ConAu 29R, ForWC 70, IntAu&W 77, –82, SmATA 2, WhoAmW 74, –58, –61, –64, –66, –68, –70, –72, –75, WrDr 76, –80, –82, –84*

Wells, Herbert George 1866-1946 *BioIn 1, –2, –3, –4, –5, –6, –7, –8, –9, –10, –11, –12, CasWL, Chambr 3, CurBio 46, DcAmSR, DcBiA, DcEnA AP, DcLEL, EncWL, EvLB, LinLib S, LongCEL, MakMC, McGEWB, MnBBF, NotNAT B, ObitOF 79, OxEng, TwCA, TwCA SUP, WhDW, WhAm 2, WhE&EA, WhLit, WhoBW&I A, WhoLA*

Wells, Herbert George *see also* Wells, H G

Wells, J Wellington 1907- *BioIn 11, –12, ConAu X, SmATA X*

Wells, J Wellington *see also* DeCamp, L Sprague

Wells, Robert L 1913- *AuBYP, BioIn 7*

Wells, Rosemary 1943- *BioIn 12, ChhPo S1, –S2, ConAu 85, ConLC 12, FourBJA, IlsBYP, IlsCB 1967, SmATA 18, TwCCW 83*

Wels, Byron G 1924- *ConAu 8NR, –61, SmATA 9*

Welsch, Roger L 1936- *ConAu 9NR, –21R*

Weltfish, Gene 1902-1980 *AmM&WS 73S, BioIn 3, –12, NewYTBS 80[port]*

Weltner, Linda R 1938- *ConAu 105*

Welty, Eudora 1909- *AmAu&B, AmNov, AmWomWr, AmWr, BioIn 1, –2, –3, –4, –5, –6, –7, –8, –9, –10, –11, –12, BlueB 76, CasWL, CelR 73, ChhPo, CnDAL, ConAu 9R, ConLC 1, –2, –5, –14, –22[port], ConNov 72, –76, –82, Conv 3, CurBio 42, –75, CyWA, DcLB 2, DcLEL 1940, DrAF 76, DrAP&F 83, EncSoH, EncWL, InWom, IntAu&W 76, –77, IntDcWB, IntWW 74, –75, –76, –77, –78, –79, –80, –81, –82, –83, LibW, LinLib L, –S, LongCTC, ModAL, ModAL SUP, NewYTBS 80[port], –83[port], Novels, OxAmL, PenC AM, RAdv 1, REn, REnAL, TwCA SUP, WebAB, –79, WebE&AL, WhDW, WhE&EA, Who 74, –82, –83, WhoAm 74, –76, –78, –80, –82, WhoAmW 74, –58, –61, –64, –66, –68, –70, –72, –81, –83, WhoS&SW 76, –78, WhoTwCL, WhoWor 74, –76, –78, –80, –82, WorAl, WrDr 76, –80, –82, –84*

Wendel, Tim 1956- *ConAu 105*

Wendt, Albert 1939- *ConAu 57, ConNov 82, IntAu&W 77, –82, WrDr 82, –84*

Wenkam, Robert 1920- *ConAu 4NR, –53, IntAu&W 82*

Wenner, Jann S 1946- *BioIn 9, –10, –11, –12, ConAu 101, CurBio 80[port], MugS, WhoAm 76, –78, –80, –82, WhoE 83*

Went, Frits W 1903- *AmM&WS 76P, –79P, –82P, BlueB 76, IntWW 74, –75, –76, –77, –78, –79, –80, –81, –82, –83, McGMS 80[port]*

Wentworth, Harold 1904- *ConAu P-1*

Werfel, Franz 1890-1945 *BiDAmM, BioIn 1, –2, –3, –4, –5, –7, –10, CasWL, ClDMEL, CmCal, CnMD, CnThe, ConAu 104, CurBio 40, –45, CyWA, DcNAA, EncSF, EncTR, EncWL, EncWT, EvEuW, LinLib L, –S, LongCTC, LuthC 75, McGEWB, McGEWD, –84[port], ModGL, ModWD, NewEOp 71, NotNAT B, Novels, ObitOF 79, OxGer, OxThe, PenC EUR, PIP&P, REn, REnWD, ScF&FL 1, TwCA, TwCA SUP, TwCLC 8[port], TwCWr, WhAm 2, WhE&EA*

Wernecke, Herbert Henry 1895- *AuBYP, BioIn 8, ConAu 5R*

Werner, Alfred 1911-1979 *Au&Wr 6, BioIn 9, –12, ConAu 89, WhAm 7, Who 74, –82, –83, WhoAm 74, –76, –78, –80, WhoAmA 73, –76, –78, –80N, –82N, WhoWorJ 72, –78*

Werner, Vivian 1921- *AuBYP SUP, ConAu 105*

Wernick, Robert 1918- *ConAu 97*

Wersba, Barbara 1932- *AuBYP, BioIn 8, –9, –11, ChlLR 3, ConAu 29R, SmATA 1, ThrBJA, TwCCW 78, –83, WrDr 80, –82, –84*

Werstein, Irving 1914-1971 *AuBYP, BioIn 7, –9, –12, ConAu 29R, –73, FourBJA, NewYTBE 71, SmATA 14*

Wertenbaker, Lael Tucker 1909- *Au&Wr 6, ConAu 3NR, –5R, ForWC 70, IntAu&W 77, –82, WhoAmW 74, –68, –70, –72, –75, WhoE 74, WrDr 76, –80, –82, –84*

Wesker, Arnold 1932- *Au&Wr 6, BiE&WWA, BioIn 6, –7, –8, –9, –10, –11, –12, BlueB 76, CasWL, CnMD, CnThe, ConAu 1R, –1NR, ConDr 73, –77, –82, ConLC 3, –5, CroCD, CurBio 62, DcLB 13[port], DcLEL 1940, EncWL, EncWT, IntAu&W 76, –77, –82, IntWW 74, –75, –76, –77, –78, –79, –80, –81, –82, –83, LinLib L, LongCEL, LongCTC, MakMC, McGEWD, –84, ModBrL, ModBrL SUP, ModWD, NewC, NotNAT, –A, OxThe, PenC ENG, PIP&P, REnWD, TwCWr, WebE&AL, Who 74, –82, –83, WhoThe 15, –16, –81, WhoTwCL, WhoWor 74, –76, –78, WorAu, WrDr 76, –80, –82, –84*

Weslager, C A 1909- *ConAu 9NR, –21R*

Weslager, Clinton Alfred 1909- *DrAS 74H, –78H, –82H, WhoAm 74, –76, –78, –80, –82, WhoE 74, –75, –77, –79, –81, –83, WhoWor 78, –80, –82*

Wesolowski, Wayne Edward 1945- *AmM&WS 79P*

Wessel, Thomas Roger 1937- *DrAS 78H*

West, Anna 1938- *ConAu 106*

West, Anthony 1914- *AmAu&B, Au&Wr 6, BioIn 2, –4, ConAu 3NR, –45, ConNov 72, –76, –82, DcIrW 1, DcLB 15, EncSF, IntAu&W 76, –77, LongCTC, ModBrL, NewC, REn, ScF&FL 1, –2, TwCA SUP, Who 82, –83, WhoAm 74, –76, –78, –80, WhoWor 74, WrDr 76, –80, –82, –84*

West, Jerry *BioIn 9, –10, ConAu X, SmATA 2*

West, Jerry *see also* Stratemeyer, Edward L

West, Jerry *see also* Svenson, Andrew E

West, Jerry Alan 1938- *BioIn 5, –6, –8, –9, –10, –11, –12, CelR 73, CmCal, NewYTBS 74, WhoAm 74, –78, –80, WhoBbl 73, WhoWest 84, WorAl*

West, Jessamyn 1907-1984 *AmWomWr, ASpks, BioIn 2, –3, –4, –5, –8, –9, –10, –11, –12, ChhPo, CmCal, ConAu 9R, ConLC 7, –17, ConNov 72, –76, –82, CurBio 77, DcLB 6[port], DcLEL 1940, DrAF 76, DrAP&F 83, InWom, IndAu 1917, IntAu&W 76, –77, LibW, LinLib LP, OxAmL, REnAL, ScF&FL 1, –2, SmATA 37N, TwCA SUP, WhoAm 74, –76, –78, –80, –82, WhoAmW 64, –66, –68, –79, –81, –83, WrDr 76, –80, –82, –84*

West, Morris 1916- *Au&Wr 6, BioIn 5, –6, –7, –8, –10, –11, –12, BlueB 76, ConAu 5R, ConLC 6, ConNov 72, –76, –82, CurBio 66, DcLEL 1940, FarE&A 78, –79, –80, –81, IntAu&W 76, –77, IntWW 74, –75, –76, –77, –78, –79, –80, –81, –82, –83, ModBrL, NewYTBS 79, –81[port], Novels, REn, TwCWr, Who 74, –82, –83, WhoAm 76, –78, –80, –82, WhoWor 74, –76, –78, WorAl, WorAu, WrDr 76, –80, –82, –84*

West, Nathanael 1903?-1940 *AmAu&B, AmWr, AtlBL, BioIn 2, –4, –5, –6, –7, –8, –9, –10, –12, CasWL, CmCal, CnMWL, ConAu X, CurBio 41, CyWA, DcLB 4, –9[port], DcLEL, DcNAA, EncWL, FilmgC, LinLib L, LongCTC, McGEWB, ModAL, ModAL SUP, Novels, OxAmL, PenC AM, RAdv 1, REn, REnAL, ScF&FL 1, TwCA, TwCA SUP, TwCLC 1, TwCWr, WebAB, –79, WebE&AL, WhDW, WhAm HSA, –4, WhoTwCL, WorAl*

West, Nathanael *see also* Weinstein, Nathan Wallenstein

West, Wallace 1900- *ConSFA, EncSF, ScF&FL 1, –2, WhoHr&F, WrDr 84*

West, Ward 1900-1978 *AmAu&B, ConAu X, SmATA X, –5, WorAu, WrDr 84*

West, Ward *see also* Borland, Harold Glen

Westall, Robert 1929- *ConAu 69, ConLC 17, IntAu&W 77, –82, SmATA 23, TwCCW 78, –83, WrDr 80, –82, –84*

Westcott, Jan Vlachos 1912- *AmAu&B,*

AmNov, BioIn 2, ConAu 1R, –2NR

Westervelt, Virginia Veeder 1914- *BioIn 11, ConAu 10NR, –61, IntAu&W 76, –77, SmATA 10, WhoAmW 74, –70, –72, –75*

Westheimer, David 1917- *AmAu&B, AmNov, Au&Wr 6, BioIn 2, –12, ConAu 1R, –2NR, DrAP&F 83, IntAu&W 76, –77, –82, ScF&FL 1, –2, SmATA 14, WhoAm 76, –78, –80, –82, WrDr 76, –80, –82, –84*

Westin, Alan F 1929?- *BioIn 8, ConAu 10NR, –13R*

Westin, Jeane Eddy 1931- *ConAu 85, WhoAmW 75, –77, –79*

Westlake, Donald E 1933- *AmAu&B, ASpks, Au&Wr 6, BioIn 9, –11, –12, ConAu 17R, ConLC 7, ConSFA, EncMys, EncSF, IntAu&W 76, NewYTBS 80[port], Novels, ScF&FL 1, TwCCr&M 80, WhoAm 82, WorAl, WrDr 76, –80, –82, –84*

Westman, Wesley Charles 1936- *AmM&WS 73S, –78S, ConAu 29R*

Westmoreland, William Childs 1914- *BioIn 5, –6, –7, –8, –9, –10, –11, –12, BioNews 74, BlueB 76, ConAu 101, CurBio 61, EncAB-H, IntWW 74, –75, –76, –77, –78, –79, –80, –81, –82, –83, LinLib S, McGEWB, PolProf J, PolProf NF, WebAB, –79, WebAMB, WhDW, WhoAm 74, –76, WhoGov 72, WhoWor 74, WorAl*

Westwood, Gwen 1915- *ConAu 25R, WrDr 76, –80, –82, –84*

Westwood, Jennifer 1940- *BioIn 11, ConAu X, –65, SmATA 10, WhoWor 80*

Wetherell, W D *DrAP&F 83*

Wetterer, Margaret K *AuBYP SUP*

Weverka, Robert 1926- *BioIn 8, ConAu 2NR, –49, ScF&FL 1, –2*

Wexler, Jerome LeRoy 1923- *BioIn 12, ConAu 73, SmATA 14, WhoAmA 78, –80, –82*

Wexley, John 1907- *AmAu&B, CnMD, ConAmA, ModWD, OxAmL, PenC AM, REn, REnAL, WhThe*

Whalen, Charles William, Jr. 1920- *AlmAP 78, AmCath 80, BiDrAC, BlueB 76, CngDr 74, –77, ConAu 105, WhoAm 74, –76, –78, –80, –82, WhoAmP 73, –75, –77, –79, –81, WhoGov 79, –72, –75, WhoMW 74, –76, –78*

Wharton, Edith 1862-1937 *AmAu&B, AmBi, AmWomWr, AmWr, ApCAB X, AtlBL, BiD&SB, BioIn 1, –2, –3, –4, –5, –6, –7, –8, –9, –10, –11, –12, CasWL, Chambr 3, ChhPo S3, CnDAL, ConAmA, ConAmL, ConAu 104, CyWA, DcAmAu, DcAmB S2, DcBiA, DcLB 4, –9[port], –12[port], DcLEL, DcNAA, EncAB-H, EncSF, EncWL, EvLB, GoodHs, HerW, InWom, IntDcWB, LibW, LinLib L, –S, LongCTC, MakMC, McGEWB, ModAL,*

*ModAL SUP, NatCAB 14, NotAW,
NotNAT B, Novels[port], OxAmL,
OxEng, PenC AM, RAdv 1, REn,
REnAL, ScF&FL 1, TwCA, TwCA SUP,
TwCBDA, TwCLC 3, –9[port], TwCWr,
WebAB, –79, WebE&AL, WhDW,
WhAm 1, WhE&EA, WhLit, WhNAA,
WhoHr&F, WhoTwCL, WomWWA 14,
WorAl*

Wharton, William 1925- *BioIn 12, ConAu 93,
ConLC 18, DcLB Y80B, WrDr 82, –84*

Whatmough, Joshua 1897-1964 *AmAu&B,
BioIn 6, ConAu 5R, WhAm 4,
WhE&EA*

Wheaton, Philip D 1916- *ConAu 104*

Whedbee, Charles H 1911- *AmBench 79*

Wheeler, Harvey 1918- *AmM&WS 73S,
BioIn 6, ConAu 1NR, –45, EncSF,
ScF&FL 1, –2, WhoAmP 73*

Wheeler, Harvey see also Wheeler, John Harvey

Wheeler, John Harvey 1918- *WhoAm 74, –76,
–78, –80, –82*

Wheeler, John Harvey see also Wheeler, Harvey

Wheeler, Keith 1911- *BioIn 6, ConAu 5R,
–7NR*

Wheeler, Michael 1943- *ConAu 9NR, –65,
WhoAmL 83*

Wheeler, Sir Mortimer 1890-1976 *BioIn 8, –11,
–12, BlueB 76, ConAu 65, –77,
CurBio 56, –76, –76N, InSci,
IntAu&W 77, IntWW 74, –75, –76, –77N,
LongCTC, NewYTBS 76, ObitOF 79,
WhDW, Who 74, WhoWor 74*

Wheeler, Richard 1922- *ConAu 8NR, –17R*

Wheeler, Thomas Gerald *EncSF, ScF&FL 1*

Wheeler, Tom 1947- *ConAu X*

Wheelock, John Hall 1886-1978 *AmAu&B,
AmLY, AnMV 1926, Au&Wr 6, BioIn 4,
–5, –9, –10, –11, BlueB 76, ChhPo, –S1,
–S2, –S3, CnDAL, ConAmA, ConAmL,
ConAu 13R, –77, ConLC 14,
ConP 70, –75, DcLEL, DrAP 75,
IntAu&W 77, IntWW 74, –75, –76, –77,
–78N, IntWWP 77, ModAL,
NewYTBS 78, ObitOF 79, OxAmL,
RAdv 1, REn, REnAL, TwCA,
TwCA SUP, WhAm 7, WhNAA,
WhoAm 74, –76, –78, WhoWor 74,
WrDr 76*

Whelan, Elizabeth 1943- *AmM&WS 79P,
–82P, BiDrAPH 79, BioIn 12,
ConAu 8NR, –57, SmATA 14*

Whelan, Gloria 1923- *ConAu 101*

Whipkey, Kenneth Lee 1932- *AmM&WS 73P,
–76P, –79P, –82P, ConAu 4NR, –53,
WhoMW 74, –76, –78, –80, –82*

Whipple, Chandler 1905- *ConAu 25R,
WhoE 74*

Whipple, Fred Lawrence 1906-
*AmM&WS 73P, –76P, –79P, –82P, AsBiEn,
Au&Wr 6, BiESc, BioIn 2, –3, –6, –7, –10,
BlueB 76, ConAu P-1, CurBio 52, InSci,*

*IntWW 74, –75, –76, –77, –78, –79, –80, –81,
–82, –83, LuthC 75, McGMS 80[port],
OxAmH, Who 74, –82, –83, WhoAm 74,
–76, –78, –80, –82, WhoGov 72,
WhoWor 74*

Whissen, Thomas Reed 1929- *DrAS 74E, –78E,
–82E*

Whitaker, David 1930- *ConAu 21R, ConSFA,
ScF&FL 1, –2*

Whitcomb, Ian 1941- *ConAu 8NR, –57,
EncPR&S 77, RkOn 78, –84,
RolSEnR 83, WhoRocM 82*

White, Alan *Au&Wr 6, ConAu 3NR, –45,
DcLEL 1940, MotPP, WrDr 76, –80, –82,
–84*

White, Anne 1896- *AmWomWr, AuBYP,
BioIn 6, –7, –9, ConAu 9R, MorJA,
SmATA 2*

White, Antonia 1899-1980 *AnObit 1980,
Au&Wr 6, BioIn 3, –4, –7, –10, –12,
BkC 5, CathA 1952, ConAu 104, –97,
ConNov 72, –76, IntAu&W 76, –77,
LongCTC, NewC, REn, Who 74,
WorAu, WrDr 76, –80*

White, Carol Hellings 1939- *ConAu 81*

White, Dale 1910- *AuBYP, ConAu X,
SmATA 3*

White, Dale see also Place, Marian Templeton

White, E B 1899- *AmWr SUP, Au&ICB,
BlueB 76, BkCL, CelR 73, ChlLR 1,
CnDAL, ConAu 13R, ConLC 10,
DcLB 11[port], –22[port], FamMS,
IntAu&W 76, –77, LinLib L, LongCTC,
ModAL, MorBMP, MorJA,
NewYTBS 76, –80[port], OxAmL,
OxAmL, PenC AM, PiP, RAdv 1, REn,
REnAL, SmATA 2, –29[port],
TwCCW 78, –83, TwCWr, WorAl,
WrDr 76, –80, –82, –84*

White, Elwyn Brooks 1899- *AmAu&B,
AuBYP, AuNews 2, BioIn 1, –3, –4, –5, –6,
–7, –8, –9, –10, –11, –12, ChhPo, –S1, –S2,
–S3, CurBio 60, DcLEL, EvLB,
IntWW 74, –75, –76, –77, –78, –79, –80, –81,
–82, –83, LinLib S, TwCA, TwCA SUP,
WebAB, –79, WhE&EA, Who 74, –82,
–83, WhoAm 74, –76, –78, –80, –82,
WhoChL, WhoWor 74*

White, Florence M 1910- *BioIn 12,
ConAu 41R, IntAu&W 76, –77,
SmATA 14*

White, Gabriel Ernest Edward Francis 1902-
*BlueB 76, Who 74, –82, –83, WhoArt 80,
–82*

White, Hilda Crystal 1917- *ConAu 5R,
ForWC 70*

White, James 1928- *ConAu 4NR, –53,
ConSFA, EncSF, IntAu&W 76, –77, –82,
ScF&FL 1, –2, WhoSciF, WrDr 76, –80,
–82, –84*

White, Jo Ann 1941- *ConAu 53*

White, Jon Manchip 1924- *ConAu 13R,*

ConNov 72, –76, ConP 70, DcLEL 1940,
DrAF 76, DrAP&F 83, DrAS 74E, –78E,
IntAu&W 76, –77, IntWWP 77,
WhoWor 78, WrDr 76, –80, –84

White, Leon S 1936- BiDrAPH 79

White, Marian E 1921-1975 AmM&WS 73S,
BioIn 11, FifIDA

White, Norval Crawford 1926- AmArch 70,
ConAu 77, WhoAm 78, –80, –82

White, Percival 1887-1970 AuBYP, BioIn 7,
–8, ConAu 1R, –2NR, WhAm 5,
WhE&EA

White, Reginald James 1905-1971 ConAu 104,
–108, WhE&EA

White, Robb 1909- AmAu&B, AuBYP,
BioIn 2, –3, –7, –9, ChlLR 3, ConAu 1R,
–1NR, JBA 51, SmATA 1, WhNAA,
WhoAm 74, –76, –78, –80, –82

White, T H 1906-1964 CnMWL, ConAu 73,
DcIrL, EncSF, LongCTC, ModBrL,
Novels, ObitOF 79, PenC ENG, RAdv 1,
REn, ScF&FL 1, SmATA 12,
TwCCW 78, –83, TwCWr, WhoHr&F,
WorAl

White, T H see also White, Terence Hanbury

White, Ted 1938- ConAu X, ConSFA,
EncSF, ScF&FL 1, –2, WhoSciF,
WrDr 84

White, Ted see also White, Theodore Edwin

White, Terence Hanbury 1906-1964 BioIn 4, –5,
–6, –7, –8, –10, –11, –12, CasWL, DcLEL,
OxEng, TelT, TwCA, TwCA SUP,
WhDW, WhAm 4, WhoChL

White, Terence Hanbury see also White, T H

White, Theodore Edwin 1938- ConAu 21R

White, Theodore Edwin see also White, Ted

White, Theodore H 1915- AmAu&B, ASpks,
Au&Wr 6, BioIn 1, –2, –3, –4, –5, –7, –8,
–9, –10, –11, –12, BlueB 76, CelR 73,
ConAu 1R, –3NR, CurBio 55, –76,
DcLEL 1940, IntAu&W 76, –77, –82,
IntWW 74, –75, –76, –77, –78, –79, –80, –81,
–82, –83, LinLib L, NewYTBS 78,
OxAmL, PolProf K, REn, REnAL,
WhoAm 74, –76, –78, –80, –82,
WhoWor 74, –78, –80, –82, WorAl,
WorAu, WrDr 76, –80, –82, –84

White, William 1910- AmAu&B, BlueB 76,
ConAu 21R, DrAS 74E, –78E, –82E,
IntAu&W 76, –77, –82, MichAu 80,
WhoAm 74, –76, –78, –80, –82, WrDr 76,
–80, –82, –84

White, William, Jr. 1934- BioIn 12,
ConAu 37R, DrAS 74H, –78H, –82H,
IntAu&W 77, –82, SmATA 16,
WhoCon 73, WhoE 81, –83, WrDr 76,
–80, –82, –84

White, William Anthony Parker 1911-1968
AmAu&B, BioIn 1, –4, –6, –8, –12,
ConAu 25R, ConAu P-1, EncMys,
ObitOF 79, ScF&FL 1, TwCA SUP

White, William Anthony Parker see also
Boucher, Anthony

Whiteford, Andrew Hunter 1913-
AmM&WS 73S, –76P, ConAu 45, FifIDA,
WhoAm 74, –76, –78, –82

Whitehead, Alfred North 1861-1947 AmAu&B,
AsBiEn, BiESc, BioIn 1, –2, –3, –4, –5, –6,
–8, –9, –10, –12, Chambr 3, DcAmB S4,
DcLEL, DcNAA, DcScB, EncAB-H,
InSci, LinLib L, –S, LongCTC, LuthC 75,
MakMC, McGEWB, NamesHP,
NatCAB 37, NewC, ObitOF 79, OxAmH,
OxAmL, OxEng, REn, REnAL, TwCA,
TwCA SUP, WebAB, –79, WhDW,
WhAm 2

Whitehill, Walter Muir 1905-1978 ConAu 6NR

Whitehouse, Arch 1895-1979 AuBYP, BioIn 7,
–8, –12, ConAu X, MnBBF, SmATA X

Whitehouse, Arch see also Whitehouse, Arthur
George

Whitehouse, Arthur George 1895-1979 AuBYP,
BioIn 7, –8, –12, ConAu 4NR, –5R, –89,
NewYTBS 79, SmATA 14, –23N

Whitehouse, Arthur George see also Whitehouse,
Arch

Whiteley, Opal Stanley 1899- BioIn 3, –6, –11,
REnAL

Whiteside, Thomas 1918?- ConAu 109

Whitfield, Stephen E ConSFA, EncSF

Whitfield, Stephen J 1942- ConAu 61,
DrAS 78H, –82H, WhoAmJ 80,
WhoWorJ 78

Whitinger, R D 1910- AuBYP, ConAu X,
SmATA 3

Whitinger, R D see also Place, Marian Templeton

Whitlock, Herbert Percy 1868-1948 AmAu&B,
BioIn 1, –2, DcNAA, InSci, NatCAB 36,
WhAm 2

Whitlock, Ralph 1914- Au&Wr 6,
ConAu 101, IntAu&W 76, –77, –82,
SmATA 35, WhoWor 76, WrDr 76, –80,
–82, –84

Whitman, Alden 1913- BioIn 7, –8, –9, –12,
ConAu 17R, IntAu&W 76, –77, WhoE 74,
–75, –77

Whitman, Edmund Spurr 1900- ConAu 17R,
WhoAm 74, –76, –78

Whitman, John 1944- ConAu 11NR, –61

Whitman, Walt 1819-1892 Alli, Alli SUP,
AmAu, AmAu&B, AmBi, AmWr, AnCL,
ApCAB, AtlBL, BbD, BiDAmM,
BiD&SB, BioIn 1, –2, –3, –4, –5, –6, –7, –8,
–9, –10, –11, –12, CasWL, CelCen,
Chambr 3, ChhPo, –S1, –S3, CnDAL,
CnE&AP, CrtT 3, –4, CyWA, DcAmAu,
DcAmB, DcAmSR, DcEnA, –AP, DcEnL,
DcLB 3, DcLEL, DcNAA, Dis&D,
EncAAH, EncAB-H, EvLB, HarEnUS,
IlEncMy[port], LinLib L, –S, McGEWB,
MouLC 4, OxAmH, OxAmL, OxCan,
OxEng, PenC AM, RAdv 1, RComWL,
REn, REnAL, SmATA 20, Str&VC,

WebAB, –79, WebE&AL, WhDW,
WorAl
Whitnell, Barbara *ConAu X*
Whitney, Alex 1922- *ConAu 53, SmATA 14*
Whitney, Charles Allen 1929- *AmM&WS 73P,*
–76P, –79P, –82P, ConAu 81, WhoAm 74,
–76, –78, –80, –82, WhoE 75, –77,
WhoGov 77, –72, –75
Whitney, Leon Fradley 1894-1973 *AmAu&B,*
AuBYP, BioIn 7, ConAu 5R, –5NR,
WhAm 6, WhNAA, WhoAm 74
Whitney, Phyllis Ayame 1903- *AmAu&B,*
AmWomWr, AuBYP, AuNews 2,
BioIn 1, –2, –7, –9, –11, –12, ConAu 1R,
–3NR, CurBio 48, EncMys, ForWC 70,
InWom, JBA 51, LibW, Novels,
SmATA 1, –30[port], TwCCW 78, –83,
TwCCr&M 80, WhoAm 74, –76, –78, –80,
–82, WhoAmW 74, –58, –61, –64, –66, –68,
–70, –72, –75, WorAl, WrDr 76, –80, –82,
–84
Whitney, Thomas Porter 1917- *AuBYP SUP,*
BioIn 10, ConAu 104, SmATA 25[port],
WhoAm 74, –76, WhoE 74, –75, –77, –79,
–81, –83, WhoWor 74, –76, –78, –80, –82
Whitridge, Arnold 1891- *AmAu&B,*
Au&Wr 6, ConAu 9R, DrAS 74H,
WhE&EA, WhoAm 74, –76, –78
Whittier, John Greenleaf 1807-1892 *Alli,*
Alli SUP, AmAu, AmAu&B, AmBi,
AmWr SUP, AnCL, ApCAB, AtlBL,
BbD, BiDAmM, BiD&SB, BioIn 1, –2, –3,
–4, –5, –6, –7, –8, –9, –10, –11, –12, CarSB,
CasWL, CelCen, Chambr 3, ChhPo, –S1,
–S2, –S3, CnDAL, CrtT 3, –4, CyAL 2,
CyWA, DcAmAu, DcAmB, DcAmSR,
DcBiPP, DcEnA, DcEnL, DcLB 1,
DcLEL, DcNAA, Dis&D, Drake,
EncAAH, EncAB-H, EvLB,
HarEnUS[port], LinLib L, –S, McGEWB,
MouLC 4, NatCAB 1, OxAmH, OxAmL,
OxEng, PenC AM, RAdv 1, REn,
REnAL, Str&VC, TwCBDA, WebAB,
–79, WebE&AL, WhDW, WhAm HS,
WorAl
Who, The *EncPR&S, –77, IlEncRk,*
RkOn 78, –84, RkOneH, RolSEnR 83
Who, The *see also* Daltrey, Roger
Who, The *see also* Entwistle, John
Who, The *see also* Moon, Keith
Who, The *see also* Townshend, Peter
Whyte, William Hollingsworth 1917- *AmAu&B,*
Au&Wr 6, BioIn 5, –8, BlueB 76,
CelR 73, ConAu 9R, CurBio 59,
DcLEL 1940, IntAu&W 76, –77, –82,
IntWW 74, –75, –76, –77, –78, –79, –80, –81,
–82, –83, REnAL, WhoAm 74, –76, –78,
–80, –82, WhoWor 74, –76, –78
Wibberley, Leonard 1915-1983 *AuBYP,*
BioIn 5, –6, –7, –9, –10, ChlLR 3, ChhPo,
ConAu 3NR, –5R, EncMys, EncSF,
IntAu&W 76, –77, –82, MorJA,

NewYTBS 83, REn, ScF&FL 1, –2,
SmATA 2, –36N, TwCCW 78, –83,
TwCCr&M 80, WhoAm 76, –78, –80, –82,
WorAu, WrDr 80, –82, –84
Wibberley, Leonard *see also* Holton, Leonard
Wibberley, Leonard *see also* O'Connor, Patrick
Wibberley, Leonard *see also* Webb, Christopher
Wickenden, Dan 1913- *AmAu&B, AmNov,*
BioIn 2, –4, CurBio 51, REnAL,
TwCA SUP
Wicker, Thomas Grey 1926- *AmAu&B,*
ASpks, BioIn 8, –9, –10, –11, ConAu 65,
WhoAm 74, –76, –78, –80, –82,
WhoS&SW 73, WhoWor 74, WorAl
Wicker, Tom 1926- *BioIn 3, –4, BlueB 76,*
CelR 73, ConAu X, ConLC 7,
CurBio 73, WrDr 76, –80, –82, –84
Wickett, William Harold, Jr. 1919- *ConAu 108,*
WhoWest 74, –76, –78, –80, –82
Wicklein, John Frederick 1924- *ConAu 106,*
WhoAm 78, –80, –82
Widder, Arthur 1928- *ConAu 5R*
Widder, Arthur *see also* Widder, John Arthur, Jr.
Widder, John Arthur, Jr. 1928- *WhoE 74*
Widder, John Arthur, Jr. *see also* Widder, Arthur
Wideman, John E 1941- *BioIn 6, BlkAWP,*
ConAu 85, ConLC 5, InB&W 80,
LivgBAA, NegAl 76, –83, SelBAA,
WhoAm 76, WhoBlA 75, –77, –80
Wiener, Harvey Shelby 1940- *ConAu 102,*
DrAS 74E, –78E, –82E
Wier, Ester 1910- *AuBYP, BioIn 6, –7, –9,*
ConAu 9R, LinLib L, SmATA 3,
ThrBJA, TwCCW 78, –83, WhoAmW 74,
–75, WrDr 84
Wiese, Kurt 1887-1974 *AmAu&B, AmPB,*
AuBYP, BioIn 1, –2, –4, –5, –7, –8, –9, –10,
ChhPo, ConAu 9R, –49, ConICB,
IlsCB 1744, –1946, –1957, –1967, JBA 34,
–51, LinLib L, REnAL, SmATA 24N, –3,
–36, TwCCW 78
Wiesel, Elie 1928- *AmAu&B, Au&Wr 6,*
AuNews 1, BioIn 8, –9, –10, –11, –12,
ConAu 5R, –8NR, ConIsC 1[port],
ConLC 3, –5, –11, CurBio 70, DrAF 76,
DrAP&F 83, EncWL, LinLib L,
NewYTBE 73, NewYTBS 81[port],
–83[port], WhoAm 74, –76, –78, –80, –82,
WhoAmJ 80, WhoE 74, WhoWorJ 72,
–78, WorAl, WorAu
Wiesenthal, Simon 1908- *BioIn 6, –7, –9, –10,*
–11, –12, ConAu 21R, CurBio 75, EncTR,
IntAu&W 77, IntWW 77, –78, –79, –80,
–81, –82, –83, WhoWor 74, –76, –78, –80,
–82, WhoWorJ 78
Wiggin, Kate Douglas 1856-1923 *Alli SUP,*
AmAu&B, AmBi, AmWom, AmWomWr,
ApCAB X, AuBYP SUP, BbD,
BiDAmEd, BiD&SB, BioIn 1, –2, –3, –4,
–6, –8, –10, –11, –12, CarSB, Chambr 3,
ChhPo, –S1, –S2, –S3, CmCal, CnDAL,
ConAmL, DcAmAu, DcAmB, DcLEL,

DcNAA, EvLB, FamAYP, FamSYP,
HerW, InWom, JBA 34, LibW,
LinLib L, –LP, –S, LongCTC, NatCAB 6,
NotAW, OxAmL, REn, REnAL, TwCA,
TwCA SUP, TwCBDA, TwCCW 78, –83,
WebAB, –79, WhAm 1, WhLit, WhoChL,
WomWWA 14, WorAl, YABC 1, –1

Wiggin, Maurice 1912- *Au&Wr 6, BioIn 8,*
–9, ConAu 5NR, –9R

Wigginton, Eliot 1942?- *AuNews 1, BioIn 10,*
–12, BioNews 74, ConAu 101

Wight, James Alfred 1916- *BioIn 10, –11, –12,*
ConAu 77, Who 82, –83, WrDr 76, –80,
–82, –84

Wight, James Alfred *see also* Herriot, James

Wilber, Donald Newton 1907- *AuBYP,*
BioIn 7, ConAu 2NR, –5R, IntAu&W 77,
–82, SmATA 35, WhoE 75, –77,
WrDr 76, –80, –82, –84

Wilbur, Richard 1921- *AmAu&B, Au&Wr 6,*
AuBYP SUP, BiE&WWA, BioIn 3, –4, –7,
–8, –9, –10, –11, –12, BlueB 76, CasWL,
ChhPo S1, –S2, –S3, CnDAL, CnE&AP,
CnMWL, ConAu 1R, –2NR, ConLC 3, –6,
–9, –14, ConP 70, –75, –80, CroCAP,
CurBio 66, DcLB 5[port], DcLEL 1940,
DrAF 76, DrAP 75, DrAP&F 83,
DrAS 74E, –78E, –82E, EncWL,
IntAu&W 77, –82, IntWW 74, –75, –76,
–77, –78, –79, –80, –81, –82, –83,
IntWWP 77, –82, LinLib L, ModAL,
ModAL SUP, NotNAT, OxAmL,
PenC AM, PIP&P, RAdv 1, REn,
REnAL, SmATA 9, TwCA SUP,
TwCWr, WebE&AL, WhoAm 74, –76,
–78, –80, –82, WhoE 74, WhoThe 15, –16,
–81, WhoTwCL, WhoWor 74, WorAl,
WrDr 76, –80, –82, –84

Wilcox, Collin 1924- *ConAu 21R, ScF&FL 1,*
TwCCr&M 80, WhoAm 82, WrDr 82,
–84

Wilcox, Preston 1923- *InB&W 80,*
WhoBlA 75, –77, –80

Wilcox, Robert Kalleen 1943- *ConAu 77*

Wilde, Oscar 1854?-1900 *Alli SUP, AtlBL,*
BbD, BiD&SB, BioIn 1, –2, –3, –4, –5, –6,
–7, –8, –9, –10, –11, –12, BrAu 19, BrWr 5,
CarSB, CasWL, Chambr 3, ChhPo, –S2,
–S3, CnE&AP, CnMD, CnThe,
ConAu 104, CrtT 3, –4, CyWA,
DcAmSR, DcBiA, DcCathB, DcEnA AP,
DcEuL, DcIrB, DcIrL, DcIrW 1,
DcLB 10[port], –19[port], DcLEL, Dis&D,
EncWL, EncWT, EvLB, FilmgC,
LinLib L, –S, LongCEL, LongCTC,
McGEWB, McGEWD, –84[port], ModWD,
MouLC 4, NewC, NewEOp 71,
NotNAT A, –B, OxEng, OxFilm, OxFr,
OxThe, PenC ENG, PIP&P, PoIre,
RAdv 1, RComWL, REn, REnWD,
ScF&FL 1, SmATA 24[port], TelT,
TwCLC 1, –8[port], WebE&AL, WhDW,

WhoChL, WhoHr&F, WorAl

Wilder, Cherry 1930- *ConAu X, EncSF,*
WrDr 84

Wilder, Laura Ingalls 1867-1957 *AmWomWr,*
AnCL, AuBYP, BioIn 1, –2, –3, –4, –5, –7,
–8, –9, –10, –11, –12, BkCL, CasWL,
ChlLR 2, ChhPo S1, CurBio 48, –57,
DcAmB S6, DcLB 22[port], FamMS,
HerW, InWom, JBA 51, LibW,
NotAW MOD, ObitOF 79, REnAL,
REnAW, SmATA 15, –29[port], Str&VC,
TwCCW 78, –83, WhAm 3, WhE&EA,
WhoChL, WorAl

Wilder, Rose 1887-1968 *AmAu&B, WhNAA*

Wilder, Rose *see also* Lane, Rose Wilder

Wilder, Thornton 1897-1975 *AmAu&B,*
AmNov, AmWr, Au&Wr 6, AuNews 2,
BiDAmM, BiE&WWA, BioIn 1, –2, –3, –4,
–5, –6, –7, –8, –9, –10, –11, –12, BlueB 76,
CasWL, CelR 73, Chambr 3, CnDAL,
CnMD, CnMWL, CnThe, ConAmA,
ConAmL, ConAu 13R, –61, ConDr 73,
–77, ConLC 1, –5, –6, –10, –15,
ConNov 72, CroCD, CurBio 43, –71,
–76N, CyWA, DcLB 4, –7[port], –9[port],
DcLEL, EncAB-H, EncWL, EncWT,
EvLB, FilmgC, IntAu&W 76, IntWW 74,
–75, –76N, LinLib L, –S, LongCTC,
McGEWB, McGEWD 84[port], ModAL,
ModAL SUP, ModWD, NewEOp 71,
NewYTBS 75, NotNAT A, –B,
Novels[port], ObitOF 79, ObitT 1971,
OxAmL, OxEng, OxThe, PenC AM, PiP,
PIP&P, RAdv 1, RComWL, REn,
REnAL, REnWD, TwCA, TwCA SUP,
TwCWr, WebAB, –79, WebE&AL,
WhDW, WhAm 6, WhE&EA, WhLit,
WhNAA, WhThe, Who 74, WhoAm 74,
WhoThe 15, WhoTwCL, WhoWor 74,
WisWr, WorAl, WorEFlm, WrDr 76

Wildman, Eugene 1938- *ConAu 25R,*
DrAP&F 83

Wiley, Farida Anna 1887- *OhA&B*

Wiley, Jack 1936- *ConAu 8NR, –61*

Wilford, John Noble, Jr. 1933- *AuBYP SUP,*
ConAu 29R, IntAu&W 76, –77, –82,
WhoAm 76, –78, –80, –82, WhoE 74, –75,
–77

Wilhelm, Kate 1928- *AmWomWr, BioIn 12,*
ConAu 37R, ConLC 7, ConSFA,
DcLB 8[port], EncSF, IntAu&W 77,
ScF&FL 1, –2, WhoAmW 70, –72,
WhoSciF, WrDr 76, –80, –82, –84

Wilhelm, Steve 1905-1967 *AmAu&B*

Wilhelmsen, Frederick D 1923- *AmCath 80,*
BioIn 3, ConAu 1R, –3NR

Wilk, Max 1920- *BioIn 10, ConAu 1R, –1NR,*
DrAP&F 83

Wilkerson, David Ray 1931- *Au&Wr 6,*
ConAu 41R

Wilkie, Katharine E 1904-1980 *AuBYP,*
BioIn 7, ConAu 21R, ForWC 70,

PolProf E, REnAL, WhoAm 74, –76, –78, –80, –82, WorAl, WorAu, WrDr 76, –80, –82, –84

Wilson, Tom 1931- *ConAu 106, SmATA 30, –33[port], WhoAm 74, –76, –78, –80, –82*

Wilton, Elizabeth 1937- *BioIn 12, ConAu 69, SingR 2, SmATA 14*

Wimmer, Helmut Karl 1925- *BioIn 8, IlsCB 1957*

Wimp, Jet *DrAP&F 83*

Windeler, Robert 1944- *ConAu 102, IntAu&W 76*

Windham, Basil *ConAu X, MnBBF, SmATA X, WhoBW&I A*

Windham, Basil *see also* Wodehouse, Pelham Grenville

Windham, Kathryn T 1918- *BioIn 12, ConAu 11NR, –69, SmATA 14*

Windsor, Patricia 1938- *ConAu 4NR, –49, SmATA 30[port], WhoAmW 83, WhoE 77, –79, WrDr 80, –82, –84*

Wing, Frances Scott 1907- *ConAu P-1, WhoAmW 74*

Wings *RkOn 78, WhoRocM 82*

Wings *see also* McCartney, Paul

Winn, Janet Bruce 1928- *ConAu 105, DrAP&F 83*

Winogrand, Garry 1928- *BioIn 7, –9, –11, –12, BnEnAmA, ConPhot, DcCAr 81, WhoAm 82, WhoAmA 78, –80, –82*

Winship, Elizabeth C 1921- *BioIn 10, ConAu 41R, WhoAmW 77, –79, –81*

Winslow, Pauline Glen *ConAu 101*

Winsor, Kathleen 1919- *AmAu&B, AmNov, BioIn 1, –2, –3, –7, ConAu 97, LongCTC, Novels, REn, REnAL, TwCWr, WhoAm 74, –76, –78, –80, –82, WhoAmW 74, –58, –68, –70, –72, WrDr 84*

Winston, Richard 1917-1979 *AuBYP SUP, BioIn 12, ConAu 25R, –93, NewYTBS 80, WhoAm 80*

Wint, Guy 1910-1969 *ConAu 1R, –3NR*

Winter, Charles A 1902- *AmM&WS 73P*

Winter, Elmer Louis 1912- *BioIn 7, –9, BlueB 76, ConAu 13R, IntYB 78, –79, –80, –81, –82, WhoAm 74, –76, –78, –80, WhoF&I 74, WhoWorJ 78, WrDr 80, –82, –84*

Winter, Ruth Grosman 1930- *ConAu 37R, ForWC 70, IntAu&W 76, WhoAm 76, –78, –80, –82, WhoAmW 74, –66, –68, –72, –75, WhoE 74, –75, –77*

Winter, William John 1912- *AuBYP*

Winterbotham, Frederick William 1897- *BioIn 12, ConAu 57, Who 74, –82, –83, WrDr 76, –80, –82, –84*

Winterfeld, Henry 1901- *ConAu 77, ScF&FL 1, ThrBJA*

Winters, Jon *ConAu X*

Winterton, Paul 1908- *BioIn 10, ConAu 5R, –6NR, EncMys, WhE&EA, WorAu, WrDr 80, –82, –84*

Winterton, Paul *see also* Garve, Andrew

Winther, Barbara 1926- *ConAu 97*

Winthrop, Elizabeth *BioIn 11, ConAu X, DrAP&F 83, SmATA 8*

Winthrop, Elizabeth *see also* Mahony, Elizabeth Winthrop

Winton, John *ConAu X, IntAu&W 76X*

Winton, John *see also* Pratt, John

Winward, Walter 1938- *Au&Wr 6, ConAu 105, IntAu&W 76*

Wise, David 1930- *AmAu&B, ConAu 1R, –2NR, WhoAm 74, –76, –78, –80, –82, WrDr 76, –80, –82, –84*

Wise, William 1923- *AuBYP, BioIn 7, –9, ChhPo, ConAu 6NR, –13R, SmATA 4*

Wise, Winifred E 1906- *AuBYP, BioIn 7, –9, ConAu 25R, ForWC 70, SmATA 2, WrDr 76, –80, –82, –84*

Wiseman, Bernard 1922- *AuBYP SUP, BioIn 9, ConAu 5R, IntAu&W 77, SmATA 4, WhoE 75, –77, WhoS&SW 78, –80, –82, WrDr 76, –80, –82, –84*

Wiseman, Thomas 1931- *Au&Wr 6, ConAu 25R, Novels*

Wisler, G Clifton 1950- *WrDr 82, –84*

Wisner, Bill 1914?-1983 *ConAu X*

Wisner, William L 1914?-1983 *AuBYP, BioIn 8, ConAu 110*

Wissmann, Ruth H Leslie 1914- *AuBYP, BioIn 7, ConAu 2NR, –5R, IntAu&W 77, WhoAmW 75*

Wister, Owen 1860-1938 *Alli SUP, AmAu&B, AmBi, AmLY, ApCAB SUP, ArizL, BiD&SB, BioIn 1, –3, –4, –5, –7, –9, –10, –12, CarSB, CasWL, Chambr 3, ChhPo, –S2, CnDAL, ConAmA, ConAmL, ConAu 108, CyWA, DcAmAu, DcAmB, DcLB 9[port], DcLEL, DcNAA, EncAAH, EncAB-H, HarEnUS, LinLib L, –S, LongCTC, NatCAB 13, Novels, OxAmL, PenC AM, RAdv 1, REn, REnAL, REnAW, ScF&FL 1, TwCA, TwCA SUP, WebAB, –79, WebE&AL, WhAm 1, WhE&EA, WhLit, WhNAA, WorAl*

Witcover, Jules 1927- *AmAu&B, ConAu 25R*

Witheridge, Elizabeth P 1907- *AuBYP SUP, BioIn 6, ConAu 97, IntAu&W 82, MinnWr*

Withey, Lynne Elizabeth 1948- *DrAS 78H, –82H*

Witt, Shirley Hill 1934- *AmM&WS 73S, –76P, BioIn 12, ConAu 5NR, –53, FifIDA, SmATA 17, WhoAmW 77, –79, –81, WhoWest 80, –82, –84*

Witton, Dorothy *AuBYP, BioIn 7, ConAu 73, MichAu 80*

Wodehouse, P G 1881-1975 *AmAu&B, AmPS, AmSCAP 66, BiDAmM, BiE&WWA, BlueB 76N, CelR 73, CmpEPM, ConAu 3NR, –45, –57, ConDr 73, ConLC 2, –5, –10, –22[port], ConNov 72,*

–76, CurBio 71, –75, –75N, EncMT,
EncSF, EncWT, LinLib L, LongCTC,
McGEWD, –84, ModBrL, ModBrL SUP,
NewC, NewCBMT, NewYTBS 75,
Novels, ObitOF 79, PenC ENG, PIP&P,
RAdv 1, REn, ScF&FL 1, –2,
SmATA 22[port], TwCWr, WebE&AL,
WhoTwCL, WorAl

Wodehouse, Pelham Grenville 1881-1975
AmSCAP 66, Au&Wr 6, AuNews 2,
BioIn 1, –2, –3, –4, –5, –6, –7, –8, –9, –10,
–11, –12, CasWL, Chambr 3, DcLEL,
EncWL, EvLB, IntWW 74, –75N,
LinLib S, MakMC, MnBBF, NotNAT A,
ObitT 1971, OxEng, TwCA, TwCA SUP,
WhDW, WhAm 6, WhE&EA, WhLit,
WhThe, Who 74, WhoAm 74,
WhoBW&I A, WhoChL, WhoWor 74

Wohlrabe, Raymond A 1900-1977 *AuBYP,*
BioIn 7, –9, ConAu 1R, –3NR, SmATA 4,
WhoPNW, WhoWest 74, WrDr 76, –80,
–82, –84

Woiwode, Larry 1941- *BioIn 8, –10,*
ConAu 73, ConLC 6, –10, ConNov 82,
DcLB 6[port], DrAF 76, DrAP 75,
DrAP&F 83, WhoAm 74, –76, –78, –80,
WrDr 80, –82, –84

Wojciechowska, Maia 1927- *AmAu&B,*
AmCath 80, Au&ICB, AuBYP, BioIn 7,
–8, –9, –10, –11, ChlLR 1, ConAu 4NR,
–9R, ConLC 26[port], CurBio 76,
DrAP&F 83, HerW, MorBMP,
NinCLC 1956, PiP, SmATA 1, –28[port],
ThrBJA, TwCCW 78, –83, WhoAm 74,
–76, –78, WhoAmW 74, –66, –68, –70, –72,
–75, WrDr 80, –82, –84

Wojciechowska, Maia *see also* Rodman, Maia

Wold, JoAnne 1938- *ConAu 61*

Wolf, Harold Arthur 1923- *AmEA 74,*
AmM&WS 73S, –78S, ConAu 13R,
WhoAm 80, –82

Wolf, Jacqueline 1928- *ConAu 109*

Wolf, Marguerite Hurrey 1914- *BioIn 11,*
ConAu 53, WhoAmW 72

Wolfe, Burton H 1932- *BioIn 10, ConAu 25R,*
DcAmSR, IntAu&W 77, –82, SmATA 5,
WhoWest 74, –76, –78, WrDr 76, –80, –82,
–84

Wolfe, Gene 1931- *BioIn 12, ConAu 6NR,*
–57, ConLC 25[port], DcLB 8, DrAF 76,
DrAP&F 83, EncSF, IntAu&W 76,
ScF&FL 1, –2, WhoMW 80, –82,
WrDr 84

Wolfe, Jean Elizabeth 1925- *WhoAmW 74, –68,*
–72, –75, –77, –79, –81, –83, WhoE 74, –75,
–77, –79, –81, –83

Wolfe, Louis 1905- *AuBYP, BioIn 7, –11,*
ConAu 3NR, –5R, ScF&FL 1, –2,
SmATA 8

Wolfe, Thomas Clayton 1900-1938 *AmAu&B,*
AmBi, AmSCAP 66, AmWr, AtlBL,
BioIn 1, –2, –3, –4, –5, –6, –7, –8, –9, –10,

–11, –12, CasWL, CnDAL, CnMD,
CnMWL, ConAmA, ConAu 104, CyWA,
DcAmB S2, DcLB DS2[port], –9[port],
DcLEL, DcNAA, EncAB-H, EncSoH,
EncWL, EncWT, EvLB, LinLib L, –S,
LongCTC, MakMC, McGEWB, ModAL,
ModWD, Novels, OxAmH, OxAmL,
OxEng, PenC AM, PIP&P, RAdv 1,
REn, REnAL, TwCA, TwCA SUP,
TwCLC 4[port], TwCWr, WebAB, –79,
WebE&AL, WhDW, WhAm 1,
WhoTwCL, WorAl

Wolfe, Thomas Kennerly, Jr. 1931- *AmAu&B,*
BioIn 12, BlueB 76, ConAu 9NR, –13R,
DcLEL 1940, IntAu&W 82, WhoAm 74,
–76, –78, –80, –82, WhoWor 74

Wolfe, Tom 1931- *AuNews 2, BioIn 7, –8, –9,*
–10, –11, –12, CelR 73, CmCal,
ConAu X, ConLC 1, –2, –9, –15,
CurBio 71, MakMC, NewYTBS 81[port],
PenC AM, WebE&AL, WhoTwCL,
WorAl, WorAu 1970, WrDr 76, –80, –82,
–84

Wolff, Ruth 1909?-1972 *BioIn 9, ConAu 37R*

Wolff, Virginia Euwer 1937- *ConAu 107*

Wolfson, Victor 1910- *BiE&WWA, BioIn 1,*
–4, ConAu 33R, NotNAT, TwCA SUP,
WhoWorJ 72, –78

Wolitzer, Hilma 1930- *BioIn 11, ConAu 65,*
ConLC 17, DrAF 76, DrAP&F 83,
SmATA 31[port], WhoAm 82, WrDr 76,
–80, –82, –84

Wolk, Allan 1936- *ConAu 77*

Wolkoff, Judie *SmATA 37*

Wollheim, Donald A 1914- *AuBYP, BioIn 7,*
ConAu 1R, –1NR, ConSFA, EncSF,
ScF&FL 1, –2, WhoAm 78, –80, –82,
WhoE 74, –75, –77, –79, WhoHr&F,
WhoSciF, WhoWor 80, WrDr 76, –80,
–82, –84

Wollstonecraft, Mary 1759-1797 *Alli, AtlBL,*
BbD, BiD&SB, BioIn 1, –2, –3, –7, –8, –9,
–10, –11, –12, BrAu, CasWL, CelCen,
Chambr 2, CrtT 4, CyEd, DcEnA,
DcEnL, DcLEL, Dis&D, GoodHs, HerW,
InWom, IntDcWB[port], NewC, OxEng,
PenC ENG, REn

Wolters, Richard A 1920- *BioIn 8, –12,*
ConAu 3NR, –5R, SmATA 35, WrDr 76,
–80, –82, –84

Womack, John, Jr. 1937- *ConAu 45,*
WhoAm 74, –76, –78, –80

Wonder, Stevie 1950?- *Baker 78, BiDAfM,*
BiDAmM, BioIn 9, –10, –11, –12,
BioNews 74, ConLC 12, CurBio 75,
DrBlPA, Ebony 1, EncJzS 70, EncPR&S,
–77, IlEncRk, InB&W 80, IntWW 78,
–79, –80, –81, –82, –83, NegAl 83[port],
NewYTBE 70, NewYTBS 75, RkOn 74,
–78, –82, –84, RolSEnR 83, WhoAm 76,

-78, -80, -82, WhoBlA 75, -77, -80, WhoRocM 82, WorAl

Wong, Jade Snow 1922- *Bioln 2, -4, -10, ConAu 109, ConLC 17, WhoAmW 58, -61, -64*

Wood, Barbara 1947- *ConAu 85*

Wood, Clement 1888-1950 *AmAu&B, AmSCAP 66, AnMV 1926, Bioln 2, -4, ChhPo, -S1, -S2, ObitOF 79, REn, REnAL, TwCA, TwCA SUP, WhAm 3, WhE&EA, WhLit, WhNAA*

Wood, Clement Biddle 1925- *ConAu 21R*

Wood, James Playsted 1905- *AmAu&B, Au&Wr 6, AuBYP, Bioln 9, ChhPo S2, ConAu 3NR, -9R, FourBJA, IntAu&W 77, -82, ScF&FL 1, SmATA 1, WhoAm 74, -76, -78, -80, -82, WrDr 76, -80, -82, -84*

Wood, Kenneth 1922- *ConAu 11NR, -69*

Wood, Laura N 1911- *AuBYP, Bioln 7, ConAu 57, SmATA X, WrDr 76, -80, -82, -84*

Wood, Laura N *see also* Roper, Laura Wood

Wood, Michael 1936- *ConAu 37R*

Wood, Nancy 1936- *Bioln 10, ConAu 9NR, -21R, SmATA 6, WhoAmW 74, -75*

Wood, Paul W 1922- *ConAu 61, WhoE 79*

Wood, Phyllis Anderson 1923- *AuBYP SUP, ConAu 37R, IntAu&W 77, SmATA 30, -33[port], WrDr 76, -80, -82, -84*

Wood-Allen, Mary 1841-1908 *DcAmAu, DcNAA, OhA&B, WhAm 1*

Woodburn, John Henry 1914- *AuBYP SUP, Bioln 11, ConAu 1R, -4NR, LEduc 74, SmATA 11*

Woodcock, George 1912- *Au&Wr 6, CaW, CanWW 70, -79, -80, -81, -83, CanWr, CasWL, ConAu 1R, -1NR, ConDr 82B, ConP 70, -75, -80, DcLEL 1940, IntAu&W 76, -77, -82, IntWW 79, -80, -81, -82, -83, IntWWP 77, ModBrL, OxCan, OxCan SUP, WhE&EA, Who 74, -82, -83, WhoAm 74, -76, -78, -80, -82, WorAu 1970, WrDr 76, -80, -82, -84*

Wooden, John R 1910- *Bioln 6, -9, -10, -11, -12, CelR 73, CmCal, CurBio 76, NewYTBE 73, WhoAm 76, -78, -80, -82, WorAl*

Woodford, Peggy 1937- *ConAu 104, SmATA 25[port], WrDr 80, -82, -84*

Woodham-Smith, Cecil 1896-1977 *Au&Wr 6, Bioln 2, -3, -4, -11, ConAu 69, -77, CurBio 55, -77, -77N, InWom, IntAu&W 76, IntWW 74, -75, -76, -77N, LongCTC, NewYTBS 77, ObitOF 79, REn, TwCA SUP, Who 74, WhoAmW 68, -70, -72, WhoWor 74, WrDr 76*

Woodman, James Monroe 1931- *ConAu 17R*

Woodman, Jim 1931- *ConAu X*

Woodman, Jim *see also* Woodman, James Monroe

Woodress, James Leslie, Jr. 1916- *ConAu 3NR, -5R, DrAS 74E, -78E, -82E, WhoAm 74, -76, -78, -80, -82, WrDr 80, -82, -84*

Woods, Donald 1933- *Bioln 12, CurBio 82[port]*

Woods, George A 1926- *AuBYP SUP, ConAu 29R, SmATA 30[port]*

Woods, Geraldine 1948- *ConAu 97, WhoBlA 80*

Woods, Harold 1945- *ConAu 97*

Woods, Stuart 1938- *Bioln 12, ConAu 93, IntAu&W 82*

Woodward, Bob 1943- *AuNews 1, Bioln 9, -12, BioNews 74, ConAu X, -69, CurBio 76, NewYTBS 80[port], WrDr 80, -82, -84*

Woodward, Robert Upshur 1943- *AuNews 1, Bioln 10, -11, -12, ConAu 69, WhoAm 74, -76, -78, -80, -82, WorAl*

Woody, Regina J 1894- *AuBYP, Bioln 6, -7, -9, ConAu 3NR, -5R, ForWC 70, IntAu&W 77, MorJA, SmATA 3, WhoAmW 74, -61, -64, -66, -68, -70, -72, -75, WhoE 74, WrDr 76, -80, -82, -84*

Woody, Robert Henley 1936- *BiDrAPH 79, ConAu 93*

Woodyard, George W 1934- *ConAu 81, DrAS 74F, -78F, -82F*

Woolf, Virginia 1882-1941 *AtlBL, Bioln 1, -2, -3, -4, -5, -6, -7, -8, -9, -10, -11, -12, CasWL, Chambr 3, CnMWL, ConAu 104, ConLCrt, -82, CurBio 41, CyWA, DcLEL, EncSF, EncWL, EvLB, GoodHs, InWom, IntDcWB[port], LinLib L, -S, LongCEL, LongCTC, McGEWB, ModBrL, ModBrL SUP, NewC, Novels[port], ObitOF 79, OxEng, PenC ENG, RAdv 1, RComWL, REn, ScF&FL 1, TwCA, TwCA SUP, TwCLC 1, -5[port], TwCWr, WebE&AL, WhDW, WhE&EA, WhoTwCL, WorAl*

Woolley, Bryan 1937- *ConAu 4NR, -49, DrAP&F 83*

Woolsey, Janette 1904- *AuBYP, Bioln 7, -9, ConAu 1R, -2NR, ForWC 70, ScF&FL 1, -2, SmATA 3, WhoAmW 68, WhoLibS 55*

Wootten, Morgan 1931- *AmCath 80, Bioln 11, -12, ConAu 101*

Worboys, Anne *ConAu 9NR, -65, WrDr 76, -80, -82, -84*

Worcester, Donald Emmett 1915- *AmAu&B, AuBYP, Bioln 7, -12, BlueB 76, ConAu 1R, -4NR, DrAS 74H, -78H, -82H, IntAu&W 76, -77, -82, SmATA 18, WhoAm 74, -76, -78, -80, -82, WhoS&SW 73, WhoWor 78, WrDr 76, -80, -82, -84*

Wordsworth, William 1770-1850 *Alli, AnCL, AtlBL, BbD, BiD&SB, BiDLA, Bioln 1,*

–2, –3, –4, –5, –6, –7, –8, –9, –10, –11, –12,
BrAu 19, BrWr 4, CasWL, CelCen,
Chambr 3, ChhPo, –S1, –S2, –S3,
CnE&AP, CrtT 2, –4, CyEd, CyWA,
DcBiPP, DcEnA, DcEnL, DcEuL,
DcLEL, Dis&D, EvLB, IlEncMy[port],
LinLib L, –S, LongCEL, LuthC 75,
McGEWB, MouLC 3, NewC, OxEng,
OxMus, PenC ENG, PoLE, RAdv 1,
RComWL, REn, Str&VC, WebE&AL,
WhDW, WorAl

Worrell, Estelle *AuBYP SUP*

Worster, Donald Eugene 1941- *ConAu 57,*
DrAS 74H, –78H, –82H

Worth, Douglas 1940- *ConAu 9NR, –65,*
DrAP 75, DrAP&F 83, IntWWP 82

Worth, Fred L 1943- *ConAu 97*

Worthy, William 1921- *InB&W 80,*
WhoBlA 77, –80

Worton, Stanley Nelson 1923- *ConAu 57,*
DrAS 74H, –78H, –82H

Wosmek, Frances 1917- *ConAu 11NR, –29R,*
SmATA 29[port], WrDr 80, –82, –84

Wouk, Herman 1915- *AmAu&B, AmNov,*
Au&Wr 6, BiE&WWA, BioIn 1, –2, –3,
–4, –5, –8, –9, BlueB 76, CnMD,
ConAu 5R, –6NR, ConLC 1, –9,
ConNov 72, –76, –82, CroCD, CurBio 52,
DcLB Y82B[port], DcLEL 1940, EncSF,
EncWL, EncWT, FilmgC, IntAu&W 76,
–77, –82, IntWW 74, –75, –76, –77, –78,
–79, –80, –81, –82, –83, LinLib L,
LongCTC, ModAL, ModWD,
NatPD 81[port], NotNAT, Novels,
OxAmL, PenC AM, REn, REnAL,
ScF&FL 1, TwCA SUP, TwCWr,
WebAB, –79, Who 74, –82, –83,
WhoAm 74, –76, –78, –80, –82,
WhoAmJ 80, WhoE 83, WhoWor 74, –76,
–78, –80, –82, WhoWorJ 72, –78, WorAl,
WrDr 76, –80, –82, –84

Wren, Percival C 1885-1941 *BioIn 1,*
CurBio 42, DcLEL, EvLB, LongCTC,
MnBBF, NewC, ObitOF 79, OxEng,
PenC ENG, REn, ScF&FL 1, TwCA,
TwCWr, WhE&EA, WhLit

Wright, Constance 1897- *Au&Wr 6,*
ConAu 13R, WrDr 76, –80, –82, –84

Wright, Gary 1943- *IlEncRk, RkOn 78,*
WhoRocM 82

Wright, Helen 1914- *AmAu&B, BioIn 4,*
ConAu 9R, CurBio 56, InSci, InWom,
ScF&FL 1, –2, WhoAm 74, –76, –78, –80,
–82, WhoAmW 74, –58, –61, –64, –66, –68,
–70, –72

Wright, James Arlington 1927-1980 *AmAu&B,*
AnObit 1980[port], AuNews 2, BioIn 9,
–10, –11, –12, ChhPo, –S1, CnE&AP,
ConAu 4NR, –49, –97, ConLC 3, –5, –10,
ConP 70, –75, –80, CroCAP,
DcLB 5[port], DcLEL 1940, DrAP 75,
IntWWP 77, ModAL, ModAL SUP,

NewYTBS 80[port], PenC AM, RAdv 1,
WebE&AL, WhAm 7, WhoAm 74, –76,
–78, –80, WhoTwCL, WorAu, WrDr 76,
–80

Wright, John Stafford 1905- *Au&Wr 6,*
ConAu 57, WhoWor 76, –78, WrDr 76,
–80, –84

Wright, Kenneth 1915- *ConAu X, –65,*
SmATA X, WrDr 84

Wright, Lawrence 1947- *ConAu 93*

Wright, Louis Booker 1899- *AmAu&B,*
Au&Wr 6, BiE&WWA, BioIn 1, –2, –3,
–8, BlueB 76, ChhPo S1, –S3, ConAu 1R,
–1NR, CurBio 50, DcLB 17[port],
DrAS 74H, –78H, –82H, IntAu&W 77,
–82, IntWW 74, –75, –76, –77, –78, –79,
–80, –81, –82, –83, NotNAT, REnAL,
WhE&EA, Who 74, –82, –83, WhoAm 74,
–76, –78, –80, –82, WrDr 76, –80, –82, –84

Wright, Nancy Means *ConAu 104,*
DrAP&F 83, IntAu&W 82

Wright, Nathan, Jr. 1923- *BioIn 9, BlkAWP,*
ConAu 37R, DrAS 74H, Ebony 1,
InB&W 80, LivgBAA, NegAl 76, –83,
SelBAA, WhoBlA 75, –77, –80, WhoE 74,
–75, –77

Wright, Richard 1908-1960 *AmAu&B,*
AmNov, AmWr, BioIn 1, –2, –3, –4, –5, –6,
–7, –8, –9, –10, –11, –12, BlkAWP, CasWL,
CnDAL, ConAu 108, ConLC 1, –3, –4, –9,
–14, –21[port], ConNov 76, CurBio 40,
–61, CyWA, DcAmB S6, DcAmSR,
DcLB DS2[port], DcLEL, DrBlPA,
Dis&D, EncAB-H, EncSoH, EncWL,
EvLB, InB&W 80, LinLib L, LongCTC,
McGEWB, ModAL, ModAL SUP,
ModBlW, NegAl 76[port], –83[port],
NotNAT A, –B, Novels[port], ObitOF 79,
ObitT 1951, OxAmL, PenC AM, PIP&P,
RAdv 1, REn, REnAL, SelBAA, TwCA,
TwCA SUP, TwCWr, WebAB, –79,
WebE&AL, WhDW, WhAm 4,
WhoTwCL, WorAl

Wright, Shannon 1956?- *BioIn 12*

Wright, Theon 1904- *ConAu 109, WhNAA*

Wrightson, Patricia 1921- *AuBYP, BioIn 8,*
–11, ChlLR 4[port], ConAu 3NR, –45,
FourBJA, ScF&FL 1, –2, SenS, SingR 1,
SmATA 8, TwCCW 78, –83, WrDr 80,
–82, –84

Wrigley, Denis *ChhPo S1, –S2, –S3*

Wrone, David R 1933- *ConAu 6NR, –57,*
WhoMW 78

Wroth, Lawrence Counselman 1884-1970
AmAu&B, BioIn 1, –9, –10, ChhPo S3,
ConAu 29R, DcAmLiB, NewYTBE 70,
OxAmL, REnAL, WhNAA

Wunsch, Josephine M 1914- *AuBYP, BioIn 8,*
ConAu 1R, ForWC 70, MichAu 80,
WrDr 76, –80, –82, –84

Wuorio, Eva-Lis 1918- *AuBYP SUP, BioIn 9,*
ConAu 77, CreCan 1, SmATA 28,

–34[port], ThrBJA

Wyatt, John 1925- *ConAu 105*

Wyatt-Brown, Bertram 1932- *ConAu 25R, DrAS 74H, –78H, –82H, WhoAm 76, –78, –80, –82*

Wyeth, N C 1882-1945 *AntBDN B, ArtsAmW, CurBio 45, ForII, SmATA 17*

Wyeth, Newell Convers 1882-1945 *AmAu&B, BioIn 1, –2, –4, –5, –7, –8, –9, –10, –12, ChhPo, –S2, –S3, ConICB, DcAmB S3, IlBEAAW, IlrAm B, IlsBYP, JBA 34, –51, ObitOF 79, OxAmH, REnAL, WebAB, –79, WhAm 2*

Wyler, Rose 1909- *AuBYP, BioIn 7, –9, –12, BkP, ConAu 93, SmATA 18, ThrBJA, WhoAmW 58, –61, –64*

Wylie, Philip 1902-1971 *AmAu&B, AmNov, BioIn 1, –2, –3, –4, –5, –7, –9, –12, ChhPo S2, CnDAL, ConAu 33R, ConAu P-2, ConNov 72, DcLB 9[port], EncMys, EncSF, EvLB, LinLib L, –S, NewYTBE 71, ObitOF 79, REn, REnAL, ScF&FL 1, –2, TwCA, TwCA SUP, TwCWr, WebAB, –79, WhAm 5, WhFla, WhoSciF*

Wyman, Bill 1941- *BioIn 12, CelR 73*

Wyman, Bill *see also* Rolling Stones, The

Wymer, Norman George 1911- *Au&Wr 6, AuBYP, BioIn 7, ConAu 104, SmATA 25, WhE&EA, WrDr 76, –80, –82, –84*

Wyndham, John 1903-1969 *BioIn 7, –8, –10, –12, ConAu X, ConLC 19, DcLEL 1940, EncSF, FilmgC, LinLib L, LongCTC, Novels, ObitOF 79, REn, ScF&FL 1, –2, TwCWr, WebE&AL, WhoSciF, WorAl, WorAu*

Wyndham, John *see also* Harris, John Benyon

Wyndham, Lee 1912-1978 *AuBYP, BioIn 6, –7, –9, –11, ConAu X, –5R, ForWC 70, IntAu&W 76, –77, –82, MorJA, SmATA X, –1, TwCCW 78, WhoAmW 58, –61, –66, –68, WhoE 74, WrDr 76*

Wyndham, Lee *see also* Hyndman, Jane Andrews

Wyss, Johann David 1743-1818 *AuBYP SUP, BioIn 1, –3, –8, CarSB, CasWL, OxGer, SmATA 27, –29, Str&VC, WhoChL*

X

Ximenes, Ben Cuellar, Jr. 1911- *ConAu 5R*

Y

Yacowar, Maurice 1942- *CanWW 83,*
ConAu 41R, DrAS 74E, –78E, –82E

Yannella, Donald 1934- *ConAu 8NR, –57,*
DrAS 78E, –82E

Yarbro, Chelsea Quinn 1942- *ConAu 9NR, –65,*
EncSF, ScF&FL 1, –2, WrDr 84

Yarrow, Philip John 1917- *Au&Wr 6,*
ConAu 13R, WrDr 76, –80, –82, –84

Yastrzemski, Carl 1939- *BioIn 5, –6, –8, –9,*
–10, –11, –12, CelR 73, ConAu 104,
CurBio 68, NewYTBE 70, –72,
NewYTBS 75, –79, –82[port], –83[port],
WhoAm 74, –76, –78, –80, –82,
WhoProB 73, WorAl

Yates, Brock Wendel 1933- *AuBYP, BioIn 7,*
–9, ConAu 9R, Ward 77F

Yates, Elizabeth 1905- *AmAu&B, AmNov,*
AmWomWr, Au&ICB, Au&Wr 6,
AuBYP, BioIn 1, –2, –3, –4, –5, –7, –9, –10,
–12, ChhPo, ConAu 1R, –6NR, –13R,
CurBio 48, InWom, IntAu&W 77,
JBA 51, MorBMP, Newb 1922, REnAL,
SmATA 4, TwCA SUP, TwCCW 78, –83,
WhoAm 74, –76, –78, –80, –82,
WhoAmW 74, –58, –61, –64, –66, –68, –70,
–72, WrDr 80, –82, –84

Yates, Madeleine 1937- *ConAu 109*

Yates, Raymond Francis 1895-1966 *Au&Wr 6,*
AuBYP, BioIn 6, –7, ConAu 110,
EncAB 38[port], MorJA,
SmATA 31[port], WhAm 4, WhE&EA,
WhLit, WhNAA

Yates, Richard 1926- *AmAu&B, BioIn 5, –10,*
ConAu 5R, –10NR, ConLC 7, –8,
–23[port], ConNov 72, –76, –82,
DcLB Y81A[port], –2, DcLEL 1940,
DrAF 76, DrAP&F 83, IntAu&W 76,
–77, LinLib L, WorAu, WrDr 76, –80,
–82, –84

Yau, John *DrAP&F 83*

Yaukey, Grace S 1899- *AmAu&B, AmNov X,*
AuBYP, BioIn 2, –8, –10, ConAu 1R,
–1NR, InWom, JBA 51, SmATA 5

Yaukey, Grace S *see also* Spencer, Cornelia

Yeakley, Marjory Hall 1908- *BioIn 12,*
ConAu 1R, –2NR, CurBio 57, InWom,
IntAu&W 77, –82, SmATA 21[port]

Yeakley, Marjory Hall *see also* Hall, Marjory

Yeakley, Marjory Hall *see also* Morse, Carol

Yeats, William Butler 1865-1939 *Alli SUP,*
AnCL, ArizL, BbD, BiD&SB, BioIn 1,
–2, –3, –4, –5, –6, –7, –8, –9, –10, –11, –12,
BrWr 6, CasWL, Chambr 3, ChhPo, –S1,
–S2, –S3, CnE&AP, CnMD, CnMWL,
CnThe, ConAu 104, CyWA, DcEnA, –AP,
DcIrB, DcIrL, DcIrW 1, DcLB 10[port],
–19[port], DcLEL, Dis&D, EncWL,
EncWT, EvLB, LinLib L, –S, LongCTC,
MakMC, McGEWB, McGEWD, –84[port],
ModBrL, ModBrL SUP, ModWD, NewC,
NewEOp 71, NotNAT A, –B, OxEng,
OxThe, PenC ENG, PIP&P, PoIre,
RAdv 1, RComWL, REn, REnWD,
TwCA, TwCA SUP, TwCLC 1, –11[port],
TwCWr, WebE&AL, WhDW, WhE&EA,
WhThe, WhoTwCL, WorAl

Yee, Min S 1938- *ConAu 101, WrDr 76, –80,*
–82, –84

Yefremov, Ivan 1907-1972 *EncSF, ScF&FL 1,*
WhoSciF

Yeo, Wilma 1918- *ConAu 25R,*
SmATA 24[port]

Yep, Laurence Michael 1948- *BioIn 10,*
ChLR 3, ConAu 1NR, –49, EncSF,
ScF&FL 1, –2, SmATA 7, TwCCW 83,
WhoAm 78, –80, –82, WrDr 84

Yerby, Frank 1916- *AmAu&B, AmNov,*
Au&Wr 6, BioIn 1, –2, –3, –4, –5, –7, –9,
–12, BlueB 76, BlkAWP, CivR 74,
ConAu 9R, ConLC 1, –7, –22[port],
ConNov 72, –82, CurBio 46, DcLEL 1940,
EncSoH, InB&W 80, IntAu&W 76, –77,
–82, IntWW 74, –75, –76, –77, –78, –79,
–80, –81, –82, –83, LinLib L, LivgBAA,
LongCTC, NegAl 76, –83, Novels[port],
PenC AM, SelBAA, TwCA SUP,
WebAB, –79, Who 74, –82, –83,
WhoAm 74, –76, –78, –80, –82, WhoBlA 75,
–77, –80, WorAl, WrDr 76, –80, –82, –84

Yerkow, Charles *AuBYP SUP*

Yermakov, Nicholas *DrAP&F 83*

Yevtushenko, Yevgeny 1933- *BioIn 6, –7, –8, –9,*
–10, –11, –12, ConAu 81, ConLC 1,
–26[port], CurBio 63, EvEuW,
IntAu&W 77, IntWW 76, LinLib L,
MakMC, McGEWB, NewYTBE 71, –72,

-73, PenC EUR, RComWL, TwCWr,
WhoTwCL, WhoWor 74, WorAl, WorAu

Yezierska, Anzia 1885-1970 AmAu&B,
AmWomWr, BioIn 2, -4, -7, -9, -12,
ConAu 89, InWom, LinLib L,
NotAW MOD, OxAmL, REnAL, TwCA,
TwCA SUP, WhAm 7

Yezzo, Dominick 1947- ConAu 53

Yglesias, Helen 1915- BioIn 9, -10, -12,
ConAu 37R, ConLC 7, -22[port],
DrAP&F 83, NewYTBS 81[port],
WhoAm 76, -78, -80, -82, WhoE 74, -75,
-77, WrDr 84

Yglesias, Rafael 1954- BioIn 9, -10,
ConAu 37R, DrAP&F 83, NewYTBE 72

Yolen, Jane 1939- AuBYP, BioIn 8, -9,
ChlLR 4[port], ChhPo S2, ConAu 11NR,
-13R, EncSF, ForWC 70, FourBJA,
ScF&FL 1, -2, SmATA 4, TwCCW 78,
-83, WhoAm 78, -80, -82, WhoAmW 83,
WrDr 80, -82, -84

York, Carol Beach 1928- AuBYP SUP,
BioIn 10, ConAu 1R, -6NR, ForWC 70,
SmATA 6, WhoAmW 64, -66

York, William 1950- ConAu 107

Yorke, Margaret 1924- Au&Wr 6,
ConAu 2NR, IntAu&W 76, -77, -82,
Novels, TwCCr&M 80, WhoWor 80,
WrDr 76, -80, -82, -84

Yoshida, Jim 1921- BioIn 9, ConAu 41R

Youd, Samuel 1922- BioIn 10, ConAu 77,
SmATA 30, WorAu

Youd, Samuel see also Christopher, John

Youman, Roger Jacob 1932- ConAu 65,
WhoAm 76, -78, -80, -82

Young, Al 1939- BioIn 8, BlkAWP,
ConAu 29R, ConLC 19, ConNov 76, -82,
ConP 70, -75, -80, DrAF 76, DrAP 75,
DrAP&F 83, LivgBAA, NegAl 83,
RAdv 1, SelBAA, WhoAm 76, -78, -80,
-82, WrDr 76, -80, -82, -84

Young, Bob 1916-1969 BioIn 7, ConAu X,
SmATA 3

Young, Bob see also Young, Robert W

Young, Carrie 1923- ConAu X

Young, Chesley Virginia 1919- AmSCAP 66,
ConAu 33R, IntAu&W 76, -77,
WhoAmW 74, -72, -75, -77, -79, -81,
WhoE 74, -75, -77, -79, -81, WrDr 76, -80,
-82, -84

Young, Dean Wayne 1938- WhoAm 78, -80,
-82

Young, Dorothea Bennett 1924- ConAu 13R,
SmATA 31

Young, Edward 1910-1964 AuBYP, ConAu X,
SmATA 3

Young, Edward see also Reinfeld, Fred

Young, James V 1936- ConAu 69

Young, Jan 1919- AuBYP, BioIn 7, -9,
ConAu X, IntAu&W 76X, -77X,
SmATA 3, WrDr 76, -80, -82, -84

Young, Jan see also Young, Janet Randall

Young, Janet Randall 1919- AuBYP, BioIn 9,
ConAu 5R, -5NR, ForWC 70,
IntAu&W 76, -77, -82, SmATA 3,
WhoAmW 75, WrDr 76, -80, -82, -84

Young, Janet Randall see also Randall, Janet

Young, John Richard AuBYP

Young, Leontine R 1910- ConAu P-1,
ForWC 70

Young, Louise B 1919- ConAu 10NR, -25R,
IntAu&W 76, -77, WrDr 76, -80, -82, -84

Young, Margaret B 1922- BkP, ConAu 21R,
InB&W 80, SelBAA, SmATA 2,
WhoAmW 74, -68, -70, -72, -75, -83,
WhoBlA 75, -77, -80, WhoE 74, -75, -77,
-79, -81

Young, Miriam 1913-1974 AuBYP, BioIn 7,
-10, ConAu 37R, -53, ScF&FL 1, -2,
SmATA 7, WrDr 76, -80

Young, Morris N 1909- AmM&WS 73P, -76P,
-79P, -82P, BioIn 8, ConAu 33R,
IntMPA 78, WhoE 77, -79, WrDr 76, -80,
-82, -84

Young, Neil 1945- BioIn 11, -12, ConAu 110,
ConLC 17, CurBio 80[port], EncPR&S,
-77, IllEncRk, RkOn 78, RolSEnR 83,
WhoAm 78, -80, -82, WhoHol A,
WhoRocM 82, WorAl

Young, Neil see also Crosby, Stills, Nash &
Young

Young, Otis E, Jr. 1925- ConAu 53,
DrAS 74H, -78H, -82H, IndAu 1917

Young, Patrick 1937- AuBYP, BioIn 8, -11,
ConAu 69, SmATA 22[port]

Young, Percy M 1912- Au&Wr 6, AuBYP,
Baker 78, BioIn 8, ConAu 13R,
IntWWM 77, OxMus, SmATA 31,
WhoMus 72

Young, Peter 1915- Au&Wr 6, ConAu 13R,
IntAu&W 76, -77, -82, Who 74, -82, -83,
WhoWor 78

Young, Robert F 1915- ConSFA, EncSF,
ScF&FL 1, -2, WhoSciF

Young, Robert W 1916-1969 AuBYP,
ConAu 5R, SmATA 3

Young, Robert W see also Randall, Janet

Young, Robert W see also Young, Bob

Young, Scott 1918- BioIn 10, CaW,
CanWW 79, -80, -81, -83, ConAu 5NR,
-9R, OxCan, OxCan SUP, SmATA 5,
TwCCW 78, WhoAm 74, -76, -78, -80,
-82, WrDr 80, -82, -84

Young, Stanley 1906-1975 AmAu&B,
Au&Wr 6, BiE&WWA, BioIn 2, -7, -10,
CathA 1930, ChhPo, ConAu 57,
CurBio 75N, DrAS 74E, IndAu 1917,
IntAu&W 76, NewYTBS 75, NotNAT,
WhAm 6, WhE&EA, WhoAm 74

Young, Whitney M 1921-1971 BioIn 6, -7, -8,
-9, -10, -11, -12, CivRSt, ConAu P-1,
CurBio 65, -71, -71N, EncAB-H, EncSoH,
InB&W 80, LinLib L, -S, McGEWB,
NatCAB 57, NegAl 76[port], -83[port],

NewYTBE 70, –71, ObitOF 79,
ObitT 1971, PolProf J, PolProf K,
SelBAA, WebAB, –79, WhAm 5, WorAl
Yourcenar, Marguerite 1903- *Au&Wr 6,*
BioIn 3, –10, –11, –12, BlueB 76,
ConAu 69, ConLC 19, CurBio 82[port],
EncWL, ForWC 70, InWom,
IntAu&W 76, –77, –82, IntDcWB,
IntWW 74, –75, –76, –77, –78, –79, –80, –81,
–82, –83, LinLib L, ModFrL,
NewYTBS 79, –81[port], REn,
WhoAm 74, –76, –78, –82, WhoAmW 74,
–61, –68, –70, –72, –75, –81, WhoFr 79,
WhoWor 74, –82, WorAu
Yurchenco, Henrietta 1916- *AuBYP SUP,*
ConAu 37R, ForWC 70, WhoAm 74, –76,
–78, –80, –82, WhoAmW 74

Z

Zacharis, John C 1936- *ConAu 73*

Zachary, Hugh 1928- *ConAu 21R,
IntAu&W 77, ScF&FL 1, WhoS&SW 73,
-75, -76, WrDr 76, -80, -82, -84*

Zagoren, Ruby 1922-1974 *AuBYP, ConAu P-1,
ForWC 70, WhoAmW 74*

Zaharias, Babe 1911?-1956 *BioIn 1, -2, -3, -4,
-5, -6, -8, -9, -10, -11, -12, CurBio 47, -56,
WhAm HSA, WhFla, WorAl*

Zaidenberg, Arthur 1903?- *AmAu&B, AuBYP,
AuBYP SUP, BioIn 7, ConAu 108,
SmATA 34[port], WhoAm 74, -76, -78,
-80, -82, WhoAmA 76, -78, -80, -82*

Zalben, Jane B 1950- *BioIn 10, ConAu 4NR,
-49, DrAP&F 83, SmATA 7, WrDr 76,
-80, -82, -84*

Zamyatin, Yevgeni 1884-1937 *CasWL,
CIDMEL, CnMD, CnMWL, DcRusL,
EncWL, EvEuW, McGEWD 84,
ModSL 1, ModWD, Novels, PenC EUR,
REn, TwCA, TwCA SUP,
TwCLC 8[port], TwCWr, WhoTwCL,
WorAl*

Zappler, Lisbeth 1930- *AuBYP SUP,
BioIn 11, ConAu 4NR, -49, SmATA 10*

Zarchy, Harry 1912- *AuBYP, BioIn 6, -7,
ConAu 1R, -2NR, MorJA,
SmATA 34[port]*

Zarem, Lewis *AuBYP, BioIn 7, EncSF,
ScF&FL 1*

Zaslavsky, Claudia 1917- *ConAu 1NR, -49,
SmATA 36*

Zassenhaus, Hiltgunt 1916- *AuNews 1,
BioIn 10, -11, ConAu 49, WhoAm 78,
-80, -82*

Zaturenska, Marya 1902-1982 *AmWomWr,
AnObit 1982, BioIn 4, -11, -12, ChhPo,
-S3, CnDAL, ConAu 105, -13R,
ConLC 6, -11, ConP 70, -75, -80,
DrAP 75, ForWC 70, NewYTBS 82,
OxAmL, PenC AM, REn, REnAL,
SixAP, TwCA, TwCA SUP, WhoAm 74,
-76, -78, -80, WhoAmW 74, -68, -70, -72,
-75, -77, WhoPolA, WrDr 76, -80, -82*

Zechlin, Ruth Hedwig Conradine 1899-
Au&Wr 6

Zei, Alki 1928- *AuBYP, ChlLR 6[port],
ConAu 77, FourBJA, SmATA 24[port],*
TwCCW 78B, -83B

Zelazny, Roger 1937- *Au&Wr 6, BioIn 12,
ConAu 21R, ConLC 21[port],
ConSFA, DcLB 8[port], DrAF 76,
DrAP&F 83, EncSF, IntAu&W 76, -77,
-82, LinLib L, Novels, ScF&FL 1, -2,
WhoAm 82, WhoHr&F, WhoSciF,
WorAl, WrDr 76, -80, -82, -84*

Zerman, Melvyn Bernard 1930- *ConAu 77,
IntAu&W 82*

Ziemian, Joseph 1922-1971 *ConAu 65*

Ziff, Gil 1938- *ConAu 106*

Zim, Herbert 1909- *AmAu&B, AmPB,
Au&Wr 6, AuBYP, BioIn 2, -3, -4, -7, -9,
BlueB 76, BkP, ChlLR 2, ChhPo S3,
ConAu 13R, CurBio 56, JBA 51,
LinLib L, SmATA 1, -30[port],
WhoAm 74, -76, -78, -80, -82, WrDr 80,
-82, -84*

Zimbardo, Philip 1933- *AmM&WS 73S, -78S,
BioIn 10, -11, ConAu 85, WhoAm 80,
-82, WrDr 80, -82, -84*

Zimmerman, Paul L 1932- *ConAu 10NR, -25R*

Zimmerman, Robert 1941- *AmAu&B,
ConAu X, IntWWP 82X, WebAB, -79*

Zimmerman, Robert *see also* Dylan, Bob

Zindel, Bonnie 1943- *ConAu 105,
SmATA 34[port]*

Zindel, Paul 1936- *AuBYP, BioIn 9, -10, -11,
-12, CelR 73, ChlLR 3, CnThe,
ConAu 73, ConDr 73, -77, -82, ConLC 6,
-26[port], CurBio 73, DcLB 7[port],
DcLEL 1940, McGEWD, -84, NatPD,
-81[port], NotNAT, SmATA 16,
TwCCW 78, -83, WhoAm 74, -76, -78,
-80, -82, WhoThe 15, -16, -81, WorAl,
WorAu 1970, WrDr 76, -80, -82, -84*

Ziner, Feenie 1921- *BioIn 7, -10, ConAu X,
DrAP&F 83, ForWC 70, SmATA 5*

Zinkin, Taya 1918- *ConAu 1R, -2NR,
IntAu&W 77, -82, WhoWor 76, -78,
WrDr 76, -80, -82, -84*

Zinn, Howard 1922- *AmAu&B,
AmM&WS 73S, -78S, BioIn 10, -11,
ConAu 1R, -2NR, DrAS 74H, -78H, -82H,
MugS, PolProf J, WhoAm 74, -76, -78,
-80, -82, WhoWor 74, WrDr 76, -80, -82,
-84*

Zinsser, Hans 1878-1940 *AmAu&B, BiHiMed, BioIn 1, -2, -3, -4, -5, -7, -9, CurBio 40, DcAmB S2, DcNAA, DcScB, InSci, LongCTC, NatCAB 36, REnAL, TwCA, TwCA SUP, WebAB, -79, WhAm 1*

Zisfein, Melvin Bernard 1926- *ConAu 108, WhoAm 74, -76, -78, -80, -82, WhoE 75, -77, WhoGov 77, -75, WhoS&SW 75, -76, WhoWor 82*

Zistel, Era *ConAu 25R*

Zizmor, Jonathan 1946?- *BioIn 12*

Zochert, Donald 1938- *ConAu 81, IntAu&W 82*

Zoffer, Gerald R 1926?-1982 *ConAu 107*

Zola, Emile 1840-1902 *AtlBL, BbD, BiD&SB, BioIn 1, -2, -3, -4, -5, -6, -7, -8, -9, -10, -11, -12, CasWL, CelCen, ClDMEL, CnThe, ConAu 104, CyWA, DcAmSR, DcBiA, DcEuL, Dis&D, EncWL, EncWT, EuAu, EvEuW, FilmgC, LinLib L, -S, LongCEL, McGEWB, McGEWD, -84, ModWD, NewC, NewEOp 71, NotNAT A, -B, Novels[port], OxEng, OxFr, OxThe, PenC EUR, RComWL, REn, REnWD, TwCLC 1, -6[port], WhoTwCL, WorAl*

Zolotow, Charlotte 1915- *AmPB, AmWomWr, AuBYP, BioIn 6, -7, -9, -10, BkP, ChlLR 2, ConAu 3NR, -5R, Dun&B 79, ForWC 70, IntAu&W 76, -77, LinLib L, MichAu 80, MorJA, PiP, SmATA 1, -35, TwCCW 78, -83, WhoAm 76, -78, -80, -82, WhoAmW 74, -66, -68, -70, -72, -75, -77, -79, -81, -83, WrDr 76, -80, -82, -84*

Zolotow, Maurice 1913- *AmAu&B, Au&Wr 6, BioIn 2, -4, ConAu 1R, -1NR, CurBio 57, REnAL, WhoAm 74, -76, -78, -80, -82, WhoWorJ 72, -78, WrDr 76, -80, -82, -84*

Zolynas, Al 1945- *ConAu 105, IntWWP 82*

Zuker-Bujanowska, Liliana 1928?- *BioIn 12*

Zulli, Floyd 1922-1980 *BioIn 4, -5, -12, ConAu 108, -37R, CurBio 58, -81N, DrAS 74F, -78F, WhoE 75*

Zumwalt, Eva 1936- *ConAu 9NR*

Zwinger, Ann 1925- *ConAu 33R, WrDr 82, -84*

KEY TO SOURCE CODES *(Continued from front endleaf)*

KEY TO SOURCE CODES *(Continued from front endleaf)*

Code	Title	Code	Title
IlDcG	An Illustrated Dictionary of Glass	*ModFrL*	Modern French Literature
IlEncJ	The Illustrated Encyclopedia of Jazz	*ModGL*	Modern German Literature
		ModLAL	Modern Latin American Literature
IlEncMy	An Illustrated Encyclopaedia of Mysticism	*ModRL*	Modern Romance Literatures
		ModSL	Modern Slavic Literatures
IlEncRk	The Illustrated Encyclopedia of Rock	*ModWD*	Modern World Drama
		MorBMP	More Books by More People
IlrAm	The Illustrator in America	*MorJA*	More Junior Authors
IlsBYP	Illustrators of Books for Young People	*MotPP*	Motion Picture Performers
		MouLC	Moulton's Library of Literary Criticism
IlsCB	Illustrators of Children's Books		
InB&W	In Black and White	*MovMk*	The Movie Makers
InSci	Index to Scientists	*MugS*	Mug Shots
InWom	Index to Women	*MusSN*	Musicians since 1900
IndAu	Indiana Authors and Their Books	*NamesHP*	Names in the History of Psychology
IntAu&W	International Authors and Writers Who's Who	*NatCAB*	The National Cyclopaedia of American Biography
IntDcWB	The International Dictionary of Women's Biography	*NatPD*	National Playwrights Directory
		NegAl	The Negro Almanac
IntEnSS	International Encyclopedia of the Social Sciences: Biographical Supplement	*NewC*	The New Century Handbook of English Literature
		NewCBMT	New Complete Book of the American Musical Theater
IntMed	International Medical Who's Who		
IntMPA	International Motion Picture Almanac	*NewEOp*	The New Encyclopedia of the Opera
IntWW	The International Who's Who	*NewRR*	The New Rock 'n' Roll
IntWWE	International Who's Who in Energy and Nuclear Sciences	*NewYHSD*	The New-York Historical Society's Dictionary of Artists in America
IntWWM	International Who's Who in Music and Musicians' Directory	*NewYTBE*	The New York Times Biographical Edition
IntWWP	International Who's Who in Poetry	*NewYTBS*	The New York Times Biographical Service
IntYB	The International Year Book and Statesmen's Who's Who	*NewYTET*	The New York Times Encyclopedia of Television
JBA	The Junior Book of Authors		
Law&B	Law and Business Directory of Corporate Counsel	*NewbC*	Newbery and Caldecott Medal Books
		Newb	Newbery Medal Books
LEduc	Leaders in Education	*NotAW*	Notable American Women
LElec	Leaders in Electronics	*NotNAT*	Notable Names in the American Theatre
LesBEnT	Les Brown's Encyclopedia to Television		
		Novels	Novels and Novelists
LibW	Liberty's Women	*ObitOF*	Obituaries on File
LinLib L	The Lincoln Library of Language Arts	*ObitT*	Obituaries from the Times
		ODwPR	O'Dwyer's Directory of Public Relations Executives
LinLib S	The Lincoln Library of Social Studies	*OhA&B*	Ohio Authors and Their Books
LivgBAA	Living Black American Authors	*OxAmH*	The Oxford Companion to American History
LongCEL	Longman Companion to English Literature	*OxAmL*	The Oxford Companion to American Literature
LongCTC	Longman Companion to Twentieth Century Literature	*OxArt*	The Oxford Companion to Art
		OxCan	The Oxford Companion to Canadian History and Literature
LuthC	Lutheran Cyclopedia		
MGM	The MGM Stock Company	*OxEng*	The Oxford Companion to English Literature
MacDCB	The Macmillan Dictionary of Canadian Biography		
		OxFilm	The Oxford Companion to Film
MakMC	Makers of Modern Culture	*OxFr*	The Oxford Companion to French Literature
McGDA	McGraw-Hill Dictionary of Art		
McGEWB	The McGraw-Hill Encyclopedia of World Biography	*OxGer*	The Oxford Companion to German Literature
McGEWD	McGraw-Hill Encyclopedia of World Drama	*OxLaw*	The Oxford Companion to Law
		OxMus	The Oxford Companion to Music
McGMS	McGraw-Hill Modern Scientists and Engineers	*OxShips*	The Oxford Companion to Ships and the Sea
MedHR	Medal of Honor Recipients		
MnBBF	The Men Behind Boys' Fiction	*OxSpan*	The Oxford Companion to Spanish Literature
MichAu	Michigan Authors		
MidE	The Middle East and North Africa	*OxThe*	The Oxford Companion to the Theatre
MinnWr	Minnesota Writers		
ModAL	Modern American Literature	*OxTwCA*	The Oxford Companion to Twentieth-Century Art
ModBlW	Modern Black Writers		
ModBrL	Modern British Literature	*PenC AM*	The Penguin Companion to American Literature
ModCmwL	Modern Commonwealth Literature		

(Continued on overleaf)

PenC CL	The Penguin Companion to Classical, Oriental, and African Literature
PenC ENG	The Penguin Companion to English Literature
PenC EUR	The Penguin Companion to European Literature
PhDcTCA	Phaidon Dictionary of Twentieth Century Art
PiP	The Pied Pipers
PlP&P	Plays, Players, and Playwrights
PoChrch	The Poets of the Church
PoIre	The Poets of Ireland
PoLE	The Poets Laureate of England
Po&Wr	The Poets & Writers, Inc. 1977 Supplement
PolProf	Political Profiles
Profile	Profiles
PrintW	The Printworld Directory
PseudAu	Pseudonyms of Authors
PueRA	Puerto Rican Authors
RAdv	The Reader's Adviser
RComWL	The Reader's Companion to World Literature
REn	The Reader's Encyclopedia
REnAL	The Reader's Encyclopedia of American Literature
REnAW	The Reader's Encyclopedia of the American West
REnWD	The Reader's Encyclopedia of World Drama
RGAfL	A Reader's Guide to African Literature
RkOn	Rock On
Rk 100	Rock 100
RolSEnR	The Rolling Stone Encyclopedia of Rock & Roll
ScF&FL	Science Fiction and Fantasy Literature
SingR	The Singing Roads
SelBAA	Selected Black American Authors
SenS	A Sense of Story
SixAP	Sixty American Poets, 1896-1944
SmATA	Something about the Author
St&PR	Standard and Poor's Register of Corporations, Directors and Executives
Str&VC	Story and Verse for Children
TelT	Tellers of Tales
TexWr	Texas Writers of Today
ThFT	They Had Faces Then
ThrBJA	Third Book of Junior Authors
TwCA	Twentieth Century Authors
TwCBDA	The Twentieth Century Biographical Dictionary of Notable Americans
TwCCW	Twentieth-Century Children's Writers
TwCCr&M	Twentieth-Century Crime and Mystery Writers
TwCLC	Twentieth-Century Literary Criticism
TwCWr	Twentieth Century Writing
TwYS	Twenty Years of Silents
UFOEn	The UFO Encyclopedia
USBiR	United States. Department of State: The Biographic Register
Vers	The Versatiles
Ward	1977 Ward's Who's Who among U.S. Motor Vehicle Manufacturers

WebAB	Webster's American Biographies
WebAMB	Webster's American Military Biographies
WebE&AL	Webster's New World Companion to English and American Literature
WhDW	Who Did What
WhAm	Who Was Who in America
WhAmP	Who Was Who in American Politics
WhE&EA	Who Was Who among English and European Authors
WhFla	Who Was Who in Florida
WhJnl	Who Was Who in Journalism
WhLit	Who Was Who in Literature
WhNAA	Who Was Who among North American Authors
WhScrn	Who Was Who on Screen
WhThe	Who Was Who in the Theatre
WhWW-II	Who Was Who in World War II
Who	Who's Who
WhoAdv	Who's Who in Advertising
WhoAm	Who's Who in America
WhoAmA	Who's Who in American Art
WhoAmJ	Who's Who in American Jewry
WhoAmL	Who's Who in American Law
WhoAmM	Who's Who in American Music
WhoAmP	Who's Who in American Politics
WhoAmW	Who's Who of American Women
WhoArab	Who's Who in the Arab World
WhoArt	Who's Who in Art
WhoAtom	Who's Who in Atoms
WhoBbl	Who's Who in Basketball
WhoBlA	Who's Who among Black Americans
WhoBox	Who's Who in Boxing
WhoBW&I	Who's Who of Boys' Writers and Illustrators
WhoCan	Who's Who in Canada
WhoChL	The Who's Who of Children's Literature
WhoColR	Who's Who of the Colored Race
WhoCon	Who's Who in Consulting
WhoCntE	Who's Who in Continuing Education
WhoE	Who's Who in the East
WhoEc	Who's Who in Economics
WhoEng	Who's Who in Engineering
WhoF&I	Who's Who in Finance and Industry
WhoFla	Who's Who in Florida
WhoFtbl	Who's Who in Football
WhoFr	Who's Who in France
WhoGen	Who's Who in Genealogy and Heraldry
WhoGolf	Who's Who in Golf
WhoGov	Who's Who in Government
WhoGrA	Who's Who in Graphic Art
WhoHcky	Who's Who in Hockey
WhoHol	Who's Who in Hollywood
WhoHr&F	Who's Who in Horror and Fantasy Fiction
WhoIns	Who's Who in Insurance
WhoJazz	Who's Who of Jazz
WhoLab	Who's Who in Labor
WhoLib	Who's Who in Librarianship (and Information Science)
WhoLibI	Who's Who in Library and Information Services
WhoLibS	Who's Who in Library Service
WhoLA	Who's Who among Living Authors of Older Nations